P9-ELQ-029

Psychology

FOURTH EDITION

ROBERT A. BARON
Rensselaer Polytechnic Institute

With the special assistance of

MICHAEL J. KALSHER

ALLYN AND BACON

BOSTON ▪ LONDON ▪ TORONTO ▪ SYDNEY ▪ TOKYO ▪ SINGAPORE

Vice President, Editor in Chief, Social Sciences: Sean W. Wakely
Developmental Editor: Elizabeth Brooks
Editorial Assistant: Jessica Barnard
Director of Field Marketing: Joyce Nilsen
Editorial-Production Administrator: Annette Joseph
Editorial-Production Service: Colophon
Text Designer: Deborah Schneck
Copyeditor: Jay Howland
Composition and Prepress Buyer: Linda Cox
Electronic Production Manager: Timothy Ries
Electronic Page Layout: Christine Thompson
Artists: Jay Alexander and Precision Graphics
Photo Researcher: Elsa Peterson Ltd.
Manufacturing Buyer: Megan Cochran
Cover Administrator: Linda Knowles
Cover Designer: Studio Nine

A Viacom Company
160 Gould Street
Needham Heights, MA 02194

Internet: www.abacon.com
America Online: keyword: College Online

Library of Congress Cataloging-in-Publication Data

Baron, Robert A.
Psychology/Robert A. Baron; with the special assistance of Michael J. Kalsher.—4th ed.
p. cm
Includes bibliographical references and indexes.
ISBN 0-205-26569-3
1. Psychology. I. Kalsher, Michael J. I. Title.
BF121.B32 1997
150—dc21

Printed in the United States of America

10 9 8 7 6 5 4 3 2 VHP 02 01 00 99 98

Dedication

To the memory of Daisy,
for whom this proverb could well have been written:

*"God could not be everywhere,
and so he made mothers"*

AND TO

Sandra, who has spent half a lifetime teaching me much
about kindness, compassion, and love

Contents

13

Health, Stress, and Coping 503

14

Psychological Disorders: Their Nature and Causes 545

Preface

Over in a far corner of my office is a small collection of books now turning yellow with age. What are they? Textbooks I bought when I was in college and decided to keep because I felt that they might prove useful. Standing tall among those books is the text I used in *my* introductory psychology course, back in the fall of 1961. "No surprise," I can almost hear you saying, "after all, you *are* a psychologist!" In fact, though, it *is* somewhat surprising that I decided to keep that particular book for the following reasons. First, when I took that course, I was a biology major; I didn't switch to psychology until the end of my junior year. Second, my introductory psychology course was a total fizzle: The professor actually read to us from the textbook and regularly bored us into a state bordering on oblivion. Looking back, though, I can see that even under those bleak circumstances, I recognized psychology as something *useful*—a field to which I'd probably want to refer again and again.

It has now been more than thirty-five years since I took that course, but I'm happy to note that my thinking in this respect has not changed; I still perceive psychology as a field that everyone can, and will, use throughout life. In my view, introductory psychology is much more than just a "pretty face"—an interesting course to be enjoyed and then forgotten. Rather, I see psychology as a body of knowledge and a way of looking at the world that everyone should take with them when their first course is over.

That idea provides a basic theme for this text. In addition to describing the knowledge base of psychology in as accurate and up-to-date a manner as possible, I've also tried to accomplish something else: I've tried to maximize the chances that students will indeed take psychology with them—that they will use this body of knowledge in dealing with the problems and challenges of their future lives. How have I tried to reach this goal? Primarily, through the steps and features described below.

New Features Relating to the Theme of "Taking Psychology with You"

To encourage readers to recognize the intrinsic usefulness and value of psychology, and so to take it with them throughout life, I've added the following new features:

BEYOND THE HEADLINES: *As Psychologists See It*

These special sections, which appear in every chapter, begin with a short excerpt from an actual news story. They then describe what psychological research (and the scientific method) has to say about the topic or issues raised in the story. The purpose is primarily to illustrate how psychology can provide important insights into virtually anything relating to human behavior. A few examples of these **Beyond the Headlines** sections:

- Warning: H-O-T Really Means $$$ When It Comes to Safety (Chapter 3)
- Drugged in Colombia (Chapter 4)
- Psychotherapist Successfully Treats Stage Fright (Chapter 5)
- It's Computer Chessmate for Chessmaster! (Chapter 7)
- The Secret of Long Life? Be Dour and Dependable (Chapter 9)
- Why Men Lose Keys—and Women Find Them (Chapter 11)
- Nursing the Funny Bone: Carol O'Flaherty Goes from Giving Shots to Needling Audiences (Chapter 15)
- Shh!! Napping Is Trying to Tiptoe into the Workplace (Chapter 17)

As you can see, these new sections touch on a very wide range of topics and lines of research in psychology.

RESEARCH METHODS: *How Psychologists Study...*

This is another new type of special section, and one I view as especially important. These **Research Methods** sections describe the methods used by psychologists to study important topics—just at the point where they are considered in the text. Research Methods sections have two major goals: (1) explaining how psychologists have uncovered the findings described in each chapter (and therefore in each major branch of psychology), and (2) illustrating how the scientific approach adopted by modern psychology can be used to study and understand virtually any aspect of behavior. Reading these sections, I believe, will give students practice in "thinking like a psychologist"—an important skill they can continue to use in the years ahead. In my opinion, discussing the methods used by psychologists to study various topics in close proximity to these topics is a much more useful approach than describing them in a separate Research Methods chapter. Some examples:

- How Psychologists Study Synaptic Transmission (Chapter 2)
- How Psychologists Study Circadian Rhythms—and Disruptions in Them (Chapter 4)
- How Psychologists Study Applications of Operant Conditioning (Chapter 5)
- How Psychologists Study the Nature of Short-Term Memory (Chapter 6)
- How Psychologists Study Development (Chapter 8)
- How Psychologists Study Aggression (Chapter 10)
- How Psychologists Study the Cognitive Basis of Intelligence (Chapter 11)
- How Psychologists Study Health-Related Behavior (Chapter 13)
- How Psychologists Study the Effectiveness of Various Forms of Therapy (Chapter 15)
- How Psychologists Study Sexism—and the "Glass Ceiling" (Chapter 16)
- How Psychologists Study Job Satisfaction (Chapter 17)

IDEAS TO TAKE WITH YOU

A special **Ideas to Take with You** feature in each chapter reviews and illustrates important ideas central to that chapter—ideas readers may find especially useful in the future. In other words, these features provide concrete illustrations of the "taking psychology with you" theme by highlighting key ideas and principles readers should remember—and use. Some examples:

- Applying Knowledge of Synaptic Transmission to Treat Psychological Disorders (Chapter 2)
- The Facts about Hypnotism (Chapter 4)
- When—and Why—Memory Sometimes Fails (Chapter 6)
- How to Reason Effectively (Chapter 7)
- Gender Differences: The Real and the Imaginary (Chapter 8)
- Aging and Cognition: Myth and Reality (Chapter 9)
- Some Tips on Winning the "Battle of the Bulge" (Chapter 10)
- Measuring Validity (Chapter 11)
- How to Recognize Depression (Chapter 14)
- When Should You Seek Therapy? (Chapter 15)
- Resisting Social Influence: Some Useful Steps (Chapter 16)
- When Will People Work Hard—or Goof Off? (Chapter 17)

MAKING PSYCHOLOGY PART OF YOUR LIFE

These sections, which appear at the end of each chapter, describe ways in which readers can apply the findings and principles of that chapter to their own lives. While similar sections were present in the previous edition, they have been modified, and several new ones have been written, to better echo the text's new major theme. A few examples of **Making Psychology Part of Your Life,** all new to this edition:

- How to Discipline Children Effectively: Avoiding Some Common Mistakes (Chapter 8)
- How to Tell When Another Person Is Lying: Nonverbal Cues and the Detection of Deception (Chapter 10)
- Managing Anger: A Key Aspect of Emotional Intelligence (Chapter 11)
- Are You a High or a Low Self-Monitor? (Chapter 12)

EXPANDED PRACTICE IN CRITICAL THINKING

Providing students with practice in critical thinking has always been a theme of this text, because thinking critically is definitely one of the skills students will take with them from introductory psychology. I have expanded this feature in the following ways:

- **Critical Thinking Questions at the end of each Beyond the Headlines section** ask readers to think about the issues raised by the topic of the news story and special section, and to reach conclusions about these topics.
- **Critical Thinking Questions at the end of each chapter** raise major issues concerning human behavior and are designed to encourage readers to "pull together" themes and findings reported in that chapter—and in other areas of psychology as well.
- **Key Questions** follow major sections in the text and are designed both to encourage students to review the materials they have just read, and to think critically about them.

- **Critical thinking questions throughout the text** ask readers to take a step back and think about the issues being discussed. Are the findings reported conclusive? Is there adequate support for a particular theory? What questions remain to be resolved? Such questions are posed in every chapter, within the text itself.

WEB

INTERACTIVITIES

The Internet and World Wide Web provide exciting opportunities for dynamic learning experiences, and I am pleased to introduce an innovative Internet-related feature with this new edition. When the reader encounters an "InterActivities" icon in the margins of the text, it is a signal to surf to this book's associated website in order to find periodically updated links to related websites featuring background information and breaking news stories, learning activities, and image and sound files. The website address is: http://www.abacon.com/baron. InterActivities will expand and update the book itself, providing additional opportunities to take psychology beyond the classroom and make it a meaningful part of the reader's life.

What Remains the Same

This book retains several features of the previous edition to which students and colleagues reacted favorably:

- *Incidents and experiences from my own life*: As in the third edition, I use these (occasionally) to help illustrate both the practical value of psychology and the unique perspective it provides on human behavior.
- *Marginal glossary*: Definitions of key terms appear in the margins, close to their occurrence in the text, as before.
- *Special labeling of all graphs and figures*: These labels help students read and interpret these illustrations. Such labels are a hallmark of all my texts, and I've received many favorable comments on them over the years.
- One additional feature deserves special note: special sections titled **Exploring Gender and Diversity.** A similar feature was included in the previous edition, but the sections in this new edition tie research on gender and diversity even more closely to the contents of each chapter—and to ongoing research throughout psychology. Some examples:

- Culture and the Perception of Pain (Chapter 3)
- Alcohol and Aggression: A Cross-Cultural Comparison (Chapter 4)
- Does Culture Influence Memory? (Chapter 6)
- Language and Culture: Revelations Based on Studies of Bilingualism (Chapter 7)
- Cross-National Differences in Mathematical Competence (Chapter 8)
- Achievement Motivation and Economic Growth (Chapter 10)
- Genetic Factors and Group Differences in IQ Scores: Ringing Down the Curtain on *The Bell Curve* (Chapter 11)
- Cultural Differences in Personality: Avoiding the Extremes (Chapter 12)
- Women and AIDS: A Rapidly Expanding Health Crisis (Chapter 13)
- Postpartum Depression: Why New Mothers Sometimes Get the Blues (Chapter 14)
- Attribution and Rape: Blaming the Victim (Chapter 16)
- Race, Gender, and Mentoring (Chapter 17)

Additional Features Worthy of Note

- *Up-to-date content:* I have always believed that a textbook should reflect a field as it is *now,* not as it was in the past. As a result, I've included the most up-to-date information I could obtain on each topic. *In fact, there are many new references from 1996 and even 1997.* Truly, I don't know how to do any better than this.
- *Displaced preface:* Many students don't bother to read prefaces, so I've included a description of the special features of the text and its major theme right in Chapter 1; that way, I feel, readers won't miss this important framework-generating information.
- *Citation of all illustrations in the text:* Nothing confuses students as much as coming upon a figure, table, or photo that has no apparent connection with the text. To avoid this problem, this book numbers every illustration and mentions it in the text. Students will know when to look at figures and tables and can quickly find them.

Changes in Content

Psychology is an ever changing field, so woe to any textbook that doesn't reflect this fact! With this point in mind, I've made many important changes in content. Here are just a few examples:

- **CHAPTER 1: Psychology: A Science . . . and a Perspective**

This chapter has been thoroughly revised to include more emphasis on the scientific method, research methods, and critical thinking. In addition, the section on Research Methods has been expanded.

- **CHAPTER 11: Intelligence: Cognitive and Emotional**

This chapter has been extensively revised; it now includes discussion of *emotional intelligence* and *practical intelligence,* and new research on *creativity.* Information on gender that was previously included in Chapter 11 has now been integrated into several other chapters (e.g., chapters 8, 9, 16).

- **CHAPTER 12: Personality: Uniqueness and Consistency in the Behavior of Individuals**

This chapter has been revised so as to devote more attention both to *personality measurement* and to *modern research* on personality.

New Topics within Chapters

In addition to these changes, literally dozens of new topics have been included—so many that I could not possibly list all of them here. Here is a small sample of these new topics:

- Discussion of advantages of the scientific method (Chapter 1)
- The scientific method in everyday life (Chapter 1)
- New findings concerning the role of neurotransmitters in disorders such as Parkinson's disease (Chapter 2)
- New findings on the effects of smell on behavior (Chapter 3)
- New evidence on the effects of hypnosis. (Chapter 4)
- How television affects daydreams and creative imagination (Chapter 4)
- New information on the neural basis of learning (Chapter 5)
- Observational learning and smoking among teenagers (Chapter 5)
- Anatomically detailed dolls and memory of childhood sexual abuse (Chapter 6)
- Intentional forgetting (Chapter 6)
- Metacognitive processing in problem solving (Chapter 7)
- Effects of social context on reasoning (Chapter 7)
- Long-term effects of temperament (Chapter 8)
- Factors that influence attachment (Chapter 8)
- Adolescent recklessness (Chapter 9)
- The role of societal events in adult development (Chapter 9)
- Caring for elderly parents (Chapter 9)
- Self-handicapping (Chapter 10)
- Cognitive motivation (Chapter 10)
- Practical intelligence (Chapter 11)
- Emotional intelligence (Chapter 11)
- Recent research on the "big five" dimensions of personality (Chapter 12)
- The unconscious (subliminal) conditioning of attitudes (Chapter 12)
- The dimensions of optimism (Chapter 13)
- Self-determination theory and weight loss (Chapter 13)
- Postpartum depression (Chapter 14)
- New information on panic attacks and social phobias (Chapter 14)
- Prescription privileges for psychologists (Chapter 15)
- Efficacy studies (Chapter 15)
- Basic principles of compliance (Chapter 16)
- The effects of overhelping (Chapter 16)
- Perceived unfairness in work settings (Chapter 17)
- Electronic performance monitoring (Chapter 17)

Ancillaries: With a Lot of Help from Some Very Good Friends

Psychology, Fourth Edition, is accompanied by a complete teaching and learning package. Each component has been carefully written to be of the highest quality with both the student and professor in mind. The key parts of this package are described below.

LEARNING AIDS FOR STUDENTS

The **Allyn and Bacon Psychology CD-ROM: "Core Concepts in Psychology"** offers a multimedia exploration into the key topics of introductory psychology. This exciting and innovative CD-ROM covers 14 core topics, and includes the following features:

- *Guided Tour*—A brief tutorial
- *Library*—Offers a resource for all key terms, animations and illustrations, video clips, study skills modules, and more. Students can browse, sort, and click on any area of interest.
- *Topic-by-Topic Exploration*—Provides Guided Question reviews, topic summaries, definitions, illustrations, and animations to enhance students' understanding of psychology's major themes and concepts. Each topic also provides a Video Focus—a short film clip with accompanying critical thinking questions. Each topic concludes with a set of multiple choice items with feedback on right and wrong answers.

Study Guide PLUS! is written by Cathy Seta and John Seta, of Wake Forest University, and Paul Paulus, of the University of Texas at Arlington. This comprehensive study guide offers a carefully structured learning system for all of the important concepts in the text. Organized around chapter learning objectives, it includes a variety of book-specific exercises, review sections, and exercises to strengthen readers' critical thinking and application skills. It provides extra vocabulary help for students who need it, as well as practice tests for each chapter, which are coordinated with the test bank that accompanies the book.

A **Practice Test Booklet** offers additional practice tests and includes answer feedback to explain why each answer is the *correct* choice. Page references to the text are also included to encourage students to review problematic areas before taking their exam.

Electronic Study Guide PLUS is a computerized study guide (for both IBM and Macintosh computers). It includes self-test items with graphics and extensive feedback and reviewing guidelines to enhance the learning process.

Computerized Study Guide is available for IBM computers and features eight enrichment modules on key topics in introductory psychology. Each module is visually enhanced with graphics to facilitate learning and encourage critical thinking.

SoundGuide for Psychology is an innovative learning tool—an audiocassette that reviews and summarizes key concepts with an interactive question-and-answer format.

Additional supplements for students include:

- *Psychologically Speaking: A Self-Assessment*, by Craig P. Donovan and Peter C. Rosato
- *Tools of Critical Thinking: Metathoughts for Psychology*, by David A. Levy
- *Psychology and Culture*, edited by Walter J. Lonner and Roy S. Malpass
- *Evaluating Psychological Information: Sharpening Your Critical Thinking Skills, Second Edition*, by James Bell
- *World of Psychology: Readings in Diversity from The Washington Post*
- *Studying Psychology: A Manual for Success*, by Robert T. Brown

The Annotated Instructor's Edition and Supplements for Instructors

The **Annotated Instructor's Edition** is designed to encourage student involvement and understanding. It includes an **instructor's section** bound into the front of the book and detailed **annotations** in the text margins. The annotations provide teaching suggestions, lecture examples, demonstrations, visual aids, learning objectives, critical thinking excercises, test bank items, and more. The Annotated Instructor's Edition should be used in conjunction with the **Instructor's Resource Manual,** which provides step-by-step instructions for all of the demonstrations and activities, as well as additional detail for many of the lecture examples. Also included are over **150 ready-to-duplicate handouts,** Chapter-at-a-Glance tables that provide a visual means for organizing the many supplementary materials available for each chapter, and an array of additional teaching aids. The Instructor's Resource Manual is also available in computerized form to allow instructors to customize it to meet their individual needs.

Allyn and Bacon's **Psychology Presentation Software,** developed by Dean Richards of California State University at Northridge, is an exciting new multimedia program designed to enhance lecture presentations. The package offers 21 core psychology topics with video animations, simulations, music, and sound effects. In addition, Allyn and Bacon's **Digital Image Archive** offers an array of full-color images that can be reproduced and used in class. **PsychScience** offers hands-on computer simulations that help explain important concepts and theories in psychology.

A Complete set of **acetate transparencies** is also available. A top-notch **computer-ready test bank** provides over 3,000 multiple choice, short-answer, and true-false questions to aid instructors in preparing exams. **Call-In** and **Fax Testing** are also available with one toll-free call to our testing center. Allyn and Bacon is proud to offer an extensive **video library** featuring high quality films on every major topic in introductory psychology. All of these supplements are keyed to the Annotated Instructor's Edition to provide the best integrated teaching package available.

All of the supplements described, and more, are available to qualified adopters of this text. Contact your Allyn and Bacon Sales Representative for more information.

Some Final Comments . . . and a Request for Help

If there's one thing I can't stand, it's a complacent, "know-it-all" attitude. So let me close by asking—sincerely and ardently—for your help. I have truly tried to improve this new edition in every way I could imagine; I have also tried to highlight the theme of "taking psychology with you"—without, I trust, overdoing it. But ultimately only you, the readers of this book, can tell me whether and to what extent I've succeeded. I truly believe the old saying "There's always room for improvement," and I will definitely *not* adopt a stand-pat attitude. So please do write, call, e-mail, or fax me with your comments. I'll listen carefully, and the chances are good that you'll see your ideas reflected in the next edition. My sincere thanks, in advance, for your help.

Robert A. Baron (left) and Michael J. Kalsher

Robert A. Baron
314 Lally
Rensselaer Polytechnic Institute
Troy, NY 12180-3590
Phone (518) 276-2864
FAX (518) 276-8661
E-mail Baronr@rpi.edu

Acknowledgments

This is the thirty-third book with my name somewhere on the cover, and people often ask me, "How do you do it?" My answer always includes two parts: (1) by spending lots of time alone, during which I enter an altered state of consciousness I describe as my "writing frenzy" (as in sharks' "feeding frenzy"); and (2) with lots of help from talented friends and colleagues. In preparing this text, as in all my writing projects, I've once again been the recipient of lots of good help. I wish to acknowledge that assistance here.

First and foremost, my sincere thanks to my good friend and colleague Michael J. Kalsher. He played a primary role in preparing several chapters, in devising the plan for the new edition, and in too many other ways for me to try to list here. In addition, he is certainly one of the few people I'd place in the category "friend for life." It was a lucky day for me when he came to interview at Rensselaer, and an even luckier one when he agreed to join our department.

Second, I wish to express my thanks to the many colleagues who read and commented on various portions of the manuscript, as well as on past editions of this book. Their comments and suggestions were exceptionally constructive and certainly shaped the final content and features of this book in important ways. They include:

George Armstrong
Bucks County Community College

Janice Beal
Prairie View A&M University

Rebecca Bigler
University of Texas–Austin

Dennis Cogan
Texas Technical University

Leslie Eckert
Mankato State University

Michael Elhert
Brigham Young University

Linda Flickinger
St. Clair County Community College

Grace Galliano
Kennesaw State College

William Gibson
North Arizona University

Alan Glaros
University of Missouri–Kansas City

Karl Haberlandt
Trinity College

Tracy Henley
Mississippi State University

Charles Kaiser
College of Charleston

Richard King
University of North Carolina–Chapel Hill

John Long
Mt. San Antonio College

Joseph Lowman
University of North Carolina–Chapel Hill

David McDonald
University of Missouri–Columbia

Kristelle Miller
University of Minnesota–Duluth

Ben Newkirk
Grossmont College

Alan Schultz
Prince George's Community College

In addition, my sincere thanks to the following colleagues who reviewed the third edition of this book:

Norman Austin
Monroe Community College

Janice Beal
Prairie View A&M University

Deborah Best
Wake Forest University

Jerry Bruce
Sam Houston State University

James Calhoun
University of Georgia

William Calhoun
University of Tennessee

Lynda Dogen
North Harris County College

William Dwyer
Memphis State University

Louis Fusilli
Monroe Community College

Grace Galliano
Kennesaw State College

Dashiel Geyen
University of Houston–Downtown

William Gibson
Northern Arizona State University

Alan Glaros
University of Missouri–Kansas City

Wayne Hall
San Jacinto College–Central

Tracy Henley
Mississippi State University

John Hensley
Tulsa Junior College

Charles Hinderliter
University of Pittsburgh

Carol Huntsinger
College of Lake County

Charles Kaiser
College of Charleston

Richard King
University of North Carolina–Chapel Hill

Clixie Larson
Utah Valley State College

Charles Levinthal
Hofstra University

Paul Levy
University of Akron

Joseph Lowman
University of North Carolina–Chapel Hill

Richard Marrocco
University of Oregon

Cameron Melville
McNeese State University

Ed Merrill
University of Alabama

Gordon Pitz
Southern Illinois University–Carbondale

Joseph Porter
Virginia Commonwealth University

Adrian Rapp
North Harris County College

Michael Robbins
University of Utah

Jerome Rosenberg
University of Alabama

Peter Rowe
College of Charleston

Richard Serkes
Tulsa Junior College–Metro Campus

Cathy Seta
Wake Forest University

Robert Siegler
Carnegie Mellon University

Mary Helen Spear
Prince George's Community College

Granville Sydnor
San Jacinto College–North

James Thomas
University of Nebraska–Omaha

Ross Thompson
University of Nebraska

John Williford
County College of Morris

I also want to extend my personal thanks to Sean Wakely, vice president and editor-in-chief at Allyn and Bacon. His support for the new edition has been unwavering, and his advice and encouragement have certainly played an important role in bringing it to fruition. I look forward to working with him for many, many years.

It's also a pleasure, once again, to express my appreciation to Beth Brooks, my developmental editor. Beth's comments and suggestions are *always* highly constructive, and are often just plain invaluable. It's a pleasure to work with someone who is at once both highly professional *and* highly sympathetic.

Next, I'd like to thank Annette Joseph, my production editor, for her outstanding help in keeping the project on track and pulling all the loose (and often maddening!) ends together.

I also wish to thank Jay Howland for a careful, intelligent, and thought-provoking job of copy-editing. She certainly helped me to combat my all-too-professorlike tendency toward wordiness, and also to clarify important points that might otherwise have "slipped between the cracks."

And speaking of slipping through the cracks, I want to take this opportunity to thank Peg Latham for her outstanding work in coordinating many elements of the production process. Her help was truly invaluable, and I look forward to working with her again in the future, too.

Finally, my thanks to several friends and colleagues for their outstanding work on various ancillaries. These are essential to helping students learn, so I'm truly indebted to these persons for their help. Mark Garrison has produced an exceptionally complete and useful set of instructor materials. Tom Jackson has prepared superior test items to accompany the text. Cathy Seta, John Seta, and Paul Paulus have once again written a top-notch study guide.

To all these truly exceptional people, and to many others too, I offer my warm personal regards.

CHAPTER OUTLINE

Psychology

A Science . . . and a Perspective

It never fails. I'm at a party, talking to someone I've just met, when they ask: "What's your field?" My answer, "I'm a psychologist," usually produces one of three different reactions. Some people—I refer to them as "believers"—show obvious pleasure and interest, and begin to ask me for my views on a wide range of issues relating to human behavior. "Do cigarette ads really make teenagers start to smoke?" "Can people really lose weight through hypnosis?" "Is depression inherited?"

A second group, which I describe as "opportunists," reacts quite differently. They seem to view our conversation as a chance to obtain free advice and counseling. They tell me about their feelings and problems, and sometimes they reveal intimate details of their lives. Then they request my advice, insights, and recommendations on these matters.

The third group, which I describe as "skeptics," wastes little time putting me in my place. They let me know, in no uncertain terms, that in their opinion psychology is not all it's cracked up to be. They often voice the opinion that *they* know more about people than any psychologist, and they remind me that they've been "doing" psychology their entire lives.

What do these experiences tell me? Primarily, two things. First, that many people—most, in fact—are deeply interested in psychology. They view it as a source of fascinating and potentially useful information about themselves and other persons, and as a source of valuable help with their personal problems. Second, these experiences also remind me that not everyone shares these views. On the contrary, the group I label "skeptics" have serious doubts about the value and usefulness of psychology.

In a sense, this book is dedicated to all three groups. For those who are already convinced of the appeal and value of psychology, it will offer an overview of a vast array of findings—helpful and intriguing information about virtually every aspect of human behavior you can imagine. For the skeptics, it will provide what I firmly believe will be a solid basis for changing their views—for coming to see psychology as the fascinating and useful field that it is.

But this book is designed to do much more than merely summarize a broad slice of psychology's varied findings: it is also directed toward the goal of providing you with a *new perspective on human behavior.* I have long believed that psychology offers far more than a collection of interesting facts; it provides a new way of thinking about your own feelings, thoughts, and actions, plus those of other persons. After reading this book, I firmly believe, *you will never think about yourself, other people, and your relations with them in quite the same way as before.* And, I also predict, this new way of thinking will enrich your life in many different ways.

I have long believed that psychology offers far more than a collection of interesting facts; it provides a new way of thinking about your own feelings, thoughts, and actions, plus those of other persons.

"What?" I can almost hear the skeptics among you saying. "Is this guy for real?" My reply to such reactions is provided by the remainder of this chapter. In it, I'll attempt to accomplish three major tasks. First, I'll explain just what psychology is and where it came from. In other words, I'll define the field, say a few words about its roots, and describe its scope as we stand on the threshold of a new century. Next, I'll briefly describe the training of psychologists and various specialties in which they work. After that, I'll turn to the *scientific method* and explain how psychologists—and you—can use it. Included here will be discussion of *critical thinking,* a careful, cautious, and open-minded approach to thinking about human behavior and many other topics. These discussions will be followed by an examination of the major *research methods* psychologists use in their efforts to add to our knowledge of human behavior. While careful research helps to answer one set of questions, the process of conducting such research raises another set of questions—ethical issues relating to the research itself. I'll consider these complex issues in another section of this chapter.

After completing these major tasks, I'll offer an overview of the special features of this book—features designed to enhance the value of this, your first college-level course in psychology. Finally, I'll provide some concrete suggestions on how to study psychology—or any other subject—effectively. Now, let's begin with an overview of modern psychology.

Modern Psychology: What It Is and Where It Came From

Have you ever seen the television program *Connections?* In it, the brilliant historian and reporter James Burke explained how seemingly unrelated and unconnected events and ideas can combine to cause major advances in technology—and improvements in human welfare. For example, he traced the development of the internal combustion engine, and therefore of the automobile, to changes in the climate in Europe in the twelfth century. How could these seemingly unrelated events be linked? Here are the intervening steps:

- In the twelfth century, the climate of Europe became, quite suddenly, much colder. This led to changes in the construction of houses; instead of single large rooms in which everyone slept and ate, houses were divided into many smaller rooms, each heated by its own fireplace. In addition, interior walls were lined with plaster and fitted with glass windows. The result: warmer rooms, which encouraged many kinds of indoor activities—including, some complained, too much lovemaking!
- Production of plaster and glass required lots of fuel, which, at the time, was wood from the forests. The result: Trees were cut at an ever increasing rate. By the fifteenth century, forests in England and several other European countries were largely gone, so the need for other fuel became critical.
- People met this need by mining coal, but coal near the surface was full of impurities and was not suitable for making glass: The impurities released when the coal was burned contaminated the glass. Coal from deeper down was better, but it could not be mined because of water in the deep shafts. The result: development of pumps employing a moving piston. Refinements of these pumps to use steam in a more efficient way led directly to the idea for a carburetor, a special device for mixing air and fuel.
- When the piston cylinder and the carburetor were combined with other, seemingly unrelated developments, the result was the internal combustion engine and then—soon after—the first practical automobiles (see Figure 1.1 on page 6).

Connections and the Emergence of Psychology

What does this excursion into history have to do with the development of psychology? Nothing directly; but it provides a good model of how the process occurred—how several trends, ideas, and developments in philosophy and several fields of science combined to produce the idea of a field that uses scientific methods to study human behavior. From philosophy came two key ideas: *empiricism,* the view that knowledge can be gathered through careful observation, and *rationalism,* the view that knowledge can be gained through logic and careful reasoning. When these ideas were combined, they produced the basic ground rules of modern science, to which we'll return below.

FIGURE 1.1

Connections between Seemingly Unrelated Events

A complex chain of seemingly unrelated events led from a change in the climate of Europe during the twelfth century to the development of the internal combustion engine. In a similar manner, the idea of a scientific field of psychology grew out of the convergence of several developments that, at first glance, might seem totally unconnected with each other.

When these new rules for investigating the world around us were put into practice, important advances in many fields of science occurred—and with gathering speed. Some of these advances—especially discoveries in the field of *physiology,* the branch of biology that studies the functions of living organisms—were directly related to the emergence of psychology. For example, during the late nineteenth century, Johannes Muller described how signals were conducted by nerves within the body; Hermann von Helmholtz reported findings on how receptors in the eyes and ears receive and interpret sensations from the outside world; and Gustav Fechner demonstrated that seemingly hidden mental events, such as perceptions, could be precisely measured. Together, these diverse lines of research converged on the following idea: *Why not use the methods of science as a basis for studying human behavior?* A famous figure in the history of psychology, Wilhelm Wundt, was an ardent believer in this idea. In addition, he was also an impressive—and persuasive—figure (see Figure 1.2). Indeed, so convincing was Wundt that in 1879 he managed to sell his colleagues at the University of Leipzig (Germany) on the validity of an independent science of psychology. We'll never know whether his colleagues fully accepted Wundt's beliefs, but they did provide the funding for the first laboratory for psychological research. By 1879, then, the idea of an independent, science-based psychology had taken shape and was spreading throughout the academic world. What was this new field like? And how did it develop in the decades that followed? Let's take a brief look at these important issues.

Psychology: From Small Beginnings . . . to a Thriving Field

Although Wundt held firmly to the idea of a scientific field of psychology, his conception of what this science should involve was quite different from that held by most psychologists today. Wundt believed that psychology should study *consciousness*—what goes on inside our minds. Consistent with this view (which was known as *structuralism* because it focused on the structure of the human mind), Wundt focused his research on such tasks as analyzing sensations, feelings, and images into their most basic parts, largely through the method of *introspection,* in which individuals describe what is going on in their own minds.

Structuralism was gradually rejected by psychologists in the United States, who moved, over a period of years, toward another idea: psychology should study only what we can *observe*—overt behavior. The most radical spokesperson for this view, known as **behaviorism,** was John B. Watson. Watson argued forcefully that only observable, overt activities can be measured in a scientific manner. Thus, only these should be part of a scientific field of psychology. In contrast, Watson held, internal events such as thoughts, images, feelings, and intentions are unmeasurable, and so should not be part of the new science.

So compelling were the arguments offered by Watson and other behaviorists, such as B. F. Skinner, that their conception of psychology defined the field for more than forty years—right up until the 1960s, when I was a graduate student working on my Ph.D. degree. The 1960s seemed to be a time of major change in many respects, and psychology was no exception to this general pattern. During that decade, psychology expanded its scope to recapture the mental events that Watson and others had written off as outside the proper domain of this field. Why did this shift take place? Again, the answer seems to involve a convergence of several independent trends.

First, advances in technology during the 1960s provided new or improved techniques for studying mental events—for instance, techniques that involved the use of computers. Computers made it possible, for example, to expose individuals to specific stimuli in a very precise manner, and then to measure the speed of their reactions, again with great precision. Researchers could use such measurements for drawing inferences about underlying mental processes (see Figure 1.3 on page 8). In a similar manner, other equipment permitted rapid and accurate measurement of subtle internal changes in bodily states such as heart rate, blood pressure, and electrical activity within the brain. Together, these new technologies offered psychologists important new tools for measuring what had been, in the past, largely unmeasurable.

Second, a growing body of scientific findings on mental processes such as memory had been quietly but steadily accumulating during the 1940s and 1950s. As this knowledge increased, it generated important new insights into the nature of these processes. When this growing body of knowledge was combined with the new research techniques described earlier, the result was something many psychologists describe as the *cognitive revolution*—a tremendous surge in interest, within psychology, in the task of studying mental events or, as psychologists prefer to term them, *cognitive processes.* You'll see the results of this "revolution" in later chapters, where we'll focus on many aspects of cognition, such as perception, dreams, moods, attitudes, problem solving, and memory.

As a result of the events described above, most psychologists now define their field as follows: **Psychology** is *the science of behavior and cognitive processes.* This is the view I'll adopt in this book; and, as will soon be clear, it is a definition that permits psychologists to study virtually every aspect of human behavior and human experience. Why? Because by the term *behavior* psychologists mean any observable action or reaction by a living organism—everything from overt actions (anything we say or do) through subtle changes in the electrical activity occurring deep within our brains. If it can be observed and measured, then it fits within the boundaries of "behavior." Similarly, by the term *cognitive processes* psychologists mean every aspect of our mental life—our thoughts, our memories, mental images, how we reason, how we make decisions and judgments, and so on. One final point: Although our definition mentions both behavior and cognitive processes, I'll use the term *behavior* to represent both, simply to avoid repeating the phrase "behavior and cognitive processes" over and over again.

FIGURE 1.2

Wilhelm Wundt, One of the Founders of Modern Psychology

Wundt was a strong advocate for an independent, scientific field of psychology. So impressive were his arguments—and his personality!—that in 1879 Wundt succeeded in founding the first laboratory for psychological research.

Behaviorism: The view that only observable, overt activities that can be measured scientifically should be studied by psychology.

Psychology: The science of behavior and cognitive processes.

Modern Psychology: Grand Issues, Key Perspectives

Several years ago, I went to the thirtieth reunion of my high school class. I hadn't been to any previous reunions, so I knew I was in for an interesting time. Would I be able to recognize my former classmates? Would they be able to recognize me? The results were mixed. Everyone had changed physically, of course; but, amazingly, I could still recognize many people. And even those who had changed so much physically that I couldn't recognize their faces still showed many of the same traits I remembered from thirty years earlier. Why do I mention this experience? Because it calls attention to one of what might be termed psychology's "grand issues"—large-scale questions or themes that seem to crosscut the field. This question, of course, has to do with *stability versus change:* To what extent do we remain stable over time, and to what extent do we change? We'll meet this issue over and over again in this book, as we address changes over time in cognitive abilities, physical functioning, personality, and other aspects of behavior (e.g., Cohen & Reese, 1994).

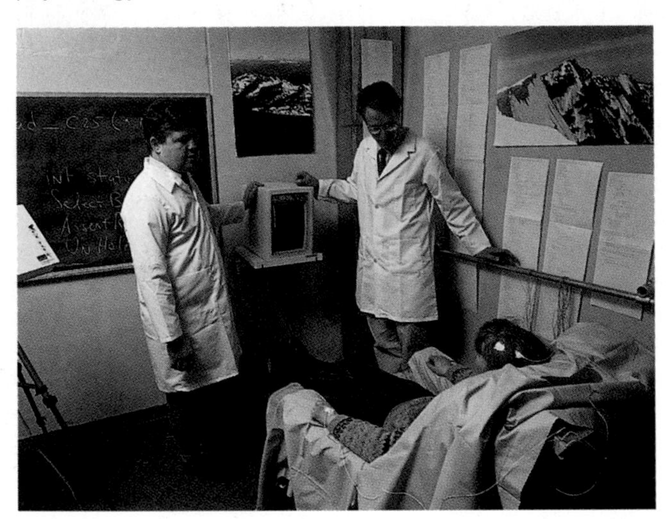

FIGURE 1.3

Computers and the Study of Cognitive Processes

Because they allow for very precise control over the presentation of stimulus materials and precise measurement of the speed of response to these materials, computers provided psychologists with a powerful new tool for studying mental (cognitive) processes—processes early behaviorists felt were beyond the scope of psychology.

A second, and closely related, theme centers around the following question: To what extent are various aspects of our behavior determined by inherited tendencies, and to what extent are they learned—shaped by experience with the world around us? This is usually known as the *nature–nurture* question, and we'll meet it repeatedly in the coming chapters. Does aggression stem primarily from innate tendencies, or is it the result of experience and "triggers" in a current situation (see Figure 1.4)? Is intelligence inherited, or shaped by early experience? Are differences in the behavior of women and men due in part to biological factors, or to the impact of contrasting child-rearing experiences and society's beliefs about gender differences? This is only a small sampling of the questions we'll examine relating to this major theme. As you'll soon see, growing evidence indicates that the answer to this question is definitely *not* one suggesting that either environment or heredity dominates; rather, many aspects of behavior seem to represent the result of complex interactions between these factors. The key question, then, is not "Which one dominates?" but rather "To what extent do nature and nurture influence specific forms of behavior—and how?"

Now for the third major theme. Answer quickly: Would you eat a piece of chocolate shaped exactly like a spider—bulging eyes, long hairy legs, fangs, and all? If you experience some reluctance, you are like many people in this situation. But now ask yourself, *Why* would you be reluctant to do so? The chocolate has no relationship to a real spider in any manner. So, why would the fact that it has been shaped to resemble a spider cause you to hesitate? The answer, in most general terms, is straightforward: in many cases, we are *not* completely rational. We know very well what the logical response or reaction would be, but our reason is overridden by our emotions. This is one illustration of a third grand theme you'll find in your study of psychology: *rationality versus irrationality*. Sometimes we do seem to operate in a largely rational manner, making decisions and reaching conclusions in accordance with the laws of logic—or, perhaps, as a computer would proceed. But in many other instances, we behave in a manner that is *not* consistent with the cold light of logic. Have you ever been overoptimistic in estimating how long

FIGURE 1.4

The Nature–Nurture Question in Action

To what extent are various aspects of behavior shaped by experience, and to what extent are they shaped by inherited tendencies? Calvin has his own answer, but his mother probably has a sharply different view.

Calvin and Hobbes **by Bill Watterson**

it would take you to complete a task? Have you ever lashed out at other people not because of something they did or said, but mainly because you were feeling rotten? If so, then you already have firsthand experience with the less than completely rational side of human behavior. This is another theme to which we'll return again and again in this book, as we examine such issues as decision making, eyewitness testimony, and social perception (how we perceive other persons and make judgments about them).

So be on the watch for these three grand issues—they are central questions that have captured the attention of psychologists for decades, and with which—I predict—the field will still be wrestling well into the next century.

Key Perspectives in Psychology: The Many Facets of Behavior Imagine the following scene: A young woman walks into the middle of a large arena, watched by a crowd of many thousands of people. Suddenly a large bull enters. The woman waves a red cape at the bull, and it charges her; she steps out of the way at the last moment, and the crowd cheers enthusiastically. Again and again the woman waves the cape and the bull charges. After many narrow but graceful escapes from the bull's horns, she kills the animal with one skilled and mercifully quick stroke of a sword (see Figure 1.5 on page 10). The crowd goes wild with admiration.

How would a psychologist interpret this intriguing situation? The answer is: from any of several different perspectives. In other words, there is a great deal going on here, and it is possible to focus on these events from different standpoints. One, known as the *behavioral* perspective, would emphasize the overt behaviors occurring—the bullfighter's actions, the charges by the bull, the reactions of the crowd. Another, the *cognitive* perspective, would focus on cognitive factors in this situation, such as the young woman's thoughts as the scene unfolds: what is passing through her mind, what strategies does she plan? How did she ever choose this career in the first place?

A third perspective would emphasize the *biological factors* that play a role in this situation. What are the emotions of the bullfighter as she faces the charging bull, what are the emotions of the crowd, and how are these reactions reflected in the participants' blood pressure, heart rate, and other bod-

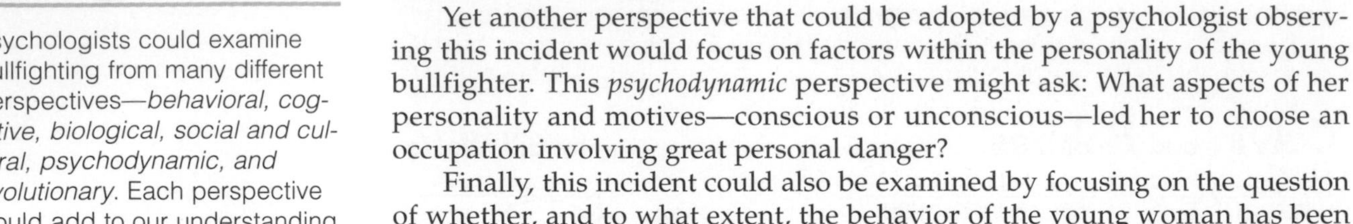

ily states? A fourth perspective would focus on *social and cultural* factors. Why, for instance, is bullfighting so popular in some cultures but not in others? How did a young woman manage to gain entry to a field that was until recently the sole domain of men?

Yet another perspective that could be adopted by a psychologist observing this incident would focus on factors within the personality of the young bullfighter. This *psychodynamic* perspective might ask: What aspects of her personality and motives—conscious or unconscious—led her to choose an occupation involving great personal danger?

Finally, this incident could also be examined by focusing on the question of whether, and to what extent, the behavior of the young woman has been influenced by inherited tendencies—from an *evolutionary* perspective. For example, do people engage in risky actions such as bullfighting because of a strong, inherited human desire for excitement and stimulation? Does bullfighting, perhaps, reflect our biological heritage as hunters (e.g., Buss, 1997)?

FIGURE 1.5

Perspectives of Modern Psychology

Psychologists could examine bullfighting from many different perspectives—*behavioral, cognitive, biological, social and cultural, psychodynamic, and evolutionary*. Each perspective would add to our understanding of these events. (See Table 1.1 for a description of these perspectives.)

The key point to remember is this: Human behavior is extraordinarily complex and is influenced by many different factors. Thus, any aspect of behavior can be examined from many different perspectives. All these perspectives can add to our understanding of behavior, so all will be represented throughout this book. (Table 1.1 summarizes these contrasting perspectives.)

Psychology in a Diverse World: The Multicultural Perspective

In 1958, when I was a high school junior, my uncle gave me an interesting book, a guide for Europeans visiting the United States for the first time. A section describing the ethnic background of the people of the United States began with the following statement: "The population of the

TABLE 1.1

Major Perspectives of Modern Psychology

As shown here, psychology studies behavior from many different perspectives.

Perspective	Description
Behavioral	Focuses on overt behavior
Cognitive	Focuses on cognitive processes such as memory, thought, reasoning
Biological	Focuses on the biological events and processes that underlie behavior
Sociocultural	Focuses on all aspects of social behavior and on the impact of cultural factors on behavior
Psychodynamic	Focuses on personality and on the role of hidden, often unconscious processes on behavior
Evolutionary	Focuses on the possible role of inherited tendencies in various aspects of behavior

United States is approximately 90 percent of European descent." How the United States—and the world!—has changed since then. Consider these statistics:

- In California, the most populous state in the United States, there is now no single majority group; rather, the population (more than 31 million) consists of many different groups, with persons of Hispanic and Asian descent showing the fastest growth in numbers.
- Current projections by the Census Bureau indicate that by the year 2050, 53 percent of the population of the United States will be of European descent, 21 percent will be Americans of Hispanic descent, 15 percent will be African Americans, and 11 percent will be Asian Americans (see Figure 1.6).
- Ethnic diversity in U.S. colleges and universities has increased greatly in recent years; approximately 78 percent of students are of European descent, 9.2 percent African American, 5.5 percent of Hispanic descent, and 4 percent Asian American; the remainder are foreign, Native American, and from other ethnic backgrounds too numerous to list here (Chronicle of Higher Education, 1992). The percentage of students who are female has also increased; and at the graduate level, females are now the recipients of the majority of advanced degrees in many fields, including psychology.
- As recently as 1970, more than 98 percent of the people living in countries such as France, Germany, and Italy were native born; today, this figure has dropped sharply, and it will continue to decrease in the face of massive migration from Eastern Europe, Africa, and Asia.

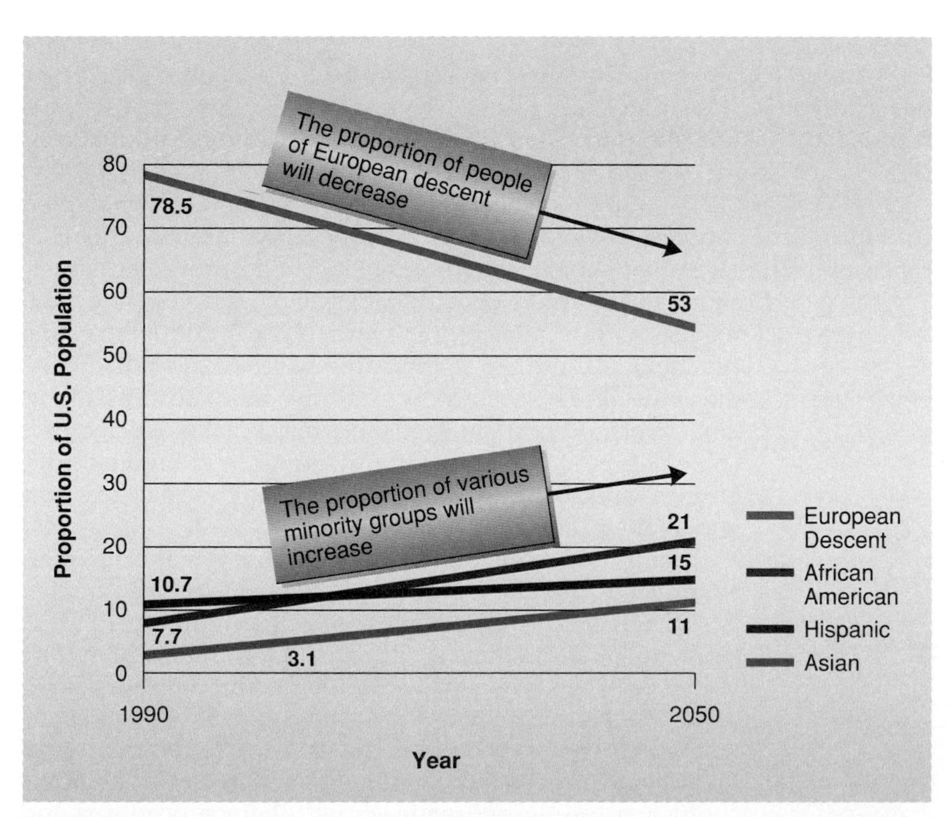

(**Source:** Based on data collected by the U.S. Department of Labor as reported by Carnevale & Stone, 1995.)

FIGURE 1.6

Increasing Diversity: Definitely the Wave of the Future in the United States

As shown here, the proportion of various minority groups is projected to increase sharply in the United States in the future. Similar trends are also occurring in many other countries.

Multicultural Perspective: In psychology, an approach that pays careful attention to the effects of ethnic and cultural factors on behavior.

- In 1950, 63.9 percent of the U.S. civilian labor force was composed of white males. By 1990 this figure had dropped to 43.1 percent, and by 2005 it is estimated that it will drop to 38.2 percent.

Similar trends have occurred around the world, as increased trade and immigration have led to increasingly diverse populations in many different countries. Psychologists are well aware of these trends, and this awareness has led, in recent years, to the adoption of an increasingly **multicultural perspective** within the field. This new perspective is reflected in a growing volume of research on the effects of ethnic and cultural factors on many aspects of behavior. Indeed, there is hardly an area of psychology in which research on such issues is not currently on the rise (e.g., Lonner & Malpass, 1994). In later chapters, therefore, we will examine topics such as these:

- Does Culture Influence Memory? (Chapter 6)
- Cross-National Differences in Mathematical Competence—Why It's Harder to Learn to Count in Some Languages Than in Others (Chapter 8)
- Life Stages and Social Events: Evidence for the View That We Are Strongly Shaped by the Events of Our Youth—the Case of the Women's Movement (Chapter 9)
- Sexual Jealousy and Aggression: Some Surprising Gender Differences (Chapter 10)
- Genetic Factors and Group Differences in IQ Scores: Ringing Down the Curtain on *The Bell Curve* (Chapter 11)
- Are There Ethnic Differences in Reactions to Psychotropic Drugs? (Chapter 15)
- Attribution and Rape: Blaming Innocent Victims (Chapter 16)
- Race, Gender, and Mentoring Leadership (Chapter 17)

In addition, psychologists' growing concern with multicultural diversity has led to the formulation of guidelines for providing psychological services (for example, counseling) to ethnically and culturally diverse populations (American Psychological Association, 1993b). These guidelines call for psychologists to recognize cultural diversity and take full account of it in all their activities. For example, psychologists must provide information to clients in forms and languages that people from different cultural groups can understand; they must be certain that psychological tests are valid for use with various ethnic groups; and in understanding psychological processes, including psychological disorders, they must recognize ethnic background and culture as important factors. In short, the guidelines insist that practicing psychologists be sensitive to cultural, ethnic, and linguistic differences and that they build awareness of these differences into all their professional activities.

In this and many other ways, psychology as a field has attempted to adopt a multicultural perspective. The situation is still not perfect—far from it (e.g., Gannon et al., 1992; Graham, 1992); but there is widespread recognition of the fact that psychologists must take careful account of growing ethnic diversity in all their activities. These include basic research, where participants should be chosen to be representative of the different groups now present in many societies, and psychological testing and counseling, where procedures and tests should be designed for and sensitive to cultural and ethnic differences.

Key Questions

- What ideas and trends converged to give rise to an independent, science-based field of psychology?
- What is the definition of psychology?
- What are the three "grand issues" about behavior with which psychology must grapple?
- What are key differences between the various perspectives adopted by psychologists—the behavioral, cognitive, biological, social and cultural, psychodynamic, and evolutionary?
- How do psychologists take account of cultural diversity in their research and in providing psychological services?

Psychologists: Who They Are and What They Do

Now that you know something about the nature and scope of psychology, let's turn briefly to two related issues: who psychologists are and what they actually do.

Who: The Training of Psychologists

The terms *psychiatrist* and *psychologist* are quite similar, so it is not surprising that many persons think they mean the same thing. In fact, though, they refer to two different groups of professionals. Psychiatrists are physicians who, after completing medical studies, specialize in the treatment of mental disorders. In contrast, psychologists receive their training in graduate programs of psychology, where they earn both a master's degree and, in most cases, either a Ph.D. or a Psy.D. (Doctor of Psychology) degree. The Ph.D. and Psy.D. degrees require a minimum of four to five years of study beyond college. In addition, psychologists who choose to specialize in certain areas of their field, such as the treatment of psychological disorders, must also complete one or more years of practical experience in a hospital, clinic, school, or business.

Clearly, then, psychologists and psychiatrists receive different kinds of training. So why are the two fields often confused? In part because many psychologists specialize in the diagnosis, study, and treatment of psychological (mental) disorders. As a result, they focus on many of the same problems and perform many of the same activities as psychiatrists. In fact, members of the two fields often work closely together in the same mental health facilities. Since only some psychologists focus on mental disorders, though, the two fields are definitely not identical.

Now that we've clarified the difference between psychologists and psychiatrists, here are a few facts about psychologists themselves:

- There are now more than 200,000 psychologists in North America alone (Fowler, 1993).

- Of these almost 50 percent are female. This represents a marked increase in the proportion of females; as recently as the 1950s, only about 10 percent of all psychologists were women (American Psychological Association, 1993a).
- At present, a majority of the Ph.D. degrees being awarded in psychology are received by women.
- As a group, psychologists are relatively young. Almost half received their Ph.D. degree between 1970 and 1979. Thus, many psychologists are in their forties or fifties.
- More than 3,000 doctoral-level degrees are awarded in psychology each year (Rosenzweig, 1992).

What: Subfields of Psychology

I have a good friend who was married to a physician for many years. She knows I'm a psychologist, and she also knows that I do *not* specialize in treating mental disorders. Yet, every now and then, she makes some remark about "my patients" and the many problems they must have. My friend's mistake illustrates the commonly held idea that all psychologists engage in counseling or therapy. This idea is not entirely wrong, since about half of all psychologists do, in fact, specialize in such activities. But there are also many other different specialties or subfields in psychology, and this means that psychologists do many different things. Table 1.2 gives a brief description of some of psychology's major subfields. As you can see from even a glance at this table, psychologists specialize in studying many different forms of behavior, and perform their work in many different settings.

I should also note that whatever their specific subfield, many psychologists engage in *research*—they work hard to acquire new information about human behavior and cognitive processes. The specific content of this research varies from subfield to subfield. For example, a *clinical psychologist* might study such topics as the effects of depression on memory (Backman, Hill, & Forsell, 1996), while a child psychologist—one who specializes in studying the behavior and development of children—might investigate the effects of stress early in life on children's later language development (e.g., Hura & Echols, 1996). Moreover, while some psychologists engage in *basic research*—research designed to increase our understanding of basic psychological processes (such as memory or learning)—other psychologists focus on *applied*

TABLE 1.2

The Major Subfields of Psychology

Psychologists specialize in studying many different aspects of behavior. The approximate percentage of all psychologists in each specialty is shown in this table; other subfields not listed separately make up the missing percentage.

Subfield	Description	Percentage
Clinical psychology	Studies diagnosis, causes, and treatment of mental disorders	43
Counseling psychology	Assists individuals in dealing with many personal problems that do not involve psychological disorders	10
Developmental psychology	Studies how people change physically, cognitively, and socially over the entire life span	5
Educational psychology	Studies all aspects of the educational process	6
Experimental psychology	Studies all basic psychological processes, including perception, learning, and motivation	14
Cognitive psychology	Investigates all aspects of cognition—memory, thinking, reasoning, language, decision making, and so on	
Industrial/organizational psychology	Studies all aspects of behavior in work settings	4
Biopsychology	Investigates the biological bases of behavior	1
Social psychology	Studies all aspects of social behavior and social thought—how we think about and interact with others	6

FIGURE 1.7

The Design of Clear Controls: An Example of Applied Psychological Research

Psychologists who specialize in *human factors* often conduct applied research on the design of controls, such as those used in operating automobiles or household appliances.

research—research designed to deal with practical problems. For example, psychologists in a specialty known as *human factors* focus on helping engineers to design equipment that is easy and convenient for human beings to use (Andre & Segal, 1993); see Figure 1.7 for an example of one situation in which such research is sorely needed!

The line between basic and applied research is far from hard-and-fast; psychologists in many subfields move back and forth, in their work, from efforts to add to our basic knowledge (basic research) to attempts to solve practical problems (applied research). In fact, these two endeavors should be, and usually are, complementary in nature.

Key Questions

- How does the training of psychologists differ from that of psychiatrists?
- What are the major subfields of psychology, and what aspects of behavior do they study?

Psychology and the Scientific Method

In a sense, we are all psychologists. From time to time, we all think about our own feelings and actions and those of other persons. Such informal efforts to make sense out of human behavior have continued for thousands of years—probably since our species first emerged on earth. As a result, we have at our disposal not only our own experience and observations, but also the collected thoughts of countless philosophers, poets, and writers. This fact leads to an intriguing—and important—question: Is the knowledge provided by psychology different, in any important way, from this accumulated "wisdom of the ages"? Or is it simply "more of the same"—the result of doing on a full-time basis what most of us do only occasionally? My reply is simple: The knowledge gathered by psychologists *is* different from that provided by intuition and common sense; it is both more accurate and more useful than knowledge of behavior acquired through informal means. Why is this so? Primarily because in their quest for greater understanding of human behavior, psychologists rely heavily on the *scientific method*. Now, to add substance to this reply, I'll explain what the scientific method is, what advantages it offers, and how it helps psychologists to think in a special way—logically and scientifically—about human behavior.

The Scientific Method: Its Basic Nature

To many people, the term *science* conjures up images of white-coated individuals working around mysterious equipment in impressive laboratories.

On the basis of such images, people often assume that the word *science* applies only to fields such as chemistry, physics, or biology. Actually, however, this term refers simply to a special approach for acquiring knowledge—an approach involving the use of several systematic methods for gathering information plus adherence to several key values or standards. Viewed in this light, the phrase *scientific method* refers simply to using these methods and adopting these values and standards in efforts to study virtually any topic—any aspect of the world around us. Since, as human beings, we too are part of the natural world, the scientific method can certainly be applied to the study of human behavior and cognition. It is this adoption of the scientific method that makes psychology a science—and that makes the information it acquires so valuable.

Since the actual procedures used to gather data by means of the scientific method are described in detail in a later section, I'll concentrate here on the values and standards that are essential components of the scientific method. Among the most important are these:

- *Accuracy:* A commitment to gathering and evaluating information about the world in as careful, precise, and error-free a manner as possible.
- *Objectivity:* A commitment to obtaining and evaluating such information in a manner that is as free from bias as humanly possible.
- *Skepticism:* A commitment to accepting findings as accurate only after they have been verified over and over again, preferably by many different scientists working independently.
- *Open-Mindedness:* A commitment to changing one's views—even views that are strongly held—in the face of evidence that shows these views to be inaccurate.

Psychology, as a field, is deeply committed to these values, and applies the scientific method in its efforts to increase our knowledge of human behavior and cognitive processes. It is primarily for this reason that it makes sense to describe psychology as a science. In short, psychology plays by the rules, and so qualifies fully as a scientific field.

At this point I should quickly note that while it is relatively easy to state the standards listed above, it is quite another matter to put them into practice. *Skepticism* is perhaps the easiest to attain, because it is built into all fields of science: scientists, psychologists included, learn, as part of their training, to say "Show me!" before accepting any statements or conclusions as true. *Accuracy* can be enhanced by the use of only the best measuring instruments available—whether these are sophisticated equipment for measuring internal bodily reactions such as blood pressure, or special tests designed to measure various aspects of personality (see Chapter 12). Implementing the values of *objectivity* and *open-mindedness,* however, require special training—and special forms of self-discipline.

Scientists, like everyone else, have personal views or attitudes (see Chapter 16) on various issues—including the ones they study. And like everyone else, scientists prefer to have their views confirmed rather than refuted. As you can readily see, this poses a potential problem any time a scientist's personal views are relevant to some aspect of her or his research. The danger is that the scientist may be tempted to conduct the research in such a manner, or to interpret the results in such a way, as to confirm these views. Such errors do not have to be conscious or overt to occur; as we'll see in later chapters, our personal views can sometimes influence our judgments or perceptions in subtle ways of which we are not aware (see Chapter 7). So all scientists—including psychologists—must always be on guard against the possibility that their own views and preferences will interfere, to some degree, with their objectivity and open-mindedness.

The Role of Theory in the Scientific Method There is one more aspect of the scientific method we should consider before concluding this discussion. In their research, scientists seek to do more than simply describe the world: they want to be able to *explain* it as well. For example, a chemist is not content merely to describe what happens when two chemicals are brought into contact with one another—she or he also wants to be able to explain *why* this reaction takes place. Similarly, a psychologist studying memory is not content merely to describe the extent to which individuals forget various kinds of information; the psychologist also wants to be able to explain *why* such forgetting occurs, and the nature of forgetting itself (which we'll examine in detail in Chapter 6). The scientific method, therefore, involves the construction of **theories**—frameworks for explaining various events or processes. The procedures involved go something like this:

1. On the basis of existing evidence, a theory that reflects this evidence is formulated.
2. This theory, which consists of some basic concepts and statements about how these concepts are related, helps to organize existing information and makes predictions about observable events. For instance, the theory might predict the conditions under which certain forms of behavior will occur.
3. These predictions, known as **hypotheses,** are then tested by actual observations—by further research.
4. If results of new observations are consistent with the theory, confidence in its accuracy is increased. If they are not, the theory is modified and further tests are conducted.
5. Ultimately, the theory is either accepted as accurate or rejected as inaccurate. Even if it is accepted as accurate, however, the theory remains open to further refinement, as additional research is conducted.

This may sound a bit abstract, so perhaps a concrete example will help. Imagine that a psychologist has formulated a theory to explain the fact that often, people seem to become trapped into "throwing good money after bad"—once they have made a decision, they feel compelled to stick with it, even if it has turned out badly. Thus, they continue to invest time, effort, and money in a losing course of action. (This is known as *escalation of commitment,* and we'll examine it in more detail in Chapter 7.) A theory designed to explain this effect might go something like this: People get trapped in bad decisions because once they have made them, they feel a strong need to justify these decisions to others. Since admitting they made a mistake runs counter to this need, they find it very hard to escape from such situations. The psychologist would now test predictions derived from this theory. For instance, one prediction might be: If people have to justify their initial decision publicly, explaining it to others, they will find it especially hard to escape from the trap of escalating commitment. If, in contrast, they don't have to justify their initial decision in this public manner, they may find it easier to escape.

Next the psychologist will conduct research to test these hypotheses. If research findings are consistent with the predictions, confidence in the theory will be strengthened; if they are not, confidence in the theory will be reduced, and the psychologist may change or, ultimately, reject the theory. This process, which lies at the core of the scientific method, is illustrated in Figure 1.8 on page 18. Many different theories relating to important aspects of human behavior will be described in later chapters. And as each is presented, I'll comment on the current state of evidence relating to these theories. So you'll soon encounter many examples of this process as it actually operates in psychology.

Theories: In science, frameworks for explaining various events or processes.

Hypotheses: Testable predictions derived from theories.

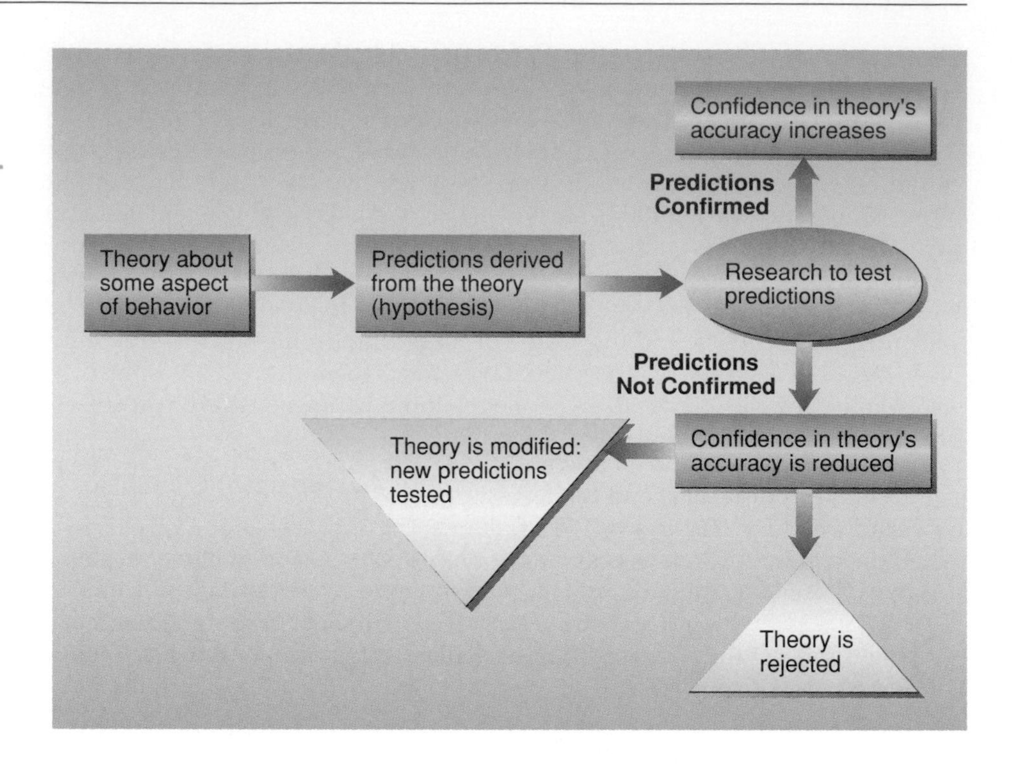

FIGURE 1.8

The Role of Theories in Psychological Research

Theories both organize existing knowledge and make predictions about how various events or processes will occur. Once theories are formulated, *hypotheses* derived from them are tested through careful research. The results of such research are used to refine existing theories and can lead ultimately to theories' acceptance as valid or their rejection as false.

Advantages of the Scientific Method: Why Common Sense Leads Us Astray

By now, you are probably convinced that using the scientific method can be difficult. If that's so, you may be wondering, then why bother? Doesn't common sense or the accumulated wisdom of the ages provide us with the answers and insights we want? Unfortunately, the answer is *no*. Common sense provides a good starting point—it often gives us interesting food for thought. But by itself, it is far from enough. In fact, on close examination, the suggestions it offers often turn out to be inconsistent and contradictory. For example, consider the following statement: "Absence makes the heart grow fonder." Do you agree? Is it true that when people are separated from those they love, they miss them and so experience increased attachment to them? Many people would answer, "Yes, that's right. Let me tell you about what happened when I was separated from my lover. . . ." But now consider the following statement: "Out of sight, out of mind." (Variation: "When I'm not near the boy/girl I love, I love the boy/girl I'm near.") How about this statement? Does it make sense? Is it true that when people are separated from those they love, they quickly find another object for their affections? Again, many people would agree. As you can see, these two views—both part of "common sense"—are contradictory. The same is true for many other informal observations about human behavior. Here are two more contradictory pairs:

> "Birds of a feather flock together" versus "Opposites attract."
>
> "Haste makes waste" versus "A stitch in time saves nine."

I could go on to list others, but by now the main point is clear: Common sense often paints a confusing and inconsistent picture of human behavior.

This is not the only reason why we must be wary of common sense, however. Another and more important one relates to the fact that unlike Mr. Spock of *Star Trek* fame, we are *not* perfect information-processing machines. On the contrary, as we'll note over and over again in this book (see Chapters 6, 7, 16), and reechoing the "grand issue" of rationality versus irrationality, our thinking is subject to several forms of errors that can lead us badly astray. Because of this fact, we simply cannot rely on informal observation, common sense, or intuition to provide us with accurate information about human behavior. Let's take a brief look at some of the sources of potential error.

The Confirmation Bias: The Temptation to Verify Our Own Views Earlier, we noted that people generally prefer to have their views confirmed rather than refuted. Don't you? Now, consider what this means when we attempt to use informal observation as a source of knowledge about human behavior. Since we prefer to have our views confirmed, we tend to notice and remember mainly information that lends support to these views—information that confirms what we already believe. This tendency is known as the **confirmation bias,** and the results of many studies indicate that it is a powerful one (e.g., Greenwald & Pratkanis, 1988; Johnson & Eagly, 1989). When the confirmation bias operates, it places us in a kind of closed system, where only evidence that confirms our existing views and beliefs gets inside; other information is often noticed (e.g., Bardach & Park, 1996), but it is quickly rejected as false. Clearly, then, the confirmation bias is one tendency that can lead us to serious errors in our efforts to understand others or ourselves.

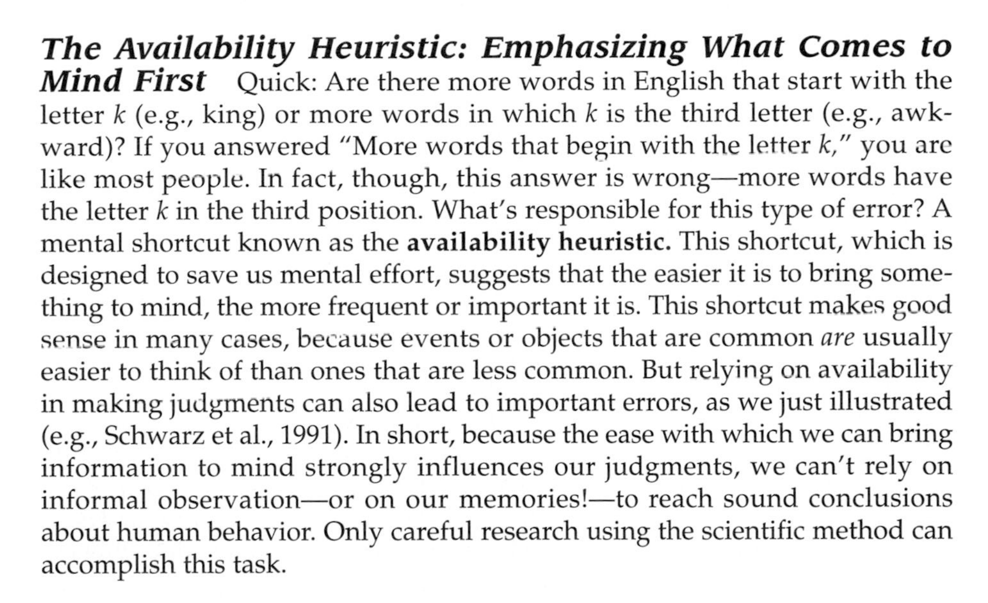

The Availability Heuristic: Emphasizing What Comes to Mind First Quick: Are there more words in English that start with the letter *k* (e.g., king) or more words in which *k* is the third letter (e.g., awkward)? If you answered "More words that begin with the letter *k*," you are like most people. In fact, though, this answer is wrong—more words have the letter *k* in the third position. What's responsible for this type of error? A mental shortcut known as the **availability heuristic.** This shortcut, which is designed to save us mental effort, suggests that the easier it is to bring something to mind, the more frequent or important it is. This shortcut makes good sense in many cases, because events or objects that are common *are* usually easier to think of than ones that are less common. But relying on availability in making judgments can also lead to important errors, as we just illustrated (e.g., Schwarz et al., 1991). In short, because the ease with which we can bring information to mind strongly influences our judgments, we can't rely on informal observation—or on our memories!—to reach sound conclusions about human behavior. Only careful research using the scientific method can accomplish this task.

Mood Effects: How We Feel Often Influences the Way We Think One day, you wake up feeling absolutely great—you are on top of the world. Another day, you wake up feeling miserable—you are really down. Will these contrasting *moods*—your current feelings—influence the way you think? Research on this topic leaves little room for doubt: Absolutely! When you are in a good mood, you will tend to think happy thoughts, remember happy events, and view everything around you in a positive light. In contrast, when you are in a bad mood, you will tend to think unhappy thoughts, remember sad events, and view everything around you negatively (e.g., Forgas, 1995). Not surprisingly, these effects of mood can strongly influence your thinking about—and conclusions concerning—human behavior. And often, it appears, we are quite unaware of the presence or magnitude of such effects (e.g., Isen & Baron, 1991).

I could continue because, as we'll see in later chapters (for instance, Chapters 7, 16), there are many other tendencies that can potentially lead us astray in our thinking (see Figure 1.9 on page 20 for a summary of the ones

Confirmation Bias: The tendency to notice and remember primarily information that lends support to our views.

Availability Heuristic: A mental shortcut suggesting that the easier it is to bring something to mind, the more frequent or important it is.

FIGURE 1.9

Aspects of Cognition That Reduce the Value of Common Sense and Intuition

The three tendencies shown here are only a few of the factors that make it risky to rely on common sense and intuition as useful guides for understanding human behavior.

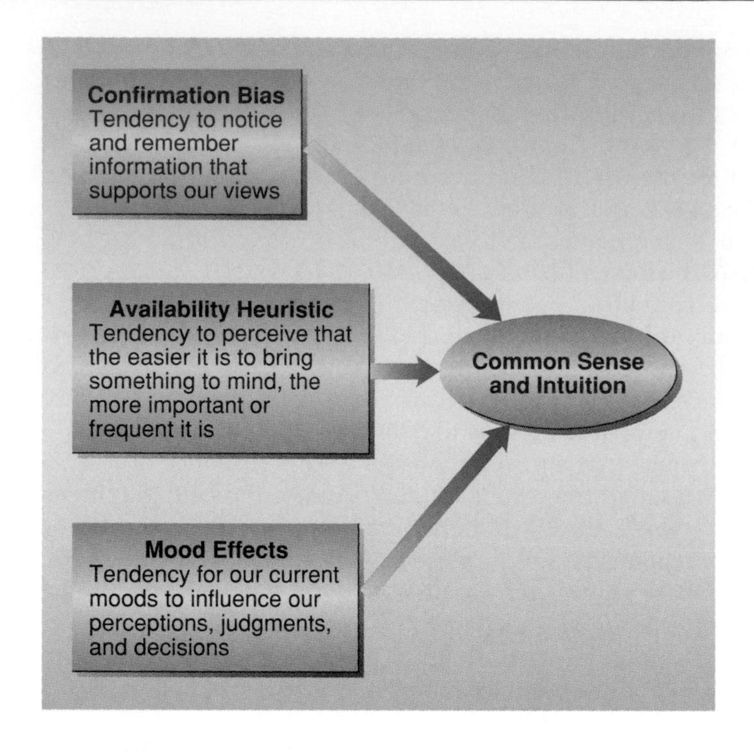

we've discussed). The main point, though, should already be clear: Because our thinking is subject to many potential sources of bias, we really can't rely on informal observation as a basis for valid conclusions about human behavior. And this, of course, is where the scientific method enters the picture: It is specifically designed to keep these and other potential sources of bias in check. By adopting the scientific method, therefore, psychologists vastly increase the probability that their efforts to attain valid information about human behavior will succeed. It is this commitment to the scientific method, more than anything else, that sets psychology apart from other efforts to understand human behavior—efforts ranging from the speculations of novelists and poets through the predictions of fortune-tellers and astrologers. Science, of course, is not the only road to truth—many would argue that philosophy and religion offer others; but psychologists firmly believe that where human behavior is concerned, science is the surest and most useful.

Key Questions

- Why can psychology be considered to be a scientific field?
- What values or guidelines are central to the scientific method?
- What is the role of theories in the scientific method?
- What's wrong with using informal observation and common sense as guides to understanding human behavior?
- What sources of potential error in our own thinking often lead us astray with respect to conclusions about behavior?
- How does the scientific method help to reduce or eliminate such errors?

The Scientific Method in Everyday Life: *Thinking Critically about Human Behavior*

"OK," I can almost hear you saying, "the scientific method is neat—it really works. But what use is it to me? I'm not going to be a psychologist or a researcher." My answer is: Even if this is so, basic understanding of the scientific method—and how it's used to study human behavior—can still offer you quite a lot. In fact, exposure to this method can be extremely useful in your everyday life. Do you remember that near the start of this chapter I promised that you would learn more than a collection of facts from your first exposure to psychology? Here's where I pay off on this claim. And the coin in which I'll do so involves **critical thinking.** What is critical thinking? It is definitely *not* "negative thinking" of the kind shown by many two-year-olds: "No," they say to anything and everything, "No! No!" *Critical thinking,* in contrast, is thinking that is critical in the sense of the basic meaning of this word: thinking that is *discerning*. (The English word *critical* comes from the Greek word *kritikos,* which means discerning.) In essence, then, critical thinking is thinking that avoids blind acceptance of conclusions or arguments and instead closely examines all assumptions, carefully evaluates existing evidence, and cautiously assesses all conclusions. In short, critical thinking mirrors the key values of the scientific method. In actual practice, critical thinking involves following guidelines such as these:

WWW WEB

- Never jump to conclusions; gather as much information as you can before making up your mind about any issue.
- Keep an open mind; don't let your existing views blind you to new information or new conclusions.
- Always ask "How?" as in "How was this evidence gathered?"
- Be skeptical; always wonder about *why* someone is making an argument, offering a conclusion, or trying to persuade you.
- Never be stampeded into accepting some view or position by your own emotions—or by arguments and appeals designed to play upon your emotions.

Perhaps the best way of illustrating critical thinking, and giving you some practice in it, is by means of a concrete example. Consider the following headline:

IS IT THE CHOCOLATE—OR ARE YOU REALLY IN LOVE?

Headlines like this one, which were common in the late 1980s and early 1990s, stirred a great deal of interest. They were based on studies reporting that people who ate a lot of chocolate experienced positive feelings—waves of euphoria similar to those they had experienced at times when they fell in love. Other reports, which also seemed to support a link between chocolate and love, cited findings indicating that persons who were depressed by romantic rejections strongly craved chocolate. To put the icing on the cake, so to speak, chemical analyses of chocolate indicated that it contains substances similar to serotonin and dopamine, which play a role in pleasure or reward centers deep in the brain (we'll discuss these in Chapter 2).

Did you read about these findings? And after doing so, did you come to believe that chocolate is indeed the "food of love"? If so, get ready for a simple lesson in critical thinking. Because many people (especially in the United States) love chocolate, it's not surprising that they found these reports very encouraging: here was a good reason for eating one of their favorite foods (see Figure 1.10 on page 22). But, unfortunately for chocolate-lovers, the scientific story didn't end there. Other research soon indicated that chocolate also contains substances that are anything but feel-good chemicals: caffeine and at least one substance known to play a role in migraine headaches. Moreover, other findings indicated that chocolate addicts didn't necessarily feel better after eating chocolate. In fact, people frequently noted that eating chocolate made them feel good for a few minutes but then left them feeling depressed. Finally, in still other studies (Rozin & Michener, 1996), persons who reported strong cravings for chocolate were fed either chocolate bars; white chocolate bars (which have none of the chemical ingredients of whole chocolate); or cocoa, from which chocolate is derived, in capsules from which

Critical Thinking: Thinking that avoids blind acceptance of conclusions or arguments and instead closely examines all assumptions, evidence, and conclusions.

all taste had been removed. Results indicated that real chocolate (either dark or white in color) reduced cravings for chocolate, while the tasteless cocoa capsules did not. Since the capsules contained all the chemicals found in chocolate bars, this was fairly conclusive evidence against the view that such chemicals played a key role in chocolate's supposed effects.

What does thinking critically about this issue suggest? That while there may be a link between chocolate and pleasant feelings for some people, the evidence concerning such a relationship is far from conclusive. Moreover, if such a link exists, it may depend more on people's liking for chocolate, and their tendency to associate this liking with other positive feelings, than with any chemical effects of chocolate itself. Jumping to the conclusion that chocolate has something like magical properties, or will enhance romantic feelings, is not justified, no matter how strongly some people would like to make this leap.

Please don't misunderstand: this example isn't presented to rain on your parade if you are a chocolate-lover—far from it. Rather, it is offered to provide you with an illustration of how critical thinking, with its emphasis on caution, skepticism, and careful evaluation of *all* existing evidence—not just the findings we prefer!—works.

But what about the benefits of critical thinking, to which I referred earlier? What, precisely, are these? Here are some of the most important:

- Practice in thinking critically will help you to think in a more sophisticated way about all aspects of human behavior—including personal health. Briefly put, critical thinking skills will help you to understand very clearly why, where human behavior or human health is concerned, there usually are no simple answers. As a result, you'll be more likely to question the kind of "quick and simple" solutions to complex human problems offered by many self-help books or audiotapes. And you will be more likely to carefully question statements to the effect that some factor causes—or cures—some disease (see Figure 1.11).
- Practice in thinking critically will help make you a more sophisticated consumer. Thinking critically about the claims advertisers make about products will give you pause—and help you to sort the hype from any underlying facts. For example, if you read an ad that says, "Our product was 57 percent better!" you'll immediately ask, "Better than *what?*"
- Practice in thinking critically will make you a more sophisticated voter. When you read or hear arguments offered by political candidates, you'll be better able to avoid jumping to conclusions, accepting unstated as-

FIGURE 1.10

Chocolate: Is It Really the Food of Love?

In the 1980s, many newspaper articles suggested that eating chocolate produced sensations similar to the feelings people experience when they fall in love. Alas! The results of scientific research did not offer strong support for this idea.

FIGURE 1.11

One Benefit of Learning to Think Critically

After you gain practice in critical thinking, you will respond even more skeptically than Robotman to statements like the one made by the TV announcer in this cartoon.

(**Source:** ROBOTMAN, reprinted by permission of Newspaper Enterprise Association, Inc.)

sumptions, or being swayed by emotional appeals. Instead, you'll focus more directly on the key issues and form your own views about these.

These are important benefits, and I believe that they are so valuable that I'll call your attention to them throughout this book in several different ways. For instance, in every chapter I'll include special sections featuring headlines like the one above. These sections, entitled Beyond the Headlines: As Psychologists See It, will indicate how psychology, with its reliance on the scientific method, can shed light upon important events occurring in the world around us. I'll also include special Critical Thinking Questions at the end of each chapter—questions designed to get you to think about the big issues raised in that chapter. The goal, of course, is to give you practice in thinking critically—carefully, cautiously, and systematically—about behavior: your own and that of others. The habit of thinking in this manner, I believe, will be one of the key benefits you'll take away with you from this book and from your first course in psychology.

Systematic Observation: A basic method of science in which events or processes in the world are observed and measured in a very careful manner.

Naturalistic Observation: A research method in which behavior is studied in the settings where it usually occurs.

Key Questions

- What is critical thinking?
- What role does it play in psychology?
- What benefits can it provide for your everyday life?

Research Methods in Psychology: *How Psychologists Answer Questions about Behavior*

Now that I've explained what modern psychology is and described both the scientific method and its relation to critical thinking, it's time to turn to another, closely related, issue: How do psychologists actually perform the task of adding to our knowledge of human behavior? (Remember: behavior means everything people do, feel, experience, or think.) In this section, we'll examine three basic procedures used by psychologists in their systematic study of human behavior: *observation* (sometimes termed *description*), *correlation*, and *experimentation*.

Observation: Describing the World around Us

One basic technique for studying behavior—or any other aspect of the world—involves carefully observing it as it occurs. Such observation is not the kind of informal observation we all practice from childhood on; rather, in science, it is observation accompanied by careful, accurate measurement. For example, scientists studying the formation of tornadoes may drive hundreds of miles in order to be present at spots where tornadoes are likely to form. They don't do this because they like to put themselves in danger, but rather because they wish to engage in careful observation of the physical events that unfold as tornadoes actually form (see Figure 1.12). The use of such **systematic observation** takes several different forms in the study of behavior.

FIGURE 1.12

Systematic Observation: One Way of Studying the World around Us

Scientists who study the formation of dangerous storms, such as tornadoes, often drive to areas where weather conditions favor the development of such storms and make careful observations of the events occurring there.

Naturalistic Observation: Observing Behavior Where It Normally Occurs Bonobo chimpanzees are a fascinating species. These small animals live in the tropical forests of Zaire and a few other spots, and they have recently been the subject of **naturalistic observation**—systematic study of behavior in natural settings (Linden, 1992).

FIGURE 1.13

Naturalistic Observation of Human Behavior

Psychologists sometimes study human behavior by observing it in public settings. For example, recent studies have used such methods to study touching in couples of various ages (e.g., Hall & Veccia, 1991).

Bonobos are interesting for several reasons. First, in contrast to many other primate species, including our own, they seem to live together in almost total harmony. Fights, bullying, and all other forms of aggression are virtually unknown. What accounts for this extremely calm and peaceful existence? One possibility involves the sexual behavior of bonobos. In contrast to other species of chimps, female bonobos are sexually receptive much of the time. In fact, they often approach males, signaling their readiness for sexual relations with more than twenty different gestures. Further, bonobos seem to use sexual relations as a means for reducing tension or anxiety: whenever they are frightened or upset, they quickly pair up and begin mating. Experts on animal behavior who have observed these chimps comment that sex seems to be one of their favorite pastimes; adult bonobos often have sexual relations twenty or more times a day!

Of course, it's a big leap from such observations to the conclusion that perhaps bonobo chimps have found the key to social harmony: Even very careful observation *cannot,* in and of itself, establish cause-and-effect relationships. But it *is* interesting to study primates' social relations as a mirror for our own societies and habits.

While naturalistic observation is often used in studies of animal behavior, it is sometimes applied to human beings as well—especially to behavior in public places such as shopping malls, hotel lobbies, and airports (e.g., Hall & Veccia, 1991; see Figure 1.13). We'll look at such research in several chapters of this book.

Case Studies: Generalizing from the Unique Every human being is unique: each of us possesses a distinctive combination of traits, abilities, and characteristics. Given this fact, is it possible to learn anything about human behavior from detailed study of one individual or perhaps of a few persons? Several famous figures in the history of psychology have contended that it is. They have adopted the **case method,** in which detailed information is gathered on specific individuals. Researchers then use this information to formulate principles or reach conclusions that, presumably, apply to much larger numbers of persons—perhaps to all human beings. By far the most famous practitioner of the case method was Sigmund Freud, who used a small number of cases as the basis for his entire theory of personality. (We'll discuss Freud's theories in Chapter 12.)

Is the case method really useful? In the hands of talented researchers such as Freud, it does seem capable of providing insights into various aspects of human behavior. Moreover, when the behavior involved is very unusual, the case method can be quite revealing. In Chapter 6, we'll see how several unique cases have added greatly to our understanding of the biological bases of memory. These cases involve individuals who have experienced specific kinds of damage to the brain and, as a result, show certain kinds of memory deficits. By studying the pattern of such memory losses, psychologists have been able to piece together a more complete picture of how memories are stored in the brain (e.g., Squire, 1991). So, much can sometimes be learned from the case method—especially when it is applied to persons who are unique in some

Case Method: A method of research in which detailed information about individuals is used to develop general principles about behavior.

manner. However, the case method suffers from several important drawbacks. First, if the persons *are* unique, it may be inappropriate to generalize from them to other human beings. Second, because researchers using the case method often have repeated and prolonged contact with the individuals they study, there is the real risk that they will become emotionally involved with these persons and so lose their scientific objectivity, at least to a degree. Because of such dangers, the case method is not widely used by psychologists today.

Survey Method: A research method in which large numbers of people answer questions about aspects of their views or their behavior.

Sampling: In the survey method, the methods used to select persons who respond to the survey.

Surveys: The Science of Self-Report At the opposite end of the scale where systematic observation is concerned is the **survey method.** Here, instead of focusing in detail upon a small number of individuals, researchers obtain a very limited sample of the behavior of large numbers of persons, usually through their responses to questionnaires. Surveys are used for many purposes—to measure attitudes toward specific issues (for example, toward health reform in the United States or toward economic reform in Russia), to measure voting preferences prior to elections, and to assess consumer reactions to new products (see Figure 1.14).

Surveys are sometimes repeated over long periods of time in order to track shifts in public opinions or actual behavior. For example, some surveys of job satisfaction—individuals' attitudes toward their jobs—have continued for several decades. And changing patterns of sexual behavior have been tracked by the Kinsey Institute since the 1940s.

The survey method offers several advantages. Information can be gathered about thousands or even hundreds of thousands of persons with relative ease. Further, since surveys can be constructed quickly, public opinion on new issues can be obtained very quickly. In order to be useful as a research tool, however, surveys must meet certain requirements. First, if the goal is to use the survey results to predict some event (for example, the outcome of an election) special care must be devoted to the issue of **sampling**—how the persons who will participate in the survey are selected. Unless these persons are representative of the larger population about which predictions are to be made (for example, predictions from a sample of voters extended to the entire voting public), serious errors can result.

Yet another issue that must be carefully addressed with respect to surveys is this: The way in which surveys are worded can exert strong effects on the outcomes obtained. For example, when asked to indicate how satisfied they are with their jobs, more than 85 percent of persons indicate that they are "satisfied" or "very satisfied." When asked whether they would choose the same job or career again, however, less than 50 percent indicate agreement! So, as experts in the survey method well know, it's often true that "the way you ask the question determines the answer you get."

In sum, the survey method can be a useful approach for studying some aspects of human behavior—especially positive and negative reactions toward almost anything—but the results obtained are accurate only to the extent that issues relating to sampling and wording are carefully addressed.

FIGURE 1.14

The Survey Method in Operation

The *survey method* is often used to gather information about the opinions of large numbers of persons. If these people are selected carefully, researchers can use their views to predict the views of entire populations.

Correlation: The Search for Relationships

At various times, you have probably noticed that some events appear to be related to each other: as one changes, the other appears to change too. For example, perhaps you have noticed that when tall, dark clouds appear in the sky, storms often follow. Or, if you listen to the evening news, you may have noticed that when interest rates rise, the stock market often falls and the sales of new homes tend to decrease. When such relationships between events exist, it is known as a **correlation**—a tendency for one aspect of the world around us to change with another aspect of the world around us. Psychologists and other scientists refer to such changeable aspects of the natural world as *variables,* since they can take different values.

From the point of view of science, the existence of a correlation between two variables can be very useful. This is so because when a correlation exists, it is possible to predict one variable from information about one or more other variables. The ability to make such *predictions*—to forecast future events from present ones—is one important goal of science; and psychologists, too, often attempt to make predictions about human behavior. To the extent such predictions can be made accurately, important benefits can be obtained. For instance, consider how useful it would be if we could predict from current information such future outcomes as a person's success in school or in various occupations, effectiveness as a parent, length of life, or likelihood of developing a serious mental disorder.

The discovery of correlations between variables allows us to make such predictions. In fact, the stronger such correlations are, the more accurate the predictions that can be made. These basic facts constitute the foundation for another important method of research—the **correlational method.** In this method, psychologists or other scientists attempt to determine whether, and to what extent, different variables are related to each other. This involves making careful observation of each variable, and then performing appropriate statistical analyses to determine whether and to what extent the variables are correlated—to what extent changes in one are related to changes in the other. Correlations range from –1.00 to +1.00, and the greater their departure from zero, the stronger the correlation in question. Thus, a correlation of –.67 is stronger than one of –.18; similarly, a correlation of +.52 is stronger than one of +.29. Positive correlations indicate that as one variable increases the other increases too. For instance, the greater the number of hours students study for their psychology tests, the higher their grades tend to be. The fact that this relationship is not perfect suggests that the correlation between these two variables—studying and grades—will be less than 1.00. Negative correlations indicate that as one variable increases, the other decreases. For example, if personal health declines as the level of stress to which individuals are related increases, then a negative correlation may exist between these two variables. (The Appendix provides more information about correlations and how they are computed.)

Psychologists often search for correlations between variables in order to be able to make accurate predictions about important aspects of behavior. To illustrate this method of research, let's consider a concrete example.

Correlation: A tendency for one aspect of the world (or one variable) to change with another aspect of the world (or variable).

Correlational Method: A research method in which researchers attempt to determine whether, and to what extent, different variables are related to each other.

The Correlational Method of Research: An Example Imagine that a researcher wished to test the following hypothesis (a prediction derived from a theory): The more positive individuals' moods, the more likely they are to help others. How could research on this hypothesis be conducted by the correlational method? While there are many possibilities, a very basic approach would involve devising some means of measuring both variables—

some way of assessing individuals' current moods and some way of assessing their willingness to help others—and then determining whether these two variables are related to each other. For example, individuals who have agreed to participate in the research could be asked to rate their current mood on a simple scale ranging from 1 (very negative) to 5 (very positive). Then they could be asked if they are willing to make a small donation to a charity; this would serve as a measure of their willingness to help. If being in a good mood does lead to increased helping, it will be observed that the better individuals' current moods, the more likely they are to make a donation.

One key advantage of the correlational method is that it can be used in natural settings as well as in the laboratory. For instance, a psychologist wishing to test the hypothesis that being in a good mood leads to greater helping could conduct a study at a large shopping mall. Here, passersby would be stopped and asked to rate their mood; then their behavior as they pass someone soliciting funds for a charity would be observed. If being in a good mood is indeed related to helping, the psychologist may observe that the happier people are, the greater the likelihood of their making a donation. In other words, the psychologist would observe a positive correlation between these two variables. Research conducted in natural settings is known as *field research;* it is often very useful, since it studies behavior in the settings where it usually occurs. In contrast, *laboratory research* is conducted in special settings that may differ in many respects from natural ones. As we'll see below, however, laboratory settings also offer important advantages.

In addition to its usefulness in natural settings, the correlational method offers several other advantages. It is often highly efficient and can yield a large amount of interesting data in a relatively short time. Moreover, it can be extended to include many different variables at once. Thus, in the study we have just described, information on the age and gender of shoppers at the mall could also be obtained. Then appropriate statistical analyses could be conducted to determine whether these variables, too, are related to helping. It is often the case that success at prediction improves as more variables are brought into the picture, so correlational research often includes measures of many different variables that, psychologists have reason to believe, may be related to each other.

While the correlational method of research offers many advantages, it also suffers from one major drawback: *The findings it yields are generally not conclusive with respect to cause-and-effect relationships.* That is, the fact that two variables are correlated, even highly correlated, does not guarantee that there is a causal link between them—that changes in one cause changes in the other. Rather, in many cases, the fact that two variables are correlated simply reflects the fact that changes in both are caused by a third variable.

For example, suppose that our researcher finds a positive correlation between individuals' ratings of their own moods and the likelihood that they will donate to a charity. Does this mean that being in a good mood causes people to help others? Common sense suggests that this is so, but other possibilities exist, too. For instance, it may be that people in a good mood have more money in their pockets—that's one reason they are in a good mood! If this is so, then the relationship between mood and helping uncovered in this research may be misleading. Both mood and helping are actually related to a third factor—personal funds available at the moment. Additional illustrations of this important fact—that even strong correlations between two variables do not necessarily mean that one variable causes the other—are presented in the **Ideas to Take with You** feature on page 28.

Key Questions

- What is the basic nature of naturalistic observation? Of the case method? The survey method?
- What is the correlational method of research, and what are some advantages it offers?
- Why doesn't the existence of a correlation between two variables necessarily indicate that one causes changes in the other?

Ideas to Take with You

Why Correlation Does Not Equal Causation

The fact that two variables are correlated—even strongly correlated—does not necessarily mean that changes in one cause changes in the other. This is true because changes in both variables may actually be related to—or caused by—a third variable. Two examples:

Observation: As weight increases, income increases.

Possible Interpretations:

1. Weight gain causes increased income.

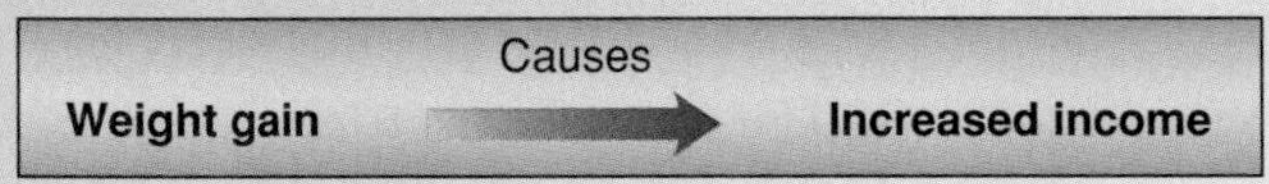

2. As people grow older, they tend to gain weight and also to earn higher incomes.

Observation: The more television people watch, the more likely they are to have a heart attack.

Possible Interpretations:

1. Watching television causes heart attacks.

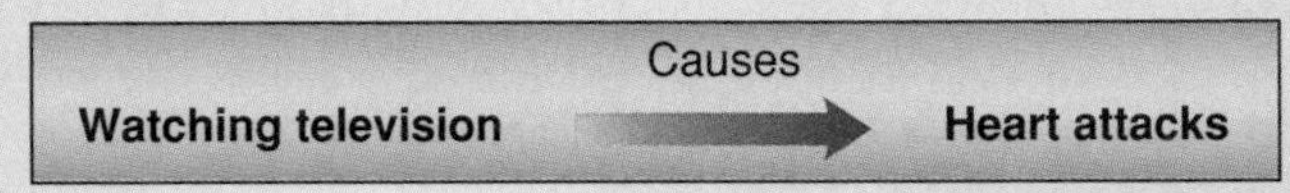

2. People who watch lots of television don't like to exercise; lack of exercise causes heart attacks.

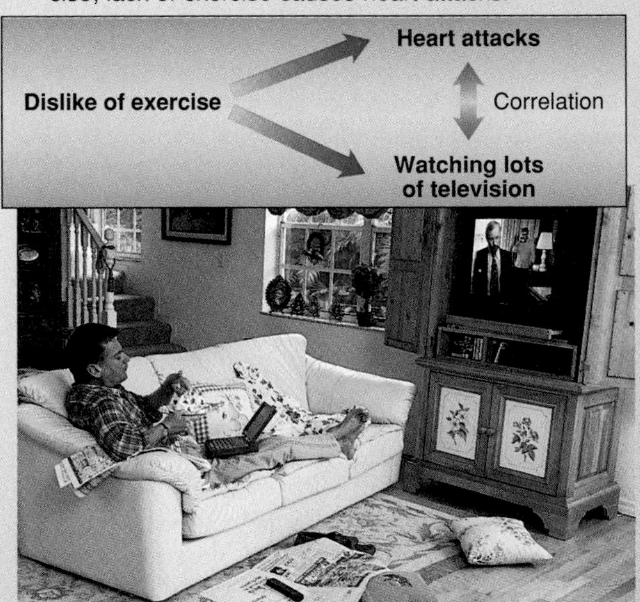

Key Conclusion: Even If Two Variables Are Strongly Correlated, This Does Not Necessarily Mean That Changes in One Cause Changes in the Other.

The Experimental Method: Knowledge through Systematic Intervention

As we have just seen, the correlational method of research is very useful and helps psychologists attain one important goal of science: being able to make accurate predictions. But it is less useful from the point of view of reaching yet another goal: *explanation.* This is sometimes known as the "why" question—the fact that scientists do not merely wish to describe the world and relationships between variables in it; they want to be able to *explain* these relationships, too. For example, while it is interesting and valuable to know that people who possess certain personality traits are more likely than others to suffer heart attacks, it is even more valuable to understand *why* this is so. What is it about these traits that causes such persons to experience heart attacks?

In order to attain the goal of explanation, it is usually important to know something about causality—the extent to which changes in one variable produce or cause changes in one or more others. How can such causal relationships be established? Primarily through another method of research known as **experimentation** or the **experimental method.** As the heading of this section suggests, experimentation involves the following strategy: One variable is changed systematically, and the effects of these changes on one or more other variables are carefully measured. If systematic changes in one variable produce changes in one or more others (and if additional conditions we'll soon consider are also met), it is possible to conclude with reasonable certainty that there is indeed a causal relationship between these variables: that changes in one do indeed cause changes in the other. Because the experimental method is so valuable in answering this kind of question, it is frequently the method of choice in psychology. But bear in mind that there is no single "best" method of research. Rather, psychologists—like all other scientists—choose the research method that is most appropriate for studying a given topic.

Experimentation: Its Basic Nature In its most basic form, the experimental method in psychology involves two key steps: (1) the presence or strength of some variable believed to affect behavior is systematically altered, and (2) the effects of such alterations (if any) are carefully measured. The logic behind these steps is as follows: If the variable that is systematically changed does indeed influence some aspect of behavior, then individuals exposed to different levels or amounts of that factor should differ in their behavior. For instance, exposure to a relatively low amount of the variable should result in one level of a behavior, while exposure to a higher amount should result in a different level, and so on.

The factor systematically varied by the researcher is termed the **independent variable,** while the aspect of behavior studied is termed the **dependent variable.** In a simple experiment, then, different groups of participants are exposed to contrasting levels of the independent variable (such as low, moderate, and high). The researcher then carefully measures their behavior to determine whether it does in fact vary with these changes in the independent variable. If it does—and if two other conditions described below are also met—the researcher can tentatively conclude that the independent variable does indeed cause changes in the aspect of behavior being measured.

To illustrate the basic nature of experimentation in psychological research, let's return to the possible effects of being in a good mood on willingness to help others. How could a psychologist study this topic by means of the experimental method? One possibility is as follows. The study would probably be

Experimentation (the Experimental Method): A research method in which researchers systematically alter one or more variables in order to determine whether such changes influence some aspect of behavior.

Independent Variable: The variable that is systematically changed in an experiment.

Dependent Variable: The variable that is measured in an experiment.

Random Assignment of Participants to Experimental Conditions: Assuring that all research participants have an equal chance of being exposed to each level of the independent variable (that is, of being assigned to each experimental condition).

conducted in a laboratory setting, because in such settings researchers can more readily control what events happen, and how and when they occur; thus, it is often easier to make systematic changes in independent variables. The psychologist could now systematically vary events known, from past research, to influence individuals' moods. For instance, participants in one condition (the positive mood condition) would perform some task and then receive positive feedback on their work (that is, praise). In contrast, those in another condition would receive neutral feedback—comments designed to have no effect on the participants' current moods. This would serve as a *control condition*—a baseline against which results in the other condition could be compared. Inclusion of such control groups is a common practice in psychological research employing the experimental method.

Following exposure to one or the other of these conditions, participants would be given an opportunity to be helpful to others in some way. They could be asked, as in the correlational study described above, to help someone; for example, to help the researcher by serving as an unpaid volunteer in further studies, or to make a donation to charity. If results now looked like those in Figure 1.15, the researcher could conclude—tentatively—that being in a good mood does indeed increase helping. It's important to remember that in this case, efforts have been made to change participants' moods (by giving them either positive or neutral feedback); in the correlational study, participants' current moods were simply measured—no effort was made to change them. By the way, research very much like this has been performed, and results indicate that this hypothesis *is* correct: The better people's current moods, the more willing they are to help others (e.g., Baron, 1997; Levine et al., 1994).

Experimentation: Two Requirements for Its Success Earlier, I referred to two additional conditions that must be met before a researcher can conclude that changes in an independent variable have caused changes in a dependent variable. Let's consider these conditions now. The first involves what is termed **random assignment of participants to experimental conditions.** This means that all participants in an experiment must have an equal chance of being exposed to each level of the independent variable. The reason for this rule is simple: If participants are *not* randomly assigned to each condition, it may later be impossible to determine whether differences

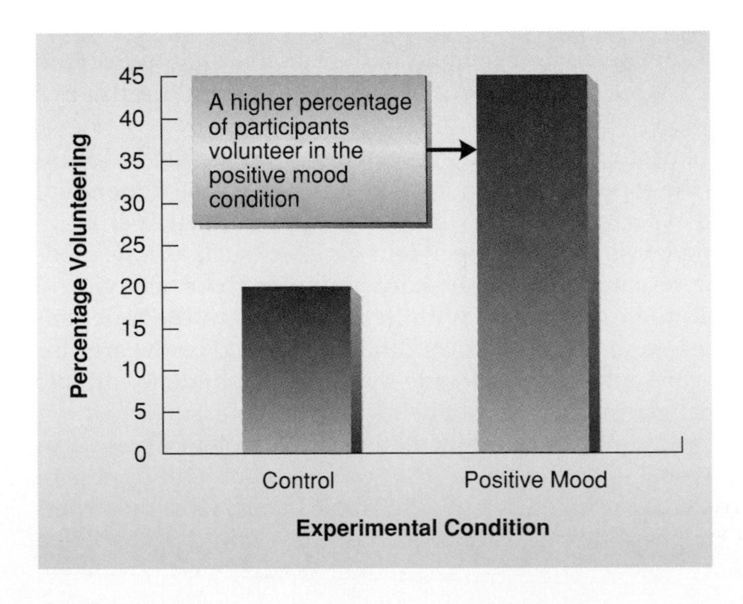

FIGURE 1.15

Experimental Research: A Simple Example

This simple experiment provides some evidence for the hypothesis that being in a good mood increases the tendency to help others.

in their behavior stem from differences they brought with them to the study, from the impact of the independent variable, or both. For instance, imagine that in the study just described, all participants assigned to the positive mood condition are members of a religious group that emphasizes the importance of helping others, while those in the control group do not belong to this church. Why did those in the positive mood condition engage in more helping? Because they were in a better mood than the persons in the control group? Because of their strong religious convictions? Because of both factors? We can't tell. If, in contrast, the members of this religious group had been randomly distributed across the two experimental conditions, their greater willingness to help would have been equally represented in both. Thus, any differences between the groups could still be attributed to the independent variable. So, as you can see, it is crucial that all participants have an equal chance of being assigned to all experimental conditions; if they do not, the potential value of an experiment may be seriously reduced.

The second condition essential for successful experimentation is as follows: Insofar as possible, all factors other than the independent variable that might also affect participants' behavior must be held constant. To see why this is so, consider what will happen if, in the study on mood and helping, persons in the positive mood condition are exposed to a stronger plea for help than those in the control condition. Again, more people in the positive mood condition volunteer. What is the cause of this result? The fact that people in this condition are in a better mood? The stronger plea for help from the experimenter? Both factors? Once again, we can't tell; and since we can't, the value of the experiment as a source of new information about human behavior is greatly reduced. In situations like this, the independent variable is said to be *confounded*, with another variable—one that is not under systematic investigation in the study. When such confounding occurs, the findings of an experiment may be largely meaningless (see Figure 1.16).

But why, you may now be wondering, would a psychologist make such a muddle of her or his own study? Why would the researcher make different kinds of requests for help in the two conditions? The answer, of course, is that the researcher certainly wouldn't do this on purpose. But suppose that the person making the requests knows the hypothesis about mood and helping and firmly believes that it is true. This belief may well exert subtle effects

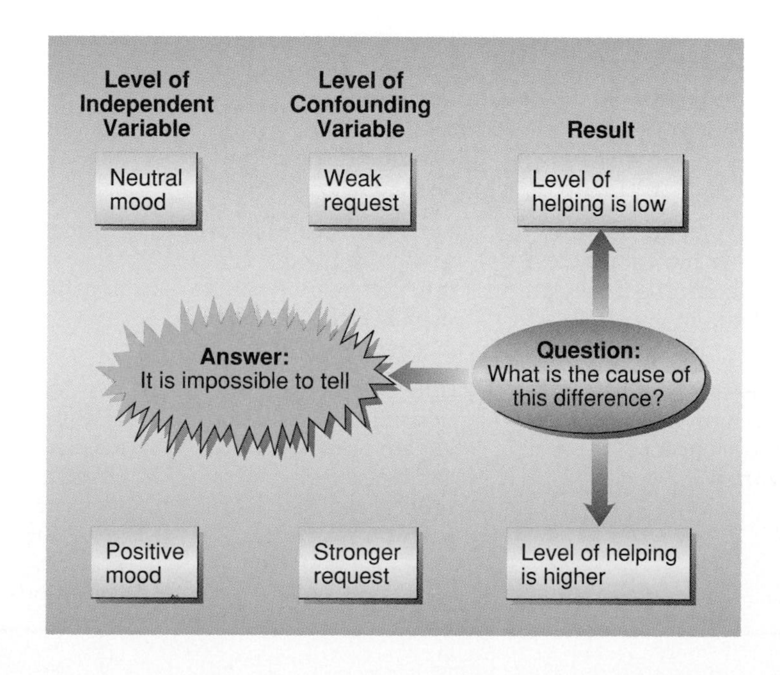

FIGURE 1.16

Confounding of Variables: A Fatal Flaw in Experimentation

The experiment illustrated here is designed to study the effects of mood on helping. The experimenter systematically varies conditions to influence participants' moods—the *independent variable*—but also, at the same time, allows *another variable* to change: The researcher makes a stronger plea for help in the positive mood condition than in the control condition. As a result, these two variables are *confounded* and it is impossible to interpret the results.

Experimenter Effects: Unintended effects, caused by researchers, on participants' behavior.

Double-Blind Procedure: Procedure in which the researchers who have contact with participants do not know the hypothesis under investigation.

on the researcher's behavior; for instance, this person may ask for participants' help a bit more fervently in the positive mood condition, where the researcher expects more helping, than in the control condition. The result: More helping does indeed occur in the positive mood condition; but this is due, at least in part, to the fact that the researcher makes stronger or more persuasive requests in this condition. In order to avoid such potential problems, which are known as **experimenter effects** (unintended effects, caused by researchers, on participants' behavior), many experiments in psychology employ a **double-blind procedure,** in which the researchers who have contact with participants do not know the hypothesis under investigation. Since they don't, the likelihood that they will influence results in the subtle ways just described are reduced. We'll describe other procedures used by psychologists to reduce factors that might interfere with the accuracy or validity of their results in the special Research Methods sections appearing in each chapter.

In sum, experimentation is, in several respects, the crown jewel among psychology's methods for answering questions about behavior. When it is

TABLE 1.3

Research Methods Used by Psychologists

As shown here, psychologists use several different research methods. Each offers a complex mixture of advantages and disadvantages, so in general the guiding rule is: Use the best and most appropriate method for studying a particular research question.

Method	Description	Advantages	Disadvantages
Systematic observation	Behavior in natural settings is studied systematically	Behavior is observed in the settings where it normally occurs	Cannot be used to establish cause-and-effect relationships; often costly and difficult to perform
Case method	A small number of persons are studied in detail	Detailed information is gathered; individuals can be studied for long periods of time	Generalizability of results is uncertain; objectivity of researcher may be compromised
Surveys	Large numbers of persons are asked questions about their attitudes or views	Large amount of information can be acquired quickly; accurate predictions of large-scale trends can sometimes be made	Generalizability may be questionable unless persons surveyed are a representative sample of a larger population
Correlational research	Researchers measure two or more variables to determine if they are related in any way	Large amount of information can be gathered quickly; method can be used in field as well as laboratory settings	Difficult to establish cause-and-effect relationships
Experimentation	The presence or strength of one or more variables is varied	Cause-and-effect relationships can be established; precise control can be exerted over other, potentially confounding variables	Results can be subject to several sources of bias (e.g., experimenter effects); generalizability can be doubtful if behavior is observed under highly artificial conditions

used with skill and care, the experimental method yields results that help us not only to answer complex questions about human behavior, but also to understand the causes of such behavior. Thus, in one sense, experimentation is psychology's ultimate answer to the question "Why?" (Please see Table 1.3 for an overview of the major research methods we have considered.)

Inferential Statistics: A special form of mathematics that allows us to evaluate the likelihood that a given pattern of findings is due to chance alone.

Replication: A basic scientific principle requiring that the results of an experiment be repeated before they are accepted with confidence.

Meta-Analysis: A statistical procedure for combining the results of many different studies in order to estimate both the direction and the magnitude of the effects of independent variables studied in these experiments.

Interpreting Research Results: Statistics as a Valuable Tool

Once an experiment has been completed, researchers must turn to the next crucial task: interpreting the results. Suppose that in the study we have been discussing, results indicate that people in a good mood do indeed offer more help than those in a neutral mood. How much confidence can we place in these results? In other words, are the differences observed real ones—ones that would be observed if the study were repeated again with other participants? This is a crucial question, for unless we can be confident that the differences are real, the results tell us little about human behavior.

One way of dealing with this question, of course, would be to repeat the study over and over again. This would work, but as you can well imagine, it would be quite costly in terms of time and effort. Another approach is to use **inferential statistics.** This is a special form of mathematics that allows us to evaluate the likelihood that a given pattern of findings, such as differences in the behavior of experimental groups, is due to chance alone. Thus, to determine whether the findings of a study are indeed real (are unlikely to have occurred by chance alone), psychologists perform appropriate statistical analyses on the data they collect. If these analyses suggest that the likelihood of obtaining the observed findings by chance is low (usually, fewer than five times in a hundred), the results are described as being *significant*. Only then are they interpreted as being of value in helping us understand some aspect of behavior.

It's important to realize that the likelihood that a given pattern of findings is a chance event is *never* zero. This probability can be very low—one chance in ten thousand, for instance—but it can never be zero. For this reason, actual replication of results by different researchers in different laboratories is usually necessary before the findings of any research project can be accepted with confidence. In other words, the basic scientific principle of **replication** is still important, even when inferential statistics are used to evaluate research findings.

Meta-Analysis and the Search for an Overall Pattern

Suppose that a specific hypothesis has been tested in many different studies. If all yield similar results, confidence in the accuracy of the hypothesis will be quite strong. But sometimes a different pattern emerges: Some studies yield one result and others yield a different pattern. What happens then? How can we combine the results of all these different experiments in order to determine whether, overall, there is support for the hypothesis? One answer involves a very powerful statistical technique known as **meta-analysis** (e.g., Bond & Smith, 1996). This procedure allows us to combine the results of many different studies in order to estimate both the direction and the magnitude of the effects of independent variables. Meta-analytic procedures are mathematical in nature, so they eliminate potential sources of error that might arise if we attempted to examine the findings of existing studies

Key Questions

- What is the basic nature of experimentation?
- Why must participants in an experiment be randomly assigned to different conditions?
- What is confounding of variables in an experiment?
- What are experimenter effects, and what is the double-blind procedure?
- What are inferential statistics, and how do they help psychologists interpret the findings of their research?
- What is meta-analysis, and what role does it play in psychologists' interpretations of the findings of many studies dealing with the same aspect of behavior?

in a more informal manner; such as, by doing a simple box count to see how many studies offer support for the hypothesis and how many do not. For instance, meta-analysis largely eliminates the all-too-human tendency to seek confirmation of our views or preferences. Overall, then, meta-analysis is a very valuable tool for psychological research, and we'll refer to it at several points in this book.

Ethical Issues in Psychological Research

Strange as it may seem, the phrase *psychological research* has an ominous ring for some people. When they hear these words, they visualize scenes in which all-knowing psychologists somehow force unwary research participants to reveal their deepest secrets and wildest fantasies, or subject participants to mysterious procedures only the psychologists understand. Do such concerns have any basis in fact? Is psychological research ever harmful to the people and animals being studied, and therefore unethical?

While I certainly don't wish to gloss over a complex and serious issue, my answer is a firm *no*. Virtually all psychological research conducted today is performed in accordance with strict ethical standards designed to ensure the safety, privacy, and well-being of all research participants. These standards, which were developed both by government agencies and by the American Psychological Association, are carefully enforced in all settings where research takes place. Thus, many safeguards are built into the system and together, these assure that the disturbing picture of psychological research outlined above has little connection to reality.

Having said this, however, I should note that two ethical issues deserving of careful attention exist. One has to do with the use of **deception**—the temporary withholding of information about a study from the persons who participate in it; the other has to do with the use of animals in psychological research.

Deception: The Ethics of Misleading Research Participants

Let's return to the study we discussed earlier—one designed to investigate the effects of being in a good mood on helping. Suppose that before the start of the study, the researcher explained the hypothesis to research participants. Would this influence the results? The chances are high that it would. Some persons might decide to "help" the researcher by confirming the hypothesis: They would agree to the request for help for this reason. Others, in contrast, would decide to play devil's advocate and would refuse to help just to disprove the hypothesis. In either case, of course, any possibility of learning something about human behavior would vanish; the study would largely be a waste of time.

In situations like this, many psychologists believe that it is necessary to withhold information about a study from participants, or even to give them misleading information, on a temporary basis. The reason behind such procedures, which are known as deception, is obvious: Researchers believe that if participants have complete information about the purposes and procedures

Deception: The temporary withholding of information about a study from participants.

of a study, their behavior will be changed by this information, and the results will be invalid.

While this reasoning is sound, the use of deception also raises important ethical issues. Is it appropriate for psychologists to withhold information from research participants, or even to mislead them? Although the issue remains somewhat controversial, most psychologists have concluded that deception is permissible, provided that two basic principles are followed. The first of these is known as **informed consent,** and requires that research participants be provided with information about all the events and procedures a study will involve before they agree to participate in it, and that they be informed that they are completely free to leave at any time (American Psychological Association, 1992).

The second principle is known as **debriefing,** and requires that research participants be given full information about all aspects of a study after they have participated in it. Debriefing ensures that participants in psychological research leave with a full understanding of its purpose, and that they receive any information that was temporarily withheld from them.

Existing evidence suggests that informed consent and thorough debriefing go a long way toward eliminating any adverse effects of temporary deception (Mann, 1994; Sharpe, Adair, & Roese, 1992). However, despite such findings, and despite the fact that most persons who have experienced temporary deception as part of research projects feel that it is justified (e.g., Smith & Richardson, 1983), some psychologists still object to its use (e.g., Rubin, 1985). They feel that deception may shake participants' faith in psychology, and may sometimes leave them with negative feelings—such thoughts as "How could I have been fooled so easily? Why didn't I figure out what was really happening?"

In view of such concerns, it is definitely unwise to take the safety or suitability of deception for granted. On the contrary, psychologists must always be on guard to protect the rights and well-being of all individuals who, by offering their time, effort, and cooperation, help advance the frontiers of psychological knowledge.

Research with Animals

If you were given a tour through the research facilities of any large psychology department, you would soon come upon rooms filled with rats, pigeons, or monkeys, plus equipment used in studying their behavior (see Figure 1.17 on page 36). At the present time, about 8 percent of all research in psychology is conducted with animals (Beckstead, 1991). Why do psychologists conduct such research? For several reasons.

First, psychologists may want to find out something about the behavior of a particular species. For instance, they may want to learn about the mating behavior of an endangered species so that its numbers can be increased through breeding programs. Second, they may want to determine whether certain principles of behavior—for example, basic principles concerning learning—apply to many different species. The most important reason for conducting research with animals, however, is the one that raises important ethical issues: some research exposes participants to conditions or treatments that could not be performed with human beings. For obvious ethical and legal reasons, researchers cannot perform operations on healthy people in order to study the roles of various parts of their brains in key aspects of behavior. Similarly, researchers cannot place human beings on diets lacking in important nutrients in order to determine how deficiencies affect their development.

Informed Consent: A principle requiring that research participants be provided with information about all the events and procedures a study will involve before they agree to participate in it.

Debriefing: Providing research participants with full information about all aspects of a study after they have participated in it.

FIGURE 1.17

Psychological Research with Animals

Only a small proportion of psychological research is conducted with animals. However, such research is very useful, especially in situations where it would be inappropriate to expose human beings to the variables being investigated (for example, deficits in nutrition).

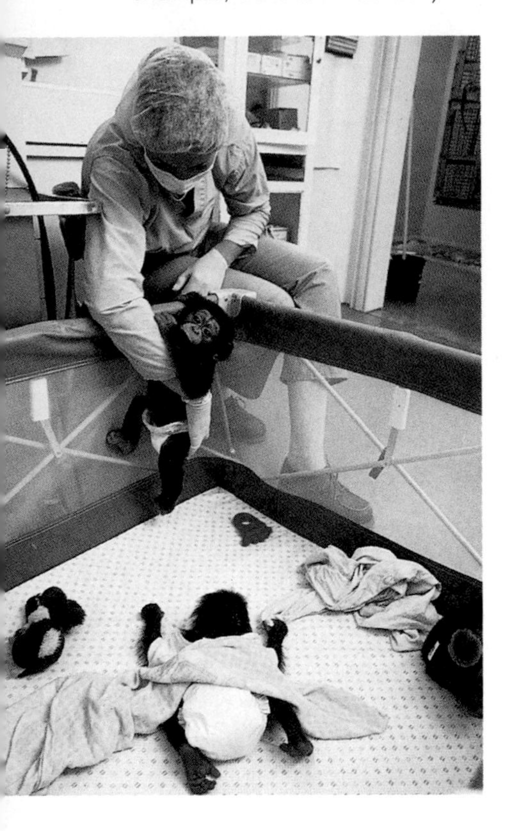

In these and many other cases, there appears to be no choice: if the research is to be conducted, it must be conducted with animals.

But is it appropriate to subject helpless rats, pigeons, and monkeys to such treatment? This is a complex issue, on which different persons have sharply contrasting views. On the one hand, supporters of animal rights contend that the procedures employed in research with animals often expose them to harsh or cruel treatment; these advocates argue that animal research is unethical. Psychologists respond to such criticism in two ways. First, they note that harsh and cruel procedures are virtually *never* used in their research; such conditions are more frequently found in medical studies—in which, indeed, researchers sometimes inject animals with dangerous microbes or give them experimental drugs in order to develop better medical procedures for treating or preventing disease. Second, psychologists note that research with animals has contributed to human welfare in many important ways. For example, it has led to improved means for treating emotional problems, controlling high blood pressure, and reducing chronic pain. In addition, psychological research with animals has increased our understanding of the neural mechanisms underlying memory loss, senility, and various addictions (Miller, 1985). Many persons would contend that these benefits far outweigh the minimal risks to animals participating in psychological research.

The issue is a complex one, though, and there are no easy answers to it. Whether the benefits of research with animals—medical or psychological—justify such studies is a value judgment, largely outside the realm of science. Only you, as an individual who thinks critically, can decide whether, and to what extent, you agree.

Ethical Issues in the Practice of Psychology

While psychologists often face complex ethical issues in their research, this is not the only source of ethical dilemmas in psychology. Such questions also arise as psychologists practice their profession—for instance, as they deliver psychological services to clients. A survey of practicing psychologists (Pope & Vetter, 1992) indicates that there are many different situations in which ethical issues or dilemmas arise. The most frequent of these have to do with questions of *confidentiality*—situations in which psychologists receive information from their clients that professional ethics require them to hold confidential, but which they also feel obligated to reveal for legal reasons. For example, one psychologist reported a distressing situation in which a client reported being raped but could not get police to believe her story. Shortly afterward, another client of the same psychologist admitted to the crime (Pope & Vetter, 1992, p. 399). Clearly, the psychologist in question faced a dilemma. Professional ethics required that the second client's information be kept confidential, but legal and moral principles suggested that it should be given to the police. What would *you* do? (I don't know what the psychologist did, because this person kept the decision confidential.)

Another frequent cause of ethical concern involves situations in which psychologists find themselves in conflicted relationships with clients; that is, situations in which a psychologist's professional role as healer is somehow inconsistent with other relationships he or she may have with a client. One therapist, for instance, reported an incident in which he sought to file a complaint against a very noisy neighbor, only to discover that the owner of the property in which the neighbor lived was one of his clients. Another, and more unsettling, cause for ethical concern centers on sexual issues—instances in which psychologists are attracted to their clients or vice versa. Clearly, the professional role of therapists (and strong ethical guidelines adopted by the

American Psychological Association) forbids sexual relationships between therapists and clients. Yet such attraction still occurs, and it places psychologists in situations filled with professional and personal peril.

These are just a few of the ethical dilemmas faced by psychologists in their efforts to assist people. Many other issues, ranging from concerns about providing expert testimony in criminal trials through the use of advertising to build one's practice, exist as well. In short, efforts to help individuals cope with life's many problems and with specific psychological disorders raise complex questions that require adherence to the highest professional standards. Truly, then, working as a psychologist can be a demanding job.

Key Questions

- What is deception, and why do many psychologists use it in their research?
- What are informed consent and debriefing?
- What ethical issues are raised by research with animals?
- What ethical dilemmas do psychologists often face in their work?

Using This Book: *A Review of Its Special Features*

Although it's a long time ago, I can remember my own first course in psychology quite well. I also remember struggling long and hard to understand many sections of the textbook we used. Because I don't want *you* to experience such difficulties, and because I want this, your first contact with psychology, to be as pleasant and beneficial as possible, I've worked hard to make this book easy to read and understand. Let me summarize some of the steps I've taken in this respect. Such information is often presented in a preface; but since most students in my classes tell me that they don't usually read these, I've decided to describe this book's special features here.

First, each chapter begins with an outline and ends with a summary. Within the text itself, key terms are printed in **dark type like this** and are accompanied by a definition. These terms are also defined in a running marginal glossary, as well as in a glossary at the end of the book. In addition, throughout each chapter I call your attention to important points and principles in special **Key Questions** sections. If you can answer these questions, that's a good sign that you understand the central points in each section. As you'll soon notice, all figures and tables are clear and simple, and most contain special labels and notes designed to help you understand them. Finally, to help you grasp concepts that students sometimes find difficult, I've included special **Ideas to Take with You** features in each chapter. These features describe important concepts or summarize several theories; the information they contain is definitely part of what you should take with you from this book and this course.

Second, in keeping with my goal of providing you with a new perspective on human behavior—one you can use in the years ahead—I've included several types of special sections. Two of these special sections are designed to give you practice in critical thinking. One is labeled **Beyond the Headlines: As Psychologists See It.** These sections take an actual headline relating to human behavior and examine it from the perspective of psychology. They illustrate both how psychologists think critically about human behavior, and how the knowledge we have acquired can shed light on important issues.

The second critical thinking–oriented section is labeled **Research Methods: How Psychologists Study. . . .** These sections describe the research methods psychologists have developed in their efforts to answer questions about many aspects of human behavior. I believe that discussing these methods in the context of the subfield where they are actually applied will help you to understand how psychology uses and adapts the scientific method to its own unique subject matter—human behavior.

A third type of special section, entitled **Exploring Gender and Diversity,** is designed to take account of psychology's growing concern both with ethnic and cultural diversity and with the far-reaching effects of gender. These sections review research findings relating to diversity and gender, and tie these topics as closely as possible to the content of chapters in which they appear.

Finally, each chapter concludes with a special section entitled **Making Psychology Part of Your Life.** These sections are designed to illustrate how you personally can apply the information in each chapter of this book to enhance your own life.

I hope that together, these features will make reading this book a stimulating and enjoyable experience. Moreover, I hope that combined with the contents of each chapter, they will help provide you with that new way of thinking about behavior that I promised at the very start. To the extent this happens, and only to that extent, I'll feel that as a psychologist, teacher, and author, I've done my part. The rest, of course, is up to you!

Making Psychology Part of Your Life

How to Study Psychology—or Any Other Subject—Effectively

Among the topics psychologists know most about are learning, memory, and motivation. (We'll examine these in Chapters 5, 6, and 10.) Fortunately, all of these topics are directly relevant to one activity you must perform as a student: studying. You must be motivated to study, must learn new materials, and must remember them accurately after they have been mastered. Knowledge gained by psychologists can be very useful to you in your efforts to accomplish these tasks (see Figure 1.18). Drawing on what psychology knows about these topics, here are some useful tips to help you get the most out of the time you spend studying.

- *Begin with an overview.* Research on memory indicates that it is easier to retain information if it can be placed within a cognitive framework—in other words, if it is clear how different pieces of information or topics relate to one another. So when you begin to study, start with an overview. Examine the outline at the start of each chapter and thumb through the pages once or twice. That way, you'll know what to expect and will already have an initial framework for organizing the information that follows.
- *Eliminate (or at least minimize) distractions.* In order for information to be entered accurately into memory, careful attention to it is necessary. This suggests that you should reduce all distractions—anything around you that will draw your attention away from the materials you are trying to learn. So, when you get down to serious studying, try to do it in a quiet place. Turn off the television or radio; put those magazines out of sight; unhook your telephone; and, if you have one, turn on a noise-reducing machine like one I've invented (it's described in Chapter 17). The result will be that it will take you less time to cover the materials you want to study.
- *Don't do all your studying at once.* All-nighters may seem to work, but in fact they are very inefficient. Research findings indicate that it is easier to learn and remember new information when such learning is spaced out over time rather than when it is

crammed into a single long session. Just as there are limits to how long you can perform a physical task without getting fatigued, there are limits to mental work, too. So do try to spread your study sessions out; in the final analysis, this will give you greater return for less overall effort.

- *Set specific, challenging goals—but make sure these are attainable.* One of the key findings of industrial/organizational psychology is that setting certain kinds of goals can increase both motivation and performance on many different tasks. This principle can be of great help to you in studying, and it's relatively easy to apply. First, set a concrete goal for each session—for example, "I'll read twenty pages and review my class notes." Merely telling yourself "I'll work until I'm tired" is less effective, because it fails to give you something concrete to shoot for. Second, try to set challenging goals, but ones you can attain. When goals are challenging, they encourage us to "stretch"—to do a little bit more. But if they are impossible to attain, they may cause us to despair—and to give up along the way. Since you are the world's greatest expert on your own limits and your own work habits, you are the best judge of what will be a challenging but attainable goal for *you*. Set such goals when you begin, and the results may surprise you.
- *Reward yourself for progress.* As you'll see in Chapter 5, people often perform various activities to attain external rewards; ones delivered to them by others. But in many cases, we can provide our own rewards; we can pat ourselves on the back for reaching goals we've set or for other accomplishments. This "pat on the back" can take many different forms: eating a favorite dessert, watching a favorite TV program, visiting friends. Again, you are the world's top expert on your own rewards, so you can readily choose ones that are appropriate. Whatever you choose, however, be sure to provide yourself with rewards for reaching your goals; you deserve it, and these intervals of pleasure will add to your efficiency.
- *Engage in active, not passive, studying.* As you probably know, it is possible to sit in front of a book or a set of notes for hours without accomplishing much—except daydreaming. In order to learn new materials and remember them, you must do mental work—that's an inescapable fact of life. You must think about the material you are reading, ask yourself questions about it, relate this new information to things you already know, and so on. To the extent you engage in such activities, you will really *learn* the materials you are studying—not merely be exposed to them. And once again, in the final analysis, this will save you time, for you'll actually accomplish more per hour of study than in any other way.

FIGURE 1.18

Improving Your Study Skills: How Psychology Can Help

Research findings in the areas of learning, memory, and motivation can help you become a more effective learner.

I know: following these guidelines sounds like a lot of . . . work! But once you master these techniques and learn to use them, the whole process will tend to get easier. And then you will learn and remember more, get better grades, and improve the value of your own education. Truly, it doesn't get much better than that.

Summary and Review of Key Questions

Modern Psychology: What It Is and Where It Came From

- **What ideas and trends converged to give rise to an independent, science-based field of psychology?** Ideas from philosophy suggesting that knowledge can be gathered through careful observation and careful reasoning combined with advances in other sciences led to the idea of a scientific field of psychology.
- **What is the definition of psychology?** Psychology is defined as the science of behavior and cognitive processes.
- **What are the three "grand issues" about behavior with which psychology must grapple?** These three issues are stability versus change, nature versus nurture, and rationality versus irrationality.
- **What are key differences between the various perspectives adopted by psychologists—the behavioral, cognitive, biological, social and cultural, psychodynamic, and evolutionary?** The behavioral perspective focuses on observable aspects of behavior. The cognitive perspective focuses on the nature of cognitive processes. The biological perspective focuses on the biological processes underlying behavior. The social and cultural perspective focuses on social interaction and various aspects of culture. The psychodynamic perspective suggests that many aspects of behavior stem from hidden forces within our personalities. The evolutionary perspective focuses on the role of inherited tendencies in behavior.
- **How do psychologists take account of cultural diversity in their research and in providing psychological services?** In their research, psychologists attempt to study the impact of cultural and ethnic factors on various aspects of behavior. In providing psychological services, they attempt to ensure that testing, therapy, and all aspects of psychological practice are sensitive to cultural and ethnic differences.

KEY TERMS

behaviorism, p. 7 • psychology, p. 7 • multicultural perspective, p. 12

Psychologists: Who They Are and What They Do

- **How does the training of psychologists differ from that of psychiatrists?** Psychologists receive Ph.D. or Psy.D. degrees in academic departments of psychology. Psychiatrists are medical doctors who specialize in the diagnosis and treatment of mental disorders.
- **What are the major subfields of psychology, and what aspects of behavior do they study?** The major subfields of psychology include cognitive psychology, developmental psychology, social psychology, psychobiology, and industrial/organizational psychology.

Psychology and the Scientific Method

- **Why can psychology be considered to be a scientific field?** Psychology can be considered to be a scientific field because in their research, psychologists employ the scientific method.
- **What values or guidelines are central to the scientific method?** Basic values of the scientific method include accuracy, objectivity, skepticism, and open-mindedness.
- **What is the role of theories in the scientific method?** Theories organize existing knowledge and make predictions that can be tested in actual research. Evidence gathered in research is used to refine a theory and can ultimately lead to the theory's acceptance as accurate or its rejection as false.
- **What's wrong with using informal observation and common sense as guides to understanding human behavior?** Common sense and intuition are not accurate guides to understanding human behavior because they often point to inconsistent or contradictory conclusions, and because they are subject to many forms of error.
- **What sources of potential error in our own thinking often lead us astray with respect to conclusions about behavior?** Important sources of error include the confirmation bias—our tendency to pay more attention to evidence that confirms our views than to evidence that refutes them; our reliance on mental shortcuts known as heuristics; and effects of our current moods on our thinking, judgments, and decisions.
- **How does the scientific method help to reduce or eliminate such errors?** The scientific method insists that researchers adhere to the values of accuracy, objectivity, skepticism, and open-mindedness.

KEY TERMS

theories, p. 17 • hypotheses, p. 17 • confirmation bias, p. 19 • availability heuristic, p. 19

The Scientific Method in Everyday Life: Thinking Critically about Human Behavior

- **What is critical thinking?** Critical thinking is thinking that avoids blind acceptance of conclusions or arguments and, instead, closely examines all assumptions, carefully evaluates existing evidence, and cautiously assesses all conclusions. In short, it is thinking that mirrors the key values of the scientific method.
- **What role does it play in psychology?** Psychologists are trained to think critically about all aspects of human behavior, and adopt this approach in their research.
- **What benefits can it provide for your everyday life?** Thinking critically can help you think in a more sophisticated and useful way about your own behavior and that of others and can help make you a more sophisticated consumer and voter.

KEY TERM

critical thinking, p. 21

Research Methods in Psychology: How Psychologists Answer Questions about Behavior

- **What is the basic nature of naturalistic observation? Of the case method? The survey method?** Naturalistic observation involves observing various aspects of behavior in natural settings. The case method involves collecting detailed information about individuals in order to develop general principles about behavior. In the survey method, large numbers of persons answer questions about aspects of their behavior or their personal views on various issues.
- **What is the correlational method of research, and what are some advantages it offers?** In the correlational method, researchers make efforts to determine whether relationships (correlations) exist between variables—that is, whether changes in one variable are accompanied by changes in another. The correlational method is easily adapted to the study of behavior in natural settings and can yield large amounts of information quickly. It can also be used to study relationships between many different variables.
- **Why doesn't the existence of a correlation between two variables necessarily indicate that one causes changes in the other?** Correlations do not ensure the existence of a causal link because changes in both variables may stem from a third variable. Thus, the two variables that are correlated may not influence each other directly.
- **What is the basic nature of experimentation?** Experimentation involves systematically altering one or more variables in order to determine whether changes in the variable(s) affect behavior.

- **Why must participants in an experiment be randomly assigned to different conditions?** Participants in an experiment must be randomly assigned to different conditions because only then is it possible to determine whether differences between the conditions stem from the independent variable or from differences among participants.
- **What is confounding of variables in an experiment?** Confounding occurs when one or more variables other than the independent variable are permitted to vary across conditions of an experiment.
- **What are experimenter effects, and what is the double-blind procedure?** Experimenter effects occur when unintentional influence is exerted by researchers on research participants. In the double-blind procedure, experimenters who interact with research participants do not know the hypothesis under investigation. As a result, the likelihood of experimenter effects is reduced.
- **What are inferential statistics, and how do they help psychologists interpret the findings of their research?** Inferential statistics are mathematical procedures that allow researchers to assess the likelihood that the results of their research occurred by chance. Only when the probability that results occurred by chance is quite low (for example, less than five times in a hundred) do psychologists accept the results of their research as being informative.
- **What is meta-analysis, and what role does it play in psychologists' interpretations of the findings of many studies dealing with the same aspect of behavior?** Meta-analysis is a statistical procedure for combining the results of many different experiments. Through meta-analysis, it is possible to determine whether, across all the studies considered, an independent variable has exerted significant effects upon behavior.

KEY TERMS

systematic observation, p. 23 • naturalistic observation, p. 23 • case method, p. 24 • survey method, p. 25 • sampling, p. 25 • correlation, p. 26 • correlational method, p. 26 • experimentation, p. 29 • independent variable, p. 29 • dependent variable, p. 29 • random assignment of participants to experimental conditions, p. 30 • experimenter effects, p. 32 • double-blind procedure, p. 32 • inferential statistics, p. 33 • replication, p. 33 • meta-analysis, p. 33

Ethical Issues in Psychological Research

- **What is deception, and why do many psychologists use it in their research?** Deception involves temporarily withholding information about an experiment from research participants. It is often used in psychological research because knowledge about the purposes of an experiment may affect participants' behavior in it.
- **What are informed consent and debriefing?** Informed consent requires that research participants be given information about all the events and procedures a study will involve before they agree to participate, and that they be told they are free to leave at any time. Debriefing requires that participants be given full information about all aspects of a study after they have participated in it.
- **What ethical issues are raised by research with animals?** Research with animals raises questions concerning the possibility that the subjects may be exposed to painful or dangerous conditions. Such conditions are very rare in psychological research. Moreover, offsetting any potential risk to animal subjects is the potential contribution of such research to human welfare.
- **What ethical dilemmas do psychologists often face in their work?** Psychologists often face ethical dilemmas concerning confidentiality of information given to them by clients, and concerning conflicted relationships (such as sexual attraction) between clients and psychologists.

KEY TERMS

deception, p. 34 • informed consent, p. 35 • debriefing, p. 35

Critical Thinking Questions

Appraisal

Most psychologists view their field as being scientific in nature. Do you agree? Explain why you accept this view.

Controversy

Do you think it is ever acceptable to withhold information about a study from persons participating in it? If not, how can researchers get around the problem that if individuals know the hypothesis under investigation, this knowledge may change their behavior?

Making Psychology Part of Your Life

Suppose that one day, you read a news story suggesting that married people who eat in fast-food restaurants several times each week are more likely to get divorced than people who rarely eat in such restaurants. How could you use critical thinking to make sense out of this surprising report?

C H A P T E R

O U T L I N E

Biological Bases of Behavior

A Look Beneath the Surface

Do you understand these words?

Are you wondering why I've begun this chapter by asking that question? The answer is simple: If you *are* reading and understanding the words on this page, then something must be happening in your brain. And that's the major theme of this chapter: All of our thoughts, feelings, and behavior originate from basic biological processes. Rapid advances in technology over the past several decades have enabled behavioral scientists to peek inside the nervous systems of living people to study these processes directly. This, in turn, has revealed ways in which biological processes interact with experience to determine how we think, feel, and act. The possibility of directly observing a functioning brain would have been viewed as science fiction only a generation ago; yet today it is a reality. Although our knowledge of

The possibility of directly observing a functioning brain would have been viewed as science fiction only a generation ago; yet today it is a reality.

the brain has not yet reached the level implied by the scene in Figure 2.1, exciting new discoveries are occurring at an astonishing pace. As we proceed through this chapter, I hope you will come to appreciate the enormous practical implications this progress holds for our understanding of the brain's many secrets.

Scientific study dedicated to unlocking the mysteries of biology and behavior is called **biopsychology** (Pinel, 1993). This term is appropriate because it accurately reflects the very broad scope of current efforts to understand how important aspects of behavior and cognition are related to complex biological processes. For example, perhaps you have wondered about such questions as these:

- What happens inside our bodies when we experience joy, anger, or sexual desire?
- How can our brains store memories of events that took place years or even decades ago?
- What happens when we dream? Make plans? Imagine future events or outcomes?
- How is our sexual orientation determined?

All these activities are related to biological events within our bodies; but what, precisely, are these events? Biopsychologists, too, are deeply interested in such questions. And although they do not yet have all the answers, they are making tremendous progress toward answering many important questions.

Of course, biopsychologists recognize that the brain does not exist in isolation, but rather performs in concert with other elements of our bodies and the physical and social environment. Armed with the tools of modern technology, behavioral scientists are hard at work, investigating how biological processes interact with environmental factors to determine how we think, feel, and act—sometimes, but not always, for the best, as we'll see later in this chapter. Fortunately, a growing body of evidence suggests that environmental factors can sometimes offset the effects of nature. Thus, while biological factors are powerful, they are not immutable.

We'll begin our discussion by examining the structure and function of neurons, the building blocks of the nervous system. As you'll soon see, understanding how neurons function—and especially how they communicate with one another—provides important insights into such diverse topics as how drugs exert their effects and how, perhaps, serious forms of mental illness develop. Recent research on the first of these topics offers important new insights into the nature of addiction to many drugs, including alcohol. Next, we will turn to the structure and function of the nervous system, devoting special attention to the brain, the marvelous organ that is ultimately responsible for consciousness—and for the fact that you are now reading and understanding these words. Discussion of the structure and function of the brain will lead us to several fascinating topics, including the surprising fact that the two sides of the brain are actually specialized for the performance of somewhat different tasks. In this section we'll also consider evidence for the possibility of sex-based differences in brain structure and function. After this, we will turn briefly to the endocrine system, internal glands regulated by the

FIGURE 2.1

Biopsychology in the Nineties

Although scientists have not yet succeeded in performing the brain transplant implied in this "Far Side" scene, they are making great strides toward understanding the biological bases of behavior.

THE FAR SIDE By GARY LARSON

"OK, Mr. Dittman, remember: That brain is only a temporary, so don't think too hard with it."

(**Source:** THE FAR SIDE copyright 1987 & 1990 FARWORKS, INC. Used with permission of UNIVERSAL PRESS SYNDICATE. All rights reserved.)

nervous system that play an important role in key aspects of behavior. We'll conclude our discussion by reviewing recent evidence that suggests how genetic and environmental factors interact to determine several important aspects of human behavior, physical and mental disorders, and even sexual orientation. Now let's discuss the structure and function of neurons.

Biopsychology: A branch of psychology interested in discovering the biological bases of our thoughts, feelings, and behaviors.

Neurons: Cells specialized for communicating information, the basic building blocks of the nervous system.

Dendrites: The parts of neurons that conduct action potentials toward the cell body.

Axon: The part of the neuron that conducts the action potential away from the cell body.

Neurons: Building Blocks of the Nervous System

Why does the following urgent message from your roommate: "Wake up—you're late for your exam!" produce overwhelming anxiety, a sinking feeling in the pit of your stomach, and a scramble to get to class? In other words, how can information reaching our ears produce sensations of panic, bodily reactions, and overt actions relating to these? The answer involves the activity of neurons—cells within our bodies that are specialized for the tasks of receiving, moving, and processing information.

Neurons: Their Basic Structure

Neurons are tremendously varied in appearance. Yet most consist of three basic parts: (1) a *cell body*, (2) an *axon*, and (3) one or more *dendrites*. **Dendrites** carry information toward the cell body, whereas the **axon** carries information away from it. Thus, in a sense, neurons are one-way channels of communication. Information usually moves from dendrites or the cell body toward the axon and then outward along this structure. A simplified diagram of a neuron is shown in Figure 2.2. Scientists estimate that the human brain may contain 100 billion neurons, or more.

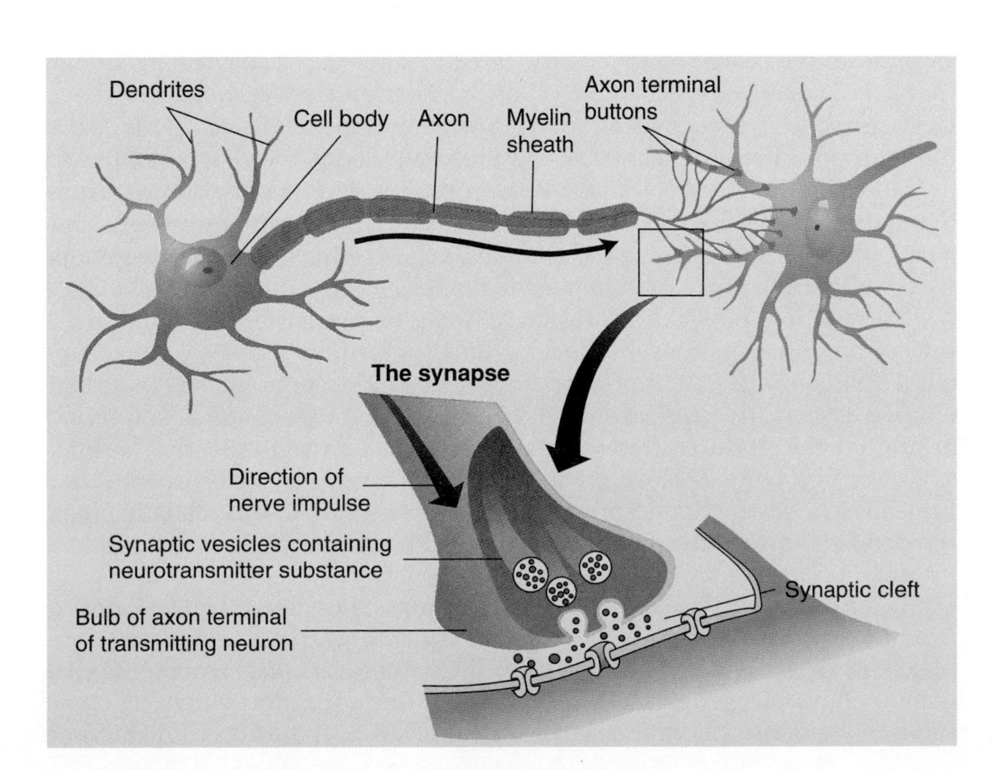

FIGURE 2.2

Neurons: Their Basic Structure

Neurons appear in many forms, but all possess the basic structures shown here: a cell body, an axon (with axon terminals), and one or more dendrites.

In many neurons the axon is covered by a sheath of fatty material known as *myelin*. The myelin sheath (fatty wrapping) is interrupted by small gaps. Both the sheath and the gaps in it play an important role in the neuron's ability to transmit information, a process we'll consider in detail shortly. Damage to the myelin sheath surrounding axons can seriously affect synaptic transmission. In diseases such as *multiple sclerosis* (MS), progressive deterioration of the myelin sheath leads to jerky, uncoordinated movement in the affected person. Richard Pryor, a noted comedian, currently suffers from MS.

The myelin sheath is actually produced by one of another basic set of building blocks within the nervous system, **glial cells**. Glial cells, which outnumber neurons by about ten to one, serve several functions in our nervous system; they form the myelin sheath around axons and perform basic housekeeping chores, such as cleaning up cellular debris. They also help form the *blood–brain barrier*—a structure that prevents certain substances in the bloodstream from reaching the brain.

Near its end, the axon divides into several small branches. These, in turn, end in round structures known as **axon terminals** that closely approach, but do not actually touch, other cells (other neurons, muscle cells, or gland cells). The region at which the axon terminals of a neuron closely approach other cells is known as the **synapse**. The manner in which neurons communicate with other cells across this tiny space is described next.

Neurons: Their Basic Function

As we consider how neurons function, two questions arise: (1) How does information travel from point to point within a single neuron, and (2) how is information transmitted from one neuron to another or from neurons to other cells of the body?

Communication within Neurons: Graded and Action Potentials The answer to the first question is complex but can be summarized as follows. When a neuron is at rest, there is a tiny electrical charge (–70 millivolts) across the cell membrane. That is, the inside of the cell has a slight negative charge relative to the outside. This electrical charge is due to the fact that several types of ions (positively and negatively charged particles) exist in different concentrations outside and inside the cell. As a result, the interior of the cell membrane acquires a tiny negative charge relative to the outside. This *resting potential* does not occur by accident; the neuron works to maintain the resting potential by actively pumping positively charged ions back outside if they enter, while retaining negatively charged ions in greater concentrations than are present outside the cell.

Stimulation, either direct (by light, heat, or pressure) or through messages from other neurons, produces **graded potentials**—a basic type of signal *within* neurons. An important feature of graded potentials is that their magnitude varies in proportion to the size of the stimulus. Thus, a loud sound or bright light produces graded potentials of greater magnitude than a softer sound or dim light. Because graded potentials tend to weaken quickly, they typically convey incoming information over short distances, usually along the dendrite toward the neuron's cell body. Please note that neurons receive information from many other cells—often from thousands of them.

If the overall pattern of graded potentials reaching the cell body is of sufficient magnitude—if it exceeds the *threshold* of the neuron in question—complex biochemical changes occur in the cell membrane, and an **action potential** is generated (please refer to Figure 2.3). During an action potential, some types of *positively charged ions* are briefly allowed to enter the cell membrane

Glial Cells: Cells in the nervous system that surround, support, and protect neurons.

Axon Terminals: Structures at the end of axons that contain transmitter substances.

Synapse: A region where the axon of one neuron closely approaches other neurons or the cell membrane of other types of cells such as muscle cells.

Graded Potential: A basic type of signal within neurons that results from external physical stimulation of the dendrite or cell body. Unlike the all-or-nothing nature of action potentials, the magnitude of graded potentials varies in proportion to the size of the stimulus.

Action Potential: A rapid shift in the electrical charge across the cell membrane of neurons. This disturbance along the membrane communicates information within neurons.

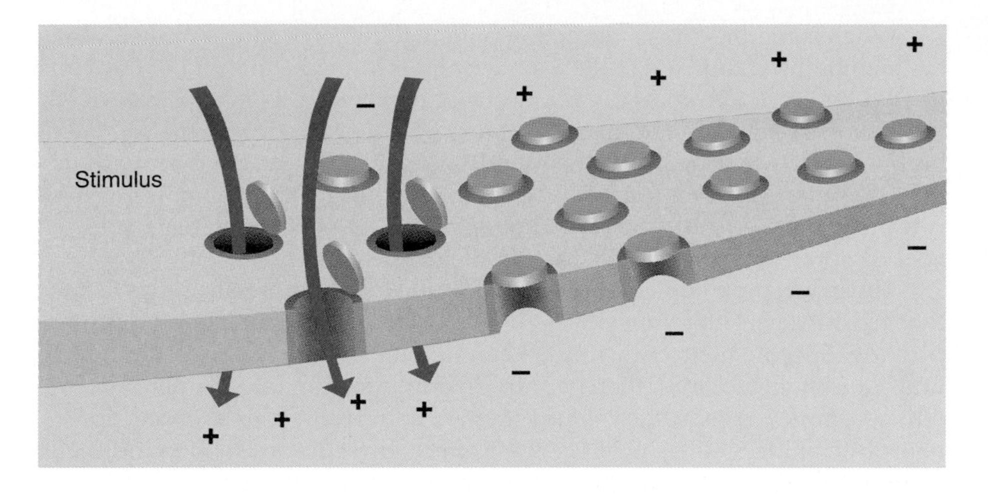

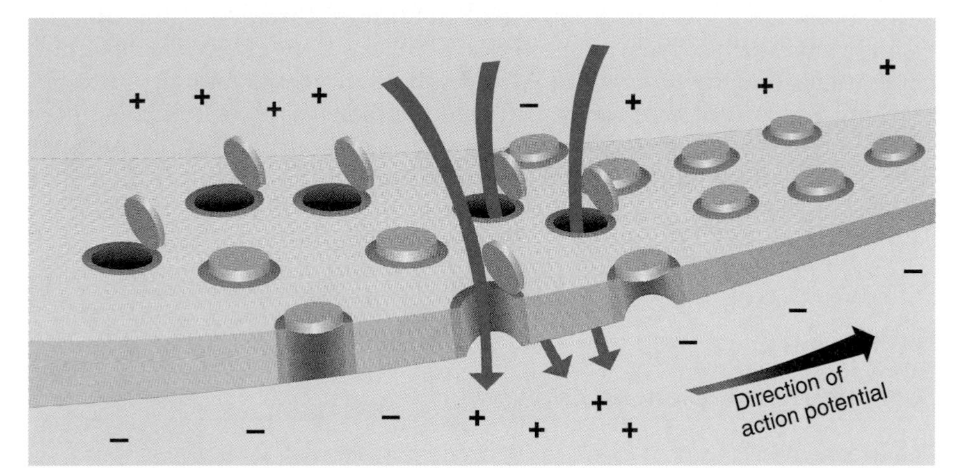

FIGURE 2.3

The Action Potential

(Top) During an action potential, positively charged particles enter the membrane through specialized ion channels, thereby momentarily eliminating the negative charge just inside the neuron's membrane. Movement of this disturbance along the membrane constitutes the action potential. (Bottom) After a brief period, however, positively charged particles are forced outside of the neuron's membrane via the ion channels.

through specialized pores called *ion channels* more readily than before. This influx of positive ions reduces and then totally eliminates the resting potential. Indeed, for a brief period of time, the interior of the cell actually attains a net positive charge relative to the outside.

After a very brief period (1 or 2 milliseconds), the neuron then actively pumps the positive ions back outside and allows other ions, which flowed outside via their own ion channels, to reenter. As a result, the resting potential is gradually restored, and the cell becomes ready to "fire" once again. Together, these swings in electric charge—from negative to positive and back again—constitute the action potential. And it is the passage of this electrical disturbance along the cell membrane that constitutes the basic signal within our nervous system.

Note, by the way, that unlike graded potentials, the action potential is an *all-or-none response*. Either it occurs at full strength or it does not occur at all; there is nothing in between. Also, the speed of conduction of an action potential is very rapid in neurons possessing a myelin sheath. In a sense, the action potential along myelinated axons jumps from one small gap in the sheath to another—openings known as **nodes of Ranvier**. Speeds along myelinated axons can reach 270 miles per hour.

Communication among Neurons: Synaptic Transmission

Earlier we saw that neurons closely approach, but do not actually touch, other neurons (or other cells of the body). How, then, does the action potential cross the gap? How does one neuron communicate with another neuron? Existing evidence points to the following answer.

Nodes of Ranvier: Small gaps in the myelin sheath surrounding the axons of many neurons.

Synaptic Vesicles: Structures in the axon terminals that contain various neurotransmitters.

Neurotransmitters: Chemicals, released by neurons, that carry information across the synapse.

When a neuron "fires," the action potential that is produced travels along the membrane of the axon to the axon terminals located at the end of the axon. Within the axon terminals are many structures known as **synaptic vesicles**. Arrival of the action potential causes these vesicles to approach the cell membrane, where they fuse with the membrane and then empty their contents into the synapse (see Figure 2.4). The chemicals thus released—known as **neurotransmitters**—travel across the tiny synaptic gap until they reach specialized receptor sites in the membrane of the other cell.

These receptors are complex protein molecules whose structure is such that neurotransmitter substances fit like chemical keys into the locks they provide. Specific neurotransmitters can deliver signals only at certain locations on cell membranes, thereby introducing precision into the nervous system's complex communication system. Upon binding to their receptors, neurotransmitters either produce their effects directly, or function indirectly through the interaction of the neurotransmitter and its receptor with other substances. It's important to note that neurotransmitters are not released exclusively into synapses; they can also be released into body fluids, which carry them to many other cells. As a result, their effects may be quite far-reaching and are not necessarily restricted to other, nearby neurons.

Whether directly or indirectly, however, neurotransmitters produce one of two effects (see Figure 2.5). If their effects are *excitatory* in nature, they help to *depolarize* (decrease the negative electrical charge of) the membrane of the

FIGURE 2.4

Synaptic Transmission: An Overview

The axon terminals found on the ends of axons contain many *synaptic vesicles*. When an action potential reaches the axon terminal, these vesicles move toward the cell membrane. Once there, the vesicles fuse with the membrane and release their contents (*neurotransmitters*) into the synapse.

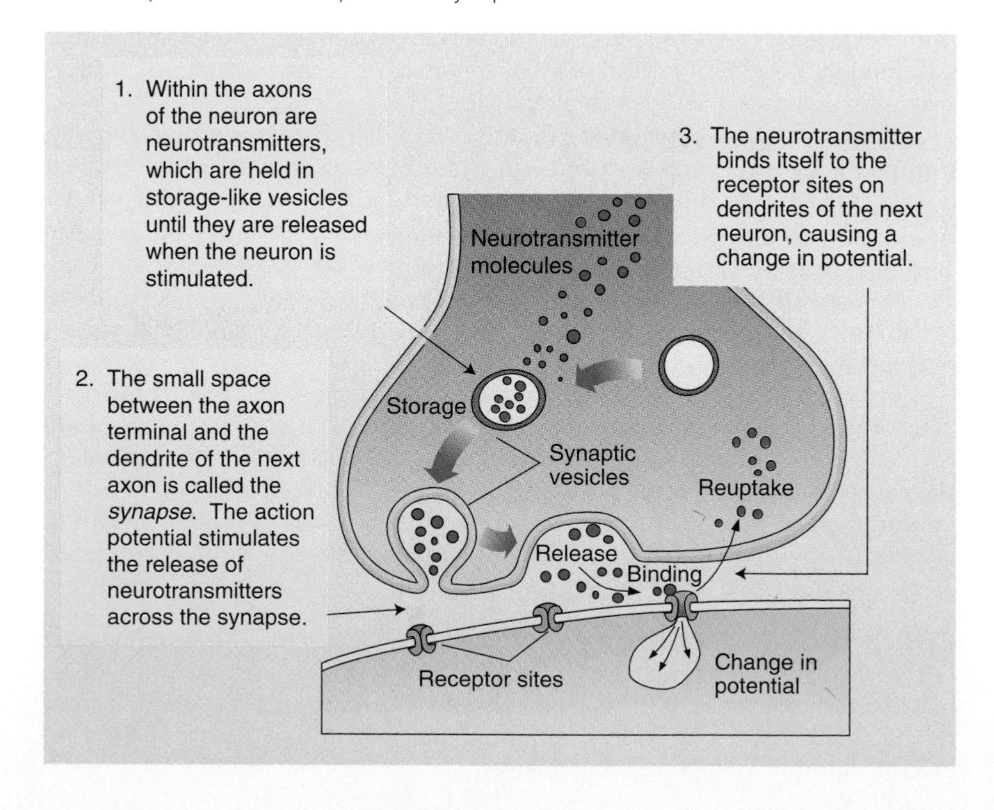

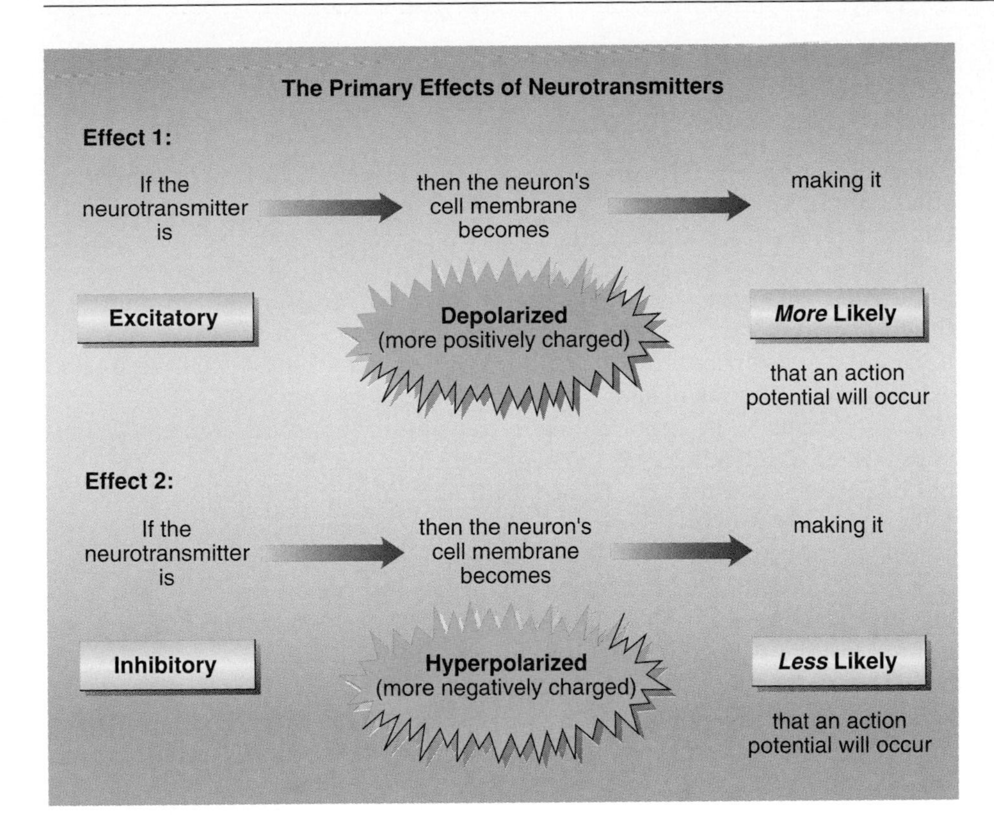

FIGURE 2.5

Neurotransmitters: Their Basic Effects

Neurotransmitters exert one of two basic effects on neurons. If the neurotransmitter is *excitatory* the neuron's cell membrane becomes depolarized (the charge becomes more positive); it increases the likelihood that an action potential will occur. In contrast, if the neurotransmitter is *inhibitory* the cell membrane of a neuron becomes hyperpolarized (the charge becomes more negative); its effects decrease the likelihood that an action potential will occur.

second neuron, making it more likely that the neuron will fire. Or the transmitter substances may produce *inhibitory* effects. In this case, they help *hyperpolarize* (increase the negative electrical charge of) the cell membrane of the second neuron, thereby making it less likely that the neuron will fire.

What happens to neurotransmitters *after* they cross the synapse from one neuron to another? The answer is relatively clear. Either they are taken back for reuse in the axon terminals of the neuron that released them, a process known as *reuptake*, or they are metabolized by various enzymes present at the synapse, and removed.

It is important to note that in my comments so far, I have greatly simplified reality by describing a situation in which one neuron contacts another across a single synapse. In fact, this rarely, if ever, happens. Most neurons actually form synapses with many others—ten thousand or more in some cases. Thus, at any given moment, most neurons are receiving a complex pattern of excitatory and inhibitory influences from many neighbors.

Whether a neuron conducts an action potential or not, then, depends on the total pattern (summation) of this input; for example, whether excitatory or inhibitory input predominates. Further, the effects of excitatory and inhibitory input can be cumulative over time, in part because such effects do not dissipate instantaneously. Thus, if a neuron that has recently been stimulated, but not sufficiently to produce an action potential, is stimulated again soon afterwards, the two sources of excitation may combine so that an action potential is generated.

In one sense, then, neurons act as tiny *decision-making* mechanisms, firing only when the pattern of information reaching them is just right. The fact that individual neurons affect and are, in turn, affected by many others strongly suggests that it is the total pattern or network of activity in the nervous system that is crucial. As we will see in later discussions, it is this intricate web of neural activity that generates the richness and complexity of our conscious experience.

Neurotransmitters: Chemical Keys to the Nervous System

The fact that transmitter substances produce either excitatory or inhibitory effects might seem to suggest that there are only two types of neurotransmitters. In fact, there are at least nine universally recognized substances known to function as neurotransmitters, and many more chemical substances appear to function as neurotransmitters. Several known neurotransmitters and their functions are summarized in Table 2.1. Although the specific roles of many transmitter substances remain largely unknown, a few have been investigated extensively. We'll look at some of these in more detail next.

Acetylcholine is an important neurotransmitter found throughout the nervous system. Acetylcholine is the neurotransmitter at most junctions between motor neurons (neurons concerned with muscular movements) and muscle cells. Anything that interferes with the action of acetylcholine can produce paralysis. South American hunters have long used this fact to their advantage by dipping their arrow tips in *curare*—a poisonous substance that occupies acetylcholine receptors. The result? Because of the paralysis induced, the hunted animal dies quickly through suffocation. Acetylcholine is also believed to play a role in attention, arousal, and memory processes. Scientists believe that the severe memory loss characteristic of persons suffering from *Alzheimer's disease* results from a degeneration of cells that produce acetyl-

TABLE 2.1

Neurotransmitters: A Summary

Neurons have been found to communicate by means of many different *neurotransmitters*. Some of these are listed and described here.

Neurotransmitter	Location	Effects
Acetylcholine	Found throughout the central nervous system, in the autonomic nervous system, and at all neuromuscular junctions.	Involved in muscle action, learning, and memory.
Norepinephrine	Found in neurons in the autonomic nervous system.	Primarily involved in control of alertness and wakefulness.
Dopamine	Produced by neurons located in a region of the brain called the substantia nigra.	Involved in movement, attention, and learning. Degeneration of dopamine-producing neurons has been linked to Parkinson's disease. Too much dopamine has been linked to schizophrenia.
Serotonin	Found in neurons in the brain and spinal cord.	Plays a role in the regulation of mood and in the control of eating, sleep, and arousal. Has also been implicated in the regulation of pain and in dreaming.
GABA (gamma-amino-butyric acid)	Found throughout the brain and spinal cord.	GABA is the major inhibitory neurotransmitter in the brain. Abnormal levels of GABA have been implicated in sleep and eating disorders.

choline. Examinations of the brains of persons who have died from this disease show unusually low levels of this substance (Coyle, Price, & DeLong, 1983).

Parkinson's Disease: A progressive and ultimately fatal disorder, caused by a deterioration of dopamine-producing neurons in the brain.

The neurotransmitter *dopamine* serves as a good example of the fact that either too little or too much of a good thing can often have profound effects—at least where neurotransmitters are concerned. In **Parkinson's disease,** a progressive and ultimately fatal disorder, afflicted persons experience a gradual onset of tremors and muscle rigidity, followed by loss of balance and difficulty initiating movements. The symptoms of Parkinson's disease are the result of progressive degeneration of dopamine-producing neurons in an area of the brain associated with motor function. Unfortunately, *too much* dopamine can also have negative effects. High levels of dopamine have been found in persons with *schizophrenia,* a severe psychological disorder that we'll discuss in Chapter 14.

Endorphins were first discovered during the 1970s by researchers studying the effects of *morphine* and other opiates. To their surprise, the researchers learned there were special receptor sites for such drugs within the brain (Hughes et al., 1975). This was indeed intriguing: Why should such receptors exist? It was soon discovered that naturally occurring substances that closely resemble morphine in physical structure are produced by the brain. These substances, known as *endorphins,* act as neurotransmitters, stimulating specialized receptor sites. Why should the brain produce such substances? Research suggests that endorphins are released by the body in response to pain or vigorous exercise and so help reduce sensations of pain that might otherwise interfere with ongoing activity (Fields & Basbaum, 1984). Additional evidence indicates that endorphins also serve to intensify positive sensations—for example, the "runner's high" many people experience after vigorous exercise.

In short, it appears that the brain possesses an internal mechanism for moderating unpleasant sensations and magnifying positive ones, and that the effects of morphine and other opiates stem, at least in part, from the fact that these drugs stimulate this naturally existing system.

This fact, and related evidence, has led to research efforts aimed at identifying drugs to alter synaptic transmission for practical purposes. In fact, understanding the process of synaptic transmission may be the key to successful treatment of various addictions and mental disorders. For examples of how knowledge of synaptic transmission has been used in the development of effective treatments for psychological disorders, please see the **Ideas to Take with You** feature on page 52. In the next section, I'll describe ways in which psychologists have used their knowledge of synaptic transmission to battle addictions to alcohol and other drugs.

Neurotransmitters: Using Knowledge of Synaptic Transmission to Treat Drug Addictions

Each day, hundreds of millions of persons use drugs to combat insomnia and to fight fatigue; to calm jittery feelings or increase energy; to chase away the blues or, perhaps, simply to get high. The explosion in recreational drug use (and abuse) during the past several decades has had devastating effects on our society, both economically and socially. Drugs affect our feelings or behavior by altering the process of synaptic transmission. They produce their effects—including the feelings of pleasure many addicts strongly crave—by changing the complex biochemical events that occur when one neuron communicates with another. In the most basic terms, such effects take one of two

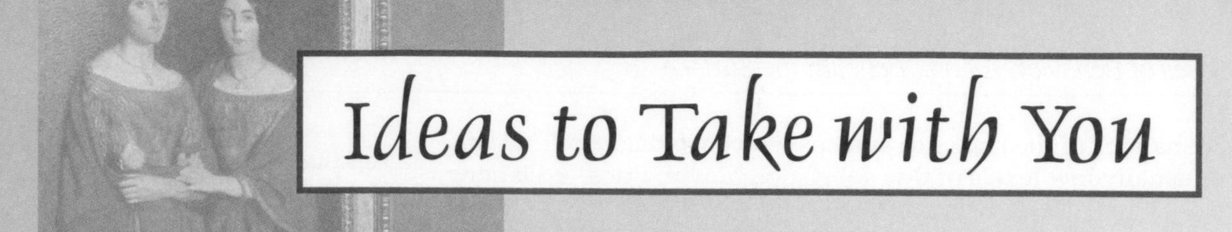

Applying Knowledge of Synaptic Transmission to Treat Psychological Disorders

As we've noted throughout this section, scientists—including biopsychologists—have learned a great deal about the nature of neural transmission in the nervous system. This knowledge is proving helpful in the treatment of many psychological disorders, as illustrated in the examples below.

Schizophrenia

A chronic disorganization of mental function that affects thinking (paranoid ideas, high distractibility), feelings (blunted affect, inappropriate reactions to social situations), and movement (from hyperactivity and excitement to bizarre postures maintained for extended periods of time).

What's Going on Here?

Schizophrenia is associated with too much dopamine in the brain.

How Is It Treated?

Schizophrenia can often be treated successfully with dopamine antagonists—drugs that block the action of dopamine at certain receptor sites in the brain.

Depression

A psychological disorder involving intense feelings of sadness, lack of energy, and feelings of hopelessness and despair.

What's Going on Here?

Some types of depression appear to be associated with decreased levels of serotonin—a neurotransmitter—in the brain.

How Is It Treated?

Successful treatment of depression has included drugs, such as Prozac, that block the reuptake of serotonin in the synapse, thereby increasing the amount of available serotonin at certain receptor sites.

Scientists are hopeful that eventually knowledge of neural transmission in the nervous system will lead to effective treatments for other physical and psychological disorders, including Alzheimer's disease, multiple sclerosis, and obsessive–compulsive disorder, to name but a few.

major forms. If a particular drug mimics, or enhances the impact of, a specific neurotransmitter at a receptor site, it is said to be an **agonist** of the neurotransmitter. If, in contrast, a drug interferes with, or inhibits the impact of, a neurotransmitter at a receptor site, it is said to be an **antagonist** of the neurotransmitter. The specific ways in which drugs can function as agonists or antagonists in synaptic transmission are summarized in Figure 2.6.

Many drugs exert their effects on behavior through one or more of these mechanisms (e.g., Kalivas & Samson, 1992). For example, cocaine seems to produce its effects by inhibiting reuptake of such neurotransmitters as dopamine, serotonin, and norepinephrine. As a result of this inhibition, the

Agonist: A chemical substance that facilitates the action of a neurotransmitter at a receptor site.

Antagonist: A chemical substance that inhibits the impact of a neurotransmitter at a receptor site.

FIGURE 2.6

Drugs: How They Influence Synaptic Transmission

Various drugs produce their effects either by facilitating (agonistic) or by interfering with (antagonistic) the operation of specific transmitter substances.

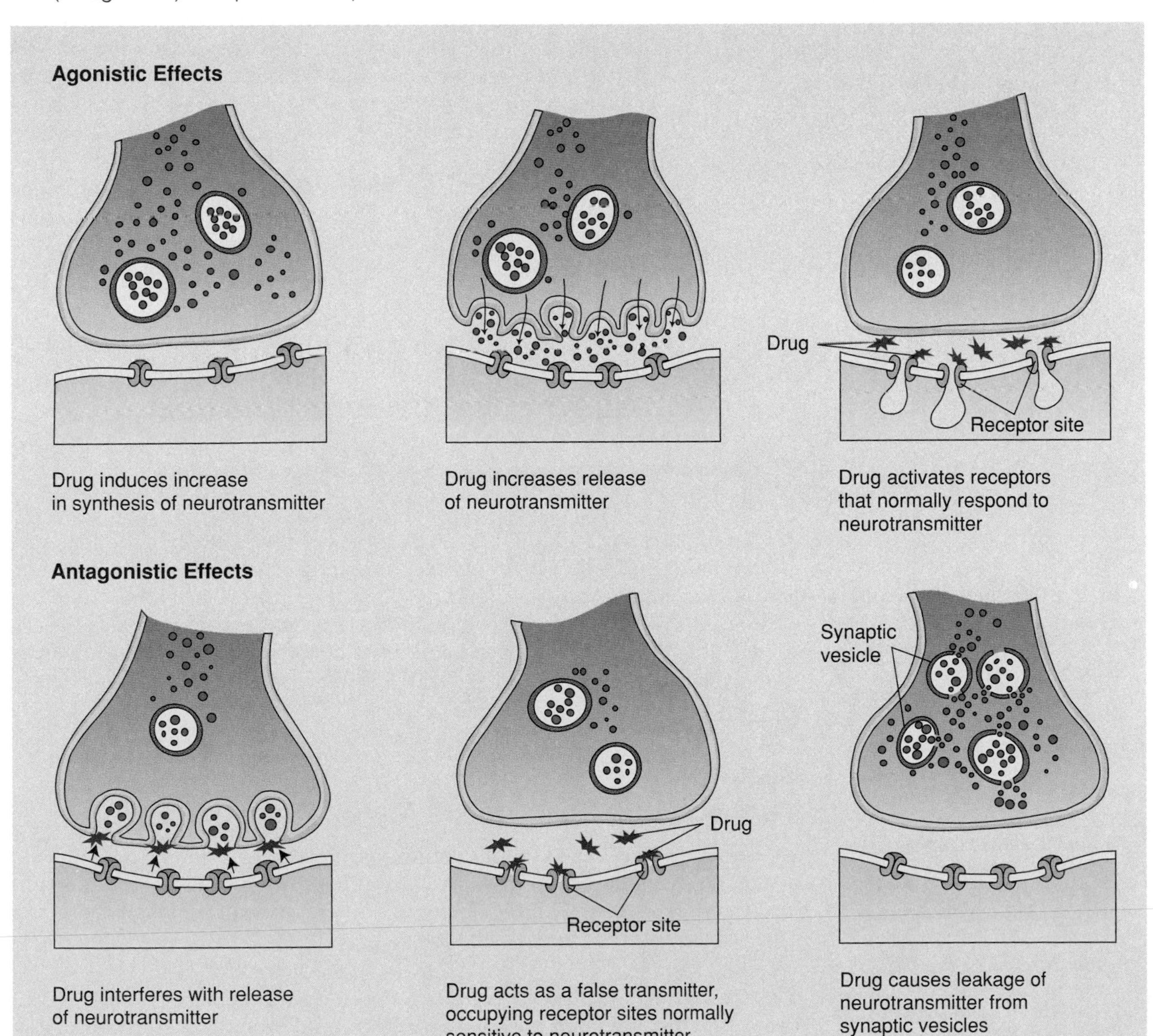

neurotransmitters remain in the synapse, where they stimulate continued activity in many neurons. This is one reason why persons taking such drugs often experience feelings of tremendous excitement and energy.

Several converging lines of evidence point to the conclusion that the addicting properties of several drugs may derive, at least in part, from their impact on naturally occurring reward circuits deep within the brain (Bozarth, 1987; Phillips & Fibiger, 1989). If this is indeed the case, then one way of combating such addictions would be to administer other drugs—ones that prevent opiates and other substances that are often abused, such as alcohol, from stimulating the reward circuits (e.g., Reid, 1996).

At this point you may be asking, "So . . . how can psychologists tell whether a drug is effective in blocking the rewarding properties of drugs like cocaine or alcohol?" Actually, psychologists have developed methods that are surprisingly straightforward, but elegant in terms of their ingenuity, as we'll see in the Research Methods section. Of course, since some of these procedures require the use of surgical procedures, animals—typically rats—serve as research subjects. This, in turn, poses another potential problem: If the goal is to determine whether a drug has addictive potential—in other words, whether taking a drug makes the rat feel good—how would you know? After all, laboratory rats rarely have anything to say. Fortunately, psychologists have discovered ways to get at these answers—without the need for talking rats.

Based on success stories like the one described in the Research Methods feature, researchers are hopeful that a new arsenal of drugs for other addictions is right around the corner. Please stay tuned.

Key Questions

- What is biopsychology?
- What do neurons do, and what are their parts?
- What are graded potentials and action potential? How do neurons communicate with one another?
- What are the effects of neurotransmitters?
- How do drugs produce their effects? What are agonists? Antagonists?

The Nervous System: Its Basic Structure and Functions

If neurons are the building blocks, then the **nervous system** is the structure they, along with other types of cells, combine to erect. The nervous system, actually a complex network of nerve cells that regulates our bodily functions and permits us to react to the external world in countless ways, deserves very careful attention. In this section I will describe the basic structure of the nervous system and will introduce several techniques psychologists use to study its complex functions.

Nervous System: The complex structure that regulates bodily processes and is responsible, ultimately, for all aspects of conscious experience.

Central Nervous System: The brain and the spinal cord.

Peripheral Nervous System: The portion of the nervous system that connects internal organs and glands, as well as voluntary and involuntary muscles, to the central nervous system.

Afferent Nerves: Nerve cells that carry information from receptors throughout the body toward the brain.

The Nervous System: Its Major Divisions

Although the nervous system functions as an integrated whole, it is viewed as having two major portions—the **central nervous system** and the **peripheral nervous system.** Figure 2.7 on page 56 presents diagrams of these and other divisions of the nervous system.

The Central Nervous System The central nervous system (CNS) consists of the brain and the spinal cord. Since I'll soon describe the structure of the brain in detail, we won't examine it here. The spinal cord runs through

■ RESEARCH METHODS ■

How Psychologists Study Synaptic Transmission

The development of tools to assess the addictive potential of drugs actually began in the 1950s when researchers attempted to determine whether electrical stimulation of a particular area of the brain would increase arousal and so facilitate learning. Quite by accident, an electrode they placed in the brain of one of their subjects (a laboratory rat) missed its mark and ended up in the limbic system instead. In retrospect, this was a lucky accident, for the effects produced by stimulation of the limbic system and hypothalamus were profound. When given weak bursts of electricity each time it entered one corner of its cage, the rat soon began to come back for more on a regular basis.

Then a brilliant idea occurred to researchers Olds and Milner: Why not implant a tiny electrode in the rats' skulls and permit the rats to provide their own brain stimulation by pushing a lever? Tests of the new procedure, termed *intracranial self-stimulation* or ICS, revealed dramatic results: Subjects would press the lever hundreds—even thousands—of times, until they literally collapsed from exhaustion (Olds, 1973; Olds & Milner, 1954). In contrast, when electrodes were placed in other locations, subjects would press the lever once, then avoid it altogether. Olds and Milner concluded that they had discovered discrete "pleasure" and "pain" circuits within the brain.

Since then, researchers have generally concluded that this "reward" circuit is a bundle of nerve fibers known as the *medial forebrain bundle* (Bozarth, 1987; Phillips & Fibiger, 1989). Low-level electrical stimulation of this circuit produces consistently higher rates of lever pressing than stimulation in other, adjacent areas. Levels of dopamine—a neurotransmitter in this system—also appear to rise after stimulation, whereas damage to this system greatly reduces self-stimulation (Fibiger et al., 1987).

Interestingly, research has also revealed that *opiates*—drugs that produce intensely pleasurable sensations for those addicted to them—appear to exert their effects, at least in part, through the same "reward" system just described. For example, rats readily learn to press a lever for small injections of cocaine or morphine, and tiny injections of these drugs directly into the terminal fields of the medial forebrain bundle increase rats' lever pressing for ICS (Goeders, Lane, & Smith, 1984). Apparently, these substances enhance the pleasure rats derive from ICS alone.

When subjects are given antagonists—chemicals that inhibit the action of neurotransmitters in this system—the rats' lever pressing is sharply reduced. These findings suggest that when activity related to dopamine or other naturally occurring neurotransmitters in the medial forebrain bundle is inhibited, opiates lose much of their appeal (Phillips, Spyraki, & Fibiger, 1982). More recent evidence has shown that the rewarding effects of several other drugs, including cocaine and amphetamines, are related to the fact that they enhance the impact of dopamine and other neurotransmitter substances (Wise & Bozarth, 1987).

Reid and his colleagues (1996) recently used the ICS procedure just described to test whether an opioid antagonist (naltrindole) could block the rewarding effects of a highly addictive recreational drug called *MDMA* or *ecstasy*. To test this possibility, the researchers first trained subjects (rats) to lever press for intracranial stimulation. Then the rats received injections of MDMA—either alone, or in combination with naltrindole. As predicted, MDMA increased rats' lever pressing for ICS. In contrast, naltrindole blocked the drug's enhancement of pressing for ICS. Please note, however, that these results are preliminary; naltrindole may not be the drug of choice to treat addictions in people. For example, it may have negative effects on the immune system. Still, the results of this, and of related research (e.g., Hubbell & Reid, 1995), show that an understanding of synaptic transmission—and access to procedures such as intracranial self-stimulation—can be helpful tools in the search for treatments effective in the war against drug abuse.

Although the findings discussed in this section are primarily based on animal research, similar results have been obtained with humans. For example, consider a study by Volpicelli and his colleagues (1992). Based on the success of previous animal research (e.g., Reid, 1990), these researchers administered the drug naltrexone (an opioid antagonist) or a placebo to two groups of persons suffering from alcohol dependence. The results showed that compared to the control group, persons in the group who received naltrexone reported much weaker cravings for alcohol, indicated that they drank less alcohol, and—most importantly—were less likely to resume drinking after the study had ended.

---

the middle of a bony column of hollow bones known as *vertebrae*. You can feel these by moving your hand up and down the middle of your back.

The spinal cord has two major functions. First, it carries sensory information to the brain via **afferent nerves** leading from receptors located throughout the body and conducts information from the brain via **efferent nerves** to muscles and glands. Second, it plays a key role in various *reflexes*. These are

Efferent Nerves: Nerve cells that carry information from the brain to muscles and glands throughout the body.

FIGURE 2.7

Major Divisions of the Nervous System

The nervous system consists of several major parts.

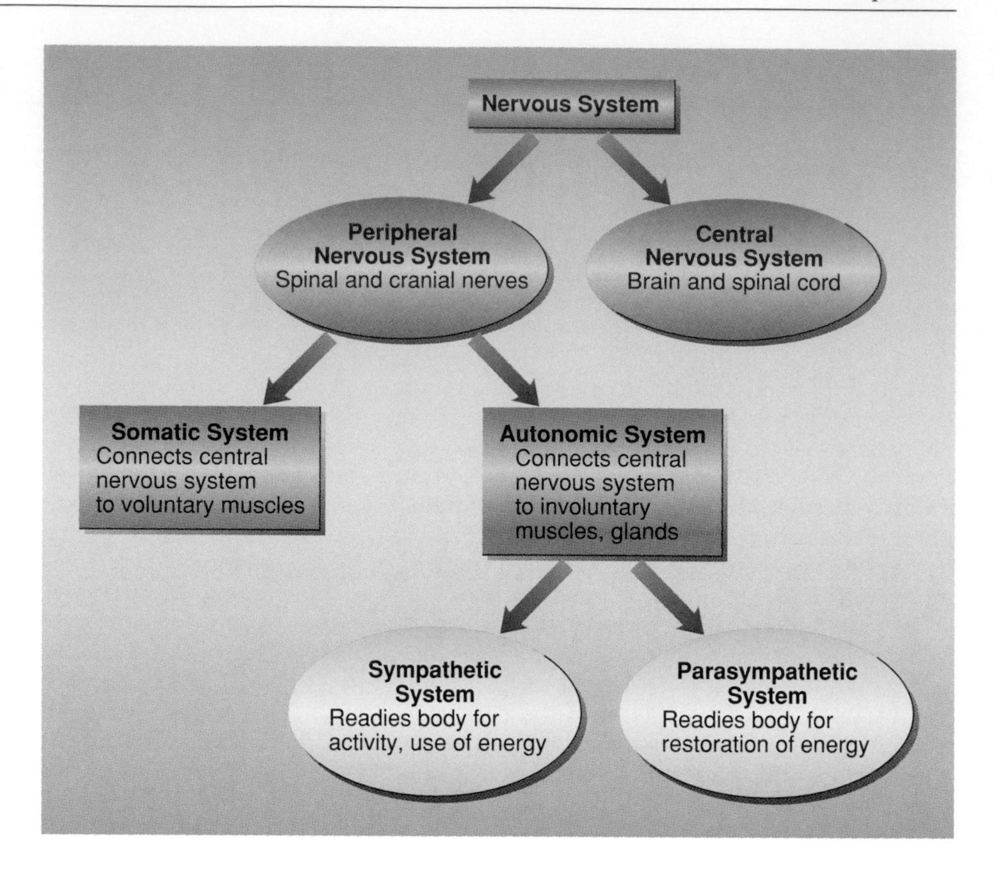

seemingly automatic actions evoked rapidly by particular stimuli. Withdrawing your hand from a hot object and blinking your eye in response to a rapidly approaching object are common examples of reflex actions. In their simplest form, reflexes involve neural circuits in which information from various receptors is carried to the spinal cord, where it stimulates other neurons known as *interneurons*. These then transmit information to muscle cells, thus producing reflex actions. But please take note: Reflexes are usually much more complex than this. Hundreds or even thousands of neurons may influence a reflex, and input from certain areas of the brain may be involved as well. However they arise, spinal reflexes offer an obvious advantage: They permit us to react to potential dangers much more rapidly than we could if the information first had to travel all the way to the brain.

The Peripheral Nervous System The peripheral nervous system consists primarily of *nerves*, bundles of axons from many neurons, which connect the central nervous system with sense organs and with muscles and glands throughout the body. Most of these nerves are attached to the spinal cord; these *spinal nerves* serve all of the body below the neck. Other nerves known as *cranial nerves* extend from the brain. They carry sensory information from receptors in the eyes and ears and other sense organs; they also carry information from the central nervous system to muscles in the head and neck.

Somatic Nervous System: The portion of the peripheral nervous system that connects the brain and spinal cord to voluntary muscles.

Autonomic Nervous System: The part of the peripheral nervous system that connects internal organs, glands, and involuntary muscles to the central nervous system.

As you can see in Figure 2.7, the peripheral nervous system has two subdivisions: the **somatic** and **autonomic nervous systems.** The somatic nervous system connects the central nervous system to voluntary muscles throughout the body. Thus, when you engage in almost any voluntary action, such as ordering a pizza or reading the rest of this chapter, portions of your somatic nervous system are involved. In contrast, the autonomic nervous system connects the central nervous system to internal organs and glands and to muscles over which we have little voluntary control—for instance, the muscles in our digestive system.

Still, we can't stop dividing things here. The autonomic nervous system, too, consists of two distinct parts. The first is known as the **sympathetic nervous system.** In general, this system prepares the body for using energy, as in vigorous physical actions. Thus, stimulation of this division increases heartbeat, raises blood pressure, releases sugar into the blood for energy, and increases the flow of blood to muscles used in physical activities. The second portion of the autonomic system, known as the **parasympathetic nervous system,** operates in the opposite manner. It stimulates processes that conserve the body's energy. Activation of this system slows heartbeat, lowers blood pressure, and diverts blood away from skeletal muscles (for example, muscles in the arms and legs) and to the digestive system. Figure 2.8 summarizes many of the functions of the sympathetic and parasympathetic divisions of the autonomic nervous system.

At first glance it might appear that these two parts of the autonomic system oppose one another in a head-on clash. In fact, they actually function in

Sympathetic Nervous System: The portion of the autonomic nervous system that readies the body for expenditure of energy.

Parasympathetic Nervous System: The portion of the autonomic nervous system that readies the body for restoration of energy.

FIGURE 2.8

The Autonomic Nervous System: An Overview

The autonomic nervous system consists of two major parts: the sympathetic and the parasympathetic nervous systems. Some of the functions of each are shown here.

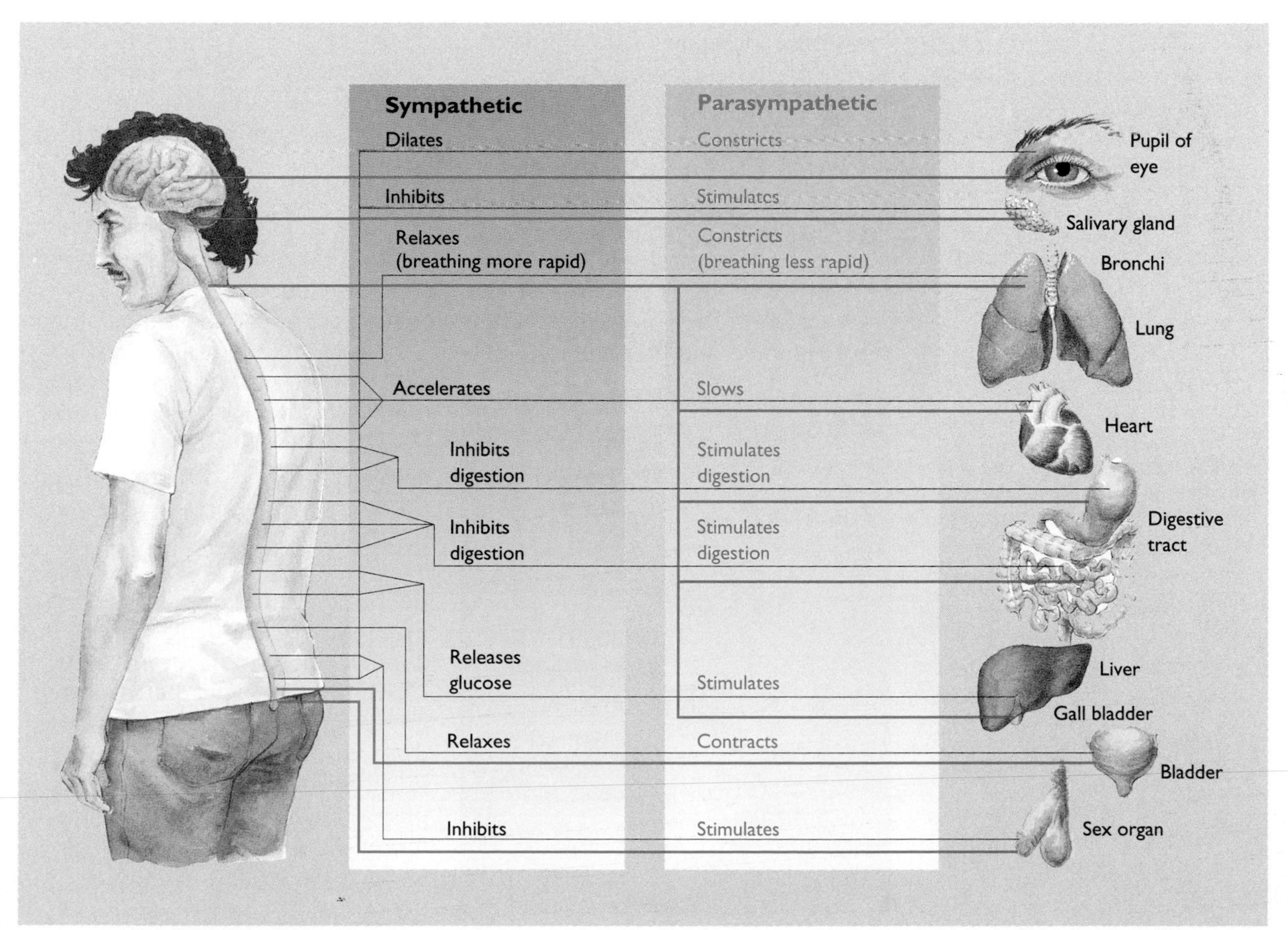

a coordinated manner. For example, after you eat a large meal on a warm day, the parasympathetic system stimulates your digestion while at the same time the sympathetic system increases sweating in order to eliminate excess heat.

Before concluding, I should emphasize that while the autonomic nervous system plays an important role in the regulation of bodily processes, it does so mainly by transmitting information to and from the central nervous system. Thus, it is the central nervous system, ultimately, that runs the show.

The Nervous System: How It Is Studied

Suppose that you are a psychologist interested in creating a map of the brain, one that reveals the brain structures and processes involved in various mental activities and behaviors. How do you get the information from which to construct your map? While there are no simple answers to this question, biopsychologists and others have devised several ingenious methods for obtaining such information.

Observing the Effects of Damage to the Brain If a particular part of the nervous system plays a role in a specific form of behavior, then damage to this area should affect the behavior in question. In perhaps the earliest method of brain research, scientists observed the behavior of persons who had suffered obvious damage to their brain or nervous system through accident. Then, following the death of these persons—sometimes years after the injury had occurred—researchers examined their brains to identify the location and extent of the brain injury. One of the most dramatic cases of severe brain injury occurred in a man named Phineas Gage during the mid-1800s. Gage suffered severe damage to his brain when an explosion drove a metal tamping rod completely through his skull (see Figure 2.9). Amazingly, Gage survived the blast—but he was never again the same person. He could no longer control his emotions and frequently exhibited fits of rage. Inspection of Phineas Gage's brain after his death showed extensive damage to the part of the brain involved in controlling emotions—a clear illustration of the intimate relationship between the brain and behavior.

In a related approach, researchers destroy portions of the brains of laboratory animals and then carefully observe the behavioral effects of such damage. For example, scientists might damage or destroy the portion of the brain assumed to be important in eating in order to determine if such procedures influence subjects' eating habits.

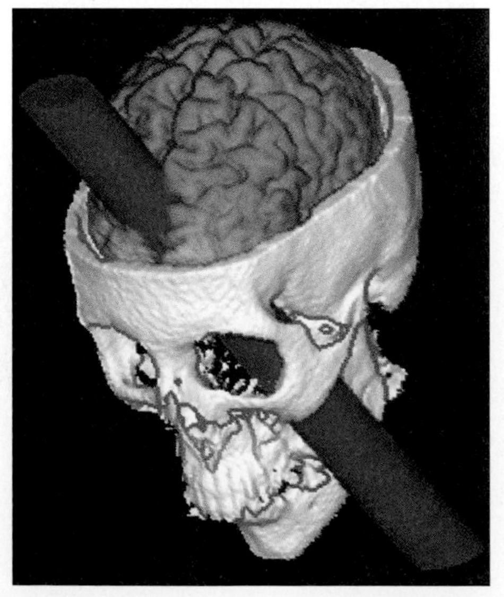

FIGURE 2.9

The Effects of Brain Damage: A Classic Case

Psychologists still marvel that Phineas Gage was able to survive the blast that hurled the tamping rod through his skull.

Psychologists have also mapped the brain's functions by using minute quantities of drugs to produce damage at specific brain sites, or to stimulate or anesthetize specific groups of neurons. If, for example, a drug that anesthetizes neurons is introduced into an area believed to play a role in speech production, we might expect the ability to speak to decrease while the drug's effects persist.

Electrical Recording and Brain Stimulation If a particular part of the brain plays a role in some form of behavior, this part should be particularly active during that behavior. Consistent with this reasoning, neuroscientists attempt to study the nervous system by recording electrical activity within the brain. Sometimes this involves measuring the electrical activity of the entire brain by means of electrodes placed at standard locations across the skull—a procedure called **electroencephalography,** or **EEG.**

In a related procedure, scientists measure the location and timing of brain activity (*event-related potentials* or ERPs) while people perform various cognitive tasks. Some research suggests the use of ERPs may be a useful diagnostic tool: ERPs may be able to yield important information about the cognitive processes of individuals at risk for various forms of psychopathology, such as Alzheimer's disease (Polich, 1993). A specific component of the ERP appears to reflect how cognitive resources are allocated in response to novel stimuli and when the memory for previous stimulus events is updated.

Electroencephalography (EEG): A technique for measuring the electrical activity of the brain via electrodes placed at specified locations on the skull.

Magnetic Resonance Imaging (MRI): A method for studying the intact brain in which technicians obtain images by exposing the brain to a strong magnetic field.

SQUID (Superconducting Quantum Interference Device): An imaging technique that captures images of the brain through its ability to detect tiny changes in magnetic fields in the brain.

Images of the Living Brain: MRIs, SQUIDs, and PETs Perhaps most exciting, however, is an alphabet soup of techniques that provide detailed images of the living brain's structures and functions. The first of these techniques is **magnetic resonance imaging,** or **MRI.** Here, images of the brain are obtained by means of a strong magnetic field. Hydrogen atoms, found in all living tissue, emit measurable waves of energy when exposed to such a field. In MRI these waves are measured and combined to form images of the brain (see Figure 2.10, left). These MRI images are impressively clear and therefore extremely useful in diagnoses of many brain disorders.

A second recently developed imaging device is called **SQUID**—short for **superconducting quantum interference device.** SQUID produces images based on its ability to detect tiny changes in magnetic fields in the brain (see Figure 2.10, right). Apparently, when neurons fire, they create an electric current. Electric currents, in turn, give rise to magnetic fields that the SQUID interprets as neural activity. Researchers have used SQUIDs in the mapping

FIGURE 2.10

Images of the Living Brain: MRI and SQUID

(Left) Magnetic resonance imaging (MRI) provides detailed images of the body's internal structures and is especially useful in diagnosing brain disorders. (Right) SQUID is a recently developed imaging device that operates by detecting tiny changes in magnetic fields in the brain.

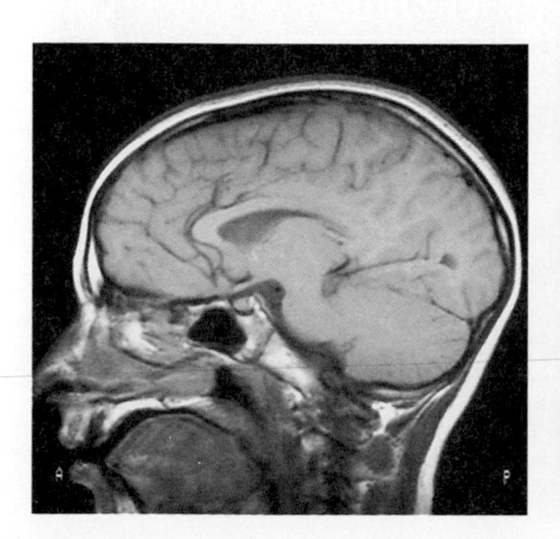

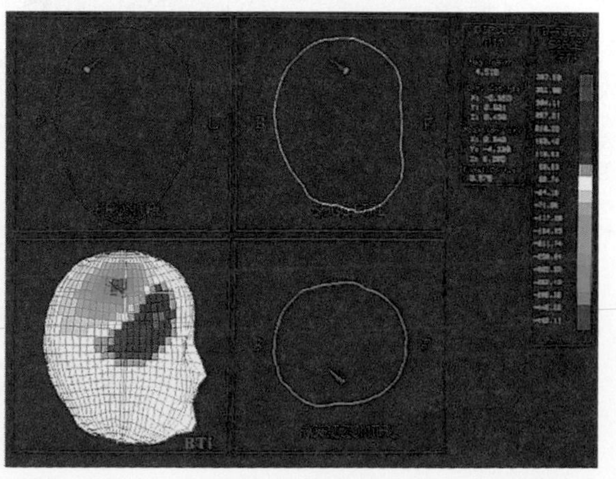

Positron Emission Tomography (PET): An imaging technique that detects the activity of the brain by measuring glucose utilization or blood flow.

of various brain functions, including construction of a representation of the hearing part of the brain.

A third high-tech method neuroscientists use to snoop on the living brain is **positron emission tomography,** or **PET,** scans. PET scans provide information regarding the metabolic activity of the brain—how active its various parts are at a given point in time. PET scans do this by measuring blood flow in various neural areas, or by gauging the rate at which glucose, the brain's fuel, is metabolized. Individuals undergoing PET scans are injected with small amounts of harmless radioactive isotopes attached to either water or glucose molecules. Blood flow (containing the radioactive water molecules) is greatest in the most active areas of the brain. Similarly, glucose is absorbed by brain cells in proportion to their level of activity, with the most active cells taking in the greatest amount of glucose. As a result, PET scans allow scientists to map activity in various parts of a person's brain as she or he reads, listens to music, or engages in a mental activity such as solving math problems.

The Nervous System: Putting Brain-Imaging Devices to Work

The development of "high-tech snoopers" has enabled researchers to apply these techniques in intriguing ways. One application involves performing brain scans on normal persons and on persons with mental disorders to detect differences in the activity of their brains (Delvenne et al., 1995; Sedvall, 1992). PET scans of persons with *obsessive–compulsive disorders* (characterized by persistent, uncontrollable intrusions of unwanted thoughts and urges to engage in ritualistic behaviors) consistently show increased activity in several areas of the brain, including the frontal lobe of the cerebral cortex—a brain region believed to be involved in impulse control and response inhibition (see Figure 2.11). Following successful pharmacologic or psychosurgical treatment, PET scans of these patients' brains show decreased activity in these areas. These findings suggest that imaging techniques may help researchers monitor the effects of treatments for a variety of mental disorders.

Imaging techniques may also reveal how the brain delegates mental tasks. In one study, researchers used a PET scanner to monitor participants' brains

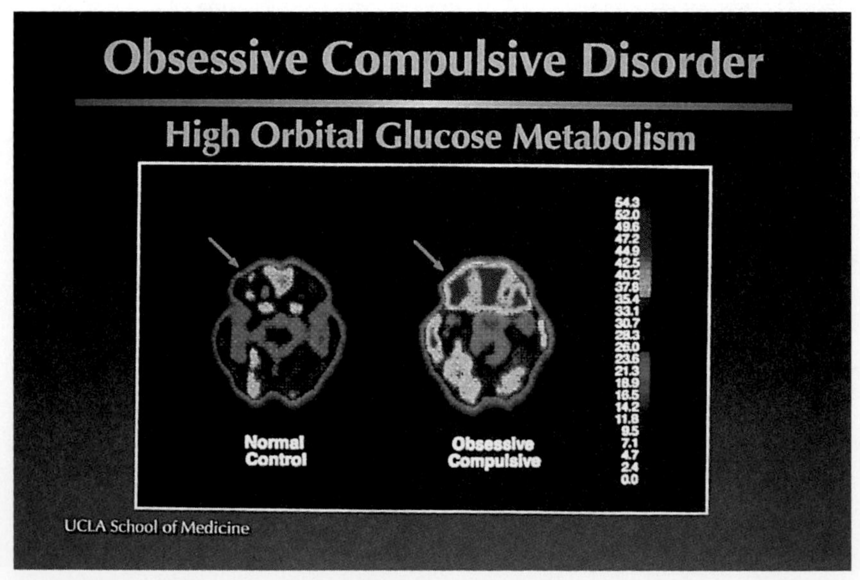

(**Source:** Courtesy of Lewis Baxter, UCLA.)

FIGURE 2.11

PET Scans: A Useful Technique for Detecting Mental Disorders

PET scans provide color-coded maps of the brain's activity. This PET scan shows the brain activity of a normal person (left side) and a patient with obsessive–compulsive disorder. Note the increased brain activity in the frontal area of the brain on the right.

while they performed a fairly simple task—signing their name with their dominant hand (Nadis, 1992). The PET scan showed a low level of activity in a region of the cortex—the region of the brain associated with higher cognitive functions such as thinking, planning, and reasoning. In contrast, a high level of activity was present in the basal ganglia, an area responsible for coordination of motor activity. When participants were asked to write their name with their *nondominant* hand, however, an opposite pattern emerged: decreased activity in the basal ganglia, but increased activity in the brain's cortex. This simple example reveals an important principle regarding how the brain delegates its resources: When we undertake a novel or complex task, a greater overall amount of mental effort is required—especially in the brain's cortex. Later, as we master a task, less mental effort is required, and responsibility for the task is shifted away from the cortex to more automatic brain regions.

Critics have raised several concerns, however, over the rapid proliferation of imaging techniques. One concern is that different persons frequently interpret the same image differently—a definite problem when these techniques are used to make important medical decisions (e.g., Coppola, Myslobodsky, & Weinberger, 1995; Sarter, Berntson, & Cacioppo, 1996). Critics also worry that researchers may tend to "overinterpret" brain images—perhaps leaping to premature conclusions regarding the nature of specific brain–behavior relationships. Still, on balance, the use of these amazing techniques has provided scientists with an important tool to increase our understanding of the many intricacies of the brain.

Key Questions

- What structures make up the central nervous system? What is the function of the spinal cord?
- What two systems make up the peripheral nervous system? What are the roles of these two systems?
- What are the functions of the sympathetic and parasympathetic nervous systems?
- How do psychologists study the nervous system?
- How are PET scans used to study the activity of the brain?

The Brain: *Where Consciousness Is Manifest*

If there can be said to be a "governing organ" of the body, it is definitely the brain. And what an amazing structure it is! Into slightly more than three pounds the brain crams an array of functions and capacities that even today computer scientists envy. After all, what computer, no matter how huge or advanced, is currently capable of (1) storing seemingly *unlimited* amounts of information for years or decades, (2) rewriting its own programs in response to new input and experience, and (3) simultaneously controlling a vast number of complex internal processes and external activities? Moreover, even if such a computer existed, it could not, as far as we can tell, reproduce the emotional experiences, imagery, insights, and creativity of the human brain.

The brain is a complex structure and can be described in many different ways. Often, though, it is divided—for purposes of discussion—into three major components: portions concerned with basic bodily functions and survival; portions concerned with motivation and emotion; and portions concerned with such complex activities as language, planning, foresight, and reasoning.

Survival Basics: The Brain Stem

Let's begin with the basics: the structures in the brain that regulate the bodily processes we share with many other life forms on earth. These structures are located in the *brain stem,* the portion of the brain that begins just above

Medulla: A brain structure concerned with the regulation of vital bodily functions such as breathing and heartbeat.

Pons: A portion of the brain through which sensory and motor information passes and which contains structures relating to sleep, arousal, and the regulation of muscle tone and cardiac reflexes.

Reticular Activating System: A structure within the brain concerned with sleep, arousal, and the regulation of muscle tone and cardiac reflexes.

Cerebellum: A part of the brain concerned with the regulation of basic motor activities.

the spinal cord and continues into the center of this complex organ (see Figure 2.12).

Two of the structures in the brain stem, the **medulla** and the **pons,** are located just above the point where the spinal cord enters the brain. Major sensory and motor pathways pass through both of these structures on their way to higher brain centers or down to effectors (muscles or glands) in other parts of the body. In addition, both the medulla and the pons contain a central core consisting of a dense network of interconnected neurons. This is the **reticular activating system,** and it has long been viewed as a part of the brain that plays a key role in sleep and arousal—a topic I'll discuss in greater detail in Chapter 4. Recent evidence, however, indicates that the reticular activating system is also concerned with many seemingly unrelated functions, such as muscle tone, cardiac and circulatory reflexes, and attention (Pinel, 1993). Thus, referring to it as a single "system," which implies a unitary function, is somewhat misleading.

The medulla also contains several *nuclei*—collections of neuron cell bodies—that control vital functions such as breathing, heart rate, and blood pressure, as well as coughing and sneezing.

Behind the medulla and pons is the **cerebellum** (refer again to Figure 2.12). It is primarily concerned with the regulation of motor activities, serving to orchestrate muscular activities so that they occur in a synchronized fashion. Damage to the cerebellum results in jerky, poorly coordinated muscle functioning. If such damage is severe, it may be impossible for a person to stand, let alone to walk or run. Recent evidence suggests the cerebellum may also play a role in certain cognitive processes, such as learning (e.g., Daum et al., 1993).

FIGURE 2.12

Basic Structure of the Human Brain

In this simplified drawing, the brain has been split down the middle to reveal its inner structure.

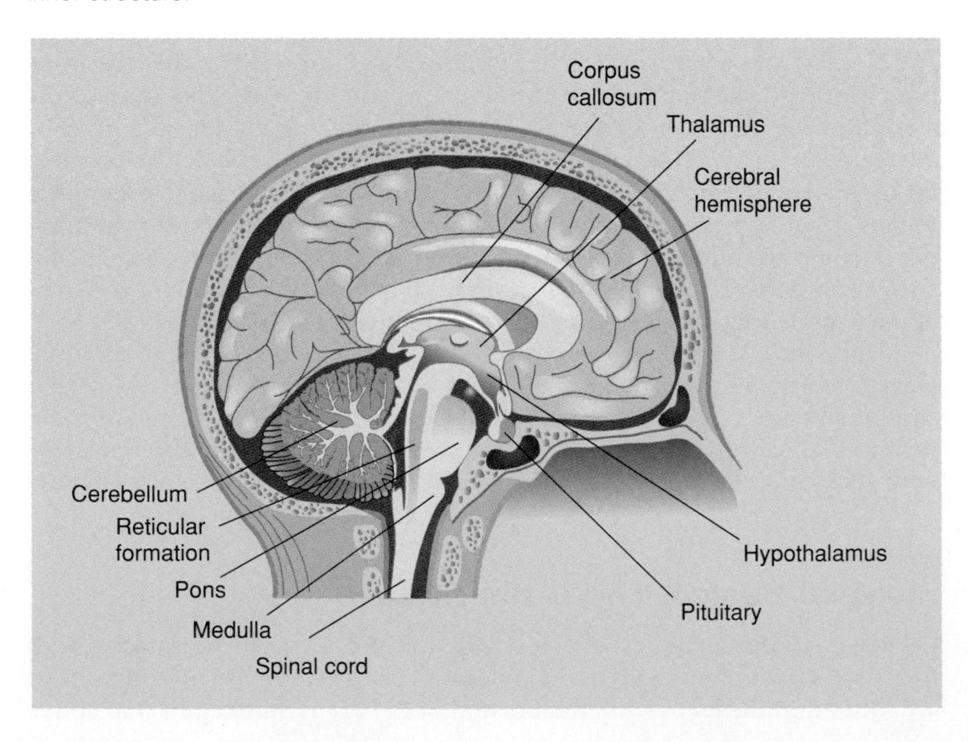

Above the medulla and pons, near the end of the brain stem, is a structure known as the **midbrain.** It contains an extension of the reticular activating system as well as information processing centers concerned with vision and hearing: the *superior colliculi* (vision) and the *inferior colliculi* (hearing). The midbrain also contains structures that play a role in such varied functions as pain perception and the guidance and control of motor movements by sensory input.

Motivation and Emotion: The Hypothalamus, Thalamus, and Limbic System

Ancient philosophers identified the heart as the center of our emotions. While this poetic belief is still reflected on many valentine cards, modern science indicates that it is wrong. If there is indeed a center for appetites, emotions, and motives, it actually lies deep within the brain in several interrelated structures, including the *hypothalamus*, the *thalamus*, and the *limbic system*.

Although the **hypothalamus** is less than one cubic centimeter in size, this tiny structure exerts profound effects. First, it regulates the autonomic nervous system, thus influencing reactions ranging from sweating and salivating to the shedding of tears and changes in blood pressure. Second, it plays a key role in *homeostasis*—the maintenance of the body's internal environment at optimal levels. Third, the hypothalamus seems to play a role in the regulation of eating and drinking. Initial studies seemed to indicate that damage to the *ventromedial* portion of the hypothalamus caused laboratory animals (usually rats) to overeat—to the point of obesity, in fact. In contrast, damage to the *lateral hypothalamus* resulted in reduced food intake and a generally reduced responsiveness to all sensory input. In short, the role of the hypothalamus seemed clear. However, these results were called into question when it was discovered that the procedures used to damage structures within the hypothalamus also destroyed fibers passing through the hypothalamus en route to other structures.

The results of more recent investigations reveal a more sharply defined role for the lateral hypothalamus: it coordinates communication between the parts of the brain that monitor and regulate aspects of the body's internal state (including thirst and hunger) and the frontal cortex—the structure responsible for planning and executing behavior (Winn, 1995). Thus, when damage is confined strictly to cells of the lateral hypothalamus, the brain continues its monitoring function, thereby detecting the need to eat or drink. However, this information does not reach the frontal cortex. As a result, the rat fails to turn this information into action. (Please see Chapter 10 for further discussion of the regulation of eating and of several eating disorders.)

The hypothalamus also plays a role in other forms of motivated behavior such as mating and aggression. It exerts this influence, at least in part, by regulating the release of hormones from the pituitary gland, which we'll consider in more detail in our discussion of the endocrine system later in this chapter.

Above the hypothalamus, quite close to the center of the brain, is another important structure, the **thalamus.** This structure consists of two football-shaped parts, one in each hemisphere. This has sometimes been called the great relay station of the brain, and with good reason. The thalamus receives input from all of our senses except olfaction (smell), performs some preliminary analyses, and then transmits the information to other parts of the brain.

Finally, we should consider a set of structures that together are known as the **limbic system.** The structures that make up the limbic system play an important role in emotion and in motivated behavior, such as feeding, flee-

Midbrain: A part of the brain containing primitive centers for vision and hearing. It also plays a role in the regulation of visual reflexes.

Hypothalamus: A small structure deep within the brain that plays a key role in the regulation of the autonomic nervous system and of several forms of motivated behavior such as eating and aggression.

Thalamus: A structure deep within the brain that receives sensory input from other portions of the nervous system and then transmits this information to the cerebral hemispheres and other parts of the brain.

Limbic System: Several structures deep within the brain that play a role in emotional reactions and behavior.

FIGURE 2.13

Principal Structures of the Limbic System

The limbic system plays an important role in emotion and motivated behavior.

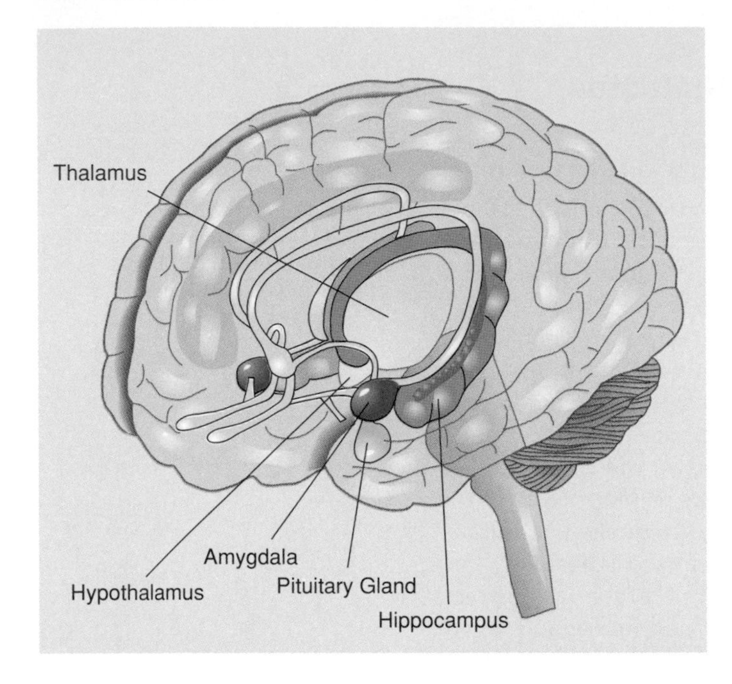

ing from danger, fighting, and sex. The largest of these structures, the **hippocampus,** plays a key role in the formation of memories (e.g., Eichenbaum & Bunsey, 1995; Gluck & Myers, 1995), a topic we'll consider in greater detail in Chapter 6. The **amygdala,** also part of the limbic system, is involved in aspects of emotional control and in the formation of emotional memories. In animals, damage to this structure can produce striking differences in behavior; for example, a typically docile cat may become uncontrollably violent. Figure 2.13 diagrams the principal structures of the limbic system.

The Cerebral Cortex: The Hub of Complex Thought

The **cerebral cortex**—the thin outer covering of the brain—seems to be the part of the brain responsible for our ability to reason, plan, remember, and imagine. In short, this structure accounts for our impressive capacity to process and transform information.

The cerebral cortex is only about one-eighth of an inch thick, but it contains billions of neurons, each connected to thousands of others. The predominance of cell bodies gives the cortex a brownish-gray color. Because of its appearance, the cortex is often referred to as gray matter. Beneath the cortex are myelin-sheathed axons connecting the neurons of the cortex with those of other parts of the brain. The large concentrations of myelin make this tissue look whitish and opaque, and hence it is often referred to as white matter. It is important to note that the cortex is divided into two nearly symmetrical halves, the *cerebral hemispheres* (see Figure 2.14). Thus, many of the structures described below appear in both the left and right cerebral hemispheres. As we'll soon see, however, this similarity in structure is not entirely matched by similarity in function. The two hemispheres appear to be somewhat specialized in the functions they perform.

The cerebral hemispheres are folded into many ridges and grooves, which greatly increase their surface area. Each hemisphere is usually described, on the basis of the largest of these grooves or *fissures,* as being divided into four distinct regions or lobes. The four lobes are: frontal, parietal, occipital, and temporal. We'll discuss each in detail next.

FIGURE 2.14

The Cerebral Cortex, Seen from Above

The left and right cerebral hemispheres are somewhat specialized in their functions.

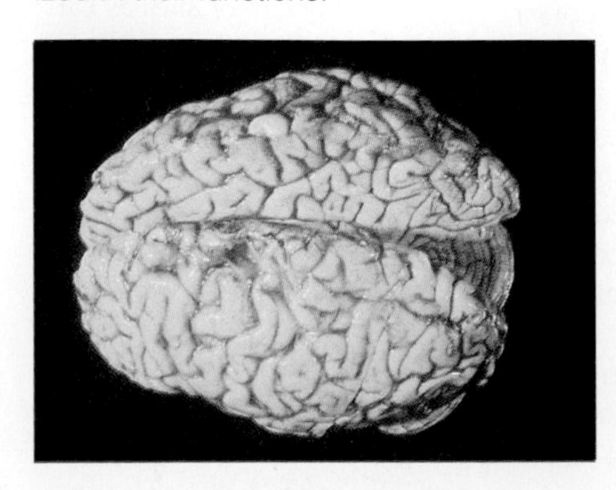

The Frontal Lobe Occupying the area of the brain nearest the face, the **frontal lobe** is bounded by the deep *central fissure*. Lying along this fissure, just within the frontal lobe, is the *motor cortex*, an area concerned with the control of body movements (see Figure 2.15). Damage to this area does not produce total paralysis. Instead, it often results in a loss of control over fine movements, especially of the fingers. This illustrates an important fact about the human brain: While a specific area may normally perform a given function, other regions can often take up the slack if an area is damaged and may gradually come to perform the same functions. Such *plasticity*, as it is often termed, is greater at a young age than after maturity, but it seems to operate to some extent throughout life.

The Parietal Lobe Across the central fissure from the frontal lobe is the **parietal lobe.** This area contains the primary *somatosensory* *cortex*, to which information from the skin senses—touch, temperature, pressure, and so on—is carried (refer to Figure 2.15). Discrete damage to this area produces a variety of effects, depending in part on whether injury occurs to the left or right cerebral hemisphere. If damage involves the left hemisphere, individuals may lose the ability to read or write, or they may have difficulty knowing where parts of their own body are located. In contrast, if damage occurs in the right hemisphere, individuals may seem unaware of the left side of their body. For example, a man may neglect to shave the left side of his face.

The Occipital Lobe The **occipital lobe** is located near the back of the head. Its primary functions are visual, and it contains a sensory area that receives input from the eyes. Local damage to this area often produces a "hole" in the person's field of vision: Objects in a particular location can't be seen, but the rest of the visual field may remain unaffected. As with other brain structures, injury to the occipital lobe may produce contrasting effects depending on which cerebral hemisphere is affected. Damage to the occipital lobe in the right hemisphere produces loss of vision in the left visual field, whereas damage to the occipital lobe in the left hemisphere produces loss of vision in the right visual field.

The Temporal Lobe Finally, the **temporal lobe** is located along the side of each hemisphere (see Figure 2.15). The location makes sense, for this

Hippocampus: A structure of the limbic system that plays a role in the formation of certain types of memories.

Amygdala: A limbic-system structure involved in aspects of emotional control and formation of emotional memories.

Cerebral Cortex: The outer covering of the cerebral hemispheres.

Frontal Lobe: The portion of the cerebral cortex that lies in front of the central fissure.

Parietal Lobe: A portion of the cerebral cortex, lying behind the central fissure, that plays a major role in the skin senses: touch, temperature, pressure.

Occipital Lobe: The portion of the cerebral cortex involved in vision.

Temporal Lobe: The lobe of the cerebral cortex that is involved in hearing.

FIGURE 2.15

Major Regions of the Cerebral Cortex

The cerebral cortex is divided into four major lobes (left drawing). Specific areas in these lobes are concerned with sensory and motor functions (right drawing).

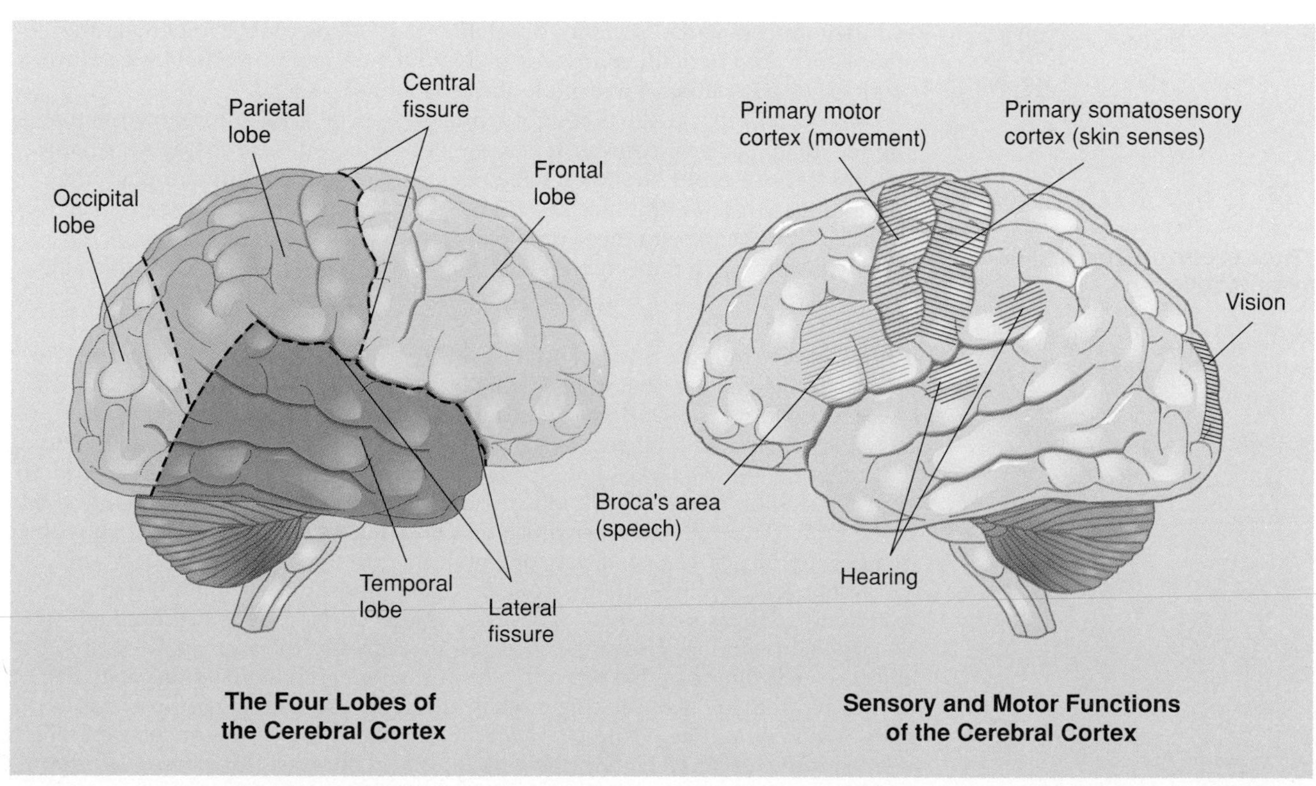

lobe is concerned primarily with hearing and contains a sensory area that receives input from the ears. Damage to the temporal lobe, too, can result in intriguing symptoms. When such injuries occur in the left hemisphere, people may lose the ability to understand spoken words. When damage is restricted to the right hemisphere, they may be able to recognize speech but may lose the ability to recognize other organizations of sound—for example, melodies, tones, or rhythms.

It is interesting to note that when added together, areas of the cortex that either control motor movements (*motor cortex*) or receive sensory input (*sensory cortex*) account for only 20 to 25 percent of the total area. The remainder is known as *association cortex* and, as its name suggests, is assumed to play a critical role in integrating the activities in the various sensory systems and in translating sensory input into programs for motor output. In addition, the association cortex seems to be involved in complex cognitive activities such as thinking, reasoning, and remembering. However, evidence concerning its role in these functions is incomplete at best (Pinel, 1993).

We'll now turn to a discussion of sex-related differences in brain structure and function in the Exploring Gender and Diversity section.

EXPLORING GENDER & DIVERSITY

The Biological Basis of Gender Differences

As we've seen throughout this chapter, basic biological processes underlie all aspects of our cognition and behavior. One age-old biological fact of life that has sparked a great deal of controversy in recent years, however, is sex. At issue is the relative contribution of *biological* sex to differences in the way that men and women think, feel, and behave. The results of a large number of studies show small differences between men and women on certain cognitive processes (e.g., Berenbaum & Hines, 1992; Law, Pellegrino, & Hunt, 1993). For example, men tend to score higher on tests of spatial ability, and they process verbal material differently than women do. Women, on the other hand, tend to hold an advantage over men on certain verbal tasks. How do psychologists attempt to explain these findings?

Research in this area has sought to identify social and cultural factors that might explain such differences. If environmental factors—including social and cultural forces—could be shown to be responsible, so the argument goes, then changing these factors should lead to the disappearance of many sex-related differences. Consistent with these predictions, many sex-related differences have sharply narrowed in the United States over the past several decades, reflecting changes in socialization, education, and employment practices that have occurred in this country.

Differences in Brain Structure and Cognitive Processes. Men and women also appear to differ in aspects of their brain structure (Hyde & Plant, 1995; Swaab, Gooren, & Hofman, 1995). Several studies have reported differences between men and women with respect to the size of certain brain structures, including the *corpus callosum* (Clarke et al., 1989). The corpus callosum is made up of more than 200 million nerve fibers and is the main link between the two hemispheres of the brain. Thus, it is not surprising that researchers would suspect the involvement of this structure in a variety of cognitive processes.

In one study, Hines and her colleagues (1992) used MRI, a brain-imaging technique, to measure the size of several regions of the corpus callosum in twenty-eight women. Then they obtained measures of the women's cognitive abilities, including a verbal test and a test of language lateralization. They hypothesized that areas of the corpus callosum reported to be larger in women than in men would be positively related to the women's scores on tests on which women typically score higher (the verbal test). In contrast, they predicted that areas reported to be larger in men than in women would be negatively related to the women's scores on tests on which men typically score higher (language lateralization). The results supported their predictions: There was a significant positive relationship between the women's scores on the verbal test and the size of a corpus callosum region reported to be larger in women. In contrast, a negative relationship was observed between scores on the language lateralization measure and the size of an area reported to be larger in men than in women.

The results of related research also suggest the existence of additional sex-based differences, which may develop early in life (e.g., Berenbaum & Hines, 1992) or may occur as people get older (e.g., Cowell et al., 1994). However, I should emphasize that these differences are typically quite small (e.g., Hyde & Plant, 1995); and for certain tasks, differences can be eliminated altogether through training and practice (Byne, 1995). Critics also point out that, overall, the range of performance on various tasks *within* each gender greatly exceeds the tiny differences in performance *between* the genders. Still, sex-related differences are provocative, in that they raise interesting questions regarding the relationship between sex differences in brain structure and sex differences in cognitive processes and behavior.

Language and the Cerebral Cortex

We have noted that many complex mental activities seem to take place in the cerebral cortex. If this is indeed the case, then it should be possible to identify areas of the cortex that are responsible for language—the abilities to speak, read, write, and so on. Not surprisingly, much research has been directed to this topic, and investigators have made considerable progress in understanding where and how the brain handles language. In the discussion that follows, I'll describe an influential model that has been proposed to explain the neural basis of language.

The Wernicke–Geschwind Model Writing in the mid-nineteenth century, Paul Broca suggested that an area of the left frontal lobe, just in front of the primary motor cortex, played a key role in processing language. Specifically, he noted that damage to this area left people able to understand speech but with reduced capacity to produce it. Broca concluded that this area of the brain contained memories for the sequence of muscular movements needed for fluent speech.

Some years later, in 1874, another researcher, Karl Wernicke, suggested that a second area, located in the left temporal lobe just behind the primary auditory cortex, also played a key role in language. Wernicke noticed that damage to this region left people able to speak but with reduced understanding of spoken or written words. In other words, such persons could speak fluently, but they could not readily understand what was said to them.

Almost one hundred years later, Norman Geschwind combined these suggestions, plus other data, into a unified model known as the **Wernicke–Geschwind theory** (Geschwind, 1972). According to this model, both areas of the cortex identified by Broca and Wernicke, pathways connecting them, and several other regions including the primary visual cortex and the primary motor cortex function together in the production and comprehension of language. Is this model accurate? Does it accurately describe how events within the brain permit us to understand and use language?

Wernicke-Geschwind Theory: A theory of how the brain processes information relating to speech and other verbal abilities.

On the one hand, consider what happens when parts of the cortex are removed for medical reasons. In some cases, surgical operations have removed areas of the brain viewed as crucial by the Wernicke–Geschwind model. Despite this fact, some patients show little disruption in their language skills, thereby calling basic assumptions of the theory into question (Rasmussen & Milner, 1975). In addition, when the brains of persons who have suffered accidental or disease-related damage during life are examined after their deaths or during medical operations, predictions of the Wernicke–Geschwind model concerning how the location of such damage should be related to language deficits are not always confirmed (Hecaen & Angelergues, 1964).

On the other hand, however, studies in which brain-imaging devices have been used to scan the brains of individuals suffering from language-related problems consistently reveal damage to either Broca's or Wernicke's area. These results provide support for the view that language is localized in specific brain regions, as predicted by this model. However, the inconsistencies noted earlier raise the possibility that individual differences in language localization may exist (Naeser et al., 1981).

Key Questions

- What structures make up the brain stem? What are their functions?
- What are the functions of the hypothalamus and thalamus?
- What is the role of the cerebral cortex?
- Are there sex differences in the sizes of brain structures? In cognitive abilities?
- How is language processed in the brain?

Lateralization of the Cerebral Cortex: Two Minds in One Body?

Look carefully at the photograph of a human brain in Figure 2.14 on page 64. Visual inspection of the two halves of the human brain depicted in the photo would lead casual observers to conclude that they are mirror images of one another. Yet a large and rapidly growing body of evidence suggests that the cerebral hemispheres of the human brain are quite different—at least with respect to their function.

In other words, the brain shows a considerable degree of **lateralization of function.** Each hemisphere seems to be specialized for the performance of somewhat different tasks. Speech is one of the most important of these. For a large majority of human beings, this crucial process is located primarily in the *left* hemisphere (Benson, 1985). In fact, taken as a whole, research on lateralization of brain functions points to the following conclusions: In many persons, though by no means all, the left hemisphere specializes in verbal activities like speaking, reading, and writing and in logical thought and the analysis of information. The right hemisphere specializes in the control of certain motor movements, in synthesis (putting isolated elements together), and in the comprehension and communication of emotion. Many studies employing diverse methods and procedures support these basic conclusions.

For purposes of summarizing, it is most convenient to divide these studies into two major categories: investigations conducted with noninjured persons and studies conducted with persons whose cerebral hemispheres have been isolated from each other through surgery. Let's now turn to a discussion of studies in each of these categories.

Lateralization of Function: Specialization of the two hemispheres of the brain for the performance of different functions.

Research with Intact (Noninjured) Persons

The most convincing evidence for lateralization of function in the cerebral hemispheres is provided by research employing the drug *sodium amytal.* When injected into an artery on one side of the neck, this drug quickly anesthetizes the cerebral hemisphere on that side, allowing researchers to investigate how the other side of the brain works. Studies using these procedures indicate that for most individuals, the left hemisphere possesses much more highly developed verbal skills than the right hemisphere. For example, when the right hemisphere is anesthetized, participants can—through the functioning of their left hemispheres—recite letters of the alphabet or days of the week, name familiar objects, and repeat sentences. In contrast, when the left hemisphere is anesthetized and only the right hemisphere is available, participants experience considerably more difficulty in performing such tasks. Further, the more complex the tasks, the greater the deficits in performance (Milner, 1974).

Additional evidence for lateralization of brain function is provided by studies using PET scan procedures. The PET scan, as you may recall, is an imaging technique that reveals which brain structures are active when people perform specific tasks. These studies indicate that when individuals speak or work with numbers, activity in the left hemisphere increases. In contrast, when they work on perceptual tasks—for instance, tasks in which they compare various shapes—activity increases in the right hemisphere (e.g., Springer & Deutsch, 1985). Interestingly, additional research suggests that while individuals are making up their minds about some issue, activity is higher in the left than in the right hemisphere (Cacioppo, Petty, & Quintanar, 1982). However, once logical thought is over and a decision has been made, heightened activity occurs in the right hemisphere, which seems to play a larger role in global, nonanalytic thought.

A third line of evidence pointing to differences between the left and right hemispheres relates to the ability to recognize and communicate emotions. Several studies (e.g., Bryden, Ley, & Sugarman, 1982) suggest that the right hemisphere is faster than the left hemisphere at recognizing signs of emotional arousal, such as facial expressions, in others. In addition, some findings indicate that the two hemispheres themselves may even play different roles in different emotional experiences (Springer & Deutsch, 1985). Apparently, the left hemisphere is more active during positive emotions, whereas the right hemisphere is more active during negative ones (Miller, 1987). Thus, individuals suffering from depression (intense negative feelings) often show higher activity in the frontal lobes of their right hemispheres than do persons not suffering from depression.

Research with Split-Brain Participants: Isolating the Two Hemispheres

Under normal conditions, the two hemispheres of the brain communicate with each other primarily through the **corpus callosum,** a wide band of nerve fibers that passes between them (Hoptman & Davidson, 1994). Sometimes, though, it is necessary to sever this link—for example, in order to prevent the spread of epileptic seizures from one hemisphere to the other. Careful study of individuals who have undergone such operations provides intriguing evidence on lateralization of function of the brain (Gazzaniga, 1984, 1985; Sperry, 1968).

For example, consider the following demonstration. A man whose corpus callosum has been cut is seated before a screen and told to stare, with his eyes as motionless as possible, at a central point on the screen. Then simple words such as *tenant* are flashed across the screen so that the letters *ten* appear to the left of the central point and the letters *ant* appear to the right. What does the man report seeing? Before you guess, consider the following fact: Because of the way our visual system is constructed, stimuli presented to the *left* visual field of each eye stimulate only the *right* hemisphere of the brain;

Corpus Callosum: A band of nerve fibers connecting the two hemispheres of the brain.

items on the *right* side of the visual field of each eye stimulate only the *left* hemisphere (see Figure 2.16).

Now, what do you think the split-brain man reports? If you said "ant," you are correct. This would be expected, since only the left hemisphere, which controls speech, can answer verbally. However, when asked to *point* to the word he saw on a list of words, the man reacts differently: He points with his left hand to the word *tenant*. So the right hemisphere has indeed seen and recognized this stimulus; it simply can't describe it in words.

Perhaps even more dramatic evidence for the existence of differences between the left and right hemispheres of the brain is provided by a recent

FIGURE 2.16

Some Intriguing Effects of Severing the Corpus Callosum

(Right) If a simple word such as *tenant* is shown to a person whose corpus callosum has been severed, the letters *ten* stimulate only the right hemisphere while the letters *ant* stimulate only the left hemisphere. The person then reports seeing *ant* (left drawing). This is because only the left hemisphere can respond to the verbal question "What do you see?" (Left) If shown a list of words and asked to point to the one seen previously, however, the split-brain person can do so correctly; he or she points to *tenant* with the left hand (right drawing). This indicates that the right hemisphere recognizes this word and can respond to it in a nonverbal manner (that is, by pointing).

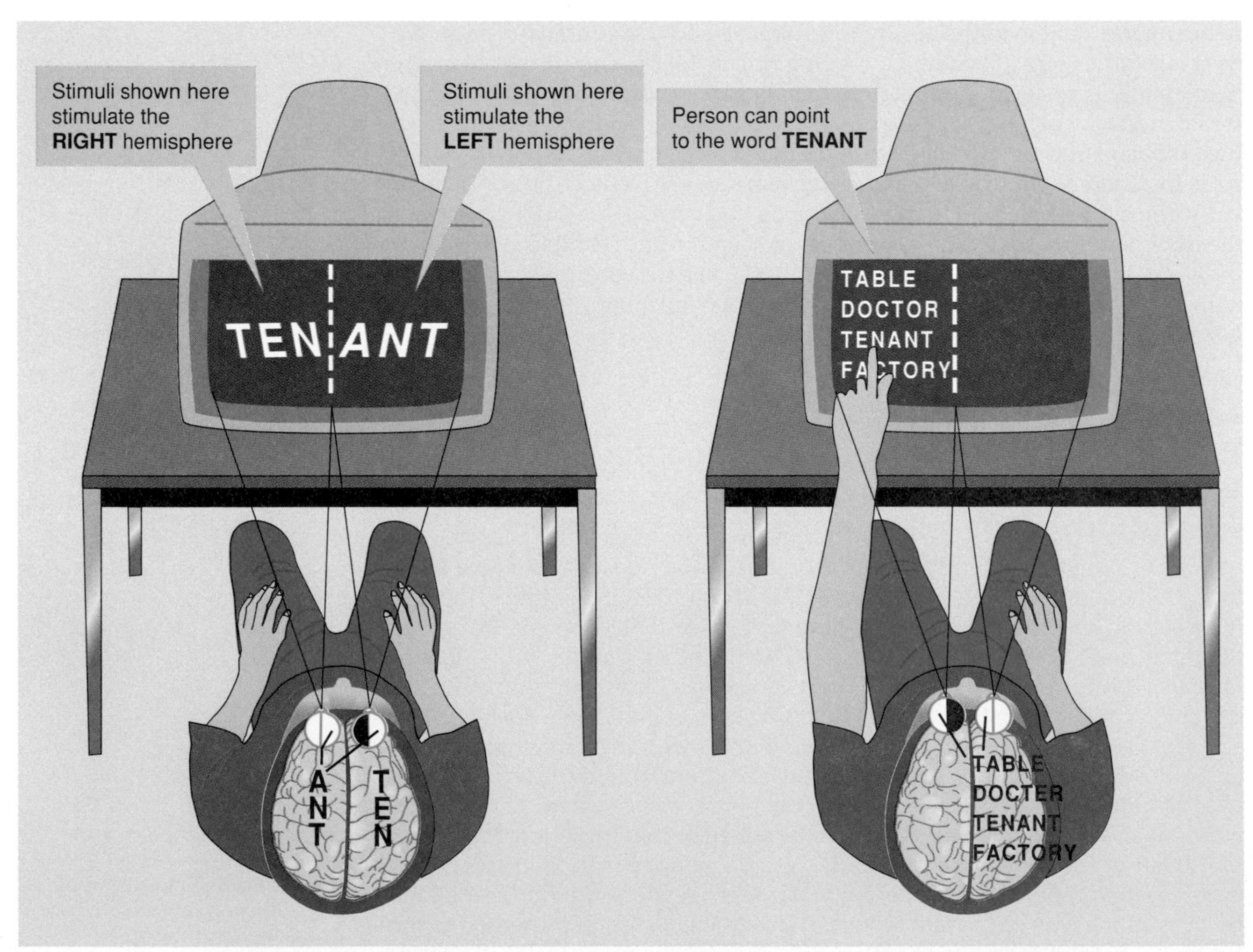

study by Metcalfe, Funnell, and Gazzaniga (1995). These researchers explored the possibility that the two hemispheres differ in the way they encode memories. Previous research had revealed that the left hemisphere not only records the details of specific events it experiences, but also constructs an interpretation of these events. This tendency may lead to "false memories," a topic we'll consider in greater detail in Chapter 6. In contrast, the right hemisphere is not so equipped, instead storing a more direct representation of the to-be-remembered information. To test their ideas, the researchers first presented a set of stimuli (e.g., children's faces) to both hemispheres of a split-brain patient. Next, the man viewed a second set of stimuli consisting of the original faces, similar faces (composites constructed from combinations of the originals), and new faces he had not seen previously. The patient's task was to indicate whether or not he had seen each face before. Because of the left hemisphere's tendency to "interpret" stored information, the researchers predicted that this hemisphere would tend to confuse similar faces (the composite faces) with the originals. The results supported their predictions: Although both hemispheres performed equally in correctly identifying the original faces, the left hemisphere tended to incorrectly classify the composite faces as ones they had seen before.

Putting the Brain Back Together Again: Multiple Resource Theory The two hemispheres of the brain show differences that are often striking (Zaidel, 1994). The existence of these differences raises interesting questions about how these separate systems coordinate their efforts to produce consciousness—the perception of continuity we have in relation to the world around us. The manner in which the brain orchestrates interaction between the two sides of the brain, however, is not always easily predicted. Some information-processing tasks require the combined efforts of both hemispheres of the brain, whereas others are carried out independently by one side of the brain.

Several recent investigations suggest that the extent of cooperation between the two sides of the brain is based on the relative costs and benefits—or efficiency—of cooperating (Hellige, 1993). One particularly important factor appears to be the difficulty of the task; performance on cognitively difficult tasks is enhanced through cooperation *between* the brain's hemispheres, whereas simple tasks are carried out more efficiently *within* a single hemisphere (Banich & Belger, 1990).

In one study, participants were asked to compare pairs of visual stimuli and to judge whether the stimuli were the same or different. The comparison tasks ranged from relatively simple visual judgments to more difficult ones. In one condition, stimulus pairs were briefly presented to only one side of the brain. In a second condition, stimulus pairs were presented so that each stimulus in the pair went to a different side of the brain. Here, participants obviously needed cooperation between the two sides of the brain to make a judgment. Of interest was whether performance would be better for a single hemisphere working alone (within-hemisphere activity) or for two hemispheres working together (between-hemispheres activity). For the simple tasks, measures of performance (reaction time and accuracy) revealed a clear within-hemisphere advantage. As task difficulty increased, however, performance was enhanced by hemispheric cooperation. This suggests that on relatively simple tasks, cooperation between the two halves of the brain may not be necessary—and, in fact, may actually hinder efficient performance.

The results just described illustrate how the brain delegates its resources in situations involving *one* task. But how about more complex situations involving multiple tasks? After all, daily life often entails doing two or more things at once. Recent evidence suggests that the brain delegates its resources not only between its two hemispheres but also *within* each hemisphere (Boles, 1992). To test the possibility of multiple resources within each side of the brain, Boles and Law (1992) used a *dual-task procedure* in which study participants performed two tasks processed by one side of the brain simultaneously. Half the task pairs were constructed such that each task used the *same* cognitive resource; for the other half, pairs consisted of tasks that used different cognitive resources.

The results were consistent with the idea that each side of the brain contains multiple cognitive resources. A decrease in performance (such as increased reaction time) was observed for task pairs that used the *same* cognitive resource. In contrast, performance of task pairs that used *different* cognitive resources was not affected. Consider how these results might apply to a real-life example: Imagine that you are steering a car while listening to the emotional voice of your distraught friend riding next to you. While both of these tasks involve the right side of the brain, separate resources are used to recognize spatial position (where your car is going) and emotion. As a result, your driving ability is unlikely to suffer from this task combination. On the other hand, steering the car while scanning a mental image of a map may spell trouble, since both tasks involve checking spatial positions and call on the same hemispheric resource. In short, apparently it *is* possible to do two things at once—as long as the tasks do not depend on the same hemispheric resource.

Key Questions

- How are the left and right hemispheres of the brain specialized for the performance of different tasks?
- What evidence supports the existence of hemispheric specialization?
- Why is it possible to perform more than one activity at once, such as listening to the radio while driving?

The Endocrine System: *Chemical Regulators of Bodily Processes*

Earlier, I mentioned that the hypothalamus plays a key role in the activities of important glands. These are the **endocrine glands,** which release chemicals called **hormones** directly into the bloodstream. Hormones exert profound effects on a wide range of processes related to basic bodily functions. Of special interest to psychologists are *neurohormones*—hormones that interact with and affect the nervous system. Neurohormones, like neurotransmitters, influence neural activity. However, because they are released into the circulatory system rather than into synapses, they exert their effects more slowly, at a greater distance, and often for longer periods of time than neurotransmitters. The locations of the major endocrine glands are shown in Figure 2.17.

The relationships between the hypothalamus and the endocrine glands are complex. Basically, though, the hypothalamus exerts its influence through the **pituitary gland** (refer to Figure 2.17). This gland is located just below the hypothalamus and is closely connected to it. The pituitary is sometimes described as the master gland of the body, for the hormones it releases control and regulate the actions of other endocrine glands.

The pituitary is really two glands in one, the *posterior pituitary* and the *anterior pituitary*. The posterior pituitary releases hormones that regulate reabsorption of water by the kidneys and, in females, the production and release of milk. It is the anterior pituitary that releases the hormones that regulate the activity of other endocrine glands. One such hormone, ACTH, stimulates the outer layer of the adrenal gland, the *adrenal cortex*, causing it

Endocrine Glands: Glands that secrete hormones directly into the bloodstream.

Hormones: Substances secreted by endocrine glands that regulate a wide range of bodily processes.

Pituitary Gland: An endocrine gland that releases hormones to regulate other glands and several basic biological processes.

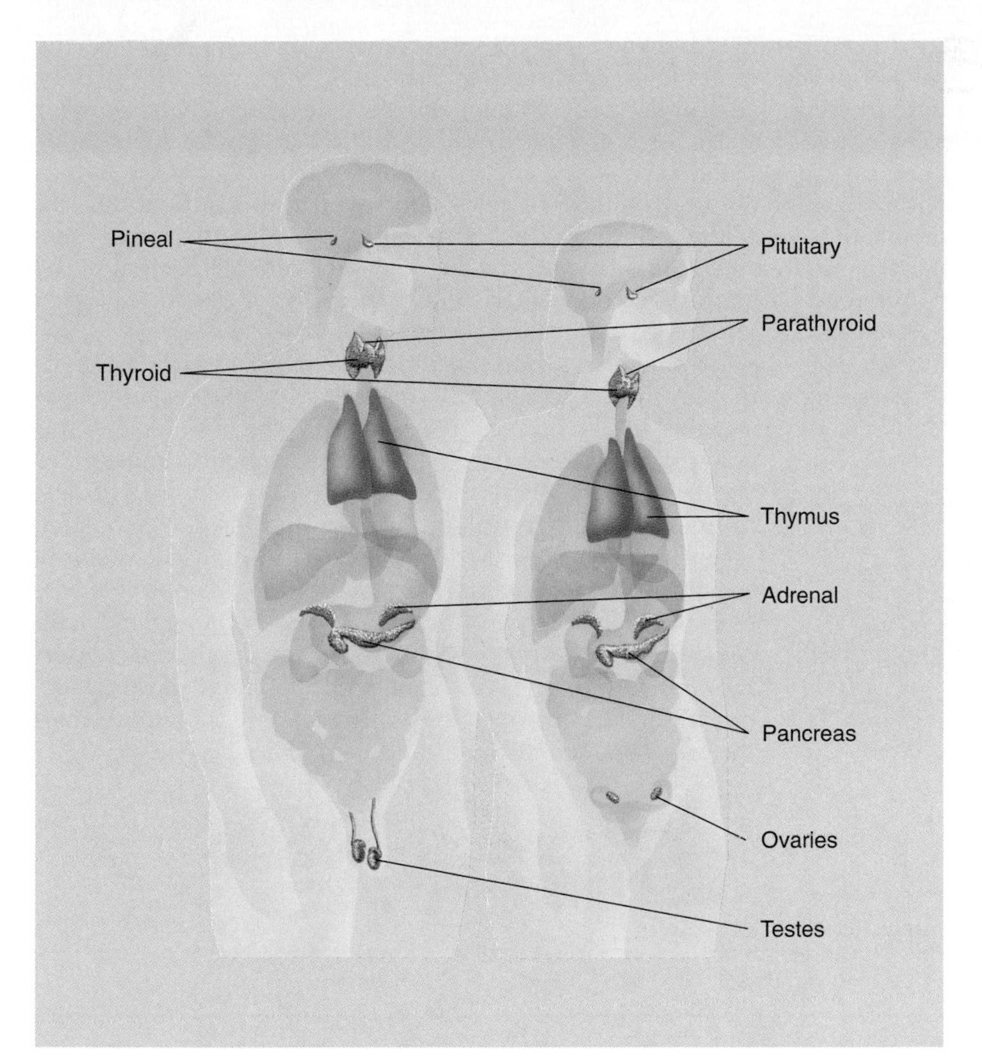

FIGURE 2.17

Location of the Endocrine Glands

Endocrine glands are found in several locations throughout the body. The hormones they produce exert important effects on many bodily processes.

to secrete cortisone. Cortisone, in turn, affects cells in many parts of the body. The pituitary also secretes hormones that affect sexual development, govern the functioning of the sexual glands (regulating the amount of hormones they release), and help control basic bodily functions relating to metabolism and excretion.

A dramatic illustration of the importance of hormones secreted by the endocrine glands is provided by a disorder known as the *congenital adrenogenital syndrome* (CAS). In this condition excessive levels of adrenal androgens (hormones that typically exist in higher concentrations in males than in females) are produced. In males, this disorder merely accelerates the onset of puberty. In females, however, the syndrome has much more disturbing effects. A female suffering from this disorder is born with external sexual organs that are distinctly masculine in appearance. If her condition is recognized at birth and she receives corrective surgery plus hormonal treatment designed to reduce levels of androgens, the girl's development may proceed normally. If, however, she does not receive treatment until her teen years, she may retain some masculine characteristics; she may describe herself as a tomboy, prefer boys' clothes, and express little interest in babies or future maternity (Ehrhardt & Meyer-Bahlberg, 1981). Since many other females also demonstrate such tendencies, however, the meaning of these findings is somewhat difficult to interpret.

In another disorder, known as the *adrenogenic insensitivity syndrome*, the cells of genetic males lack receptors for androgens. Such persons are born with genitals that are distinctly female, and they develop as what appear to be normal females. As noted by Money and Ehrhardt (1972), their childhood play, goals, sexual behavior, and maternal interests all conform to patterns traditionally seen among females. However, these individuals are unable to have children, since they lack ovaries and other internal female sexual organs. Treatment for such persons includes surgical enlargement of the vagina and psychological counseling to help them cope with the fact that because of their condition, they cannot become pregnant.

Together, the adrenogenital syndrome and adrenogenic insensitivity syndrome suggest that hormones secreted by the endocrine glands, and especially by the *gonads* or sex glands, exert important effects on social and cognitive as well as on physical development. However, as we'll see in Chapter 8, the development of *gender identity*—individuals' recognition of their sex and the effects of such recognition on later development—is influenced by many social and environmental variables. Thus, the possible role of biological factors in this process should be viewed with considerable caution. Nevertheless, these syndromes underscore the importance of the endocrine glands and the various different hormones they secrete. Table 2.2 summarizes the major endocrine glands and their effects.

Key Questions

- How does the endocrine system influence aspects of our behavior?
- What role does the endocrine system play in shaping gender-specific behaviors?

TABLE 2.2

The Endocrine System: A Summary of Its Major Effects

Hormones of the endocrine glands and their major effects.

Gland	Effects or Functions It Regulates
Adrenal Glands	
Adrenal medulla	Produces *epinephrine* and *norepinephrine.* Both play an important role in reactions to stress (e.g., increased heartbeat, raised blood pressure).
Adrenal cortex	Produces hormones that promote release of sugar stored in the liver. Also regulates the excretion of sodium and potassium.
Gonads	
Ovaries	Produce hormones responsible for secondary sex characteristics of females (e.g., breast development); also regulate several aspects of pregnancy.
Testes	Produce hormones responsible for secondary sex characteristics of males (e.g., beard growth); also affect sperm production and male sex drive.
Pancreas	Produces hormones (e.g., insulin, glucagon) that regulate metabolism.
Parathyroid	Produces hormones that regulate levels of *calcium* and *phosphate* within the body (these substances play an important role in the functioning of the nervous system).
Pituitary Gland	
Anterior	Controls activity of gonads; regulates timing and amount of body growth; stimulates milk production in females.
Posterior	Releases hormones that control contractions of the uterus during birth and the release of milk from mammary glands; also regulates excretion of water.
Thyroid	Produces *thyroxin,* which regulates rate of metabolism and controls growth.

Heredity and Behavior

Heredity: Biologically determined characteristics passed from parents to their offspring.

Chromosomes: Threadlike structures containing genetic material, found in nearly every cell of the body.

Genes: Biological "blueprints" that shape development and all basic bodily processes.

Mitosis: Cell division in which chromosome pairs split and then replicate themselves so that the full number is restored in each of the cells produced by division.

By now, the basic theme of this chapter should be clear: that behavior and consciousness are manifestations of complex biological processes within our bodies. If this is true, and virtually all psychologists assume that it is, then it certainly makes sense to consider the relationship of **heredity**—biologically determined characteristics—to behavior. After all, many aspects of our biological nature are inherited; so in an indirect manner, and always through the filter of our experience and environmental factors, heredity can indeed influence behavior (Rushton, 1989a, 1989b). In this final section, then, we'll examine several aspects of heredity that appear to be relevant to understanding the biological bases of behavior.

Genetics: Some Basic Principles

Every cell of your body contains a set of biological blueprints that enable it to perform its essential functions. This information is contained in **chromosomes,** strandlike structures found in the nuclei of all cells (see Figure 2.18). Chromosomes are composed of a substance known as DNA, short for deoxyribonucleic acid. DNA, in turn, is made up of several simpler components arranged in the form of a double helix—something like the twisting water slides found by the sides of large swimming pools. Chromosomes contain thousands of **genes**—segments of DNA that serve as basic units of heredity. Our genes, working in complex combinations and in concert with forces in the environment, ultimately determine all aspects of our biological makeup.

Most cells in the human body contain forty-six chromosomes, existing in pairs (refer to Figure 2.18). When such cells divide, the chromosome pairs split; then, after the cells have separated, each chromosome replicates itself so that the full number is restored. This kind of cell division is known as **mitosis.** In contrast, sperm and ova—the male and female sex cells, or *gametes*—contain only twenty-three chromosomes. Thus, when they join to form a fertilized ovum from which a new human being will develop, the full number (forty-six) is attained. For each of us, then, half of our genetic material comes from our mother and half from our father.

These basic mechanisms explain why persons who are related resemble one another more than persons who are totally unrelated, and also why the closer the familial tie between individuals, the more similar they tend to be physically. The closer such links are, the greater the proportion of chromosomes and genes family members share. And since genes determine many aspects of physical appearance, similarity increases with closeness of relationship. Thus, siblings (children of the same parents) tend to be more alike than cousins (the children of siblings). In the case of identical twins, or *monozygotic twins*, a single fertilized egg splits in two and forms two children; in contrast, nonidentical or *fraternal* twins grow from two eggs fertilized by

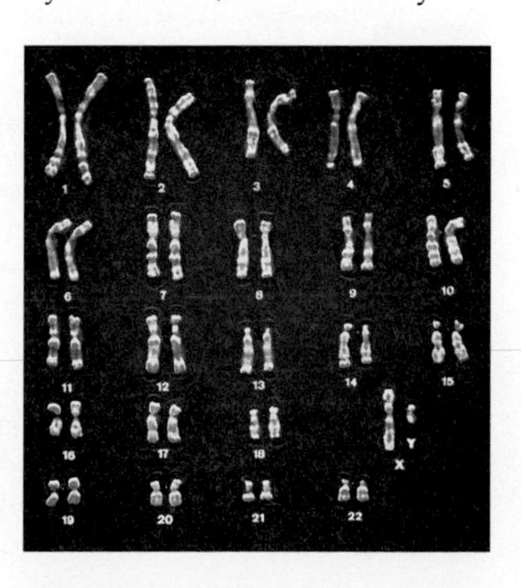

FIGURE 2.18

DNA: Mapping Our Genetic Heritage

Chromosomes are composed of DNA (deoxyribonucleic acid). Each human cell contains twenty-three pairs of chromosomes. The twenty-third pair determines sex. In males, the twenty-third pair contains one X and one Y chromosome (shown here); in females, the twenty-third pair contains two X chromosomes.

two different sperm. Because identical twins share all of their genes, they are usually remarkably similar in appearance. They are surprisingly similar in other respects as well, including their religious beliefs, their television viewing preferences, and even their grief responses (e.g., Segal & Bouchard, 1993).

Remarkable progress has been made toward detecting genetic involvement in a variety of physical and mental disorders. For example, researchers recently discovered the gene that causes **Huntington's disease,** a rare, progressive neuromuscular disorder. Persons afflicted with Huntington's disease experience a gradual onset of uncontrollable, jerky movements in their limbs. Unfortunately, there is at present no cure for Huntington's disease (Pinel, 1993). Children of an affected person have a 50 percent chance of inheriting the gene that causes this disorder. Ironically, the onset of symptoms usually appears after age forty—long after most parents have their children, and therefore too late for them to reconsider their decision. Although scientists are not yet sure how the gene actually causes Huntington's disease, it is now possible to detect the gene's presence before the onset of symptoms (e.g., Giordani et al., 1995; Rothland et al., 1993) and, more importantly, in time to let parents avoid passing the lethal gene to their children.

Merely possessing a particular gene, however, does not ensure that a specific effect will follow. Genes do not directly control behavior or other aspects of life—as we'll see later in this section. Instead, genes exert their influence only indirectly, through their influence on chemical reactions in the brain or other organs. These reactions, in turn, may depend on certain environmental conditions. One example is **phenylketonuria (PKU),** a genetically based disorder in which persons lack the enzyme necessary to break down *phenylalanine*—a substance present in many foods. Affected persons on a normal diet tend to accumulate phenylalanine in their bodies. This, in turn, interferes with normal development of the brain and leads to mental retardation, seizures, and hyperactivity (Nyhan, 1987). Altering environmental conditions, however, can prevent this chain of events. Hospitals now routinely screen infants' blood for high levels of phenylalanine. If PKU is detected during the first few weeks of life, babies placed on a diet low in phenylalanine do not develop the PKU symptoms. Dietary restrictions can then be relaxed in late childhood, after the majority of brain development is complete.

As you might suspect, however, most human traits are determined through more than one gene. In fact, hundreds of genes acting in concert with environmental forces are involved in shaping complex physical or cognitive abilities (Lerner, 1993; McClearn et al., 1991). Whatever the specific mechanisms involved, it seems clear that there may be a genetic component in many aspects of behavior—including sexual orientation, a possibility we consider in greater detail in the Beyond the Headlines section.

Huntington's Disease: A genetically based fatal neuromuscular disorder characterized by the gradual onset of jerky, uncontrollable movements.

Phenylketonuria (PKU): A genetically based disorder in which persons lack the enzyme to break down phenylalanine, a substance present in many foods. The gradual buildup of phenylalanine contributes to subsequent outcomes that include retardation.

Nature–Nurture Controversy: Argument regarding the relative contributions of genetic factors (nature) and environmental factors (nurture) to aspects of behavior and cognitive processes.

Disentangling Genetic and Environmental Effects: Research Strategies

At this point I can almost hear you wondering, "How do psychologists assess the relative contributions of heredity and experience to various aspects of behavior?" This question has been the source of debate among psychologists for many years and is often referred to as the **nature–nurture controversy,** an issue we'll consider next.

As we saw earlier in this chapter, psychologists are often quite resourceful in devising ways to study aspects of behavior. Efforts to assess the relative contributions of genetic and environmental factors to various forms of behavior have often involved comparisons between identical twins who were separated early in life and raised in contrasting environments. Because such

Beyond the Headlines

As Psychologists See It

Biology Breathes New Life into Old Controversy

Gay Newlyweds Seek Parity

Los Angeles, California—DATELINE NBC, Friday, May 17, 1996:

Mounting evidence pointing to a biological basis for homosexuality—leads gays to demand equal access to marital benefits.

Sean and Rob, both gay males, exchanged wedding vows in the presence of an ordained minister, family, friends, and *Dateline NBC*. Like a growing number of gay couples, Sean and Rob feel they should have the same rights as heterosexual couples. What is the basis for their claim? They point to mounting evidence that homosexuality may not be merely a lifestyle preference, shaped by environmental circumstances, but instead a natural outcome of basic biological processes, perhaps coded in the genes.

But how is sexual orientation determined? Is it biologically determined, and therefore immutable?

Evidence for a Biological Basis of Sexual Orientation

A number of studies have reported neuroanatomical and neurochemical differences between homosexual and heterosexual persons (Gladue, 1994). For example, comparison of the size and shape of the *suprachiasmatic nucleus*, an area of the brain involved in coordinating hormonal functions, has shown differences between homosexual and heterosexual men, but striking similarity between homosexual men and heterosexual women. Differences have also been detected in several other brain structures (e.g., LeVay, 1991; Swaab, Gooren, & Hofman, 1995), as well as in levels of sex-related hormones and their precursors (Banks & Gartrell, 1995; Collaer & Hines, 1995).

Researchers have also explored homosexuality as a genetically inherited trait, typically by studying twins. The rationale? If homosexuality has a genetic component, then concordance for homosexuality (the chances that if one twin is gay, the other is too) should be highest among identical twins. In one study, Bailey and Pillard (1991) examined concordance rates in a group of gay men, each of whom had an identical twin, a non-identical male twin, or an adopted brother. As predicted, 52 percent of the identical twins were both gay, compared to 22 percent of the nonidentical twins and 11 percent of the adopted brothers. A similar pattern of results was obtained for a group of homosexual women (Bailey et al., 1993).

Scientists have also tried to locate a possible homosexual gene directly (Turner, 1995). In an intriguing study, Hamer and colleagues (1993) traced a group of gay men's family histories and discovered a relatively high incidence of homosexuality among the men's mothers' male relatives—a clear signal that the gene might be located on the X chromosome (the only chromosome inherited exclusively from the mother).

Looking for Facts in All the Wrong Places?: Nurture Revisited

Careful review of the evidence supporting a biological explanation of sexual orientation has revealed serious inconsistencies (e.g., Byne, 1995). For example, some studies report differences between homosexuals and heterosexuals; others do not. Further, even in instances in which consistent differences were discovered, scientists still have no definitive evidence that actually links differences in structure or neurochemistry to specific behaviors (Byne, 1995; Swaab, Gooren, & Hofman, 1995). Based on these findings, researchers have been forced to consider, once again, the possibility that sexual orientation is the product of both biological and environmental forces. Interestingly, most gay persons report *knowing they were different* from their same-sex peers during childhood. This reported feeling forms the basis of a theory proposed by psychologist Daryl Bem. Termed the "exotic leads to erotic" theory, Bem's theory attempts to show how both biology *and* experience interact to determine sexual orientation (Bem, 1996).

According to Bem, biological variables, such as genes, do not determine sexual orientation directly, but instead shape childhood temperaments that predispose some children to prefer male-typical activities, such as rough-and-tumble play, and others to prefer female-typical activities. Over time, *gender-conforming* children—those who prefer sex-typical activities—begin to feel different from their opposite-sex peers. In contrast, *gender-nonconforming* children—those who prefer sex-atypical activities—begin to feel different from their same-sex peers, perceiving them as dissimilar and perhaps exotic.

Bem claims that every child—conforming or nonconforming—experiences heightened nonspecific arousal in the presence of peers from whom he or she feels different. Later on, that arousal may be transformed into romantic attraction. Although at this point Bem's theory is just that, a theory, it appears consistent with available evidence from both camps—nature and nurture. Still, given the complexity of sexual orientation, only time—and additional systematic research—will determine the theory's accuracy.

Critical Thinking Questions

1. Based on the evidence presented in this section, do you feel that Rob and Sean are justified in their efforts to achieve equal rights for same-sex marriages?
2. Do you believe that Bem's "exotic leads to erotic" theory adequately explains sexual orientation?

twins have identical genes, as we've already noted, any differences between them must be due to contrasting experiences and environments. And to the extent that identical twins demonstrate similarity in various behaviors, despite being raised in different environments, the greater the contribution of genetic factors to such behaviors. Research of this type (e.g., Bouchard, 1987; Bouchard et al., 1990) has yielded some surprising findings. Even identical twins reared in very different environments show remarkable similarities (Hershberger, Lichtenstein, & Knox, 1994; Lykken et al., 1992).

Some intriguing evidence for such similarity is provided by a study conducted by Lykken and his colleagues (1993). These researchers explored the possibility that genetic factors play a role in determining people's interests in occupations and hobbies. Lykken and his colleagues administered standard measures of occupational and leisure interests to more than nine hundred pairs of twins: identical twins raised together, identical twins raised apart, or nonidentical twins raised together. The researchers reasoned that if interests in these activities are, at least in part, an inherited characteristic, then identical twins—either raised together or raised apart—should show more similarity in their interests than nonidentical twins (even when they are raised together). As predicted, there was a greater similarity of occupational and leisure-time interests among both groups of identical twins (raised together and raised apart) than among nonidentical twins.

Also intriguing was the finding that the *degree* of similarity of interests between identical twins in the two groups (raised together or raised apart) was nearly the same. If the effects of experience—being raised in a common family environment—contribute to the development of interests, then we should expect to see greater similarity of interests between identical twins raised together than between identical twins raised apart. Note that the identical twins raised apart had been separated since they were only a few months old and had spent most of their lives in different homes, leading different lives. The results of this study, however, suggest that the effects of being raised together did *not* play a significant role in shaping their interests. Lykken and his colleagues caution, however, that genes do not determine our behavior—or interests—directly. Instead, it is more likely that genes contribute to aspects of our physical makeup and personality, which in turn predispose us to prefer certain activities to others. This may help explain—at least in part—why some people opt for sports while others prefer the challenges of pursuits such as playing chess or listening to Mozart.

Key Questions

- How do genetic factors influence behavior?
- What are some examples of genetically based diseases?
- How is sexual orientation determined?
- What evidence supports the possibility that genetic factors influence aspects of our behavior?

Making Psychology Part of Your Life

Traumatic Brain Injury: Using Psychology to Enhance Quality of Life

If you were asked to guess the odds that you will be involved in a life-threatening accident during your lifetime, what would you guess? You may be surprised to learn the odds are fifty–fifty. In fact, one of the biggest threats facing young adults is severe trauma to some portion of their nervous systems—from severe blows sustained in contact sports such as hockey or football, to injuries sustained in automobile crashes (see Figure 2.19). Because of the prevalence of these traumas, the chances are likely that you may even know someone who has suffered such an injury.

After reading this chapter, you should have no trouble understanding why a discussion of brain injuries is included here. There is an intimate relationship between the activity of the nervous system and the capacity to think, feel, and behave. Damage to the brain will have corresponding effects on all of these abilities. In other words, the consequences of injury to the brain aren't confined to the *physical* repercussions of injury-producing events, but often result in profound *psychological* ones as well (Gainotti, 1993). Indeed, some people who have sustained such injuries report that in certain respects, living with a damaged brain can be a fate worse than death.

The term often used to refer to severe instances of head injury is **traumatic brain injury** or **TBI** (Prigatano, 1992). The damages that result from TBI are often diffuse and variable in scope. Some portions of the damage may be extensive enough to be discovered by brain-imaging devices, whereas others may be microscopic and thus escape detection. The damage also tends to extend to regions throughout the brain, making it difficult for psychologists and other health professionals to predict with precision the type or extent of psychological disturbances that are likely to occur. This, in turn, makes it difficult to design effective treatments for persons who have sustained a TBI (Armstrong, 1991).

Psychologists have developed rehabilitation programs that attempt to accommodate the unique circumstances of brain-injured people (Armstrong, 1991). One of the most important ingredients in a successful treatment program appears to be structure, including an environment arranged to reduce frustration and increase the probability that the person's efforts to cope will meet with success. For example, a common source of frustration among brain-injured persons is the inability to anticipate future events. Providing a structure that allows these persons to focus their efforts one step at a time increases the chances they will meet with success. This sets the stage for greater accomplishments later on. Another advantage of structure is that it limits the number of things these persons must attend to at one time, and thereby reduces the confusion (and frustration) TBI patients experience while making choices. A final—but critical—ingredient of successful treatment of TBI has to do with how the intervention is applied; the chances of success are increased when treatment begins soon after injury, when family members are actively involved, and when the procedures are applied consistently over time.

In short, thanks to advances in our understanding of the complex interactions between biological processes and behavior, psychologists can improve the quality of life among persons who have suffered traumatic brain injury. It's important to realize, however, that the approach outlined here helps persons who have suffered TBI to deal more effectively with their disabilities—it does not restore their former physical and cognitive abilities.

FIGURE 2.19

Traumatic Brain Injury: A Preventable Tragedy

Injuries to the brain can often be prevented—simply through appropriate use of protective equipment.

Summary and Review of Key Questions

Neurons: Building Blocks of the Nervous System

- **What is biopsychology?** Biopsychology is the branch of psychology concerned with discovering the biological processes that give rise to our thoughts, feelings, and actions.
- **What do neurons do, and what are their parts?** Neurons are cells specialized for receiving, processing, and moving information. They are made up of a cell body, an axon, and one or more dendrites.
- **What are graded potentials and action potentials? How do neurons communicate with one another?** Graded potentials occur in response to a physical stimulus or stimulation by another neuron; they weaken quickly, and their strength is directly proportional to the intensity of the physical stimulus that produced them. Action potentials are rapid changes in the electrical properties of the cell membranes of neurons. They constitute a basic mechanism by which information travels through the nervous system. Neurons communicate across tiny gaps (synapses) that separate them by means of neurotransmitters.
- **What are the effects of neurotransmitters?** Neurotransmitters produce one of two effects: Excitatory effects cause a depolarization in the nerve cell membrane, making it more likely that an action potential will be generated; inhibitory effects hyperpolarize the cell membranes, making it less likely that the cell will fire.
- **How do drugs produce their effects? What are agonists? Antagonists?** Many drugs produce their effects by influencing synaptic transmission. Agonists are drugs that facilitate the impact of neurotransmitters at specific receptors; drugs that inhibit their impact are termed antagonists. Growing evidence suggests that knowledge of neurotransmitter systems can be applied to solve important practical problems, including drug and alcohol abuse and certain mental disorders.

KEY TERMS

biopsychology, p. 45 • neurons, p. 45 • dendrites, p. 45 • axon, p. 45 • glial cells, p. 46 • axon terminals, p. 46 • synapse, p. 46 • graded potential, p. 46 • action potential, p. 46 • nodes of Ranvier, p. 47 • synaptic vesicles, p. 48 • neurotransmitters, p. 48 • Parkinson's disease, p. 51 • agonist, p. 53 • antagonist, p. 53

The Nervous System: Its Basic Structure and Functions

- **What structures make up the central nervous system? What is the function of the spinal cord?** The central nervous system includes the brain and the spinal cord. The spinal cord carries sensory information from receptors of the body to the brain via afferent nerve fibers and carries information from the brain to muscles and glands via efferent nerve fibers. It also plays an important role in reflexes.
- **What two systems make up the peripheral nervous system? What are the roles of these two systems?** The peripheral nervous system consists of the somatic and autonomic nervous systems. The somatic nervous system connects the brain and spinal cord to voluntary muscles throughout the body; the autonomic nervous system connects the central nervous system to internal organs and glands and to muscles over which we have little voluntary control.
- **What are the functions of the sympathetic and parasympathetic nervous systems?** The sympathetic nervous system prepares the body for using energy, whereas the parasympathetic nervous system activates processes that conserve the body's energy.
- **How do psychologists study the nervous system?** Psychologists use several methods for studying the nervous system, including observation of the effects of brain damage, electrical or chemical stimulation of the brain, and several modern imaging techniques.
- **How are PET scans used to study the activity of the brain?** PET scans have been used to show how the brain's activities change as people perform various mental activities and to detect brain activity differences between normal persons and persons with mental disorders, such as obsessive–compulsive disorders. PET scans reveal that the brain expends less energy on a task once it has mastered that particular task.

KEY TERMS

nervous system, p. 54 • central nervous system, p. 54 • peripheral nervous system, p. 54 • afferent nerves, p. 54 • efferent nerves, p. 55 • somatic nervous system, p. 56 • autonomic nervous system, p. 56 • sympathetic nervous system, p. 57 • parasympathetic nervous system, p. 57 • electroencephalography (EEG), p. 59 • magnetic resonance imaging (MRI), p. 59 • SQUID (superconducting quantum interference device), p. 59 • positron emission tomography (PET), p. 60

The Brain: Where Consciousness Is Manifest

- **What structures make up the brain stem? What are their functions?** The brain stem includes the medulla, the pons, and the cerebellum and is concerned primarily with the regulation of basic bodily functions. The cerebellum, however, may be involved in higher cognitive processes, such as learning.
- **What are the functions of the hypothalamus and thalamus?** The hypothalamus is a brain structure involved in the regulation of motivated behavior and emotion. The thalamus serves as a relay station, directing afferent messages to appropriate brain regions.
- **What is the role of the cerebral cortex?** The cerebral cortex is the hub for higher mental processes such as thinking, planning, reasoning, and memory.
- **Are there sex differences in the sizes of brain structures? In cognitive abilities?** Some evidence suggests a relationship between sex differences in the size of regions of the corpus callosum and sex differences in several cognitive abilities, including verbal fluency and language lateralization. However, most differences in cognitive abilities are small, and the differences within a gender are usually larger than the differences between men and women.
- **How is language processed in the brain?** The Wernicke-Geschwind model suggests that language processing may be localized in specific regions of the brain. Support for this model comes from studies in which brain-imaging devices have been used to scan the brains of individuals suffering from language-related problems. These studies usually report damage to either Broca's or Wernicke's area.

KEY TERMS

medulla, p. 62 • pons, p. 62 • reticular activating system, p. 62 • cerebellum, p. 62 • midbrain, p. 63 • hypothalamus, p. 63 • thalamus, p. 63 • limbic system, p. 63 • hippocampus, p. 65 • amygdala, p. 65 • cerebral cortex, p. 65 • frontal lobe, p. 65 • parietal lobe, p. 65 • occipital lobe, p. 65 • temporal lobe, p. 65 • Wernicke–Geschwind theory, p. 67

Lateralization of the Cerebral Cortex: Two Minds in One Body?

- **How are the left and right hemispheres of the brain specialized for the performance of different tasks?** In most persons, the left hemisphere specializes in verbal activities and in logical thought and analysis. The right hemisphere specializes in the comprehension and communication of emotion and in the synthesis of information. The right hemisphere may be more accurate in recalling certain types of stored information.
- **What evidence supports the existence of hemispheric specialization?** Evidence for hemispheric specialization has been obtained from studies of people with intact brains and from research on split-brain individuals.
- **Why is it possible to perform more than one activity at once, such as listening to the radio while driving?** Within each hemisphere of the brain, cognitive processes may operate inde-

pendently, allowing us to do two tasks at once—as long as the tasks do not depend on the same cognitive resource.

KEY TERMS

lateralization of function, p. 68 • corpus callosum, p. 69

The Endocrine System: Chemical Regulators of Bodily Processes

- **How does the endocrine system influence aspects of our behavior?** Hormones released by the endocrine glands exert far-reaching effects on bodily processes and, in turn, on important aspects of behavior.
- **What role does the endocrine system play in shaping gender-specific behaviors?** Genetically based hormonal disturbances such as congenital adrenogenital syndrome (CAS) may play a role in shaping gender-specific behaviors.

KEY TERMS

endocrine glands, p. 72 • hormones, p. 72 • pituitary gland, p. 72

Heredity and Behavior

- **How do genetic factors influence behavior?** Genetic factors influence behavior via genes—biological blueprints located on chromosomes. Genes do not control behavior or other aspects of life directly. Instead, genes exert their influence only indirectly, through their influence on chemical reactions in the brain or other organs.
- **What are some examples of genetically based diseases?** Two well-known genetically based diseases are Huntington's disease and phenylketonuria (PKU). The mental retardation that often accompanies PKU can be prevented by avoidance of foods containing phenylalanine.
- **How is sexual orientation determined?** Research now supports the view that both genetic and environmental factors play a role in the development of sexual preference.
- **What evidence supports the possibility that genetic factors influence aspects of our behavior?** Research comparing identical twins raised together or apart suggests that genetic factors play a role in many aspects of behavior.

KEY TERMS

heredity, p. 75 • chromosomes, p. 75 • genes, p. 75 • mitosis, p. 75 • Huntington's disease, p. 76 • phenylketonuria (PKU), p. 76 • nature–nurture controversy, p. 76 • traumatic brain injury (TBI), p. 79 (in text)

Critical Thinking Questions

Appraisal

A primary theme of this chapter is that our thoughts, feelings, and actions stem from basic biological processes. Do you think that all of our conscious experience can be reduced to electrochemical events? If so, why? If not, offer an alternative view.

Controversy

Evidence presented in this chapter suggests that sexual orientation may be linked to structural features of the brain present at birth, or even earlier. Given this strong possibility, what ethical and social implications does this hold? A related issue pertains to the fact that scientists are now able to detect if certain genetic abnormalities are present in the developing fetus. What ethical issues does this raise? What are your views on these issues?

Making Psychology Part of Your Life

Perhaps you know someone who has suffered traumatic brain injury. Now that you understand the difficult path such a person faces during rehabilitation, can you think of ways in which you can use the information in this chapter to improve the TBI patient's quality of life?

CHAPTER

OUTLINE

Sensation and Perception

Making Contact with the World around Us

Have you ever wondered why certain smells trigger vivid memories? Why bathwater that initially "scalds" us feels soothing only moments later? Why the moon looks larger on the horizon than when it is directly overhead? Whether ESP really exists? If you've wondered about issues like these, then you're already aware that making sense of the world around us is complicated business. Indeed, the mystery of how we sense and interpret events in our environment constitutes one of the oldest areas of study in psychology. Careful psychological research conducted over the past hundred years has shown that we do not understand the external world in a simple, automatic way. Rather, we actively construct our interpretation of sensory information through several complex processes.

To clarify how we make sense of the world around us, psychologists

The mystery of how we sense and interpret events in our environment constitutes one of the oldest areas of study in psychology.

distinguish between two key concepts: sensation and perception. The study of **sensation** is concerned with the initial contact between organisms and their physical environment. It focuses on describing the relationship between various forms of sensory stimulation (including electromagnetic and sound waves and physical pressure) and how these inputs are registered by our sense organs (the eyes, ears, nose, tongue, and skin). In contrast, the study of **perception** is concerned with identifying the processes through which we interpret and organize sensory information to produce our conscious experience of objects and relationships among objects. It is important to remember that perception is not simply a passive process of decoding incoming sensory information. If this were the case, we would lose the richness of our everyday stream of conscious experiences.

The dual processes of sensation and perception play a role in virtually every topic we will consider in later chapters. For these reasons, we will devote careful attention to them here. We'll begin by exploring in detail how the receptors for each sensory system transduce raw physical energy into an electrochemical code. As we'll soon note, our sensory receptors are exquisitely designed to detect various aspects of the world around us. As part of our discussion, we'll consider the role of cultural factors in one very important aspect of our sensory processes—the sensation of pain. Next, we'll turn our attention to the active process of perception. Here, we'll focus on how the brain integrates and interprets the constant flow of information it receives from our senses. In our discussion of perception, we'll also consider the contributions of heredity and experience to our perception of the world around us. Finally, we'll conclude by examining the evidence supporting one intriguing aspect of perception—the possibility of extrasensory perception, or *psi*.

Sensation: The Raw Materials of Understanding

The sight of a breathtaking sunset, the taste of ice-cold lemonade on a hot day, the piercing sound of heavy metal music, the soothing warmth of a steamy bath—exactly how are we able to experience these events? (See Figure 3.1.) As you may recall from Chapter 2, all of these sensory experiences are based on complex processes occurring within the nervous system. This fact highlights an intriguing paradox: Although we are continually bombarded by various forms of physical energy, including light, heat, sound, and smells, our brain cannot directly detect the presence of these forces. Rather, it can only respond to intricate patterns of action potentials conducted by *neurons,* special cells within our bodies that receive, move, and process sensory information. Thus, a critical question is how the many forms of physical energy impacting our sensory systems are converted into signals our nervous system can understand.

Highly specialized cells known as **sensory receptors,** located in our eyes, ears, nose, tongue, and elsewhere, are responsible for accomplishing this coding task. Thus, sights, sounds, and smells that we experience are actually the product of **transduction,** a process in which the physical properties of stimuli are converted into neural signals that are then transmitted to our brain via specialized sensory nerves. To illustrate how our nervous system makes

Sensation: Input about the physical world provided by our sensory receptors.

Perception: The process through which we select, organize, and interpret input from our sensory receptors.

Sensory Receptors: Cells specialized for the task of transduction—converting physical energy (light, sound) into neural impulses.

Transduction: The translation of physical energy into electrical signals by specialized receptor cells.

FIGURE 3.1

Experiencing the World around Us: The Role of Our Sensory Processes

Our ability to experience events such as the ones pictured here are the result of complex processes occurring within the nervous system.

sense out of the surging sea of physical energies in our environment, we'll begin by focusing on two critical concepts: *thresholds* and *sensory adaptation.*

Sensory Thresholds: How Much Stimulation Is Enough?

Try to focus on all of the sensory information impacting you at this moment—the sights, sounds, smells, tastes, the feel of the clothing against your skin. Although we are immersed in sensory information, we thrive rather than drown. Our bodies seem well prepared to deal with this ocean of information; so well prepared that when deprived of all sensory input—in a condtion termed *sensory deprivation*—our brains may produce hallucinations to fill the void (Sekuler & Blake, 1990). But what is the slightest amount of stimulation that our sensory systems can detect? In other words, how much physical stimulation is necessary in order for us to experience a sensation? Actually, this threshold turns out to be impressively low for most aspects of sensation. We can hear a watch tick twenty feet away in a quiet room; we can smell a single drop of perfume in an empty three-room apartment; and on a clear dark night, we can see a dim candle thirty miles away (Galanter, 1962).

Although our receptors are remarkably efficient, they do not register all the information available in the environment at any given moment. We are able to smell and taste certain chemicals but not others; we hear sound waves only at certain frequencies; and our ability to detect light energy is restricted to a relatively narrow band of wavelengths. The range of physical stimuli that we and other species can detect seems to be designed in a way that maximizes survival potential. For instance, human survival is tied to our unique capacity for spoken language. Thus, it is not surprising that our auditory system is best at detecting sound frequencies that closely match the frequencies of human speech (Coren & Ward, 1989).

Absolute Thresholds: "Was It Really There?" For more than a century, psychologists have conducted studies to determine the level of sensitivity in each sensory system. To do this, they have used a variety of procedures called *psychophysical methods.* These procedures allow psychologists to determine the smallest magnitude of a stimulus that can be reliably discriminated from no stimulus at all 50 percent of the time; this is called the **absolute threshold.** To understand how absolute thresholds for our sensory systems have been explored, consider the following example. Suppose researchers at

Absolute Threshold: The smallest amount of a stimulus that we can detect perfect ly 50 percent of the time.

the Jaw Breaker Chewing Gum Company have discovered a new way to make the flavor in gum last forever. The process is simple and inexpensive but has a minor flaw—a critical ingredient, substance SOUR, escapes detection when in low concentrations, but in larger concentrations makes the gum taste terrible.

To determine the absolute threshold for detection of SOUR, Jaw Breaker researchers select several concentrations; the lowest is clearly below threshold (nobody tastes the SOUR), and the highest causes the tasters to spit out the gum. Then volunteers chew many samples of gum with different concentrations of SOUR. The concentration at which the volunteers detect SOUR 50 percent of the time is the absolute threshold, suggesting that the concentration of SOUR in the final product should fall somewhat *below* this level.

Absolute Thresholds: Some Complications We often assume there is a direct relationship between the presence of a physical stimulus and the resulting sensation. Thus, given a stimulus of sufficient intensity, we should always be able to detect its presence. Unfortunately, the SOUR example shows that this relationship is not so simple. Why? One reason is that our sensitivity to stimuli changes from moment to moment. A stimulus we can detect at one time will not necessarily be detected later. For this reason, psychologists have arbitrarily defined the absolute threshold as that magnitude of physical energy we can detect 50 percent of the time.

Although this definition takes account of fluctuations in our sensitivity to various stimuli, it does not explain *why* such fluctuations occur. There are actually several reasons. First, aspects of our body's functions are constantly changing in order to maintain our body's internal environment at optimal levels, a state termed *homeostasis*. It is not surprising that as a result of these changes, the sensitivity of our sensory organs to external stimuli also varies. Second, motivational factors such as the rewards or costs associated with detecting various stimuli also play a role. For example, the outcome of the SOUR study might have changed if the participants had been faced with the prospect of being fired for a wrong decision.

Signal detection theory suggests that complex decision mechanisms are involved whenever we try to determine if we have or have not detected a specific stimulus (Swets, 1992). For instance, imagine that you are a radiologist. While scanning a patient's X-ray, you think you detect a faint spot on the film, but you're not quite sure. What should you do? If you conclude that the spot is an abnormality, you must order more scans or tests—an expensive and time-consuming alternative. If further testing reveals an abnormality, such as cancer, you may have saved the patient's life. If no abnormality is detected, though, you'll be blamed for wasting resources and unnecessarily upsetting the patient. Alternatively, if you decide the spot is *not* an abnormality, then there's no reason to order more tests. If the patient remains healthy, then you've done the right thing. If the spot is really cancerous tissue, the results could be fatal.

Your decision in this scenario is likely to be influenced by the rewards and costs associated with each of the alternatives. Because of the potentially deadly consequences, as well as the potential for a significant malpractice suit against you and the hospital, you may be tempted to order more tests—even if the spot on the X-ray is extremely faint. But what if the tests are extremely painful to the patient, or what if the patient's insurance company has made it clear they will not pay for the tests? The fear of making a decision that could make the patient suffer needlessly, or could ruin the person financially, may weigh more heavily in the balance; you may not report the spot unless you are quite certain you saw it.

Signal Detection Theory: A theory suggesting that there are no universal absolute thresholds for sensations. Rather, detection of a stimulus depends on its physical energy and on internal factors such as the relative costs and benefits associated with detecting the stimulus.

In summary, deciding whether we have detected a given stimulus is not always easy. These decisions often involve much more than a simple determination of the relationship between the amount of physical energy present in a stimulus and the resulting psychological sensations.

Difference Thresholds: Are Two Stimuli the Same or Different? A good cook tastes a dish, then adds salt to it, then tastes it again to measure the change. This illustrates another basic question relating to our sensory capacities: How much change in a stimulus is required before a shift can be noticed? Psychologists refer to the amount of change in a stimulus required for a person to detect it as the **difference threshold.** Obviously, the smaller the change we can detect, the greater our sensitivity. In other words, the difference threshold is the amount of change in a physical stimulus necessary to produce a **just noticeable difference (jnd)** in sensation. As it turns out, our ability to detect differences in stimulus intensity depends on the magnitude of the initial stimulus; we easily detect even small changes in weak stimuli, but we require much larger changes before we notice differences in strong stimuli. If you are listening to your favorite tunes at a low sound intensity, even small adjustments to the volume are noticeable. But if you are listening to very loud music, much larger changes are required before a difference is apparent. As you might guess, we are also more sensitive to changes in some types of stimuli than to changes in others. For example, we are able to notice very small shifts in temperature (less than one degree Fahrenheit) and in the pitch of sounds (a useful ability for people who tune musical instruments), but we are somewhat less sensitive to changes in loudness or in smells.

Stimuli Below Threshold: Can They Have an Effect? For decades **subliminal perception** has been a source of controversy. The question is whether we can sense or be affected by subthreshold stimuli that remain outside our conscious awareness (Greenwald, 1992; Merikle, 1992). Subliminal perception first captured the public's attention in the 1950s when a clever marketing executive announced he had embedded subliminal messages like "Eat popcorn" and "Drink Coke" into a then popular movie. Supposedly, the embedded messages were flashed on the screen in front of movie audiences so briefly (a fraction of a second) that audience members were not aware of them. Popular press reports claimed that sales of both products in theater lobbies increased substantially right after the messages (Brean, 1958). Although the executive later confessed to the hoax (no messages were actually presented), many people remained convinced that subliminal messages could be powerful sources of persuasion.

During the 1980s, public attention was again drawn to the issue of subliminal perception when concerned parents and religious leaders expressed outrage over the presence of "evil messages" recorded backward (this is known as *backward masking*) and embedded into songs on rock albums. The issue came to a head in a highly publicized trial in which the heavy metal band Judas Priest was accused of embedding subliminal satanic messages promoting suicide on their album *Stained Class.* The subliminal messages were alleged to be instrumental in the shotgun suicides of two young men. The judge in the case dismissed the charges against the rock band, citing a lack of scientific evidence that the subliminal messages actually *caused* the shootings (*Vance et al. v. Judas Priest et al.*, 1990).

Is it possible that subliminal messages exert powerful influences on behavior? A recent study on this topic seems to suggest the answer is no (Smith & Rogers, 1994). In one experiment, the researchers asked a group of college students to monitor a series of television commercials for the message "choose this." The embedded message was presented long enough for participants to detect it (33 milliseconds) but was sufficiently brief that it occasionally slipped past unnoticed. The message was presented in some versions of the commercials but was absent in others. Whenever participants detected

Difference Threshold: The amount of change in a stimulus required before a person can detect the shift.

Just Noticeable Difference (jnd): The smallest amount of change in a physical stimulus necessary for an individual to notice a difference in the intensity of a stimulus.

Subliminal Perception: The presumed ability to perceive a stimulus that is below the threshold for conscious experience.

Sensory Adaptation: Reduced sensitivity to unchanging stimuli over time.

the message, they pressed a key on a computer keyboard. The researchers then carefully examined instances in which the message was presented *and* detected (*supraliminal perception*) and instances in which the message was presented but *not* detected (*subliminal perception*). Of primary interest was the impact, if any, these messages exerted on the participants' memory of or feelings toward the products, services, or ideas presented in the commercials. The results did *not* provide strong support for the possibility of subliminal perception. In fact, neither type of message had a significant effect on participants' intentions to purchase the products, use the services, or adopt the ideas. Further, compared to the effects of the supraliminal messages—the ones participants actually detected—the effects of the subliminal messages were truly tiny.

The fact that this and related studies fail to find support for the use of subliminal messages has not slowed the current explosion of self-help materials that offer to help you lose weight, stop smoking, get smarter, or improve your memory. Their manufacturers often claim that the effectiveness of these products is due to the presence of subliminal messages. Are these claims true? As we've seen throughout this section, systematic evidence seems to cast doubt on this possibility (Greenwald et al., 1991; Urban, 1992). Instead, improvements appear to stem from other factors, such as motivation and expectations—not from the effects of subliminal perception.

FIGURE 3.2

Sensory Adaptation

At first icy water feels freezing, but later it feels refreshing.

Sensory Adaptation: "It Feels Great Once You Get Used to It"

I have vivid memories of summer camping trips I took as a young boy with my friends. On particularly hot afternoons we would cool off with a dip in an icy mountain lake or stream. Although the initial shock of the icy water was overpowering, as illustrated in Figure 3.2, it eventually felt refreshing. This experience illustrates the process of **sensory adaptation,** the fact that our sensitivity to an unchanging stimulus tends to decrease over time. When we first encounter a stimulus, like icy water, our temperature receptors fire vigorously. Soon, however, they fire less vigorously; and through the process of sensory adaptation, the water then feels just right.

Sensory adaptation has some practical advantages. If it did not occur, we would constantly be distracted by the stream of sensations we experience each day. We would not adapt to our clothing rubbing our skin, to the feel of our tongue in our mouth, or to bodily processes such as eye blinks and swallowing. However, sensory adaptation is not always beneficial and can even be dangerous. After about a minute, our sensitivity to most odors drops by nearly 70 percent. Thus, in situations where smoke or harmful chemicals are present, sensory adaptation may actually reduce our sensitivity to existing dangers. In general, though, the process of sensory adaptation allows us to focus on changes in the world around us, and that ability to focus on and respond to stimulus change is usually what is most important for survival.

Now that we've considered some basic aspects of sensation, let's examine in detail each of the major senses: vision, hearing, touch, smell, taste, and the kinesthetic and vestibular senses.

Key Questions

- What is the primary function of our sensory receptors?
- What does the term *absolute threshold* refer to, and why is signal detection theory important?
- What is a difference threshold?
- Can subliminal messages affect our behavior?
- What is the role of sensory adaptation in sensation?

Vision

Light, in the form of energy from the sun, is part of the fuel that drives the engine of life on earth. Thus, it is not surprising that we possess exquisitely adapted organs for detecting this stimulus: our eyes. Indeed, for most of us, sight is the most important way of gathering information about the world. Figure 3.3 on page 90 shows a simplified diagram of the human eye.

The Eye: Its Basic Structure

How is light energy converted into signals our brain can understand? The answer lies in the basic structure of the eye. It is in the eye that light energy is converted into a neural code understandable to our nervous system. Light rays first pass through a transparent protective structure called the **cornea** and then enter the eye through the **pupil,** a round opening whose size varies with lighting conditions: the less light present, the wider the pupil opening (refer to Figure 3.3). These adjustments are executed by the **iris,** the colored part of the eye, which is actually a circular muscle that contracts or expands to let in varying amounts of light. After entering through the pupil, light rays pass through the **lens,** a clear structure whose shape adjusts to permit us to focus on objects at varying distances. When we look at a distant object, the lens becomes thinner and flatter; when we look at a nearby object, the lens becomes thicker and rounder. Light rays leaving the lens are projected on the **retina** at the back of the eyeball. As illustrated in Figure 3.4 on page 91, the lens bends light rays in such a way that the image projected onto the retina is actually upside down and reversed; but the brain reverses this image, letting us see objects and people correctly.

The retina is actually a postage stamp–sized structure that contains two types of light-sensitive receptor cells: about 6.5 million **cones** and about 100 million **rods.** Cones, located primarily in the center of the retina in an area called the **fovea,** function best in bright light and play a key role both in color vision and in our ability to notice fine detail. In contrast, rods are found only outside the fovea and function best under lower levels of illumination, so rods help us to see in a darkened room or at night. At increasing distances from the fovea, the density of cones decreases and the density of rods increases. Once stimulated, the rods and cones transmit neural information to other neurons called *bipolar cells.* These cells, in turn, stimulate other neurons, called *ganglion cells.* Axons from the ganglion cells converge to form the **optic nerve** and carry visual information to the brain. Interestingly, no receptors are present where this nerve exits the eye, so there is a **blind spot** at this point in our visual field. Try the exercise in Figure 3.5 on page 91 to check your own blind spot.

Cornea: The curved, transparent layer through which light rays enter the eye.

Pupil: An opening in the eye, just behind the cornea, through which light rays enter the eye.

Iris: The colored part of the eye; adjusts the amount of light that enters by constricting or dilating the pupil.

Lens: A curved structure behind the pupil that bends light rays, focusing them on the retina.

Retina: The surface at the back of the eye containing the rods and cones.

Cones: Sensory receptors in the eye that play a crucial role in sensations of color.

Rods: One of the two types of sensory receptors for vision found in the eye.

Fovea: The area in the center of the retina in which cones are highly concentrated.

Optic Nerve: A bundle of nerve fibers that exit the back of the eye and carry visual information to the brain.

Blind Spot: The point in the back of the retina through which the optic nerve exits the eye. This exit point contains no rods or cones and is therefore insensitive to light.

Light: The Physical Stimulus for Vision

At this point we will consider some important facts about light, the physical stimulus for vision. First, the light that is visible to us is only a small portion of the electromagnetic spectrum. This spectrum ranges from radio waves at the slow or long-wave end to cosmic rays at the fast or short-wave end (see Figure 3.6 on page 92).

FIGURE 3.3

The Human Eye

Light filters through layers of retinal cells before striking receptors (rods and cones) located at the back of the eye and pointed away from the incoming light. The rods and cones then stimulate bipolar cells, which, in turn, stimulate the ganglion cells. The axons of these cells form the fibers of the optic nerve.

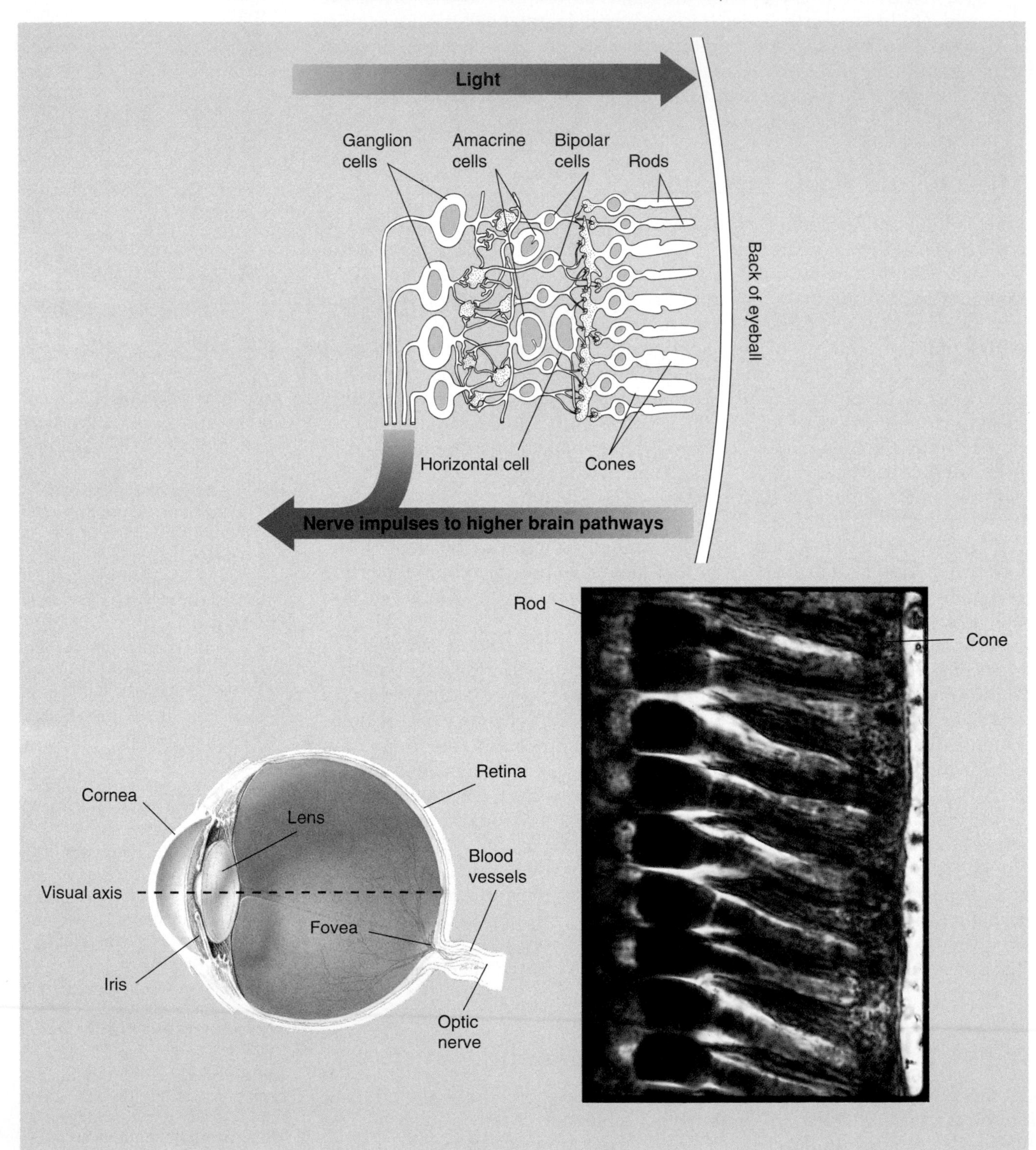

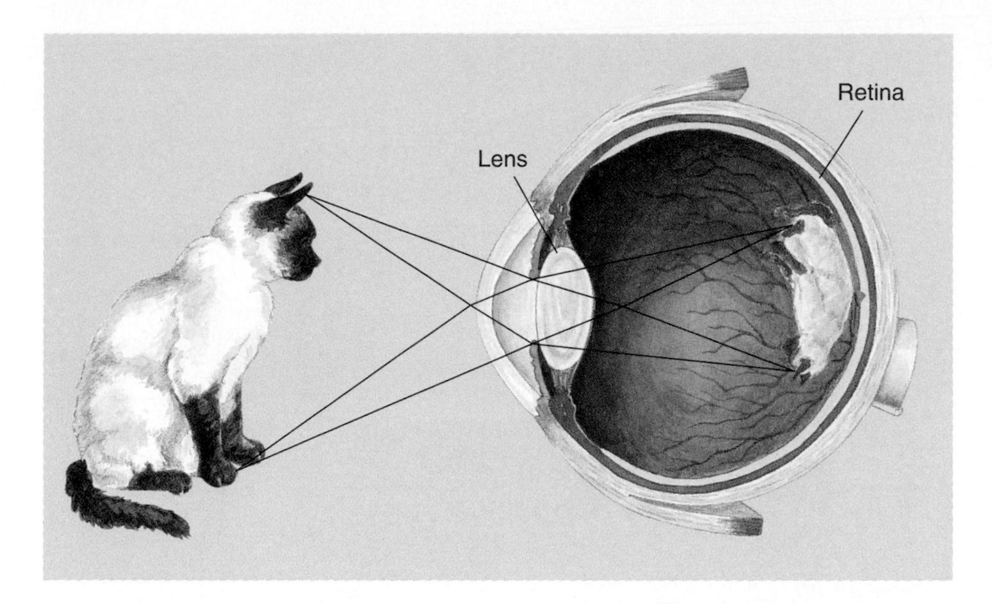

FIGURE 3.4

The Upside-Down and Reversed Image Projected onto the Retina

The lens bends light rays entering the eye so that the image projected onto the retina is upside down and reversed: Light rays from the top of an object are projected onto receptors at the bottom of the retina, and light rays from the left side of an object are projected onto receptors on the right side of the retina. Our brain rearranges this information and enables us to see the object correctly.

Second, certain physical properties of light contribute to our psychological experiences of vision. **Wavelength,** the distance between successive peaks and valleys of light energy, determines what we experience as **hue** or color. As shown in Figure 3.6 on page 92, as wavelength increases from about 400 to 700 nanometers (a nanometer is one billionth of a meter), our sensations shift from violet through blue (shorter wavelengths), green, yellow, orange (medium wavelengths), and finally red (longer wavelengths). The intensity of light, the amount

FIGURE 3.5

The Blind Spot

To find your blind spot, close your left eye and focus your right eye on the A. Slowly move the page toward and away from your right eye until the dark spot on the right disappears. The image of this dot is now being projected onto the blind spot—the region of the retina where there are no rods or cones. Now follow the same procedure for the B and the C. What do you see?

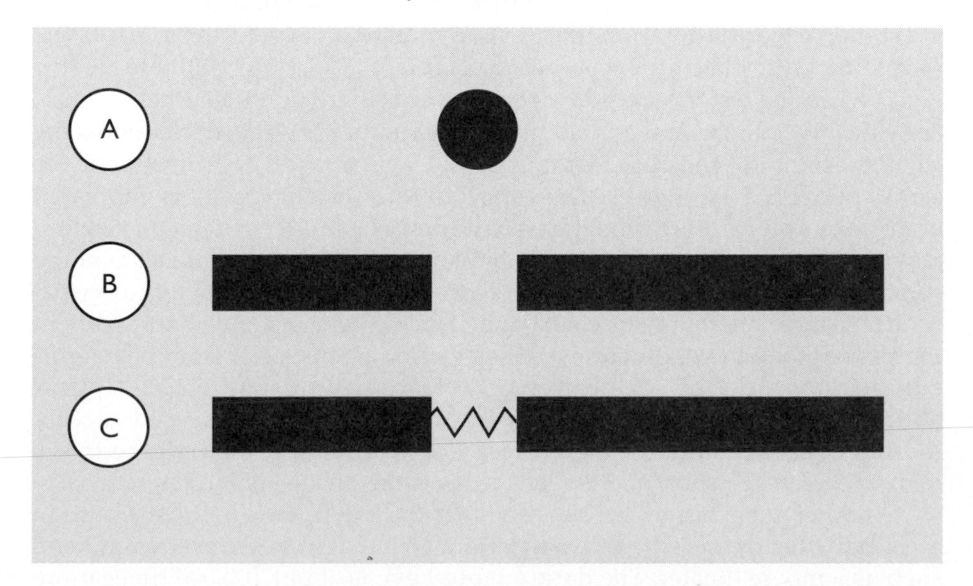

Wavelength: The peak-to-peak distance in a sound or light wave.

Hue: The color that we experience due to the dominant wavelength of a light.

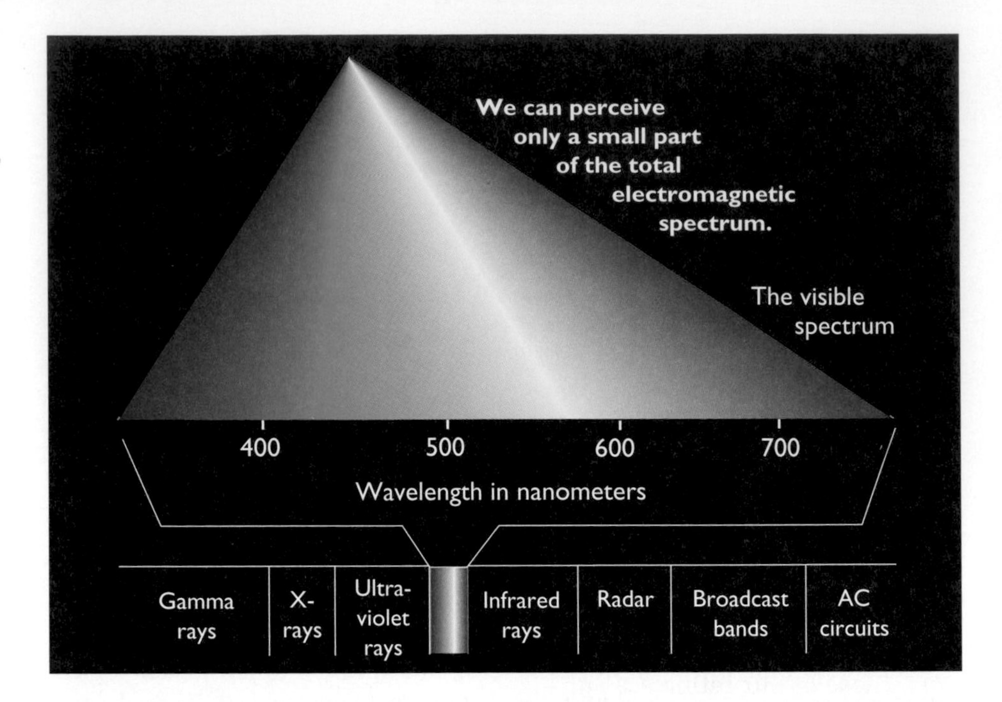

FIGURE 3.6

The Electromagnetic Spectrum

Visible light occupies only a narrow band in the entire spectrum.

of energy it contains, is experienced as **brightness.** The extent to which light contains only one wavelength, rather than many, determines our experience of **saturation;** the fewer the number of wavelengths mixed together, the more saturated or "pure" a color appears. For example, the deep red of an apple is highly saturated, whereas the pale pink of an apple blossom is low in saturation.

Brightness: The physical intensity of light.

Saturation: The degree of concentration of the hue of light. We experience saturation as the purity of a color.

Acuity: The visual ability to see fine details.

Nearsightedness: A condition in which the visual image entering our eye is focused slightly in front of our retina rather than directly on it. Therefore near objects can be seen clearly, while distant objects appear fuzzy or blurred.

Farsightedness: A condition in which the visual image entering our eye is focused behind rather than directly on the retina. Therefore close objects appear out of focus, while distant objects are in clear focus.

Dark Adaptation: The process through which our visual system increases its sensitivity to light under low levels of illumination.

Basic Functions of the Visual System: Acuity, Dark Adaptation, and Eye Movements

Our visual system is remarkably sensitive and can detect even tiny amounts of light. However, another important aspect of vision is **acuity,** the ability to resolve fine details. Two types of visual acuity are measured. The first is *static visual acuity (SVA),* our ability to discriminate different objects when they are stationary or static, as on the familiar chart at an eye doctor's office. The second measure of acuity is *dynamic visual acuity (DVA),* our ability to resolve detail when the test object and/or the viewer is in motion (Houfman, House, & Ryan, 1981). In general, our ability to discriminate objects decreases as the *angular velocity* of the object—the speed at which an object's image moves across our retina—increases. This aspect of our visual capacity is important in, for example, a professional baseball player's ability to detect a sizzling fastball out of the corner of his eye on his way to hitting a grand slam home run. If you wear eyeglasses or contact lenses designed to improve your visual acuity, chances are that your visual deficit stems from a slight abnormality in the shape of your eye. If your eyeball is too long, you suffer from **nearsightedness,** in which you see near objects clearly, but distant objects appear blurry. This occurs because the image entering your eye is focused slightly in front of the retina rather than directly on it. Similarly, in **farsightedness,** your eyeball is too short and the lens focuses the image behind the retina.

Another aspect of visual sensitivity is **dark adaptation,** the increase in sensitivity that occurs when we move from bright light to a dim environment, such as a movie theater. The dark-adapted eye is about 100,000 times more sensitive to light than the light-adapted eye. Actually, dark adaptation occurs in two steps. First, within five to ten minutes, the cones reach their maximum sensitivity. After about ten minutes, the rods begin to adapt; they complete this process in about thirty minutes (Matlin & Foley, 1992).

Eye movements also play a role in visual acuity. To appreciate the importance of the ability to move your eyes, just imagine how inefficient it would be to read a book or play your favorite sport if your eyes were stuck in one position. In order to change the direction of your gaze, you would have to move your entire head.

Eye movements are of two basic types: *version movements,* in which the eyes move together in the same direction, and *vergence movements,* in which the lines of sight for the two eyes converge or diverge. As we'll discover later in this chapter, vergence movements are crucial to our ability to perceive distance and depth. Three types of version movements are *involuntary movements, saccadic movements,* and *pursuit movements.*

At the end of this sentence, stop reading and stare at the last word for several seconds. Did your eyes remain motionless or did they tend to move about? The eye movements you probably experienced were *involuntary;* they occurred without your conscious control. These movements ensure that the stimuli reaching our rods and cones are constantly changing. Like other sensory receptors, those in our retina are subject to the effects of sensory adaptation; if involuntary movements did not occur, we would experience temporary blindness whenever we fixed our gaze on any object for more than a few seconds.

Saccadic movements are fast, frequent jumps by the eyes from one fixation point to the next. Saccadic movements are apparent in reading or driving. Both the size of the jumps and the region seen during each fixation maximize the information we glean while reading (Just & Carpenter, 1987; McConkie & Zola, 1984). The saccadic movements of good readers move smoothly across the materials being read; those of poor readers are shorter and move backward as well as forward (Schiffman, 1990). Research suggests that our attention—what we're focused on at the moment—is the force that guides the location and duration of each fixation (Hoffman & Subramaniam, 1995; Rayner & Raney, 1996).

Finally, *pursuit movements* are smooth movements used to track moving objects, as when you watch a plane fly overhead and out of sight.

Color Vision

A world without color would be sadly limited; for color—vivid reds, glowing yellows, restful greens—is a crucial part of our visual experience. For many people, though, some degree of color deficiency is a fact of life. Nearly 8 percent of males and 0.4 percent of females are less sensitive than the rest of us either to red and green or to yellow and blue (Nathans, 1989). And a few individuals are totally color blind, experiencing the world only in varying shades of white, black, and gray. Intriguing evidence on how the world appears to people suffering from color weakness has been gathered from rare cases in which individuals have normal color vision in one eye and impaired color vision in the other (e.g., Graham & Hsia, 1958). For example, one such woman indicated that to her color-impaired eye, all colors between red and green appeared yellow, while all colors between green and violet seemed blue.

There are two leading theories to explain our rich sense of color. The first, **trichromatic theory,** suggests that we have three different types of cones in our retina, each of which is maximally sensitive, though not exclusively so, to a particular range of light wavelengths—a range roughly corresponding to blue (400–500 nanometers), green (475–600 nanometers), or red (490–650 nanome-

Saccadic Movements: Quick movements of the eyes from one point of fixation to another.

Trichromatic Theory: A theory of color perception suggesting that we have three types of cones, each primarily receptive to particular wavelengths of light.

Negative Afterimage: A sensation of complementary color that we experience after staring at a stimulus of a given hue.

Opponent-Process Theory: Theory that describes the processing of sensory information related to color at levels above the retina. The theory suggests that we possess six different types of neurons, each of which is either stimulated or inhibited by red, green, blue, yellow, black, or white.

ters). Careful study of the human retina suggests that we do possess three types of receptors, although as Figure 3.7 shows, there is a great deal of overlap in each receptor type's sensitivity range (DeValois & DeValois, 1975; Rushton, 1975). According to trichromatic theory, our ability to perceive colors results from the joint action of the three receptor types. Thus, light of a particular wavelength produces differential stimulation of each receptor type, and it is the overall pattern of stimulation that produces our rich sense of color. This differential sensitivity may be due to genes that direct different cones to produce pigments sensitive to blue, green, or red (Nathans, Thomas, & Hogness, 1986).

Trichromatic theory, however, fails to account for certain aspects of color vision, such as the occurrence of **negative afterimages**—sensations of complementary colors that occur after one stares at a stimulus of a given color. For example, after you stare at a red object, if you shift your gaze to a neutral background, sensations of green may follow. Similarly, after you stare at a yellow stimulus, sensations of blue may occur. (Figure 3.8 demonstrates a negative afterimage.)

The **opponent-process theory** addresses phenomena such as negative afterimages more effectively than trichromatic theory, by accounting for what happens after the cones in the retina transmit their information to the bipolar and ganglion cells. This theory suggests that we possess six kinds of cells that play a role in sensations of color (DeValois & DeValois, 1975). Two of these handle red and green: One is stimulated by red light and inhibited by green light, whereas the other is stimulated by green light and inhibited by red. This is where the phrase *opponent process* originates. Two additional types of cells handle yellow and blue; one is stimulated by yellow and inhibited by blue, while the other shows the opposite pattern. The remaining two types handle black and white—again, in an opponent-process manner. Opponent-process theory can help explain the occurrence of negative afterimages (Jameson & Hurvich, 1989). The idea is that when stimulation of one cell in an opponent pair is terminated, the other is automatically activated. Thus, if the original stimulus viewed was yellow, the afterimage seen would be blue. Each opponent pair is stimulated in different patterns by the three types of cones. It is the overall pattern of such stimulation that yields our complex and eloquent sensation of color.

FIGURE 3.7

Three Types of Receptors Contribute to Our Perception of Color

Color vision appears to be mediated by three types of cones, each maximally (but not exclusively) sensitive to wavelengths corresponding to blue, green, and red.

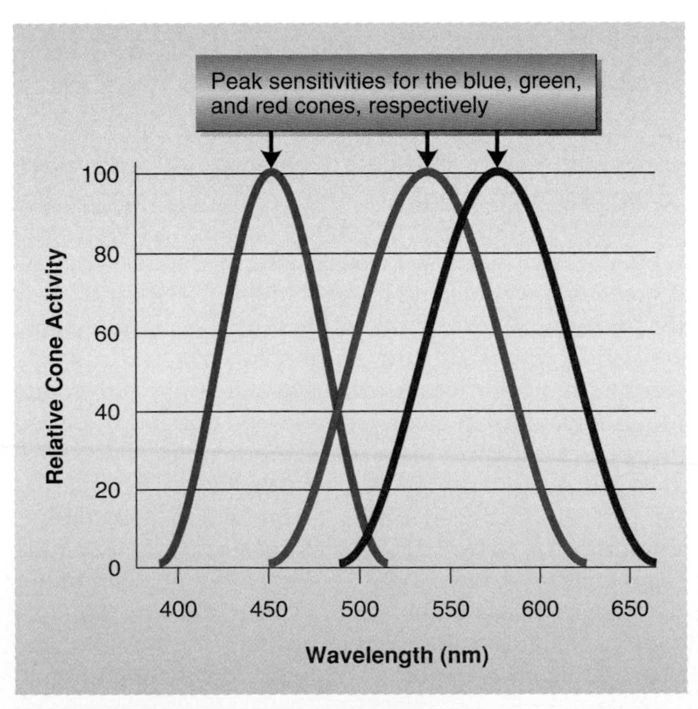

(**Source:** Adapted from MacNichol, 1964.)

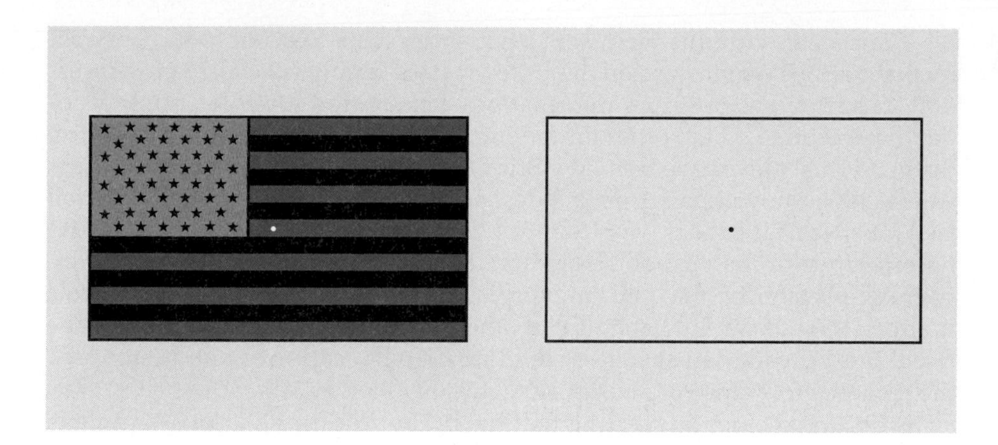

FIGURE 3.8

Demonstration of a Negative Afterimage

Stare at the object on the left for about one minute. Then shift your gaze to the blank space at the right. Do you see a negative afterimage?

Although these theories competed for many years, we now know that both are necessary to explain our impressive ability to respond to color. Trichromatic theory explains how color coding occurs in the cones of the retina, whereas opponent-process theory accounts for processing in higher-order nerve cells (Coren & Ward, 1989; Hurvich, 1981; Matlin & Foley, 1992). We'll now turn to a discussion of how visual information is processed by the brain.

Vision and the Brain: Processing Visual Information

Our rich sense of vision does not result from the output of single neurons, but instead from the overall pattern of our sensory receptors. In other words, there is more to vision than meets the eye. But how, then, do the simple action potentials of individual neurons contribute to our overall conscious experience? To help answer this question, let's consider how the brain "invents" our visual world.

At one time it was believed that visual scenes in our environment were impressed onto our retinas, much like images on photographic plates, and then sent directly to the brain. We now know this view is wrong, however. The visual world we perceive results from a complex division of labor that only *begins* in the retina. In other words, it is only light that enters our eyes—we really see with our brains.

Our understanding of the initial stages of this process was greatly advanced by the Nobel Prize–winning series of studies conducted by Hubel and Wiesel (1979). These researchers conducted studies on **feature detectors**—neurons at various levels in the *visual cortex*, an area located at the back of the brain, that respond primarily to stimuli possessing certain features. Their work revealed the existence of three types of feature detectors. One group of neurons, known as **simple cells,** responds to bars or lines presented in certain orientations (horizontal, vertical, and so on). A second group, **complex cells,** responds maximally to moving stimuli, such as a vertical bar moving from left to right or a tilted bar moving from right to left. Finally, **hypercomplex cells** respond to even more complex features of the visual world, such as length, width, and even aspects of shape such as corners and angles.

These findings led scientists to the intriguing possibility that the brain processes visual information hierarchically. According to this view, groups of neurons analyze simpler aspects of visual information and send their results to other groups of neurons for further analysis. At successive stages in this process, increasingly complex visual information is analyzed and compiled—eventually producing the coherent and flowing scenes that constitute our perception of the world around us (Zeki, 1992).

Feature Detectors: Neurons at various levels within the visual cortex that respond primarily to stimuli possessing certain features.

Simple Cells: Cells within the visual system that respond to specific shapes presented in certain orientations (horizontal, vertical, etc.).

Complex Cells: Neurons in the visual cortex that respond to stimuli moving a particular direction and having a particular orientation.

Hypercomplex Cells: Neurons in the visual cortex that respond to complex aspects of visual stimuli, such as width, length, and shape.

Blindsight: A rare condition, resulting from damage to the primary visual cortex, in which individuals report being blind yet respond to certain aspects of visual stimuli as if they could see.

Prosopagnosia: A rare condition in which brain damage impairs a person's ability to recognize faces.

Consistent with this view, some evidence seems to point to the possibility that various regions within the cortex may be highly specialized to process only certain types of visual information—one region for color, another for depth perception, yet another for motion, and so on. In fact, more than thirty distinct visual areas have been identified (Felleman & Van Essen, 1991). Other studies have shown, however, that destruction of areas thought to be specialized for specific functions—for example, processing color information—doesn't necessarily eliminate color perception. Research now suggests another intriguing possibility: that cells in our visual cortex may play a dynamic role in processing visual information; in other words, their function may not be fixed, but instead may change depending on what captures our attention or the personal relevance of a visual stimulus (Schiller, 1994).

Additional clues suggesting that the brain processes various aspects of visual information separately come from case studies of persons with visual disorders like **blindsight,** a rare condition that results from damage to the primary visual cortex. Studies of persons with blindsight have revealed some startling facts about how the brain processes visual information. Persons with blindsight are able to respond to certain aspects of visual stimuli, such as color or movement, as if they could see; yet, paradoxically, they are completely unaware of the stimuli and deny having "seen" anything (Gazzaniga, Fendrich, & Wessinger, 1994; Weiskrantz, 1995). A related disorder, termed **prosopagnosia,** provides further evidence that the visual system operates much like a computer, assembling bits of visual information at various locations in the brain. In prosopagnosia, persons lose the ability to recognize well-known faces but still retain relatively normal vision in other respects (Schweinberger, Klos, & Sommer, 1995). This "computer" model explains why we can lose certain visual abilities—like recognizing faces—while other abilities, including the ability to perceive form, motion, or color, remain largely unaffected (Barbur et al., 1993; Zeki, 1992).

Taken together, these findings have important implications for our understanding of visual perception. First, they suggest that the visual system is quite *selective;* certain types of visual stimuli stand a greater chance of reaching the brain and undergoing further processing. Second, since nature is rarely wasteful, the existence of cells specially equipped to detect certain features of the external world suggests that these feature detectors may be the building blocks for many complex visual abilities, including reading and identifying subtly varied visual patterns such as faces. Finally, as illustrated by disorders such as blindsight and prosopagnosia, "seeing" the world is a complex process—one that requires precise integration across many levels of our visual system.

Key Questions

- What are the basic structures of the eye, and what is the physical stimulus for vision?
- What are the basic functions of the visual system?
- How do psychologists explain color perception?
- Why is visual perception a hierarchical process?
- What are the basic building blocks of visual perception?

Hearing

The melody of a baby's laughter, the roar of a jet plane, the rustling of leaves on a crisp autumn day—clearly, we live in a world full of sound. And, as with vision, human beings are well equipped to receive many sounds in their environment. A simplified diagram of the human ear is shown in Figure 3.9; please refer to it as you proceed through the discussion below.

FIGURE 3.9

The Human Ear

A simplified diagram of the human ear. Sound waves (alternating compressions and expansions in the air) enter through the external auditory canal and produce slight movements in the eardrum. This, in turn, produces movements in fluid within the cochlea. As this fluid moves, tiny hair cells shift their position, thus generating the nerve impulses we perceive as sound.

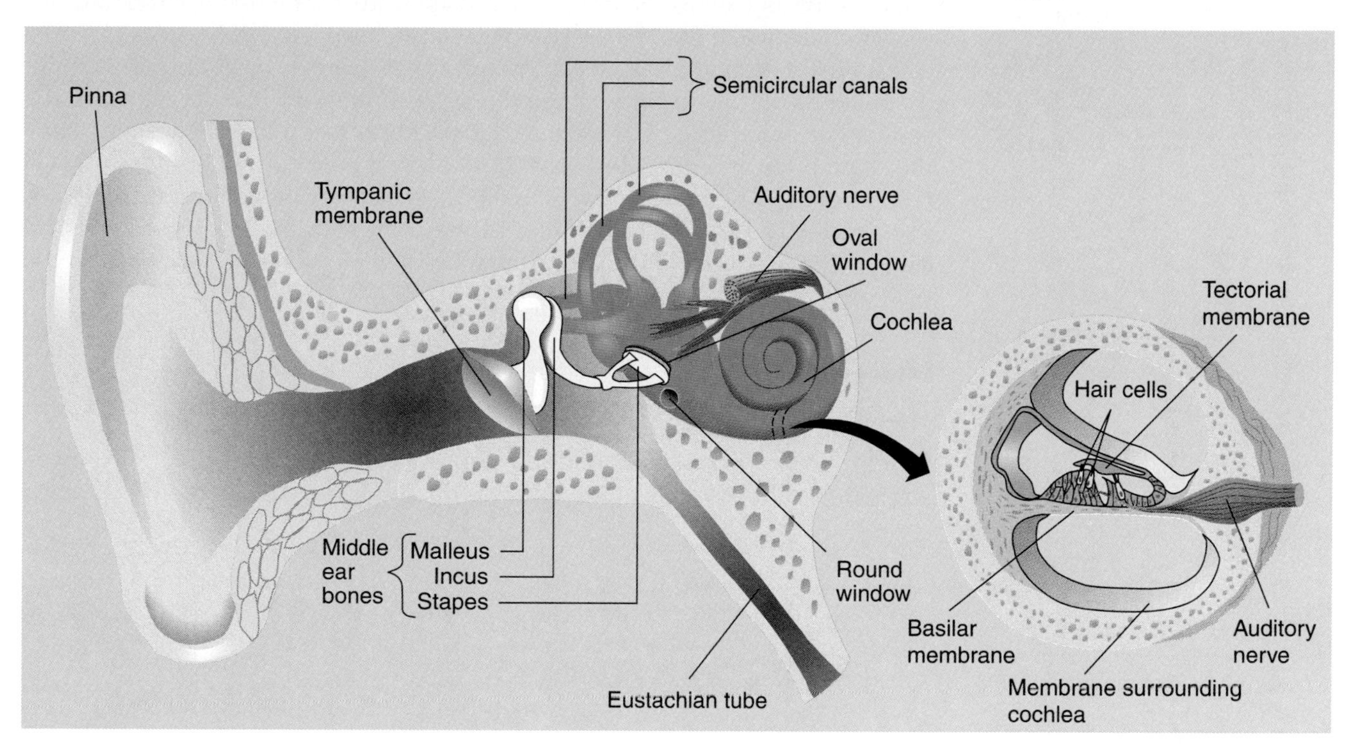

The Ear: Its Basic Structure

Try asking a friend, "When did you get your pinna pierced?" The response will probably be a blank stare. **Pinna** is the technical term for the visible part of our hearing organ, the *ear.* However, this is only a small part of the entire ear. Inside the ear is an intricate system of membranes, small bones, and receptor cells that transform sound waves into neural information for the brain. The *eardrum,* a thin piece of tissue just inside the ear, moves ever so slightly in response to sound waves striking it. When it moves, the eardrum causes three tiny bones within the *middle ear* to vibrate. The third of these bones is attached to a second membrane, the *oval window,* which covers a fluid-filled, spiral-shaped structure known as the **cochlea.** Vibration of the oval window causes movements of the fluid in the cochlea. Finally, the movement of fluid bends tiny *hair cells,* the true sensory receptors of sound. The neural messages they create are then transmitted to the brain via the *auditory nerve.*

Sound: The Physical Stimulus for Hearing

In discussing light, we noted that relationships exist between certain of light's physical properties, such as wavelength and intensity, and psychological aspects of vision, like hue and brightness. Similar relationships exist for sound, at least with respect to two of its psychological qualities: *loudness* and *pitch.*

Pinna: The external portion of the ear.

Cochlea: A portion of the inner ear containing the sensory receptors for sound.

Pitch: The characteristic of a sound that is described as high or low. Pitch is mediated by the frequency of a sound.

Timbre: The quality of a sound, resulting from the complexity of a sound wave; timbre helps us distinguish the sound of a trumpet from that of a saxophone.

Sound waves consist of alternating compressions of the air, or, more precisely, of the molecules that compose air. The greater the *amplitude* (magnitude) of these waves, the greater their loudness to us (see Figure 3.10). The rate at which air is expanded and contracted constitutes the *frequency* of a sound wave, and the greater the frequency, the higher the **pitch.** Frequency is measured in terms of cycles per second, or hertz (Hz), and humans can generally hear sounds ranging from about 20 Hz to about 20,000 Hz. In Making Psychology Part of Your Life, at the end of this chapter, we'll explore the benefits as well as the dangers of the sounds that emanate from a quintessential device of the 1990s—personal stereo headsets.

A third psychological aspect of sound is its **timbre,** or quality. This quality depends on the mixture of frequencies and amplitudes that make up the sound. For example, a piece of chalk squeaking across a blackboard may have the same pitch and amplitude as a note played on a clarinet, but it will certainly have a different quality. In general, the timbre of a sound is related to its complexity—how many different frequencies it contains. Other physical aspects of the source of the sound may be involved as well, however, so the relationship is not simple (refer to Figure 3.10).

Pitch Perception

When we tune a guitar or sing in harmony with other people, we demonstrate our ability to detect differences in pitch. Most of us can easily tell when

FIGURE 3.10

Physical Characteristics of Sound

Our perception of sounds is determined by three characteristics. *Loudness* depends on the amplitude or the height of the sound waves; as amplitude increases, the sound appears louder. *Pitch* is determined by the frequency of the sound waves—the number of sound waves that pass a given point per second. *Timbre* is the quality of the sound we perceive and helps us distinguish the sound of a flute from the sound of a saxophone.

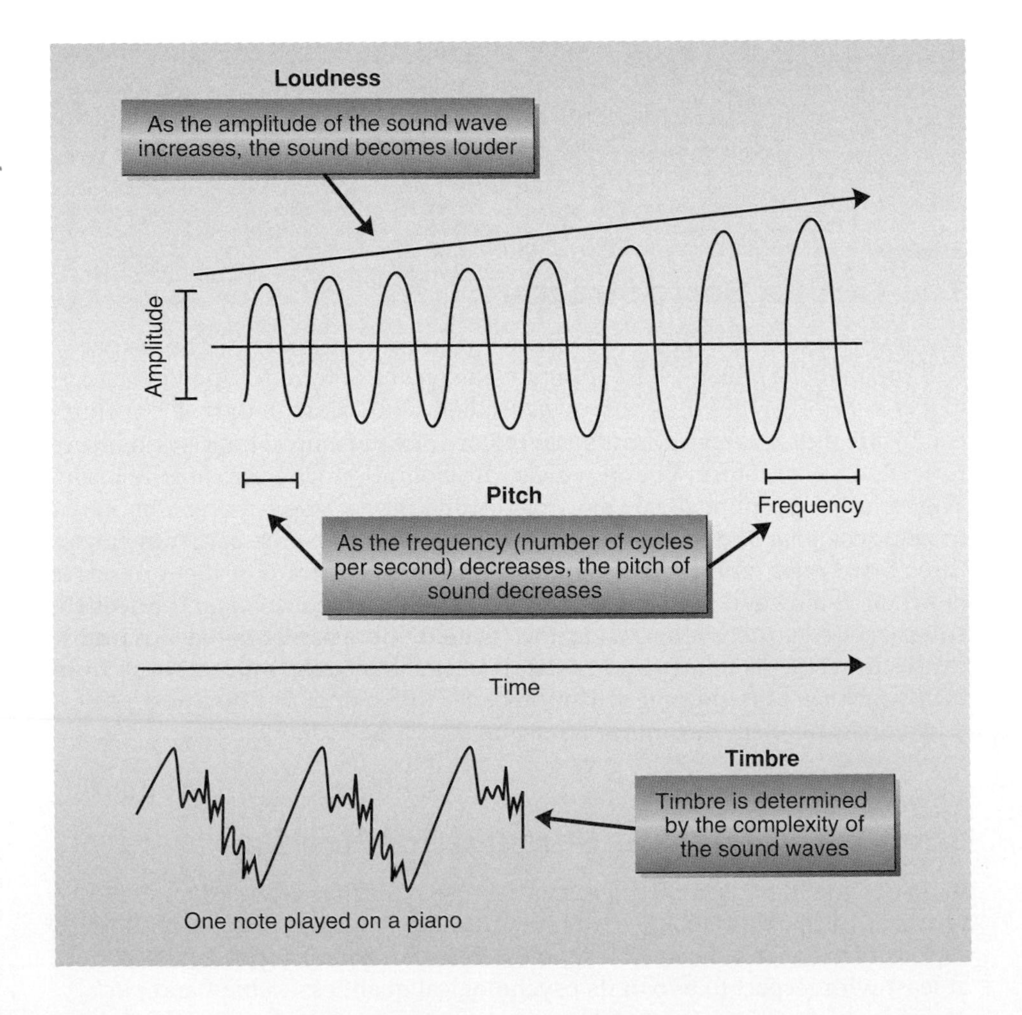

two sounds have the same pitch and when they are different. But how do we manage to make such fine distinctions? Two explanations, based on two different mechanisms, seem to provide the answer.

Place theory (also called the *traveling wave theory*) suggests that sounds of different frequencies cause different places along the *basilar membrane* (the floor of the cochlea) to vibrate. These vibrations, in turn, stimulate the hair cells—the sensory receptors for sound. Actual observations have shown that sound does produce pressure waves and that these waves peak, or produce maximal displacement, at various distances along the basilar membrane, depending on the frequency of the sound (Békésy, 1960). High-frequency sounds cause maximum displacement at the narrow end of the basilar membrane near the oval window, whereas lower frequencies cause maximal displacement toward the wider, farther end of the basilar membrane. Unfortunately, place theory does not explain our ability to discriminate among very low-frequency sounds—sounds of only a few hundred cycles per second—because displacement on the basilar membrane is nearly identical for these sounds. Another problem is that place theory does not account for our ability to discriminate sounds whose frequencies differ by as little as 1 or 2 Hz; for these sounds, too, basilar membrane displacement is nearly identical.

Frequency theory suggests that sounds of different pitch cause different rates of neural firing. Thus, high-pitched sounds produce high rates of activity in the auditory nerve, whereas low-pitched sounds produce lower rates. Frequency theory seems to be accurate up to sounds of about 1,000 Hz—the maximum rate of firing for individual neurons. Above that level, the theory must be modified to include the *volley principle*—the assumption that sound receptors for other neurons begin to fire in volleys. For example, a sound with a frequency of 5,000 Hz might generate a pattern of activity in which each of five groups of neurons fires 1,000 times in rapid succession; that is, in volleys.

Since our daily activities regularly expose us to sounds of many frequencies, both theories are needed to explain our ability to respond to this wide range of stimuli. Frequency theory explains how low-frequency sounds are registered, whereas place theory explains how high-frequency sounds are registered. In the middle ranges, between 500 and 4,000 Hz, the range that we use for most daily activities, both theories apply.

Sound Localization

You are walking down a busy street filled with many sights and sounds. Suddenly a familiar voice calls your name. You instantly turn in the direction of this sound and spot one of your friends. How do you know where to turn? Research on **localization**—the ability of the auditory system to locate the source of a given sound—suggests that several factors play a role.

The first is the fact that we have two ears, placed on opposite sides of our head. As a result, our head creates a *sound shadow,* a barrier that reduces the intensity of sound on the "shadowed" side. Thus, a sound behind us and to our left will be slightly louder in our left ear. The shadow effect is strongest for high-frequency sounds, which have difficulty bending around the head, and may produce a difference in intensity of 30 decibels or more in the ear farthest away (Phillips & Brugge, 1985). The placement of our ears also produces a slight difference in the time it takes for a sound to reach each ear. Although this difference is truly minute—often less than one millisecond—it provides an important clue to sound localization.

What happens when sound comes from directly in front or directly in back of us? In this instance, we often have difficulty determining the location of the sound source, since the sound reaches both our ears at the same time.

Place Theory: A theory suggesting that sounds of different frequency stimulate different areas of the basilar membrane, the portion of the cochlea containing sensory receptors for sound.

Frequency Theory: A theory of pitch perception suggesting that sounds of different frequencies (heard as differences in pitch) induce different rates of neural activity in the hair cells of the inner ear.

Localization: The ability of our auditory system to determine the direction of a sound source.

Key Questions

- What is the physical stimulus for hearing?
- How do psychologists explain pitch perception?
- How do we localize sound?

Head movements can help resolve a problem like this. By turning your head, you create a slight difference in the time it takes for the sound to reach each of your ears—and now you can determine the location of the sound and take appropriate action (Moore, 1982).

In summary, our auditory system is ideally constructed to take full advantage of a variety of subtle cues. When you consider how rapidly we process and respond to such information, the whole system seems nothing short of marvelous in its efficiency.

Touch and Other Skin Senses

The skin is our largest sensory organ and produces the most varied experiences: everything from the pleasure of a soothing massage to the pain of an injury. Actually, there are several skin senses, including touch (or pressure), warmth, cold, and pain. As there are specific sensory receptors for vision and hearing, it seems reasonable to expect this to be true for the various skin senses as well—one type of receptor for touch, another for warmth, and so on. And microscopic examination reveals several different receptor types, which led early researchers to suggest that each receptor type produced a specific sensory experience. However, the results of research conducted to test this prediction were disappointing; specific types of receptors were *not* found at spots highly sensitive to touch, warmth, or cold. Other studies have also shown that many different types of receptors often respond to a particular stimulus. Therefore, the skin's sensory experience is probably determined by the total pattern of nerve impulses reaching the brain.

Have you ever wondered why certain areas on your body are more sensitive than others? As it turns out, the receptors in skin are not evenly distributed; the touch receptors in areas highly sensitive to touch, such as our face and fingertips, are much more densely packed than receptors in less sensitive areas, such as our legs. Additionally, areas of the skin with greater sensitivity also have greater representation in higher levels of the brain.

The physical stimulus for touch is a stretching of or pressure against receptors in the skin. In most instances we discover the texture of an object through active exploration—using our fingertips or other sensitive areas of our body. Psychologists distinguish between *passive touch,* in which an object comes in contact with the skin, and *active touch,* in which we place our hand or other body part in contact with an object. We are considerably more accurate at identifying objects through active than through passive touch, in part because of feedback we receive from the movement of our fingers and hands when exploring an object (Matlin & Foley, 1992). Psychologists have discovered, however, that when people's fingers make contact with an object for as little as 200 milliseconds, without active exploration but with hints about what types of objects are likely to be present, people are very accurate at identifying the object (Klatzky & Lederman, 1995).

It is noteworthy that the sense of touch is intimately interconnected with our other senses, including vision. This point is illustrated by a recent study in which three groups—blindfolded sighted persons, persons blind since birth, and blind persons who had lost their sight later in life—were asked to identify raised line drawings of common objects (fruit, furniture, vehicles, body parts) through touch alone (Heller et al., 1996). The researchers reasoned that if visual experience is important to our sense of touch, sighted persons and persons who had lost their vision later in life (late blind) should outperform persons blind since birth (congenitally blind). In general, these predictions were supported; the sighted and late blind persons were more accurate than congenitally blind persons at identifying objects through touch alone (see Figure 3.11). Closer inspection, however, revealed that this performance difference was apparent only for objects unfamiliar to the congenitally blind persons; their ability to identify *familiar* objects was equal to the levels of performance of the other groups. Let's now turn to a discussion of how the sense of touch helps us experience pain.

FIGURE 3.11

Interconnections between the Senses

The importance of the sense of touch is clearly evident in this scene. Blind persons depend greatly on touch to navigate their environment.

Pain: Its Nature and Control

Pain plays an important adaptive role; without it, we would be unaware that something is amiss with our body or that we have suffered some type of injury. Determining the mechanisms for pain sensation has been particularly difficult, because unlike the other sensory processes that we have studied, pain sensation has no specific stimulus (Besson & Chaouch, 1987). However, sensations of pain do seem to originate in *free nerve endings* located throughout the body: in the skin, around muscles, and in internal organs.

Actually, two types of pain seem to exist. One can best be described as quick and sharp—the kind of pain we experience when we receive a cut. The other is dull and throbbing—the pain we experience from a sore muscle or an injured back. The first type of pain seems to be transmitted through large myelinated sensory nerve fibers (Campbell & LaMotte, 1983). You may recall from Chapter 2 that impulses travel faster along myelinated fibers, and so it makes sense that sharp sensations of pain are carried via these fiber types. In contrast, dull pain is carried by smaller unmyelinated nerve fibers, which conduct neural impulses more slowly. Both fiber types synapse with neurons in the spinal cord that carry pain messages to the thalamus and other parts of the brain (Willis, 1985).

Pain Perception: The Role of Physiological Mechanisms

The discovery of the two pain systems described above led to the formulation of an influential view of pain known as the **gate-control theory** (Melzack, 1976). Gate-control theory suggests that there are neural mechanisms in the spinal cord that sometimes close, thus preventing pain messages from reaching the brain. Apparently, pain messages carried by the large fibers cause this "gate" to close, while messages carried by the smaller fibers—the ones related to dull, throbbing pain—cannot. This may explain why sharp pain is relatively brief, whereas an ache persists. The gate-control theory also helps to explain why vigorously stimulating one area to reduce pain in another sometimes works (Matlin & Foley, 1992). Presumably, tactics such as rubbing the skin near an injury, applying ice packs or hot-water bottles, and even acupuncture stimulate activity in the large nerve fibers, closing the spinal "gate" and reducing sensations of pain.

Gate-control theory has been revised to account for the importance of several brain mechanisms in the perception of pain (Melzack, 1993). For example, our current emotional state may interact with the onset of a painful stimulus to alter the intensity of pain we experience. The brain, in other words, may affect pain perception by transmitting messages that either close the spinal "gate" or keep it open. The result: When we are anxious, pain is intensified;

Gate-Control Theory: A theory of pain suggesting that the spinal cord contains a mechanism that can block transmission of pain to the brain.

and when we are calm and relaxed, pain may be reduced. Gate-control theory has spurred the development of innovative treatment techniques, such as the use of neural stimulation devices to relieve pain (Abram, 1993). We'll explore the influence of additional factors on the experience of pain—including culture—in the Exploring Gender and Diversity section below.

Pain Perception: The Role of Cognitive Processes In cases of persistent excruciating pain, people sometimes seek relief through potentially addictive drugs such as morphine, or through measures as extreme as

EXPLORING GENDER & DIVERSITY

Culture and the Perception of Pain

Imagine the following scene: You are in the midst of an ancient tribal ceremony. Nearly a hundred warriors are seated cross-legged on the ground of a smoke-filled lodge. Their attention is riveted on two persons, an old man and a young one, standing face-to-face at the center of the room. Only a low, rhythmic drumbeat breaks the silence. Sunlight through the lodge's apex penetrates the smoke, revealing what comes next. Using an eagle's talon, the old man rips the skin above the younger man's chest, then inserts lengths of bone horizontally through each of the wounds. Amazingly, the young man's stoic expression remains unchanged. Loops of rope are then secured around the bones and the young man is hoisted into the air, where he is allowed to dangle—until the bones tear through the skin or he becomes unconscious (see Figure 3.12).

Sound like a sadistic late-night horror show? It's actually a description of *"Swinging to the Pole,"* a ceremony practiced by the Lakota, Sioux, and Cheyenne tribes in which warriors demonstrated their courage and ability to withstand tremendous pain. This ceremony and similar ones in other cultures have led to intriguing questions about the nature of pain (Weisenberg, 1982). Although we commonly view pain as something automatic and universal, large cultural differences in the interpretation and expression of pain do exist, as illustrated in the "swinging" scene above. But what is the basis for these differences?

FIGURE 3.12

Cultural Differences in Pain Perception

As suggested by this photo, there appear to be large cultural differences in the interpretation and expression of pain.

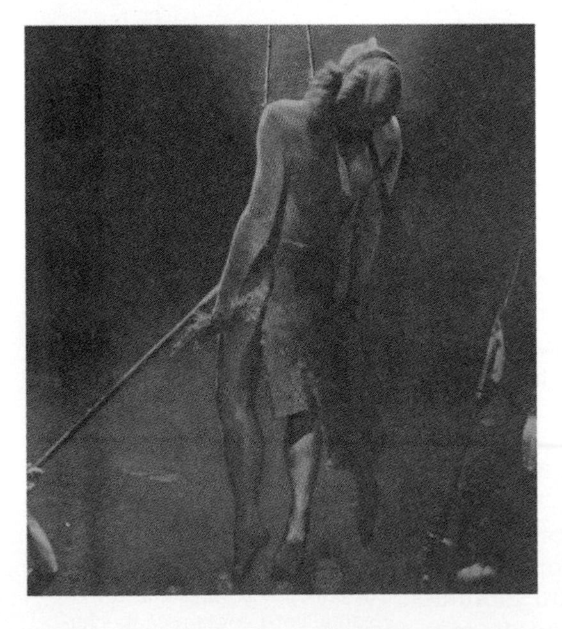

At first glance, it is tempting to conclude that cultural differences in *pain threshold*—physical differences—are the cause. After all, many of us could never endure such torture. However, no consistent experimental evidence supports this view (Zatzick & Dimsdale, 1990). Instead, observed cultural differences in the capacity to withstand pain—or not—seem to be perceptual in nature and to reflect the powerful effects of social learning (Morse & Morse, 1988). For example, honor and social standing among the Bariba of West Africa are tied closely to stoicism and the ability to withstand great pain (Sargent, 1984). Thus, both Bariba men and women are expected to suffer pain silently. And as you might expect, their language contains few words for the expression of pain. Additional environmental factors may also play a role in determining our perceptions of pain. For example, some evidence suggests that persons exposed to harsh living or working conditions become more stoical than those who work or live in more comfortable circumstances (Clark & Clark, 1980).

In sum, the evidence suggests that pain may, in fact, be universal—at least in some respects. Specifically, differences in pain perception seem to result from the powerful effects of social learning, not from physical differences.

surgery to sever nerve pathways. Fortunately, the recognition that pain stems from both physical and psychological causes has led to development of less drastic means of relief—such as a group of therapies collectively termed *cognitive–behavioral procedures* (Novy et al., 1995; Turk, 1994). These procedures are based on the fact that our thoughts, feelings, and beliefs—as well as our overt responses—before, during, and after painful episodes can dramatically influence our perceptions of pain (Turk & Rudy, 1992).

To appreciate the important role of cognitive processes in pain perception, let's consider a recent study by Montgomery and Kirsch (1996). These researchers explored the possibility that *placebos*—chemically inert substances that a person *believes* will help—would be effective in reducing perceptions of pain. Participants in the study were told they would be involved in testing a new topical anesthetic for its pain-reducing effect. The fictitious pain reliever, Trivaricane, was actually a harmless but medicinal-smelling mixture of iodine, oil of thyme, and water. The mixture was dispensed from a medicine bottle labeled "Trivaricane: Approved for research purposes only." To complete the impression, the researchers wore surgical gloves as they applied the mixture to either the left or the right index finger of each participant. After waiting a brief period of time to allow the "medication" to take effect, the researchers applied equal intensities of a painful stimulus (pressure) to both left and right fingers. As predicted, the placebo was effective in reducing the participants' perceptions of pain; ratings of pain intensity and unpleasantness were significantly lower for "treated" than for "untreated" fingers. These results illustrate the important role cognitive processes play in determining the extent to which we experience pain.

As a longtime runner, I have used these and related techniques to deal with the pain associated with my training. For example, I'm careful not to focus on the discomfort I sometimes feel while running; instead I think about something pleasant, such as a relaxing dip in the pool upon my return. Of course, I'm careful to avoid overdoing it. Pain can be a warning sign that we are pushing our bodies to—and beyond—their limit. For additional information on pain perception and on how psychologists study the role of cognitive processes in pain, please see the Research Methods section on page 104.

Key Questions

- What is the physical stimulus for touch?
- Where does the sensation of pain originate?
- What is the basis for cultural differences in pain perception?
- What role do cognitive processes play in the perception of pain?

Smell and Taste: The Chemical Senses

Although smell and taste are separate senses, we'll consider them together for two reasons. First, both respond to substances in solution—that is, substances that have been dissolved in a fluid or gas, usually water or air. That is why smell and taste are often referred to as the *chemical senses.* Second, in everyday life, these two senses are interrelated.

Smell and Taste: How They Operate

The stimulus for sensations of smell consists of molecules of various substances contained in the air. Such molecules enter the nasal passages, where they dis-

▪ RESEARCH METHODS ▪

How Psychologists Study the Effects of Negative Thinking on Pain Perception

We've already noted that cognitive processes play a significant role in pain perception. A cognitive element that seems particularly important is the extent to which we think negative thoughts, often termed *catastrophizing,* while in pain (Turk & Rudy, 1992). Research has shown that reducing or interrupting such thoughts can greatly improve our ability to cope with pain (Chaves & Brown, 1987; Turner & Clancy, 1986). At this point I can almost hear you saying, "Okay—I can buy the idea that negative thinking may affect our perceptions of pain; that makes perfect sense. But how do psychologists *know* what we're thinking? And how do they relate a person's thoughts or feelings to their pain?"

Although none of the psychologists that I know are mind readers, most are resourceful at solving this type of measurement problem. Consider a recent study by Sullivan and his colleagues (Sullivan, Bishop, & Pivik, 1995). These researchers attempted to quantify the relationship between negative thoughts and pain. To accomplish their goal, the researchers first constructed the *Pain Catastrophizing Scale (PCS)*—a survey designed to measure people's negative thoughts about pain, such as the tendency to dwell on negative thoughts, to exaggerate the potential threat of painful stimuli, and to experience feelings of helplessness. High scorers on the PCS are people with a greater tendency toward negative thoughts (catastrophizers), whereas low scorers are people with a lesser tendency toward such thinking (noncatastrophizers). After completing the PCS, participants were subjected to a *cold pressor test,* a standard procedure used to induce intense but temporary pain in laboratory settings. Participants immersed their arm in a container of icy water for about a minute—the point at which most people can no longer withstand the pain. At several points during the test, the researchers asked the participants to rate the pain they felt on a scale from 1 (no pain) to 10 (excruciating pain). Following the cold pressor test, participants were asked to report all the thoughts and feelings they experienced during their chilling experience. As shown in Figure 3.13, participants who scored highest on the PCS—the catastrophizers—reported more negative thoughts while in pain than the noncatastrophizers. Further, although both groups reported increasing levels of pain over time, the catastrophizers reported more pain throughout the immersion period.

The results of this research have several important implications. First, they demonstrate that psychologists are

FIGURE 3.13

Negative Thinking and Pain

Participants who received high scores on the Pain Catastrophizing Scale—catastrophizers—reported greater pain during the ice-water immersion and more negative thoughts while in pain. These results underscore the role of cognitive processes in the perception of pain.

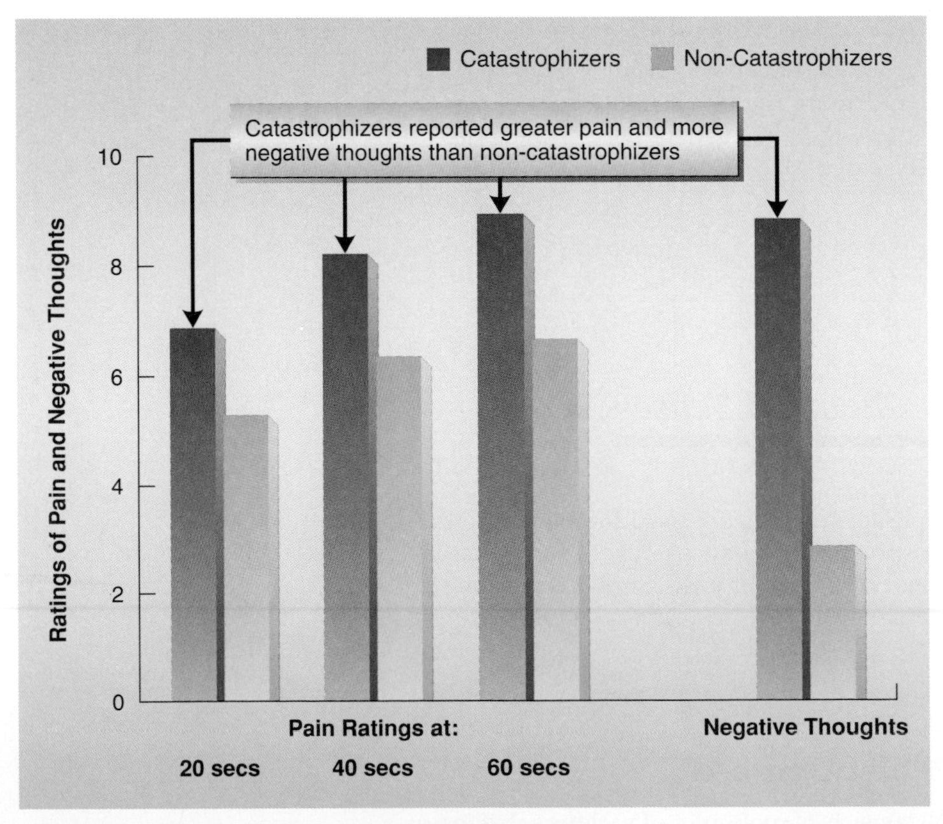

(**Source:** Based on data from Sullivan, Bishop, & Pivik, 1995.)

resourceful when it comes to measuring important aspects of our cognitive processes. In this case, participants' scores on the PCS were strongly related to their ratings of pain and the extent to which they catastrophized—engaged in negative thinking about their pain. These results also suggest that the PCS may be a useful tool to predict who is likely to exhibit strong distress in reaction to painful medical procedures, such as chemotherapy. Identifying these persons *before* such procedures would enable health care professionals to help them cope with pain more effectively.

solve in moist nasal tissues. This brings them in contact with receptor cells contained in the *olfactory epithelium* (see Figure 3.14). Human beings possess only about 10 million of these receptors. (Dogs, in contrast, possess more than 200 million receptors.) Nevertheless, our ability to detect smells is impressive. To appreciate this, consider a "scratch-and-sniff" smell survey in which six different odors were embedded separately onto panels measuring about 1.75 by 1.25 inches. Amazingly, less than 1 ounce of each odor was needed to place these smells onto 11 million copies of the survey (Gibbons, 1986; Gilbert & Wysocki, 1987).

Our olfactory senses, however, are restricted in terms of the range of stimuli to which they are sensitive, just as our visual system can detect only a small portion of the total electromagnetic spectrum. Our olfactory receptors can detect only substances with molecular weights—the sum of the atomic weights of all atoms in an odorous molecule—between 15 and 300 (Carlson, 1994). This explains why we can smell the alcohol contained in a mixed drink, with a molecular weight of 46, but cannot smell table sugar, with a molecular weight of 342.

Several theories have been proposed to explain how smell messages reach the brain. *Stereochemical theory* suggests that substances differ in smell because they have different molecular shapes (Amoore, 1970, 1982). Unfortunately, support for this theory has been mixed; nearly identical molecules can have extremely different fragrances, whereas substances with very different chemical structures can produce very similar odors (Engen, 1982; Wright, 1982). Other theories have focused on isolating "primary odors," similar to the basic hues in color vision. But these efforts have been unsuccessful, because there is often disagreement in people's perceptions of even the most basic smells. In short, scientists do not yet fully understand how the brain interprets smell, but research in this intriguing area is ongoing. We'll now turn to a discussion of the other chemical sense—taste.

The sensory receptors for taste are located inside small bumps on the tongue known as papillae. Within each papilla is a cluster of *taste buds* (see Figure 3.15 on page 106). Each taste bud contains several receptor cells. Human beings possess about 10,000 taste buds. In contrast, chickens have only 24, while catfish would win any taste bud–counting contest—they possess more than 175,000, scattered over the surface of their body. In a sense, catfish can "taste" with their entire skin (Pfaffmann, 1978).

People generally believe that they can distinguish a large number of flavors in foods. But in fact, there appear to be only four basic tastes: sweet, salty, sour, and bitter. Why, then, do we perceive many more? The answer lies in the fact that we are aware

FIGURE 3.14

The Receptors for Smell

Receptors for our sense of smell are located in the olfactory epithelium, at the top of the nasal cavity. Molecules of odorous substances are dissolved in moisture present in the nasal passages. This brings them into contact with *receptor cells* whose neural activity gives rise to sensations of smell.

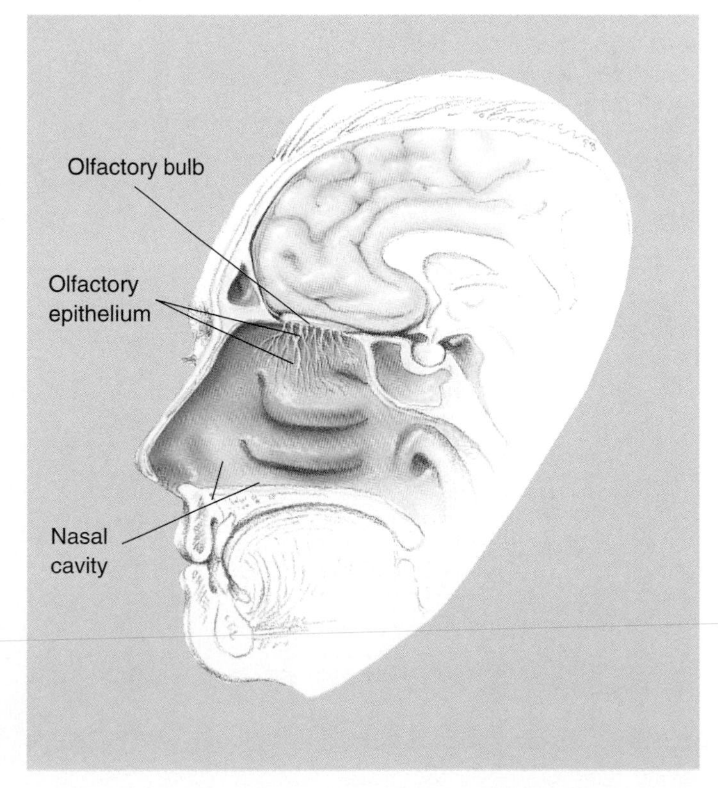

not only of the taste of the food but of its smell, its texture, its temperature, the pressure it exerts on our tongue and mouth, and many other sensations. When these factors are removed from the picture, only the four basic tastes remain (see Figure 3.15).

Smell and Taste: Some Interesting Facts

Perhaps because they are more difficult to study, the senses of smell and taste have received far less attention from researchers than vision and hearing. However, this does not imply that these senses are not important. Indeed, individuals who have lost their sense of smell (a state known as anosmia) often become deeply depressed; some even commit suicide (Douek, 1988).

Despite the relative lack of research effort, many interesting facts have been uncovered about smell and taste. For example, it appears that we are not very good at identifying different odors (Engen, 1986). When asked to identify thirteen common fragrances (such as grape, smoke, mint, pine, and soap), individuals were successful only 32 percent of the time. Even when brand-name products or common odors are used, accuracy is still less than 50 percent. Some research suggests that we lack a well-developed representational system for describing olfactory experiences (Engen, 1987). In other words, we may recognize a smell without being able to name the odor in question—a condition sometimes called the "tip-of-the-nose" phenomenon (Lawless & Engen, 1977; Richardson & Zucco, 1989). And some experiments

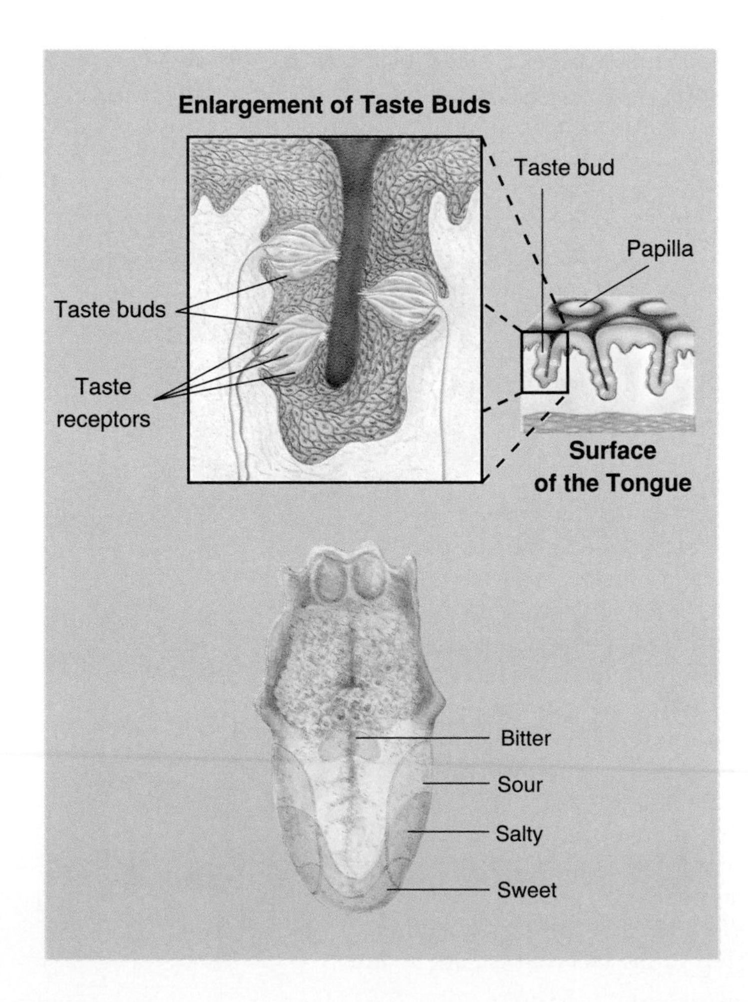

FIGURE 3.15

Sensory Receptors for Taste

Taste buds are located inside small bumps on the surface of the tongue known as papillae; within each taste bud are a number of individual receptor cells. Also shown are the areas of the tongue most sensitive to the four basic tastes: sweet, salty, sour, and bitter.

have shown that when odorants are associated with experimenter-provided verbal and visual cues, participants' long-term ability to recognize odors is enhanced (Lyman & McDaniel, 1986, 1987).

Actually, although our ability to identify specific odors is limited, our memory of them is impressive (Schab, 1991). Once exposed to a specific odor, we can recognize it months or even years later (Engen & Ross, 1973; Rabin & Cain, 1984). This may be due, in part, to the fact that our memory for odors is often coded as part of memories of a more complex and significant life event (Richardson & Zucco, 1989). For example, the delicious aroma of freshly made popcorn may elicit images of your favorite movie theater.

Knowledge about the chemical senses, especially smell, can also have important practical implications—a fact that has not escaped manufacturers of scented products. In the United States alone, sales of fragranced products exceed $19 billion annually (Foderaro, 1988). Commercial success has led to numerous claims regarding the potential benefits of fragrances. For example, practitioners of a field called *aromatherapy* claim that they can successfully treat a wide range of psychological problems and physical ailments by means of specific fragrances (Tisserand, 1977). Moreover, a growing number of companies have installed equipment that introduces various fragrances into the heating and air-conditioning systems of their buildings. Supposedly, the fragrances yield a variety of benefits: Fragrances such as lemon, peppermint, and basil lead to increased alertness and energy, whereas lavender and cedar promote relaxation and reduce tension after high-stress work periods (Iwahashi, 1992). Although little scientific evidence for such claims exists, the concept poses an intriguing question: Can fragrance influence human behavior in measurable ways? A growing body of evidence indicates the answer is yes.

In a recent study, Mike Kalsher and I (Baron & Kalsher, 1996) examined whether the use of pleasant ambient fragrance might be a cost-effective way to combat *drowsy driving*—a significant cause of deaths and injuries in this country (Peters et al., 1995). Previous research had shown that fragrance can enhance alertness and also increase performance on certain cognitive tasks (e.g., Baron & Bronfen, 1994; Baron & Thomley, 1994; Kaneda et al., 1994). To test the possibility that a pleasant fragrance would increase alertness and therefore enhance driving performance, participants in the study took part in a simulated driving task. The driving task was performed under varying conditions, including the presence or absence of a pleasant ambient lemon fragrance found to increase alertness in previous research (Baron & Thomley, 1994). The results indicated that performance on the task was significantly enhanced by the presence of a pleasant fragrance, suggesting that the use of fragrance may be an inexpensive but effective tool for maintaining alertness among persons engaged in potentially dangerous activities such as driving.

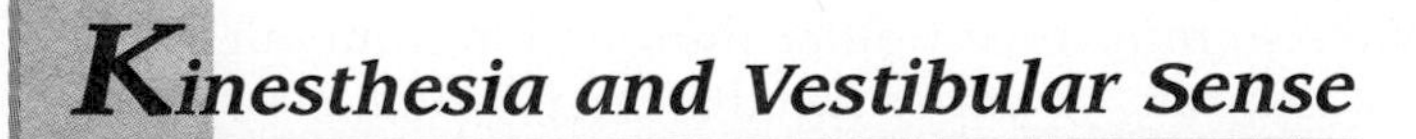

Kinesthesia and Vestibular Sense

One night while driving, you notice flashing lights on the roadside ahead. Because traffic has slowed to a crawl, you get a close look at the situation as you pass by. A state trooper is in the process of administering a sobriety test to the driver of a car he has pulled over. The driver's head is tilted back at an angle, and he is trying to touch each of his fingers to his nose but

FIGURE 3.16

Kinesthesis and the Vestibular Sense: Applying Knowledge of Basic Sensory Processes to Driver Safety

Alcohol and other drugs can impair many aspects of our sensory processes—including our kinesthetic and vestibular senses. Here, a suspected drunk driver undergoes a field sobriety test.

is having great difficulty doing so (see Figure 3.16). This example illustrates the importance of our *kinesthetic* and *vestibular senses*—two important but often ignored aspects of our sensory system.

Kinesthesia is the sense that gives us information about the location of our body parts with respect to each other and allows us to perform movements—from simple ones like touching our nose with our fingertips to more complex ones required for gymnastics, dancing, or driving an automobile. Kinesthetic information comes from receptors in joints, ligaments, and muscle fibers (Matlin & Foley, 1992). When we move our body, these receptors register the rate of change of movement speed as well as the rate of change of the angle of the bones in our limbs, then transform this mechanical information into neural signals for the brain. We also receive important kinesthetic information from our other senses, especially vision and touch. To demonstrate how your kinesthetic sense system draws on other senses, try the following experiment: Close your eyes for a moment and hold your arms down at your sides. Now, without looking, touch your nose with each of your index fingers—one at a time. Can you do it? Most people can, but only after missing their nose a time or two. Now try it again with your eyes open. Is it easier this way? In most instances it is, because of the added information we receive from our visual sense.

Whereas kinesthesia keeps our brain informed about the location of our body parts with respect to each other, the **vestibular sense** gives us information about body position, movement, and acceleration—factors critical for maintaining our sense of balance (Schiffman, 1990). We usually become aware of our vestibular sense after activities that make us feel dizzy, like amusement park rides that involve rapid acceleration or spinning motions.

The sensory organs for the vestibular sense are located in the inner ear (see Figure 3.17). Two fluid-filled *vestibular sacs* provide information about the body's position in relation to the earth by tracking changes in linear movement. When our body accelerates (or decelerates) along a straight line, as when we are in a bus that is starting and stopping, or when we tilt our head or body to one side, hair cells bend in proportion to the rate of change in our motion. This differential bending of hair cells causes attached nerve fibers to discharge neural signals that are sent to the brain.

Kinesthesia: The sense that gives us information about the location of our body parts with respect to each other and allows us to perform movement.

Vestibular Sense: Our sense of balance.

Three fluid-filled *semicircular canals,* also in the inner ear, provide information about rotational acceleration of the head or body along three principal axes. Whenever we turn or rotate our head, the fluid in these canals begins to move and causes a bending of hair cells. Because these structures are arranged at right angles to each other, bending is greatest in the semicircular canal corresponding to the axis along which the rotation occurs. Note that the vestibular system is designed to detect changes in motion rather than constant motion. For example, it helps us to detect the change in acceleration that accompanies takeoff in an airplane, but not the constant velocity that follows.

Key Questions

- What is the physical stimulus for smell?
- Where are the sensory receptors for taste located?
- What are the practical benefits of using ambient pleasant fragrance to solve real-world problems?
- What information does our kinesthetic sense provide to the brain?
- What information does the vestibular sense provide to the brain?

We also receive vestibular information from our other senses, especially vision—a fact that can produce queasy consequences if the information from these senses is in conflict (Jefferson, 1993). Developers of a realistic "Back to the Future" ride at Universal Studios in Florida discovered this fact when riders in their DeLorean simulator suffered from motion sickness. Apparently, the visual effects were not synchronized with the movements the riders felt. Once reprogrammed, however, the simulator conveyed the developers' initial intent—the sensation of flying through space and time. Please refer

FIGURE 3.17

The Structures Underlying Our Sense of Balance

Shown here are the organs of our kinesthetic and vestibular senses. Structures in the two *vestibular sacs* provide information about the positions of the head and body with respect to gravity by tracking changes in linear movement, whereas those in the *semicircular canals* provide information about *rotational acceleration* around three principal axes.

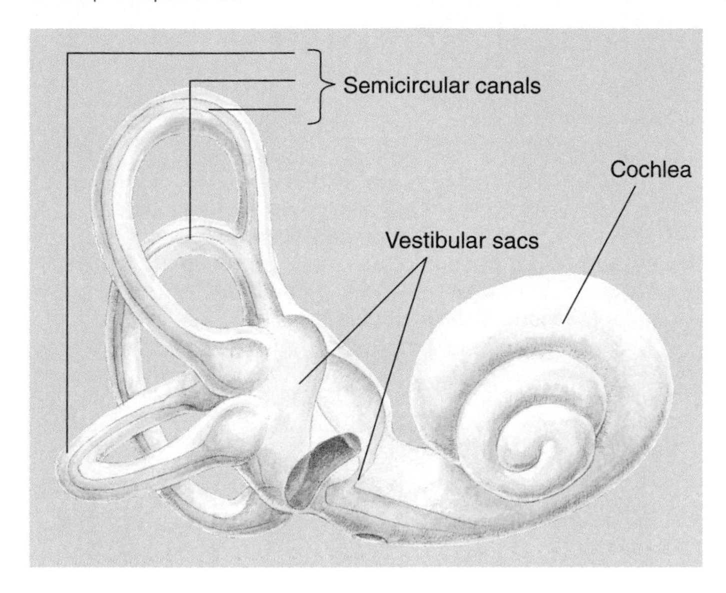

to the **Ideas to Take with You** feature on page 110 for additional information on how the various senses contribute to our conscious experience.

Perception: Putting It All Together

Up to this point, we have focused on the sensory processes that convert raw physical stimulation into usable neural codes: vision, hearing, touch, taste, smell, and the kinesthetic and vestibular senses. But you may now be wondering how this array of action potentials contributes to the richness of conscious experience. Stop for a moment and look around you. Do you see a meaningless swirl of colors, brightnesses, and shapes? Probably not. Now turn on the radio and tune it to any station. Do you hear an incomprehensible babble of sounds? Certainly not (unless, of course, you've tuned to a foreign-language or heavy metal station). In both cases, you "see" and "hear" more than the raw sensations that stimulate the receptors in your eyes, ears, and other sense organs; you see recognizable objects and hear understandable words or music. In other words, transmission of sensory information from sensory receptors to the brain is only part of the picture. Equally important is the process of perception—the way in which we *select, organize,* and *interpret* sensory input to achieve a grasp of our surroundings. The remainder of this chapter concerns some basic principles that influence perception.

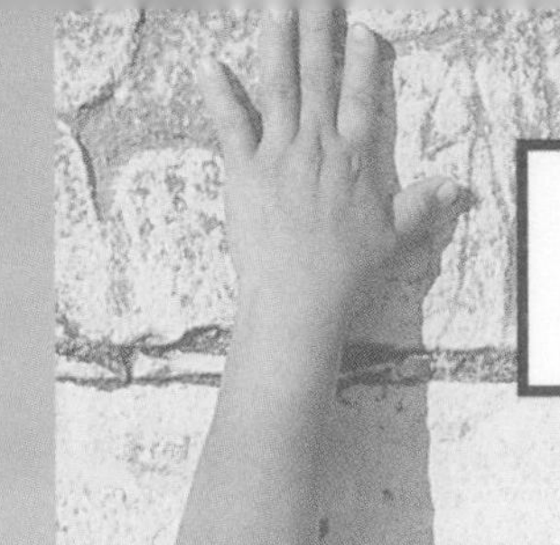

Ideas to Take with You

It's Not Just a Game Any More: Practical Applications of Virtual Reality

Virtual reality is a term used to describe the recently developed technology that puts people in computer-generated worlds that look and feel like the real thing. The development of *virtual reality* comes on the heels of advances in our understanding of how information from the various senses described in this chapter contributes to our conscious experience. The term *virtual reality* conjures up for many of us images of arcade video games or the use of 3-D lenses at movies. Scientists, however, have discovered practical applications of virtual reality to help solve problems of everyday life. A few examples:

Medicine

The development of "virtual" operating rooms has allowed doctors—working with advanced robotics—to perform life-saving operations, often at great distances from their patients.

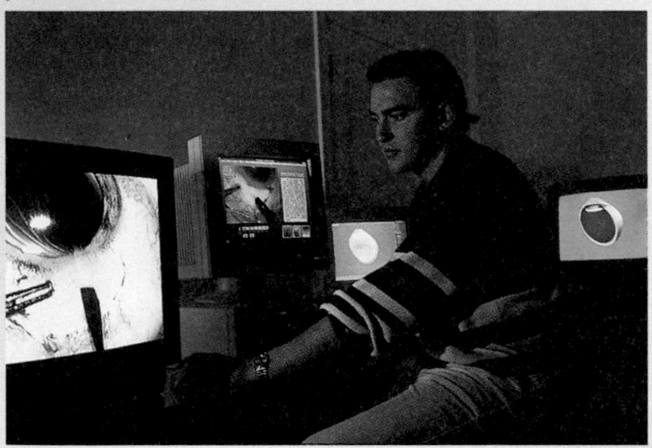

Training

Psychologists collaborate with computer scientists to design virtual reality training systems for use in safety-sensitive occupations. The obvious advantage is that these systems allow people to gain proficiency at performing critical aspects of their jobs—while guaranteeing the possibility of a second chance should they fail.

Entertainment

Manufacturers of video games and amusement park owners incorporate virtual reality into the design of their products and services to give us the thrill of a lifetime!

Perception: The Focus of Our Attention

Based on the preceding discussion, you may realize that your attention, or mental focus, captures only a small portion of the visual and auditory stimuli available at a given moment, while ignoring other aspects. But what about information from our other senses? By shifting the focus of our attention, we may suddenly notice smells, tastes, and tactile sensations that were outside our awareness only moments ago. For example, if you're absorbed in a good book or watching a suspenseful movie, you may not notice the delightful aroma of a freshly baked pie—at least until the cook says, "Dessert is ready!"

One thing is certain—we cannot absorb all of the available sensory information in our environment. Thus, we *selectively attend* to certain aspects of our environment while relegating others to the background (Johnston & Dark, 1986). Selective attention has obvious advantages, since it allows us to maximize information gained from the object of our focus while reducing sensory interference from other irrelevant sources (Matlin & Foley, 1992). Unfortunately, selective attention to one thing may mean neglect of another. For a firsthand understanding of the power of selective attention, watch someone who is completely absorbed in a suspenseful novel or a thrilling sports event. Studies have shown that people can focus so intently on one task that they fail to notice other events occurring simultaneously—even very salient ones (Becklen & Cerone, 1983; Cherry, 1953). We are, however, faced with many everyday situations in which we must cope with multiple conflicting inputs. Think back to the last time you were at a crowded party with many conversations going on at once. Were you able to shut out all voices except for that of the person you were talking to? Probably not. Our attention often shifts to other aspects of our environment, such as a juicy bit of conversation or a mention of our own name (Moray, 1959). This is often referred to as the *cocktail party phenomenon* and illustrates one way in which we deal with the demands of divided attention.

Although we control the focus of our attention, at least to some extent, certain characteristics of stimuli can cause our attention to shift suddenly. Features such as contrast, novelty, stimulus intensity, color, and sudden change tend to attract our attention. As you might expect, the ability to shift the focus of our attention to detect such changes plays a crucial survival role in aspects of our everyday life by alerting us to immediate natural dangers in our environment—enabling us, for example, to leap back onto the curb when we glimpse a speeding car out of the corner of our eye. You can probably imagine hundreds of ways in which attentional processes help you to avoid peril. But what about hazards for which there are no sensory cues available? One of the most deadly examples of such a hazard is radioactivity. The radioactive particles emitted by certain materials are colorless and odorless and thus cannot be detected through our normal sensory receptors; even a limited exposure, however, can have deadly consequences. In such cases, people need *warnings*—information displays that attempt to influence behavior through the information they present. In the Beyond the Headlines section on page 112, we'll examine how aspects of our sensory and perceptual processes have figured prominently in the development of warnings.

Perception: Some Organizing Principles

Look at the illustrations in Figure 3.20 on page 114. Instead of random smatterings of black and white, you can probably discern a familiar figure in each. But how does our brain allow us to interpret these confused specks as a dog and a horseback rider? The process by which we structure the input from our

Gestalt Psychologists: German psychologists intrigued by our tendency to perceive sensory patterns as well-organized wholes, rather than as separate, isolated parts.

sensory receptors is called *perceptual organization.* Aspects of perceptual organization were first studied systematically in the early 1900s by **Gestalt psychologists**—German psychologists intrigued by certain innate tendencies of the human mind to impose order and structure on the physical world and to perceive sensory patterns as well-organized wholes, rather than as separate, isolated parts (*Gestalt* means "whole" in German). These scientists outlined several principles that influence the way we organize basic sensory input into whole

Beyond the Headlines

As Psychologists See It

McDonald's Is Fighting Over More Than Just Spilled Coffee

Los Angeles, California—Have you ever heard the old saying, "There's no sense in crying over spilled milk"? This adage was amended recently for the 90s to: "Don't cry over spilled coffee—especially if you get $1.4 million for your troubles." That was the amount of money awarded to a woman for burns she suffered after spilling hot coffee from a McDonald's restaurant on herself.

Warning: H-O-T Really Means $$$ When It Comes to Safety

Was the decision to award this amount—or any amount of money—justified? Critics claim that lawsuits such as the one just mentioned are turning the legal system into a lottery. They claim it is simply a matter of common sense to recognize the potential hazards of hot liquids, including coffee. They also point out that McDonald's has met its obligation to customers by providing a printed warning message on its coffee cups (see Figure 3.18). Therefore, while sympathetic to the woman's injuries, critics of this lawsuit attribute the burns to the woman's own careless behavior.

Her supporters argue, however, that McDonald's and other companies have an obligation to alert their customers to potentially hazardous products (Allen, 1995). Indeed, supporters of the coffee lawsuit point to a long list of pending cases that stem from similar incidents. Apparently, one of the reasons for the large number of burn injuries is the high temperature of the coffee served at McDonald's, significantly higher than the temperatures of coffee served by other fast-food restaurants. Lawsuit proponents add that the printed warning message currently found on McDonald's cups is poorly designed, and therefore will not be effective in alerting customers to the potential dangers of handling hot coffee.

The purpose of warnings is to inform people of potential hazards and, more importantly, to change their behavior; to direct people to perform behaviors that keep them safe and to deter them from unsafe behaviors they might otherwise perform (see Figure 3.19). Warnings can be effective, but their ability to influence behavior depends on many factors—including both physical features of the warnings themselves and characteristics of the people who view them (Wogalter & Young, 1993).

To be effective, warnings should meet several criteria (Wogalter & Laughery, 1996). First, warnings must be conspicuous relative to their surroundings. In other words, they should be *attention-getting* to compete with other sights and sounds present in the environments in which we work and play. Second, warnings must be understood by the persons to whom they are directed. Often this includes children; persons who are not well educated; non-English-speaking readers and speakers; and persons with visual handicaps, such as some elderly people. Third, warnings should be designed to overcome preexisting beliefs and attitudes. Persons familiar with the use of a product are less likely to look for safety information than persons using the product for the first time. Why? Because their experience—repeated successful use of a product without injury—decreases their perceptions of hazard. Finally, people must be convinced that the potential benefits of complying with the warning outweigh the costs of doing so.

FIGURE 3.18

Consumer Product Warnings: Are They Effective?

McDonald's alerts customers to the potential hazards of hot coffee by printing the warning shown below on their cups.

Therefore, warnings should be designed to motivate people to engage in safe behaviors or to avoid unsafe ones.

Can warnings make a difference in getting us to act more safely? The results of systematic research suggest the answer is yes. In one study, Wogalter and Young (1991) examined the effects of warning modality (whether the warning was visual or auditory) on compliance behavior. Participants performed a chemistry demonstration task involving the measuring and mixing of what they thought were hazardous chemicals. Included in the instructions was the following message: *"WARNING: Wear gloves and mask while performing the task to avoid irritating fumes and possible irritation of skin."*

Participants received this warning in one of three ways: in printed form, orally (presented by the experimenter or by an audiotape), or both (printed instructions and oral presentation). Not surprisingly, compliance was highest when the warning was presented in both printed and oral form. Why? Our conscious experience depends on input from *all* of our senses, so presentation of critical information to multiple sensory modalities may enhance a warning's effectiveness. Additionally, auditory warnings may have added advantages, not yet considered. They can be lifesavers for blind people and they can be heard from any direction. So next time you encounter a warning—one that could possibly save your life—proceed with *CAUTION.*

Critical Thinking Questions

1. In light of the findings mentioned in this feature, do you believe that warnings can be effective in alerting us to potential hazards in our environment? Are warnings effective in getting us to act safely?
2. Suppose that you were called upon to design a warning that would be effective in changing the behavior of your peers. What steps would you follow in its development?

FIGURE 3.19

Protecting the Public: Improving Instructional Warnings

Research has shown that carefully designed warnings can be effective in attracting our attention and changing our behavior. How would you rate the potential effectiveness of the warning depicted here?

BIZARRO By DAN PIRARO

"WARNING: DO NOT USE THIS PRODUCT AS A STEP STOOL TO REACH SHARP OBJECTS ON A HIGH SHELF. DO NOT SET ON FIRE AND LEAVE ON CARPET. DO NOT GRIND INTO SAWDUST AND INGEST. DO NOT MELT WITH ACID AND INHALE FUMES. DO NOT STRIKE REPEATEDLY AGAINST YOUR HEAD. DO NOT DROP FROM BRIDGE ONTO PASSING MOTORISTS.
INJURIES RESULTING FROM IMPROPER USE OF THIS PRODUCT WILL NOT BE THE RESPONSIBILITY OF THE MANUFACTURER."

3 LEGGED FOOT STOOL
3 LEGGED FOOT STOOL

PIRARO

(**Source:** The "Bizarro" cartoon by Dan Piraro is reprinted courtesy Chronicle Features, San Francisco, California. All rights reserved.)

FIGURE 3.20

Perceptual Organization

Look carefully at each of these figures. What do you see? Our perceptual processes often allow us to perceive shapes and forms from incomplete and fragmented stimuli.

patterns (gestalts). Some of these are described below. You could say that the Gestalt psychologists changed our perceptions about the nature of perception.

Figure and Ground: What Stands Out? By looking carefully at Figure 3.21, you can experience a principle of perceptual organization known as the **figure–ground relationship.** What this means, simply, is that we tend to divide the world around us into two parts: *figure,* which has a definite shape and a location in space; and *ground,* which has no shape, seems to continue behind the figure, and has no definite location. The figure–ground relationship helps clarify the distinction between sensation and perception. While the pattern of sensory input generated in our receptors remains constant, our perceptions shift between the two figure–ground patterns in Figure 3.21; thus, we may see either the young or the old woman, but not both. Note that the principles of perceptual organization apply to the other senses, too. For instance, consider how the figure–ground relationship applies to audition: during a complicated lecture, you become absorbed in whispered gossip between two students sitting next to you; the professor's voice becomes background noise. Suddenly you hear your name and realize the professor has asked you a question; her voice has now become the sole focus of your attention, while the conversation becomes background noise.

Figure–Ground Relationship: Our tendency to divide the perceptual world into two distinct parts: discrete figures and the background against which they stand out.

Laws of Grouping: Simple principles describing how we tend to group discrete stimuli together in the perceptual world.

Grouping: Which Stimuli Go Together? The Gestaltists also called attention to a number of principles known as the **laws of grouping**—basic ways in which we group items together perceptually. Several of these laws are illustrated in Figure 3.22 on page 116. As you can see, the laws of grouping do offer a good description of our perceptual tendencies.

The principles outlined by Gestalt psychologists are not, however, hard-and-fast rules. They are merely descriptions of ways in which we perceive the

FIGURE 3.21

A Demonstration of Figure–Ground

What do you see when you look at this drawing? You probably see either an old woman or a young woman. Because this is an ambiguous figure, your perceptions may switch back and forth between these two possibilities.

world around us. Whether these principles are innate, as the Gestaltists believe, or learned, as some newer evidence suggests, is still open to debate. In any case, principles of perceptual organization are readily visible in the natural world, and they are effective in helping us organize our perceptual world.

Constancies and Illusions: When Perception Succeeds—and Fails

Perception, we have seen, is more than the sum of all the sensory input supplied by our eyes, ears, and other receptors. It is the active selection, organization, and interpretation of such input. It yields final products that differ from raw, unprocessed sensations in important ways. Up to now, this discussion has focused on the benefits of this process. But perception, like any other powerful process, can be a double-edged sword. On the one hand, perception helps us adapt to a complex and ever changing environment. On the other hand, perception sometimes leads us into error. To see how, let's consider *constancies* and *illusions.*

Perceptual Constancies: Stability in the Face of Change Try this simple demonstration. Hold your right hand in front of you at arm's length. Next, move it toward and away from your face several times. Does its size seem to change? Probably not. The purpose of this demonstration is to illustrate the principles of perceptual **constancies**—our tendency to perceive aspects of the world as unchanging despite changes in the sensory input we receive from them. The principle of **size constancy** relates to the fact that the perceived size of an object remains the same when the distance is varied, even though the size of the image the object casts on the retina changes greatly. Under normal circumstances, such constancy is impressive. Consider, for example, seeing a friend you are meeting for lunch walking toward you, though still several blocks away. Distant objects—including cars, trees, and people—cast tiny images on your retina. Yet you perceive them as being of normal size. Two factors seem to account for this tendency: size–distance invariance and relative size.

The principle of *size–distance invariance* suggests that when estimating the size of an object, we take into account both the size of the image it casts on our retina and the apparent distance of the object. From these data we almost

Constancies: Our tendency to perceive physical objects as unchanging despite shifts in the pattern of sensations these objects induce.

Size Constancy: The tendency to perceive a physical object as having a constant size even when the size of the image it casts on the retina changes.

Laws of Similarity

Tendency to perceive similar items as a group

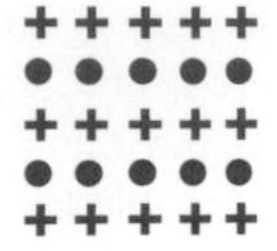

Laws of Proximity

Tendency to perceive items located together as a group

Laws of Common Region

Tendency to perceive objects as a group if they occupy the same place within a plane

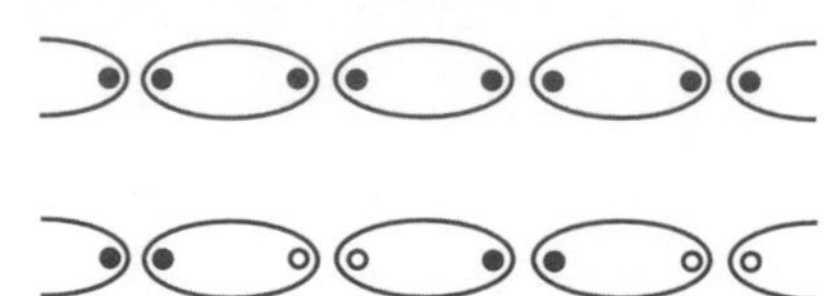

Law of Good Continuation

Tendency to perceive stimuli as part of a continuous pattern

Law of Closure

Tendency to perceive objects as whole entities, despite the fact that some parts may be missing or obstructed from view

Laws of Simplicity

Tendency to perceive complex patterns in terms of simpler shapes

FIGURE 3.22

Laws of Perceptual Grouping

We seem to possess strong tendencies to group stimuli together in certain ways. Several of these *laws of grouping* are illustrated here.

Relative Size: A visual cue based on comparison of the size of an unknown object to objects of known size.

Shape Constancy: The tendency to perceive a physical object as having a constant shape even when the image it casts on the retina changes.

Brightness Constancy: The tendency to perceive objects as having a constant brightness even when they are viewed under different conditions of illumination.

instantly calculate the object's size. Only when the cues that normally reveal an object's distance are missing do we run into difficulties in estimating the object's size (as we'll see in our discussion of illusions below). We also notice the **relative size** of an object compared to objects of known size. This mechanism is especially useful for estimating the size of unfamiliar things.

But size is not the only perceptual feature of the physical world that does not correspond directly with the information transmitted by our sensory receptors. The principle of **shape constancy** refers to the fact that the perceived shape of an object does not alter as the image the object casts on the retina changes (see Figure 3.23). For example, all of us know that coins are round; yet we rarely see them that way. Flip a coin into the air: although you continue to perceive the coin as being round, the image that actually falls onto your retina constantly shifts from a circle to various forms of an ellipse.

The principle of **brightness constancy** refers to the fact that we perceive objects as constant in brightness and color, even when they are viewed under different lighting conditions. Thus, we will perceive a sweater as dark green whether indoors or outdoors in bright sunlight. Brightness constancy apparently prevails because objects and their surroundings are usually lighted by the same illumination source, so changes in lighting conditions occur simultaneously for both the object and its immediate surroundings. As long as the changes in lighting remain constant for both object and surround, the neural message reaching the brain is unchanged. Brightness constancy breaks down, however, when changes in lighting are not equivalent for both the object and its surroundings (Sekuler & Blake, 1990).

FIGURE 3.23

Shape Constancy: A Simple Example

The principle of shape constancy allows us to recognize this object as a rectangular door, despite the fact that the image cast on the retina changes as the door opens or closes.

Although most research on perceptual constancies has focused on size, shape, and brightness, constancy pervades nearly every area of perception, including our other senses. For example, imagine listening to elevator music while riding on an elevator en route to a dental appointment on the top floor of an office building. When one of your favorite oldies from the mid-1970s begins, you can't believe what they've done to "your song." Nonetheless, you are still able to recognize it, despite differences in its loudness, tone, and pitch.

Whatever their basis, perceptual constancies are highly useful. Without them, we would spend a great deal of time and effort reidentifying sensory information in our environments each time we experienced the information from a new perspective. Thus, the gap between our sensations and the perceptions provided by the constancies is clearly beneficial.

Illusions: When Perception Fails We've seen that perception organizes sensory information into a coherent picture of the world around us. Perception can also, however, provide false interpretations of sensory information. Such cases are known as **illusions,** a term used by psychologists to refer to incorrect perceptions. Actually, there are two types of illusions: those due to physical processes and those due to cognitive processes (Matlin & Foley, 1992). Illusions due to distortion of physical conditions include *mirages,* in which you perceive things that aren't really there—like the water you often seem to see on the dry road ahead of you. Our focus, however, will be on the latter types of illusions—those involving cognitive processes.

Illusions: Instances in which perception yields false interpretations of physical reality.

Countless illusions related to cognitive processes exist, but most fall into two categories: illusions of *size* and illusions of *shape* or *area* (Coren et al., 1976). Natural examples of two well-known size illusions are presented in Figure 3.24; as you can see, their effects are powerful. But why do illusions occur? What causes our interpretation of such stimuli to be directly at odds with physical reality? Some evidence suggests that illusions generally have multiple

FIGURE 3.24

Powerful Illusions of Size

(Left) The horizontal–vertical illusion stems from our tendency to perceive objects higher in our visual field as more distant. This illusion helps explain why the St. Louis Gateway falsely appears taller than it is wide (its height and width are actually equal). (Right) In the Ponzo illusion, the line in the distance appears larger, although both lines are actually the same size.

FIGURE 3.25

The Müller–Lyer Illusion

(A) In the Müller–Lyer illusion, lines of equal length appear unequal; the line with the wings pointing outward looks longer than the line with the wings pointing inward. (B) Now carefully examine the vertical line in each of the photographs. Which line is longer? Most people perceive the vertical line in the photo on the right as longer, although careful measurement shows they are exactly the same length.

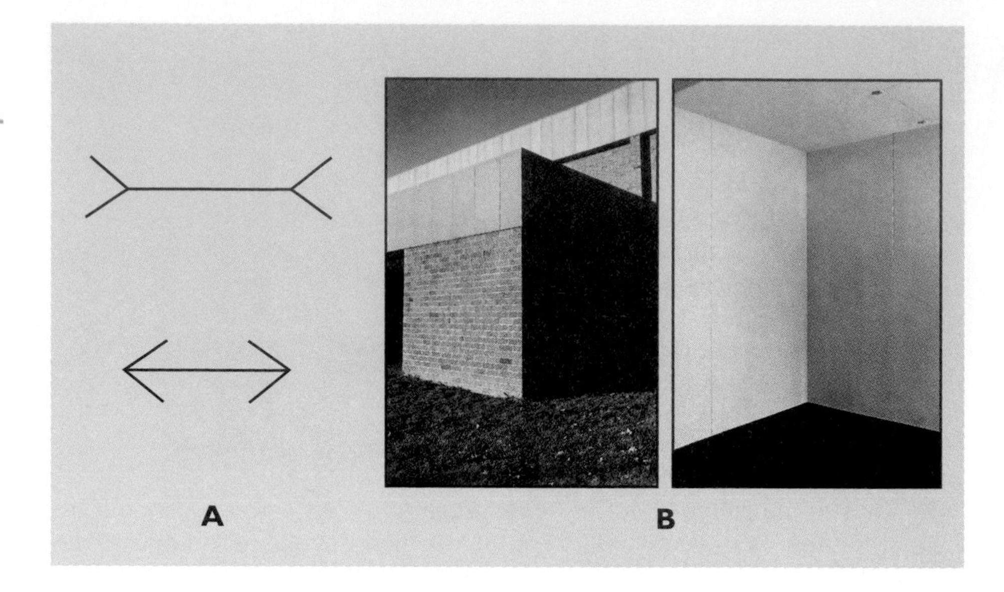

causes (Schiffman, 1990). However, one explanation is provided by the *theory of misapplied constancy.* This theory suggests that when looking at illusions, we interpret certain cues as suggesting that some parts are farther away than others. Our powerful tendency toward size constancy then comes into play, with the result that we perceptually distort the length of various lines (see Figure 3.25). Learning also plays an important role in illusions, as shown in the architectural examples of the *Müller–Lyer illusion* in Figure 3.25. Past experience tells us that the corner shown in the photo on the right should be farther away than the corner in the photo on the left. Therefore, although the size of the retinal image cast by the vertical lines in both photos is identical, we interpret the vertical line as longer in the photo on the right. Moreover, learning seems to affect the extent to which our perception is influenced by illusions: many visual illusions decline in magnitude following extended exposure—although they do not decline altogether (Greist-Bousquet, Watson, & Schiffman, 1990).

FIGURE 3.26

Illusions of Area or Shape

Illusions of area or shape can be quite powerful. (A) In this drawing, known as the Poggendorf illusion, which of the three lines on the right continues the line on the left? Check your answer with a ruler. (B) In this drawing, are the horizontal lines straight or bent in the middle? Again, check for yourself. (C) Finally, in this drawing, are the letters tilted or vertical? When you check, you'll understand that sometimes you can't believe what you think you see.

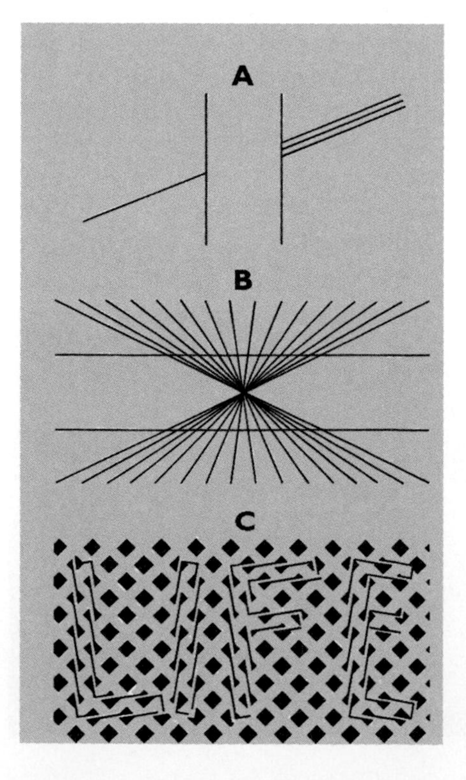

Another type of illusion is that of *area* or *shape.* If you've ever wondered why the moon looks bigger at the horizon (about 30 percent bigger) than at its highest point in the sky, then you are familiar with the most famous area illusion—the *moon illusion.* Why does the moon illusion occur? In part, because when the moon is near the horizon, we can see that it is farther away than trees, houses, and other objects. When it is overhead at its zenith, such cues are lacking. Thus, the moon appears larger near the horizon because there are cues available that cause us to perceive that it is very far away. Once again, our tendency toward size constancy leads us astray.

Like illusions of size or area, shape illusions (see Figure 3.26) can influence perception—sometimes producing some unsettling consequences. Consider a real-world example involving the *Poggendorf illusion* (see drawing A in Figure 3.26). In this illusion, a line disappears at an angle behind a solid figure, reappearing at the other side—at what seems to be the incorrect position. As reported by Coren and Girgus (1978), in 1965 two airplanes were about to arrive in New York City, and because of the Poggendorf illusion, they perceived that they were on a collision course. Both pilots changed their path to correct for what they perceived as an error, and thus the planes collided. The result was four deaths and forty-nine injuries—all because of an illusion.

One final point: Illusions are not limited to visual processes. Indeed, there are numerous examples of illusions for our other sensory modalities, including touch and audition (Sekuler & Blake, 1990; Shepard, 1964). One well-known illusion that you can demonstrate for yourself is that of touch temperature. First, place one hand in a container of hot water and the other hand in cold water. Then place *both* hands in a container of lukewarm water. What do you feel? Most people experience a dramatic difference in perceived temperature between the two hands; the hand initially placed in hot water feels the lukewarm water as cool, whereas the hand initially placed in cold water feels it as hot. How do we explain this illusion? When we touch an object, the temperature of the area of our skin in contact with it shifts toward that of the object's surface. So when we perceive an object to be warm or cool, our experience stems partly from the temperature difference between the object and our skin, not solely from the actual temperature of the object.

Key Questions

- Why is selective attention important?
- Why is it important to consider sensation *and* perception in the development of warnings?
- What role do Gestalt principles play in perceptual processes?
- What are perceptual constancies?
- What are illusions?

Some Key Perceptual Processes: Pattern and Distance

Perception is a practical process, for it provides organisms with information essential to survival in their normal habitat. The specific nature of this information varies greatly with different species. For example, frogs must be able to detect small moving objects in order to feed on insects, whereas porpoises require sensory input that enables them to navigate turbulent and murky ocean waters. Nonetheless, it is probably safe to say that virtually all living creatures need information concerning (1) what's out there and (2) how far away it is. Humans are no exception to this general rule, and we possess impressive perceptual skills in both areas.

Pattern Recognition: What's Out There? Your ability to read the words on this page depends on the ability to recognize small black marks as letters and collections of such marks as words (Ittelson, 1996). How do we accomplish this task? An early explanation for this phenomenon suggested that we have many **templates,** or specific patterns stored in our memories for various visual stimuli that we encounter. Thus, if a visual stimulus—say a letter—matches one of the templates, we recognize it; if it does not, we search for another that does match. But this *template-matching theory* is impractical, because it would require that we store an almost infinite number of these templates in our memories. Additionally, this theory does not explain our ability to read at rates exceeding hundreds of words per minute, to detect moving objects, or to recognize visual stimuli almost instantly, even when they're viewed from different perspectives (Pinker, 1984).

Templates: Specific patterns stored in our memories for various visual stimuli that we encounter.

A related but more viable explanation, referred to as *prototype-matching theory,* suggests that we automatically compare each letter (and perhaps word) to abstract representations of these stimuli in our memories known as **prototypes.** According to this view, we have a prototype in memory for each letter of the alphabet, based on all examples of the letter previously encountered. Thus, recognition is dependent on finding a correct match between the stimulus letter or word and a previously seen prototype. Please note that a prototype is not an exact match or a template for some visual stimulus, but a general pattern that lets us recognize a letter even when it is distorted. While some evidence supports this view (e.g., Franks & Bransford, 1971), the physiological details of this approach are not well developed (Matlin & Foley, 1992).

Two other approaches are the bottom-up and top-down theories of pattern recognition. As their names imply, these adopt somewhat opposite perspectives on the basic question of how we recognize patterns of visual stimuli. The *bottom-up approach* suggests that our ability to recognize specific patterns, such as letters of the alphabet, is based on simpler capacities to recognize and combine correctly lower-level features of objects, such as lines, edges, corners, and angles. Bottom-up theories suggest that pattern recognition is constructed from simpler perceptual abilities through a discrete series of steps (Hummell, 1994; Marr, 1982). One currently popular view on this topic suggests that a type of basic building block essential to pattern recognition consists of a group of three-dimensional cylinders called *geons* (Biederman, 1987). Apparently, a small set of geons, when assembled according to specific rules, can be combined to form any object. Thus, we accomplish pattern recognition by matching features of an object to geon representations of this information in memory (Biederman, 1987; Hummell, 1994). Although additional research is necessary to confirm the accuracy of this view of pattern recognition, the geon concept does help explain our efficiency at recognizing not only objects but also complex scenes (Schyns & Oliva, 1994).

In contrast, the *top-down approach* emphasizes the fact that our expectancies play a critical role in shaping our perceptions. We often proceed in accordance with what our past experience tells us to expect, and therefore we don't always analyze every feature of most stimuli we encounter. Although top-down processing can be extremely efficient (think about the speed with which you can read this page), it can also lead us astray. Nearly everyone has had the experience of rushing over to another person who appears to be an old friend, only to realize he or she is actually a stranger. In such cases, our tendency to process information quickly from the top down can indeed produce errors.

Which of these theories is correct? Research indicates that both processes play a role in pattern recognition (Matlin & Foley, 1992). When we have strong expectations or we are in a familiar context, we often opt for speed and adopt a top-down approach. However, when we are dealing with unfamiliar situations or stimuli, bottom-up processing often dominates. In many situations, both processes may occur at once. In summary, our efforts to make sense out of the world around us tend to take whatever form is most efficient in a given context.

Distance Perception: How Far Away Is It? Our impressive ability to judge depth and distance exists because we make use of many different cues in forming such judgments. These cues can be divided into two categories, *monocular* and *binocular,* depending on whether they can be seen with only one eye or require the use of both eyes.

Monocular cues to depth or distance include the following:

1. *Size cues:* The larger the image of an object on the retina, the larger the object is judged to be; in addition, if an object is larger than other objects, it is often perceived as closer.
2. *Linear perspective:* Parallel lines appear to converge in the distance; the greater this effect, the farther away an object appears to be.

Prototypes: Representations in memory of various objects or stimuli in the physical world.

Monocular Cues: Cues to depth or distance provided by one eye.

3. *Texture gradient:* The texture of a surface appears smoother as distance increases.
4. *Atmospheric perspective:* The farther away objects are, the less distinctly they are seen—smog, dust, haze get in the way.
5. *Overlap* (or interposition): If one object overlaps another, it is seen as being closer than the one it covers.
6. *Height cues* (aerial perspective): Below the horizon, objects lower down in our field of vision are perceived as closer; above the horizon, objects higher up are seen as closer.
7. Motion parallax: When we travel in a vehicle, objects far away appear to move in the same direction as the observer, whereas close objects move in the opposite direction. Objects at different distances appear to move at different velocities.

Binocular Cues: Cues to depth or distance provided by the use of both eyes.

We also rely heavily on **binocular cues**—depth information based on the coordinated efforts of both eyes. Binocular cues for depth perception stem from two primary sources:

1. *Convergence:* In order to see close objects, our eyes turn toward one another; the greater this movement, the closer such objects appear to be.
2. *Retinal disparity* (binocular parallax): Our two eyes observe objects from slightly different positions in space; the difference between these two images is interpreted by our brain to provide another cue to depth. Figure 3.27 contains a *stereogram*—a pattern of dots in which we can perceive 3-D images, thanks in part to retinal disparity.

These lists of monocular and binocular cues are by no means exhaustive. By using the wealth of information provided by these and other cues (Schiffman, 1990), we can usually perceive depth and distance with great accuracy.

Key Questions

- What are the bottom-up and top-down theories of pattern recognition?
- What are geons? What is their role in object recognition?
- How are we able to judge depth and distance?

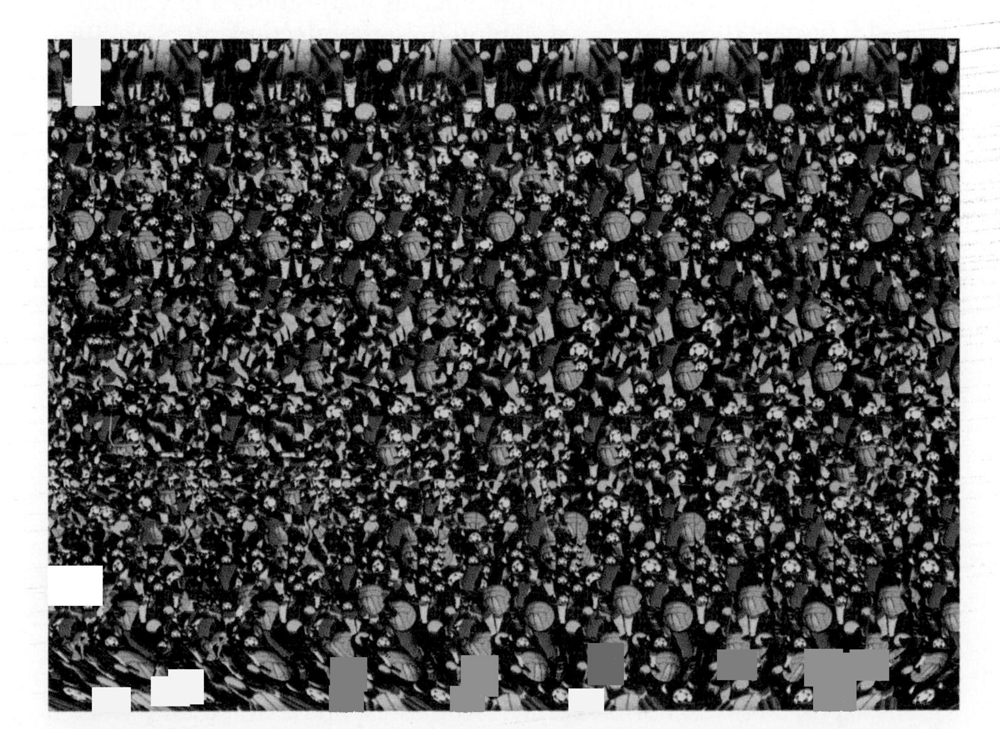

FIGURE 3.27

Retinal Disparity and Stereograms

Retinal disparity is the basis for our perception of 3-D images in stereograms. Hold the book right up to your nose and very, very slowly pull the book away from your face. Look through the image and try not to blink. A 3-D picture will magically appear. What do you see? Hint: Do you like soccer?

The Plasticity of Perception: To What Extent Is It Innate or Learned?

Imagine a man blind from birth whose sight is suddenly restored through a miraculous operation. Will his visual world be the same as yours or mine? Will it be orderly and consistent with his expectations? Or will he experience a chaotic swirl of colors, brightnesses, and meaningless shapes? This is an intriguing question that has often served as the basis for exploring the *nature–nurture controversy,* an issue you may recall from Chapters 1 and 2. In other words, to what extent are aspects of perception learned or hereditary?

Perception: Evidence That It's Innate

Evidence that perception is innate stems from two lines of research. The first involves people like the one described above—people born blind (or blinded soon after birth) whose sight is later restored through medical procedures. If perception is innate, then such persons should be able to see clearly immediately after recovery from surgery. Although cases like this are few in number and the results often vary, many of these individuals can make at least partial sense out of the visual world soon after their sight is restored. For example, they can detect and follow moving objects, suggesting that some aspects of visual perception may indeed be innate (Von Senden, 1960). However, individuals who regain their vision later in life never seem to attain fully normal visual perception. In addition, certain complications require us to be cautious in making even limited interpretation of these findings. For example, it is difficult to know precisely when recovery from a medical procedure is sufficient to allow for "normal" vision. This leaves open the question of when the patient should be tested for perceptual abilities.

Additional evidence suggesting that perception is innate is provided by research with very young participants, such as babies only a few hours or days old. Systematic research has explored numerous perceptual abilities, particularly auditory and visual abilities, that are present at birth or shortly afterward (Schiffman, 1990). In one such study, infants slightly more than three days old were exposed to squares of colored light (blue, green, yellow, red) and to gray light of equal brightness. The results showed that infants spent more time looking at every one of the colored stimuli than at the gray—an indication that ability to perceive color is present soon after birth (Adams, 1987). Studies like this one suggest that some aspects of perception are innate or at least that they appear early in life.

Perception: Evidence That It's Learned

On the other hand, there is considerable evidence for the view that key aspects of perception are learned. In a famous series of studies, Blakemore and Cooper (1970) raised kittens in darkness except for brief periods, during which the kittens were exposed to either horizontal or vertical stripes. When later released from their restricted environment, the kittens showed what seemed to be permanent effects of their earlier experience. Those exposed only to vertical lines would respond to a long black rod when it was held in an upright position but ignored it when it was held horizontally. In contrast, kittens exposed only to horizontal lines would respond to a rod only when it was held in a horizontal position, ignoring it when presented vertically. Despite the fact that the kittens' visual systems were undamaged—at least in any measurable physical sense—their restricted visual experience appeared to produce permanent perceptual deficits.

Please note, however, that recent research shows that organisms may compensate for such deficits through enhanced abilities in their other senses. For example, recent evidence suggests that binocularly deprived cats develop improved auditory localization abilities compared to normal control subjects. Apparently the brain, at least in cats, possesses the capacity to reorganize itself to compensate for the loss (Rauschecker, 1995). Whether humans exhibit similar capabilities is still a topic of debate. However, it is common to hear of instances in which blind persons develop heightened capabilities in their other senses.

Additional evidence for the role of learning in perception comes from studies in which human volunteers wear special goggles that invert their view of the world and reverse right and left. Such persons initially experience difficulty in carrying out normal activities with their goggles on, but soon adapt and do everything from reading a book to flying a plane (Kohler, 1962). These findings, and others, suggest that we do indeed learn to interpret the information supplied by our sensory receptors.

Must We Resolve the Nature–Nurture Controversy?

The findings we've reviewed thus far offer no simple resolution to the nature–nurture issue, and other studies involving both animals and humans are equally inconclusive. Some studies show that certain aspects of visual perception seem to be present without previous sensory experience, whereas other aspects develop only through experience with the external world (Wiesel, 1982).

Confronted with this mixed evidence, most psychologists accept that perception is influenced both by innate factors and by experience. For example, consider the case of a fifty-year-old man who regained his sight after forty-five years of blindness (Sacks, 1993). Careful testing revealed that the man could detect visual features such as letters, objects, and colors and could perceive motion, suggesting the influence of nature. However, the man could not "see" in the true sense. Learning even simple visual relationships required great effort, since most of his knowledge of the world had come to him through the sense of touch.

To summarize, perception is plastic in the sense that it can be, and often is, modified by our encounters with physical reality. Perception may also, however, be strongly affected by innate tendencies and principles. So the answer to the question "Must we resolve the nature–nurture controversy?" is a resounding *no,* since it is clear that learning *and* biology both play critical roles in perception. We'll now turn to a controversial topic in psychology—extrasensory perception.

Extrasensory Perception: *Perception without Sensation?*

Have you ever wondered if we have a "sixth sense"? In other words, can we gain information about the external world without use of our five basic senses? Many persons believe we can and accept the existence of

extrasensory perception—literally, perception without a basis in sensation. The first and most basic question we can ask about ESP is "Does it really exist?" Bem and Honorton (1994) have recast this question in terms of a hypothetical process known as **psi.** These researchers define psi as unusual processes of information or energy transfer that are currently unexplained in terms of known physical or biological mechanisms (Bem & Honorton, 1994). What precisely is psi? And is there any evidence for its existence? In this section we will discuss some of the evidence regarding this intriguing topic.

Psi: What Is It?

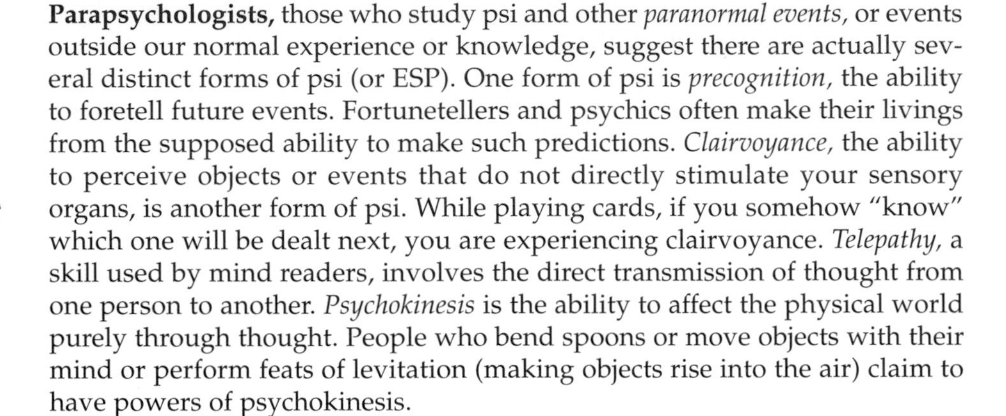

Parapsychologists, those who study psi and other *paranormal events,* or events outside our normal experience or knowledge, suggest there are actually several distinct forms of psi (or ESP). One form of psi is *precognition,* the ability to foretell future events. Fortunetellers and psychics often make their livings from the supposed ability to make such predictions. *Clairvoyance,* the ability to perceive objects or events that do not directly stimulate your sensory organs, is another form of psi. While playing cards, if you somehow "know" which one will be dealt next, you are experiencing clairvoyance. *Telepathy,* a skill used by mind readers, involves the direct transmission of thought from one person to another. *Psychokinesis* is the ability to affect the physical world purely through thought. People who bend spoons or move objects with their mind or perform feats of levitation (making objects rise into the air) claim to have powers of psychokinesis.

Psi: Does It Really Exist?

The idea of a mysterious sixth sense is intriguing, and many people are passionately convinced of its existence (Bowles & Hynds, 1978). But does psi really exist? Most psychologists are skeptical about the existence of psi for several reasons. The first, and perhaps the most important, reason for doubting its existence is the repeated failure to replicate instances of psi; that is, certain procedures yield evidence for psi at one time but not at others. Indeed, one survey failed to uncover a single instance of paranormal phenomena that could be reliably produced after ruling out alternative explanations such as fraud, methodological flaws, and normal sensory functioning (Hoppe, 1988). Moreover, it appears that the more controlled studies of psi are, the less evidence for psi they provide (Blackmore, 1986).

Second, present-day scientific understanding states that all aspects of our behavior must ultimately stem from biochemical events, yet it is not clear what physical mechanism could account for psi. In fact, the existence of such a mechanism would require restructuring our view of the physical world.

Third, much of the support for psi has been obtained by persons already deeply convinced of its existence. As we noted in Chapter 1, scientists are not immune to being influenced in their observations by their own beliefs. Thus, while studies suggesting that psi exists may represent a small sample of all research conducted on this topic, perhaps only the few experiments yielding positive results find their way into print; perhaps the many "failures" are simply not reported.

Parapsychologists have attempted to increase the rigor of their research through the use of the *ganzfield procedure*—a technique used to test for telepathic communication between a *sender* and a *receiver*. Receivers in the ganzfield procedure are placed in a comfortable chair in a soundproof room. Translucent Ping-Pong ball halves are taped over the receivers' eyes, and

Extrasensory Perception: Perception without a basis in sensory input.

Psi: Unusual processes of information or energy transfer that are currently unexplained in terms of known physical or biological mechanisms. Included under the heading of psi are such supposed abilities as telepathy (reading others' thoughts) and clairvoyance (perceiving unseen objects or unknown events).

Parapsychologists: Individuals who study psi and other paranormal events.

headphones are placed over their ears. A red floodlight directed toward the eyes produces a homogenous visual field, and white noise is played through the headphones to mask any outside noises.

The sender is usually secluded in a separate room and asked to concentrate on a "target" visual stimulus, such as a photograph or brief videotape. Simultaneously, the receiver provides an ongoing verbal report of mental images that he or she experiences. After about thirty minutes, the receiver is presented with several stimuli and, without knowing which was the target stimulus on which the sender concentrated, is asked to rate the extent to which each stimulus matches the imagery he or she experienced during the ganzfield period. If receivers give high ratings to target stimuli, it is assumed to be evidence for psi.

Psi research employing the ganzfield procedure is currently under way (e.g., Bem & Honorton, 1994). However, most psychologists remain highly skeptical that such research will yield support for the existence of psi (Hymen, 1994).

Key Questions

- How are the concepts *nature* and *nurture* related to perception?
- How do most psychologists view the possibility of extrasensory perception or psi?

Making Psychology Part of Your Life

Listen While You Work: The Potential Benefits—and DANGERS—of Stereo Headsets

Do you recall the old Disney tune "Whistle While You Work"? The gist of the song is that whistling, humming, or just listening to music can often make a job go by faster and seem easier. Intriguing new evidence on this topic suggests that the Seven Dwarfs may have been right all along—music can yield some important benefits, at least where work is concerned. Although a large number of studies have confirmed that the presence of background music in the workplace can have beneficial effects (Sundstrom, 1986), not all people exposed to it are pleased. Indeed, some people find that music distracts them from their work, while others find it annoying (Uhrbock, 1961). The relatively recent introduction of the personal stereo headset, however, may have provided the means to reintroduce music to the workplace.

Personal Stereo Headsets: Let's Turn Down the Sound

In one recent study, Oldham and his colleagues arranged for one group of employees to use stereo headsets during the workday while their fellow employees did not (Oldham et al., 1995). The researchers' purpose was to determine if the use of individual headsets to provide music at work would be beneficial to the employees who wished to listen, while avoiding some of the problems associated with background office music. To test this possibility, the researchers assessed a variety of measures, including the employees' on-the-job performance. The results indicated that personal stereo headsets afforded important practical benefits to the employees who used them; listening to music improved aspects of their workers' mood, their outlook toward the organization, and their productivity, compared to those of employees who did not listen (see Figure 3.28 on page 126).

Please note, however, that observed improvements in performance were only for relatively simple jobs; as job complexity increased, performance actually decreased. These results suggest that listening to music at work can be beneficial—at least to people who enjoy it. They also show, however, that it may be prudent to discourage this practice among persons who perform complex jobs requiring focused mental effort.

While it is clear that the use of stereo headsets can have positive effects on those who use them, I want to alert you to some potential problems associated with the use of these devices. One problem is that stereo headsets can produce sound intense enough to cause

FIGURE 3.28

Music to the Ears: Reintroducing Personal Stereo Headsets into the Workplace

Following the introduction of stereo headsets at work, work performance increased significantly among employees who chose to use them. These results suggest that listening to music at work may have some practical benefits, such as more productivity.

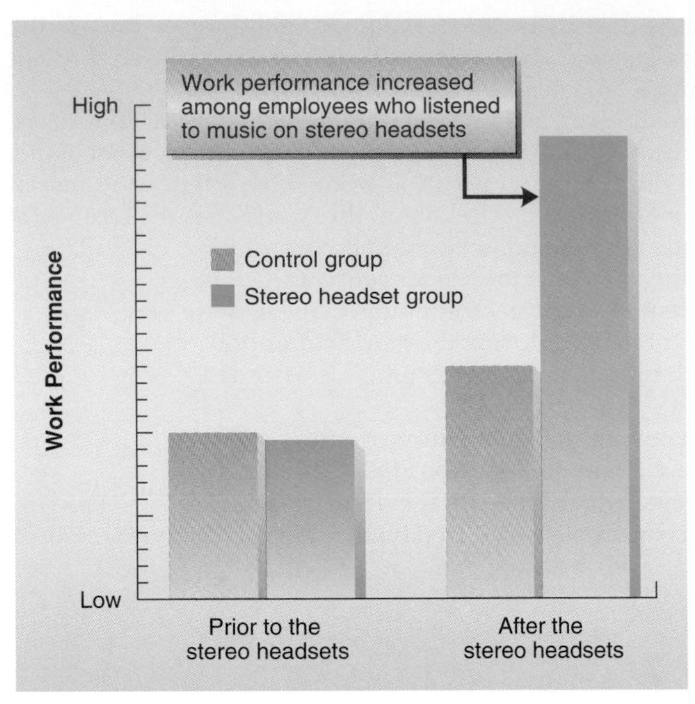

(**Source:** Based on data from Oldham et al., 1995).

varying degrees of hearing loss (Rice, Breslin, & Roper, 1987). For example, exposure to 90-decibel sound levels—the level of noise that might be present in a crowded restaurant—can produce significant short-term hearing loss after only one and one-half hours of sound exposure. If you are not already convinced of the potential dangers of stereo headsets, consider the results of a study in which researchers examined fifty personal stereo headsets to determine if they had the potential to damage hearing. The decibel levels were measured at three volume settings: one-third, two-thirds, and full volume (Navarro, 1990). The results showed that headsets produce an average of 87 decibels at one-third of their full volume, 100 decibels at two-thirds of their full volume, and 108 decibels at full volume. These results should make it clear that personal stereo headsets have the potential to produce serious hearing loss—even at seemingly low volume settings, particularly among persons who listen to them often and for extended periods of time. Indeed, some evidence suggests that habitual use of stereo headsets at high volumes does result in *tinnitus,* or ringing of the ears, and increases the risk of permanent hearing loss (Lee et al., 1985 Rice, Breslin, & Roper, 1987;).

So next time you get the urge to pump up the volume of your portable headset while walking, jogging, or working—do yourself a favor by turning down the sound. The hearing you save may be your own.

Summary and Review of Key Questions

Sensation: The Raw Materials of Understanding

- **What is the primary function of our sensory receptors?** Sensory receptors transduce raw physical energy into neural impulses, which are then interpreted by our central nervous system.
- **What does the term *absolute threshold* refer to, and why is signal detection theory important?** The absolute threshold is the smallest magnitude of a stimulus that can be detected 50 percent of the time. Signal detection theory helps to separate sensitivity from motivational factors.
- **What is a difference threshold?** The term *difference threshold* refers to the amount of change in a stimulus required for a person to detect the change.
- **Can subliminal messages affect our behavior?** Most careful research fails to show any meaningful effects of subliminal messages on aspects of our cognitive processes or behavior.
- **What is the role of sensory adaptation in sensation?** Sensory adaptation serves a useful function by allowing us to focus on important changes in our environment.

KEY TERMS

sensation, p. 84 • perception, p. 84 • sensory receptors, p. 84 • transduction, p. 84 • absolute threshold, p. 85 • signal detection theory, p. 86 • difference threshold, p. 87 • just noticeable difference (jnd), p. 87 • subliminal perception, p. 87 • sensory adaptation, p. 88

Vision

- **What are the basic structures of the eye, and what is the physical stimulus for vision?** Light rays first pass through the cornea and then enter the eye through the pupil. Adjustments to lighting conditions are executed by the iris. The lens is a clear structure whose shape adjusts to permit us to focus on objects at varying distances. Light rays leaving the lens are projected onto the retina at the back of the eyeball. The physical stimulus for vision consists of electromagnetic wavelengths that stimulate the rods and cones in the retina.
- **What are the basic functions of the visual system?** The basic functions of the visual system include acuity, dark adaptation, and eye movements. Acuity is the ability to see fine details. Dark adaptation is the increase in sensitivity that occurs when we move from bright light to a dim environment. Various types of eye movements are crucial to our ability to track moving objects and to perceive distance and depth.
- **How do psychologists explain color perception?** Our rich sense of color stems from mechanisms at several levels of our nervous system. Two leading theories that explain how we perceive color are trichromatic theory and opponent-process theory.
- **Why is visual perception a hierarchical process?** Visual perception is a hierarchical process because increasingly complex visual information is analyzed and compiled at successive stages—eventually yielding a coherent and flowing visual world.
- **What are the basic building blocks of visual perception?** The basic building blocks of visual perception begin with feature detectors—neurons in the visual cortex that respond when particular types of stimuli, with characteristic features, are detected.

KEY TERMS

cornea, p. 89 • pupil, p. 89 • iris, p. 89 • lens, p. 89 • retina, p. 89 • cones, p. 89 • rods, p. 89 • fovea, p. 89 • optic nerve, p. 89 • blind spot, p. 89 • wavelength, p. 91 • hue, p. 91 • brightness, p. 92 • saturation, p. 92 • acuity, p. 92 • nearsightedness, p. 92 • farsightedness, p. 92 • dark adaptation, p. 92 • saccadic movements, p. 93 • trichromatic theory, p. 93 • negative afterimage, p. 94 • opponent-process theory, p. 94 • feature detectors, p. 95 • simple cells, p. 95 • complex cells, p. 95 • hypercomplex cells, p. 95 • blindsight, p. 96 • prosopagnosia, p. 96

Hearing

- **What is the physical stimulus for hearing?** The physical stimulus for hearing is sound waves, which stimulate tiny hair cells in the cochlea.
- **How do psychologists explain pitch perception?** Place theory and frequency theory help explain how we perceive pitch.
- **How do we localize sound?** The "sound shadow" created by our head causes sound to reach one ear slightly faster than the other. This small time difference helps us localize the source of sound.

KEY TERMS

pinna, p. 97 • cochlea, p. 97 • pitch, p. 98 • timbre, p. 98 • place theory, p. 99 • frequency theory, p. 99 • localization, p. 99

Touch and Other Skin Senses

- **What is the physical stimulus for touch?** The physical stimulus for touch is a stretching of or pressure against receptors in the skin.
- **Where does the sensation of pain originate?** Sensations of pain originate in free nerve endings throughout the body.
- **What is the basis for cultural differences in pain perception?** Cultural differences in pain perception appear to be the result of learning, not physical differences.
- **What role do cognitive processes play in the perception of pain?** Negative thinking while in pain, referred to as *catastrophizing*, can increase the perceived intensity of pain.

KEY TERM

gate-control theory, p. 101

Smell and Taste: The Chemical Senses

- **What is the physical stimulus for smell?** The physical stimulus for sensations of smell consists of molecules that stimulate receptors in the nose.
- **Where are the sensory receptors for taste located?** The sensory receptors for taste are located in papillae on the tongue.
- **What are the practical benefits of using ambient pleasant fragrance to solve real-world problems?** The use of pleasant fragrances can increase alertness among persons engaged in potentially dangerous activities, such as driving.

Kinesthesia and Vestibular Sense

- **What information does our kinesthetic sense provide to the brain?** Kinesthesia informs the brain about the location of body parts with respect to each other.
- **What information does the vestibular sense provide to the brain?** The vestibular sense provides information about body position, movement, and acceleration.

KEY TERMS

kinesthesia, p. 108 • vestibular sense, p. 108

Perception: Putting It All Together

- **Why is selective attention important?** Selective attention reduces interference from irrelevant sensory sources.
- **Why is it important to consider sensation *and* perception in the development of warnings?** The effectiveness of warnings depends on both sensory and perceptual processes.
- **What role do Gestalt principles play in perceptual processes?** The Gestalt principles of perceptual organization help us to structure the input from our sensory receptors.

- **What are perceptual constancies?** Perceptual constancies are principles describing our ability to perceive aspects of the world as unchanging despite variations in the information reaching our sensory receptors, such as information about size, shape, or brightness.
- **What are illusions?** *Illusion* is a term used by psychologists to refer to errors in interpreting sensory information.
- **What are the bottom-up and top-down theories of pattern recognition?** The bottom-up theory suggests that pattern recognition stems from our ability to recognize and combine basic visual features. In contrast, top-down theory emphasizes the role that expectations play in shaping our perceptions.
- **What are geons? What is their role in object recognition?** Geons are basic cylindrical shapes that, when combined according to rules, can be used to form any object. Some evidence suggests that geons are the basis of our representation of objects in memory.
- **How are we able to judge depth and distance?** Judgments of depth and distance result from both monocular and binocular cues.

KEY TERMS

gestalt psychologists, p. 112 • figure–ground relationship, p. 114 • laws of grouping, p. 114 • constancies, p. 115 • size constancy, p. 115 • relative size, p. 116 • shape constancy, p. 116 • brightness constancy, p. 116 • illusions, p. 117 • templates, p. 119 • prototypes, p. 120 • monocular cues, p. 120 • binocular cues, p. 121

The Plasticity of Perception: To What Extent Is It Innate or Learned?

- **How are the concepts *nature* and *nurture* related to perception?** Both nature and nurture are important determinants of the ways we perceive the world around us. Nature refers to genetic influences on perception, whereas nurture refers to the relative effects of the environment and learning.

Extrasensory Perception: Perception without Sensation?

- **How do most psychologists view the possibility of extrasensory perception or psi?** Most psychologists remain highly skeptical about its existence and await the results of further careful research.

KEY TERMS

extrasensory perception, p. 124 • psi, p. 124 • parapsychologists, p. 124

Critical Thinking Questions

Appraisal

Many psychologists would agree that conscious experience is nothing more than the result of the brain's efforts to integrate information received from the senses. Do you agree? Why? If not, offer an alternative view.

Controversy

Recent studies employing the ganzfield procedure have eliminated many of the methodological flaws present in earlier research and have demonstrated some weak evidence for psi. Still, most psychologists remain highly skeptical of the possibility of a mysterious "sixth sense." Does psi exist? Or is it more likely that subsequent research will uncover additional flaws in these studies?

Making Psychology Part of Your Life

Knowing something about the way in which we receive and process sensory information is useful for a variety of practical reasons. For example, the finding that ambient pleasant fragrance can increase alertness in drowsy drivers could also be applied to other potentially dangerous situations in which alertness is critical. Can you think of other ways in which you can benefit from such knowledge?

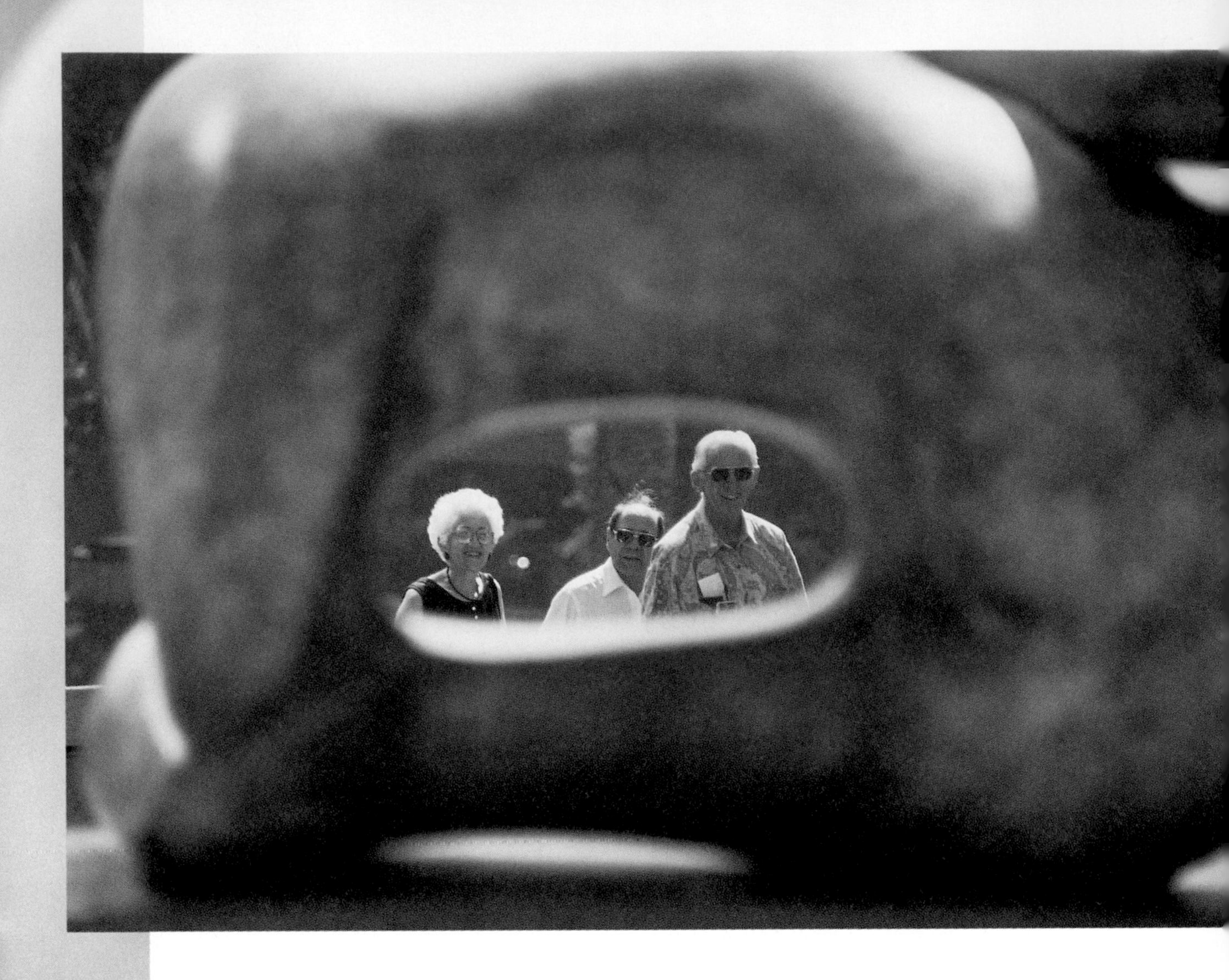

CHAPTER OUTLINE

States of Consciousness

Do you feel more alert and energetic in the morning or in the evening? Have you ever daydreamed while another person was talking to you so that when they were finished, you had no idea what they had said? Have you ever stood in front of a mirror brushing your teeth while your thoughts were far away? If so, you already know that every day, we all experience different **states of consciousness**—varying levels of awareness of our internal states and the world around us. And when we go to sleep at night (perhaps to dream) or take some drug that affects the way we feel, these changes in consciousness are even more dramatic in scope. Being familiar with these shifts, however, doesn't necessarily help us understand them. Can we really do two or more things at the same time? And if so, how? *Why* are we more alert at some times during the day than at others, and what effects do such changes have on our behavior? What happens when we fall asleep? What, precisely, *are* dreams, and do they have any meaning? How do various drugs affect our emotions, perceptions, and cognition?

Given the obvious impact of states of consciousness on many aspects of our behavior, they are clearly an important topic for the field of psychology. As I noted in Chapter 1, however, consciousness was largely written out of the field for several decades, primarily because early behaviorists believed that psychology should study only overt, observable behavior. Since consciousness cannot be directly seen or measured, they concluded that it was not a suitable topic for scientific study. As we'll see throughout this chapter, however, those behaviorists were wrong: While states of consciousness can't be observed in the same direct manner as, for instance, running through a maze, they *can* be studied scientifically in other ways. As the methods for accomplishing this task emerged, more and more psychologists turned their attention to studying various aspects of consciousness, with the result that today we know a great deal about this fascinating topic.

We all experience different states of consciousness—varying levels of awareness of our internal states and the world around us.

In this chapter we'll proceed as follows. First, we'll examine the biological roots for at least some of our shifting patterns of consciousness: *biological rhythms*. These are natural cyclical changes in many basic bodily processes and mental states that occur over the course of a day or over longer periods of time. Next, we'll consider several aspects of *waking consciousness*. Included here will be discussions of the degree of conscious control we exert over our own behavior, and of the nature and effects of *daydreams* and *fantasies*. After that, we'll turn to what is perhaps the most profound regular shift in consciousness we experience: *sleep*. Here, of course, we'll also consider the nature of dreams and what functions, if any, they may serve. Our next topic will be *hypnosis*, and we'll ask whether this procedure actually produces dramatic changes in consciousness. Finally, we'll conclude with a discussion of *consciousness-altering drugs* and how, perhaps, they produce their effects.

Biological Rhythms: *Tides of Life—and Conscious Experience*

I've known for many years that I'm a "morning person": I rarely have trouble waking up, and I feel most alert and energetic early in the day. After lunch, though, I often experience a sharp drop in alertness from which I don't recover until late afternoon. What about you? When do *you* feel most alert and energetic? Whatever your answer, it's clear that most of us do experience regular shifts in these respects each day. Psychologists and other scientists refer to such changes as **biological rhythms**—regular fluctuations in our bodily processes over time. Many of these fluctuations occur over the course of a single day and are therefore known as **circadian rhythms** (from the Latin words for "around" and "day"). As the woman in Figure 4.1 realizes, circadian rhythms can exert important effects on us in many respects, so they are worth considering in many different contexts. I should note that other biological rhythms take place within shorter periods of time. For example, many people become hungry every two or three hours (at least while they are awake). And as we'll soon see, during sleep, periods of dreaming seem to occur roughly at ninety-minute intervals. Finally, some biological rhythms

States of Consciousness: Varying degrees of awareness of ourselves and the external world.

Biological Rhythms: Cyclic changes in bodily processes.

Circadian Rhythms: Cyclic changes in bodily processes occurring within a single day.

occur over longer periods, such as the twenty-eight day menstrual cycle experienced by women. Since circadian rhythms have been the focus of most research, however, we'll focus primarily on these.

BOTTOM LINERS

"Sorry I'm late ... I forgot to set my inner clock."

(**Source:** © Tribune Media Services, Inc. All Rights Reserved. Reprinted with permission.)

FIGURE 4.1

Circadian Rhythms and Being on Time

Do you find it easy to wake up at the same time each morning—even without an alarm clock? If so, circadian rhythms relating to sleep play a key role.

Circadian Rhythms: Their Basic Nature

Most people are aware of fluctuations in their alertness, energy, and moods over the course of a day, and research findings indicate that such shifts are closely related to changes in underlying bodily processes (e.g., Moore-Ede, Sulzman, & Fuller, 1982). Daily cycles occur in the production of various hormones, in core body temperature, in blood pressure, and in several other processes. For many persons, these functions are highest in the late afternoon and evening, and lowest in the early hours of the morning. Large individual differences in this respect exist, however, so the pattern varies greatly for different persons.

As you might expect, these cyclic fluctuations in basic bodily functions—and in our subjective feelings of alertness—are related to task performance. In general, people do their best work when body temperature and other internal processes are at or near their personal peaks. However, this link appears to be somewhat stronger for physical tasks than for mental ones—especially tasks that require considerable thought and cognitive effort (Daniel & Potasova, 1989).

Circadian Rhythms: What Mechanism Underlies Them?

If bodily processes, mental alertness, and performance on many tasks change regularly over the course of the day, it seems reasonable to suggest that we possess some internal biological mechanism for regulating such changes. In other words, we must possess one or more biological "clocks" that time various circadian rhythms. While there is not as yet total agreement on the number or nature of these internal clocks, existing evidence points to the conclusion that one structure—the **suprachiasmatic nucleus,** located in the hypothalamus—plays a key role in this respect (Moore & Card, 1985). In fact, it may act as a kind of superclock, keeping other internal clocks synchronized with one another (Lewy, Sack, & Singer, 1992). This nucleus responds to visual input from the eyes and either stimulates or inhibits activity in the pineal gland. This gland secretes *melatonin,* a hormone with far-reaching effects. Melatonin exerts a sedative effect, reducing activity and increasing fatigue.

Exposure to daylight stimulates the suprachiasmatic nucleus, and this, in turn, reduces the secretion of melatonin. In contrast, darkness enhances it. Thus, we tend to feel alert and active during the day but tired when it is dark. Evidence that the suprachiasmatic nucleus acts as a biological clock is provided by research indicating that when this structure is damaged or when neural pathways connecting it to the eyes are destroyed, circadian rhythms disappear (Moore & Card, 1985).

Suprachiasmatic Nucleus: A portion of the hypothalamus that seems to play an important role in the regulation of circadian rhythms.

Morning Person: Individual who experiences peak levels of energy and physiological activation relatively early in the day.

Night (Evening) Person: Individual who experiences peak levels of energy and physiological activation relatively late in the day.

Another intriguing fact has emerged from research in which volunteers live in caves or other environments totally removed from clocks, the rising and setting of the sun, and other cues we normally use to keep track of time. Under these conditions, most persons seem to shift toward a "day" of about twenty-five hours (Moore-Ede, Sulzman, & Fuller, 1982). In other words, each day they rise and go to sleep a little later; and all their activities—and peaks in bodily functions such as temperature and blood pressure—shift as well.

Individual Differences in Circadian Rhythms: Are You a Morning Person or a Night Person?

Before reading further, please answer the questions in Table 4.1. How did you score? If you answered "Day" to eight or more questions, the chances are good that you are a **morning person.** If, instead, you answered "Night" to eight or more questions, you are probably a **night (evening) person.** Morning people feel most alert and active early in the day, while night people experience peaks in alertness and energy in the afternoon or evening. Such differences are more than purely subjective. Studies comparing morning and evening persons indicate that the two groups differ in several important

TABLE 4.1

Are You a Morning Person or a Night Person?

If you answer "Day" to eight or more of these questions, you are probably a morning person. If you answer "Night" to eight or more, you are probably a night person.

Respond to each of the following items by circling either "Day" or "Night":		
1. I feel most alert during the	Day	Night
2. I have most energy during the	Day	Night
3. I prefer to take classes during the	Day	Night
4. I prefer to study during the	Day	Night
5. I get my best ideas during the	Day	Night
6. When I graduate, I would prefer to find a job during the	Day	Night
7. I am most productive during the	Day	Night
8. I feel most intelligent during the	Day	Night
9. I enjoy leisure-time activities most during the	Day	Night
10. I prefer to work during the	Day	Night

(**Source:** Based on items from Wallace, 1993.)

ways. Morning people have a higher overall level of adrenaline than night people; thus, they seem to operate at a higher overall level of activation (e.g., Akerstedt & Froberg, 1976). Similarly, morning people experience peaks in body temperature earlier in the day than night people (Wallace, 1993).

That these differences in alertness and bodily states translate into important effects on behavior is indicated by a study conducted by Guthrie, Ash, and Bendapudi (1995). These researchers reasoned that students who are morning persons would get higher grades in early-morning classes than students who are night (evening) persons. To test this hypothesis, the researchers had several hundred college students complete a questionnaire similar to the one in Table 4.1; on the basis of the replies, they classified the students as either morning or evening persons. Then, at the end of the semester, they obtained the students' grades in all their classes—those that began at 8:00 or 8:30 a.m., and those that began later in the day. As you can see from Figure 4.2, students classified as morning persons obtained higher grades in early morning classes than in later classes; the opposite was true for students clas-

FIGURE 4.2

Circadian Rhythms and Grades

As shown here, students who were classified as being morning persons obtained higher grades in early-morning classes than in later classes. In contrast, students classified as being night (evening) persons obtained higher grades in classes held later in the day than in early-morning classes.

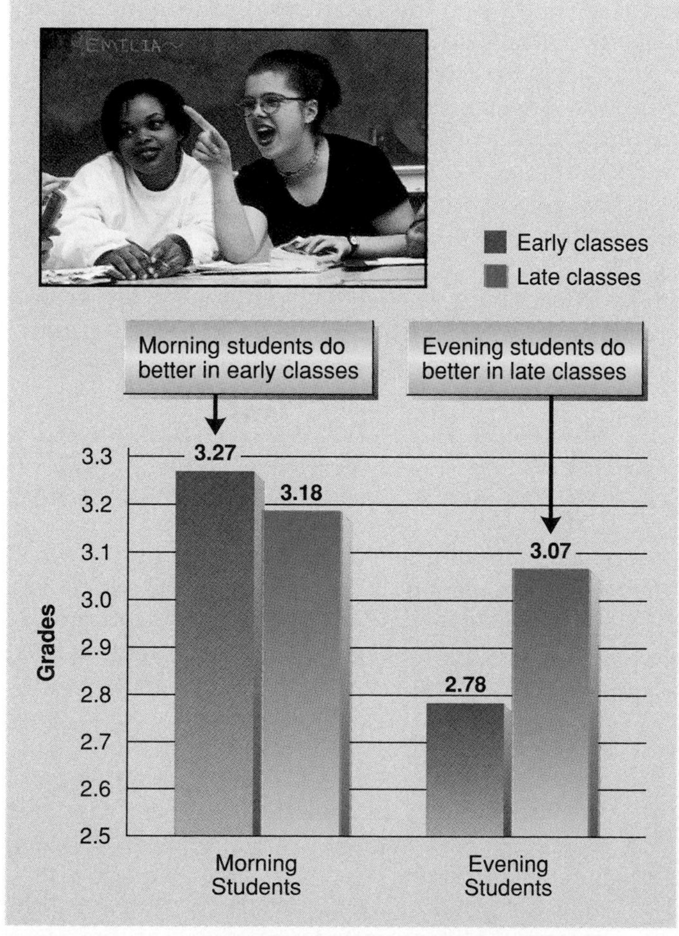

(**Source:** Based on data from Guthrie, Ash, & Bendapudi, 1995.)

Diary Approach: A method of research in which individuals report on various aspects of their behavior on a regular basis for several days, weeks, or even months.

sified as being evening persons, who obtained higher grades in classes that begin later in the day. (Morning persons obtained higher grades overall, but this was largely attributable to their better performance in early morning classes.) The practical implications of these findings seem clear: Determine whether you are a morning or night person, and then try—to the extent this is possible—to schedule your classes accordingly. The benefits to your grade point average may be considerable.

Disturbances in Circadian Rhythms: Jet Lag and Shift Work

Under normal conditions, the existence of circadian rhythms poses no special problems; we are aware of these daily fluctuations in our alertness and energy, and we adjust our activities accordingly. There are two situations, however, in which circadian rhythms may get badly out of phase with events in our lives—with potentially serious consequences for us.

The first of these occurs as a result of travel. When we fly across several time zones, we may experience considerable difficulty in adjusting our internal clock to the new location—an effect known as *jet lag*. Persons suffering from jet lag feel tired, dull, and generally out of sorts; as one of my friends puts it, "After I take a long flight, all systems are no-go for several days." Research on circadian rhythms indicates that in general it is easier to reset our biological clocks by delaying them than by advancing them. In other words, we experience less disruption when we fly to a time zone where it is *earlier* than the one in which we normally live, than when we fly to one where it is *later*. So, for instance, if you live on the East Coast of the United States and fly to California, where it is three hours earlier, you simply stay up a few extra hours and then go to sleep. In contrast, if you live in California and fly to the East Coast, where it is three hours later, you may experience greater disruption—and take longer to adjust your internal clock. Why is this so? Perhaps because of our tendency to shift toward a twenty-five-hour day. Moving to a time zone that is earlier is compatible with this tendency, while moving to one where it is later—and so your "day" is shorter—is inconsistent with it (see Figure 4.3).

A second cause of difficulties with respect to circadian rhythms is shift work in which individuals must work at times when they would normally be sleeping (for instance, midnight to 8:00 a.m.). This is an important issue, because at the present time, about 20 percent of all employees in the United States and several other countries work at night (usually from 11:00 p.m. or midnight until 7:00 or 8:00 a.m.; Fierman, 1995). To make matters worse, shift workers often face a schedule in which they work on one shift for a fairly short period (say a week), get two days off, and then work on another shift. The effects of swing shifts—alternating periods of day and night work—are, for many people, quite unsettling. And the reason is clear: Such individuals have to reset their biological clocks over and over again, and this process is draining, both physically and psychologically (e.g., Czeisler, Moore-Ede, & Coleman, 1982). For more information on the effects of shift work and on how psychologists study circadian rhythms, please see the Research Methods section.

FIGURE 4.3

Jet Lag: A Hazard of Modern Life

As shown here, jet lag is more likely when you fly to a time zone that is later than the one in which you normally live than when you fly to a time zone where it is earlier.

▪ RESEARCH METHODS ▪

How Psychologists Study Circadian Rhythms—and Disruptions in Them

In most industrialized countries there are strict government regulations concerning the maximum number of hours employees can work and the amount of rest time they must have after each work period. The underlying assumption behind such regulations is that work leads to fatigue and other adverse effects, and that people need time off for recovery. This is an eminently reasonable assertion, and no one would argue seriously with it. But how much rest time do people need? And does this differ as a function of the kind of shift on which they have been working (for instance, day, evening, or night shift)? Psychologists believe that answers to such questions can be acquired only through systematic research. But how can such research be conducted? How can we determine how quickly people recover from a period of work, and whether such recovery differs across different shifts? One answer involves a research method used to study disruptions in circadian rhythms—and several other topics as well: a method known as the **diary approach.**

In this method, participants in a study are asked to report on various aspects of their behavior over a period of several days, weeks, or even months. Recent investigations, making use of technological advances in computers, provide participants with special devices that signal them as to when to report on their own behavior, and in some cases permit them to enter their reactions directly onto the device. Use of these devices ensures that data will be collected in a systematic and accurate manner. Perhaps the best way of illustrating the diary approach, and its usefulness in studying the effects of circadian rhythms, is by examining a recent study that used this approach.

In this investigation, a team of psychologists (Totterdell et al., 1995), attained the cooperation of a group of nurses who worked on rotating shifts. Each nurse was given a pocket computer and asked to use it to report on specific aspects of his or her own behavior several times a day for twenty-eight days. At specified times, the nurses provided information on their sleep (e.g., when they went to sleep, when they woke up, the quality of their sleep) and on their current moods (e.g., how cheerful, calm, and alert they felt). On workdays, they also rated their own performance and stress every two hours. Finally, every two hours, they also completed measures of their mental alertness—for example, a reaction-time task, which measured how quickly they could respond to various stimuli.

The researchers then analyzed these data to determine how performance changed over successive workdays, and how it changed during the rest days that followed each work shift. Given the wealth of data gathered, results were complex; but here are some of the most important conclusions:

- Alertness, calmness, and sleep quality were worse on the first rest day following night shift work than on the first rest day following day or evening shifts.
- Several aspects of mood and performance were worse on the first day of a night shift if this shift began after several days of rest than if it began after only one day of rest.
- Several aspects of mood and performance deteriorated over successive night shift periods; in other words, the adverse effects of working the night shift seemed to cumulate over time.

Together, these findings underscore the potentially harmful effects of working on the night shift—especially when individuals must alternate between day work and night work. In addition, they indicate that more days off after night shifts may not be the best way to counter such effects. Apparently, this is the case because after several days of rest, individuals' circadian rhythms become readjusted to a normal day schedule, thus making it harder for them to begin night work once again. If you've ever found it harder to wake up for early-morning classes after spring break, when you got used to staying up and sleeping later, you are already familiar with such effects.

In sum, the findings obtained by Totterdell and his associates (1995) by means of the diary approach suggest that the best solution to swing shifts may *not* be what common sense, and government regulations, require—giving employees several days of rest between shifts. Instead, the best approach may be a combination of lengthening the amount of time people spend on each shift (several weeks or months instead of just a week or two) and recruiting groups of employees who are willing to stay permanently on the night shift. Extra rest after working the night shift may help people feel better; but if they must soon return to this shift, the costs of readjusting to it may be greater than the benefits of any extra time off.

Research on the effects of shift work using the diary method and other techniques points to unsettling conclusions: shift work—and especially swing shifts—often leads to poorer on-the-job performance and increased rates of industrial accidents, and can also exert adverse effects on personal health (e.g., Lidell, 1982; Meijmann, van der Meer, & van Dormolen, 1993). Can anything be done to reduce these harmful effects? I have already mentioned two steps that seem useful—keeping employees on the same shift for several weeks, rather than only one (e.g., Czeisler, Moor-Ede, & Coleman, 1982), and hiring people who are willing to work the night shift on a permanent basis. Other procedures still in early stages of development involve adjusting indoor lighting during night shifts so that it simulates the changing pattern of natural light during the course of a day (e.g., Noble, 1993). Thus, lighting in offices and factories is relatively subdued early in the workshift, just as sunlight is relatively weak early in the morning. Later, indoor lighting gradually increases and then weakens, in a pattern similar to that of sunlight. While data concerning the effectiveness of these procedures is still being gathered, early results are promising, at least with respect to increased feelings of well-being and reduced on-the-job errors among employees.

Key Questions

- What are biological rhythms? What are circadian rhythms?
- How do morning persons and night persons differ?
- What effects do jet lag and shift work have on circadian rhythms?
- How do psychologists use diary studies to study circadian rhythms and disruptions in them?

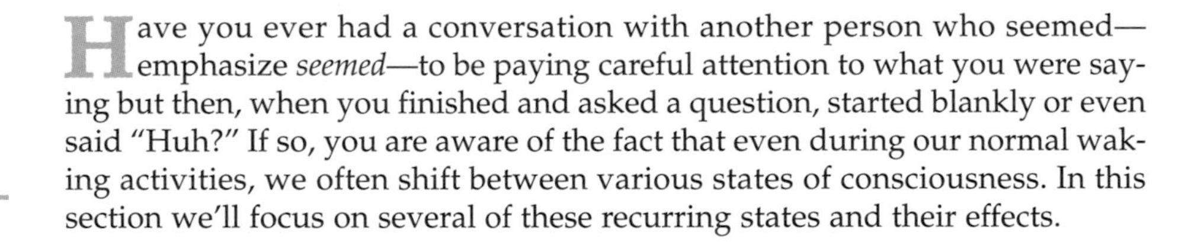

Waking States of Consciousness

Have you ever had a conversation with another person who seemed—emphasize *seemed*—to be paying careful attention to what you were saying but then, when you finished and asked a question, started blankly or even said "Huh?" If so, you are aware of the fact that even during our normal waking activities, we often shift between various states of consciousness. In this section we'll focus on several of these recurring states and their effects.

Controlled and Automatic Processing: The Limits of Attention

Earlier, I noted that we often perform more than one task at the same time—for example, brushing our teeth while we think about many other things, or talking to another person as we cook some dish. How can we do this? The answer involves the fact that we have two contrasting ways of controlling ongoing activities—two different levels of attention to, or conscious control over, our own behavior (Logan, 1985, 1988).

The first level uses very little of our *information-processing capacity,* and seems to occur in an automatic manner with very little conscious awareness on our part. Psychologists refer to this as **automatic processing,** and it *does* seem to be automatic. For this reason, several different activities, each under automatic control, can occur at the same time (e.g., Shiffrin & Dumais, 1981; Shiffrin & Schneider, 1977). You demonstrate such automatic processing every time you drive and listen to the radio at the same time: Both activities can occur simultaneously because both involve automatic processing (see Figure 4.4).

FIGURE 4.4

Automatic Processing in Action

When activities are well practiced, we can perform them automatically, without using much of our information-processing capacity. The person shown here can engage in two activities at once because they are both well-learned—but the risks of doing so are high, and I certainly recommend against such behavior.

In contrast, **controlled processing** involves more effortful and conscious control of behavior. In controlled processing you direct careful attention to the task at hand and concentrate on it. Processing of this type consumes significant cognitive resources; as a result, only one task requiring controlled processing can usually be performed at a time.

Research on the nature of automatic and controlled processing suggests that these two states of consciousness differ in several respects. First, behaviors that have come under the control of automatic processing are performed more quickly and with less effort than ones that require controlled processing (e.g., Logan, 1988). In addition, acts that have come under automatic processing—usually because they are well practiced and well learned—can be initiated without conscious intention; they are triggered in a seemingly automatic manner, by specific stimuli or events (e.g., Norman & Shallice, 1985). In fact, it may be difficult to inhibit such actions once they are initiated. If you ever played Simple Simon as a child, you are well aware of this fact. After following many commands beginning "Simple Simon says do this," you probably also responded to the similar command, "Do this." Why? Because your imitation of the leader's actions was under automatic control, and you obeyed—without conscious thought—even when you should have refrained from doing so.

Is either of these types of processing superior? Not really. Automatic processing is rapid and efficient, but it can be relatively inflexible—precisely because it is so automatic. Controlled processing is slower but is more flexible and open to change. In sum, both play an important role in our efforts to deal with information from the external world. One final point: Automatic and controlled processing are not hard-and-fast categories, but rather ends of a continuous dimension. On any given task, individuals may operate in a relatively controlled or a relatively automatic manner.

Daydreams and Fantasies: Self-Induced Shifts in Consciousness

Stop! What are you thinking right now? Are your thoughts focused on the words in this book? Or have they wandered off somewhere into your own private world, so that your eyes are scanning the pages but your mind is focused largely on other matters? Whether that's true or not, you certainly know that sometimes you do indeed have **daydreams**—thoughts and images that you yourself generate internally (Singer, 1975). When these daydreams become intense enough to affect our own emotions, they are sometimes termed **fantasies** (e.g., Jones & Barlow, 1990). What are these daydreams and fantasies like, and what—if any—function do they serve? Let's see what psychologists have discovered about these issues.

The Content of Daydreams and Fantasies What was the content of *your* last daydream? If you are like most people, it probably fit under one of the following categories: success or failure (you imagined receiving straight A's or failing an important exam), aggression or hostility (you imagined getting even with someone for something he or she did to you), sexual or romantic fantasies (I'll return to these below), guilt (you tortured yourself about something you should have done—or shouldn't have done), or problem solving (you imagined yourself working on some task or solving some problem). Of course, many other themes exist; these are merely the ones that have been found to be most common (e.g., Klinger, 1990).

The Sources of Daydreams: Internal and External Research findings indicate that from time to time almost everyone has daydreams; just

Automatic Processing: Processing of information with minimal conscious awareness.

Controlled Processing: Processing of information with relatively high levels of conscious awareness.

Daydreams: Imaginary scenes and events that occur while an individual is awake.

Fantasies: Intense and vivid daydreams.

FIGURE 4.5

Television: What Is It Doing to Children?

Research findings indicate that watching television can increase daydreaming, but that TV may reduce viewers' creative imagination as well as their ability to generate novel or unusual ideas.

as, we'll soon see, everyone dreams when asleep. What is the source of these experiences? To a large extent, they are self-induced: They are the result of turning our thoughts to images that are based on memory—or on our imagination (Singer, 1975). But since memory is a reflection of our past experience, it is clear that daydreams can be influenced, to a degree, by external events. One such influence involves television. Many developmental psychologists have expressed concern over the possibility that television, because it involves passive reception of information shown on the screen, may reduce both children's tendency to daydream and their *creative imagination*—their ability to generate many different novel or unusual ideas (e.g., Singer, Singer, & Rapaczynski, 1984; Viemero & Paajanen, 1992). Numerous studies have been performed to investigate this possibility, and a careful review of the evidence by Valkenburg and van der Voort (1994) suggests that television may indeed influence both daydreaming and creative imagination in children, but in different ways.

With respect to daydreaming, most studies suggest that television may actually *encourage* daydreaming among children, and in adults too (e.g., McIlwraith et al., 1991). That is, the more television children watch, the greater the frequency of their daydreams. This seems to be the case because television provides the raw materials from which people can construct daydreams—it provides vivid images and new information from which people can then assemble absorbing inner musings.

In contrast, however, the overwhelming weight of existing evidence suggests that television exerts a chilling effect on creative imagination. The more television people watch, the lower their creative imagination, as measured by teacher ratings of their creativity or by their performance on standard tests of creative imagination (for example, coming up with unusual uses for an everyday object). How television exerts such effects is not yet clear, but it seems possible that important factors include the rapid pace of television (which leaves viewers little time to engage in their own thoughts) and the fact that watching television is largely a passive process (which discourages the mental effort needed for creative imagination). In any case, the overall picture is not encouraging: Television seems to encourage children (and adults) to withdraw into their own inner world, and at the same time reduces their capacity to cope creatively with unexpected situations or problems. To the extent these findings are verified in further research, they sound an alarm for parents (see Figure 4.5).

Sexual Fantasies: Their Nature and Effects As I noted earlier, nearly everyone has daydreams; and growing evidence indicates that for most people, these sometimes take the form of **sexual fantasies**—mental images that are sexually arousing or erotic to the individual who has them (Leitenberg & Henning, 1995). In fact, studies in which individuals report on their fantasies indicate that more than 95 percent of both women and men report that they have had such fantasies at some time or other (e.g., Pelletier & Herold,

Sexual Fantasies: Mental images that are sexually arousing or erotic to the individual who has them.

1988). Thus, while men report having more sexual fantasies each day than women, such fantasies are common for both genders. This does not mean that the content of sexual fantasies is identical for women and men, however. On the contrary, some gender differences do appear in this respect. For instance, men's erotic fantasies seem to contain more explicit visual imagery and anatomic detail, while women's fantasies contain greater reference to affection, more emotions, and a story line. Similarly, males, more than females, fantasize about having more than one sexual partner. A third difference involves submission fantasies: More females report having these than males. But don't misunderstand: Submission fantasies do not necessarily involve being enslaved or forced to have sex against one's will. On the contrary, most such fantasies described by females involve scenes in which a man the woman finds sexually attractive is irresistibly stimulated by the woman's sexual appeal, then uses just enough force to overcome her token resistance. In fact, the sex is mutually consensual and mutually enjoyable (e.g., Bond & Mosher, 1986).

What function do sexual fantasies serve? Both women and men report that they use such fantasies to increase their own arousal, and therefore their own sexual pleasure. Moreover, this strategy seems to work: People who report frequent sexual fantasies also report engaging in greater sexual activity—and enjoying it more—than people who report fewer sexual fantasies (Leitenberg & Henning, 1995). So, in sum, sexual fantasies appear to be a normal part of sexual life for most persons, and pose problems of personal adjustment only if they focus on inappropriate partners (e.g., children) or activities (e.g., forced sexual contact).

Key Questions

- What is the difference between automatic processing and controlled processing?
- What are daydreams? What are some of the major themes they contain?
- How are daydreams influenced by television watching?
- What are sexual fantasies? How do they differ for women and men?

Sleep: The Pause That Refreshes?

What single activity occupies more of your time than any other? While you may be tempted to say "studying" or "working," think again. The correct answer is probably **sleep**—a process in which important physiological changes and slowing basic bodily functions are accompanied by major shifts in consciousness. Most people spend fully one-third of their entire lives asleep (Dement, 1975; Webb, 1975). It stands to reason that any activity that occupies so much of our time must be important, so efforts to understand the nature of sleep have continued in psychology for several decades. What has this research revealed? Let's take a closer look.

Sleep: How It Is Studied

Everyone would agree that when we sleep, we are in a different state of consciousness than when we are awake. But what is sleep really like? This is a difficult question to answer, since during sleep we are generally less aware of ourselves and our surroundings than at other times. For this reason, asking people about their own experience with sleep is not a very useful technique for studying it. Fortunately, a much better approach exists. As a person moves from a waking state to deep sleep, complex changes in the electrical

Sleep: A process in which important physiological changes (e.g., shifts in brain activity, slowing of basic bodily functions) are accompanied by major shifts in consciousness.

activity of the brain occur. These changes can be measured with great precision, and the resulting record—known as an **electroencephalogram** (**EEG** for short)—reveals much about the nature of sleep. Thus, in much research on this process, volunteers are fitted with electrodes so that researchers can study their EEGs as well as other changes in bodily functions such as respiration, muscle tone, heart rate, and blood pressure. The changes that occur as the volunteers fall asleep and continue sleeping are then recorded and serve as a basic source of information about many aspects of sleep.

Sleep: Its Basic Nature

What has sleep research revealed? A picture of sleep that goes something like this. When you are fully awake and alert, your EEGs contain many *beta waves:* relatively high-frequency (14 to 30 cycles per second), low-voltage activity. As you enter a quiet, resting state—for example, after getting into bed and turning out the light—beta waves are replaced by **alpha waves,** EEG activity that is somewhat lower in frequency (8 to 13 cycles per second) but slightly higher in voltage. As you begin to fall asleep, alpha waves are replaced by even slower, higher-voltage **delta waves.** The appearance of delta waves seems to reflect the fact that increasingly large number of neurons are firing together, in a synchronized manner.

Although such phrases as "drifting off to sleep" suggest that the onset of sleep is gradual, it is actually quite sudden. One instant you are awake and aware of your surroundings; the next you are asleep, no longer experiencing such awareness. Sleep is not entirely an either–or phenomenon, however. EEG records obtained from thousands of volunteers indicate that sleep can actually be divided into four stages. The transition from wakefulness to sleep occurs with the onset of Stage 1 sleep. During this stage, a mixed but relatively slow, low-voltage EEG pattern emerges. Breathing slows, muscle tone decreases, and the body generally relaxes. At this level, individuals can be readily awakened by external stimuli. If they are not, they move into Stage 2 (Webb, 1975). During this stage the brain emits occasional short bursts of rapid, high-voltage waves known as sleep spindles. In Stage 2, sleepers are much more difficult to awaken. Stage 2 is followed by Stages 3 and 4. As shown in Figure 4.6, these stages are marked by the increasing appearance of slow, high-voltage delta waves, and by a further slowing of all bodily functions (Dement, 1975). Almost everyone shows the same pattern of shifts as they fall asleep, and departures from this pattern are often a sign of physical or psychological disorders (e.g., Empson, 1984).

So far, the picture I have presented probably seems consistent with your own subjective experience of sleep. About ninety minutes after the process begins, however, several dramatic changes occur, as individuals enter a distinct phase known as **REM (rapid eye movement) sleep.** During this phase the electrical activity of the brain changes rapidly; it now closely resembles that shown when people are awake. Delta waves disappear, and fast, low-voltage activity returns. Sleepers' eyes begin to move about rapidly beneath their closed eyelids, and there is an almost total suppression of activity in body muscles.

These observable shifts in brain activity and bodily processes are accompanied, in many cases, by one of the most dramatic aspects of sleep: *dreams.* Individuals awakened during REM sleep often report dreaming. In some cases, eye movements during such sleep seem to be related to the content of dreams (Dement, 1975). It is as if dreamers are following the action in their dreams with their eyes. The relationship between rapid eye movements and dream content is uncertain, however, so it is best to view this as an intriguing but as yet unverified possibility.

Electroencephalogram (EEG): A record of electrical activity within the brain. EEGs play an important role in the scientific study of sleep.

Alpha Waves: Rapid, low-amplitude brain waves that occur when individuals are awake but relaxed.

Delta Waves: High-amplitude, slow brain waves that occur during several stages of sleep, but especially during Stage 4.

REM (Rapid Eye Movement) Sleep: A state of sleep in which brain activity resembling waking restfulness is accompanied by deep muscle relaxation and movements of the eyes. Most dreams occur during periods of REM sleep.

FIGURE 4.6

Sleep Stages

As individuals fall asleep, the electrical activity in their brains changes in an orderly manner. Note the changes that occur as people fall asleep and then move through four major sleep stages.

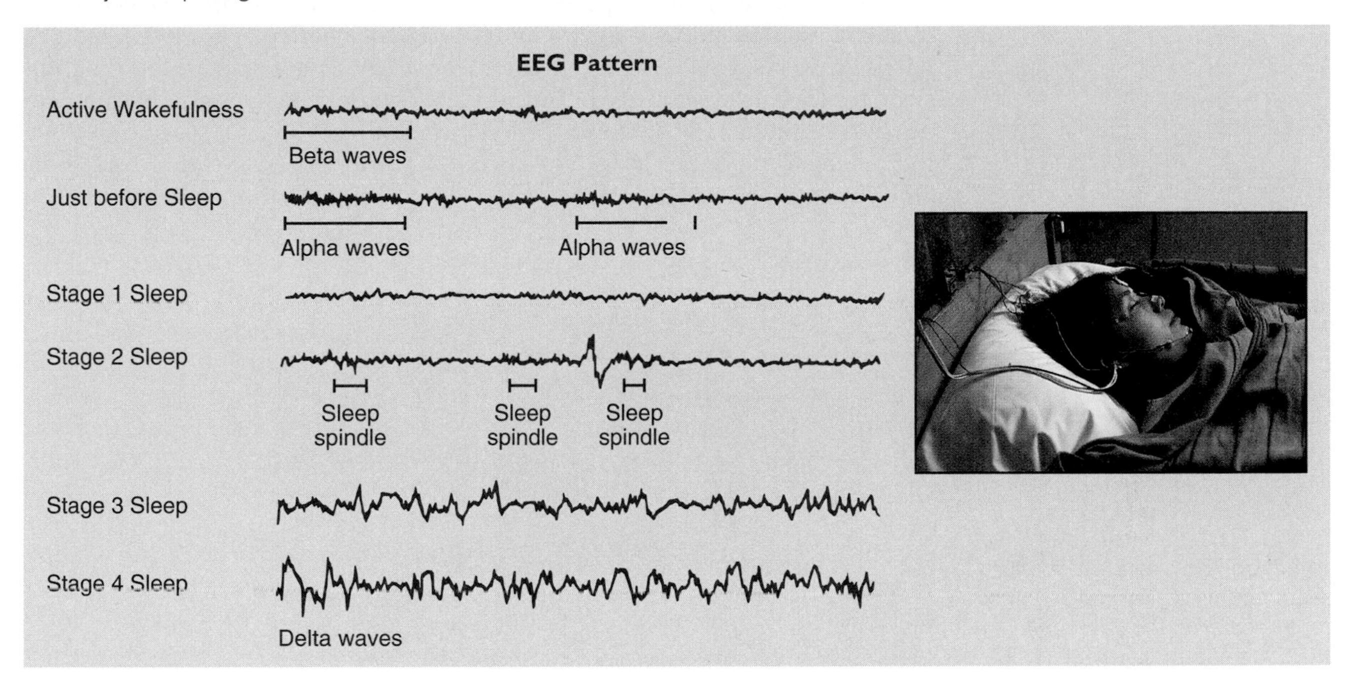

Periods of REM sleep continue to alternate with the other stages of sleep throughout the night. The duration is variable, but the REM periods tend to increase in length toward morning, while the amount of time spent in Stage 4 tends to decrease. Thus, while the first REM period may last only five to ten minutes, the final ones—from which many people awake—may last thirty minutes or more (Hartmann, 1973; Kelly, 1981).

It is interesting to note that patterns of sleep do change somewhat with age. Newborn infants sleep sixteen hours a day or more, and spend about 50 percent of their time in REM sleep. Both figures drop rapidly, so that by the time we are teenagers, total sleep time has fallen to slightly more than eight hours, with REM sleep making up about 20 percent of this figure (less than two hours). Total sleep time continues to decrease as we age, dropping to six hours or less after age fifty; however, the proportion of this time spent in REM sleep remains fairly constant (see Figure 4.7 on page 144).

Sleep: What Functions Does It Serve?

Any activity that fills as much of our lives as sleep must serve important functions. But what, precisely, are these? Several possibilities exist. The first, and perhaps most obvious, is that sleep serves primarily a restorative function, allowing us to rest and recover from the wear and tear of the day's activities. While this view seems consistent with the fact that we *do* often feel rested and restored after a good night's sleep, there is little direct evidence for it. Even prolonged deprivation of sleep does not seem to produce large or clear-cut effects on behavior. For example, in one demonstration, seventeen-year-old Randy Gardner stayed awake for 264 hours and 12 minutes—eleven entire days! His motivation for doing this was simple: He wanted to earn a place in the *Guinness Book of Records,* and he did. Although he had some difficulty staying awake this long, he remained generally alert and active throughout the entire period. After completing his ordeal, Randy slept a mere 14 hours. Then he returned to his usual 8-hour cycle. Further, he seemed to suffer no lasting physical or psychological harm from his long sleepless period.

More systematic studies of the effects of sleep deprivation have been conducted with both animals and people (e.g., Rechtschaffen et al., 1983). Studies with human subjects have asked volunteers to gradually reduce their nightly sleep by, for example, thirty minutes every two or three weeks. These procedures continue until the volunteers report that they do not want to reduce their sleep any further. Results indicate that most people can reduce their amount of sleep to about five hours per night (Mullaney et al., 1977).

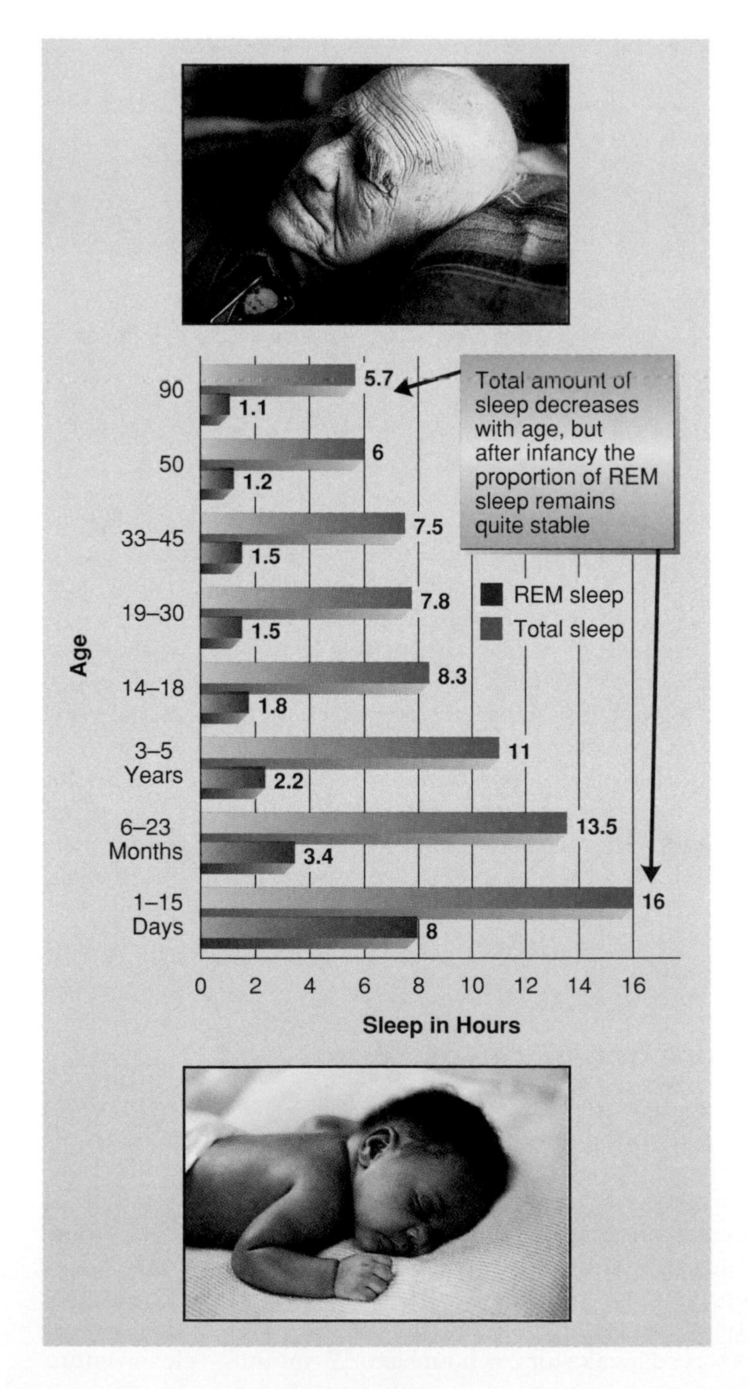

FIGURE 4.7

Changing Patterns of Sleep over the Life Span

Infants sleep sixteen hours a day or more and spend about half that time in REM sleep. Total sleep decreases as we age, dropping to only about six hours each night for older persons. However, the proportion of REM sleep remains fairly constant.

Moreover, no reductions in their performance on various tasks, no negative shifts in mood, and no harmful effects on health seem to result from such reductions. The major changes observed involve sleep itself. After reducing their sleep to five hours or less, participants demonstrate increased *sleep efficiency*—they fall asleep very quickly, and they spend a higher proportion of time in Stage 4 sleep. It is as if they have learned to compress their sleep into a shorter period of time. Research with animals yields similar effects: sleep deprivation does not produce large or obvious effects. Clearly, these findings do *not* provide strong support for the view that sleep serves mainly a restorative function.

A second possible function of sleep emphasizes the relationship of sleep to circadian rhythms—cyclic changes in bodily processes during the day. According to this view, sleep is merely the neural mechanism that has evolved to encourage various species, including our own, to remain inactive during those times of day when they do not usually engage in activities related to their survival. As one well-known sleep researcher (Webb, 1975) has put it, sleep is nature's way of keeping us quiet at night, a dangerous time for our ancestors—and for us—since we are not equipped with sensory capacities suited for nighttime activity.

Yet another possibility is that only certain components of sleep are crucial. For example, it has been suggested that perhaps it is REM sleep that is essential to our health and well-being, and that being deprived of such sleep will induce harmful effects. While some findings are consistent with this view, other studies suggest that the only effect of depriving individuals of REM sleep is to increase the amount of such sleep on subsequent nights (Webb & Agnew, 1967).

So where does all this leave us? Most experts believe that sleep serves both the restorative and the circadian functions noted above (e.g., Borbely et al., 1989). In support of this reasoning, some findings indicate that the amount of time people spend in slow-wave sleep is related to how long they have been awake, while the amount of time they spend in REM sleep is related mainly to circadian rhythms (Knowles et al., 1990). Further, there is an important relationship between sleep and waking moods. The more effectively people sleep, the more positive are their waking moods, and the less anxiety they experience (Berry & Webb, 1985). So, in sum, sleep does seem to serve important functions. Falling asleep is a function of both restorative and circadian factors, and sleep itself fulfills needs related to both.

Sleep Disorders: No Rest for Some of the Weary

Do you ever have trouble falling or staying asleep? If so, you are in good company: almost 40 percent of adults report that they sometimes have these problems—known, together, as **insomnia** (Bixler et al., 1979). Such problems seem to increase with age and are somewhat more common among women than men. While many people report insomnia, however, it is not clear that the incidence of this problem is as high as these self-reports might suggest. When the sleep habits of people who claim to be suffering from insomnia are carefully studied, it turns out that many of them sleep as long as people who do not complain of insomnia (Empson, 1984). This does not mean that such persons are faking; rather, it is possible that although they attain an amount of sleep that falls within normal limits (6.5 hours or more per night), this may not be enough to meet their individual needs. Further, the quality of their sleep may be disturbed in ways not yet measured in research. Still, such arguments aside, it does appear that many people who believe that their sleep is

Insomnia: The inability to fall asleep or to maintain sleep once it is attained.

Somnambulism: A sleep disorder in which individuals actually get up and move about while still asleep.

Night Terrors: Extremely frightening dreamlike experiences that occur during non-REM sleep.

Apnea: A sleep disorder in which sleepers stop breathing several times each night, and thus wake up.

Hypersomnias: Disorders involving excessive amounts of sleep or an overwhelming urge to fall asleep.

Narcolepsy: A sleep disorder in which individuals are overcome by uncontrollable periods of sleep during waking hours.

somewhat inadequate may actually be getting as much sleep, and sleeping about as well, as others.

On the other hand, insomnia is quite real for many persons, at least occasionally. What can you do if you encounter this problem? The following tactics may prove helpful:

- Read something pleasant or relaxing just before going to sleep.
- Arrange your schedule so you go to sleep at the same time each night.
- Take a warm bath or have a massage before going to sleep.
- Avoid coffee or tea late in the day.
- Exercise every day, but not just before going to sleep.
- Don't smoke.
- Don't nap during the day.
- Don't worry; almost everyone experiences difficulty falling asleep sometimes, so don't be overly concerned unless the problem persists for more than a few days.
- If, despite these measures, you find yourself tossing and turning, get up and read, work, or watch television until you feel drowsy. Lying in bed and worrying about your loss of sleep is definitely *not* the answer!

By the way, despite the promises of advertisements, sleeping pills—prescription or nonprescription—are not usually an effective sleep aid. They may induce sleep at first, but tolerance to these pills develops quickly so that larger and larger doses are needed. Further, some drugs used for this purpose interfere with REM sleep, and this can lead to other sleep disturbances.

While insomnia is the most common sleep disorder, it is not the only one. Several other *disorders of initiating and maintaining sleep* (DIMS for short) exist. First, there are disorders of arousal. The most dramatic of these is **somnambulism**—walking in one's sleep. This is less rare than you might guess; almost 25 percent of children experience at least one sleepwalking episode (Empson, 1984). A second, related disorder is **night terrors.** Here, individuals—especially children—awaken from deep sleep with signs of intense arousal and powerful feelings of fear. Yet they have no memory of any dream relating to these feelings. Night terrors seem to occur mainly during Stage 4 sleep. In contrast, *nightmares,* which most of us have experienced at some time, occur during REM sleep and often can be vividly recalled. Both somnambulism and night terrors appear to be linked to disturbances in the functioning of the autonomic system, which plays a key role in regulating brain activity during sleep.

Another disturbing type of sleep disorder is **apnea.** Persons suffering from sleep apnea actually stop breathing when they are asleep. This causes them to wake up; and since the process can be repeated hundreds of times each night, apnea can seriously affect the health of persons suffering from it.

Other sleep disorders involve **hypersomnias,** in which affected persons appear to sleep too much. The most serious of these is **narcolepsy,** a condition in which individuals suddenly fall deeply asleep in the midst of waking activities. Such spells are sometimes accompanied by almost total paralysis and are often triggered by a strong emotion. Thus, when a person with narcolepsy becomes excited or upset, he or she may suddenly fall down in a deep sleep.

What causes sleep disorders? For some persons insomnia seems to involve disturbances in the internal mechanisms that regulate body temperature. As noted in our discussion of circadian rhythms, core body temperature usually drops

Key Questions

- How do psychologists study sleep?
- What are the major stages of sleep?
- What happens during REM sleep?
- What are the effects of sleep deprivation?
- What functions does sleep seem to serve?
- What are some of the most common sleep disorders?
- What steps help promote a good night's sleep?

to low levels during sleep. In persons suffering from insomnia, however, this fails to happen, so their bodies remain in a waking state in this respect (Sewitch, 1987).

Other causes of sleep disorders may involve disturbances of the biological clock within the hypothalamus (the suprachiasmatic nucleus). This clock interacts with other structures of the brain—such as serotonin-producing portions of the reticular activating system and parts of the forebrain just in front of the hypothalamus—to regulate all circadian rhythms, including the sleep–waking cycle. Any disturbances in these complex and delicately balanced mechanisms can result in sleep disorders.

Dreams: "Now Playing in Your Private, Inner Theater . . . "

What is the most dramatic aspect of sleep? For many persons, the answer is obvious: **dreams**—those jumbled, vivid, sometimes enticing and sometimes disturbing images that fill our sleeping minds. What are these experiences? Why do they occur? Let's first consider some basic facts about dreams, and then turn to the answers to these questions provided by psychological research.

Dreams: Some Basic Facts Answer each of the following questions. Then consider the answers given—which reflect our current knowledge about dreams.

1. *Does everybody dream?* The answer seems to be *yes.* While not all people remember dreaming, EEG recordings and related data indicate that everyone experiences REM sleep. Moreover, if awakened during such periods, even people who normally don't recall dreaming often report vivid dreams.
2. *How long do dreams last?* Many people believe that dreams last only an instant, but in fact dreams seem to run on "real time": the longer they seem to last, the longer they really are (Dement & Kleitman, 1957).
3. *Can external events become part of dreams?* Yes, at least to a degree. For example, Dement and Wolpert (1958) sprayed water on volunteers who were in the REM stage of sleep. When they woke them up, more than half the sleepers reported water in their dreams.
4. *When people cannot remember their dreams, does this mean that they are purposely forgetting them, perhaps because they find the content disturbing?* Probably not. Research on why people can or cannot remember their dreams indicates that this is primarily a function of what they do when they wake up. If they lie quietly in bed, actively trying to remember a dream, they have a good chance of remembering it. If, instead, they jump out of bed and start the day's activities, the chances of recalling the dream are reduced. While we can't totally rule out the possibility of some kind of repression—that is, motivated forgetting—there is little evidence for its occurrence.
5. *Do dreams foretell the future?* As you can probably guess, there's no evidence whatsoever for this idea.
6. *Do dreams express unconscious wishes?* Many people believe that they do; but again, there is no convincing scientific evidence for this view. Please see our discussion of this topic below.

Now that we've considered some basic facts about dreams, let's turn to several views concerning their nature and function.

Dreams: Cognitive events, often vivid but disconnected, that occur during sleep. Most dreams take place during REM sleep.

Dreams: The Psychodynamic View Let's begin with the idea that dreams express unconscious wishes or impulses. This idea has existed for centuries, but its influence was greatly increased by Sigmund Freud, who felt that dreams provide a useful means for probing the unconscious—all those thoughts, impulses, and wishes that lie outside the realm of conscious experience. In dreams, Freud believed, we can give expression to impulses and desires we find unacceptable during our waking hours. Thus, we can dream about gratifying illicit sexual desires or about inflicting painful tortures on persons who have made us angry—thoughts we actively repress during the day.

Freud carefully analyzed the dreams of his patients, and he reported that in this manner he frequently gained important insights into the causes of his patients' problems. So fascinating were his reports of these experiences as a therapist, and so filled with conviction, that many people quickly accepted Freud's claims; and such beliefs about the meaning of dreams are definitely alive and well today. Despite this fact, these beliefs are *not* supported by convincing scientific evidence. On the contrary, Freud left us with no clear-cut rules for interpreting dreams and no way of determining whether such interpretations are accurate. In view of these facts, few psychologists currently accept the view that dreams offer a unique means for exploring the unconscious. Instead, most accept one of the alternative views we will now consider.

Dreams: The Physiological View If dreams aren't reflections of hidden wishes or impulses, what are they? Another answer is provided by what is sometimes known as the *physiological view* of dreams (Hobson, 1988). According to this perspective, dreams are merely our subjective experience of what is, in essence, random neural activity in the brain. Such activity occurs while we sleep simply because a minimal amount of stimulation is necessary for normal functioning of the brain and nervous system. Dreams then represent efforts by our cognitive systems to make sense out of this random neural activity (Foulkes, 1985; Hobson, 1988).

Dreams: The Cognitive View Another explanation of dreams carries somewhat further these suggestions concerning our cognitive systems' efforts to interpret neural activity while we sleep. This perspective, proposed by Antbrobus (1991), suggests that two facts about REM sleep are crucial to understanding the nature of dreams: (1) During REM sleep areas of the brain in the cerebral cortex that play a role in waking perception, thought, and regulation of motor processes are highly active; (2) yet at the same time, during REM sleep there is massive inhibition of input from sensory systems and muscles (these are suppressed). As a result, Antrobus (1991) reasons, the cortical structures or systems that normally regulate perception and thought have only their own activity as input. The result is that this activity forms the basis for the imagery and ideas in dreams (see Figure 4.8).

Does this mean that dreams are meaningless? Not at all. Since they represent interpretations of neural activity by our own brain, they reflect aspects of our memories and waking experience. Convincing evidence for connections between dreams and important events in our lives is provided by the fact that persons attempting to make important changes in their own behavior—for example, to quit smoking or drinking—often report having **dreams of absent-minded transgression**—DAMIT dreams for short (e.g., Gill, 1985). In such dreams, people suddenly notice that they have carelessly or absent-mindedly slipped into the habit they wish to break—they are smoking or drinking without having planned to do so. This realization leads to feelings of panic or guilt in the dream. In many cases, the dreamers awake at that point feeling very

Dreams of Absent-Minded Transgression: Dreams in which persons attempting to change their own behavior, as in quitting smoking, see themselves slipping into the unwanted behavior in an absent-minded or careless manner.

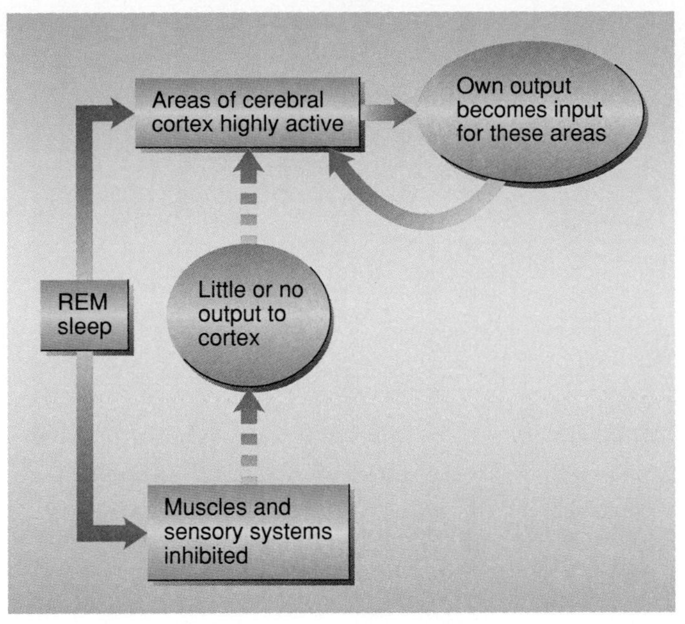

(**Source:** Based on suggestions by Antrobus, 1991.)

FIGURE 4.8

Dreams: A Cognitive Perspective

According to one view, dreams occur because during REM sleep, areas of the brain that play a key role in waking perception and thought are highly active while at the same time there is massive inhibition of input from sensory systems and muscles. As a result, the cortical systems that normally regulate perception and thought have only their own activity as input. The interpretation of this activity forms the basis for dreams.

disturbed. Interestingly, having such dreams is positively related to success in breaking the habits in question. For example, in one study on people who were attempting to quit smoking, those who reported DAMIT dreams were successful in breaking this habit more often than persons who did not report such dreams (Hajek & Belcher, 1991). Apparently, these individuals found the dreams so disturbing that the DAMIT experience strengthened their resolve to quit. These findings suggest that what is happening in people's dreams *is* sometimes linked to what is happening in their lives and that, moreover, some kinds of dreams can actually influence subsequent behavior. In such instances, the content of dreams does indeed have meaning.

Key Questions

- During what stage of sleep do dreams usually occur?
- Do most people dream? How long do dreams last?
- How do the psychodynamic, physiological, and cognitive views of dreams differ?
- What are dreams of absent-minded transgression, and what do they tell us about the meaning of dreams?

Hypnosis: *Altered State of Consciousness . . . or Social Role Playing?*

A few years ago I went to a local county fair. There were lots of attractions, but the one that drew the largest crowds by far was the demonstration of hypnotism (see Figure 4.9 on page 150). The hypnotist—who looked like anyone's grandfather—called for volunteers and quickly gathered about twenty people of all ages on the stage. Within a few minutes, he had put the volunteers into what he described as a "deep trance" and had them doing some very strange things. He told one young woman to imagine that she was a rooster, and that it was now dawn. The result? She crowed at the top of her lungs. He told two young men that they were famous ballerinas and were dancing for the Queen of England; they took off doing circles around the stage. In his grand finale, he put everyone on the stage back into a deep trance just by snapping his fingers. (He had previously suggested to them, while

FIGURE 4.9

Hypnotism: A Crowd Pleaser?

Demonstrations of hypnotism have been popular at fairs and on the stage for centuries. Even today, when many people are much more sophisticated about human behavior, hypnotists continue to attract large crowds.

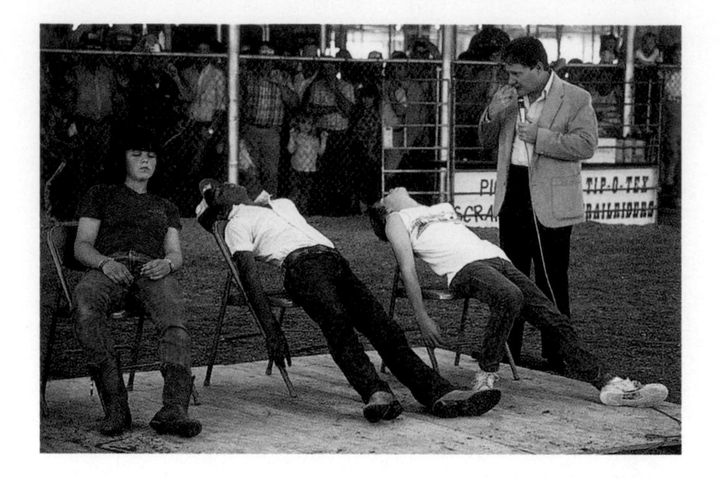

they were under hypnosis, that they would react like this.) Then he told them all that whenever he said the word "turnip," they would fall deeply asleep. He brought them out of the trance and engaged them in conversation. Then suddenly, without warning, he uttered the magic word "turnip." Most of his subjects immediately slumped over in their chairs in what seemed to be deep, restful sleep.

After the show, everyone in our group turned to me, as the psychologist-in-residence, and asked what I thought. Is hypnotism real? Were the people on the stage really in a trance, or were they somehow faking? "Complicated," I replied. "Complicated." And now let me explain why I gave this answer—and how psychologists interpret the strange phenomenon of **hypnosis:** a special type of interaction between two persons in which one (the hypnotist) induces changes in the behavior, feelings, or cognitions of the other (the subject) through suggestions.

Hypnosis: How It's Done and Who Is Susceptible to It

Let's start with two basic questions: (1) How is hypnotism performed? (2) Is everyone susceptible to it? With respect to the first, standard hypnotic inductions usually involve *suggestions* by the hypnotist that the person being hypnotized feels relaxed, is getting sleepy, and is unable to keep his or her eyes open. Speaking continuously in a calm voice, the hypnotist suggests to the subject that she or he is gradually sinking deeper and deeper into a relaxed state—not sleep, but a state in which the person will not be able to do, think, or say anything without input from the hypnotist. Another technique involves having the subject concentrate on a small object, often one that sparkles and can be rotated by the hypnotist. The result of such procedures, it appears, is that some people enter an altered state of consciousness. But hypnosis is definitely not sleep—EEG recordings from hypnotized persons resemble those of normal waking, not any of the sleep stages described earlier (Wallace & Fisher, 1987).

Hypnosis: An interaction between two persons in which one (the hypnotist) induces changes in the behavior, feelings, or cognitions of the other (the subject) through suggestions. Hypnosis involves expectations on the part of subjects and their attempts to conform to social roles (e.g., the role of hypnotized person).

Now for the second question: Can everyone be hypnotized? The answer seems clear: Large individual differences in hypnotizability exist. About 15 percent of adults are highly susceptible (as measured by their response to a graded series of suggestions by the hypnotist); 10 percent are highly resistant; the rest are somewhere in between. In addition, it appears that several traits are related to hypnotic susceptibility (Silva & Kirsch, 1992). Specifically, persons who are susceptible to hypnotism tend to:

- Have vivid, frequent fantasies
- Be high in visual imagery
- Be high in the trait of absorption—the tendency to become deeply involved in sensory and imaginative experiences
- Be dependent on others and seek direction from them
- Expect to be influenced by hypnotic suggestions and believe that these will have a powerful effect on them
- Experience more or stronger *dissociative experiences*—experiences in which some portion of the self or memory is split off from the rest

The greater the extent to which individuals possess these tendencies, the greater, in general, is their susceptibility to hypnosis. Recent evidence suggests that this is the case because such persons, to a greater extent than others, can readily imagine the effects suggested by the hypnotist and so tend to translate these into their own behavior (Silva & Kirsch, 1992).

Hypnosis: Contrasting Views about Its Nature

Now let's consider a more complex question: Is hypnosis real? In other words, does it produce actual changes in consciousness and other psychological processes? Systematic research on hypnosis has led to the formulation of several contrasting views concerning this issue.

The Social–Cognitive or Role-Playing View The first of these approaches, known as the **social–cognitive** or **role-playing view of hypnosis,** suggests that in fact there is nothing strange or mysterious about hypnosis. On the contrary, the effects it produces are simply a reflection of a special type of relationship between the hypnotist and the subject. According to this perspective, persons undergoing hypnosis have generally seen many movies and read stories about hypnosis. Thus, they have clear ideas about what it involves and what, supposedly, will happen to them when hypnotized. These views lead such persons to play a special *social role*—that of *hypnotic subject.* This role implies that they will be "in the hypnotist's power," unable to resist the hypnotist's suggestions. When they are then exposed to hypnotic inductions—instructions to behave in certain ways or to experience specific feelings—they tend to obey, since this is what the social role they are enacting indicates *should* happen. Further, they often report experiencing the changes in perceptions and feelings that they *expect* to experience (e.g., Lynn, Rhue, & Weekes, 1990; Spanos, 1991).

It's important to note that this view does *not* imply that persons undergoing hypnosis engage in conscious efforts to fool others—that they are faking. On the contrary, they sincerely believe that they are experiencing an altered state of consciousness and that they have no choice but to act and feel as the hypnotist suggests (Kinnunen, Zamansky, & Block, 1994). But these behaviors and experiences are due primarily to their beliefs about hypnosis and the role of hypnotic subject rather than to the special skills of the hypnotist or their entry into an altered state of consciousness.

Social–Cognitive or Role-Playing View of Hypnosis: A view suggesting that effects produced by hypnosis are the result of hypnotized persons' expectations about and their social role as "hypnotized subject."

Neodissociation Theory of Hypnosis: A theory suggesting that hypnotized individuals enter an altered state of consciousness in which consciousness is divided.

The Neodissociation View The second major approach to hypnosis—known as the **neodissociation theory**—is very different. It suggests that hypnosis operates by inducing a split or dissociation between two basic aspects of consciousness: an *executive function,* through which we regulate our own behavior, and a *monitoring function,* through which we observe it.

According to Hilgard (1986, 1993), the most influential supporter of this view, these two aspects of consciousness are normally linked. Hypnosis, however, breaks this bond and erects a cognitive barrier—often referred to as *hypnotic amnesia*—that prevents experiences during hypnosis from entering into normal consciousness. The result is that persons who are hypnotized are indeed in a special altered state of consciousness, in which one part of their mind accepts suggestions from the hypnotist, while the other part—which Hilgard terms "the hidden observer"—observes the procedures without participating in them. Because of the split in consciousness produced by hypnosis, this theory suggests these two cognitive mechanisms are no longer in direct contact with each other. So, for example, if hypnotized persons are told to put their arms into icy water but informed that they will experience no pain, they will obey and will report no discomfort. If asked later to describe their feelings in writing, however, they may indicate that they *did* experience feelings of intense cold (Hilgard, 1979).

More recently, Bowers and his associates (e.g., Bowers, 1992; Woody & Bowers, 1994) have modified this view by suggesting that hypnotism does not necessarily split consciousness. Rather, it simply weakens control by the executive function over other aspects of consciousness. Thus, these subsystems can be invoked directly by the hypnotist's suggestions in an automatic manner that is not mediated by normal cognitive mechanisms.

Which of these views is correct? Existing evidence presents a complex picture (e.g., Noble & McConkey, 1995; Reed et al., 1996). On the one hand, most evidence seems to favor the social–cognitive view, and this is the position adopted by most psychologists. That is, it appears that most of the unusual or bizarre effects observed under hypnosis can readily be explained in terms of hypnotized persons' beliefs in the effects of hypnotism and their efforts—not necessarily conscious—to behave in accordance with these expectations. On the other hand, there are some findings that do seem to suggest that there may be a bit more to hypnotism than this: that it may indeed involve a distinct, and in some ways unusual, state of consciousness (e.g., Noble & McConkey, 1995). Let's look briefly at both types of evidence.

Evidence for the Social–Cognitive View First, let's consider the effects of hypnotism on perception. Under hypnosis, some persons seem to experience dramatic changes in their ability to perceive various stimuli. For example, as I noted earlier, they may report little pain even when exposed to painful stimuli such as ice-cold water (Spanos et al., 1990). Further, when told by the hypnotist that they will not be able to perceive certain stimuli that are presented to them, or—alternatively—that they will "perceive" stimuli that are *not* actually there, many persons report such effects (e.g., Miller & Bowers, 1993). In other words, they seem to experience mysterious changes in perception. Are such shifts real? Or are the hypnotized persons merely reporting what they think the hypnotist wants them to report? Careful research on these effects offers strong support for the latter conclusion. For instance, in several studies, Spanos and his colleagues (Spanos et al., 1992) have used the following procedures.

Individuals are exposed to a tone they can readily hear on three different occasions. After hearing it the first time, they rate its loudness. Then they are hypnotized and told that they will not be able to hear it. When the tone is presented again, they do tend to rate it lower in loudness than on the first trial. Now comes the crucial part. Before the tone is presented again, some (those in a *demand instruction* group) are told that they have probably slipped back into hypnosis and probably won't be able to hear the tone very well. In contrast, those in a *control* group are not given these instructions. Spanos reasons that if persons in the demand instruction group rate the tone as lower than those in the control group, this provides strong evidence that hypnotized persons do *not* actually experience changes in perception; rather, they are simply reporting what they think the hypnotist wants to hear (they are responding to what psychologists term *demand characteristics*). Results have strongly supported this latter conclusion (see Figure 4.10). Thus, it appears that changes in perception under hypnosis do not represent actual changes in how people perceive the world; rather, they are the result of people's expectations and their desire to live up to their role of hypnotized subject.

In a similar manner, other effects attributed to hypnosis—for example, distortions in memory induced by a hypnotist's suggestions—have been found to be largely the result of hypnotized persons' expectations and their desire to do what the hypnotist wants them to do. For example, when told that they will remember events that didn't happen, hypnotized persons often report such false memories. When offered a monetary reward for being accurate, however, they no longer make such errors (Murrey, Cross, & Whipple, 1992).

Taken together, such findings seem to offer support for the social–cognitive view of hypnosis: the view that the effects of hypnotism stem primarily from hypnotized persons' beliefs about hypnotism, plus their tendency to meet the hypnotist's expectations (Green & Lynn, 1995).

And Yet . . . Some Evidence for the Neodissociation View

Now, having noted that most scientific evidence argues against the view that hypnosis produces dramatic shifts in consciousness, I must report that there are a few findings consistent with the opposite point of view—findings that seem to provide support for some version of the neodissociation theory (e.g., Reed et al., 1996). Perhaps the most dramatic findings offering support for the neodissociation view are those from research in which hypnotized persons are told that they have undergone a sex change—that they are now female if they were male, or male if they were female (e.g., McConkey, 1991). Consider a study by Noble and McConkey (1995) that used such procedures.

In this investigation, two groups of persons previously identified as being (1) exceptionally or (2) highly susceptible to hypnosis were hypnotized and

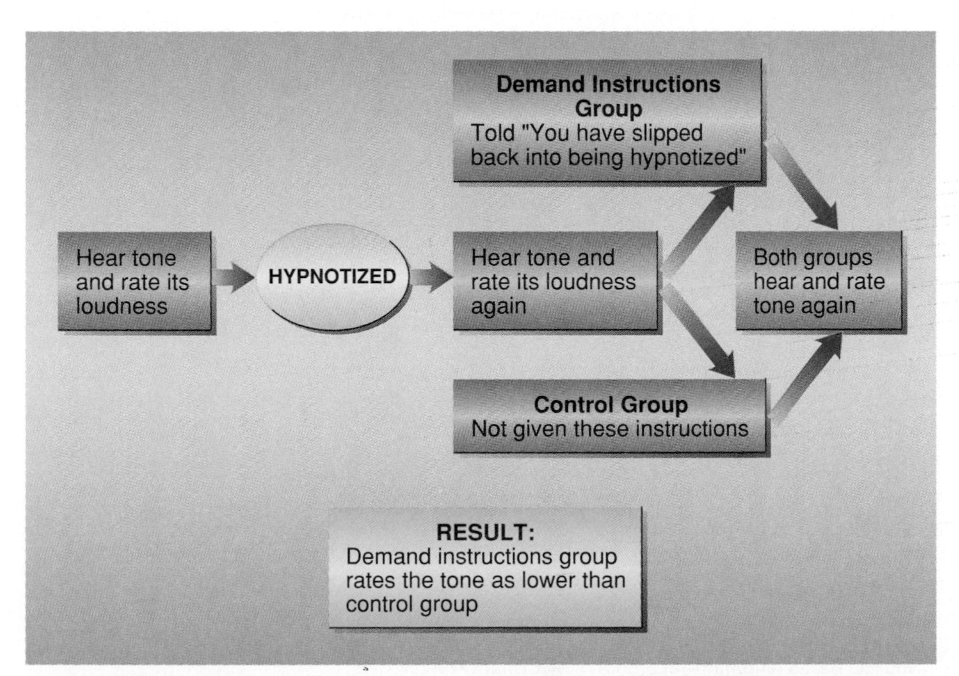

(**Source:** Based on suggestions and data from Spanos, Burgess, & Perlini, 1992.)

FIGURE 4.10

One Technique for Testing the Social–Cognitive View of Hypnosis

Many of the effects produced by hypnotism may be the result of hypnotized persons' expectations and their efforts to play the social role of "hypnotized subject."

told that they had undergone a sex change. Persons in a third group, previously found to be low in susceptibility to hypnosis, were not hypnotized; but they were given the same suggestion and told to *simulate* the reactions they would have if they had been hypnotized. Following these procedures, all participants were asked to indicate their sex. As expected, almost all persons in all three groups gave responses consistent with the hypnotic suggestion: they reported a sex change.

Now came the most interesting part of the study: The participants' reports that they had undergone a sex change were challenged in two different ways. First, the participants were told that a doctor had examined them and said that they had not undergone a sex change. They were then asked to indicate how they would respond. Second, they were shown their own image on a television monitor and asked again about their current biological sex. Noble and McConkey reasoned that if persons who had been hypnotized and those who were merely simulating reacted differently to these two challenges, then evidence for actual shifts in perception—and therefore for real changes in consciousness under hypnosis—would be obtained. This is just what happened. For example, a higher proportion of persons exceptionally susceptible to hypnosis than of those in the other two groups maintained their belief in a sex change when it was challenged by a physician. Similarly, a higher proportion of the exceptionally susceptible persons—"virtuosos"—maintained their belief in a sex change when confronted with their own image on a television monitor. Moreover, a higher proportion of these virtuosos changed their name to match the sex change (see Figure 4.11).

Findings such as these suggest that hypnotism can, perhaps, produce actual changes in perception among some persons, and may therefore represent an altered state of consciousness. The important point to emphasize,

FIGURE 4.11

Hypnotism: Some Surprising Results

When persons who are exceptionally susceptible to hypnotism (virtuosos) are told under hypnosis that they have undergone a sex change, they accept this suggestion and resist later efforts to change it. In contrast, persons who are less susceptible to hypnosis, or nonhypnotized participants who have been asked to simulate being hypnotized, surrender their belief in a sex change more readily. These findings seem to suggest that hypnosis may indeed produce actual changes in perception or consciousness among some people.

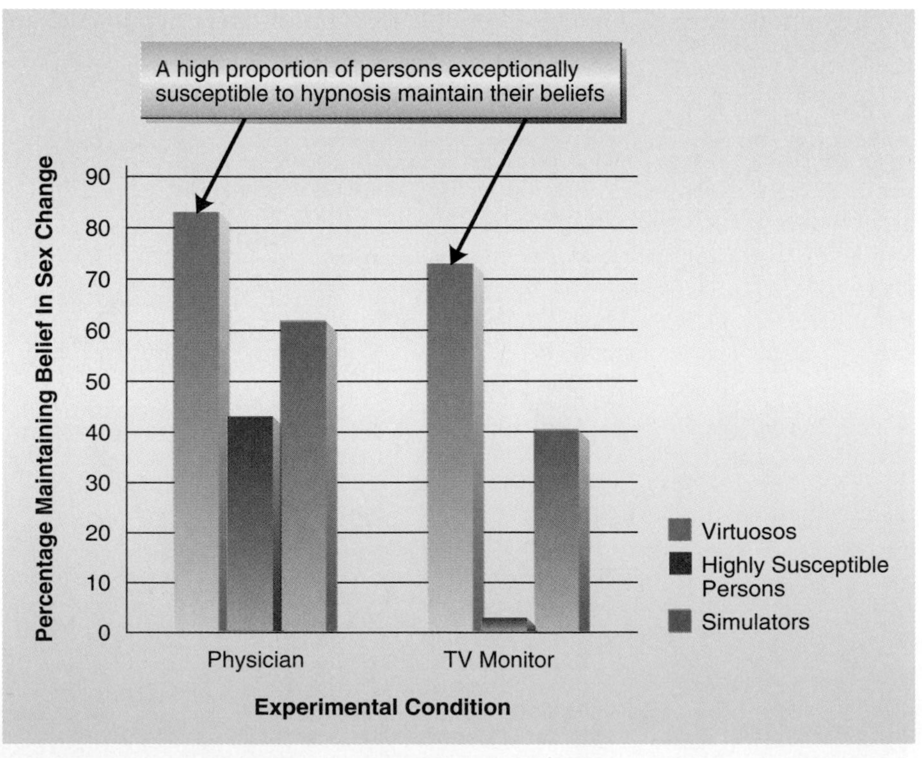

(**Source:** Based on data from Noble & McConkey, 1995.)

however, is captured by the phrase *some persons.* If such effects exist—and it is by no means certain that they do—then they appear to occur among only a relatively small number of persons, those who are exceptionally susceptible to hypnosis and the suggestions it involves. In contrast, most persons—an overwhelming majority—react to hypnosis largely in terms of their beliefs and expectations about it, and do *not* seem to enter an altered state of consciousness. Please see the **Ideas to Take with You** on page 156 for an overview of these ideas, which—I hope!—you'll remember when you read or hear about hypnosis in the years ahead.

Key Questions

- What is hypnosis?
- How do the social–cognitive and neodissociation views of hypnosis differ?
- What evidence supports the social–cognitive view?
- Is there any evidence for the neodissociation view? If so, what is this evidence?

Consciousness-Altering Drugs: *What They Are and What They Do*

Have you ever taken aspirin for a headache? Do you drink coffee or soft drinks to boost your alertness or energy? If so, you are in good company: each day, many millions of persons all around the world use drugs to change the way they feel—to alter their moods or states of consciousness. Much of this use of consciousness-altering drugs is completely legal—aspirin and soft drinks are freely available everywhere, and many other drugs are consumed under a doctor's supervision. In many cases, however, people use drugs that are illegal, or use legal ones to excess. The effects of doing so can be both dramatic and tragic, so in this final section of this chapter, we'll consider several issues relating to the use of consciousness-altering drugs.

Drugs: Chemical compounds that change the functioning of biological systems.

Consciousness-Altering Drugs: Some Basic Concepts

Let's begin with some basic issues. First, what are **drugs?** One widely accepted definition states that drugs are compounds that, because of their chemical structure, change the functioning of biological systems (Grilly, 1989). *Consciousness-altering drugs,* therefore, are drugs that produce changes in consciousness (Wallace & Fisher, 1987).

Suppose you went to your medicine cabinet and conducted a careful inventory of all the drugs present. How many would you find? Unless you are very unusual, quite a few (see Figure 4.12). Many of these drugs are probably perfectly legal and can be obtained in any pharmacy without a prescription (for example, aspirin). Others are proba-

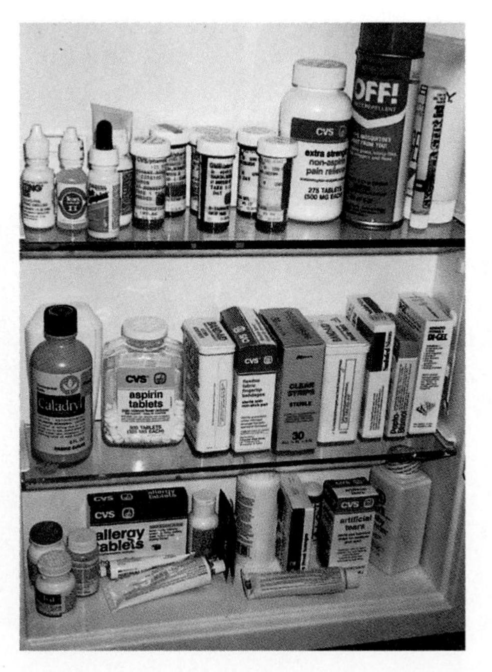

FIGURE 4.12

My Family Medicine Cabinet

My family medicine cabinet contains quite a few drugs, prescription and nonprescription. How does your own medicine cabinet compare?

Ideas to Take with You

The Facts about Hypnotism

Scientific research on hypnotism points to the following conclusions. Please keep them in mind whenever you encounter this controversial topic.

Do hypnotists have special powers that enable them to bend other persons to their will?

No, unless being very persuasive is viewed as a "special power." Hypnotists' effects on their subjects can be explained in terms of well-known psychological processes, such as persuasion and the subjects' expectations that the hypnotist will be able to influence them.

Does hypnotism produce an altered state of consciousness?

Most evidence indicates that it does not, unless a strong desire on the part of the hypnotized persons to act in accordance with their expectations and to play the role of hypnotized subject is viewed in these terms.

Are hypnotized persons faking?

No, most evidence indicated that such persons are not consciously faking; they believe that the effects they experience or report are real.

Will hypnotized persons do things they ordinarily would not do?

To some extent, they will. Persons who are hypnotized will often do or say things they would normally view as silly or inappropriate. And while they may resist a hypnotist's suggestions to engage in actions that are potentially dangerous or harmful, they may be induced to perform such behaviors if they believe strongly enough that the hypnotist can control their will.

Are some people more susceptible to hypnotism than others?

Absolutely. Such differences are large: while some individuals are highly susceptible to hypnosis, others cannot be hypnotized at all.

How can you prevent someone from hypnotizing you?

The best protection against being hypnotized is simply to maintain your skepticism about hypnotism and its effects on you. If you don't expect to be affected by a hypnotist, you probably won't be.

bly drugs prescribed by a physician. Using drugs in both categories is generally both safe and appropriate. The term **drug abuse,** therefore, applies only to instances in which people take drugs purely to change their moods, and in which they experience impaired behavior or social functioning as a result (Wallace & Fisher, 1987).

Unfortunately, when people consume consciousness-altering drugs on a regular basis, they often develop **dependence**—they come to need the drug and cannot function without it. Two types of dependence exist. One, **physiological dependence,** occurs when the need for the drug is based on organic factors, such as changes in metabolism. This type of dependence is what is usually meant by the term *drug addiction.* However, people can also develop **psychological dependence,** in which they experience strong desires to continue using the drug even though, physiologically, their bodies do not need it. As we'll soon see, several psychological mechanisms probably contribute to such dependence. Physiological and psychological dependence often occur together, magnifying individuals' cravings for and dependence on specific drugs.

Continued use of a drug over a prolonged period of time often leads to drug **tolerance**—a physiological reaction in which the body requires larger and larger doses in order to experience the same effects. For example, I once had a friend who drank more than twenty cups of coffee each day. He didn't start out this way; rather, he gradually increased the amount of coffee he consumed over the years until he reached the level where, we joked, he sloshed as he walked! In some cases, one drug increases tolerance for another; this is known as **cross-tolerance.**

Psychological Mechanisms Underlying Drug Abuse: Contrasting Views

At first glance, drug abuse is a puzzling form of behavior. Use of drugs, after all, carries considerable risk of harm. Why, then, do so many people engage in this behavior? Let's consider several possibilities.

The Learning Perspective: Rewarding Properties of Consciousness-Altering Drugs Several explanations for why people use consciousness-altering drugs derive from basic principles of learning—principles we'll consider in detail in Chapter 5. One approach suggests that people use such drugs because doing so feels good; in other words, the effects produced by the drugs are somehow rewarding (Wise & Bozarth, 1987). Evidence supporting this view is provided by many studies indicating that animals will self-administer many of the same drugs that people abuse, presumably because they find the effects of these drugs rewarding (Young & Herling, 1986).

On the other side of the coin, use of consciousness-altering drugs has also been attributed to the fact that these substances reduce *negative* feelings such as stress, anxiety, or physical discomfort. Thus, people take drugs to reduce negative feelings rather than simply to generate positive ones (Cooper et al., 1995). This explanation is especially applicable when individuals have become dependent on a drug; the negative symptoms they experience when it is no longer consumed—known as *withdrawal*—may provide a powerful incentive to obtain the drug at all costs.

The Psychodynamic Perspective: Coping with Unconscious Fears and Desires As we saw in Chapter 1, the psychodynamic perspective views human behavior as stemming from unconscious conflicts among hidden aspects of personality. This perspective suggests another

Drug Abuse: Instances in which individuals take drugs purely to change their moods, and in which they experience impaired behavior or social functioning as a result.

Dependence: Strong need for a particular drug and inability to function without it.

Physiological Dependence: Strong urges to continue using a drug based on organic factors such as changes in metabolism.

Psychological Dependence: Strong desires to continue using a drug even though it is not physiologically addicting.

Tolerance: Habituation to a drug, causing larger and larger doses to be required to produce effects of the same magnitude.

Cross-Tolerance: Increased tolerance for one drug that develops as a result of taking another drug.

explanation for drug abuse: Perhaps individuals use drugs to reduce the anxiety generated by such inner turmoil. While this is an intriguing idea, it is very difficult to test scientifically. Thus, it currently receives little attention from psychologists.

The Social Perspective: Drug Abuse and Social Pressure A third perspective suggests that drug abuse can be understood largely in terms of social factors. According to this view, individuals—especially adolescents and young adults—use consciousness-altering drugs because it is the "in" thing to do. Their friends use these drugs, and they believe that if they do too, this will enhance their social image. Evidence for this view has recently been reported by Sharp and Getz (1996). These researchers asked several hundred students to complete a questionnaire designed to measure their use of alcohol, their motivation to gain others' liking, and their perceptions of their own success at *impression management*—making a good impression on others. The researchers found that persons who reported using alcohol regularly did, in fact, report stronger motivation to gain others' liking and higher perceived success at impression management than persons who did not use alcohol frequently. These findings offer support for the view that some people do use alcohol—and perhaps abuse it—as a tactic of impression management, one means of looking good in the eyes of others.

The Cognitive Perspective: Drug Abuse as Automatic Behavior Do you remember reading about the distinction between automatic and controlled processing earlier in this chapter? This distinction forms the basis for yet another perspective on drug abuse. According to this view, the cognitive systems controlling many aspects of obtaining and consuming various drugs may take on the character of automatic processes. To the extent this occurs, drug use becomes quick and relatively effortless, occurs without conscious intention, is difficult to inhibit, and may even take place in the absence of conscious awareness. Once individuals have used a drug on numerous occasions, then, they may find themselves responding almost automatically to external cues—for example, to a specific environment in which they have often enjoyed this drug, such as a bar, or to specific sights and smells, such as the aroma of a burning cigarette. In a similar manner, they may respond automatically to internal cues or emotions, such as wanting to celebrate or feeling tired or out of sorts. These cues may trigger people's tendencies to use drugs, and they may find themselves doing so before they realize it, even without any strong urge to take a drug (Tiffany, 1990).

Which of these perspectives is most accurate? Most psychologists favor a view that combines the learning, social, and cognitive perspectives. Drug abuse, it appears, stems from a combination of factors; and this—sadly—is one reason why it is so difficult to combat.

Key Questions

- What are drugs? What is drug abuse?
- What are physiological and psychological dependence on drugs?
- How does the learning perspective explain drug abuse?
- How does the social perspective explain drug abuse?
- How does the cognitive perspective explain drug abuse?

Consciousness-Altering Drugs: An Overview

Depressants: Drugs that reduce activity in the nervous system and therefore slow many bodily and cognitive processes. Depressants include alcohol and barbiturates.

While many different drugs affect consciousness, most seem to fit under one of four major headings: *depressants, stimulants, opiates,* or *psychedelics* and *hallucinogens.*

Depressants Drugs that reduce both behavioral output and activity in the central nervous system are called **depressants.** Perhaps the most important of these is *alcohol*, a likely candidate for the most widely consumed drug in the world. Small doses seem, subjectively, to be stimulating—they induce feelings of excitement and activation. Larger doses, however, act as a depressant. They dull the senses so that feelings of pain, cold, and other forms of discomfort become less intense. This is why alcohol was widely used to deaden the pain of medical operations before more effective painkillers became available. Large doses of alcohol interfere with coordination and with the normal functioning of our senses (see Table 4.2 on page 162), often with tragic results for motorists. Alcohol also lowers social inhibitions so that after consuming large quantities of this drug, people become less restrained in their words and actions and more likely to engage in dangerous forms of behavior such as aggression. But cultural factors seem to play an important role in such effects, as described in the Exploring Gender and Diversity section below. Alcohol seems to produce its pleasurable effects by stimulating special receptors in the brain. Its depressant effects may stem from the fact that it interferes with the capacity of neurons to conduct nerve impulses, perhaps by affecting the cell membrane directly.

Barbiturates: Drugs that act as depressants, reducing activity in the nervous system and behavior output.

Barbiturates, which are contained in sleeping pills and relaxants, constitute a second type of depressant. First manufactured in the late nineteenth century, these drugs depress activity in the central nervous system and reduce activation and mental alertness. How these effects are produced is not certain, but some evidence suggests that barbiturates may reduce the release of excitatory neurotransmitters by neurons in many different locations. Initially, high doses of barbiturates can produce feelings of relaxation and euphoria—a kind of drunkenness without alcohol. They often go on to produce confusion, slurred speech, memory lapses, and reduced ability to concentrate. Wide swings of emotion, from euphoria to depression, are also common. Extremely large doses can be fatal, because they result in paralysis of centers of the brain that regulate breathing. This is a real danger, because tolerance to barbiturates gradually develops, leading individuals to use larger doses of these drugs.

Because some barbiturates induce sleep, people often try to use them to treat sleep disorders such as insomnia. However, these drugs do not seem to produce normal sleep. They suppress REM sleep, and this sleep stage may rebound sharply after individuals stop taking the drugs.

Alcohol and Aggression: A Cross-Cultural Comparison

Does consuming alcohol make people aggressive? Scientific evidence on this issue suggests that it does, especially in situations where the individuals involved have been exposed to some kind of provocation (Baron & Richardson, 1994). However, such effects are not inevitable: under conditions where individuals believe that aggression is inappropriate or can lead to punishment, persons who have consumed alcohol are not necessarily more aggressive than those who have not (e.g., Leonard, 1989). These latter findings raise another question: Are the effects of alcohol on aggression largely the result of the impact of this drug on the nervous system? Or do cultural factors, such as beliefs about the impact of alcohol on aggression, play a role too? A study by Lindman and Lang (1994) offers support for the latter view.

In this investigation, more than one thousand students in eight different countries (Belgium, Finland, France, Italy, Panama, Poland, Spain, the United States) completed questionnaires designed to measure their beliefs about the effects of alcohol on aggression and on many other aspects of behavior—for instance, effects on mood, irritability, attention seeking, and wild or noisy behavior. Results indicated the existence of large differences across the eight countries. For instance, students in the United States, Spain, Belgium, and Panama believed that there was a strong link between consuming alcohol and behaving aggressively. In contrast, students in France, Italy, and Poland perceived a much weaker relationship between these variables. And more important, these beliefs were apparently translated into overt behavior: Students in the United States and Panama, for instance, reported having observed more instances of alcohol-related aggression during the last year than those in France or Italy.

These findings suggest that cultural factors do play an important role in the relationship between alcohol and aggression. Consciousness-altering drugs certainly do affect the nervous system, and so our perceptions of the world around us. But the impact of these effects on our overt behavior is often filtered through cognitive factors, which may include the beliefs and values of our culture. The result: Individuals' tendency to attribute their own or others' aggressive behavior to the impact of alcohol and other drugs may differ greatly around the world.

Stimulants Drugs that produce the opposite effects of depressants—feelings of energy and activation—are known as **stimulants.** Included in this category are **amphetamines** and **cocaine.** Both of these stimulants inhibit the reuptake of the neurotransmitters dopamine and norepinephrine. As a result, neurons that would otherwise stop firing continue to respond. Such drugs raise blood pressure, heart rate, and respiration—signs of activation produced by the sympathetic nervous system. In addition, stimulants yield short periods of pleasurable sensations, twenty to forty minutes during which users feel extremely powerful and energetic. Users pay dearly for such feelings, however; for as the drug wears off, they often experience an emotional crash involving anxiety, depression, and fatigue.

In the past, cocaine was widely praised as a valuable medical drug and was added to many patent medicines. Freud believed that it was useful in treating such illnesses as asthma, indigestion, and even addiction to alcohol or other drugs. But continued use of cocaine can produce harmful effects, including a loss of appetite and intense feelings of anxiety, so it is clearly a dangerous drug.

Cocaine is usually consumed by *snorting,* a process in which it is inhaled into each nostril. There it is absorbed through the lining of the nose directly into the bloodstream. Cocaine can also be swallowed, usually in liquid form, but this produces weaker effects. When cocaine is heated and treated chemically, a form known as **crack** is produced. This can be smoked, and when it is, the drug affects the brain almost instantly. This produces a high during which individuals experience powerful feelings of energy, confidence, and excitement. While cocaine is not usually considered to be addicting, it often produces strong psychological dependence. And crack appears to have much stronger effects of this type. In order to obtain it, heavy users turn to prostitution, theft, and anything else they can think of that will provide enough money for the next dose.

Other stimulants in common use include *caffeine,* found in coffee, tea, and many soft drinks, and *nicotine,* found in tobacco. Many experts view nicotine as highly addicting, and there has recently been a great deal of controversy in the United States over charges that large tobacco companies have sometimes increased the amount of nicotine in cigarettes in order to hook smokers more strongly. Whether these charges are true or not, it is clear that once people begin smoking on a regular basis, many find it almost impossible to stop (see Figure 4.13). So please think carefully before *you* start down this path.

Opiates Among the most dangerous drugs in widespread use are the **opiates.** These drugs include opium, morphine, heroin, and related synthetic drugs. Opium is derived from the opium poppy—remember the scene in *The*

Stimulants: Drugs that increase activity in the nervous system (e.g., amphetamines, caffeine, nicotine).

Amphetamines: Drugs that act as stimulants, increasing feelings of energy and activation.

Cocaine: A powerful stimulant that produces pleasurable sensations of increased energy and self-confidence.

Crack: A derivative of cocaine that can be smoked. It acts as a powerful stimulant.

Opiates: Drugs that induce a dreamy, relaxed state and, in some persons, intense feelings of pleasure. Opiates exert their effects by stimulating special receptor sites within the brain.

For Better or For Worse® **by Lynn Johnston**

FIGURE 4.13

Smoking: A One-Way Street for Most People

Like the character in this cartoon, many people find it almost impossible to stop smoking once they start. That's an important point to remember before you take up this practice.

Wizard of Oz where Dorothy and the Cowardly Lion fall asleep in a field of beautiful poppies? Morphine is produced from opium, while heroin is obtained from morphine. Opiates produce lethargy and a pronounced slowing of almost all bodily functions. These drugs also alter consciousness, producing a dreamlike state and, for some people, intensely pleasurable sensations. The costs associated with these thrills are high, however. Heroin and other opiates are extremely addicting, and withdrawal from them often produces agony for their users. Growing evidence indicates that the brain produces substances (opioid peptides or endorphins) closely related to the opiates in chemical structure and also contains special receptors for them (Phillips & Fibiger, 1989). This suggests one possible explanation for the pain experienced by opiate users during withdrawal. Regular use of opiates soon overloads endorphin receptors within the brain. As a result, the brain ceases production of these substances. When the drugs are withdrawn, endorphin levels remain depressed. Thus, an important internal mechanism for regulating pain is disrupted (Reid, 1990b). To make matters worse, tolerance for opiates such as heroin increases rapidly with use, so physiological addiction can occur very quickly.

Psychedelics and Hallucinogens Perhaps the drugs with the most profound effects on consciousness are the **psychedelics,** drugs that alter sensory perception and so may be considered mind-expanding, and **hallucinogens,** drugs that generate sensory perceptions for which there are no external stimuli. The most widely used psychedelic drug is *marijuana.* Use of this drug dates back to ancient times; indeed, marijuana is described in a Chinese guide to medicines from the year 2737 B.C. Marijuana was widely used in the United States and elsewhere for medical purposes as late as the 1920s. It could be found in almost any drugstore and purchased without a prescription. It was often prescribed by physicians for headaches, cramps, and even ulcers. Starting in the 1920s, however, the tide of public opinion shifted, and by 1937 marijuana was outlawed completely in the United States. When smoked or eaten—for example, in cookies—marijuana produces moderate arousal in the form of increased blood pressure and pulse rate; a perceived increase in the intensity of various stimuli such as sounds, colors, or tastes; and distortion in the sense of time. Unfortunately, marijuana also interferes with the ability to judge distances, an effect that can lead to serious accidents when users of the drug drive a car or operate machinery. Other effects reported by some, but not all, users include reduced inhibitions, increased sexual pleasure (which may simply reflect increased sensitivity to a wide range of stimuli), and feelings of relaxation.

Psychedelics: Drugs that alter sensory perception and so may be considered mind-expanding (e.g., marijuana).

Hallucinogens: Drugs that generate sensory perceptions for which there are no external stimuli (e.g., LSD).

Marijuana is in widespread use throughout the world, mostly as a recreational drug. There have been few studies of its long-term effects, although the research that has been performed reports few adverse effects (e.g., Page, Fletcher, & True, 1988). Yet continued use of marijuana does pose certain dan-

LSD: A powerful hallucinogen that produces profound shifts in perception; many of these are frightening in nature.

gers. First, the perceptual distortions it produces can result in tragedy when users drive or operate power machinery. Second, because it is an illegal drug in many nations, marijuana is often blended with other substances, with the result that users never know exactly what they are getting. Third, there is some indication that long-term use of marijuana may result in shifts in personality toward passivity and a general lack of motivation (Baumrind, 1984). These potential risks should be carefully weighed against the potential pleasures some people report obtaining from this drug.

More dramatic effects are produced by *hallucinogens*—drugs that produce vivid hallucinations and other perceptual shifts. Of these, the most famous is **LSD** (lysergic acid diethylamide), or *acid.* After taking LSD, many persons report profound changes in perceptions of the external world. Objects and

TABLE 4.2

Effects of Consciousness-Altering Drugs: A Summary

The effects of many different consciousness-altering drugs are summarized here.

Depressants: Reduce behavioral output and activity in the central nervous system		
Alcohol: Deadening of pain Reduced coordination Interference with normal functioning of senses Reduced social inhibitions	**Barbiturates:** Reduced mental alertness; confusion; euphoria; memory lapses; suppression of REM sleep	
Stimulants: Induce feelings of energy and activation		
Amphetamines: Elevation of blood pressure, heart rate, respiration Feelings of alertness and energy, followed by depression as effects wear off	**Caffeine:** Mild feelings of increased alertness Mild diuretic effect (increased urination)	**Cocaine and derivatives:** (including crack): Feelings of tremendous power and energy Intense pleasure Psychological dependence (cocaine) Powerful addiction (crack)
Opiates: Produce lethargy and slowing of many bodily functions; induce dreamlike state and pleasurable sensations		
Opium: Deadening of pain Dreamlike state Pleasurable feelings Powerful addiction	**Morphine:** Effects similar to those of opium but even stronger	**Heroin:** Effects like those of opium and morphine, but with intensified pleasurable sensations Powerful addiction
Psychedelics and Hallucinogens: Psychedelics alter sensory perception; hallucinogens generate sensory perceptions for which there are no external stimuli		
Psychedelics (e.g., marijuana): Moderate arousal Increased intensity of various stimuli Distortions in sense of time Diminished ability to judge distances For some people, feelings of increased sexual pleasure and relaxation	**Hallucinogens** (e.g., LSD): Profound changes in perceptions Blending of sensory experiences Sense of menace in ordinary situations Effects that vary greatly within and among individuals	

people seem to change color and shape; walls may sway and move; and many sensations seem to be more intense than normal. There may also be a strange blending of sensory experiences so that colors produce feelings of warmth or cold, while music yields visual sensations. Such effects may sound exciting, but many others produced by LSD are quite negative. Objects, people, and even one's own body may seem distorted or threatening. Users may experience deep sorrow or develop intense fear of close friends and relatives. Perhaps worst of all, the effects of the drug are unpredictable; there is no way of knowing in advance whether LSD will yield mostly pleasant or mostly unpleasant effects. In fact, the same person may experience radically different effects at different times. Unless you are willing to gamble with your own health, therefore, LSD is certainly a drug to avoid. For information on another dangerous consciousness-altering drug, please see the Beyond the Headlines section below. And for an overview of the effects of many different drugs, see Table 4.2.

Beyond the Headlines

As Psychologists See It

Drugged in Colombia: Street Thugs Dope Unwitting Victims

Taking Candy from Strangers Ill-Advised in Bogota

Albany Times Union, May 11, 1996—Bogota, Colombia—If you thought cocaine was bad news, wait until you hear about Burundanga.

Burundanga is a kind of Colombian voodoo powder obtained from a common local plant. . . . Used for hundreds of years by Native Americans in religious ceremonies, the powder when ingested causes victims to lose their will and memory, sometimes for days. . . .

It seems that everyone in Bogota knows someone who has been victimized by the drug. . . . In one common scenario, a person will be offered a soda or drink laced with the substance. The next thing the person remembers is waking up miles away, extremely groggy and with no memory of what happened. People soon discover that they handed over jewelry, money, or car keys, and sometimes have even made multiple bank withdrawals for the benefit of their assailants. "The victim can't say no; he has no will and becomes very open to suggestion. It's like a chemical hypnotism," says Dr. Uribe. "From the moment it's given, the victim remembers absolutely nothing of what happened. . . ."

Frightening stuff, eh? A drug that totally destroys the will, turning those who take it into chemical slaves with no will of their own. The article goes on to cite several disturbing incidents in which people have been victimized by this drug. In one, for example, an architect accepted a candy from two strangers. He woke up the next day to discover that he had made thirteen withdrawals from the bank—all of which he gave to the criminals who had drugged him. In even more horrifying cases, young women are given this drug by criminals who then proceed to abuse them sexually. When they wake up, several days later, they have no memories of what happened to them and can't identify their attackers.

These are frightening events, and the article concludes by warning all visitors to Colombia to avoid talking to strangers and never to leave their food or drinks unprotected—someone may dump Burundanga into them! How do psychologists react to such reports? Certainly with concern—but also with a healthy dash of skepticism. Is there such a thing as a drug that, in a single dose, totally destroys the will? If so, it is unlike any other drug known at the present time. And closer examination reveals that Burundanga is closely related to *scopolamine,* a drug that has been used for many years as a sedative and to combat motion sickness. How, then, could it turn human beings into mindless robots with no will of their own? There seems to be no scientific basis for predicting such effects.

Perhaps most important, the article consists of informal reports by persons who have either been the victim of this drug or witnessed its effects. As you can readily see, this is *not* scientific evidence for the claimed effects. Perhaps Burundanga has these effects; perhaps—but it is also possible that the claims are exaggerated, or that the drug was mixed with other substances, or that only certain people are susceptible to its effects: the list goes on and on. What we have here, in essence, is a series of informal observations that the report then uses to draw a strong conclusion. Psychologists would certainly be interested in this report—it suggests the possible existence of a drug with powerful consciousness-altering effects. But they—and you—should require more convincing evidence before jumping to the conclusion that Burundanga actually produces these effects. The moral: Yes, certainly take the precautions suggested if you happen to visit Colombia. You don't want to take a chance on being drugged by strangers, and this practice appears to be one common form of crime in that country. But pending scientific study, remain skeptical about the claims that this drug has effects unlike those of any other now known.

Critical Thinking Questions

1. How could the actual effects of Burundanga be tested?
2. What kind of evidence would be required before we could conclude that this drug does indeed temporarily destroy the human will?
3. How do Burundanga's reported effects compare with those claimed for hypnotism?

A Note on the Psychology of Drug Effects

In my comments so far, I may have given you the impression that each drug always produces specific effects. Before concluding, I should point out that this is not entirely accurate. While specific drugs do generally produce the effects described above, drugs' impacts may vary, depending on many other factors.

First, as we saw in the case of alcohol, the impact of a drug is often determined by expectations. If users expect a drug to produce certain effects (for instance, to increase their sex drive or reduce their anxiety), such effects are much more likely to occur than if users do not anticipate them.

Second, drug effects depend on users' physical states. Some people are naturally more tolerant of various drugs than others, so in these people it takes a larger dose to produce the effects others experience from smaller doses. In addition, the effects of a specific drug may depend on whether the person taking it is fatigued or well rested, whether he or she has recently eaten, and many other factors.

Third, the effects of various drugs depend on previous experience. First-time users of alcohol or tobacco generally report very different reactions to these substances than people who have used them for quite some time. The same is true for many other drugs that alter mood or consciousness.

Finally, the influence of a given drug depends on what other drugs users are also taking. In medicine, careful physicians check on the possibility of *drug interactions,* in which the impact of a drug is altered by the presence of other drugs, before issuing prescriptions. People who take various illegal drugs, however, rarely consider possible interactions between them—sometimes with tragic results.

In sum, the influence of drugs on feelings, behavior, and consciousness is neither certain nor fully predictable. Many factors can determine the magnitude and direction of such effects. This is yet another reason why, where drugs are concerned, the basic guideline should always be *caution.*

Key Questions

- What are the effects of depressants?
- Do cultural factors play a role in the effects of alcohol on behavior?
- What are the effects of stimulants? Opiates? Psychedelics? Hallucinogens?
- What factors influence the behavioral effects of a given drug?

Meditation: Procedures designed to produce altered states of consciousness in which awareness of and contact with the external world are reduced.

Meditation: Changing Your Own Consciousness

Over the centuries, travelers from Europe who visited India returned with amazing tales about the strange abilities of *yogis*—members of special religious orders. Such persons, the travelers reported, could walk barefoot over hot coals and lie on beds of nails without experiencing pain. Further, it was reported, some could enter a self-induced trance in which they could even bring their own hearts to a virtual stop!

Were such reports true? Existing evidence is mixed, at best, but one fact *is* clear; there are indeed techniques through which at least some individuals can produce important shifts in their own consciousness, and in which they are less responsive than usual to the external word (Shapiro, 1980). Several techniques for producing such changes exist, but among these **meditation** is by far the most popular.

Why would you—or anyone else—want to use this technique? Because, it appears, doing so can help to counter the adverse effects of stress—a topic we'll consider in detail in Chapter 13. In fact, some research on the effects of meditation suggests that heartbeat, oxygen consumption, and other bodily processes do in fact slow down during meditation (e.g., Wallace & Benson, 1972). Similar effects can be produced simply by resting, but some evidence indicates that larger shifts in physiological processes—and in consciousness—are produced by meditation (Benson & Friedman, 1985). So, in essence, meditation may offer one safe and relatively convenient means for taking a brief break from the strains of everyday life—a break that can help you feel refreshed and ready for the tasks that are sure to follow when you resume your regular routine.

Fortunately, learning to meditate is not difficult. In fact, by practicing the steps below, you can soon learn to bring on a relaxed state—a potentially beneficial change in your own consciousness. Here's how to proceed:

- **First, find a quiet, isolated spot.** Meditation doesn't require lots of time, but it *does* require you to focus your attention inward, away from the outside world. The first step, then, is finding a location where you can be alone and undisturbed for twenty minutes to a half an hour (see Figure 4.14).
- **Choose a word or set of words on which you can concentrate.** Focusing on a specific word that you repeat to yourself over and over again—silently or in a very low voice—can help you shift your attention inward. The trick is to clear your mind of everything else and to focus only on the word or phrase you have chosen as you repeat it over and over. (This word or phrase is often referred to as a mantra.)
- **Gain practice in meditating.** The hardest part of meditation is learning to keep your thoughts from slipping away from your mantra, back to the worries, cares, and concerns of everyday life. At first you may find this difficult, but if you practice and really try, you can quickly acquire such self-discipline. Start with a short period—say, five minutes or so—and then gradually increase your meditating time as you gain practice.
- **Examine how you feel after meditating.** As you gain practice in meditating, compare how you feel at the end of each session with how you felt at the beginning. Many people report that they experience feelings of relaxation and a relief of tension.
- **Meditate for about twenty minutes each day, or whenever you feel especially tense.** As you master the skill of focusing your attention on your chosen word and screening out other distracting thoughts, gradually increase your period of meditation to about twenty minutes.

FIGURE 4.14

Meditation: One Way to Change Your Own Consciousness

Millions of persons around the world engage in some form of meditation. Many of these people report that meditation helps to make them feel calmer, happier, and more in control of their lives. Can you obtain such benefits? You may want to try meditation yourself to find out.

Summary and Review of Key Questions

Biological Rhythms: Tides of Life—and Conscious Experience

- **What are biological rhythms? What are circadian rhythms?** Biological rhythms are regular fluctuations in our bodily processes. Circadian rhythms are biological rhythms that occur within a single day.
- **How do morning persons and night persons differ?** Morning persons feel most alert and energetic early in the day. Night (evening) persons feel most alert and energetic late in the day.
- **What effects do jet lag and shift work have on circadian rhythms?** Travel across time zones and shift work can produce disturbances in circadian rhythms. Knowledge of circadian rhythms suggests effective ways of avoiding such disturbances.
- **How do psychologists use diary studies to study circadian rhythms and disruptions in them?** In diary studies individuals record their own moods, physical states, and performance at regular intervals. Using such information, psychologists can determine how various aspects of behavior change over the course of a day or, sometimes, over longer periods of time.

KEY TERMS

states of consciousness, p. 132 • biological rhythms, p. 132 • circadian rhythms, p. 132 • suprachiasmatic nucleus, p. 133 • morning person, p. 134 • night (evening person), p. 134 • diary approach, p. 136

Waking States of Consciousness

- **What is the difference between automatic processing and controlled processing?** In automatic processing, we perform activities without directing conscious attention to them. In controlled processing, we direct conscious attention to various activities.
- **What are daydreams? What are some of the major themes they contain?** Daydreams are thoughts and images that we generate internally. Common themes in daydreams include success or failure, aggression or hostility, sexual or romantic fantasies, guilt, and problem solving.
- **How are daydreams influenced by television watching?** Television seems to encourage daydreaming, perhaps by providing individuals with exciting images from which they can construct their daydreams. However, it seems to discourage creative imagination, the ability to generate many novel or unusual ideas.
- **What are sexual fantasies? How do they differ for women and men?** Sexual fantasies consist of mental images that are sexually arousing or erotic to the individual who has them. The sexual fantasies of women and men appear to differ in several respects. Men's erotic fantasies contain more explicit visual imagery and more frequently feature more than one partner; women's fantasies often contain greater reference to affection and emotions, a story line, and more reference to themes of submission.

KEY TERMS

automatic processing, p. 139 • controlled processing, p. 139 • daydreams, p. 139 • fantasies, p. 139 • sexual fantasies, p. 140

Sleep: The Pause That Refreshes?

- **How do psychologists study sleep?** Researchers often study sleep by examining EEG changes—changes in electrical activity in the brain—that occur as people fall asleep.
- **What are the major stages of sleep?** There appear to be four major stages of sleep, each successive stage showing shifts in the EEG and reduced awareness of the outside world. In addition, there is another distinct stage of sleep—REM sleep.
- **What happens during REM sleep?** During REM sleep the EEG shows a pattern similar to that of waking, but the activity of body muscles is almost totally suppressed. Most dreams occur during REM sleep.
- **What are the effects of sleep deprivation?** Although people undergoing sleep deprivation report feeling tired and irritable, they can function quite well even after long sleepless periods.
- **What functions does sleep seem to serve?** Growing evidence indicates that sleep serves important functions related to restoration of bodily resources and to basic circadian rhythms.
- **What are some of the most common sleep disorders?** Insomnia is difficulty in falling or staying asleep; somnambulism is walking in one's sleep; narcolepsy is a tendency to fall suddenly into a deep sleep in the midst of waking activities.
- **What steps help promote a good night's sleep?** Steps that may help you get a good's night sleep include these: read something pleasant or relaxing just before going to sleep; arrange your schedule so you go to sleep at the same time each night; take a warm bath or have a massage before going to sleep; avoid coffee or tea late in the day; exercise every day, but not just before going to sleep; don't smoke; don't nap during the day.
- **During what stage of sleep do dreams usually occur?** Dreams usually occur during REM sleep.
- **Do most people dream? How long do dreams last?** Almost everyone dreams. The longer dreams seem to be, the longer they last in actual time.
- **How do the psychodynamic, physiological, and cognitive views of dreams differ?** The psychodynamic view, made famous by Freud, suggests that dreams reflect suppressed thoughts, wishes, and impulses. The physiological view suggests that dreams reflect the brain's interpretation of random neural activity that occurs while we sleep. The cognitive view holds that dreams result from the fact that many systems of the brain are active during sleep while input from muscles and sensory systems is inhibited.
- **What are dreams of absent-minded transgression, and what do they tell us about the meaning of dreams?** In dreams of absent-minded transgression, individuals who are trying to change their own behavior—for example, to stop smoking or drinking alcohol—dream that they have performed the unwanted behaviors in an absent-minded manner, without meaning to do so. These DAMIT dreams suggest that there are sometimes significant links between dreams and waking behavior.

KEY TERMS

sleep, p. 141 • electroencephalogram (EEG), p. 142 • alpha waves, p. 142 • delta waves, p. 142 • REM (rapid eye movement) sleep, p. 142 • insomnia, p. 145 • somnambulism, p. 146 • night terrors, p. 146 • apnea, p. 146 • hypersomnias, p. 146 • narcolepsy, p. 146 • dreams, p. 147 • dreams of absent-minded transgression, p. 148

Hypnosis: Altered State of Consciousness . . . or Social Role Playing?

- **What is hypnosis?** Hypnosis involves a special type of interaction between two persons in which one (the hypnotist) induces changes in the behavior, feelings, or cognitions of the other (the subject) through suggestions.
- **How do the social–cognitive and neodissociation views of hypnosis differ?** The social–cognitive view suggests that the effects of hypnosis stem from the hypnotized person's expectations and his or her efforts to play the role of hypnotized subject. The neodissociation view suggests that the effects of hypnotism stem from a split in consciousness in which executive cognitive functions (those that allow us to control our own behavior) are separated from other cognitive functions (those that allow us to observe our own behavior).
- **What evidence supports the social–cognitive view?** The social–cognitive view is supported by the finding that persons

who are led to believe that they have "slipped back into hypnosis" but are not hypnotized often behave like those who have been hypnotized.

- **Is there any evidence for the neodissociation view? If so, what is this evidence?** Some evidence offers support for the neodissociation view. For instance, it has been found that when persons who are exceptionally susceptible to hypnosis are given the suggestion that they have undergone a sex change, they resist even very strong evidence contrary to this suggestion.

KEY TERMS

hypnosis, p. 150 • social–cognitive or role-playing view of hypnosis, p. 151 • neodissociation theory of hypnosis, p. 151

Consciousness-Altering Drugs: What They Are and What They Do

- **What are drugs? What is drug abuse?** Drugs are substances that, because of their chemical structure, change the functioning of biological systems. Drug abuse involves instances in which people take drugs purely to change their moods, and in which they experience impaired behavior of social functioning as a result.
- **What are physiological and psychological dependence on drugs?** In physiological dependence, strong urges to continue using a drug are based on organic factors, such as changes in metabolism. In psychological dependence, people experience strong desires to continue using a drug even though it is not physiologically addicting.
- **How does the learning perspective explain drug abuse?** The learning perspective suggests that people abuse drugs because they find the experience rewarding or because these drugs help to lessen stress, anxiety, and other negative feelings.
- **How does the social perspective explain drug abuse?** The social perspective suggests that people abuse drugs because of strong social pressures to do so, or because they believe that doing so will enhance their social image.
- **How does the cognitive perspective explain drug abuse?** The cognitive perspective proposes that drug abuse may be at least in part an automatic behavior triggered by the presence of external cues.
- **What are the effects of depressants?** Depressants reduce both behavioral output and activity in the central nervous system. Important depressants include alcohol and barbiturates.
- **Do cultural factors play a role in the effects of alcohol on behavior?** Yes. For example, in cultures where it is widely believed that consuming alcohol leads to aggression, such effects are actually observed. In cultures where this belief is weaker or absent, however, there is no clear link between alcohol consumption and aggression.
- **What are the effects of stimulants? Opiates? Psychedelics? Hallucinogens?** Stimulants produce feelings of energy and activation. Opiates produce lethargy and pronounced slowing of many bodily functions, but also induce intense feelings of pleasure in some persons. Psychedelics such as marijuana alter sensory perception, while hallucinogens such as LSD produce vivid hallucinations and other bizarre perceptual effects.
- **What factors influence the behavioral effects of a given drug?** A specific dose of a given drug may have very different effects for the same person at different times, depending on such factors as the person's expectations, physical state, and other drugs he or she has taken recently.

KEY TERMS

drugs, p. 155 • drug abuse, p. 157 • dependence, p. 157 • physiological dependence, p. 157 • psychological dependence, p. 157 • tolerance, p. 157 • cross-tolerance, p. 157 • depressants, p. 158 • barbiturates, p. 159 • stimulants, p. 160 • amphetamines, p. 160 • cocaine, p. 160 • crack, p. 160 • opiates, p. 160 • psychedelics, p. 161 • hallucinogens, p. 161 • LSD, p. 162 • meditation, p. 164

Critical Thinking Questions

Appraisal

Most psychologists believe that states of consciousness can be studied in a scientific manner. Do you agree? Or do you feel that this is stretching the definition of psychology, "the science of behavior," beyond the breaking point? Why do you hold the opinion that you do?

Controversy

Hypnosis is one of the most controversial topics of research in the study of states of consciousness. Many psychologists doubt that hypnosis produces an altered state of consciousness. Yet there is some evidence consistent with the view that it does. What are your views? What kind of evidence would help to resolve this issue once and for all?

Making Psychology Part of Your Life

Now that you have some basic understanding of states of consciousness, can you think of ways in which you can put this information to practical use? For example, how might you change your own daily schedule so as to take advantage of high points in your own circadian rhythms? What can you do to help improve your sleep? Will you be less willing to "experiment" with various drugs or to refrain from smoking now that you know more about the risks these actions may involve? List at least three ways in which you can put the information in this chapter to practical use in your own life.

CHAPTER OUTLINE

Learning

How We're Changed by Experience

Is it possible to locate precisely where learning takes place in the brain? Have you ever gotten ill after eating a favorite food—and then wondered why, even years later, just the thought of that food makes you feel queasy? Can people overcome severe stage fright? How do animals at Sea World learn to perform complex sequences of behaviors, while your dog does not seem to comprehend even simple commands like "sit"? Does watching violence on television cause children to perform violent acts? If you've wondered about issues like these, then you are already familiar with one of the most basic topics in psychology—*learning.* Indeed, the learning process is crucial to all organisms, including people, since it helps us adapt to changing conditions in the world around us.

In this chapter we'll examine several basic principles that help to explain how many forms of behavior are affected by experience. Psychologists refer to these effects on behavior as learning. Specifically, they define **learning** as *any relatively permanent change in behavior, or behavior potential, produced by experience.* Several aspects of this definition are noteworthy. First, the term *learning* does not apply to temporary changes in behavior such as those stemming from fatigue, drugs, or illness. Second, it does not refer to changes resulting from maturation—the fact that you change in many ways as you grow and develop. Third, learning can result from *vicarious* as well as from direct experiences; in other words, you can be affected by observing events and behavior in your environment as well as by participating in them (Bandura, 1986). Finally, the changes produced by learning are not always positive in nature. As you well know, people are as likely to acquire bad habits as good ones.

Learning is a key process in human behavior. Indeed, learning appears to play an important role in virtually every activity we perform.

There can be no doubt that learning is a key process in human behavior. Indeed, learning appears to play an important role in virtually every activity we perform—from mastering complex skills to falling in love. Although the effects of learning are diverse, many psychologists believe that learning occurs in several basic forms: *classical conditioning, operant conditioning,* and *observational learning.* We'll begin with *classical conditioning,* a form of learning in which two stimulus events become associated in such a way that the occurrence of one event reliably predicts the occurrence of the other. Classical conditioning is the basis for many learned fears, including stage fright, and also helps explain how we acquire aversions to certain foods or beverages. Next, we'll turn to *operant conditioning,* a form of learning in which organisms learn associations between behaviors and stimuli that precede them (antecedents) or follow them (consequences). Here, we'll see how psychologists have applied basic operant principles to promote certain behaviors, such as recycling and occupational safety, and to discourage others, such as self-injury. Finally, we'll explore *observational learning,* a form of learning in which organisms learn by observing the behaviors—and the consequences of the behaviors—of others around them.

Classical Conditioning: *Learning That Some Stimuli Signal Others*

Imagine that during a very hectic semester, you find yourself with a class schedule that leaves absolutely no time for lunch. After a few days, you lose your ability to concentrate during your afternoon classes because all you can think about is food. A friend tells you about a vending area where she buys microwaveable snacks, including popcorn. As it turns out, this solution works out well; you love popcorn, it is ready in only a few minutes, and you find that it is even possible to do other things while the popcorn is popping—like cram for tests—because a loud beep from the microwave signals when the popcorn is done. When you open the door of the microwave, the delightful aroma of freshly popped popcorn rushes out, causing you to salivate in anticipation of eating it. After several days, however, your mouth waters immediately after the beep, before you actually open the door to the microwave. Why should this occur? After all, at this point you can neither see nor smell the popcorn. The reason is actually fairly simple: The beep is

Learning: Any relatively permanent change in behavior (or behavior potential) resulting from experience.

always followed by the aroma and taste of the popcorn, so the beep comes to serve as a signal. Just hearing the beep, you expect the smell and taste of the popcorn to follow, and you react accordingly (see Figure 5.1).

The situation just described is a common example of **classical conditioning,** the first type of learning that we will consider. In classical conditioning, a physical event—termed a **stimulus**—that initially does not elicit a particular response gradually acquires the capacity to elicit that response as a result of repeated pairing with a stimulus that can elicit a reaction. Learning of this type is quite common and seems to play a role in such varied reactions as strong fears, taste aversions, some aspects of sexual behavior, and even racial or ethnic prejudice (Baron & Byrne, 1997). Classical conditioning became the subject of careful study in the early twentieth century, when Ivan Pavlov, a Nobel Prize–winning physiologist from Russia, identified it as an important behavioral process.

Classical Conditioning: A basic form of learning in which one stimulus comes to serve as a signal for the occurrence of a second stimulus. During classical conditioning, organisms acquire information about the relations between various stimuli, not simple associations between them.

Stimulus: A physical event capable of affecting behavior.

FIGURE 5.1

Classical Conditioning: A Simple Example

At first, the microwave's beep may startle you and cause you to look toward its source, but it will probably not cause you to salivate. After the beep has been paired with the aroma and taste of fresh popcorn on several occasions, however, you may find that you salivate to the beep alone. This "mouthwatering" reaction is a result of classical conditioning.

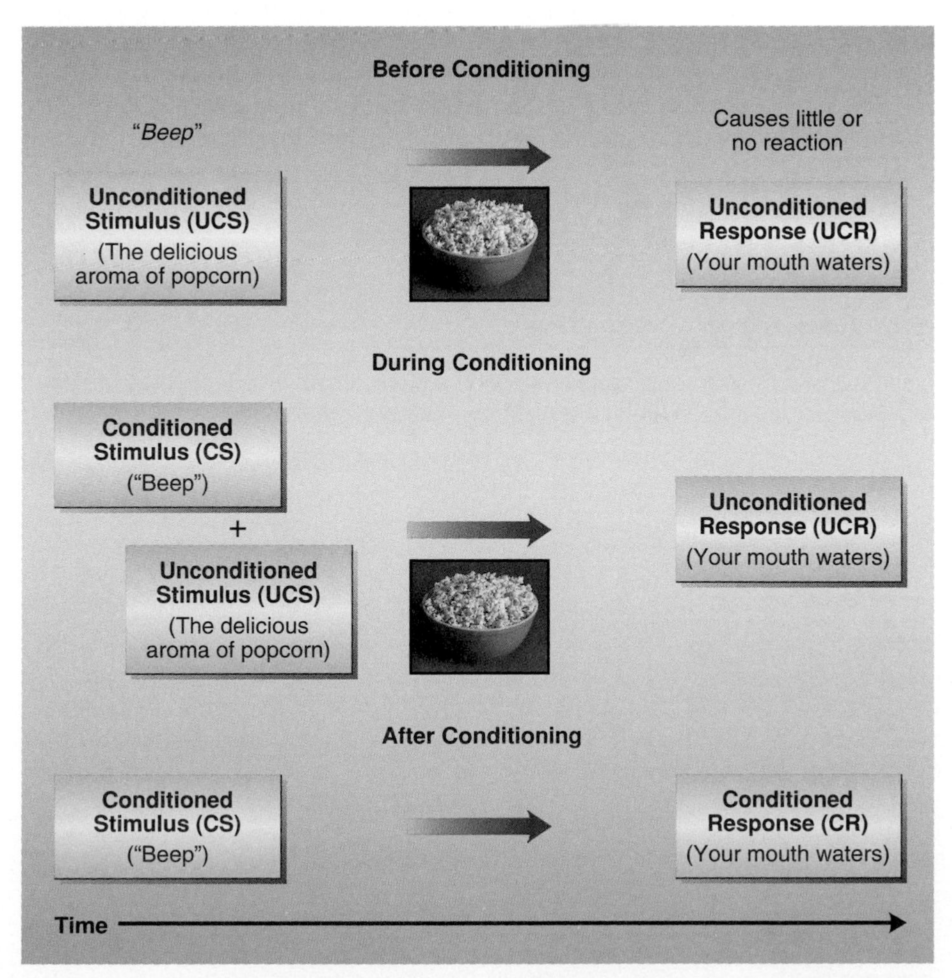

Unconditioned Stimulus (UCS): In classical conditioning, a stimulus that can evoke an unconditioned response the first time it is presented.

Unconditioned Response (UCR): In classical conditioning, the response evoked by an unconditioned stimulus.

Conditioned Stimulus (CS): In classical conditioning, the stimulus that is repeatedly paired with an unconditioned stimulus.

Conditioned Response (CR): In classical conditioning, the response to the conditioned stimulus.

Pavlov's Early Work on Classical Conditioning: Does This Ring a Bell?

Pavlov did not actually set out to investigate classical conditioning. Rather, his research focused on the process of digestion in dogs (see Figure 5.2). During his investigations Pavlov noticed a curious fact: Similar to the popcorn example described above, the dogs in his studies often began to salivate when they saw or smelled food but *before* they actually tasted it. Some even salivated at the sight of the pan where their food was kept or at the sight or sound of the person who usually brought it. This suggested to Pavlov that these stimuli had somehow become signals for the food itself: The dogs had learned that when the signals were present, food would soon follow.

Pavlov quickly recognized the potential importance of this observation and shifted the focus of his research accordingly. The procedures that he now developed were relatively simple. On *conditioning trials,* a neutral stimulus that had previously been shown to have no effect on salivation—a bell, for example—was presented. This was immediately followed by a second stimulus known to produce a strong effect on salivation: dried meat powder placed directly into the dog's mouth. The meat powder was termed the **unconditioned stimulus (UCS),** because its ability to produce salivation was automatic and did not depend on the dog's having learned the response. Similarly, the response of salivation to the meat powder was termed an **unconditioned response (UCR);** it too did not depend on previous learning. The bell was termed a **conditioned stimulus (CS),** because its ability to produce salivation depended on its being paired with the meat powder. Finally, salivation in response to the bell was termed a **conditioned response (CR).**

The basic question was whether the sound of the bell would gradually elicit salivation in the dogs as a result of its repeated pairing with the meat

FIGURE 5.2

Early Research on Conditioning

Ivan Pavlov, a Russian physiologist who won a Nobel Prize in 1904 for his work on digestion, is best known for his research on classical conditioning.

powder. In other words, would the bell elicit a conditioned response when it was presented alone? The answer was clearly *yes*. After the bell had been paired repeatedly with the meat powder, the dogs salivated upon hearing it, even when the bell was not followed by the meat powder.

Acquisition: The process by which a conditioned stimulus acquires the ability to elicit a conditioned response through repeated pairings of an unconditioned stimulus with the conditioned stimulus.

Classical Conditioning: Some Basic Principles

Let's turn now to the principles that govern the occurrence of classical conditioning.

Acquisition: The Course of Classical Conditioning In most instances, classical conditioning is a gradual process in which a conditioned stimulus gradually acquires the capacity to elicit a conditioned response as a result of repeated pairing with an unconditioned stimulus. This process—termed **acquisition**—proceeds quite rapidly at first, increasing as the number of pairings between conditioned and unconditioned stimulus increases. However, there is a limit to this effect; after a number of pairings of CS and UCS, acquisition slows down and finally levels off.

Although psychologists initially believed that conditioning was determined primarily by the number of conditioned–unconditioned stimulus pairings, we now know that this process is affected by other factors. As shown in Figure 5.3, one such factor is *temporal arrangement* of the CS–UCS pairings.

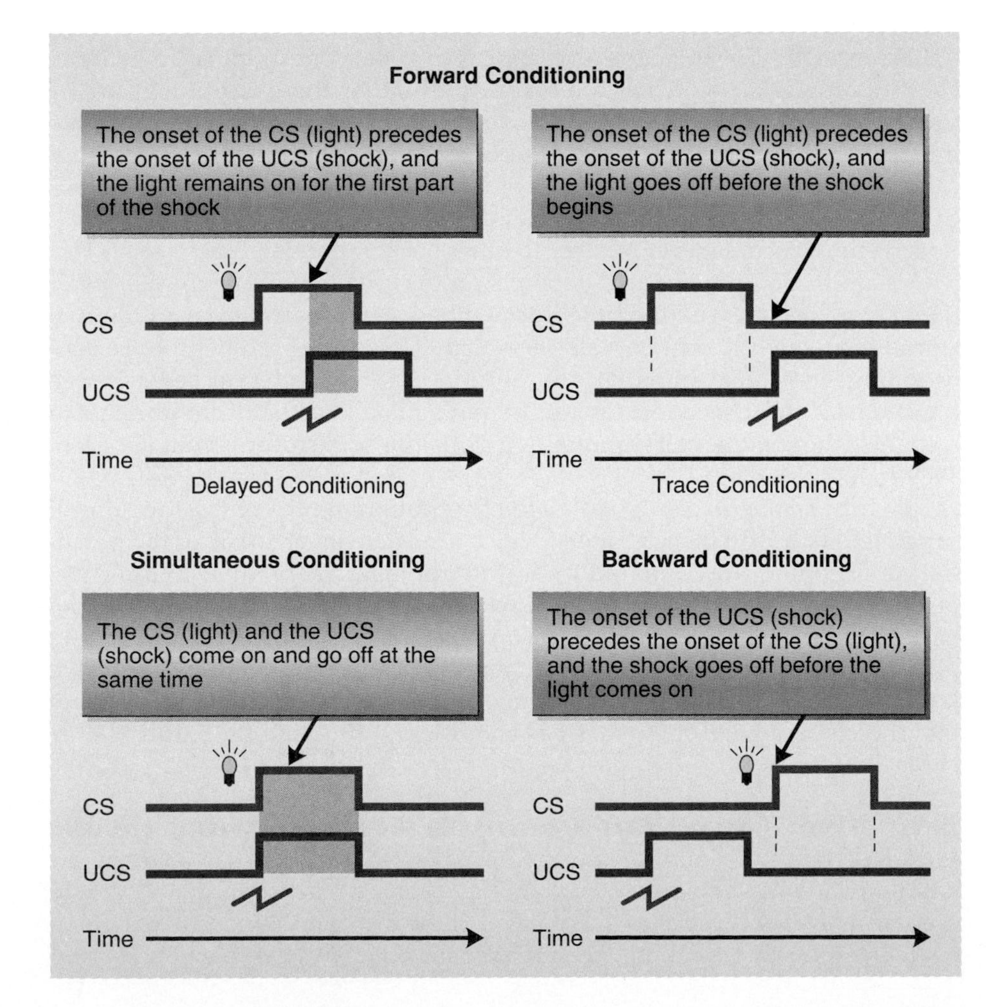

FIGURE 5.3

Temporal Arrangement of the CS and UCS Affects the Acquisition of a Conditioned Response

Four CS–UCS temporal arrangements commonly used in classical conditioning procedures are shown above. *Temporal* means time-related: the extent to which a conditioned stimulus precedes or follows the presentation of an unconditioned stimulus. *Delayed conditioning* generally produces the most rapid rate of learning. *Simultaneous* and *backward conditioning* are usually the least effective procedures.

Temporal means time-related: the extent to which a conditioned stimulus precedes or follows the presentation of an unconditioned stimulus. The first two temporal arrangements shown, **delayed conditioning** and **trace conditioning,** are examples of what is termed *forward conditioning,* since the presentation of the conditioned stimulus (light) always precedes the presentation of the unconditioned stimulus (shock). They differ, however, in that the CS and the UCS overlap to some degree in *delayed* conditioning, but not in trace conditioning. Two other temporal arrangements are **simultaneous conditioning,** in which the conditioned and unconditioned stimuli begin and end at the same time; and **backward conditioning,** in which the unconditioned stimulus precedes the conditioned stimulus.

Research suggests that *delayed conditioning* is generally the most effective method for establishing a conditioned response. This is because the conditioned stimulus often plays an important role in predicting forthcoming presentations of the unconditioned stimulus (Lieberman, 1990). To illustrate this point, consider the following example: You are taking a shower when suddenly the water turns icy cold. Your response—a startle reaction to the cold water—is an unconditioned response. Now imagine that just before the water turns cold, the plumbing makes a slight grinding sound. Because this sound occurs just before and overlaps with the onset of the icy water, delayed conditioning can occur. If this situation is repeated several times, you may acquire a startle reaction to the slight grinding sound; it serves as a conditioned stimulus. In contrast, suppose you do not hear the sound until after the water turns cold, as in backward conditioning, or until the precise instant at which it turns cold, as in simultaneous conditioning. In these cases, you will probably not acquire a startle reaction to the grinding sound, because it provides no information useful in predicting the occurrence of the icy water.

Several additional factors also appear to affect conditioning. In general, conditioning is faster when the *intensity* of either the conditioned or the unconditioned stimulus increases. However, it is not necessarily the absolute intensity of a stimulus that is most important to the conditioning process, but rather its relative intensity or degree of contrast with other background stimuli (Kamin, 1965). In other words, conditioning is more likely when conditioned stimuli stand out in relation to other background stimuli.

Second, conditioning also depends on the *conditioned stimulus–unconditioned stimulus* interval: the time interval between presentations of the two stimuli. Extremely short intervals—less than 0.2 second—rarely produce conditioning. In animal research, the optimal CS–UCS interval seems to be between 0.2 and 2 seconds; longer intervals make it difficult for animals to recognize the conditioned stimulus as a signal for some future event (Gordon, 1989).

Finally, *familiarity* can greatly affect conditioning. In contrast to stimuli selected for study in the laboratory, which are often novel, many of the potential conditioning stimuli found in the environment are familiar to us. Thus, our day-to-day experiences often teach us that certain stimuli, such as the background noise usually present in an office setting or the odors ordinarily present in our homes, do not predict anything unusual. In other words, we learn that these stimuli are largely irrelevant, which makes it highly unlikely that these stimuli will come to act as conditional stimuli in the future (Baker & Mackintosh, 1977).

Delayed Conditioning: A form of forward conditioning in which the presentation of the unconditioned stimulus (UCS) begins while the conditioned stimulus (CS) is still present.

Trace Conditioning: A form of forward conditioning in which the onset of the conditioned stimulus (CS) precedes the onset of the unconditioned stimulus (UCS) and the CS and UCS do not overlap.

Simultaneous Conditioning: A form of conditioning in which the conditioned stimulus (CS) and the unconditioned stimulus (UCS) begin and end at the same time.

Backward Conditioning: A type of conditioning in which the presentation of the unconditioned stimulus (UCS) precedes the presentation of the conditioned stimulus (CS).

Extinction: Once Conditioning Is Acquired, How Do We Get Rid of It?

Suppose you are one of several executives in a large marketing firm. You and your coworkers have been working night and day to prepare a proposal crucial to the survival of the firm, and things are not going well. Over the past week the president of the company has chewed you out at least a dozen times. Now, whenever you hear the unmistakable sound of his approaching footsteps, your heart starts racing and your mouth gets dry, even though he has not yet reached your office. Fortunately, the story has a happy ending—the company's directors are impressed by the proposal, and your boss is no longer angry when he enters your office. Will you continue to react strongly to his footsteps? In all likelihood, you won't. Gradually, his footsteps will cease to elicit the original conditioned response from you. The eventual decline and disappearance of a conditioned response in the absence of an *un*conditioned stimulus is known as **extinction.**

The course of extinction, however, is not always entirely smooth. Let's consider the behavior of one of Pavlov's dogs to see why this is true. After many presentations of a bell (conditioned stimulus) in the absence of meat powder (unconditioned stimulus), the dog no longer salivates in response to the bell. In other words, extinction has occurred. But if the CS (the bell) and the UCS (the meat powder) are again paired after the conditioned response of salivation has been extinguished, salivation will return very quickly—a process termed **reconditioning.**

Or suppose that after extinction, the experiment is interrupted: Pavlov is caught up in another project that keeps him away from his laboratory and the dog for several weeks. Now will the sound of the bell, the conditioned stimulus, elicit salivation? The answer is yes, but the reaction will be in a weakened form. The reappearance of the reaction after a time interval is referred to as **spontaneous recovery.** If extinction is then allowed to continue—that is, if the sound of the bell is presented many times in the absence of meat powder—salivation to the sound of the bell will eventually disappear.

Generalization and Discrimination: Responding to Similarities and Differences Suppose that because of several painful experiences, a child has acquired a strong conditioned fear of hornets—whenever she sees one or hears one buzzing, she shows strong emotional reactions and heads for the hills. Will she also experience similar reactions to other flying insects, such as flies? She almost certainly will, because of a process called **stimulus generalization,** the tendency of stimuli similar to a conditioned stimulus to elicit similar conditioned responses (Honig & Urcuioli, 1981; Pearce, 1986). As you can readily see, stimulus generalization often serves a useful function. In this example, it may indeed save the girl from additional stings. The red lights that we encounter at certain intersections while driving also illustrate the important function served by stimulus generalization; even though these signals often vary in brightness or shape, we learn to stop in response to all of them, and it's a good thing we do.

Many other species also turn the existence of stimulus generalization to their advantage. For example, some totally harmless insects resemble more dangerous species in coloring and so ward off would-be predators. Similarly, some frogs that would make a tasty mouthful for birds show markings highly similar to those of poisonous species, increasing their chances of survival.

Although stimulus generalization can serve an important adaptive function, it is not always beneficial and in some cases can be dangerous. For example, because of many pleasant experiences with parents and other adult relatives, a young child may become trusting of all adults through stimulus generalization; but this process will not be beneficial if it extends to certain strangers. You can understand why stimulus generalization can be maladaptive—even deadly. Fortunately, most of us avoid such potential problems through **stimulus discrimination**—a process of learning to respond to certain stimuli but not to others. A few years ago a friend was badly bitten by a dog. Until that incident she had had no fear of dogs. Because she was so

Extinction: The process through which a conditioned stimulus gradually loses the ability to evoke conditioned responses when it is no longer followed by the unconditioned stimulus.

Reconditioning: The rapid recovery of a conditioned response to a CS–UCS pairing following extinction.

Spontaneous Recovery: Following extinction, return of a conditioned response upon reinstatement of CS–UCS pairings.

Stimulus Generalization: The tendency of stimuli similar to a conditioned stimulus to evoke conditioned responses.

Stimulus Discrimination: The process by which organisms learn to respond to certain stimuli but not to others.

Key Questions

- What is learning?
- What is classical conditioning?
- Upon what factors does acquisition of a classically conditioned response depend?
- What is extinction?
- What is the difference between stimulus generalization and stimulus discrimination?

frightened by the attack, I was concerned that the incident would generalize to other breeds of dogs—perhaps even to her own dog. Thanks to stimulus discrimination, however, this didn't happen; my friend becomes fearful only when she encounters the breed of dog that bit her.

Classical Conditioning: The Neural Basis of Learning

Now that we've discussed the basic principles of classical conditioning, let's turn to another question that has puzzled scientists for many years—what is the neural basis of learning? In other words, what actually happens in the brain during classical conditioning, or in other forms of learning? Actually, psychologists have started to unravel this mystery, at least for relatively simple forms of behavior (Daum & Schugens, 1996). Several converging lines of evidence seem to indicate that the *cerebellum* and related brain circuitry play a significant role in learning (see Figure 5.4). As you may recall from Chapter 2, the cerebellum is a structure in the brain well known for its role in helping us to maintain our sense of balance and coordinate movements. But what is the evidence for the cerebellum's role in the acquisition of conditioned responses?

First, electrical recordings of the brains of laboratory animals show that the rate of neural firing of cells in the cerebellum predicts the onset of a conditioned response. Second, researchers have shown that electrical stimulation of specific pathways into the cerebellum can elicit the occurrence of both conditioned and unconditioned responses. Finally, when structures in the cerebellum of animals are surgically destroyed, previously learned associations can be severely disrupted, and the ability to learn new associations eliminated altogether (Thompson & Krupa, 1994).

FIGURE 5.4

The Neural Basis of Learning: The Role of the Cerebellum

Growing evidence shows that the cerebellum plays an important role in classical conditioning.

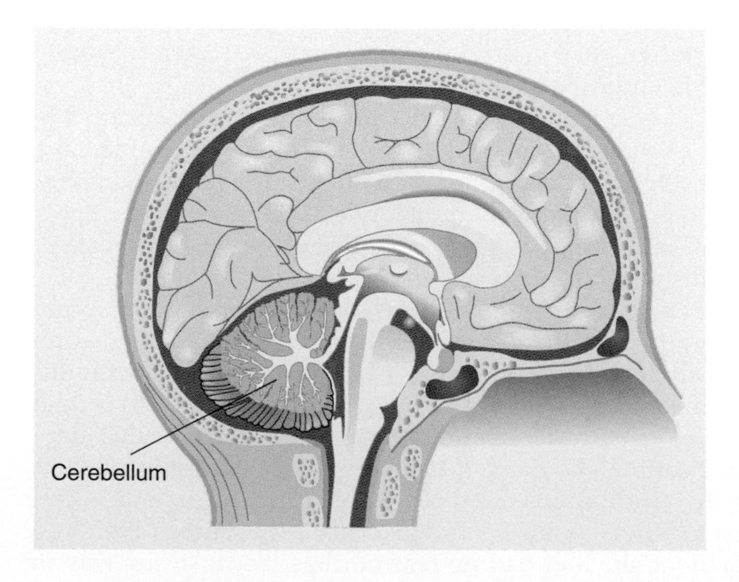

Studies of humans who have sustained damage to their cerebellum reveal a similar pattern of results. For example, careful research indicates that it is extremely difficult to establish conditioned responses with these persons. They blink normally (UCR) in response to a puff of air to the eye (UCS), indicating that their motor functions and ability to respond to external stimulation remain intact. However, efforts to establish a conditioned response to, say, a light or a tone are usually unsuccessful (Daum & Schugens, 1996; Topka et al., 1993). Related research has also revealed that the ability to acquire conditioned eye-blink responses seems to fade with age. Researchers believe that age-related declines in the number and efficiency of certain cells in the cerebellum may be the cause (Woodruff-Pak & Thompson, 1988).

In short, these findings provide strong evidence that the cerebellum plays a significant role in classical conditioning—at least for the relatively simple stimulus relationships just described. Additional intriguing research on more complex aspects of conditioning suggests a more complicated picture, including the involvement of other brain structures (e.g., Myers et al., 1996). Although scientists are just beginning to understand the complex relationship between brain functions and behavior, it is clear that our knowledge of the neural basis of learning is expanding at a rapid pace.

Classical Conditioning: Exceptions to the Rules

When psychologists began the systematic study of learning, around the turn of the century, they noticed that some species could master certain tasks more quickly than others could. Such findings sparked little interest, though, because early researchers saw their task as that of establishing general principles of learning—principles that applied equally well to all organisms and to all stimuli. For several decades it was widely assumed that such principles existed. Beginning in the 1960s, however, some puzzling findings began to accumulate. These results suggested that not all organisms learn all responses or all associations between stimuli with equal ease.

The most dramatic evidence pointing to such conclusions was reported by Garcia and his colleagues (Braverman & Bronstein, 1985; Garcia, Hankins, & Rusiniak, 1974). In perhaps the most famous of these studies, Garcia and Koelling (1966) allowed two groups of rats to sip saccharin-flavored water from a device that emitted a bright flashing light and a loud clicking noise (conditioned stimuli) whenever the rats licked the water. While both groups were drinking, one group of rats was exposed to X rays that later made them sick (an unconditioned stimulus); the other group received painful shocks to their feet (an unconditioned stimulus). Traditional principles of classical conditioning suggest that *both* groups of rats should have learned to avoid all three stimuli—the flavored water, the bright light, and the clicking noise. After all, for both groups, these stimuli were followed by a strong unconditioned stimulus (either X rays or a painful shock). But this was not what Garcia and Koelling found. Rats exposed to the painful shock learned to avoid the light and noise, but not the flavored water; rats that were made to feel ill learned to avoid the flavored water, but not the light or noise (see Figure 5.5 on page 178). In short, it seems that rats—and other organisms—are predisposed to associate nausea and dizziness with something they've consumed (the flavored water) and to associate pain with something they've seen or heard (the bright light and clicking noise). Similar findings from many different studies (e.g., Braverman & Bronstein, 1985) suggest that acquisition of a conditioned response does not occur with equal ease for different stimuli.

FIGURE 5.5

Biological Constraints and Characteristics of the CS and UCS Affect the Acquisition of a Conditioned Response

Rats quickly acquired an aversion to a flavored water when it was followed by X rays that made them ill, but they did *not* readily acquire an aversion to the flavored water when it was followed by an electric shock. In contrast, rats learned to avoid a light–noise combination when it was paired with shock, but *not* when it was followed by X rays. These findings indicate that classical conditioning cannot be established with equal ease for all stimuli and for all organisms.

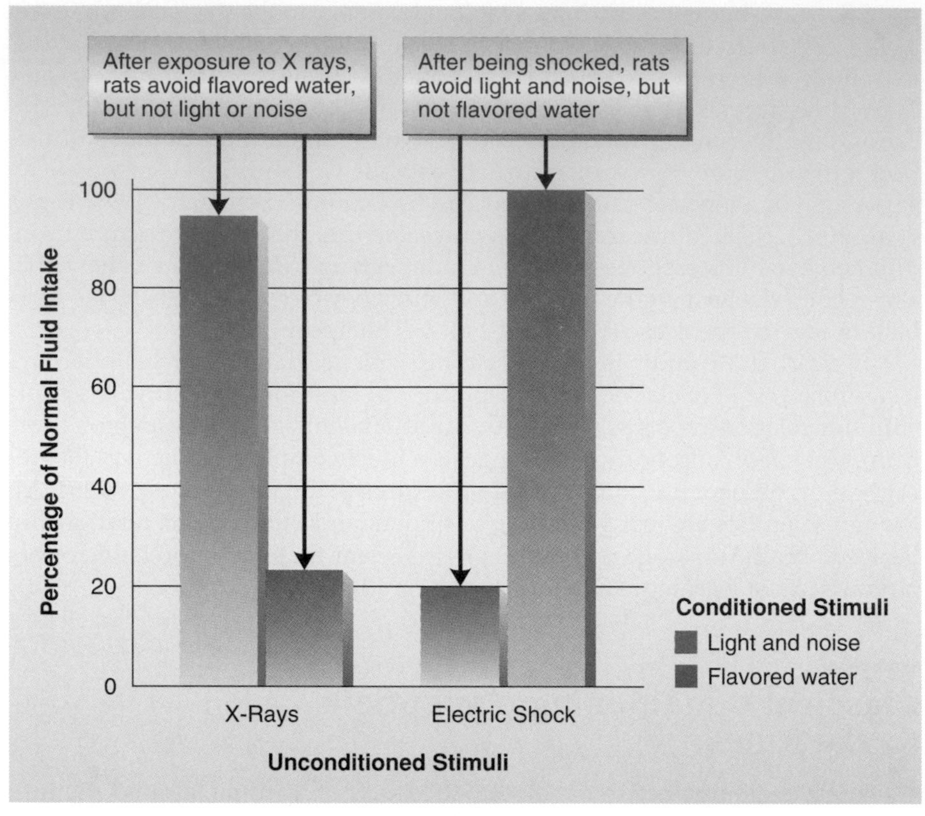

(**Source**: Based on data from Garcia & Koelling, 1966.)

Another intriguing outcome that emerged from Garcia and Koelling's study is also noteworthy: Although the rats who received the X rays did not get sick immediately, they still acquired an aversion to the taste of the flavored water. This finding contradicted the widely held belief that classical conditioning can occur only if the unconditioned stimulus follows the conditioned stimulus within a very short interval. I'll discuss learned taste aversions in greater detail shortly.

Further research has also shown that in regard to conditioning, important differences exist among species. Because of these **biological constraints on learning,** types of conditioning readily accomplished by some species are only slowly acquired by others. And often, the types of conditioning most readily accomplished by a species are the very ones it needs to survive in its normal habitat (Shettleworth, 1993). For example, rats eat a varied diet and are most active at night. Thus, it is especially useful for them to be able to associate specific tastes with later illness, since in many cases they can't see the foods they eat. In contrast, birds depend heavily upon vision for finding food. For a bird it is more useful to be able to form associations between visual cues and later illness (Wilcoxon, Dragoin, & Kral, 1971).

Biological Constraints on Learning: Tendencies of some species to acquire some forms of conditioning less readily than other species do.

Conditioned Taste Aversion: A type of conditioning in which the UCS (usually internal cues associated with nausea or vomiting) occurs several hours after the CS (often a novel food) and leads to a strong CS–UCS association in a single trial.

Conditioned Taste Aversions: Breaking All the Rules? As I've just noted, one of the clearest demonstrations of an exception to the rules of traditional classical conditioning involves what is termed **conditioned taste aversion**—a learned aversion to a particular food, based on feelings of illness following its ingestion. Conditioned taste aversions are important for survival because they inhibit the repeated ingestion of dangerous and toxic substances in animals' natural environment. Surveys show that food or beverage aversions are very common among humans (Logue, Logue, & Strauss, 1983; Logue, Ophir, & Strauss, 1981). Such aversions are unusually strong and can occur despite our thoughts about the actual cause of our illness. For example, many people report that even though they are convinced that a particular food or beverage was not the cause of the illness that followed, they continue to experience a taste aversion to that substance (Seligman & Hager, 1972).

The way in which these powerful associations are formed differs from most classical conditioning in several important respects. First, a conditioned taste aversion can usually be established with a single CS–UCS pairing, termed *one-trial learning,* in contrast to the many pairings involved in most Pavlovian conditioning. Second, conditioned taste aversions have been reported when the conditioned stimulus was presented hours before the occurrence of the unconditioned stimulus. In contrast, most instances of conditioning require a CS–UCS interval of not more than a few seconds. Finally, conditioned taste aversions are extremely resistant to extinction; in fact, they may last a lifetime.

FIGURE 5.6

Preventing Learned Taste Aversions: Putting Knowledge about Classical Conditioning to Work

Understanding classical conditioning can help solve many practical problems—such as the formation of learned taste aversions during cancer treatments.

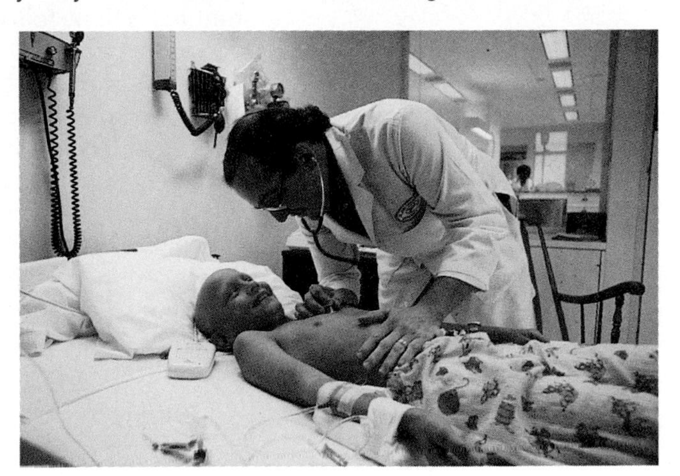

Conditioned taste aversions create serious problems for some people. For example, radiation and chemotherapy used to treat cancer often cause nausea or vomiting as a side effect (Burish & Carey, 1986). Thus, cancer patients may acquire taste aversions to food ingested before therapy sessions (see Figure 5.6). Several studies have in fact shown that conditioned taste aversions are common among patients receiving chemotherapy (Bernstein, 1978). Radiation and chemotherapy patients can take steps to reduce the likelihood of developing a conditioned taste aversion, however. First, patients receiving chemotherapy should arrange their meal schedules to decrease the chances of establishing an association between ingestion of the food and illness; the interval between their meals and chemotherapy should be as long as possible. Second, patients should eat familiar food, avoiding new or unusual foods before therapy. Because familiar foods have already been associated with feeling good, it is less likely that cancer patients will acquire an aversion to them. Finally, since the strength of a conditioned response is related to the intensity of the conditioned stimulus, patients should eat bland foods and avoid strongly flavored ones.

Our knowledge regarding learned taste aversions has also been used to help Western ranchers reduce the loss of livestock to predators such as wolves and coyotes (Garcia, Rusiniak, & Brett, 1977; Gustavson et al., 1974). By establishing a conditioned taste aversion for cattle and sheep, ranchers have been able to save livestock without having to kill the predators. To create the taste aversion, ranchers lace small amounts of mutton or beef with lithium chloride, a substance that causes dizziness and nausea. The predators eat the bait, become sick several hours later, and, as a result, learn to avoid sheep or cattle. One caution should be noted, however; some research has shown that taste aversions may be limited to the contexts in which they were established (Bonardi, Honey, & Hall, 1990; Nakajima, obayashi, & Imada, 1995). In other words, taste aversions established at one location may not extend to other places. Thus, ranchers should take this possibility into account when planning interventions to control predators.

Key Questions

- Where in the brain does classical conditioning take place?
- Is classical conditioning equally easy to establish with all stimuli for all organisms?
- How do we acquire conditioned taste aversions?

Classical Conditioning: A Cognitive Perspective

During his early conditioning experiments, Pavlov (1927) observed a curious thing. A dog was conditioned to the ticking of a metronome, which had been previously paired with the presentation of food. When the metronome was turned off, the dog sat in front of the machine and proceeded to whine and beg. Why? If conditioning involves only the development of an association between conditioned and unconditioned stimuli, then the dog should have responded only when the conditioned stimulus was presented. The fact that the dog appeared to beg for the ticking sound suggests that classical conditioning involves more than just a simple association. In fact, this and several related findings point to the following conclusion: Regular pairing of a conditioned stimulus with an unconditioned stimulus provides subjects with valuable *predictive* information; it indicates that whenever a conditioned stimulus is presented, an unconditioned stimulus will shortly follow. Thus, as conditioning proceeds, subjects acquire the *expectation* that a conditioned stimulus will be followed by an unconditioned stimulus; that is, a cognitive process takes place.

In this context, the dog's behavior is easy to understand. During conditioning, the dog learned that the ticking of the metronome signaled the delivery of food. Then, without any warning, this fickle machine stopped working. Obviously, something had to be done to get it started, so the dog acted on its expectancies; it whined and begged for the metronome to tick again. The idea that cognitive processes involving expectation play a role in classical conditioning is a thesis supported by several types of evidence (Rescorla & Wagner, 1972). First, conditioning fails to occur when unconditioned and conditioned stimuli are paired in a random manner. With random pairings, subjects cannot acquire any firm expectation that an unconditioned stimulus will indeed follow presentation of a conditioned stimulus. Therefore, for conditioning to occur, the CS–UCS pairing must be consistent.

Second, the cognitive thesis is supported by a phenomenon known as *blocking*—the fact that conditioning to one stimulus may be prevented by previous conditioning to another stimulus. For example, suppose that a dog is initially conditioned to a tone. After repeated pairings with presentation of meat powder, the tone becomes a conditioned stimulus, capable of causing the dog to salivate. Then a second stimulus, a light, is added to the situation. It too occurs just before the presentation of food. If classical conditioning occurs in an automatic manner, simply as a result of repeated pairings of a conditioned stimulus with an unconditioned stimulus, then the light too should become a conditioned stimulus: It should elicit salivation when presented alone. In fact, this does not happen. Why? Again, an explanation in terms of expectancies is helpful. Since the meat powder is already predicted by the tone, the light provides no new information. Therefore, it is of little predictive value to the subjects and fails to become a conditioned stimulus.

These findings suggest that classical conditioning involves much more than the formation of simple associations between specific stimuli. Indeed, modern views of conditioning conceive of it as a complex process in which organisms form rich representations of the relationships among a variety of factors—including many aspects of the physical setting or context in which the conditioned and unconditioned stimuli are presented (Rescorla, 1988; Swartzentruber, 1991).

I should add that this cognitive perspective on classical conditioning has also been extended to several of the basic principles of conditioning. For example, one theory of stimulus generalization suggests that memory and other cognitive processes play an important role (Pearce, 1986; Shettleworth, 1993). During conditioning, organisms form a representation in memory of the stimuli that preceded the unconditioned stimulus. When they then encounter different stimuli at later times, they compare these with the information stored in memory. The greater the similarity between current stimuli and such memory representations, the stronger the response now evoked. In short, both memory and active comparison processes play a role in what might at first seem to be an automatic function.

The suggestion that cognitive processes are important in human classical conditioning is not surprising. After all, we all have expectancies about what events go together or are likely to follow one another. But it may surprise you to learn that processes like memory and active comparison also occur in animals. Although this possibility would have been unheard of even as recently as the 1970s, growing evidence suggests that animals, like humans, form mental representations of events in the world around them (Cook, 1993; Wasserman, 1993). We'll consider cognitive processes in greater detail in Chapter 7.

FIGURE 5.7

Classical Conditioning: Useful for Practical Purposes

Classical conditioning has many practical applications.

"GO RUN THE ELECTRIC CAN OPENER SO HE'LL GET OFF MY CHAIR."

(**Source:** George Crenshaw/Post Dispatch Features.)

Classical Conditioning: Turning Principles into Action

Much of the discussion in this chapter has focused on basic principles of classical conditioning, many of them derived from laboratory research involving animals. Before concluding, however, I should call attention to the fact that knowledge of these principles has been put to many practical uses to help people, as illustrated by the cartoon in Figure 5.7.

Classical Conditioning and Phobias One of the earliest applications was reported in a study, now a classic in psychology, conducted by John B. Watson and his assistant, Rosalie Raynor, in 1920. Watson and Raynor (1920) demonstrated through their work with "little Albert" that human beings can sometimes acquire strong fears—termed **phobias**—through classical conditioning. In this study, an eleven-month-old child named Albert was shown a white laboratory rat (see Figure 5.8). Albert's initial reactions to the

FIGURE 5.8

Classical Conditioning and Phobias

Psychologist John Watson and his assistant Rosalie Raynor used classical conditioning to establish a fear of small, furry objects in an infant known as "little Albert."

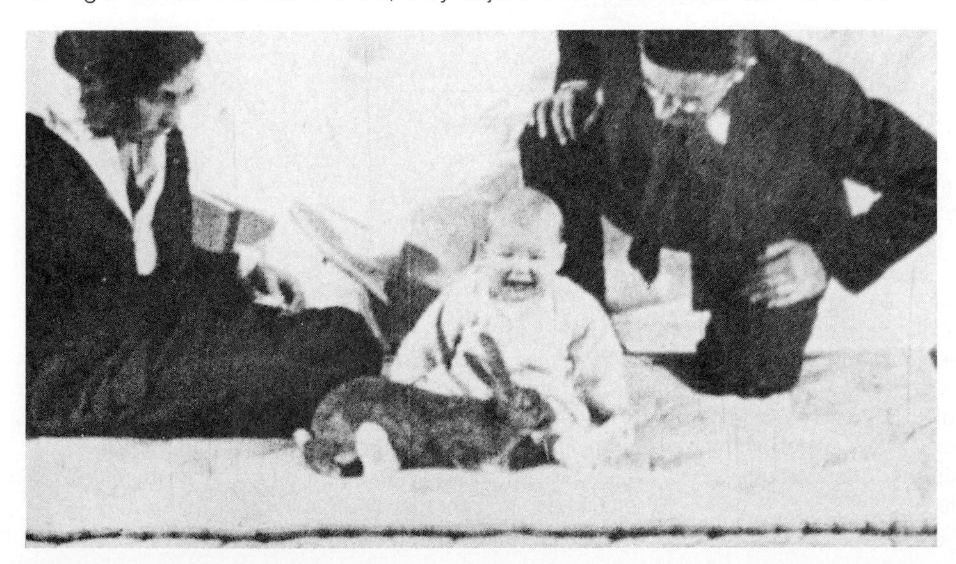

Phobias: Intense, irrational fears of objects or events.

Flooding: Procedures for eliminating conditioned fears based on principles of classical conditioning. During flooding an individual is exposed to fear-inducing objects or events. Since no unconditioned stimulus then follows, extinction of fears eventually takes place.

rat were positive: He smiled and attempted to play with it. Just as he reached out for the rat, though, an iron bar was struck to make a loud noise right behind his ear. Albert jumped, obviously very upset by the startling noise. After several more pairings of the rat (conditioned stimulus) and the loud noise (unconditioned stimulus), Albert cried hysterically and tried to crawl away whenever he saw the rat—or any other small, furry object—even when there was no loud noise.

Fortunately, knowledge of how phobias like little Albert's occur has led to the development of several effective procedures for reducing these reactions (Davey, 1992). In one procedure, termed **flooding,** a person suffering from a specific fear may be forced to confront the fear-eliciting stimulus without an avenue of escape (Gordon, 1989; Morganstern, 1973). For example, a therapist may persuade a person who has an irrational fear of heights to walk onto a high bridge and may keep the person there for a while—under careful supervision, of course. Because no harm results from this experience, the person may eventually become less fearful of heights. In cases where fear-provoking thoughts are too painful to deal with directly, *systematic desensitization*—a progressive technique designed to replace anxiety with a relaxation response—has proved effective (Wolpe, 1958, 1969). A person undergoing this procedure is asked to describe fearful situations. Then, starting with the least anxiety-producing situation, the person alternately visualizes situations and relaxes. Gradually, the individual learns to relax while imagining situations that are increasingly more threatening. Please see the Beyond the Headlines section for more information on the use of classical conditioning to treat phobias.

Beyond the Headlines

As Psychologists See It

Psychotherapist Successfully Treats Stage Fright

Exotic New Cure, or Window Dressing on Tried and True Techniques?

NEW YORK, N.Y.—ABC 20/20, July 12, 1996—If you suffer from stage fright or other forms of performance anxiety, psychotherapist Joyce Ashley claims to have the answer to your problem. Most, if not all, instances of performance anxiety can be traced to childhood trauma—claims Ashley.

During a recent episode of ABC's *20/20,* psychotherapist Joyce Ashley described the procedure she's developed to treat severe cases of stage fright, an immobilizing form of performance anxiety that afflicts millions of people in this country. The physical symptoms of stage fright include sweaty palms, shaky hands, rapid pulse, a narrowing of the visual field, and difficulty in breathing. If you've personally experienced stage fright, then you can probably appreciate the pain some people endure—even when their intended audience is only a handful of close friends. According to Ashley, therapists can successfully treat performance anxiety by helping afflicted persons to identify childhood incidents in which they felt humiliated (perhaps while performing skits in front of parents or friends), then to overcome the trauma stemming from these events.

To illustrate the effectiveness of this approach, *20/20* filmed a group of patients undergoing treatment for their stage fright. Ashley began the session by asking the participants to imagine themselves in an anxiety-producing situation. For most persons in the group this meant conjuring up images of themselves speaking in front of an audience. When they were asked to report how they felt, their responses were quite predictable—they felt awful. At this point, Ashley did something that surprised her patients: She acknowledged their discomfort but calmly asked them to relax while hanging on to the disturbing image a little longer.

Then she helped each participant reconstruct memorable childhood events that led to feelings of humiliation, including recalling the person who put them down. For most participants this was a parent, usually their mother. Ashley then asked the patients to reenact the scene, playing two different parts: themselves (as a child) and the person who humiliated them. Her purpose? To help the members of the group confront the situations and people allegedly responsible for their fear—or at least to confront the memories of these events—directly.

In other words, the participants were encouraged to "rewrite the script." Ashley claims that her therapy is simply a vehicle that she provides her patients to help them reassert their control over themselves and their behavior. Is the treatment successful? Apparently, many of Ashley's patients successfully overcome their stage fright. For example, both of the women filmed for the *20/20* episode succeeded in conquering their fears; one woman is now a successful public speaker, the other a flawless reader of biblical passages at church. At this point, it should be evident that certain aspects of Ashley's therapy are neither new nor revolutionary. Instead, I hope you recognize that the therapeutic steps just described closely resemble two techniques for treating conditioned fears described earlier in this chapter: *systematic desensitization* and *flooding.*

Although it is difficult to assess whether asking people to relive their childhood traumas is a key ingredient in overcoming conditioned fears, the overall goal of Ashley's therapy *is* clear: to weaken existing associations between speaking in public—or the mere thought of doing so—and feelings of humiliation. The moral: Remain skeptical whenever you hear of "new" or "revolutionary" treatment procedures, such as the one headlined in this section. Moreover, take care to look beyond the headlines to identify the real substance of the solution—in this case, well-documented techniques based on principles of classical conditioning.

Critical Thinking Questions

1. Do you think the psychotherapist is correct in her assessment that most cases of stage fright stem from traumatic childhood experiences? If yes, why? If not, why?
2. Is it possible to verify the accuracy of Ashley's patients' memories of childhood events?
3. What factors, in your opinion, play the most important roles in helping people to overcome their fears of public speaking?

Classical Conditioning and Drug Overdose Knowledge of conditioning processes has also helped explain some instances of drug overdose. For example, it is well known that certain drugs become less effective over time. But why does this occur? One possibility is that when a person uses drugs repeatedly in a particular context, the stimuli in that environment become conditioned stimuli and come to elicit a conditioned response (Siegel, 1983, 1984). For certain addictive drugs, this conditioned response can be just the opposite of the unconditioned response (Siegel, 1975; Siegel et al., 1982).

An experiment conducted by Siegel and his colleagues (1982) supported this theory. In the study, rats received injections of either heroin or placebo on alternating days, in alternating environments. Then all subjects received a single high—potentially fatal—dose of heroin. One group received this dose in the environment in which they'd previously received heroin, the other group in the environment in which they'd previously received the placebo. A control group that had previously received only placebo were also injected with the high dose of heroin. The results? First, more subjects with previous drug experience survived than control group subjects; apparently, tolerance resulted from the early nonlethal injections. Second, and more interesting, mortality differed between the drug-experience groups: mortality was highest among those receiving the injection in the environment previously associated with the placebo—*not* with heroin. Taken together, these facts suggest that cues associated with the heroin environment served as conditioned stimuli and prepared the rats' bodies partially to counteract the effects of the lethal injection; the placebo environment did not provide such cues. Indeed, drug users who have nearly died following drug use commonly report something unusual about the environment in which they took the drug (Siegel, 1984).

FIGURE 5.9

Classical Conditioning and the Immune System

Research suggests that classical conditioning may play a role in both suppressing and enhancing aspects of the immune system. Perhaps someday these principles will be useful to persons whose immune systems are compromised because of diseases such as AIDS.

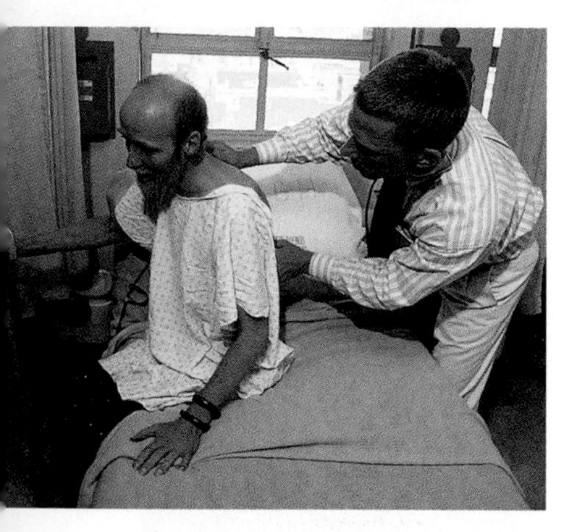

Often these environmental differences are quite subtle, a fact that emphasizes the powerful effects produced by conditioning. These results may also have implications for drug treatment: The environments to which former drug users return often contain cues that may produce drug-related conditioned responses, such as withdrawal symptoms and drug cravings (Ehrman et al., 1992). Knowledge of classical conditioning processes may help health professionals arrange environments that minimize relapse among former drug users—by eliminating the cues that trigger conditioned responses.

Classical Conditioning and the Immune System Research evidence suggests that it may be possible to affect aspects of the immune system through classical conditioning (Ader et al., 1993; Husband et al., 1993). In one recent study, Alvarez-Borda and her colleagues (1995) used classical conditioning to enhance specific immune functions in a group of rats. The researchers first divided the rats into two groups. On conditioning day, one group of rats was allowed to drink a distinctive beverage—saccharin-flavored water (the CS)—before receiving an injection of a substance (the UCS) known to raise the level of certain antibodies in their systems. A second group of rats received only water before receiving the same injection. As predicted, both groups showed an enhanced immune response (UCR) to the injection. Then, after the effects of the injection had faded (more than a month later), the researchers tested to see if conditioning had taken place. Half of the rats that had been exposed to saccharin-flavored water during conditioning were again exposed to saccharin-flavored water, while the other half received only water. The group that had received only water during conditioning also received water during the test trial. The researchers' predictions were supported: Reexposure to the saccharin-flavored water (the CS) resulted in a significant elevation of antibodies in these rats, despite the fact that no further injections (the UCS) were given. In contrast, there was no enhanced immune response in the other groups; measurements indicated that antibody levels in these rats were not significantly different from levels assessed prior to conditioning. Although these results are only preliminary, and require replication in additional studies, and in different species, they clearly show that conditioning can exert powerful effects on the immune system—in the absence of the original substance that produced it. As you may have guessed already, the implications of these results are enormous. Indeed, they offer tremendous hope to people whose health is compromised due to depressed immune systems; for example, persons who are HIV positive or have AIDS (see Figure 5.9).

Key Questions

- How do modern views of classical conditioning differ from earlier perspectives?
- What is blocking?
- What is flooding? Systematic desensitization?
- How can we employ classical conditioning principles to solve problems of everyday life?

Operant Conditioning: *Learning Based on Consequences*

A nightly television news program recently devoted a segment to the growing use of vulgar language by children and young adults in this country. Among the primary causes cited were the usual suspects: the prevalence of obscene language in movies, television, and televised sports. However, the program also indicated another possibility often overlooked: parents. Filmed interviews with two families clearly illustrated the important role that parents can play in determining their children's choice of language. In one family, the use of vulgar language by the children—or by their visiting playmates—was simply not tolerated. Further, the children were not allowed to watch television programs or movies containing objectionable language. Not surprisingly, the children in this family rarely used foul language. Contrast this scenario with the practices of the second family, in which a five-year-old boy's obscenities produced very different consequences—including remarks such as "Isn't that cute?" or mild admonitions such as "Oh Andrew, you shouldn't talk like that!"

"That's exactly what he wants you to do, Al. Can't you see this is just a ploy to get attention? Don't give him the satisfaction of knowing that his behavior upsets you."
(**Source:** CLOSE TO HOME copyright 1993 & 1996 John McPherson. Reprinted with permission of UNIVERSAL PRESS SYNDICATE. All rights reserved.)

FIGURE 5.10

Operant Conditioning: Learning Based on Consequences

Operant conditioning is a form of learning in which behavior is maintained, or changed, through consequences. What consequences are maintaining the behavior problems depicted in this scene?

What's going on here? The answer is probably obvious: The children's behavior in each case was consistent with the consequences it produced (see Figure 5.10). Andrew's behavior received a lot of positive attention that encouraged further vulgar language. In contrast, the use of objectionable language by the children in the other family met with negative consequences and, as a result, rarely occurred. In both instances, however, the children's behaviors were influenced by the use of *operant conditioning*.

The Nature of Operant Conditioning: Consequential Operations

In situations involving **operant conditioning,** the probability that a given response will occur changes depending on the consequences that follow it. Psychologists generally agree that these probabilities are determined through four basic procedures, two of which strengthen or increase the rate of behavior and two of which weaken or decrease the rate of behavior. Procedures that strengthen behavior are termed *reinforcement,* whereas those that *suppress* behavior are termed *punishment.*

Reinforcement There are two types of **reinforcements:** positive reinforcement and negative reinforcement. *Positive reinforcement* involves the impact of **positive reinforcers**—stimulus events or consequences that strengthen responses that precede them. In other words, if a consequence of some action increases the probability that the action will occur again in the future, that consequence is functioning as a positive reinforcer. Some positive reinforcers seem to exert these effects because they are related to basic biological needs. Such *primary reinforcers* include food when we are hungry, water when we are thirsty, and sexual pleasure. In contrast, other events acquire their capacity to act as positive reinforcers through association with primary reinforcers. As illustrated in Figure 5.11 on page 186, such *conditioned reinforcers* include money, status, grades, trophies, and praise from others.

Preferred activities can also be used to reinforce behavior, a principle referred to as the **Premack principle.** If you recall hearing "You must clean

Operant Conditioning: A process through which organisms learn to repeat behaviors that yield positive outcomes or permit them to avoid or escape from negative outcomes.

Reinforcement: The application or removal of a stimulus to increase the strength of a specific behavior.

Positive Reinforcers: Stimuli that strengthen responses that precede them.

Premack Principle: The principle that a more preferred activity can be used to reinforce a less preferred activity.

FIGURE 5.11

Conditioned Reinforcers in Action

Conditioned reinforcers, as depicted here, acquire their capacity to act as positive reinforcers through association with primary reinforcers.

your room before you can watch TV" or "You must eat your vegetables before you get dessert" when you were growing up, then you're already familiar with this principle. As you can guess, the Premack principle is a powerful tool for changing behavior.

Please note that a stimulus event that functions as a positive reinforcer at one time or in one context may have a different effect at another time or in another place. For example, food may serve as a positive reinforcer when you are hungry, but not when you are ill or just after you finish a large meal. Also, at least where people are concerned, many individual differences exist. Clearly, a stimulus that functions as a positive reinforcer for one person may fail to operate in a similar manner for another person. We will return to this important point later on in this chapter.

Negative reinforcement involves the impact of **negative reinforcers**—stimuli that strengthen responses that permit an organism to avoid or escape from their presence. Thus, when we perform an action that allows us to escape from a negative reinforcer that is already present or to avoid the threatened application of one, our tendency to perform this action in the future increases. Some negative reinforcers, such as intense heat, extreme cold, or electric shock, exert their effects the first time they are encountered, whereas others acquire their impact through repeated association.

There are many examples of negative reinforcement in our everyday lives. For example, imagine the following scene. On a particularly cold and dark winter morning, you're sleeping soundly in a warm, comfortable bed. Suddenly, the alarm clock across the room begins to wail. Getting out of your cozy bed is the last thing you want to do, but you find the noise intolerable. What do you do? If you get up to turn off the alarm—or, on subsequent mornings, get up early to avoid hearing the sound of the alarm altogether—your behavior has been *negatively* reinforced. In other words, your tendency to perform actions that allow you to escape from or avoid the sound of the alarm clock has increased. Another everyday example of negative reinforcement occurs when parents give in to their children's tantrums—especially in public places, such as restaurants and shopping malls. Over time, the parent's tendency to give in may increase, because doing so stops the screaming. To repeat, then, *both positive and negative reinforcement are procedures that strengthen or increase behavior.* Positive reinforcers are stimulus events that strengthen responses that precede them, whereas negative reinforcers are aversive stimulus events that strengthen responses that lead to their termination or avoidance.

Negative Reinforcers: Stimuli that strengthen responses that permit an organism to avoid or escape from their presence.

Punishment: The application or removal of a stimulus so as to decrease the strength of a behavior.

Punishment In contrast to reinforcement, **punishment** aims to weaken or decrease the rate of a behavior. As with reinforcement, there are two types of punishments: positive punishment and negative punishment. In *positive punishment*, behaviors are followed by aversive stimulus events termed *punishers*. In such instances, we learn not to perform these actions because aversive consequences—punishers—will follow. And this highlights a point about which there is often much confusion. Contrary to what common sense seems to suggest, punishment is *not* the same as negative reinforcement. Here is an example to illustrate the difference. Imagine that you are driving home in a hurry, exceeding the speed limit. A sick sensation creeps into your stomach as you become aware of flashing lights and a siren. A state trooper has detected your speeding. Your eyes bug out when you see how much the ticket will cost you; and after paying that fine, you obey the posted speed limit. This is an example of the impact of *punishment*—an unpleasant outcome follows your speeding, so the chances that you will speed in the future *decrease*. Now imagine that a year later you are again caught speeding. Apparently the punishment suppressed your speeding behavior only temporarily. Because you are a past offender, the judge handling your case gives you an interesting choice: Either attend a monthlong series of driver education classes or lose your driver's license. In order to avoid losing your license, you attend every class. This is an example of *negative reinforcement:* You attend the driver education classes to *avoid* an aversive event—the loss of your license.

In *negative punishment*, the rate of a behavior is weakened or decreased by the aversiveness of loss of potential reinforcements (Catania, 1992; Millenson & Leslie, 1979). For example, parents frequently attempt to decrease the frequency of certain behaviors of their teenagers (e.g., hitting younger siblings or talking back to parents) by temporarily denying them access to positive reinforcers—such as driving the family car on weekend dates. A common form of negative punishment is "time-out," a procedure you may have experienced as a youngster growing up. Thus, both positive and negative punishment are procedures that weaken or decrease behavior. Table 5.1 on page 188 summarizes positive reinforcement, negative reinforcement, positive punishment, and negative punishment.

Key Questions

- What is operant conditioning?
- What are examples of primary reinforcers? Of conditioned reinforcers?
- Which operant techniques strengthen behavior? Weaken behavior?
- How do negative reinforcement and punishment differ?

Operant Conditioning: Some Basic Principles

In classical conditioning, organisms learn associations between stimuli; certain stimulus events predict the occurrence of others that naturally trigger a specific response. In addition, the responses performed are generally *involuntary*. In other words, they are *elicited*—pulled out of the organism—by a specific unconditioned stimulus in an automatic manner; for example, salivation to the taste of food, blinking of the eyes in response to a puff of air.

In operant conditioning, in contrast, organisms learn associations between particular *behaviors* and the consequences that follow them. Additionally, the responses involved in operant conditioning are more voluntary and are *emitted* by organisms in a given environment. In order to understand the nature of this form of conditioning, then, we must address two basic questions: (1) Why are certain behaviors emitted in the first place? (2) Once behaviors occur, what factors determine the frequency with which they are repeated?

Shaping and Chaining: Getting Behavior Started and Then Putting It All Together Many of the behaviors that we perform each day require little conscious effort on our part. In fact, we perform many of them flawlessly without even trying. But what about new forms of behavior

TABLE 5.1

Reinforcement and Punishment: An Overview

Positive and negative reinforcement are both procedures that strengthen behavior. Positive and negative punishment are both procedures that weaken behavior.

Procedure	Stimulus Event	Effects	Behavioral Outcomes
Positive reinforcement	Application of a desirable stimulus (e.g., food, sexual pleasure, praise)	Strengthens responses that precede occurrence of stimulus	Organisms learn to perform responses that produce positive reinforcers
Negative reinforcement	Removal or postponement of an undesirable (aversive) stimulus (e.g., heat, cold, harsh criticism)	Strengthens responses that permit escape from or avoidance of stimulus	Organisms learn to perform responses that permit them to avoid or escape from negative reinforcers
Positive punishment	Application of an undesirable (aversive) stimulus	Weakens responses that precede occurrence of stimulus	Organisms learn to suppress responses that lead to unpleasant consequences
Negative punishment	Loss or postponement of a desirable stimulus	Weakens responses that lead to loss or postponement of reinforcement	Organisms learn to suppress responses that lead to loss or postponement of reinforcement

with which we are unfamiliar? How are these behaviors initially established? The answer involves a procedure known as shaping.

In essence, **shaping** is based on the principle that a little can eventually go a long way. Participants receive a reward for each small step toward a final goal—the target response—rather than only for the final response. At first, actions even remotely resembling the target behavior—termed *successive approximations*—are followed by a reward. Gradually, closer and closer approximations of the final target behavior are required before the reward is given. This sounds simple, but does it actually work? Absolutely. For example, when a baby suddenly blurts out the sound "Mmmuuhh," the parents are ecstatic. They immediately lavish attention and affection on the child and do so each time the baby repeats the sound; all the baby's other relatives do the same. But what happens over time? Although initially the family responds enthusiastically to any sound the child makes, gradually they respond only to sounds that approximate actual words. Shaping, then, helps organisms acquire, or construct, new and more complex forms of behavior from simpler behavior.

Shaping: A technique in which closer and closer approximations of desired behavior are required for the delivery of positive reinforcement.

Chaining: A procedure that establishes a sequence of responses, which lead to a reward following the final response in the chain.

What about even more complex sequences of behavior, such as the exciting water routines performed by dolphins and killer whales at Sea World? (see Figure 5.12). These behaviors can be cultivated by a procedure called **chaining,** in which trainers establish a sequence, or chain, of responses, the last of which leads to a reward. Trainers usually begin chaining by first shaping the final response. When this response is well established, the trainer shapes responses earlier in the chain, then reinforces them by giving the animal the opportunity to perform responses later in the chain, the last of which produces the reinforcer. Shaping and chaining obviously have important implications for human behavior. For example, when working with a beginning student, a skilled dance teacher or ski instructor may use shaping techniques to establish basic skills, such as performing a basic step or standing on the skis without falling down, by praising simple accomplishments. As training progresses, however, the student may receive praise only when he or she successfully completes an entire sequence or chain of actions, such as skiing down a small slope.

FIGURE 5.12

A Simple Demonstration of Shaping and Chaining

The dual processes of shaping and chaining help to explain the development of complex behavior. Please note that *complex*, however, is a relative term—relative to the abilities and limitations of each organism.

Shaping and chaining techniques can produce dramatic effects. But can they be used to establish virtually any form of behavior in any organism? If you recall our earlier discussion of biological constraints on classical conditioning, you can probably guess the answer: no. Just as there are *biological constraints* on classical conditioning, there are constraints on forms of learning based on consequences, or shaping. Perhaps this is most clearly illustrated by the experience of two psychologists, Keller and Marian Breland (1961), who attempted to put their expertise in techniques of operant conditioning to commercial use by training animals to perform unusual tricks and exhibiting them at state fairs. At first, things went well. Using standard shaping techniques, the Brelands trained chickens to roll plastic capsules holding prizes down a ramp and then peck them into the hands of waiting customers; they taught pigs to deposit silver dollars into a piggy bank. As time went by, though, these star performers gradually developed some unexpected responses. The chickens began to seize the capsules and pound them against the floor, and the pigs began to throw coins onto the ground and root them about instead of making "deposits" in their bank. In short, despite careful training, the animals showed what the Brelands termed *instinctive drift*—a tendency to return to the type of behavior they would show under natural conditions. So operant conditioning, like classical conditioning, is subject to biological constraints. While the power of positive and negative reinforcers is great, natural tendencies are important, too, and can influence the course and results of operant conditioning in many cases.

The Role of Reward Delay in Impulsiveness and Procrastination: Two Sides of the Same Coin? Operant conditioning usually proceeds faster as the *magnitude* of the reward that follows each response increases. But the effectiveness of rewards can be dramatically affected by *reward delay*—the amount of time that elapses before the reward is delivered. In general, longer delays produce poorer levels of performance. A study by Capaldi (1978), for example, examined how reward delay affected running behavior in two groups of rats. Although both groups received the same amount and quality of food on each trial, one group received the reward immediately and the other group received it after a ten-second delay. As you might guess, subjects in the immediate-reward group performed better than subjects in the delayed-reward group.

The effects of reward delay are also evident in humans. For example, children will often choose smaller, immediate rewards over rewards of greater value that they must wait to receive, a tendency sometimes referred to as *impulsiveness* (Logue, 1988). But are children more impulsive than adults? The results of a study by Green, Fry, and Myerson (1994) seem to suggest that they are. These researchers asked three groups of participants—sixth graders, college students, and older adults—to make a series of hypothetical choices between smaller amounts of money they could receive immediately, and larger amounts of money they could receive later. For example, a sample choice might be: "Would you prefer $1,000 in five years or $650 right now?" The results showed clear differences between the groups: The sixth graders made significantly more impulsive choices than the college students, who, in turn, made more impulsive choices than the older adults. Please note, however, that adults, too, frequently engage in impulsive behavior—even when the long-term consequences of their impulsiveness are deadly. Smokers and heavy drinkers, for instance, choose the immediate pleasures they derive from smoking or consuming alcoholic beverages over the potentially negative consequences they may suffer later on, such as cancer (Rachlin, 1995; Steele & Josephs, 1990).

Is it possible to counteract the powerful effects of reward delay? Some research suggests that prevention may be the key. In a typical study of reward delay, people are given a choice between a smaller reward that is available immediately and a larger reward whose delivery is postponed for some period of time (Mazur, 1987). If the wait for the larger reward is lengthy, it is understandable why a person might instead choose the smaller-but-sooner alternative. However, if the time frame is shifted so that the smaller reward is still available before the larger one, but access to both rewards is relatively far off in the future, people generally choose the larger alternative (Kirby & Herrnstein, 1995). In other words, when both reward options are relatively distant events, people tend to be more rational in their decisions. However, as access to the smaller reward draws near, people's impulsive tendencies seem to overpower their earlier decision to hold out for the better reward; as time passes, many people switch their preference to the smaller reward—the one that will become available first. Here is where prevention comes in. Getting people to make a commitment ahead of time, and helping them to stick with this decision, may help reduce the effects of reward delay.

The processes underlying impulsive behavior also seem to describe another type of behavior you may be familiar with: *procrastination*—the tendency to put off until tomorrow what we should do today. To illustrate this point, consider the choice procrastinators must make; they must decide between performing a smaller, less effortful task now and tackling a larger, more effortful task later on. Although the most efficient decision in terms of time and effort is obvious—do the less effortful task now—research shows that people, and animals, often choose the more delayed alternative, even when it leads to more work. For example, in a recent study, Mazur (1996) placed pigeons in a situation where they chose between two courses of action, both of which led to the same amount of food reinforcement. They could choose to perform a relatively easy task (eight key pecks on a colored light) right away, or to perform a more difficult task (up to thirty key pecks) that they could put off for a little while. Which option did they choose? Surprisingly, most pigeons chose to procrastinate—despite the fact that procrastination led to more work for the same amount of reward. Although these results seem counterintuitive in many respects, they do seem to provide an accurate reflection of the choices people often make.

Schedules of Reinforcement: Different Rules for Delivery of Payoffs Through experience, you may already realize that under natural conditions reinforcement is often an uncertain event. Sometimes a given response yields a reward every time it occurs, but sometimes it does not. For example, smiling at someone you don't know may produce a return smile and additional positive outcomes. On other occasions it may be followed by a suspicious frown or other rejection. Similarly, putting a coin in a soda machine usually produces a soft drink. Sometimes, though, you merely lose the money.

In these cases, the occurrence or nonoccurrence of reinforcement seems to be random or unpredictable. In many other instances, though, it is governed by rules. For example, paychecks are delivered on certain days of the month; free pizzas or car washes are provided to customers who have purchased a specific amount of products or services. Do such rules—known as **schedules of reinforcement**—affect behavior? Several decades of research by B. F. Skinner and other psychologists suggest that they do. Many different types of schedules of reinforcement exist (Ferster & Skinner, 1957; Honig & Staddon, 1977). We'll concentrate on several of the most important ones here.

The simplest is called the **continuous reinforcement (CRF) schedule,** in which every occurrence of a particular behavior is reinforced. For example, if a rat receives a food pellet each time it presses a lever, or a small child receives twenty-five cents each time he ties his shoes correctly, both are on a continuous reinforcement schedule. As you might imagine, continuous reinforcement is useful for establishing or strengthening new behaviors.

Other types of schedules, however, termed *partial* or *intermittent reinforcement,* are often more powerful in maintaining behavior. In the first of these, known as a **fixed-interval schedule,** the occurrence of reinforcement depends on the passage of time; the first response made after a specific period has elapsed brings the reward. When placed on schedules of this type, people generally show a pattern in which they respond at low rates immediately after delivery of a reinforcement, but then gradually respond more and more as the time when the next reward can be obtained approaches. A good example of behavior on a fixed-interval schedule is provided by students studying. After a big exam, little if any studying takes place. As the time for the next test approaches, the rate of such behavior increases dramatically.

Reinforcement is also controlled mainly by the passage of time in a **variable-interval schedule.** Here, though, the period that must elapse before a response will again yield reinforcement varies around some average value. An example of behavior on a variable-interval schedule of reinforcement is provided by employees whose supervisor checks their work at irregular intervals. Since the employees never know when such checks will occur, they must perform in a consistent manner in order to obtain positive outcomes, such as praise, or avoid negative ones, such as criticism. This is precisely what happens on variable-interval schedules: Organisms respond at a steady rate, without the kind of pauses observed on fixed-interval schedules. An important procedure that is arranged according to a variable-interval schedule is random drug testing of individuals in safety-sensitive jobs—people whose impaired performance could endanger the lives of others, such as airline pilots or operators at nuclear reactor sites. Random drug testing is also common in many collegiate and professional sports. Because they cannot predict the day on which the next test will occur, these individuals may be more likely to refrain from using drugs that could impair their work performance.

Reinforcement is determined in a very different manner on a **fixed-ratio schedule.** Here, reinforcement occurs only after a fixed number of responses. Individuals who are paid on a piecework basis, in which a fixed amount is paid for each item produced, are operating according to a fixed-ratio schedule. Generally, such schedules yield a high rate of response, though with a tendency toward a brief pause immediately after each reinforcement. The pauses occur because individuals take a slight breather after earning each unit of reinforcement. People who collect beverage containers, office paper waste, and other recyclable materials for the money they bring are behaving according to a fixed-ratio schedule (see Figure 5.13 on page 192).

Finally, on a **variable-ratio schedule,** reinforcement occurs after completion of a variable number of responses. Since organisms confronted with a variable-ratio schedule cannot predict how many responses are required before reinforcement will occur, they usually respond at high and steady rates.

Schedules of Reinforcement: Rules determining when and how reinforcements will be delivered.

Continuous Reinforcement Schedule: A schedule of reinforcement in which every occurrence of a particular behavior is reinforced.

Fixed-Interval Schedule: A schedule of reinforcement in which a specific interval of time must elapse before a response will yield reinforcement.

Variable-Interval Schedule: A schedule of reinforcement in which a variable amount of time must elapse before a response will yield reinforcement.

Fixed-Ratio Schedule: A schedule of reinforcement in which reinforcement occurs only after a fixed number of responses have been emitted.

Variable-Ratio Schedule: A schedule of reinforcement in which reinforcement is delivered after a variable number of responses have been emitted.

FIGURE 5.13

Applying Schedules of Reinforcement to Solve Problems of Everyday Life

Returning empty beverage containers for the money they bring is an example of behavior controlled through a fixed-ratio schedule of reinforcement.

The effect of such schedules on human behavior is readily apparent in gambling casinos, where high rates of responding occur in front of slot machines and other games of chance. Variable-ratio schedules also result in behaviors that are highly resistant to extinction—ones that persist even when reinforcement is no longer available. In fact, resistance to extinction is much higher after exposure to a variable-ratio schedule of reinforcement than it is after exposure to a continuous reinforcement schedule. This phenomenon is known as the *partial reinforcement effect* and seems to occur for the following reason: When reinforcement has been infrequent and intermittent in its delivery, people or other organisms may continue to respond after all reinforcement has ended, because it is difficult for them to recognize that reinforcement is no longer available. Under a variable-ratio schedule, many responses are not followed by reinforcement. Many golfers are well acquainted with the partial reinforcement effect; for each great shot they hit, they hit many more poor ones, yet they continue to play the game. Suppose that a golfer fails to hit even one good shot over the course of an entire season—will she continue to play? The chances are good that she will. As summarized in Figure 5.14 and evident throughout the preceding discussion, different schedules of reinforcement produce distinct patterns of responding. Each schedule helps describe how the delivery of consequences affects our behavior.

Concurrent Schedules of Reinforcement and the Matching Law Many psychologists readily admit that the schedules of reinforcement just described do not fully account for the complex forms of human behavior observed in everyday life (e.g., Hanisch, 1995; Pierce & Epling, 1994). Each day people are faced with alternatives and must choose one to the exclusion of others. For example, on a given evening, students must choose between doing homework and other behaviors they could do instead, such as going out with friends, talking on the telephone, doing their laundry, or watching TV. This example describes a **concurrent schedule of reinforcement:** a situation in which a person's behavior is free to alternate continuously between two or more responses, each having its own schedule of reinforcement (Catania, 1992). This type of schedule has been used to study choice behavior in both animals and humans (e.g., Elsmore & McBride, 1994; Pierce & Epling, 1994).

To illustrate, let's consider a typical animal experiment involving a concurrent schedule of reinforcement in which a rat is free to press lever A or lever B at any time, or to press neither. Furthermore, the rat may distribute its presses between the two levers as it chooses. Now suppose the consequences of pressing each lever (e.g., food reward) are arranged according to distinct variable-interval schedules of reinforcement. How will the rat distribute its lever presses? The rate of responding on each lever will tend to match the rate of reinforcement each lever produces. In other words, the rat will distribute its behavior between alternatives in such a way that maximizes the reinforcement it receives for its efforts. This phenomenon has been termed the *matching law* (Herrnstein, 1961).

Concurrent Schedule of Reinforcement: A situation in which behaviors having two or more different reinforcement schedules are simultaneously available.

Although this is a relatively simple example of choice behavior, the matching law can be extended to explain more complex forms of behavior,

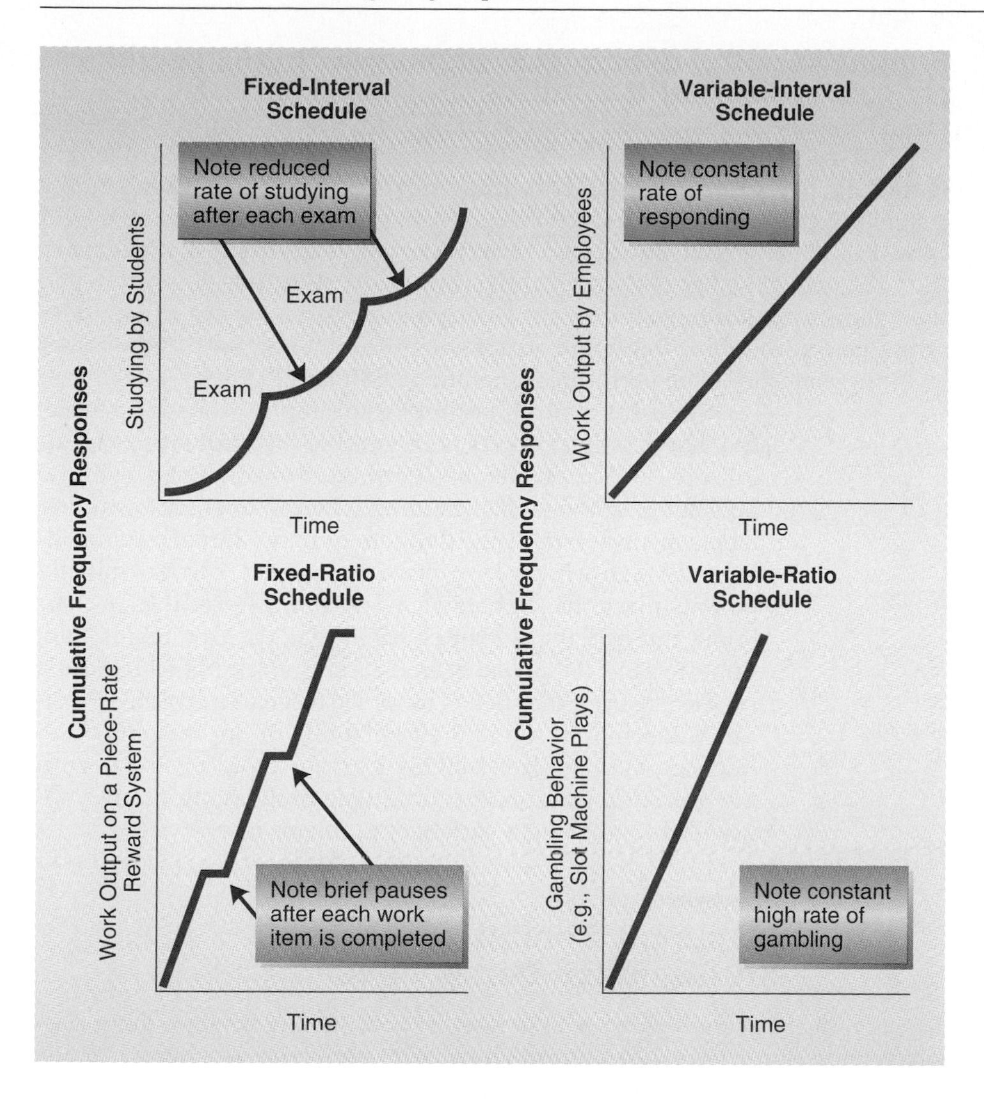

FIGURE 5.14

Schedules of Reinforcement: A Summary of Their Effects

Rates of responding vary under different schedules of reinforcement. The steeper the line in each diagram, the higher the rate at which responses are performed.

too. According to Herrnstein (1970), we don't usually choose between just two alternatives—A (doing homework) and B (going out with friends); instead, we choose between doing homework and all other available alternatives. This helps to explain why particular events are reinforcing at certain times, but not at others. For instance, on a particular Friday night, cleaning your room may not seem so bad if nothing else is going on. In contrast, the same chore may be unappealing if there is something better to do.

Application of the matching law to human behavior has several important implications. First, it forces behavioral researchers to view behavior somewhat differently—as one response choice among many potential alternatives. Analyzing behavior as choice may help psychologists improve their understanding of how people allocate responses in everyday life. Second, as we've already noted, research on the matching law helps explain why certain reinforcers are attractive at certain times, but not at others. Finally, recognizing that people evaluate reinforcement value against the context of all reinforcements available could lead to the development of more effective behavioral interventions. For instance, by increasing the relative attractiveness of desired responses, it may be possible to eliminate undesirable or destructive behavior without the need for punishment. However, consequences are not the only determinants of behavior. As we'll see in the next section, stimuli that precede behavior and signal the availability of certain consequences are also important.

Discriminative Stimulus: Stimulus that signals the availability of reinforcement if a specific response is made.

Stimulus Control: Consistent occurrence of a behavior in the presence of a discriminative stimulus.

Learned Helplessness: Feelings of helplessness that develop after exposure to situations in which no effort succeeds in affecting outcomes.

Stimulus Control of Behavior: Signals about the Usefulness (or Uselessness) of Responses Imagine you are a rat in an experimental chamber. Over the past few days, you have learned to press a lever in order to receive food pellets. One morning you notice the presence of a light in the box that is turned on and off with some regularity. The light is actually a signal: You will be rewarded with food if you press the lever when the light is on, but not when the light is off. Over time, you learn to press the lever in the presence of the light—termed a **discriminative stimulus**—but not when the light is turned off. In short, your lever-pressing behavior has come under **stimulus control** of the light; you are obeying the light's signal as to whether lever pressing should be performed or omitted (Skinner, 1938).

Stimulus control has important implications for people, too. For example, one type of graphic discriminative stimulus, the *Mr. Yuk* sticker, has been used to prevent accidental poisonings among small children who can't yet read warning labels or understand the dangers of many household products (see Figure 5.15). How do Mr. Yuk stickers work? Initially parents place the stickers on all poisonous products in their home and explain to their children that Mr. Yuk means "No, don't touch." Then, each time a child attempts to handle a product bearing the sticker, he or she receives a scolding. Soon Mr. Yuk comes to signal the availability of unpleasant consequences, and children quickly learn to avoid products with Mr. Yuk stickers. In short, stimulus control has important implications for solving a variety of problems in everyday life.

Key Questions

- What are shaping and chaining?
- How does reward delay affect operant conditioning?
- What are schedules of reinforcement?
- When is the use of continuous reinforcement desirable, and when should other reinforcement schedules be used?
- What are concurrent schedules of reinforcement and the matching law?
- What is a discriminative stimulus, and what is stimulus control?

Operant Conditioning: A Cognitive Perspective

Do cognitive processes play a role in operant conditioning as they do in classical conditioning? This continues to be a point on which psychologists disagree. Operant psychologists (also referred to as behaviorists) have contended that there is no need to introduce cognition into the picture: If we understand the nature of the reinforcers available in a situation and the schedules on which they are delivered, we can accurately predict behavior. But many other psychologists believe that no account of operant conditioning can be complete without attention to cognitive factors such as perceptions, beliefs, evaluations, and expectancies (e.g., Colwill, 1993). Several types of evidence support this conclusion.

Learned Helplessness: Throwing in the Towel When Nothing Seems to Work Perhaps the most dramatic evidence for the role of cognitive factors in operant conditioning is the existence of a phenomenon known as **learned helplessness:** the lasting effects produced by exposure to situations in which nothing an organism does works—no response yields reinforcement or provides escape from negative events. After such experience, both people and animals seem literally to give up. And here is the unsettling part: If the situation changes so that some responses will work, organisms in a state of learned helplessness never discover this fact. Rather, they remain in a seemingly passive state and simply don't try (Seligman, 1975; Tennen & Eller, 1977). Although it is not clear why learned helplessness occurs (McReynolds, 1980), it seems impossible to explain it entirely in terms of contingent relations between individual responses and the consequences they produce. Rather, some evidence suggests that organisms learn a general

FIGURE 5.15

Applying Stimulus Control to Prevent Accidental Poisonings

Stimulus control can help solve important problems of everyday life—in this case, preventing accidental poisonings among very small children.

(**Source**: Permission to use Mr. Yuk symbol given by Children's Hospital of Pittsburgh.)

expectation of helplessness that transfers across situations, even if they do gain control over their environment (Maier & Jackson, 1979).

Research on learned helplessness seems to suggest that its onset stems partly from our perceptions of control; when we begin to believe that we have no control over our environment or our lives, we stop trying to improve our situations (Dweck & Licht, 1980). For example, many children growing up in urban slums perceive they have little control over their environment and even less hope of escaping it. As a result of learned helplessness, they may simply resign themselves to a lifetime of disenfranchisement, deprivation, and exclusion. However, not all people respond in this way, which suggests that other factors must also be involved. As we'll note in Chapter 12, people differ in many specific ways—and different personality traits may make people more, or less, prone to learned helplessness (Minor, 1990).

The results of a study by Minor and his colleagues (1994) seem to support this possibility. These researchers examined whether individual differences on one trait—*neophobia*—would help predict learned helplessness among subjects (rats) exposed to varying levels of inescapable electric shock. Neophobia is a tendency to withdraw from anything unfamiliar, such as new people, places, or objects. The researchers reasoned that since neophobic rats are less able to cope with stressful conditions than nonneophobic rats, these subjects might also be less resilient in the face of experiences that can lead to learned helplessness. The investigators measured neophobia by giving each rat a choice between remaining in a familiar box and exploring a much larger, unfamiliar enclosure into which the box was placed. The rat's neophobia "score" was the relative amount of time it spent exploring the new enclosure. Each rat then received either 0, 60, or 120 painful, inescapable shocks to its tail. In general, a greater number of shocks increases the likelihood that learned helplessness will occur.

On the following day, the researchers tested for evidence of learned helplessness by exposing the rats, once again, to painful shocks. This time, however, the rats could easily escape. Learned helplessness was gauged by the amount of time it took the rats to escape—or by whether they attempted to do so at all. The results of this study can be summarized as follows. First, consistent with the view that learned helplessness stems partly from perceptions of loss of control, the rats' escape behavior was directly related to the number of inescapable shocks they had received. The greater the number of inescapable shocks they received, the longer it took them to escape.

Second, and perhaps more interestingly, neophobia appeared to predict the occurrence of learned helplessness, at least for the group receiving the intermediate number (60) of shocks. Among the rats in this group, learned helplessness (longer escape times) was most likely to occur among the neophobic rats. In contrast, their nonneophobic counterparts appeared to be unfazed by their "shocking" experience. The escape times among these rats closely resembled those of the rats who were never exposed to inescapable shocks.

Not surprisingly, scores on the neophobia measure did not predict the occurrence of learned helplessness among rats who initially received the greatest number (120) of inescapable shocks. In fact, on test day, most of the rats in this group didn't even try to escape, despite the fact they could do so easily. In summary, these findings suggest the existence of characteristics that make some people, and apparently some animals, more resistant to learned helplessness than others. They also show, however, that under extreme circumstances even the most resilient individuals may eventually succumb to learned helplessness (see Figure 5.16). In Chapter 9 we'll consider several additional factors that seem to explain why some people are more resilient than others under difficult circumstances.

FIGURE 5.16

Learned Helplessness: The Role of Individual Differences

Research evidence suggests that certain individual differences may make some people more, or less, susceptible to learned helplessness.

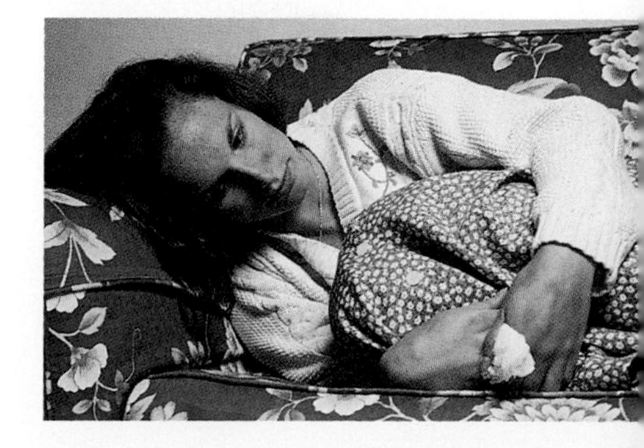

I'm Getting Paid What? Beliefs about Schedules of Reinforcement Several studies indicate that in some cases people's beliefs about schedules of reinforcement may exert stronger effects on behavior than do the schedules themselves. For example, in one study (Kaufman, Baron, & Kopp, 1966), three groups of participants performed a task that was rewarded on a variable-interval schedule; the period between reinforcements varied, but averaged one minute. One group was told the schedule would be in effect. Two other groups were given false information: members of one group were told that they would be rewarded every minute, a fixed-interval schedule; people in the other group were told that they would be rewarded after an average of 150 responses, a variable-ratio schedule. Although all groups actually worked on the same schedule, large differences in their behavior emerged. Those who thought they were working on a variable-ratio schedule showed a high rate of responses: 259 per minute. Those told they would be rewarded on a fixed-interval schedule showed a very low rate of 6 responses per minute; and those who were correctly informed that they would work on a variable-interval schedule showed an intermediate rate of 65 responses per minute. As suggested by Bandura (1986, p. 129), people's behavior may sometimes be more accurately predicted from their beliefs than from the actual consequences they experience.

Evidence That It's All Relative: The Contrast Effect Some evidence suggests that our behavior is influenced not only by the level of rewards we receive, but by our evaluation of rewards relative to our experiences with previous rewards. Studies have shown that shifts in the amount of reward we receive can dramatically influence performance, a temporary behavior shift termed the *contrast effect* (e.g., Crespi, 1942; Flaherty & Largen, 1975; Shanab & Spencer, 1978). For example, when laboratory animals are shifted from a small reward to a larger reward, there is an increase in their performance to a level higher than that of subjects consistently receiving the larger reward. This increase is known as a positive contrast effect. Conversely, when subjects are shifted from a large reward to a smaller reward, their performance decreases to a level lower than that of subjects receiving only the smaller reward—a negative contrast effect. But positive and negative contrast effects are transient. Thus, the elevated or depressed performances slowly give way to performance levels similar to those of control animals that receive only one level of reward.

The existence of contrast effects indicates that level of reward alone cannot always explain our behavior and that experience with a previous level of reward—and consequent expectancies—can dramatically affect our performance. Contrast effects also help explain certain instances of our everyday behavior. For example, following an unexpected raise in salary or a promotion, a person is initially elated, and his or her performance skyrockets—at least for a while. Then, after the novelty wears off, performance falls to a level equal to that of others already being rewarded at the same level.

Tolman's Cognitive Map: A Classic Study in the History of Psychology Finally, evidence suggests that cognitive processes play an important role in operant conditioning among animals, as well. In a study by Tolman and Honzik (1930), rats were trained to run through a complicated maze. One group, the reward group, received a food reward in the goal box at the end of the maze on each of their daily trials. A second group, the no-reward group, never received a reward. The third group, the no-reward/reward group, did not receive a food reward until the eleventh day of training. As illustrated in Figure 5.17, rats in the reward group showed a steady improvement in per-

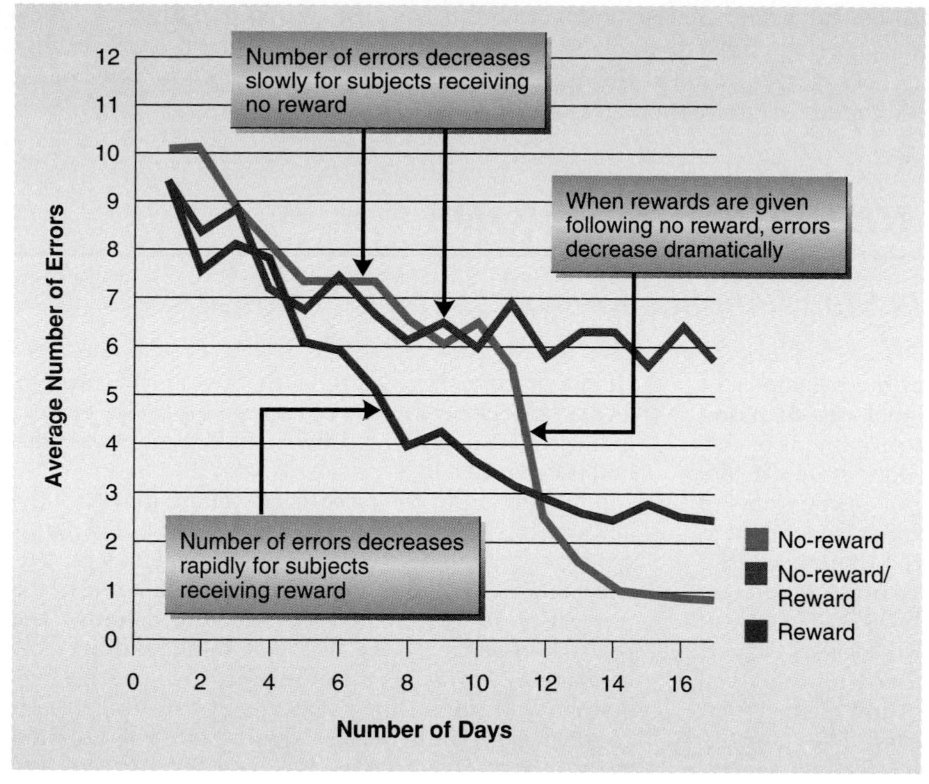

(**Source**: Based on data from Tolman & Honzik, 1930).

FIGURE 5.17

The Role of Cognitive Processes in Animal Learning

Performance of rats in the no-reward/reward group improved dramatically immediately after the introduction of the food reward. Because the improvement was so dramatic, these data suggest that the animals "learned" something during previous trials—even though they received no reward for their efforts. Tolman used this as evidence for the importance of cognitive processes in learning, suggesting that the rats may have formed a "cognitive map."

formance, decreasing the number of errors they made in reaching the goal box. Rats in the no-reward group showed only a slight improvement in performance. Rats in the no-reward/reward group showed performance similar to those in the no-reward group—for the first ten days. However, their performance improved dramatically immediately after the introduction of the food reward. In fact, as of day 12 their performance was as good as that of rats who had been rewarded for their performance all along.

How do we account for these results? An explanation based on reinforcement alone is not sufficient; the dramatic improvement in the performance of the third group was too sudden. Obviously, the rats had learned something in the previous trials. Tolman and others point to these data, and the results of other studies (e.g., Colwill & Rescorla, 1985, 1988), as evidence for the importance of cognitive processes in learning. In fact, Tolman theorized that the rats may have formed what he termed a *cognitive map*—a mental representation of the maze. Although the existence of such maps has not yet been clearly established (e.g., Dyer, 1991; Wehner & Menzel, 1990), a growing body of evidence supports the view that animals do in fact form mental representations of their environments—perhaps even memories of them.

Systematic research by Capaldi and his colleagues points to the possibility that animals form memories of rewards they've received in the past (Capaldi, 1996; Capaldi, Birmingham, & Alptekin, 1995). According to this view, distinctive reward events produce distinctive reward memories. Reward event memories apparently serve two important purposes. First, they function as discriminative stimuli, directing the animal's behavior by signaling when, or if, future responses will lead to reinforcement. Second, reward memories serve a response-enhancing function. In other words, the memories associated with bigger rewards lead to greater increases in responding than memories of small rewards or nonreward. Although we do not yet fully

Applied Behavior Analysis: A field of psychology that specializes in the application of operant conditioning principles to solve problems of everyday life.

understand their precise nature, one thing is clear: Cognitive processes play an important and active role in animal learning as well as in human learning.

For details of a real-life application of operant conditioning in humans, see the Research Methods feature below.

RESEARCH METHODS

How Psychologists Study Applications of Operant Conditioning

You may have guessed by now that the principles of operant conditioning are powerful tools for changing many aspects of behavior. A major proponent of this approach to learning was B. F. Skinner (1904–90). Skinner is well known for his outspoken criticisms of cognitive psychology. Although Skinner never denied the existence of mental events, he felt that measuring these processes was irrelevant to accurate prediction and control of behavior (Skinner, 1938, 1971). He instead insisted that people could determine the causes of most forms of behavior by identifying the environmental conditions, or contingencies, supporting the behavior and could then manipulate these conditions to influence the behavior in desired directions. Skinner's views dominated the focus of psychological research for many years, leading to the development of a distinct branch of psychology called **applied behavior analysis.** Research efforts in this area are directed primarily toward solving problems of everyday life. Before we review several significant contributions of applied behavior analysis, let's first examine how these researchers study behavior.

How Applied Behavior Analysts Study Behavior

The research method used by applied behavior analysts is actually a four-step process. These steps can be summarized by the acronym *DO-IT,* proposed by psychologist Scott Geller (1996). Since the primary focus here is on altering observable behavior or the outcomes of behavior, it is not surprising that the first step in the process is to clearly *define* the target behaviors to be changed. Doing so allows researchers to develop procedures to *observe* how often the behaviors occur under existing (or baseline) conditions. Once a stable measure of the behaviors has been obtained, researchers *intervene* to change the target behaviors in desired directions. For example, they may begin to reward behaviors they wish to increase, or they may withhold rewards that follow inappropriate behaviors they wish to decrease. Or they may alter aspects of the physical environment to encourage or discourage certain behaviors. Finally, it is important to test the impact of the intervention by continuing to observe and record the target behaviors during the intervention, and beyond. Testing provides researchers with evidence of the intervention's impact and its effectiveness over time. To illustrate this process, let's consider a recent study that used the DO-IT process to investigate a growing problem in this country—graffiti (Watson, 1996).

In their study, the researchers set out to reduce the amount of graffiti on the walls of three public bathrooms, each located in a different building on a university campus. The proliferation of graffiti had forced the university to repaint these rooms repeatedly. The researchers began by objectively defining graffiti; in this case, it was defined as the number of distinct markings on each wall. For example, letters and punctuation each counted as separate marks; a happy face was counted as five marks—one for the circle depicting the head and one each for the two eyes, nose, and mouth.

Next, the researchers began observing: They made daily counts of graffiti to determine its baseline level of occurrence. Figure 5.18 shows the cumulative number of markings observed in each bathroom across consecutive observation days. Then the researchers introduced an intervention they felt might help reduce the proliferation of graffiti. The intervention consisted of taping on each bathroom wall a sign that read: "A local licensed doctor has agreed to donate a set amount of money to the local chapter of the United Way for each day this wall remains free of any writing, drawings, or other markings. Your assistance is greatly appreciated in helping to support your United Way."

As shown in Figure 5.18, the intervention was successful. After the posters were introduced, no further marking occurred on any of the walls. Moreover, the bathrooms remained free of graffiti at each of three monthly follow-ups, suggesting that the posters were a cost-effective solution to this problem. Please note that the posters were introduced into the three bathrooms *sequentially.* The reason for this procedure was to ensure that any changes observed in the occurrence of graffiti were due to the intervention (the posting of the signs) and not to other, unrelated factors. Specifically, following the introduction of the poster into the first bathroom, graffiti ceased to occur there, but continued to occur in the other two bathrooms. Similarly, following the introduction of the poster into the second bathroom, graffiti ceased to occur there, but continued to occur in the third bathroom. In short, this sequential procedure—termed a *multiple-baseline design*—increases our confidence that the poster was the cause of the abrupt change in the amount of graffiti observed.

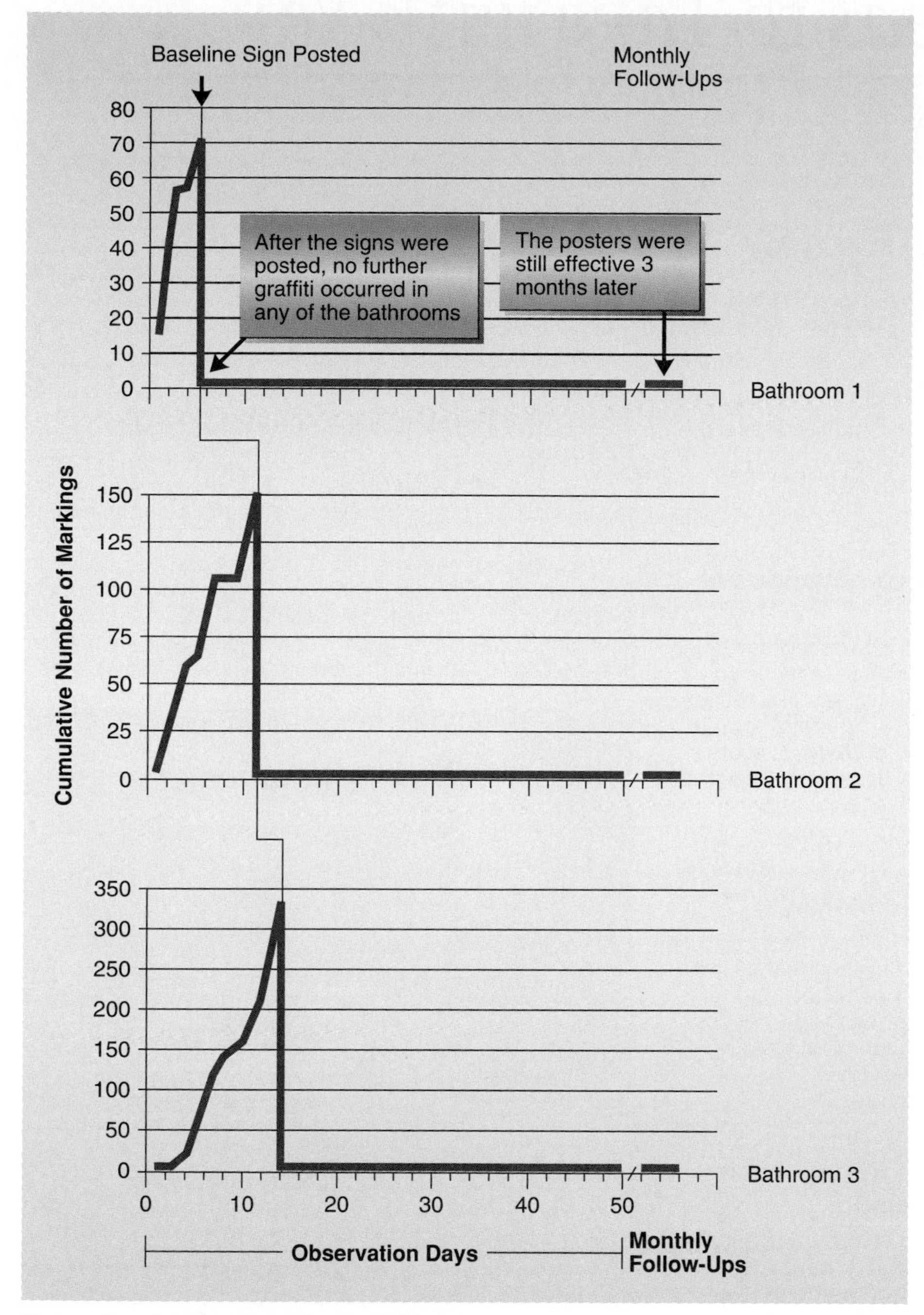

(**Source**: Based on data from Watson, 1997.)

FIGURE 5.18

Applied Behavior Analysis in Action

This graph shows the cumulative number of graffiti markings across observation days in three public restrooms. Before the intervention, a significant amount of graffiti was occurring in each of the bathrooms. After the intervention, however, no more graffiti occurred. Follow-up observations showed that the walls of the bathrooms remained graffiti-free three months later. Please note that the sequential introductions of the posters into the three bathrooms make it more likely that the reduction in graffiti resulted from the contents of the posters, not from other factors.

Caution: The fact that the posters were useful in these particular bathrooms does not ensure the same outcome elsewhere, such as in shopping malls or on subway cars. Nevertheless, the DO-IT process remains a useful tool for systematically studying behavior and the effects of behavior-change interventions. Please refer to the **Ideas to Take with You** feature on page 200 for an example of how to make the DO-IT process work for you.

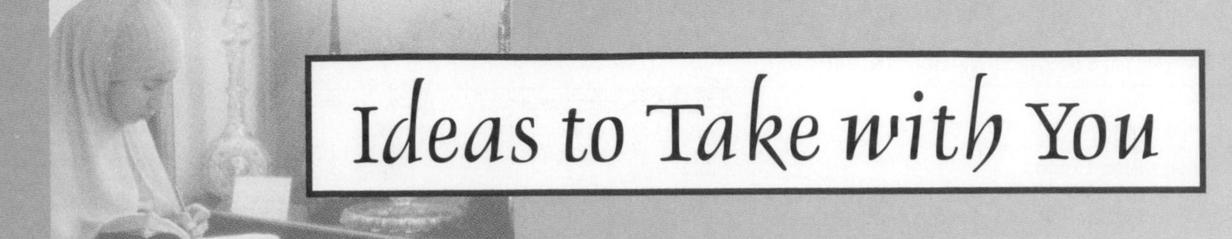

Applying the DO-IT Process to Increase Studying Behavior

The DO-IT process can be applied to a wide variety of everyday behaviors, including some that may be important to you. To illustrate this point, let's apply the DO-IT process to studying—a topic I'm sure you're familiar with.

DEFINE the target behaviors or outcomes of behavior you wish to change.

In this case, studying might include the following: the amount of time spent reading or working on homework assignments, the number of pages or chapters read each day, or the number of homework problems completed. It might also include outcomes of behavior, such as scores on quizzes and tests and grades on homework assignments.

OBSERVE the behaviors systematically across time.

Next, begin to keep score. Develop a system that allows you to consistently track each of the behaviors (or outcomes of behaviors) you have targeted. Some people find that graphing or charting this information is a useful way to see how these behaviors change over time.

INTERVENE in a way you feel will motivate you to improve your study habits.

Designing and implementing a successful intervention often involves setting a series of smaller or short-term goals. Begin by setting a goal to work toward; for example, a certain number of hours per week devoted to studying, or a specific number of chapters completed per week. Then select a reward to give yourself upon achieving your goal.

TEST to see if the intervention was successful.

Continue to track your progress. Doing so will allow you to see how the target behaviors, and important outcomes of these behaviors, change over time.

As you can see, the DO-IT process can be applied to many important target behaviors. Interestingly, students frequently report that competing behaviors—such as watching TV or goofing off—tend to decrease over time, leaving additional time for more productive activities.

Let's now turn to a discussion of additional ways in which applied behavior analysts have applied operant conditioning principles to solve several important problems of everyday life.

Biofeedback: A technique that enables people to monitor and self-regulate certain bodily functions through the use of specialized equipment.

Applying Operant Conditioning: Can We Make a Difference?

Because positive and negative reinforcement exerts powerful effects on behavior, procedures based on operant conditioning have been applied in many practical settings—so many that it would be impossible to describe them all here. An overview of some of these uses will suffice, though.

First, principles of operant conditioning have been applied to the field of education. One of the most impressive operant-based teaching techniques involves the use of computers in the classroom—often termed *computer-assisted instruction,* or *CAI.* In CAI students interact with sophisticated computer programs that provide immediate reinforcement of correct responses. With certain restrictions, these programs are paced according to each student's progress (Ross & McBean, 1995). The effectiveness of CAI as an instructional tool is even more impressive when students are exposed to an instructor who models the use of these programs in advance. Some evidence suggests that students may learn to take greater responsibility for their own performance under CAI than under teacher-led instruction, because they view computers as impersonal and therefore fairer. With the color graphics, synthesized speech, and other effects available on videodisc, CAI instruction may add excitement and enhance motivation for learning (e.g., Kritch, Bostow, & Dedrick, 1995).

A second intriguing area of application of operant conditioning is **biofeedback**—a technique in which sophisticated equipment allows people to monitor and then alter bodily responses not usually susceptible to voluntary control, such as skin temperature, muscle tension, blood pressure, and electrical activity of the brain. For example, with biofeedback equipment ongoing increases or decreases in muscle tension are reflected by concomitant changes in a light or tone. A patient undergoing biofeedback then monitors this information and uses it to alter muscular tension. Biofeedback has been used successfully to treat a broad range of ailments, including headaches (Arena et al., 1995; Hermann, Kim, & Blanchard, 1995), high blood pressure (Dubbert, 1995), muscle tics and chronic lower back pain (Newton et al., 1995; O'Connor, Gareau, & Borgeat, 1995), depression in alcoholics (Saxby & Peniston, 1995)—and even sexual dysfunction (Palace, 1995).

Third, principles of operant conditioning have been applied in interventions for solving socially significant issues in our communities, such as crime, energy conservation and recycling, health care issues, consumer affairs, and safety promotion (Geller, 1995, 1996; Green et al., 1987).

Finally, techniques of operant conditioning have been applied to many issues and problems in work settings—for example, to improve the performance of employees (e.g., George & Hopkins, Luthans, Paul, & Baker, 1981; 1989; Petty, Singleton, & Connell, 1992) and in the development of flexible work schedules (Winett & Neale, 1981). In one study, Petty and his colleagues (1992) demonstrated that a group incentive program improved the productivity of employees in a division of an electric utility company, thereby reducing the cost of electricity to the customers. Moreover, employees perceived that the incentive plan increased teamwork and encouraged greater employee involvement in decision making. Clearly, both organizations and their workers can profit greatly from closer attention to basic principles of operant conditioning.

Key Questions

- What evidence supports the involvement of cognitive factors in operant conditioning?
- Why is knowledge of operant conditioning important?

Observational Learning: Learning from the Behavior and Outcomes of Others

You are at a formal dinner party. Arranged at your place are five different forks, including two of a shape you've never seen before. Which ones do you use for which dishes? You have no idea. In order to avoid making a complete fool of yourself, as the first course arrives, you watch the other guests. When several reach unhesitatingly for one of the unfamiliar forks, you do the same. Now, thank goodness, you can concentrate on the food.

Even if you have not had an experience quite like this, you have probably encountered situations in which you have acquired new information, forms of behavior, or even abstract rules and concepts from watching other people (see Figure 5.19). Such **observational learning** is a third major way we learn, and it is a common part of everyday life (Bandura, 1977, 1986). Indeed, a large body of research findings suggest that observational learning can play a role in almost every aspect of behavior. A few examples:

- A student chef watches while an experienced chef prepares a soufflé; under the guidance of this person, she then tries to prepare one herself.
- A couple watches a television program that shows step by step how to remodel a bathroom. The following day, the couple sets out to remodel their own.
- A child watches his parents wash dishes, do the laundry, cook meals, and go to their jobs each morning. From such experience, he forms an impression that married couples share the responsibilities of running a household.

In these and countless other instances, we appear to learn vicariously, merely by watching the actions of other persons and the consequences others experience. More formal evidence for the existence of observational learning has been provided by hundreds of studies, many of them performed with children. Perhaps the most famous of these studies are the well-known "Bobo doll" experiments conducted by Bandura and his colleagues (e.g., Bandura, Ross, & Ross, 1963). In these studies one group of nursery-school children saw an adult engage in aggressive actions against a large inflated Bobo doll. The adult who was serving as a model knocked the doll down, sat on it, insulted it verbally, and repeatedly punched it in the nose. Another group of children were exposed to a model who behaved in a quiet, nonaggressive manner. Later, both groups of youngsters were placed in a room with several toys, including a Bobo doll. Careful observation of their behavior revealed that those who had seen the aggressive adult model often imitated this person's behavior: They too punched the toy, sat on it, and even uttered verbal comments similar to those of the model. In contrast, children in the control group rarely if ever demonstrated such actions. While you may not find these results surprising, they may be significant in relation to the enduring controversy over whether children acquire new ways of aggression through exposure to violent television programs and movies. We'll return to this issue below. For the moment, let's consider the nature of observational learning itself.

FIGURE 5.19

Acquiring New Skills through Observational Learning

Acquiring new skills by observing the behavior of others is a common part of everyday life.

Observational Learning: Some Basic Principles

Observational Learning: The acquisition of new forms of behavior, information, or concepts through exposure to others and the consequences they experience.

Given that observational learning exists, what factors and conditions determine whether, and to what extent, we acquire behaviors, information, or concepts from others? According to Bandura (1986), who is still the leading expert on this process, four factors are most important.

First, in order to learn through observation you must direct your *attention* to appropriate models—that is, to other persons performing an activity. And, as you might expect, you don't choose such models at random but focus most attention on people who are attractive to you; on people who possess signs of knowing what they're doing, such as status or success; and on people whose behavior seems relevant to your own needs and goals (Baron, 1970).

The second essential factor is *retention,* or memory, of what the persons have said or done. Only if you can retain some representation of their actions in memory can you perform similar actions at later times or acquire useful information from your models.

Third, you need to be able to convert these memory representations into appropriate actions. Bandura terms this aspect of observational learning *production processes.* Production processes depend on (1) your own physical abilities—if you can't perform the behavior in question, having a clear representation of it in memory is of little use; and (2) your capacity to monitor your own performance and adjust it until it matches that of the model.

Finally, *motivation* plays a role. We often acquire information through observational learning but do not put it into immediate use in our own behavior. You may have no need for the information, as when you watch someone tie a bow tie but have no plans to wear one yourself. Or the observed behaviors may involve high risk of punishment or be repugnant to you personally, as when you observe an ingenious way of cheating during an exam but don't want to try it yourself. Only if the information or behaviors acquired are useful will observers put them to actual use. Figure 5.20 summarizes factors affecting observational learning.

As you can see, observational learning is a complex process—far more complex than mere imitation—and plays an important role in many aspects

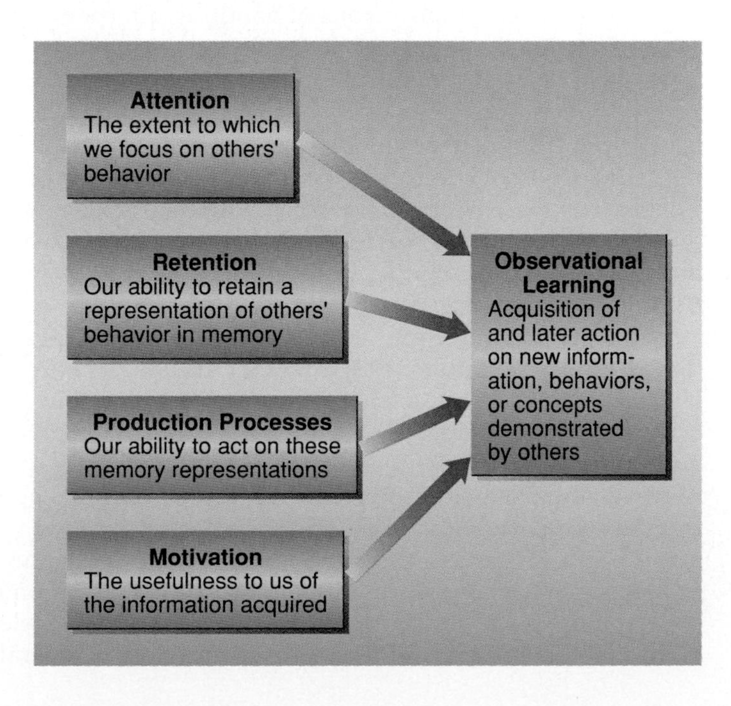

FIGURE 5.20

Key Factors in Observational Learning

Observational learning is affected by several factors or subprocesses. The most important of these are summarized here.

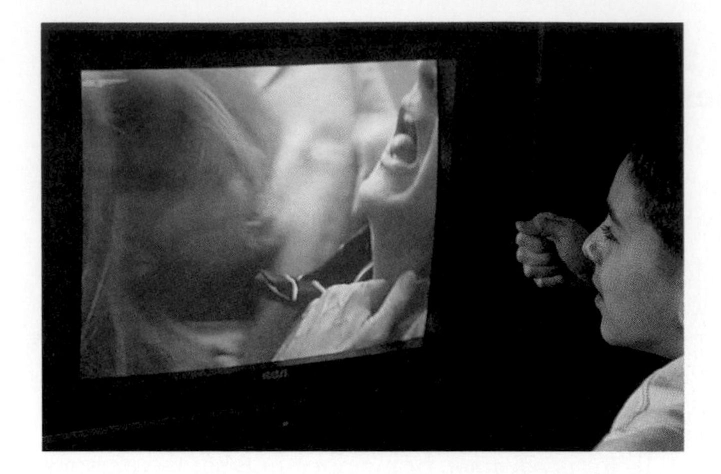

FIGURE 5.21

Observational Learning and Aggression

Some experts worry that exposure to violence on television and in movies may encourage children to perform violent acts.

of behavior. This point is perhaps most forcefully illustrated by the controversy that has persisted in psychology, and in society as a whole, since the early 1960s: the questions of whether children, and perhaps even adults, are made more aggressive by long-term exposure to violence on television shows or in movies.

Observational Learning and Aggression

A large body of evidence suggests that aggression may indeed be learned through observation (Baron & Richardson, 1994; Centerwall, 1989; Snyder, 1991; Wood, Wong, & Chachere, 1991). Apparently, when children and adults are exposed to new ways of aggressing against others—techniques they have not previously seen—they may add these new behaviors to their repertoire. Later, when angry, irritated, or frustrated, they may put such behaviors to actual use in assaults against others. Of course, exposure to media violence, whether on the evening news or in movies or television programs, has other effects as well (see Figure 5.21). Media violence may convey messages that violence is an acceptable means of handling interpersonal difficulties; after all, if heroes and heroines can do it, why not viewers? It may elicit additional aggressive ideas and thoughts, convincing viewers, for example, that violence is even more common than it really is (Berkowitz, 1984). And it may also lessen emotional reactions to aggression and the harm it produces, so that such violence comes to seem less upsetting or objectionable (Thomas, 1982). When these effects are coupled with new behaviors and skills acquired through observational learning, the overall impact may contribute to an increased tendency among many persons to engage in acts of aggression (Eron, 1987; Zillman & Weaver, 1997).

It is important to note that not all findings support such conclusions (Freedman, 1986; Widom, 1989) and that the effects of exposure to media violence, when they occur, seem to be modest in scope. Given the fact that many children spend more time watching television, playing violent video games, and, more recently, surfing the Web than they do any other single activity, however, the potential influence of such experience on behavior seems worthy of careful attention. In Chapter 10 I'll return to the topic of aggression and discuss additional factors that seem to motivate aggressive behavior.

Research has also studied the effects of television on behavior in other areas of life. In one study, for instance, observations of television depictions of automobile drivers and their passengers during several viewing seasons revealed that most of these persons were rarely shown belted (Geller, 1988). Moreover, the most probable real-life consequences of crashes for unbelted vehicle occupants—serious injury or death—were almost never shown on TV. In response to this, Geller initiated a nationwide campaign designed to bring public attention to the nonuse of safety belts on TV. As part of this campaign, Geller and his students encouraged children to write letters to their television heroes, requesting that they use safety belts. In one instance, more than eight hundred students from Olympia, Washington, wrote buckle-up requests to a star on a then popular action show. Interestingly, the star increased his on-screen belt use dramatically following the letter-writing campaign.

It is noteworthy that safety-belt use on television shows *increased* over the three-year period of the study, consistent with changes in national safety-belt use statistics. Because television shows enjoy such a massive viewing audience, often millions of viewers, efforts to depict exemplary behavior among network stars—like safe driving—could potentially save millions of lives.

Observational Learning: Some Interesting Applications

As you can see from the previous discussions, the effects of observational learning on our behavior can, indeed, be powerful—and not always for the good. For example, observational learning may contribute to the development of unhealthy behaviors, including smoking, especially among adolescents (Hahn et al., 1990). Acceptance by peers is intensely important to persons in this age group, so it is possible that observing peers who smoke contributes to adolescents' own decisions to start smoking (Hawkins, Catalano, & Miller, 1992). Recent evidence seems to indicate this is true. In one study, Aloise-Young, Graham, and Hansen (1994) surveyed several thousand seventh graders to assess their smoking habits and the smoking habits of their peers. They also asked participants if they cared how their friends would react if they used drugs or alcohol. Finally, they assessed whether each student was already a member of a social group (group members) or not (outsiders). Then, during the following school year, they surveyed the students as eighth graders to determine their smoking status. Which of these students was most likely to have started smoking? Because peer acceptance is so important to twelve- and thirteen-year-olds, Aloise-Young and her colleagues predicted that the "outsiders," teens who had not yet been accepted into a friendship group, would be influenced to a greater extent by the behavior of their peers than would teens already in a friendship group. Their predictions were confirmed. The results showed that the "outsiders" were much more likely to emulate the behavior of others—and hence to begin smoking—than participants who were group members. In fact, outsiders whose best friend smoked in the seventh grade were twice as likely to begin smoking than outsiders whose friends did not smoke. In contrast, this pattern of peer influence was not evident among teens who were already part of a group.

Although the results of this study highlight the potential negative effects of observational learning, there is a large body of evidence showing that peer influence can also be used to promote more productive behaviors. In one recent study, Werts, Caldwell, and Wolery (1996) examined whether mildly retarded children enrolled in a regular classroom could acquire skills by having their nonhandicapped peers model the skills for them (as shown in Figure 5.22). The skills included spelling their name, using a calculator to perform simple arithmetic, and sharp-

FIGURE 5.22

Modeling Appropriate Behaviors Can Make a Difference

Handicapped students can frequently learn important skills simply by watching the behavior of their peers.

ening a pencil. Each of the skills was broken down into simpler sets of tasks that the peer tutors learned to perform and describe accurately. The students were required to master performance on one set of tasks before moving onto the next step in the chain. Through this procedure, each participant acquired useful skills in a relatively short period of time (less than a month). It is noteworthy that the time the peers spent modeling the behaviors averaged about five minutes per day—suggesting that observational learning can be an efficient tool in the learning process.

To summarize, then, observational learning plays an important role in many aspects of behavior. Please see the Exploring Gender and Diversity section below for more information on this topic.

Key Questions

- What is observational learning?
- What factors determine the extent to which we acquire new information through observational learning?
- In what forms of behavior does observational learning play a role?
- In what ways can observational learning be used to solve problems of everyday life?

EXPLORING GENDER & DIVERSITY

Learning to Avoid "Culture Shock"

Much of our understanding of the world around us—including our language and customs—comes to us through observation of the behaviors of others around us. Psychologists have applied principles of observational learning to help solve a problem of growing concern: preparing people for "culture shock."

As the United States and other countries move toward a global economy, companies throughout the world are faced with a difficult challenge. They must prepare their employees for the business environment of the 1990s—an environment that requires a broad range of skills and the ability to interact effectively with persons from other cultures (Adler & Bartholomew, 1992; Feldman & Tompson, 1993). Dramatic differences in language, customs, and lifestyle often lead to unintended misunderstandings between persons from different cultural backgrounds. Behaviors that are acceptable in one country may be quite offensive to persons from another country (see Figure 5.23). For example, consider differences in social greetings. When a young man is introduced to a young woman in Argentina, he is expected to kiss her lightly on the cheek; but this greeting would be considered quite impolite in Japan and many other countries. Ignorance of cultural differences has long been cited as a chief cause of misunderstandings between persons of different cultural backgrounds (Harris, 1979).

To soften the effects of culture shock, companies that conduct business abroad have scrambled to develop cross-cultural training programs. The goal of these programs is to help a company's representatives learn appropriate, sensitive, and consistent behavior. Initial efforts to prepare employees for cross-cultural assignments focused on a cognitive approach, in which trainees received factual information about a particular country (Fielder, Mithell, & Triandis, 1971).

More recently, however, experts in the area of cross-cultural training have advocated an "experiential" approach based on behavioral modeling (Black & Mendenhall, 1990). In the behavioral modeling approach, trainees first watch films in which models exhibit the correct behaviors in a problem situation. Then the trainees participate in a role-playing exercise to test their knowledge. Finally, they receive constructive feedback regarding their performance. But are such programs effective?

FIGURE 5.23

Observational Learning: Adapting to Diversity

Observing the behaviors of persons from different cultures can help us avoid social gaffes and acquire social skills that will be important in a global economy.

Research evidence suggests that the answer is yes. In one study, Harrison (1992) compared the effectiveness of several approaches to cross-cultural training: one group of participants got culture-relevant information only; another group was given behavioral modeling training only; a third received both forms of training; and a fourth, the control group, got no training. The results showed that participants who received both forms of training—information and behavioral modeling—performed best on measures of culture-specific knowledge and on a behavioral measure.

These findings, and those of other related studies, illustrate the important role that observational learning plays in alleviating the effects of culture shock. Observational learning initially enables us to perform behaviors appropriate to our own culture, but it can also help us adapt to the demands of a rapidly changing world.

Making Psychology Part of Your Life

Getting in Shape: Applying Psychology to Get Fit and Stay Fit

Although it is well known that keeping fit is important to good health, a recent report from the U.S. Surgeon General also suggests that staying in shape may help offset some less healthy behaviors—such as smoking, drinking alcohol, or overeating. Apparently, people who overindulge but exercise regularly (see Figure 5.24 on page 208) may be less at risk for premature death than people who appear fit but are couch potatoes. Do you need to get back into shape? Or lose a pound or twenty? Why not make learning principles a part of your fitness system—the *true* breakfast of champions? Establishing your fitness program using the learning principles we've discussed in this chapter will help you hit the diet and exercise trail running.

First, it is important to set your sights realistically. Don't try to lose all twenty pounds in one week, or try to run ten miles the first time out. Why not? If you recall our discussion of reinforcement and punishment, you'll recognize that overdoing at the outset will actually punish your efforts, making it even more difficult to stay with your program. If you've tried and failed to stick with a diet or exercise program in the past because of this, you can probably appreciate the point.

Instead, remember that a little can go a long way. So set yourself up for small wins by taking advantage of the principle of *shaping*—rewarding yourself initially with modest rewards for successive approximations in the direction of your ultimate exercise and weight-reduction goals. Then slowly increase the amount of exercise that you do or the cumulative amount of weight that you lose, building on each of your previous successes. Also, take care in your selection of rewards—choose rewards that are desirable but consistent with your goals. For example, if you are trying to lose weight, reward yourself with a movie or clothes with a smaller waist size—not with a hot fudge sundae.

Third, specify the amount and intensity of the exercise you will do or the amount of weight you intend to lose—and write it down. Some people find that it is helpful to chart their progress in order to give themselves accurate and immediate *feedback* that will serve to reinforce or punish their behavior. Also, by placing the chart in a prominent place for yourself and your friends and family to see, you can take advantage of both *positive and negative reinforcement*. For example, you can work to receive the positive attention that will come your way when your chart shows progress. Negative reinforcement may also help, because posting your progress publicly may cause you to work to avoid the negative comments you may get if you are tempted to "take a day off . . . just because."

Fourth, *stimulus control* can help set the stage for healthy responses. So avoid situations in which you may be tempted to consume unhealthy food or bever-

FIGURE 5.24

Types of Moderate Exercise

A recent Surgeon General's report on physical activity and health suggests that regular, moderate physical activity—like the examples listed above—is the key to good health.

Examples of Moderate Amounts of Activity	
Washing and waxing a car for 45–60 minutes	**Less vigorous, more time**
Washing windows or floors for 45–60 minutes	
Playing volleyball for 45 minutes	
Playing touch football for 30–45 minutes	
Gardening for 30–45 minutes	
Wheeling self in wheelchair for 30–40 minutes	
Walking 1.75 miles in 35 minutes	
Basketball (shooting baskets) for 30 minutes	
Bicycling 5 miles in 30 minutes	
Dancing fast (social) for 30 minutes	
Pushing a stroller 1.5 miles in 30 minutes	
Raking leaves for 30 minutes	
Walking 2 miles in 30 minutes (15 min./mile)	
Water aerobics for 30 minutes	
Swimming laps for 20 minutes	
Wheelchair basketball for 20 minutes	
Basketball (playing a game) for 15–20 minutes	
Bicycling 4 miles in 15 minutes	
Jumping rope for 15 minutes	
Running 1.25 miles in 15 minutes (10 min./mile)	
Shoveling snow for 15 minutes	
Stair walking for 15 minutes	**More vigorous, less time**

(**Source**: Based on information from at-a-glance companion document to Physical Activity and Health: A Report of the Surgeon General.)

age; instead, begin going to places and meeting people that are likely to occasion healthy responses. For example, by joining a health club, YMCA, or other *active* organization, you will be more likely to exercise and eat healthily.

Finally, take advantage of the principles of *observational learning* by identifying people with traits and skills that you admire. By observing and then emulating their behavior, you may become more efficient in reaching your goals. So make psychology a part of your fitness system—to get fit and stay fit!

Summary and Review of Key Questions

Classical Conditioning: Learning That Some Stimuli Signal Others

- **What is learning?** Learning is any relatively permanent change in behavior (or behavior potential) produced by experience.
- **What is classical conditioning?** Classical conditioning is a form of learning in which neutral stimuli—stimuli initially unable to elicit a particular response—come to elicit that response through their association with stimuli that are naturally able to do so.
- **Upon what factors does acquisition of a classically conditioned response depend?** Acquisition is dependent upon the temporal arrangement of the conditioned stimulus–unconditioned stimulus pairings, the intensity of the CS and UCS relative to other background stimuli, and the familiarity of potentially conditioned stimuli present.
- **What is extinction?** Extinction is the process through which a conditioned stimulus gradually ceases to elicit a conditioned response when it is no longer paired with an unconditioned stimulus. However, this response can be quickly regained through reconditioning.
- **What is the difference between stimulus generalization and stimulus discrimination?** Stimulus generalization allows us to apply our learning to other situations; stimulus discrimination allows us to differentiate among similar but different stimuli.
- **Where in the brain does classical conditioning take place?** Research shows that the cerebellum, a structure in the brain involved in balance and coordination, plays a key role in the formation of simple forms of classically conditioned responses.
- **Is classical conditioning equally easy to establish with all stimuli for all organisms?** Because of biological constraints that exist among different species, types of conditioning readily accomplished by some species are acquired only slowly—or not at all—by others.
- **How do we acquire conditioned taste aversions?** Conditioned taste aversions are usually established when a food or beverage (conditioned stimulus) is paired with a stimulus that naturally leads to feelings of illness (unconditioned stimulus). Conditioned taste aversions can be established after a single CS–UCS pairing.
- **How do modern views of classical conditioning differ from earlier perspectives?** Modern views of classical conditioning emphasize the important role of cognitive processes. A large body of research suggests that conditioning is a complex process in which organisms form representations of the relationships among a variety of factors—including many aspects of the physical setting or context in which the conditioned and unconditioned stimuli are presented.
- **What is blocking?** In blocking, conditioning to one stimulus is prevented by previous conditioning to another stimulus.
- **What is flooding? Systematic desensitization?** Flooding and systematic desensitization are procedures used to extinguish fears established through classical conditioning. In flooding, a person is forced to come into contact with fear-eliciting stimuli without an avenue of escape. Cases in which fearful thoughts are too painful to deal with directly are treated by systematic desensitization—a progressive technique designed to replace anxiety with a relaxation response.
- **How can we employ classical conditioning principles to solve problems of everyday life?** Basic principles of classical conditioning have been used to solve a variety of everyday problems, including phobias (learned fears) and unexplained instances of drug overdose. Classical conditioning processes may also play a role in suppressing or enhancing aspects of the immune system.

KEY TERMS

learning, p. 170 • classical conditioning, p. 171 • stimulus, p. 171 • unconditioned stimulus (UCS), p. 172 • unconditioned response (UCR), p. 172 • conditioned stimulus (CS), p. 172 • conditioned response (CR), p. 172 • acquisition, p. 173 • delayed conditioning, p. 174 • trace conditioning, p. 174 • simultaneous conditioning, p. 174 • backward conditioning, p. 174 • extinction, p. 175 • reconditioning, p. 175 • spontaneous recovery, p. 175 • stimulus generalization, p. 175 • stimulus discrimination, p. 175 • biological constraints on learning, p. 178 • conditioned taste aversion, p. 178 • phobias, p. 181 • flooding, p. 182

Operant Conditioning: Learning Based on Consequences

- **What is operant conditioning?** In operant conditioning, organisms learn the relationships between certain behaviors and the consequences they produce.
- **What are examples of primary reinforcers? Of conditioned reinforcers?** Primary reinforcers include food, water, and sexual pleasure; conditioned reinforcers include money, status, and praise.
- **Which operant techniques strengthen behavior? Weaken behavior?** Both positive and negative reinforcement strengthen or increase behavior. In contrast, positive and negative punishment suppress or weaken behavior.
- **How do negative reinforcement and punishment differ?** Both negative reinforcement and punishment involve aversive events. They differ, however, in terms of their effects on behavior. In negative reinforcement behaviors that allow an organism to escape from an aversive event, or to avoid it altogether, are *strengthened.* In punishment an aversive event *weakens* the behavior it follows.
- **What are shaping and chaining?** Shaping is useful for establishing new responses by initially reinforcing behaviors that resemble the desired behavior, termed *successive approximations.* Chaining is a procedure used to establish a complex sequence or chain of behaviors. The final response in the chain is trained first; then, working backwards, earlier responses in the chain are reinforced by the opportunity to perform the last response in the chain, which leads to a reward.
- **How does reward delay affect operant conditioning?** When asked to choose between a smaller-but-sooner and a larger-but-later reward—and when both options are relatively distant events—people often choose the latter option. As access to the smaller reward draws near, however, people's *impulsive* tendencies tend to overpower their earlier decision to hold out for the delayed (but better) reward. Getting people to make a commitment ahead of time may help reduce this tendency. People exhibit a similar tendency when faced with a choice between performing a smaller, less effortful task now and performing a larger, more effortful task later on: they *procrastinate,* choosing the more delayed alternative, even when it leads to more work.
- **What are schedules of reinforcement?** Schedules of reinforcement are rules that determine when a response will be reinforced. Schedules of reinforcement can be time-based or event-based, fixed or variable. Each schedule of reinforcement produces a characteristic pattern of responding.
- **When is the use of continuous reinforcement desirable, and when should other reinforcement schedules be used?** A continuous reinforcement schedule is desirable for establishing new behaviors; partial or intermittent reinforcement schedules are more powerful in maintaining behavior.
- **What are concurrent schedules of reinforcement and the matching law?** In a concurrent schedule, an organism's behavior is free to alternate between two or more responses, each of which has its own schedule of reinforcement. The matching law suggests that an organism distributes its behavior between response alternatives in such a way as to maximize the reinforcement obtained from each alternative.
- **What is a discriminative stimulus, and what is stimulus control?** Discriminative stimuli signal the availability of spe-

cific consequences if a certain response is made. When a behavior occurs consistently in the presence of a discriminative stimulus, it is said to be under stimulus control.

- **What evidence supports the involvement of cognitive factors in operant conditioning?** Studies of learned helplessness, beliefs about reinforcement, contrast effects, and memory of reward events support the conclusion that cognitive factors play an important role in operant conditioning.
- **Why is knowledge of operant conditioning important?** Procedures based on operant conditioning principles can be applied to address many problems of everyday life—for example, in improving classroom instructional technology; in the development of interventions to solve community-based problems such as crime, health care, and safety; and to improve employee performance in the workplace.

KEY TERMS

operant conditioning, p. 185 • reinforcement, p. 185 • positive reinforcers, p. 185 • Premack principle, p. 185 • negative reinforcers, p. 186 • punishment, p. 186 • shaping, p. 188 • chaining, p. 188 • schedules of reinforcement, p. 191 • continuous reinforcement schedule, p. 191 • fixed-interval schedule, p. 191 • variable-interval schedule, p. 191 • fixed-ratio schedule, p. 191 • variable-ratio schedule, p. 191 • concurrent schedule of reinforcement, p. 192 • discriminative stimulus, p. 194 • stimulus control, p. 194 • learned helplessness, p. 194 • applied behavior analysis, p. 198 • biofeedback, p. 201

Observational Learning: Learning from the Behavior and Outcomes of Others

- **What is observational learning?** Observational learning is the acquisition of new information, concepts, or forms of behavior through exposure to others and the consequences they experience.
- **What factors determine the extent to which we acquire new information through observational learning?** In order for observational learning to be effective, we must pay attention to those modeling the behavior, remember the modeled speech or action, possess the ability to act upon this memory, and have the motivation to do so.
- **In what forms of behavior does observational learning play a role?** Observational learning plays an important role in countless types of everyday behavior, including aggression.
- **In what ways can observational learning be used to solve problems of everyday life?** Observational learning is important in many aspects of life, including work; for example, it can be used in training programs designed to help workers interact more effectively with people from different cultural backgrounds.

KEY TERM

observational learning, p. 203

Critical Thinking Questions

Appraisal

Psychologists are moving increasingly toward a cognitive view of the learning process. Do you think this movement is appropriate, or is there still a role for the views of operant psychologists?

Controversy

Growing evidence suggests that animals form mental representations of their environments, including memories, that are analogous to those formed by human beings. Does this mean that animals think? What are your views on this issue? What are the implications of this theory of animal learning?

Making Psychology Part of Your Life

Knowing something about principles of learning is very useful to persons who wish to get into shape or lose weight. But these are only two ways in which these principles can be applied to solve problems of everyday life. Can you think of others?

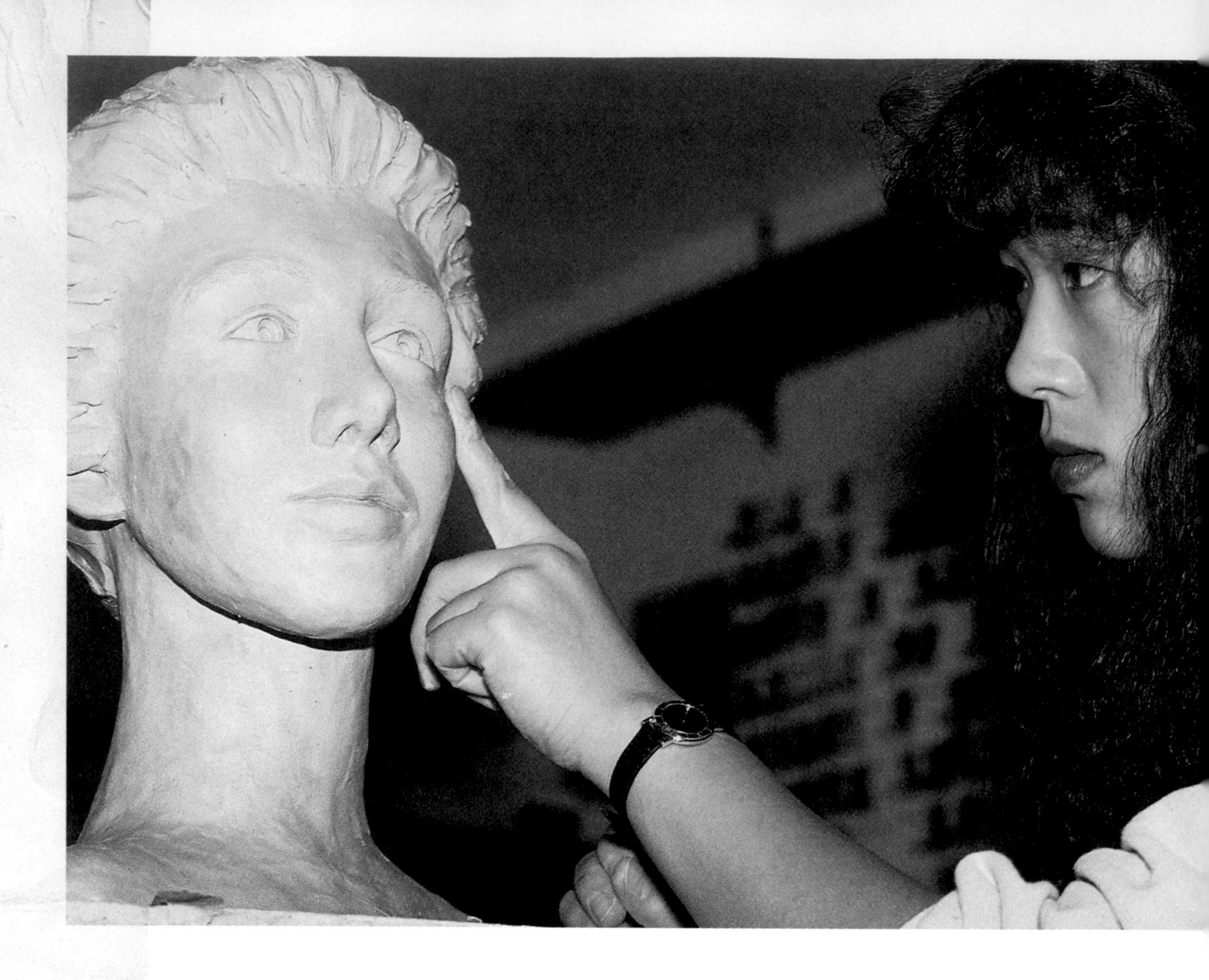

CHAPTER OUTLINE

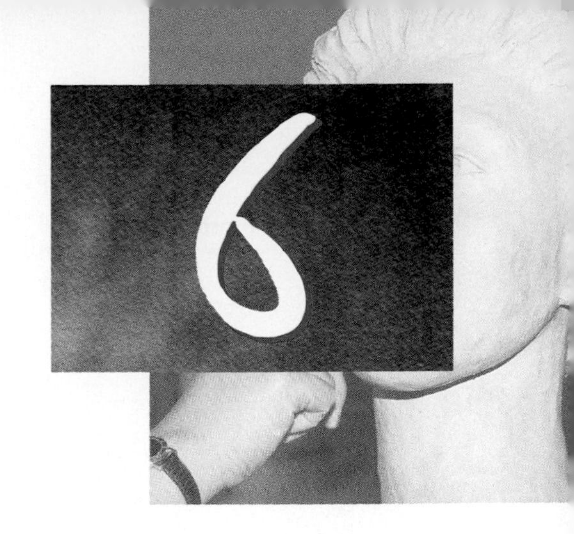

Memory

Of Things Remembered . . . and Forgotten

Can you remember your first day on campus? Your most recent visit to the dentist? The teachers you had in grade school? Your first date? Although these events and people date back months or even years, you can probably bring vivid images of them to mind. Now, answer quickly: Is any building shown on the back of a $5 bill (or the equivalent in your own currency if you don't live in the United States or Canada)? What about a $20 bill—whose face is shown on the front? Although you've seen these objects many, many times, you may have some difficulty in answering. Similarly, have you ever had problems finding your car after parking it at a shopping mall or forgotten someone's name minutes after being introduced to the person (see Figure 6.1 on page 214)? And what about this one: At least ten times each day, I put my eyeglasses down somewhere—and then can't find them!

Memory: The capacity to retain and later retrieve information.

Experiences like this indicate that memory—our cognitive system for storing and retrieving information—is indeed, as the saying goes, a funny thing. It allows us to retain vivid and often accurate memories of events for months, years, or even decades. Yet just when we need it most, it seems to let us down.

Because it is clearly a crucial aspect of cognition, memory has long been a topic of study in psychology. In fact, memory was the focus of some of the earliest systematic work in the field—studies conducted more than one hundred years ago by Hermann Ebbinghaus (1885). Using himself as a subject, Ebbinghaus memorized and then recalled hundreds of *nonsense syllables*—meaningless combinations of letters, such as teg or pxt. Some of his findings about the nature of memory and forgetting have withstood the test of time and are valid even today. For example, Ebbinghaus found that at first we forget materials we have memorized quite rapidly but that later, forgetting proceeds more slowly.

It is probably correct to say that psychologists now know more about memory than about any other basic aspect of cognition.

While Ebbinghaus's studies were ingenious in many respects, modern research on memory has gone far beyond these simple beginnings. In fact, it is probably correct to say that psychologists now know more about memory than about any other basic aspect of cognition. To provide you with an overview of this intriguing body of knowledge, we'll proceed as follows. First, we'll consider the picture of human memory that has emerged from psychological research—a picture suggesting that we possess three different systems for storing and later retrieving (remembering) information. Next, we'll explore the nature of *forgetting*—how and why information is lost from memory. Third, we'll focus on memory in *natural contexts*—how memory operates in daily life, outside the confines of the experimental laboratory. Here, we'll examine such topics as *autobiographical memory*—memory of events and expe-

FIGURE 6.1

Memory: Far from Perfect!

As suggested by this cartoon, we are frequently unable to retrieve information we'd like to remember.

"As I get older, I find I rely more and more on these sticky notes to remind me."

(**Source:** Drawing by Levin; © 1996 The New Yorker Magazine, Inc.)

riences in our own lives—and *distortion* and *construction* in memory. We'll conclude by considering several memory disorders and what these disorders, plus other research, tell us about the biological nature of memory.

Human Memory: The Information-Processing Approach

Have you ever operated a personal computer? If so, you already know that computers, like people, have memories. In fact, most have two different types of memory: a temporary, working memory (known as *random access memory*) and a larger and more permanent memory in which information is stored for longer periods of time (a hard drive). Do the memories of computers operate like those of human beings? Almost certainly not. Consider the following differences: Unless you correctly specify the precise nature and location of information you want to find—for instance, a specific file—computers are unable to recover it. In contrast, you can often find information in your own memory even on the basis of a partial description. Similarly, if information is lost from a computer, it is often permanently gone—or at least can be recovered only with considerable difficulty. In contrast, you can fail to remember a fact or information at one time but then remember it readily at another. And you can often remember part of the information you want, even if you can't remember all of it. So, clearly, human memory and computer memory are *not* identical.

Yet many researchers have found computer memory to be useful as a working model for human memory. Both types of memory, after all, must accomplish the same basic tasks: (1) **encoding,** or converting information into a form that can be entered into memory; (2) **storage,** or retaining information over varying periods of time; and (3) **retrieval,** or locating and accessing specific information when it is needed at later times. Please don't misunderstand: The fact that computers and human memory deal with the same basic task in no way implies that they operate in the same manner. They certainly do not. Thus, you should view this **information-processing approach,** with its emphasis on encoding, storage, and retrieval, mainly as a useful and convenient way of discussing memory—not as a claim that human memory and computer memory operate in the same way.

Human Memory: A Basic Model

So, what kind of model of human memory does this general approach yield? One like that in Figure 6.2 on page 216. Perhaps the most surprising aspect of this model is that it suggests that in fact we possess not one but *three* distinct systems for storing information—three different kinds of memory, if you like. One of these, known as *sensory memory*, provides temporary storage of information brought to us by our senses. If you've ever watched someone wave a flashlight in a dark room and perceived trails of light behind it, you are familiar with the operation of sensory memory.

A second type of memory is known as *short-term memory* or *working memory*. Short-term memory holds relatively small amounts of information for brief periods of time, usually thirty seconds or less. This is the memory system you use when you look up a phone number and dial it.

Encoding: The process through which information is converted into a form that can be entered into memory.

Storage: The process through which information is retained in memory.

Retrieval: The process through which information stored in memory is located.

Information-Processing Approach: An approach to understanding human memory that emphasizes the encoding, storage, and later retrieval of information.

FIGURE 6.2

Human Memory: How Psychologists See It

Most psychologists accept a model of human memory like the one shown here. This model involves three distinct memory systems, plus mechanisms through which information moves between them.

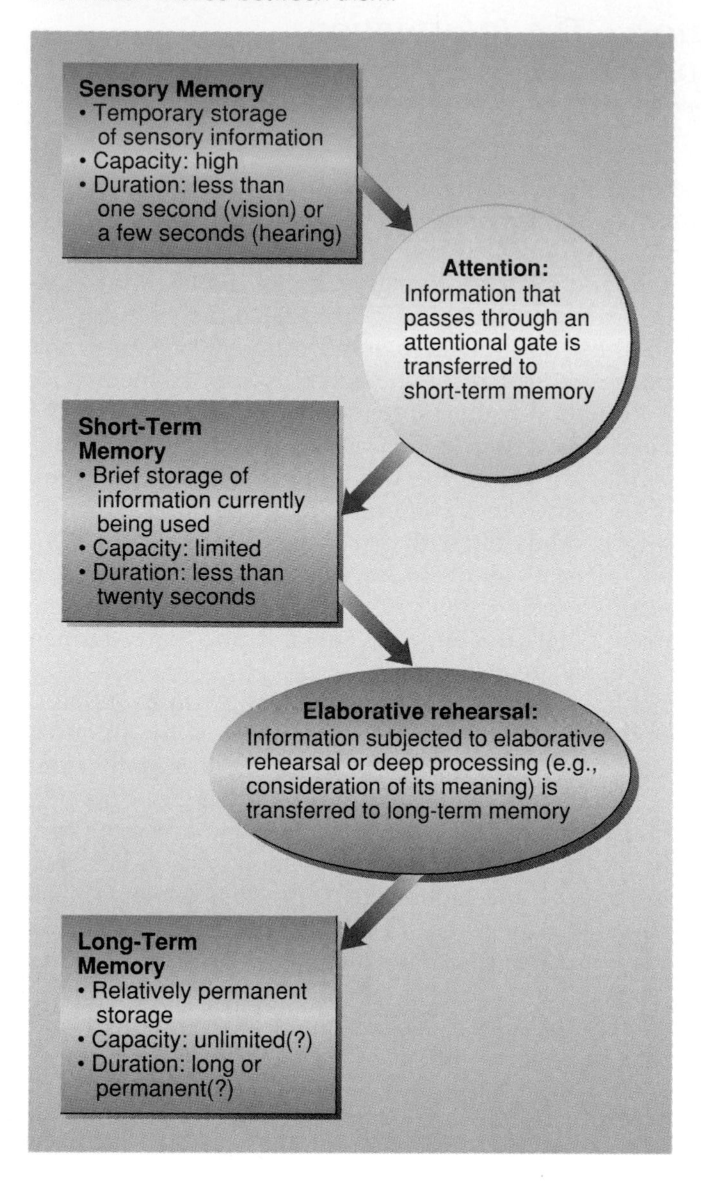

Our third memory system, *long-term memory,* allows us to retain vast amounts of information for very long periods of time. It is this memory system that permits you to remember events that happened a few hours ago, yesterday, last month—or many years in the past. And it is long-term memory that allows you to remember the capital of your state or country, the name of the president, and the information in this book—and to bring such information into consciousness when it is needed, as during an examination.

How does information move from one memory system to another? We'll examine this complex question in more detail below; but in general terms, this involves the operation of *active control processes* that serve as filters, determining which information will be retained. For example, information in sensory memory enters short-term memory when it becomes the focus of our attention; sensory impressions that do not engage attention fade and quickly disappear. So where memory is concerned, **selective attention**—our ability to pay attention to only some aspects of the world around us while largely ignoring others—often plays a crucial role (Johnston, McCann, & Remington, 1995; Posner & Peterson, 1990).

In contrast, information in short-term memory enters long-term storage through *elaborative rehearsal*—when we think about its meaning and relate it to other information already in long-term memory. Unless we engage in such cognitive effort, information in short-term memory quickly fades away and is lost.

Selective Attention: Our ability to pay attention to only some aspects of the world around us while largely ignoring others.

Semantic Memory: General, abstract knowledge about the world.

Episodic Memory: Memories of events that we have experienced personally (sometimes termed *autobiographical memory*).

Procedural Memory: Information we cannot readily express verbally—for example, information necessary to perform various skilled motor activities such as riding a bicycle.

Types of Information in Memory

If memory is a system (or, as we have just seen, several systems) for retaining information, a key question is: What types of information does memory store? The world, and our experience in it, is incredibly diverse, so this is a more complex question than you might guess. After careful study, however, psychologists have concluded that most information in memory can be classified as falling into one of three distinct categories.

The first kind of information in memory is general, abstract knowledge about the world, and it is referred to as **semantic memory.** How far is it from New York to London? Who is the prime minister of Russia? Are shrimp crustaceans or mollusks? And whatever they are, how long does it take to cook them? The answers to these and countless other questions are contained in semantic memory. Semantic memory allows us to represent and mentally operate on objects or situations that are not present and not open to examination by our senses. As Endel Tulving, one expert on memory, puts it (1993, p. 687): "The owner of a semantic memory system can think about things that are not here now."

A second type of information we retain involves specific events that we have experienced personally. This is known as **episodic memory,** or autobiographical memory. It is episodic memory that allows us, in a sense, to travel back in time. When was the last time you went to a movie? What happened on your last birthday? Information pertaining to these and countless other aspects of your own experience are contained in episodic memory. In essence, it is a record of the things you've seen, done, and heard, along with information about *when* these happened.

Finally, we retain information relating to the performance of various tasks. Do you know how to ride a bicycle? Tie a necktie? Play the piano? If so, then you are well aware of the **procedural memory** system—a memory system holding information that we can't put into words but that allows us to carry out countless activities.

As you can readily guess, we often require—and use—information of all three types at once. Consider what happens when you take an examination. First, you draw on facts stored in semantic memory. Second, you are using complex motor skills such as writing, which are represented in procedural memory. And as you take the exam, you may think about experiences with other examinations. For instance, you may remember that you actually lowered your score on another exam by changing many of your answers. As you remember this, you may refrain from changing some of your answers on this test. In many situations, then, we use all three types of information at once. (Please see Figure 6.3 on page 218 for a summary of the kinds of information held in semantic, episodic, and procedural memory.)

Key Questions

- What tasks are involved in encoding, storage, and retrieval?
- What are sensory memory, short-term memory, and long-term memory?
- What are semantic memory, episodic memory, and procedural memory?

Semantic Memory
Abstract, factual information about the world

Episodic Memory
Information about events we have experienced in our own lives

Procedural Memory
Information necessary to perform various tasks involving skilled movement

FIGURE 6.3

Semantic Memory, Episodic Memory, and Procedural Memory

Semantic memory consists of factual information. Episodic memory stores information about events we have experienced in our own lives. Procedural memory enables us to perform skilled activities such as riding a bicycle.

Sensory Memory, Short-Term Memory, and Long-Term Memory: *Our Basic Memory Systems*

Now that you have a basic idea of how psychologists think about human memory, let's take a closer look at the three memory systems described briefly above—sensory memory, short-term memory, and long-term memory. In this section I'll describe how each system carries out the basic tasks of memory—encoding information (that is, entering it into storage), retaining such information, and retrieving it when it is needed.

Sensory Memory: The Gateway to Consciousness

You are waiting in a busy airport. Many activities are occurring around you: people are rushing about, passengers are moving through security, people are talking, laughing, crying, hugging one another. You glance at a large video monitor containing flight information and then look away. As soon as you do, you look back, because something about it seemed different—what was it? Sighing, you realize that what has changed is information about your own flight: It is delayed again!

This incident may seem at first to have more to do with the pain of modern travel than with memory, but think again: What made you glance back at the screen? The answer involves what is in a sense our simplest memory system: **sensory memory.** This system holds representations of information from our senses very briefly—just long enough for us to determine that some aspect of this input is worthy of further attention. Without such memory, you would have had no reason to look back at the video monitor. As soon as your eyes moved away from it, all traces of the screen and its contents would have vanished. In this and countless other situations, sensory memory is very useful. Without it, we'd be able to react only to those stimuli reaching us at a given instant.

Sensory Memory: A memory system that retains representations of sensory input for brief periods of time.

How much can sensory memory hold? And how long does such information last? Existing evidence suggests that the capacity of sensory memory is quite large; indeed, it may hold fleeting representations of virtually everything we see, hear, taste, smell, or feel (Reeves & Sperling, 1986). These representations are retained for only brief periods of time, however. Visual sensory memory seems to last for less than a second, while acoustic sensory memory lasts for no more than a few seconds (Cowan, 1984). How do we know this is true? From ingenious studies such as the one performed by Sperling (1960) that is now viewed as a classic in the field.

Short-Term Memory: A memory system that holds limited amounts of information for relatively short periods of time.

In this study participants were shown nine letters arranged in rows of three on a card. These stimuli were shown very briefly—for only 50 milliseconds (0.05 second). Participants were then asked to report all the letters they could remember seeing. Under these procedures, the participants' memory was not impressive: They could recall only about four or five of the nine letters shown. However, they reported the impression that right after seeing the card, they could remember all of the letters; but the visual image faded quickly, so by the time they had named four or five letters, the rest were completely gone. To determine if this was actually happening, Sperling used an inventive technique. Immediately after presentation of the letters, he sounded a tone that was either high, medium, or low in pitch. The high tone meant that participants should report letters in the first row, the medium tone indicated that they should report the second row, and so on. Results were clear: Under these conditions, the participants showed near-perfect scores. So all the information on the card was present in sensory memory, but then quickly faded away. How long does such information last? To answer this question, Sperling repeated the above procedures but delayed presentation of the tone for various periods of time. Results indicated that sensory memory is indeed brief. When the tone was delayed only 0.10 second (100 milliseconds), participants' performance dropped sharply; when it was delayed for an entire second, their ability to remember the letters all but disappeared.

These findings, confirmed in many later studies, point to two conclusions. Sensory memory exists, and it can store an impressive amount of information. But it is very fleeting. Where sensory memory is concerned, then, it appears to be a matter of "now you see (hear) and remember it, now you don't."

Key Questions

- What kind of information does sensory memory hold?
- How long does such information last in sensory memory?

Short-Term Memory: The Workbench of Consciousness

Imagine that as you are walking along, you see a car come weaving down the street. It turns at the corner, but as it does, it hits the side of a car parked there. "Hit and run!" you think to yourself, and quickly you look at the license plate as the car moves out of view. You don't have a pen handy, so you repeat the plate number to yourself in an attempt to remember it: "GS6087," you murmur over and over again. Just then someone rushes out from a nearby store and begins to shout: "Oh no! He hit my car! Where did he go?" Then this person turns to you and asks: "Did you get the license number?" You think for a moment—but quickly realize that although you *did* know the number a minute ago, you've already forgotten it. All you can remember is the "GS" part. What's happening here? A clear illustration of the operation of **short-term memory,** a memory system that holds a limited amount of information for brief periods of time. Despite its limitations, however, short-term memory is very important. Indeed, many experts on memory view it as a kind of workbench for consciousness—a cognitive system for temporarily holding information you are using or processing right now. That's why another term for short-term memory is *working memory.*

Serial Position Curve: The greater accuracy of recall of words or other information early and late in a list than of words or information in the middle of the list.

Evidence for the Existence of Short-Term Memory Everyday experience offers strong support for the existence of short-term memory and the view that it is distinct from long-term memory; every time you look up a telephone number but then forget it before you can finish dialing, you have informal proof that this memory system is real. There is also a great deal of scientific evidence for the existence of the short-term memory system.

The Serial Position Curve Suppose that someone read you a list of unrelated words and then asked you to recall as many as possible in any order you wished. Which words would you be most likely to remember? Research findings indicate that you would be more likely to remember words at the beginning and at the end of the list than words in the middle (see Figure 6.4). Why does this effect, known as the **serial position curve,** occur? One possible answer involves the existence of two memory systems. Presumably, you remember the last words you heard very well—a *recency effect*—because they are still present in short-term memory when you are asked to recall them. And you remember the words at the start of the list because they have already been entered into long-term memory. Words in the middle, in contrast, have vanished from short-term memory but are not present in long-term memory. The result? You remember few of them at this point in time. Many studies have obtained results consistent with this reasoning, so the serial position curve provides support for the existence of two distinct memory systems, one of which retains information for short periods of time—a matter of seconds.

The Word-Length and Word-Similarity Effects A related finding is that memory span for immediate recall is greater for lists of short words than for lists of longer words—a finding known as the *word-length effect*. Existing evidence indicates that this is due to the fact that long words take more time to pronounce; this, in turn, interferes with the rehearsal that is needed to maintain information in short-term memory (e.g., Longoni, Richardson, & Aiello, 1993).

Additional evidence for the existence of short-term memory is provided by the *word-similarity effect*—the finding that memory span for immediate

FIGURE 6.4

The Serial Position Curve

When people try to recall a list of unrelated words, they usually remember more words from the beginning and end of the list than from the middle. This serial position curve provides evidence for the existence of two distinct memory systems: short-term memory and long-term memory.

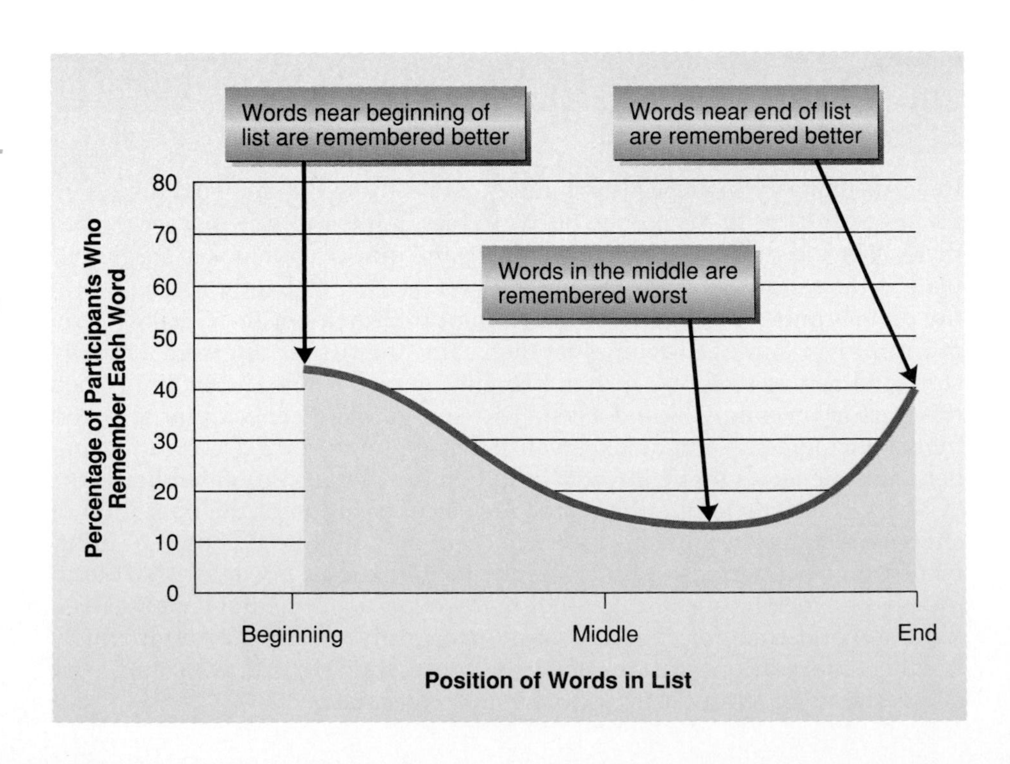

recall is greater for words that do not sound alike than for words that do sound alike. Apparently, words are recorded in short-term memory in terms of how they sound, and similar-sounding words produce confusion that interferes with memory. Together, these findings as well as others provide a compelling case for the existence of a distinct short-term memory system (Cowan, Wood, & Borne, 1994).

Short-Term Memory: Its Basic Operation Now let's turn to some of the basic features of short-term memory. How does it operate? How much information does it hold, and for how long?

First let's consider how short-term memory operates. A growing body of evidence indicates that where verbal information is concerned, short-term memory consists of two basic components: a *phonological store* of representations of words, reflecting how they sound, and a *rehearsal mechanism* that refreshes the contents of the phonological store through repetition of these words (Baddeley, 1992). If you've ever tried to keep a phone number, license-plate number, or list of grocery items in mind by saying it to yourself over and over again, you are already familiar with these components. Only by rehearsing the items—saying them to yourself out loud or subvocally—can you keep them in short-term memory.

How do we know that these two components exist? Partly from studies that indicate that preventing individuals from engaging in such rehearsal eliminates the word-length effect but does not eliminate the word-similarity effect (Schweickert, Guentert, & Hersberger, 1990). The word-length effect is related to rehearsal, but not to the information actually stored in short-term memory. More direct, and dramatic, evidence for the existence of these two components of short-term memory is provided by studies designed to determine whether different parts of the brain are active during the performance of tasks relating to these two components. The methods used by researchers to examine this possibility are described in the Research Methods section on page 222.

How much can short-term memory hold? The answer turns out to be something like seven to nine separate pieces of information. However, each of these "pieces" can contain several separate bits of information—bits that are somehow related and can be grouped together into meaningful units. When this is the case, each piece of information is described as a *chunk*, and the total amount of information held in chunks can be quite large. For example, consider the following list of letters: IBFIMBWBMATWIAC. After hearing or reading these letters once, how many could you remember? Probably no more than about seven. But imagine that instead, the letters were presented as follows: FBI, IBM, BMW, TWA, CIA. Could you remember more now? In all likelihood you could, because now the letters are grouped in meaningful chunks—the initials of famous organizations. Because of the process of *chunking*, short-term memory can hold a larger amount of information than you might guess, even though it can retain only seven to nine separate items at once.

How long does information in short-term memory last? The answer is clear: not very long. Unless it is actively *rehearsed* (repeated again and again), information entered into short-term memory fades quickly. Indeed, if individuals are prevented from rehearsing—for example, by being asked to count backwards—the information may be almost totally gone within twenty seconds (e.g., Peterson & Peterson, 1959). So if you want to keep a phone number, a license plate number, a new acquaintance's name, or any other piece of information in short-term memory, there's only one solution: Rehearse, rehearse, and then rehearse some more.

Key Questions

- What are the serial position curve, the word-length effect, and the word-similarity effect?
- How much information can short-term memory hold, and for how long?
- What are the two basic components of short-term memory?

■ RESEARCH METHODS ■

How Psychologists Study the Nature of Short-Term Memory

Short-term memory is by its very nature a fleeting thing. Under normal conditions it holds information for only a few seconds. How, then, can psychologists study it in detail? And more specifically, how can they determine whether it really consists of two major components—a temporary phonological storage system and a rehearsal mechanism, through which such information is maintained in short-term memory? While there are several ways of conducting such research, perhaps the most dramatic—and convincing—involves studying the brain itself. Are these two components of short-term memory actually reflected in activity in different brain regions? Research designed to answer this question is possible because of the development of techniques for scanning brain activity that were described in Chapter 2. One of these techniques—*positron emission tomography*—or PET for short—has proved extremely useful in this regard (e.g., Paulseu, Frith, & Frackowiak, 1993).

As an example of such research—and to illustrate the scientific reasoning it involves—let's consider a recent study by Awh and his colleagues (Awh et al., 1996). In this study, participants performed tasks specifically designed to help separate the storage and rehearsal mechanisms of short-term memory. The basic task was this: The participants saw a series of capital letters on the screen of a computer, each presented for 500 milliseconds (0.5 second). In one condition (the *two-back* condition), they were then asked, 2.5 seconds later, to indicate whether or not each letter they saw was identical to the one presented two letters previously. The researchers reasoned that this task would require both components of short-term memory—both storage of letters seen and rehearsal. Participants in two other conditions performed somewhat different tasks that were designed to help separate these components. One group (the *search control* condition) were merely asked to indicate whether each letter they saw was the same as the first letter in the entire series. This, presumably, would not require activation of either component of short-term memory. Participants in the other group (the *rehearsal control* condition) were asked simply to look at each letter and rehearse it silently until the next one appeared. This task would, presumably, require activation of the rehearsal mechanism. As participants performed these tasks, the researchers scanned their brains by means of PET to see which areas were most active.

Now, here's the crucial scientific logic: Brain activation in the two-back condition should provide information about brain regions involved in both storage and rehearsal components of short-term (working) memory. Subtracting activation in the rehearsal control condition from that in the two-back condition should provide an indication of which brain regions are involved in storage, since only the rehearsal component would be activated in the rehearsal control group. Subtracting activation in the search control from that in the two-back condition and comparing the result with the first subtraction (two-back condition minus the rehearsal control) should provide information on the regions involved in rehearsal (see Figure 6.5 for a summary of this reasoning).

FIGURE 6.5

Scientific Reasoning about Short-Term Memory

One task (two-back) requires both components of short-term memory: storage and rehearsal. Another task (rehearsal control) requires only rehearsal. Subtracting brain activation during the rehearsal control task from brain activation during the two-back task provides information on regions of the brain required by the storage component; this is what's left after activation required for rehearsal is removed. A third task (search control) requires neither component. Subtracting activation during this task from activation during the task requiring both components, and comparing the result with the first subtraction indicates two-back condition minus the rehearsal control during the rehearsal control task, indicates which brain regions are required during rehearsal.

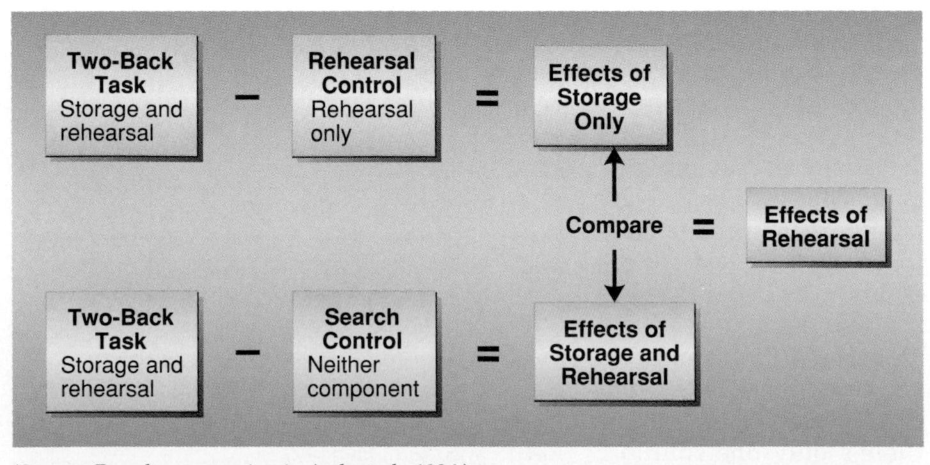

(**Source:** Based on reasoning in Awh et al., 1996.)

If a comparison of the results of these subtractions of activity revealed different patterns, this would provide evidence for the view that there are two components of short-term memory, and that different parts of the brain are involved in them.

Results of the Awh study indicated that different areas of the brain were indeed differentially active during the three tasks. In particular, findings pointed to the conclusion that the posterior parietal cortex is crucial for the storage of information in short-term memory, while portions of the brain that play a role in actual speech play a key role in the rehearsal component—more frontal areas of the brain such as Broca's area and premotor areas (see Chapter 2).

Findings such as these suggest that the two components of short-term memory established by other research methods are reflected in contrasting patterns of brain activity. In a sense, then, methods for scanning the intact, functioning human brain provide us with a unique window on consciousness. No, we can't "see" short-term memory directly; but we *can* see the patterns of brain activity that underlie it, and the components of which it is composed. Personally, I think it would be hard to ask for more.

Long-Term Memory: The Storehouse of Consciousness

Can you remember your first trip to the dentist? Your first-grade teacher? Your first pet? The chances are good that you can; even though these memories have to do with events that occurred long ago. The fact that you retain these memories points to the existence of a third memory system—one that permits us to store vast quantities of information in a relatively permanent manner. This system is known as **long-term memory,** and research evidence concerning its accuracy is nothing short of startling. In one study, for example, Standing, Canezio, and Haber (1970) presented 2,560 color slides to participants at the rate of one slide each ten seconds. Later, they presented slides in pairs, each pair consisting of one slide participants had already seen and one they had not. The participants' task was to point to the slides they had seen earlier. Despite the enormous number of items shown, they were accurate almost 90 percent of the time!

Yet we have all had experiences in which we could not remember some item or piece of information, no matter how hard we tried. To make matters worse, at such times we often feel that the information we want is somewhere "in there" but lies just beyond our reach. This is known as the **tip-of-the-tongue phenomenon,** and research findings indicate that it is quite real. For example, when individuals are given the definition of an uncommon English word such as *sampan, geode,* or *charisma* and report that they can almost think of the word, they are quite successful in supplying its first letter and in indicating how many syllables it has (Brown & McNeill, 1966). To add to our frustration at such times, we often find ourselves repeatedly coming up with related but incorrect responses (Reason & Lucas, 1984). These tend to be words that are more common than the one we want, and as we think of them repeatedly, they tend to strengthen still further in consciousness until they totally block all efforts to remember the word we really want. If we then give up, however, some kind of search often continues—and later, quite unexpectedly, the missing item may suddenly appear in consciousness. These everyday experiences indicate that the information being sought is indeed present in memory but can't be located. As we'll soon see, *retrieval* is indeed a crucial process where long-term memory is concerned.

So, we are left with a mixed picture of long-term memory. On the one hand, it is impressive in its capacity to store huge quantities of information for long periods of time. On the other hand, it often lets us down just when we seem to need it most—for example, when we are taking an exam or delivering an important speech. How does this memory system operate? How is

Long-Term Memory: A memory system for the retention of large amounts of information over long periods of time.

Tip-of-the-Tongue Phenomenon: The feeling that we can almost remember some information we wish to retrieve from memory.

information entered into long-term memory and later retrieved? These are among the questions we'll now consider.

Long-Term Memory: Its Basic Operation The first question we should address is this: How does information enter long-term memory from short-term memory? The answer seems to involve a process we have already discussed: rehearsal. In this case, though, the rehearsal does not consist simply of repeating what we wish to remember over and over again. Rather, for information to enter long-term memory, **elaborative rehearsal** seems to be necessary. This is rehearsal requiring cognitive effort; it can include thinking about the meaning of the new information and attempting to relate it to information already in memory. For example, if you wish to enter the facts and findings presented in a section of this chapter into long-term memory, it is not enough merely to state them over and over again. Instead, you should think about what they mean and how they relate to things you already know.

If elaborative rehearsal is required for information to enter long-term memory, then anything that interferes with such rehearsal should also interfere with long-term memory. Many factors produce such interference, but one with which many people have had direct experience is alcohol: when consumed in sufficient quantities, this drug impairs long-term memory (Birnbaum & Parker, 1977), perhaps by interfering with the processes through which information is entered into long-term memory (Yuille & Tollestrup, 1990).

Another factor that has been found to interfere with long-term memory is *depression*—a psychological disorder involving intense sadness, lack of energy, and feelings of hopelessness and despair (e.g., Burt, Zembar, & Niederehe, 1995). Persons suffering from this disorder tend to show impaired memory on many different tasks. Perhaps even more disturbing, recent findings indicate that such effects occur even among persons who are not depressed, but who show some of the symptoms of depression (Forsell et al., 1993). For example, consider a recent study by Backman, Hill, and Forsell (1996). These researchers asked persons aged seventy-five or older who were *not* clinically depressed to perform a memory task in which common words (e.g., child, pencil, horse) were presented either rapidly (2 seconds per word) or slowly (5 seconds per word). After seeing the words, participants were asked to recall as many of them as possible. Results indicated that those who showed some of the symptoms of depression—especially symptoms relating to a lack of motivation, such as loss of energy, lack of interest, and difficulties in concentrating—performed worse than those who did not have such symptoms (see Figure 6.6). Since lack of motivation may be linked to lower rates of elaborative rehearsal, which requires considerable cognitive effort, these findings can be viewed as closely linked to the basic functioning of long-term memory.

Levels of Processing: Cognitive Effort and Long-Term Memory The concept of elaborative rehearsal is closely related to an influential model of long-term memory that we have not yet considered—the **levels of processing view** (Craik & Lockhart, 1972). Craik and Lockhart contend that rather than concentrating on the structure of memory and the different systems it involves, it might be more useful to focus on the processes that contribute to remembering. According to these researchers, information can be processed in several different ways, ranging from relatively superficial *shallow processing* through more effortful and lasting *deep processing*. Shallow processing might involve merely repeating a word or making a simple sensory judgment about it—for example, do two words or letters look alike? A deeper level of processing might involve more complex comparisons—for

Elaborative Rehearsal: Rehearsal in which the meaning of information is considered and the information is related to other knowledge already present in memory.

Levels of Processing View: A view of memory suggesting that the greater the effort expended in processing information, the more readily it will be recalled at later times.

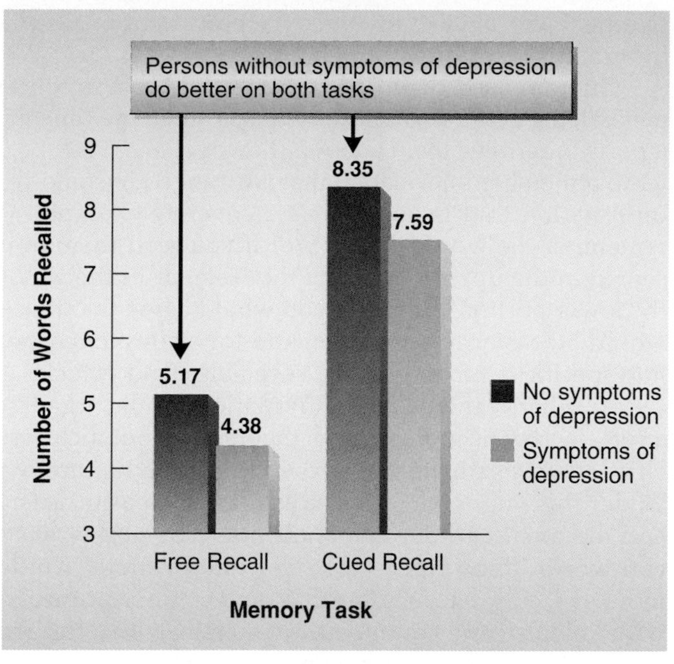

(**Source:** Based on data from Backman, Hill, & Forsell, 1996.)

FIGURE 6.6

Memory and Subclinical Depression

Elderly persons who were not depressed in a clinical sense but who showed some of the symptoms of depression—especially symptoms relating to a lack of motivation—performed worse than elderly persons who did not have these symptoms.

example, do two words rhyme? A much deeper level of processing would include attention to meaning—for instance, do two words have the same meaning? Does a word make sense when used in a specific sentence?

Considerable evidence suggests that the deeper the level of processing that takes place when we encounter new information, the more likely the information is to enter long-term memory. For example, in a well-known study, Craik and Tulving (1975) presented unrelated words and asked participants one of three kinds of questions about each word: Was the word written in capital or lowercase letters? Did the word rhyme with another word? Did the word fit within a given sentence? After answering a large number of such questions, participants were asked whether each word in a list was one they had already seen or was new. Results offered support for the levels of processing view. The deeper the level of processing performed by participants, the slower their responses—but the more accurate their decisions.

While such findings are compatible with the levels of processing model, there are still some difficulties with this model that cannot be overlooked. For example, it is difficult to specify in advance just what constitutes a deep versus a shallow level of processing. Second, it is not clear that a person can read a word over and over again and not be aware of, or think about, its meaning. In fact, several forms of processing may occur at once. Because of these potential confusions, it is difficult to speak about discrete levels of processing.

Despite such problems, there can be little doubt that the levels of processing view has added to our understanding of long-term memory, and especially to our knowledge of how information is entered into this system.

Retrieval: Locating Information in Long-Term Memory As I've already noted, long-term memory has a huge capacity and can retain information for very long periods of time—perhaps indefinitely. Does this make it a perfect memory system? Definitely not. All too often we are unable to remember information just when we need it. Only later—maddeningly!—does it sometimes appear in our consciousness. What is the cause of such difficulties? The answer involves the process of *retrieval*—our ability to locate information previously stored in memory.

One principle that plays an important role in retrieval is *organization*. In general, the better organized materials are at the time they are stored, the easier it is to retrieve them later on (Bower et al., 1969). So, for instance, it is easier to remember information that is arranged in some systematic manner than information that is not. Here's a concrete example: Would it be easier to remember the words in Table 6.1 if you read them in the way they are presented in the upper portion of the table, or in the way they are presented in the lower portion? Probably you would agree that those in the lower portion would be easier to remember, and for a simple reason: They are organized into specific *categories*—fruits, vegetables, and vehicles.

Another way in which information can be organized is in terms of *hierarchies*—classification systems that move from inclusive to increasingly specific levels. For instance, at the top of one hierarchy might be "animals." Under this might be various divisions such as insects, crustaceans, reptiles, and mammals. Under mammals might be herbivores (cows, sheep, goats), carnivores (lions, tigers, weasels), and primates. Under primates might be monkeys, chimpanzees, gorillas, and so on. Another hierarchy might begin with "plants" and continue from there. Clearly, information organized into hierarchies is easier to remember than information that is not. Other kinds of organization exist, too, but the key point remains the same: One key to effective retrieval of information from long-term memory is organization. Organizing information requires extra effort, but it appears that the benefits in terms of later ease of retrieval make this effort well worthwhile.

Retrieval Cues: Stimuli That Help Us Remember Imagine that after an absence of several years, you return to a place where you used to live. On your arrival, memories of days gone by come flooding back, with no apparent effort on your part to bring them to mind. You remember incidents you had totally forgotten, conversations with people you haven't seen in years, even the weather during your last visit. Have you ever had this kind of experience? If so, you are already familiar with the effects of what psychol-

TABLE 6.1

The Role of Organization in Memory

Would you find it easier to memorize the items in this list if they were presented randomly, as in the upper half of the table, or if they were presented in an organized manner, as in the lower half? Probably you would find the latter task easier, because it is generally easier to remember information that is organized in some logical manner.

broccoli	apple	parsley
elevator	bus	submarine
bicycle	potato	grapes
watermelon	lemon	turnip
Fruits	**Vegetables**	**Vehicles**
watermelon	broccoli	elevator
apple	potato	bicycle
lemon	parsley	bus
grapes	turnip	submarine

ogists term **retrieval cues.** These are stimuli that are associated with information stored in memory and so can help bring it to mind at times when it cannot be recalled spontaneously. Such cues can be aspects of the external environment—a place, sights or sounds, even smells (Hirsch, 1992; Richardson & Zucco, 1989).

Many studies point to the important effect of retrieval cues on long-term memory. Perhaps the most intriguing research on this topic involves what is known as **context-dependent memory:** the fact that material learned in a particular environment or context is easier to remember in a similar context or environment than it is in a very different one. Many illustrations of this effect exist, but one of the most intriguing—and unusual—is a study conducted by Godden and Baddeley (1975).

In this experiment, participants were experienced deep-sea divers. They learned a list of words either on the beach or beneath fifteen feet of water. Then they tried to recall the words, either in the same environment in which they had learned them or in the other setting. Results offered clear support for the impact of context—in this case, physical setting. Words learned on land were recalled much better in this location than under water, and vice versa. Interestingly, additional findings suggest that it is not necessary actually to be in the location or context where information was first entered into long-term memory; merely imagining this setting may be sufficient (Smith, 1979). In other words, we seem capable of generating our own context-related retrieval cues. So if you study for an exam in your room and then take the exam in a very different setting, it may be helpful to imagine yourself back in your room when you try to remember specific information; doing so may provide you with additional, self-generated retrieval cues.

State-Dependent Retrieval External cues are not the only ones that can serve as aids to memory, however; a growing body of evidence indicates that our own internal states can sometimes play this role, too. The most general term for this kind of effect is **state-dependent retrieval,** which refers to the fact that it is often easier to recall information stored in long-term memory when our internal state is similar to that which existed when the information was first entered into memory. For example, suppose that while studying for an exam, you drink lots of coffee. Thus, the effects of caffeine are present while you memorize the information in question. On the day of the test, should you also drink lots of coffee? The answer appears to be yes—and not just for the boost in alertness this may provide; being in the same physical state may provide you with retrieval cues that may help boost your performance (Eich, 1985).

Mood-Dependent Memory Recently, a related effect known as **mood-dependent memory** has been the focus of increasing research attention. This term refers to the possibility that what you remember while in a given mood may be determined in part by what you learned when previously in that mood. For instance, if you stored some information in long-term memory when in a good mood, then you are more likely to remember this information when in a similar mood. Mood-dependent memory is often distinguished from **mood congruence effects,** which suggest that we are more likely to store or remember positive information when in a positive mood and negative information when in a negative mood—in other words, that we notice or remember information that is congruent with our current moods (Blaney, 1986). A simple way to think about this distinction is to remember that in mood-dependent memory, the nature of the information doesn't matter; only your mood at the time when you learned it and your mood when

Retrieval Cues: Stimuli associated with information stored in memory that can aid in its retrieval.

Context-Dependent Memory: The fact that information entered into memory in a particular context or setting is easier to recall in that context, or in a similar context, than in others.

State-Dependent Retrieval: The greater ease of retrieval of information stored in long-term memory when our internal state is the same as it was when the information was first entered into memory.

Mood-Dependent Memory: The finding that what we remember while in a given mood may be determined in part by what we learned when previously in that same mood.

Mood Congruence Effects: Our tendency to notice or remember information congruent with our current mood.

FIGURE 6.7

Mood Congruence Effects and Mood-Dependent Memory

Mood-dependent memory refers to the fact that when we are in a given mood, we tend to remember information we entered into memory—when in that mood. We remember this information regardless of whether it is consistent or inconsistent with our current mood. In contrast, *mood congruence effects* refer to our tendency to notice and remember information that is consistent with our current mood.

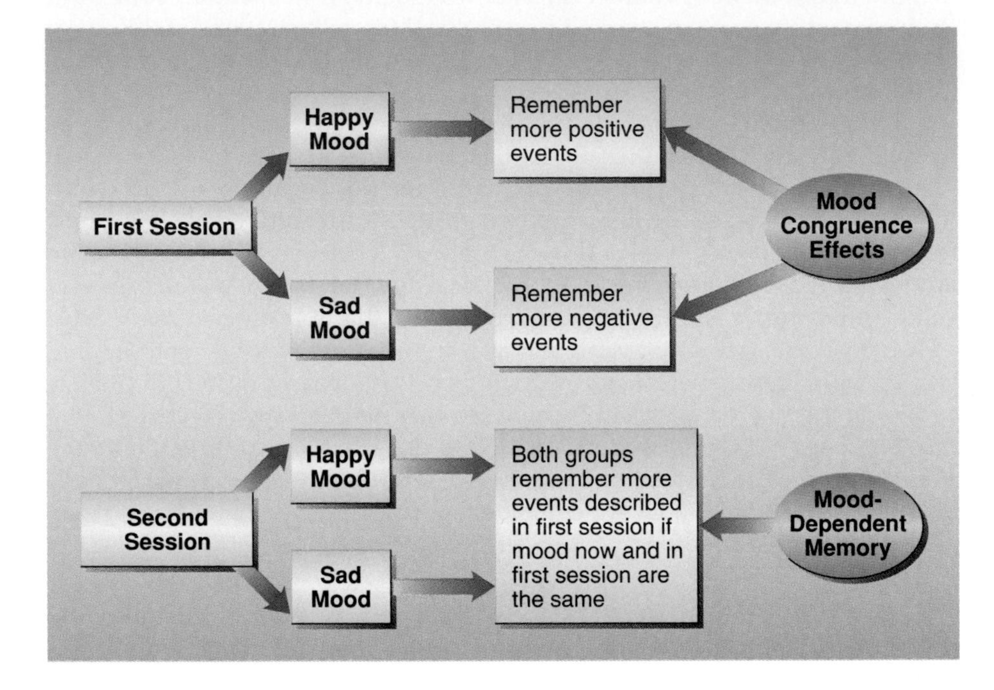

you try to recall it are relevant. In mood congruence effects, in contrast, the affective nature of the information—whether it is emotionally positive or negative—is crucial (see Figure 6.7).

Recent findings confirm the existence of mood-dependent memory (e.g., Eich, 1995). However, it seems to occur only under specific conditions (Eich, 1995). For instance, mood-dependent memory effects are more likely to occur when the moods we experience while entering information into long-term memory are strong ones and when we generate the items stored in memory rather than merely have them presented to us (e.g., Eich, Macaulay, & Ryan, 1994). The existence of mood-dependent memory has important implications. For instance, such effects help explain why depressed persons have difficulty in remembering times when they felt better (Schachter & Kihlstrom, 1989): Being in a very negative mood now, they tend to remember information they entered into memory when in the same mood—and this information relates to feeling depressed. This is important because being able to remember what it felt like *not* to be depressed can play an important part in successful recovery from this problem. We'll return to depression and ways of coping with it in Chapters 14 and 15. For information concerning another aspect of retrieval from long-term memory, see the Beyond the Headlines section.

Key Questions

- How does information move from short-term to long-term memory?
- What roles do levels of processing and organization play in long-term memory?
- What are retrieval cues, and what role do they play in long-term memory?
- How do mood-dependent memory effects and mood congruence effects differ?

Beyond the Headlines

As Psychologists See It

The Scent of Romantic Ardor?

Thanksgiving Aromas Give Some Feasters a Real Happy Holiday

Wall Street Journal, April 22, 1996—Thanksgiving may never be the same. According to recent research, the smells of this once-pious Pilgrim feast could end up inciting celebrations of a different kind. The nutmeg- and cinnamon-laced scents of pumpkin pie not only whet the appetite, but also arouse male ardor. So claims Alan R. Hirsch, a Chicago-based neurologist and psychiatrist. Dr. Hirsch took 25 student volunteers and covered their noses with scent-soaked surgical masks. He then measured their responses, monitoring their blood pressure and penile blood flow. He had theorized that flowery perfumes would stimulate the volunteers. As a control, he compared perfume with cinnamon rolls. Cinnamon rolls won. . . . "Maybe the odors acted to induce a Pavlovian response that recalled girlfriends or wives, and the mood-state recurred," Dr. Hirsch offered. "We call this olfactory-induced nostalgic response. . . ." Dr. Hirsch next tried to replicate the work with 31 volunteers aged 18 to 64, exposing each man to 30 scents from baby powder to musk, from chocolate to roasting meat. The least arousal was sparked by the sharp scents of cranberry and pink grapefruit. The most rampant response—a 40 percent increase in blood flow—was registered when men inhaled the unexpected blend of pumpkin pie and lavender.

Intriguing, I'm sure you'll agree—food-related odors stimulate sexual arousal among males, and to a much greater extent than the sweet, flowery, or spicy smells of expensive perfumes (see Figure 6.8 on page 230). And the effect, it appears, may have something to do with memory. In fact, Dr. Alan Hirsch, the medical researcher who performed this and many other ingenious studies on the effects of odors, points to two possibilities: (1) These smells serve as retrieval cues, reminding men of their wives and girlfriends; and/or (2) these smells put the men into a good mood, thus stimulating positive memories, such as ones related to sexual activities.

How do psychologists react to such suggestions—and to this kind of research? With interest, of course, but also with a healthy degree of scientific skepticism. First, who were the volunteers in this research? There were only fifty-six of them altogether, and it's not clear why they agreed to participate in these studies. Were they men with a special interest in the sense of smell, or with special sensitivity to various aromas? Similarly, how did they react to procedures in which they inhaled various fragrances through a face mask while having blood flow to their sexual organs measured? This is a very unusual state of affairs, and one in which the researchers' expectations could potentially be transmitted to the participants. Could the men see Dr. Hirsch's face as they sniffed the various fragrances? Did Dr. Hirsch or his nurses say anything to the participants as they inhaled the various aromas? And assuming that none of these problems existed, *why* did certain aromas increase arousal more than others? Why, for instance, would the smell of pumpkin pie cause men to remember their girlfriends or wives rather than, say, Thanksgiving dinners with their families? Alternatively, if these smells served to put participants into a good mood, did they influence arousal through mood congruence effect, mood-dependent memory, or both?

As you can see, this research raises many questions—many more, in fact, than it answers.

So, while it certainly describes a novel and inventive way of studying a topic related to memory, it definitely does *not* provide the kind of conclusive evidence psychologists seek in their own research. Spicy smells may indeed be one of the many languages of love, but this research, as it stands, can't tell us with the degree of certainty scientific inquiry demands.

FIGURE 6.8

The Food of Love?

Some findings suggest that men are sexually aroused by the aroma of several food-related smells (e.g., cinnamon, pumpkin pie). However, pending the completion of further, confirming research, most psychologists remain somewhat skeptical about the possibility of a strong link between certain smells and passion-inducing memories.

Critical Thinking Questions

1. Participants in this research sniffed many different fragrances. Could the order in which these were presented have influenced the results?
2. Participants knew that this research was concerned with studying their reactions to various fragrances. Could this knowledge have influenced their behavior in any way? How?
3. How could further research separate the possible roles of mood-dependent memory and mood congruence effects with respect to the men's responses to various odors?

Forgetting from Long-Term Memory

When are we most aware of memory? Typically, when it fails—when we are unable to remember information that we need at a particular moment. Given this fact, it is not surprising that the first systematic research on memory, conducted by Herman Ebbinghaus, was concerned with forgetting. As you may recall, Ebbinghaus experimented on himself and studied the rate at which he forgot nonsense syllables. The results of his studies suggested that forgetting is rapid at first but slows down with the passage of time.

Modern research has generally confirmed Ebbinghaus's findings where meaningless materials such as nonsense syllables are concerned, but suggests that we are much better at remembering other and more meaningful types of information. For example, Bahrick (1984) asked college professors to identify the names and faces of former students who had taken a single course with them. Even after more than eight years, the professors were quite successful in recognizing the students' names and in matching their names with photos of them. Similarly, it is clear that many complex skills, such as swimming, driving a car, riding a bicycle, or playing a musical instrument, are retained over long periods of time, even if we have little opportunity to practice them. In contrast, other skills—ones requiring associations between specific stimuli and responses, called *discrete skills*—are subject to much greater forgetting. Thus, a few months after learning how to perform a procedure for reviving heart attack victims, most persons have forgotten many of the steps and actions it involves (McKenna & Glendon, 1985). And many other complex skills, such as typing, show a similar pattern. What, then, accounts for forgetting? Why is information firmly entered in long-term memory sometimes lost, at least in part, with the passage of time? Several explanations have been offered; here, we'll focus on the two that have received the most attention. After that, we'll examine a third and sharply contrasting view of forgetting—*repression*—and its bearing on the tragedy of childhood sexual abuse (Bowers & Fanvolden, 1996). Finally, we'll turn to the nature of *intentional forgetting*—instances in which we purposely attempt to "clean house" and eliminate information that's no longer needed from long-term memory (Johnson, 1994).

The Trace Decay Hypothesis: Forgetting with the Passage of Time

Perhaps the simplest view of forgetting is that information entered into long-term memory fades or decays with the passage of time. This suggestion is consistent with our informal experience: Often, information acquired quite some time ago is more difficult to remember than information learned only recently. Yet considerable evidence suggests that decay is probably *not* the key mechanism in forgetting.

First, consider a famous early study by Jenkins and Dallenbach (1924). They asked two individuals to learn a list of ten nonsense syllables. In one condition, both persons then went directly to sleep. In another, they continued with their normal activities. The participants' recall of the nonsense syllables was tested after one, two, four, and eight hours. Results indicated that forgetting was more rapid when the participants stayed awake than when they went to sleep. These findings argue against the view that forgetting is primarily the result of gradual decay of information over time.

Can you see any problems with this study that raise doubts about its results? Here's one: When participants went to sleep after learning the nonsense syllables, they had studied them in the evening. When they stayed awake, they had studied the nonsense syllables in the morning. Thus, differences in circadian rhythms (Chapter 4) may have played a role in the obtained results. Indeed, sleep during the day does not seem to reduce forgetting as reported by Jenkins and Dallenbach.

However, other research, in which animals have been kept awake but prevented from moving about and engaging in normal activities, also indicated that forgetting is not merely a matter of the passage of time. In one such study, Minami and Dallenbach (1946) taught cockroaches to avoid a dark compartment by giving them an electric shock whenever they entered it. After the subjects had mastered this simple task, they were either restrained in a paper cone or permitted to wander around a darkened cage at will. Results again argued against the trace decay hypothesis. Roaches permitted to move about showed more forgetting over a given period of time than those who were restrained.

Forgetting as a Result of Interference

If forgetting is not a function of the passage of time, then what *is* its source? The answer currently accepted by most psychologists focuses on *interference* between items of information stored in memory. Such interference can take two different forms. In **retroactive interference,** information currently being learned interferes with information already present in memory. If learning how to operate a new computer program causes you to forget how to oper-

Retroactive Interference: Interference with retention of information already present in memory by new information being entered into memory.

ate one you learned previously, you are experiencing the effects of retroactive interference. In **proactive interference,** in contrast, previously learned information present in long-term memory interferes with information you are learning at present. Suppose you have learned how to operate one VCR; now you buy a new one, which requires different steps for recording a television program. If you now make mistakes by trying to operate the new VCR in the same way as your old one, you are experiencing the impact of proactive interference (see Figure 6.9).

FIGURE 6.9

Retroactive and Proactive Interference

In *retroactive interference,* information currently being learned interferes with retention of previously acquired information. In *proactive interference,* information learned previously interferes with retention of new information.

Retroactive Interference

Information being learned currently → Interferes → Information learned previously

Proactive Interference

Information being learned currently ← Interferes ← Information learned previously

A large body of evidence offers support for the view that interference plays a key role in forgetting from long-term memory (e.g., Tulving & Psotka, 1971). For example, in many laboratory studies, the more similar the words or nonsense syllables participants are to learn from different lists, the more interference occurs among them, and the poorer the participants' recall of these materials (Gruneberg, Morris, & Sykes, 1988). So interference, in one form or another, appears to be the key culprit when we forget information from long-term memory rather than simply experiencing difficulty in locating it.

Repression: "What's Too Painful to Remember, We Simply Choose to Forget"

Have you ever heard the song "The Way We Were"? If so, you know that the heading of this subsection quotes one line from it: "What's too painful to remember, we simply choose to forget." This line could almost serve as a basic definition of the term **repression**—the active elimination from consciousness of memories or experiences we find threatening. As we'll see in Chapter 12, the concept of repression played a key role in Sigmund Freud's theory of human personality and in his view of the causes of psychological disorders. Freud contended that repressed memories are pushed into hidden recesses of the unconscious mind, where they remain, festering and causing many psychological problems, until they are brought back into consciousness by the probings of a skilled therapist.

The existence of repression is widely accepted by psychologists and psychiatrists, as well as by society generally (Loftus & Herzog, 1991). Partly because of this fact, it has featured prominently in many dramatic trials focusing on charges of *early childhood sexual abuse.* In these trials, repression has sometimes been offered as an explanation for the fact that the abused persons failed to remember their terrible experiences until many years later—and remembered them then only as a result of careful questioning by trained therapists.

Are such claims accurate? And, more to the point, are the "memories" reported during therapy really accurate? Did such persons really experience these devastating events—ones they could not remember until helped to do so by their therapist? This is a complex question. Many of the cases occurred so long ago that concrete, objective evidence is difficult, if not impossible, to obtain. In addition, as noted by Loftus (1993), a leading expert on memory, there are several reasons for viewing at least some of these claims with a healthy degree of skepticism.

First, despite its widespread acceptance, there is still very little scientific evidence for the existence of repression. Most support for the theory of repression derives from case studies. While these are often fascinating, they do not,

Proactive Interference: Interference with the learning or storage of current information by information previously entered into memory.

Repression: The active elimination from consciousness of memories or experiences we find threatening.

as we saw in Chapter 1, provide conclusive scientific evidence on the issues they address. Indeed, existing evidence for repression as an important aspect of memory is so weak that one researcher (Holmes, 1990, p. 97) has suggested that use of the concept of repression in psychological reports should be preceded by this statement: "Warning: The concept of repression has not been validated with experimental research and its use may be hazardous to the accurate interpretation of behavior."

Second, the fact that many therapists believe strongly in the existence of repression and in its role in psychological disorders indicates that in some instances, at least, therapists may act in ways that lead clients to report repressed memories even if they don't really have them. In other words, therapists may *suggest* such memories, often in a subtle and unintentional manner (Bowers & Fanvolden, 1996). For example, a therapist who believes in the powerful impact of repressed memories might say something like this to a client: "You know, in my experience a lot of people who are struggling with the same kinds of problems as you had painful experiences as children—they were beaten or even molested. I wonder if anything like that ever happened to you?" Faced with such questions and the *demand characteristics* they imply (subtle pressures to tell the therapist what she or he wants to hear), some clients may begin to search their memories for traces of traumatic early events (see Figure 6.10). As we'll soon see, this search can lead a person to generate memories that weren't there or to distort ones that do exist so that they are consistent with what the therapist seems to be suggesting (Haugaard et al., 1991; Loftus & Coan, 1995).

FIGURE 6.10

Repressed Memories: Are They Always Real?

As we'll see in more detail in Chapter 15, therapy involves a complex relationship between the client and therapist. If a therapist believes strongly in the existence and importance of repressed memories, she or he may *suggest* these to the client, thus setting the stage for the construction of false memories.

Third, even if they are not undergoing therapy and do not hear their therapists talk about repressed memories, many people may be influenced by media reports indicating that both early sexual abuse and repressed memories of these experiences are quite common. As a result of exposure to such accounts, persons suffering from various psychological problems may begin to wonder if their own problems stem from such causes—and perhaps to conclude that they do—even if this is *not* the case.

Finally, growing evidence (Bowers & Farvolden, 1996) suggests that repression of truly traumatic events is rare—such events are simply too disturbing and generate too many intrusive thoughts to be entirely pushed from memory.

I am certainly *not* suggesting that repressed memories never exist or that they can't be accurate. There is no doubt that childhood sexual abuse is a disturbingly frequent occurrence (e.g., Keary & Fitzpatrick, 1994). However, there do seem to be sufficient questions about the nature of repression, and sufficient evidence that some "memories" of traumatic events can be unintentionally constructed, to suggest the need for caution (Koocher et al., 1995). As Loftus (1993) has put it, we must be careful to avoid assuming that *all* reports of repressed memories of childhood abuse are accurate. If we make such an assumption, we run the risk of falsely convicting at least some innocent persons of crimes they never committed.

Intentional Forgetting: Removing Inaccurate or Useless Information from Memory

Suppose that after shopping at large mall, you walk out into the parking lot to find your car. You head for the location where you remember parking it, only to find it's not there (see Figure 6.11 on page 234). "Oh yeah," you say to yourself, "that's where I parked *last* time I was here. Now where did I put it *this* time?" And then you try to push out of your mind the memory of where you parked your car before so you can remember where it is today. In situa-

FIGURE 6.11

Intentional Forgetting and the "Lost Car" Effect

Have you ever had the experience shown here—being unable to remember where you parked your car in a huge parking lot? If so, this may have stemmed, at least in part, from a failure of *intentional forgetting*—you didn't successfully forget where you parked last time!

tions like this, you are engaging in **intentional forgetting**—you try to remove, or at least ignore, some information in long-term memory not because you find it to be frightening or painful, as in repression, but simply because it is inaccurate or no longer useful.

While forgetting where you parked your car last week may seem like a trivial task, intentional forgetting actually has important implications in many situations. During trials, for instance, jurors are sometimes told by the judge: "Strike that information from the record—pay no attention to it." In other words, the jurors are instructed to forget about something they have heard in the courtroom. Similarly, when interviewers attempt to choose among several job applicants after meeting them, they try to forget about the gender, race, and ethnic background of the applicants; such factors are presumably irrelevant to choosing the best person and should not be remembered during the decision process.

How do we manage to accomplish such tasks? Existing evidence suggests that several factors may play a role. First, in some situations, we expect that we will want to get rid of some information in the near future. This is true when we park our car and find it; we don't need to remember where it was on this occasion again—in fact, such information might lead to confusion. In such cases, we seem to go about the initial stage of *encoding* in a special way. Specifically, we tag or label the soon-to-be-forgotten information so that we can recognize it as such. As a result, we find it easy to recognize and eliminate such information when it is no longer needed (Johnson, 1994).

In other situations, we don't know in advance that we'll want to forget some information at a future time, so we can't encode it in a special way. However, when we realize that this information is no longer useful or valid, we may focus on inhibiting retrieval of it. If it comes to mind, we quickly reject it rather than thinking about it. As the information is not used and is not rehearsed, it may weaken or at least become harder to bring into consciousness.

How successful are we at carrying out intentional forgetting? Quite successful, it appears. But we can't always accomplish this task: a large body of evidence on how we form judgments about other persons (see Chapter 16) suggests that often we can't totally ignore or "forget" others' gender, racial identity, age, attractiveness, or other factors (e.g., Kenney, 1994). Such information remains in memory and can influence our reactions to people, and our decisions about them, even when we try to ignore it. In many instances, though, we are successful in removing unwanted, irrelevant, and useless information from memory, thereby reducing the possibility that it will exert negative effects upon us or our behavior.

Prospective Memory: Forgetting What We're Supposed to Do

Have you ever forgotten to turn in a class assignment on time? Have you ever promised to stop by the store to buy some items, but then forgotten to do so? Such incidents involve **prospective memory**—remembering that we are supposed to perform some action at a certain time. This aspect of memory has important practical effects. Missing an important meeting can have serious consequences for one's career—or one's social life; forgetting to take a prescribed medicine at certain times of the day can adversely affect one's health (Ley, 1988).

Why do we experience this type of forgetting? The answer seems to involve at least two factors. First, such forgetting is closely related to motiva-

Intentional Forgetting: Efforts to remove, or at least ignore, information in long-term memory that is inaccurate or no longer

Prospective Memory: Remembering to perform certain activities at specific times.

tion. We tend to forget appointments or errands that are relatively unimportant to us, or that we view as unpleasant burdens, while remembering the ones we view as important or pleasurable (Winograd, 1988). For example, many dentists—including mine!—phone their patients a day or two in advance to remind them of their appointments; if they don't, many patients forget to show up. In contrast, few hairdressers find this necessary.

Second, prospective memory, like other forms of memory, involves the impact of retrieval cues. We remember to perform those activities that we build into the structure of our days in such a way that we are reminded of them by various cues. We remember to go to the supermarket, the dry cleaners, and the bank on the way home because we take a route that passes each of these businesses. The route itself provides vivid reminders—retrieval cues—for prospective memory. Other cues we use to improve our prospective memory are internal, relating to the passage of time (Harris & Wilkins, 1982). At first we check our watch frequently, in order to "calibrate" our internal time-measuring mechanism. Then, in the middle of the waiting period, we perform fewer checks. Later, as the time for performing some activity—such as removing a cake from the oven or leaving for a meeting—approaches, we check clocks and watches with increasing frequency. The result: We have a continuing series of cues that remind us of the activity we must perform and when it should occur (Ceci, Baker, & Bronfenbrenner, 1988). If such retrieval cues are absent—if, for instance, we forget to wear our watch—prospective memory, too, may fail.

Key Questions

- Why does forgetting from long-term memory occur?
- What is retroactive interference? Proactive interference?
- What is repression, and what role does it play in forgetting of traumatic events such as childhood sexual abuse?
- What is intentional forgetting?
- What is prospective memory?

Memory in Natural Contexts

Much of the research mentioned so far has involved the performance of relatively artificial tasks, such as memorizing nonsense syllables or lists of unrelated words. While we do sometimes perform tasks of this kind outside the laboratory—for instance, as a student, you sometimes memorize lists of terms or definitions used in a specific course and nowhere else—we generally apply our memory systems to very different tasks in our daily lives. Let's see what psychologists have discovered about how memory functions in these natural contexts.

Autobiographical Memory: Remembering the Events of Our Own Lives

How do we remember information about our own lives? Such **autobiographical memory** (also known, as I mentioned earlier, as *episodic memory*) has long been of interest to psychologists. While autobiographical memory has been studied in several different ways—for example, by means of questionnaires in which individuals answer detailed questions about their lives (Baddeley, 1990)—perhaps the most dramatic approach has involved the use of *diary studies*, in which individuals keep detailed diaries of events in their lives. (As I noted in Chapter 4, this method has also been used to study biological rhythms.)

Autobiographical Memory: Memory for information about events in our own lives (also known as *episodic memory*).

In one well-known study using this approach, the Dutch psychologist Willem Wagenaar (1986) kept a diary for six years. Each day he recorded one or two incidents, carefully indicating who was involved, what happened, and where and when each event took place. Wagenaar rated each incident in terms of whether it was something that happened often or rarely, and he also indicated the amount of emotional involvement he experienced. During the course of the study, he recorded a total of 2,400 incidents. Then he tested his own memory for each, over a period of twelve months. The results, while complex, generally indicated that autobiographical memory is affected by many of the same variables as other forms of memory—for example, by retrieval cues and emotional states. Since diary studies are conducted under more natural, if less controlled, conditions than typical studies of memory, and since they examine memory for everyday events rather than for lists of words or nonsense syllables, they are certainly useful in one crucial respect: They offer support for the view that the findings of research on memory can indeed be generalized beyond the confines of the psychological laboratory.

Infantile Amnesia: Forgetting the Events of Our Earliest Years

What is your earliest memory? Mine involves an incident during a heat wave, when my father and I went up to the roof of an apartment building where we lived. I can vividly remember asking him: "Daddy, when will this end?" According to my parents, this incident must have occurred before I was four, because my father stopped going up to the roof after that time. (I still hate summer heat, by the way.) If you are like me—and most people—your earliest memory probably dates from your third or fourth year of life, although a few people report even earlier memories. This fact raises an interesting question: Why can't we remember events from the first two or three years of our lives? Our inability to do so is known as **infantile amnesia** (Howe & Courage, 1993) and is quite puzzling. It is obvious that we do retain information we acquire during the first years of life, for it is then that we learn to walk and to speak. So why is autobiographical memory absent during this period?

Until recently, two explanations were widely accepted. According to the first, autobiographical memory is absent early in life because the brain structures necessary for such memory are not sufficiently developed at this time (Moscovitch, 1985). A second possibility involves the absence of language skills. Since we can't verbalize very effectively during the first two years of life, and since language plays a key role in long-term memory, it is not at all surprising that we can't remember specific events from this period (Baddeley, 1990).

While both of these explanations make sense, recent findings suggest that neither is entirely accurate. Contrary to widespread belief, infants do seem to possess relatively well-developed memory abilities. For example, even one-day-old infants seem capable of imitating some actions shown by adults (Meltzoff, 1990). Further, they show considerable ability to remember various events (e.g., Goodman et al., 1991).

In view of such findings, it does not seem reasonable to explain infantile amnesia in terms of infants' lack of memory abilities. What, then, *does* account for this effect? According to Howe and Courage (1993), the answer may lie in the fact that it is not until somewhere between our second and third birthdays that most of us develop a clear *self-concept*. And without this concept, we lack the personal frame of reference necessary for autobiographical memory. In other words, we cannot remember events that happened to us because we have no clear sense of ourselves as distinct individuals.

Infantile Amnesia: Our inability to remember experiences during the first two or three years of life, probably because we do not possess a well-developed self-concept during this period.

When do we acquire a clear self-concept? Sometime around the age of two. Before this time, for example, babies show considerable interest in their own reflection in a mirror (see Figure 6.12) but will not attempt to clean a spot of coloring that has been placed on their nose. By the time babies are eighteen months to about two years of age, however, most do attempt to clean this spot, thus indicating that they recognize their own image (Lewis et al., 1989).

In sum, some evidence suggests that infantile amnesia may actually be a misleading term. Our inability to report autobiographical memories from the first two years of life seems to reflect the absence of a clearly defined self-concept rather than deficits in our memory systems. In view of this evidence, it might be more appropriate to refer to this gap in our autobiographical memories not as a period of "infantile amnesia" but as a period of "infantile nonself."

FIGURE 6.12

Infantile Amnesia: One Possible Cause

Until we have a clear self-concept, we can't store autobiographical memories. This is why most people can't remember events that happened to them before they were about three years old.

Flashbulb Memories: Memories That Don't Fade—or Do They?

Think back over the last year. What was the most surprising or unusual event that you can remember reading or hearing about? Now, once you've identified this event, answer the following question: Can you remember what you were doing and where you were when you first learned about this event? If so, then you have firsthand evidence for what Brown and Kulik (1977) term **flashbulb memories**—vivid memories of what we were doing at the time of an emotion-provoking event.

Are such memories accurate? Can we really remember what we were doing or where we were at the time of dramatic events? Growing evidence suggests that this is one of those cases in which common sense is wrong. The surprising thing about flashbulb memories is not that they are so accurate but rather that they are actually quite *in*accurate (Neisser, 1991). For example, in one study on this topic, students were asked, the day after the space shuttle *Challenger* exploded, how they had first heard this news. Three years later, the same persons were asked to recall this information again. Most were sure that they could remember; but in fact, about one third of their accounts were completely wrong. Why do such errors occur? Perhaps because the strong emotions present when flashbulb memories are formed interfere with accurate encoding (Forgas & Bower, 1988). Whatever the mechanism, it is clear that flashbulb memories are another intriguing aspect of autobiographical memory.

Key Questions

- What is autobiographical memory?
- What is infantile amnesia?
- What are flashbulb memories?

Memory Distortion and Memory Construction

One of your friends has just seen a popular film and describes it to you. It sounds great, so you go to see it. When you do, you find that the film does not seem to be at all like what your friend described. The plot is different, and your friend seems to have left out some important details while adding others that you don't notice. What has happened? One possibility is that your friend misled you on purpose. But another and more likely possi-

Flashbulb Memories: Vivid memories of what we were doing at the time of an emotion-provoking event.

Schemas: Cognitive frameworks representing our knowledge and assumptions about specific aspects of the world.

bility is that your friend's description of the film fell prey to two basic kinds of errors that frequently affect memory in natural contexts: *distortion*—alterations in what is remembered and reported—and *construction*—the addition of information that was not actually present or, in some cases, the creation of "memories" of events or experiences that never took place.

Distortion and the Influence of Schemas

Like the cartoon character in Figure 6.13, we have all had experience with memory distortion. For example, when we look back on our own behavior in various situations, we often tend to perceive it in a favorable light; we remember that we said or did the "right" thing, even if this wasn't the case. Similarly, when thinking about other persons, we often remember their behavior as closer to our overall impressions of them, or to stereotypes of the groups to which they belong, than is actually true.

Distortions in memory also occur in response to false or misleading information provided by others. If someone's comments suggest a fact or detail that is not present in our memories, we may add that fact or detail (Loftus, 1992). Unfortunately, such effects often occur during trials, when attorneys pose *leading questions* to witnesses—questions that lead the witnesses to "remember" what the attorneys want them to remember. For example, during a trial an attorney may ask a witness, "Was the getaway car a light color or a dark color?" While the witness may not remember seeing a getaway car, the question puts subtle pressure on this person to answer—to make a choice. And once the answer is given, it may be incorporated into the witness's memories and tend to distort them. Leading questions are also used by police during the questioning of suspects and often help police to wring confessions from these persons (Kassin & Kiechel, 1996). I'll return to such effects in a discussion of eyewitness testimony below.

What accounts for memory distortions? In many cases they seem to involve the operation of **schemas**—cognitive structures representing our knowledge and assumptions about aspects of the world (Wyer & Srull, 1994). Schemas are developed through experience and act something like mental scaffolds, providing us with basic frameworks for processing new information and relating it to existing knowledge—including knowledge held in long-term memory.

Once schemas are formed, they exert strong effects on the way information is encoded, stored, and later retrieved. These effects, in turn, can lead to important errors or distortions in memory. Perhaps such effects are most apparent with respect to encoding. Current evidence suggests that when schemas are initially being formed—for example, when you are first learning about the activities, roles, and responsibilities of being a college student—information inconsistent with the newly formed schema is easier to notice and encode than information consistent with it. Such inconsistent information is surprising and thus seems more likely to become the focus of attention. After the schema has been formed and is well developed, in contrast, information *consistent* with it becomes easier to notice and hence to remember (e.g., Stangor & Ruble, 1989). It is the operation of schemas that, in part, accounts for the fact that in many cases we are more likely to notice and remember information that supports our beliefs about the world than information that challenges them.

So, what role might schemas play in your friend's account of the film? Suppose that the movie is about a group of scientists striving to discover a cure for a fatal disease, but one of the scientists is secretly working for a large drug company that wants to obtain the cure for

FIGURE 6.13

Remembering What We Want to Remember

As shown here, we often remember what we want to remember, or what puts us in a favorable light.

(**Source:** ZIGGY © 1996 ZIGGY AND FRIENDS, INC. Dist. by UNIVERSAL PRESS SYNDICATE.

its own use. Your friend fails to mention this crucial fact. Why? Perhaps because the idea of a scientist selling out for personal gain doesn't fit with your friend's strongly established schema for scientists. This may not be the cause of the errors in this particular case, but it is indicative of the way in which schemas can lead to distortion in long-term memory.

Another important cause of distortion in memory involves motivation: We often distort our memories in order to bring them "in line" with our current motives. For example, suppose that you like someone; this may lead you to want to remember positive information about him or her. Conversely, if you dislike someone, you want to remember negative information about this person. Effects of this kind have recently been observed in a careful series of studies conducted by McDonald and Hirt (1997). These researchers had participants watch an interview between two students. Liking for one of the two individuals was varied by having this stranger act in a polite, a rude, or a neutral manner. When later asked to recall information about this person's grades (information that was provided during the interview), those who were induced to like the stranger distorted their memories so as to place him or her in a more favorable light, while those induced to dislike the stranger showed the opposite pattern. In this and many other situations, then, our memories can be distorted by our current motives.

Memory Construction: Remembering What Didn't Happen

Unfortunately, distortion is not the only type of error that can affect memory of everyday events. Such memory is also affected by *construction*—our tendency to fill in the details when recalling events, or even to remember experiences we never actually had or information to which we were never actually exposed. As one expert on memory has put it (Kihlstrom, 1994, p. 341), "Memory is not so much like reading a book as it is like writing one from fragmentary notes." In other words, we often construct our memories from incomplete information. I had a startling experience with memory construction a few years ago, when I visited my parents. I asked my father what had become of my great-grandfather's uniform, the one he wore when he was a soldier in Europe in the 1890s. My father was puzzled and asked how I knew about the uniform. When I answered that I remembered seeing it on many occasions as a child, he retorted that that was impossible: The uniform was thrown away when *he* was a teenager, many years before I was born. I was shocked, because I vividly recalled seeing it. I realize now, though, that despite what my memory told me (and still tells me!), I never actually saw the uniform; what I was remembering was my grandfather's descriptions of it and of how my great-grandfather looked when wearing it.

While this incident is trivial, memory construction can sometimes have far more important—and unsettling—effects. In fact, as we'll soon see, memory construction can play an important role in legal proceedings involving charges of *child sexual abuse* and in the testimony of *eyewitnesses* to various crimes (Loftus, 1993). Before turning to these effects, however, let's address a basic issue concerning constructed memories: How persistent are they? In other words, once formed, can they be readily changed and, perhaps, corrected? A growing body of scientific evidence points to a disturbing conclusion: False memories may be very difficult to change. Among young children, in fact, they may be more persistent than real memories (Reyna & Titcomb, 1996). Evidence for this conclusion has been reported in many different studies, but one of the most convincing is research reported by Brainerd, Reyna, and Brandse (1995).

These psychologists exposed kindergarten children (average age 5 years, 9 months) and third-grade children (average age 8 years, 11 months) to lists of sixty common nouns (e.g., table, tree, house). Then the researchers read to the children half these words, plus additional words not presented on the first occasion. The children's task was to indicate whether they had heard each word before. The researchers repeated these procedures one week later, to see if false memories—instances in which the children said "Yes, I heard it before" when in fact they hadn't—persisted. In fact, as you can see from Figure 6.14, the false memories did persist; moreover, among the older children false alarms actually tended to be more persistent than hits—instances in which children were correct in their reports.

Brainerd and his colleagues confirmed these results in two additional studies. The results further indicated that when the word lists encouraged children's tendencies to think in terms of the *gist*—the underlying meanings of the words—by replacing some of the words with the names of their categories (for instance, *animal* instead of *cat, color* instead of *red*), these tendencies grew stronger. Under these conditions, younger as well as older children showed greater persistence of false alarms (memory errors).

Very similar results have been reported in a recent study in which children observed staged events, responded to an immediate test of their memory for these events, then responded again one week later. Again, there was a significant tendency for false memories to persist more strongly than correct ones (Pool, update). These findings and those in related research (Weekes et al., 1992) suggest that memory construction can sometimes pose a serious threat to our efforts to attain accuracy in our reports of past events. And this, in turn, has important implications for the two important legal contexts mentioned previously—accusations of child sexual abuse and the testimony of eyewitnesses to crimes and accidents. Let's take a closer look at both.

Memory Construction and Charges of Child Sexual Abuse

Child sexual abuse is a frightening and detestable crime. Instead of caring for and nurturing young children, some adults prey upon them, using them as objects of their own sexual desires. We'll discuss child sexual abuse and

FIGURE 6.14

The Persistence of False Memories

Children in two age groups heard lists of common words (e.g., table, tree, house) and then, in an immediate test of memory, indicated whether they had heard these words when they were mixed with other words they had not previously heard. As expected, the children made many errors, reporting "Yes, I heard it before" for words they had not actually heard. When the children were retested one week later, these errors tended to persist and in fact, for the older group, were more persistent than accurate memories.

First Session:

Children hear list of common words.

Then they hear some of these words and others and indicate whether they heard each word before.

Results: They make many errors (report having heard words they did not actually hear "false memories").

Second Session:

Children hear lists of words again one week later.

They indicate whether they heard these words before.

Results: Errors they made during the first session tend to persist; children report, again, that they heard words that were *not* presented during the first session.

For older children these "false memories" are more persistent than "hits" (accurate memories).

(**Source:** Based on findings reported by Brainerd, Reyna, & Brandse, 1995.)

its devastating effects in Chapter 9. Here, we'll focus on the possibility that some charges of child sexual abuse result in part from constructed (false) memories. One famous case of this kind occurred several years ago in the state of Washington. In this highly publicized case, two young women accused their father of having sexually abused them for many years. At first their father denied the charges. Under repeated questioning by police and attorneys, however, he began to report "recovered memories" of the crimes. Gradually, he "remembered" many of the scenes described by his daughters, then even supplied new ones they had not described. Were these reports accurate? Or were they false memories, constructed in response to the repeated suggestion that he had committed the crimes?

To find out, a trained psychologist, Richard Ofshe, used some ingenious procedures. First, he made up a completely false story in which the defendant forced his son and daughter to have sex (Loftus, 1993; Ofshe, 1992). The story was constructed in such a manner that it could not possibly be accurate. When it was presented to the father, he at first denied it—but then reported that he could "remember" the events as described. His children, too, ultimately confirmed the story, even though it could not have been true.

While some charges of child sexual abuse seem to be false, this in no way implies that most are based on constructed memories. On the contrary, child sexual abuse is all too real and all too frequent (Kendall-Tackett, Williams, & Finkelhor, 1993). But these findings do suggest the need for caution in assessing the accuracy of such charges.

One aid to evaluating the possibility that young children are being sexually abused by adults is the use of *anatomically detailed dolls*—dolls that show male and female genitals (Koocher et al., 1995). It has been suggested that these dolls help young children, whose verbal skills are often minimal, to describe what has happened to them. And in fact the dolls are now frequently used by psychologists and other professionals for this purpose (e.g., Conte et al., 1991). Unfortunately, however, there are potential dangers associated with the use of such dolls. The presence of anatomical details may lead very young children to report events that never happened to them. For example, consider a study by Bruck, Ceci, and Francoeur (1994). These researchers questioned three-year-old children for whom there was no suspicion of child sexual abuse about what had happened to them during a medical examination by their regular pediatrician; the children's mothers were present during the entire examination and observed all medical procedures. For half the children the examination included touching of the buttocks and genitals by the doctor and for half it did not. The children in both groups were later questioned about these events both with and without an anatomically detailed doll. Results indicated that when the researcher pointed to the buttocks and genital area of an anatomically detailed doll, fully 50 percent of the children who had *not* been touched there by their doctor indicated that they had. And for children who had been touched, fully 75 percent reported that the doctor had penetrated their bodies with his or her fingers, whereas in fact this did not occur. Fortunately, such errors do not appear to occur among older children. Still, these findings suggest that anatomically detailed dolls should be used with extreme caution, because the detail they contain may lead children to construct and report false memories in response to leading questions about what has happened to them.

Eyewitness Testimony: Is It as Accurate as We Believe?

Eyewitness testimony—evidence given by persons who have witnessed a crime or accident—plays an important role in many trials. At first glance, this makes a great deal of sense: What better source of information about a crime than the persons who actually saw it? After reading the previous discussions of potential sources of errors, distortion, and construction in memory, how-

Eyewitness Testimony: Information provided by witnesses to crimes or accidents.

ever, you may already be wondering about an important question: Is such testimony as accurate as many people believe?

The answer provided by careful research is clear: Eyewitnesses to crimes are far from infallible. In fact, they often falsely identify innocent persons as criminals (Wells, 1993), make mistakes about important details of a crime (Loftus, 1991), and sometimes even report "remembering" events they did not actually see (Haugaard et al., 1991). Do you remember the *leading questions* tactic discussed earlier in this chapter? This is just one of several ways in which eyewitnesses to crimes can be led, by their own erroneous memories and by the tactics of attorneys, to report inaccurate or totally false information. Because jurors and even judges tend to place great weight on the testimony of eyewitnesses, such errors can have serious consequences. Innocent persons may be convicted of crimes they did not commit—or, conversely, persons guilty of serious crimes may be wrongly cleared of the charges against them. Indeed, recent evidence indicates that the single largest factor accounting for such miscarriages of justice is faulty eyewitness testimony (Wells, 1993). Can anything be done to enhance eyewitnesses' accuracy? Fortunately, several procedures seem useful in this regard:

- Asking eyewitnesses to report everything they can remember
- Asking eyewitnesses to describe events from several different perspectives and in several different orders, not just the one in which events actually occurred
- Asking eyewitnesses to imagine themselves back at the scene and to reconstruct as many details as possible

Why do these procedures help? Perhaps because they provide eyewitnesses with increased retrieval cues; and as we've seen repeatedly, such cues often do help us to remember specific information.

Interestingly, simply asking eyewitnesses over and over again to recall what they saw does not seem to help (Turtle & Yuille, 1994). While repeated attempts at remembering do sometimes yield increased reports of details, errors also increase, so there is no overall gain in accuracy.

What about hypnosis—can it help to improve accuracy? You may have read in your local newspaper about instances in which eyewitnesses have undergone hypnosis in an attempt to increase their recall for the events they presumably saw. Unfortunately, there is little evidence that such procedures work. Eyewitnesses have occasionally reported new information while hypnotized, but it is unclear whether these effects stemmed from hypnosis or from differences in the way the witnesses were questioned while in this state. For example, while hypnotized, some witnesses have been forcefully instructed to "make a real effort" to remember. This kind of urging rather than hypnosis itself may have been responsible for improvements in memory—if improvements actually occurred.

To conclude: Existing evidence suggests that eyewitnesses are not as accurate a source of information as the public, attorneys, police, and juries often assume. Several techniques can assist eyewitnesses in remembering information they noticed and entered into memory; but if information was never entered into memory in the first place, such procedures will *not* prove helpful. In many cases, then, it is best to view eyewitness testimony as an imperfect and potentially misleading source of information about reality.

For an overview of potential pitfalls where memory is concerned, please see the **Ideas to Take with You** feature. And for a consideration of the effects of cultural differences on memory, see Exploring Gender and Diversity on page 245.

Key Questions

- What are schemas, and what role do they play in memory distortion?
- What are false memories, and how persistent are they?
- What role do false memories play in charges of childhood sexual abuse?
- How accurate is eyewitness testimony?

Ideas to Take with You

When—and Why—Memory Sometimes Fails

Retroactive Interference

We sometimes forget information we want to retain because new information interferes with it.

EXAMPLE: You learn the rules of a new board game, and as you do, you forget the rules for another, similar game that you learned to play before.

Repression

We sometimes forget information in memory because it is threatening or disturbing.

EXAMPLE: You forget that you met a certain person because when you met that person something very embarrassing happened to you.

Intentional Forgetting

We sometimes forget information we believe to be inaccurate or useless—only to find that we do need it at a later time.

EXAMPLE: You intentionally forget a phone number you have memorized because you think that you won't need it again. Then you discover that you do need it.

Prospective Forgetting

We sometimes forget to do things we are supposed to do at a particular time because they are unpleasant or because we lack sufficient retrieval cues to remind us to do them.

EXAMPLE: You forget about a dental appointment because in fact you really don't want to visit the dentist and because you don't have any cues reminding you of your appointment.

Infantile Amnesia

We can't remember events that happened to us early in life because they occurred before we had a well-developed self-concept.

EXAMPLE: You can't remember a big birthday party your parents had for you when you were two because at that time you had no clear self-concept.

Memory Distortion

We distort information stored in memory.

EXAMPLE: When you were eight years old, you had a part in a class play. You remember that you did quite well in this role, but your friends tell you that in fact you forgot your lines. You have unconsciously distorted your memory of the event so as to put yourself in a good light in your own consciousness.

Memory Construction

We construct false memories—memories of events that never happened or experiences we never had.

EXAMPLE: You remember receiving a toy you really liked as a present from your aunt. Now you learn that this toy wasn't even on the market at the time you remember receiving it; this is a false memory constructed on the basis of other information.

The Biological Bases of Memory: How the Brain Stores Knowledge

Let's begin with a simple but necessary assumption: When you commit information to memory, something must happen in your brain. Given that memories can persist for decades, it is only reasonable to suggest that this "something" involves relatively permanent changes within the brain. But where, precisely, do these changes occur? And what kinds of alterations do they involve? These questions have fascinated—and frustrated—psychologists for decades. Now, however, thanks to the development of tools and methods such as those described in the Research Methods section earlier in this chapter, answers have finally begun to emerge (e.g., Paller, Kutas, & McIsaac, 1995). Let's see what research on these issues has revealed.

Amnesia and Other Memory Disorders: Keys for Unlocking the Biology of Memory

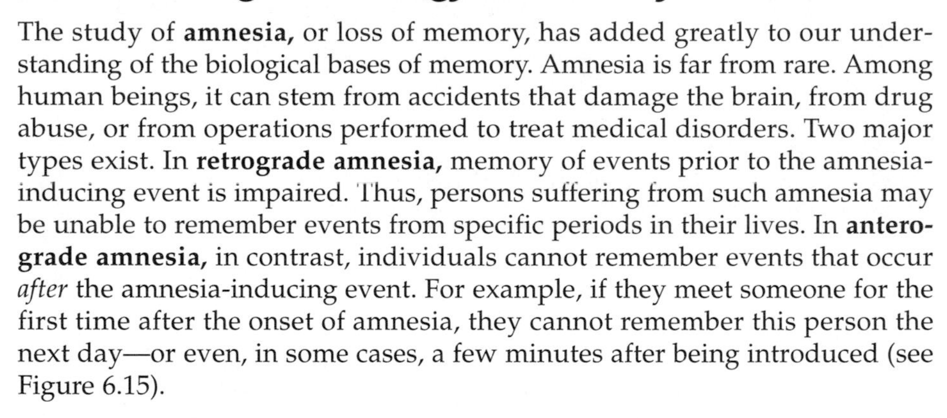

The study of **amnesia,** or loss of memory, has added greatly to our understanding of the biological bases of memory. Amnesia is far from rare. Among human beings, it can stem from accidents that damage the brain, from drug abuse, or from operations performed to treat medical disorders. Two major types exist. In **retrograde amnesia,** memory of events prior to the amnesia-inducing event is impaired. Thus, persons suffering from such amnesia may be unable to remember events from specific periods in their lives. In **anterograde amnesia,** in contrast, individuals cannot remember events that occur *after* the amnesia-inducing event. For example, if they meet someone for the first time after the onset of amnesia, they cannot remember this person the next day—or even, in some cases, a few minutes after being introduced (see Figure 6.15).

H.M. and the Role of the Medial Temporal Lobes Let's begin with the dramatic case of H.M.—an individual whose amnesia has been studied by psychologists since the 1950s. In 1953, at the age of twenty-seven, H.M. underwent an operation to remove the medial portion of both temporal lobes of his brain. The reason for this operation was to stop seizures; H.M. suffered from an extreme form of epilepsy. The operation almost completely cured H.M.'s seizures, but it produced both retrograde and anterograde amnesia (Milner, Corkin, & Teuber, 1968). H.M.'s retrograde amnesia was relatively minor; he could remember all of the past except for the most recent year or two. His anterograde amnesia, however, was profound. For example, he could read the same magazine over and over again with continued enjoyment, because as soon as he put it down, he forgot what was in it. Similarly, when his family moved, he could not find his way back to the new location even after several months of practice.

H.M. seemed quite normal in many respects. He could carry on conversations, repeat seven numbers from memory, and perform simple arithmetic tasks without paper and pencil. So both his short-term and his long-term memory systems seemed to be intact. His major problem seemed to be an inability to transfer new information from short-term memory to long-term memory. As a result, it was as if he had become suspended in time on the day in 1953 when he regained his health but lost his memory functions (Graf & Schachter, 1985).

Amnesia: Loss of memory stemming from illness, accident, drug abuse, or other causes.

Retrograde Amnesia: Loss of memory of events that occurred before an amnesia-inducing event.

Anterograde Amnesia: The inability to store in long-term memory information that occurs after an amnesia-inducing event.

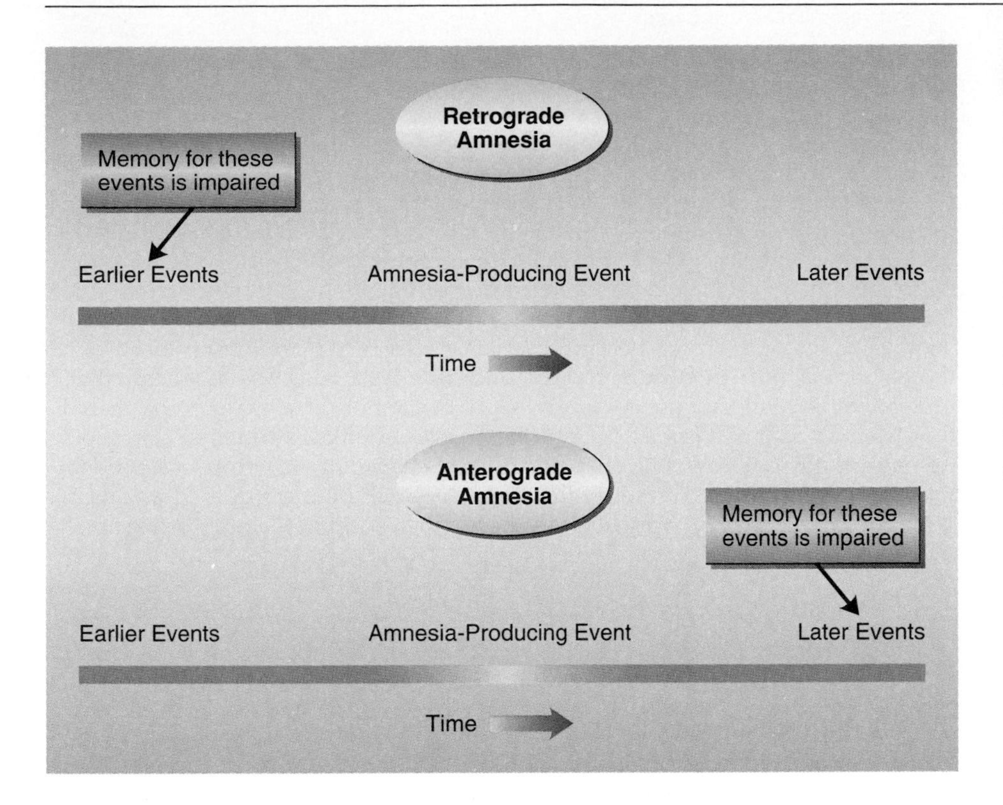

FIGURE 6.15

Two Kinds of Amnesia

In *retrograde amnesia*, memory of events prior to the amnesia-inducing event is impaired—people forget things that happened to them in the past. In *anterograde amnesia*, memory of events occurring after the amnesia-inducing events is impaired—people can't remember things that happen to them after the onset of their amnesia.

EXPLORING GENDER & DIVERSITY

Does Culture Influence Memory?

Memory is a very basic aspect of cognition, so in one sense we might expect it to operate in much the same manner among human beings everywhere. As far as we can tell, this is true: No matter where they live and in what culture, people all around the world have the same basic memory abilities. This does not mean, however, that memory is unaffected by culture. In fact, as noted by Mistry and Rogoff (1994), there are many ways in which such effects might occur. First, consider the kinds of information people try to remember in different cultures. In many industrialized societies, students learn as part of their education to remember lists of unrelated terms or definitions; they also practice entering abstract information such as mathematical equations and chemical equations into their memories. In nonindustrialized, traditional societies, in contrast, individuals have little if any practice with such tasks. People in these societies, too, commit large amounts of information to memory; but most of it is directly linked to their daily lives. For instance, they don't learn the names of plants and animals they never see, but they *do* memorize the names of large numbers of plants and animals that *are* a part of everyday life.

Second, consider the act of remembering itself. Children in industrialized societies practice memorizing because they know they may be asked to retrieve memorized information during examinations—a context far removed from the situations in which such information might actually be used. Children in traditional societies, in contrast, never practice such skills; they too retrieve large amounts of information from memory, but only in the contexts where this information is actually put to use.

Third, because of their formal education, children in industrialized societies are familiar with special kinds of interactions with adults—interactions in which the adult (as teacher or examiner) asks them specific questions about information they have committed to memory. This rarely if ever happens in traditional societies; in such societies children may never have interacted with adults in this manner, and may feel quite inhibited about answering direct questions from them. For instance, consider the culture of the Maya people of Central America (Rogoff & Mistry, 1985). In this culture it is viewed as very rude for children to answer questions from adults in a direct manner. Rather, they must say, "So I have been told . . ." to avoid appearing to know more than the adult—which would be the height of bad manners in that culture.

In short, for children raised in traditional cultures, the very act of remembering has a different meaning than it has for children raised in industrialized societies—a meaning closely linked to cultural values and practices. Thus, it is not surprising that when tested on standard memory tasks used in research in industrialized countries, such youngsters often perform more poorly. Most psychologists do not interpret these findings as evidence that children from traditional cultures have inferior memories, but rather as a reflection of the fact that they have different experiences with the use of memory. The main point, then, is this: Memory is indeed a basic cognitive process, but like every other aspect of human behavior, it occurs against a cultural backdrop. If we ignore cultural factors and influences, we run the risk of confusing culture-produced differences with ones relating to memory abilities themselves—and that would be inappropriate indeed.

What does the case of H.M. tell us about the biological bases of memory? Since it was portions of his temporal lobes that were removed, these findings suggest that these lobes—or structures within them—play a key role in the *consolidation of memory*—the process of shifting new information from short-term to longer-term storage. Research has confirmed this conclusion and has identified one structure in the temporal lobes—the *hippocampus*—as crucial in this respect, at least where spatial memories are concerned.

The Biological Bases of Explicit Memory and Implicit Memory Throughout this chapter, we have focused primarily on what might be termed *intentional memory*—memory that permits us to remember information that has been stored as a result of previous learning and that we actively try to bring to mind. Psychologists refer to this as **explicit memory,** since we can describe its contents verbally, in fairly specific terms. (Both episodic and semantic memory, which we considered earlier, fall under this general heading.) There is another kind of memory, however, that is also important—a kind of memory that involves being able to use information without necessarily being able to put it into words. This is known as **implicit memory,** and it operates in subtle ways. (Procedural memory, which we considered earlier, is one kind of implicit memory.) For instance, suppose you see a series of words. Then you are shown another series containing some of these words along with others that you didn't see previously. This second list is presented so quickly that it's hard for you to recognize the words shown. Will you do better at identifying the words you saw before than the new ones? Research findings indicate that you will, and such effects provide one demonstration of the operation of implicit memory (e.g., Gabrieli et al., 1995).

Explicit Memory: Memory for information that has been stored as a result of previous learning—information that we actively try to bring to mind and that we can express verbally.

Implicit Memory: Memory for information that we cannot express verbally. (See also *procedural memory*.)

Now, here's where things get interesting. Many persons suffering from amnesia do very poorly on tests of explicit memory—they can't recognize or recall information they have seen very recently. However, their implicit memory does not seem to be affected: They perform as well as normal persons on tasks such as the one described above. Such deficits in explicit memory appear to be linked to damage to the hippocampus, a portion of the temporal lobes (Knowlton, Ramus, & Squire, 1992).

What about implicit memory—is it related to other parts of the brain? Research evidence indicates that this is the case. Specifically, persons who have had portions of their *occipital lobe* removed for medical reasons sometimes show deficits in implicit memory, while maintaining their explicit memory largely intact (e.g., Gabrieli et al., 1995). So in sum, existing evidence points to two conclusions: (1) We do seem to possess two distinct kinds of memory, explicit and implicit; and (2) the functioning of these memory systems is related to different portions of the brain. For this reason, damage to different portions of the brain, as a result of accidents or medical procedures, can produce very different—and sometimes very surprising—effects on memory.

Amnesia as a Result of Korsakoff's Syndrome Individuals who consume large amounts of alcohol for many years sometimes develop a serious illness known as **Korsakoff's syndrome.** The many symptoms of Korsakoff's syndrome include sensory and motor problems as well as heart, liver, and gastrointestinal disorders. In addition, the syndrome is often accompanied by both anterograde amnesia and severe retrograde amnesia. Patients cannot remember events that took place even many years before the onset of their illness. Careful medical examinations of such persons' brains after their death indicate that they have experienced extensive damage to portions of the thalamus and hypothalamus. This suggests that these portions of the brain play key roles in long-term memory. The case of N.A. provides additional evidence for this conclusion.

N.A. was serving in the U.S. Air Force when he experienced a tragic accident. His roommate was making thrusts with a miniature fencing sword when N.A. suddenly turned around in his chair. The blade penetrated his right nostril and damaged his brain. The results of this accident were both immediate and striking. N.A. could no longer form verbal memories—he couldn't recall someone's name after meeting them, or information he had just read. However, he *could* still form visual memories—he could recognize an object he had seen previously (Squire, 1987). What was the cause of his memory deficit? A brain scan revealed that N.A. had suffered damage to the mediodorsal nucleus of the thalamus. (We discussed the nature of such scans in Chapter 2.) While other causes of N.A.'s problem cannot be entirely ruled out, these findings suggest that the mediodorsal nucleus may play an important role in long-term memory.

The Amnesia of Alzheimer's Disease One of the most tragic illnesses to strike human beings in the closing decades of life is **Alzheimer's disease.** This illness occurs among 5 percent of all people over age sixty-five. It begins with mild problems, such as increased difficulty in remembering names, phone numbers, or appointments. Gradually, though, patients' conditions worsen until they become totally confused, are unable to perform even simple tasks like dressing or grooming themselves, and experience an almost total loss of memory. In the later stages, patients may fail to recognize their spouse or children. Careful study of the brains of deceased Alzheimer's patients has revealed that in most cases they contain tiny bundles of *amyloid beta protein,* a substance not found in similar concentrations in normal brains. Growing evidence (Yankner et al., 1990) suggests that this substance causes damage to neurons that project from nuclei in the basal forebrain to the hippocampus and cerebral cortex (Coyle, 1987). These neurons transmit information primarily by means of the neurotransmitter acetylcholine, so it appears that this substance may play a key role in memory. Further evidence that acetylcholine-based systems are important is provided by the fact that the brains of Alzheimer's patients contain lower than normal amounts of acetylcholine. In addition, studies with animal subjects in which the acetylcholine-transmitting neurons are destroyed suggest that this does indeed pro-

Korsakoff's Syndrome: An illness caused by long-term abuse of alcohol; often involves profound retrograde amnesia.

Alzheimer's Disease: An illness primarily afflicting individuals over the age of sixty-five and involving severe mental deterioration, including retrograde amnesia.

duce major memory problems (Fibiger, Murray, & Phillips, 1983). However, very recent evidence suggests that other neurotransmitters are also involved, so the picture is more complex than was previously assumed.

In sum, evidence obtained from the study of various memory disorders indicates that specific regions and systems within the brain play important roles in our ability to transfer information from short-term to long-term storage and to retain it in long-term memory for extended periods of time. Table 6.2 presents an overview of the findings we have discussed.

TABLE 6.2

The Brain and Memory: A Summary of Current Knowledge

Existing evidence indicates that several areas of the brain and several biological systems within it play important roles in memory.

Brain Structure or System	Current Findings as to Role in Memory
Temporal lobes; hippocampus	Play key roles in transfer of information from short-term memory to long-term memory.
Temporal lobes; hippocampus	Damage to these areas produces deficits in explicit memory.
Portions of occipital lobes	Damage to these areas produces deficits in implicit memory.
Thalamus; hypothalamus	Damage to these structures plays a role in the amnesia observed in Korsakoff's syndrome.
Acetylcholine-based systems in the brain, especially those projecting from basal forebrain to hippocampus and cerebral cortex.	Disturbance of these systems plays a role in the amnesia observed in Alzheimer's disease.

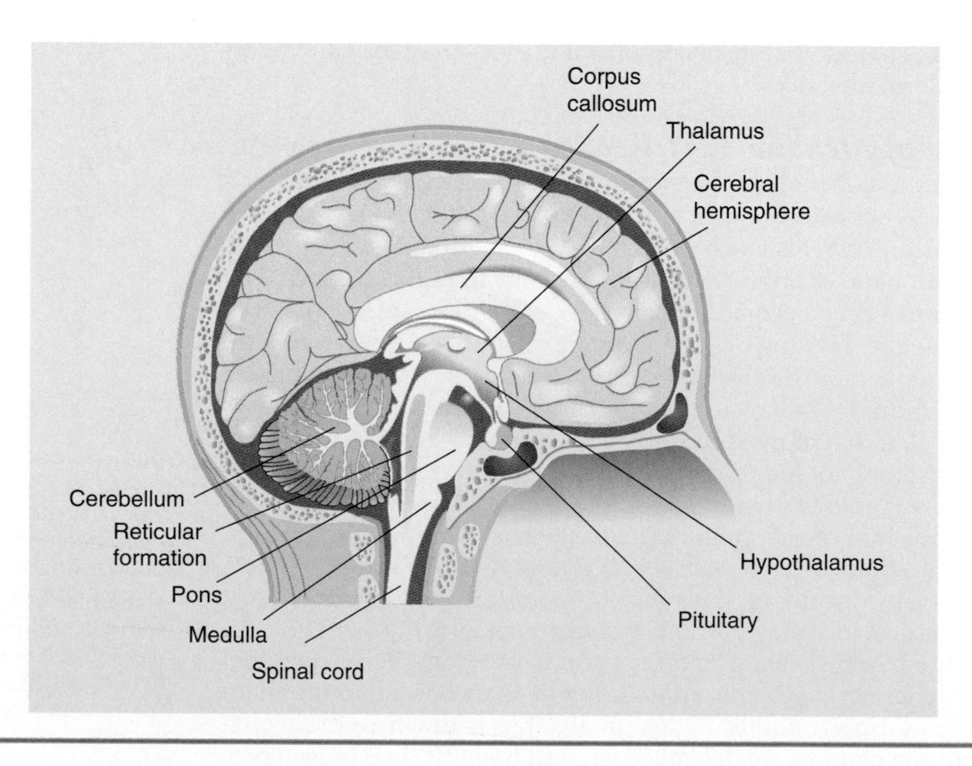

Memory and the Brain: A Modern View

Earlier I noted that "something" must happen within the brain when we enter information into memory. What is that "something"? Existing evidence is still too limited to permit us the luxury of final conclusions, but the picture emerging from ongoing research is something like this. The formation of long-term memories involves changes in the rate of production or release of specific neurotransmitters. Such changes increase the ease with which neural information can move within the brain and may produce *localized neural circuits.* Evidence for the existence of such circuits, or *neural networks,* is provided by research in which previously learned conditioned responses are eliminated when microscopic areas of the brain are destroyed—areas that, presumably, contain the neural circuits formed during conditioning (Thompson, 1989).

Long-term memory may also involve changes in the actual structure of neurons—changes that strengthen communication across specific synapses (Teyler & DeScenna, 1984). For instance, after learning experiences, the shape of dendrites in specific neurons may be altered, and these alterations may increase the neurons' responsiveness to certain neurotransmitters. Some of these changes may occur very quickly, while others may require considerable amounts of time. This, perhaps, is one reason why newly formed memories are subject to disruption for some period after they are formed (Squire & Spanis, 1984).

In sum, it appears that we are now entering an exciting period; armed with new and sophisticated research techniques, psychologists and other scientists may finally be able to unravel the biochemical code of memory. When they do, the potential benefits for persons suffering from amnesia and other memory disorders will probably be immense.

Key Questions

- What are retrograde amnesia and anterograde amnesia?
- What role does the hippocampus play in long-term memory?
- What are explicit and implicit memory? Are they related to different parts of the brain?
- What are Korsakoff's syndrome and Alzheimer's disease? What do they tell us about the biological bases of memory?

Making Psychology Part of Your Life

Improving Your Memory: Some Useful Steps

How good is your memory? If you are like most people, your answer is probably "Not good enough!" At one time or another, most of us have wished that we could improve our ability to retain facts and information. Fortunately, with a little work, almost anyone can learn to remember more information more accurately. Here are some suggestions you can readily put to use:

1. **Really think about what you want to remember.** If you wish to enter information into long-term memory, it is important to think about it. Ask questions about it, consider its meaning, and examine its relationship to information you already know. In other words, engage in "deep processing." Doing so will help make the new information part of your existing knowledge frameworks—and will increase your chances of remembering it later.

2. **Pay careful attention to what you want to remember.** Remember the demonstration at the start of this chapter—the one involving $5 and $20 bills? If so, you realize that unless you pay careful attention to information you want to remember, it stands little chance of really getting "in"—into long-term

memory. So be sure to direct your full attention to information you want to remember. True, this involves a bit of hard work. But in the long run, it will save you time and effort.

3. **Minimize interference.** Interference is a major cause of forgetting; and in general, the more similar materials are, the more likely they are to produce interference. In practical terms, this means that you should arrange your studying so that you don't study similar subjects one right after the other. Instead, work on subjects that are unrelated; the result may be less interference between them—and, potentially, better grades.

4. **Use visual imagery and other mnemonics.** You've probably heard the saying "A picture is worth a thousand words." Where memory is concerned, this is sometimes true; it is often easier to remember information associated with vivid mental images (e.g., Gehring & Toglia, 1989). You can put this principle to use by adopting any one of several different mnemonics—tactics for improving memory. One of these, the method of loci, involves linking points you want to remember with visual images arranged in some familiar order. For instance, suppose you want to remember the points in a speech you will soon make. You can imagine walking through some familiar place, say your own home. Then form a series of images in which each item you wish to remember is placed in a specific location. Perhaps the first point is, "The greenhouse effect is real." You might imagine a large, steamy greenhouse right outside your front door. The next point might be, "Cutting down the rain forest is increasing the greenhouse effect." For this one, you might imagine a large cut-down tree in your living room. You'd form other images, in different locations, for the other points you want to make. Then, by taking an imaginary walk through your house, you can "see" each of these images and so remember the points in your speech.

5. **Give yourself extra retrieval cues.** Remember the concept of state-dependent retrieval? As I noted previously, you can use this principle to provide yourself with extra retrieval cues and so help to enhance your memory. For instance, if you studied for a test while in one physical state, try to be in the same state when you take the test. Similarly, use the principle of mood-dependent memory. If you learned some material while in a given mood and then want to remember it, try to put yourself in the same mood. This is not as hard as it sounds: You can often vary your own mood by imagining happy or sad events. The point is that if your mood matches the mood you were in when you learned the information, your memory for the information may be improved.

6. **Develop your own shorthand codes**. When I learned the names of the nine planets, I did so by the first-letter technique, in which the first letter of each word in a phrase stands for an item to be remembered. In this case, the phrase was "Mary's Violet Eyes Make John Stay Up Nights Pondering" (for Mercury, Venus, Earth, Mars, Jupiter, Saturn, Uranus, Neptune, and Pluto). This can be a very useful technique if you need to remember lists of items.

I could list additional techniques for enhancing your memory, but most would be related to the points already described. Whichever techniques you choose, you will find that making them work does require effort. In memory training, as in any other kind of self-improvement, it appears that "No pain, no gain" holds true.

Summary and Review of Key Questions

Human Memory: The Information-Processing Approach

- **What tasks are involved in encoding, storage, and retrieval?** Encoding involves converting information into a form that can be entered into memory. Storage involves retaining information over time. Retrieval involves locating information when it is needed.
- **What are sensory memory, short-term memory, and long-term memory?** Sensory memory holds fleeting representations of our sensory experiences. Short-term memory holds a limited amount of information for short periods of time. Long-term memory holds large amounts of information for long periods of time.
- **What are semantic memory, episodic memory, and procedural memory?** Semantic memory consists of general information about the world. Episodic memory is information about experiences we have had in our own lives. Procedural memory is nonverbal information that allows us to perform various motor tasks, such as riding a bicycle or playing the piano.

KEY TERMS

memory, p. 214 • encoding, p. 215 • storage, p. 215 • retrieval, p. 215 • information-processing approach, p. 215 • selective attention, p. 217 • semantic memory, p. 217 • episodic memory, p. 217 • procedural memory, p. 217

Sensory Memory, Short-Term Memory, and Long-Term Memory: Our Basic Memory Systems

- **What kind of information does sensory memory hold?** Sensory memory holds representations of information brought to us by our senses.
- **How long does such information last in sensory memory?** These representations generally last for less than a second.
- **What are the serial position curve, the word-length effect, and the word-similarity effect?** The serial position curve is the phenomenon whereby items near the beginning and end of a list are remembered more accurately than items near the middle. The word-length effect is our tendency to have greater immediate recall for lists of short words than for lists of longer words. The word-similarity effect is our tendency to have greater immediate recall for words that do not sound alike than for words that do sound alike.
- **How much information can short-term memory hold, and for how long?** Short-term memory can hold seven to nine separate items or chunks, generally for twenty seconds or less.
- **What are the two basic components of short-term memory?** Short-term memory involves a memory store that holds the information and a rehearsal mechanism that refreshes it through rehearsal.
- **How does information move from short-term to long-term memory?** Information moves from short-term to long-term memory through the process of elaborative rehearsal.
- **What roles do levels of processing and organization play in long-term memory?** Research findings indicate that the deeper the level of processing and the better organized the material stored in memory, the better information is recalled from long-term memory.
- **What are retrieval cues, and what role do they play in long-term memory?** Retrieval cues are stimuli associated with information stored in long-term memory; they help us bring such information to mind.
- **How do mood-dependent memory effects and mood congruence effects differ?** Mood-dependent memory effects indicate that what we remember while in a given mood is determined, in part, by what we learned when previously in that mood. Mood congruence effects involve the tendency to store or remember information consistent with our current moods.

KEY TERMS

sensory memory, p. 218 • short-term memory, p. 219 • serial position curve, p. 220 • long-term memory, p. 223 • tip-of-the-tongue phenomenon, p. 223 • elaborative rehearsal, p. 224 • levels of processing view, p. 224 • retrieval cues, p. 227 • context-dependent memory, p. 227 • state-dependent retrieval, p. 227 • mood-dependent memory, p. 227 • mood congruence effects, p. 227

Forgetting from Long-Term Memory

- **Why does forgetting from long-term memory occur?** Forgetting from long-term memory results mainly from interference.
- **What is retroactive interference? Proactive interference?** Retroactive interference occurs when information currently being learned interferes with information already present in memory. Proactive interference occurs when information already present in memory interferes with the acquisition of new information.
- **What is repression, and what role does it play in forgetting of traumatic events such as childhood sexual abuse?** Repression is the active elimination from consciousness of memories or experiences we find threatening. It has been suggested that memories of traumatic events such as childhood sexual abuse are often repressed and will be remembered only when brought back into consciousness by the probings of a trained therapist.
- **What is intentional forgetting?** Intentional forgetting involves efforts to remove, or at least ignore, information in long-term memory that is inaccurate or no longer useful.
- **What is prospective memory?** Prospective memory involves remembering to perform certain activities at certain times.

KEY TERMS

retroactive interference, p. 231 • proactive interference, p. 232 • repression, p. 232 • intentional forgetting, p. 234 • prospective memory, p. 234

Memory in Natural Contexts

- **What is autobiographical memory?** Autobiographical memory contains information about our own lives.
- **What is infantile amnesia?** Infantile amnesia is our inability to recall events from the first two to three years of life.
- **What are flashbulb memories?** Flashbulb memories are memories connected to dramatic events in our lives.

KEY TERMS

autobiographical memory, p. 235 • infantile amnesia, p. 236 • flashbulb memories, p. 237

Memory Distortion and Memory Construction

- **What are schemas, and what role do they play in memory distortion?** Schemas are cognitive structures representing our knowledge and assumptions about some aspect of the world. Once formed, they influence the ways in which we process new information—what we notice, what we store in memory, and what we remember. This can lead to memory distortion.
- **What are false memories, and how persistent are they?** False memories are memories of events that never happened or experiences that we never had. Research findings suggest that in some instances, these constructed memories may be more persistent than real ones.
- **What role do false memories play in charges of childhood sexual abuse?** Growing evidence suggests that some charges of early childhood sexual abuse made by adults may in fact be based on false memories—that the events the individuals describe never actually occurred. Rather, they are constructed in

response to suggestions from therapists, attorneys, or other persons.

- **How accurate is eyewitness testimony?** The testimony of eyewitnesses to various crimes appears to be far less accurate than is widely believed.

KEY TERMS

schemas, p. 238 • eyewitness testimony, p. 241

The Biological Bases of Memory: How the Brain Stores Knowledge

- **What are retrograde amnesia and anterograde amnesia?** Retrograde amnesia involves loss of memory of events prior to the amnesia-inducing event. Anterograde amnesia is loss of ability to remember events that occur after the amnesia-inducing event.
- **What role does the hippocampus play in long-term memory?** The hippocampus seems to play a crucial role in the consolidation of memory—the process of shifting new information from short-term to longer-term storage.
- **What are explicit and implicit memory? Are they related to different parts of the brain?** Explicit memory permits us to remember information that has been stored in memory, that we actively try to bring to mind and that can be described verbally. Implicit memory allows us to use stored information without necessarily being able to express it in words. Existing evidence suggests that the hippocampus may play an important role in explicit memory, while the occipital lobe may play an important role in implicit memory.
- **What are Korsakoff's syndrome and Alzheimer's disease? What do they tell us about the biological bases of memory?** Korsakoff's syndrome is a serious illness caused by long-term abuse of alcohol which involves profound retrograde amnesia. Persons suffering from this illness often have damage to portions of the thalamus and hypothalamus, so these brain structures appear to be linked to amnesia. Alzheimer's disease involves severe mental deterioration, including retrograde amnesia. It may be linked to damage in neurons projecting from the basal forebrain to the hippocampus and cerebral cortex.

KEY TERMS

amnesia, p. 244 • retrograde amnesia, p. 244 • anterograde amnesia, p. 244 • explicit memory, p. 246 • implicit memory, p. 246 • Korsakoff's syndrome, p. 247 • Alzheimer's disease, p. 247

Critical Thinking Questions

Appraisal

At the present time, most psychologists accept the view that studying human memory from an information-processing perspective is very useful. Do you agree? Or do you feel that this view omits important aspects of memory that have nothing to do with computers and how they work?

Controversy

Public concern with childhood sexual abuse has increased greatly in recent years, as many people have come forward with claims that they were subjected to such treatment. Growing evidence indicates, however, that some charges of this type are false—that they are based on false memories suggested by therapists, attorneys, and others. What steps, if any, do you think should be taken to protect innocent persons against such charges, while also protecting the rights of persons who have actually suffered sexual abuse?

Making Psychology Part of Your Life

Now that you know how fallible and prone to errors memory can be, can you think of ways in which you can put this knowledge to use? In other words, can you think of situations in your own life where you may be less willing to rely on your memory in making judgments or decisions than was true in the past? And if so, what steps can you take in those situations to improve the accuracy of your judgments or decisions?

CHAPTER OUTLINE

Cognition

Thinking, Deciding, Communicating

Why is it that some people are great thinkers, while others are merely average? What happens in the brain during thought? Will computers ever become as smart as people? Do animals think? These and related questions have to do with **cognition**—a general term used to describe thinking and many other aspects of our higher mental processes. Where cognition is concerned, thinking and reasoning are only part of the picture. Have you ever agonized over an important decision, carefully weighing the advantages and disadvantages of potential alternatives? In all probability you have, perhaps in terms of selecting a college, choosing a major, or deciding between courses of action. To make the right decision you probably *thought* long and hard about the various alternatives; you tried to *reason* your way to a conclusion about their relative merits; and finally you made

Cognition: The mental activities associated with thought, knowledge, and memory.

some sort of *decision*. We perform these activities many times each day, and in a variety of contexts. It is on these and related issues that we'll focus in the present chapter.

We'll begin our discussion by examining the nature of *thinking*, an activity that involves the manipulation of mental representations of various features of the external world. Thinking includes *reasoning*—mental activity through which we transform available information in order to reach conclusions. We'll also look at an intriguing question that would definitely *not* have been included in this book twenty years ago: Do animals think? Next, we'll turn to *decision making*, the process of choosing between two or more alternatives on the basis of information about them. Here we'll explore different factors that influence the decision-making process. Third, we'll examine several aspects of *problem solving*, which typically involves processing information in various ways in order to move toward desired goals. Finally, we'll examine an aspect of cognition that provides the basis for much of the activity occurring in each of the processes listed so far: *language*. It is through language that we can share the results of our own cognition with others and receive similar input from them. We'll also consider new evidence suggesting the possibility that other species may also possess several basic elements of language.

Have you ever agonized over an important decision, carefully weighing the advantages and disadvantages of potential alternatives?

One additional point: As we'll soon see, our abilities to think, reason, make decisions, and use language are impressive in many respects. But they are far from perfect. As is true for memory, our cognitive activities are subject to many forms of error: When we think, reason, make decisions, solve problems, and use language, we do not always do so in ways that would appear completely rational to an outside observer (Hawkins & Hastie, 1990; Johnson-Laird, Byrne, & Tabossi, 1989). As we examine each aspect of cognition, therefore, I'll call attention to these potential sources of distortion, because understanding the nature of such errors can shed important light on the nature of the cognitive processes they affect (Smith & Kida, 1991).

Thinking: *Forming Concepts and Reasoning to Conclusions*

What are you thinking about right now? If you've answered the question, then it's safe to say that at least to some extent you are thinking about the words on this page. But perhaps you are also thinking about a snack, the movie you saw last night, the argument you had with a friend this morning—the list could be endless. At any given moment in time, consciousness contains a rapidly shifting pattern of diverse thoughts, impressions, and feelings. In order to try to understand this complex and ever changing pattern, psychologists have often adopted two main strategies. First, they have focused on the basic elements of thought—how, precisely, aspects of the external world are represented in our thinking. Second, they have sought to determine the manner in which we *reason*—how we attempt to process available information cognitively in order to reach specific conclusions.

Basic Elements of Thought: Concepts, Propositions, Images

Concepts: Mental categories for objects or events that are similar to one another in certain respects.

What, precisely, does thinking involve? In other words, what are the basic elements of thought? While no conclusive answer currently exists, it appears that our thoughts consist largely of three basic components: *concepts, propositions,* and *images.*

Concepts: Categories for Understanding Experience What do the following objects have in common: a country home, a skyscraper, a grass hut? Although they all look different, you probably have no difficulty in replying—they are all buildings. Now, how about these items: a Ford Explorer, the space shuttle *Discovery*, an elevator? Perhaps it takes you a bit longer to answer, but soon you realize that they are all vehicles (see Figure 7.1). The items in each of these groups look different from one another, yet in a sense you perceive—and think about—them as similar, at least in certain respects. The reason you find the task of answering these questions relatively simple is that you already possess well-developed concepts for both groups of items.

Concepts are mental categories for objects, events, experiences, or ideas that are similar to one another in one or more respects. Concepts play a central role in our task of understanding the world around us and representing it mentally. For example, imagine that in conversation a friend uses the term *zip drive.* You've never heard it before, so you ask what she means. When she replies, "It's a speedy, high-capacity portable hard drive useful for backing up files on your computer and transferring large numbers of computer files from one computer to another," you're home free. You already have a concept for "hard drive" and immediately place this new term in that category. Now you can think about it quite efficiently: You know that it stores large numbers of computer files, that it is portable, and that it can help accomplish

FIGURE 7.1

Concepts: Mental Categories for Diverse but Related Objects

What do these objects have in common? You probably have no difficulty labeling them "vehicles." This is because you already have well-developed concepts for such items.

certain tasks, such as helping you to avoid losing information in the event of a computer crash. In this and countless other situations, concepts allow us to represent a lot of information about diverse objects, events, or ideas in a highly efficient manner.

Artificial and Natural Concepts Is a tomato a fruit or a vegetable? Many people would answer, "a vegetable." Botanists, however, classify it as a fruit, because it contains seeds and its structure is definitely more like that of apples and pears than those of potatoes or spinach. This fact illustrates the important distinction between what psychologists term artificial (or logical) concepts and natural concepts. **Artificial concepts** can be clearly defined by a set of rules or properties. Thus, a tomato is a fruit because it possesses the properties established by botanists for this category. Similarly, as you learned in geometry, a figure can be considered to be a triangle only if it has three sides whose angles add to 180 degrees, and can be a square only if all four sides are of equal length and all four angles are 90 degrees. Such artificial concepts are very useful in many areas of mathematics and science.

In contrast, **natural concepts** have no fixed or readily specified set of defining features. They are fuzzy around the edges. Yet they more accurately reflect the state of the natural world, which rarely offers us the luxury of hard-and-fast, clearly defined concepts. For example, consider the following questions:

Is chess a sport?

Is a pickle a vegetable?

Is a psychologist a scientist?

Is someone who helps a terminally ill person commit suicide a murderer?

As you can readily see, these all relate to common concepts: sport, vegetable, science, crime. But what specific attributes are necessary for inclusion in each concept? If you find yourself puzzled, don't be surprised; the boundaries of natural concepts are somewhat indistinct.

Such natural concepts are often based on **prototypes**—the best or clearest examples (Rosch, 1975). Prototypes emerge from our experience with the external world, and new items that might potentially fit within their category are then compared with them. The more attributes new items share with an existing prototype, the more likely they are to be included within the concept. For example, consider the following natural concepts: *clothing, art.* For clothing, most people think of items like shirts, pants, or shoes. They are far less likely to mention wet suits, mink coats, or coats of armor. Similarly, for art, most people think of paintings, drawings, and sculptures. Fewer think of artwork such as the light show at Disney World.

In determining whether a specific item fits within a natural concept, then, we seem to adopt a *probabilistic* strategy. The more similar an object or event is to others already in the category, especially to the prototype for the category, the more likely we are to include the new item within the concept. In everyday situations, therefore, concept membership is not an all-or-nothing decision; rather, it is graded, and items are recognized as fitting within a category to a greater or lesser degree (Medin & Ross, 1992).

Artificial Concepts: Concepts that can be clearly defined by a set of rules or properties.

Natural Concepts: Concepts that are not based on a precise set of attributes or properties, do not have clear-cut boundaries, and are often defined by prototypes.

Prototypes: The best or clearest examples of various objects or stimuli in the physical world.

Concepts: How They Are Represented That concepts exist is obvious. But how are they represented in consciousness? No firm answer to this question exists, but several possibilities have been suggested. First, concepts may be represented in terms of their features or attributes. As natural concepts are formed, the attributes associated with them may be stored in memory. Then, when we encounter a new item, we compare its attributes with the ones we have already learned about. The closer the match, the more likely we are to include the item within the concept.

A second possibility is that natural concepts are represented, at least in part, through **visual images:** mental pictures of objects or events in the external world. When considering whether chess is a sport, did you conjure up an image of two players bending intently over the board while an audience looked on? If so, you can readily see how visual images may play a role in the representation of natural concepts. I'll have more to say about the role of such images in thought later in this discussion.

Finally, it is important to note that concepts are closely related to *schemas,* cognitive frameworks that represent our knowledge of and assumptions about the world (see Chapter 6). Like schemas, natural concepts are acquired through experience and also represent information about the world in an efficient summary form. However, schemas appear to be more complex than concepts; each schema contains a broad range of information and may include a number of distinct concepts. For example, each of us possesses a *self-schema,* a mental framework holding a wealth of information about our own traits, characteristics, and expectations. This framework, in turn, may contain many different concepts, such as intelligence, attractiveness, health, and so on. Some of these are natural concepts; so the possibility exists that natural concepts are represented, at least in part, through their links to schemas and other broad cognitive frameworks.

To sum up, concepts may be represented in the mind in several ways. Whatever their precise form, concepts certainly play an important role in thinking and in our efforts to make sense out of a complex and ever changing external world.

Visual Images: Mental pictures or representations of objects or events.

Propositions: Sentences that relate one concept to another and can stand as separate assertions.

Propositions: Relations between Concepts Thinking is not a passive process; it involves active manipulation of internal representations of the external world. As we have already seen, the representations that are mentally manipulated are often concepts. Frequently, thinking involves relating one concept to another, or one feature of a concept to the entire concept. Because we possess highly developed language skills, these cognitive actions take the form of **propositions**—sentences that relate one concept to another and can stand as separate assertions. For example, consider the following propositions:

Politicians are often self-serving.

This is a very interesting book.

Frozen yogurt is not as sweet as ice cream.

Concepts play a key role in each: *politicians* and *self-serving* in the first; *book* and *interesting* in the second; *frozen yogurt, sweet,* and *ice cream* in the third. Moreover, each sentence indicates some kind of relationship between the concepts or between the concepts and one or more of their features. For example, for many people a self-serving tendency is one feature of the concept *politician.* Research evidence indicates that much of our thinking involves the formulation and consideration of such propositions. Thus, propositions can be considered one of the basic elements of thought.

Images: Mental Pictures of the World Look at the drawing in Figure 7.2. Now cover it up with a piece of paper and answer the following questions:

1. Was there a flag? If so, in what direction was it fluttering?
2. Was there a tiller (handle) attached to the rudder?
3. Was there a porthole? On which side of the boat?

FIGURE 7.2

Mental Scanning of Visual Images

When shown a drawing such as this one and then asked questions about it, most people take longer to estimate the distance between the flag and the rudder than between the flag and the porthole.

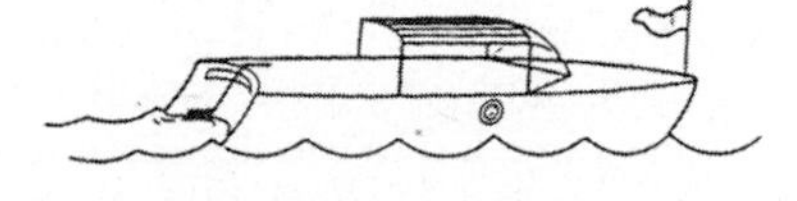

(**Source:** Based on an illustration used by Kosslyn, 1980.)

You probably answered all of these questions quite easily. But how? If you are like most people, you formed a visual image of the boat. Then, when asked about the flag, you focused on that part of your image. Next, you were asked to think about the rudder, at the opposite end of the boat. Did you simply jump to that end of the boat, or did you scan the entire image? Research findings indicate that you probably scanned the entire image: After being asked about some feature near the front of the boat, most people take longer to answer a question about a feature near the back than to respond concerning a feature somewhere in the middle (Kosslyn, 1980). Such findings suggest that once we form a mental image, we think about it by scanning it visually just as we would if it actually existed. Other findings support this conclusion. For example, when asked to estimate distances between locations on a familiar university campus, the farther apart the places indicated, the longer people take to make their estimates (Baum & Jonides, 1979).

Other findings, however, indicate that our use of visual images in thinking is not precisely like that of actual vision (Pylyshyn, 1981). In one study, for example, participants were asked to imagine carrying either a cannonball or a balloon along a familiar route (Intons-Peterson & Roskos-Ewoldsen, 1988). Not surprisingly, the participants took longer to complete their imaginary journeys when carrying the heavy object. So perhaps we don't simply "read" the visual images we generate; if we did, participants in this study should have been able to move through the imagined route equally fast in both conditions. The fact that they could not indicates that visual images are embedded in our knowledge about the world, and are interpreted in light of such knowledge rather than simply scanned.

Whatever the precise mechanisms through which they are used, mental images serve important purposes in the thinking process. People report using images for understanding verbal instructions, by converting the words into mental pictures of actions; for increasing motivation, by imagining successful performance; and for enhancing their own moods, by visualizing positive events or scenes (Kosslyn et al., 1991). Clearly, then, visual images constitute another basic element of thinking.

Key Questions

- What are concepts?
- What is the difference between artificial and natural concepts?
- What are propositions and images?
- What is verbal protocol analysis?

For more information on how psychologists study various aspects of thinking, please see the Research Methods section below.

RESEARCH METHODS

How Psychologists Study Cognitive Processes

People think—that's obvious. But how do psychologists measure *what* someone is thinking? After all, it is difficult to assess cognition directly. For example, what goes on in your mind as you grapple with a tough decision? What mental processes are involved when you try to determine the meaning behind a warm smile from an attractive person you'd like to meet? Or how do the cognitive processes of expert problem solvers differ from those of persons who are less skilled in this regard? Issues like these have led to the development of techniques that help psychologists understand the nature of various cognitive processes—such as thinking and memory—by measuring performance on tasks thought to involve these processes. One widely used cognitive assessment tool is *reaction time*—the amount of time it takes a person to react to a particular stimulus; an example would be pressing a computer key as quickly as possible each time a randomly occurring STOP sign icon appears on a computer screen. By varying the requirements of a cognitive task, such as the task's difficulty or the number of mental steps involved, psychologists can use differences in reaction time, or in the number or types of errors people commit, to make inferences regarding the nature of the underlying mental processes involved.

Perhaps the most interesting technique for studying cognitive processes, however, is **verbal protocol analy-**

sis. Participants in studies using this technique are asked to give continuous verbal reports, or to "think aloud," while making a decision or solving a problem (Ericsson & Simon, 1993). Verbal protocol analysis can provide information difficult to obtain by other means—most importantly, information about the types of knowledge people access while performing a particular task. This technique has the advantage of providing an ongoing record of the thinking *process,* rather than a single measure obtained at the end of the process (Crutcher, 1994; Payne, 1994).

How is the information obtained through the use of verbal protocols analyzed? By combining data obtained from many participants, psychologists are able to pinpoint meaningful patterns in the verbal protocol data. For example, researchers might note instances in which certain types of thoughts seem to occur consistently at a certain point as people attempt to solve a difficult problem. Or participants might be asked to report their thoughts while imagining themselves in a social situation; for example, at a party where two people they know are talking about them (Davison, Navarre, & Vogel, 1995). In the party example, analysis of the participants' reports might reveal important differences in responses based on age, gender, or other characteristics of interest to the researchers.

Verbal protocols can also be broken down into shorter segments to reveal the mental processes that underlie certain parts of a task. Research examining the "think-aloud" procedure has shown that the information obtained is typically consistent with the results obtained through the use of other well-known cognitive assessment techniques, such as reaction time or error data (Ericsson & Simon, 1993).

In one recent study, Blessing and Ross (1996) used verbal protocol analysis to examine ways in which experienced problem solvers differ from less-skilled problem solvers. One way in which expert and novice problem solvers are known to differ is the extent to which they rely on the surface content and deep structures of word problems (Chi, Feltovich, & Glaser, 1981). *Surface Structure* refers to the specific descriptions used to convey word problems, whereas *deep structure* refers to the underlying principles or mathematical equations needed to solve them. Some evidence indicates that experts do not focus on the context in which a problem is presented, but instead concentrate on discovering the problem's deep structure. In contrast, novices do not search for deep structure, but instead spend their time examining the problem's surface content.

Despite these findings, Blessing and Ross (1996) hypothesized that the experts do not ignore the suface structure of a problem altogether, but rather use this information—when relevant—as a clue to the type of problem it is and its solution. To test this possibility, the researchers asked experts (highly skilled math students) to solve word problems and to think aloud as they solved each one. Three versions of each problem were constructed so that the surface content was either appropriate, neutral, or inappropriate with respect to the problem's deep structure. Consistent with the researchers' predictions, participants spent the *least* amount of time solving problems whose surface structure matched its deep structure.

Even more interesting, however, were the results of the think-aloud protocol. These results indicated that participants presented with the "matching" version of each problem stated either the correct answer or the key equation(s) necessary to solve it almost immediately after reading the problem. In contrast, participants who solved the other ("neutral" or "nonmatching") versions of the same problem did not solve the problem in the same way. Because the clues provided by their problems' specific descriptions were *not* appropriate to the problems' deep structure, these participants were forced to translate each sentence of their word problem sequentially; as a result, it took them longer to solve the problem.

To summarize, these results illustrate the usefulness of verbal protocol analysis. Please note, however, that the think-aloud approach is not without its problems (Payne, 1994). First, as you might expect, verbal protocol analysis can be extremely time-consuming. Second, data obtained via this technique may reflect what participants believe they "should" be saying rather than the true underlying cognitive processes involved in a task. Finally, critics point out that asking participants to verbalize their thoughts may fundamentally alter the mental processes of interest. Still, the use of verbal protocol analysis, in conjunction with other well-established methods, can provide an important window into the inner workings of the mind.

Reasoning: Transforming Information to Reach Conclusions

One task we often face in everyday life is **reasoning:** drawing conclusions from available information. More formally, in reasoning we make cognitive transformations of appropriate information in order to reach specific conclusions (Galotti, 1989). How do we perform this task? And to what extent are we successful at it—in other words, how likely are the conclusions we reach to be accurate or valid?

Verbal Protocol Analysis: A technique for studying cognitive processes in which participants are asked to talk aloud while making a decision or solving a problem.

Reasoning: Cognitive activity that transforms information in order to reach specific conclusions.

Formal versus Everyday Reasoning First, it's important to draw a distinction between *formal reasoning* and what might be described as *everyday reasoning*. In formal reasoning, all the required information is supplied, the problem to be solved is straightforward, there is typically only one correct answer, and the reasoning we apply follows a specific method. One important type of formal reasoning is **syllogistic reasoning**—reasoning in which conclusions are based on two propositions called premises. For example, consider the following syllogism:

Premise: All people who are churchgoers are honest.

Premise: All politicians are churchgoers.

Conclusion: Therefore, all politicians are honest.

Is the conclusion correct? According to the rules of formal reasoning, it is. But you may find it hard to accept—and the reason for the problem should be obvious. At least one of the premises is incorrect: there is no strong evidence that all politicians attend church. This simple example illustrates an important point: Formal reasoning can provide a powerful tool for processing complex information, but *only* when its initial premises are correct.

In contrast to formal reasoning, *everyday reasoning* involves the kind of thinking we do in our daily lives: planning, making commitments, evaluating arguments. In such reasoning some of the premises are implicit, or unstated. Others may not be supplied at all. The problems involved often have several possible answers, which may vary in quality or effectiveness; and the problems themselves are not self-contained—they relate to other issues and questions of daily life (Hilton, 1995). For example, imagine that you have a problem with your next-door neighbor. You and your neighbor share a driveway leading to your garages. It is narrow, so only one car at a time can pass. Lately, your neighbor has taken to parking her car midway down the driveway, next to her side door. This prevents you from putting your own car in your garage. You begin to reason about this situation in order to understand why your neighbor is doing this. One potential premise might be "She has been quite ill lately"; a second might be "People who are ill are weak and don't want to walk a lot." These could lead to the conclusion "Although she is a nice person, she is too ill to be considerate." Other premises, however, are also possible: "She has been quite ill lately" coupled with "But she has gotten a lot better" and "People who look as healthy as she does don't mind walking." Your conclusion then might be quite different: "She is using her recent illness as an excuse for being irresponsible."

Notice that in this situation, the premises are not specified for you, as in syllogisms; you must generate them for yourself. And many different premises are possible. The ones you choose will probably depend on numerous factors, including your recent experiences with other neighbors, with people who are ill, and so on. Finally, when you do reach a conclusion, it is not easy to determine whether it is correct or whether others, too, might be accurate.

Everyday reasoning, then, is far more complex and far less definite than formal syllogistic reasoning. Since it is the kind we usually perform, however, it is worthy of careful attention.

Reasoning: Some Basic Sources of Error How good are we at reasoning? Unfortunately, not as good as you might guess. Several factors, working together, seem to reduce our ability to reason effectively.

Syllogistic Reasoning: A type of formal reasoning in which two premises are used as the basis for deriving logical conclusions.

The Role of Mood States You may not be surprised to learn that the way we feel—our current moods or emotions—can dramatically reduce our ability to reason effectively (Forgas, 1995). Most of us have experienced situations in which we've lost our cool—and, unfortunately, our ability to reason effectively as well. You may be surprised to learn, however, that *positive* moods can also reduce our ability to reason effectively. In one recent study, Oaksford and colleagues (1996) used brief film clips to induce either positive, negative, or neutral moods in the study participants. Following the mood induction, all participants in the study attempted to solve a difficult analytical task. Interestingly, the participants in the positive mood condition required significantly *more* trials to solve the problem than participants in the other groups. How do we account for these results? Apparently, inducing positive mood states makes more, and more diffuse, memories available to us—definitely an asset if the task at hand requires a creative solution. Solving analytical tasks like the one used in this study, however, relies less on long-term memory retrieval and more on the ability to work through the discrete steps necessary to solve the problem. In short, a positive mood state does not guarantee that our ability to reason effectively will be enhanced. (See Chapter 10 for additional information on the effects of mood on cognitive processes.)

The Role of Beliefs Reasoning is often influenced by emotion-laden beliefs. For example, imagine that a person with deeply held convictions against the death penalty listens to a speech favoring capital punishment. Suppose that the arguments presented by the speaker contain premises the listener can't readily refute, and thus point to the conclusion that the death penalty is justified for the purpose of preventing further social evil. Yet the listener totally rejects this conclusion. Why? Because of his or her passionate beliefs and convictions against the death penalty, the listener may alter the meaning of the speaker's premises or "remember" things the speaker never really said. This, of course, serves to weaken the speaker's conclusion. Such effects can arise in many ways. Whatever your views on this particular issue, the general principle remains the same: When powerful beliefs come face to face with logical arguments, it is often the latter that give way. We'll consider the powerful effects of emotion again in Chapter 10.

The Social Context Social context can also exert powerful effects on reasoning (Hilton, 1995). To illustrate this, consider the following example: While entering a restaurant—one you've never tried before—you ask a couple who are leaving, "How was it?" If they reply, "It was great!" what do you conclude? After all, the couple did not comment directly on the quality of the food, the service, or the atmosphere inside the restaurant. However, from a variety of contextual variables—the tantalizing aromas emanating from the restaurant, the fact that many people are eating there, the unmistakable look of satisfaction on the couple's faces (or on the faces of other people leaving the restaurant), and the enthusiasm in their voices—you probably conclude that your chances of experiencing a delightful meal are good. But this may not be sound reasoning. Clearly, aspects of the social context contribute significantly to the accuracy of the conclusions we reach. We'll consider some of these factors again in Chapter 16.

The Confirmation Bias: Searching for Positive Evidence To illustrate another source of error in reasoning, let's consider our anti–death penalty person once again. Suppose that over several weeks he or she encounters numerous magazine articles; some report evidence confirming the usefulness of the death penalty, while others report evidence indicating that capital punishment is ineffective in terms of deterring crime. As you can readily guess, the individual will probably remember more of the articles that support the anti–death penalty view. In fact, there is a good chance that this person will read only these articles, or will read these articles more carefully

Confirmation Bias: The tendency to pay attention primarily to information that confirms existing views or beliefs.

Hindsight Effect: The tendency to assume that we would have been better at predicting actual events than is really true.

than the ones arguing in favor of capital punishment. To the extent that this happens, it demonstrates the **confirmation bias**—our strong tendency to test conclusions or hypotheses by examining only, or primarily, evidence that confirms our initial views (Baron, 1988; Klayman & Ha, 1987). Because of the confirmation bias, individuals often become firmly locked into their conclusions; after all, when this bias operates, it prevents people from even considering information that might call their premises, and thus their conclusions, into question (see Figure 7.3).

Hindsight: The "I knew it all along" Effect Revisited Have you ever heard the old saying "Hindsight is better than foresight"? What it means is that after specific events occur, we often have the impression that we could have predicted or actually did predict them. This is known in psychology as the **hindsight effect:** the tendency to judge events as more predictable after their occurrence than in foresight (Fischoff, 1975).

A dramatic real-life illustration of this effect was provided by the launch of the Hubble space telescope in the spring of 1990. Shortly after the telescope reached orbit, it was discovered to have a serious defect. Within a few days of this discovery, several officials stated that they had known all along that this might happen; in fact, the problem resulted from a failure to conduct certain tests of the telescope that they had personally recommended. Were these individuals correct? Existing evidence on the hindsight effect casts considerable doubt on this possibility. In many studies, conducted in widely different contexts, learning that an event occurred causes individuals to assume that they could have predicted it more accurately than is really the case (Christensen-Szalanski & Willham, 1991; Mitchell, Russo, & Pennington, 1989).

Can anything be done to counteract the hindsight effect? There are several possibilities. For example, if individuals are asked to explain a reported outcome along with other possible outcomes that did *not* occur, they are better able to recall their actual views before learning of the event, and this reduces the hindsight effect (Davies, 1987; Slovic, Fischoff, & Lichtenstein, 1977). Other people may also reduce the hindsight effect by calling attention to the fact that they too were surprised by the event and that it was indeed truly difficult to predict (Mazursky & Ofir, 1996; Wasserman, Lempert, & Hastie, 1991). In sum, it does appear that we can combat our strong tendency to assume that we are better at predicting events than is truly justified. And to the extent that we avoid tendencies to flawed thinking, our ability to reason effectively may be enhanced. Please refer to the **Ideas to Take with You** feature for tips to help you reason more effectively.

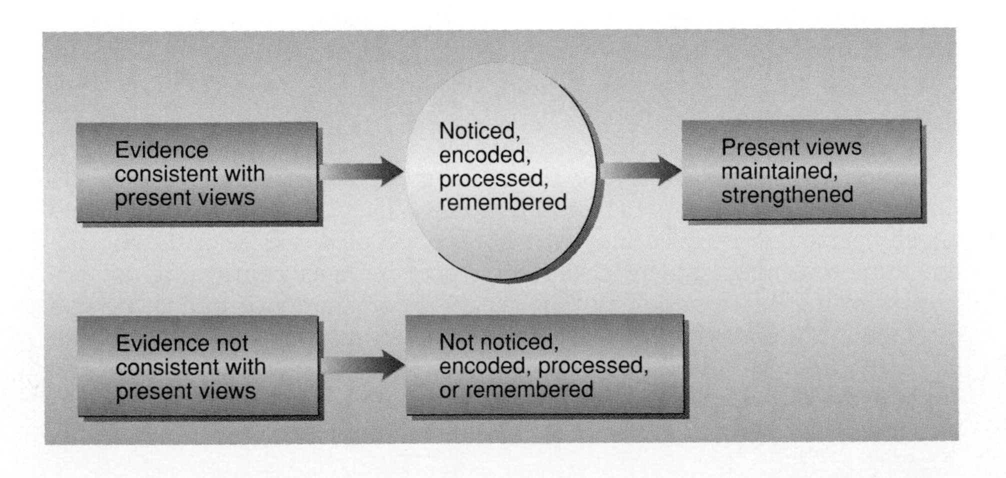

FIGURE 7.3

The Confirmation Bias

The confirmation bias leads individuals to test conclusions or hypotheses by examining primarily—or only—evidence consistent with their initial views. As a result, these views may be maintained regardless of the weight of opposing evidence.

Ideas to Take with You

How to Reason Effectively

Each day we face a succession of events that require the use of our wits—in other words, our ability to reason. Several factors can greatly reduce our ability to reason effectively, however, thereby placing us at risk for making bad decisions. To reduce the chances that you'll fall prey to one or more of these factors, consider the following suggestions.

MOOD STATES: Feeling Too Good or Too Bad Can Spell Trouble

Most people's mood states fluctuate over time—that's normal. When it comes to reasoning, however, extremes in emotional states can be bad news. Losing your cool, for instance, can result in decisions you may regret later. Yet, being in a good mood also has its advantages and disadvantages. Performance on creative tasks seems to be enhanced by a positive mood state, but performance on analytic tasks is diminished. So beware of making important decisions or trying to solve difficult problems when you are unhappy or angry—or when you're walking on air.

PERSONAL BELIEFS: Try to Focus on the Facts

Personal beliefs can cause us to ignore or overreact to a point of view on an issue about which we feel strongly. Protect yourself from this potential source of error by asking yourself whether you are responding to the facts—or to your personal beliefs.

THE SOCIAL CONTEXT: Filling in the Gaps

Social conventions can cause our reasoning to go astray because of our tendency to view all information through the filter of our personal experience. For example, we may interpret a message quite differently depending on who said it, how we choose to interpret the intended meaning, and the setting in which we hear the message.

THE CONFIRMATION BIAS: Failure to Consider Alternative Views

The confirmation bias is our tendency to pay attention primarily—or exclusively—to information that supports our own preexisting attitudes or opinions. To combat this tendency, seek out information from all points of view, and then carefully weigh the merits of each argument.

Animal Cognition: Do Animals Really Think?

That human beings possess cognitive abilities, such as the abilities to think, reason, and plan, is obvious. But how about other species—do animals have similar abilities? So far, our discussions in this chapter have implied that cognitive processes are, for the most part, a human attribute. After all, it is difficult for most of us to picture animals thinking or performing other complex mental activities. And for many years this view prevailed among some behavioral researchers as well (Blumberg & Wasserman, 1995).

Several developments, however, have led to a reevaluation of these initial conclusions. For example, as discussed in Chapter 5, many instances of animal learning have been encountered that cannot be explained solely through conditioning (e.g., Capaldi, 1996; Tolman & Honzik, 1930). Also, growing evidence suggests that animals *do* form complex mental representations of their environments, a cognitive activity that helps them adapt to changing conditions they often face in nature (Cook, 1993; Shettleworth, 1993). Finally, earlier studies of animal cognition often used tasks designed to assess features of *human* cognition; in other words, these procedures may not have been optimal for studying the cognitive processes of animals (Hulse, 1993).

A more recent view—termed the *ecological approach*—focuses on how animals solve the kinds of cognitive problems that are important to their survival; for example, finding their way around, assessing the status of food and other resources in the environment, and recognizing and avoiding danger when it is present (Shettleworth, 1993). In other words, the ecological approach tests for the presence of cognitive processes appropriate to a particular species.

Assessing Cognitive Processes of Animals: Establishing Equivalent Procedures Although it is apparent that animals differ from human beings in important ways, there are many similarities among species as well. Establishing commonality of cognitive processes in different species, however, requires the creation of comparable testing conditions (Wasserman, 1993). To determine whether animals and humans possess similar cognitive abilities, researchers have devised procedures that allow direct comparisons between them.

One cognitive ability that has been well established in human beings—but not in nonhuman species—is the ability to perform mental rotation of visual forms (Shepard & Metzler, 1971). To test mental rotation, people first view a *sample stimulus*—say the letter R. They are then shown two *comparison stimuli*—rotated versions of the same stimulus and of its mirror image. Their task is to determine which of the comparison stimuli matches the sample. To do so, participants must first mentally rotate both stimuli to a normal position. The time required to select the correct stimulus usually varies directly with the amount of mental rotation required.

To test whether baboons are capable of mentally rotating visual stimuli, Vauclair, Fagot, and Hopkins (1993) developed a procedure appropriate to the abilities of baboons (see Figure 7.4). Their subjects (baboons) first viewed a sample shape (such as the letter F) that was flashed briefly on a screen. Then two comparison shapes that were rotated 0, 60, 120, 180, 240, or 300 degrees were presented. One of the comparison shapes always matched the sample; the other comparison shape was its mirror image. The baboons' task was to use a joystick to

FIGURE 7.4

Animal Cognition: A Sample Test Environment

The upper portion of the figure shows the apparatus used to assess baboons' ability to rotate visual stimuli mentally. The baboons were trained to use the joystick to indicate which of two rotated comparison stimuli (bottom right) matched a sample stimulus (bottom left). The comparison stimuli consisted of the "correct match" and its mirror image.

(**Source:** From an article by J. Vauclair, J. Fagot, and W. D. Hopkins, in *Psychological Science*, Vol. 4, 1993. Reprinted with the permission of Cambridge University Press.)

select the comparison shapes that matched the original samples. Each correct response produced a small food reward.

The results showed that baboons were able mentally to rotate visual stimuli, an ability that some researchers had previously believed was beyond the capacity of nonhuman species. Moreover, the baboons' performance varied directly with the degree of rotation of the comparison stimuli—a finding that closely paralleled the performance of humans on the same task. Taken together, the results of these studies, as well as others, suggest that when appropriate methods are used, other animal species demonstrate cognitive abilities that are similar in many respects to those of humans.

Key Questions

- What is the process of reasoning? How does formal reasoning differ from everyday reasoning?
- What forms of error and bias can lead to faulty reasoning?
- What is the ecological approach to animal cognition?

Making Decisions: Choosing among Alternatives

Reasoning is hard work; in fact, it's an activity many people try to avoid. In some respects, though, reasoning is less difficult than another cognitive task you perform many times each day: **decision making.** From the moment you wake up until you turn out the light at night, life presents a continuous series of choices. What to wear, what to eat for breakfast, whether to attend a class or meeting, whether to speed up so you can get through that yellow traffic light—the list of everyday decisions is endless. And at intervals we face much more important decisions: what school to attend, what job to accept, what house to buy, whether to continue or end a long-term relationship.

If you were a perfectly rational decision maker, you would make each of these choices in a cool, almost mathematical way. You would consider (1) the utility or value to you of the outcomes each alternative might yield and (2) the probability that such results would actually occur. Then, taking these two factors into account, you would make your decision on the basis of **expected utility**—the product of the value and the probability of each possible outcome. As you probably know from your own experience and through observing the behavior of others, however, people don't usually pause to reason in such a systematic manner. Instead, they often make decisions informally, on the basis of hunches, intuition, or the opinions of others (Christenfeld, 1995). And even if you did try to make decisions in a perfectly rational way, you would quickly find that even this would not provide a fail-proof method. For example, both the values you attached to various outcomes and your estimates concerning their probability might shift over time. Let's consider several factors that influence the decision-making process, making it less rational or effective than might otherwise be the case.

Decision Making: The process of choosing among various courses of action or alternatives.

Expected Utility: The product of the subjective value of an event and its predicted probability of occurrence.

Heuristics: Mental rules of thumb that permit us to make decisions and judgments in a rapid and efficient manner.

Heuristics: Using Quick—but Fallible—Rules of Thumb to Make Decisions

Where cognition is concerned, human beings definitely follow the path of least resistance whenever possible. Since making decisions is hard work, it is only reasonable to expect people to take shortcuts in performing this activity. One group of cognitive shortcuts is known as **heuristics**—rules of thumb that reduce the effort required, though they may not necessarily enhance the

Availability Heuristic: A cognitive rule of thumb in which the importance or probability of various events is judged on the basis of how readily they come to mind.

quality or accuracy of the decisions reached (Kahneman & Tversky, 1982). Heuristics are extracted from past experience and serve as simple guidelines for making reasonably good choices quickly and efficiently. We'll focus on the three heuristics that tend to be used most frequently.

Availability: What Comes to Mind First? Let's start with the **availability heuristic:** the tendency to make judgments about the frequency or likelihood of events in terms of how readily examples of them can be brought to mind. This shortcut tends to work fairly well, because the more readily we can bring events to mind, the more frequent they generally are; but it can lead us into error as well.

A good example of the availability heuristic in operation is provided by a study conducted by Tversky and Kahneman (1974). They presented participants with lists of names like the one in Table 7.1 and then asked whether the lists contained more men's or women's names. Although the numbers of male and female names were equal, nearly 80 percent of the participants reported that women's names appeared more frequently. Why? Because the women named in the lists were more famous, so their names were more readily remembered and brought to mind.

The availability heuristic also influences many people to overestimate their chances of being a victim of violent crime, being involved in an airplane crash, or winning the lottery. Because such events are given extensive coverage in the mass media, people can readily bring vivid examples of them to mind. The result: They conclude that such outcomes are much more frequent than they really are (Tyler & Cook, 1984).

Representativeness: Assuming That What's Typical Is Also Likely You have just met your next-door neighbor for the first time. On the basis of a brief conversation, you determine that he is neat in his appear-

TABLE 7.1

The Availability Heuristic in Operation

Does this list contain more men's or women's names? The answer may surprise you: The number of male and female names is about equal. Because of the *availability heuristic*, however, most people tend to guess that female names are more numerous. The reason: The women listed are more famous than the men, so it is easier to bring their names to mind, and this leads to overestimates of their frequency in the list.

Read this list, then decide if it contains more men's or women's names.	
Louisa May Alcott	Pearl Buck
John Dickson Carr	Amy Lowell
Emily Dickinson	Robert Lovett
Thomas Hughes	Edna St. Vincent Millay
Laura Ingalls Wilder	George Jean Nathan
Jack Lindsay	Allan Nevins
Edward George Lytton	Jane Austen
Margaret Mitchell	Henry Crabb Robinson
Michael Drayton	Joseph Lincoln
Edith Wharton	Emily Brontë
Henry Vaughan	Arthur Hutchinson
Kate Millet	James Hunt
Eudora Welty	Erica Jong
Richard Watson Gilder	Brian Hooker
Harriet Beecher Stowe	

ance, has a good vocabulary, seems very well read, is somewhat shy, and dresses conservatively. Later, you realize that he never mentioned what he does for a living. Is he more likely to be a business executive, a dentist, a librarian, or a waiter? One quick way of making a guess is to compare him with your image of typical members of each of these occupations. If you proceeded in this fashion, you might conclude that he is a librarian, because his traits seem to resemble those of your image of librarians, and especially those of your image of the prototypical librarian, more closely than the traits of waiters, dentists, or executives. If you reasoned in this manner you would be using the **representativeness heuristic.** In other words, you would be making your decision on the basis of a relatively simple rule: The more closely an item—or event, object, or person—resembles the most typical examples of some concept or category, the more likely it is to belong to that concept or category.

Although making judgments or decisions on the basis of representativeness saves cognitive effort, it can also be a source of serious errors. In particular, use of this heuristic sometimes causes us to ignore forms of information that could potentially prove very helpful. The most important of these is information relating to *base rates*—the relative frequency of various items or events in the external world. Returning to your new neighbor, there are many more businessmen than male librarians. Thus, of the choices given, the most rational guess might be that your neighbor is a business executive. Yet because of the representativeness heuristic, you might well decide that he is a librarian and reach a false conclusion (Tversky & Kahneman, 1974).

Anchoring-and-Adjustment: Reference Points That May Lead Us Astray The day I received my driver's license, I began to shop for my first car. After a long search, I found the car of my dreams. The major question, of course, was "How much will it cost?" A totally rational person would have located this information in the *Blue Book,* which lists the average prices paid for various used cars in recent months. But did I proceed in this fashion? Absolutely not. Given our strong tendency to follow the path of least resistance (and the fact that the *Blue Book* is not readily available everywhere), I tried a different approach. I asked the seller what he wanted for the car, then proceeded to bargain from there. At first glance, this may seem like a reasonable strategy. But think again. If you adopt it, as I did when I purchased that car, you have allowed the seller to set a *reference point*—a figure from which your negotiations will proceed. In the case of a used car, if the reference point is close to the *Blue Book* price, all well and good. If it is much higher, though, you may end up paying more for the car than it is really worth—as I did.

In such cases, decisions are influenced by what is known as the **anchoring-and-adjustment heuristic:** a mental rule of thumb for reaching decisions by making adjustments in information that is already available. The basic problem with the anchoring-and-adjustment heuristic is that the adjustments are often insufficient in magnitude to offset the impact of the original reference point. In this case, the reference point was the original asking price. In other contexts, it might be a performance rating assigned to an employee, a grade given to a term paper, or a suggested asking price for a new home (Diekmann et al., 1996; Northcraft & Neale, 1987).

The influence of heuristics appears to be quite strong and occurs unintentionally and unconsciously. New evidence on this topic suggests that completely arbitrary numbers can anchor people's judgments—even when these numbers are irrelevant to the decision at hand (Wilson et al., 1996). Fortunately, research indicates that the anchoring-and-adjustment heuristic can be reduced in the case of experts working on tasks with which they are very familiar (Frederick & Libby, 1986; Smith & Kida, 1991). So, while the impact of such potential sources of error is strong, it is not irresistible; it can be reduced by expertise and experience.

Representativeness Heuristic: A mental rule of thumb suggesting that the more closely an event or object resembles typical examples of some concept or category, the more likely it is to belong to that concept or category.

Anchoring-and-Adjustment Heuristic: A cognitive rule of thumb for decision making in which existing information is accepted as a reference point but then adjusted in light of various factors.

Framing and Decision Strategy

Imagine that a rare tropical disease has entered the United States and is expected to kill 600 people. Two plans for combating the disease exist. If plan A is adopted, 200 people will be saved. If plan B is adopted, the chances are one in three that all 600 will be saved but two in three that no one will be saved. Which plan would you choose?

Now consider the same situation with the following changes. Again, there are two plans. If plan C is chosen, 400 people will definitely die; if plan D is chosen, the chances are one in three that no one will die, but two in three that all 600 will die. Which would you choose now?

If you are like most respondents, you probably chose plan A in the first example but plan D in the second example (Tversky & Kahneman, 1981). Why? Plan D is just another way of stating the outcomes of plan B, and plan C is just another way of stating the outcome of plan A. Why, then, do you prefer plan A in the first example but plan D in the second? Because in the first example the emphasis is on *lives saved,* while in the second the emphasis is on *lives lost*. In other words, the two examples differ in what psychologists term **framing**—the presentation of information about potential outcomes in terms of gains or in terms of losses. When the emphasis is on potential gains (lives saved), research indicates that most people are *risk averse.* They prefer avoiding unnecessary risks. Thus, most choose plan A. In contrast, when the emphasis is on potential losses (deaths), most people are *risk prone;* they prefer taking risks to accepting probable losses. As a result, most choose plan D.

Framing effects have been found to be quite general in scope. For example, negotiators tend to evaluate offers from their opponents more favorably, and to make more actual concessions, if they are urged to think about potential gains than if they are urged to think about potential losses that may result from such concessions (Neale & Bazerman, 1985).

Recent evidence suggests, however, that the framing effects observed in previous studies may stem partly from the scenarios used to induce them (Jou, Shanteau, & Harris, 1996; Wang, 1996). Specifically, careful examination of the disease example just described reveals that it is arbitrary in the sense that it does not provide a rationale for the relationship *between* the potential gains and losses. People usually have a general understanding about how events are related based on schemas, a term we discussed in Chapter 6. When events we encounter cannot be fit into a schema—as in the disease scenario above—then the relationship between the events may not be apparent. To test this possibility, Jou and his colleagues (1996) asked participants in their study to read either the original disease examples or the same ones revised to include a rationale that explained why a choice must be made. The rationale indicated that saving some proportion of lives would require sacrificing other lives because of limited resources. The researchers reasoned that including this rationale would clarify the relationship between lives saved and lives lost, which in turn might reduce the effects of framing. As shown in Figure 7.5, the researchers' predictions were confirmed. The framing effects were quite apparent for participants who read the original disease examples. Consistent with the results of previous research, when the choice was framed in terms of lives saved, they were risk averse; when the choice was framed in terms of lives lost, they were risk prone. In contrast, the effects of framing did not occur among participants who read the revised examples. Additional research suggests that people's attitudes toward a disease can also influence the effects of framing (Rothman & Salovey, 1997). These results suggest that the effects of framing, though powerful, are not immutable; they are affected by people's attitudes and they can be offset when people are given a more complete picture of the choices to be made.

Framing: Presentation of information concerning potential outcomes in terms of gains or in terms of losses.

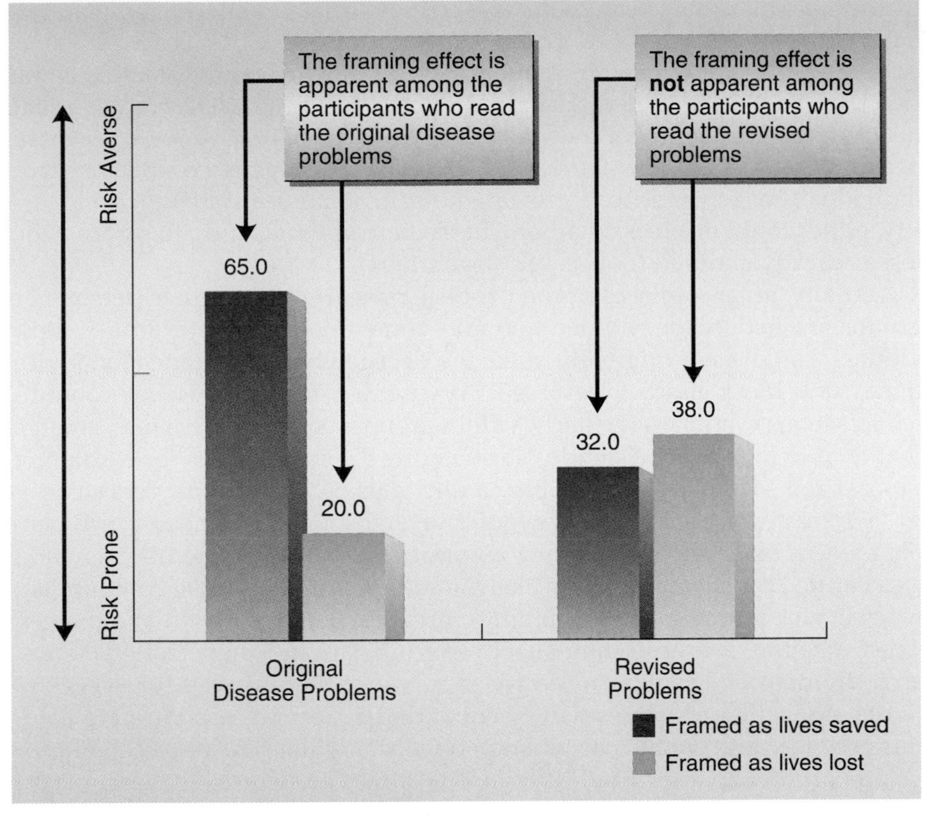

(**Source:** Based on data from Jou et al., 1996.)

FIGURE 7.5

Understanding the Effects of Framing

The effects of framing are evident among participants who read the original disease problem: These participants were risk averse when it was framed positively (lives saved), but risk prone when the same problem was framed negatively. The effects of framing disappeared, however, when participants were given a rationale that helped them understand the relationship between lives saved and lives lost.

Escalation of Commitment: Getting Trapped in Bad Decisions

Have you ever heard the phrase "throwing good money after bad"? It refers to the fact that in many situations, persons who have made a bad decision—one that yields negative consequences—tend to stick to it even as the evidence for its failure mounts. In fact, they may decide to commit additional time, effort, and resources to the failing course of action in order—they hope—to turn the situation around. This tendency to become trapped in bad decisions is known as **escalation of commitment** and is all too common in many spheres of life. Escalation of commitment helps explain the tendencies of many investors to hold on to what are clearly bad investments, and it underlies situations in which people remain in troubled marriages or relationships long after these have begun to yield more pain than happiness (Brockner & Rubin, 1985; Staw & Ross, 1989). In these and many other cases, people do indeed seem to become trapped in bad decisions with no simple or easy means of getting out.

Escalation of Commitment: Why Does It Occur? Escalation of commitment is both real and widespread. But why, precisely, does it occur? Research suggests that escalation of commitment probably stems from several different factors (Staw & Ross, 1989). Early in the process, decisions are based primarily on rational factors. People choose particular courses of action because they believe that these will yield favorable outcomes. When things go wrong and negative results occur, it is at first quite reasonable to continue. After all, temporary setbacks are common, and it is often necessary to increase one's effort or investment to attain a favorable outcome (Staw & Ross, 1987).

Escalation of Commitment: The tendency to become increasingly committed to bad decisions even as losses associated with them increase.

In addition, there may be considerable costs associated with changing an initial decision before it has had a chance to succeed.

As negative outcomes continue to mount, however, other factors come into play. First, as indicated above, individuals feel responsible for the initial decision and realize that if they now back away from or reverse it, they will be admitting to a mistake (Larrick, 1993). Indeed, as negative results increase, individuals may experience a growing need to obtain *self-justification*—to justify, either to themselves or others, both their previous judgments and the losses already endured (Bobocel & Meyer, 1994).

Finally, in later phases of the process, pressures from other persons or groups affected by the bad decision may come into play. For example, individuals who did not originally make the decision but have gone along with it may now block efforts to reverse it because they too have become committed to actions it implies. Similarly, within groups, political forces may emerge that tend to lock the decision in place. Figure 7.6 summarizes the escalation process and several factors that play a role in its occurrence and persistence.

Fortunately, researchers have found several conditions under which people are less likely to escalate their commitment to a failed course of action (see Figure 7.6). First, people are likely to refrain from escalating commitment when available resources to commit to further action are limited and the evidence of failure is overwhelmingly obvious (Garland & Newport, 1991). Thus, an individual or a group can decide in advance that if losses reach certain limits, no further resources will be squandered. Second, escalation of commitment is unlikely to occur when people can *diffuse their responsibility* for being part of a poor decision (Whyte, 1991). In other words, the less we feel personally responsible for making a bad decision, the less we may be motivated to justify our mistake by investing additional time, efforts, or money. Thus, a helpful strategy is to assign the tasks of making decisions and implementing them to different persons. Together, these steps can help both individuals and groups to avoid getting trapped in costly spirals that magnify the harmful effects of poor decisions (but see Chapter 16 for another aspect of diffusion of responsibility).

FIGURE 7.6

Escalation of Commitment: An Overview

Early in the escalation-of-commitment process, there may be a rational expectation of a positive outcome. As losses occur, however, people are reluctant to admit their errors and seek self-justification. Later, external factors may strengthen tendencies to stick to the initial bad decision. However, other conditions may reduce the likelihood of escalation of commitment.

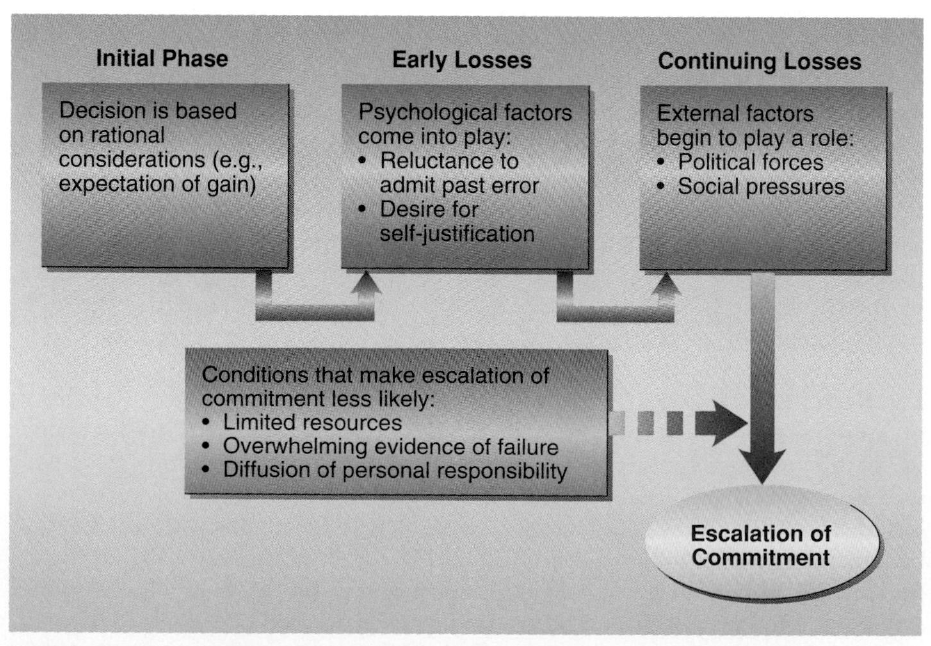

(**Source:** Based on suggestions by Staw & Ross, 1989; and Garland & Newport, 1991.)

Naturalistic Decision Making: Making Choices in the Real World

Naturalistic Decision Making: A movement toward studying decision making as it occurs in applied or real-world settings.

In recent years researchers who study decision making have shifted their efforts away from the laboratory and into applied settings. This newer emphasis on studying decision making as it occurs in the real world has been termed **naturalistic decision making** (Orasanu & Connolly, 1993). This approach contributes to the study of decision making in several ways (Cannon-Bowers, Salas, & Pruitt, 1996). First, it focuses attention on how people bring their experience to bear in making decisions. After all, people differ in many ways, and these differences contribute to the type and the quality of decisions they make. Second, naturalistic decision making broadens the focus from a single decision "event" to include elements of the decision context. Much of what is known about decision making is based on controlled laboratory studies in which participants read a brief story and then make a decision based on its contents. The stories are often contrived and without context—and therefore have little real meaning to participants who read them. Researchers now question whether much of this laboratory research bears any relationship to decision making in everyday life (Fischhoff, 1996). Finally, naturalistic decision making emphasizes the dynamic nature of decision making and takes into account the complexity of modern decision environments—including the potentially enormous costs of making bad decisions, both in terms of money and loss of life.

Although naturalistic decision making is a relatively new development, its application has led to fuller, and perhaps more accurate, descriptions of the decision-making process as it unfolds in environments in which the accuracy of decisions is paramount. Examples of such environments include military and health care settings, the courtroom, and even on an oil-drilling platform in the North Sea (Flin, Slaven, & Stewart, 1996; Kaempf et al., 1996; Pennington & Hastie, 1993; Pierce, 1996).

The shift toward studying decision making in naturalistic settings has had another, unexpected effect as well. As I indicated above, some previous research on decision making has been called into question. The reason? The discovery that several key findings derived from laboratory research may not accurately depict decision making in the natural environment (e.g., Fischhoff, 1996). To illustrate this point, let's consider one of the most widely reported findings: that people tend to ignore the relative frequency of various events when making decisions, instead of opting for simpler heuristics. This tendency is referred to as the *base-rate problem*. That is, if given a general description of a person and then asked to judge whether the person is a surgeon or engineer, many people tend to rely on the *representativeness heuristic*—making their judgment merely on the basis of how closely the description matches the central features of each occupation, and ignoring the fact that there are many more engineers than surgeons.

But recent evidence seems to indicate that we've been oversold on the base-rate problem and that people *do* consider base rates in their decisions (e.g., Koehler, 1996). Some researchers have argued that laboratory tasks are often contrived and lack contextual information that people have available to them when making judgments in everyday life. They add that experience may also play a role; as people gain experience with specific types of judgments, they are more likely to consider base rates in their decisions. Finally, in certain instances, it may be prudent to ignore base rates. Similar criticisms have been leveled at other well-documented find-

Key Questions

- What are heuristics?
- What are the availability, representativeness, and anchoring-and-adjustment heuristics, and what roles do they play in reasoning?
- What is framing, and how does it relate to decision making?
- How does escalation of commitment affect decision making?
- What is naturalistic decision making, and what is its usefulness?

ings, including the effects of framing on decision making, a topic described earlier in this section (Jou et al., 1996). To summarize, naturalistic decision making represents a bold step toward discovering how people make decisions in real-world settings. Stay tuned for additional developments in this rapidly growing field—they are certain to come.

Problem Solving: *Finding Paths to Desired Goals*

Imagine that you are a parent whose son is attending college in another state. You've asked him to keep in touch, but long periods go by without a word—by either phone or mail. You phone him repeatedly, but all you get is his answering machine. What do you do? Several possibilities exist. You could call his friends and ask them to urge him to get in touch with you. You could leave a message that, you hope, will cause him to phone. Or—and here's the interesting one—you could try something like this: You write a letter to your son in which you mention that you've enclosed a check—but you don't enclose one. Is the problem solved? In all probability, yes. Your son will no doubt call to find out what happened to the check.

While you may not have any children, there is little doubt that you have encountered situations that resemble this one in basic structure: You would like to reach some goal, but there is no simple or direct way of doing so. Such situations involve **problem solving,** efforts to develop responses that permit us to attain desired goals. In this section we'll examine the nature of problem solving, techniques for enhancing its effectiveness, and factors that interfere with its successful execution. (Please note that we'll consider *creativity*—the ability to produce new and unusual solutions to various problems—in Chapter 11).

Problem Solving: An Overview

What does problem solving involve? Psychologists are not totally in agreement on this basic issue (e.g., Lipshitz & Bar-Ilan, 1996), but many believe that four major aspects, as summarized in Figure 7.7, are central.

First, we must *understand* the problem—figure out just what issues, obstacles, and goals are involved. In the example above, the immediate problem boils down to this: You want to find some way of inducing your son to contact you. But identifying the problems we face is not always so simple. For example, suppose your car won't start. Why? Is it a bad battery? Bad ignition? Lack of fuel? Until you identify the problem, it is difficult to move ahead with its solution.

Second, we must *formulate potential solutions.* While this too might seem fairly simple, it is actually very complex (Treffinger, 1995). Solutions do not arise out of a cognitive vacuum; they require thinking critically about a problem, and they depend heavily on the information at our disposal—information stored in long-term memory that can be retrieved (see Chapter 6). The more information available, the greater the number and the wider the scope of potential solutions we can generate. Formulating a wide range of possible solutions is an extremely important step in effective problem solving. (Yet even when abundant information is available, several tendencies and potential sources of bias can cause us to overlook useful solutions and get stuck on less productive ones.)

Problem Solving: Efforts to develop or choose among various responses in order to attain desired goals.

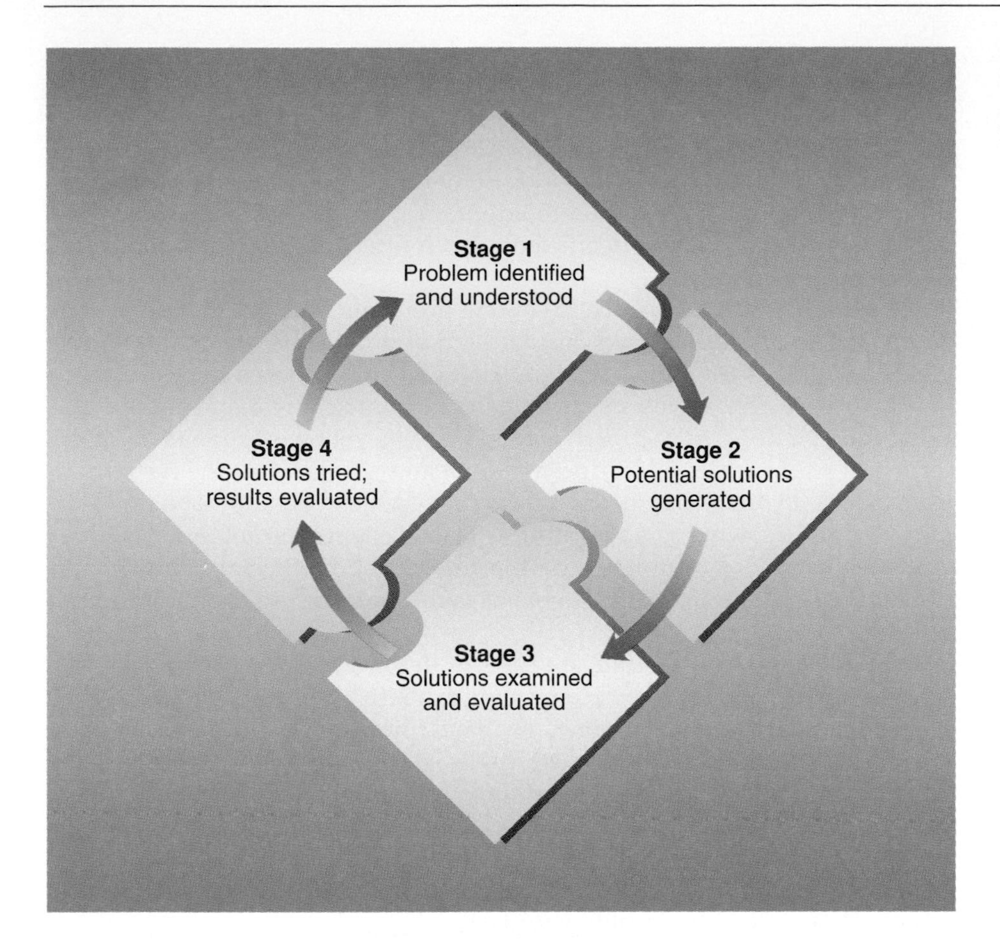

FIGURE 7.7

Problem Solving: An Overview

Effective problem solving involves four stages. First, the problem must be identified and understood. Next, potential solutions must be generated. Third, these must be examined and evaluated. Finally, solutions must be tried and their effectiveness evaluated.

Third, we must *evaluate* each alternative and the outcomes it will produce. Will a given solution work—bring us closer to the goal we want? Are there any serious obstacles to its use? Are there hidden costs that will make a potential solution less useful than it seems at first? These are considerations that must be taken into account.

Finally, we must *try* potential solutions and evaluate them on the basis of the effects they produce. All too often, a potential solution is only partially effective: It brings us closer to where we want to be but doesn't solve the problem completely or finally. The tantalizing letter strategy described above illustrates this point. Yes, it may induce a response from the erring child on this occasion. But it does not guarantee that he will write or phone more frequently in the future. So it constitutes only a partial solution to the problem. In this case it is easy to recognize that the solution will be only a partial one. In many other situations, though, it is difficult to know how effective a potential solution will be until it is implemented. Thus, careful assessment of the effects of various solutions is another key step in the problem-solving process.

Methods for Solving Problems: From Trial and Error to Heuristics

Suppose that you are using a friend's computer to complete a term paper due tomorrow. You decide to take a break and then you realize—with panic—that you don't remember how to save, or put in memory, what you've written with this word processor. You think for a moment, then try hitting one of the keys, but nothing happens. You try another key; again no result. You hit a third one and the message "Find What?" appears on the screen. Now you

Trial and Error: A method of solving problems in which possible solutions are tried until one succeeds.

Algorithm: A rule that guarantees a solution to a specific type of problem.

Means–Ends Analysis: A technique for solving problems in which the overall problem is divided into parts and efforts are made to solve each part in turn.

Analogy: A strategy for solving problems based on applying solutions that were previously successful with other problems similar in underlying structure.

decide to try a combination of keys. You are still trying, and still in a panic, when your friend arrives and rescues you.

This incident illustrates a problem-solving technique you have certainly used yourself—**trial and error**. Trial and error involves trying different responses until, perhaps, one works. Sometimes this is all you can do: You don't have enough information to adopt a more systematic approach. But such an approach is not very efficient, and it offers no guarantee that you'll find a useful solution.

A second general approach to solving problems involves the use of **algorithms.** These are rules for a particular kind of problem that will, if followed, yield a solution. For example, imagine that you are supposed to meet a friend at a restaurant. Try as you may, you can't remember the name of the place. What can you do? One approach is to get out the yellow pages and see if this refreshes your memory. If it doesn't, you can try calling all the restaurants listed to ask if your friend made a reservation (which you know she was planning to do). Following this algorithm—"Call every restaurant in the book"—will eventually work; but it is time-consuming and inefficient. A much more effective way of solving many problems is through the use of an appropriate *heuristic*.

Heuristics, as you'll recall, are rules of thumb we often use to guide our cognition. With respect to problem solving, heuristics involve strategies suggested by prior experience—ones we have found useful in the past. These may or may not work in the present case, so a solution is not guaranteed. But what heuristics lack in terms of certainty they gain in efficiency: They often provide useful shortcuts. In the case of the forgotten restaurant, you might begin by assuming that your friend probably chose a restaurant close to where she lives. This simple rule could eliminate many of the most distant restaurants and considerably simplify your task.

One heuristic we often employ is known as **means–ends analysis** (or subgoals analysis). This involves dividing the problem into a series of smaller pieces or subproblems. Each of these is then solved, and the distance between our original state and the goal is reduced in a step-by-step fashion. Finally, we sometimes attempt to solve problems through the use of **analogy**—by applying techniques that worked in similar situations in the past. For example, imagine that while driving through an unfamiliar town, you are suddenly seized by an uncontrollable desire for a Big Mac. You don't know your way around this town, but you know from past experience that many McDonald's restaurants are located near busy interstate highways. Applying this knowledge, you follow signs showing the way to the nearest interstate. If you are then rewarded by the sight of the famous golden arches, you have solved the problem through analogy. Intriguing new evidence on this topic seems to suggest that people frequently solve problems through the use of analogy—although they may remain unaware that they've done so (Burns, 1996; Schunn & Dunbar, 1996). To summarize, selecting an appropriate strategy is critical to effective problem solving.

Key Questions

- How do psychologists define problem solving?
- What are two general approaches to problem solving?
- What role do heuristics play in problem solving?

Facilitating Effective Problem Solving: The Role of Metacognitive Processing

Try to recall the last time you were faced with a difficult problem: solving a challenging math problem, determining why your car wouldn't start, finding an error in your checkbook. What steps did you follow in trying to solve the problem? Did you find it helpful to talk through the problem, either aloud or to yourself? People commonly report that talking things out hastens the process of finding the solution. But does doing so really help? Research on this topic suggests that it does—but only indirectly (e.g., Berry & Broadbent, 1984).

Apparently, talking through a problem helps divert attention away from the problem's content and toward the process—what you are *doing* to solve the problem. In other words, talking through a problem may facilitate your ability to solve the problem by expanding your level of awareness—in a sense, allowing you to observe yourself engaged in the problem-solving process. This process has been termed **metacognitive processing** (Berardi-Coletta et al., 1995). Some evidence suggests that metacognitive processing activates processes that lead to more effective problem solutions (Dominowski, 1990).

Metacognitive Processing: An expanded level of awareness that allows us, in a sense, to observe ourselves in the problem-solving process.

Does metacognitive processing improve performance on problem-solving tasks? The results of a recent study by Berardi-Coletta and her colleagues (1996) seem to suggest it does. Although this study was complex, it can be summarized as follows. In one experiment, participants were allowed to practice solving progressively more difficult versions of a playing-card problem, then were tested on the most difficult one. The problem involved ordering a set of playing cards so that when the cards were dealt they appeared in a prescribed order (ace, one, two, three, etc.). What made the problem difficult was a complicated dealing rule. During the practice trials, participants were assigned to one of three groups: a group in which the experimenters induced metacognitive processing by asking participants process-oriented questions as they practiced ("How are you deciding on a way to work out the order for the cards?"); a group in which participants were asked problem-focused questions ("What is the goal of the problem?"); or a control group in which participants merely worked on the problem with no additional instructions or discussion. The results indicated that the participants in the metacognitive condition performed best on the task, taking the least number of trials to obtain the correct solution. In contrast, participants in the problem-focused group performed worst, requiring the most trials to solve the problem. These results indicate that talking through a problem can be useful—especially when it leads to metacognitive processing and a focus on the problem-solving *process*. They also highlight the fact that focusing solely on the problem can have detrimental effects—in this case, making reaching a solution more difficult. Please note that merely talking aloud is not enough. Rather, verbalization must be process-oriented to trigger metacognitive processing. So the next time you're faced with a difficult problem—talk it out.

Factors That Interfere with Effective Problem Solving

Sometimes, despite our best efforts, we are unable to solve problems. In many cases our failure stems from obvious causes, such as lack of necessary information or experience. We may also lack internal frameworks that allow us to represent the problem situation fully and effectively. As a result, we don't know which variables or factors are most important, and we spend lots of time "wandering about," using an informal type of trial and error (Johnson, 1985). In other cases, though, difficulties in solving problems seem to stem from more subtle factors. Let's consider some of these now.

Functional Fixedness: Prior Use versus Present Solutions

Suppose you want to use the objects shown in Figure 7.8 on page 278 to attach the candle to a wall so that it can stand upright and burn properly. What solution(s) do you come up with? If you are like most people, you may mention

FIGURE 7.8

Solving Complex Problems

How can you attach the candle to a wall so that it stands upright and burns normally, using only the objects shown here?

using the tacks to nail the candle to the wall or attaching it with melted wax (Duncker, 1945). While these techniques may work, they overlook a much more elegant solution: emptying the box of matches, attaching the box to the wall, and placing the candle on it (see Figure 7.9). Described like this, the solution probably sounds obvious. Then why don't most people think of it? The answer has to do with **functional fixedness**—our strong tendency to think of using objects only in ways they have been used before. Because most of us have never used an empty box as a candle holder, we don't think of it in these terms and so fail to hit upon this solution. Interestingly, if the matchbox in this problem is shown empty, people are much more likely to think of using it as a candle holder (Weisberg & Suls, 1973); it doesn't take much to overcome such mental blind spots. But unless we can avoid functional fixedness, our ability to solve many problems can be seriously impaired.

Mental Set: Sticking to the Tried and True Another factor that often gets in the way of effective problem solving is **mental set.** This is the tendency to stick with a familiar method of solving particular types of problems—one that has worked before. Since past solutions have in fact succeeded, this is certainly reasonable, at least up to a point. Difficulties arise, however, when this tendency causes us to overlook other more efficient approaches. The powerful impact of mental set was first demonstrated by Luchins (1942) in what is now a classic study. Luchins presented study participants with the problems shown in Table 7.2, which involve using three jars of different sizes to measure amounts of water. If you work through the first two or three items, you will soon discover that you can solve them all by following this simple formula: Fill jar B, and from it fill jar A once and jar C twice. The amount of water remaining in jar B is then the desired amount.

Because this formula works for all items, subjects in Luchins's study tended to stick with it for all seven problems. But look at item 6: It can be solved in a simpler way. Just fill jar A, then from it fill jar C. The amount remaining in jar A is precisely what's required (20 units). A simple solution also exists for item 7; see if you can figure it out. Do you think many of the subjects in Luchins's experiment noticed these simpler solutions? Absolutely not. When they reached item 6, almost all continued to use their old tried-and-true formula and overlooked the more efficient one.

Similar effects occur in many other contexts. For example, commuters often continue to take the same crowded roads to work each day because they have always done so; they don't even consider alternate routes that might seem less direct but are easier to travel. In these and many other situations, sliding into mental ruts can indeed prove costly.

Functional Fixedness: The tendency to think of using objects only as they have been used in the past.

Mental Set: The impact of past experience on present problem solving; specifically, the tendency to retain methods that were successful in the past even if better alternatives now exist.

Artificial Intelligence: A branch of science that studies the capacity of computers to demonstrate performance that, if it were produced by human beings, would be described as showing intelligence.

TABLE 7.2

Mental Set: Another Potential Deterrent to Problem Solving

How can you use three jars, A, B, and C, each capable of holding the amounts of liquid shown, to end up with one jar holding the exact amount listed in the right-hand column? See the text for two possible solutions.

	Amount Held by Each Jar			
Problem	Jar A	Jar B	Jar C	Goal (amount of water desired)
1	24	130	3	100
2	9	44	7	21
3	21	58	4	29
4	12	160	25	98
5	19	75	5	46
6	23	49	3	20
7	18	48	4	22

Artificial Intelligence: Can Machines Really Think?

If we can someday hold ordinary conversations with computers, and if they can do many other things we usually attribute to human intelligence, an interesting question arises: Does it make sense to say that computers are intelligent? This question lies at the heart of **artificial intelligence**—an interdisciplinary branch of science in which psychologists study the capacity of computers to demonstrate performance that, if it were produced by human beings, would be described as showing intelligence. (We will examine the nature of intelligence in more detail in Chapter 11.)

How much intelligence do computers show? Actually, quite a lot. Modern computers carry out complex computations at blinding speeds, often performing millions of computations per second—a capability far beyond that of mere mortals. It is therefore not surprising that computers are more proficient than people at doing repetitive tasks requiring speed and accuracy. Consider, for example, the "pharmacy robot"—a computer system designed to stock and retrieve prescription drugs quickly and efficiently in hospital settings. How efficient is the system? It apparently even bills the patients! Because computers such as the pharmacy robot are tireless and can perform specific tasks with amazing speed, they are better suited than human beings for certain rigidly defined tasks.

Computers are also useful in situations deemed too dangerous for humans. For example, a computerized robot was recently used to retrieve two flight recorders from a plane that crashed into the Atlantic Ocean offshore of the Dominican Republic (World-wide: The Navy recovered, 1996). Locating the recorders was necessary to determine the cause of the crash. Why was the help of the robot needed? The recorders were eventually found in water 7,200 feet deep—a depth too great for humans to survive. As you might guess, computers are quite useful in this type of situation.

FIGURE 7.9

Functional Fixedness: How It Interferes with Problem Solving

Because of functional fixedness, surprisingly few people think of using the tacks to attach the box to the wall as a candle holder.

Neural Networks: Computer systems modeled after the brain and made up of highly interconnected elementary computational units that work together in parallel.

Language: A system of symbols, plus rules for combining them, used to communicate information.

However, efforts to demonstrate computer intelligence with regard to language—clearly an important human capability—have had somewhat mixed results. On one hand, the language abilities demonstrated by computers are remarkable. For example, banks, credit unions, and credit card companies now regularly use computerized voice recognition systems to handle certain business transactions, such as customer calls to check account balances. Even more impressive are computers that can converse with their owners and carry out a variety of tasks, including booking airline reservations. These complex machines possess large vocabularies, grasp syntax well enough to allow them to understand normal sentences, and know when to ask relevant questions if they do not understand or do not have enough information to act (Rensberger, 1993).

On the other hand, though, it has proved frustratingly difficult to teach computers to comprehend many of the subtleties of human speech. And many ordinary activities, that most people take for granted, such as understanding everyday conversation, exceed the capabilities of even the most powerful of today's computers. In response to these and related issues, researchers have designed computers that imitate the way in which the brain—perhaps the most powerful computer in the universe—operates. Whereas most computers process information in a sequential fashion, the brain processes the input from all of our senses simultaneously through a complex network of highly connected neurons. The new computer systems, called **neural networks,** are structures consisting of highly interconnected elementary computational units that work together in parallel (Denning, 1992; Levine, 1991). The primary advantage of neural networks comes not from the individual units themselves but from the overall pattern resulting from millions of these units working together. In addition, neural networks have the capacity to learn from experience by adjusting the strength of the output from individual units based on new information. Although research on neural networks is still in its infancy, information obtained thus far has yielded insight into how the brain operates.

The Beyond the Headlines section digs deeper into one specialized area of artificial intelligence.

Where does all this leave us with respect to artificial intelligence? Most psychologists who specialize in this field would readily admit that early predictions about the capacities of computers to show such characteristics as intention, understanding, and consciousness were greatly overstated (Levine, 1991; Searle, 1980). However, these specialists note that computers are indeed exceptionally useful in the study of human cognition and can, in certain contexts, demonstrate performance that closely resembles that of intelligent human beings. In general, while you may not soon meet a robot who can speak with you in a fluent manner like the ones in films, the chances are good that computers and other machines will continue to become more "intelligent" with the passage of time.

Key Questions

- What is metacognitive processing, and how does it contribute to more effective problem solving?
- What factors can interfere with effective problem solving?
- What is artificial intelligence?

Language: The Communication of Information

At present many experts agree that what truly sets us apart from other species of animals is our use of **language**—our ability to use an extremely rich set of symbols, plus rules for combining them, to communi-

Beyond the Headlines

As Psychologists See It

It's Computer Checkmate for Chessmaster!

New York—Chess aficionados throughout the world are reeling upon receiving the news that chess champion Garry Kasparov succumbed to an IBM supercomputer known as "Deep Blue." In a previous match with Deep Blue in 1996, Kasparov lost the opening game, but adjusted his playing style to exploit weaknesses in the computer's play, winning the second, fifth, and sixth games and earning ties in the other two. However, Kasparov was not so fortunate in their May 1997 rematch. After exchanging wins in the first two games and earning ties in games three, four, and five, Deep Blue slaughtered Kasparov in the final, and deciding, game of the match—forcing him to resign after just one hour and 19 moves of play.

Machine Bests Human—Experts Say It Was Only a Matter of Time

What makes Deep Blue so formidable? Sheer brute force; in other words, the computer's ability to select the best possible move by evaluating the consequences of various moves far more deeply into a game than a human player can (Peterson, 1996). During their most recent match, Deep Blue was evaluating about 200 million positions every second, assessing strengths and weaknesses and the various pieces' capacity for attack and defense. To put this into perspective, consider that a typical person evaluates about one position per second; Kasparov can evaluate two, maybe three. In short, it was style versus power. And at least in the second match, power won out (see Figure 7.10 on page 282).

Please note, however, that not even Deep Blue's massive computing capabilities allow it to foresee every possible sequence of chess moves. Deep Blue's computing capabilities are much more modest in scope, limited to foreseeing the moves and countermoves possible within the next ten to fifteen moves—still an impressive feat. Although Kasparov cannot match Deep Blue's massive computing capabilities, he does retain several advantages over Deep Blue—at least for now.

First, Kasparov can predict what the general shape of a game will be many moves into the future (Gobet & Simon, 1996a). For example, as his 1996 match against Deep Blue progressed, Kasparov used this advantage increasingly to maneuver the computer into situations that played to his strengths—strategy and overall knowledge of the game—rather than ones that favored sheer computing capability (Weber, 1996).

Still, grand masters such as Kasparov are no slouches when it comes to the computing process. The world's very best chess players are able to store in memory as many as 50,000 board configurations in memory—including the locations of each of the individual pieces (Chase & Simon, 1973). Moreover, these memories are quickly accessible as they become relevant to the game, thereby eliminating the need to consider thousands of less promising alternatives. To illustrate this point, consider the results of a recent study by Gobet and Simon (1996b). These researchers asked chess players of varying abilities (grand master, expert, club player) to briefly view a series of chessboard configurations on a computer screen (5 seconds per configuration) and then reconstruct each of the configurations from memory. There were two different types of configurations included in the series: real chessboard configurations and ones consisting of pieces generated randomly. The researchers reasoned that if chess expertise stems, at least in part, from a unique memory for chess configurations, then performance in reconstructing these configurations should vary by chess-playing ability. In contrast, performance in reconstructing irrelevant (randomly generated) configurations should not differ by ability level. The researchers' predictions were confirmed: The best chess players clearly outperformed their less skilled counterparts when reconstructing *actual* chess configurations, but not when reconstructing the randomly generated ones.

These results highlight a second, and perhaps more important, advantage for Kasparov: the fact that he could learn both as a game progressed and between games. This enabled Kasparov to adjust his style of play to take advantage of weaknesses displayed by his opponent. Playing Deep Blue forced Kasparov into an uncharacteristic style of play, most evident in the first game of the match. During subsequent games he learned to be more precise in judging the quality of his chess positions. He also learned to attack gradually, increasing his advantage in small increments, until his ability to foresee the remaining moves—including the likely outcome of the game—matched Deep Blue's. Will Deep Blue's successors routinely overtake the best human players? Based on Deep Blue's recent victory, its creators say it is only a matter of time.

Critical Thinking Questions

1. Are the tremendous computing capabilities of Deep Blue evidence that computers are intelligent? If yes, why? If no, what additional characteristics would cause you to change your mind?
2. What cognitive skills allowed Kasparov to outwit Deep Blue?

FIGURE 7.10

Man Versus Machine: Kasaparov Meets His Match

Although world chess champ Garry Kasparov eventually defeated IBM's Deep Blue in 1996, he was beaten by a much improved Deep Blue during their rematch in May 1997.

cate information. While the members of all species communicate with one another in some manner, and while some species may use certain features of language, the human ability to use language far exceeds that of any other organism on earth. In this final section we'll examine the nature of language and its relationship to other aspects of cognition.

Language: Its Basic Nature

Language uses symbols for communicating information. In order for a set of symbols to be viewed as a language, however, several additional criteria must be met.

First, information must be transmitted by the symbols: The words and sentences must carry *meaning*. Second, although the number of separate sounds or words in a language may be limited, it must be possible to combine these elements into an essentially infinite number of sentences. Finally, the meanings of these combinations must be independent of the settings in which they are used. In other words, sentences must be able to convey information about other places and other times. Only if all three of these criteria are met can the term *language* be applied to a system of communication. In actual use, language involves two major components: the *production* of speech, and its *comprehension*.

Phonemes: A set of sounds basic to a given language.

Morphemes: The smallest units of speech that convey meaning.

Syntax: Rules about how units of speech can be combined into sentences in a given language.

The Production of Speech All spoken language consists of **phonemes,** a set of basic sounds; **morphemes,** the smallest units of speech that convey meaning; and **syntax,** rules about how these units can be combined into sentences.

English has forty-six separate phonemes: vowels, *a, e, i, o,* and *u;* consonants, such as *p, m, k,* and *d;* and blends of the two. Other languages have more or fewer basic sounds. Further, different languages often employ different groups of phonemes. Sounds used in one language may be absent in another, although learning the phonological structure of one language may increase one's chances of proficiency in a second language (Holm & Dodd, 1996).

English has about 100,000 morphemes. Some of these are words; others, such as the plural *s* or prefixes such as *un* or *sub,* are not. The number of English words is greater still—about 500,000. And the number of possible combinations of these words, or sentences, is for all practical purposes infinite.

Speech Comprehension Have you ever listened to a conversation between two people speaking a foreign language you didn't know? If so, you may recall that it seemed very confusing. In part, this confusion results from the fact that when you listen to a language you don't speak, you can't recognize the boundaries between words.

Even in our own language, not all speech is equally easy to interpret. For example, sentences containing *negatives (not, no)* are more difficult to understand than sentences without them (Clark & Chase, 1972). Also, ambiguous sentences—those with two or more possible meanings—are harder to understand than unambiguous sentences (Mistler-Lachman, 1975). Compare "Last night I saw an alligator in my pajamas" with "Last night I saw an alligator while wearing my pajamas." Clearly, the first is harder to understand than the second. Incidentally, such ambiguity is far from rare; newspaper headlines often show this characteristic. Does "Homeless Appeal to Mayor" mean that homeless people are making an appeal to the mayor for help or that the mayor finds homeless people personally attractive? The first possibility is much more likely, but from the structure of the sentence, it's really not possible to tell.

Surface Structure and Deep Structure Suppose that I introduce you to my friend Stuart and say, "Meet Stuart; he's my oldest friend." Do I mean that he is the oldest person with whom I am friends, or that I have been friends with him longer than with anyone else? In all probability, you can tell from the context. If Stuart is about my age (which he is!), you might conclude—correctly—that I've been friends with him longer than anyone else. (In fact, we've been friends since we were seven years old.) If, however, Stuart is much older than I am, you might conclude that the first meaning applies: He's the oldest person I call "friend."

This simple example illustrates one aspect of the difference between what linguists such as Noam Chomsky (1968) describe as the **surface structure** and **deep structure** of language. Surface structure refers to the actual words people use and what's readily apparent about them, whereas deep structure refers to the information that underlies a sentence and gives it meaning. Another way of seeing this distinction is by considering sentences that are grammatically correct but totally devoid of meaning. For example, consider the sentence, "Dark purple ideas eat angrily." It is perfectly correct in terms of grammar but has no meaning whatsoever. In view of such facts, Chomsky and others have argued that we can never understand the true nature of spoken language by focusing only on words and grammatical rules. Rather, we must search for underlying meaning and the ways in which people translate, or transform, this into overt speech. While some psychologists question the validity of the distinction between surface and deep structure, most agree that it is useful to look beyond verbal behavior and rules of grammar in order to examine the cognitive representations on which speech is based. In this sense, the distinction Chomsky proposed has proven useful.

Surface Structure: The actual words of which sentences consist.

Deep Structure: Information that underlies the form of a sentence and is crucial to its meaning.

The Development of Language

Throughout the first weeks of life, infants have only one major means of verbal communication: crying. Within a few short years, however, children progress rapidly to speaking whole sentences and acquire a vocabulary of hundreds or even thousands of words. Some of the milestones along this remarkable journey are summarized in Table 7.3. Although we'll consider other developmental issues in more detail in Chapter 8, this section will focus on two questions relating to the development of language: What mechanisms play a role in this process? And how, and at what ages, do children acquire various aspects of language skills?

Theories of Language Development: Some Contrasting Views The *social learning view* suggests one mechanism for the rapid acquisition of language. This view proposes that speech is acquired through a combination of operant conditioning and imitation. Presumably, children are praised or otherwise rewarded by their parents for making sounds approximating those of their native language. Moreover, parents often model sounds, words, or sentences for them. Together, this view contends, these basic forms of learning contribute to the rapid acquisition of language.

A sharply different view has been proposed by linguist Noam Chomsky (1968): the *innate mechanism view*. According to Chomsky, language acquisition is at least partly innate. Human beings, he contends, have a built-in neural system that provides them with an intuitive grasp of grammar—a language acquisition device. In other words, humans are prepared to acquire language and do so rapidly for this reason.

Finally, a *cognitive theory* offered by Slobin (1979) recognizes the importance of both innate mechanisms and learning. This theory suggests that chil-

TABLE 7.3

Language Development: Some Milestones

Children develop language skills at an amazing pace. Please note: These approximate ages are only *averages;* individual children will often depart from them to a considerable degree.

Average Age	Language Behavior Demonstrated by Child
12 weeks	Smiles when talked to; makes cooing sounds
16 weeks	Turns head in response to human voice
20 weeks	Makes vowel and consonant sounds while cooing
6 months	Progresses from cooing to babbling that contains all sounds of human speech
8 months	Repeats certain syllables (e.g., "ma-ma")
12 months	Understands some words: may say a few
18 months	Can produce up to fifty words
24 months	Has vocabulary of more than fifty words; uses some two-word phrases
30 months	Has vocabulary of several hundred words; uses phrases of three to five words
36 months	Has vocabulary of about a thousand words
48 months	Has mastered most basic elements of language

dren possess certain information-processing abilities or strategies that they use in acquiring language. These are termed *operating principles* and seem to be present, or to develop, very early in life. One such operating principle seems to be "Pay attention to the ends of words"—children pay more attention to the ends than to the beginnings or middles of words. This makes sense, because in many languages suffixes carry important meanings. Another principle is "Pay attention to the order of words." And indeed, word order in children's speech tends to reflect that of their parents. As word order differs greatly from one language to another, this, too, is an important principle.

Which of these theories is correct? At present, all are supported by some evidence, but none seems sufficient by itself to account for all aspects of language development. For example, the social learning view is supported by research showing that parents provide differentiating feedback to their children, praising or rewarding them for correct grammar and syntax and correcting them when they make mistakes (Bohannon & Stanowicz, 1988). And, in every culture, children's speech resembles that of their parents in many important ways, so learning does seem to play an important role. Critics maintain, however, that parental feedback may be too infrequent to account fully for the observed rapidity of language acquisition (Gordon, 1990; Pinker, 1989).

Turning to the possibility of an innate language acquisition device, some findings suggest that there may be a *critical period* for language development during which children find it easiest to acquire various language components (Elliot, 1981). If for some reason children are not exposed to normal speech at this time, they may find it increasingly difficult to master language (De Villiers & De Villiers, 1978). The possibility of a critical period for language development is also supported by research on adults who communicate via American Sign Language. Adults who acquire sign language early in life seem to be more proficient, on average, than those who learn to sign later in life (Meier, 1990). Still, critics of this view have noted several of its weaknesses. For example, details regarding the neural structure and precise function of the "language acquisition device" remain somewhat vague.

Given this mixed pattern of evidence, it is probably safest to conclude that language development is the result of a complex process involving several aspects of learning, many cognitive processes, and perhaps various genetically determined mechanisms as well.

Basic Components of Language Development

Although the underlying mechanisms of language development remain to be clarified, much is known about how this process unfolds. Basically, it includes progress in three distinct but interrelated areas: **phonological development**—development of the ability to pronounce the sounds and words of one or more languages; **semantic development**—learning to understand the meaning of words; and acquisition of **grammar**—the rules by which words are arranged into sentences in a given language.

Phonological Development: Development of the ability to produce recognizable speech.

Semantic Development: Development of understanding of the meaning of spoken or written language.

Grammar: Rules within a given language indicating how words can be combined into meaningful sentences.

Babbling: An early stage of speech development in which infants emit virtually all known sounds of human speech.

Phonological Development: The Spoken Word

At some point between three and six months, babies begin babbling. At first **babbling** contains a rich mixture of sounds, virtually every sound used in human speech. Indeed, research suggests that babies only a few months old can distinguish sounds from many different languages (Werker & Desjardins, 1995). By nine or ten months, however, the range of babbling narrows and consists mainly of sounds used in the language of the child's native culture. From this point to the production of the first spoken word is a relatively short step, and most children accomplish it by their first birthday.

Between the ages of one and two, childrens' vocabularies increase rapidly; for instance, by the time they are eighteen months old, many toddlers have a vocabulary of fifty words or more. What are these words? Generally, they include the names of familiar objects important in the children's own lives—for instance, foods (*juice, cookie*), animals (*cat, dog*), toys (*block, ball*), body parts (*ear, eye*), clothing (*sock, hat, shoe*), and people (*momma, dadda*). Children make the most of these words, often using them as *holophrases*—single word utterances that communicate much meaning, especially when combined with pointing and other gestures. For example, if a child wants some chocolate syrup, she may point to the refrigerator while saying "milk," thus indicating that she wants some milk with syrup in it. At this time, children's pronunciation leaves much to be desired; many of their words take a simple form, consisting of a consonant and a vowel. So the child described above might say "mih" instead of "Milk." They often have difficulty with consonant clusters, two or more consonants. I remember, for instance, that when my daughter was in this age group (between one and two years old), she referred to the stairs in the house as "tairs," and to her blanket as "banky."

What about verbs—words describing action—when do children acquire these? Until recently, it was widely assumed that acquisition of such words follows the acquisition of nouns—words referring to specific objects (e.g., Gentner, 1982). However, recent evidence suggests that in some cultures, this order may be reversed. For instance, Tardif (1996) found that in their naturalistic speech, Chinese children twenty-two months old actually used more verbs than nouns in their everyday speech. Thus, the order in which children acquire nouns and verbs may vary somewhat from culture to culture, and further research is needed to determine precisely why this is so.

Semantic Development: The Acquisition of Meaning Children's vocabulary increases rapidly after they reach the age of two, and they learn many new words each day. Thus, by the time they are six, most have a vocabulary of several thousand words. They don't simply learn new words, however; they also learn new types of words—ones that allow them to communicate a much richer range of thoughts and ideas. Thus, they acquire understanding of negatives such as "no" and how to use these in sentences. Similarly, they acquire many adjectives and propositions—words that allow them to be more specific in describing their own thoughts and the world around them. They start with simple adjectives such as "little," "good," and "bad," but soon move on to ones with more specific meaning such as "high," "low," "narrow," and "wide," "in front of," and "behind." Children also learn to use question words—words that allow them to ask for information from others in efficient and specific ways: Why? When? Who? Where? These are key words children acquire between the ages of two and three.

While children increase their vocabulary very rapidly (they have to move fast to learn thousands of new words in just a few years!), they often demonstrate several interesting forms of error. One such error involves overextensions—a tendency to extend the meaning of a word beyond its actual usage. For instance, eighteen-month-olds may use the word "raisin" to refer to all small objects—flies and pebbles as well as raisins themselves. Similarly, they may use "meow" as a shorthand word for all small furry animals—dogs as well as cats. They also show underextensions too—limiting the meaning of a word more than is appropriate. For instance, they may think that the word "cat" refers to the family's pet cat and to no others

The Development of Grammar Every language has *grammar*, a set of rules dictating how words can be combined into sentences. Children must learn to follow these rules, as well as to utter sounds that others can recognize as words. At first grammar poses little problem, since, as noted above, children's earliest speech uses single words, often accompanied by pointing and other gestures. By the time most children are two, two-word sentences make their appearance—a pattern sometimes known as *telegraphic speech.* For instance, a child who wants a book may say "give book," and then—if this doesn't produce the desired action—switch to another two-word utterance: "Daddy give." Youngsters can pack quite a bit of meaning into these simple phrases by changing the inflection—"Go swim!" to indicate that they are going for a swim or "Go swim?" in order to ask permission for taking a swim.

Children's grasp of grammar continues to increase as they move to longer sentences of three words or more (generally between the ages of two and three). They add inflections to their words—endings that carry meaning, such as the letter *s* to indicate more than one object (plurals) and endings that change the tense of a verb (e.g., *ed* to indicate that something happened in the past, as in "He picked up the ball" rather than "He pick up the ball.)

From this, children move on to an increasing grasp of their language's grammar, and to the production of ever more complex sentences. They begin to link two or more ideas in a single utterance (e.g., Clark & Clark, 1977), and gradually learn to understand, and use, sentences in which important ideas are implied or understood rather than directly stated. For instance, what does the following sentence mean to you? "Stacey promised Jason to bring the book." As an adult, you understand that Stacey will bring the book; she has promised to do so. Three-year-olds, however, may misinterpret it as meaning that Jason will bring the book because they don't fully understand that the word "promised" refers to Stacey. As they grow older, they learn to unravel this and other mysteries of grammar.

In sum, language development is definitely a continuing feature of cognitive development throughout childhood. Given the complexity it involves, and its central role in many aspects of cognition, this is far from surprising.

The Role of Nonverbal Communication in Language Development Have you ever heard the saying "Actions speak louder than words?" This phrase underlies new evidence showing that the *nonverbal* communication that occurs between young children as they play may be an important building block of certain forms of spoken language. At about two years of age, children begin to imitate the behavior of their peers; for example, a two-year-old may imitate the behavior of a peer who just kicked a ball. Repeated instances of this nonverbal interaction may lead the two toddlers to coordinate their efforts, kicking or throwing the ball to each other. Later on, words that help coordinate and direct their play activities gradually replace the use of nonverbal cues (Eckerman, 1993). In other words, children come to recognize the connection between the words and the actions. Children typically receive their first exposure to coordinated activities through games like pat-a-cake with their parents. Although parents initially control much of the activity of these games, children quickly learn their part.

To illustrate how the emergence of basic skills necessary to engage in coordinated activities with others facilitates spoken language, let's consider a recent study by Eckerman and Didow (1996). These researchers examined the types of verbal and nonverbal communication that occurred between same-age pairs of toddlers as they played. The toddler pairs were 16, 20, 24, 28, and 32 months of age. The researchers' purpose was to determine the age at which verbal communication emerges and how it relates to coordinated *non*verbal play behaviors. They reasoned that if coordinated nonverbal activities form the basis of later verbal behavior, then speech that accompanies these activities should increase with age and occur most frequently in situations requiring coordinated action, such as in a game of "follow the leader," but less frequently in situations that do not require coordinated action (playing together with two of the same toy) or when children play by themselves.

FIGURE 7.11

Nonverbal Interactions during Play: An Important Step Toward Verbal Communication

Measures of discussions between pairs of toddlers as they played indicated that speech used to direct or alter the other child's behavior occurred most frequently during coordinated activities, such as games, and less frequently when the children played with either the same or different toys.

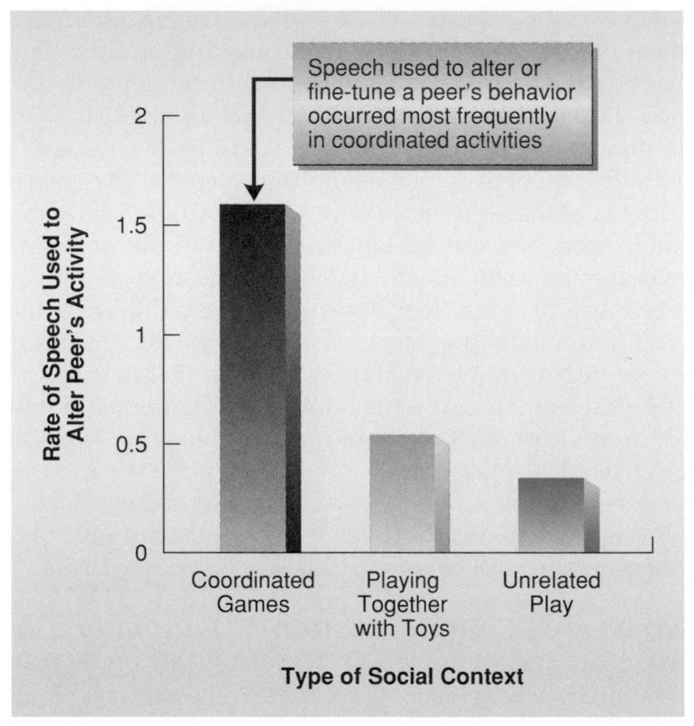

(**Source:** Based on data from Eckerman & Didow, 1996.)

The researchers' predictions were confirmed. With increasing age, the toddlers directed more of their discussions toward one another and to their mutual activities. Further, as indicated in Figure 7.11, speech relevant to coordinated play, such as "It's my turn" or "Play ball," occurred much more often during periods of time in which the toddlers were engaged in joint activities. To summarize, these findings indicate that the development of certain forms of spoken language may arise, at least in part, from basic forms of nonverbal interaction that take place between children. We'll now turn to some basic aspects of the relationship between language and thought.

Language and Thought: Do We Think What We Say or Say What We Think?

Although we often have vivid mental images, most of our thinking seems to involve words. This fact raises an intriguing question: What is the precise relationship between language and thought? One possibility, known as the **linguistic relativity hypothesis,** suggests that language shapes or determines thought (Whorf, 1956). According to this view, people who speak different languages may perceive the world in different ways because their thinking

Linguistic Relativity Hypothesis: The view that language shapes thought.

is determined, at least in part, by the words available to them. For example, Eskimos, who have many different words to describe snow, may perceive this aspect of the physical world differently from English-speaking people, who have only one word.

The opposing view is that thought shapes language. This position suggests that language merely reflects the way we think—how our minds work. Which position is more accurate? While the issue is far from resolved, existing evidence seems to argue against the linguistic relativity approach (Miura & Okamoto, 1989). If this approach were correct, people who speak a language that has few words to describe colors should have greater difficulty in perceiving various colors than people who speak a language rich in color words. But research designed to test such possibilities has generally failed to support them. In one experiment Rosch (1973) studied natives of New Guinea. Their language, Dani, has only two color names: *mola,* for bright, warm colors, and *mili,* for dark, cool ones. Rosch found that despite this fact, Dani speakers perceived colors in much the same manner as persons who speak English, a language containing many color words.

So, while it may indeed be easier to express a particular idea or concept in one language than another, this in no way implies that our thoughts or perceptions are strongly shaped by language. On the contrary, basic aspects of human perception and thought seem to be very much the same around the world, regardless of spoken language. For additional information on the role of thought and language in behavior, please refer to the Exploring Gender and Diversity section below.

Language and Culture: Revelations Based on Studies of Bilingualism

EXPLORING GENDER & DIVERSITY

The current worldwide push toward a global economy has resulted in massive changes, not only in activities related to commerce but in terms of the impact these activities have on people. An interesting outcome of this globalizing trend has been a sharp rise in the numbers of people who emigrate to other countries in response to new opportunities, or to escape oppressive living conditions. Countries throughout the world—including the United States—are currently absorbing large numbers of immigrants and refugees from many parts of the world. Because of this trend, experts predict that by the middle of the next century, minorities who now constitute 18 percent of the U.S. population will account for nearly half (Basic Behavioral Science Task Force, 1996).

Why are psychologists concerned with this issue? Because the rapid increase in cultural diversity will undoubtedly bring with it the potential for many mental health challenges; for example, potential conflicts that may arise between immigrant and indigenous populations as the immigrants attempt to assimilate into the new culture. At the root of such conflicts, of course, are differences these people bring with them—most notably their language and culture.

A group of immigrants who have been of particular interest to psychologists who study these issues are *bilinguals*—people who regularly use both English and another language. Why? One reason is that English and the native languages of immigrants are often associated with very different cultures. As a result, studies of bilingual individuals provide opportunities for researchers to observe the ways in which people change as they shift between languages. Interestingly, many bilinguals report that the way they think and feel is greatly affected by the current cultural context—including the language they are using to communicate. The tendency of immigrant bilinguals to think and behave in accordance with the expectations of the culture that is associated with the language they are currently speaking is termed the *culture-affiliation hypothesis* (Matsumoto, 1994). For example, the children of immigrant parents may speak their native language at home, and as a result may also respond in ways consistent with the social rules of that culture when they are at home. In contrast, they may behave quite differently when they are out with their friends or in other social situations in which English is spoken.

Additional evidence on this topic seems to support the culture-affiliation hypothesis. For example, bilinguals score very differently on personality measures, depending on whether they respond to these measures in English or in their native language (Dinges & Hull, 1992). Similar results have been reported in studies investigating differences in how bilinguals perceive emotion. In one study, Matsumoto and Assar (1992) asked bilingual participants to look at facial expressions and judge what emotions were being expressed and the intensity of the emotions. The participants made these judgements at two different times: once in English (their second language) and once in Hindi (their native language). The results indicated that the accuracy of their judgments was greater in English; however, the emotions expressed were judged as more intense in Hindi. These results are important in that they illustrate the powerful ways in which language—and the culture in which language is embedded—influences our everyday experience.

Language in Other Species

Members of nonhuman species communicate with one another in many ways. Bees do a complex dance to indicate the distance to and direction of a food source; birds sing songs when seeking to attract a mate; seagoing mammals in the wild, such as whales, communicate with one another through complex patterns of sounds. But what about language? Are we the only species capable of using this sophisticated means of communication? Until the 1970s there seemed little question that this was so. Early efforts to teach chimpanzees to speak failed miserably. For example, during the 1940s Keith and Cathy Hayes raised a chimp named Vicki from infancy in their home and provided her with intensive speech training; but she was eventually able to utter only a few simple words such as *mama*, *papa*, and *cup*.

These disappointing results were due in part to the fact that nonhuman primates (and other animals) lack the vocal control necessary to form words, and hence *spoken* language. But as we saw earlier in our discussion of animal cognition, it is not always appropriate to ask animals to do what people do. The ability to speak is not essential for the use of language. For example, persons who have lost the power of speech through accident or illness can still communicate by writing or sign language. The fact that chimps cannot learn to speak, then, does not rule out the possibility that they or other animals can learn to use some form of language.

The findings reported by several teams of researchers seem to indicate that this may be so. Beatrice and Allen Gardner succeeded in teaching Washoe, a female chimp, to use and understand almost two hundred words in American Sign Language (ASL), which is used by many deaf persons (Gardner & Gardner, 1975). After several years of practice, Washoe learned to respond to simple questions and to request actions such as tickling and objects such as food.

Research with gorillas, too, has yielded what some interpret as evidence for the ability to use language. Francine Patterson (1978) taught Koko, a female gorilla, a vocabulary of several hundred signs. Patterson reported that Koko showed great flexibility in using signs, constructing original sentences, remembering and describing past events, and even creating her own signs for new objects and events. Interestingly, Koko learned to use language in complex and all-too-human ways, such as bending the truth to her own advantage. In one incident she jumped on a sink and pulled it out from the wall. When asked if she had caused this damage, she accused one of the researchers of being responsible.

In what may be the most surprising evidence of all, Irene Pepperberg has trained an African gray parrot named Alex to use speech in what appear to be highly complex ways (Stipp, 1990). Alex can name more than eighty objects and events, frequently requests things he wants ("I want shower"), and has been known to give directions to his human trainers. But does Alex really understand the words he uses? Professor Pepperberg (1990) believes that he does. On one occasion Alex was given an apple for the first time. He immediately labeled it "banerry," and he stuck with this word despite her best efforts to teach him "apple." Her explanation: Apples taste somewhat like bananas and look something like cherries, so Alex had chosen a word that from his perspective was quite appropriate.

Are We the Only Species Capable of Using Language? Some Recent Findings Based on the evidence presented thus far, you may now be ready to conclude that members of these species can indeed use language (see Figure 7.12 on page 292). Please note, however, that this conclusion has been the source of great controversy. Many psychologists believe that the animals in these studies, while exhibiting impressive learning, are not really demonstrating use of language (Davidson & Hopson, 1988; Terrace, 1985). For instance, close examination of the procedures used to train and test the animals suggests that their trainers may often unintentionally provide subtle cues that help animals respond correctly to questions. It also appears that in some cases trainers may have overinterpreted the animals' responses, reading complex meanings and intentions into relatively simple signs. Finally, it is still unclear whether animals are capable of mastering several basic features of human languages; for example, *syntax*—the rules by which words are arranged to form meaningful sentences—and *generativity*—the ability to combine a relatively limited number of words into unique combinations that convey a broad range of meanings.

Studies involving other species of animals, including bonobos (a rare type of chimpanzee) and dolphins, have addressed these and related issues. For example, consider the language abilities demonstrated by a twelve-year-old bonobo named Kanzi (Savage-Rumbaugh et al., 1989). While attempting to teach Kanzi's mother to use an artificial language made up of abstract visual symbols, psychologist Sue Savage-Rumbaugh noticed that Kanzi (then an infant) had learned several symbols just by watching. Intrigued by the possibilities raised by this discovery, Savage-Rumbaugh and her colleagues continued to train Kanzi in this informal way—speaking to him throughout the day, while simultaneously pointing to the corresponding word symbols on portable language boards they carried with them. Kanzi quickly learned to combine the symbol-words to request tasty snacks and preferred activities, such as watching Tarzan movies.

Since then, Kanzi has demonstrated a grasp of grammatical concepts, and he now comprehends several hundred spoken words. In one experiment, Savage-Rumbaugh and her colleagues compared Kanzi and a 2-year-old girl in terms of their ability to respond to commands expressed in spoken sentences (Savage-Rumbaugh et al., 1992). The sentences consisted of familiar words that were combined to produce commands that Kanzi and the little

FIGURE 7.12

Language in Other Species: Can We Talk to the Animals?

A growing body of evidence suggests that certain species of animals, such as chimpanzees, can grasp many aspects of language, including comprehension of spoken messages.

girl had never heard before. Surprisingly, Kanzi's progress in comprehending the novel commands paralleled the little girl's throughout most of the experiment, although her language abilities eventually surpassed Kanzi's (his ability topped out at the level of an average $2^1/_2$-year-old child). More importantly, though, the use of strict control procedures ruled out the possibility that Kanzi was responding to subtle cues from his trainers, a criticism leveled against many early demonstrations of animal language. For instance, a one-way mirror prevented Kanzi from seeing who gave him the commands, and persons recording his responses wore headphones to prevent them from hearing the requests. Psychologists are now more willing to accept that Kanzi was responding solely to the requests.

But what about more complex features of language? Are animals capable of grasping these concepts, too? Psychologist Louis Herman believes the answer is yes. Herman and his colleagues taught a female dolphin named Akeakamai—Ake for short—an artificial language in which sweeping hand gestures are the words (Herman, Richards, & Wolz, 1984). Each gesture symbolizes either an *object* such as "Frisbee," an *action* such as "fetch," or a *description of position* such as "over" or "left." Ake has learned more than fifty of these gesture-words. To test whether Ake is capable of comprehending complex features of language, the researchers established a set of rules on word order and the grammatical function of each type of gesture. They discovered that Ake comprehends word order and syntax in word sequences up to five gestures. For example, RIGHT BASKET LEFT FRISBEE FETCH instructs Ake to take the Frisbee on her left to the basket on her right. More impressively, though, when familiar gestures are rearranged to form novel commands—ones Ake has never seen before—she continues to respond correctly.

Herman has continued to probe Ake's language comprehension through the use of *anomalous sentences*—sentences that are grammatically incorrect, use nonsense words, or make impossible requests, such as asking her to fetch an immovable object. These procedures are often used to test children's comprehension of language. In one instance Herman and his colleagues issued a series of commands to Ake that consisted of either grammatically correct sequences or anomalous sequences (Herman, Kuczaj, & Holder, 1993). Interestingly, Ake was highly accurate in responding to requests that were grammatically correct and rarely refused to carry them out. In contrast, she refused nearly all of the anomalous requests, making no attempt to respond to them. It appeared as if Ake recognized that the requests were "silly," a response often observed in children who are presented with anomalous sentences. Although dolphins may be a long way from achieving a level of language proficiency on par with that of adult human beings, it is clear that they are capable of comprehending features of language that go beyond the forms of behavior observed in the earlier studies of animal language.

Research with these highly intelligent animals suggests that language may not be a uniquely human possession, but rather a continuum of skills that different species of animals exhibit to varying degrees. However, many critics remain unconvinced (Gisiner & Schusterman, 1992). The results of further studies will undoubtedly shed additional light on this controversial issue. In the meantime, the question of whether we'll soon "talk with the animals" remains largely unresolved.

Key Questions

- What abilities are involved in the production of language, and how is language acquired in humans?
- What factors are involved in language acquisition?
- How does nonverbal communication facilitate later verbal behavior?
- What is the linguistic relativity hypothesis?
- Do animals possess language?

Making Psychology Part of Your Life

Making Better Decisions

Have you ever made a bad decision—one that you later wished you could change? Such errors in judgment may prove quite costly. Here are some guidelines for increasing the chances that many of your decisions will be good ones—or at least as free from sources of error and bias as possible.

1. **Don't trust your own memory,** or **beware of availability**. When we make decisions, we can do so only on the basis of the information available to us. Be careful! The information that comes most readily to mind is not always the most useful or revealing (Kahneman & Tversky, 1982). When you face an important decision, therefore, jog your memory in several ways and, if time permits, consult written documents or sources before proceeding. As noted in Chapter 6, memory often plays tricks on us; relying on a quick scan of it when making an important decision can be risky.
2. **Don't take situations at face value,** or **question all anchors**. In many decision-making situations the stage is set long before we come on the scene. The asking price for a house or car is set by the seller, the number of meetings for a committee has been determined by its chair, and so on. While you can't always change such givens, you should at least recognize them for what they are and question whether they make sense. If you don't raise such questions, you will probably accept these "anchors" implicitly and then offer only minor adjustments to them (Northcraft & Neale, 1987).
3. **Remain flexible,** or **don't fall in love with your own decisions**. Making decisions is effortful, so once a decision is made we tend to heave a sigh of relief and to stick with it—through thick and thin. Then, before we know it, we may have too much invested to quit. In other words, we may be trapped in a situation where we ought to change our initial decision and cut our losses but where, instead, we continue down the path to ruin—or at least to negative outcomes (Brockner & Rubin, 1985). Don't let this happen! It's always difficult to admit a mistake, but doing so is often far better than sticking to a losing course of action.
4. **Consider all options.** When you make a decision, you must choose among the available options. But what, precisely, are your options? Start by gathering as much information as you can and then use it to generate as many potential options as possible. Doing so can often suggest choices or courses of action that you did not think of at first.

Summary and Review of Key Questions

Thinking: Forming Concepts and Reasoning to Conclusions

- **What are concepts?** Concepts are mental categories for objects, events, or experiences that are similar to one another in one or more respects.
- **What is the difference between artificial and natural concepts?** Artificial concepts can be clearly defined by a set of rules or properties. Natural concepts cannot; they are usually defined in terms of prototypes—the most typical category members.
- **What are propositions and images?** Propositions (sentences that can stand as separate assertions) are useful for relating one concept to another, or relating one feature of a concept to the entire concept. Images (mental pictures of the world) are another basic element of thinking.
- **What is verbal protocol analysis?** Cognitive researchers on using verbal protocol analysis ask study participants to "think aloud" while making a decision or solving a problem. This technique provides information about the types of knowledge people access while performing a particular task.
- **What is the process of reasoning? How does formal reasoning differ from everyday reasoning?** Reasoning involves transforming available information in order to reach specific conclusions. Formal reasoning derives conclusions from specific premises. In contrast, everyday reasoning is more complex and less clear-cut.
- **What forms of error and bias can lead to faulty reasoning?** Reasoning is subject to several forms of error and bias. It can be distorted by emotions and/or beliefs; by the social contents; by our tendency to focus primarily on evidence that confirms our beliefs, or confirmation bias; and by our tendency to assume that we could have predicted actual events more successfully than is really the case, or the hindsight effect.
- **What is the ecological approach to animal cognition?** The ecological approach focuses on how animals solve the kinds of cognitive problems that are important to their survival.

KEY TERMS

cognition, p. 256 • concepts, p. 257 • artificial concepts, p. 258 • natural concepts, p. 258 • prototypes, p. 258 • visual images, p. 259 • propositions, p. 259 • verbal protocol analysis, p. 261 • reasoning, p. 261 • syllogistic reasoning, p. 262 • confirmation bias, p. 264 • hindsight effect, p. 264

Making Decisions: Choosing among Alternatives

- **What are heuristics?** We do not make all decisions on the basis of expected utility—the product of the probability and the subjective value of each possible outcome. Instead, we often use heuristics, or mental rules of thumb.
- **What are the availability, representativeness, and anchoring-and-adjustment heuristics, and what roles do they play in reasoning?** The availability heuristic is our tendency to make judgments about the frequency or likelihood of various events in terms of how readily they can be brought to mind. The representativeness heuristic is the tendency to assume that the more closely an item resembles the most typical examples of some concept, the more likely it is to belong to that concept. The anchoring-and-adjustment heuristic is the tendency to reach decisions by making adjustments to reference points or existing information.
- **What is framing, and how does it relate to decision making?** Decisions can be strongly affected by framing, the presentation of information about possible outcomes in terms of gains or losses.
- **How does escalation of commitment affect decision making?** People often become trapped in bad decisions through escalation of commitment, an effect that derives from reluctance to admit past mistakes and a desire to justify past losses.
- **What is naturalistic decision making, and what is its usefulness?** Naturalistic decision making refers to the study of decision making in real-world settings. Proponents argue that this approach has several advantages over laboratory research: It focuses attention on how decision makers bring their experience to bear in making a decision, it broadens the focus from a single decision "event" to a focus on the decision context, and it emphasizes the dynamic nature of decision making and takes into account the complexity of modern decision environments.

KEY TERMS

decision making, p. 267 • expected utility, p. 267 • heuristics, p. 267 • availability heuristic, p. 268 • representativeness heuristic, p. 269 • anchoring-and-adjustment heuristic, p. 269 • framing, p. 270 • escalation of commitment, p. 271 • naturalistic decision making, p. 273

Problem Solving: Finding Paths to Desired Goals

- **How do psychologists define problem solving?** Problem solving involves efforts to develop or choose among various responses in order to attain desired goals.
- **What are two general approaches to problem solving?** One common problem-solving technique is trial and error. Another is the use of algorithms—rules that will, if followed, yield solutions in certain situations.
- **What role do heuristics play in problem solving?** Heuristics are rules of thumb suggested by our experience that often provide useful shortcuts in problem solving.
- **What is metacognitive processing, and how does it contribute to more effective problem solving?** Metacognitive processing involves expanding our level of awareness—in a sense, observing ourselves engaged in the problem-solving process. Metacognition seems to activate processes that lead to more effective problem solutions, such as a focus on the actual problem-solving process.
- **What factors can interfere with effective problem solving?** Both functional fixedness (the tendency to think of using objects only as they have been used before) and mental sets (tendencies to stick with familiar methods) can interfere with effective problem solving.
- **What is artificial intelligence?** Artificial intelligence is an interdisciplinary field concerned with the capacity of computers to demonstrate "intelligent" performance.

KEY TERMS

problem solving, p. 274 • trial and error, p. 276 • algorithm, p. 276 • means–ends analysis, p. 276 • analogy, p. 276 • metacognitive processing, p. 277 • functional fixedness, p. 278 • mental set, p. 278 • artificial intelligence, p. 278 • neural networks, p. 280

Language: The Communication of Information

- **What abilities are involved in the production of language, and how is language acquired in humans?** Language involves the ability to use a rich set of symbols, plus rules for combining these, to communicate information. It includes the abilities to produce and to comprehend speech. Language seems to involve more than mere spoken words and rules of grammar, or surface structure; the underlying meaning, or deep structure, is important too. Existing evidence on language development suggests that language is acquired by children through complex interactions among (1) social learning, (2) innate mechanisms, and (3) cognitive mechanisms.
- **What basic components are involved in language acquisition?** Language acquisition involves phonological development—learning to produce the sounds of words; semantic development—learning to understand the meaning of words; and

acquisition of grammar—the rules through which words can be combined into sentences in a given language.

- **How does nonverbal communication facilitate later verbal behavior?** Nonverbal communication that occurs between young children as they play helps them perform coordinated actions. Later, words that help coordinate and direct their play activities gradually replace the nonverbal cues.
- **What is the linguistic relativity hypothesis?** According to the linguistic relativity hypothesis, language shapes or determines thought. Existing evidence does not offer strong support for this hypothesis.
- **Do animals possess language?** Growing evidence suggests that some species of animals, including bonobo chimpanzees and dolphins, are capable of grasping basic aspects of language including word order and grammar; but these findings remain highly controversial.

KEY TERMS

language, p. 280 • phonemes, p. 282 • morphemes, p. 282 • syntax, p. 282 • surface structure, p. 283 • deep structure, p. 283 • phonological development, p. 285 • semantic development, p. 285 • grammar, p. 285 • babbling, p. 285 • linguistic relativity hypothesis, p. 288

Critical Thinking Questions

Appraisal

Throughout this chapter, we've seen that human thought processes are less than optimal in several important respects. For instance, relying on heuristics frequently leads to flawed decision making. And we often fall prey to biases that lead us astray in our ability to think and reason effectively. How can psychology help people reduce or eliminate the effects of these errors?

Controversy

The results of many studies demonstrate that animals are capable of grasping important aspects of language that many believed were beyond their capabilities. Do you think it is possible that in the coming years scientists will discover ways to "talk with the animals"? If so, why? If not, why not?

Making Psychology Part of Your Life

Now that you understand the basic nature of cognitive processes and the many factors that affect them, can you think of ways in which you can use this knowledge to improve your problem-solving abilities? Name several specific steps you could take to become more proficient in this regard.

CHAPTER OUTLINE

Human Development I

The Childhood Years

Can you remember what it was like to be a child? To look up—literally!—to adults (see Figure 8.1 on page 298). To look at a page filled with words and only be able to read some of them? To play your way through summers that seemed endless, followed by the excitement of a new school year? If so, then you probably realize that, to paraphrase an old advertisement, "You've come a long, long way." As psychologists would put it, you've changed *physically, cognitively,* and *socially*. And such *change* is the basic theme of this chapter and the next one. In these chapters we'll review some of the major findings of the field of **developmental psychology**—the branch of psychology that focuses on the many ways we change throughout life. In this chapter, we'll concentrate on changes during **childhood**—the years between birth and adolescence. In the next chapter, we'll examine

Developmental Psychology: The branch of psychology that focuses on the many ways we change throughout life.

Childhood: The period between birth and adolescence.

changes occurring during adolescence and adulthood. In both units, the general plan will be to consider changes in the three categories mentioned above: physical, cognitive, and social development.

These changes often occur together, however, so this division is mainly for purposes of clarity and convenience; it is *not* intended to suggest that clear boundaries exist between these interrelated processes. In fact, an additional topic to which we'll devote special attention—*gender*—involves changes in all three dimensions. With respect to gender, which refers to a given society's beliefs about the traits and behavior of males and females, we'll consider the development of *gender identity* (the process through which children learn that they belong to one of the two sexes) and *gender differences* (the question of whether, and to what extent, males and females actually differ in their behavior).

To what extent do various aspects of our development represent an unfolding of "biological scripts," largely determined by our genes, and to what extent can they be affected by experience and the external world around us?

One more point before we begin. In Chapter 1 I described two of psychology's "grand issues" as involving the *nature–nurture controversy* and the question of *stability versus change*. While these issues relate to many areas of psychology (we've already discussed them in Chapters 2 and 3), they are especially relevant to the study of human development. To what extent do various aspects of our development represent an unfolding of "biological scripts," largely determined by our genes, and to what extent can they be affected by experience and the external world around us? Developmental psychologists often grapple with these complex issues (e.g., Collaer & Hines, 1995), and they'll arise over and over again in this chapter.

Physical Growth and Development

When does human life begin? In one sense, this is a philosophical or religious issue, outside the realm of science. From a purely biological point of view, though, your life as an individual began when one of the millions of sperm released by your father during sexual intercourse fertilized an *ovum* deep within your mother's body. The product of this union was barely 1/175

FIGURE 8.1

Human Development: A Long—and Interesting!—Journey

Can you remember when you had to bend your head back to look up at adults? Do you recall what it was like *not* to be able to read? If so, you realize how much you've changed in the intervening years.

of an inch in diameter—smaller than the period at the end of this sentence. Yet packed within this tiny speck were the genetic blueprints—twenty-three chromosomes from each of your parents—that guided all your subsequent physical growth.

The Prenatal Period

Fertilization begins the *prenatal period* (the period prior to birth). After fertilization, the ovum moves through the mother's reproductive tract until it reaches the womb or *uterus*. This takes several days, and during this time the ovum divides frequently. Ten to fourteen days after fertilization, the ovum becomes implanted in the wall of the uterus. For the next six weeks it is known as the **embryo** and develops rapidly. By the third week the embryo is about one fifth of an inch (one-half centimeter) long, and the region of the head is clearly visible. By the end of the eighth week the embryo is about one inch long, and a face as well as arms and legs are present. By this time, too, all major internal organs have begun to form; and some, such as the sex glands, are already active. The nervous system develops rapidly, and simple reflexes begin to appear during the eighth or ninth week after fertilization.

During the next seven months the developing child—now called a **fetus**—shows an increasingly human form. The external genitals take shape, so the sex of the fetus is recognizable by the twelfth week. Fingernails and toenails form, hair follicles appear, and eyelids that open and close emerge. By the end of the twelfth week the fetus is 3 inches (7.6 centimeters) long and weighs about 3/4 ounce (21 grams). By the twentieth week it is almost 10 inches (25 cm) long and weighs 8 or 9 ounces (227–255 g). By the twenty-fourth week all the neurons that will be present in the brain have been produced. The eyes are formed and are sensitive to light by the end of the twenty-fourth to twenty-sixth week.

During the last three months of prenatal development, the fetus gains about 8 ounces each week. By the seventh and eighth months, it appears to be virtually fully formed. However, if born prematurely, it may still experience difficulties in breathing. At birth, babies weigh more than 7 pounds (3.17 kilograms) on average and are about 20 inches (50.8 cm) long (see Figure 8.2 on page 300).

Cognitive abilities also appear to take shape during the prenatal period (see, e.g., Smotherman & Robinson, 1996). In an ingenious series of studies, DeCasper and his colleagues (e.g., DeCasper & Fifer, 1980; DeCasper & Spence, 1986) arranged for expectant mothers to read *The Cat in the Hat* to their unborn children two times each day during the last six weeks of pregnancy. At the end of that period, the heart rate of each fetus was measured as recordings of the familiar story and of an unfamiliar story were played. Results indicated that the familiar story produced a slight decrease in fetal heart rate, while the unfamiliar one produced a slight increase, thus indicating that the fetuses could distinguish between—or at least react differently to—these two stimuli.

Prenatal Influences on Development

Under ideal conditions, development during the prenatal period occurs in an orderly fashion, and the newborn child is well equipped at birth to survive outside its mother's body. Unfortunately, however, conditions are not always ideal. Many environmental factors can damage the fetus and interfere with normal patterns of growth. Such factors are known as **teratogens,** and their impact can be devastating (e.g., Bookstein et al., 1996).

Embryo: The developing child during the second through the eighth week of prenatal development.

Fetus: The developing child during the last seven months of prenatal development.

Teratogens: Factors in the environment that can harm the developing fetus.

FIGURE 8.2

Prenatal Development

These photos show different stages in prenatal development—and a newborn infant.

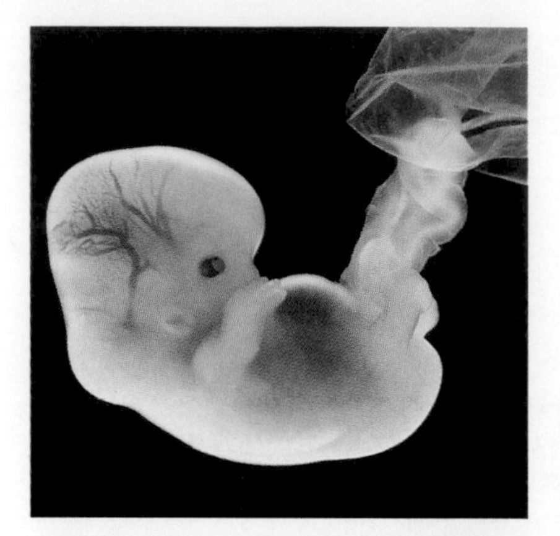

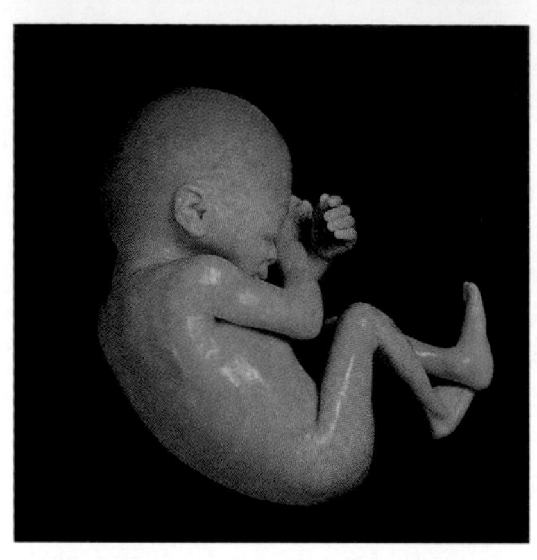

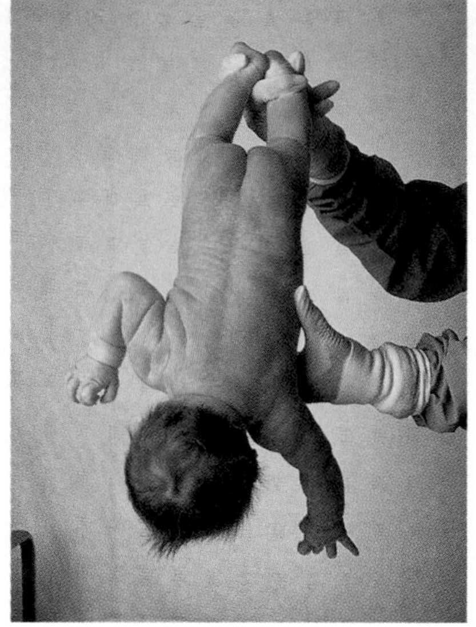

Disease During Pregnancy The blood supply of the fetus and that of its mother come into close proximity in the **placenta,** a structure within the uterus that protects and nourishes the growing child. As a result, disease-producing organisms present in the mother's blood can sometimes infect the fetus. Tragically, diseases that exert only relatively minor effects on the mother can be very serious for the fetus. For example, *rubella,* or German measles, can cause blindness, deafness, or heart disease in the fetus if the mother contracts this illness during the first four weeks of pregnancy. Other diseases that can be transmitted to the fetus include chicken pox, mumps, tuberculosis, malaria, syphilis, and herpes (Samson, 1988).

Since the early 1980s, two other illnesses, genital herpes and AIDS (acquired immune deficiency syndrome), have been added to this list. Genital herpes is usually transmitted during birth, when the newborn comes into contact with lesions present in the mother's genitals. When newborns contract this disease, they may suffer many harmful effects, ranging from paralysis and brain damage through deafness and blindness; the disease is fatal for many babies (Rosenblith, 1992). AIDS, in contrast, can be transmitted to the fetus prior to birth, as well as during the birth process. About one-third of women who carry the AIDS virus in their bodies transmit it to their infants (Valleroy, Harris, & Way, 1990). Tragically, few babies born with AIDS survive until their first birthday.

Placenta: A structure that surrounds, protects, and nourishes the developing fetus.

Prescription and Over-the-Counter Drugs The use of drugs by the mother can also exert important effects on the fetus. Excessive use of aspirin, a drug most people take without hesitation, can result in harm to the fetus's circulatory system (Kelsey, 1969). Caffeine, the stimulant found in coffee, tea, and many soft drinks, can slow fetal growth, contribute to premature birth (Jacobson et al., 1984), and produce increased irritability in newborns whose mothers have consumed large amounts of this drug (Aaronson & MacNee, 1989).

Illegal Drugs The use of illegal drugs such as heroin, cocaine, and crack has risen to epidemic proportions in many countries, and the results are nothing short of tragic for developing fetuses. Infants born to heroin-addicted mothers suffer from many problems, including respiratory disease and physical malformations. It is estimated that almost 400,000 babies addicted to cocaine or its derivatives are born in the United States each year (Reid, 1990), and these infants, too, suffer from many problems, including breathing difficulties, low birth weight, and physical defects (Chasnoff et al., 1989).

The Fetal Alcohol Syndrome Although consumption of alcohol is legal in most countries, the harm alcohol can produce when it is abused is just as devastating as that of illegal drugs. Children born to mothers who make heavy use of this drug sometimes suffer from a disorder known as the *fetal alcohol syndrome,* or *FAS* (Julien, 1992). This includes an abnormally small head, irritability, hyperactivity, retarded motor and mental development, and heart defects (Bookstein et al., 1993).

How much alcohol must a pregnant woman consume, and how often, before such effects are produced? This is a complex question and is still under investigation (e.g., Bookstein et al., 1996). However, some findings suggest that even very small amounts (e.g., the amount of alcohol in one to three drinks) can, if taken early in pregnancy, produce some harmful effects on the fetus, such as slight reductions in IQ, reaction time, and attention span (Barr et al., 1990).

Smoking While the percentage of adults who smoke has decreased in the United States and several other nations, this figure is increasing in many parts of the world (see Chapter 13). Moreover, the proportion of *women* who smoke is definitely on the rise. From the point of view of fetal development, this is unfortunate, for smoking by pregnant women has many harmful effects on the fetus and newborn child. These include decreased birth weight and size and increased risk for miscarriage and stillbirth (Wen et al., 1990). Maternal smoking may also interfere with cognitive development in early childhood (Sexton, Fox, and Hebel, 1990).

In sum, many factors can adversely affect development during the prenatal period, and prospective mothers should carefully consider the potential risks before engaging in actions that may put their unborn children at risk.

For information on yet another potential source of danger to developing fetuses—and perhaps to the entire human species—please see the Beyond the Headlines section on page 302.

Physical and Perceptual Development during Our Early Years

Physical growth is rapid during infancy. Assuming good nutrition, infants almost triple in weight (to about 20 pounds or 9 kilograms) and increase in body length by about one third (to 28 or 29 inches, 71 to 74 centimeters) during the first year alone.

Newborns possess a number of simple reflexes at birth. They can follow a moving light with their eyes, suck on a finger or nipple placed in their mouth, and turn their head in the direction of a touch on the cheek. In addition, they can grasp a finger placed in their palms and will make stepping motions if held so that their feet barely touch a flat surface. Their ability to

Beyond the Headlines

As Psychologists See It

Synthetic Chemicals in the Environment May Be Wreaking Havoc with the Endocrine Systems of Humans and Animals

Natural History, March 1996.—In July 1991, a group of scientists . . . gathered . . . to discuss their concerns about hormone-disrupting chemicals in the environment. They were disturbed by mounting evidence that synthetic compounds found in pesticides and industrial chemicals were wreaking havoc with endocrine systems. The scientists shared information on a broad range of species with problems that ranged from thyroid dysfunction, decreased fertility, and gross birth deformities to feminization of males, masculinization of females, and compromised immune systems. . . . The scientists concluded that the substances had the potential to cause large-scale dysfunction in humans as well as other species.

Hormonal Sabotage?

Scary stuff—and it gets even worse. One of the main culprits, it appears, is the chemical DES (diethylstilbestrol), which is used by the ton in animal feed because it increases growth. As a result, it may be present in many foods eaten by pregnant women. How does DES interfere with endocrine systems? Apparently, by acting as a hormone. First, it binds with sites throughout the body that are normally responsive to estrogen, an important naturally occurring hormone found in much higher levels in females than males. Not only does DES occupy such sites; it appears to stimulate them more strongly or effectively than do naturally occurring hormones. Second, it appears to circumvent mechanisms that normally protect the developing fetus from excess exposure to estrogen. This mechanism involves blood proteins that soak up excess estrogen. These proteins can't bond with DES, so it remains biologically active in the fetal blood supply.

What does this do to the fetus? Research on this issue is just beginning; but in animals the effects of DES appear to produce several kinds of cancers and several kinds of reproductive-system problems, ranging from undescended testicles to abnormal sperm and reduced fertility (e.g., Colborn, Dumanoski, & Myers, 1996). And in humans some findings suggest that DES and related chemicals may be linked to vaginal cancers and to a decline in human sperm counts that may be occurring throughout the world (although very recent findings call this latter result into question).

Other chemicals similar to DES in their action are currently being used in large amounts; in the United States alone, for instance, almost 450 million pounds of one type—alkylphenon polyethoxylates—are being fed to animals and used in industrial processes. And perhaps worst of all, recent findings suggest that such chemicals may actually leach slowly out of plastic cups and plates—and even from dental fillings (Science News, 1996)—all long considered to be totally safe.

Where does all this leave us? With a new and potent cause for alarm, of course; but also with the clear message that a great deal of additional research is needed. If chemicals that serve many useful functions also disrupt endocrine systems in the developing human fetus, we need to know this fact, and also how such effects are produced. Stay tuned, because this is one issue that is unlikely to go away in the years ahead.

Critical Thinking Questions

1. Suppose that DES and other chemicals do indeed interfere with the normal development of the human fetus; does this mean that such chemicals should be totally banned? And if they are, should farmers and others who depend on them be compensated in any way?
2. Some findings indicate that human sperm counts have declined sharply in the past fifty years (although this remains uncertain). If such declines turn out to be real and if they continue, human reproduction may become impossible within a few generations. Should we wait for further evidence before taking action against environmental chemicals that may cause such effects? Or should we proceed now, because the risks of waiting are simply too high?

move about and reach for objects is quite limited, but this changes quickly. Within a few months they can sit and crawl. And as harried parents quickly learn, most infants are quite mobile by the time they are fourteen or fifteen months old. Figure 8.3 summarizes several milestones of motor development. It's important to keep in mind that the ages shown are merely *average* values. Departures from them are of little importance unless they are quite extreme.

After the initial spurt of the first year, the rate of physical growth slows considerably; both boys and girls gain about 2 to 3 inches (5 to 10 cm) and 4 to 7 pounds (2 to 4 kg) per year. The rate accelerates during adolescence, when both sexes experience a *growth spurt* lasting about two years.

Learning Abilities of Newborns Can newborns show the kinds of learning discussed in Chapter 5? Evidence concerning *classical conditioning* suggests that they can, but primarily with respect to stimuli that have survival value for babies. For example, infants only two hours old readily learn to associate gentle stroking on the forehead with a sweet solution, and after these two stimuli have been paired repeatedly, they will show sucking responses to the stroking (the conditioned stimulus); (Rosenzstein & Oster, 1988). In contrast, human infants do not readily acquire conditioned fears

(**Source:** Frankenburg and Dodds, 1992.)

FIGURE 8.3

Milestones of Motor Development

Some highlights of motor development. Please note that the ages shown are only *averages*. Most children will depart from them to some extent, and such variations are of little importance unless they are extreme.

FIGURE 8.4

Newborn Infant Imitating Adult Facial Expressions

Research by Dr. Nadja Reissland-Burghart has shown that newborns only a few minutes old can imitate two facial expressions: widened and pursed lips.

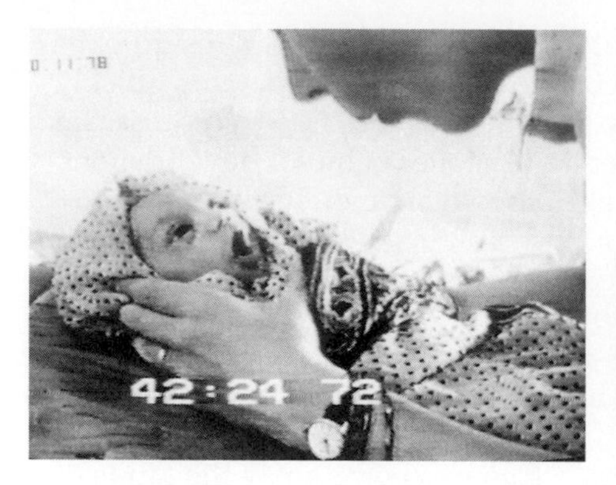

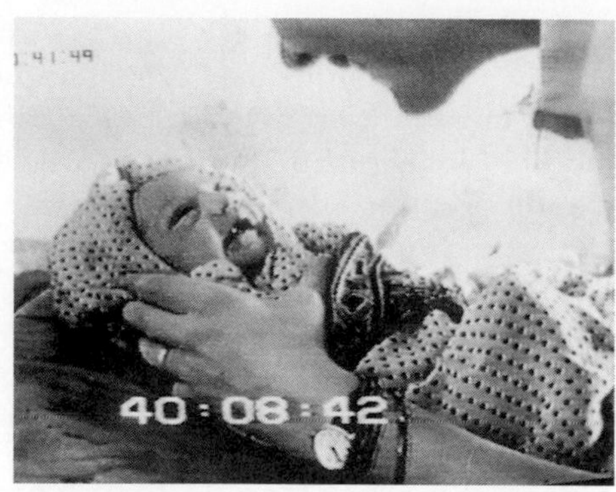

until they are at least eight months old. Remember little Albert in Chapter 5, who acquired fear of a rabbit (the conditioned stimulus) after it was paired with a loud noise (the unconditioned stimulus)? He was eleven months old at the time the study was conducted.

Turning to *operant conditioning,* there is evidence that newborns can readily show this basic kind of learning. For example, they readily learn to suck faster to see visual designs or hear music and human voices (Sansavini, Bertonicini, and Giovanelli, 1997). And by the time infants are two months old, they can learn to turn their heads to the side on which their cheek is gently brushed in order to gain access to a bottle of sugar water (e.g., Siquelande & Lipsitt, 1966).

Additional evidence indicates that newborns are capable of *imitation*. In a series of famous studies, Meltzoff and his colleagues (e.g., Meltzoff & Moore, 1977, 1989) demonstrated that infants only twelve to twenty days of age could imitate facial gestures shown by an adult—for example, sticking out their tongues or opening their mouths. Indeed, in one well-conducted study, infants tested only a few minutes after birth showed imitation of two facial expressions: widened lips and pursed lips (Reissland, 1988; see Figure 8.4). While such imitation seems to occur for only a few movements or actions, and may disappear after infants are a few weeks old, the fact that newborns can show any degree of imitation of adult behavior is both intriguing and impressive.

Perceptual Development How do infants perceive the world around them? Do they recognize form, see color, and perceive depth in the same manner as do adults? Infants can't talk, so it is necessary to answer such questions through indirect methods, such as observing changes in behaviors they *can* perform when exposed to various stimuli—for instance, differences in sucking responses or in bodily functions such as heart rate. Developmental psychologists reason that if infants show different reactions to different stimuli, then they can indeed distinguish between the stimuli at some level. For example, it has been found that after infants have seen a visual stimulus several times, they spend less time looking at it when it is presented again than they do at a new stimulus they have never seen before. This fact provides a means for determining whether infants can detect a difference between two stimuli. If they can, then after seeing one stimulus repeatedly, infants should spend less time looking at it than at a different stimulus when both are presented together. If they cannot tell the two stimuli apart, then they should look at both equally. Studies based on this reasoning have found that newborns can distinguish between different colors (Adams, 1987), odors (Balogh & Porter, 1986), tastes (Granchrow, Steiner, & Daher, 1983), and sounds (Morrongiello & Clifton, 1984). Moreover, infants as young as two or three days old have been found to show differential patterns of sucking in response to what seems to be quite subtle differences in the sound of human speech. Even at this tender age, infants show more vigorous sucking (high-amplitude sucking) to words that are spoken with changing patterns of stress—for instance, ma*ma* versus *ma*ma—than to the same words when they are spoken with a constant pattern of stress (Sansavini, Bertoncini, & Giovanelli, 1997). Infants as young as three days old will turn their eyes and heads in the direction of a sound (Bargones & Werner, 1994; Eimas & Tarter, 1979).

One sound to which they are especially attentive is—not surprisingly—that of their own names. When can infants recognize their name; that is, distinguish it from other, similar sounds? Apparently, by the time they are only a few months old. In a study that investigated this issue, Mandel, Jusczyk and Pisoni (1995) exposed infants who were between four and five months of age to the sound of their own name and to other names that had either the same pattern of stress as their own name or an opposite pattern of stress. For example, if an infant were named "Christ*ine*," a similar-stress name was "Mi*chelle*" while an opposite stress one was "*Co*rey." During the testing session, the infants' attention was attracted to the center of a four- by six-foot panel by a flashing green light. A red light was mounted to the left or right of the panel center. When it flashed, it was followed by the sound of either the infant's name or another name coming from a speaker on the same side as the flashing light. The amount of time they spent looking in the direction of the speaker from which these sounds came was recorded. As you can see from Figure 8.5, the infants spent significantly more time looking in the direction of their own names than in the direction of names with the same stress pattern as theirs, and they spent the least time looking in the direction of names with the opposite pattern. These findings, of course, don't indicate whether the infants understand the meaning of their names—the fact that these words refer to them. But they *can* recognize their names and respond differentially to them.

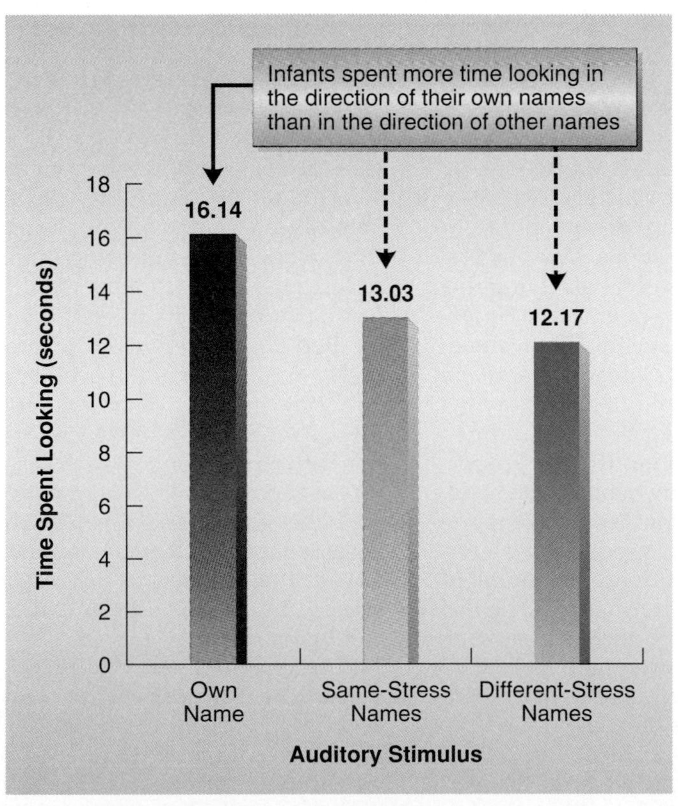

(**Source:** Based on data from Mandel, Jusczyk, & Pisoni, 1995.)

FIGURE 8.5

Evidence That Infants Can Recognize Their Own Names

As shown here, infants only a few months old spent more time looking in the direction of the sound of their own names than in the direction of other names.

FIGURE 8.6

The Visual Cliff

Infants six or seven months old refuse to crawl out over the deep side of the visual cliff. This indicates that they can perceive depth.

Infants also show impressive abilities with respect to recognizing *form* or *pattern*. In now classic research on this topic, which I remember reading about when *I* was taking introductory psychology, Fantz (1961) showed babies six months old a variety of visual patterns. By observing how long they looked at each pattern, he determined that the babies had a clear preference for patterned as opposed to plain targets and that they seemed to prefer the human face over all other stimuli tested. Later research indicated that recognition of faces may develop even earlier. By two months of age, infants prefer a face with features in normal locations over one with scrambled features (Maurer & Barrera, 1981). By three months, they can distinguish between their mother's face and that of a stranger, and even distinguish one stranger's face from another (Maurer & Young, 1983).

The ability to perceive depth, too, seems to develop rapidly. Early studies on *depth perception* employed an apparatus known as the *visual cliff* (Gibson & Walk, 1960). As you can see in Figure 8.6, the patterned floor drops away on the deep side of the "cliff"; but a transparent surface continues across this drop, so there is no drop in the surface—and no real danger. Yet human infants six or seven months old refuse to crawl across the deep side to reach their mothers, thus indicating that they perceive depth by this time. Does this ability appear even before six months? Since younger infants can't crawl across the cliff even if they want to, this research method can't answer that question. But other research, using different methods, indicates that depth perception may first appear when infants are only three months old (e.g., Yonas, Arterberry, & Granrud, 1987).

Before turning to cognitive development in infants and children, let's take a look, in the Research Methods section below, at the basic procedures used by psychologists to study many aspects of human development.

RESEARCH METHODS

How Psychologists Study Development

How can we obtain systematic evidence on the course of human development and the many factors that affect it? Developmental psychologists employ several different methods for answering such questions. One of these is **longitudinal research,** which involves studying the same individuals for extended period of time (see Figure 8.7). For example, suppose that a psychologist wanted to investigate the effects on children's later development of being bullied—of being victimized in some way by another child (Olweus, 1995). Using the longitudinal method, the researcher could first identify two groups of children—ones who were currently being bullied and ones who were not. The psychologist would compare aspects of the behavior of these groups now—for instance, the children's level of confidence, the number of friends they have, their school performance. Then the researcher would study the same children on several future occasions—for instance, midway through each of the next five school years. In this way, the psychologist could obtain evidence on the effects of being bullied.

Longitudinal research offers several important advantages. Because the same people are studied over long periods of time, it may be possible to draw conclusions about how specific events influence the course of subsequent development. For instance, if youngsters being bullied showed drops in their confidence over time, while those not being bullied did not show such reductions, these findings would suggest that bullying has harmful effects on self-assurance. However, this method also suffers from several potential disadvantages. First, there is the problem referred to as *subject attrition*—the loss of participants over the course of time. Families may move, children may be transferred to a different school; in such cases, the participants are no longer available to take part in the study. Another problem is *practice effects*. Children who are tested or observed repeatedly may become very familiar with the kinds of tasks used in the research—or may even be affected by them. As a result, the findings may be difficult to interpret.

Another and very different way of studying human development is **cross-sectional research.** Here, researchers compare children of different ages at one point in time, to see if they differ in certain ways. Returning to our study of the effects of being bullied, a psychologist might study the behavior of children who are five, six,

FIGURE 8.7

Basic Methods of Developmental Research

Developmental psychologists use the two methods of research shown here to study many aspects of human development. In *longitudinal research* the same persons are studied repeatedly over time. In *cross-sectional research* persons of different ages are studied at the same time.

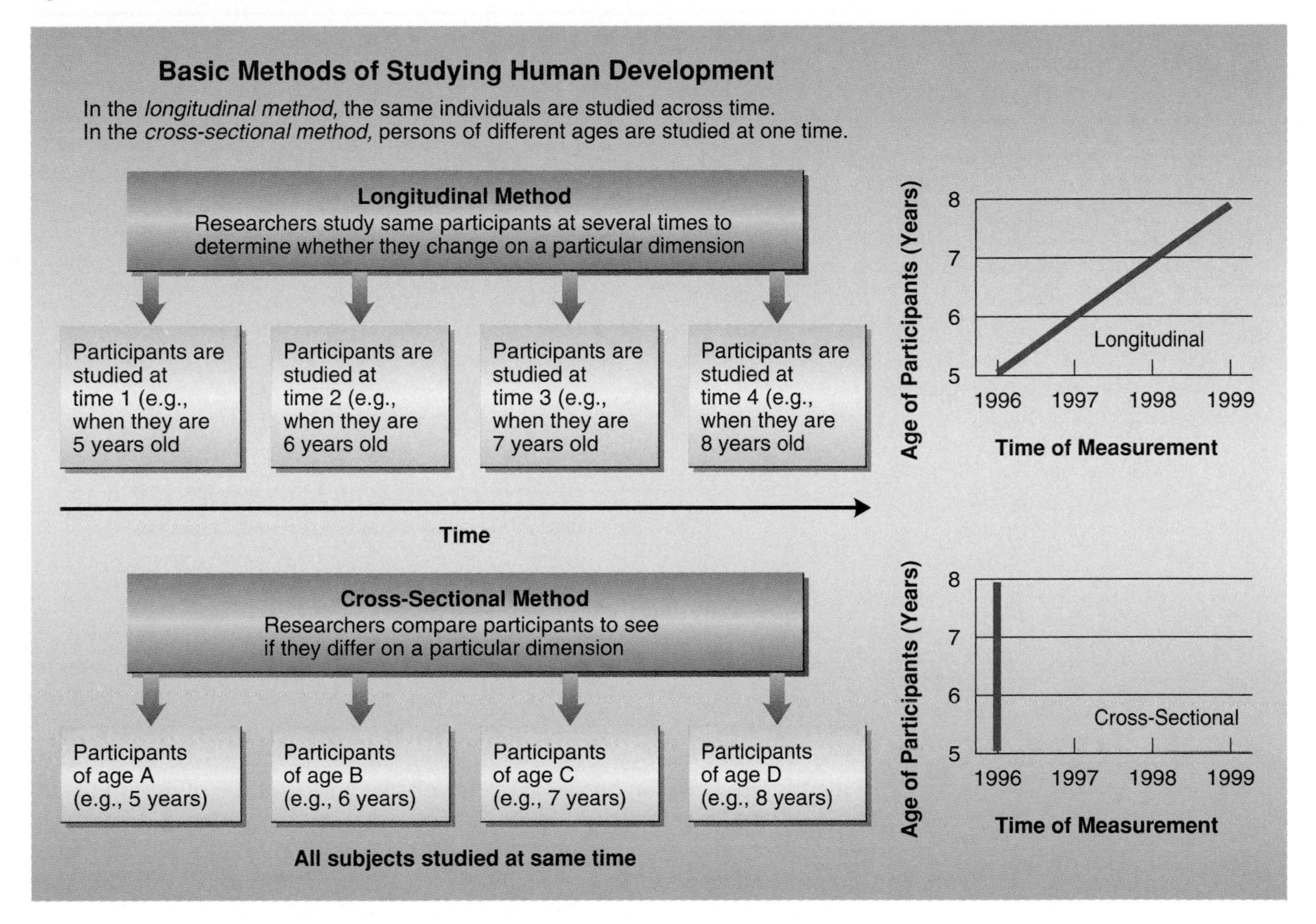

seven, and eight years old, comparing youngsters who are being bullied and those who are not within each age group.

Such research offers several advantages. It can be conducted much more quickly than longitudinal research. Since all the children are studied at one time, we don't have to wait months or years to see what happens as they grow older. However, it too has certain disadvantages. Perhaps the most important of these involve what are known as **cohort effects.** That is, differences between groups of persons of different ages may derive not only from differences in age and from changes in development related to age, but also from the fact that the groups were born at different times and have been exposed to contrasting life experiences or cultural conditions. Such differences may be small among children who are currently five, six, seven, and eight years old. But suppose we are comparing people who are sixty-five, forty-five, and twenty-five? Clearly, the life experiences of these groups may differ greatly; and these different experiences, not increasing age, may be largely responsible for many of the differences between the groups.

Faced with the mixed picture of advantages and disadvantages outlined above, developmental psychologists tried to devise approaches that combine the advantages of longitudinal and cross-sectional research while minimizing the disadvantages of both. One such approach is known as the **longitudinal–sequential design.** It involves studying several samples of people of different ages over a prolonged period of time—months or even years. In other words, this technique combines major aspects of both longitudinal and cross-sectional research. Since each sample of participants is studied across time, changes within each can be attributed to development. But since several such samples are studied, researchers can also assess the impact of cohort effects, by comparing groups born in different years with one another *when they are the same age*. Any differences between them can then reasonably be attributed to cohort effects—to the fact that participants were born in different years and have, as a result, had different life experiences. Another advantage of such designs is that they allow for both longitudinal and cross-sectional comparisons. If the results for both are the same, then we can be quite confident about the validity of these findings. While the longitudinal–sequential design still faces problems of participant attrition, practice effects, and the like, it does offer an additional means for untangling some of the interwoven strands of culture and individual change. In this respect it constitutes another useful research tool for developmental psychologists.

Key Questions

- What environmental factors can adversely affect the development of the fetus?
- How does research suggest that some chemicals may threaten the future of our entire species?
- What perceptual abilities are shown by infants?
- What are the three basic methods used by psychologists to study human development?

As I noted earlier, infants have sophisticated abilities to interpret complex input from their senses shortly after birth. How do babies and children then integrate such information into cognitive frameworks for understanding the world? This is the question we will consider next.

Cognitive Development: Changes in Our Ability to Understand the World around Us

Do children think, reason, and remember in the same manner as adults? Until well into the twentieth century, it was widely assumed that they do. In many societies, it was assumed that while adults are superior mentally, just as they are physically, the cognitive processes of children and adults are basically very similar.

These assumptions were vigorously challenged by the Swiss psychologist Jean Piaget. On the basis of careful observations of his own and many other children, Piaget concluded that in several respects children do *not* think or reason like adults: Their thought processes are different not only in degree but in kind. Piaget's theory of *cognitive development* contains many valuable insights and has guided a great deal of research. Thus, we'll consider it in detail here. But it is important to realize at the start that many psychologists no longer accept this theory as accurate. In recent years Piaget's theory has been seriously challenged by several newer approaches—ones based firmly on advances in several areas of psychology (e.g., Gopnik, 1996). So, after considering Piaget's theory and modern assessments of it, we'll review what is perhaps the most influential of these newer views of cognitive development—a view based on the kind of *information-processing* perspective described in Chapter 6.

Longitudinal Research: Research in which the same individuals are studied across relatively long periods of time.

Cross-Sectional Research: Research comparing groups of persons of different ages in order to determine how certain aspects of behavior or cognition change with age.

Cohort Effects: Differences between persons of different ages stemming from the fact that they have experienced contrasting social or cultural conditions.

Longitudinal–Sequential Design: A research method in which several groups of individuals of different ages are studied across time.

Stage Theory: Any theory proposing that all human beings move through an orderly and predictable series of changes.

Piaget's Theory: An Overview

Piaget's theory of cognitive development is a **stage theory**—a type of theory suggesting that all human beings move through an orderly and predictable series of changes. We'll have reason to examine other stage theories in our discussions of adult development (see Chapter 9) and personality (see Chapter 12). However, I should point out that many psychologists today question the ideas, basic to such theories, that (1) all human beings move through a set series of stages; (2) they move from one stage to another at specific ages; and (3) the order of such progress is unchanging (Flavell, 1985). There simply seems to be too much variability among individuals to enable us to assume such a high degree of orderliness in human development.

Having clarified this point, let's consider Piaget's theory. Central to it is the assumption—often known as *constructivism*—that children are active thinkers who are constantly trying to construct more accurate or advanced understanding of the world around them (e.g., Siegler & Ellis, 1996). Piaget believed that the mechanism responsible for children's movement through the various stages of cognitive development he described is **adaptation**—a process in which individuals build mental representations of the world through direct interaction with it. In other words, children come to construct increasingly advanced and accurate representations of the world through their experience in it. Adaptation, in turn, involves two basic components. The first of these is **assimilation,** our tendency to fit new information into existing mental frameworks—to understand the world in terms of existing concepts and schemas. For instance, if a child goes to a zoo, sees a porpoise, and says, "Look at the fish!" this is an example of assimilation. The second process is **accommodation,** our tendency to alter existing concepts or mental frameworks in response to new information or new recognizable dimensions of the external world. If the same child later comes to realize that not all animals that swim in the water are fish, this illustrates accommodation. Piaget believed that it is the tension between these two components that fosters adaptation and cognitive development—our progress through ever more complex conceptions of the world around us. Now let's look at the various stages of cognitive development Piaget described.

The Sensorimotor Stage: Learning to Represent the World Internally Piaget suggested that the first stage of cognitive development lasts from birth until somewhere between eighteen and twenty-four months. During this period, termed the **sensorimotor stage,** infants gradually learn that there is a relationship between their actions and the external world. They discover that they can manipulate objects and product effects. In short, they acquire a basic grasp of the concept of *cause and effect*. For example, they learn that if they make certain movements—for instance, shaking their leg—specific effects follow (for example, toys suspended over their crib also move), and they begin to "experiment" with various actions, to see what effects they will produce.

Throughout the sensorimotor period, Piaget contended, infants seem to know the world only through motor activities and sensory impressions. They have not yet learned to use mental symbols or images to represent objects or events. This results in some interesting effects. For example, if an object is hidden from view, four-month-olds will not attempt to search for it. For such infants, "out of sight" is truly "out of mind." By eight or nine months of age, however, they *will* search for hidden objects. They have acquired a basic idea of **object permanence**—the fact that objects continue to exist even when they are hidden from view.

The Preoperational Stage: Growth of Symbolic Activity Some time between the ages of eighteen and twenty-four months, Piaget suggested, babies acquire the ability to form mental images of objects and events. At the same time, language develops to the point at which a young child begins to think in terms of verbal symbols—words. These developments mark the end of the sensorimotor period and the start of Piaget's second stage—the **preoperational stage.**

During this stage, which lasts until about age seven, children are capable of many actions they could not perform earlier. For instance, they demonstrate **symbolic play,** in which they pretend that one object is another—for

Adaptation: In Piaget's theory of cognitive development, a process in which individuals build mental representations of the world through direct interaction with it.

Assimilation: In Piaget's theory, the tendency to understand new information in terms of existing mental frameworks.

Accommodation: In Piaget's theory, the modification of existing mental frameworks to take account of new information.

Sensorimotor Stage: In Piaget's theory, the earliest stage of cognitive development.

Object Permanence: The fact that objects continue to exist when they pass from view.

Preoperational Stage: In Piaget's theory, a stage of cognitive development during which children become capable of mental representations of the external world.

Symbolic Play: Play in which children pretend that one object is another object.

FIGURE 8.8

Make-Believe Play

When children engage in make-believe play, they demonstrate that they can represent everyday activities mentally.

instance, that a pencil is a rocket, or a dinner roll is a frog. One variant of this is *make-believe play,* in which youngsters pretend to perform various activities they have seen adults perform, such as reading, working with tools, cutting the lawn, and so on (see Figure 8.8).

While the thought processes of preoperational children are more advanced than those in the preceding stage, Piaget emphasized that preoperational thought processes are still immature in several respects. First, they show considerable **egocentrism;** children at the preoperational stage have difficulty understanding that others may perceive the world differently than they do (Piaget, 1975). For example, if a two-year-old is shown a card with a picture of a dog on one side and a cat on the other, and the card is positioned upright between the child and the researcher, many children do not seem to realize that they and the adult see different pictures.

Children in the preoperational stage also seem to lack understanding of relational terms such as *lighter, larger, softer*. Further, they lack a grasp of *seriation*—the ability to arrange objects in order along some dimension. Finally, and most important, they lack understanding of what Piaget terms the principle of **conservation**—knowledge that certain physical attributes of an object remain unchanged even though the outward appearance of the object is altered. For example, imagine that a four-year-old is shown two identical lumps of clay. One lump is then flattened into a large pancake as the child watches. Asked whether the two lumps still contain the same amount of clay, the child may answer no. Similar findings occur when children of this age watch water from one of two identical tall containers being poured into a shorter but wider one. When asked whether the remaining tall container and the newly filled shorter one contain the same amount of water, children again answer no.

The Stage of Concrete Operations: The Emergence of Logical Thought

By the time they are six or seven (or perhaps even earlier, as we'll see below), most children can solve the simple problems described above. According to Piaget, their mastery of conservation marks the beginning of a third major stage known as the stage of **concrete operations.**

During this stage, which lasts until about the age of eleven, many important skills emerge. Children gain understanding of relational terms and seriation. They come to understand *reversibility*—the fact that many physical changes can be undone by a reversal of the original action. Children who have reached the stage of concrete operations also begin to engage in what Piaget described as *logical thought*. If asked, "Why did you and your mother go to the store?" they reply, "Because my mother needed some milk." Younger children, in contrast, may reply, "Because afterwards, we came home."

The Stage of Formal Operations: Dealing with Abstractions as Well As Reality

At about the age of twelve, Piaget suggested, most children enter the final stage of cognitive development—the stage of **formal operations.** During this period, major features of adult thought make their appearance. While children in the earlier stage of concrete operations can think logically, they can do so only about concrete events and objects. In contrast, those who have reached the stage of formal operations can think abstractly; they can deal not only with the real or concrete but with possibilities—events or relationships that do not exist, but can be imagined.

Egocentrism: The inability of young children to distinguish their own perspective from that of others.

Conservation: Understanding that certain physical attributes of an object remain unchanged even though its outward appearance changes.

Concrete Operations: In Piaget's theory, a stage of cognitive development occurring roughly between the ages of seven and eleven. It is at this stage that children become aware of the permanence of objects.

Formal Operations: In Piaget's theory, the final stage of cognitive development, during which individuals may acquire the capacity for deductive or propositional reasoning.

During this final stage, children become capable of what Piaget termed **hypothetico–deductive reasoning.** This involves the abilities to formulate hypotheses about some aspect of the external world, and to think logically about abstractions, such as symbols and propositions.

Hypothetico–Deductive Reasoning: In Piaget's theory, a type of reasoning first shown by individuals during the stage of formal operations. It involves the ability to formulate hypotheses about some aspect of the external world, and to think logically about abstractions such as symbols.

While the thinking of older children or adolescents closely approaches that of adults, however, Piaget believed that it still falls short of the adult level. Thus, older children, and especially adolescents, often use their new reasoning abilities to construct broad theories about human relationships, what makes a given behavior right or wrong, and political systems. The reasoning behind these views may be logical in the sense of meeting the formal requirements of logic, but the theories themselves are often flawed because the young people who construct them don't know enough about these complex matters to do a thorough job.

One final—but crucial—point: While people who have reached the stage of formal operations are *capable* of engaging in advanced forms of thought, there is no guarantee that they will actually do so. Such thinking requires lots of cognitive effort, so it is not surprising that adolescents, and adults too, often slip back into less advanced modes of thought (Kuhn, 1989).

Table 8.1 provides a summary of the major stages in Piaget's theory.

Piaget's Theory: A Modern Assessment

All theories in psychology are subject to careful scientific testing, but grand theories such as Piaget's require especially careful assessment because they are so sweeping in nature. What do the results of research on Piaget's theory reveal? Briefly, that although the theory is insightful in many respects, it def-

TABLE 8.1

Major Stages in Piaget's Theory

According to Piaget, we move through the discrete stages of cognitive development listed here.

Stage	Age	Major Accomplishments
Sensorimotor	0–2 years	The child develops basic ideas of cause and effect and object permanence.
Preoperational	2–6 or 7 years	The child begins to represent the world symbolically.
Concrete Operations	7–11 or 12 years	The child gains understanding of principles such as conservation; logical thought emerges.
Formal Operations	12–adult	The adolescent becomes capable of several forms of logical thought.

FIGURE 8.9

The Use of Mental Symbols by Young Children

Three-year-olds who watch an adult hide a miniature toy in a model of a room can later find a real toy that has been hidden in the same location in a full-size room. This indicates that these young children can already use *mental symbols* effectively.

initely does *not* provide a fully accurate account of cognitive development. In particular, existing evidence suggests that Piaget's theory is incorrect—or at least requires major revision—with respect to three issues: (1) the ages at which infants and preschoolers achieve many milestones of cognitive development, (2) the discreteness of stages of cognitive development, and (3) the importance of social interactions between children and caregivers in cognitive growth.

The Case of the Competent Preschooler With respect to the first of these issues, growing evidence indicates that Piaget seriously underestimated the cognitive abilities of infants and young children (e.g., Siegal & Peterson, 1996). For example, toddlers as young as eighteen months seem able to infer others' desires or preferences (Repacholi & Gopnik, 1997). This is much younger than Piaget's theory would predict. Similarly, even infants 4.5 months of age seem to possess a basic grasp of object permanence (Baillargeon, 1987). And children as young as three show some understanding of *conservation*—they recognize that certain physical attributes of an object can remain unchanged even though the outward appearance is altered (Cuneo, 1980). Finally, even three-year-olds show quite sophisticated use of mental symbols—they can understand that an object may be an abstract symbol representing something other than itself (e.g., Pratt & Garton, 1993). For instance, in a series of ingenious studies, DeLoache and her colleagues (e.g., DeLoache, 1995) had children two to three years old watch as a researcher hid a miniature toy in a small model of a room (see Figure 8.9). Then the children were taken to a full-size room highly similar to the model and were asked to find the toy. If the children could use symbols, they should be able to find the toy without any difficulty: They should realize that the small room represented the large room in certain respects. In fact, three-year-olds do quite well at this task. (Slightly younger children—about two and a half—often fail, however; they cannot yet use symbols and therefore do not realize that they have any way of knowing where the toy is hidden.) Piaget's theory predicts that children would have to be older to use symbols in this way; so in this respect, as in many others, it underestimates the abilities of young children.

Discrete Stages in Cognitive Development Piaget proposed that cognitive development passes through discrete stages and that these are *discontinuous*—children must complete one stage before entering another. Most research findings, however, indicate that cognitive changes occur in a more gradual manner. Rarely does an ability entirely absent at one age appear suddenly at another. Further, these changes are often *domain specific;* children may be advanced with respect to some kinds of thinking, but far less advanced with respect to others (Gopnik, 1996).

The Social Context of Cognitive Development While Piaget certainly recognized the importance of social interactions in cognitive development, they were not central to his theory. A growing body of evidence, however, suggests that interactions between children and adults may play a key role in at least some kinds of cognitive growth (e.g., Rogoff, 1990). For instance, such interactions call children's attention to particular aspects of the environment, and so increase the likelihood that children will acquire certain kinds of knowledge and therefore certain ways of looking at the world. As noted recently by Gopnik (1996), a child who plays with mixing bowls provided by caregivers will certainly be gathering evidence about different sorts of activities than a child who plays with toy arrows or spears. Similarly, verbal interactions between parents and children can play an important role in cognitive development (Bivens & Berk, 1990; Vygotsky, 1987). Perhaps the key point is that cognitive development is not an automatic unfolding of stages but rather a process, in which progress can be—and often is—affected by social experiences (e.g., Behrend, Rosengren, & Perlmutter, 1992).

In sum, there is now general agreement among developmental psychologists that in certain respects Piaget's theory is inaccurate. Despite its shortcomings, however, there is no doubt that this theory—and especially the research methods Piaget developed to test his views—has profoundly altered our ideas about how children think and reason (e.g., Brainerd, 1996). In this sense, certainly, Piaget's work has made a lasting contribution to psychology—and to our understanding of several important issues.

Key Questions

- What are the major stages in Piaget's theory, and what cognitive abilities do infants, children, and adolescents acquire as they move through these stages?
- In what three respects does Piaget's theory appear to be inaccurate?

Cognitive Development: An Information-Processing Perspective

While Piaget's theory remains influential even today, several other approaches to the study of cognitive development have emerged in recent years (e.g., Gopnik, 1996). Perhaps the most influential of these is known as the *information-processing* approach. (Recall our discussion of the information-processing model of memory in Chapter 6.) This view suggests that it is very useful to view the human mind as an active information-processing system. Psychologists who adopt this perspective seek to understand how children's capacities to process, store, retrieve, and actively manipulate information increase with age (Case, 1991). Because the information-processing approach is supported by a rapidly growing body of evidence, it merits our careful attention.

Sensory Processing: Efficiencies in Perceiving the External World Earlier in this chapter, I noted that even newborns possess considerable ability to perceive the world around them. Children's skills in this respect improve rapidly over the years, however. The information-processing approach suggests that such improvements include increasing abilities to notice subtle features of the external world—for example, not just the difference between a human face and a jumbled pattern, but the differences between individual faces (e.g., Lewkowicz, 1996).

In addition, cognitive growth involves the development of increasingly sophisticated cognitive frameworks or *schemas* for interpreting new stimuli. Newborns seem to possess impressive abilities to construct such frameworks (Langlois, Roggmann, & Reisser-Danner, 1990; Walton & Bower, 1993), and these increase rapidly with time. As these cognitive frameworks, and the capacity to form them, develop, children can interpret complex stimuli in an increasingly efficient way. To put it simply, they have better and better mental frameworks for holding such information and for interpreting it.

Attention: From Unfocused Scanning to Focused Planfulness
If you've ever observed very young children, you know that they are readily distracted. They seem unable to focus their attention exclusively on whatever task they are currently performing. As they grow older, children acquire an increasing ability to concentrate, and to know which stimuli are the ones

Attention-Deficit Hyperactivity Disorder: A psychological disorder in which children are unable to concentrate their attention on any task for more than a few minutes.

on which they should focus (e.g., Gibson & Rader, 1979). Thus, by the time they are about seven years old, they can learn to tune out such distractions as music or other background stimuli. Since our information-processing capacities are quite limited (see Chapters 6 and 7), this growing ability to focus on the most important aspects of a given situation offers important advantages.

In addition, as they grow older, children acquire greater skills in *planfulness*—active decision making about where and how to direct their attention. By the time they are five, preschoolers can search for a lost object by retracing their steps in an orderly sequence (Wellman, Somerville, & Haake, 1979). And by the time they are nine, they can plan activities in detail, even search for various kinds of shortcuts (Gauvain & Rogoff, 1989).

Unfortunately, not all children show increasing ability to focus their attention. Some—those suffering from **attention-deficit hyperactivity disorder** (ADHD for short)—seem almost totally unable to concentrate on any task for more than a few minutes. As a result, they become bored in school and cause many problems for teachers, classmates, and themselves. They talk during quiet periods, ignore social rules, leave their seats, and generally create one disturbance after another (see Figure 8.10; Henker & Whalen, 1989).

ADHD children have normal intelligence, but they show deficits in their ability to focus their attention. They literally can't seem to sit still, and are readily distracted by irrelevant information. Unfortunately, such problems do not go away with age: One recent study followed children with this disorder for sixteen years and found that a substantial proportion (more than 11 percent) still had such problems as adults (Manuzza, Klein, Bessler, Malloy, & LaPadula, 1993).

What are the causes of this disorder? Heredity seems to play a role; children whose parents or siblings have ADHD are more likely to experience this problem themselves than children in whose families ADHD is absent (Biederman et al., 1992). ADHD also seems to be related to many other factors, too, including exposure to lead (Needleman, Schell, Bellinger, Leviton, & Allred, 1990), and such family variables as poverty and a lack of praise and other forms of positive reinforcement at home (Pfiffner & O'Leary, 1993). Fortunately, ADHD can be effectively treated with medication and with special forms of therapy, so there is definitely hope for such children, if they receive appropriate care (Pelham, Milich, & Dixon, 1992).

FIGURE 8.10

Attention-Deficit Hyperactivity Disorder

Children who suffer from attention-deficit hyperactivity disorder literally can't sit still. As a result, they often disrupt their classrooms.

Memory: Improving Strategies, Improving Performance

Memory is a key aspect of cognition, so it is not surprising that it improves in many ways as children mature (e.g., Nelson, 1995). For instance, short-term memory develops rapidly during the first year of life. Infants younger than about eight months of age seem to forget the location of an object that they see hidden if they cannot reach for it immediately. However, by the time they are about fifteen months old, they remember the object's location even if they cannot reach for it until ten seconds have elapsed (Bell & Fox, 1992). This indicates that their ability to hold information in short-term memory has increased greatly in these few months. Another change involves infants' increasing use of various strategies for retaining information in short-term memory. Rehearsal is perhaps the most important of these. As you might expect, five- and six-year-olds are much less likely than adults to repeat information to themselves as they try to memorize it. By the time children are eight years old, however, they can do this much more effectively. Interestingly, even very young children use strategies—although not necessarily rehearsal—to improve their memories. For instance, when trying to remember information, they point at it, stare at, or name it; they will engage in such activities as long as they can understand *why* they are being asked to remember some-

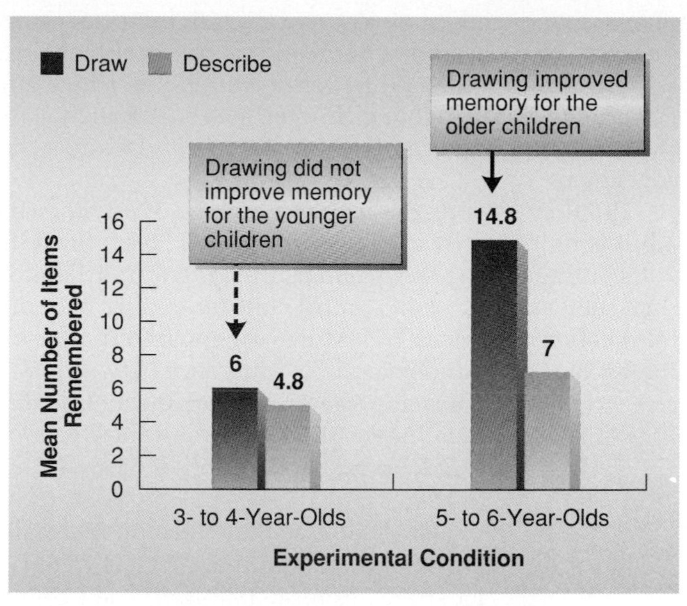

(**Source:** Based on data from Butler, Gross, & Hayne, 1995.)

FIGURE 8.11

Drawing as an Aid to Memory for Young Children

Children five to six years old who drew pictures of events they experienced were later able to recall more of these events than children who were simply asked to describe them verbally. Similar effects did not occur for children three to four years old, however. These findings suggest that drawing is an aid to memory, but only for children five years old or older.

thing. If such motivation is lacking, then they don't spontaneously adopt these memory-enhancing strategies (e.g., Wellman, Ritter, & Flavell, 1975).

With respect to long-term memory, it is clear that as children mature, the amount of information they have entered into memory grows considerably. Moreover, such information becomes better organized, primarily into various *schemas*—cognitive frameworks that help individuals organize existing information and both interpret and store new information. The overall result is that new information is processed more efficiently, and memory improves in several respects. Such effects are illustrated by an intriguing study conducted by Butler, Gross, and Hayne (1995).

These researchers exposed children in two age groups—three to four years old and five to six years old—to an exciting series of events involving a visit to a fire station. One day later, half the children in each age group were asked to tell a researcher what had happened during the visit. The other half, in contrast, were asked to draw pictures of what happened. Then, a month later, all the children were asked to describe verbally what happened during their visit. As shown in Figure 8.11, the five- to six-year-olds who drew the events remembered more than those who simply described them orally. However, similar results did not occur among the three- to four-year-olds. These findings illustrate the kinds of improvements in memory abilities that children experience as they grow older. However, as is true for adults (see Chapter 6), they remain susceptible to distortion and error in this respect. For instance, five- and six-year-olds exposed to suggestions that a visitor to their classroom engaged in various actions—such as tearing a book—readily reported having witnessed these events even though they never occurred (Leichtman & Ceci, 1995). As I noted in Chapter 6, such *false reports* can have devastating effects if they refer to sexual abuse by adults.

Metacognition: Thinking about—and Understanding—Thinking Another important aspect of cognitive development that fits very well with the information-processing approach involves **metacognition:** what we know about our own cognitive processes or, in other words, what we think about thinking, know about the process of knowing, and remember about remembering! Such knowledge is very helpful, for it tells us what would be most useful to know in a given situation. For instance, as a result

Metacognition: Awareness and understanding of our own cognitive processes.

of our understanding of our own cognitive processes, we can generate such thoughts as these: "I'd better read this paragraph again; I didn't understand it the first time," or "I'd better make a note of that information—it seems important." Clearly, young children lack such insights in comparison to older children and adults. Yet they are not totally lacking where metacognition is concerned.

Children as young as eighteen months of age appear to recognize that an adult is imitating their behavior, and will "test" the adult to see if she or he will continue doing so (Asendorpf, Warkentin, & Baudonniere, 1996). By the time they are four or five, most children realize that other people can hold false beliefs (Harris, 1991). Moreover, most four-year-olds—and even some three-year-olds—understand the difference between telling a lie and making a mistake (Siegal & Peterson, 1996). These and related findings suggest that children rapidly acquire a fairly sophisticated understanding of their own and others' cognitive process.

Gradually, as they develop increasing understanding of how their own minds operate, children acquire new and better strategies for maximizing their cognitive efficiency. They combine various strategies for enhancing attention and memory, monitor their progress toward chosen goals, and examine their understanding of information and feedback as it is received. In short, they become increasingly capable of *self-regulation* with respect to their cognitive processes as well as other aspects of their behavior. Another aspect of children's growing cognitive capacities is described in the Exploring Gender and Diversity section below.

Key Questions

- According to the information-processing perspective, what does cognitive development involve?
- What changes occur in children's ability to focus their attention and to enhance their own memory as they grow older?
- What is metacognition?
- Why do Chinese children have an advantage over American children with respect to mathematics even before they enter school? (see below)

EXPLORING GENDER & DIVERSITY

Cross-National Differences in Mathematical Competence: Why It's Harder to Learn to Count in Some Languages Than in Others

Although many children—and adults!—report finding mathematics a difficult subject, being able to deal with numbers and other mathematical concepts is crucial for success in many activities. It is interesting to note, therefore, that Asian children generally outscore U.S. children in tests of mathematical achievement. The fact that these differences occur quite early in life—even before children enter school (e.g., Stevenson & Stigler, 1992)—has led some persons to speculate about the potential contribution of genetic factors to such differences. However, recent research points to a much more obvious explanation: These differences may stem in part from differences between English and some Asian languages, especially Chinese.

In both English and Chinese, the first ten numbers consist of an unordered set of names—one can't predict that *nine* would follow *eight* in English or that *jiu* would follow *ba* in Chinese. Beyond ten, however, Chinese number names follow a consistent rule; for instance, the Chinese term for *eleven* is literally "ten one." In English, in contrast, numbers between ten and twenty follow a less straightforward rule. So it is possible that Chinese children outperform American children in tests of mathematics partly because their language provides them with an early advantage in this respect.

This possibility has been tested by Miller and his colleagues (1995) in a study conducted with American children ages three to five living in Illinois and Chinese children of the same ages living in Beijing. Children in both countries performed two tasks: an abstract counting task in which they were asked to count as high as possible, and an object-counting task in which they counted objects (small stones) arranged in random patterns. Results confirmed the pre-

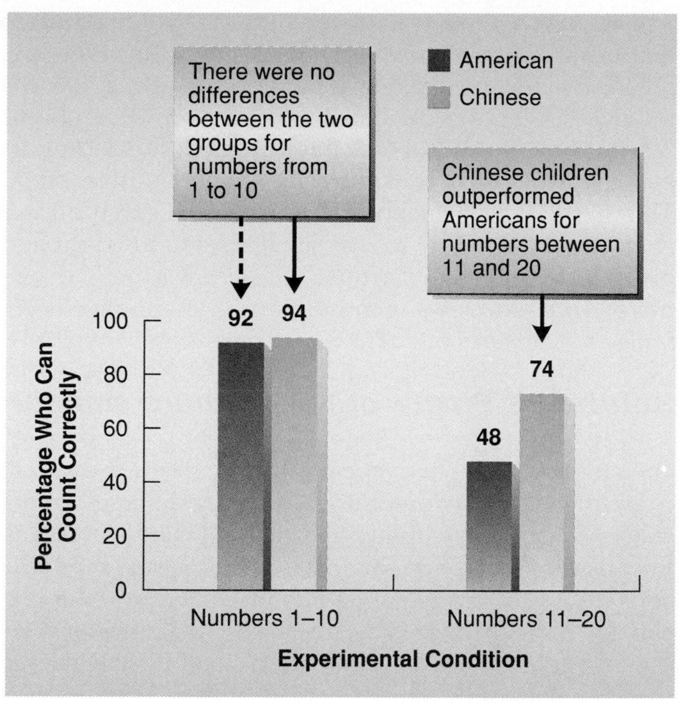

(**Source:** Based on data from Miller et al., 1995.)

FIGURE 8.12

Language and Cross-National Differences in Mathematical Competence

Young Chinese children outperformed American children in terms of counting, but only for numbers between eleven and twenty. One possible explanation is that the English language follows less systematic rules than Chinese for constructing numbers in this range.

diction that the Chinese children would outperform their American counterparts on both tasks. In addition, closer analysis revealed a possible reason for such differences: The two groups did not differ with respect to the proportion of children who could count to ten—but significant differences emerged for the numbers between eleven and twenty, with Chinese children doing better than the Americans (see Figure 8.12). Similarly, while the Chinese children bested the American youngsters when asked to count relatively large sets of objects (fourteen to seventeen), no such differences emerged for smaller sets.

These findings, and those of related research, serve to underscore the important contribution of language and other cultural factors to cognitive development. Chinese students begin their study of mathematics with an edge provided by their language, while English-speaking youngsters in the United States seem to start with a language-based source of confusion. Needless to say, many other factors, including differences in the educational systems of the two countries, soon come into play. But learning to count is the first task children must accomplish with respect to mathematics, so these early differences could help set the pattern for what follows—and for the important cross-national differences that continue to show up throughout the school years.

Moral Development: Reasoning about "Right" and "Wrong"

Is it ever right to cheat on an exam? What about "fudging" your income taxes? Would it ever be right to lie to another person—for example, to tell someone that you like her new dress when you really hate it? Suppose you eat at a restaurant and find that one expensive item has not been included in your bill; would it be right to keep quiet about it and pay the reduced bill? As adults we often ponder such *moral questions*—issues concerning what is right and what is wrong in a given context. And as adults, we realize that such matters are often complex. Whether a given action is acceptable or unacceptable may depend on many factors, including the specific circumstances involved, legal considerations, and our own personal code of ethics.

But how do children deal with such issues? They, too, must make moral judgments. Is their reasoning about such matters similar to that of adults? This is the key question addressed in research on **moral development**—changes in the ability to reason about what is right and what is wrong in a given situation (e.g., Carlo et al., 1996; Carpendale & Krebs, 1995). While many different views of moral development have been proposed, the most famous is a theory offered by Lawrence Kohlberg (1984).

Kohlberg's Stages of Moral Understanding Building on earlier ideas proposed by Piaget (1932/1965), Kohlberg studied boys and men and suggested that human beings move through three distinct levels of moral reasoning, each divided into two separate stages. In order to determine the stage of moral development participants had reached, Kohlberg asked them to consider imaginary situations which raised moral dilemmas for the persons involved. Participants then indicated the course of action they would choose, and explained why. According to Kohlberg, it is the explanations, *not* the decisions themselves, that are crucial, for it is the reasoning displayed in these explanations that reveals individuals' stages of moral development. One such dilemma is as follows:

A man's wife is ill with a special kind of cancer. There is a drug that may save her, but it is very expensive. The pharmacist who discovered this medicine will sell it for $2,000, but the man has only $1,000. He asks the pharmacist to let him pay part of the cost now and the rest later, but the pharmacist refuses. Being desperate, the man steals the drug. Should he have done so? Why?

Let's consider the kinds of reasoning that would reflect the three major levels of moral reasoning proposed by Kohlberg; see Table 8.2 for an overview of all the stages he described.

The Preconventional Level At the first level of moral development, the **preconventional level,** children judge morality largely in terms of consequences: Actions that lead to rewards are perceived as good or acceptable; ones that lead to punishments are seen as bad or unacceptable. For example, a child at this level might say, "The man should not steal the drug, because if he does, he'll be punished."

The Conventional Level As cognitive abilities increase, Kohlberg suggests, children enter a second level of moral development, the **conventional level.** Now they are aware of some of the complexities of the social order and judge morality in terms of what supports and preserves the laws and rules of their society. Thus, a child at this stage might reason: "It's OK to steal the drug, because no one will think you are bad if you do. If you don't, and let your wife die, you'll never be able to look anyone in the eye again."

The Postconventional Level Finally, in adolescence or early adulthood many—though by no means all—individuals enter a third level known as the **postconventional level,** or principled level. Persons who attain this stage often believe that certain obligations and values transcend the rules or laws of society. The principles such individuals follow are abstract and ethical, not concrete like the Ten Commandments, and are based on inner conscience rather than on external sources of authority. For example, persons at this stage of moral development might argue for stealing the drug as follows:

Moral Development: Changes that occur with age in the capacity to reason about the rightness or wrongness of various actions.

Preconventional Level (of morality): According to Kohlberg, the earliest stage of moral development, in which individuals judge morality in terms of the effects produced by various actions.

Conventional Level (of morality): According to Kohlberg, a stage of moral development during which individuals judge morality largely in terms of existing social norms or rules.

Postconventional Level (of morality): According to Kohlberg, the final stage of moral development, in which individuals judge morality in terms of abstract principles.

TABLE 8.2

Kohlberg's Theory of Moral Development: A Summary

According to Kohlberg, we move through the stages of moral development described here.

Level/Stage	Description
Preconventional Level	
Stage 1: Punishment-and-obedience orientation	Morality judged in terms of consequences
Stage 2: Naive hedonistic orientation	Morality judged in terms of what satisfies own needs or those of others
Conventional Level	
Stage 3: Good boy–good girl orientation	Morality judged in terms of adherence to social rules or norms with respect to personal acquaintances
Stage 4: Social order–maintaining orientation	Morality judged in terms of social rules or laws applied universally, not just to acquaintances
Postconventional Level	
Stage 5: Legalistic orientation	Morality judged in terms of human rights, which may transcend laws
Stage 6: Universal ethical principle orientation	Morality judged in terms of self-chosen ethical principles

"If the man doesn't steal the drug, he is putting property above human life; this makes no sense. People could live together without private property, but a respect for human life is essential." In contrast, they might argue for not stealing the drug: "If the man stole the drug, he wouldn't be blamed by others but would probably blame himself, because he would have violated his own standards of honesty and hurt another person for his own gain."

Evidence Concerning Kohlberg's Theory Do we really pass through the series of stages described by Kohlberg, becoming increasingly sophisticated in our judgments of morality? Some findings are consistent with this view, at least in its broad outlines. As suggested by Kohlberg, individuals do generally seem to progress through the stages of moral reasoning he described, moving from less sophisticated to increasingly sophisticated modes of thought (e.g., Walker, 1989). Other findings, however, suggest that Kohlberg's theory, while providing important insights into moral development, requires major revisions in several respects.

Gender Differences in Moral Development Soon after Kohlberg presented his views, psychologist Carol Gilligan criticized the theory strongly on the grounds that it was biased against women (e.g., Gilligan, 1982). She noted that many women do not base moral judgments on the principles of justice emphasized by Kohlberg; rather, they base them on what she termed *care-based principles*—concerns over relationships, caring, and the promotion of others' welfare. Because moral reasoning based on such considerations is scored as relatively immature in Kohlberg's theory, Gilligan charged that Kohlberg's approach undervalued the moral maturity of females.

Are such charges accurate? Evidence on this issue is mixed, but overall, fails to provide clear support for Gilligan's suggestions. Several studies comparing the moral development of males and females have failed to uncover the differences predicted by Gilligan; indeed, if anything, females have scored *higher* not lower than males (e.g., Thoma, 1986; Walker, 1991). Further, it appears that contrary to Gilligan's suggestions, females do *not* seem to base their moral reasoning solely, or even primarily, on care-based concerns. While females do show a tendency to make more care-based judgments than males, this occurs primarily for personal moral dilemmas they have experienced themselves; this tendency does *not* appear to affect females' judgments on other types of questions, including the ones used originally by Kohlberg (e.g., Wark & Krebs, 1996). So, overall, there is little evidence for important differences between males and females with respect to moral development or moral reasoning. Instead, it appears that if such differences exist, they are quite subtle and restricted in scope, occurring only with respect to specific kinds of moral dilemmas.

Consistency of Moral Judgments Kohlberg's theory, like other stage theories, suggests that as people grow older, they move through a successive series of discrete stages. Given this framework, it would be predicted that at any point in time, individuals' moral reasoning across a wide range of moral dilemmas should be consistent—it should reflect the stage they have reached. Do people show such consistency? The answer appears to be no. For example, in one recent study on this issue, Wark and Krebs (1996) asked college students to respond to the moral dilemmas developed by Kohlberg and also to describe real-life dilemmas they had experienced or witnessed—dilemmas that had affected them personally, and dilemmas they knew about but which had not affected them personally. For these real-life dilemmas, the students also described their moral reasoning: their thoughts about the issues, what they felt was the right course of action, and so on. Results indicated that contrary to Kohlberg's theory, participants showed little consistency across the various types of moral dilemmas. In fact, only 24 percent obtained the same global "stage score" (e.g., Stage 3, Stage 4; refer to Table 8.2) across all three types of dilemmas. A large majority of participants, fully 85 percent, made judgments that ranged across three different stages. So, contrary to what Kohlberg's theory suggests, people do not show a high degree of consistency reflecting a specific stage of moral reasoning.

Cultural Factors and Moral Development Finally, it's important to note that the stages described by Kohlberg, and steady movement through them, do not appear in all cultures. For example, in cross-cultural studies carried out in many countries (Taiwan, Turkey, Mexico), it has sometimes been found that persons from tribal or rural village backgrounds are less likely to reach Stage 5 reasoning than persons from urban or more advantaged backgrounds (e.g., Nisan & Kohlberg, 1982; Simpson, 1974). These findings suggest that Kohlberg's work may, to an extent, be "culture-bound": It is biased against persons from ethnic groups and populations different from the ones he originally studied. Whether, and to what degree, this is true, remains uncertain, but it is clear that cultural factors play an important role in shaping moral development, and should be taken fully into account in our efforts to understand this important topic.

Key Questions

- What are the major stages of moral development described by Kohlberg's theory?
- What do research findings indicate with respect to gender differences in moral reasoning?
- Do cultural factors have any impact on moral development?

Social and Emotional Development: Forming Relationships with Others

Cognitive development is a crucial aspect of human growth, but it does not occur in a social vacuum. As infants and children are acquiring the capacities to think, reason, and use language, they are also gaining the basic experiences, skills, and emotions that permit them to form close relationships and interact with others effectively in many settings. How does such *social and emotional development* occur? What are some of its crucial milestones? We'll focus next on these and related questions. (We'll consider aspects of *personality development*, including an influential theory proposed by Erikson, in Chapter 9.)

Emotional Development and Temperament

At what age do infants begin to experience and demonstrate specific emotions? They can't describe their subjective feelings, of course, so efforts to answer these questions have focused mainly on discrete *facial expressions*—outward signs of distinct emotions. Research on emotional development has documented that such expressions appear within the first few months of life (Kavanagh, Zimmerberg, & Fein, 1992). Infants as young as two months old demonstrate *social smiling* in response to human faces. They show laughter by the time they are three or four months old (Sroufe & Waters, 1976). And other emotions, such as anger, sadness, and surprise, also appear quite early and are readily recognizable to adults.

Interestingly, some expressions appear before others, or at least are more common at early ages. For example, following medical inoculations, two-month-old infants show pain expressions more frequently than anger expressions (Izard et al., 1980). A few months later, however, they show anger expressions more often than pain. These findings, and many others, underscore an important point: *Emotional development and cognitive development occur simultaneously, and there are many connections between them.* The finding that anger expressions in response to painful experiences become more common during the first eighteen months of life can be interpreted, for instance, as reflecting infants' growing ability to understand who or what has caused their discomfort.

As they grow older, infants also acquire increasing capacities to "read" the emotional expressions of others. At three months, they become upset when their mothers show an immobile facial expression (Tronick, 1989). By eight or ten months, they actively seek information about other people's feelings and begin to demonstrate **social referencing**—using others' reactions to appraise uncertain situations. Thus, after a fall, a one-year-old will look at its caregivers and, depending on *their* reactions, will cry or laugh (Walden & Ogan, 1988; see Figure 8.13 on page 322).

Finally, children also grow in the ability to regulate their own emotional reactions and to express these to others. Infants have very little capacity to do this, but within a few years, they begin to engage in active efforts to understand and regulate their own feelings. If you have ever seen a four-year-old cover his or her eyes while watching a frightening television show or film, you have witnessed such efforts directly: The children involved are trying to regulate their own feelings by preventing exposure to something they don't like! Children's abilities to regulate their emotions increase through the grade-

Social Referencing: Using others' reactions to appraise an uncertain situation or experience.

FIGURE 8.13

Social Referencing in Action

Young children often look at adults after a fall in order to determine whether to laugh or cry. They use adults' reactions as a basis for deciding how to react to many events.

school years, as does the range of strategies available to them for expressing these feelings—for communicating them to others (e.g., Saarni, 1993). By the time they are ten, therefore, most children are quite adept at these tasks. For instance, they have learned to express sadness, both verbally and nonverbally, in order to gain sympathy and support, and to withhold or disguise anger in order to avoid adult disapproval for such reactions (e.g., Zeman & Shipman, 1996). Progress in both these tasks—regulating and expressing emotions—plays a key role in children's ability to form increasingly complex social relationships, a topic to which we'll soon return.

Temperament: Individual Differences in Emotional Style

Think back over the many people you have known during your life. Can you remember someone who is usually happy, cheerful, and upbeat? And can you remember someone who is just the opposite of this—a person who is usually reserved, quiet, and gloomy? Psychologists refer to such stable individual differences in characteristic mood, activity level, and emotional reactivity as **temperament** (e.g., Stifter & Fox, 1990). Growing evidence suggests that these differences are present very early in life—perhaps at birth (e.g., Kagan & Snidman, 1991; Seifer et al., 1994). In fact, systematic research suggests that most infants can be divided into three basic categories with respect to temperament (Thomas & Chess, 1989). Those in the first category, about 40 percent of infants, are described as *easy children*. They quickly establish regular routines in infancy, are generally cheerful, and adapt easily to new experiences. About 10 percent are *difficult children*. They are irregular in daily routines, are slow to accept new situations or experiences, and show negative reactions more than other infants (see Figure 8.14). Finally, about 15 percent can be described as *slow-to-warm-up children*. They are relatively inactive and apathetic and show mild negative reactions when exposed to unexpected events or new situations. The remaining 35 percent of infants cannot be readily classified under one of these headings.

Interestingly, while girls and boys don't differ with respect to problems relating to temperament during the first three years of life, such differences begin to appear, and to widen, after that age: Boys show a higher incidence of "difficult" behaviors (Prior et al., 1993). In fact, such changes in the frequency of temperament-related problems are only part of a much larger pattern in which, by the time they enter school, boys show much higher rates with respect to what have been termed *externalizing disorders*—problems relating to overt behavior, such as hyperactivity and conduct disorders—than do girls (Keenan & Shaw, 1997). This advantage for girls persists until adolescence, when they begin to experience higher rates of *internalizing disorders*—depression and mood disturbances—than do boys (e.g., Agnold & Rutter, 1992). We'll return to the nature and possible origins of such problems in Chapter 14.

How stable are such differences in temperament? Research findings present a mixed picture. On the one hand, some studies indicate that certain dimensions of temperament—attentiveness, activity level, and irritability—are quite stable (e.g., Rothbart & Ahadi, 1994): Children who are high on these

Temperament: Stable individual differences in the quality and intensity of emotional reactions.

"Noah, I'm tired of doing battle with you!"

(**Source:** Drawing by Koren; © 1986 The New Yorker Magazine, Inc.)

FIGURE 8.14

Temperament: The Difficult Child

Some infants show a pattern of behavior sometimes described as *difficult*. Like Noah, they are often hard to handle.

dimensions at four months of age tend to be high on them months or even years later, while those who are low on these dimensions at four months remain relatively low as they grow older. On the other hand, additional studies indicate that long-term stability in various aspects of temperament may occur only in persons who are relatively extreme on these dimensions (e.g., Saarni, 1993). So, although temperament may be influenced by genetic factors and tends to be quite stable for some people, it *can* be altered by experience for others.

Whatever the relative contributions of genetic and environmental factors to temperament, individual differences in emotional style have important implications for social development. For example, a much higher proportion of difficult than easy children experience behavioral problems later in life (Chess & Thomas, 1984). They find it more difficult to adjust to school, to form friendships, and to get along with others. In addition, many highly reactive children demonstrate *shyness* as they grow older and enter an increasingly broad range of social situations. Finally, there is growing evidence that some aspects of temperament can influence the kind of bonds infants form with their caregivers—and hence important aspects of their personality and even their abilities to form close relationships with other persons when they are adults (Shaver & Brennan, 1992; Shaver & Hazan, 1994). Given the importance of bonds with caregivers, our earliest social ties, let's turn to this topic now.

Attachment: The Beginnings of Love

Do infants love their parents? They can't say so directly, but by the time they are six or seven months old, most appear to have a strong emotional bond with the persons who care for them (Ainsworth, 1973; Lamb, 1977). This strong affectional tie between infants and their caregivers is known as attachment and is, in an important sense, the first form of love we experience toward others. What are the origins of this initial form of love? How can it be measured? These are among the questions developmental psychologists have sought to answer in their research on attachment.

The Measurement and Origins of Attachment That infants form strong attachments to the persons who care for them is obvious to anyone who has ever watched what happens when they are separated from their caregivers. I remember my daughter Jessica's reactions when her mother and I had to leave her with some friends in order to travel to another state to search for a new home. She was only six months old at the time. To this day, I can still hear her anguished, heartbreaking cries as we left. And I can also vividly remember her reactions when we returned after an absence of several days. She came to me very willingly, and clung to me with all her strength. But her mother—that was another matter. It took several days before Jessica seemed to forgive her.

WEB

Actually, infants' reactions to such separations play a central role in one procedure psychologists use to measure attachment. This is known as the **strange situation test,** and it is based on a theory proposed by Bowlby (1969) suggesting that attachment involves a balance between infants' tendencies to seek to be near their caregivers, and their willingness to explore new environments. The quality of attachment, Bowlby contended, is revealed by the degree to which the infant behaves as if the caregiver, when present, serves as a secure base of operations—provides comfort and reassurance; and by the effectiveness of infant–caregiver interactions when the caregiver returns after a separation. How does the strange situation test work? The major steps are outlined in Table 8.3. In essence, it involves careful observations of babies' reactions in response to a series of events involving their caregivers. For example, does the baby cry when its mother leaves the room and he or she is left with a stranger? How does the baby react when she returns? Does the baby appear more confident in her presence despite the presence of the stranger?

Research using these procedures has found that infants differ in the quality or style of their attachment to their caregivers. In fact, most show one of four distinct patterns of attachment. In strange situation studies with infants and their mothers, about 67 percent of American middle-class infants show **secure attachment.** They may or may not cry on separation from their mothers; but if they do, it is because of the mother's absence, and when she returns, they actively seek contact with her and stop crying very quickly. About 20 percent show **avoidant attachment**. They don't cry when their mother leaves, and they react to the stranger in much the same way as to their mother. When the mother returns, they typically avoid her or are slow to greet her. About 10 percent of American middle-class infants show a different pattern known as **resistant attachment**. Before separation, these infants seek contact with their mother. After she leaves and then returns, however, they are angry and push her away; and many continue to cry even after she picks them up. Finally, about 5 percent of infants show **disorganized attachment** (also termed **disoriented attachment**). When reunited with their mothers, these babies show disorganized or even contradictory responses. They look away from the mother while being held or approach her with a lack of emotion; and they often adopt odd, frozen postures after being comforted.

The existence of these distinct patterns of attachment raises an intriguing—and important—question: What factors influence attachment and the particular form it takes? One factor that was long assumed to play a central role is referred to as *maternal sensitivity*—a mother's (or other caregiver's) alertness to infant signals, appropriate and prompt responses to these, flexi-

Attachment: A strong affectional bond between infants and their caregivers.

Strange Situation Test: A procedure for studying attachment in which a caregiver leaves a child alone with a stranger for several minutes and then returns.

Secure Attachment: A pattern of attachment in which infants actively seek contact with their caregiver, and take comfort from the caregiver's presence when he or she returns in the strange situation test.

Avoidant Attachment: A pattern of attachment in which babies don't cry when their caregiver leaves in the strange situation test, and are slow to greet their caregiver when this person returns.

Resistant Attachment: A pattern of attachment in which infants reject and refuse to be comforted by their caregiver after the caregiver leaves them in the strange situation test.

Disorganized or Disoriented Attachment: A pattern of attachment in which infants show contradictory reactions to their caregiver after being reunited with the caregiver in the strange situation test.

TABLE 8.3

Sequence of Events in the Strange Situation Test

The strange situation test is used to study infants' attachment to their caregivers (typically, their mothers). Researchers carefully observe the baby's reactions to each of the events described here.

Episode	Persons Present	Duration	Events/ Procedures
1	Caregiver and baby	30 seconds	Experimenter brings caregiver and baby to room; leaves
2	Caregiver and baby	3 minutes	Baby plays; caregiver seated
3	Caregiver, baby, stranger	3 minutes	Stranger enters, talks to caregiver
4	Stranger and baby	3 minutes (or less)	Caregiver leaves room; stranger remains, offers comfort to baby
5	Caregiver and baby	3 minutes (or more)	Caregiver returns, greets baby, offers comfort
6	Baby alone	3 minutes (or less)	Caregiver leaves room
7	Stranger and baby	3 minutes (or less)	Stranger enters room, offers comfort
8	Caregiver and baby	3 minutes	Caregiver returns, offers comfort

(**Source:** Adapted from Ainsworth et al., 1978.)

bility of attention and behavior, appropriate level of control over the infant, and so on. It was long assumed that caregivers who showed a high degree of maternal sensitivity would be more likely to produce secure attachment in their infants than caregivers who did not, and some research findings offered support for this view (e.g., Isabella, 1993). However, recent evidence suggests that maternal sensitivity may actually play a somewhat smaller role in determining infants' attachment, and that other factors, such as infant temperament, may actually be more important (e.g., Rosen & Rothbaum, 1993).

For instance, in research conducted by Seifer and his colleagues (Seifer et al., 1996; Seifer & Schiller, in press), infants' attachment to their mothers was studied when the infants were six months, nine months, and twelve months old. Observations of attachment were made both in the laboratory (by means of the strange situation test) and in the infants' homes (through careful study of their behavior). Researchers made observations of infant temperament and maternal sensitivity in the infants' homes and carefully analyzed many hours of videotapes. Results indicated that, as the researchers expected, maternal sensitivity was only weakly related to infants' attachment style. Certain aspects of infants' temperament, however, were more strongly related to attachment. Specifically, infants who were difficult and those who often expressed negative or unhappy moods were less likely to show secure attachment than infants who were not difficult and did not show negative moods.

How did these differences in temperament affect attachment? Perhaps infants who, by temperament, are happy and seek contact with their mothers evoke sensitive caregiving behaviors from their mothers, and this in turn contributes to secure attachment. Whatever the specific mechanisms involved, however, one fact seems clear: Several different factors, ranging from parents' responsiveness to their children's needs to parents' memories of their own childhood attachment experiences (e.g., Ijzendoorn, 1995), probably influence attachment.

The Long-Term Effects of Attachment Style Do differences in patterns of attachment have effects that persist beyond infancy? A growing body of evidence indicates that they do. During childhood, youngsters who are securely attached to their caregivers are more sociable, better at solving certain kinds of problems, more tolerant of frustration, and more flexible and persistent in many situations than children who are insecurely attached (i.e., ones who show avoidant, resistant, or disorganized attachment) (Belsky & Cassidy, 1995; Pastor, 1981). Further, securely attached children seem to experience fewer behavioral problems during later childhood (Fagot & Kavanagh, 1990).

Perhaps even more surprising, some findings suggest that differences in attachment style in infancy may have strong effects on the kinds of relationships individuals form when they are adults (e.g., Hazan & Shaver, 1990). People who were avoidantly attached to their caregivers as infants seem to worry constantly about losing their romantic partners; they didn't trust their caregivers as infants, and they don't trust spouses or lovers when they are adults. Similarly, persons who showed resistant or ambivalent (i.e., disorganized) attachment as infants seem to be ambivalent about romantic relationships, too: They want them, but they fear them as well, because they perceive their partners as distant and unloving. In contrast, persons who were securely attached to their caregivers as infants seek closeness in their adult relationship and are comfortable with having to depend on their partners (Shaver & Hazan, 1994). In a sense, then, it seems that the pattern of our relationships with others is set—at least to a degree—by the nature of the very first relationship we form, attachment to our caregivers.

How can experiences with our earliest relationship influence our behavior as adults? One possibility was suggested by Bowlby (1969, 1988). He proposed that infants with different attachment styles learn to filter information differently. Specifically, those who are securely attached see themselves as lovable, others as caring, and the world as basically benevolent. In contrast, those who are not securely attached view themselves as unlovable, other persons as uncaring, and the world as a dangerous and threatening place. And then they behave in ways that tend to confirm these views.

Recent findings offer support for this reasoning. For example, Belsky, Spritz, and Crnic (1996) found that securely attached three-year-olds showed a tendency to remember positive events in puppet shows they had seen, while three-year-olds who were not securely attached tended to remember negative events. These findings, and those of related research, suggest that attachment—the first kind of love we experience—may have profound effects on our self-concept and our view of the world: effects that shape the nature and course of all our later relationships. Having said that, however, I should quickly add that such patterns are definitely *not* set in stone. Individuals who, because of unhappy experiences with attachment early in life, tend to mistrust others *can* change these tendencies through participation in close and happy adult relationships (Shaver & Brennan, 1992). Once again, therefore, we see the complex interaction between nature (e.g., temperament) and nurture (parents' behavior toward their children, the course of adult relationships) that is a basic theme of human development.

Contact Comfort and Attachment: The Soft Touch of Love

Before concluding, it's important to consider an additional factor that seems to play a key role in attachment. This is *close physical contact* between infants and their caregivers. Such contact—known as *contact comfort*—involves the hugging, cuddling, and caresses infants receive from their caregivers, and it seems to be an essential ingredient in attachment. The research that first established this fact is a classic in the history of psychology and was conducted by Harry Harlow and his coworkers.

When Harlow began his research, infant attachment was the farthest thing from his mind. He was interested in testing the effects of brain damage on learning. Since he could not perform such experiments with humans, he chose to work with rhesus monkeys. To prevent the baby monkeys from catching various diseases, Harlow raised them alone, away from their mothers. This led to a surprising observation. Many of the infants seemed to become quite attached to small scraps of cloth present in their cages. They would hold tightly to these "security blankets" and protest loudly when they were removed for cleaning. This led Harlow to wonder whether the babies actually needed contact with soft materials.

To find out, he built two artificial "mothers." One consisted of bare wire, while the other possessed a soft terrycloth cover. Conditions were then arranged so that the monkey babies could obtain milk only from the wire mother. According to principles of conditioning, they should soon have developed a strong bond to this cold wire mother; after all, she was the source of all their nourishment. To Harlow's surprise, this did not happen. The infants spent almost all their time clinging tightly to the soft cloth-covered mother and left her to visit the wire mother only when driven by pangs of hunger (see Figure 8.15 on page 328).

Additional and even more dramatic evidence that the infants formed strong bonds to the soft mothers was obtained in further research (e.g., Harlow & Harlow, 1966), in which monkey babies were exposed to various forms of rejection by their artificial mothers. Some of the mothers blew them away with strong jets of air; others contained metal spikes that suddenly appeared from inside the cloth covering and pushed the infants away. None of these actions had any lasting effects on the babies' attachment. They merely waited until the periods of rejection were over and then clung to their cloth mother as tightly as before.

On the basis of these and related findings, Harlow concluded that a monkey baby's attachment to its mother rests, at least in part, on her ability to satisfy its need for contact comfort—direct contact with soft objects. The satisfaction of other physical needs, such as that for food, is not enough.

Do such effects occur among human babies as well? Some studies seem to suggest that they may. For example, two- and three-year-old children placed in a strange room play for longer periods of time without becoming

FIGURE 8.15

Harlow's Studies of Attachment

Although the wire "mothers" used in Harlow's research provided monkey babies with nourishment, the babies preferred the soft cloth-covered mothers that provided contact comfort.

distressed when they have a security blanket present than when it is absent (Passman & Weisberg, 1975). In fact, they play almost as long as they do when their mother is in the room. These findings suggest that for blanket-attached children, the presence of this object provides the same kind of comfort and reassurance as that provided by their mothers. So human infants, too, may have a need for contact comfort, and the gentle hugs, caresses, and cuddling they obtain from their mothers and other caregivers may play a role in the formation of attachment.

School and Friendships: Key Factors in Social Development

In Chapter 17 I'll point out that adults spend more of their waking time at work than in any other context. For children, the same could be said of school: They spend more of their time in school and in school-related activities (homework, sports, social events) than in any other setting. Clearly, then, children's experiences in school play an important role in their social and emotional development. In school, children do not merely acquire information that contributes to their cognitive growth; they also have the opportunity to acquire, and practice, many social skills. They learn to share, to cooperate, to work together in groups to solve problems. And, perhaps most important of all, they acquire growing experience in forming and maintaining **friendships**—relationships involving strong mutual affective (emotional) ties between two persons (see Figure 8.16).

How do friendships differ from other relationships children have with their peers? A recent review

FIGURE 8.16

School: A Key Setting for Social Development

In school, children acquire and practice many skills essential to effective social development. In addition, they form *friendships*—relationships with other children that involve close affective ties.

of many studies dealing with this topic (Newcomb & Bagwell, 1995) indicates that the following are generally true of children's friendships:

- Friends have stronger affective ties to each other than they have to other peers.
- Friends cooperate with and help each other more than they do other peers.
- Friends may have conflicts with each other, but are more concerned with resolving such disputes than is true with respect to other peers.
- Friends see themselves as equals and engage in less intense competition and fewer attempts at domination with each other than with other peers.
- Friends are more similar to each other than to other peers, and also express more mutual liking, closeness, and loyalty.

Additional evidence indicates that friendships contribute in important ways not only to social and emotional development but to cognitive growth as well. With respect to social development, friendships give children an opportunity to learn and practice skills needed for effective interpersonal relationships, such as closeness and loyalty. With respect to emotional development, friendships give children opportunities to experience intense emotional bonds with people other than their caregivers, and to express these feelings in their behavior. With respect to cognitive functioning, research evidence indicates that friends are more likely than other peers to exchange ideas and to share reactions; and these exchanges of ideas can enhance cognitive growth. In one recent study, for instance, Teasley (1995) found that pairs of fourth graders (about ten years old) who were instructed to talk with their partners as they worked on a task (discovering how a "mystery key" on a computer worked) solved this problem more quickly than children who were told to work quietly, without talking. Findings such as these offer support for the conclusion that friendship can help children acquire skills useful in solving many problems.

In sum, through a wide range of experiences in school—and especially the formation of friendships—children expand their social and emotional skills, and acquire the skills needed for forming close and lasting relationships with others.

Key Questions

- At what age do infants first show recognizable facial expressions?
- How do children's abilities to regulate their own emotions develop?
- What is temperament, and what role does it play in later development?
- What is attachment, and how is it measured?
- What factors affect attachment between infants and their caregivers?
- How does attachment influence later social development?
- What role do children's friendships play in their social, emotional, and cognitive development?

Gender: *Gender Identity and Gender Differences*

My daughter was born in 1970, and although much of that hectic day is a blur in my memory, I do remember one scene very vividly. I was sitting in the waiting room when the nurse came out with a bundle in her arms and announced: "Professor Baron, you are the father of a baby girl!" I must have looked shocked; because, laughing she opened my daughter's blanket and said, "Look! See for yourself!" For me, this scene is vivid proof of the fact that at birth, society immediately classifies us as either *female* or *male* on the basis of our biologically determined sex.

The term **gender,** however, involves much more than this. Every society has preconceived notions about what it means to be male or female—what traits each sex possesses; psychologists term these **gender stereotypes** (e.g.,

Friendships: Relationships involving strong mutual affective (emotional) ties between two persons.

Gender: The supposed traits and behavior of males and females as defined by a given society.

Gender Stereotypes: Cultural beliefs about differences between women and men.

FIGURE 8.17

Gender Roles and Stereotypes

Every culture has *gender roles*—expectations concerning the roles people of each gender should play—and *gender stereotypes*—beliefs about the traits of each gender. As you can see, not all persons behave in ways predicted by these beliefs.

Unger & Crawford, 1992). Further, all societies have more or less clearly defined **gender roles**—expectations concerning the roles people of each sex should fill and the ways in which the genders are supposed to behave (e.g., Deaux, 1993; see Figure 8.17). Such expectations come into play as soon as a nurse or physician announces, "It's a boy!" or "It's a girl!" And they continue to influence us, and our behavior, throughout life. So gender is clearly an important aspect of development and worthy of our special attention. In this section, therefore, I'll focus on gender. Specifically, I'll examine two topics that have received a great deal of attention from psychologists: **gender identity**—how children acquire the understanding that they belong to one gender, or the other, and **gender differences**—how, quite apart from the beliefs held by a given society, females and males actually differ.

Gender Identity: Some Contrasting Views

At what age does a child become aware of being a girl or a boy? Existing evidence suggests that this process begins very early in life. By the time they are two, many children have learned to use *gender labels* appropriately; they refer to themselves as a boy or a girl and correctly label others in this manner. However, they are still uncertain about the stability of gender. When asked, "Could you ever become a daddy?" many little girls below the age of three and a half say yes, and little boys indicate that they could become a mother. Between three and a half and four and a half, however, children begin to understand the stability of gender over time—**gender constancy.**

Through what process do children acquire gender identity? Several different theories have been proposed. According to the *social learning theory*, two kinds of learning are involved: observational learning and operant conditioning. Many studies on observational learning indicate that children tend to imitate models they perceive as similar to themselves more than models they perceive as different (e.g., Bandura, 1986; Baron, 1970). Thus, it is not surprising that over time, children gradually come to match the behaviors of their same-sex parents more and more. Such imitation, of course, is actively

Gender Roles: Beliefs about how males and females are expected to behave in many situations.

Gender Identity: Children's understanding of the fact that they are male or female.

Gender Differences: Differences between females' and males' behavior. Often, perceptions of these differences are exaggerated by *gender stereotypes*.

Gender Constancy: The stability of gender over time.

reinforced by adults who make such comments as "Just like her Mommy!" or "Just like his Daddy!" As children become increasingly aware of their own behavior and these similarities, the idea that they belong to one gender or the other emerges with increasing clarity.

An alternative view of how children acquire gender identity has been proposed by Bem (1984). This approach, known as **gender schema theory,** focuses primarily on the cognitive mechanisms underlying gender identity. It suggests that acquisition of such identity rests in part on the emergence of *gender schemas*. These are cognitive frameworks reflecting children's experiences with their society's beliefs about the attributes of males and females, such as instructions from their parents, observations of how males and females typically behave, and so on. Gender schemas develop, in part, because adults call attention to gender even in situations where it is irrelevant; for instance, teachers say, "Good morning, boys and girls!" Recent findings indicate that when children are exposed to environments in which adults label and refer to gender frequently, they quickly acquire gender schemas as well as gender stereotypes of traits and occupations (e.g., Bigler, 1995).

Gender Schema Theory: A theory that children develop a cognitive framework reflecting the beliefs of their society concerning the characteristics and roles of males and females; this gender schema then strongly affects the processing of new social information.

Once gender schemas take shape, they influence children's processing of many forms of social information (Martin & Little, 1990). For example, children with firmly established gender schemas tend to categorize the behavior of others as either masculine or feminine. Similarly, they may process and recall behaviors consistent with their own gender schemas more easily than ones not consistent with them. In short, for children possessing such schemas, gender is a key concept or dimension, one they often use in attempts to make sense out of the social world, and one that becomes linked in important ways to their self-concept.

Existing evidence suggests that both social learning views and cognitive views of gender identity add to our understanding of this important process. Thus, they should be viewed as complementary rather than as conflicting points of view.

Gender Differences: Do Males and Females Really Differ, and If So, How?

Each semester, when I get to the topic of prejudice, I ask the students in my class this question: "Suppose you had a female boss—would she act any differently from a male boss?" What kind of answers do you think I receive? Do you think my students tell me, "Get real, Baron—there *are* no differences." No way. What they usually do—both male and female students—is provide me with a long list of ways in which female bosses differ from male bosses. For instance, my students often tell me, "Female bosses are more interested in being liked; male bosses focus on getting the job done." And often several students state that "Female bosses try to get consensus before making decisions; males listen to input, but then they just do whatever they want."

What my students are telling me, of course, is that they believe that males and females really do differ in important ways where behavior is concerned. To what extent do these views reflect persistent *gender stereotypes*—cultural beliefs about differences between women and men—and to what extent do they reflect actual differences? The answer provided by psychological research is anything but simple. In essence, though, it boils down to this: *Yes, there are indeed some differences between males and females with respect to many aspects of behavior, but in general, the magnitude of such differences is overestimated by prevailing gender stereotypes. Further, differences between individuals within a given gender are generally far greater than differences between genders* (Bettancourt & Miller, 1996; Voyer, Voyer, & Bryden, 1995). Let's take a closer look at some specific findings. After we do, we'll turn to the important question of the origin of such differences.

Gender Differences in Social Behavior First, let's consider possible differences between males and females with respect to social behavior. Many gender stereotypes relate to social behavior—for example, the beliefs that females are *nurturant* and *emotionally sensitive* while males are *aggressive* and *dominant*. Do such differences in social behavior actually exist? Research findings paint a mixed picture. First, with respect to *emotional expression*, it does appear that in general females are more adept than males at recognizing others' emotions from *nonverbal cues*—facial expressions, body language, and so on. And females are also better at sending messages about their own feelings nonverbally (e.g., DePaulo, 1992; DePaulo et al., 1996).

WWW WEB

What about *aggression*—are males actually more aggressive than females? Here, it appears, the answer depends on what kind of aggression we are considering. With respect to *physical aggression*—overt assaults on others—males are indeed more aggressive than females, especially in the absence of strong provocation (Bettancourt & Miller, 1996). When strong provocation is present, however, differences between males and females tend to be much smaller. But people aggress against others in many different ways, and some of these are *indirect*—actions such as spreading rumors about other people, giving them the cold shoulder, failing to defend them when they are criticized by others, and so on. Research findings indicate that females are actually *more* likely to engage in such indirect forms of aggression than males (e.g., Bjorkqvist, Osterman, & Kaukiainen, 1992).

Another aspect of social behavior where large gender differences have often been assumed to exist is *susceptibility to social influence*. Females, because they want to be pleasing, are assumed to be more susceptible to persuasion or influence than males. In fact, however, existing evidence provides little evidence for such differences (e.g., Graziano et al., 1993). Females do seem to be more influenced by evaluative feedback from others (e.g., Roberts & Nolen-Hoeksema, 1990); but overall, they are *not* more readily influenced than males.

In sum, there do appear to be some minor differences in the social behavior of males and females, but these are small in size and very limited in scope.

Gender Differences in Cognitive Abilities It is widely assumed that females have higher verbal abilities than males and that males surpass females in mathematics and in tasks involving *spatial abilities*—accurate perception of the movements of objects in space, mental rotation of objects, and so on. Do these differences exist? Research on this question suggests that once again, such differences—if they do exist—are smaller than gender stereotypes suggest (e.g., Hyde, Fennema, & Lamon, 1990; Voyer, Voyer, & Bryden, 1995). Further, the magnitude of cognitive differences has tended to decrease in recent years, especially among adolescents (Feingold, 1992). On the whole, there appear to be few if any differences between females and males with respect to many aspects of cognition.

Gender Differences in Psychological Adjustment One area of behavior where sizable gender differences have been found, however, involves certain aspects of psychological adjustment. For example, around the world, females are more than twice as likely as males to suffer from some form of *depression* (e.g., Nolen-Hoeksema, 1990). They are much more likely to experience such symptoms as persistent feelings of sadness; loss of energy; and reduced pleasure in activities that are normally enjoyable, such as eating and sexual relations. In addition, females are more likely than males to suffer from various forms of *eating disorders*, such as *anorexia nervosa* (self-starvation) and *bulimia* (binge eating and purging); see Chapter 14.

Why are females more likely than males to experience depression? Many psychologists point not to biological or hormonal factors but to social factors; for example, the fact that females, because of a lack of power, status, and income, are more likely than males to experience feelings of *helplessness*—an important forerunner of depression (Strickland, 1992). Similarly, it is primarily females who seem to bear the brunt of many societies' current insistence that one must be slim to be attractive. Given this fact, it is not surprising that females suffer more than males from psychological disorders relating to this standard (Williamson, Cubic, & Gleaves, 1993).

The **Ideas to Take with You** feature on page 334 summarizes key information on gender differences—and generally supports the conclusion that while some gender differences do seem to exist, they are smaller in magnitude, less numerous in number, and more limited in scope than gender stereotypes suggest.

Gender Differences: A Note on Their Possible Origins

At several points in the preceding discussion of gender differences, I referred to explanations of these differences emphasizing social and cultural factors. That was no accident because, in general, psychologists believe that behavioral differences between males and females probably stem in large measure from social and cultural causes. As I indicated earlier, all societies have beliefs about the supposed traits of females and males; and as a result of such views, societies often adopt contrasting socialization practices for the two genders. In other words, parents, teachers, and other adults often treat male and female children differently because of gender stereotypes suggesting that boys and girls are—and should be—different in many respects (e.g., Etaugh & Liss, 1992; Stoppard & Gruchy, 1993). I vividly remember my father telling me, when, as a boy of about five, I broke into tears after falling and hurting my knee, "Boys don't cry—stop that sniveling!" I don't have any sisters, but I never noticed my uncles telling my female cousins the same thing; on the contrary, when *they* cried, they were picked up and comforted. Parents teach their children lessons like these over and over again, and such lessons are often repeated by television shows and movies. Given this constant exposure to cultural stereotypes concerning supposed gender differences, it is not surprising that there are some differences in the behavior of males and females. On the contrary, what's surprising is that such differences are not even larger or more numerous than they are.

The Potential Role of Biological Factors To repeat: Most psychologists attribute gender differences in behavior largely to social and cultural factors. This does not imply, however, that biological factors play no role in such differences. In fact, some evidence suggests that such factors may contribute, to some degree, to a few differences in behavior between males and females.

We have already considered this issue in Chapter 2, where we saw that some findings point to the possible existence of subtle differences between the brains of females and males (e.g., Hyde & Plant, 1995; Swaab, Gooren, & Hofman, 1995). As you may recall, it appears that the corpus callosum, the broad band of neurons that connects the two hemispheres of the brain, may differ in males and females. For instance, some portions of this structure are larger in women than in men, and it appears that such differences may be related in some manner to the fact that females are slightly superior to males with respect to some verbal abilities (e.g., Hines et al., 1992).

In addition, other findings indicate that gonadal hormones—hormones

Ideas to Take with You

Gender Differences: The Real and the Imaginary

Research findings indicate that the behavior of females and males may differ in some respects. However, these differences are smaller in magnitude and less frequent than gender stereotypes suggest.

Social Behavior

AGGRESSION: Males are more physically aggressive than females, especially in the absence of provocation. In the presence of provocation, such differences are slight. Females engage in *indirect* forms of aggression more often than males.

FRIENDSHIPS: Females report being more satisfied with their friendships and are more likely to discuss feelings with their friends. Males report that their friendships are based on shared interests or activities.

SEXUAL BEHAVIOR: Males assign greater weight than females to physical beauty in selecting romantic partners; females assign greater weight than males to success, status, and personality.

LEADERSHIP: Few if any differences exist. Females may be slightly more likely than males to make decisions through consensus.

Psychological Adjustment

DEPRESSION: Females experience depression more often than males.

EATING DISORDERS: Females are more likely than males to experience eating disorders.

Cognitive Abilities

VERBAL ABILITIES: Females score slightly higher than males.

SPATIAL ABILITIES: Males score slightly higher than females.

Differences of both types seem to be decreasing.

produced by the ovaries and testes—influence prenatal and childhood development and thus contribute to some differences in the behavior of males and females (e.g., Collaer & Hines, 1995). For instance, some females are born with a condition known as *congenital adrenal hyperplasia,* in which their own pituitary glands secrete abnormally high levels of *androgen*—a male sex hormone. Careful studies of these females suggest that as children, they sometimes show a pattern in which they engage in the kind of rough, active outdoor play more typically shown by boys than by girls, coupled with reduced interest in makeup, feminine clothing, and doll play (e.g., Dittman et al., 1990). These females also sometimes show reduced interest in child care or in having children, and may show enhanced spatial skills (e.g., Hampson, Rovet, & Altmann, 1994). In short, it is almost as if their early exposure to high doses of male hormones have "masculinized" their behavior to some extent.

A very different pattern is shown by males who, because they have reduced levels of enzymes required for androgen synthesis, experience a deficit of this hormone prior to puberty. They are often born with female-appearing genitalia, and are typically raised as girls. At puberty, however, they undergo changes associated with being male, such as deepening of the voice and masculinization of their genitals. What happens at this time? They reverse their previous sexual identity and show a shift in interests to typical male patterns—for instance, lessened interest in clothing (e.g., Herdt & Davidson, 1988). While there are many complexities in interpreting the results of such research, they do tend to point to the conclusion that hormonal factors play some role in gender differences.

To conclude: While most evidence suggests that gender differences in behavior stem primarily from social and cultural factors, the possibility that biological factors, too, play a role cannot be ruled out—and should not be ignored. Even if biological factors *do* play a role in such differences, however, this is no way indicates that that gender differences are unmodifiable, predetermined, or irresistible—far from it. Biological factors are far from dominant and actually appear to constitute only a small part of the total picture.

Key Questions

- How do children acquire gender identity—the understanding that they are male or female?
- What gender differences in behavior have been reported in systematic research?
- What are the relative roles of social and cultural factors on the one hand, and biological factors on the other, with respect to gender differences?

Making Psychology Part of Your Life

How to Discipline Children Effectively: Avoiding Some Common Mistakes

Do you have children, or do you plan to have children sometime in your future? Choosing to be a parent is one of the most important choices of your life, for it is one of the few decisions that cannot be unmade. Once you are a parent, you are one for life. In addition, raising children in today's complex and often threatening world is one of the most demanding and difficult jobs anyone can undertake. Given these facts, and the huge investment in time, love, and resources that most parents make in their children, it's important to be as effective as possible in this role. Psychology has much to offer in this regard, because being a successful parent involves many different skills.

One of the most important of these skills is the ability to discipline your children effectively—to train them to behave in accordance with rules you establish. What are such rules? While they certainly vary from family to family, almost all parents would agree that they want their children to follow rules like these:

- Don't hurt other people.
- Do what your parents tell you to do.
- Don't play with the telephone.
- Come home on time.
- Do your homework.
- Don't fight with your brothers or sisters.

How can parents get their children to follow such rules? Psychologists who have studied this issue (e.g., O'Leary, 1995) have found that the answer involves two parts. First, to discipline their children effectively, parents must use appropriate and effective techniques—approaches that work. Successful approaches include (1) being consistent; (2) avoiding excessively harsh forms of punishment; (3) avoiding excessive laxness (allowing children to get away with practically anything); (4) being receptive to bargaining, so that compromises acceptable to both parents and children can be found; and (5) showing affection when enforcing discipline so that children feel that they are loved even when being reprimanded.

Second, and perhaps even more important, parents must learn to avoid common discipline mistakes—errors that undermine their own efforts to regulate their children's behavior (e.g., Kendziora & O'Leary, 1993). What are such mistakes? Here is an overview of the ones that are most important:

Laxness Laxness involves establishing but then failing to enforce rules—or even worse, positively reinforcing behavior that violates the rules. What children learn from this is simple: The rules don't really count; they are simply words that can be ignored.

Overreactivity This involves reacting too strongly to violations of parental rules—reacting with anger, irritability, and harsh punishment. Spanking and other forms of physical force are especially dangerous, since they may teach children that it is perfectly acceptable to harm other people in order to get one's way (e.g., Kochanska, 1993). Overreactivty often occurs when parents react not to a child's behavior but to their own frustration or annoyance—feelings that often stem from sources other than the child.

Verbosity Verbosity involves engaging in lengthy verbal interactions about misbehavior, even when this is ineffective. Verbosity may be ineffective because the children on the receiving end are too young to understand the abstract principles being described, or because they are in an emotional state that makes it impossible for them to listen and absorb the message.

Perhaps concrete examples of discipline mistakes will help. Imagine a parent who has stated the rule "Don't make a fuss while we are in stores." Yet, her four-year-old daughter begins to whine, nag, and cry while she is at the supermarket. The mother responds by trying to distract the daughter—first by showing her new snack foods, then by buying one. The mother has made the error of laxness, and her child learns that the rule is meaningless: If she whines and cries, her mother will do what she wants.

As an example of overreactivity, consider a parent who comes home from a very bad day at the office, only to find that the furnace has broken down and that the phone bill is twice as high as usual. He is feeling very frustrated and angry, so when his son spills his milk at the dinner table, the father loses his temper, shouts angrily at the boy, slaps him, and sends him to bed without supper. In this case, the father has overreacted to a fairly trivial incident—and perhaps taught his son that it is O.K. to take it out on others when feeling frustrated or annoyed.

Needless to say, avoiding these and many other mistakes in disciplining children is far from easy. But it is well worth parents' efforts to learn to recognize and avoid such pitfalls. If they do, they will be able to teach their children the kind of self-discipline and moral values they want to transmit. If they don't, they will still teach the children many lessons about these important areas of life—but the lessons will not be the ones the parents *want* to teach.

Summary and Review of Key Questions

Physical Growth and Development

- **What environmental factors can adversely affect the development of the fetus?** Diseases, drugs, alcohol, and smoking by prospective mothers are all among teratogens that can harm the developing fetus.
- **How does research suggest that some chemicals may threaten the future of our entire species?** Some chemicals—especially DES—seem to mimic the effects of natural hormones. As a result, they can disrupt normal fetal development. Recent findings indicate that such chemicals may be contributing to sharply reduced sperm counts among males, and so may endanger human reproduction.
- **What perceptual abilities are shown by infants?** Infants can distinguish among different colors, sounds, and tastes, and they prefer certain patterns, such as the features on the human face.
- **What are the three basic methods used by psychologists to study human development?** In longitudinal research, the same individuals are studied for extended periods of time. In cross-sectional research, persons of different ages are studied at the same time. In longitudinal–sequential research, persons of different ages are studied over extended periods of time.

KEY TERMS

developmental psychology, p. 298 • childhood, p. 298 • embryo, p. 299 • fetus, p. 299 • teratogens, p.299 • placenta, p. 300 • longitudinal research, p. 308 • cross-sectional research, p. 308 • cohort effects, p. 308 • longitudinal–sequential design, p. 308

Cognitive Development: Changes in Our Ability to Understand the World around Us

- **What are the major stages in Piaget's theory, and what cognitive abilities do infants, children, and adolescents acquire as they move through these stages?** During the sensorimotor stage, infants acquire basic understanding of the links between their own behavior and the effects it produces—cause and effect. During the preoperational stage, infants can form mental representations of the external world, but show egocentrism in their thinking. During the stage of concrete operations, children are capable of logical thought and show understanding of conservation. During the stage of formal operations, children and adolescents can think logically.
- **In what three respects does Piaget's theory appear to be inaccurate?** Piaget's theory is inaccurate in that it underestimates the cognitive abilities of young children, overstates the importance of discrete stages, and underestimates the importance of language and social interactions.
- **According to the information-processing perspective, what does cognitive development involve?** According to this approach, cognitive development involves the increasing ability to process, store, retrieve, and manipulate information.
- **What changes occur in children's ability to focus their attention and to enhance their own memory as they grow older?** Children become better able to ignore distractions and to focus their attention on tasks they are currently performing. They develop increasingly sophisticated schemas, acquire increased capacity to rehearse information they want to memorize, and greatly expand their domain-specific knowledge.
- **What is metacognition?** Metacognition is awareness and understanding of our own cognitive processes.
- **Why do Chinese children have an advantage over American children with respect to mathematics even before they enter school?** Chinese children acquire an advantage because their language follows a more straightforward rule with respect to the names for numbers between eleven and twenty.
- **What are the major stages of moral development described by Kohlberg's theory?** At the preconventional level, morality is judged largely in terms of its consequences. At the conventional level, morality is judged in terms of laws and rules of society. At the postconventional level, morality is judged in terms of abstract principles and values.
- **What do research findings indicate with respect to gender differences in moral reasoning?** Contrary to suggestions by Gilligan, there is little evidence that males and females differ in moral reasoning or attain different levels of moral development.
- **Do cultural factors have any impact on moral development?** Cultural factors do appear to influence moral development. Depending on the society in which they live, individuals learn to make moral judgments on the basis of different criteria.

KEY TERMS

stage theory, p. 308 • adaptation, p. 309 • assimilation, p. 309 • accommodation, p. 309 • sensorimotor stage, p. 309 • object permanence, p. 309 • preoperational stage, p. 309 • symbolic play, p. 309 • egocentrism, p. 310 • conservation, p. 310 • concrete operations, p. 310 • formal operations, p. 310 • hypothetico–deductive reasoning, p. 311 • attention-deficit hyperactivity disorder, p. 314 • metacognition, p. 315 • moral development, p. 318 • preconventional level, p. 318 • conventional level, p. 318 • postconventional level, p. 318

Social and Emotional Development: Forming Relationships with Others

- **At what age do infants first show recognizable facial expressions?**

Infants show discrete facial expressions as early as two months of age.

- **How do children's abilities to regulate their own emotions develop?** As they grow older, children acquire increasing abilities to avoid disturbing stimuli and to adjust their expectations.
- **What is temperament, and what role does it play in later development?** Temperament is defined as stable individual differences in the quality and intensity of emotional reactions. It plays a role in characteristics such as shyness, in attachment, and in several kinds of childhood behavioral problems; it may even influence the nature of adult romantic relationships.
- **What is attachment, and how is it measured?** Attachment is the strong emotional bond between an infant and its caregiver. It is measured by the strange situation test, in which infants' reactions to being separated from their caregiver are studied, and through careful observation of infants' behavior in their own homes.
- **What factors affect attachment between infants and their caregivers?** Attachment is influenced by infants' temperament and by several other factors, including parents' responsiveness to children's needs and contact comfort.
- **How does attachment influence later social development?** Children who are securely attached to their caregivers are more sociable, better at solving some problems, more tolerant of frustration, and more flexible and persistent in many situations than children who are not securely attached. In addition, persons who were securely attached to their caregivers as infants seem more capable of forming close, lasting relationships than persons who did not have secure attachments in infancy.
- **What role do children's friendships play in their social, emotional, and cognitive development?** Children's friendships, which are often formed in school, provide them with opportunities to acquire and practice essential social skills, such as sharing, cooperation, and closeness. Friendships also provide children with opportunities to experience and express intense emotions, and friendships promote cognitive growth by encouraging exchanges of ideas.

KEY TERMS

social referencing, p. 321 • temperament, p. 322 • attachment, p. 324 • strange situation test, p. 324 • secure attachment, p. 324 • avoidant attachment, p. 324 • resistant attachment,

p. 324 • disorganized or disoriented attachment, p. 324 • friendships, p. 329

Gender: Gender Identity and Gender Differences

- **How do children acquire gender identity—the understanding that they are male or female?** Children acquire gender identity through both social learning and the development of gender schemas.
- **What gender differences in behavior have been reported in systematic research?** Research findings indicate that there are small and subtle differences between males and females with respect to several aspects of social behavior (e.g., aggression, the ability to send and read nonverbal cues), sexual behavior (e.g., the criteria for mate selection), cognitive abilities (e.g., spatial abilities), and psychological adjustment (e.g., the incidence of depression).
- **What are the relative roles of social and cultural factors on the one hand, and biological factors on the other, with respect to gender differences?** Most psychologists believe that gender differences in behavior stem primarily from social and cultural factors, such as contrasting socialization experiences for females and males. However, some evidence suggests that biological factors such as subtle differences in brain structure and the impact of gonadal hormones may also play some role.

KEY TERMS

gender, p. 329 • gender stereotypes, p. 329 • gender roles, p. 330 • gender identity, p. 330 • gender differences, p. 330 • gender constancy, p. 330 • gender schema theory, p. 331

Critical Thinking Questions

Appraisal

Physical, cognitive, and emotional/social development occur simultaneously. Given this fact, does it make sense to study each separately?

Controversy

Suppose further research confirms that synthetic chemicals fed to animals and sprayed on crops to speed their growth are exerting effects on human fetuses, and on human children as well. Should these chemicals be banned, even though banning them would raise the price of meat?

Making Psychology Part of Your Life

Many parents worry about the effects on their children of television, movies, and other forms of the mass media. Do you think that such concerns are justified? And if so, what should be done? In other words, should there be some kind of censorship or government control over the content of such programs to help reduce any harmful effects on children?

CHAPTER OUTLINE

Human Development II

Adolescence, Adulthood, and Aging

Imagine that one day, a scientist invents a time machine. You enter it and are transported twenty-five years into the future, where you encounter . . . yourself! Assuming that this meeting between you and yourself does not cause a violent explosion, what will you find? Will you recognize your older self? Will your future self have the same personality characteristics as you do now? Will this person share your attitudes, beliefs, and feelings? In short, will this future self be *you*, or someone who is, in many respects, a stranger?

These are intriguing questions, and they relate to one of psychology's grand themes—*stability versus change*. When I began my career, back in the 1960s, most psychologists engaged in the study of human development would probably have emphasized *stability*. "Yes," they would have noted,

> **A growing body of research findings indicates that we change in many ways as we proceed along life's journey—that in reality, the physical alterations we all recognize as part of growing older are only the highly visible tip of a much larger iceberg.**

"we do change physically throughout life. But our major traits, our cognitive abilities, and basic aspects of our social behavior remain much the same throughout our adult years." Now, however, the pendulum of scientific opinion has swung somewhat toward the *change* side of the equation. A growing body of research findings indicates that we change in many ways as we proceed along life's journey—that in reality, the physical alterations we all recognize as part of growing older are only the highly visible tip of a much larger iceberg (e.g., Duncan & Agronick, 1995; Friedman et al., 1995).

In this chapter, therefore, we'll focus on human development in the years after childhood—during *adolescence,* the period between puberty (sexual maturation) and entry into adult life, and during *adulthood,* the remaining decades of our lives. As in Chapter 8, we'll examine changes during these periods under three major headings: *physical, cognitive,* and *social and emotional* development. In addition, since *aging, death, and bereavement* (mourning for loved ones who have died) are basic facts of human life, these topics, too, will be part of our discussion.

Adolescence: Between Child and Adult

When does childhood end and adulthood start? Because development is a continuous process, there are no hard-and-fast answers to these questions. Rather, every culture decides for itself just where the dividing line falls. Many cultures mark this passage with special ceremonies, like those shown in Figure 9.1. In many countries, however, the transition from child to adult takes place more gradually during a period known as **adolescence.**

Adolescence has traditionally been viewed as beginning with the onset of **puberty,** a rapid spurt in physical growth accompanied by sexual maturation, and as ending when individuals assume the responsibilities associated with adult life—marriage, entry into the workforce, and so on (Rice, 1992). Again, though, I wish to stress the fact that different cultures have sharply contrasting ideas about this issue, and even about whether a distinct period of adolescence exists. In the United States, for instance, the idea of a separate period of adolescence did not gain widespread acceptance until well into the twentieth century. Before that time, children were called on to perform various jobs as soon as they were physically large enough to do so, and they assumed the roles and responsibilities of adult life gradually. Now, in contrast, adolescence is a distinct period in the lives of young people. Further, in recent years it has shown signs of expanding at both ends. Children enter this phase at ever earlier ages—perhaps because of early maturation (possibly brought on, in part, by the hormone-mimicking chemicals described in Chapter 8). Similarly, as suggested by the cartoon in Figure 9.2 on page 344, many people currently delay the time at which they accept responsibilities associated with adult life, such as full-time work, marriage, or full financial independence (Duff, 1996). Such trends emphasize the facts that the definition of adolescence is largely a social one, determined by each culture, and that ideas about this phase of life can—and do—change greatly within a given culture over time.

Adolescence: A period beginning with the onset of puberty and ending when individuals assume adult roles and responsibilities.

Puberty: The period of rapid change during which individuals reach sexual maturity.

FIGURE 9.1

From Adolescent to Adult

In many cultures the transition from adolescent to adult is marked by special ceremonies, such as those shown here.

Physical Development during Adolescence

The beginning of adolescence is signaled by a sudden increase in the rate of physical growth. While this *growth spurt* occurs for both sexes, it starts earlier for girls (at about age ten or eleven) than for boys (about age twelve or thirteen). Before this spurt, boys and girls are similar in height; in its early phases, girls are often taller than boys; after it is over, males are several inches taller on average than females.

This growth spurt is just one aspect of *puberty*, the period of rapid change during which individuals of both genders reach sexual maturity. During puberty the *gonads*, or primary sex glands, produce increased levels of sex hormones, and the external sex organs assume their adult form. Girls begin to *menstruate* and boys start to produce sperm. In addition, both sexes undergo many other shifts relating to sexual maturity. Boys develop facial and chest hair and their voices deepen. Girls experience breast enlargement and a widening of their hips; both sexes develop pubic hair. There is great individual variability in all these aspects of development. Most girls begin to menstruate by the time they are thirteen; but for some this process does not start until considerably later, and for others it may begin as early as age seven or eight (Coleman, 1997). Most boys begin to produce sperm by the time they are fourteen or fifteen; but again, for some the process may start either earlier or later.

Facial features, too, often change during puberty. Characteristics associated with childhood, such as large eyes, a high forehead, round cheeks, and a small chin, give way to a more adult appearance (Berry, 1991; Berry & McArthur, 1986). As we'll see in a later discussion of what makes people phys-

FIGURE 9.2

Delaying Entry into Adulthood

In many societies, increasing numbers of persons are delaying the time at which they assume full adult responsibilities, such as moving into their own home and becoming fully self-supporting.

"Your mother and I think it's time you got a place of your own. We'd like a little time alone before we die."

(**Source:** Drawing by Koren; © 1995 The New Yorker Magazine, Inc.)

ically attractive (see Chapter 16), some members of both genders retain relatively childlike facial features, and for females such "baby-faced" appearance can be a plus; many males find it attractive (Cunningham et al., 1995). Being "baby-faced" does not confer such advantages on males, however.

Gender differences also exist with respect to the effects of early sexual maturation. Early-maturing boys seem to have a definite edge over those who mature later. They are stronger and more athletic and often excel in competitive sports. Partly as a result of these advantages, they tend to be more self-assured and popular and are often chosen for leadership roles (Blyth, Bulcroft, & Simmons, 1981). In contrast, early sexual maturation can have negative implications for females. Early-maturing girls are taller than their classmates—frequently taller than boys of their own age—and their increased sexual attractiveness may invite envy from classmates and unwanted sexual advances from older persons (Peterson, 1987). In short, the timing of puberty can play an important role in adolescents' developing self-identities and so in their later social development.

Cognitive Development during Adolescence

As we saw in Chapter 8, adolescents become capable of logical thought. Yet despite this fact, Piaget and other psychologists who have studied cognitive development believe that adolescents' thinking still falls short of that of adults in some respects. Adolescents often use their newfound cognitive skills to construct sweeping theories about various aspects of life; but these theories are somewhat naive, because adolescents lack sufficient information and experience to formulate sophisticated views. Similarly, they continue to show tendencies toward *egocentrism*, often assuming, rigidly, that no other views but their own are reasonable.

The idea that adolescents' thinking is different from that of adults is echoed by many other theorists. For example, Elkind (1967) suggested that adolescents often go seriously astray when they try to imagine the thoughts of other persons. Adolescents often assume that their feelings and thoughts are totally unique—that no one else on the planet has ever had experiences like theirs. Elkind describes this as the *personal fable*, and believes that it is responsible for the difficulties many parents and teachers experience when trying to communicate with teenagers: No matter what the parents say, the adolescents assume that it doesn't apply to them, because they are *different* and *unique*.

While many findings offer support for the view that the thinking of adolescents does indeed differ from that of adults in several respects, perhaps the most intriguing findings in this respect have to do with questions of whether—and to what extent—adolescents think about *risk* differently from adults.

Adolescent Recklessness: Do Adolescents Think Differently Than Adults Do about Risk? Consider these facts:

- In Rio de Janeiro, Brazil, adolescents "surf" on the tops of rapidly moving trains, standing upright with their arms extended.

- On Truk Island in the South Pacific, male teenagers often go spear fishing where large sharks are common.
- Among sexually active teenagers, less than half use contraceptives on a regular basis.
- In the United States, teenagers are 5.11 percent of all drivers but constitute 13.87 percent of all traffic fatalities (National Association of Independent Insurers, 1996).

FIGURE 9.3

Adolescent Recklessness

Adolescents often engage in high-risk behaviors that seem reckless to adults. Several factors probably contribute to this tendency to "live dangerously."

In short, adolescents take a lot of risks—they behave in ways that appear downright reckless to adults (see Figure 9.3), a pattern sometimes known as **adolescent recklessness.** Why? One possibility is that young people believe they are *invulnerable*—that they can't be harmed or suffer injury. I certainly remember feeling this way when I was a teenager. In fact, my friends and I often engaged in actions that make me shiver when I remember them now, almost forty years later—crazy stunts like walking barefoot across the extremely slippery top of a dam over which water was flowing, and where one false step would have plunged us more than one hundred feet to jagged rocks below. Yet careful research on the idea that adolescents feel invulnerable suggests that in reality, they are no more prone to this illusion than adults (e.g., Quadrel, Fischoff, & Davis, 1993). Why, then, do teenagers engage in so many risky behaviors? According to one psychologist who has studied this issue in detail (Arnett, 1995), several factors play a role.

First, adolescents are high in a characteristic known as **sensation seeking**—the desire to seek out novel and intense experiences (e.g., Zuckerman, 1990). Many high-risk behaviors—driving very fast, experimenting with drugs, "living dangerously" where sex is concerned—yield such experiences, and this is what adolescents crave. Second, adolescents do indeed engage in egocentric thinking that leads them to the conclusion that they are somehow "special." Thus, although they don't feel invulnerable, they do tend to believe that what happens to other people probably won't happen to them. For instance, when asked to estimate the probability of becoming pregnant, adolescent girls who have engaged in sex without contraception show a strong tendency to underestimate this likelihood—sometimes with serious consequences (e.g., Arnett, 1992). Finally, adolescent males tend to be aggressive compared to adults, and their aggression often shows up in dangerous driving and criminal behavior—two activities that are certainly reckless and put them at considerable risk.

In the United States today, unfortunately, these sensation-seeking tendencies are often combined with what Arnett describes as *broad socialization*—social practices that encourage individuality and autonomy with a minimum of personal restraint. Who engages in such broad socialization? Nearly everyone and everything with which adolescents have contact. Families often allow adolescents to do pretty much what they please; the media often send the message "Do it *now;* gratify your impulses wherever and whenever they arise." In a similar manner, the legal system is often reluctant to impose harsh sanctions on adolescents who engage in reckless behavior; after all, they are minors. And schools have generally dropped many restrictions such as dress codes. You'll probably find this shocking, but when I was in high school, not only was it required that boys wear slacks and girls skirts or dresses; there were also "silent passings" in which we moved from one class to another without uttering a word. (These were used when, in the judgment of the principal, there was too much noise in the hallways.) I'm not defending these policies—from the perspective of the late 1990s, they do seem excessive. But they were part of a larger effort by society, at the time, to restrain adolescents from expressing their sensation-seeking, egocentric, and aggressive tenden-

Adolescent Recklessness: The tendency for adolescents to engage in forms of behavior that are dangerous or reckless.

Sensation Seeking: The desire to seek out novel and intense experiences.

Key Questions

- What is puberty, and what physical changes does it bring?
- Why do adolescents often engage in reckless behavior?

cies. Such restraints did, indeed, restrict personal freedom; but it's just possible that they saved many young lives, too.

In any case, it is clear that at present, adolescents engage in many forms of reckless behavior. As I'll note in a later section, when this factor is combined with several others that are not of their own making, today's teenagers do indeed seem to be a generation at considerable risk.

Social and Emotional Development during Adolescence

It would be surprising if the major physical and cognitive changes occurring during adolescence were not accompanied by equally major changes in social and emotional development. What are these changes like? Let's see what research on these topics has revealed.

Emotional Changes: The Ups and Downs of Everyday Life

It is widely believed that adolescents are wildly emotional—they experience huge swings in mood and turbulent outbursts of emotion. Is this belief correct? To a degree, it is. In several studies on this issue, large numbers of teenagers wore beepers and were signaled at random times throughout an entire week. When signaled, they entered their thoughts and feelings in a diary. Results indicated that they did show more frequent and larger swings in mood than those shown by older persons (e.g., Csikszenthmihalyi & Larson, 1984). Moreover, these swings occurred very quickly, sometimes within only a few minutes. Older people also show shifts in mood, but theirs tend to be less frequent, slower, and smaller in magnitude.

Other widely accepted views about adolescent emotionality, however, do not appear to be correct. For instance, it is often assumed that adolescence is a period of great stress and unhappiness. In fact, most adolescents report feeling quite happy and self-confident, *not* unhappy or distressed (Diener & Diener, 1996). Moreover, and again contrary to prevalent views, most teenagers report that they enjoy relatively good relations with their parents. They agree with them on basic values, on future plans, and on many other matters (Bachman, 1987). There are some points of friction, of course. Teenagers often disagree with their parents about how they should spend their leisure time and how much money they should have or spend; and to some extent parents and teenagers disagree about sexual behavior, although the gap is not nearly as large as you might imagine (Kelley & Byrne, 1992). In general, though, teenagers are happier and get along better with their parents than is widely assumed.

Social Development: Friendships, Goals and Beliefs, and the Quest for Identity While most adolescents report mainly positive relations with their parents, such family-based relationships are only a part of the total picture in the social development of adolescents. *Friendships*, primarily with members of their own gender but also with members of the other gender, become increasingly important. In fact, most adolescents are part of extensive *social networks* consisting of many friends and acquaintances. Girls tend to have somewhat larger networks than boys, and these networks tend to become smaller and more exclusive as adolescents grow older (Urberg et al., 1995); but for most teenagers, forming friendships and learning about trust and intimacy within them are important aspects of social development.

Since having lots of friends and being popular are increasingly important outcomes for adolescents, it is not surprising that young people soon acquire clear *social goals*—ends they want to achieve in their social relationships. Further, they also form beliefs about how they can attain these goals (e.g., Berndt & Savin-Williams, 1993). What are these goals and strategies like? A study performed recently by Jarvinen and Nicholls (1996) provides some revealing answers.

These researchers asked several hundred high school freshmen (about fourteen years old) to describe their social goals by indicating the extent to which they agreed or disagreed with statements describing a wide range of outcomes. All of the questions began with the phrase "When I'm with people my own age, I like it when . . ." or "I dislike it when. . . ." Careful analysis of the students' replies indicated that they sought six major goals in their social relations. For each general goal, an example of the kinds of statements reflecting the goal is provided below:

- Dominance: "I like it when they are afraid of me."
- Intimacy: "I like it when I can tell them my private thoughts."
- Nurturance: "I like it when I can make their lives easier."
- Leadership: "I like it when I'm in charge."
- Popularity: "I like it when everyone wants me for a friend."

Do these goals sound familiar? They probably do, because these are very much like the kinds of social goals we continue to seek throughout life.

How did the adolescents plan to reach these goals? Another part of the study asked them to indicate the extent to which they agreed or disagreed with statements about strategies for getting along well with others. The major strategies identified were: *Be sincere* (e.g., never pretend to be something you aren't); *have high status* (e.g., be really good looking or good at sports, or have lots of money); *be responsible* (do your homework, work hard); *pretend to care* (pretend to like everyone; tell people what they want to hear); *entertain* (be good at small talk, tell good jokes); *be tough* (push people around; be the toughest). Again, I'm sure these strategies sound familiar; in fact, we'll meet them again in Chapter 16, when we discuss the topic of *social influence* (how people try to get others to do what they want them to do).

Interestingly, some gender differences also emerged in both goals and strategies. For instance, as you can see from Figure 9.4 on page 348, adolescent males were more interested in attaining the goals of dominance and leadership, while females were more interested in intimacy and nurturance. Also, males tended to see social success as stemming mainly from having status, entertaining others, and being tough, while females often viewed such success as dependent on being sincere. As you can see, these findings are consistent with some of the gender differences we discussed in Chapter 8; and once again, although differences do seem to exist, they are not very large.

Friendships and social success also play an important role in another key aspect of social development during adolescence—the quest for a *personal identity*. This process is a key element in a famous theory of psychosocial development proposed by Erik Erikson (1950, 1987)—a theory well worthy of a closer look.

Erikson's Eight Stages of Life Erikson's theory deals with development across the entire life span, so I could have introduced it in Chapter 8. But adolescence in some ways is a bridge between childhood and adulthood, so it makes sense to examine the theory here; we can look back to topics we covered previously, and ahead to ones we'll discuss later in this chapter.

Erikson's theory is, like Piaget's, a *stage* theory: It suggests that all human beings pass through specific stages or phases of development. In contrast to Piaget's theory, however, Erikson's is concerned primarily with social rather than cognitive development. Erikson believed that each stage of life is marked

FIGURE 9.4

Gender Differences in Adolescent Social Goals

As shown here, male adolescents express stronger interest in attaining social goals such as dominance and leadership, while female adolescents express more interest in attaining the goals of intimacy and nurturance.

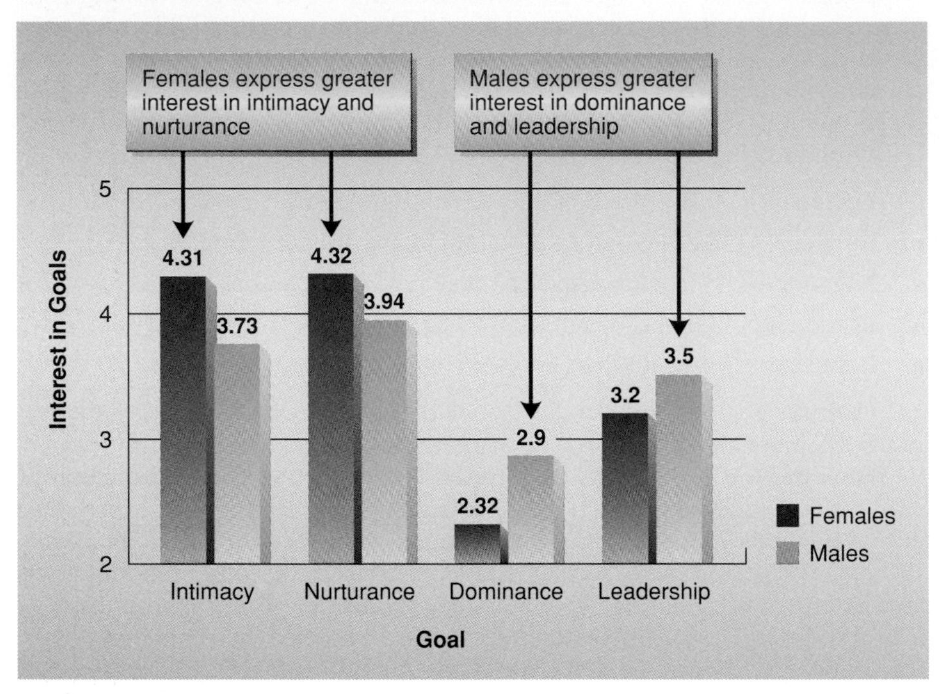

(**Source**: Based on data from Jarvinen & Nicholls, 1996.)

by a specific crisis or conflict between competing tendencies. Only if individuals negotiate each of these hurdles successfully can they continue to develop in a normal, healthy manner.

The stages in Erikson's theory are summarized in Table 9.1. The first four occur during childhood; one takes place during adolescence; and the final three occur during our adult years. The initial stage, which occurs during the first year of life, centers on the crisis of *trust versus mistrust*. Infants must trust others to satisfy their needs. If these needs are not met, infants fail to develop feelings of trust in others and remain forever suspicious and wary.

The next crisis occurs during the second year of life and involves *autonomy versus shame and doubt*. During this time, toddlers are learning to regulate their own bodies and to act in independent ways. If they succeed in these tasks, they develop a sense of autonomy. But if they fail, or if they are labeled as inadequate in some manner by the persons who care for them, they may experience shame and doubt their abilities to interact effectively with the external world.

The third stage unfolds during the preschool years, between the ages of three and five. The crisis at this time involves what Erikson terms *initiative versus guilt*. During these years, children are acquiring many new physical and mental skills. Simultaneously, however, they must develop the capacity to control their impulses, some of which lead to unacceptable behavior. If a child strikes the right balance between feelings of initiative and feelings of guilt, all is well. However, if initiative overwhelms guilt, children may become too unruly for their own good; if guilt overwhelms initiative, they may become too inhibited.

TABLE 9.1

Erikson's Eight Stages of Psychosocial Development

According to Erikson, we move through eight stages of psychosocial development during our lives. Each stage centers on a specific crisis or conflict between competing tendencies.

Crisis/Phase	Description
Trust versus mistrust	Infants learn either to trust the environment (if needs are met) or to mistrust it.
Autonomy versus shame and doubt	Toddlers acquire self-confidence if they learn to regulate their bodies and act independently. If they fail or are labeled as inadequate, they experience shame and doubt.
Initiative versus guilt	Preschoolers (aged 3–5) acquire new physical and mental skills but must also learn to control their impulses. Unless a good balance is struck, they become either unruly or too inhibited.
Industry versus inferiority	Children (aged 6–11) acquire many skills and competencies. If they take pride in these, they acquire high self-esteem. If they compare themselves unfavorably with others, they may develop low self-esteem.
Identity versus role confusion	Adolescents must integrate various roles into a consistent self-identity. If they fail to do so, they may experience confusion over who they are.
Intimacy versus isolation	Young adults must develop the ability to form deep, intimate relationships with others. If they do not, they may become socially or emotionally isolated.
Generativity versus self-absorption	Adults must take an active interest in helping and guiding younger persons. If they do not, they may become preoccupied with purely selfish needs.
Integrity versus despair	In the closing decades of life, individuals ask themselves whether their lives had any meaning. If they can answer *yes,* they attain a sense of integrity. If they answer *no,* they experience despair.

The fourth and final stage of childhood occurs during the early school years, when children are between six and eleven or twelve years of age. This stage involves the crisis of *industry versus inferiority*. During these years, children learn to make things, use tools, and acquire many of the skills necessary for adult life. Children who successfully acquire these skills form a sense of their own competence; those who do not may compare themselves unfavorably with others and suffer from low self-esteem.

Now we come to the crucial stage in Erikson's theory for this discussion of adolescence: the crisis of *identity versus role confusion*. At this time of life, teenagers ask themselves, "Who am I?" "What am I *really* like?" "What do I want to become?" In other words, they seek to establish a clear *self-identity*—to understand their own unique traits and what is really of central importance to them. These, of course, are questions individuals ask themselves at many points in life. According to Erikson, though, during adolescence it is crucial that these questions be answered effectively. If they are not, individuals may drift along, uncertain of where they want to go or what they wish to accomplish.

Adolescents adopt many different strategies to help them resolve their own personal identity crises. They try out many different roles—the good girl/boy, the rebel, the dutiful daughter/son, the athlete, the supercool operator—and join many different social groups. They consider many possible *social selves*—different kinds of persons they might potentially become (Markus & Nurius, 1986). Out of these experiences, they gradually piece

Key Questions

- What goals do adolescents often seek in their friendships?
- According to Erikson, what is the most important crisis faced by adolescents?
- How do psychologists study children's and adolescents' social behavior?

together a cognitive framework for understanding themselves—a *self-schema*. Once formed, this framework remains fairly constant and serves as a guide for adolescents in many different contexts.

The remaining three stages in Erikson's theory relate to crises we face as adults. We'll return to them in our later discussions of adult development. They are summarized in Table 9.1.

How do developmental psychologists study the social behavior of children and adolescents? For information on one newly developed technique, please see the Research Methods section below.

RESEARCH METHODS

How Psychologists Study the Social Behavior of Children and Adolescents

In their efforts to study cognitive development, psychologists focus on the abilities and achievements of single individuals: How much can they remember? How do they reason about moral dilemmas? What factors influence their decisions? Researchers can investigate various aspects of cognitive development under controlled laboratory conditions by asking study participants to work on tasks designed to test memory, reasoning, and so on. Although such tasks are not exactly like the ones people perform in their everyday lives, most psychologists believe that they do tap basic aspects of cognition; thus, results obtained with them can be generalized outside the confines of the research laboratory.

FIGURE 9.5

Studying Social Behavior Where It Naturally Occurs

In order to study aspects of social behavior such as *aggression* in natural contexts, psychologists have developed research methods that use high-tech equipment such as the latest video cameras and wireless microphones.

Social behavior, on the other hand, presents a very different situation. Such behavior, by definition, involves interactions between two or more persons (see Chapter 16). And it is sometimes difficult to observe certain aspects of it in laboratory settings. How do friendships form (e.g., Berndt, 1992)? What makes specific individuals popular (Jarvinen & Nicholls, 1996)? Questions such as these can sometimes only be answered through *naturalistic observation* of behavior in the settings where it normally occurs.

In past decades, such observation involved watching children and adolescents as they interacted with one another and recording their actions on special forms or checklists. More recently, however, developmental psychologists have adapted modern technology for use in the study of social development. One form of social behavior that cannot be studied very readily in the laboratory, and to which such methods seem highly applicable, is *aggression*—actions by children or adolescents designed to harm others in some manner (e.g., Bjorkqvist, Osterman, & Kaukianainen, 1992). To study such behavior, developmental psychologists use video cameras and wireless microphones. As you probably know from your own experience, such devices are now smaller and lighter than ever before. As a result, it is possible to equip children with wireless microphones and to videotape their behavior as they play in natural settings—for example, in school playgrounds, on streets, or in parks. Although studies using such methods are very recent, they have already begun to yield important findings. For instance, Pepler and Craig (1995) found that aggression between children and adolescents is even more common than was previously believed. In fact, they discovered that even among children rated as nonaggressive by their teachers and peers, verbal aggression occurs once every five minutes and physical aggression once every eleven minutes, on average, while children are at play (see Figure 9.5). Among highly aggressive youngsters, rates are even higher: once every three and eight minutes, respectively, for verbal and physical aggression. Other findings are beginning to shed new light on what factors lead to aggressive reactions—and on how teachers, parents, and other adults can effectively reduce their occurrence (e.g., Coie & Jacobs, 1993).

Of course, such methods are far from perfect; they raise important ethical issues, such as whether it is appropriate to wire children for sound and listen in on their conversations, even if they consent to such procedures. Similarly, if researchers observe an incident in which one child seems likely to harm another, can they sit idly by and allow such actions to occur? Shouldn't the researchers intervene or at least alert the children's teacher? Doing so may interfere with the ongoing research, but may also prevent harm. So, as is true with all research methods, there are drawbacks as well as pluses. However, the use of modern sound and video equipment to study social behavior does provide developmental psychologists with one more useful technique for finding out how—and why—we change with the passing years.

Adolescence in the Late 1990s: A Generation at Risk?

Just recently, I reread a book by the famous novelist Pearl S. Buck—a book I first read when I was an adolescent. This novel (*Dragon Seed*) describes the Japanese invasion of China during the 1930s. The story focuses on one family and tells how the invasion brought death and suffering, in one form or another, to all of its members. For instance, the youngest son, aged fifteen, was brutally raped by Japanese soldiers when they failed to find any women in the family's house (the women had already fled to the relative safety of a nearby Christian mission). After this horrendous experience, the boy left home to join rebels in the nearby hills. What's the point of all this? Simply to emphasize the fact that there have been—and continue to be—many periods in the world's history when adolescents have been placed at great risk by war, revolution, plagues, and other frightening and tragic events.

While these events differ greatly, they all can be viewed as catastrophes that arise suddenly and come largely from outside a given culture. Today's adolescents, it can be argued, face a set of different but perhaps equally harmful threats—ones arising from *within* their own cultures. These problems have increased everywhere, but they are perhaps most serious in the United States. Consider a few facts:

- In the last forty-five years, the number of children being raised in fatherless homes has quadrupled (Burrell, 1996).
- Adolescents living in the United States are fifteen to twenty times more likely to die from homicide then their counterparts living in other developed countries (Baron & Richardson, 1994).
- Between 1960 and 1995, the proportion of adolescents suffering from sexually transmitted diseases increased more than fourfold.
- Adolescent females in the United States have a higher risk of pregnancy than adolescents in any other developed country (e.g., Ambuel, 1995).
- The rate of suicide among ten- to fourteen-year-olds has tripled in recent years; it has doubled among fifteen- to nineteen-year-olds (United States Bureau of the Census, 1991).

These and related statistics suggest that today's adolescents face a new set of circumstances—ones very different from those that confronted previous generations. Let's take a closer look at the nature of some of the factors that seem to threaten the welfare of teenagers.

Divorced, Parent-Absent, and Blended Families At present, about half of all marriages in the United States and many other countries end in divorce. This means that a large proportion of children and adolescents will spend at least part of their lives in a one-parent family—typically with their mothers (Norton & Moorman, 1987). Adolescents react to divorce with fear, anxiety, and guilt. They become angry at the remaining parent, wondering, "What did she/he do to make Mommy/Daddy leave?" And sometimes they blame themselves: "Why doesn't he love me anymore?"

The effects of divorce on adolescents' emotional well-being depend on many different factors, including the quality of the care they received before the divorce (Raphael et al., 1990) and the nature of the divorce itself—whether amicable or filled with anger and resentment. The more negative the feelings of the parents toward each other, the more likely is emotional harm to the adolescent (e.g., McCall, 1994).

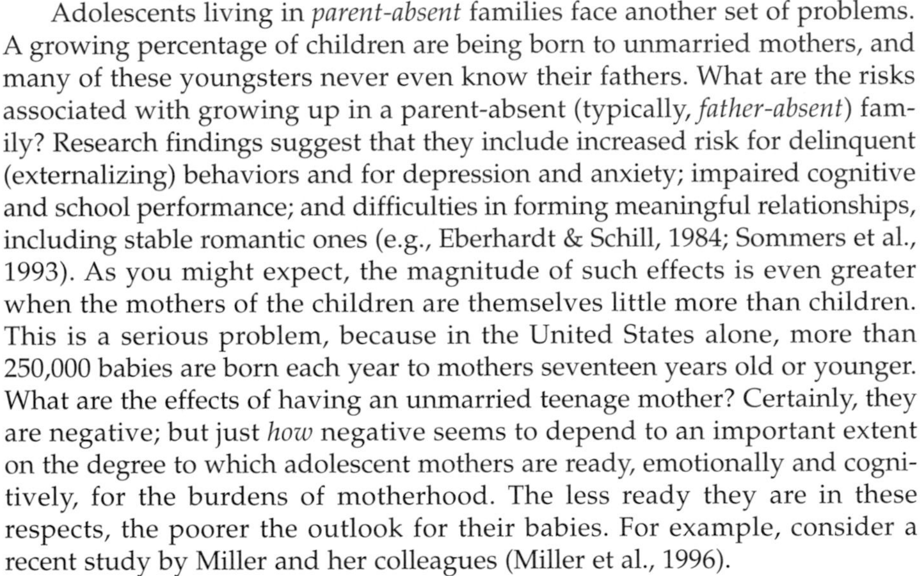

Adolescents living in *parent-absent* families face another set of problems. A growing percentage of children are being born to unmarried mothers, and many of these youngsters never even know their fathers. What are the risks associated with growing up in a parent-absent (typically, *father-absent*) family? Research findings suggest that they include increased risk for delinquent (externalizing) behaviors and for depression and anxiety; impaired cognitive and school performance; and difficulties in forming meaningful relationships, including stable romantic ones (e.g., Eberhardt & Schill, 1984; Sommers et al., 1993). As you might expect, the magnitude of such effects is even greater when the mothers of the children are themselves little more than children. This is a serious problem, because in the United States alone, more than 250,000 babies are born each year to mothers seventeen years old or younger. What are the effects of having an unmarried teenage mother? Certainly, they are negative; but just *how* negative seems to depend to an important extent on the degree to which adolescent mothers are ready, emotionally and cognitively, for the burdens of motherhood. The less ready they are in these respects, the poorer the outlook for their babies. For example, consider a recent study by Miller and her colleagues (Miller et al., 1996).

These researchers interviewed pregnant adolescent girls and asked them to complete questionnaires designed to measure their knowledge about children and the style of parenting they expected to adopt after their baby was born (e.g., how much attention they would pay to their children, whether and to what extent they would use physical punishment). The researchers then used these measures to estimate the extent to which the young mothers-to-be were cognitively ready to be parents—the extent to which they knew what this role would require and how to perform it effectively.

What effects would the mothers' cognitive readiness have on the development of their babies? To find out, the researchers returned when the children were three years old and administered standard measures of cognitive development and language development. Results were clear: The less ready for parenthood the mothers had been more than three years earlier, the poorer the children's performance. Specifically, the poorer the children's cognitive and language development, and the more likely the children were to show depression and anxiety. When we consider the fact that few adolescent girls are truly ready for the burdens and responsibilities of parenthood combined with the large number of babies being born to such mothers, the implications are nothing short of alarming.

What can be done to reduce the number of unplanned births among teenagers? Most psychologists would emphasize such steps as providing teenagers with information about the risks and personal costs of pregnancy, or even, perhaps, making birth control information and devices available to them. In one state, however, a very different approach has recently been adopted:

Idaho teenagers who become pregnant and seek state-funded assistance are being charged as criminals under an old law banning sexual relations between unmarried persons (see Figure 9.6; Hardy, 1996). Fathers, as well as mothers, have been charged and sentenced to terms in prison (although these are generally suspended). Needless to say, these efforts are highly controversial and seem unlikely to succeed. But they do suggest the depth of society's exasperation with this particular form of irresponsible behavior by teenagers.

FIGURE 9.6

Adolescent Mothers: Ready for the Burdens?

Each year, hundreds of thousands of adolescent girls become mothers in the United States. Unfortunately, many are not prepared for the responsibilities of motherhood, either emotionally or cognitively. In one state (Idaho), a highly controversial approach to this problem has been adopted: Teenagers who become pregnant and the fathers of their children are being prosecuted as criminals.

Dysfunctional Families: The Intimate Enemy During the 1950s, television shows in the United States painted a glowing picture of family life. A caring, loving mother, a kind and wise father, considerate siblings—even as a teenager I knew that there was a sizable gap between these images and reality. For many of today's adolescents, however, it's not so much a gap as a chasm. Many teenagers find themselves in what are known as **dysfunctional families**—families that do not meet children's needs and which, in fact, may do them serious harm (Amato, 1990; McKenry, Kotch, & Browne, 1991). Some dysfunctional families are neglectful of or even mistreat children. For example, consider what it is like for adolescents growing up in homes where one or both parents abuse alcohol or other drugs. And try to imagine what it is like for youngsters with parents who suffer from serious psychological problems—problems that may cause them to act in unpredictable, abusive, or even physically threatening ways (e.g., Ge et al., 1995). Clearly such parents do not provide the kind of guidance, consistent control, and support needed for successful development. Recent findings indicate that when these factors are lacking, children and adolescents are at increased risk for a wide range of problems, such as drug abuse and *externalizing behaviors;* for example, stealing, disobedience at home and at school, and overt aggression (Stice & Barrera, 1995).

An even more disturbing form of maltreatment is **sexual abuse**—sexual contact or activities forced on children or adolescents. Unfortunately, sexual abuse is far from rare (Kendall-Tackett, Williams, & Finkelhor, 1993); indeed, large numbers of children become the victims of such betrayal by adults every year. In fact, one recent survey indicated that among pregnant teenagers in the United States, 66 percent had experienced sexual abuse prior to their pregnancy (Ambuel, 1995). Such experiences can produce severe psychological harm. Common among adolescent victims of sexual abuse are depression, withdrawal, running away, and substance abuse (Morrow & Sorell, 1989). The likelihood and magnitude of these harmful effects increase with the frequency and duration of the abuse; when the perpetrator is a close family member, such as father, mother, or sibling; and when overt force is involved (Kendall-Tackett, 1991). Clearly, then, sexual abuse is a very serious problem requiring both energetic prevention efforts and compassionate treatment for its victims.

Overcoming the Odds: Adolescent Resilience Children, it has sometimes been said, are like weeds: They can grow and flourish even in very harsh environments. Some support for this view is provided by studies of children and adolescents who, despite their exposure to truly devastating conditions, develop into competent, confident, healthy adults (Jessor, 1993; Taylor, 1991). Such persons are described as showing **resilience in development:** Somehow, they manage to buck the odds and rise far above the harmful environments they must confront. How do they manage to accomplish this task? Research findings point to the conclusion that they do so because of several *protective factors*—factors that, together, serve to buffer resilient indi-

Dysfunctional Families: Families that do not meet the needs of children and in fact do them serious harm.

Sexual Abuse: Sexual contact or activities forced on children or adolescents by other persons, usually adults.

Resilience in Development: The capacity of some adolescents raised in harmful environments to somehow rise above these disadvantages and achieve healthy development.

FIGURE 9.7

Factors Contributing to Adolescent Resilience

The factors summarized here have been found to contribute to *resilience in development*—the ability to develop normally even in potentially harmful environments.

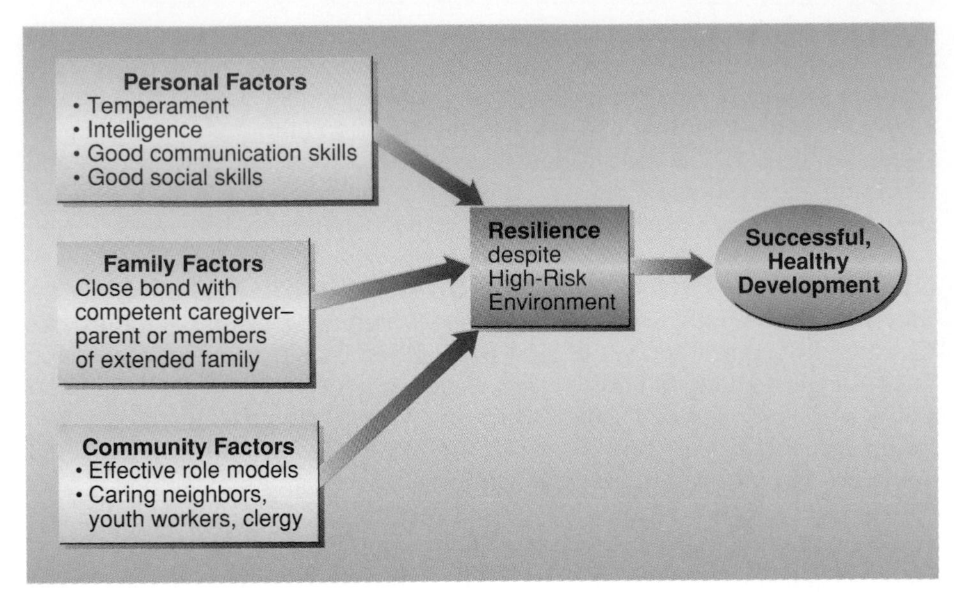

(**Source**: Based on suggestions by Werner, 1995.)

viduals against conditions that would ordinarily be expected to undermine their chances. What are these factors? Research findings (e.g., Werner, 1995) point to the following conclusions.

First, resilience in development stems from protective factors within the individuals themselves. Careful study of such youngsters suggests that they possess traits and temperament that elicit positive responses from many caregivers. They are active, affectionate, good-natured, and easy to deal with. Their "easy" temperament allows them to recruit the help of many competent adult caregivers, who contribute willingly to their development. In addition, such youngsters are often highly intelligent and have good communication and problem-solving skills. The result: They get along well with others and form friendships easily; and these factors, too, contribute to their resilience.

Second, such children and adolescents also benefit from protective factors within their families. Even in a dysfunctional family environment, they have the opportunity to establish a close bond with at least one competent and emotionally stable person. This gives them the sense of trust Erikson views as so crucial to healthy growth. In many cases these bonds are formed not with mothers or fathers, but with other persons in an extended family. What is crucial is not the biological relationship between the adolescent and the adult or adults in question, but rather the fact that these adults serve as models, and provide encouragement for autonomy and initiative.

Finally, resilient youngsters often benefit from protective factors in their community. Favorite teachers are often positive role models for them. Caring neighbors, youth workers, clergy, and others—all can help give adolescents at risk the boost they need to rise above the poverty, shattered homes, and parental instability that mark their early lives. (See Figure 9.7 for a summary of these protective factors.)

When children and adolescents benefit from such protective factors, they *can* beat the odds and develop into competent, confident, responsible, and caring adults—good parents and role models for their own children (Werner, 1995). Clearly, then, providing as many of these protective factors as possible would seem to be a high-priority task for any society that wishes to nurture its children—and so assure its own future stability.

Key Questions

- What are some of the major threats to the well-being of adolescents in the United States today?
- What factors contribute to adolescent resilience—the ability to rise above conditions that threaten healthy development?

Adulthood and Aging

If you live for an average number of years, you will spend more than 70 percent of your life as an adult. How will you change during that period? Obviously, in many different ways. Before turning to these changes, however, let's pause to consider some contrasting views concerning the nature of adult development as a process.

Contrasting Views of Adult Development: Internal Crises, External Life Events, or Active Development Regulation?

The driving mechanism behind change during adulthood has been the subject of considerable debate. On the simplest level, it is possible to argue that we change mainly as a function of the process of living. Small adjustments in response to the everyday events of life may, over time, combine into major change. While this suggestion seems reasonable, psychologists who study adult development have often adopted two other perspectives on adult development. These are sometimes known as the *crisis* (or *stage*) *approach* and the *life-event model*. A third approach, proposed very recently, focuses on the process of *developmental regulation*—individuals' efforts to influence their own development while at the same time adapting to the inevitable facts of growing older.

The Crisis Approach: Erikson's Theory, Part Two We have already reviewed what is certainly the most famous crisis-oriented theory of adult development, the one proposed by Erik Erikson. As you will recall, Erikson (1987) proposed that development proceeds through a series of distinct stages, each defined by a specific crisis. These crises, in turn, result from the fact that as individuals grow older, they confront new combinations of biological drives and societal demands. The biological drives reflect individual growth and physical change, while the societal demands reflect the expectations and requirements of society for people at different ages. During adulthood, Erikson suggested, we pass through three major crises.

Erikson described the first of these as the crisis of *intimacy versus isolation*. During late adolescence and early adulthood, individuals must develop the ability to form deep, intimate relationships with others. This does not mean merely sexual intimacy; rather, it involves the ability to form deep emotional attachments to others. In short, this first crisis of adult life centers on the capacity to *love*—to care deeply and consistently for others. People who fail to resolve it successfully will live in isolation, unable to form truly intimate, lasting relationships.

Erikson called the second crisis of adult life the crisis of *generativity versus self-absorption:* the need for individuals to overcome selfish, self-centered concerns and to take an active interest in helping and guiding the next generation. For parents, such activities are focused on their children. After the children are grown, however, the tendency toward generativity may involve serving as a *mentor* or guide for members of the younger generation, helping them in their careers and lives. People who do not become parents can express generativity by providing help and guidance to young people—students, younger coworkers, nieces and nephews, and so on. Individuals who successfully resolve this crisis and turn away from total absorption with their own lives discover new meaning. People who do not resolve this crisis successfully become absorbed in their own lives and gradually cut themselves off from an important source of growth and satisfaction.

Erikson termed the final crisis of adult development *integrity versus despair*. As people reach the final decades of life, they look back and ask, "Did my life have any meaning?" "Did my being here really matter?" If they are able to answer *yes* and to feel that they reached many of their goals, they attain a sense of integrity. If, instead, they find their lives to be lacking in such dimensions, they may experience intense feelings of despair. As we'll see later, successful resolution of this final crisis can have important effects on how individuals come to terms with their own mortality—the inevitable fact of death—and on their psychological and physical health during the final years of life.

WEB

In sum, according to Erikson and others who view adult development in terms of discrete phases or stages, the major force behind change is a series of crises or transitions we face as we mature and grow older. The way in which we deal with each of these turning points then determines the course and nature of our lives from that point on.

Life-Event Models: Changes in Response to the Occurrence and the Timing of Key Events A sharply different perspective on adult development is offered by the *life-event model*. This approach suggests that people change and develop in response to specific events in their lives and to the times at which these occur. During childhood and even adolescence, such theories acknowledge, development does occur largely in response to an internal *biological clock* that sets the pace of development. During our adult years, however, development occurs in response to important life events such as graduation from school, beginning a career, marriage, parenthood, promotions, and retirement. Thus, development becomes tied much more closely to a *social clock* than to a biological one.

Several life-event models divide important occurrences into two categories: events that are expected, or *normative*, and ones that are unexpected, or *nonnormative* (Neugarten, 1987). Normative events include the ones mentioned above—graduation from school, marriage, parenthood, and so on. Among nonnormative events are divorce, traumatic accidents, the sudden death of loves ones, and the unexpected loss of a long-term job (an increasingly common event in the late 1990s). Normative events, although very important, are generally less stressful and less disruptive than nonnormative ones. The timing of life events, too, is very important (Neugarten, 1987). Most people in a given society expect certain life events to occur during specific periods. In the United States, for example, graduation from college usually occurs when people are in their early twenties, and marriage often follows within a few years of this event—although this pattern seems to be changing. If events occur when they are unexpected—for example, the death of a spouse when a couple is quite young—the stress associated with such life events can be greatly magnified (see Figure 9.8).

FIGURE 9.8

The Timing of Life Events

When important events occur at times when they are not expected to occur—for example, if one becomes a widow or widower while young—they can be quite stressful. As shown here, however, not all departures from the standard pattern are disruptive.

Developmental Regulation: Adjusting Our Goals as We Age A third approach to adult development, proposed very recently (Heckhausen & Schulz, 1995; Heckhausen, 1997), focuses on the fact that throughout life, individuals pursue goals and try to regulate both their own lives and their own development. As they grow older, however, they realize that some goals are no longer attainable. As a result, they may change their goals, making them more appropriate to their actual age, and also tend to become more flexible in terms of adjusting their goals to match the changing realities of adult life. For example, as they grow older, individuals often recognize that certain career goals are less and less likely to be met, so they tend to give this up as unrealistic. Similarly, as they age, many persons shift from focusing on goals concerning *gains* in various areas of life—work and family, to name just two—to goals focusing on avoiding losses in these areas. Growing evidence lends support to these suggestions, so it appears that adult development can also be understood in terms of individuals' active efforts to regulate their own development and come to terms with the changing realities of life in one's 40s, 50s, 60s, and so on (Heckhausen, 1997).

In sum, contrasting perspectives about development during our adult years hold, respectively, that (1) such change occurs in response to a series of internal conflicts or crises, (2) it occurs in response to specific life events and timing of these events, or (3) it occurs partly as a result of individuals' active efforts to regulate their own development. While all these views provide insights into the nature of adult development, many psychologists strongly question the idea that all human beings pass through a discrete series of stages or phases. For this reason, many currently prefer or emphasize either a life-event approach or an approach emphasizing developmental regulation. However, we do seem to be concerned with different tasks at different points in our lives; so Erikson's approach, too, appears to offer insights into change during our adult years. For information on how specific events occurring in a society can also influence adult development, please see the Exploring Gender and Diversity section below.

Life Stages and Societal Events: Evidence for the View That We Are Strongly Shaped by the Events of Our Youth

EXPLORING GENDER & DIVERSITY

All through my childhood, my parents told me stories about events they experienced during World War II. This was hardly surprising, because my father was in the U.S. Air Force and my mother traveled all over the United States in order to be with him until he was sent to England and France. In contrast, though, my grandparents often told me stories about the Great Depression and how it affected their lives. Why did these two generations of my closest relatives focus on different events? One possibility is this: They did so because the experiences we have when we are young—during adolescence and early adulthood—play an especially crucial role in shaping our later development. This is not a new idea; it is closely related to Erikson's belief that events occurring when we are about seventeen to twenty-five years old have a profound influence on our social identity—our sense of who we are. And this idea also fits with other views about the origins of *cohort effects*—differences between groups of people born at different times who had contrasting life experiences as a result of being raised during different decades (e.g., Braungart & Braungart, 1990; Mannheim, 1972). Consistent with this view, I can now see that most of the stories I told my own daughter as she was growing up were about the Vietnam War—an event of great importance to people in my own generation.

Is this view really accurate? Do events in our society that occur when we are young play a special role in our later development? A creative study by Duncan and Agronick (1995) offers clear evidence in support of this suggestion. These researchers reasoned that if this idea about societal events is accurate, then women who were adolescents or young adults when the women's movement emerged in the late 1960s would view it as more important, and be influenced by this movement to a greater extent, than women who were somewhat older at this time. To test this hypothesis, they asked female college graduates of different ages to describe the societal events that were most important in their own lives. As expected, participants generally mentioned events that occurred when they were adolescents or young adults as the most influential. The nature of these varied with the age of the women: Those who graduated from college in

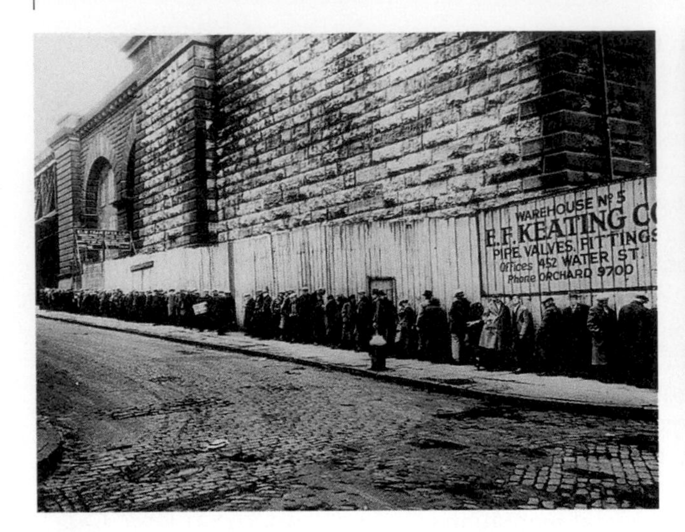

FIGURE 9.9

Societal Events Often Shape Development

When asked to name the societal events that were most important in their own lives, women of different ages identified different events. In general, the events they named were ones that occurred when they were adolescents or young adults. The oldest group identified events such as the Great Depression of the 1930s; younger women named the Civil Rights movement of the late 1950s and early 1960s; and the youngest group pointed to the women's movement of the 1960s and 1970s.

the 1940s chose the Depression and World War II. Those who graduated during the 1950s mentioned the Civil Rights movement and the Kennedy presidency; while those who graduated during the 1960s mentioned the women's movement, AIDS, and issues relating to the environment. Regardless of the specific issues they identified, in almost all cases, the participants pointed to events occurring during their early adult years as the most influential (see Figure 9.9).

That these events really *were* influential in shaping the women's later lives is indicated by other findings reported by Duncan and Agronick (1995). They compared women who rated the women's movement as very influential in their own lives with those who rated it lower in this respect; and they found that at midlife, women in the former group had attained higher work status and income levels and were more confident, assertive, and socially poised. (Both groups had experienced this societal event when in early adulthood or shortly thereafter.)

In sum, it appears that what happens in the world around us when we are young really does matter: Events occurring in our society at this time exert lasting effects on our later development. Perhaps such effects, to a much greater extent than mere differences in age, help explain why persons belonging to different generations sometimes tend to see the world through very different eyes.

Physical Change during Our Adult Years

Looking through a family photo album—one that spans several decades—can be a very revealing experience. There, staring out at you with youthful faces, are your grandparents, parents, aunts, and uncles—and yourself (see Figure 9.10). When you compare their current appearance (or your own) with that in the photos, the scope of the physical changes that occur during the adult years comes sharply into focus.

Physical Change during Early Adulthood Physical growth is usually complete by the time people leave their teens; but for some parts of the body, the process of aging actually begins long before this time. For example, the lenses in our eyes begin to lose flexibility by the time we are only twelve or thirteen years old. For some people, the tissues supporting their teeth have already begun to recede and weaken even before they have attained full physical maturity. So aging, like growth, is a continuous process that starts very early in life.

FIGURE 9.10

Physical Change over the Life Span

As these photos of the author at ages four, seventeen, and fifty-three show, we all change tremendously in appearance over the course of our lives.

Such change occurs quite slowly at first, but then proceeds more rapidly in later decades. Muscular strength, reaction time, sensory acuity, and heart action and output are all at or near their peak through the mid-twenties and then decline—slowly—through the mid-thirties. Many members of both genders do experience considerable weight gain during early adulthood, and some men undergo significant hair loss. By and large, however, physical change is both slow and minimal during this period of life.

Physical Change during Midlife By the time they are in their forties, most people are all too aware of the age-related changes occurring in their bodies. *Cardiac output,* the amount of blood pumped by the heart, decreases noticeably, and the walls of the large arteries lose some degree of flexibility. As a result, less oxygen can be delivered to working muscles within a given period of time, and even people who exercise regularly become aware of some decline in this respect. They simply can't do quite as much as they once could. The performance of other major organ systems, too, declines, and an increasing number of people experience difficulties with digestion. Other changes are readily visible when middle-aged people look in the mirror: thinning and graying hair, bulges and wrinkles in place of the sleek torso and smooth skin of youth. Huge individual differences exist in the rate at which such changes occur, however. While some persons in their forties and fifties closely match common stereotypes concerning middle age (see Figure 9.11 on page 360), others retain much of their youthful appearance and vigor during this period of life.

Among the most dramatic changes occurring during middle adulthood is the **climacteric**—a period of several years during which the functioning of the reproductive system and various aspects of sexual activity change greatly. While both sexes experience the climacteric, its effects are more obvious for females, most of whom experience **menopause**—cessation of the menstrual cycle—in their late forties or early fifties. During menopause the ovaries stop producing estrogens, and many changes in the reproductive system occur: thinning of the vaginal walls, reduced secretion of fluids that lubricate the vagina, and so on. Since females no longer release ova, pregnancy is no longer possible. In the past, menopause was considered to be a stressful process for many women. Now, however, it is widely recognized that cultural factors play a key role in reactions to menopause and its effects, and that for most women around the world it is definitely *not* a disturbing or anxiety-provoking event (e.g., Datan, Antonovsky, & Moaz, 1984).

Among men the climacteric involves reduced secretion of testosterone and reduced functioning of the *prostate gland,* which plays a role in semen formation. In many men the prostate gland becomes enlarged, and this may interfere not only with sexual functioning but with urination. Men often expe-

Climacteric: A period during which the functioning of the reproductive system and various aspects of sexual activity change greatly.

Menopause: Cessation of the menstrual cycle.

rience reduced sexual drive at this time of life; although sperm production decreases, many men are still capable of fathering children.

So far, this picture of physical change during midlife may sound discouraging; strength, beauty, and vigor all decline during this period. But remember: While some physical decline is inevitable during the middle decades of life, both the magnitude and the rate of such decrements are strongly influenced by individual lifestyle. In fact, growing evidence suggests that factors such as physical exercise, personal nutrition, and effective stress management may be better predictors of physical vigor and health than biological age (Roskies, 1987). A fifty-year-old who exercises regularly, eats a balanced diet, doesn't smoke, and avoids weight gain may score higher on many tests of physical fitness than a twenty-five-year-old who gets no exercise, lives on fast food, smokes heavily, and is very overweight. So yes, aging is a fact of life; but no, it's not necessary to say good-bye to vigor, health, and energy in one's thirties or forties. We can maintain health and well-being much longer than was once believed—provided we are willing to make the effort to do so.

FIGURE 9.11

Middle Age: Is It Always Like This?

Contrary to what this cartoon suggests, many middle-aged adults retain much of their youthful vigor and even some of their youthful appearance.

(**Source:** Drawing by R. Chast; © 1994 The New Yorker Magazine, Inc.)

Physical Changes in Later Life

Average age in many countries is currently rising at a steady pace. In the United States, for example, the proportion of the population sixty-five or older has risen from about four or five percent in 1900 to about 12 or 13 percent now; and this figure will increase to almost 20 percent when the baby-boom generation born during the 1950s and 1960s turns sixty-five. This trend brings sharply into focus the question of physical changes during the later decades of life, for the nature of these changes has important implications for health care systems throughout the world.

What picture emerges from research on physical changes in later life? A mixed but somewhat encouraging one. Stereotypes suggesting that people in their sixties, seventies, and eighties are generally frail, in poor health, and unable to take care of themselves turn out to be largely false. A very large proportion of Americans in these age groups report excellent or good health. And these are not simply overoptimistic self-reports. It appears that most people below the age of eighty *are* in reasonably good health and are not much more likely than middle-aged people to suffer from *chronic illnesses*—ones that are long-term, progressive, and incurable (United States Department of Health and Human Services, 1989). Further, even in their seventies and eighties, a large majority of people do not receive hospital care during any given year (Thomas, 1992). In short, the picture of older persons that emerges, at least in developed countries like the United States, is quite encouraging.

One additional point should not be overlooked: While many physical changes do occur with increasing age, it is crucial to distinguish between those that are the result of **primary aging**—changes caused by the passage of time and, perhaps, genetic factors—and those that result from **secondary aging**—changes due to disease, disuse, or abuse of our bodies. Bearing this point in mind, let's briefly examine some of the physical changes that are the result of primary aging.

Primary Aging: Changes in our bodies caused by the passage of time and, perhaps, genetic factors.

Secondary Aging: Physical changes due to disease, disuse, or abuse of our bodies.

Several of these involve decrements in *sensory abilities*. As people age, they experience declines with respect to vision, hearing, smell, taste, and other senses. *Visual acuity*, as measured by the ability to read letters on a standard eye examination chart, drops off sharply after age seventy. In addition, many people experience such changes as slower *dark adaptation* and reduced ability to notice moving targets, such as cars on a highway (Long & Crambert, 1990).

Similarly, auditory sensitivity decreases with age, especially among persons who have worked in noisy environments (Corso, 1977). Declines occur, too, in abilities to identify specific tastes and smells, although these declines do not become noticeable until after age seventy-five (Spence 1981). There is also a general slowing in reflexes and in the speed of responding generally, so *reaction time* increases with age (Spirduso & MaCrae, 1990). Again, however, there are large individual differences: A specific seventy-year-old may still respond more quickly than a specific forty-year-old.

Many of these changes have important implications for everyday activities. For example, consider driving. Accident rates are high among young drivers—perhaps because of the tendency toward recklessness we considered earlier—and then fall to much lower levels through much of adult life. But accident rates rise sharply once again above the age of seventy-five or eighty (Cerelli, 1989). I've seen these statistics in action in my own father's driving. He is close to eighty, and in the past five years, he has gotten into more accidents than he did in the preceding thirty. The same process is at work in other contexts where quick responses are required—for example, in operating dangerous machinery. As reaction time slows, the chance of dangerous accidents rises. Here again, however, the rate at which such changes occur varies greatly from individual to individual.

Key Questions

- How do stage theories (such as Erikson's), life-event theories, and the developmental-regulation approach explain the changes we experience during our adult years?
- At what age are we most influenced by the events occurring in our society?
- What physical changes do men and women experience during early and middle adulthood?
- What physical changes occur in later life?

Cognitive Change during Adulthood

That people change physically across the entire life span is obvious: We can readily see such changes with our own eyes. But what about *cognition?* Do adults change in this respect as well? Our cognitive abilities rest ultimately on biological processes—events occurring within our brains (see Chapters 2 and 6); so it is reasonable to expect some declines in cognitive functioning with age. On the other hand, as we grow older, we also gain in experience, practice with various tasks, and our overall knowledge base. Can these changes compensate for inevitable biological decline? The issue of whether, and how, our cognitive functioning changes with age is more complex than you might at first guess.

Aging and Memory First, let's consider the impact of aging on memory. Research on short-term memory indicates that older people seem able to retain just as much information in this limited-capacity system as young ones—seven to nine separate items (Poon & Fozard, 1980). However, when information in short-term memory must be processed—as, for example, when you try to solve anagrams (word puzzles) in your head—older persons sometimes perform more poorly than younger ones (Babcock & Salthouse, 1990). In addition, if they must perform several short-term memory tasks in a row, older persons often show a greater decline on later tasks than young persons (e.g., Shimamura & Jurica, 1994). Apparently, as we grow older, our ability to deal with the effects of *proactive interference*—interference with materials we are currently entering into short-term memory from materials we entered earlier—declines (e.g., Shimamura et al., 1995).

Turning to long-term memory, it appears that where relatively meaningless information such as nonsense syllables is concerned, young people do sometimes have an edge. This is especially true with respect to *recall*—the ability to bring previously memorized information to mind. Performance on such tasks does seem to decline with age (Hultsch & Dixon, 1990). Such differences are smaller and less consistent with respect to *recognition*—the ability simply to tell whether or not information being presented has been presented before. Still, for many tasks involving long-term memory, there does seem to be some decline in performance with increasing age.

Such effects are less apparent, however, when the information being committed to memory is meaningful—for instance, when it has some connection to individuals' everyday life or to information they want to remember. Here differences between younger and older persons are much smaller and in some studies do not appear at all (e.g., May, Hasher, & Stoltzfus, 1993).

If you have found the information presented so far somewhat encouraging, you will *really* like what comes next. All of the evidence pointing to declines in memory with increasing age has been gathered in studies performed with what have been termed "standard" groups of participants—people who do not engage in strenuous cognitive activities as part of their careers or daily lives—in other words, persons in ordinary walks of life. What about persons who do engage in such activities—who stretch their minds and memories on a daily basis? If mental exercise produces benefits corresponding to those stemming from physical exercise, we might expect that such persons would *not* show declines in memory with age.

In fact, this is precisely what research findings reveal. For instance, in a well-conducted study on this issue, Shimamura and his colleagues (1995) compared the performance on several different memory tasks of university professors in three age groups: professors whose average ages were 38.4 years, 52.2 years, and 64.7 years. The researchers also included undergraduate students and a group of "standard" older persons (average age 66.5 years) in the study. All participants performed several memory tasks: a *paired-associates* task in which they were asked to remember randomly formed pairs of names (e.g., Edward and Nancy); a test of *working memory* in which they were shown an array of visual patterns and asked, on each trial, to point to a different pattern than they had pointed to before; and a *prose recall* task in which they were asked to recall passages dealing with various topics that were read to them once. Results indicated that on the paired-associates task performance decreased with age for both the professors and the "standard" participants. On the test of working memory, however, professors did *not* show an increasing number of errors as the task continued; and on the prose recall task, all three groups of professors—young, middle-aged, and older—performed at the same level. In contrast, for the standard groups, old participants performed more poorly than young ones on both working memory and prose recall (see Figure 9.12).

These findings, and those of related studies, indicate that declines in memory are *not* an inevitable aspect of aging. On the contrary, if we remain intellectually active and exercise our mental abilities, they may be less likely to decline, or may decline to a lesser degree, than if we are mental couch potatoes. So in this respect as in many others, our fate is at least partly in our own hands—if we are willing to expend the effort to seize it!

Aging and Intelligence: Decline or Stability? In the past it was widely believed that intelligence increases into early adulthood, remains stable through the thirties, but then begins to decline as early as the forties. This view was based largely on cross-sectional research that compared the performance of persons of different ages on standard tests of intelligence. Results indicated that in general, the older persons were, the lower their scores tended to be (Schaie, 1974; Thomas, 1992). Unfortunately, such cross-sectional research suffers from a serious drawback. Differences between various groups of participants can stem from factors other than their respective ages, such as differences in education or health. In order to eliminate such

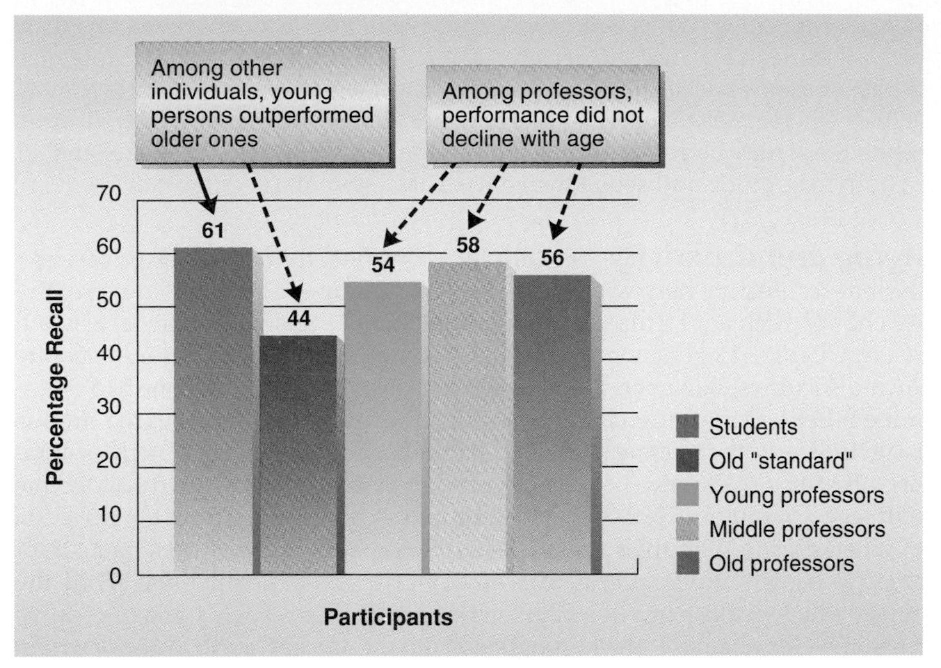

(**Source:** Based on data from Shimamura et al., 1995).

FIGURE 9.12

Evidence That Memory Does Not Necessarily Decline with Age

Three groups of university professors—young, middle-aged, and older—showed approximately the same level of performance on a test of prose recall. These and other findings indicate that persons who frequently engage in strenuous cognitive activities do not experience declines in several aspects of memory with increasing age.

problems, more recent research on aging and intelligence has often employed a longitudinal design. In such research, as you probably recall from Chapter 8, the same persons are tested at several different times over a period of years to see whether there are consistent changes in their performance.

The results of studies using longitudinal procedures have yielded a more positive picture than the earlier cross-sectional studies. Instead of declining sharply with age, many intellectual abilities seem to remain quite stable across the entire life span. In fact, they show relatively little change until persons are well into their sixties, seventies, or beyond. Moreover, some abilities even seem to increase. For example, Schaie and his colleagues (Schaie, 1986, 1990, 1993) have tested thousands of people ranging in age from twenty-five to eighty-one at seven-year intervals. Results clearly indicate that various components (as measured by one standard test of intelligence) remain remarkably stable throughout adult life. Indeed, even at age eighty fewer than half of the persons studied showed any declines during the preceding seven years. Only on tasks involving speed of reasoning do there appear to be consistent declines in performance. Because these drops in performance may reflect increased reaction time—which is known to decline with age (e.g., Shimamura et al., 1995)—there is little if any indication of a general decrease in intelligence with age.

While such findings are encouraging, they are not the entire story. As I'll explain in Chapter 11, standardized intelligence tests may not capture all aspects of adult intelligence. The distinction between *crystallized* and *fluid intelligence* is especially relevant here. **Crystallized intelligence** refers to those aspects of intelligence that draw on previously learned information as a basis for making decisions or solving problems. Classroom tests, vocabulary tests, and many social situations in which we must make judgments or decisions about other persons draw on crystallized intelligence. In contrast, **fluid intelligence** includes the abilities to form concepts, reason, and identify similarities. Research focusing on these two types of intelligence suggests that fluid intelligence increases into the early twenties and then gradually declines. In contrast, crystallized intelligence tends to increase across the entire life span

Crystallized Intelligence: Aspects of intelligence that draw on previously learned information as a basis for making decisions or solving problems.

Fluid Intelligence: Aspects of intelligence that involve forming concepts, reasoning, and identifying similarities.

(e.g., Lerner, 1990; Willis & Nesselroade, 1990). Similarly, there may be little or no decline in *practical intelligence*—the ability to solve everyday problems. In fact, it seems possible that such intelligence, which is very important, may actually increase with age (e.g., Sternberg et al., 1995; see Chapter 11). In sum, while there may be some declines in intelligence with age, these are smaller in both magnitude and scope than age-related stereotypes suggest.

Aging and Creativity Finally, let's consider *creativity*—cognitive activity that results in a new way of viewing or solving a problem. Does creativity change with age? This is a difficult question to answer, because, as we'll see in Chapter 11, this concept is easier to define than to measure. Despite such difficulties, however, there have been several studies designed to determine whether creativity changes with age. Cross-sectional research on this issue indicates that, as measured by standard laboratory tasks (such as coming up with novel ways of using everyday objects), creativity does decline with age (Simonton, 1990). However, other research, focused on the question of when during their lives scientists, authors, poets, and painters make their creative contributions, points to somewhat different conclusions. While the age at which peak creativity occurs varies greatly across fields, many creative persons—for example, psychologists—make their key contributions when they are in their forties and fifties (Simonton, 1990). Further, while the number of creative accomplishments decreases with age, their *quality* does not.

Where does all this leave us? With, I believe, an overall pattern of evidence suggesting that few intellectual abilities decline sharply with age. Some do decrease—especially ones closely related to speed of responding. But others remain quite stable over many years, and others may actually increase as individuals gain in experience. My conclusion: Aging is inevitable, but our minds can and often do remain active until the very end of life. For a summary of what we currently know about the effects of aging on cognition, please see the **Ideas to Take with You** feature.

Key Questions

- What changes in memory occur as we age?
- How do intelligence and creativity change over the life span?

Social Change in Adulthood: Tasks and Stages of Adult Life

Did you ever envy adults when you were a child? I remember having such feelings. Many times, I would think, "I can't wait until I grow up, so I can . . . " and then complete the sentence with phrases such as "stay up as late as I want," "eat whatever I want," "have my own car," and so on. I assumed, as many children do, that one day I would suddenly be converted into an adult and that from that point on, I'd enjoy all the privileges of being totally grown-up. Now, a lot older and—I hope—at least a little wiser, I realize that change actually continues throughout life. While we are declared legally "adult" at a specific age, that's far from the end of the process. On the contrary, we move through many different roles and many different tasks on life's journey. What are these changes like? An influential theory proposed by Levinson (1986) offers some insights.

Life Structure: In Levinson's theory of adult development, the underlying pattern or design of a person's life.

Levinson's Stages of Adult Life Let's begin with a crucial aspect of Levinson's theory—a concept he calls the **life structure.** This term refers to the underlying patterns of a person's life at a particular time: an evolving cognitive framework reflecting an individual's views about the nature and

Ideas to Take with You

Aging and Cognition: Myth and Reality

Short-Term Memory

Short-term (working) memory declines somewhat with age because of the increasing impact of proactive interference; information already in memory interferes with storage of new information.

Long-Term Memory

Memory for meaningless information declines somewhat with age, especially in the case of *recall.* There are smaller declines for *recognition* memory, and for more meaningful materials. Among persons who frequently engage in intellectual activities—those who "exercise" their cognitive systems—declines are much smaller or nonexistent.

Intelligence

Many components of intelligence do *not* decline with age.

Crystallized intelligence—aspects that draw on previously learned information—may actually increase with age.

Fluid intelligence—abilities to form concepts, reason, identify similarities—may decline slowly with increasing age.

Practical intelligence—may increase with age.

Creativity

Creativity may decline with age in some fields, but not in others; this depends on the specific kinds of intellectual tasks performed in a given field.

meaning of his or her life. Work and family are usually central to the life structure, but it may include other components as well—for example, a person's racial or ethnic background, or important external events that provide a backdrop for life, such as economic boom or depression. According to Levinson, individuals have different life structures at different times during their adult years and move from one to another through *transition periods* lasting about five years.

Levinson divides our adult years into four major *eras,* each with its characteristic life structure, and each separated from the next by a transition period. These eras are summarized in Figure 9.13. As you can see, the first transition occurs between the *preadult era,* the time before we are adults, and early adulthood. Taking place between the ages of seventeen and twenty-two, this transition involves establishing one's independence, both financial and emotional. Many people pass through this transition during their college years; other accomplish it when they accept their first job or enter military service. In either case, the transition is marked by such events as establishing a separate residence and learning to live on one's own.

Once this initial transition is complete, individuals enter *early adulthood.* Two key components of their life structure at this time are what Levinson terms the **dream** and the **mentor.** The dream is a vision of future accomplishments—what a person hopes to achieve in the years ahead. Mentors are older and more experienced individuals who help to guide young adults. Both the dream and the mentor play an important part in our early adult years.

At about age thirty, Levinson suggests, many people experience what he terms the *age thirty transition.* At this time, individuals realize that they are nearing the point of no return: If they remain in their present life course, they will soon have too much invested to change. Faced with this fact, they reexamine their initial choices and either make specific changes or conclude that they have indeed chosen the best course.

Now, after the relative calm of the closing years of early adulthood, individuals move into another potentially turbulent transitional period—the **midlife transition.** For most people, this occurs somewhere between the ages of forty and forty-five. *Middle adulthood* is a time when many people must come to terms for the first time with their own mortality. Up until this period, most people view themselves as "still young." After age forty, however, many come to view themselves as the older generation. Levinson's findings suggest that for many persons this realization leads to a period of emotional turmoil. They take stock of where they have been, the success of their past choices, and the possibility of reaching their youthful dreams. This leads to the formation of a new life structure—one that takes account of the individual's new position in life and may involve new elements such as a change in career direction, divorce, or a redefinition of one's relationship with one's spouse. In this new life structure, the individual perceives herself or himself as middle-aged, with all that this implies.

Many persons experience another period of transition between ages fifty and fifty-five, a transition in which they consider modifying their life structure once again—for example, by adopting a new role in their career or by coming to view themselves as a grandparent as well as a parent. However, this transition is often less dramatic than one that occurs somewhere between the ages of sixty and sixty-five. This **late-adult transition** marks the close of the middle years and the start of *late adulthood.* During this transition, individuals must come to terms with their impending retirement and the major life changes it will bring. As they move through this period of readjustment, their life structure shifts to include these changes. They come to see themselves as persons whose working career is over, or almost over, and who will now have much more leisure time to pursue hobbies and other interests.

Dream: In Levinson's theory of adult development, a vision of future accomplishments—what a person hopes to achieve in the years ahead.

Mentor: Older and more experienced individual who helps guide young adults.

Midlife Transition: In Levinson's theory of adult development, a turbulent transitional period occurring between the ages of forty and forty-five.

Late-Adult Transition: In Levinson's theory of adult development, a transition in which individuals must come to terms with their impending retirement.

FIGURE 9.13

Levinson's Theory of Adult Development

According to Levinson's (1986) theory of adult development, individuals move through distinct *eras* of life, each separated from the next by a turbulent *cross-era transition* period.

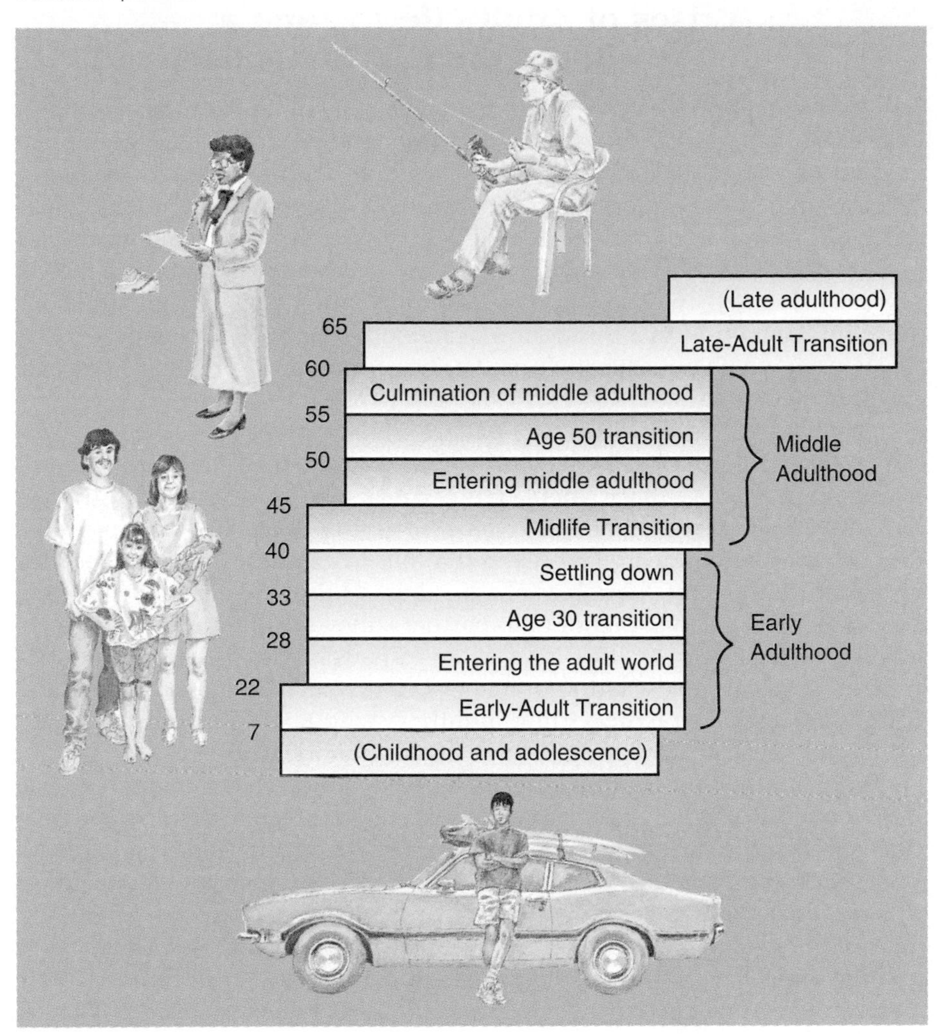

Levinson's Theory: Is It Accurate? In several respects Levinson's picture of social development during our adult years seems to match our commonsense ideas about this process. Relatively long periods of stability are punctuated by shorter, turbulent periods in which we come to terms with changes in our goals, status, and outlook. However, it's important to note that Levinson based his theory primarily on extensive interviews with only forty participants—all men, and all ages thirty-five to forty-five. Critics argue that this is too small and too restricted a sample on which to base such a sweeping framework (Wrightsman, 1988). In addition, of course, it is uncertain whether Levinson's suggestions apply to women as well as men. Women in many societies face a different set of issues and problems as they age. For instance, women, more than men, have the responsibility of caring for their elderly parents; and women, if they have remained at home during at least a portion of child rearing, may find a larger hole in their lives when the youngest child departs—the "empty-nest" effect. We'll return to some of these issues

Key Questions

- In Levinson's theory, what is the life structure and what are the major eras of adult life?
- What criticisms have been directed against Levinson's theory?

below; here, it's important to note that Levinson's theory, though interesting and insightful, remains largely unverified and may be quite incomplete with respect to adult development among females.

Crises of Adult Life . . . and a Little about Personal Happiness

Levinson's theory is a *stage theory*—it suggests that all persons pass through a series of eras and transitions. In contrast, many other researchers have focused on major *events* of adult life and how we are affected by these. Echoing a theme we explored with respect to adolescents—risks to their well-being—I'll now focus on three events that can be viewed as major *crises* of adult life: *divorce, caring for elderly parents,* and *unemployment*. But since there's a lot more to life than crises and the emotional stress they generate. I'll conclude this section with a discussion of personal *happiness,* focusing on the questions of whether most people are happy or unhappy with their lives, and why this may be so.

Divorce Divorce rates in the United States and many other countries are at very high levels. In fact, about half of all first marriages end in divorce (Glick, 1989). Clearly, divorce is a very upsetting event for most persons. Families are shattered, a relationship that has lasted years or even decades has ended, and a difficult process of adjusting to life alone must begin. While these effects are devastating for both partners, they are often much worse for females, who usually shoulder most of the responsibilities for raising the children, often under greatly reduced financial circumstances. Indeed, legislation designed to reduce the proportion of fathers who fail to pay child support has recently been enacted in the United States and other countries.

What are the causes of divorce? Long-term studies have compared couples who remain happily married with those who ultimately divorce, and provide insights into this important question. On the positive side, people who report being happy in their marriage indicate that they agree with their spouse on aims, goals, and even sex; that they genuinely *like* their spouse; that they are committed to the relationship and want it to succeed; that they share many positive experiences with their spouse; and that they are proud of their spouse's achievements (Fincham & Bradbury, 1993; Lauer & Lauer, 1985).

In contrast, couples who divorce recognize and are disturbed by dissimilarities between them—basic disagreements about goals, lifestyles, sex, and many other matters (Levinger, 1988). Persons in unhappy marriages report high levels of boredom in their relationship and say that their spouse no longer fills their needs for affection, esteem, or approval (e.g., Cottrell, Eisenberg, & Speicher, 1992). In addition, they often have strong feelings of *sexual jealousy*—concerns that their spouse is transferring, or will soon transfer, his or her affections to another person (Buunk, 1995).

Other factors associated with divorce include low income, a brief courtship, unrealistic expectations about the relationship, and pregnancy at the time of marriage (Kurdek, 1993). Finally, there is even some indication that the tendency to get divorced is affected by genetic factors. In one study on this issue, McGue and Lykken (1992) compared the divorce rates of hundreds of monozygotic (identical) and dizygotic (nonidentical) twins whose parents were or were not divorced. They found that among monozygotic twins, if one twin was divorced, it was likely that the other twin, too, was divorced; this tendency for twins to be similar with respect to divorce was much weaker among dizygotic twins—who, of course, do not share an identical genetic makeup. How can genetic factors influence divorce? McGue and Lykken (1992) suggest that some individuals may inherit personal characteristics that make it difficult for them to maintain long-term relationships. These characteristics remain to be identified, but it seems possible that they are related to temperament; as we saw in Chapter 8, some children are "difficult"—fussy, irritable, and hard to soothe. Perhaps such traits continue into adult life and make the persons who possess them poor choices as marriage partners—and likely candidates for divorce. At present there is no firm evidence for such conclusions, but they do seem to fit with the results of many studies on temperament and its effects on attachment (e.g., Shaver & Hazan, 1994).

Caring for Elderly Parents You have probably heard a great deal about the "baby boom" generation. This is the generation born between 1946 and 1964, which is now the largest single segment of the population in the United States and many other countries. Baby boomers in the United States enjoyed many advantages because they grew up during a period of relative prosperity. As a result, they have high expectations concerning the lifestyle they will lead. This has led to an intriguing development: Unlike previous generations, many baby boomers remain financially dependent on their parents long after they leave home (Duff, 1996). A much higher proportion than in the past continues to receive money—often substantial sums—from their parents, even as the boomers move into their forties and fifties. Despite such changes, there is one responsibility many baby boomers are now beginning to face, which is a key crisis of adult life: caring for their aging parents (see Figure 9.14).

Although I'm not a baby boomer (I was born in 1943), I came face-to-face with this problem myself when my wife's mother became seriously ill. As is typical, much more of the burden of caring for my mother-in-law was borne by my wife than by her brother. The result: Our lives were seriously disrupted as my wife flew back and forth between South Carolina, where she grew up and her parents live, and upstate New York. The emotional and financial burdens of caring for aging parents can be tremendous, regardless of whether they are in a nursing home or living at home. Government programs help to defer the costs, and the hospice movement—a network of organizations that care for terminally ill patients—is of major assistance. But clearly, this remains one of the crises of adult life, and one almost all people ultimately face.

FIGURE 9.14

Caring for Aging Parents: One Crisis of Adult Life

At some point during middle age, most persons find that they must begin to care for their elderly parents. The emotional and financial burdens of this task often constitute an important crisis of adult life.

Unemployment As I'll note again in Chapter 17, work is one of the most central activities in most people's lives. When asked "Who are you?" a large proportion of employed adults reply in terms of their job or occupation (Greenberg & Baron, 1997). Thus, it is not surprising that losing a job—or even the prospect of losing a job—is very stressful for most people (Konovsky & Brockner, 1993). Unfortunately, this is an increasingly common experience for adults in the 1990s. In the United States and else-

where, many companies have greatly reduced the number of persons they employ through a process known as *downsizing* (sometimes euphemistically called *rightsizing*; Hendricks, 1992). How big a problem is this trend? The following statistic should give you a clear idea: *Since 1979, the largest companies in the United States have eliminated more than 4.4 million jobs* (Swerzgold, 1993). The result is that the term *downsizing* has taken on a very frightening meaning for tens of millions of working women and men, who worry every day where the corporate ax will fall next and whether, if it does, they will be able to find another job (Stewart, 1995).

One new feature of this widespread loss of jobs is that, for the first time since the Great Depression of the 1930s, it has fallen heavily on white-collar employees. Being unemployed is a new and devastating experience for people who formerly held excellent jobs and enjoyed numerous fringe benefits. Many of these newly unemployed are males in their forties and fifties, and because being employed is so central to their self-concept, their self-esteem is torn to shreds by the experience of being unemployed (see Figure 9.15). Indeed, studies on the effects of unemployment (e.g., Winefield & Tiggemann, 1991) indicate that this experience has negative effects on both the psychological and the physical health of the persons who experience it. Fortunately, there are steps individuals can take to cope with this problem and to assure that if their own job is eliminated, they can bounce back quickly. We'll examine these in the Making Psychology Part of Your Life section at the end of this chapter.

Subjective Well-Being: Who Is Happy and Why Quick—answer this question: "How satisfied with your life are you? Are you very satisfied? Satisfied? Not very satisfied? Not at all satisfied?" What was your

FIGURE 9.15

The Devastating Effects of Unemployment

When individuals who have had good jobs for many years lose their jobs through downsizing, the experience can be devastating to their self-esteem. Unfortunately, massive layoffs by many large companies made this an all-too-common experience in the 1990s.

reply? If you are like most people—a large majority, in fact—you probably indicated that you are satisfied with your own life. In fact, recent studies (e.g., Diener & Diener, 1996; Myers & Diener, 1995) suggest that something like 80 percent of all people who answer this question report being satisfied. In other words, they report relatively high levels of what psychologists term **subjective well-being**—personal happiness. Moreover, this seems to be true all over the world, across all age groups, at all income levels above grinding poverty, among relatively unattractive persons as well as among attractive ones (Diener, Wolsic, & Fujita, 1995), and in all racial and ethnic groups (e.g., Myers & Diener, 1995). Of course, some differences exist: Married people generally report being somewhat more satisfied with their lives than single persons (Lee, Seccombe, & Shehan, 1991), and people in some countries—for instance, the United States—report being happier and more satisfied with their lives than those in others—Japan and France, to name just two (Veenhoven, 1993). But amazingly, even among persons who are severely disabled (Hellmich, 1995); persons who belong to racial and ethnic minorities that have been the target of long-standing prejudice, such as African Americans (Myers & Diener, 1995); and persons who have just enough money to buy the necessities of life (Inglehart, 1990), large majorities report being satisfied with their lives.

Subjective Well-Being: Personal happiness.

Do such results stem, at least in part, from the way in which subjective well-being is measured? In other words, would different results be obtained if individuals were asked to rate their personal happiness in other ways? Apparently not. To test this possibility, Diener and Diener (1996) compared the results obtained with several different measures of subjective well-being. These included the single-question self-report measure described above ("How satisfied with your life are you these days?"); ratings of individuals' happiness by members of their family and friends; an *experience-sampling* measure, in which individuals were beeped at random times during the day and asked to report their current moods; and a measure of whether individuals remembered more positive or more negative events in their own lives. As you can see from Figure 9.16 on page 372, no matter what kind of measure was used, large majorities reported high levels of subjective well-being.

While such findings are certainly encouraging, they raise an intriguing question: *Why* are people so satisfied with their own lives? Research on this issue has just begun, so no firm answers are yet available. However, two possibilities seem promising. First, it may be the case that high levels of subjective well-being reflect the fact that most people are in a relatively good mood most of the time. Being in a good mood is adaptive from the point of view of survival, because it helps negative events or experiences stand out and be noticed; and of course these are the events that require our attention.

Second, feeling happy may be important for motivating behavior. Only when people are in a relatively positive state can they approach and explore new situations and stimuli, and seek out new contacts with others. We'll discuss motivation in detail in Chapter 10; but if you think about how everything seems to be a great effort on days when you are feeling "down," you will see why feeling happy may be important for many of our activities (Diener & Diener, 1996).

Whatever the precise reasons, it does seem clear that most people are satisfied with their lives and express relatively high levels of subjective well-being. Despite the many negative events that occur during our adult years, therefore, we tend to retain a degree of optimism and a positive outlook on life. Fortunately for us, the poet Theodosia Garrison was correct when she wrote: "The hardest habit of all to break / Is the terrible habit of happiness."

Key Questions

- What differences exist between the behaviors of happily married couples and those of couples who ultimately divorce?
- What are the effects of unemployment on the psychological and physical health of persons who lose their jobs?
- To what extent are people satisfied with their lives, and does such happiness vary greatly across different groups?
- What factors may explain the prevalence of high levels of subjective well-being?

FIGURE 9.16

Who Is Happy? Most Persons, It Appears

No matter what kind of measure is used, most people report fairly high levels of personal happiness or *subjective well-being.*

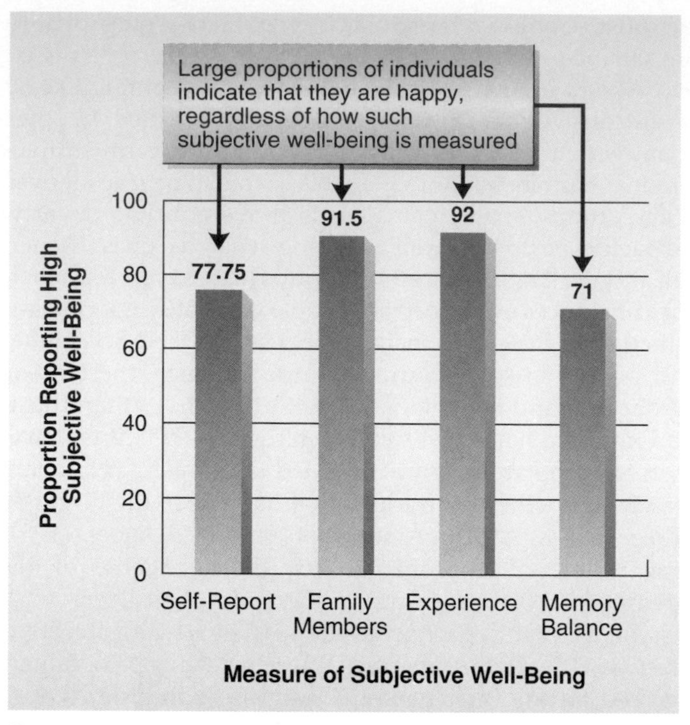

(**Source**: Based on data from Diener & Diener, 1996.)

Aging, Death, and Bereavement

Since ancient times, human beings have searched for the "Fountain of Youth"—some means of prolonging youth, and life, indefinitely. But, sad to relate, such dreams have remained only illusions; while life and health *can* be prolonged (see Chapter 13), there is no way to live forever. In this section we'll consider several questions relating to the close of life: (1) What, specifically, are the causes of aging and death? (2) How do terminally ill people react to their own impending death? and (3) how do survivors cope with the loss of their loved ones?

Theories of Aging: Contrasting Views about Why We Grow Old

Many different views about the causes of aging have been proposed, but most fall under one of two major headings: *wear-and-tear theories* and *genetic theories.*

Wear-and-Tear Theories of Aging: Theories suggesting that aging results from the continual use of cells and organs in our bodies.

Wear-and-Tear Theories of Aging The first group of views, **wear-and-tear theories of aging,** suggests that we grow old because various parts of our bodies, or the cells of which they are composed, wear out. One such theory emphasizes the role of *free radicals*—atoms that are unstable because they have lost electrons. According to this theory, these highly unstable particles are continuously produced by body metabolism; once formed, they react violently with other molecules in cells, thus producing damage. When this damage affects DNA, free radicals can interfere with basic aspects of cell maintenance and repair. The theory proposes that this damage cumulates over time, thus producing the declines associated with aging. Other wear-and-tear theories focus on different mechanisms, but the outcome—cumulative damage to cells and organs—is much the same.

Indirect evidence for wear-and-tear theories of aging is provided by individuals who repeatedly expose their bodies to harmful substances or conditions—for instance, large doses of alcohol, various drugs, or harsh environments. Such persons often show premature signs of aging, presumably because they have overloaded their bodies' capacity for internal repairs.

Genetic Theories A second group of theories attribute physical aging primarily to genetic programming. According to **genetic theories of aging,** every living organism contains some kind of built-in biological clock that regulates the aging process. Where is this clock located? Recent findings suggest that it may involve, at least in part, strips of DNA that cap the ends of our chromosomes—**teleomeres** (Gladwell, 1996). Each time a cell divides, the teleomere becomes shorter; when it reaches some critical point, the cell can no longer divide, and this may contribute to the aging process. For instance, in skin cells, when the teleomeres are shortened to a critical length, the cells cannot divide, so normal repair processes that keep the skin healthy and young-looking begin to break down. Another genetic theory, *gene mutation theory,* suggests that genetic mutations that interfere with normal cell functioning occur throughout our lives. When these mutations reach high levels, death results.

Support for genetic theories is provided by the finding that certain cells do indeed divide only a set number of times before dying. Moreover, no environmental conditions seem capable of altering this number.

Which of all these genetic and wear-and-tear theories is most accurate? None is supported by sufficient evidence to be viewed as conclusive. The best scientific guess at present is that aging is caused by several different mechanisms and results from a complex interplay between environmental and genetic factors.

Meeting Death: Facing the End of Life

What is death? The answer to this question is more complex than you might suspect. First, there are several kinds of death. *Physiological death* occurs when all physical processes that sustain life cease. *Brain death* is defined as a total absence of brain activity for at least ten minutes. *Cerebral death* means cessation of activity in the cerebral cortex. And *social death* refers to a process through which other people relinquish their relationships with the deceased (Thomas, 1992).

Second, there are complex ethical issues connected with death. Should dying patients have the right to choose their hour of death? Should physicians be allowed to help such individuals die? And if people have the right to choose, must they express this right before they are seriously ill, in *living wills?* As you may know, these issues have received a great deal of attention in the United States lately, partly because of the efforts of one physician, Dr. Jack Kevorkian (sometimes known as "Doctor Death"). He has campaigned long and hard for laws that guarantee terminally ill patients the right to choose when to die (see Figure 9.17 on page 374). These are complex questions, only partly within the realm of science. I raise them here simply to remind you that death involves much more than a biological event.

Genetic Theories of Aging: Theories that attribute physical aging primarily to genetic programming.

Teleomeres: Strips of DNA that cap the ends of chromosomes, and which seem to regulate the number of times a cell can divide.

FIGURE 9.17

Death on Demand?

Should individuals have the right to die when they choose—for instance, to end medical treatment that is sustaining their lives? Dr. Jack Kevorkian, a physician sometimes known as "Dr. Death," has worked vigorously to make this option legal for terminally ill patients.

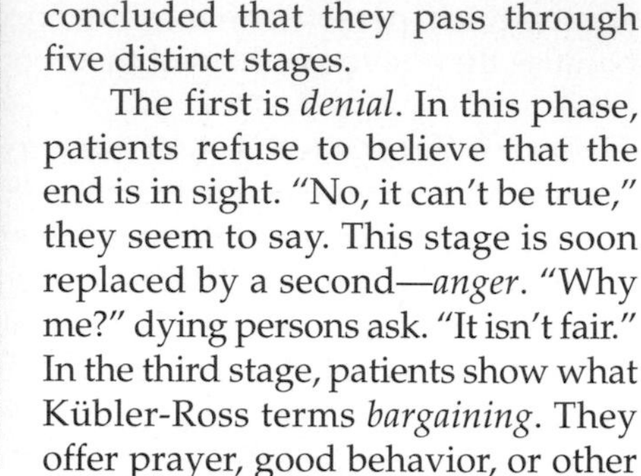

But given that death is the inevitable end of life, how do persons confronted with their own impending death react? Perhaps the most famous study of this subject was conducted in the late 1960s by Elizabeth Kübler-Ross (1969). She studied terminally ill patients and, on the basis of extensive interviews with them, concluded that they pass through five distinct stages.

The first is *denial*. In this phase, patients refuse to believe that the end is in sight. "No, it can't be true," they seem to say. This stage is soon replaced by a second—*anger*. "Why me?" dying persons ask. "It isn't fair." In the third stage, patients show what Kübler-Ross terms *bargaining*. They offer prayer, good behavior, or other changes in lifestyle in exchange for a postponement of death. Unfortunately, such efforts cannot alter physical realities; so when it becomes apparent that their best efforts to make a deal with death have failed, many dying persons enter a stage of *depression*.

That's not the end of the process, however. According to Kübler-Ross, many people ultimately move into a final stage she labels *acceptance*. At this stage, dying persons are no longer angry or depressed. Instead, they seem to accept their impending death with dignity; they concentrate on saying goodbye to important persons in their lives and putting their affairs in good order.

Although these findings are comforting and appealing, they have not been confirmed by other researchers. For example, Aronoff and Spilka (1984–1985) videotaped terminally ill patients at various points during their illness and examined their facial expressions for evidence of Kübler-Ross's five stages. They found an increase in sad expressions over time, but no evidence that these persons became calmer or happier as their deaths approached. Other researchers have found somewhat different patterns, such as expressions of hope throughout a terminal illness (Metzger, 1980). In view of these findings, and in light of the fact that Kübler-Ross used relatively informal methods in her research (she is a psychiatrist, not a psychologist), it seems best to view her conclusions with caution. They are intriguing, and they certainly hold out hope that many of us can meet death in a dignified manner. However, they cannot be viewed as scientifically valid unless they are confirmed by further research.

What factors are related to longevity—living a long life? For some information on this issue, please see the Beyond the Headlines section.

Bereavement: Coming to Terms with the Death of Loved Ones

My grandfather was almost ninety-three when he died, and he was healthy and vigorous almost until the end. But one day he said something I'll remember the rest of my life: "Bobby, I feel so alone. Almost everyone I loved is gone." He was correct; by the time he died, his wife, his sister, and all his lifelong friends were long gone. So my grandfather had more than his share of **bereavement**—grieving for the loss of persons who were dear to him.

Bereavement: The process of grieving for the persons we love who die.

Beyond the Headlines

As Psychologists See It

The Secret of Long Life? Be Dour and Dependable

New York Times, November 11, 1993—Score one for those pious voices of prudence; being cautious and somewhat dour is a key to longevity, according to a 60-year study of more than 1,000 men and women. Those who were conscientious as children were 30 percent less likely to die in any given year of adulthood than their most freewheeling peers. But those who were ebullient in childhood fared less well in life's roulette wheel; they were about 6 percent more likely to die in any given year than the least cheerful children. . . .

Personality and the Human Lifespan

Interesting—a link between personality and longevity? Can this be so? In this case, the headline is accurate. It is based on the results of a longitudinal study of 1,528 bright California boys and girls that began in 1921. These individuals, who were about eleven years old when the study began, have been tested repeatedly for more than seventy-five years. The length of this study provides psychologists with the opportunity to determine whether aspects of personality, and many other factors, are related to how long people live. In a recent report summarizing findings through the mid-1990s, Friedman and his colleagues (Friedman et al., 1995) reported that one significant predictor of longevity was an aspect of personality known as *conscientiousness*. We'll return to this, and other aspects of personality, in more detail in Chapter 12. Briefly, however, conscientiousness refers to the tendency to be neat, orderly, and dependable. Conscientious children, for instance, get their homework done on time and keep their rooms neat. They set goals and fulfill them, and they generally don't take many risks. In the California study, persons high in this characteristic have been fully *30 percent less likely to die in any given year* than persons low in this trait. Why should conscientiousness be related to living a long time? Perhaps because people high in conscientiousness are less likely to drink alcohol to excess, to smoke, and to engage in other behaviors that put their own health at risk. While this is certainly true up to a point, it does not seem to be the entire story, because even when such factors are taken into account, persons high in conscientiousness still seem to live longer. So perhaps conscientiousness is a reflection of some underlying biological factor that itself is linked to long life.

Other findings of the study indicate that parental divorce may be another significant predictor of longevity. Regardless of personality, participants whose parents divorced have tended to die younger than those whose parents did not divorce. When this factor is combined with personality, dramatic results emerge: Men who were low in conscientiousness in childhood and whose parents divorced when they were children showed a 40 percent probability of dying by age seventy. In contrast, for men who were high in conscientiousness and whose parents did not divorce, this probability was less than 30 percent (see Figure 9.18 on page 376).

In sum, longevity seems to be affected by many different factors—and, contrary to what many medical reports seem to suggest, regular exercise and low cholesterol levels are not all of them. On the contrary, how long we live seems to be linked to aspects of our personality and to events we experience early in life.

Critical Thinking Questions

1. The participants in research conducted by Friedman and his colleagues are a highly selected group of persons—all far above average intelligence, and all raised in California. Do you think that these factors may have influenced the findings of the research?
2. Certain aspects of personality seem to be related to longevity. Do you think that individuals can change their own personalities in order to cultivate more of the traits linked to living a long life?

FIGURE 9.18

Predicting Longevity

Research findings indicate that certain aspects of personality and certain life events can significantly affect how long we live. As shown here, men who were low in conscientiousness and whose parents divorced when they were children had a greater chance of dying by age seventy than men who were high in conscientiousness and whose parents did not divorce.

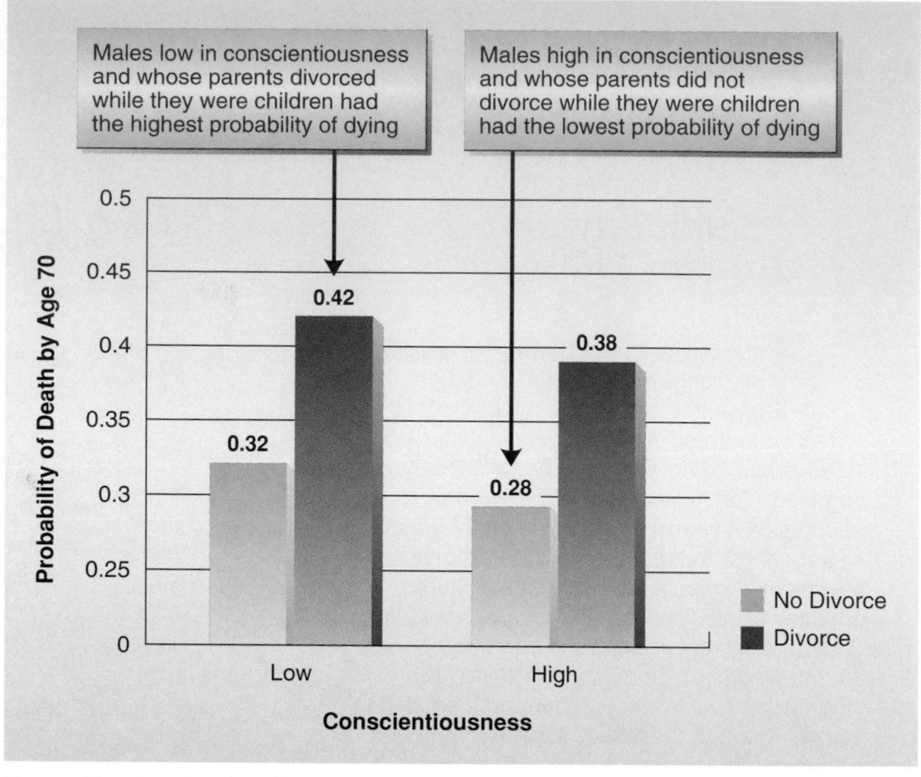

(**Source:** Based on data from Friedman et al., 1995.)

Because bereavement is an experience most adults have, it has been studied in detail by psychologists (Norris & Murrell, 1990). This research suggests that bereavement is a process in which individuals move through a series of discrete stages. The first is *shock*—a feeling of numbness and unreality. This is followed by stages of *protest* and *yearning*, in which bereaved persons resent the loss of their loved one and fantasize about the loved one's return. These reactions are often followed by deep *despair*, which can last a year or more—a period when bereaved persons feel that life is not worth living. Finally, bereaved persons usually enter a state of *detachment and recovery*, in which they separate themselves psychologically from the loved person who has died (e.g., Hart et al., 1995) and go on with their lives. Even during this stage, however, painful bouts of grieving may recur on birthdays, anniversaries, and other occasions that remind the bereaved person of his or her loss.

Recent research on bereavement has focused on how persons who care for individuals dying from AIDS react to their loss. For instance, in one study on this issue, Folkman and her colleagues (Folkman et al., 1996) interviewed the male partners/caregivers of gay male AIDS patients on several occasions: one month before the partner's death; shortly after his death; and three, five, and seven months later. During these interviews the researchers collected data on many factors that might play a role in bereavement and in the caregiver's coming to terms with grief, such as his physical and mental health, his personal traits, and the social resources available to him (e.g., support from family, friends, and/or other individuals and agencies in the community). Results indicated that grief declined during the course of the study, as caregivers came to terms with the loss of someone they loved. The speed with which this process occurred, however, was influenced by many factors. For example, starting out with a very high level of grief or depression prior to the partner's death and finding positive meaning in the process of caregiving led to faster declines in grief after the partner's death. In contrast, being HIV positive oneself, having been in a long-term relationship with the partner, and blaming oneself for events during caregiving led to slower declines in grief and depression. Interestingly, although the participants in this study were homosexual males, many of the findings obtained are very similar to those of studies of bereavement in spouses, parents, and children (e.g., Wortman, Carnelley, & Kessler, 1994).

Taken as a whole, the findings reported by Folkman and her colleagues (1996) and those of other researchers suggest that bereavement is a painful process, but one from which most persons recover within a year. The loss of persons we love is one of the true sorrows of life; but, as one Italian saying puts it, "Life," nevertheless, "continues."

Key Questions

- How do wear-and-tear and genetic theories account for aging and death?
- According to Kübler-Ross, what stages do terminally ill persons pass through when confronting their own death?
- What psychological and social factors have recently been found to play a role in longevity?
- What are the major stages of bereavement?
- What factors influence the bereavement of male partners/caregivers of men who die from AIDS?

Making Psychology Part of Your Life

Preparing for Tomorrow's Job Market Today

In recent years, up to 30 percent of new college graduates have either failed to find a job or been forced to accept one for which they were overqualified. Faced with the uncertainties of today's and tomorrow's job market, are there any steps you can take to increase your chances? Fortunately, there are. Several of these are summarized below. While they can't guarantee that you'll get the job you want, they *can* give you an edge in an increasingly competitive world.

1. **Choose a field with a future.** The job market is changing—rapidly. This means that if you want a good job, you must choose your field carefully. Specifically, you should consider a career in areas of the economy that promise to grow rapidly. What are these? Fields such as computer engineering, physical therapy, teaching (especially special education and preschool), occupational therapy, speech pathology, and—I'm happy to report—psychology. These are not the only fields where growth is forecast, but they are the ones in which the most growth is expected to take place in the foreseeable future.
2. **Focus on small and medium-sized companies.** In the past, many graduates sought jobs with large companies—those with a big reputation and lots of glamour. Unfortunately, those are precisely the companies that have downsized most in recent years. A better bet, then, is smaller and less well-known companies, which also happen to be growing the fastest.
3. **Be ready to work for a foreign-owned company.** In the United States and many other countries, multinational corporations are expanding their operations. Working for a foreign-owned company means that you must learn much about another culture and how it conducts business; but it may open many opportunities for you, both at home and abroad.
4. **Consider part-time or contract work as a way to get started.** As companies have downsized, they have hired part-time and contract (self-employed) persons to fill the gaps. The advantages to companies are obvious: Such employees usually don't receive expensive fringe benefits. However, it is often the case that when the people in a company like a part-time or contract worker, they manage to hire this person full-time. So don't reject part-time or temporary work: It is often a way to get your foot in the door.
5. **Think of any job as a potential learning experience.** The days when individuals were hired by a company and stayed with it for their entire career are largely over. This means that you should think of your career as a series of jobs, each of which provides you with opportunities to expand your skills and knowledge. The greater your knowledge and experience, the more desirable you will be as a potential employee. So keep this approach in mind as you search for a job.

Summary and Review of Key Questions

Adolescence: Between Child and Adult

- **What is puberty, and what physical changes does it bring?** Puberty, the most important feature of physical development during adolescence, is a period of rapid change and growth during which individuals attain sexual maturity.
- **Why do adolescents often engage in reckless behavior?** Recent findings indicate that such behavior does not necessarily stem from feelings of invulnerability on the part of adolescents. Instead, it seems to stem from their tendencies toward sensation seeking, egocentric thinking, and aggressiveness.
- **What goals do adolescents often seek in their friendships?** Goals adolescents seek include dominance, intimacy, nurturance, leadership, and popularity. Teenagers believe that these social goals can be reached through specific strategies, although both goals and strategies differ somewhat between the two genders.
- **According to Erikson, what is the most important crisis faced by adolescents?** Erikson suggests that this crucial crisis is that of identity versus role confusion: the need to establish a clear self-identity.
- **How do psychologists study children's and adolescents' social behavior?** In recent studies, researchers have employed video cameras and wireless microphones to study adolescent social behavior in the settings where it normally occurs.
- **What are some of the major threats to the well-being of adolescents in the United States today?** These threats include the effects of growing up in families in which the parents are divorced, with one or both parents absent, or in dysfunctional families where children are exposed to various forms of neglect or abuse.
- **What factors contribute to adolescent resilience—the ability to rise above conditions that threaten healthy development?** Factors contributing to resilience include personal characteristics that make adolescents easy to get along with; family-based factors, including a close bond with one or more competent, emotionally stable caregivers; and community-based factors such as supportive teachers, neighbors, or clergy.

KEY TERMS

adolescence, p. 342 • puberty, p. 342 • adolescent recklessness, p. 345 • sensation seeking, p. 345 • dysfunctional families, p. 353 • sexual abuse, p. 353 • resilience in development, p. 353

Adulthood and Aging

- **How do stage theories such as Erikson's, life-span theories, and the developmental regulation approach explain the changes experienced during our adult years?** Stage theories propose that we move through distinct stages during our adult years. Life-event theories view adult development as tied to important events occurring in our lives. The developmental regulation approach suggests that adult development occurs partly as a result of individuals' active efforts to regulate their own development by changing their goals and adjusting to the changing realities of adult life.
- **At what age are we most influenced by the events occurring in our society?** Recent findings indicate that we are most influenced by events occurring when we are adolescents or young adults. For example, women who were in these age groups when the modern women's movement started report being most influenced by this important societal event.
- **What physical changes do men and women experience during early and middle adulthood?** By and large, physical change is both slow and minimal during early adulthood. Reduced physical functioning and decreased vigor plus changes in appearance begin during middle adulthood. In addition, both women and men experience changes in their reproductive systems during midlife.
- **What physical changes occur in later life?** Among the many physical changes occurring in later life are declines in sensory abilities and a slowing of reflexes.
- **What changes in memory occur as we age?** Short-term (working) memory does not decline with age, but it becomes more subject to proactive interference. Recall of information from long-term memory does decline somewhat, but such effects are greater for meaningless than for meaningful information. Recent findings indicate that individuals who are mentally active experience smaller declines in memory functioning with age.
- **How do intelligence and creativity change over the life span?** There may be some declines in some aspects of intelligence with age, but these are smaller and more limited in scope than was once widely believed. There appears to be little or no decline in creativity with age.
- **In Levinson's theory, what is the life structure, and what are the major eras of adult life?** According to Levinson, the life structure is an underlying pattern or framework reflecting an individual's views about his or her life at a given time. Our life structure often changes as we move through four major life eras: the preadult era, early adulthood, middle adulthood, and late adulthood.
- **What criticisms have been directed against Levinson's theory?** Levinson's theory is based on a small sample of men, so it is unclear whether his findings apply to women as well.
- **What differences exist between the behaviors of happily married couples and those couples who ultimately divorce?** Happily married couples express more agreement on goals, lifestyles, and sex than unhappy couples. Further, happily married individuals view their spouse as a friend and share many interests with this person.
- **What are the effects of unemployment on the psychological and physical health of persons who lose their jobs?** Being unemployed can undermine individuals' self-esteem and can also have negative effects on psychological and physical health.
- **To what extent are people satisfied with their lives, and does such happiness vary greatly across different groups?** A large majority of individuals report that they are satisfied with their lives—they experience high levels of subjective well-being. This is true across many different groups—people of different ages, living in different countries, with different income levels, and in different life circumstances.
- **What factors may explain the prevalence of high levels of subjective well-being?** Being in a positive mood may be a dominant tendency for most persons. Further, being in a positive mood may be necessary for many forms of motivated behavior.

KEY TERMS

climacteric, p. 359 • menopause, p. 359 • primary aging, p. 360 • secondary aging, p. 360 • crystallized intelligence, p. 363 • fluid intelligence, p. 363 • life structure, p. 364 • dream, p. 366 • mentor, p. 366 • midlife transition, p. 366 • late-adult transition, p. 366 • subjective well-being, p. 371

Aging, Death, and Bereavement

- **How do wear-and-tear and genetic theories account for aging and death?** Wear-and-tear theories suggest that aging results from the fact that cells and organs in our bodies wear out with continued use. In contrast, genetic theories suggest that we possess biological clocks that limit longevity.
- **According to Kübler-Ross, what stages do terminally ill persons pass through when confronting their own death?** Kübler-Ross reported five stages: denial, anger, bargaining, depression, and acceptance.
- **What psychological factors and social experiences have recently been found to play a role in longevity?** Certain aspects of personality—especially conscientiousness—and cer-

tain social experiences, such as the divorce of one's parents, seem to play a role in the length of life.

- **What are the major stages of bereavement?** These include shock, protest and yearning, despair, and finally detachment and recovery.
- **What factors influence the bereavement of male partners/caregivers of men who die from AIDS?** Male caregivers of partners with AIDS recover from their grief more quickly if they start out with very high levels of grief and depression, and if they perceive positive value in their caregiving. Their recovery from grief is slowed if they have had a long-term relationship with the AIDS patient, if they blame themselves for events during the caregiving period, and if they themselves are HIV positive.

KEY TERMS

wear-and-tear theories of aging, p. 372 • genetic theories of aging, p. 373 • teleomeres, p. 373 • bereavement, p. 374

Critical Thinking Questions

Appraisal

The changes we experience during childhood are truly huge. Do you think that the changes we experience during our adult years are as great? (Rem-ember: We spend many more years as adults than as children.)

Controversy

Some psychologists believe that today's adolescents face a unique set of risks and dangers. Do you agree? Or do you think that adolescents have always been exposed to many factors that can adversely influence their development—and their future lives?

Making Psychology Part of Your Life

On the basis of what you've learned from this chapter, can you think of actions *you* can take to increase the chances that your adult life will be happy, productive, and healthy? What about the possibility of taking various steps to increase your own longevity—can you formulate several of these, too?

CHAPTER OUTLINE

Motivation and Emotion

Why are some people driven to seek success and achievement, while others are satisfied with whatever life happens to send their way? Why do some people gain weight even when dieting, while others hold a constant weight easily, without any special efforts? What makes some movie scenes, written passages, and articles of clothing so sexually arousing? Can we use subtle cues from others' facial expressions or body posture to tell when they are lying? Do our expectations shape our reactions to new experiences, so that we like what we *expect* to like and dislike what we expect to dislike? And how about the impact of our moods on our decisions and judgments? Are we more likely to evaluate the world around us—including other people—more favorably when we are in a good mood than when we are in a bad mood? Questions such as these relate to what might be described as the "feeling" side of life, or, as psychologists would put it, to the topics of *motivation* and *emotion*.

The term *motivation* refers to internal processes that serve to activate, guide, and maintain our behavior. Understanding motivation often helps us answer the question "Why?" as in "Why do other people behave as they do?" or "Why do people persist in certain courses of action, even when these don't seem to yield any obvious or immediate rewards?" Clearly, motivation is relevant to several of the questions raised above—differences between highly ambitious and unambitious people, regulation of body weight, the nature of sexual arousal, and so on.

Understanding motivation often helps us answer the question "Why?" as in "Why do other people behave as they do?"

Emotion, in contrast, refers to complex reactions consisting of (1) physiological responses such as changes in blood pressure and heart rate; (2) subjective cognitive states—the feelings we describe as happiness, anger, sorrow, or disgust; and (3) expressive reactions that reflect these internal states, such as changes in facial expressions or posture. It is on the last of these components—expressive reactions—that we often focus when trying to answer the question "Is that person lying or telling the truth?" (De Paulo et al., 1996). Emotions play a crucial role in many aspects of behavior, including personal health (see Chapter 13) and psychological disorders (see Chapter 14). In addition, as suggested by the question about the impact of our moods on our decisions or judgments, emotions interact with and influence many aspects of cognition (e.g., Forgas, 1995).

This chapter will provide you with an overview of what psychologists currently know about these two important topics. Starting with *motivation,* we'll consider contrasting theories about its basic nature. Next, we'll examine several important forms of motivation: *hunger, sexual motivation,* and *aggressive motivation.* In addition, we'll also consider two motives that, as far as we can tell, are unique to human beings: *achievement* and the *cognitive motivation*—motivation to engage in and enjoy complex cognitive activities (Cacioppo et al., 1996).

After these discussions, we'll turn to the topic of *emotion*. Again, we'll start by examining several theories about its nature. Then we'll turn to the physiological bases of emotion. Third, we'll consider the expression and communication of emotion—how emotional reactions are reflected in external behavior. Finally, we'll take at a look at the complex relationships between emotion and cognition—how feelings shape thoughts and thoughts shape feelings.

Motivation: The Activation and Persistence of Behavior

Consider the following events (see Figure 10.1):

A group of young women and men hurl themselves out of a plane. Then, as they fall toward earth, they join hands and form a circle. After that, they divide into pairs and swing round and round each other in a kind of dance. Only at the last minute do they open parachutes and glide safely to the ground.

FIGURE 10.1

Motivation: A Useful Concept for Explaining Behavior

Why do people engage in behaviors like these—behaviors for which there is no obvious reward in the immediate situation? The concept of *motivation* often adds to our understanding of such actions.

Employees of a large company remain on strike for many weeks, despite the fact that no matter how large the settlement they may ultimately win, it will not be enough to compensate them for the wages and benefits they have lost during the strike.

A man spends long hours working on complex word puzzles that require a great deal of concentration. He receives no rewards for solving these puzzles; in fact, he is often frustrated by being unable to solve them.

How can such actions be explained? On the face of it, they are somewhat puzzling. Why would people voluntarily jump out of a plane and risk their lives playing games as they fall toward earth? Why would workers remain on strike even though their action offers no chance of real economic benefits? Why would someone exert so much effort solving puzzles? One answer to such questions is this: These actions occur because the persons involved are *motivated* to perform them. In other words, they are responding to their own **motivation**—internal processes that can't be directly observed but which are real, nevertheless, and which serve to activate, guide, and maintain people's actions. Whenever the causes of a specific form of behavior can't be readily observed in the immediate situation, many psychologists believe that it is reasonable to explain them in terms of various motives. While there is general agreement in psychology on this basic point, there has been considerable *disagreement* about the nature of motivation itself, as reflected in the contrasting theories described below.

Theories of Motivation: Some Major Perspectives

In psychology, before there was the concept of *motivation*, there was **instinct theory.** In other words, before psychologists attempted to explain behavior in terms of motivation, they attempted to do so through reference to various **instincts**—innate patterns of behavior that are universal in a species, independent of experience, and elicited by specific stimuli or conditions. For a time, this approach was quite popular. William James (1890), one of the founders of American psychology, included on his list of basic instincts *pugnacity, acquisitiveness* (greed), *sympathy*, and *curiosity*. And Sigmund Freud suggested that many complex forms of behavior—everything from aggression to love—stem from inherited, biologically determined instincts.

Do instincts really play a major role in human behavior? Most psychologists today doubt that they do. Moreover, most believe that instincts are not very useful from the point of view of understanding motivation. The basic problem is this: In many cases, the existence of an instinct was inferred from

Motivation: Internal processes that activate, guide, and maintain behavior over time.

Instinct Theory: A theory of motivation suggesting that many forms of behavior stem from innate urges or tendencies.

Instincts: Patterns of behavior assumed to be universal in a species.

Drive Theory: A theory of motivation suggesting that behavior is "pushed" from within by drives stemming from basic biological needs.

Homeostasis: A state of physiological balance within the body.

the very behavior it was supposed to explain. For example, take the case of *aggression,* a form of behavior we'll examine later in this chapter. Why do human beings frequently attack others? The answer provided by James, Freud, and many others was simple: Because human beings possess a powerful aggressive instinct. So far, so good. But how do we know that they possess this instinct? Because aggression is so frequent. I'm sure you can see that this is a circular process in which the existence of an instinct is inferred from observations of behavior that presumably stem from it. As recognition of this basic flaw in the instinct approach increased, support for this theory waned, and it was soon replaced by other, more sophisticated views of motivation.

Drive Theory: Motivation and Homeostasis What do being hungry, being thirsty, being too cold, and being too hot have in common? One answer is that they are all unpleasant states and often cause us to do something to reduce or eliminate them. This basic fact provides the foundation for a major approach to motivation known as **drive theory.** According to drive theory, biological needs arising within our bodies create unpleasant states of arousal—the feelings we describe as hunger, thirst, fatigue, and so on. In order to eliminate such feelings and restore a balanced physiological state known as **homeostasis,** we engage in certain activities (Winn, 1995). Thus, according to drive theory, motivation is basically a process in which various biological needs *push* (drive) us to actions designed to satisfy these needs (see Figure 10.2). Behaviors that work—ones that help reduce the appropriate drive—are strengthened and tend to be repeated (see Chapter 5). Those that fail to produce the desired effects are weakened and will not be repeated when the drive is present once again.

In its original form, drive theory focused primarily on biological needs and the drives they produce. Soon, though, psychologists extended this model to other forms of behavior not so clearly linked to basic needs, such as drives for stimulation, status, achievement, power, and stable social relationships (Baumeister & Leary, 1995).

Drive theory persisted in psychology for several decades; indeed, it has not been totally discarded even today. However, most psychologists believe that this approach suffers from several major drawbacks. Contrary to what drive theory seems to suggest, human beings often engage in actions that *increase* rather than reduce various drives. For example, people sometimes skip snacks when hungry in order to lose weight or to maximize their enjoyment of a special dinner. Similarly, many people watch or read erotic materials in

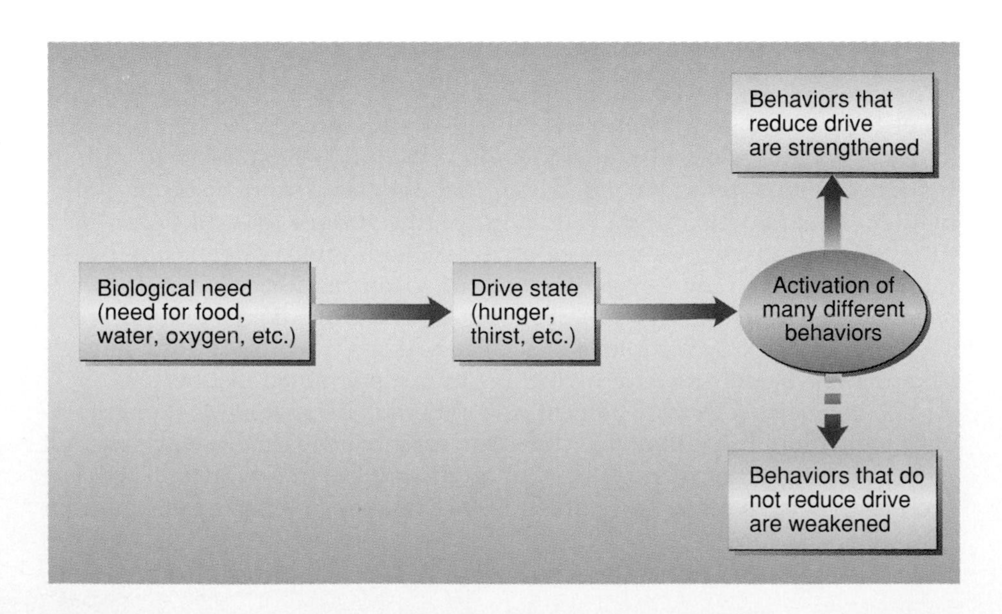

FIGURE 10.2

Drive Theory: An Overview

According to *drive theory,* biological needs lead to the arousal of *drives,* which activate efforts to reduce them. Behaviors that are successful in reducing drives are strengthened and tend to be repeated when the drive is aroused again. Behaviors that fail to reduce the drive are weakened and are less likely to recur when the drive is aroused once again.

order to increase their sexual excitement, even when they don't anticipate immediate sexual gratification (e.g., Kelley & Byrne, 1992). In view of such evidence, most psychologists now believe that drive theory, by itself, does not provide a comprehensive framework for understanding human motivation.

Arousal Theory: A theory of motivation suggesting that human beings seek an optimal level of arousal, not minimal levels of arousal.

Yerkes–Dodson Law: The suggestion that the level of arousal beyond which performance begins to decline is a function of task difficulty.

Arousal Theory: Seeking Optimum Activation When it became clear that people sometimes seek to increase rather than reduce existing drives, an alternative theory of motivation known as **arousal theory** was formulated (Geen, Beatty, & Arkin, 1984). This theory focuses on *arousal,* our general level of activation. Arousal varies throughout the day from low levels during sleep to much higher ones when we are performing strenuous tasks or activities we find exciting. Arousal theory suggests that what we seek is not minimal levels of arousal, but rather *optimal arousal*—a level of arousal that is best suited to our personal characteristics and whatever activity in which we are currently engaged. So, for example, if you are knitting, whittling, or reading, a low level of arousal will be optimal and will be preferred. If you are competing in a sports event, a much higher one will be best.

Many studies offer at least indirect support for arousal theory. For example, there *is* often a close link between arousal and performance (Weiner, 1989). For many tasks, in fact, performance increases as arousal rises, *up to some point;* Beyond that level, further increases in arousal actually reduce performance (see Figure 10.3). But it is often difficult to determine in advance just what level of arousal will be optimal for a given task or situation. In general, it has been suggested, the more difficult the task, the lower the level of arousal beyond which reductions in performance begin to occur. This suggestion is known as the **Yerkes–Dodson law,** and it does seem to apply in many situations. However, other factors aside from task difficulty also seem to play a role. For instance, large individual differences exist with respect to optimal arousal level. At one extreme are persons who prefer and seek high

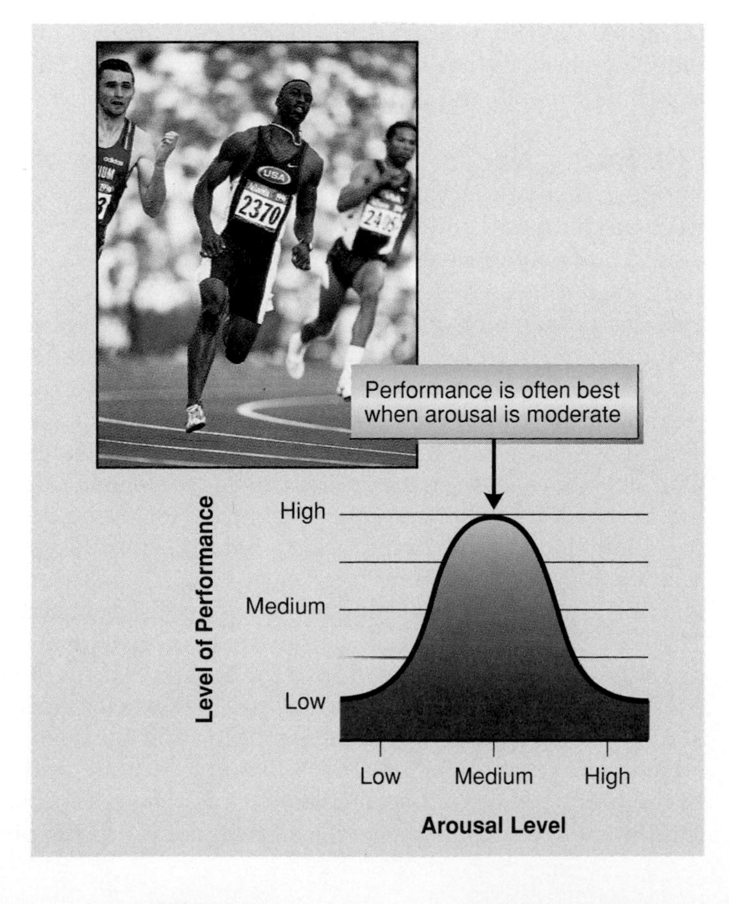

FIGURE 10.3

Arousal and Performance

Across a wide range of tasks, performance increases as arousal rises to moderate levels. Beyond some point, however, optimal levels of arousal are exceeded, and performance declines.

levels of activation—people like the sky divers described at the start of this chapter (Zuckerman, 1990). At the other extreme are persons who prefer much lower levels of arousal. Thus, while arousal theory does provide useful insights into the nature of motivation, it has important limitations, too.

Expectancy Theory: A Cognitive Approach Why are you reading this book? Not, I'd guess, to reduce some biological need. Rather, you are probably reading it because doing so will help you to reach important goals: gaining useful and interesting knowledge, earning a high grade on the next exam, graduating from college. In short, your behavior is determined by your expectancies, or thoughts about future outcomes, and by how your current actions can help you get wherever it is that you want to go in life. This basic point underlies another major theory of motivation, **expectancy theory.**

This theory suggests that motivation is not primarily a matter of being pushed from within by various urges or drives; rather it is more a question of being *pulled* from without by expectations of attaining desired outcomes. Such outcomes, known as **incentives,** can be almost anything we have learned to value—money, status, the approval of others, to name just a few. In other words, while drive theory focuses mainly on the stick in the familiar carrot-and-stick notion, expectancy theory focuses more on the carrot. Why do people engage in complex, effortful, or even painful behaviors—such as working many hours on their jobs, studying long into the night, or performing strenuous exercises? Expectancy theory answers: Because they believe that doing so will yield the outcomes they wish to attain.

Expectancy theory has been applied to many aspects of human motivation, but perhaps it has found its most important applications as an explanation of **work motivation**—the tendency to expend energy and effort on one's job (Locke & Latham, 1990). Research findings in the field of *industrial/organizational psychology* indicate that people will work hard at their jobs only when they believe that doing so will improve their performance (known as *expectancy* in the theory), that good performance will be recognized and rewarded (known as *instrumentality* in the theory), and that the rewards provided will be ones they want (known as *valence*). We'll have more to say about expectancy theory and its uses in Chapter 17.

Maslow's Needs Hierarchy: Relations Among Motives

Suppose that you were very hungry and very cold; could you study effectively under these conditions? Probably not. Your hunger and feelings of cold would probably prevent you from focusing on the task of learning new materials, even if these were quite interesting to you. Observations like this suggest that human motives may exist in a *hierarchy,* so that we must satisfy those that are more basic before moving on to ones that are less linked to biological needs. This point is central to a theory of motivation proposed by Abraham Maslow (1970). At the base of the **hierarchy of needs,** Maslow describes *physiological needs* such as those for food, water, oxygen, and sleep. One step above these are *safety needs:* needs for feeling safe and secure in one's life. Above the safety needs are *social needs,* including needs to have friends, to be loved and appreciated, and to belong—to fit into a network of social relationships (e.g., Baumeister & Leary, 1995).

Maslow refers to physiological, safety, and social needs as *deficiency needs.* They are the basics and must be satisfied before higher levels of motivation or *growth needs,* can emerge. Above the social needs in the hierarchy Maslow proposes are *esteem needs:* the needs to develop self-respect, gain the approval of others, and achieve success. Ambition and the need for achievement, to which we'll return later, are closely linked to esteem needs. Finally, at the top of the hierarchy are *self-actualization needs.* These involve the need for self-fulfillment—the desire to become all that one is capable of being. Self-actual-

Expectancy Theory: A theory of motivation suggesting that behavior is "pulled" by expectations of desirable outcomes.

Incentives: Rewards individuals seek to attain.

Work Motivation: The tendency to expend energy and effort on one's job or on a specific task.

Hierarchy of Needs: In Maslow's theory of motivation, an arrangement of needs from the most basic to those at the highest levels.

ization needs include concerns not only with one's selfish interests, but also with issues that affect the well-being of others, and even of all humanity. Figure 10.4 provides an overview of Maslow's theory.

Maslow's theory is intuitively appealing, but research designed to test it has yielded mixed results. Some results suggest that growth needs do come into play only after people have satisfied lower-level needs (e.g., Betz, 1982). But other findings indicate that people sometimes seek to satisfy higher-order needs even when needs lower in the hierarchy have not been met (e.g., Williams & Page, 1989). So the idea that needs arise and are satisfied in a particular order has not been confirmed. For this reason, Maslow's theory should be viewed mainly as an interesting but unverified framework for understanding motivation. (See Table 10.1 on page 388 for an overview of the theories of motivation discussed in this section.)

Hunger Motivation: The motivation to obtain and consume food.

Key Questions

- Why did psychologists largely reject instinct theory?
- According to drive theory, what is the basis for various motives?
- Why is expectancy theory described as a cognitive theory of motivation?
- What are the basic ideas behind Maslow's needs hierarchy theory?

Hunger: Regulating Our Caloric Intake

Mahatma Gandhi, one of the founders of modern India, once remarked: "Even God cannot speak to a hungry man except in terms of bread." By this he meant that when people are hungry, **hunger motivation,** the urge to obtain and consume food, takes precedence over all others—a view consistent with Maslow's needs hierarchy. If you have ever had the experience of going without food for even a single day, you know how strong feelings of hunger can be, and what a powerful source of motivation they can provide. But where do such feelings come from? And how do we manage to regulate the amount of food we consume so that, for most persons, body weight remains fairly stable over long periods of time? Let's see what psychologists have discovered about these and related questions.

The Regulation of Eating: A Complex Process Consider the following fact: If you consume just twenty extra calories each day (less than the number in a single small carrot), you will gain about two pounds a year—twenty pounds in a decade. How do people keep caloric input and output closely balanced and so avoid such outcomes? One answer, of course, is that in many cases, they don't: People do gain weight despite their best efforts to avoid doing so. We'll return to why this happens below. For most people, however, a balance *is* struck between needs and caloric intake, so weight remains relatively stable. What mechanisms contribute to this balance? As we saw in Chapter 2, part of the answer involves the *hypothalamus,* which plays a role in both eating and satiety (knowing when we've had enough), and also, through its links with portions of the cerebral cortex, in our ability to adapt to changing environmental conditions such as shifts in the foods available to us (Winn, 1995).

The regulation of eating involves much more than this, however. In fact, it seems to involve a complex system of regulatory mechanisms located not only in the hypothalamus, but in the liver and other organs of the body as well. These systems contain special *detectors,* cells that respond to variations in the concentration of several nutrients in the blood. One type of detector responds to the amount of *glucose* or blood sugar. Other detectors respond to levels of *protein,* and especially to certain amino

FIGURE 10.4

Maslow's Needs Hierarchy

According to Maslow (1970), needs exist in a hierarchy. Only when lower-order needs are satisfied can higher-order needs be activated.

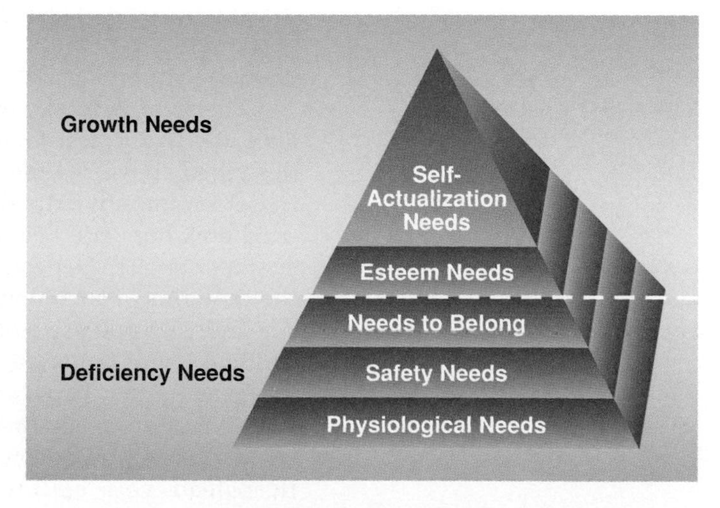

TABLE 10.1

Theories of Motivation: An Overview

As shown here, many different perspectives on motivation have been proposed.

Theory of Motivation	Key Assumptions	Strengths/Weaknesses
Instinct Theory	Specific forms of behavior stem from universal instincts.	Behaviors used as a basis for inferring instincts are also used as support for their existence—circular reasoning.
Drive Theory	Biological needs produce unpleasant states of arousal, which people then seek to reduce.	People sometimes try to *increase* their drives, not reduce them.
Arousal Theory	Arousal (general level of activation) varies throughout the day and can motivate many forms of behavior; people seek *optimal* arousal, not low arousal.	Arousal is only one of many factors that influence motivated behavior.
Expectancy Theory	Behavior is "pulled" by expectations of desired outcomes rather than "pushed" from within by biologically based drives.	Focus on cognitive processes in motivation is an emphasis consistent with that of modern psychology; widely used to explain *work motivation*.
Maslow's Needs Hierarchy	Needs exist in a hierarchy; higher-level needs cannot be activated until lower-level needs are satisfied.	Very little research support exists for key assumptions of the theory.

acids. This is why we feel full after eating a meal high in protein, such as a steak, even though the level of glucose in our blood remains relatively low. Finally, other detectors respond to *lipids,* or fats. Again, even if glucose levels are low, when the amount of lipids circulating in the blood is high, we do not feel hungry.

Complex as this may sound, it is still not the entire picture. In addition, eating and hunger are also strongly affected by the smell and taste of food and by feedback produced by chewing and swallowing. As we consume food, information from taste and smell receptors, and from muscles in our mouth and throat, provides feedback that helps us determine when we have eaten enough (e.g., Stellar, 1985).

The sight of food, too, is important. Foods that are attractive in appearance are hard to resist and may even overwhelm the regulatory mechanisms described above, leading us to overeat. Cultural facts also play a major role in determining what, when, and how much we eat. Would you munch on fried grasshoppers? Sea urchins? Octopus cooked in its own ink? How about snails or snake? Depending on the culture in which you have been raised, the thoughts of such items may induce hunger pangs or feelings of disgust. According to one psychologist (Rozin 1996), such feelings may arise from our implicit belief that "we are what we eat" coupled with our own culture's views about the characteristics of various potential foods. If you live in a culture that defines octopuses as slimy and dangerous predators just waiting to seize unwary swimmers, you may find the idea of eating them unpleasant. If, instead, your culture views octopuses as inoffensive creatures closely related to lobsters, you may find them quite appetizing. In any case, it is clear that there is a complex interaction between physiological mechanisms and cognitive ones where the regulation of eating by human beings is concerned.

Factors in Weight Gain: Why Some Persons Experience Difficulty in the Long-Term Regulation of Body Weight

There can be little doubt that in the 1990s—at least in Western cultures—thin is in. In the United States alone, consumers spend huge sums each year on products and programs related to weight loss. Despite these efforts, however, many people lose "the battle of the bulge." In fact, as shown in Figure 10.5, a large proportion of adults in the United States are overweight (their actual weight exceeds their ideal weight by at least 5 percent), and this figure rises greatly as people grow older (Harris Poll, 1995). Why? Several factors seem to play a role.

First, part of the problem involves the effects of learning. Many people acquire eating habits that are very likely to generate excess pounds. They learn to prefer high-calorie meals that are rich in protein and fats—Big Macs and Whoppers, for instance. Further, they learn to associate the act of eating with many different contexts and situations. If you feel a strong urge to snack every time you sit down in front of the television set or movie screen, you already know about such effects. The desire to eat can be classically conditioned (see Chapter 5); cues associated with eating when we are hungry can acquire the capacity to prompt eating when we are *not* hungry.

Genetic factors, too, are important. Individuals differ greatly in terms of their *basal metabolic rate*—the number of calories their bodies require at rest within a given period of time. Persons of the same age and weight performing the same daily activities can differ greatly in this respect, with the result that one person may require almost twice as many calories as another to maintain a stable weight.

A third factor that seems to play an important role in the regulation of weight among humans involves the effects of stress. How do *you* react to stress—for example, to the stress caused by an important exam, a fight with your parents, or a traffic ticket? If you are like most people, your appetite

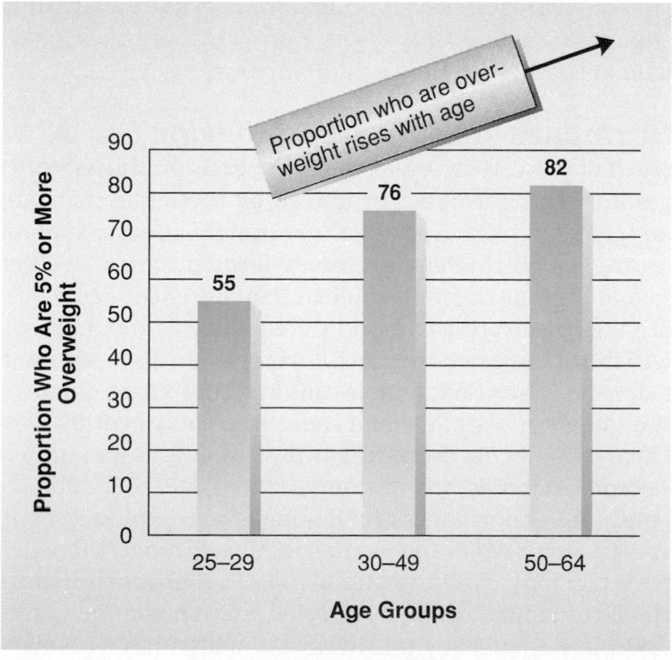

(**Source:** Based on data from a Harris Poll, 1995.)

FIGURE 10.5

Heavy News for Americans

Although the results of surveys differ, most indicate that a substantial proportion of Americans are overweight. The figures shown here indicate the percentage in each age group who are more than 5 percent above their ideal weight.

probably decreases at such times. Those unpleasant feelings in the pit of your stomach make eating unattractive, at least temporarily. Overweight persons, however, often react in the opposite manner: They tend to eat *more* during periods of stress.

Yet another factor that seems to contribute to unwanted weight gain involves an intriguing difference between people who are obese and those who are not. Several studies indicate that overweight persons respond more strongly to external cues relating to food (Rodin & Slochower, 1976). They report feeling hungrier in the presence of food-related cues—the sight or smell of foods—than do persons of normal weight, and they find it harder to resist eating when tasty foods are available (Rodin, 1984). And, of course, modern societies expose such individuals to many food cues all day long.

Taking all these factors together, it is not surprising that many people experience difficulties in regulating their weight over the long term. There are simply too many variables or conditions that, together, can overwhelm the mechanisms that establish and maintain a balance between our internal needs and the food we consume. (For some suggestions that may help you to win the battle against the expanding waistline, please see the **Ideas to Take with You** feature.) We'll examine two serious eating disorders—*anorexia nervosa,* in which individuals starve themselves and lose dangerous amounts of weight, and *bulimia,* a condition involving a repeated cycle of binge eating and purging—in Chapter 14.

Key Questions

- What factors play a role in the regulation of eating?
- What factors override this regulatory system, so that many people do not maintain a stable weight?

Sexual Motivation: The Most Intimate Motive

Suppose that voyagers from another planet arrived on Earth and visited large cities in many different countries. What would they see? Among other things, large numbers of advertisements designed to attract attention through the use of sex-related images (see Figure 10.6 on page 392). So common are such displays, in fact, that the alien visitors might quickly conclude that human beings are obsessed with this topic. While advertisements may well exaggerate our interest in sex, it is clear that **sexual motivation**—our motivation to engage in sexual activity—is a powerful one. Let's see what psychologists have discovered about such motivation.

Hormones and Sexual Behavior As we saw in Chapter 9, the onset of puberty involves rapid increases in the activity of the sex glands, or **gonads.** The hormones produced by these glands have many effects on the body; and in many species, they strongly affect sexual motivation. In fact, sex hormones exert what are usually termed *activation effects*—in their presence sexual behavior occurs, while in their absence sexual behavior does not occur or takes place with a very low frequency. For example, in rats, the species in which the link between sex hormones and sexual behavior has been most extensively studied, females show receptivity to males only at times during their menstrual cycle when concentrations of certain sex hormones are high. Once these levels drop—regardless of whether mating has resulted in fertilization—females are no longer receptive. Additional evidence for a link between sex hormones and mating is also provided by the fact that for many species, removal of the ovaries totally eliminates female sexual receptivity to males. Removal of the testes in males produces similar though somewhat less clear-cut results. In many species, then, hormones produced by the gonads do indeed play a key role in sexual motivation (Rissman, 1995).

Sexual Motivation: Motivation to engage in various forms of sexual relations.

Gonads: The primary sex glands.

Ideas to Take with You

Some Tips on Winning the "Battle of the Bulge"

Research on factors related to weight gain suggests that the steps outlined here may help you maintain a constant weight, despite the many temptations of modern life.

Avoid High-Calorie Snack Foods

A handful of potato chips or a small order of french fries can contain hundreds of calories. Yet, these snacks don't tend to make you feel full. Avoid such foods as much as possible.

Don't Eat Out of Habit When You Aren't Hungry

It's all too easy to get into the habit of eating whenever you watch TV, study, or sit down to talk with friends. If you must munch on something, eat a piece of fruit, or drink some coffee or tea. These drinks contain natural substances that tend to reduce appetite.

Drink Water with Your Meals

In the late 1980s the amount of soft drinks consumed by the average American surpassed the amount of water drunk—and the curves have continued to diverge. Each glass of Coke, Pepsi, or whatever can contain almost 200 calories. So ignore the ads and sip water when you are thirsty; the waistline you protect will be your own!

Avoid Temptation!

If you see attractive foods (or smell them), they are often hard to resist. Try to stay out of the reach of such temptations as much as possible.

Exercise!

Not only does exercise burn calories and improve your personal health, it often helps to control your appetite by giving you the natural feelings of well-being people often seek in "comfort foods." You don't have to be an athlete to obtain such effects—even moderate exercise such as walking can do the trick.

Human beings—and to some degree other primates—are an exception to this general pattern. Although research findings indicate that many women report substantial changes in sexual desire over the course of their menstrual cycle, these changes do *not* occur at times when hormones such as estrogen are at peak levels (Zillmann, Schweitzer, & Mundorf, 1994). On the contrary, peaks of sexual desire or interest seem to occur when such hormones are at relatively low levels. Further, many women continue to engage in and enjoy sexual relations after menopause, when the hormonal output of their ovaries drops sharply. And in men, there is little evidence of a clear link between sexual responsiveness and blood levels of sex hormones such as testosterone (Byrne, 1982).

This is not to say, however, that sex hormones play no role in human sexual motivation. Among males, there is some evidence that testosterone levels are associated with differences in sexual arousal. For example, men with high levels of testosterone become aroused more quickly by erotic films than those with relatively low levels (Lange et al., 1980). In general, though, the link between sex hormones and sexual motivation appears to be far less clear-cut and less compelling for human beings than is true for many other species.

Other chemical substances within the body may also play a role. Research findings suggest that when human beings are sexually attracted to another person, their brain produces increased amounts of several substances related to amphetamines. As you may recall from Chapter 4, amphetamines are stimulants; so the increased production of amphetaminelike substances such as phenylethylamine (PEA) may account for the fact that many people describe strong sexual attraction—the first stage in falling in love—as a feeling that "sweeps them away." As one researcher puts it, "love is a natural high" (Walsh, 1993).

FIGURE 10.6

Sex: A Modern Obsession?

Magazine ads, billboards, television commercials—all make lavish use of sexy models in an effort to sell their products. The result: We are surrounded by such images much of the time.

In sum, there does appear to be a biochemical side to love, but we are only just beginning to understand it. While sex hormones are not as clearly linked to sexual motivation in humans as in other species, there is some evidence that other substances produced by our bodies do play a role in such motivation, and even in romantic love.

Human Sexual Behavior: Some Basic Facts Until the 1960s the only source of scientific information about human sexual motivation was that provided by surveys: Large samples of individuals were simply asked to report on their sexual behavior and experiences (e.g., Kinsey et al., 1953; Kinsey, Pomeroy, & Martin, 1984). Results were varied, but the surveys generally pointed to one key conclusion: Where sexual behavior is concerned, individual differences are enormous. Some people reported little or no interest in sex and indicated that they had been celibate for years, while others reported engaging in sexual relations with a large number of partners and having three or more orgasms every day.

Starting in the 1960s, however, another source of information about human sexual motivation became available: direct and systematic observation of actual sexual activities. The first and still the most famous project of this kind was conducted by Masters and Johnson in the mid-1960s (Masters & Johnson, 1966). These researchers observed and recorded the reactions of several hundred volunteers of both sexes as they engaged in sexual intercourse or masturbation. More than ten thousand cycles of arousal and satisfaction were studied. The results yielded important insights into the nature of human sexuality. Perhaps the clearest finding was the fact that both males and females move through four distinct phases during sexual behavior.

First, they enter the *excitement phase*. During this phase, many physiological changes indicative of growing sexual excitement occur. The penis and clitoris become enlarged, vaginal lubrication increases, and nipples may become erect in both sexes. If sexual stimulation persists, both women and men enter the *plateau phase*. The size of the penis increases still further, and the outer third of the vagina becomes engorged with blood, reducing its diameter. Muscle tension, respiration, heart rate, and blood pressure all rise to high levels.

After a variable period of direct stimulation, both males and females approach the *orgasmic phase*. This consists of several contractions of the muscles surrounding the genitals, along with intense sensations of pleasure. The pattern of contractions, including their timing and length, is virtually identical in females and males.

The most striking difference between the two sexes occurs during the final *resolution phase*. For males, orgasm is followed by a reduction in sexually and physiological arousal. Males then enter a *refractory period* during which they cannot be sexually aroused or experience another orgasm. Among females, in contrast, two distinct patterns are possible. They too may experience a reduction in sexual and physiological arousal. If stimulation continues, however, they may experience additional orgasms.

The basic pattern just described seems to apply to all human beings. However, practically everything else varies from one society to another. Different cultures have widely different standards about such matters as (1) the age at which sexual behavior should begin, (2) the frequency with which it should occur, (3) physical characteristics considered attractive or sexy, (4) the particular positions and practices that are acceptable, (5) the proper time and setting for sexual relations, (6) the persons who are appropriate partners, and (7) the number of partners individuals should have at one time or in succession. So, to repeat: Where human sexuality is concerned, *variability* is definitely the central theme.

Human Sexual Behavior: What's Arousing and Why Clearly, sexual motivation plays an important role in human behavior. But what, precisely, stimulates sexual arousal? In certain respects, the same events or stimuli that produce arousal in other species. First, direct physical contacts—various forms of touching and foreplay—generate arousal. Second, there is some evidence that human beings, like other organisms, can be sexually aroused by certain naturally occurring odors.

For example, one study found that approximately 20 percent of males appear to be sexually stimulated by the scents of *copulins*, chemicals found in vaginal secretions (Hassett, 1978). More recently, some scientists have reported that natural substances known as *pheromones* can produce sexual attraction and arousal in both males and females (Bishop, 1996; Blakeslee, 1993). For more information on this topic—and on the possibility that wearing perfume or colognes containing human pheromones can make you more attractive to the opposite sex—please see the Beyond the Headlines section on page 394.

One potential source of sexual motivation, however, does seem to set human beings apart from other species: real or imagined erotic stimuli and images. Unlike other species, human beings possess the capacity to generate their own sexual arousal on the basis of erotic fantasies or daydreams

(Leitenberg & Henning, 1995; recall our discussion in Chapter 4). And many people respond strongly to *erotic materials* containing either visual images or verbal descriptions of sexual behavior. There is no evidence that other species respond in these ways, so our highly developed cognitive capacities do seem to play an important role in human sexual motivation. In many cases, in fact, they may play the most important role. As one famous researcher put it, "The mind is the only true erogenous zone" (Byrne, 1992).

Beyond the Headlines

As Psychologists See It

Can We Sniff Our Way to Emotional Health?

Sixth-Sense Therapy Path to Be Reported: Data Hint Humans Can Get Chemical Messages

Wall Street Journal, April 11, 1996—Researchers are expected to report the first evidence that a long-forgotten sixth sense in humans may offer a new pathway to the brain for treating a long list of emotional and mental disorders.

The new study is bound to raise controversy because it claims that humans, like many animals, can receive odorless chemical messages called pheromones from each other, a sense that most scientists have assumed was lost to evolution long ago. . . .

In a set of experiments to be published soon, scientists with a small, closely held company called Pherin Corp. will report that when they exposed a tiny mysterious spot inside the nose (the vomeronasal organ) to a synthetic pheromone, they changed the levels of certain hormones circulating in the blood. . . .

Even more startling, the chemicals extracted from male skin activated only the vomeronasal organs (VNOs) of females, while the extracts from female skin activated only the VNOs of the male volunteers. Further research found that the extracts from one sex promoted a feeling of well-being in the other sex. As a result, Dr. Berlinger formed Erox Corp., which produces male and female perfumes in which the odorless pheromones are mixed with conventional perfume odors. . . .

A new "sixth sense"? "Odorless" substances that can affect us through the vomeronasal organ? Perfumes that make us more sexually attractive because they contain chemical messengers (pheromones)? Sounds interesting—but how much scientific evidence is there for these claims?

Unfortunately, not much. First, although psychologists and other scientists have known for decades about the presence of the vomeronasal organ inside the nose, there is as yet little evidence that the VNO is sensitive to "odorless" substances—ones that can be carried by the air, but which we can't detect through our normal sense of smell (see Chapter 3). Second, even if this organ can respond to airborne molecules, it is not clear what substances might stimulate it in this manner. Only naturally produced pheromones? Other chemicals too? At present, we don't know. Third, many of the studies conducted to date either appear to be informal in nature, or have not yet been published. I myself have been investigating the effects of pleasant fragrances for many years—for example, such questions as whether applicants who wear perfume or cologne to a job interview receive higher (or lower) ratings (e.g., Baron, 1983), and whether the presence of pleasant fragrances in the air produces mild enhancements in people's current moods, thereby influencing their performance on some tasks or their willingness to help strangers (Baron, 1997; Baron & Bronfen, 1994). As part of this work, I have often tried to obtain information about the research mentioned in this newspaper article. The result? I've been told that it was not available for public distribution. Since the free exchange of information is crucial to all fields of science, this has led me to wonder whether in this case, commercial interests—such as promoting perfumes and colognes that supposedly make their wearers sexually irresistible—have taken precedence over finding out whether such effects are, in any sense, real (see Figure 10.7).

FIGURE 10.7

The Secret of Sexual Attractiveness?

Promoters of products containing human pheromones claim that these scents will enhance the sexual attractiveness of people who use them. Little scientific evidence exists for such claims, however.

Please don't misunderstand: I'm not arguing that the VNO has no functions; that humanpheromones do not exist; or that if they do exist, they have no effects. Rather, I'm simply noting that until research findings relating to the claims described above are published in high-quality scientific journals and are held up to the same kind of careful scrutiny that *all* scientific research must survive, we should view them with a healthy degree of skepticism. In short, I'm definitely not turning up my nose at this research—but I'm not rushing to accept it, either.

Critical Thinking Questions

1. What kind of evidence would be needed to prove that the vomeronasal organ has real functions—that it provides us with a "sixth sense"?
2. Why do you think claims about this organ and about the effects of human pheromones have *not* been published in top-notch scientific journals?
3. If human pheromones are found to exist, do you think they will be shown to exert very powerful effects on sexual attraction and arousal? Or will they turn out to be less important than other factors that influence these processes?

Sexual Orientation Estimates vary, but it appears that about 2 percent of all adults are exclusively **homosexual** in their sexual orientation: They engage in sexual relations only with members of their own sex (Kelley & Byrne, 1992; see Figure 10.8 on page 396). In addition, 2 to 3 percent of each sex are **bisexual** to some degree: They seek out and enjoy sexual contact with members of both sexes. The remainder of the population is **heterosexual** and engages in sexual relations only with members of the opposite sex. What factors influence or determine sexual orientation? In other words, why are some persons homosexual, while most others are exclusively heterosexual? We have already examined some of the research relating to this issue in Chapter 2. As you may recall, existing evidence, taken together, suggests that many factors probably play a role—genetic factors (Bailey & Pillard, 1991, 1993; Gladue, 1994; Turner, 1995); behaviors and feelings during childhood (Johnston & Bell, 1995); and individual differences in temperament, which predispose children to prefer activities associated with one gender or the other (Bem, 1996; see Chapter 2). In sum, therefore, we do not yet have any-

Homosexual (Sexual Orientation): A sexual orientation in which individuals prefer sexual relations with members of their own sex.

Bisexual (Sexual Orientation): A sexual orientation in which individuals seek and enjoy sexual contact with members of both sexes.

Heterosexual (Sexual Orientation): A sexual orientation in which individuals prefer sexual relations with members of the opposite sex.

FIGURE 10.8

Homosexual Marriage

In recent years, homosexuals of both genders have campaigned for legal recognition of their long-term relationships: They want governments to formally recognize homosexual marriages. This issue remains controversial today.

thing approaching a complete understanding of the origins of a homosexual sexual orientation; but we are definitely making progress toward this goal.

Key Questions

- What role do hormones play in human sexual motivation?
- What are the major phases of sexual activity?
- What is a key difference between human beings and other species with respect to sexual arousal?
- Is there any scientific evidence for the role of pheromones in human sexual behavior?
- What factors appear to play a role in determining sexual orientation?

Aggressive Motivation: The Most Dangerous Motive

War. Murder. Rape. Child abuse. In the 1990s no one—neither tourists visiting popular attractions nor government employees at work at their desks—seems safe from acts of violence. Consider a few statistics:

- In the United States in one year (1992), there were 6,621,140 crimes of violence (United States Department of Justice, 1994).
- In that same year there were 140,930 forcible rapes and 657,500 assaults that resulted in injury to the victim (United States Department of Justice, 1994)—more than one rape every 5 minutes and one assault every 28 seconds.
- Nearly 1,400 cases of fatal child abuse are reported in the United States each year (Daro & McCurdy, 1992); in addition, tens of thousands of children are treated for what are termed "unintended injuries," many of which may actually be the result of abuse by their parents or other adults (Peterson & Brown, 1994).
- Cases of *familicide*—instances in which individuals murder their spouse and one or more of their children—are far from rare; in fact, in England and Wales, one out of every 72 homicide victims dies in such crimes (Wilson & Daly, 1996).

Facts such as these suggest that **aggressive motivation**—the desire to inflict harm on others—plays an all-too-common role in human behavior. While human beings don't always express aggressive motivation overtly, they frequently do; that is, they engage in various forms of **aggression** against others—efforts to harm them in some manner (Baron & Richardson, 1994). Here, we'll examine some contrasting perspectives concerning the origins of aggression, and a few of the factors that seem to influence its occurrence.

Aggressive Motivation: The desire to harm or injure others in some manner.

Aggression: Behavior directed toward the goal of harming another living being who wishes to avoid such treatment.

The Roots of Aggression: Innate or Learned? Is aggression an inherited and unavoidable human tendency? Looking at the statistics above, you may be tempted to assume that it is; and if you do, you will not be alone in this conclusion. After witnessing the horrible carnage of World War I, Freud concluded that human beings possess a powerful built-in tendency to harm others. While this view has been shared by many other scientists—for example, Konrad Lorenz, the famous *ethologist*—it is definitely *not* widely accepted by psychologists at the present time (e.g., Anderson, Anderson, & Deuser, 1996; Berkowitz, 1993). Most psychologists today believe that aggression, like many other forms of motivation, is elicited by a wide range of external events and stimuli. In other words, it is often "pulled" from without rather than "pushed" or driven from within by irresistible, perhaps inherited tendencies. Why do the experts now hold this view? Partly because several findings argue strongly against the existence of universal, innate human tendencies toward aggression. Perhaps the most telling of these is the finding that rates of violent crimes differ tremendously in different cultures. For instance, in many developed countries rates of violent crimes are much lower than those reported for the United States, while in some developing nations rates are even higher (Kutchinsky, 1992; Osterman et al., 1994). In fact, murder rates are more than one hundred times higher in some countries than in others (Scott, 1992). Such huge differences in the incidence of aggression suggest that aggressive behavior is strongly influenced by social and cultural factors; and that even if it stems in part from innate tendencies, these are literally overwhelmed by social conditions and other factors.

If aggression does not stem primarily from inherited tendencies, the next question is obvious: What factors *do* influence its occurrence? Decades of careful research have yielded an increasingly clear answer (e.g., Baron & Richardson, 1994). While it would be impossible to summarize the results of all this research here, we can at least take a brief look at several factors that have been found to play an important role in eliciting overt aggression.

Social Factors and Aggression Try to remember the last time you lost your temper. What made you blow your cool? The chances are quite good that your aggressive motivation stemmed from the actions of another person. In other words, your aggression stemmed primarily from social factors. For instance, the other person may have done something that blocked or thwarted you from reaching your goals—in other words, this person may have *frustrated* you. For many years psychologists viewed **frustration** as *the* major cause of aggression (Dollard et al., 1939). Research findings indicate, however, that in fact frustration is just one of many different social causes of aggression, and perhaps not the strongest one. Further, when exposed to severe frustration, many people become depressed rather than aggressive (e.g., Berkowitz, 1989). Thus, contrary to one famous view known as the *frustration–aggression hypothesis,* frustration does not always produce aggression. However, when individuals feel not only that their interests have been thwarted, but that someone has thwarted them arbitrarily and without good cause—that they have been treated *unfairly*—frustration can indeed be a powerful cause of aggression. In fact, feelings of injustice have recently been found to play an important role in instances of **workplace violence**—violent outbursts in which employees attack and even kill other persons with whom they work (e.g., Baron & Neuman, 1996; Folger & Baron, 1996).

Another social factor that often plays a role in aggression is direct provocation from another person. Verbal insults or physical actions interpreted as aggressive in nature often lead the party on the receiving end to reciprocate, with the results that a powerful aggression–counteraggression spiral develops (e.g., Ohbuchi & Ogura, 1984).

Frustration: The blocking of ongoing, goal-directed behavior.

Workplace Violence: Violent outbursts in which employees attack and even kill other persons with whom they work.

FIGURE 10.9

Media Violence: One Factor in Human Aggression

A large body of evidence indicates that regular exposure to *media violence* can increase aggression among viewers. Yet despite this fact, the level of violence in films and television shows continues to increase—and to become more graphic.

Finally, I should note that a large body of evidence indicates that exposure to violence in the media—television, movies, and so on—has been found to increase aggression on the part of viewers (e.g., Huesmann, 1994). Such results have been obtained in literally hundreds of studies, so this is one of the most consistent—and perhaps important—findings of research on aggression. Apparently, when people witness scenes in which characters assault one another, they may learn that such actions are an appropriate response to provocation or frustration—and that, moreover, aggression often succeeds. In addition, people may learn new ways of aggressing against others, and may experience reductions in their own restraints against such behavior. Perhaps most alarming of all, exposure to a steady diet of media violence can lead individuals to become desensitized to the harm produced by violence: Scenes in which others are harmed cease to have any emotional impact on them. As you can see, the implications of such findings are frightening for any society in which large numbers of people regularly watch scenes like the one shown in Figure 10.9. I should add that related research indicates that exposure to scenes in films and television programs that combine violence with sexually arousing images may be one important factor contributing to *sexually aggressive behavior* (Nagayama Hall & Barongan, 1997).

For information on yet another social factor that plays an important role in aggression, see the Exploring Gender and Diversity section below.

EXPLORING GENDER & DIVERSITY

Sexual Jealousy and Aggression: Some Surprising Gender Differences

As I noted earlier, millions of wives are assaulted by their husbands each year in the United States alone (Russell, 1988). When these battered women are asked why their husbands assaulted them, many have a simple answer: "Jealousy!" And growing evidence indicates that they are correct (Wilson & Daly, 1996). **Sexual jealousy**—a perceived threat to a romantic relationship from a rival for one's partner—does appear to be a very potent cause of aggression. Individuals who feel that their lover has "done them wrong" by flirting—or worse—with another person often experience strong feelings of anger, and frequently think about or actually engage in actions designed to punish their lover, the rival, or both (Buss et al., 1992; Parrott, 1991; Sharpsteen, 1991).

Do males and females differ in such reactions, and in the tendency to translate sexual jealousy into assaults against their spouse or lover? On the basis of the findings mentioned above, you might assume that males experience stronger jealousy and are more likely to become aggressive. And indeed, the incidence of husbands assaulting wives is much higher than the reverse (e.g., Wilson & Daly, 1996). But remember: Males are generally much stronger than females and have often had much more experience with aggression. So the fact that men are more likely to assault women than vice versa doesn't necessary mean that males experience stronger sexual jealousy; perhaps females experience jealousy that is just as strong, and have equally powerful motives to punish their mates, but they simply lack the strength or expertise to do so. In fact, the findings of several studies suggest that this may be so (e.g., Paul, Foss, & Galloway, 1993).

Sexual Jealousy: A negative state aroused by a perceived threat to a sexual relationship with another person.

Consider an experiment conducted by de Weerth and Kalma (1993). These researchers asked a large number of students enrolled in a social psychology course at a university in the Netherlands to indicate how they would react if they learned that their current lover was having an affair with another person. As you can see from Figure 10.10, females reported they would be more likely to respond with verbal and physical abuse of their lover, or to cry and demand

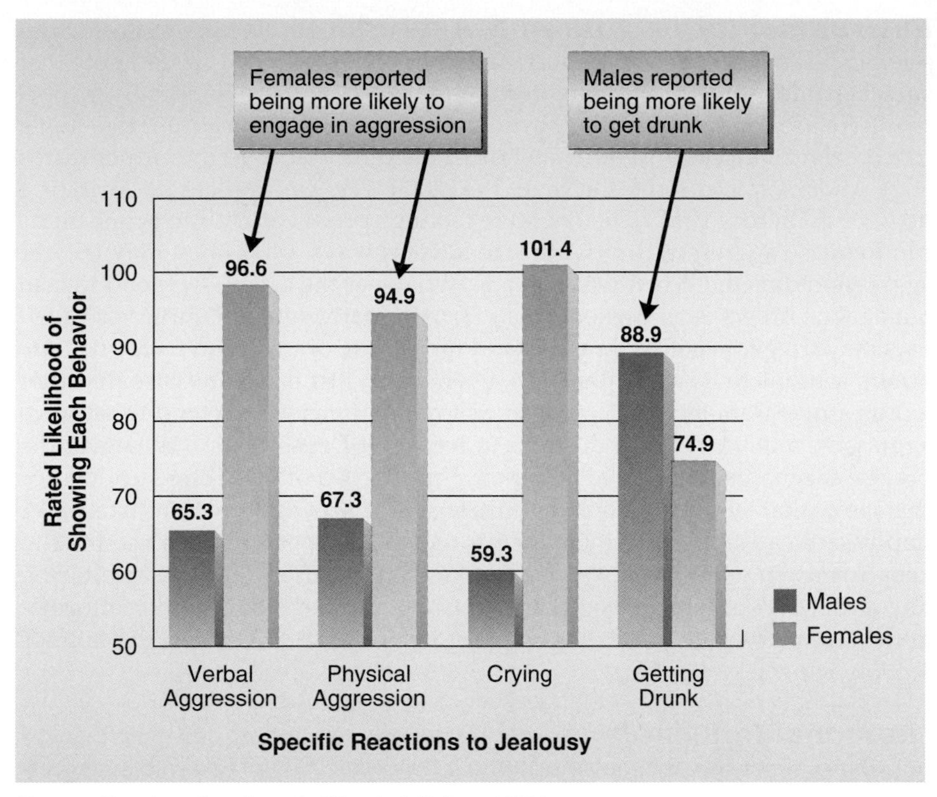

(**Source:** Based on data from de Weerth & Kalma, 1993.)

FIGURE 10.10

Gender Differences in Sexual Jealousy

As shown here, in one study in the Netherlands, female university students indicated that they would be more likely than males to respond aggressively to sexual infidelity by their lover.

an explanation. In contrast, males indicated that they would be more likely to get drunk!

Similar results have been obtained in several other studies (e.g., Paul et al., 1993), so this gender difference appears to be a real one. What accounts for its existence? One possibility is suggested by the perspective of *evolutionary psychology,* which we encountered in Chapter 1 (e.g., Buss). According to this perspective, contrasting biological forces may underlie male and female sexual jealousy. For females, such jealousy may focus primarily on the potential loss of resources needed for child rearing. Throughout most of human evolution, females have been dependent on males for the resources needed to raise children. In this context, a wandering mate might decide ultimately to wander off completely, taking these precious resources with him. The result: Females react very strongly to male sexual infidelity. For males, in contrast, sexual jealousy may rest primarily on concern over paternity. If their mate has sexual relations with other men, they may find themselves—perhaps unknowingly—in the uncomfortable situation of raising other men's children. In the past, this was a strong basis for male sexual jealousy. In Western societies today, however, the advent of effective contraceptives has made it much less likely that women will become pregnant by other men, even if they have affairs with them. As a result, de Weerth and Kalma (1993, p. 275) contend, men may now have weaker reasons for experiencing sexual jealousy than was true in the past. For women, however, the basis for such reactions may be largely unchanged. The overall result? Stronger reactions to sexual infidelity on the part of women than among men.

I should quickly add that this is only one possible explanation for recent findings pointing to greater jealousy-induced aggression by females than by males. Many other explanations also exist; for example, norms suggesting that males should not aggress against females, even when strongly provoked. Whatever the precise explanation, it is clear that sexual jealousy is a strong impetus to aggression for both genders, and that in this respect the "green-eyed monster" continues to live up to its fearful reputation.

Aggression Machine: A device used in the laboratory study of human aggression.

Environmental Factors and Aggression While social factors seem to be among the most important causes of aggression, I should note that such behavior sometimes stems from other causes as well. Especially important here are conditions in the physical environment that cause individuals to experience discomfort—for instance, uncomfortably high temperatures (e.g., Anderson, Deuser, & DeNeve, 1995; Bell, 1992) or unpleasant, irritating noise (e.g., Baron, 1994). The negative feelings produced by such conditions can increase aggressive motivation in several ways. First, they may trigger aggression directly: When we feel bad—whatever the cause—we tend to lash out against others (e.g., Berkowitz, 1993). Alternatively, such unpleasant feelings may trigger negative thoughts and memories, or may lead us to attribute others' actions to hostile intentions, even when this is not the case. In other words, unpleasant feelings may lead us to think in ways that tend to produce aggressive motives (e.g., Anderson, Anderson, & Deuser, 1996). Whatever the precise mechanism involved, research findings do offer strong support for the view that environmental conditions that we find uncomfortable or unpleasant can sometimes increase our tendencies to aggress—something to keep firmly in mind the next time you are caught in traffic on a sweltering day and feel your temper beginning to fray around the edges. (For information on how psychologists study aggression, please see the Research Methods section below.)

Hormonal Influences Finally, some research findings suggest that sex hormones, especially the male hormone *testosterone,* may play a role in aggression. Drugs that reduce testosterone levels in violent human males seem to reduce their aggression; and among prisoners, testosterone levels tend to be higher among those who have committed unprovoked violent crimes than among those who have committed nonviolent crimes (Dabbs, 1992; Dabbs et al., 1995). These findings do *not* suggest that high testosterone levels, in and of themselves, stimulate overt aggression. However, they do point to the conclusion that individual differences with respect to these and perhaps other biochemical processes can play some role in such behavior.

In sum, aggressive motivation, and the overt aggression it produces, stems from many different factors (e.g., Baron & Richardson, 1994). Identifying these factors is an essential first step toward the goal of reducing the frequency of human violence. However, the number of variables involved suggests that achieving this objective will be far from an easy or simple task.

Key Questions

- Why do psychologists generally reject the view that aggression stems from innate factors?
- What are some important social factors that facilitate aggression?
- Are there any gender differences in sexual jealousy and in its effects on aggression?
- What are some important environmental causes of aggression?
- What is the aggression machine, and how is it used to study aggression?

■ *RESEARCH METHODS* ■

How Psychologists Study Aggression

Whether we like it or not, aggression is an important part of the human experience. At one time or another, almost everyone experiences anger and the intense desire to aggress against others. It is not surprising, then, that psychologists have studied aggression for many years. But *how,* precisely, can such behavior be investigated? As you can readily see, researchers who want to study aggression face a paradox: On the one hand, they wish to examine a form of behavior that is, by definition, potentially dangerous. On the other, they cannot expose research participants to the risk of harm—doing so would be unethical, and probably illegal too. How can this dilemma be resolved? One answer—which remains somewhat controversial even today—emerged during the 1960s. At that time, two famous psychologists, Arnold Buss and Stanley Milgram, hit upon the same basic approach at virtually the same time. Both reasoned as follows: Why not develop procedures in which research participants are told that they can harm another person in some manner, when in fact they cannot? In short, why not use temporary deception (see Chapter 1) to convince participants that they can aggress against another person, and then measure their willingness to do so under varying conditions?

While both Buss and Milgram developed procedures based on this reasoning, Buss applied his technique primarily to the study of aggression—voluntarily harming another person when such actions are not required. Milgram, in contrast, applied his approach mainly to the study of what he termed *destructive obedience*—harming another person in response to direct orders from a source of authority. We'll return to Milgram's chilling research in Chapter 16; here, we'll focus on Buss's procedures.

Buss's research on aggression involved the following events. Research participants were told that they were participating, along with another person, in a study dealing with the effects of punishment on learning. One of them would serve as a *teacher,* and the other as a *learner*. The teacher would present various materials to the learner; and on occasions when the learner made a correct response, the teacher would reward this person by flashing a light indicating "Correct." When the learner made an error, however, the teacher would deliver an electric shock as punishment. These shocks would be delivered by means of a device like the one shown in Figure 10.11, which soon came to be known as the **aggression machine.** Participants were told that the higher the number of the button they pushed, the stronger the shock to the learner, and that the longer they held the button down, the longer this pulse would last.

That is what participants were told. In reality, however, the learner was an assistant working with the researcher, and this person *never received any electric shocks*, no matter what the participants did. During the course of the session, the learner made many prearranged errors. On each of these occasions, then, participants faced a choice: They could inform the learner of the error by choosing the mildest shock button on the aggression machine—a shock so weak that, as the experimenter explained, "almost no one can even feel it." Or they could choose higher-numbered buttons that supposedly delivered more and more intense shocks. (Participants received a fairly mild but slightly unpleasant "sample" shock, purportedly delivered by button number 3; given the strength of this shock, those from buttons 8, 9, and 10 would be strong indeed.) On each occasion when the learner made an error, the choice was the participants': they could aggress or not, as they wished.

What did participants do? As you can guess, this depended very much on other conditions in the study—conditions that might, researchers using these procedures guessed, be related to human aggression. For instance, it was found that if the learner (the accomplice) had acted in a rude or condescending manner toward participants, they tended to choose higher-numbered shocks than if this person had behaved in a courteous and pleasant manner. Similarly, it was found that if the study took place under uncomfortably hot temperatures, participants sometimes tended to choose higher-numbered buttons. I could go on, but by now you probably get the picture: The *aggression machine* appeared to be a tool that could be used to investigate the potential effects of many different variables on aggression.

Now for a key question: Did these procedures really measure human aggression? Critics argued that they were too artificial to provide a valid measure, and that few research participants would believe that they could actually harm the learner. Psychologists who used these procedures responded by noting that in fact most participants *did* believe that they could actually hurt the learner (Berkowitz & Donnerstein, 1982). Further, they called attention to the finding, repeated in several studies, that people with a prior history of aggressive behavior often chose stronger shocks than persons without such a history (e.g., Gully & Dengerink, 1983; Wolfe & Baron, 1971). More recently, Anderson and Bushman (in press) have noted that if relationships between variables uncovered in laboratory studies of aggression are similar to the relation-

FIGURE 10.11

The Aggression Machine

The device shown here has been used to study aggression in many laboratory studies. Participants are told that they can deliver shocks (or other unpleasant stimuli) of varying intensity to another person by pushing buttons on this machine; the higher the number of the button pushed, the stronger the shock. (In fact, however, there are no shocks and no one is ever harmed.)

ships between these variables observed in real-world settings, this provides strong support for the validity of the laboratory methods. And in fact this is often the case. For example, in laboratory studies *and* in natural settings, males are more aggressive than females; similarly, in both kinds of settings, being anonymous increases aggression.

Together, such findings seem to indicate that the method devised by Buss provides one useful means for studying aggression—or at least aggressive intent, which is the heart of aggressive motivation. Certainly this method (and ones related to it) is far from perfect: Some people probably don't believe that they can deliver painful stimuli to the victim. However, if nothing else, Buss's procedures gave psychologists a new tool for studying aggression; and this tool led researchers to investigate many variables that had previously been ignored—everything from the impact of uncomfortable heat (the "long hot summer" effect) through the effects of exposure to erotic materials (e.g., Anderson, Anderson, & Deuser, 1996; Baron & Richardson, 1994). In this respect, these procedures did contribute to our understanding of an important form of behavior. And that, of course, is *the* task of modern psychology.

Achievement Motivation: The desire to accomplish difficult tasks and meet standards of excellence.

Need for Cognition: Motivation for engaging in effortful cognitive activities.

Thematic Apperception Test: A psychological test used to assess individual differences in several different motives, such as achievement motivation and power motivation.

Achievement Motivation and Cognitive Motivation: Two Complex Human Motives

Hunger, sex, aggression—these are motives we share with many other forms of life. There are some motives, however, that, as far as we can tell, are unique to our own species. In this section and the next we'll examine two of these motives: **achievement motivation** (often termed *need for achievement*)—the desire to accomplish difficult tasks or excel—and motivation to engage in complex cognitive activity, or **need for cognition** (Cacioppo et al., 1996).

Achievement Motivation: The Quest for Excellence

Individuals differ greatly in the desire for achievement. For some persons, accomplishing difficult tasks and meeting high standards of excellence are extremely important. For others, just getting by is quite enough. How can differences in this motive be measured? What are their effects? Psychologists have studied both issues.

Measuring Achievement Motivation While several different methods have been used to measure achievement motivation, most are based on the **thematic apperception Test (TAT).** This test consists of a series of ambiguous pictures similar to the one shown in Figure 10.12. Drawings used for this purpose show, for example, a boy at a desk, an engineer at a drawing board, a couple sitting on a bench, two women in a laboratory, a couple engaged in a trapeze act. Persons taking the test are asked to make up stories about the pictures. These stories are then scored for the presence of achievement-related content according to carefully developed scoring manuals (e.g., Smith, 1992). The result is a score for achievement motivation; if the researchers wish, they can obtain scores for several other motives as well (e.g., *power motivation*—the desire to exert influence over others). While the TAT continues to be used in its original form, Winter (1983) has also developed a technique for scoring achievement motivation directly from any type of verbal material, without the need for ambiguous pictures or story construction. Winter's technique can be applied to speeches or to books or any other written material. This has permitted psychologists to study the achievement motivation of political and military leaders and to compare achievement motivation across many different societies—with some fascinating results, as I'll describe in the following section.

FIGURE 10.12

Measuring Achievement Motivation

Persons taking the *thematic apperception test* are asked to make up stories about the ambiguous scenes; the amount of achievement-related imagery in these stories is then scored.

Effects of Achievement Motivation Do individual differences in achievement and power motivation really matter? In other words, do persons high and low in these motives have contrasting life experiences? Growing evidence suggests that they do. As you might expect, individuals high in achievement motivation tend to get higher grades in school, earn more rapid promotions, and attain greater success in running their own businesses than persons low in such motivation (Andrews, 1967; Raynor, 1970). Interestingly, recent findings suggest that achievement motivation, in combination with several other factors, may affect success in school and elsewhere in the same manner across various ethnic and cultural groups (Rowe, Vazsonyi, & Flannery, 1995). In other words, success may stem from factors that are much the same regardless of one's ethnic or cultural background.

Persons high in achievement motivation differ from persons low in this motive in two other respects. First, persons high in achievement motivation tend to seek tasks that are moderately difficult and challenging. The reason why they tend to avoid very easy tasks is obvious: Such tasks don't pose enough challenge for persons high in achievement motivation. But why do achievement-motivated individuals prefer tasks that are *moderately* challenging to ones that are extremely difficult? Because the chances of failing on extremely difficult tasks is too high; such persons want success above everything else (e.g., McClelland, 1985).

Another characteristic of persons high in achievement motivation is that they have a stronger-than-average desire for feedback on their performance: They want to know how well they are doing so that they can adjust their goals to make these challenging—but not impossible. Because of this desire for feedback, persons high in achievement motivation tend to prefer jobs in which rewards are closely related to individual performance—*merit-based pay systems*. They generally don't like working in situations where everyone receives the same across-the-board raises regardless of their performance (e.g., Turban & Keon, 1993).

Finally, as you might expect, persons high in achievement motivation tend to excel in performance under conditions where their achievement motive is activated (e.g., McClelland, 1995). Situations in which they are challenged to do their best, are confronted with difficult goals, or in which they compete against others, are grist for the mill of high-achievement persons, and these persons generally rise to the occasion in terms of excellent performance.

For information suggesting that achievement motivation can influence the fortunes of nations as well as individuals, please see the Exploring Gender and Diversity section below.

Achievement Motivation and Economic Growth

EXPLORING GENDER & DIVERSITY

That the economic fortunes of nations rise and fall over time is obvious. When I took high school economics in the late 1950s, our teacher showed us many graphs indicating that the United States was truly the dominant economic power in the world: It accounted for a majority of the world's output of steel, automobiles, and electricity, to name just a few important items. Today, of course, such graphs tell a very different story. The United States no longer accounts for most of the world's production in these areas; and in recent years, the U.S. rate of growth has been exceeded by that in several Asian countries. What factors contribute to such trends? Most persons (including economists) would list such factors as the price and availability of natural resources, labor costs, and government policies that encourage growth. To this list, psychologists would add another factor: national differences in achievement motivation.

While achievement motivation is certainly an individual process, some evidence points to the conclusion that average levels of this motive vary sharply across cultures. For example, in classic research on this topic, McClelland (1985) analyzed children's stories in twenty-two different cultures with respect to the degree to which the stories showed themes of achievement motivation. He then related these levels of achievement motivation to two measures of economic development: average income per person in each society, and electrical production per person. The major finding was clear: Achievement motivation scores were highly correlated with economic growth. In other words, the greater the emphasis placed on achievement in the stories told to children in various nations, the more rapid the economic growth in these nations as the children grew up.

While you may find these results surprising, they have been confirmed repeatedly. For example, in a massive study involving more than 12,000 participants in forty-one different countries, Furnham, Kirkcaldy, and Lynn (1994) examined the relationship between a wide range of attitudes closely related to achievement motivation, and two indicators of economic growth: gross domestic product (the amount of income produced by a country) and growth rate (percentage of increase in economic output from year to year). Results showed a significant relationship between achievement-related attitudes and economic growth. For instance, across all countries studied, attitudes toward competitiveness were a significant predictor of economic growth: The stronger these attitudes, and therefore the higher the achievement motivation, the greater the rate of growth.

These findings, and those reported in several earlier studies, support McClelland's original conclusion that a nation's economic success is related, at least in part, to the level of achievement motivation among its citizens. Of course, such research is correlational in nature, so we can't be certain that differences in achievement motivation across various cultures *cause* differences in economic growth. However, the fact that achievement motivation does influence individual performance and success suggests that investigating cultural differences in this motive may indeed provide us with insights into why certain countries suddenly rise to economic prominence at particular times in their history.

Cognitive Motivation: "I Think, Therefore I Am . . . Happy?" Before reading further, answer the questions in Table 10.2. (Instructions for entering and scoring your answers accompany the table.)

What were your results? If you obtained a score of 40 or more, you are probably high in another motive—motivation for engaging in effortful cognitive activities, *need for cognition.* If you scored 20 or lower, you are probably relatively low in this motive. Do you like to work on crossword puzzles? Do you like to read books or magazines that make you think about complex issues? Do you like activities that require careful reasoning, such as solving mathematical problems or writing computer programs? These are the kind of activities persons high in need for cognition tend to enjoy. In contrast, they are not preferred activities for persons low in need for cognition.

Please don't misunderstand: Being high in need for cognition does not necessarily imply being high in intelligence, and being low in this motive does not necessarily imply being low in intelligence. In fact, need for cognition is only modestly related to verbal intelligence, and it may not be closely related at all to other aspects of intelligence we'll consider in Chapter 11 (e.g., Petty & Jarvis, 1996). However, because enjoying effortful cognition can contribute to success in some intellectual activities, need for cognition does appear to be related—again, modestly—to such outcomes as high school and college grade point average (correlations averaging around +.20; Waters & Zakarjsek, 1990).

TABLE 10.2

Measuring Cognitive Motivation

The items shown here are similar to those on one test of the *need for cognition.* To obtain your score, add the numbers you entered for items 1, 4, 5, 7, and 9. Then convert the numbers you entered for items 2, 3, 6, 8, and 10 as follows: 1 becomes 5, 2 becomes 4, 3 remains 3, 4 becomes 2, and 5 becomes 1. Then add the numbers for the two sets of items together. If you scored 40 or above, you are high in need for cognition.

For each item below, indicate the extent to which it is true of you. Write one of these numbers next to each item:

1 = The statement is completely false with respect to you.
2 = The statement is mostly false with respect to you.
3 = The statement is neither false nor true with respect to you.
4 = The statement is mostly true with respect to you.
5 = The statement is completely true with respect to you.

1. I like situations that require a lot of thinking.
2. Thinking is not my idea of fun.
3. I prefer doing things that require little thought to things that challenge my ability to think.
4. I really enjoy tasks that involve coming up with new solutions to problems.
5. I like to work on puzzles.
6. I think only as much as I have to.
7. I feel lots of satisfaction after completing a task that requires mental effort.
8. Learning new ways to think doesn't interest me very much.
9. I like to think about abstract issues.
10. I prefer short-term daily projects to long-term ones.

What other effects do differences in cognitive motivation exert? Many of these have to do with how persons high or low on this dimension react to persuasive communications—messages aimed at changing their attitudes from advertisers, politicians, public service organizations and others. (We'll examine persuasion in detail in Chapter 16.) For instance, after hearing such messages, persons high in need for cognition tend to remember more of the information the persuasive messages contain than persons low in need for cognition (e.g., Boehm, 1994). Perhaps more important, persons high and low in need for cognition also seem to differ in how they react to such messages. Persons high in need for cognition tend to think carefully about the arguments presented; thus, whether and to what extent they are influenced by persuasive messages depends heavily on the quality of the arguments offered—whether these are well reasoned, well supported, and so on (e.g., Priester & Petty, 1995). In contrast, persons low in need for cognition are more influenced by other aspects of persuasive messages—for instance, the source of the message and how attractive this source is.

Finally, individuals high in need for cognition think more about a wide range of situations, including social ones. For example, they want to understand themselves and their feelings, and to understand why other persons behave the way they do and why they react to others in certain ways (e.g., Lassiter, Briggs, & Slaw, 1991). In short, like the people shown in Figure 10.13, they spend a lot of time thinking about and trying to make sense out of the world around them. Persons low in need for cognition also seek such understanding, but they often use shortcuts to attaining it—they more readily accept the explanations or interpretations of "experts" or celebrities, and they tend to use the kind of heuristics I described in Chapter 7. In sum, the motivation to engage in effortful cognitive activity is an important one, with wide-reaching effects on many aspects of behavior.

Key Questions

- What is achievement motivation, and how is it measured?
- What are the effects of achievement on individual behavior and on the economic fortunes of countries?
- What is need for cognition? What are its effects?

Intrinsic Motivation: How, Sometimes, to Turn Play into Work

Individuals perform many activities simply because they find them enjoyable. Everything from hobbies to gourmet dining to lovemaking fits within this category. Such activities may be described as stemming from **intrinsic motivation;** we perform them because of the pleasure they yield, not because they lead to external rewards. But what happens if people are given external rewards for performing such activities—if, for example, they are paid for sipping vintage wines or for pursuing their favorite hobby? Research findings suggest that they may then actually experience reductions in intrinsic motivation. In other words, they may become *less* motivated to engage in such activities. Why? One explanation goes something like this. When people consider their own behavior, they now conclude that they chose to perform the activities in question partly to obtain the external reward—not simply because they enjoyed the activities. To the extent they reach that conclusion, they may then view their own interest in these activities as lower than was previously the case. In short, when provided with an external reward for performing some activity they enjoy, people may shift from viewing their own behavior as stemming from intrinsic motivation ("I do it because I enjoy it") to perceiving it as stemming from external rewards ("I do it partly because of the external rewards I receive").

FIGURE 10.13

Need for Cognition

People who are high in cognitive motivation *(need for cognition)* tend to spend lots of time thinking—trying to make sense out of the complex world around them.

(**Source:** Drawing by Leo Cullum; ©1988 The New Yorker Magazine, Inc.)

Many studies support this reasoning. In such research, some participants were provided with extrinsic rewards for engaging in a task they initially enjoyed, while others were not. When later given an opportunity to perform the task, those who received the external rewards showed reduced motivation to do so (Deci, 1975; Lepper & Green, 1978). These results have important implications for anyone seeking to motivate others by means of rewards—parents, teachers, managers. The findings suggest that if the target persons already enjoy various activities, offering them rewards for performing those activities may lower their intrinsic motivation and so, ultimately, produce the surprising effect of reducing rather than enhancing performance!

Fortunately, additional evidence suggests that this is not always the case, and that intrinsic and extrinsic motivation are not necessarily incompatible (Deci & Ryan, 1985; Rigby et al., 1992). In fact, if external rewards are viewed as signs of recognition rather than as bribes (Rosenfeld, Fogler, & Adelman, 1980), and if the rewards provided are large and satisfying, intrinsic motivation may be enhanced rather than reduced (Lepper & Cordova, 1992; Ryan, 1982).

In addition, research findings indicate that individuals can "buffer" themselves against reductions in intrinsic motivation by engaging in a strategy known as *self-handicapping* (Berglas & Jones, 1978; Rhodewalt & Fairfield, 1991). In this strategy, individuals provide themselves with ready explanations for poor performance—explanations they offer before performing some task. If you've ever said, before beginning some activity, "I really didn't sleep well last night," or "I'm really not feeling too great today," you have used self-handicapping. The goal is to be able to explain away poor performance by pointing to various external factors that could potentially diminish your effectiveness.

Intrinsic Motivation: Motivation to perform activities because they are rewarding in and of themselves.

Emotions: Reactions consisting of physiological reactions, subjective cognitive states, and expressive behaviors.

How is this strategy related to intrinsic motivation? Deppe and Harackiwiecz (1996) suggest that by using self-handicapping with respect to tasks they think they'll enjoy, individuals can protect themselves against reductions in intrinsic motivation that might result from poor performance. By being able to "explain away" poor performance, they maintain their enjoyment of the task, and so their intrinsic motivation. To test this reasoning, Deppe and Harackiweicz conducted a study in which persons who were known to be high or low in the tendency to use self-handicapping (based on results of a test of this tendency) played an enjoyable, intrinsically motivating pinball game. Before playing the game, they were given an opportunity to practice as much as they wished on a related task; as expected, high self-handicappers practiced *less* than others, thus giving themselves a ready explanation for poor performance on the pinball task. They played the pinball game either under conditions where they competed against an opponent or under noncompetitive conditions. The researchers predicted that the effects of self-handicapping might be stronger in the competitive situation.

After the participants played the pinball task, the experimenter left the room, remarking as she did: "While I'm gone, feel free to do whatever you want; hang out, play pinball, or whatever." The amount of time participants then played the pinball game was observed, and this constituted the measure of their intrinsic motivation to play this game. As you can see from Figure 10.14 on page 408, results offered support for the major predictions: In the competitive condition, high self-handicappers played the pinball game longer than low self-handicappers; in the noncompetitive condition, there were no significant differences between the two groups.

These results indicate that if individuals want to protect their intrinsic motivation from possible reductions, they can readily do so. Moreover, since most of us become expert at self-handicapping early in life, it appears that we have effective techniques for doing so readily at our disposal. In short, we can prevent the conversion of play into work in at least some situations, if we are willing to exert the cognitive effort required to do so.

Key Questions

- What is intrinsic motivation?
- Why is intrinsic motivation sometimes reduced when individuals receive external rewards for performing activities they enjoy?
- What is self-handicapping, and how can it protect against reductions in intrinsic motivation?

Emotions: *Their Nature, Expression, and Impact*

Can you imagine life without **emotions**—without joy, anger, sorrow, or fear? What would such an existence be like—a life without any feelings? If you've seen any of the *Star Trek* movies, you know that Mr. Spock, who

FIGURE 10.14

Self-Handicapping and Intrinsic Motivation

Under conditions where they were competing with another person, participants high in self-handicapping spent more time playing a pinball machine when they were free to choose any activity they wished than did persons low in self-handicapping. These findings suggest that self-handicapping can protect individuals from reductions in intrinsic motivation resulting from concern over poor performance on a task.

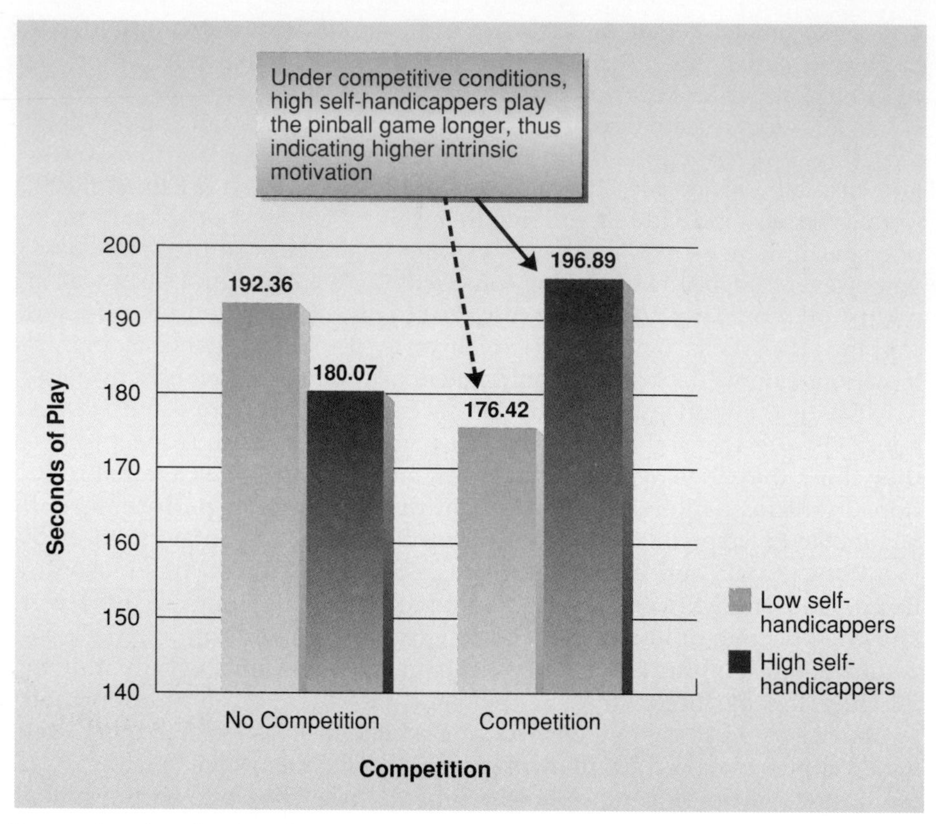

(**Source:** Based on data from Deppe & Harackiewicz, 1996.)

prided himself on being completely lacking in emotions, often suffered greatly from this deficit—thereby proving, of course, that he was *not* totally devoid of human feelings! So while we can imagine a life without emotions, few of us would choose such an existence.

But what, precisely, are emotions? The closer we look, the more complex these reactions seem to be. There is general agreement among scientists who study emotions, however, that they involve three major components: (1) physiological changes within our bodies—shifts in heart rate, blood pressure, and so on; (2) subjective cognitive states—the personal experiences we label as emotions; and (3) expressive behaviors—outward signs of these internal reactions (Tangney et al., 1996; Zajonc & McIntosh, 1992).

In this discussion, we'll first look at several contrasting theories of emotion. Second, we'll consider the physiological basis of emotions. Third, we'll examine how emotions are expressed. Finally, we'll examine the complex interplay between emotions and cognition—how feelings shape thought and thought shapes feelings.

The Nature of Emotions: Some Contrasting Views

Many different theories of emotions have been proposed, but among these, three have been most influential. These are known, after the scientists who proposed them, as the *Cannon–Bard, James–Lange,* and *Schachter–Singer* theories. A fourth theory—the *opponent-process theory*—offers additional insights into the nature of emotion and is also deserving of our attention.

Cannon–Bard Theory: A theory of emotion suggesting that various emotion-provoking events simultaneously produce subjective reactions labeled as emotions and physiological arousal.

James–Lange Theory: A theory of emotion suggesting that emotion-provoking events produce various physiological reactions and that recognition of these is responsible for subjective emotional experiences.

The Cannon–Bard and James–Lange Theories: Which Comes First, Action or Feeling? Imagine that in one of your courses, you are required to make a class presentation. As you walk to the front of the room, your pulse races, your mouth feels dry, and you can feel beads of perspiration on your forehead. In short, you are terrified. What is the basis for this feeling? Contrasting answers are offered by the Cannon–Bard and James–Lange theories of emotion.

Let's begin with the **Cannon–Bard theory,** because it is consistent with our own commonsense beliefs about emotions. This theory suggests that various emotion-provoking events induce *simultaneously* the subjective experiences we label as emotions and the physiological reactions that accompany them. Thus, in the situation just described, the sight of the audience and of your professor, pen poised to evaluate your performance, causes you to experience racing heart, a dry mouth, and other signs of physiological arousal *and,* at the same time, to experience subjective feelings you label as fear. In other words, this situation stimulates various portions of your nervous system so that both arousal, mediated by your *autonomic nervous system* (discussed in Chapter 2), and subjective feelings, mediated by your cerebral cortex and other portions of the brain, are produced.

The **James–Lange theory,** in contrast, offers a more surprising view of emotion. It suggests that subjective emotional experiences are actually the *result of* physiological changes within our bodies. In other words, you feel frightened when making your speech *because* you notice that your heart is racing, your mouth is dry, and so on. As William James himself put it (1890, p. 1066): "We feel sorry because we cry, angry because we strike, and afraid because we tremble." (See Figure 10.15 for a comparison of these two theories.)

Which of these theories is most accurate? Until recently, most evidence seemed to favor the Cannon–Bard approach: Emotion-provoking events produce both physiological arousal and the subjective experiences we label as emotions. Now, however, the pendulum of scientific opinion has moved somewhat toward greater acceptance of the James–Lange approach—the view that we experience emotions because of our awareness of physiological reactions to various stimuli or situations. What evidence supports this view? Several lines of research point in this direction. First, studies conducted with highly sophisticated equipment indicate that different emotions are indeed

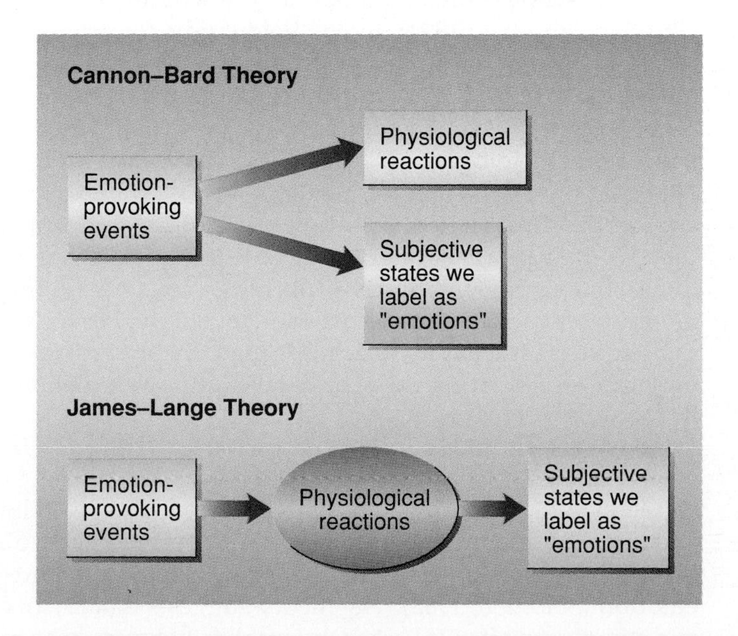

FIGURE 10.15

Two Major Theories of Emotion

According to the *Cannon–Bard theory,* emotion-provoking stimuli simultaneously evoke physiological reactions and the subjective states we label as emotions. According to the *James–Lange theory,* emotion-provoking events evoke physiological reactions, and it is our awareness of these that we label as emotions.

associated with different patterns of physiological activity (Levenson, 1992). Not only do various emotions *feel* different, it appears; they are reflected in somewhat different patterns of bodily changes, including contrasting patterns of brain and muscle activity (Ekman, Davidson, & Friesen, 1990; Izard, 1992).

Second, support for the James–Lange theory is also provided by research on the **facial feedback hypothesis** (Laird, 1984; McCanne & Anderson, 1987). This hypothesis suggests that changes in our facial expressions sometimes produce shifts in our emotional experiences rather than merely reflecting them. In other words, as James would suggest, we feel happier when we smile, sadder when we frown, and so on. While there are many complexities in examining this hypothesis, the results of several studies offer support for its accuracy (e.g., Ekman et al., 1990). So there may be a substantial grain of truth in the James–Lange theory (Zajonc, Murphy, & Inglehart, 1989). Subjective emotional experiences *do* often arise directly in response to specific external stimuli, as the Cannon–Bard view suggests. However, consistent with the James–Lange theory, they can also be generated by changes in and awareness of our own bodily states—even, it appears, by changes in our current facial expressions (Ekman, 1992).

Schachter and Singer's Two-Factor Theory Strong emotions are a common part of daily life, but how do we tell them apart? How do we know that we are angry rather than frightened, sad rather than surprised? One potential answer is provided by a third theory of emotion. According to this view, known as the **Schachter–Singer theory** or the **two-factor theory** of emotion, emotion-provoking events produce increased arousal (Schachter & Singer, 1962). In response to feelings of arousal, we search the external environment in order to identify the causes of our feelings. The factors we then select play a key role in determining the label we place on our arousal, and so in determining the emotion we experience. If we feel aroused after a near miss in traffic, we will probably label our emotion as "fear" or perhaps "anger." If, instead, we feel aroused in the presence of an attractive person, we may label our arousal as "attraction" or even "love." In short, we perceive ourselves to be experiencing the emotion that external cues, and our interpretation of them, suggest that we should be feeling. This view of emotions is described as a two-factor theory because it considers both arousal and the cognitive appraisal we perform in our efforts to identify the causes of such arousal.

Many studies provide support for the Schachter–Singer theory (Reisenzein, 1983; Sinclair et al., 1994). In one field study, for example, Dutton and Aron (1974) arranged conditions so that male hikers encountered an attractive female research assistant either on solid ground or while crossing a swaying suspension bridge high above a rocky gorge. Later, the researchers asked the men to rate their attraction to the assistant. The Schachter–Singer theory predicts that those who met the assistant on the swaying bridge would be more aroused, and that to the extent they attributed this arousal to the assistant, they would report finding her more attractive. This is precisely what was found. In fact, not only did the hikers who met her on the bridge rate her as more attractive, they were also more likely to call her for a date. Findings such as these suggest that the Schachter–Singer theory provides important insights into the process through which we label our own emotions.

Opponent-Process Theory: Action and Reaction to Emotion

Have you ever noticed that when you experience a strong emotional reaction it is soon followed by the opposite reaction? Elation is followed by a letdown, and anger is often followed by calm, or even by regret over one's previous outbursts. This relationship is the focus of the **opponent-process theory of emotion** (Solomon, 1982). The theory suggests that (1) an emotional reaction to a stimulus is often followed automatically by an opposite reaction, and (2)

Facial Feedback Hypothesis: A hypothesis indicating that facial expressions can influence as well as reflect emotional states.

Schachter–Singer Theory: A theory of emotion suggesting that our subjective emotional states are determined, at least in part, by the cognitive labels we attach to feelings of arousal; also known as **two-factor theory.**

Opponent-Process Theory of Emotion: A theory suggesting that an emotional reaction is followed automatically by an opposite reaction.

repeated exposure to a stimulus causes the initial reaction to weaken and the opponent process, or opposite reaction, to strengthen.

For example, consider a surgeon who initially experiences very positive emotions each time she successfully completes a lifesaving operation. Later, though, she experiences a subsequent emotional letdown. Gradually her positive reactions decrease, while the letdown intensifies or occurs sooner after each medical procedure. The result: She may gradually reduce the number of operations she performs or, at least, become increasingly bored with and indifferent to her work.

Opponent-process theory provides important insights into drug addiction. For instance, heroin users initially experience intense pleasure followed by unpleasant sensations of withdrawal. With repeated use of the drug, the pleasure becomes less intense and the unpleasant withdrawal reactions strengthen (Marlatt et al., 1988). In response, addicts begin to use the drug not for the pleasure it provides, but to avoid the negative feelings that occur when they *don't* use it.

In sum, opponent-process theory suggests that a law of physics—every action produces a reaction—may apply to emotions as well. Many emotional responses produce reactions, and such cycles can have important effects on many aspects of our behavior.

Key Questions

- How do the Cannon–Bard and James–Lange theories of emotion differ?
- What is the Schachter–Singer theory of emotion?
- What is the opponent-process theory of emotion?

The Physiology of Emotion

As you may recall from Chapter 2, the physiological reactions that accompany emotions are regulated by the two parts of the *autonomic nervous system*. Activation of the *sympathetic* nervous system readies the body for vigorous activity, producing such reactions as increases in heart rate, blood pressure, and respiration. In contrast, activation of the *parasympathetic* nervous system influences activity related to restoration of the body's resources. Blood is diverted away from large muscles and to the digestive organs, and digestion itself is facilitated. As we saw earlier, research findings indicate that different emotions are associated with somewhat different patterns of physiological reactions; so the fact that emotions such as anger, joy, and disgust feel very different subjectively does appear to reflect different biological reactions, at least to a degree.

In addition, growing evidence suggests that different emotions are related to contrasting patterns of activation in the cerebral cortex (Davidson, 1992). For more than a hundred years, medical reports have indicated that persons who experience damage to the left hemisphere often develop deep depression, while those with damage to the right hemisphere show euphoria (Robinson et al., 1984). These cases suggest that positive feelings may be centered mainly in the left hemisphere, while negative ones are centered mainly in the right hemisphere. Recent studies using recordings of electrical activity in the brain (EEGs; see Chapter 2) tend to confirm this possibility. When watching films designed to elicit happiness or amusement, individuals generally show greater activation in the left than in the right cortex. In contrast, when watching films designed to elicit disgust, they show greater activation in the right cortex (Davidson, 1992; Tomarken, Davidson, & Henriques, 1990).

Large individual differences in these patterns exist (e.g., Henriques & Davidson, 1991) but, taken as a whole, current findings suggest that the cerebral hemispheres show some degree of specialization with respect to emotions. Positive feelings such as happiness are associated with greater activation in the left hemisphere, while negative ones such as sadness are associated with greater activation in the right hemisphere. In brain activity

FIGURE 10.16

Lie Detectors: A Reliable Guide to Truth?

Lie detectors measure change in physiological reactions during questioning. The pattern of such changes supposedly reveals the truthfulness of a person's answers. However, because individuals can readily alter their physiological reactions, it is uncertain whether lie detectors provide a valid means for detecting lies.

as well as in heart rate and other bodily processes, then, there appear to be strong links between our subjective emotional experiences and our physiological states.

Can Physiological Reactions Be Used to Detect Lies? If different emotions are associated with contrasting physiological reactions, including different patterns of activity in the two hemispheres of the brain, an intriguing possibility arises. People often experience different emotions when lying than when telling the truth—so perhaps we can use these contrasting physiological patterns to assess the truthfulness of what they say. This is the central idea behind the use of *polygraphs,* or "lie detectors"—devices that record several different physiological reactions at once (see Figure 10.16). Lying, presumably, is more emotionally exciting than telling the truth. So if individuals show greater arousal while responding to questions about which they might be expected to lie than in responding to questions about which they have no reason to lie, perhaps this indicates that they are indeed lying. For example, suppose, using a standard lie-detector procedure known as the *control question technique,* we ask a woman suspected of a crime whether she committed it. She answers, "No"; but the needles on the polygraph show larger reactions than when she is asked a *control question* such as "Have you ever lied to another person?" Since the reaction to the key, or *relevant,* question is larger, it might be concluded that she is lying. In contrast, innocent persons who know they did not commit the crime may well show a larger reaction to the control question (Saxe, 1994).

Can deception be separated from truth in this fashion? There are several grounds for skepticism in this respect. First, so-called lie detectors really measure only *arousal;* the relationship of arousal to lying remains uncertain. Indeed, accomplished con artists may show little or no emotional response when telling huge lies. Second, people can and do influence their physiological reactions in many ways (Lykken, 1985; Zajonc & McIntosh, 1992). For example, try this simple exercise. Take your pulse. After you've measured it, take it again; but this time, slow your breathing and emphasize exhaling. Did your pulse change? For many people, it slows down. Persons taking lie-detector tests can change their breathing, tense their muscles, and do other things that affect the readings.

Finally, differential reactions by persons lying and persons telling the truth would be expected to occur only to the extent that both groups believe that the polygraph works—that it really can determine whether their answers are honest or dishonest (Saxe, 1994). If dishonest persons are skeptical but honest persons believe that lie detectors work, persons telling the truth may actually show *larger* reactions than those who are lying.

Recognizing such problems, many states have banned the use of lie-detector test results as evidence in court proceedings. While many psychologists agree with these actions, some studies do suggest that the accuracy of polygraphs can be increased through the use of improved procedures. In one of these, known as the *directed lie technique,* the persons being tested are instructed to lie in response to some control questions so that comparisons can be made between their truthful and deceitful responses. It is expected that innocent persons will show larger reactions when lying in response to control questions than will guilty persons, because lying is a more unusual and upsetting behavior for them. Some research findings suggest that the accuracy of polygraph tests is indeed increased by such improved testing procedures (Honts, 1994). Still, despite such evidence, most psychologists remain skeptical about the overall value of lie detectors and recognize that using them to evaluate individuals' honesty can be a very risky business.

Key Questions

- Are different emotions associated with contrasting patterns of physiological reactions?
- Are different emotions related to different patterns of brain activity?
- Do lie detectors provide a valid means of determining whether individuals are lying?

The External Expression of Emotion: Outward Signs of Inner Feelings

Emotions are a private affair. No one, no matter how intimate with us they are, can truly share our subjective inner experiences. Yet, we are able to recognize the presence of various emotions in others, and we are able to communicate our own feelings to them as well. How does such communication occur? A large part of the answer involves **nonverbal cues**—outward signs of others' internal emotional states shown in their facial expressions, body posture, and other behaviors.

Nonverbal Cues: The Basic Channels Several decades of research on nonverbal cues suggests that this kind of communication occurs through several different *channels* or paths simultaneously. The most revealing of these consist of *facial expressions, body movements and posture,* and *touching.*

Unmasking the Face: Facial Expressions as Clues to Others' Emotions More than two thousand years ago, the Roman orator Cicero stated that "the face is the image of the soul." By this he meant that feelings and emotions are often reflected in the face and can be read there from specific expressions. Modern research suggests that Cicero, and many other observers of human behavior, were correct: It *is* possible to learn much about others' current moods and feelings from their facial expressions. In fact, it appears that six different basic emotions are represented clearly, and from an early age, on the human face: anger, fear, sadness, disgust, happiness, and surprise (Ekman, 1992). In addition, recent findings suggest that another emotion—contempt—may also be quite basic (e.g., Rosenberg & Ekman, 1995). However, agreement on what specific facial expression represents contempt is less consistent than that for the other six emotions just mentioned.

Until recently, it was widely assumed that basic facial expressions such as those for happiness, anger, or disgust are universal—that they are recognized by people all over the world as indicating those specific emotions (e.g., Ekman & Friesen, 1975). In other words, it was assumed that a smile is a clear sign of happiness and a frown a clear sign of sadness in every culture. Some research, however, has called this assumption into question (Russell, 1994, 1995). These studies indicate that while facial expressions may indeed reveal much about others' emotions, interpretations of such expressions are also affected by the context in which the expressions occur, and by various situational cues. For instance, if participants in a study are shown a photo of a face exhibiting what would normally be judged as fear, but are also read a story suggesting that the person in the photo is actually showing anger, many describe the face as showing *this* emotion—not fear (see Figure 10.17 on page 414; Carroll & Russell, 1996). Findings such as these suggest that facial expressions may not be as universal in terms of providing clear signals about underlying emotions as was previously assumed. These findings are somewhat controversial, however, so at present it would be unwise to reach firm conclusions about this issue.

Body Language: Gestures, Posture, and Movements Try this simple demonstration: First, remember some incident that made you angry—the angrier the better. Think about it for a minute. Now try to remember another incident, one that made you feel happy—again, the happier the bet-

Nonverbal Cues: Outward signs of individuals' emotional states shown in their facial expressions, body posture, and other behaviors.

FIGURE 10.17

Facial Expressions

What emotion is this woman experiencing? In the absence of any further information, you would probably say "fear." However, what if you learned that she showed this expression upon learning that she would not be seated in a restaurant, even though she had a reservation?

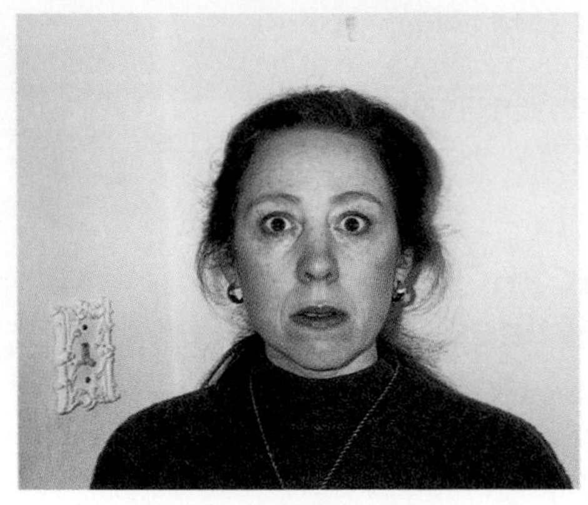

ter. Did you change your posture or move your hands, arms, or legs as your thoughts shifted from the first incident to the second? The chances are good that you did, for our current mood or emotion is often reflected in the posture, position, and movement of our body. Together, such nonverbal behaviors are termed **body language,** and they can provide several kinds of information about others' emotions.

First, frequent body movements—especially ones in which a particular part of the body does something to another part, such as touching, scratching, or rubbing—suggest emotional arousal. The greater the frequency of such behavior, the higher a person's level of arousal or nervousness seems to be (Harrigan et al., 1991).

Larger patterns of movements involving the whole body can also be informative. Such phrases as "she adopted a *threatening posture*" and "he greeted her with *open arms*" suggest that different body orientations or postures can be suggestive of contrasting emotional reactions. In fact, research by Aronoff, Woike, and Hyman (1992) confirms this possibility. These researchers first identified two groups of characters in classical ballet: ones who played dangerous or threatening roles (e.g., Macbeth, the Angel of Death, Lizzie Borden) and ones who played warm, sympathetic roles (Juliet, Romeo). Then they examined examples of dancing by these characters in actual ballets to see if they adopted different kinds of postures. Aronoff and his colleagues predicted that the dangerous, threatening characters would show more diagonal or angular postures, while the warm, sympathetic characters would show more rounded postures; and results strongly confirmed this hypothesis. These and related findings (e.g., Lynn & Mynier, 1993) indicate that body movements or postures can sometimes provide important information about others' emotions.

Finally, more specific information about others' feelings are often provided by **gestures**—body movements carrying specific meanings in a given culture. For example, in several countries, holding one's hand with the thumb pointing up is a sign of "Okay." Similarly, seizing one's nose between the thumb and index finger is a sign of displeasure or disgust. Gestures vary greatly from culture to culture; but every human society seems to have at least some gestures, and they are used in many different contexts.

Touching: The Most Intimate Nonverbal Cue Suppose that while you were talking with another person, she or he touched you briefly. What information would this convey? How would you react? The answer to both questions is "It depends." And what it depends on is several factors relating to who does the touching—a friend or a stranger, a member of your own or the other gender; the nature of the touching—brief or prolonged, gentle or rough; and the context in which it takes place—a business setting, social gathering, a doctor's office. Depending on such factors, touch can suggest affection, sexual interest, dominance, caring, or even aggression. Despite these complexities, growing evidence indicates that when one person touches another in a manner that is considered acceptable in that context, positive reactions generally result (Alagna, Whitcher, & Fisher, 1979; Smith, Gier, & Willis, 1982). Consider, for example, an ingenious field study conducted by Crusco and Wetzel (1984).

These researchers enlisted the aid of waitresses who agreed to treat customers in one of three different ways when giving them their change: They did not touch the customers, they touched them briefly on the hand, or they

Body Language: Nonverbal cues involving body posture or movement of body parts.

Gestures: Movements of various body parts that convey a specific meaning to others.

touched them for a longer period of time on the shoulder. Crusco and Wetzel predicted that in this context, touching would be viewed as sign of friendliness, and so would increase tipping. Results confirmed this hypothesis: Both a brief touch on the hand (about one-half second) and a longer touch on the shoulder (one second or slightly more) significantly increased tipping over the no-touch control condition. These findings, and those of more recent research, indicate that touching, like other actions that convey friendliness to customers (such as drawing a smiling face on the back of checks; e.g., Rind & Bordia, 1996), produce one result waitpersons want: larger tips.

Key Questions

- What emotions are clearly shown by facial expressions? What do research findings indicate about the universality of such expressions?
- What information about others' emotions is conveyed by body language? By touching?

Emotion and Cognition: How Feelings Shape Thought and Thought Shapes Feelings

Earlier, I asked you to recall incidents that made you feel angry and happy. When you thought about these events, did your mood also change? The chances are good that it did, for in many instances our thoughts seem to exert strong effects on our emotions. This relationship works in the other direction as well. Being in a happy mood often causes us to think happy thoughts, while feeling sad tends to bring negative memories and images to mind. In short, there are important links between *emotion* and *cognition*—between the way we feel and the way we think. Let's take a brief look at some of the evidence for such links (e.g., Forgas & Fiedler, 1996).

How Affect Influences Cognition Does **affect**—our current mood—influence the way we think? The findings of many different studies indicate that such effects do in fact occur, and that our current moods influence many aspects of cognition. First, it has been found that our moods, or *affective states* as they are often termed (Isen, 1993; Isen & Baron, 1991), influence our perception of ambiguous stimuli. In general, we perceive and evaluate these stimuli more favorably when we are in a good mood than when we are in a negative one. For example, when asked to interview job applicants whose qualifications are ambiguous—neither very strong nor very weak—research participants assign higher ratings to applicants when they (the interviewers) are in a positive mood than when they are in a negative mood (e.g., Baron, 1987, 1993).

Second, positive and negative moods exert a strong influence on memory. In general, it appears that there is often a good match between our current mood and what we remember and also think about: When we are feeling happy, we tend to retrieve happy ideas and experiences from memory and to think happy thoughts, while when we are in a negative mood, we tend to retrieve negative information from memory and to think unhappy thoughts (see the discussion of mood-dependent memory in Chapter 6; Seta, Hayes, & Seta, 1994).

These are not the only ways in which affect influences cognition, however. Other findings indicate, for example, that feeling happy can sometimes increase creativity—perhaps because being in a happy mood activates a wider range of ideas or associations, and creativity involves combining these into new patterns. A study conducted by Estrada, Isen, and Young (1995) clearly illustrates such effects.

In this investigation, participants were physicians working at a large hospital. The doctors were asked to evaluate a medical case and, at the same time, to complete a test of creativity. For some participants, the packet of materials they received also contained some candy—a small, unexpected gift designed to give them a small "mood boost." The other participants did not

Affect: A person's current mood.

receive this small gift. The creativity test involved coming up with a word that was related to three other words (e.g., club gown mare ______ [answer: night]). This test has been found to provide one useful measure of creativity (Mednick, Mednick, & Mednick, 1964).

Estrada and his colleagues (1995) predicted that the small gift of candy would increase the physicians' creativity; and in fact, as shown in Figure 10.18, this is what was found. Those who received the candy answered more questions correctly than those who did not. Since accurately diagnosing complex medical problems often involves recognizing links between test results and symptoms that do not at first appear to be related, these findings suggest that physicians' affective states may play some role in their success at this crucial task. Obviously, to the extent this is so, there are important implications for the quality of medical treatment.

How Cognition Influences Affect Most research on the relationship between affect and cognition has focused on how feelings influence thought. However, there is also compelling evidence for the reverse—the impact of cognition on affect. I mentioned one aspect of this relationship in discussing the two-factor theory of emotion proposed by Schachter and Singer (1962). As you may recall, their theory suggests that often we don't know our own feelings or attitudes directly. Rather, since these internal reactions are often somewhat ambiguous, we look outward—at our own behavior or other aspects of the external world—for clues about our feelings' essential nature. In such cases, the emotions or feelings we experience are strongly determined by the interpretation or cognitive labels we select.

A second way in which cognition can affect emotions is through the activation of *schemas* containing a strong affective component. For example, if we label an individual as belonging to some group, the schema for this social category may suggest what traits he or she probably possesses. In addition, it may also tell us how we *feel* about such persons. Thus, activation of a strong

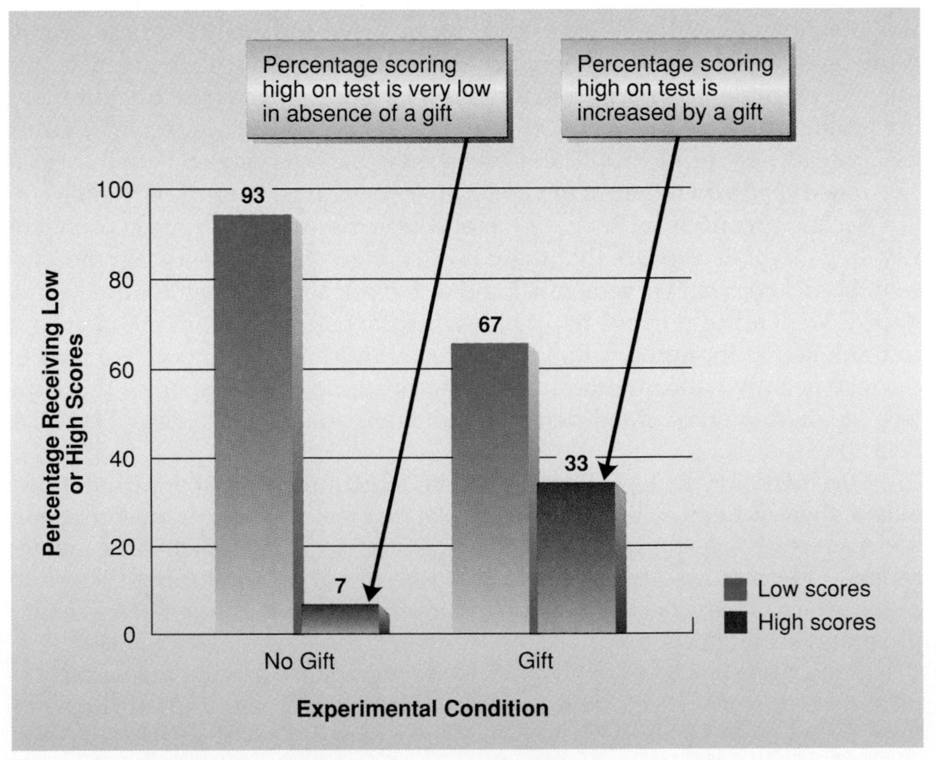

(**Source:** Based on data from Estrada, Isen, & Young, 1995.)

FIGURE 10.18

Affective States and Creativity

After receiving a small, unexpected gift (some candy), more physicians scored high on one widely used test of creativity. These findings suggest that being in a positive mood can sometimes increase creativity.

racial, ethnic, or religious schema or stereotype may exert powerful effects upon our current feelings or moods. (Please see Chapter 16 for more information on this topic.)

Third, our thoughts can often influence our reactions to emotion-provoking events. For example, anger and resulting aggressive motivation can often be reduced by apologies and other information that help explain why others have treated us in a provocative manner (Ohbuchi, Kameda, & Agari, 1989). Further, anger can sometimes be reduced—or even prevented—by techniques such as thinking about events *other* than those that generate anger (Zillmann, 1993). In such instances, the effects of cognition on feelings can have important social consequences.

A fourth way in which cognition influences affect involves the impact of *expectancies* on our reactions and judgments. When individuals hold expectations about how they will react to a new event or stimulus, these expectations often shape their perceptions of, and feelings about, the event or stimulus when they do encounter it (e.g., Wilson et al., 1989). For example, when people expect that they will dislike a new food, they often show visible signs of displeasure even before they put it into their mouths. Conversely, when people expect to enjoy a film, joke, or story, they are very likely to do so even if they might have had weaker positive reactions in the absence of such expectations. Indeed, it appears that expectancies can even shape our memories of events so that we recall them as more (or less) pleasant than they actually were, in line with what we expected them to be like (Wilson & Klaaren, 1992). In such cases, expectations—an aspect of our cognition—may be a more important determinant of our current emotions than reality itself.

Microexpressions: Fleeting facial expressions that occur very quickly and may reveal individuals' true emotional reactions to events or situations.

Interchannel Discrepancies: Inconsistencies between cues from different basic channels of nonverbal communication.

Key Questions

- In what ways do our affective states influence cognition?
- In what ways does cognition influence our affective states?

Making Psychology Part of Your Life

How to Tell When Another Person Is Lying: Nonverbal Cues and the Detection of Deception

Every violation of truth is not only a sort of suicide in the liar, but is a stab at the health of human society.—Ralph Waldo Emerson

It is sad but true that everyday life presents us with many temptations to lie to others. And in fact, research findings indicate that all too often we yield to these temptations. One recent study of lying found that college students typically tell about two lies per day, most of which are designed to enhance their social image or advance their selfish interests (DePaulo et al., 1996). But lies between friends or acquaintances are often quite benign when compared to the lies told by professionals—persons who earn their living by influencing others—such as con artists, salespersons, and politicians, to name a few (see Figure 10.19 on page 418).

Given these facts, it seems important for us to be able to tell when another person is lying—without the aid of a polygraph machine! Fortunately, the findings of a large body of research on nonverbal communication can prove very useful in this respect. Much of

FIGURE 10.19

Lying: A Part of Everyday Life

In some fields—for example, sales, politics, and negotiations—individuals earn their living by lying to others.

this research has focused on what psychologists term the *detection of deception*, and the results of this work provide us with several important clues that can help us determine whether another person is lying. Before turning to these specific nonverbal cues, however, we should ask *why* it's possible to use such information—even in the case of highly skilled liars.

The answer centers in the fact that because there are many different *channels* of nonverbal communication, it's virtually impossible for anyone to monitor and control all of these channels at once (DePaulo, Epstein, & Wyer, 1993). For this reason, even persons who lie frequently, and are highly practiced at this task, often reveal the fact that they are lying through *some* channel of nonverbal cues. For example, if they focus on regulating their facial expressions and eye contact, then the fact that they are lying may be revealed through their body movements and posture, or through changes in the nonverbal aspects of speech—the tone of their voice, and related cues.

Now that we've clarified this issue, let's turn to the specific clues *you* can use to help decide whether another person is being honest with you.

One nonverbal cue that can be very helpful in this respect is **microexpressions.** These are fleeting facial expressions lasting only a few tenths of second. Such reactions appear on the face very quickly after an emotion-provoking event and are difficult to suppress (Ekman, 1985). As a result, they can be quite revealing about others' true feelings or emotions. So when you have reason to suspect that another person may be lying, say something you think they'll find surprising or upsetting, and *watch their face very carefully as you say it*. If you see one expression that is followed very quickly by another, different one, watch out: The person may be trying to deceive you.

A second nonverbal cue we can use is known as **interchannel discrepancies.** These are inconsistencies between nonverbal cues from different basic channels. Such inconsistencies result from the fact that, as we noted earlier, persons who are lying find it difficult to control all these channels at once. For example, a defendant who is lying on the witness stand may succeed in managing her facial expressions and in maintaining a high level of eye contact with the jury. At the same time, however, she may demonstrate postural shifts on body movements that reveal that she is experiencing a high level of emotional arousal.

A third nonverbal cue involves nonverbal aspects of people's speech—aspects sometimes known as *paralanguage*. When people lie, the pitch of their voices often rises (Zuckerman, DePaulo, & Rosenthal, 1981), and they tend to speak more slowly and with less fluency. In addition, they engage in more *sentence repairs*—instances in which they start a sentence, interrupt it, and then start again (Stiff et al., 1989). So listen carefully: If you observe these changes in another person's voice, he or she may be lying.

Fourth, deception is frequently revealed by various aspects of eye contact. Persons who are lying often blink more frequently and show pupils that are more dilated than those of persons who are telling the truth. They may also show an unusually low level of eye contact—or, surprisingly, an unusually high one, as they attempt to feign honesty by looking others right in the eye (Kleinke, 1986).

Finally, persons who are lying sometimes show exaggerated facial expressions. They smile more—or more broadly—than usual, show greater sorrow, and so on than is typical for them in this kind of situation. A prime example: Someone says no to a request you've made and then shows exaggerated regret. This is a good sign that the reasons they have given you for the no may not be accurate.

Through careful attention to these nonverbal cues, we can often tell when others are lying—or merely trying to hide their true feelings from us. Our performance in this respect is far form perfect; skillful liars do often succeed in deceiving us. But their task will be made more difficult if you pay careful attention to the clues described above.

Summary and Review of Key Questions

Motivation: The Activation and Persistence of Behavior

- **Why did psychologists largely reject instinct theory?** They rejected instinct theory because it involved circular reasoning.
- **According to drive theory, what is the basis for various motives?** Drive theory suggests that motivation is a process in which various biological needs push (drive) us to actions designed to satisfy them.
- **Why is expectancy theory described as a cognitive theory of motivation?** Expectancy theory is a cognitive theory because it suggests that behavior is motivated by expectancies concerning the outcomes that will result from specific actions.
- **What are the basic ideas behind Maslow's needs hierarchy theory?** Maslow's theory suggests that needs exist in a hierarchy and that higher-level motives cannot be activated until lower-level ones are satisfied.
- **What factors play a role in the regulation of eating?** Eating is regulated by complex biochemical systems within the body involving detector cells in the hypothalamus and elsewhere; it is also affected by the sight of food, by feedback from chewing and swallowing, and by cultural factors.
- **What factors override this regulatory system, so that many people do not maintain a stable weight?** Many factors tend to override this system, including the impact of learning (e.g., associating eating with specific contexts), responses to food-related cues, genetic factors (a predisposition to gain weight), and reactions to stress.
- **What role do hormones play in human sexual motivation?** Sex hormones seem to play only a subtle and relatively minor role in human sexual motivation; other chemicals produced within the body may play a more important role.
- **What are the major phases of sexual activity?** During sexual activity both males and females move through a series of distinct phases: excitement, plateau, orgasm, and resolution.
- **What is a key difference between human beings and other species with respect to sexual arousal?** In contrast to other species, human beings can be sexually aroused by self-generated fantasies and by exposure to erotic stimuli.
- **Is there any scientific evidence for the role of pheromones in human sexual behavior?** At present there is little if any scientific evidence for such effects.
- **What factors appear to play a role in determining sexual orientation?** At present it appears that many factors may play a role, including genetic factors, early experiences, and differences in temperament.
- **Why do psychologists generally reject the view that aggression stems from innate factors?** Psychologists reject this view because of huge variations in the incidence of aggression across different cultures. Such variations suggest that social and cultural factors play key roles in aggression.
- **What are some important social factors that facilitate aggression?** Aggression is increased by some forms of frustration, by direct provocation, and by exposure to media violence.
- **Are there any gender differences in sexual jealousy and in its effects on aggression?** Research findings indicate, surprisingly, that females seem to experience stronger sexual jealousy and a greater tendency to aggress against their mates than do males.
- **What are some important environmental causes of aggression?** Environmental factors that influence aggression include uncomfortably high temperatures, irritating noise, crowding—any factors that tend to induce negative moods or feelings.
- **What is the aggression machine, and how is it used to study aggression?** The aggression machine is a device used to measure aggression under laboratory conditions. It contains a series of buttons that can be pushed to, supposedly, deliver shocks of varying intensity to another person. In fact, no shocks or other unpleasant stimuli are ever delivered.
- **What is achievement motivation, and how is it measured?** Achievement motivation is the desire to meet standards of excellence or to outperform others. It is measured by the thematic apperception test and by the content of verbal materials.
- **What are the effects of achievement on individual behavior and on the economic fortunes of countries?** Individuals high in achievement motivation tend to excel in school and in running their own businesses. Some research findings indicate that the higher the level of achievement motivation in a given society, the greater its economic success.
- **What is need for cognition? What are its effects?** Need for cognition is the motivation to engage in and enjoy complex cognitive activities. Persons high in this motive tend to receive higher grades in school, think more, and to pay closer attention to the quality of arguments in persuasive appeals than persons low in this motive.
- **What is intrinsic motivation?** Intrinsic motivation is motivation to perform some activity simply because it is enjoyable.
- **Why is intrinsic motivation sometimes reduced when individuals receive external rewards for performing activities they enjoy?** When individuals receive rewards for performing activities they enjoy, they reach the conclusion that they perform these activities not solely because they like them, but also because of the external rewards for doing so.
- **What is self-handicapping, and how can it protect against reductions in intrinsic motivation?** Self-handicapping is a strategy in which individuals provide themselves in advance with good excuses for poor performance. Individuals who use self-handicapping protect themselves against reductions in intrinsic motivation that may follow from poor performance on a task.

KEY TERMS

motivation, p. 383 • instinct theory, p. 383 • instincts, p. 383 • drive theory, p. 384 • homeostasis, p. 384 • arousal theory, p. 385 • Yerkes–Dodson law, p. 385 • expectancy theory, p. 386 • incentives, p. 386 • work motivation, p. 386 • hierarchy of needs, p. 386 • hunger motivation, p. 387 • sexual motivation, p. 390 • gonads, p. 390 • homosexual, p. 395 • bisexual, p. 395 • heterosexual, p. 395 • aggressive motivation, p. 396 • aggression, p. 396 • frustration, p. 397 • workplace violence, p. 397 • sexual jealousy, p. 398 • aggression machine, p. 400 • achievement motivation, p. 402 • need for cognition, p. 402 • thematic apperception test (TAT), p. 402 • intrinsic motivation, p. 407

Emotions: Their Nature, Expression, and Impact

- **How do the Cannon–Bard and James–Lange theories of emotion differ?** The Cannon–Bard theory suggests that emotion-provoking stimuli simultaneously elicit physiological arousal and the subjective cognitive states we label as emotions. The James–Lange theory suggests that emotion-provoking stimuli induce physiological reactions and that these form the basis for the subjective cognitive states we label as emotions.
- **What is the Schachter–Singer theory of emotion?** The Schachter–Singer theory suggests that when we are aroused by emotion-provoking stimuli, we search the external environment for the causes of our feelings of arousal. The causes we select then determine our emotions.
- **What is the opponent-process theory of emotion?** The opponent-process theory suggests that strong emotional reactions are followed by opposite emotional reactions, and that (partly as a result) our reactions to emotion-provoking stimuli tend to decrease over time.
- **Are different emotions associated with contrasting patterns of physiological reactions?** Research findings indicate that different emotions are indeed associated with contrasting patterns of physiological reactions.

- **Are different emotions related to different patterns of brain activity?** Recent findings indicate that positive emotional reactions are associated with greater activity in the left cerebral hemisphere, while negative emotional reactions are associated with greater activity in the right cerebral hemisphere.
- **Do lie detectors provide a valid means of determining whether individuals are lying?** Some findings suggest that when used with carefully refined methods, lie detectors can yield valid information about lying. However, because the reactions measured by such devices are subject to faking, most psychologists remain skeptical about the usefulness of lie detectors.
- **What emotions are clearly shown by facial expressions? What do research findings indicate about the universality of such expressions?** Research findings indicate that clear facial expressions exist for anger, fear, sadness, disgust, happiness, and surprise. Recent studies indicate that such expressions, while informative, may not be as universal in meaning as was previously assumed.
- **What information about others' emotions is conveyed by body language? By touching?** Body language provides information about others' overall level of arousal, about their reactions to us, and about specific reactions they may be having. Touching can convey a wide range of information, including affection, sexual interest, dominance, caring, or even aggression.
- **In what ways do our affective states influence cognition?** Our affective states can influence our perception of ambiguous stimuli, our memory, decisions and judgments we make, and our creativity.
- **In what ways does cognition influence our affective states?** Cognition can influence our affective states by activating schemas containing strong affective components; by shaping our interpretation of emotion-provoking events; and through the impact of expectancies, which can shape our affective reactions to new stimuli or experiences.

KEY TERMS

emotions, p. 407 • Cannon–Bard theory, p. 409 • James–Lange theory, p. 409 • facial feedback hypothesis, p. 410 • Schachter–Singer theory, p. 410 • opponent-process theory of emotion, p. 410 • nonverbal cues, p. 413 • body language, p. 414 • gestures, p. 414 • affect, p. 415 • microexpressions, p. 417 • interchannel discrepancies, p. 417

Critical Thinking Questions

Appraisal

Motivation is by definition a hidden, internal process: We can measure its effects, but we can't "see" it directly. Given this fact, do you think that we can ever obtain full understanding of motivation and the roles it plays in overt behavior?

Controversy

Although many psychologists remain skeptical about the value of lie detectors, they continue to receive widespread attention and are even used by some police departments. Do you think that these devices can ever yield truly valid information about whether people are lying? Or should we rely, instead, on other sources of information, such as nonverbal cues?

Making Psychology Part of Your Life

Now that you know more about the causes of human aggression, do you think the evidence gathered by psychologists who study this topic can be used to design practical techniques for reducing such behavior? And what about you: Can you use what you now know to protect yourself against aggressive outbursts—either your own or those of others?

CHAPTER OUTLINE

Intelligence

Cognitive and Emotional

When I was nine years old, I had a friend named Johnny. He was a year older than I was and, I thought, also about ten times as smart. Johnny knew everything—or, at least, everything that seemed important to a ten-year-old boy. He knew all about fishing; the name and batting average of every major-league player; how to do scientific "experiments"; and, perhaps most important of all, the best places to buy ice cream. He also knew about things I didn't even know existed. Johnny had a telescope and showed me the craters of the moon; he knew the names of different kinds of rocks and how they were formed. He told me about fossils, and even had a few in his room. Johnny was quick, too: He could think, reason, and argue circles around me. Yes, Johnny was quite a friend—and something of an idol for me. We stayed friends for about a year; then, much to my dismay, he left my school to attend one for gifted children. I still saw him sometimes, but this school was at the other end of the city, so he was gone most of the day. What a loss!

A few years later my family moved, and I lost track of Johnny completely—although I always half expected to read about him in the newspapers as he rose to fame and fortune. It was not until decades later that, quite by accident, I learned more about his fate. Sad to say, it wasn't a happy one. Yes, Johnny had been brilliant—everyone recognized that. But somehow he had still managed to go completely off the track. He started getting into trouble in high school, where he used his persuasive skills to mastermind several instances of senseless vandalism. Despite these troubles, he was accepted by a prestigious university; but he quickly became bored with his classes and began experimenting with drugs. Johnny dropped out of college in his junior year and began a life of white-collar crime: fraud, swindles, confidence rackets—you name it, he tried it. He got away with these schemes for a while, but ultimately his arrogant belief that everyone else was stupid caught up with him, and he spent many years in jail. It was a sad ending for one of my childhood heroes.

By itself, a high level of intelligence is not a guarantee of success, accomplishment, or personal happiness.

Why do I start with this unhappy tale? Because it illustrates two points I want to emphasize at the very beginning of this discussion: (1) *Yes,* intelligence is indeed an important human characteristic—after all, it was Johnny's high intelligence that made him so quick and so knowledgeable. But (2) *no,* by itself, a high level of intelligence (or at least the kind of intelligence shown by Johnny) is *not* a guarantee of success, accomplishment, or personal happiness. Indeed, as we'll see throughout this chapter, intelligence is only a part of the total picture where such desirable outcomes are concerned.

But what, precisely, *is* intelligence? How can it be measured? Is there only one kind of intelligence, or are there many? To what extent is intelligence influenced by genetic factors—and to what extent by environmental factors, such as our unique life experience? These are the kinds of questions psychologists have sought to answer in their research on human intelligence, and we'll address all of them in this chapter. Specifically, our discussion of human intelligence will proceed as follows.

First, we'll examine several different perspectives on the nature of intelligence—contrasting views about what it is and how it operates. Next, we'll consider some of the ways in which intelligence is measured: psychological tests, measures of basic cognitive processes, and even measures of various aspects of neural functioning. This will be followed by a discussion of *reliability* and *validity,* two important requirements for any psychological test. This discussion will lead us, quite logically, to consideration of several complex ethical and social issues relating to the measurement of intelligence—for instance, whether intelligence tests are biased against minority groups. Next, we'll focus on a topic that has long been the subject of careful study in psychology but which has recently become the center of heated debate once again: To what extent do individual differences in intelligence stem from genetic and from environmental factors? This same question also applies to *group differences* in intelligence, so we'll examine that topic, too. After that, we'll turn to a new perspective on intelligence—the view that intelligence is shown not only in cognitive activities such as thinking and reasoning, but in our abilities to deal effectively with the emotional side of life. The ability to recognize and manage our own emotions and those of other persons is known as *emotional intelligence* and has recently been the subject of a great deal of research attention by psychologists (Goleman, 1995). Finally, we'll conclude by briefly examining *creativity*—a characteristic that is related to, but not identical with, intelligence (e.g., Sternberg & Lubart, 1996).

Intelligence: Contrasting Views of Its Nature

Intelligence: Individuals' abilities to understand complex ideas, to adapt effectively to the environment, to learn from experience, to engage in various forms of reasoning, to overcome obstacles by careful thought.

In everyday life, we often make judgments about where other people—and we ourselves—stand along many different dimensions: attractiveness, ambition, energy, patience, friendliness, honesty, to name just a few. One of the most important dimensions on which we make such comparisons, however, is *intelligence*. Most languages have many adjectives to describe people with varying degrees of intelligence—for instance, *smart, brilliant, clever, cunning, wise* on the positive end, and *dumb, foolish, stupid,* and *silly* on the other. Moreover, for most people, their level of intelligence is closely linked to their self-concept, so comments to the effect that they are *not* highly intelligent are often "fighting words."

It seems clear, then, that we attach considerable importance to individual differences in this respect. But to what, precisely, does the term **intelligence** refer? The answer to this question is somewhat tricky, because intelligence, like love, is easier to recognize than to define. Further, as we'll soon see, intelligence is expressed in many different ways and seems to take many different forms. As a working definition, however, we can adopt the one offered recently by a distinguished panel of experts (Neisser et al., 1966): Intelligence refers to *individuals' abilities to understand complex ideas, to adapt effectively to the environment, to learn from experience, to engage in various forms of reasoning, to overcome obstacles by careful thought.*

Why do we place so much importance on evaluating others' (and our own) intelligence? Partly because we believe that intelligence is related to many important aspects of behavior: how quickly we can master new tasks and adapt to new situations, how successful we will be in school and in various kinds of jobs, and even how well we can get along with others (e.g., Sternberg et al., 1995; see Figure 11.1). As we'll soon see, these commonsense ideas are correct, at least to a degree. Various measures of intelligence *are* related to important life outcomes such as success in school, job performance, social status, and income (Neisser et al., 1996). However, such relationships between intelligence and life outcomes are far from perfect: Many other factors, too, play a role.

In any case, the fact that intelligence influences many important aspects of behavior has led psychologists to study the nature and origins of this characteristic for many decades. Let's now take a look at some of the contrasting views of intelligence that have emerged from this work.

FIGURE 11.1

Intelligence and Life Outcomes

We attach a great deal of importance to intelligence because we believe that it is closely related to many important life outcomes; for instance, success in school, learning new tasks, and getting along well with others.

Intelligence: Unitary or Multifaceted?

Is intelligence a single characteristic, or does it consist of several distinct parts? In the past, psychologists who studied intelligence often disagreed sharply on this issue. In one camp were scientists who viewed intelligence as mainly a general, unified capacity—a single characteristic or dimension along which people vary. One early supporter of this view was Spearman (1927), who believed that performance on any cognitive task depended on a primary general factor (which he termed *g* for *general*) and on one or more specific factors relating to that particular task. Spearman based this view on the following finding: Although tests of intelligence often contain different kinds of items designed to measure different aspects of intelligence, scores on these items often correlate highly. This suggested to Spearman that no matter how intelligence was demonstrated, it was related to a single, primary factor.

In contrast to this view, other researchers believed that intelligence was composed of many separate abilities that operated more or less independently. Thus, according to this *multifactor* view, a given person can be high in some components of intelligence but low in others, and vice versa. One early supporter of this position was Thurstone (1938), who suggested that intelligence was composed of seven distinct primary mental abilities. Included in his list were *verbal meaning*—understanding ideas and word meanings; *number*—speed and accuracy in dealing with numbers; and *space*—the ability to visualize objects in three dimensions.

Which of these views of intelligence has prevailed? Most modern theories of intelligence adopt a position somewhere in between these opposite views. They recognize that intelligence may involve a general ability to handle a wide range of cognitive tasks and problems, as Spearman suggested, but also that intelligence *is* expressed in many different ways, and that persons can be high in some abilities but low in others. As examples of this modern approach, let's briefly consider two influential views of intelligence.

Gardner's Theory of Multiple Intelligences

In formulating their views of intelligence, most researchers have focused primarily on what might be described as "normal" children and adults: persons who neither exceed nor fall below what most of us would view as "average" levels of intelligence. Howard Gardner (1983) argued that this approach was limiting psychology's view of intelligence. A better tactic, he suggested, would be to study not only persons in the middle of the intelligence dimension, but also ones at the extremes—acclaimed geniuses and those whose cognitive functioning is impaired—as well as experts in various domains and those who might be described as possessing special mental "gifts." For instance, consider the young gymnasts who competed in the 1996 Olympics. Watching these youngsters, I was often truly amazed by the feats they could perform. Is their extraordinary ability simply the result of grueling training? Or does their performance also show a special kind of intelligence—something very different from the verbal fluency we usually associate with the term *intelligence,* but perhaps just as important?

Gardner (1983) would argue strongly for the latter view. In fact, to aspects of intelligence most of us readily recognize (such as the verbal, mathematical, and spatial abilities studied by Thurstone) Gardner's theory of multiple intelligences added such components as *musical intelligence*—the kind shown by one of my friends who, without any formal training, can play virtually any tune on the piano; *bodily–kinesthetic intelligence*—the kind of intelligence shown by the Olympic athletes in Figure 11.2; and *interpersonal intelligence*—

for instance, the ability to understand other persons and get along well with others. (I'll return to this latter topic in detail in the discussion of *emotional intelligence*.)

In sum, Gardner's theory proposes that there are several important types of intelligence—and that we must understand each in order to get the big picture where this important human characteristic is concerned.

FIGURE 11.2

Skilled Athletic Performance: Another Kind of Intelligence?

Gardner's theory of multiple intelligences views performance such as that shown here as evidence for a high level of *bodily–kinesthetic intelligence.*

Sternberg's Triarchic Theory: The Value of Practical Intelligence

Another important modern theory of intelligence is one proposed by Robert Sternberg (Sternberg, 1985; Sternberg et al., 1995). According to this theory, known as the **triarchic theory** of intelligence, there are actually three basic types of human intelligence. The first, known as *componential* or *analytic* intelligence, involves the abilities to think critically and analytically. Persons high on this dimension usually excel on standard tests of academic potential and make excellent students. It's a good bet that your professors are high on this aspect of intelligence. The second type of intelligence, known as *experiential* or *creative* intelligence, emphasizes insight and the ability to formulate new ideas. Persons who rate high on this dimension excel at zeroing in on what information is crucial in a given situation, and at combining seemingly unrelated facts. This is the kind of intelligence shown by many scientific geniuses and inventors, such as Einstein, Newton, and—some would say—Freud. For example, Johannes Gutenberg, inventor of the printing press, combined the mechanisms for producing playing cards, pressing wine, and minting coins into his invention; thus, he showed a high level of creative intelligence.

Sternberg terms the third type of intelligence *contextual* or **practical intelligence,** and in some ways it is the most interesting of all. Persons high on this dimension are intelligent in a practical, adaptive sense—they have what many would term "street smarts." Like the young woman shown in Figure 11.3 on page 428, they are adept at solving the problems of everyday life. For example, consider the following story, cited by Sternberg and Lubart (1995) as an example of high practical intelligence.

In Tallahassee, Florida (home of Florida State University), the city provides trash containers to all residents. Garbage collectors used to retrieve each full container from the resident's backyard, bring the container to the truck, empty it, and then return it to its original location. This system continued until one day a newly hired employee considered the situation—and realized that the amount of work involved could be cut almost in half through one simple but ingenious change. Can you guess the solution he devised? Here it is: After the collectors emptied each trash container, they would take it to the next yard (instead of returning it to its original location). There, it would replace the full container that would then be brought to the truck. All the city trash cans were identical, so it made no difference to each household which trash can they received back; but this simple step *saved one entire trip to each backyard for the trash collectors.*

Triarchic Theory: A theory suggesting that there are three basic forms of intelligence: componential, experiential, and contextual (practical) intelligence.

Practical Intelligence: Intelligence useful in solving everyday problems.

FIGURE 11.3

Practical Intelligence in Action

The young woman in this cartoon has shown what Sternberg and other researchers would describe as *practical intelligence.* As a result, she gets to keep her job!

"Pam here is the winner of our 'How small a salary can I live on?' essay contest. The rest of you are fired."

(**Source:** Drawing by Ed Fisher; ©1996 The New Yorker Magazine, Inc.)

According to Sternberg, solving practical problems like this requires a different kind of intelligence from that required for success in school or other intellectual pursuits. Specifically, Sternberg notes that solving problems related to academic tasks requires that individuals work on problems formulated by others, that are of little interest to them, and that are disconnected from the problem solver's ordinary experience. In contrast, solving problems of everyday life—the kind requiring high practical intelligence—involves working on problems that are unformulated or in need of reformulation, that are of personal interest to the problem solver, and that are directly related to everyday experience.

What evidence suggests that practical intelligence is indeed different from componential intelligence—the kind necessary for academic success? Sternberg points to several forms of support for this view. First, when asked to describe the characteristics of intelligent individuals, persons stopped at random in supermarkets, libraries, and train stations tend to make a distinction between these two types of intelligence. In other words the "person in the street" recognizes the existence of these two important forms of intelligence (Sternberg et al., 1981). Second, growing evidence suggests that while componential intelligence may peak relatively early in life—perhaps in our forties or fifties—practical intelligence continues to grow throughout the life span (see our discussion of aging and intelligence in Chapter 9). Finally, there are many instances in which individuals who show high levels of practical intelligence do not score above average on standard measures of academic intelligence. For instance, consider workers in a milk plant who had to assemble orders for delivery—orders consisting of many different dairy products in different-sized containers. This task involved reaching for the various products and putting them together in a large container. Careful study of the behavior of persons experienced in this job indicated that they used complex strategies for minimizing the number of moves required to complete a given order (Scribner, 1986). The assemblers had little formal education, and there was no correlation between their work performance and scores on standard tests of intelligence. Yet they certainly showed high practical intelligence (e.g., Scribner, 1986).

How do persons high in practical intelligence go about solving problems? In part, Sternberg and his colleagues suggest (Sternberg et al., 1995), through the use of **tacit knowledge.** Tacit knowledge is very different from formal academic knowledge, which often involves memorizing definitions, formulas, and other information. In contrast, tacit knowledge has three major characteristics: (1) It is *action-oriented*; (2) it allows individuals to achieve goals they personally value; and (3) it is usually acquired without direct help from others (Horvath et al., in press). The term *action-oriented* refers to the fact that such knowledge involves "knowing how" to do something rather than "knowing that" (for instance, "knowing how" to persuade someone to do what one wishes, rather than "knowing that" the circumference of the earth is roughly 25,000 miles). Tacit knowledge is also *practically useful*—it helps individuals attain goals they want to reach. Thus, it is not subject to the criticism, often voiced by students, that "This stuff is not relevant—I can't use it!" Finally, such knowledge is often acquired on one's own, largely because it is often unspoken—individuals must recognize tacit knowledge, and its value, for themselves. For instance, no one may tell an employee that getting help from a more senior person (having this person act as a *mentor*) will aid his or her career; but the employee may recognize this fact independently and act on it.

Tacit Knowledge: Knowledge that plays an important role in practical intelligence. Such knowledge is action-oriented and goal-directed, and is usually acquired without direct help from others.

Because it is a basic part of practical intelligence, tacit knowledge is an important predictor of success in many areas of life—from getting along well with others to success in one's career. For instance, in research on the effects of tacit knowledge, Williams and Sternberg (in press) found that the greater individuals' store of tacit knowledge, the higher their salary and the greater their number of promotions. In fact, tacit knowledge was almost as good a predictor of these outcomes as years of education and years of job experience.

In sum, growing evidence suggests that there is more to intelligence than the verbal, mathematical, and reasoning abilities that are often associated with academic success. Practical intelligence, too, is important and contributes to success in many areas of life. As a final demonstration of the fact that there are indeed many kinds of intelligence, construct a list of ten famous people currently in the news (e.g., Bill Clinton, Madonna, Bill Gates), and for each ask yourself, "What kinds of intelligence do they show?" You'll probably come up with very different patterns for each.

Key Questions

- What is intelligence?
- What is Gardner's theory of multiple intelligences?
- What is Sternberg's triarchic theory of intelligence?
- What is practical intelligence? Tacit knowledge?

Measuring Human Intelligence: From Tests to Underlying Psychological Processes . . . and Beyond

In 1904, when psychology was just emerging as an independent field, members of the Paris school board approached Alfred Binet with an interesting request: Could he develop an objective method for identifying children who were mentally retarded, so that they could be removed from the regular classroom and given special education? Binet was already at work on related topics, so he agreed, enlisting the aid of his colleague, Theodore Simon.

In designing this test Binet and Simon were guided by the belief that the items used should be ones children could answer without special training or

Stanford–Binet Test: A widely used individual test of intelligence.

study. They felt that this was important because the test should measure the ability to handle intellectual tasks—*not* specific knowledge acquired in school. To attain this goal, Binet and Simon decided to use items of two basic types: ones so new or unusual that none of the children would have prior exposure to them, and ones so familiar that almost all youngsters would have encountered them in the past. For example, children were asked to perform the following tasks:

Follow simple commands or imitate simple gestures.

Name objects shown in pictures.

Repeat a sentence of fifteen words.

Tell how two common objects are different.

Complete sentences begun by the examiner.

The first version of Binet and Simon's test was published in 1905 and contained thirty items. Much to the two authors' pleasure, it was quite effective: With its aid, schools could readily identify children in need of special help. Encouraged by this success, Binet and Simon broadened the scope of their test to measure variations in intelligence among all children. This revised version, published in 1908, grouped items by age, with six items at each level between three and thirteen years. Items were placed at a particular age level if about 75 percent of children of that age could pass them correctly.

Binet's tests were soon revised and adapted for use in many countries. In the United States, Lewis Terman, a psychologist at Stanford University, developed the **Stanford–Binet test**—a test that was soon put to use in many different settings. Over the years the Stanford–Binet has been revised several times (see Figure 11.4). One of the features of the Stanford–Binet that contributed to its popularity was the fact that it yielded a single score assumed to reflect an individual's level of intelligence—the now famous (some would say *infamous*) IQ.

FIGURE 11.4

The Stanford–Binet Test

A recent version of the Stanford–Binet test yields a rating of overall intelligence that is based on scores of four types of mental activity: verbal reasoning, quantitative reasoning, abstract visual reasoning, and short-term memory. Scores on each of these components are based on subtests designed to measure more specific mental abilities.

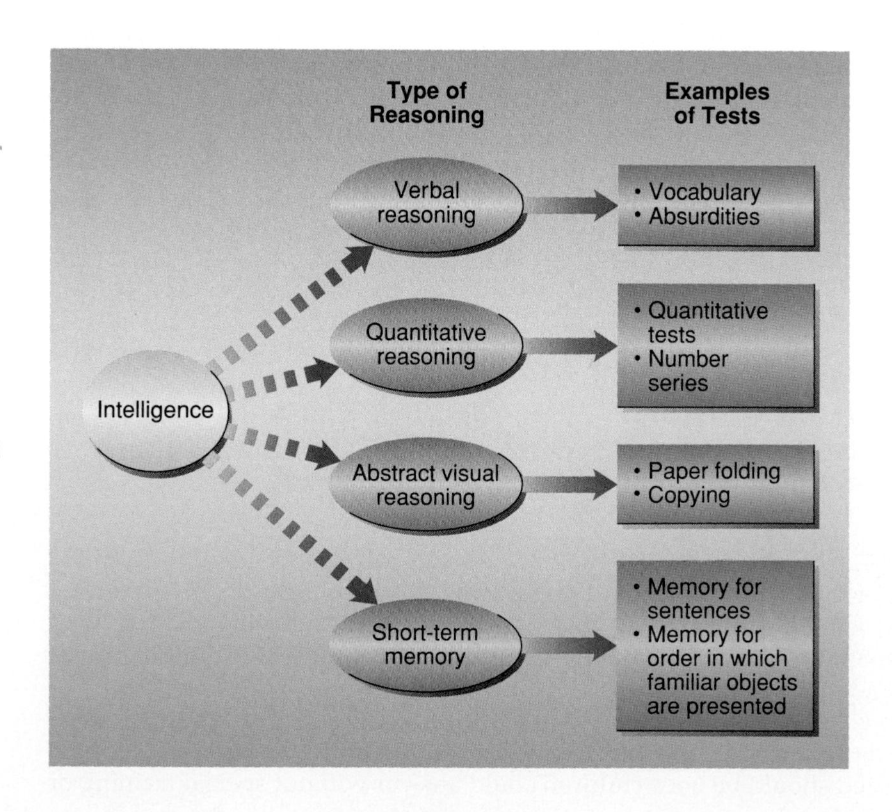

IQ: Its Meaning Then and Now

Originally, the letters **IQ** stood for *intelligence quotient,* and a "quotient" is precisely what the scores represented. To obtain an IQ score, an examiner divided a student's "mental age" by his or her chronological age, then multiplied this number by 100. For this computation, mental age was based on the number of items a person passed correctly on the test: Test takers received two months' credit of mental age for each item passed. If an individual's mental and chronological ages were equal, an IQ of 100 was obtained; this was considered to be an average score. IQs above 100 indicated that a person's intellectual age was greater than her or his chronological age—in other words, that the individual was more intelligent than typical students of the same age. In contrast, numbers below 100 indicated that the individual was less intelligent than her or his peers.

Perhaps you can already see one obvious problem with this type of IQ score: At some point, mental growth levels off or stops, while chronological age continues to grow. As a result, IQ scores begin to decline after the early teen years! Partly because of this problem, IQ scores now have a different meaning. They simply reflect an individual's performance relative to that of persons of the same age who have taken the same test. Thus, an IQ above 100 indicates that the person has scored higher than the average person in her or his age group, while a score below 100 indicates that the person has scored lower than average.

The Wechsler Scales

As noted above, the tests developed by Binet and later adapted by Terman and others remained popular for many years. They do, however, suffer from one major drawback: All are mainly verbal in content. As a result, they pay little attention to the fact that intelligence can be revealed in nonverbal activities as well. For example, an architect who visualizes a majestic design for a new building is demonstrating a high level of intelligence; yet no means for assessing such abilities was included in early versions of the Stanford–Binet test.

To overcome this and other problems, David Wechsler devised a set of tests for both children and adults that include nonverbal, or *performance,* items as well as verbal ones, and that yield separate scores for these two components of intelligence. Wechsler began with the view that intelligence is *not* a unitary characteristic, shown only through verbal and mathematical reasoning. However, he developed these tests at a time when the multifaceted nature of intelligence was not yet well understood, and it is not clear that Wechsler's various subtests actually do measure different aspects of intelligence. Despite such problems, the Wechsler tests are currently among the most frequently used individual tests of intelligence. An overview of the subtests that make up one of the Wechsler scales, the *Wechsler Adult Intelligence Scale–Revised* (WAIS–R for short) is presented in Table 11.1 on page 432.

Wechsler believed that differences between scores on the various subtests could be used to diagnose serious psychological disorders (see Chapter 14). Research on this possibility has yielded mixed results at best, however.

A Wechsler test for children, the *Wechsler Intelligence Scale for Children* (WISC), has also been developed; it too is in widespread use. Patterns of scores on the subtests of the WISC are sometimes used to identify children suffering from various *learning disabilities.* Some findings indicate that children who score high on certain subtests, such as Picture Completion and

IQ: Originally, "intelligence quotient," a number that examiners derived by dividing an individual's "mental age" by his or her chronological age. Now IQ simply indicates an individual's level of performance on an intelligence test relative to those of other persons their age.

TABLE 11.1

Subtests of the Wechsler Adult Intelligence Scale

This widely used test of adult intelligence includes the subtests described here.

Test	Description
Verbal Tests	
Information	Examinees are asked to answer general information questions, increasing in difficulty.
Digit Span	Examinees are asked to repeat series of digits read out loud by the examiner.
Vocabulary	Examinees are asked to define thirty-five words.
Arithmetic	Examinees are asked to solve arithmetic problems.
Comprehension	Examinees are asked to answer questions requiring detailed answers; answers indicate their comprehension of the questions.
Similarities	Examinees indicate in what way two items are alike.
Performance Tests	
Picture Completion	Examinees indicate what part of each picture is missing.
Picture Arrangement	Examinees arrange pictures to make a sensible story.
Block Design	Examinees attempt to duplicate designs made with red and white blocks.
Object Assembly	Examinees attempt to solve picture puzzles.
Digit Symbol	Examinees fill in small boxes with coded symbols corresponding to a number above each box.

Object Assembly, but lower on others, such as Arithmetic, Information, and Vocabulary, are more likely to have learning disabilities than children with other patterns of scores (Aiken, 1991). Once again, however, not all findings point to such conclusions, so the value of the WISC for this kind of diagnosis remains somewhat uncertain.

Individual Tests of Intelligence: Some Practical Uses Individual tests of intelligence are costly: They must be administered one-on-one by a psychologist or other trained professional. Why, then, do these tests continue in widespread use? The answer is that these tests have several practical uses and provide benefits that help to offset their obvious costs. The most important of these uses involves identification of children at the extremes with respect to intelligence—those who suffer from some degree of *mental retardation,* and those who are *intellectually gifted.*

Mental Retardation: Considerably below-average intellectual functioning combined with varying degrees of difficulty in meeting the demands of everyday life.

Mental retardation refers to considerably below-average intellectual functioning combined with varying degrees of difficulty in meeting the demands of everyday life (Aiken, 1991; Wielkiewicz & Calvert, 1989). As shown in Figure 11.5, persons with mental retardation are typically described according to four broad categories of retardation: mild, moderate, severe, and profound. Individuals' level of retardation is determined by at least two factors: their test scores *and* their success in carrying out activities of daily living expected of persons their age. As you can guess, persons whose retardation is in the "mild" category can usually learn to function quite well. One of the children of my next-door neighbors fits into this category. As a result of special classes and training, he is now able to hold down a job and to function quite well in many situations. In fact, like many other persons who suffer from mild mental retardation, he is an exceptionally sweet and pleasant young man.

Down Syndrome: A genetically caused condition that results in mental retardation.

What causes mental retardation? In some cases it can be traced to genetic abnormalities such as **Down syndrome,** which is caused by the presence of an extra chromosome; persons with Down syndrome usually have IQs below 50. Mental retardation can also result from environmental factors, such as inadequate nutrition or use of drugs or alcohol by mothers during pregnancy, infections, toxic agents, and traumas resulting from a lack of oxygen during birth. Most cases of mental retardation, however, cannot readily be traced to specific causes.

Intelligence tests have also been used to identify the *intellectually gifted*—persons whose intelligence is far above average (Friedman et al., 1995; Terman, 1954). The most comprehensive study on such persons was begun by Lewis Terman in 1925. (I discussed this study in Chapter 9.) The study followed the lives of 1,528 children with IQs of 130 or above to determine the relationship between high intelligence and occupational success and social adjustment. As a group, these gifted persons experienced high levels of success. They earned more academic degrees, attained higher occupational status and salaries, experienced better personal and social adjustment, and were healthier than the average adult in their age group. These results refuted the commonly held belief that intellectually gifted persons are social or emotional weaklings—nerds who miss out on all the fun of life. (I should quickly note

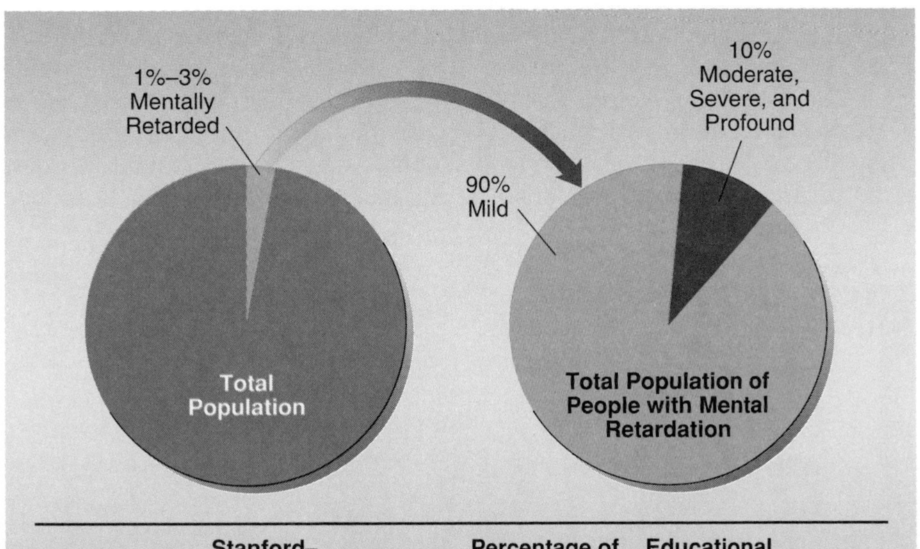

Classification	Stanford–Binet IQ Score	Wechsler IQ Score	Percentage of the Mentally Retarded	Educational Level Possible
Mild	52–68	55–69	90	Sixth grade
Moderate	36–51	40–54	6	Second to fourth grade
Severe	20–35	25–39	3	Limited speech
Profound	Below 20	Below 25	1	Unresponsive to training

FIGURE 11.5

Degrees of Mental Retardation

Degree of mental retardation is often identified according to IQ scores. In general, an IQ below 70 suggests some level of retardation. IQ scores are not the only consideration, however; the individual's capacity to function adequately in everyday life is also important.

that these findings were obtained primarily for males in the study; because of restricted opportunities for females at the time, many of the women did not pursue careers outside the home and could not, therefore, attain similar achievements as a result of their high intelligence.)

Group Tests of Intelligence

Both the Stanford–Binet and the Wechsler scales are *individual* tests of intelligence: They are designed for use with one person at a time. Obviously, it would be much more efficient if *group* tests could be administered to large numbers of people at once. The need for such tests was driven home at the start of World War I, when the armed forces in the United States suddenly faced the task of screening several million recruits. In response to this challenge, psychologists such as Arthur Otis developed two tests: *Army Alpha* for persons who could read (remember, this was back in 1917), and *Army Beta* for persons would could not read or who did not speak English. These early group tests proved highly useful. For example, they were used to select candidates for officer training school, and they did accurately predict success in such training.

A far more controversial use of group tests of intelligence took place during the 1920s, when, in response to the urgings of psychologists Henry Goddard and others, the United States adopted legislation requiring that all potential immigrants be tested for intelligence. As a result, millions of persons arriving at Ellis Island—now a national park—were tested; and some were refused entry on the basis of low scores (see Figure 11.6). Such testing suffered from many problems: Often, the tests were not administered under standard conditions or by trained examiners; also, the tests were designed for people from American culture and so were strongly biased against the immigrants tested, most of whom came from Southern and Eastern Europe. So this episode can be considered to be one of the first instances in which intelligence tests were widely misused.

In succeeding decades many other group tests of intelligence were developed. Among the more popular of these are the *Otis tests,* such as the Otis–Lennon School Ability Test (Otis & Lennon, 1967); the *Henmon–Nelson Tests* (Nelson, Lamke, & French, 1973); and the *Cognitive Abilities Test* (CAT; Thorndike & Hagen, 1982). All are available in versions that can be administered to large numbers of persons. The advantages offered by such tests soon

FIGURE 11.6

Group Tests of Intelligence: One Controversial Use

During the 1920s, group intelligence tests were administered to millions of persons wishing to immigrate to the United States. Such testing was required by legislation designed to prevent "mentally defective" persons from entering the country. The racial and ethnic prejudice reflected in such testing made it a very controversial use of intelligence tests.

made them very popular, and they were put to routine use in many school systems. During the 1960s, though, this practice was called into serious question and became the focus of harsh criticism. While there were many reasons for this controversy, the most serious was the charge that such tests were unfair to children from disadvantaged backgrounds—especially youngsters from certain minority groups. We'll return to these objections in a later section.

The Cognitive Basis of Intelligence: Measuring Intelligence through Processing Speed

"Quick study," "quick-witted," "fast learner"—phrases such as these are often used to describe people who are high in intelligence, both academic and practical. Such expressions suggest that being intelligent involves being able to process information quickly. Is there any scientific evidence for this view? In fact, there is. In recent years, psychologists interested in studying intelligence have moved beyond tests such as the Stanford–Binet and Wechsler scales in an attempt to identify the basic cognitive mechanisms and processes that underlie intelligence—and that enable people to obtain high scores on intelligence tests (e.g., Ceci, 1990; Deary, 1995). This has led to two major developments. First, several tests that are based on the findings of cognitive psychology, and our growing understanding of many aspects of cognition, have been developed (Naglieri, 1997). Among these the most noteworthy are the *Kaufman Assessment Battery for Children* and the *Kaufman Adult Intelligence Test* (e.g., Kaufman & Kaufman, 1993), and the *Woodcock–Johnson Test of Cognitive Abilities* (Woodcock & Johnson, 1989). The Woodcock–Johnson Test, for instance, attempts to measure important aspects of both fluid and crystallized intelligence.

Second, a growing body of research has focused on the finding that the speed with which individuals perform simple perceptual and cognitive tasks is often correlated with scores on intelligence tests (Neisser et al., 1996; Vernon, 1987). For example, significant correlations (on the order of –.30 to –.40) have often been found between various measures of *reaction time* and scores on intelligence tests (see, e.g., Deary & Stough, 1996). A recent and informative study using such measures is one conducted by Fry and Hale (1996).

These investigators wished to investigate the possibility that one reason why *fluid intelligence* increases with age is that **processing speed**—the speed with which individuals can process information—rises with age. Such increments in processing speed, in turn, increase working memory, and this leads to increments in fluid intelligence. (As you may recall from our discussion in Chapter 9, fluid intelligence involves the abilities to form concepts, reason, and identify similarities; it is distinct from *crystallized intelligence,* which relates to use of previously learned information.)

To test their ideas, Fry and Hale (1996) had children and young adults ranging in age from seven to nineteen perform several tasks designed to measure processing speed. For all these tasks, the researchers asked participants to respond as quickly as possible. For example, one of the tasks involved a simple *disjunctive reaction-time task:* Two vertical arrows were flashed on a computer screen, pointing in either the same or different directions. Participants pushed a key as quickly as possible to indicate their "same/different" judgment. Another task involved determining, as quickly as possible, whether two simple geometric forms were the same or different in shape. The investigators obtained a single index of processing speed for each participant by averaging speeds across the various tasks.

Processing Speed: The speed with which a person can process information.

FIGURE 11.7

Processing Speed, Working Memory, and Fluid Intelligence

Growing evidence indicates that as children grow older, their processing speed increases. These gains in processing speed underlie improvements in working memory; and this, in turn, leads to gains in fluid intelligence.

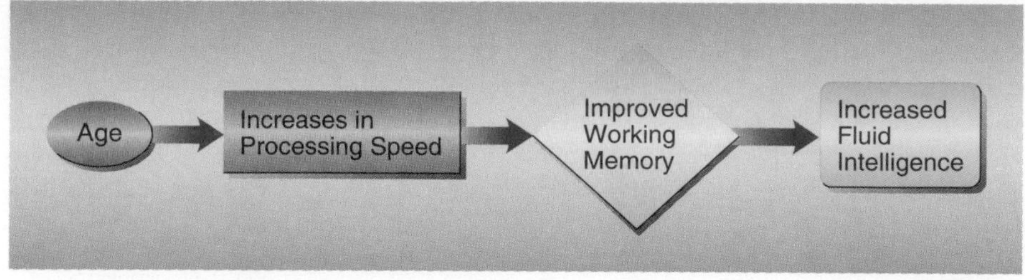

(**Source:** Based on suggestions by Fry & Hale, 1996.)

To measure working memory, Fry and Hale (1996) had participants perform several tasks—for instance, recalling digits (numbers) they had viewed for brief periods of time. As you may recall from our discussion of memory in Chapter 6, working memory (short-term memory) is a kind of memory that allows us to hold limited amounts of information in consciousness for relatively brief periods of time. It is, in a sense, the memory system in which information currently in our conscious mind is initially processed. The researchers also assessed fluid intelligence by means of one standard measure (the standard Raven Progressive Matrices; Court & Raven, 1983).

Results provided strong support for the view that as children grow older, their processing speed increases, and that these increments in processing speed increase the capacity of working memory. The increased capacity of working memory, in turn, contributes to increments in fluid intelligence (see Figure 11.7). In addition, of course, these findings also indicate that processing speed is an important component of intelligence. Being able to "think fast," it appears, is indeed one basic aspect of human intelligence.

While reaction-time measures of processing speed appear to provide one useful means for measuring intelligence and understanding its nature, a somewhat different approach seems even more promising in this respect—see the Research Methods section below.

RESEARCH METHODS

How Psychologists Study the Cognitive Basis of Intelligence

Science, as I noted in Chapter 1, is not concerned simply with observing various events: It seeks to *understand* or *explain* them as well. For this reason, psychologists are not content with simply being able to measure human intelligence—they want to understand the mechanisms and processes that contribute to it. Toward this end, several lines of research have converged on the speed of mental operations or processing as a basic component of intelligence. The faster individuals can perform basic cognitive operations, it is reasoned, the more intelligent they will be in many different contexts.

At first glance, measures of reaction time seem to offer a useful means for estimating such speed. However, as noted recently by Deary and Stough (1996), there appear to be some serious drawbacks to such measures. While they are indeed correlated with scores on intelligence tests, these correlations are not as strong as might be expected (e.g., Deary & Stough, 1996). Further, it has proved more difficult to relate reaction-time measures to basic aspects of cognitive activity than was initially assumed (Brody, 1993). Finally, because reaction-time tests tap speed of responding (e.g., pushing one of two buttons) as well as speed of mental processes, scores on these measures may be affected by factors unrelated to intelligence.

Because of these problems, many researchers have turned to a different kind of measure of the speed of mental operations—**inspection time.** This measure reflects the minimum amount of time a particular stimulus must be exposed for individuals to make a judgment about it that meets some preestablished criterion of accuracy. The shorter the duration time necessary for individuals to attain a given level of accuracy, presumably, the faster the speed of important aspects of their cognitive (mental) operations. To measure inspection time, psychologists often use procedures in which indi-

FIGURE 11.8

Inspection Time: How It's Measured

To measure inspection time, psychologists ask research participants to indicate whether the longer side is on the left or the right. Participants are *not* told to respond as quickly as possible; rather, they are instructed to take their time and to be accurate. Inspection time is measured in terms of the time they require in order to make such decisions at some predetermined level of accuracy.

viduals are shown simple drawings, like the one in Figure 11.8, and are asked to indicate (for example) whether the longer side is on the left or right. They are *not* told to respond as quickly as possible. Rather, they are instructed to take their time and to be accurate. Inspection time is measured by the time they take to make such decisions at a prespecified level of accuracy—for example, 85 percent.

What does inspection time measure? Presumably, the amount of time individuals require for the intake of new visual information. Supporters of this measure argue that this task—perceiving new information—is basic to all higher-level mental operations in human thought (e.g., Deary, 1995; Deary & Stough, 1996). Further, they note that this measure is closely related to current theories of perception and decision making—theories emphasizing that new visual information is perceived in discrete samples, then combined into judgments such as "I see it" or "I don't see it."

Growing evidence indicates that inspection time is indeed closely related to intelligence, as measured by standard tests. In fact, inspection time scores and scores on such tests correlate –.50 or more (e.g., Kranzler & Jensen, 1989). Additional support for the value of this measure is provided by the findings that improvements in inspection-time measures may be one cause of increases in IQ scores with age (Deary, 1995).

In sum, inspection time appears to be a very promising measure for probing the nature of human intelligence—for understanding the basic cognitive processes that underlie this important characteristic. And since understanding a process is often an essential first step toward being able to change it in beneficial ways, this is valuable progress indeed.

The Neurological Basis of Intelligence: Intelligence and Neural Efficiency

In Chapter 2 I noted that everything we do, think, or feel rests, in an ultimate sense, on neurochemical events occurring in our brains. If that is indeed true—and virtually all psychologists believe that it is—then an intriguing possibility arises: Can we trace individual differences in intelligence to differences in neural functioning? The answer suggested by a growing body of evidence is yes (e.g., Mattarazzo, 1992; Vernon, 1993). A clear illustration of the kind of evidence pointing to this conclusion is provided by a study conducted by Reed and Jensen (1993).

These researchers recorded evoked potentials (electrical responses to visual stimuli) in the brains of 147 male volunteers. The researchers obtained the average latency (delay) with which these potentials followed presentation of the visual stimuli for each volunteer; then they divided this number by the length of the volunteer's head (from front to back) to obtain a measure of the speed with which nerve impulses were conducted in the visual system. They then correlated this measure, known as *nerve conduction velocity,* with scores on a standard test of intelligence (again, the Raven Progressive Matrices). Results were impressive: The higher this measure of neural speed in a participant, the higher was the participant's measured intelligence.

Inspection Time: The minimum amount of time a particular stimulus must be exposed for individuals to make a judgment about it that meets some preestablished criterion of accuracy.

Additional research has used PET brain imaging (Chapter 2) to examine metabolic activity in the brain during cognitive tasks (e.g., Haier et al., 1996). Presumably, if intelligence is related to efficient brain functioning, then the more intelligent people are, the less energy their brains should expend while working on various tasks. This prediction has been confirmed; the brains of persons scoring highest on written measures of intellectual ability *do* expend less energy when these individuals perform complex cognitive tasks than lower scorers' brains do.

Finally, and perhaps most surprising of all, it has been found that there is a link between brain structure and intelligence (Andreason et al., 1993). Specifically, scores on standard measures of intelligence such as the Wechsler Adult Intelligence Scale are related to the size of certain portions of the brain, including the left and right temporal lobe and the right and left hippocampus. Moreover, this is true even when corrections are made for individuals' overall physical size.

In sum, it appears that the improved methods now available for studying the brain and nervous system are beginning to establish the kind of links between intelligence and physical structures that psychologists have long suspected to exist. Such research is very recent, so it is still too soon to reach firm conclusions. It does appear, though, that we are on the verge of establishing much firmer links between intelligence—a crucial aspect of mind—and body than has ever been true before.

Key Questions

- What was the first individual test of intelligence, and what did scores on it mean?
- What are the Wechsler scales?
- What is inspection time, and what does it measure?
- What findings suggest that intelligence is related to neural functioning and brain structure?

Reliability and Validity: *Basic Requirements for All Psychological Tests*

Suppose that in preparation for a summer at the beach, you decide to go on a diet to lose 10 pounds. Your current weight is 135, and for two weeks you skip desserts and engage in extra exercise. Then you step onto your bathroom scale to see how you've done. Much to your surprise, the needle reads 139; you've actually *gained* 4 pounds! How can this be? Perhaps you made a mistake. So you step back on the scale. Now it reads 134. You get off and step onto it again; the needle swings to 131. At this point, you realize the truth: Your scale is *unreliable*—the numbers it shows change even though your weight, obviously, doesn't change from one instant to the next.

This is a simple illustration of a very basic but important point. Measuring devices, whether they are bathroom scales or psychological tests, must have high **reliability:** They must yield the same result each time they are applied to the same quantity. If they don't, they are essentially useless. But how do we know whether and to what extent any measuring device, or any psychological test, is reliable? In fact, several different methods exist for assessing a test's reliability.

Assessing Reliability: Internal Consistency and Test–Retest Reliability

If we wish to develop a test that measures a psychological characteristic such as intelligence, then it is important to establish that all the items on the test actually measure the same characteristic—that the test has what psychologists call *internal consistency*. One way to assess such internal consistency involves dividing the test in two equivalent parts, such as the first and second halves or odd- and even-numbered items, and then comparing people's scores on each part. If the test is internally consistent, then the correlation

Reliability: The extent to which any measuring device (including a psychological test) yields the same result each time it is applied to the same quantity.

between each individual's scores on the two parts should be positive and high. If it is, then the test is high in **split-half reliability.** If it is not, then some of the items may be measuring different things, and the test may be unreliable in one important sense. There are several statistical formulas for measuring internal consistency, but one of the most widely used is known as *coefficient alpha*. This formula simultaneously considers all the possible ways of splitting the test into halves—a process that can be completed very rapidly on high-speed computers.

Split-Half Reliability: The correlation between an individual's scores on two equivalent halves of a test.

Test–Retest Reliability: A measure of the extent to which individuals' scores on a test remain stable over time.

Internal consistency is not the only measure of reliability in intelligence tests, however. Another involves assessing the extent to which scores change or remain the same over time. Psychologists measure such **test–retest reliability** by having the same persons take a test at different times. The more similar a given person's scores on these occasions are, the higher is the test–retest reliability. Since intelligence is a characteristic that would not be expected to change over time—unless, of course, something fairly dramatic such as a serious illness or injury intervenes—high test–retest reliability is a requirement of all tests of human intelligence.

While test–retest reliability is important, it does suffer from one drawback you will probably find obvious: If people take the same test on two or more occasions, their scores may change because of *practice effects*. To reduce this problem, psychologists often use *alternate forms* of the same test–two different forms that cover the same material and, presumably, measure the same characteristic. Figure 11.9 provides an overview of the basic methods used to assess both split-half reliability and test–retest reliability.

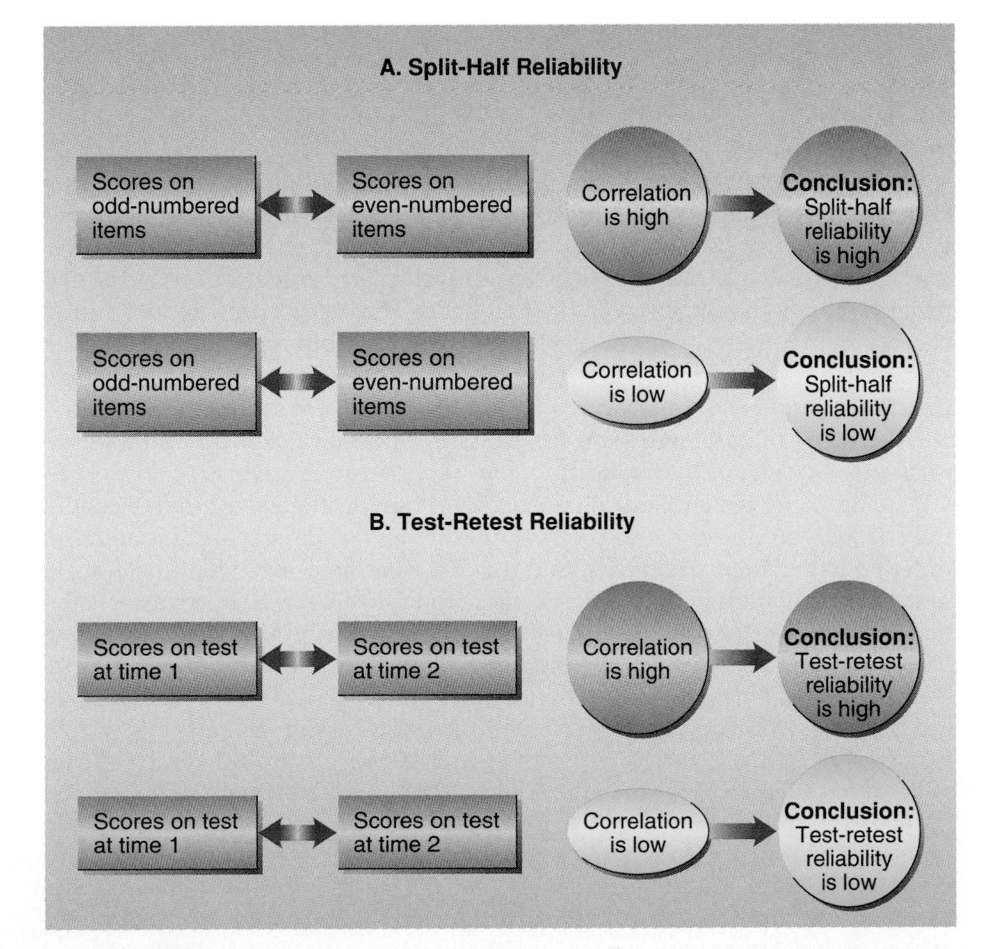

FIGURE 11.9

Measures of Reliability

To be useful, psychological tests must be *reliable*. Two important types of reliability are illustrated here.

Validity: Do Tests Measure What They Claim to Measure?

On a recent visit to one of our local malls, I noticed a new machine outside one of the stores. A sign on the front read, "Test Your Sex Appeal!" I was fascinated, so I read further. According to the instructions, if I inserted a quarter and pushed some buttons, the machine would rate my appeal to members of the opposite sex. Do you think the machine was really capable of measuring sex appeal? The answer is obvious, if a little disappointing: No way! After all, how could this device tell persons who used it how they would be perceived by others? Psychologists would say that machines like this—and any other measuring devices that claim to measure something they do not—are low in **validity,** the ability to measure what they are supposed to measure.

The same principle applies to psychological tests: They are useful only to the extent that they really measure the characteristics they claim to measure. Thus, an intelligence test is useful only to the extent that it really measures intelligence. How can we determine whether a test is valid? Through several different methods. One of these is known as **content validity,** and refers to the extent to which items on the test are related in a straightforward way to the characteristic we wish to measure. For example, if an intelligence test consisted of measurements of the length of people's ears or the sharpness of their teeth, we would probably conclude that it was low in content validity: These measurements seem totally unrelated to what we mean by the term *intelligence*.

Another type of validity is known as **criterion-related validity** and is based on the following reasoning: If a test actually measures what it claims to measure, then persons attaining different scores on it should also differ in terms of behaviors (criteria) that are relevant to the characteristic being measured. For example, we might expect that scores on an intelligence test would be related to such aspects of behavior as grades in school and success in various occupations.

Two kinds of criterion-related validity that are often measured by psychologists are *predictive validity* and *concurrent validity*. To measure predictive validity, psychologists use scores on a test taken now to predict *later* performance on some criterion measure. For example, administrators of a training program might use scores on an intelligence test to predict participants' future success in the program. To measure concurrent validity, psychologists relate scores on a test taken now to *current* performance on some criterion. Thus, they might relate students' scores on the test to current school performance. See the **Ideas to Take with You** feature for a summary of the methods used to assess various kinds of validity.

In sum, any psychological test is useful only to the extent that it is both reliable and valid—to the extent that the test yields consistent scores and that independent evidence confirms that it really does measures what it claims to measure. How do intelligence tests stack up in this respect? In terms of reliability, the answer is: quite well. The tests I have described do yield consistent scores and do possess internal consistency. The question of validity, however, is much more controversial. As I've already noted, most widely used tests of intelligence were designed to assess what Sternberg and others would describe as *academic intelligence*—the kind of cognitive skills and abilities needed for success in school and related activities. They were *not* designed to measure practical intelligence; indeed, as we saw earlier, persons high in practical intelligence do not necessarily score high on standard tests of academic intelligence. So tests such as the Stanford–Binet and the Wechsler scales have, at best, limited validity; they measure only one aspect of intelligence and so are related only to aspects of behavior that reflect such intelligence.

Validity: The extent to which a test actually measures what it claims to measure.

Content Validity: The extent to which items on a test are related in a straightforward way to the characteristic the test aims to measure.

Criterion-Related Validity: The extent to which scores on a test are related to behaviors (criteria) that are relevant to the characteristics the test purports to measure.

Ideas to Take with You

Measuring Validity

No psychological test is useful unless it actually measures what it claims to measure—that is, unless it has high *validity.* Here are some basic ways to assess this important requirement.

Content Validity: The extent to which items on a test are related in a straightforward way to the characteristic the test supposedly measures.

HIGH CONTENT VALIDITY

The flight simulator here provides a valid test of the abilities needed to pilot a plane, because the behaviors it requires are closely related to those needed by pilots during actual flight. Thus, it has a high level of content validity.

LOW CONTENT VALIDITY

In the past, employers used various kinds of "aptitude tests" to select candidates for various jobs. Often, the content of these tests had little or nothing to do with what people actually did in these jobs. Often, the content of these tests had little or nothing to do with what people actually did in these jobs. As a result, such tests were low in content validity.

Criterion-Related Validity: The extent to which scores on a test are related to some observable behavior (criterion) relevant to the characteristic the test purports to measure.

HIGH CRITERION-RELATED VALIDITY

Scores on several standard tests of academic intelligence are correlated with success in school. It would be expected that persons with high academic intelligence would succeed in academic pursuits; therefore, correlations indicate that the tests have high criterion-related validity.

LOW CRITERION-RELATED VALIDITY

At one time it was believed that intelligence could be estimated from measurements of people's skulls. In fact, no relationship was found to exist between such measurements and various criteria indicative of intelligence, such as success in school or job performance. Thus, the criterion-related validity of such "test" was very low (or nonexistent).

Another issue relating to validity arises with respect to group tests of intelligence. Here the key question is this: In view of the fact that such tests were designed for use with persons belonging to one cultural or ethnic group (typically, persons of European descent), are the tests suitable for use with persons from other ethnic backgrounds? Let's take a closer look at this important question.

Intelligence Testing and Public Policy: Are Intelligence Tests Fair?

Concern over the question of fairness in group intelligence testing has been aroused, at least in part, by the following fact: In the United States and elsewhere, people belonging to several ethnic and racial minorities—for instance, in the United States, African Americans, Native Americans, and Hispanic Americans—generally score lower on group tests of intelligence than those belonging to the majority group—in the United States, Caucasians of European descent (Neisser et al., 1996). Indeed, in the past, persons belonging to such ethnic and racial minorities often showed average scores as much as ten to fifteen points lower than those of persons of European descent. The size of this gap appears to have decreased in recent years, at least where African Americans are concerned (e.g., Grissmer et al., 1994), but the gap has not entirely vanished.

What factors contribute to such group differences? We'll examine these in detail in a later section, but I should note here that many critics believe that one important factor is the strong **cultural bias** built into group intelligence tests. Because these tests were developed by and for persons belonging to a particular culture, individuals from other backgrounds may be at a disadvantage when taking them.

Are such concerns valid? Careful examination of the items used on intelligence tests suggests that to a degree they are. Many items assume that all children have had the opportunity to acquire certain kinds of information. Unfortunately, this is not always true for children from disadvantaged or minority backgrounds, who may never have had the chance to acquire the knowledge being tested. To the extent this is so, they cannot answer correctly no matter how high their intelligence.

Going farther, some psychologists (e.g., Helms, 1992) have argued that intelligence tests may suffer from other, more subtle forms of cultural bias as well. For instance, the tests often incorporate what some have described as a *Eurocentric perspective*—an implicit acceptance of European values and standards (Helms, 1989). European cultures generally place a high value on logical thinking, for example, and often view answers as being either right or wrong. As a result, children from European-descended cultural backgrounds accept these values and search for the correct answers when taking intelligence tests. In contrast, children from other backgrounds—for example, African American youngsters—may be less likely to assume that answers are either right or wrong. As a result, they may spend time reasoning about the *extent* to which each possible answer is correct, and this may tend to reduce their scores. At the present time no direct evidence for the accuracy of such suggestions exists; but they do raise unsettling possibilities that should be carefully investigated.

Cultural Bias: The tendency of items on a test of intelligence to require specific cultural experience or knowledge.

In an effort to eliminate cultural bias from intelligence tests, some psychologists have attempted to design *culture-fair* tests. Such tests attempt to include only items to which all groups, regardless of ethnic or racial background, have been exposed. Because many minority children in the United States are exposed to languages other than standard English, these tests tend to be nonverbal in nature. I referred previously to one of these—the **Raven Progressive Matrices** (Raven, 1977). This test consists of sixty "matrices," or groups of items, of varying difficulty, each containing a logical pattern or design with a missing part (see Figure 11.10). Individuals select the item that completes the pattern from several different choices. Because the Raven test and ones like it focus primarily on *fluid intelligence*—basic abilities to form concepts, reason, and identify similarities—these tests seem less likely to be subject to cultural bias than other kinds of intelligence tests. However, it is not clear that these tests totally eliminate the subtle kinds of bias described earlier.

Raven Progressive Matrices: A popular test of intelligence that was designed to be relatively free of cultural bias.

Perhaps, ultimately, the solution to designing intelligence tests that are totally free from cultural bias may involve increased use of basic measures of cognitive functioning such as *processing speed* or *inspection time*, or even of measures that focus on physiological factors such as nerve conduction velocity (as described earlier). Such measures would assess basic processes that underlie intelligence—processes that presumably should be much the same in all human beings, regardless of cultural background. I should hasten to add, however, that at present this approach is merely an intriguing but untested possibility. Such measures are still too new and still too uncertain in terms of their validity for anyone to suggest that they will provide *the* answer to this continuing puzzle. They do, however, provide one promising means for reaching a goal on which all psychologists agree: the development of tests of intelligence that do not place *any* group of persons at an unfair disadvantage.

Key Questions

- What is reliability, and how do psychologists attempt to measure it?
- What is validity, and how do psychologists attempt to measure it?
- What is cultural bias, and how may it affect scores on standard intelligence tests?

FIGURE 11.10

The Raven Progressive Matrices: One "Culture-Fair" Test of Intelligence

The items shown here are similar to those on one widely used test of intelligence that was designed to be relatively free from cultural bias: the Raven Progressive Matrices.

An Example of a Test Item on a Culture-Fair Test

This culture-fair test does not penalize test takers whose language or cultural experiences differ from those of the urban middle or upper classes. Subjects are to select, from the six samples on the right, the patch that would complete the pattern. Patch number 3 is the correct answer. (Adapted from the Raven Standard Progressive Matrices Test.)

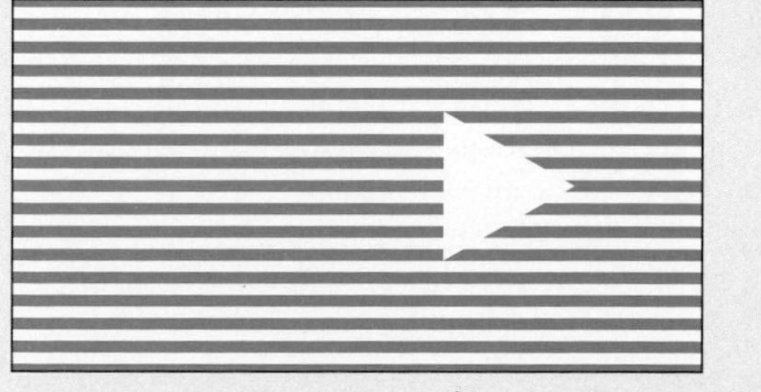
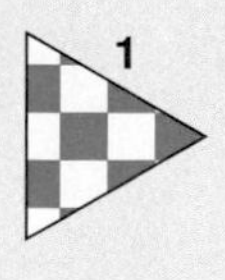

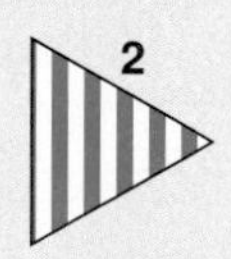

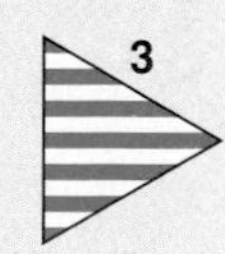

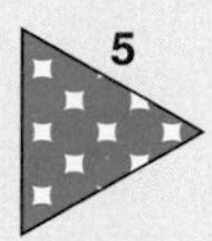

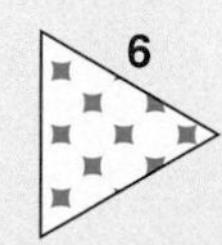

Human Intelligence: The Role of Heredity and the Role of Environment

That people differ in intelligence is obvious. *Why* such differences exist is quite another matter. Are they largely a matter of heredity—differences in the genetic materials and codes we inherit from our parents? Or are they primarily the result of environmental factors—conditions in the world around us that affect our intellectual development? I'm sure you know the answer: Both types of factors are involved. Human intelligence is clearly the result of the complex interplay between genetic factors and a wide range of environmental conditions (e.g., Plomin & Bergeman, 1991). Let's now consider some of the evidence pointing to this conclusion.

Evidence for the Role of Heredity

Several lines of research offer support for the view that heredity plays an important role in human intelligence. First, consider findings with respect to family relationship and measured IQ. If intelligence is indeed determined in part by heredity, we would expect that the more closely two persons are related, the more similar their IQs will be. This prediction has generally been confirmed (e.g., McGue et al., 1993; Neisser et al., 1996). For example, the IQs of identical twins raised together correlate almost +0.90, those of brothers and sisters

FIGURE 11.11

Correlations Between IQ Scores of Persons of Varying Relationships

The closer the biological relationship of two individuals, the higher the correlation between their IQ scores. This finding provides support for the role of genetic factors in intelligence.

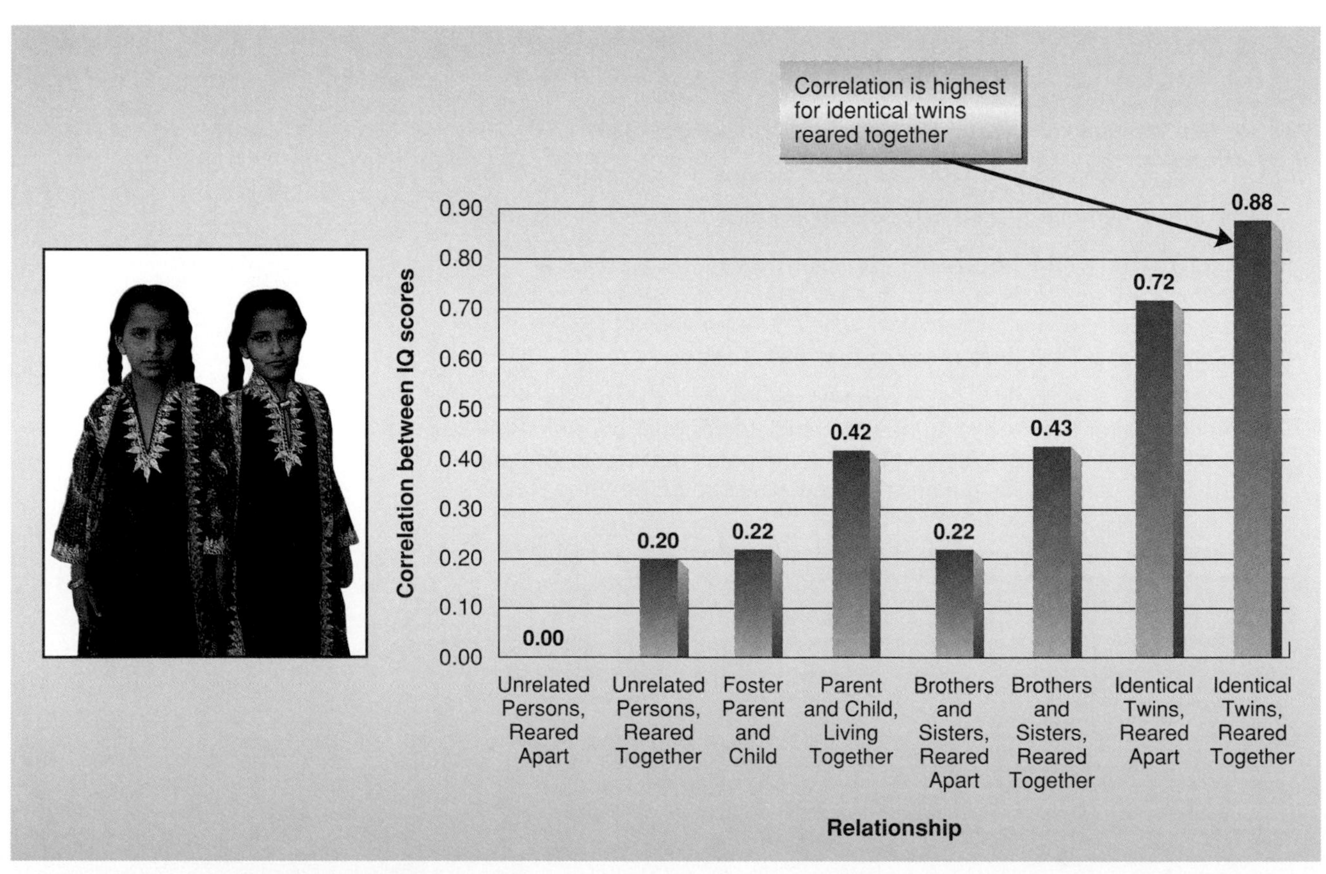

(**Source:** Based on data from Bouchard & McGue, 1981.)

about +0.50, and those of cousins about +0.15 (see Figure 11.11). (Remember: Higher correlations indicate stronger relationships between variables.)

Additional support for the impact of heredity on intelligence is provided by studies involving adopted children. If intelligence is strongly affected by genetic factors, the IQs of adopted children should resemble those of their biological parents more closely than those of their adoptive parents. In short, the children should be more similar in IQ to the persons from whom they received their genes than to the persons who raised them. This prediction, too, has been confirmed. While the IQs of adopted children correlate about +0.40 to +0.50 with those of the children's biological parents, they correlate only about +0.10 to +0.20 with those of their adoptive parents (Jencks, 1972; Munsinger, 1978). Be aware, though, that not all studies have yielded such results. Further, in some investigations, the IQs of adopted children have been observed to become increasingly similar to those of their adoptive parents over time (Scarr & Weinberg, 1976). These latter findings indicate that environmental factors, too, play an important role.

FIGURE 11.12

Identical Twins Reared Apart

The IQ scores of identical twins separated at birth and raised in different homes are highly correlated. This finding provides evidence for the impact of genetic factors on intelligence.

Perhaps the most dramatic evidence for the role of genetic factors in intelligence has been provided by research on identical twins separated early in life who were then raised in different homes (e.g., Bouchard et al., 1990). Such persons have identical genetic inheritance but have been exposed to different environmental conditions—in some cases, sharply contrasting conditions; so studying their IQs provides a powerful means for comparing the roles of genetic and environmental factors in human intelligence. The results of such research are very clear: The IQs of identical twins reared apart (often, from the time they were only a few days old) correlate almost as highly as those of identical twins reared together. Moreover, such individuals are also amazingly similar in many other characteristics, such as physical appearance, preferences in dress, mannerisms, and even personality (see Figure 11.12). Clearly, these findings point to an important role of heredity in intelligence and in many other aspects of psychological functioning.

On the basis of these and other findings, some researchers have estimated that the **heritability** of intelligence—the proportion of the variance in intelligence within a given population that is attributable to genetic factors—ranges from about 35 percent in childhood to as much as 75 percent in adulthood (McGue et al., 1993). Why does the contribution of genetic factors to intelligence increase with age? Perhaps because as individuals grow older, their interactions with their environment are shaped less and less by the impacts of their families or their social origins, and more and more by the characteristics they bring with them to their environments. In other words, as they grow older, individuals are increasingly able to choose or change their environments so that these permit expression of their genetically determined tendencies and preferences (Neisser et al., 1996). Whatever the precise origin of the increasing heritability of intelligence with age, there is little doubt that genetic factors do indeed play an important role in intelligence throughout life.

Evidence for the Role of Environmental Factors

Genetic factors are definitely *not* the entire picture where human intelligence is concerned, however. Other findings point to the conclusion that environ-

Heritability: The proportion of the variance in a trait within a given population that is attributable to genetic factors.

mental variables, too, are of great importance. One such finding is that IQ scores have risen substantially around the world at all age levels in recent decades. This is sometimes known as the *Flynn effect*, after the psychologist who first reported it (Flynn, 1987). Such increases have averaged about three IQ points per decade, but in some countries they have been even larger. In the Netherlands, for instance, the average IQ of nineteen-year-olds increased more than eight points between 1972 and 1982. What accounts for this increase? Since it seems unlikely that massive shifts in human heredity have occurred during this time period, a more reasonable explanation seems to lie in changing environmental conditions. Urbanization has increased all over the world, with the result that growing numbers of people are being exposed, through television and other media, to an increasing amount of information. Similarly, there have been improvements both in nutrition and in educational opportunities in many countries (e.g., Lynn, 1990; see Figure 11.13). To the extent that these variables are responsible for the increase in IQ, of course, this provides strong support for the role of environmental factors in human intelligence.

Additional evidence for the role of environmental factors in intelligence is provided by the findings of studies of *environmental deprivation* and *environmental enrichment*. With respect to deprivation, it has been found that intelligence can be reduced by the absence of certain forms of environmental stimulation early in life (Gottfried, 1984). In terms of enrichment, removing children from sterile, restricted environments and placing them in more favorable settings seems to enhance their intellectual growth (e.g., Skeels, 1938, 1966). For example, in one of the first demonstrations of the beneficial impact of an enriched environment on IQ, Skeels (1966) removed thirteen children, all about two years old, from an orphanage in which they received virtually no intellectual stimulation—and virtually no contact with adults—and placed them in the care of a group of retarded women living in an institution. After a few years, Skeels noted that the children's IQs had risen dramatically—29 points on average. Interestingly, Skeels also obtained IQ measures of children who had remained in the orphanage and found that on average, these had actually dropped by 26 points—presumably as a result of continued exposure to the impoverished environment at the orphanage. Twenty-five years later, the thirteen children who had experienced the enriched environment

FIGURE 11.13

Worldwide Gains in IQ: One Reason Why They May Be Occurring

In many parts of the world, both children and adults are receiving more education than ever before. This may be one factor contributing to recent worldwide gains in IQ scores.

were all doing well; most had graduated from high school, found a job, and married. In contrast, those in the original control group either remained institutionalized or were functioning poorly in society.

While more recent—and more carefully controlled—efforts to increase intelligence through environmental interventions have not yielded gains as dramatic as those reported by Skeels (1966), some of these programs *have* produced beneficial results. For example, in one such study, known as the *Venezuelan Intelligence Project*, hundreds of seventh-grade children from disadvantaged backgrounds were exposed to special school programs designed to improve their thinking skills. This intervention produced significant gains in the children's scores on many tests (Herrnstein et al., 1986). In another program, the *Carolina Abecedarian Project* (Campbell & Ramey, 1994), children were provided with enriched environments from early infancy through preschool. The test scores of these youngsters were higher than those of children who did not benefit from this intervention, and remained higher even at age twelve, seven years after the end of the program. Together, findings such as these suggest that improving the environment in which children live can indeed affect their IQs.

A fourth source of evidence for the impact on intelligence of environmental factors is provided by the finding, in many studies, that the longer students remain in school, the higher their IQ scores tend to be (e.g., Ceci, 1991). While this finding could also be interpreted as suggesting that it is the more intelligent people who choose to remain in school, several facts point to the conclusion that staying in school may actually benefit intelligence. For example, it has been found that students who attend school regularly score higher on intelligence tests than students who attend irregularly. Similarly, when children of nearly identical age but who are one grade apart in school are compared, those who have attended school longer have higher average IQs. (This difference in grade levels occurs because all school systems have a cutoff date for birthdays, and only children born before that date can start school in a given year.)

Additional support for the role of environmental factors in intelligence comes from research showing that many biological factors that children encounter while growing up can affect their intelligence. Prolonged malnutrition can adversely affect IQ (e.g., Sigman, 1995), as can exposure to lead either in the air or in lead-based paint—which young children often eat because it tastes sweet (e.g., Baghurst et al., 1992). We have already examined the adverse effects of factors such as alcohol and drugs on the physical health of developing fetuses; here I simply want to add that research findings indicate that these factors can also adversely affect intelligence (e.g., Neisser et al., 1996). To conclude, then, many forms of evidence support the view that intelligence is determined, at least in part, by environmental factors.

Environment, Heredity, and Intelligence: Summing Up

In sum, there is considerable evidence that *both* environmental and genetic factors play a role in intelligence. This is the view accepted by almost all psychologists, and there is little controversy about it. Greater controversy continues to exist, however, concerning the *relative* contribution of each of these factors. Do environmental or genetic factors play a stronger role in shaping intelligence? As I noted earlier, existing evidence seems to favor the view that genetic factors may account for more of the variance in IQ scores within a given population than environmental factors (e.g., McGue et al., 1993; Neisser et al., 1996). Many people, including psychologists, are made somewhat uneasy by this conclusion, in part because they assume that characteristics that are heritable—ones that are strongly influenced by genetic factors—cannot readily be changed. *It's important to recognize that this assumption is false.* For instance, consider height: This is a characteristic that is highly heritable—one that is influenced by genetic factors to a greater extent than intelligence is. Yet despite this fact, average heights have increased in many countries as nutrition has improved. So here is a case of a trait that is strongly determined by genetic factors, yet is still responsive to shifts in environmental conditions.

The same thing is almost certainly true for intelligence. Even if it is influenced by genetic factors, it can still be affected by environmental conditions. For this reason, programs designed to enrich the intellectual environments of children from disadvantaged backgrounds may still produce beneficial results. Whether such programs have the desired effects or not is an empirical question open to scientific study; however, there is no reason to assume in advance that enrichment programs cannot succeed because intelligence is influenced by genetic factors. Heredity, in short, should not be viewed as a set of biological shackles, nor as an excuse for giving up on children who are at risk because of poverty, prejudice, or neglect.

Key Questions

- What evidence suggests that intelligence is influenced by genetic factors?
- What evidence suggests that intelligence is influenced by environmental factors?
- Can characteristics that are highly heritable be influenced by environmental factors?

Group Differences in Intelligence Test Scores: *Why They Occur*

Earlier I noted that there are sizable differences in the average IQ scores of various ethnic groups. In the United States and elsewhere, members of various minority groups score lower, on average, than members of the majority group. Why do such differences occur? I've already described one possibility: the argument that standard IQ tests suffer from *cultural bias*. Here, I'll expand upon this earlier discussion by examining several other potential causes for such *group differences* in intelligence test scores. In addition, I'll briefly examine the possibility that *gender differences* in intelligence, too, exist.

Possible Causes of Group Differences in IQ Scores

While many different factors may contribute to group differences in IQ scores, three, in addition to test bias, have received the greatest amount of attention: *socioeconomic factors*, *cultural factors*, and *genetic factors*.

Socioeconomic Factors In the United States and many other countries, members of minority groups have, on average, much lower income than persons belonging to the majority group. Further, much larger proportions of several ethnic minorities live below the poverty line (Neisser et al., 1996). Since poverty is associated with many factors that can exert adverse effects on intelligence—for instance, poorer nutrition, inadequate prenatal care, and substandard schools—it seems possible that economic disadvantage may be one important cause of lower IQ scores among ethnic minorities (see Figure 11.14).

FIGURE 11.14

Poverty and IQ

Growing up under conditions of severe poverty may exert harmful effects on the IQ scores of children. This may be one factor contributing to group differences in IQ.

When children in various ethnic groups who are closely matched in terms of socioeconomic status are compared, however, differences still exist: Those of Asian descent score highest, those of European descent score lower, and those of African descent score lowest (e.g., Loehlin, Lindzey, & Spuhler, 1975; Lynn, 1996). This suggests that while socioeconomic factors contribute to group differences in IQ scores, other factors, as yet unknown, may also play some role.

Cultural Differences Another possibility is that certain aspects of the cultures to which minority persons belong interfere in subtle ways with their test performance. For instance, according to Boykin (1994), several features of African American culture conflict with features of the majority culture in the United States, and therefore with practices in American schools. For instance, while the majority culture insists that children work alone and sit still and quietly in class, African American culture emphasizes sharing work and high levels of expressiveness and movement. The result, Boykin (1994) contends, is that African Americans find school an unpleasant environment and quickly become alienated from the educational process. This, he argues, tends to reduce their test scores.

Another, and related, factor that may adversely affect the test scores of minorities involves what some psychologists describe as the effects of belonging to *castelike minorities* (e.g., Ogbu, 1994). The nature of such minorities is best captured, perhaps, by the Indian concept of "untouchables." The caste concept implies that persons are assigned to the castelike minority in an involuntary manner, that their membership in this minority is permanent, and that they will experience sharply restricted opportunities because of belonging to this minority. Ogbu (1994) argues that in the United States, many African Americans feel that they have been assigned to such a castelike minority and that they can never escape from it. The result: They grow up convinced that no matter what they do, they will never share in the "American dream." In terms of expectancy theory (see Chapter 10), these African Americans grow up with low expectancies, believing that effort on their part will *not* result in better outcomes. This leads them to reject academic achievement and other forms of behavior described as "acting white"; and these reactions, in turn, tend to lower their test scores.

Do such factors actually contribute to lower test scores among minority groups? At present, there is very little direct evidence on this issue. However, given the powerful impact of cultural factors and expectancies on many other forms of behavior, it seems quite reasonable to expect that the results of future studies may well confirm these suggestions, at least to a degree.

The third potential cause of group differences in IQ scores listed above—genetic factors—is both important and intensely controversial. I will examine it in the special Exploring Gender and Diversity section below.

EXPLORING GENDER & DIVERSITY

Genetic Factors and Group Differences in IQ Scores: Ringing Down the Curtain on The Bell Curve

In 1994 a highly controversial book entitled *The Bell Curve* was published. Because the book was written by two well-known psychologists (Richard Herrnstein and Charles Murray), it received immediate attention in the popular press and soon became a best-seller. The book focused on human intelligence. It covered many aspects of this topic, but the most controversial portions dealt with what is known as the **genetic hypothesis**—the view that group differences in intelligence are due, at least in part, to genetic factors.

In *The Bell Curve,* Herrnstein and Murray (1994) voiced strong support for this view. They noted, for instance, that there are several converging sources of evidence for "a genetic factor in cognitive ethnic differences" (p. 270) between African Americans and white Americans and between other ethnic groups as well. Proceeding from this premise, they suggested that intelligence may not be readily modifiable through changes in environmental conditions; the authors proposed, therefore, that efforts to raise the IQ scores of disadvantaged minorities through special programs were probably a waste of effort. In their own words, "Taken together, the story of attempts to raise intelligence is one of high hopes, flamboyant claims, and disappointing results. For the foreseeable future, the problems of low cognitive ability are not going to be solved by outside interventions to make children smarter" (p. 389).

As you can imagine, these suggestions were challenged vigorously by many psychologists (e.g., Sternberg, 1995). These critics argued that much of the reasoning in *The Bell Curve* was flawed, and that the book overlooked many important findings. Perhaps the harshest criticism centered on the book's contention that because *individual* differences in intelligence are strongly influenced by genetic factors, *group* differences are, too. Several researchers took strong exception to this reasoning (e.g., Schultze, Karie, & Dickens, 1996; Sternberg, 1995). They noted that in fact this contention would be accurate only if the environments of the various groups being compared were identical. Under those conditions, it could be argued that differences between the groups stemmed, at least in part, from genetic factors. In reality, however, the environments in which the members of various ethnic groups exist are *not* identical. As a result, it is a mistake to assume that differences between them with respect to IQ scores stem from genetic factors, even if we know that individual differences in such scores *are* strongly influenced by these factors. Perhaps this point is best illustrated by a simple analogy.

Imagine that a farmer plants two fields with seeds that are known to be genetically identical. In one field, the farmer fertilizes, waters, and cultivates the crop very carefully. In the other, the farmer does none of these things, and also removes key nutrients needed for growth. Several months later, there are large differences between the plants growing in the two fields, *despite the fact that their genetic makeup is identical*. In a similar manner, it is entirely possible that differences in the IQ scores of various groups occur because of contrasting life environments, and that genetic factors play little if any role in such group differences.

So where does all this leave us? With the conclusion that although we know fairly certainly that individual differences in IQ scores are influenced by genetic

Genetic Hypothesis: The view that group differences in intelligence are due, at least in part, to genetic factors.

factors, we *don't* know whether this is also true with respect to group differences. While a few researchers continue to insist that sufficient evidence exists to conclude that genetic factors play a role (e.g., Rushton, 1997), most take strong exception to this view and contend that the evidence pointing to this possible conclusion is relatively weak (e.g., Neisser, 1997). As one researcher put it (Sternberg, 1995, p. 260): "Herrnstein and Murray do not have a very good understanding of the factors that influence [*group differences in*] IQ. Neither does anyone else . . . , but most psychologists are more willing to admit to the fact that factors affecting IQ are still poorly understood." (Italics added.) Or, as I'd put it, while *The Bell Curve* has certainly tolled—the book has sold tens of thousands of copies and received a great deal of public attention—from the standpoint of scientific knowledge, it definitely does *not* ring true.

Gender Differences in Intelligence

Do males and females differ in intelligence? Overall, they score virtually identically on standard tests of this characteristic (e.g., Lynn, 1994). However, a few subtle differences do seem to exist with respect to certain components of intelligence. First, females tend to score higher than males with respect to verbal abilities—such tasks as naming synonyms (words with the same meaning) and verbal fluency (e.g., naming words that start with a given letter). Females also score higher than males on college achievement tests in literature, spelling, and writing (e.g., Stanley, 1993). Such differences are relatively small and seem to be decreasing (Feingold, 1992), but they do appear, even in very careful meta-analyses performed on the results of many different studies.

In contrast, males tend to score somewhat higher than females on visual–spatial tasks such as mental rotation or tracking a moving object through space (Law, Pellegrino, & Hunt, 1993). You may be able to demonstrate such differences for yourself by following the instructions in Figure 11.15. Ask sev-

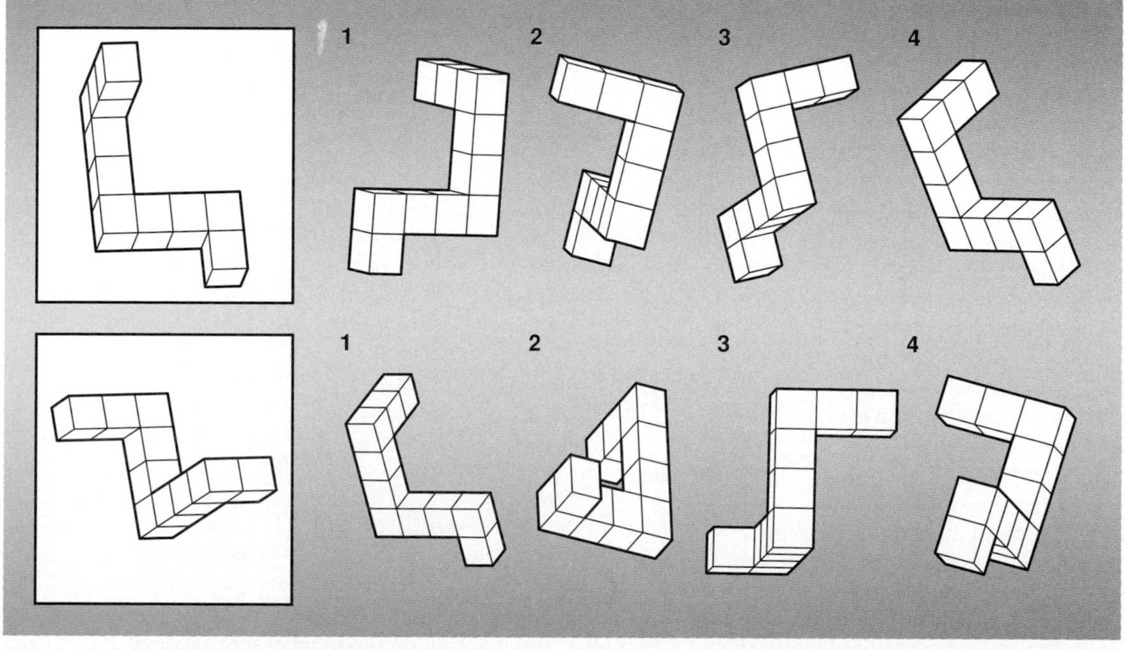

(**Source:** Adapted from Azar, 1996.)

FIGURE 11.15

Gender Differences in Visual–Spatial Abilities

Males tend to score somewhat higher than females on tasks such as this one. Try it with your friends. Do the males do better, or find it easier, than the females? Which figure (or figures) on the right shows (show) the figure on the left in a different position? Answers: Top row: 1, 3; Bottom row: 2, 3

Key Questions

- What roles do socioeconomic and cultural factors play in group differences in IQ scores?
- In *The Bell Curve* the authors argue that because individual differences in IQ are highly heritable, group differences in IQ must also be highly heritable. How do most psychologists view this argument?
- Do any gender differences with respect to intelligence exist? If so, what is the possible origin of such differences?

eral male and female friends to try their hand at the task it involves. You may find that the males find this slightly easier (and perhaps more enjoyable) than the females. However, gender differences in performing visual–spatial tasks, like almost all gender differences, are far smaller than gender stereotypes suggest; so if you do observe any difference, it is likely to be a small one. For one intriguing explanation of gender differences with respect to spatial abilities, see the Beyond the Headlines section below.

Beyond the Headlines

As Psychologists See It

Why Men Lose Keys—and Women Find Them

Gender Differences in Spatial Abilities May Be Linked to Our Heritage of Hunting and Gathering

APA Monitor, August, 1996, p. 32.

"I can't find my keys."
"They're on your dresser."
"I looked on my dresser. They're not there."
"Yes they are. They're on the left side, next to your book and under your yellow shirt."
"Oh, there they are!"

If you guessed that it's a man who can't find his keys and a woman who tells him where to look, you'd most likely be right. Many of us can recall similar episodes from our own lives. At the root of such dialogues is a story that might allow women to join men on an equal footing in the realm of spatial abilities. . . . Researchers at York University speculate that women simply excel at different types of spatial skills. Women surpass men in learning and remembering the location of objects. . . .

Have you ever had experiences like the one described in the clipping? I certainly have: At least three times a day, it seems, I ask my wife to find something *I* can't find—and she does so with ease. Such experiences have led me—and, I suspect, many other males too—to believe that women have some kind of mystical power that allows them to find lost or misplaced objects. Now research findings are helping to resolve this puzzle. Irwin Silverman and Marion Eals, two psychologists at York University, reasoned that perhaps gender differences in spatial abilities reflect the different kinds of tasks performed by women and men throughout much of human history. Before the development of civilization—which began only some ten thousand years ago—our species lived by hunting and gathering: Men hunted and women foraged for edible plants. According to Silverman and Eals, these tasks required different spatial abilities. Hunters (males) needed to be able to orient themselves in relation to objects or places at great distances from each other so that they could pursue prey over unfamiliar ground. In contrast, gatherers (females) needed to be able to remember the locations of plants so that they could find them again each growing season. The result, the two psychologists rea-soned, is that men are better at tasks such as rotating objects in their minds, while women are better at remembering the locations of objects.

To test this reasoning, Silverman and Eals performed a series of studies in which male and female participants performed several tasks in a small office. In one condition, participants were told to try to remember the location of various objects in the room, while in another condition, no mention was made of this additional task. When later tested for naming the objects and indicating their locations, women outperformed men in both conditions. However, the difference was much larger in the condition where participants were *not* told to try to remember this information (Azar, 1996).

Needless to add, the question of whether differences in the spatial abilities of females and males are actually the result of our species' evolutionary history cannot be resolved through such research—ingenious though it is. However, such research does provide important insights into gender differences in this important aspect of intelligence, and in this respect is both interesting and valuable.

Critical Thinking Questions

1. What other methods might be used to test the hypothesis that women are actually better than men at locating objects?
2. Since it is impossible to determine whether such gender differences in spatial abilities actually stem from evolution, are such explanations useful from a scientific point of view?

Emotional Intelligence: *The Feeling Side of Intelligence*

Do you remember my friend Johnny—the genius who failed? I was quite young at the time we were friends, but when I remember those long-ago days, I think I can see *why* he had so many problems later in life. First and foremost, Johnny came across as arrogant: He was smart and he knew it, and—even worse—he often rubbed it in. He did this directly with his friends, telling us how little we knew. With adults he used a different tactic, adopting an insolent manner that said—without words—"You're older and bigger, but *I'm still smarter*." No wonder he got into so many conflicts with teachers. In addition, Johnny was what I'd now describe as *emotionally unstable*. His moods swung widely and quickly from one extreme to another. More important, he seemed incapable of restraining his impulses; when he wanted something, he wanted it *now;* waiting was for others, not for him. I'm sure that this was one of the characteristics that got him into serious trouble in college and later life. Finally, although he was smooth and charming when he wanted to be, Johnny was not really interested in other people. He paid little or no attention to others' feelings and formed only temporary, shallow relationships. I often had the feeling that I was a mere convenience for him: We lived in the same building, so he included me in his plans because I was handy and also because I let him run the show. So, taking everything into account, I'm not really surprised that Johnny didn't live up to his bright promise. He was brilliant, all right, but only in certain respects; in other ways he was truly backward.

This discussion of my friend leads me to the topic of this section—another kind of intelligence, quite distinct from that measured by IQ tests. Daniel Goleman (1995), in yet another best-selling book about intelligence, recently described this kind of intelligence as **emotional intelligence.** Basically, such intelligence can be defined as a cluster of traits or abilities relating to the emotional side of life—abilities such as recognizing and managing one's own and others' emotions, motivating oneself and restraining impulses, and handling interpersonal relationships in an effective manner (Goleman, 1995). Growing

Emotional Intelligence: A form of intelligence relating to the emotional side of life such as the ability to recognize and manage one's own and others' emotions, to motivate oneself and restrain impulses, and to handle interpersonal relationships effectively.

evidence suggests that such skills are important for personal success and for having a happy, productive life. In other words, as I've already noted at several points in this chapter, it is not enough to be bright in an academic sense (that is, to have a high IQ); other aspects of intelligence are crucial too. Let's take a closer look at the major components of emotional intelligence and how they influence important forms of behavior.

Major Components of Emotional Intelligence

Goleman (1995) suggests that emotional intelligence consists of five major parts: (1) knowing our own emotions, (2) managing our emotions, (3) motivating ourselves, (4) recognizing the emotions of others, and (5) handling relationships. Each of these components of emotional intelligence, he contends, plays an important role in shaping our life outcomes so each is worthy of our careful attention.

Knowing Our Own Emotions As I noted in Chapter 10, emotions are often powerful reactions—so it would seem at first glance that everyone ought to be able to recognize their own feelings. As suggested by the cartoon in Figure 11.16, however, this is not always the case. Some persons are highly aware of their own emotions and their thoughts about them, while others seem to be almost totally oblivious to their feelings. What are the implications of such differences? First, to the extent individuals are not aware of their own feelings, they cannot make intelligent choices: How can they tell whom to date or marry, what job to take, which house or car to buy, or even what to order in a restaurant? Second, because such persons aren't aware of their own emotions, they are often low in *expressiveness*—they don't show their feelings clearly through their facial expressions, their body language, or the other cues most of us use to recognize others' feelings (Malandro, Barker, & Barker, 1994). Clearly, this can have adverse effects on their interpersonal relationships. For these reasons, then, this first component of emotional intelligence is quite important.

FIGURE 11.16

Knowing Our Own Emotions: A Key Aspect of Emotional Intelligence

As suggested by this cartoon, individuals differ greatly with respect to awareness of their own emotions.

"Oh, and your feelings have been trying to get in touch with you."

(**Source:** Drawing by Wm. Hamilton; ©1989 The New Yorker Magazine, Inc.)

Managing Our Own Emotions Have you ever lost your temper or cried when you didn't want to show such reactions? Have you ever done something to cheer yourself up when you felt anxious or depressed? If so, you are already aware of the fact that we often try to *manage* our emotions—to regulate both their nature and their intensity (e.g., Zillmann, 1996). Doing so is very important both for our own mental health and from the point of view of interacting effectively with others. For instance, consider persons who simply cannot control their temper; are they bound for success and a happy life? No. In all likelihood, they will be avoided by many people and will *not* get the jobs, promotions, or lovers they want.

Perhaps one of the most important tasks we undertake with respect to managing our emotions is that of countering negative moods: overcoming feelings of melancholy or depression. Persons who are high in emotional intelligence have many effective tactics for accomplishing this goal (e.g., Tice &

Baumeiseter, 1993). For instance, they participate in activities they enjoy, such as eating a favorite food, listening to enjoyable music, taking a warm bath, or buying themselves or someone they love a gift. Alternatively, they may arrange to experience a small triumph or easy success, such as finishing some household chore, or simply washing their hair and putting on makeup. Persons low in this aspect of emotional intelligence, in contrast, have fewer tactics for countering depression or other negative moods up their sleeves. As a result, they experience such states more often and for longer periods of time. (Please see the Making Psychology Part of Your Life section at the end of this chapter for more information on emotional intelligence.)

Motivating Ourselves The great inventor Thomas Edison once remarked that success requires "one percent inspiration and ninety-nine percent perspiration." Do you agree? While inspiration or creativity is certainly important (see the next section of this chapter), I'm inclined to believe that Edison was right. By "perspiration," however, I mean more than simply hard work: I also include aspects of emotional intelligence such as being able to motivate oneself to work long and hard on a task (see Figure 11.17); remaining enthusiastic and optimistic about the final outcome; and being able to delay gratification—to put off receiving small rewards now in order to get larger ones later on (e.g., Shoda, Mischel, & Peake, 1990).

How important are such skills? Consider the following facts: Asian Americans often outperform other groups in the United States on tests like the SAT (Scholastic Aptitude Test) and the GRE (the Graduate Record Exam, required for entry into many graduate schools). Further, they outperform other groups in terms of occupational success and in the proportion who hold high-level jobs (Flynn, 1991); the figure is 55 percent for Chinese Americans and 46 percent for Japanese Americans but only 34 percent for Americans of European descent (Neisser et al., 1996). On the basis of such outcomes, you might assume that Asian Americans would outscore other groups in terms of IQ. In fact, however, this is *not* the case; their IQ scores are quite close to average (Lynn, 1996). Why, then, do they excel in so many ways? Apparently because they are very high in motivation—and in the ability to motivate themselves. To the extent extra effort pays off in improved performance, this aspect of emotional intelligence can yield handsome rewards.

Recognizing Others' Emotions I have a friend who is long-winded even for a professor. Once he begins to tell you something—a story, his political views, how to cook some dish—he continues regardless of what you do or say. I've watched my friend drone on as the people to whom he is talking give him cue after cue that they are no longer interested in what he's saying. My friend is a brilliant engineer and a bright, with-it person generally, so on one occasion I asked him: "Didn't you notice that they were losing interest?" His reply: "No . . . what makes you say that? How could you tell?"

My friend, as you can guess, is relatively low in another important aspect of emotional intelligence: being able to recognize the emotions of others. This basic skill could well be described as the ability to read *nonverbal cues*, since it is primarily through such cues that people generally communicate their feelings (e.g., Carroll & Russell, 1996). This ability is crucial in many situations, because unless we know how others are reacting or feeling, it's difficult to interact with them in an effective way. Persons who are high in this skill

FIGURE 11.17

Self-Motivation: Another Key Component of Emotional Intelligence

Being able to motivate oneself to work long and hard on a task while remaining enthusiastic about it is, according to Goleman (1995), a key component of emotional intelligence.

are often very effective as salespersons or politicians: they can readily sense how others are reacting to their words or actions, and they adjust these accordingly. Just watch a successful salesperson in operation, and you'll see a clear example of this type of emotional intelligence. Such persons watch their customers intently, noticing every fleeting sign that might suggest whether they like or dislike some item or feature, and how they are responding to the salesperson's words. Persons who are high in this aspect of emotional intelligence don't merely recognize others' reactions, however. They also *manage* them; they often do whatever it takes to induce in others the kinds of reactions they want—such as a positive attitude toward a product or a liking for themselves as a political candidate. In these and many other contexts, this component of emotional intelligence can be quite valuable.

Handling Relationships Some people seem to have a knack for getting along with others: Most people who meet them like them, and as a result, they have many friends and often enjoy high levels of success in their careers. In contrast, others seem to make a mess of virtually all their personal relationships: Try as they may, they just can't seem to get along with others. According to Goleman (1995), such differences reflect another aspect of emotional intelligence or, as some researchers would phrase it, *interpersonal intelligence* (Hatch, 1990).

What does such intelligence involve? Such skills as being able to coordinate the efforts of several people, to negotiate solutions to complex interpersonal problems, and to form relationships with others—often by being a good "team player." Again, such skills are clearly distinct from the ones needed for getting good grades or scoring high on tests of intelligence, but they often play a key role in important life outcomes.

Emotional Intelligence in Action: Building Successful Intimate Relationships

When asked what they want in life, most young people include "a happy long-term relationship with someone I love" high on their list (Hales, 1996). Yet statistics with respect to the success of such relationships are nothing short of alarming. For couples who married in 1920, the divorce rate was about 18 percent; for couples who married in 1950, it approached 30 percent. Couples who married in 1990 face about a 70 percent chance that their relationship will end unhappily (Gottman, 1993). Is emotional intelligence relevant to these statistics? And could emotional intelligence help improve the odds for what start out as loving couples? Growing evidence suggests positive answers to both questions.

Long-term studies of couples indicate that in many cases difficulties arise from the fact that, as the title of a recent book put it, *Men Are from Mars, Women Are from Venus*; that is, the two sexes have acquired different, and in some cases conflicting, emotional skills. Overall, females clearly have the edge with respect to such skills: They enter long-term relationships with more sophisticated understanding of their own and others' feelings and of how information about feelings can be communicated (Brody & Hall, 1993). Because of contrasting socialization practices, males are generally taught to ignore others' emotions and their own, while females learn to direct more attention to such reactions. Such differences are clearly illustrated in situations where one of a group of children is hurt while at play. Among boys, the injured person is urged to get out of the way and stop crying so the game can continue; I remember literally crawling off a playing field myself on several occasions, shouting as I did, "I'm going, I'm going!" Among girls, in contrast, the game stops while everyone gathers around to help the one who is hurt and crying (Goleman, 1995).

These differences in emotional style—one might say emotional intelligence—influence the behavior of partners in marriages and other intimate relationships. For instance, because they are less skilled at recognizing and expressing emotions, males react to criticisms from their spouses with intense feelings—ones they can't readily manage. The result? They often resort to "stonewalling"—going blank emotionally and withdrawing from the conversation. Their wives or partners are dismayed by such behavior and, as a result, may redouble their assault in order to get *some* reaction. Needless to say, such tactics often backfire, and they may start a spiral of anger and ill will that can permanently damage the relationship. The other side of the coin is that men often fail to tell their partners how they are reacting to things the partners do or say, thus providing little guidance to them. In addition, because men are often "solutions-oriented" rather than "feelings-oriented," they may grasp at the first solution that pops into their heads, and so short-circuit a full discussion of difficulties in the relationship.

In sum, it appears that both genders can profit from fine-tuning where emotional intelligence is concerned. Men need to learn that when a woman voices a criticism, it may be motivated by love. Criticism often represents an attempt by the woman to improve the relationship, so men must learn to avoid reacting so strongly to such remarks that they become incapable of profiting from them. In contrast, women should recognize the fact that men are especially sensitive to criticism and often have difficulty regulating their emotional reactions to critical remarks. Thus, women should generally use comments milder in nature than ones they themselves might readily tolerate.

In concluding this section, I should add that intimate relationships are only one context in which emotional intelligence is important. Such intelligence also plays a crucial role in the world of business, where high emotional intelligence may be a better predictor of career success than high academic intelligence (e.g., Sternberg et al., 1995). And as we'll see in Chapter 13, it may also play an important role in personal health and in the effectiveness of the health care system: Physicians high in emotional intelligence may be more successful in treating their patients than physicians who are low in such intelligence. In sum, the commonsense notion that there is more to intelligence than "book smarts" seems to be correct; and one of the most important aspects of that "other" kind of intelligence appears to be emotional intelligence.

Key Questions

- What is emotional intelligence?
- What role does emotional intelligence play in success and personal happiness?
- What role does emotional intelligence play in long-term intimate relationships?

Creativity: Generating the Extraordinary

Suppose you were asked to name people high in creativity—who would be on your list? Many people would name such famous figures as Albert Einstein, Leonardo da Vinci, Thomas Edison, and Sigmund Freud. What do these diverse individuals have in common? All were responsible for producing something—a theory, an invention—that was viewed as unexpected and *new*. More formally, psychologists generally define **creativity** as involving the ability to produce work that is both novel (original, unexpected) and appropriate (it works—it is useful or meets task constraints; e.g., Lubart,

Creativity: The ability to produce work that is both novel and appropriate.

FIGURE 11.18

Creativity in Action?

While the action shown here is certainly new and different, it isn't very practical. Therefore, it doesn't really meet psychologists' definition of *creativity*.

HEINRICH COULD ALWAYS BE RELIED UPON TO SERVE COFFEE IN HIS OWN INIMITABLE STYLE.

(**Source:** Drawing by Glen Baxter; ©1991 The New Yorker Magazine, Inc.)

1994). By this definition, does the action shown in Figure 11.18 illustrate creativity? Probably not, because while it is certainly original, it really isn't practical! The U.S. Patent Office applies the same criteria to patent applications: Not only must an idea be new, but it must be practical too. (I currently hold three U.S. patents, so I have learned about this process firsthand; a product based on my patents is shown in Chapter 17.)

Clearly, creativity is important; in a sense, it is responsible for all of the advances made by our species since it emerged on the planet. It is somewhat surprising to learn, therefore, that until recently, creativity was *not* the subject of extensive study by psychologists. Why not? One important reason was that although several methods for measuring creativity existed—for instance, asking individuals to come up with as many uses for everyday objects as possible (known as the Unusual Uses Test; Guilford, 1950) or to formulate as many ways of improving a product as possible (Torrance, 1974)—none of these measures seemed to be completely satisfactory. They did not seem to capture all aspects of creativity as it occurs in real-life situations (Sternberg & Lubart, 1996). Another problem was the fact that the concept of creativity was associated, in many people's minds, with factors outside the realm of science—for instance, with vague notions of "the creative spirit." This made psychologists somewhat reluctant to address this topic.

During the past two decades, however, this situation has changed, and rapid advances have been made in our understanding of creativity. Because creativity is clearly related to certain aspects of intelligence, and because it is an important topic in its own right, I'll now describe what psychologists have discovered about this fascinating topic. (We considered creativity briefly in Chapter 9, as part of our discussion of aging.)

Contrasting Views of Creativity

A basic question about creativity is "What factors underlie its occurrence?" Until recently different branches of psychology offered contrasting answers. Cognitive psychologists, for example, tended to focus on the basic processes that underlie creative thought. Research findings indicate that such processes as retrieval of information from memory, association, synthesis, transformation, and categorical reduction (mentally assigning objects to basic categories) may all play a role in creativity. In contrast, social psychologists generally focused on the personality traits that make people creative and the environmental conditions that either encourage or discourage creativity (e.g., Simonton, 1994).

While these approaches have certainly added to our understanding of creativity, most researchers now believe that even more can be learned through what is termed a **confluence approach**—an approach based on the idea that for creativity to occur, multiple factors must converge (Amabile, 1983). For example, according to an influential confluence model of creativity proposed by Lubart (e.g., Lubart, 1994), creativity requires a confluence of six distinct resources:

- *Intellectual abilities:* The ability to see problems in new ways, the ability to recognize which of one's ideas are worth pursuing, and persuasive skills—the ability to convince others of these new ideas.
- *Knowledge:* Enough knowledge about a field to move it forward.
- *Certain styles of thinking:* Both a preference for thinking in novel ways and an ability to see the big picture—to think globally as well as locally.

Confluence Approach: A view of creativity suggesting that for creativity to occur, multiple factors must converge.

- *Personality attributes:* Such traits as willingness to take risks and tolerance for ambiguity.
- *Intrinsic, task-focused motivation:* Creative people usually love what they are doing and find intrinsic rewards in their work.
- An environment that is supportive of creative ideas.

Only when all of these conditions are present, Sternberg and his colleagues argue, can a high level of creativity emerge (Sternberg & Lubart, 1996; see Figure 11.19).

Recent Research on Creativity: Evidence for the Confluence Approach

Is there any support in scientific research for the confluence view of creativity described above? Absolutely. For example, consider one recent study by Lubart and Sternberg (1995). In this study, forty-eight adults ranging in age from eighteen to sixty-five were asked to produce creative products in each of four domains: writing, art, advertising, and science. For example, in the art category they were asked to produce drawings showing "hope" and "rage" and to depict "the earth from an insect's point of view." With respect to advertising, they were asked to design television ads for "bow ties" and "the Internal Revenue Service." All the participants' work was then rated by several persons for overall creativity, novelty, and perceived effort. Participants also completed a measure of fluid intelligence, a measure of thinking style, and two personality measures.

Results indicated, first, that there was considerable agreement among raters: They agreed on what was creative and what was not creative. This is an important finding, because it indicates that creativity can be studied scientifically. Second, creativity in one domain (art, writing, and so on) was only moderately related to creativity in other domains. Thus, as common sense suggests, people can be creative in one area but not in another. Third, intellectual ability, thinking style, and personality were all significantly related to creativity. Additional research (e.g., Sternberg et al., 1997), indicated that—

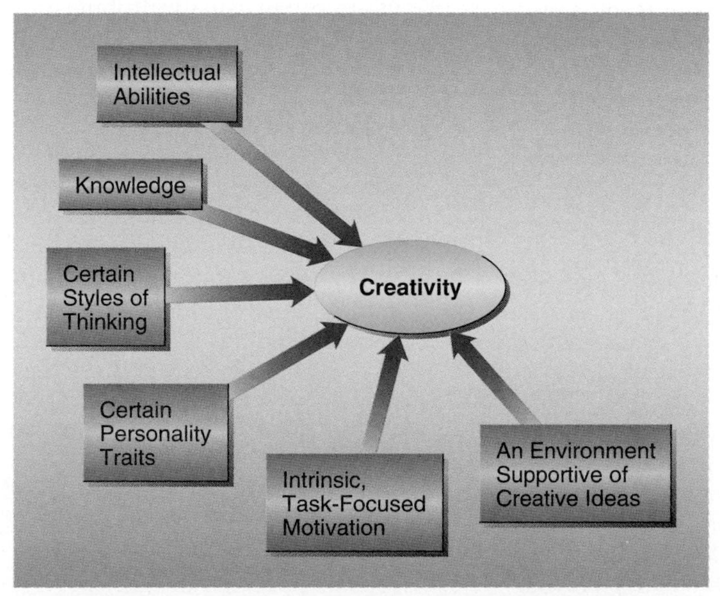

(**Source:** Based on suggestions by Sternberg & Lubart, 1996.)

FIGURE 11.19

Creativity: A Confluence Approach

According to modern *confluence theories*, creativity can emerge only when several different conditions are present or converge.

Key Questions

- What is creativity?
- What are confluence theories, and what factors do they view as essential to creativity?
- What evidence offers support for the confluence approach?

consistent with theoretical predictions—willingness to take intellectual risks was also related to creativity.

Taken together, these findings and the findings of other recent studies offer support for the confluence approach. For creativity to occur, it appears, many factors must converge. None of these factors is unusual in and of itself; but together they produce outcomes and results that are, in some cases, extraordinary.

Making Psychology Part of Your Life

Managing Anger: A Key Aspect of Emotional Intelligence

In discussing emotional intelligence, I noted that one key aspect of such intelligence is the ability to manage our own emotions. Perhaps the most difficult emotion of all to manage is anger, which all too often erupts into open rage. You probably know from your own experience that once it starts, anger tends to be self-perpetuating—and sometimes self-amplifying, too. What begins as mild irritation can quickly move into strong anger and then, if we don't take active steps to stop it, a virtual emotional explosion. What can you do to avoid such outcomes—to manage your own anger more effectively? Here are some useful steps.

- **Stop the process early.** Because anger is self-amplifying, it is easier to break the annoyance–anger–rage cycle early on. So if you feel yourself getting angry and feel that this emotion is inappropriate or might get out of hand, take one of the actions described below as soon as possible. Delay can be quite costly in terms of your ability to break this cycle.
- **Try a cooling-off period.** If possible, leave the scene, change the subject, or at least stop interacting with the other person. Doing so can give your emotional arousal a chance to dissipate, *as long as you don't use this time to mull over the causes of your anger*. So if you do try a cooling-off period, it's important also to use the next step below.
- **Do something to get yourself off the anger track.** If you think angry thoughts, you will remain angry—and perhaps become even angrier. It's important to do something to get your mind *off* the causes of your anger. Here's where the *incompatible response* approach, a technique I developed some years ago (e.g., Baron, 1983, 1993), can come in handy. This technique suggests that it is difficult, if not impossible, to remain angry in the presence of stimuli that cause us to experience some incompatible emotion—for example, humorous materials that make us laugh. You can readily use this technique to control your own anger: Just expose yourself as quickly as possible to stimuli you know will induce pleasant feelings incompatible with anger. Your anger may quickly vanish.
- **Seek positive explanations for the things others say or do that make you angry.** When others make us angry, we usually attribute their actions to insensitivity, selfishness—or worse. If, instead, you try to come up with other explanations for the words or actions that have made you angry, this may greatly reduce your annoyance. Did the other person mean to say something that hurt your feelings? Perhaps she or he didn't realize the implications of what they said. If you concentrate on interpretations like this, your anger may quickly dissipate.
- **Whatever you do, don't rely on "catharsis"—on getting it out of your system.** A large body of research findings indicates that giving vent to anger does *not* usually reduce it. On the contrary, as I noted above, expressing anger tends to fan the flames, not drown them. So, whatever else you do, *don't follow your impulse to give the other person a dirty look, to shout, or to pound your fist*. Doing so will only make the situation worse. A little restraint is definitely in order.

Summary and Review of Key Questions

Intelligence: Contrasting Views of Its Nature

- **What is intelligence?** *Intelligence* refers to individuals' abilities to understand complex ideas, to adapt effectively to the environment, to learn from experience, to engage in various forms of reasoning, and to overcome obstacles by careful thought.
- **What is Gardner's theory of multiple intelligences?** This is a view suggesting that there are several different kinds of intelligences, such as verbal, mathematical, musical, and bodily–kinesthetic intelligence.
- **What is Sternberg's triarchic theory of intelligence?** Sternberg's theory suggests that there are three basic kinds of intelligence: componential, experiential, and contextual (practical).
- **What is practical intelligence? Tacit knowledge?** Practical intelligence is intelligence useful in solving everyday problems. Tacit knowledge, the kind of knowledge often used by persons high in practical intelligences, is action- and goal-oriented and is independently acquired.

KEY TERMS

intelligence, p. 425 • triarchic theory, p. 427 • practical intelligence, p. 427 • tacit knowledge, p. 429

Measuring Human Intelligence: From Tests to Underlying Psychological Processes . . . and Beyond

- **What was the first individual test of intelligence, and what did scores on it mean?** The first individual test of intelligence was devised for schoolchildren by Binet and Simon. It yielded a "mental age," and testers then derived an IQ (intelligence quotient) score by dividing mental by chronological age and multiplying by 100.
- **What are the Wechsler scales?** The Wechsler scales are individual tests of intelligence for children and adults that seek to measure several aspects of intelligence—performance components as well as verbal components of intelligence.
- **What is inspection time, and what does it measure?** Inspection time is the minimum amount of time a particular stimulus must be exposed for individuals to make a judgment about it that meets some preestablished criterion of accuracy.
- **What findings suggest that intelligence is related to neural functioning and brain structure?** Research findings indicate that scores on standard tests of intelligence are correlated with nerve conduction velocity and also with the size of certain portions of the brain.

KEY TERMS

Stanford–Binet test, p. 430 • IQ, p. 431 • mental retardation, p. 432 • Down syndrome, p. 433 • processing speed, p. 435 • inspection time, p. 437

Reliability and Validity: Basic Requirements for All Psychological Tests

- **What is reliability, and how do psychologists attempt to measure it?** Reliability is the extent to which a test yields the same results each time it is applied to the same quantity. Measures of reliability include internal consistency and test–retest reliability.
- **What is validity, and how do psychologists attempt to measure it?** Validity is the extent to which a test measures what it purports to measure. Measures of validity include content validity and criterion-related validity.
- **What is cultural bias, and how may it affect scores on standard intelligence tests?** *Cultural bias* refers to the extent to which intelligence tests place members of minority groups at a disadvantage because the tests were developed for use with members of the majority group. Such bias may adversely affect the scores of persons from various minorities.

KEY TERMS

reliability, p. 438 • split-half reliability, p. 439 • test–retest reliability, p. 439 • validity, p. 440 • content validity, p. 440 • criterion-related validity, p. 440 • cultural bias, p. 442 • Raven Progressive Matrices, p. 443

Human Intelligence: The Role of Heredity and the Role of Environment

- **What evidence suggests that intelligence is influenced by genetic factors?** Evidence for the role of genetic factors is provided by the finding that the more closely related persons are, the higher the correlation in their IQ scores; by research on adopted children; and by research on identical twins separated early in life and raised in different homes.
- **What evidence suggests that intelligence is influenced by environmental factors?** Evidence for the role of environmental factors is provided by the worldwide rise in IQ scores in recent decades (the Flynn effect), by studies of environmental deprivation and enrichment, by demonstrations of the beneficial effects of special environmental interventions, and by the fact that the longer children remain in school, the higher their IQs.
- **Can characteristics that are highly heritable be influenced by environmental factors?** Traits that are highly heritable can be strongly influenced by environmental factors. For example, height is highly heritable, yet average height has increased in many countries as a result of improved nutrition.

KEY TERM

heritability, p. 445

Group Differences in Intelligence Test Scores: Why They Occur

- **What role do socioeconomic and cultural factors play in group differences in IQ scores?** Socioeconomic factors such as poverty appear to exert adverse effects on IQ scores. Cultural factors, such as being assigned to a "castelike minority" and holding values that are different from those of the majority, can cause minority children to feel alienated from the educational process and so can reduce their IQ scores.
- **In *The Bell Curve* the authors argue that because individual differences in IQ are highly heritable, group differences in IQ must also be highly heritable. How do most psychologists view this argument?** Most psychologists reject this view, because they realize that it would be valid only if the environmental conditions experienced by various groups were identical in all respects.
- **Do any gender differences with respect to intelligence exist? If so, what is the possible origin of such differences?** Females tend to score higher than males with respect to verbal abilities, while males tend to score higher in visual–spatial abilities (e.g., mental rotation of objects). Recent findings suggest that gender differences with respect to visual–spatial abilities may reflect the evolutionary history of our species: Men were generally hunters while women were generally gatherers, tasks requiring somewhat different spatial abilities.

KEY TERM

genetic hypothesis, p. 450

Emotional Intelligence: The Feeling Side of Intelligence

- **What is emotional intelligence?** Emotional intelligence is a cluster of traits or abilities relating to the emotional side of life—abilities such as recognizing and managing one's own emotions, motivating oneself and restraining impulses, recognizing and managing others' emotions, and handling interpersonal relationships in an effective manner.

- **What role does emotional intelligence play in success and personal happiness?** Growing evidence suggests that emotional intelligence plays an important role in these and other life outcomes.
- **What role does emotional intelligence play in long-term intimate relationships?** The abilities to understand one's own emotions and those of one's partner, as well as to communicate such feelings effectively, appear to be crucial ingredients for successful intimate relationships.

KEY TERM

emotional intelligence, p. 453

Creativity: Generating the Extraordinary

- **What is creativity?** Creativity involves the ability to produce work that is both novel (original, unexpected) and appropriate (it works—it is useful or meets task constraints).
- **What are confluence theories, and what factors do they view as essential to creativity?** Confluence theories suggest that for creativity to occur, multiple factors must converge. Among the factors such theories view as crucial for creativity are certain intellectual abilities (e.g., the ability to see problems in new ways), knowledge of a given field, certain styles of thinking (e.g., a preference for thinking in novel ways), certain personality traits (e.g., a willingness to take risks), intrinsic motivation, and an environment supportive of creative ideas.
- **What evidence offers support for the confluence approach?** Recent findings indicate that all of the factors mentioned by confluence theories are significant predictors of creativity across many different domains (e.g., writing, art, science).

KEY TERMS

creativity, p. 457 • confluence approach, p. 458

Critical Thinking Questions

Appraisal

Psychologists have long assumed that intelligence is a crucial dimension along which people differ. Do you think this assumption is justified? Or do you think that other characteristics are even more important?

Controversy

Growing evidence indicates that practical intelligence and emotional intelligence may be just as important in determining success and happiness as academic intelligence. Yet school systems throughout the world tend to focus on fostering academic intelligence. Do you think this should be changed? Should schools devote more attention to helping children develop practical and emotional intelligence?

Making Psychology Part of Your Life

Now that you understand some of the basic requirements of all psychological tests, do you think you will be more skeptical of the kinds of questionnaires many magazines publish, which claim to measure various traits? (I hope so.) Why should you view these "tests" with caution? Under what conditions could you view them as useful or informative?

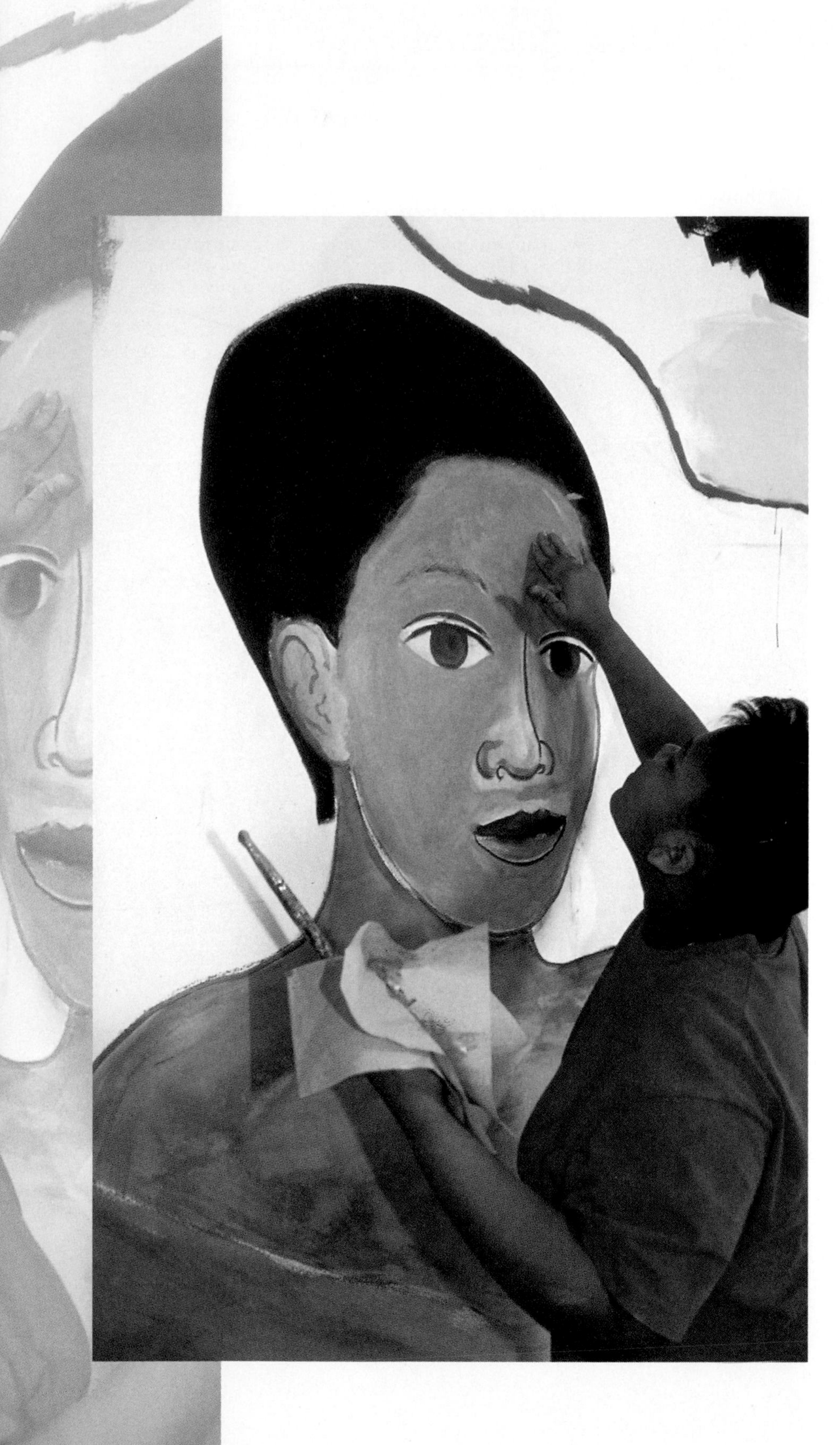

CHAPTER OUTLINE

12

Personality

Uniqueness and Consistency in the Behavior of Individuals

When I was in the fifth grade, our teacher decided that we should all have "Pen Pals"—children our own age in another state with whom we would correspond. Each of us drew the name of our Pen Pal from a large bag; then we were supposed to write letters to them, which our teacher would read and mail. "What should we write?" I remember several members of the class asking. "Tell your new friend all about yourself," our teacher answered. "Tell them what kind of person you are—what makes you unique."

I'm not sure she realized it, but our teacher was giving us a very challenging task: describing the essence of our uniqueness as individuals in a few short sentences. How would you handle this task today? Could you list the traits and characteristics that make you unique? If so, you would be describing your **personality**—what psychologists generally define as an individual's unique and relatively stable patterns of behavior, thoughts, and emotions (e.g., Carver & Scheier, 1992; Nelson & Miller, 1995; Zuckerman, 1995).

Interest in personality is as old as civilization: Ancient philosophers and poets often speculated about why individuals were unique, and why they differed from one another in so many ways. It was not until the emergence of a scientific field of psychology, however, that personality became the focus of systematic research and revealing answers to these ancient questions began to emerge. What have psychologists learned about personality from their research? And how can you use this information to gain insight into your own personality and the personalities of others? These are the central themes of the present chapter. To acquaint you with psychology's findings about personality, our discussion will proceed as follows. First, I'll consider what is perhaps the most basic question we can ask about personality: Is it real? In other words, do people really show consistency in their behavior over time and across situations, or is our belief that they do merely a kind of cognitive or perceptual error? Since this chapter exists, you can probably guess the answer: Yes, personality *is* real. But please read on, because the overall picture is far from simple, and considering this basic question provides a useful introduction to the study of personality.

Interest in personality is as old as civilization: Ancient philosophers and poets often speculated about why individuals were unique, and why they differed from one another in so many ways.

After addressing the question of the reality of personality, I'll describe several major *theories of personality*—grand and sweeping conceptual frameworks offered by some of the true giants in the history of psychology. A word of caution: While these theories make for fascinating reading, few of them are currently accepted as accurate by psychologists. As a group, though, they do call our attention to important issues worthy of careful attention. For each theory, I'll first describe it, then present some research evidence relating to it, and finally offer an evaluation of its current status. After examining these theories of personality, we'll turn to another basic question: how personality is measured. Finally, I'll provide you with the flavor of modern research on personality by examining recent findings concerning several specific traits—ones viewed by psychologists as having important effects on behavior (e.g., Kilduff & Day, 1994; Zuckerman, 1995). (Because the research methods used to study each of the theories covered are discussed along with each theory, I have not included a separate Research Methods section in this chapter.)

Personality: Is It Real?

In our everyday life, we behave as though personality is a fact: We expect others—and ourselves—to demonstrate consistency in behavior across different situations and over long periods of time. In other words, once we conclude that a specific person (ourself included) possesses certain traits—that, for instance, she or he is *friendly, neat, impulsive,* and *good-natured*—we expect that person generally to behave in ways consistent with these traits. This raises an intriguing question: Does such consistency really exist? Some psychologists have argued that it does not—that behavior is largely determined by external factors rather than by stable traits (Mischel, 1985). According to

Personality: An individual's unique and relatively stable patterns of behavior, thoughts, and feelings.

these critics, the very concept *personality* is misleading, because the kind of stability it implies does not really exist. On the contrary, individuals behave very differently in different situations; our perception that people possess specific traits and behave in accordance with those traits much of the time is largely an illusion, stemming from our desire to simplify the task of understanding others (Kunda & Nisbett, 1986; Reeder, Fletcher, & Furman, 1989).

While these arguments are intriguing ones, the weight of existing evidence seems to be against them: Personality, defined in terms of stable behavior tendencies, is indeed real. Many studies indicate that people *do* show at least a moderate degree of consistency with respect to many aspects of behavior (e.g., Pulkinen, 1996; Woodall & Matthews, 1993). Some of these research projects have continued for more than fifty years, studying the same people from early childhood to old age; and in general they have reported an impressive amount of consistency in at least some traits (e.g., Heatherton & Weinberger, 1994). In other words, the traits individuals show today are also likely to present tomorrow—even if "tomorrow" occurs years or even decades in the future (see Figure 12.1). Moreover, a growing body of evidence suggests that some aspects of personality are influenced by genetic factors, as well as life experiences and the environment (e.g., Vernon et al., 1997). Indeed, recent findings suggest that genetic factors may account for as much as fifty percent of individual variability in the tendency to behave aggressively (Miles & Carey, 1997).

FIGURE 12.1

Personality: Consistency in Behavior over Time

As suggested by this cartoon, personality does seem to be real: Traits individuals show at one time in life are likely to persist unless something intervenes to change them.

(**Source:** Drawing by Chas. Addams; ©1984 The New Yorker Magazine, Inc.)

Having said that, I should quickly note that such consistency over long periods of time does *not* exist for all traits or in all persons (Tice, 1989). In fact, the extent to which people show such consistency across time and situations may itself be an important aspect of personality (Koestner, Bernieri, & Zuckerman, 1992): Some people are more consistent than others! Also, the existence of stable traits in no way implies that situational factors are not important. On the contrary, most psychologists agree that *both* traits and situations shape behavior. Individuals do have traits that predispose them to behave in certain ways—for instance, to be friendly, neat, and good-natured. Whether these tendencies actually appear in overt behavior, however, depends on many situational factors. If situations permit, then traits and dispositions may well be expressed in overt behavior. If situations make it very costly or difficult for these characteristics to appear, they may not.

For instance, consider a man who strongly prefers to be neat. This trait may show up in how he dresses, in his personal grooming, in the way he arranges his room, in how often he washes his car, and many other ways. But suppose a river floods near where the man lives; after the disaster is over, there is mud and grime everywhere. Faced with these conditions, this person *can't* be neat—or, at least, as neat as he would prefer. In fact, he may give up trying to keep his shoes, his clothes, or even the floors of his home clean, because it is impossible to do so. This is a case in which personal traits are overridden by the external world. In sum, and to conclude this initial discussion: Personality is indeed real and does influence behavior, providing that external factors permit such influence to occur.

Key Questions

- What is personality, and does it really exist?
- What role do personality traits and situational factors play in influencing human behavior?

The Psychoanalytic Approach: Messages from the Unconscious

Quick: Before you took this course, who would you have named as the most famous psychologist in history? If you are like most students I have known, your answer would probably be *Freud.* Sigmund Freud is by far the most famous figure in the history of psychology. Why is this so? The answer lies in several provocative and influential theories he proposed—theories that focus on personality and the origins of psychological disorders. Before turning to his theories, however, it seems appropriate to spend a moment or two on Freud the individual—on *his* personality, if you will.

Freud the Person

Freud was born in what is now part of the Czech Republic, but when he was four years old, his family moved to Vienna, and he spent almost his entire life in that city. As a young man, Freud was highly ambitious and decided to make a name for himself as a medical researcher. He became discouraged with his prospects in this respect, however, and soon after receiving his medical degree, he entered private practice. It was during this period that he formulated his theories of human personality and psychological disorders.

Freud's mother was his father's second wife, and she was much younger than her husband. In fact, she was only twenty-one when Freud was born. Although she had several other children, Sigmund was the first and always remained her favorite. Among the Freud children, only Sigmund had his own room; and when his sister's piano practice disturbed his study, her lessons were stopped and the piano sold. Freud's relationship with his father, in contrast, was cold and distant. Indeed, he even arrived late at his father's funeral and missed most of the service. At the age of twenty-six, Freud married Martha Bernays. The marriage was a happy one and produced six children. Freud had a powerful personality and, as he developed his theories, attracted numerous followers. In many cases these supporters began as ardent disciples but then came to question some aspects of Freud's work. Freud was intolerant of such criticism and often had angry breaks with once cherished students. One disciple, however, never broke with him: his daughter Anna, who became a famous psychologist in her own right.

Freud loved antiques and collected statues and figurines from ancient civilizations throughout his life. His collection filled the walls and shelves of his office—even the top of his desk (see Figure 12.2). Each morning the first thing he did was to reach over and affectionately pat one or more of his stone sculptures. Freud recognized a connection between his hobby and his work; he told many of his patients that his search for hidden memories in their unconscious minds was similar to the excavation of a buried ancient city. Freud

FIGURE 12.2

Freud the Collector

Sigmund Freud is clearly a major figure in the history of psychology. As shown here, he was an enthusiastic collector of antiques, covering the shelves of his office with items he had acquired.

smoked heavily (he is often shown with a large cigar in his hand), and he contracted cancer of the mouth. This caused him great pain, and starting in 1923 he underwent numerous operations for his disease. Ultimately these interfered with his speech and ended his career as a public speaker. Freud's native language was German, but he spoke and wrote English quite fluently.

Like many people of Jewish descent, Freud found it necessary to flee the Nazis, and in 1938 he left Vienna for England. He died there of throat cancer the next year. Many biographies of Freud have been written, and several draw connections between his theories and his personal life experiences—for example, his close relationship with his mother and his distant relationship with his father. Whether such links actually exist remains open to debate. What *is* certain, however, is that this complex, brilliant, and dominating man exerted a powerful impact upon many of our ideas about personality and psychological disorders.

Freud's Theory of Personality

Freud entered private medical practice soon after graduating from medical school. A turning point in his early career came when he won a research grant to travel to Paris to observe the work of Jean-Martin Charcot, who was then using hypnosis to treat several types of mental disorders. When Freud returned to Vienna, he worked with Joseph Breuer, a colleague who was using hypnosis in the treatment of *hysteria*—a condition in which individuals experienced physical symptoms, such as blindness, deafness, or paralysis of arms or legs, for which there seemed to be no underlying physical cause. Out of these experiences, and out of his growing clinical practice, Freud gradually developed his theories of human personality and mental illness. His ideas were complex, and touched on many different issues. With respect to personality, however, four topics are most central: levels of consciousness, the structure of personality, anxiety and defense mechanisms, and psychosexual stages of development.

Levels of Consciousness: Beneath the Iceberg's Tip Freud viewed himself as a scientist, and he was well aware of research on sensory thresholds (see Chapter 3). In fact, he believed that his psychological theories were just a temporary measure and would ultimately be replaced by knowledge of underlying biological and neural processes (Zuckerman, 1995). In any case, Freud applied to the task of understanding the human mind some of the then emerging ideas about sensory thresholds and the possibility of responding to stimuli we can't report perceiving. He soon reached the startling conclusion that most of the mind lies below the surface—below the threshold of conscious experience. Above this threshold is the realm of the *conscious*. This includes our current thoughts: whatever we are thinking about or experiencing at a given moment. Beneath this conscious realm is the much larger *preconscious*. This contains memories that are not part of current thoughts but can readily be brought to mind if the need arises. Finally, beneath the preconscious, and forming the bulk of the human mind, is the *unconscious:* thoughts, desires, and impulses of which we remain largely unaware. Although some of this material has always been unconscious, Freud believed that much of it was once conscious but has been actively *repressed*—driven from consciousness because it was too anxiety-provoking. For example, Freud contended that shameful experiences or unacceptable sexual or aggressive urges are often driven deep within the unconscious. The fact that we are not aware of these thoughts and feelings, however, in no way prevents them from affecting our behavior. Indeed, Freud believed that many of the symptoms experienced by his patients were disguised and indirect reflections of repressed thoughts and desires. This is why one major goal of **psychoanalysis**—the method of treating psychological disorders devised by Freud—is to bring repressed material back into consciousness. Presumably, once such material is made conscious, it can be dealt with more effectively, and important causes of mental illness may be removed.

As we noted in Chapter 4, Freud believed that one way of probing the unconscious was through the *interpretation of dreams.* In dreams, Freud believed, we give expression to impulses and desires we find unacceptable during our waking hours. Unfortunately, as we saw in that earlier discussion, there is little scientific evidence for this view.

The Structure of Personality: Id, Ego, and Superego

Do you know the story of Dr. Jekyll and Mr. Hyde? If so, you already have a basic idea of some of the key structures of personality described by Freud. He suggested that personality consists largely of three parts: the *id,* the *ego,* and the *superego* (see Figure 12.3). As we'll soon see, these correspond roughly to *desire, reason,* and *conscience.*

The **id** consists of all our primitive, innate urges. These include various bodily needs, sexual desire, and aggressive impulses. According to Freud, the id is totally unconscious and operates in accordance with what he termed the **pleasure principle:** It wants immediate, total gratification and is not capable of considering the potential costs of seeking this goal. In short, the id is the Mr. Hyde of our personality—although, in contrast to this character, it is more appropriately described as *unrestrained* rather than as purely evil.

Unfortunately, the world offers few opportunities for instant pleasure. Moreover, attempting to gratify many of our innate urges would soon get us into serious trouble. It is in response to these facts that the second structure of personality, the **ego,** develops. The ego's task is to hold the id in check until conditions allow for satisfaction of its impulses. Thus, the ego operates in accordance with the **reality principle:** It takes into account external conditions and the consequences of various actions and directs behavior so as to maximize pleasure *and* minimize pain. The ego is partly conscious but not entirely so; thus, some of its actions—for example, its eternal struggle with the id—are outside our conscious knowledge or understanding.

The final aspect of personality described by Freud is the **superego.** It too seeks to control satisfaction of id impulses; but, in contrast to the ego, it is concerned with *morality*—with whether various actions that could potentially satisfy id impulses are right or wrong. The superego permits us to gratify such impulses only when it is morally correct to do so—not simply when it is safe or feasible, as required by the ego. So, for example, it would be the superego, not the ego, that would prevent a stockbroker from altering a computer program and thereby transferring funds from his clients' accounts into his own account, even though he knew he could get away with this action.

The superego is acquired from our parents and through experience, and it represents our internalization of the moral teachings and norms of our society. Unfortunately, such teachings are often quite inflexible and leave little room for gratification of our basic desires—they require us to be good all the time, like Dr. Jekyll. Because of this fact, the ego faces another difficult task: It must strike a balance between our primitive urges (the id) and our learned moral constraints (the superego). According to Freud, this constant struggle among id, ego, and superego plays a key role in personality and in many psychological disorders.

Psychoanalysis: A method of therapy based on Freud's theory of personality, in which the therapist attempts to bring repressed unconscious material into consciousness.

Id: In Freud's theory, the portion of personality concerned with immediate gratification of primitive needs.

Pleasure Principle: The principle on which the id operates, according to which immediate pleasure is the sole motivation for behavior.

Ego: In Freud's theory, the part of personality that takes account of external reality in the expression of instinctive sexual and aggressive urges.

Reality Principle: The principle according to which the ego operates, in which the external consequences of behavior are considered in the regulation of expression of impulses from the id.

Superego: According to Freud, the portion of human personality representing the conscience.

Anxiety and Defense Mechanisms: Self-Protection by the Ego

In its constant struggle to prevent the eruption of dangerous id impulses, the ego faces a difficult task. Yet for most people, most of the time,

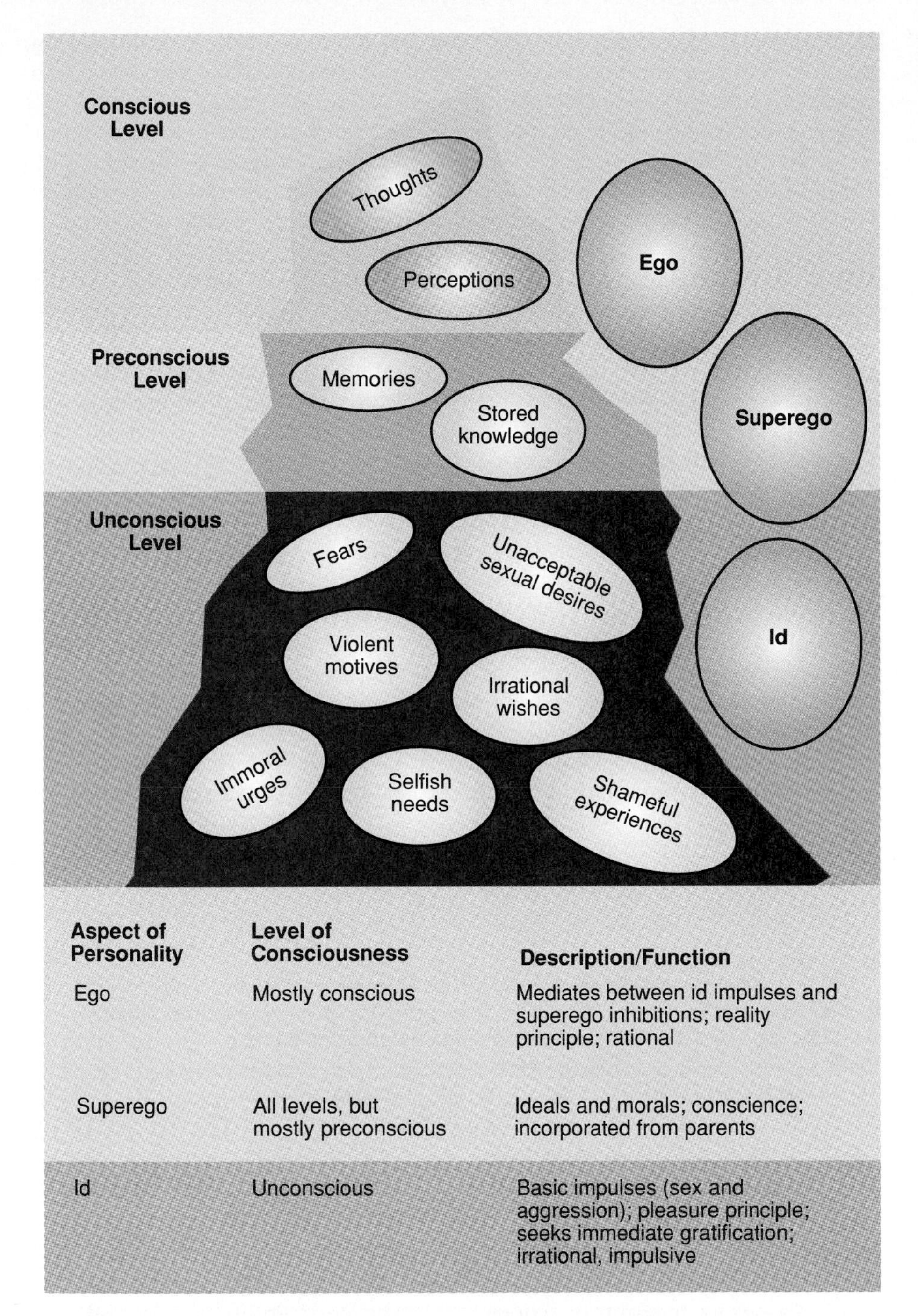

Aspect of Personality	Level of Consciousness	Description/Function
Ego	Mostly conscious	Mediates between id impulses and superego inhibitions; reality principle; rational
Superego	All levels, but mostly preconscious	Ideals and morals; conscience; incorporated from parents
Id	Unconscious	Basic impulses (sex and aggression); pleasure principle; seeks immediate gratification; irrational, impulsive

FIGURE 12.3

Freud's Views about Levels of Consciousness and the Structure of Personality

Freud believed that the human mind has three distinct levels: the conscious, preconscious, and unconscious. He also believed that personality involves three important structures: id, ego, and superego, which correspond very roughly to desire, reason, and conscience.

the ego succeeds. Sometimes, though, id impulses grow so strong that they threaten to get out of control. For example, consider the case of a middle-aged widow who finds herself strongly attracted to her daughter's boyfriend. She hasn't had a romantic attachment in years, so her sexual desire quickly rises to high levels. What happens next? According to Freud, when her ego senses that unacceptable impulses are about to get out of hand, it experiences **anxiety**—intense feelings of nervousness, tension, or worry. These feelings occur because the unacceptable impulses are getting closer and closer to consciousness, as well as closer and closer to the limits of the ego's ability to hold them in check.

At this point, Freud contended, the ego may resort to one of several different **defense mechanisms.** These are all designed to keep unacceptable impulses from the id out of consciousness and to prevent their open expression.

Anxiety: In Freudian theory, unpleasant feelings of tension or worry experienced by individuals in reaction to unacceptable wishes or impulses.

Defense Mechanisms: Techniques used by the ego to keep threatening and unacceptable material out of consciousness and so to reduce anxiety.

Sublimation: A defense mechanism in which threatening unconscious impulses are channeled into socially acceptable forms of behavior.

Psychosexual Stages of Development: According to Freud, an innate sequence of stages through which all human beings pass. At each stage, pleasure is focused on a different region of the body.

Libido: According to Freud, the psychic energy that powers all mental activity.

Fixation: Excessive investment of psychic energy in a particular stage of psychosexual development; this results in various types of psychological disorders.

Defense mechanisms take many different forms. For example, in **sublimation,** the unacceptable impulse is channeled into some socially acceptable action. Instead of trying to seduce the young man, as Freud would say the widow's id wants to do, she might "adopt" him as a son and provide financial support to further his education. Other defense mechanisms are described in Table 12.1. While they differ in form, all serve the function of reducing anxiety by keeping unacceptable urges and impulses from breaking into consciousness.

Psychosexual Stages of Development Now we come to what is perhaps the most controversial aspect of Freud's theory of personality: his ideas about its formation or development. Freud's views on this topic can be grouped under the heading **psychosexual stages of development:** innately determined stages of sexual development through which, presumably, we all pass, and which strongly shape the nature of our personality. Before turning to the stages themselves, however, we must first consider two important concepts relating to them: *libido* and *fixation.*

Libido refers to the instinctual life force that energizes the id. Release of libido is closely related to pleasure, but the focus of such pleasure—and the expression of libido—changes as we develop. In each stage of development, we obtain different kinds of pleasure and leave behind a small amount of our libido; this is the normal course of events. If an excessive amount of libido energy is tied to a particular stage, however, **fixation** results. Fixation can stem from either too little or too much gratification during a stage, and in either case the result is harmful. Since the individual has left too much "psychic energy" behind, less is available for full adult development. The outcome may be an adult personality reflecting the stage or stages at which fixation

TABLE 12.1

Defense Mechanisms: Reactions to Anxiety

Freud believed that when the ego feels that it may be unable to control impulses from the id, it experiences anxiety. To reduce such feelings, the ego uses various *defense mechanisms* such as the ones described here.

Defense Mechanism	Its Basic Nature	Example
Repression	"Forgetting"—or pushing from consciousness into unconsciousness—unacceptable thoughts or impulses	A woman fails to recognize her attraction to her handsome new son-in-law.
Rationalization	Conjuring up socially acceptable reasons for thoughts or actions based on unacceptable motives	A young woman explains that she ate an entire chocolate cake so that it wouldn't spoil in the summer heat.
Displacement	Redirecting an emotional response from a dangerous object to a safe one	A man redirects anger from his boss to his child.
Projection	Transferring unacceptable motives or impulses to others	A man who feels strong hostility toward a neighbor perceives the neighbor as being hostile to him.
Regression	Responding to a threatening situation in a way appropriate to an earlier age or level of development	A student asks a professor to raise his grade; when she refuses, the student throws a temper tantrum.

has occurred. To put it another way, if too much energy is drained away by fixation at earlier stages of development, the amount remaining may be insufficient to power movement to full adult development. Then an individual may show an immature personality and several psychological disorders.

Now back to the actual stages themselves. According to Freud, as we grow and develop, different parts of the body serve as the focus of our quest for pleasure. In the initial **oral stage,** lasting until we are about eighteen months old, we seek pleasure mainly through the mouth. If too much or too little gratification occurs during this stage, an individual may become *fixated* at it. Too little gratification results in a personality that is overly dependent on others; too much, especially after the child has developed some teeth, results in a personality that is excessively hostile, especially through verbal sarcasm and "biting" forms of humor (see Figure 12.4).

FIGURE 12.4

Fixation at the Oral Stage

According to Freud, individuals who receive too much gratification during the oral stage—especially after they have developed teeth!—may develop into hostile adults who frequently use biting humor and sarcasm such as that used by comic Roseanne Barr.

The next stage occurs in response to efforts by parents to toilet train their children. During the **anal stage,** the process of elimination becomes the primary focus of pleasure. Fixation at this stage stemming from overly harsh toilet-training experiences may result in individuals who are excessively orderly or *compulsive*—they can't leave any job unfinished and strive for perfection in everything they do. In contrast, fixation stemming from very relaxed toilet training may result in people who are undisciplined, impulsive, and excessively generous. Freud himself might well be described as compulsive; even when he was seriously ill, he personally answered dozens of letters every day—even letters from total strangers asking his advice (Benjamin & Dixon, 1996).

At about age four the genitals become the primary source of pleasure, and children enter the **phallic stage.** Freud speculated that at this time we fantasize about sex with our opposite-sex parent—a phenomenon he termed the **Oedipus complex** (after Oedipus, a character in ancient Greek literature who unknowingly killed his father and then married his mother). Fear of punishment for such desires then enters the picture. Among boys, the feared punishment is castration, leading to *castration anxiety.* Among girls, the feared punishment is loss of love; in both cases, these fears being about resolution of the Oedipus complex and identification with the same-sex parent. In other words, little boys give up sexual desires for their mothers and come to see their fathers as models rather than as rivals, while little girls give up their sexual desires for their father and come to see their mothers as models.

Perhaps one of Freud's most controversial suggestions is the idea that little girls experience *penis envy* stemming from their own lack of a male organ. Freud suggested that because of such envy, girls experience strong feelings of inferiority and envy—feelings they carry with them in disguised form even in adult life. As you can readily guess, these ideas are strongly rejected by virtually all psychologists.

After resolution of the Oedipus conflict, according to Freud, children enter the **latency stage,** during which sexual urges are at a minimum. Finally, during puberty adolescents enter the **genital stage.** During this stage pleasure is again focused on the genitals. Now, however, lust is blended with affection, and people become capable of adult love. Remember: According to Freud, progression to this final stage is possible only if serious fixation has *not* occurred at earlier stages. If such fixation exists, development is blocked and various disorders result. The major stages in Freud's theory are summarized in Figure 12.5 on page 474.

Oral Stage: In Freud's theory, a psychosexual stage of development during which pleasure is centered in the region of the mouth.

Anal Stage: In Freud's theory, a psychosexual stage of development in which pleasure is focused primarily on the anal zone.

Phallic Stage: In Freud's theory, a psychosexual stage of development during which pleasure is centered in the genital region. It is during this stage that the Oedipus complex develops.

Oedipus Complex: In Freud's theory, a crisis of psychosexual development in which children must give up their sexual attraction for their opposite-sex parent.

Latency Stage: In Freud's theory, the psychosexual stage of development that follows resolution of the Oedipus complex. During this stage sexual desires are relatively weak.

Genital Stage: In Freud's theory, the final psychosexual stage of development—one in which individuals acquire the adult capacity to combine lust with affection.

FIGURE 12.5

The Psychosexual Stages of Development Described by Freud

According to Freud, all human beings pass through a series of discrete *psychosexual stages of development.* At each stage pleasure is focused on a particular part of the body. Too much or too little gratification at any stage can result in *fixation* and can lead to psychological disorders.

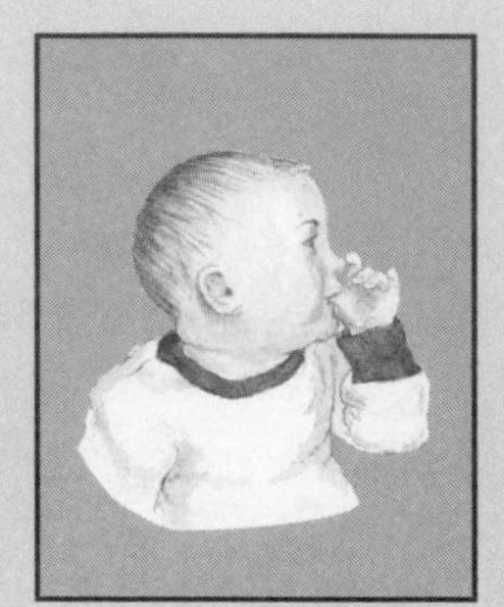

Oral 0–2
Infant achieves gratification through oral activities such as feeding, thumb sucking, and babbling.

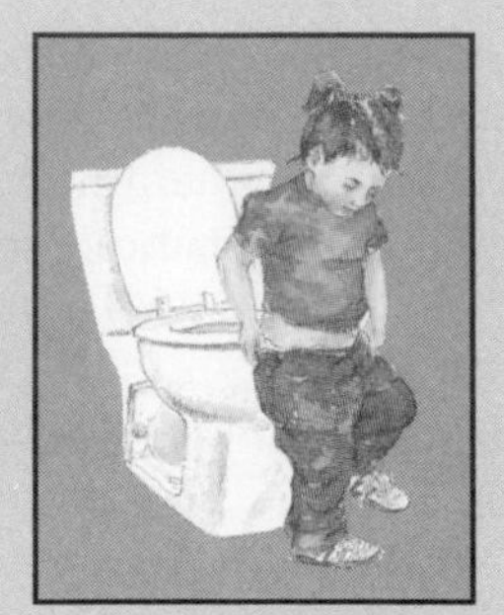

Anal 2–3
The child learns to respond to some of the demands of society (such as bowel and bladder control).

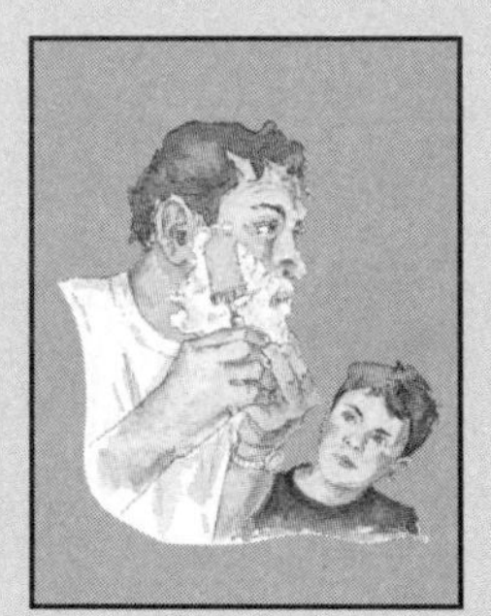

Phallic 3–7
The child learns to realize the differences between males and females and becomes aware of sexuality.

Latency 7–11
The child continues his or her development but sexual urges are relatively quiet.

Genital 11–adult
The growing adolescent shakes off old dependencies and learns to deal maturely with the opposite sex.

Research Related to Freud's Theory: Probing the Unconscious

Freud's theories contain many intriguing ideas; and as you probably know, several of these have entered into pop culture—people everywhere talk about the unconscious, repressed impulses, and the struggle among id, ego, and superego. It's not surprising, therefore, that psychologists have investigated several of these ideas—at least the ones that *can* be studied through scientific means. We have already discussed the scientific status of Freud's ideas about dreams in Chapter 4; as you may recall, at present there is virtually no scientific evidence to support his belief that dreams carry messages from the unconscious.

Another of Freud's ideas about the unconscious, however, has fared somewhat better: His contention that our feelings and behavior can be strongly affected by information we can't bring to mind and can't describe verbally—information buried in the unconscious. Research in many fields of psychology suggests that to some extent this is true (e.g., Bornstein, 1992). For instance, consider research on what is known as the *subliminal conditioning of attitudes.* The term *subliminal* means "below threshold," and in such research the following question has been studied: Can stimuli we can't perceive (because they are presented so briefly) still influence our reactions to various objects, including, perhaps, other people?

To test this possibility, Krosnick and his colleagues have conducted several studies using the following procedures (e.g., Krosnick et al., 1992). Participants in these studies were shown photos of a female stranger engaged in routine daily activities—walking into her apartment, shopping in a grocery, sitting in a restaurant. Each photo was shown for two seconds. Immediately before each photo was presented, participants were also exposed to other photos previously demonstrated to produce either positive or negative feelings. For instance, photos that generated negative feelings included a bloody shark and open-heart surgery; ones that produced positive feelings included happy people playing cards and a smiling bridal couple. These affect-inducing photos were flashed on the screen for very brief periods of time—less than a tenth of a second. In fact, they were shown so briefly that participants could not even tell whether they were words or photos, let alone what scenes they showed. In other words, they were presented *subliminally.* After viewing these stimuli, participants were asked to indicate their attitudes toward the woman shown in the photos and to rate her on a variety of trait dimensions (unfriendly–friendly, cruel–kind, considerate–thoughtless).

Krosnick and his colleagues reasoned that if participants' attitudes toward the stranger were influenced by exposure to emotion-provoking photos they couldn't report seeing, this would provide evidence for the view that our reactions to others can sometimes be affected by feelings or images of which we are not aware. As you can see from Figure 12.6, results supported this hypothesis: Participants who saw photos that induced positive feelings rated the stranger more favorably than those who saw photos that induced negative feelings. While these findings certainly don't address Freud's ideas about repressed impulses, they do, when combined with other findings (e.g., Bornstein, 1992), support the view that our behavior is sometimes influenced by thoughts, ideas, or feelings we can't bring to mind—by information present in the unconscious, as Freud would put it.

Key Questions

- According to Freud, what are the three levels of consciousness?
- In Freud's theory, what are the three basic parts of personality?
- According to Freud, what are the psychosexual stages of development?
- Do research findings support Freud's views about the unconscious?

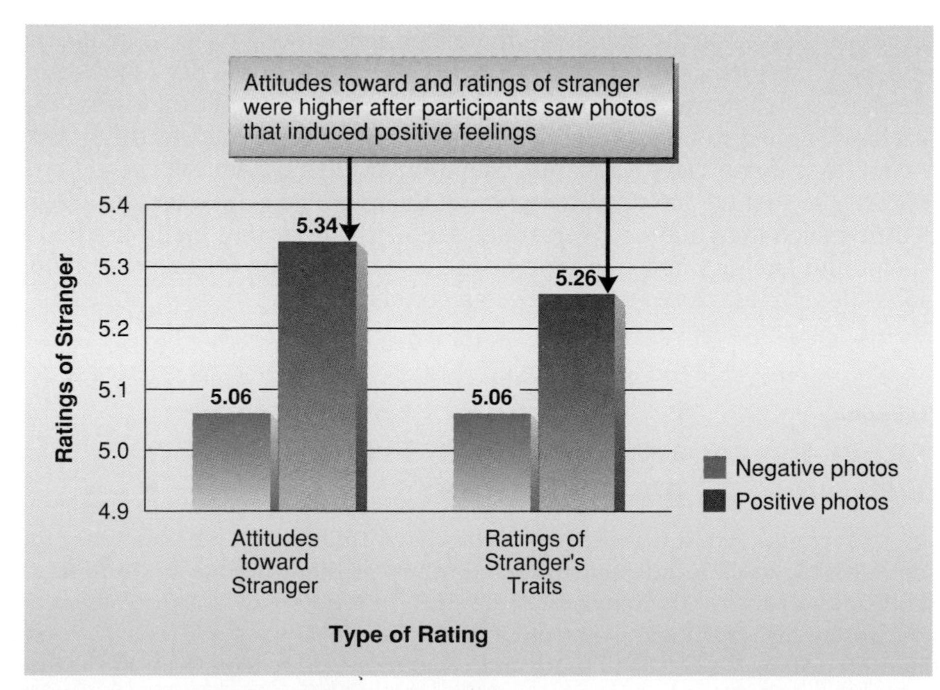

(**Source:** Based on data from Krosnick et al., 1992.)

FIGURE 12.6

The Unconscious Mind at Work: Subliminal Conditioning of Attitudes

Participants who saw photos that induced positive feelings rated a stranger more favorably than those who saw photos that induced negative feelings. This was true even though these photos were shown so briefly that participants could not describe their contents. In a sense, ratings of the stranger were influenced by information that Freud would describe as being present in the unconscious mind.

Freud's Theory: An Overall Evaluation

As noted earlier, Freud's place in history is assured; his ideas and writing have exerted a profound impact on society. But what about his theory of personality? Is it currently accepted by most psychologists? As you can probably guess from my earlier comments, the answer is *definitely not,* and the reasons are clear. First, many critics have noted that Freud's theory is not really a scientific theory at all. True, as we just saw, some of his ideas, or hypotheses derived from them, can be tested. But many concepts in his theory cannot be measured or studied systematically. How, for instance, can one go about observing an *id,* a *fixation,* or the psychic energy contained in the *libido?* As I noted in Chapter 1, a theory that cannot be tested is largely useless, and this criticism applies to many of Freud's ideas.

Second, as we have already seen, several of Freud's proposals are not consistent with the findings of modern research; for instance, his ideas about the meaning of dreams. Third, in constructing his theory, Freud relied heavily on a small number of case studies—no more than a dozen at most. Almost all of these persons came from wealthy backgrounds and lived in a large and sophisticated city within a single culture. Thus, they were not representative of human beings generally. Moreover, Freud indicated that he accepted for study and treatment only persons he viewed as particularly good candidates for successful therapy; and he himself recorded and later analyzed all of the information about these cases. Clearly, these are *not* the kind of procedures required for construction of a valid scientific theory.

Finally, and perhaps most important of all, Freud's theories contain so many different concepts that they can explain virtually any pattern of behavior in an after-the-fact manner. If a theory can't be shown to be false, then it is largely useless; and this does seem to be the case with Freud's views.

For these and other reasons, Freud's theory of personality is not currently accepted by most psychologists. Yet several of his insights—especially his ideas about levels of consciousness and about the importance of anxiety in various psychological disorders—*have* contributed to our understanding of human behavior in general, and of personality in particular. Also, recall that Freud viewed his theories as stopgap measures—frameworks that would become unnecessary as advances in neuroscience took place. So, while his theories don't measure up to the rigorous standards of science required by modern psychology, he himself might have answered that they were not really designed to do so. In reply to criticism of his theories, he might ask, "And do you now have a full understanding of the biochemical bases of personality so that we can do away with my theories?" (e.g., Zuckerman, 1995). Putting such imaginary conversations aside, it is clear that Freud has had a major and lasting impact on psychology and on society; for this reason, his ideas deserve the close attention I've given them here.

Other Psychoanalytic Views: Freud's Disciples . . . and Defectors

Neo-Freudians: Personality theorists who accepted basic portions of Freud's theory but rejected or modified other portions.

Whatever else Freud was, he was certainly an intellectual magnet. Over the course of several decades, he attracted many brilliant people as students or colleagues. Most of them began by accepting Freud's views. Later, however, they often disagreed with some of his major assumptions. Let's see why these **neo-Freudians** broke with Freud, and what they had to say about the nature of personality.

FIGURE 12.7

The Young Hero: An Archetype

According to Jung, all human beings possess a *collective unconscious.* Information stored there is often expressed in terms of *archetypes*—representations of key aspects of human experience such as *the hero* (shown here), *mother, father,* and so on.

Jung: The Collective Unconscious Perhaps the most bitter of all the defections Freud experienced was that of Carl Jung—the follower Freud viewed as his heir apparent. Jung shared Freud's views concerning the importance of the unconscious, but contended that there is another part to this aspect of personality that Freud overlooked: the **collective unconscious.** According to Jung, the collective unconscious holds experiences shared by all human beings—experiences that are, in a sense, part of our biological heritage. The contents of the collective unconscious, in short, reflect the experiences our species has had since it originated on earth. The collective unconscious finds expression in our minds in several ways, but among these, **archetypes** are the most central to Jung's theory. These are manifestations of the collective unconscious that express themselves when our conscious mind is distracted or inactive; for example, during sleep or in dreams or fantasies (e.g., Neher, 1996). The specific expression of archetypes depends in part on our unique experiences as individuals, but in all cases such images are representations of key aspects of the human experience—*mother, father, wise old man, the sun, the moon, God, death,* and *the hero* (see Figure 12.7). It is because of these shared innate images, Jung contended, that the folklores of many different cultures contain similar figures and themes.

Two especially important archetypes in Jung's theory are known as **animus** and **anima.** The animus is the masculine side of females, while the anima is the feminine side of males. Jung believed that in looking for a mate, we search for the person onto whom we can best project these hidden sides of our personality. When there is a good match between such projections and another person, attraction occurs.

Another aspect of Jung's theory was his suggestion that we are all born with innate tendencies to be concerned primarily either with ourselves or with the outside world. Jung labeled persons in the first category **introverts** and described them as being hesitant and cautious; introverts do not make friends easily and prefer to observe the world rather than become involved in it. Jung labeled persons in the second category **extroverts.** Such persons are open and confident, make friends readily, and enjoy high levels of stimulation and a wide range of activities. While many aspects of Jung's theory have been rejected by psychologists—especially the idea of the collective unconscious—the dimension of introversion–extroversion appears to be one of major importance; it is included in several *trait theories* we'll consider in a later section (although in these modern theories the term is spelled extr*a*version).

Collective Unconscious: In Jung's theory, a portion of the unconscious shared by all human beings.

Archetypes: According to Jung, inherited manifestations of the collective unconscious that shape our perceptions of the external world.

Anima: According to Jung, the archetype representing the feminine side of males.

Animus: According to Jung, the archetype representing the masculine side of females.

Introverts: In Jung's theory, individuals who are hesitant and cautious and do not make friends easily.

Extroverts: In Jung's theory, individuals who are open and confident and make friends readily.

Karen Horney and Alfred Adler Two other important neo-Freudians were Karen Horney and Alfred Adler. Horney was one of the few females in the early psychoanalytic movement, and she disagreed strongly with Freud over his view that differences between men and women stemmed largely from innate factors—for example, from anatomical differences resulting in penis envy among females. Horney contended that each sex has attributes admired by the other, and that neither should be viewed as superior *or* inferior. In addition, she maintained that psychological disorders did not stem from fixation of psychic energy, as Freud thought, but rather from disturbed interpersonal relationships during childhood. In a sense, therefore, she emphasized the importance of social factors in shaping personality—a view echoed by modern psychology.

Alfred Adler also disagreed very strongly with Freud, but over somewhat different issues. In particular, Adler emphasized the importance of feelings of inferiority, which he believed we experience as children because of our small size and physical weakness. He viewed personality development as stemming primarily from our efforts to overcome such feelings through compensation, or what Adler termed **striving for superiority.** Like Horney and other neo-Freudians, Adler also emphasized the importance of social factors in personality; for instance, he called attention to the importance of birth order. Only children, he suggested, are spoiled by too much parental attention, while first-borns are "dethroned" by a second child. Second-borns, in contrast, are competitive, because they have to struggle to catch up with an older sibling.

By now the main point should be clear: Neo-Freudians, while accepting many of Freud's basic ideas, did not agree with his emphasis on innate patterns of development. On the contrary, they perceived personality as stemming from a complex interplay between social factors and the experiences we have during childhood, primarily in our own families. While the theories proposed by neo-Freudians are not widely accepted by psychologists today, they did serve as a kind of bridge between the provocative views offered by Freud and more modern conceptions of personality. In this respect, at least, they made a lasting contribution.

Key Questions

- According to Jung, what is the collective unconscious?
- To what aspects of Freud's theory did Horney object?
- According to Adler, what is the role of feelings of inferiority in personality?

Humanistic Theories: Emphasis on Growth

Id versus ego, Jekyll versus Hyde—on the whole, psychoanalytic theories of personality take a dim view of human nature, contending that we must struggle constantly to control our bestial impulses if we are to function as healthy, rational adults. Is this view accurate? Many psychologists doubt that it is. They believe that human strivings for growth, dignity, and self-determination are just as—if not more—important in the development of personality than the primitive motives Freud emphasized. Because of their more optimistic views concerning human nature, such views are known as **humanistic theories** (Maslow, 1970; Rogers, 1977, 1982). These theories differ widely in the concepts on which they focus, but share the following characteristics.

First, they emphasize *personal responsibility.* Each of us, these theories contend, is largely responsible for what happens to us. Our fate is mostly in our own hands; we are *not* mere chips driven here and there by dark forces within our personalities. Second, while these theories don't deny the importance of past experience, they generally focus on the present. True, we may be influenced by traumatic events early in life. Yet these do *not* have to shape our entire adult lives, and the capacity to overcome early troubles and to go on from there is both real and powerful. Third, humanistic theories stress the importance of *personal growth.* People are not, such theories argue, content

Striving for Superiority: Attempting to overcome feelings of inferiority. According to Adler, this is the primary motive for human behavior.

Humanistic Theories: Theories of personality emphasizing personal responsibility and innate tendencies toward personal growth.

with merely meeting their current needs. They wish to progress toward "bigger" goals such as becoming the best they can be. Only when obstacles interfere is the process of personal growth interrupted. A key goal of therapy, therefore, should be to remove obstacles that prevent natural growth processes from proceeding. As examples of humanistic theories, we'll now consider the views proposed by Carl Rogers and Abraham Maslow.

Rogers's Self Theory: Becoming a Fully Functioning Person

Carl Rogers planned to become a minister, but after taking several courses in psychology, he changed his mind and decided instead to focus on human personality—and why it sometimes goes off the track. The theory Rogers formulated played an important role in the emergence of humanistic psychology and remains influential even today.

One central assumption of Rogers's theory was this: Left to their own devices, human beings show many positive characteristics and move, over the course of their lives, toward becoming **fully functioning persons.** What are such persons like? Rogers suggested that they are people who strive to experience life to the fullest, who live in the here and now, and who trust their own feelings. They are sensitive to the needs and rights of others, but do not allow society's standards to shape their feelings or actions to an excessive degree. "If it feels like the right thing to do," such people reason, "then I should do it." Fully functioning people aren't saints; they can—and do—lose their tempers or act in ways they later regret. But throughout life, their actions become increasingly dominated by constructive impulses. They are in close touch with their own values and feelings and experience life more deeply than most other persons.

If all human beings possess the capacity to become fully functioning persons, why don't they all succeed? Why, in short, aren't we surrounded by models of health and happy adjustment? The answer, Rogers contends, lies in the anxiety generated when life experiences are inconsistent with our ideas about ourselves—in short, when a gap develops between our **self-concept** (our beliefs and knowledge about ourselves) and reality or our perceptions of it. For example, imagine a young girl who believes that she is very likable and makes friends easily. One day she happens to overhear a conversation between two neighbors who describe her as moody and difficult to get along with. She is crushed; here is information that is highly inconsistent with her self-concept. As a result of this experience, anxiety occurs, and she adopts one or more psychological defenses to reduce it. The most common of these defenses is *distortion*—changing our perceptions of reality so that they *are* consistent with our self-concept. For example, the girl may convince herself that the two people talking about her don't know her well, or that they themselves have serious problems. Another defense process is *denial;* the girl may refuse to admit to herself that she heard the conversation or that she understood what these people were saying.

In the short run, such tactics are successful: They help reduce anxiety. Ultimately, however, they produce sizable gaps between an individual's self-concept and reality. The larger such gaps, Rogers contends, the greater an individual's maladjustment—and personal unhappiness (see Figure 12.8 on page 480). Rogers suggested that distortions in the self-concept are common because most people grow up in an atmosphere of *conditional positive regard.* They learn that others, such as their parents, will approve of them only when they behave in certain ways and express certain feelings. As a result, many people are forced to deny the existence of various impulses and feelings, and their self-concepts become badly distorted.

Fully Functioning Persons: In Rogers's theory, psychologically healthy persons who enjoy life to the fullest.

Self-Concept: All the information and beliefs individuals have about their own characteristics and themselves.

FIGURE 12.8

Gaps between Our Self-Concept and Our Experience: A Cause of Maladjustment in Rogers's Theory

According to Rogers, the larger the gap between an individual's self-concept and reality, the poorer this person's psychological adjustment.

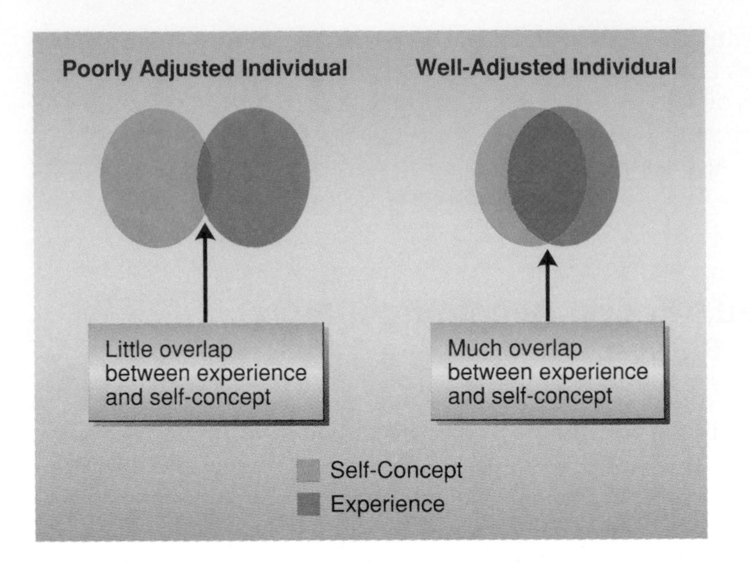

How can such distorted self-concepts be repaired, so that healthy development can continue? Rogers suggests that therapists can help accomplish this goal by placing individuals in an atmosphere of **unconditional positive regard**—a setting in which they understand that they will be accepted by the therapist *no matter what they say or do.* Such conditions are provided by *client-centered therapy,* a form of therapy we'll consider in detail in Chapter 15. Here, I wish simply to emphasize that such therapy is closely linked to Rogers's theory of personality and seeks to remove obstacles interfering with healthy development. Remove these barriers, Rogers contends, and individuals will move once again toward the goal they naturally seek: becoming fully functioning persons.

Maslow and the Study of Self-Actualizing People

Another influential humanistic theory of personality was proposed by Abraham Maslow (1970). We have already described a portion of Maslow's theory, his concept of a *needs hierarchy,* in Chapter 10. As you may recall, this concept suggests that human needs exist in a hierarchy ranging from *physiological needs* on the bottom through *self-actualization needs* at the top. According to Maslow, lower-order needs must be satisfied before we can turn to more complex, higher-order needs (Neher, 1991).

The needs hierarchy, however, is only part of Maslow's theory of personality. Maslow has also devoted much attention to the study of people who, in his terms, are *psychologically healthy.* These are individuals who have attained high levels of **self-actualization**—a state in which people reach their fullest true potential. What are such persons like? In essence, much like the fully functioning persons described by Rogers. Self-actualized people accept themselves for what they are; they recognize their shortcomings as well as their strengths. Being in touch with their own personalities, they are less inhibited and less likely to conform than most of us. Self-actualized people are well aware of the rules imposed by society, but feel greater freedom to ignore them than most persons. Unlike most of us, they seem to retain their childhood wonder and amazement with the world. For them, life continues to be an exciting adventure rather than a boring routine. Finally, self-actualized persons sometimes have what Maslow describes as **peak experiences**—instances in which they have powerful feelings of unity with the universe

Unconditional Positive Regard: In Rogers's theory, a therapeutic atmosphere that communicates that a person will be respected or loved regardless of what he or she says or does.

Self-Actualization: In Maslow's theory, a state of personal development in which individuals reach their maximum potential.

Peak Experiences: According to Maslow, intense emotional experiences during which individuals feel at one with the universe.

and feel tremendous waves of power and wonder. Such experiences appear to be linked to personal growth, for after them, people report feeling more spontaneous, more appreciative of life, and less concerned with the problems of everyday life. Examples of people Maslow describes as fully self-actualized are Thomas Jefferson, Albert Einstein, and Eleanor Roosevelt.

Research Related to Humanistic Theories: Studying the Self-Concept

At first glance it might seem that humanistic theories, like psychoanalytic ones, would not be readily open to scientific testing. In fact, however, the opposite is true. Humanistic theories were proposed by psychologists, and a commitment to empirical research is one of the true hallmarks of modern psychology. For this reason, several concepts that play a key role in humanistic theories have been studied quite extensively. Among these, the one that has probably received most attention is the idea of the *self-concept,* which is so central to Rogers's theory.

Research on the self-concept has addressed may different issues—for instance, how our self-concept influences our perception of and interpretation of new information (e.g., Klein & Loftus, 1988). A very basic question in such research has been: Just what does our self-concept include—of what kind of information is it composed? To find out, Rentsch and Heffner (1994) asked several hundred college students to give twenty different answers to the question "Who am I?" Careful analysis of these data indicated that while the contents of each person's self-concept are unique, the basic structure remains much the same. All of us seem to include information in the categories shown in Figure 12.9—information about our traits, our beliefs, what makes us unique, and so on.

Still other research on the self-concept has examined the question of whether we possess a single self-concept or several self-concepts—ideas about not only what kind of person we are *now,* but what kind of person we

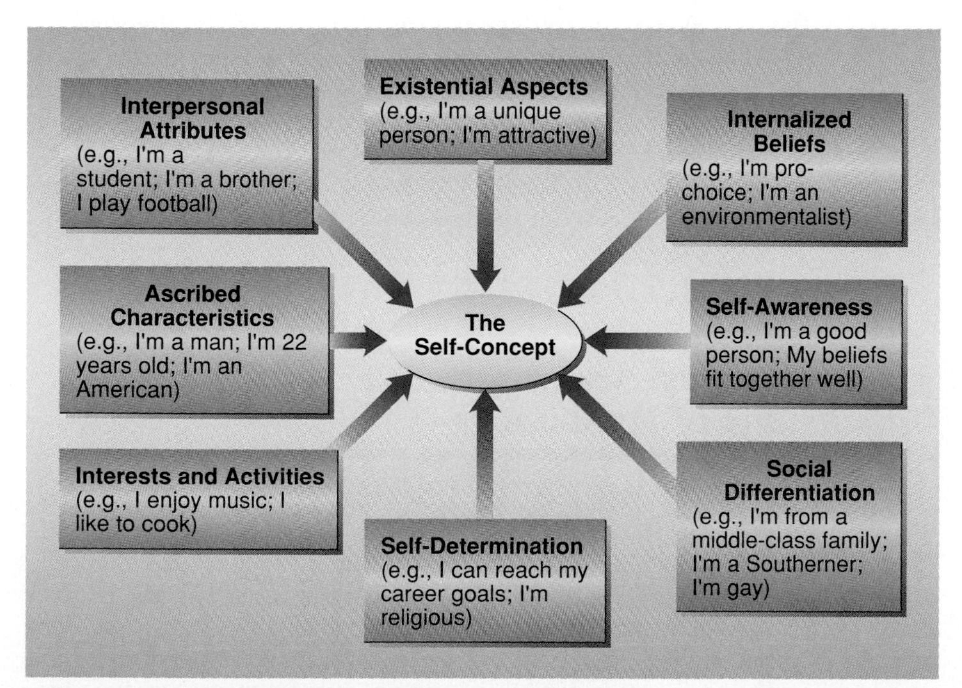

(**Source:** Based on findings reported by Rentsch & Heffner, 1994.)

FIGURE 12.9

Contents of the Self-Concept: Shared Categories

Research findings indicate that while each person's self-concept is unique, almost everyone's self-concept contains information relating to the categories shown here.

might become in the future (Markus & Nurius, 1986). Research findings favor the latter conclusion: Most people can imagine several possible future selves that differ from each other to some extent (Symons & Johnson, 1997). Moreover, persons who can imagine many possible selves rather than just one or a few appear to be able to cope more readily with traumatic life events (Morgan & Janoff-Bulman, 1994). Together, these and other findings indicate that Rogers and other humanistic theorists were correct in assigning the self-concept an important role in personality.

Humanistic Theories: An Evaluation

Humanistic theories hit psychology like a cyclone in the 1960s and 1970s. Many psychologists dissatisfied with the pessimistic nature of Freud's views quickly adopted the new theories as a framework for understanding personality. As with all storms, however, interest in the humanistic approaches rose to a peak and then gradually diminished. Have these theories left a lasting impact? Definitely. Several of the ideas first proposed by Rogers, Maslow, and other humanistic theorists have entered into the mainstream of psychology. As I noted above, the self or self-concept has remained a major focus of research for many years (e.g., Baumeister, 1993). Similarly, the view that behavior stems more from positive forces such as tendencies toward personal growth than from primitive sexual and aggressive urges has done much to restore a sense of balance to current views of personality.

But humanistic theories have also been subject to strong criticism. First, many psychologists are uncomfortable with the strong emphasis, in these theories, on personal responsibility or *free will*. Humanistic theories propose that individuals are responsible for their own actions and can change these if they wish to do so. To an extent, this is certainly true. Yet this emphasis on free will conflicts with determinism, the idea that behavior is determined by numerous factors and can be predicted from them. Such determinism is one of the cornerstones of modern scientific psychology.

Second, many key concepts of humanistic theories are loosely defined. What, precisely, is self-actualization? A peak experience? A fully functioning person? Until such terms are clearly defined, it is difficult to conduct systematic research on them. Despite such criticisms, the impact of humanistic theories has persisted, and does indeed constitute a lasting contribution to our understanding of human personality.

Key Questions

- How does the view of human beings proposed by humanistic theories of personality differ from that of psychoanalytic theories?
- According to Rogers, why do many individuals fail to become fully functioning persons?
- In Maslow's theory, what is self-actualization?
- What is the self-concept?

Trait Theories: Seeking the Key Dimensions of Personality

When we describe other persons, we often do so in terms of specific **personality traits**—stable dimensions of personality along which people vary. This strong tendency to think about others in terms of specific characteristics is reflected in **trait theories** of personality. Such theories focus on identifying key dimensions of personality—the most important ways in which people differ. The basic idea behind this approach is as follows: Once we identify the key dimensions along which people differ, we can measure how *much*

Personality Traits: Specific dimensions along which individuals' personalities differ in consistent, stable ways.

Trait Theories: Theories of personality that focus on identifying the key dimensions along which people differ.

they differ and can then relate such differences to many important forms of behavior.

Unfortunately, this task sounds easier than it actually is. Human beings differ in an almost countless number of ways (see Figure 12.10). How can we determine which of these are most important and stable? The scope of the problem was first suggested by a famous study conducted by Allport and Odbert (1936). By consulting a standard dictionary, they identified fully *17,953* words in English referring to specific traits. Even when words with similar meanings were combined, 171 distinct traits remained. How can we hope to deal with this multitude of traits? One solution is to search for *clusters*—groups of traits that seem to go together. We'll now take a brief look at two theories that have adopted this approach. Then we'll turn to evidence suggesting that in the final analysis, the number of key traits or dimensions of personality is actually quite small—perhaps no more than five.

FIGURE 12.10

Personality Traits: The Dimensions along Which People Differ

Human beings differ from each other along many different dimensions. A key task for psychologists who study personality is that of identifying the most important of these dimensions or *traits.*

Allport's Central, Secondary, and Cardinal Traits

If you have a successful older sister or brother, you can empathize with Gordon Allport: He grew up in the shadow of his brother Floyd, who was a famous social psychologist. Gordon, in contrast, chose personality as the focus of his own career.

On the basis of his research, Allport concluded that personality traits could be grouped in several major categories. Of least importance are **secondary traits,** which exert relatively weak effects on behavior. More important are **central traits**—the five to ten traits that together best account for the uniqueness of an individual's personality. Finally, Allport noted that a few people are dominated by a single all-important **cardinal trait.** A few examples of such persons and the cardinal traits that seemed to drive their personalities: Napoleon (ambition), Florence Nightingale (empathy), Machiavelli (lust for power), and Don Juan (just plain lust).

Perhaps an even more important aspect of Allport's theory of personality is his concept of **functional autonomy** (Allport, 1965)—the idea that patterns of behavior that are initially acquired under one set of circumstances, and which satisfy one set of motives, may later be performed for very different reasons. For example, initially a child may learn to read because this pleases his teachers and parents and because failure to do so is punished. Later in life, however, the same person may read because he has come to enjoy reading in and of itself—in terms of our discussion in Chapter 10, reading is intrinsically motivated. Notice how this contrasts with Freud's view that the roots of adult personality are planted firmly in the soil of childhood—that, as Freud himself put it (quoting Wordsworth), "The child is the father [mother] of the man [woman]." For Allport, such connections are not necessarily present; our adult behavior may spring from roots entirely different from those that gave rise to our childhood behavior.

Secondary Traits: According to Allport, traits that exert relatively weak effects upon behavior.

Central Traits: According to Allport, the five or ten traits that best describe an individual's personality.

Cardinal Trait: According to Allport, a single trait that dominates an individual's entire personality.

Functional Autonomy: In Allport's theory, maintenance of patterns of behavior by motives other than the ones originally responsible for the behavior's occurrence.

Cattell's Surface and Source Traits

Another well-known advocate of the trait approach is Raymond Cattell. He and his colleagues have focused on the task described earlier: identifying the basic dimensions of personality. Instead of beginning with hunches or insights, however, Cattell has used a very different approach. He has conducted extensive research in which literally thousands of persons responded to measures designed to reflect individual differences on hundreds of traits. These responses were then subjected to a statistical technique known as *factor analysis*. This technique reveals patterns in the extent to which various traits are correlated. In this manner, factor analysis can help identify important clusters of traits—ones that seem to be closely linked to one another. As such clusters are identified, Cattell reasoned, the number of key traits in human personality can be reduced until we are left with those that are truly central.

Using this approach, Cattell and his associates (e.g., Cattell & Dreger, 1977) have identified sixteen **source traits**—dimensions of personality that he believes underlie differences in many other, less important *surface traits*. A few of the source traits identified by Cattell: cool versus warm, easily upset versus calm and stable, not assertive versus dominant, trusting versus suspicious, and undisciplined versus self-disciplined. It is not yet clear whether Cattell's list is actually valid, but at least it is considerably briefer than previous ones.

The "Big Five" Factors: The Basic Dimensions of Personality?

This discussion of trait theories began with what seemed to be a fairly simple question: What are the key dimensions of human personality? By now you realize that this issue is more complex than it seems. Fortunately, though, this is one instance in which I do *not* have to say, "We don't yet have an answer." Research conducted during the past twenty years has begun to converge on an encouraging conclusion: In fact, there may be only five key or central dimensions of personality (e.g., Costa & McCrae, 1994; Zuckerman, 1994). These are sometimes labeled the "big five," and they can be described as follows:

1. **Extraversion:** A dimension ranging from sociable, talkative, fun-loving, affectionate, and adventurous at one end to retiring, sober, reserved, silent, and cautious at the other (see Figure 12.11).
2. **Agreeableness:** A dimension ranging from good-natured, gentle, cooperative, trusting, and helpful at one end to irritable, ruthless, suspicious, uncooperative, and headstrong at the other.
3. **Conscientiousness:** A dimension ranging from well-organized, careful, self-disciplined, responsible, and precise at one end to disorganized, careless, weak-willed, and neglectful at the other.
4. **Emotional Stability:** A dimension ranging from poised, calm, composed, and not hypochondriacal at one end to nervous, anxious, excitable, and hypochondriacal at the other.
5. **Openness to experience:** A dimension ranging from imaginative, sensitive, intellectual, and polished at one end to down-to-earth, insensitive, crude, and simple at the other.

How basic and therefore important are the "big five" dimensions? Although there is far from complete agreement on this point (e.g., Zuckerman, 1995), many researchers indicate that these dimensions are indeed very basic ones. This is indicated, in part, by the fact that these dimensions are ones to which most people in many different cultures refer in describing themselves

Source Traits: According to Cattell, key dimensions of personality that underlie many other traits.

Extraversion: One of the "big five" dimensions of personality; ranges from sociable, talkative, fun-loving at one end to sober, reserved, cautious at the other.

Agreeableness: One of the "big five" dimensions of personality; ranges from good-natured, cooperative, trusting at one end to irritable, suspicious, uncooperative at the other.

Conscientiousness: One of the "big five" dimensions of personality; ranges from well-organized, careful, responsible at one end to disorganized, careless, unscrupulous at the other.

Emotional Stability: One of the "big five" dimensions of personality; ranges from poised, calm, composed at one end to nervous, anxious, excitable at the other.

Openness to Experience: One of the "big five" dimensions of personality; ranges from imaginative, sensitive, intellectual at one end to down-to-earth, insensitive, crude at the other.

(Funder & Colvin, 1991). Also, we can often tell where individuals stand along at least some of these dimensions from an initial meeting of only a few minutes. Researchers have conducted several studies in which strangers met and interacted briefly, then rated each other on measures of the big five dimensions. When the researchers compared these ratings by strangers with ratings by other people who knew the participants very well (e.g., their parents or best friends), they found a substantial amount of agreement on at least some of the big five dimensions (e.g., Funder & Sneed, 1993; Watson, 1989). For instance, strangers who met each other for a few minutes were quite accurate in rating one another with respect to the dimensions of extraversion and conscientiousness. While this may seem surprising, it actually fits quite well with our informal experience. Think about it: If someone met *you* for the first time, could he or she tell right away whether you are friendly and outgoing or shy and reserved? Whether you are neat and orderly or impulsive and disorganized? The answer offered by research findings is clear: They probably could!

FIGURE 12.11

Extraversion: One of the "Big Five" Dimensions of Personality

People high in extraversion are sociable, fun-loving, adventurous, and often highly expressive.

Research on Trait Theories: Effects of the "Big Five"

If the big five dimensions of personality are really so basic, then it is reasonable to expect that they will be related to important forms of behavior. In fact, many studies indicate that this is the case. As noted recently by Hogan, Hogan, and Roberts (1996), individuals' standing on the big five dimensions is closely linked to important outcomes, such as success in performing many jobs. For example, in one large-scale study, Barrick and Mount (1993) examined the results of more than two hundred separate studies in which at least one of these dimensions was related to job performance. Several interesting findings were uncovered. First, *conscientiousness* was found to be a good predictor of performance for all types of jobs. Second, for people in managerial and sales positions, *extraversion* was highly related to job success. This is consistent with the popular image of successful salespersons, who are generally viewed as being sociable and outgoing. Finally, other research (e.g., McDaniel & Frei, 1994) indicates that agreeableness and emotional stability are good predictors of success in customer service jobs; for example, for someone working in customer support at a software company.

In sum, existing evidence indicates that the big five dimensions are indeed basic and important ones where human personality is concerned. No, they are not all there is to personality; but yes, they are dimensions we notice, and they are related to important life outcomes. See the **Ideas to Take with You** feature on page 486 for more information about the big five personality dimensions and their bearing on your own life. And for an intriguing illustration of traits in action, please see the Beyond the Headlines section on page 487.

Key Questions

- What are central traits? Source traits?
- What are the "big five" dimensions of personality?
- What do research findings indicate about the effects of the big five dimensions?

Trait Theories: An Evaluation

At present, most research on personality by psychologists occurs within the context of the trait approach. Instead of seeking to propose and test grand theories such as the ones offered by Freud, Jung, and Rogers, most personality psychologists currently direct their effort to the task of understanding specific traits (e.g., Friedman et al., 1993; Kring, Smith, & Neale, 1994). This trend is due both to the success of the trait approach and to the obvious shortcomings of the theories described in earlier sections of this chapter.

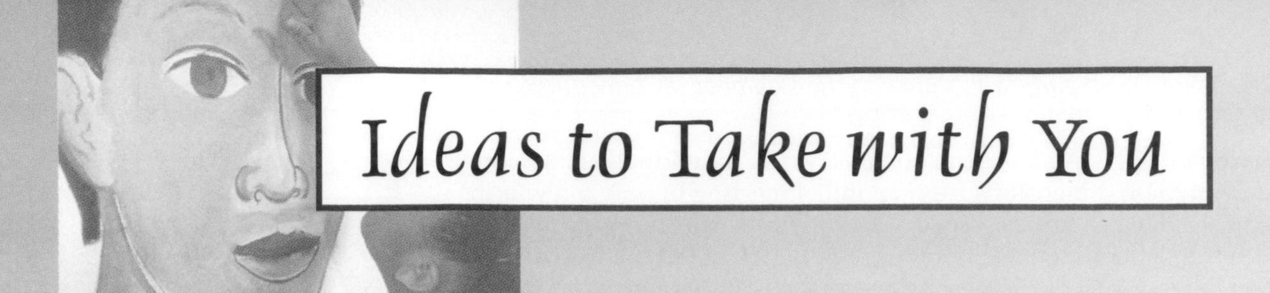

The "Big Five" Personality Dimensions and Some of Their Effects

EXTRAVERSION: The extent to which people are outgoing and impulsive as opposed to reserved and cautious.

People high on this dimension often make friends more easily and tend to be successful in fields requiring lots of contact with strangers (e.g., sales).

AGREEABLENESS: The extent to which people are cooperative, trusting, and easy to get along with as opposed to uncooperative, suspicious, and difficult.

People high in agreeableness tend to have few problems getting along with others.

CONSCIENTIOUSNESS: The extent to which people are neat, self-disciplined, and organized as opposed to sloppy, lacking in self-discipline, and disorganized.

People high in conscientiousness tend to get things done on time; they do well in fields requiring high levels of neatness and organization.

EMOTIONAL STABILITY: The extent to which people are calm, composed, and stable as opposed to nervous, anxious, and unstable.

People high in emotional stability are able to cope with high levels of stress better than persons low in emotional stability.

OPENNESS TO EXPERIENCE: The extent to which people are imaginative and open to new experiences as opposed to insensitive and reluctant to have new experiences.

People high in openness to experience are creative and often get along well with people from cultures different from their own.

Beyond the Headlines

As Psychologists See It

Litigation as a Way of Life

California Woman Has Sued Stores, Drivers, Tenants As Legal System Stood By

Wall Street Journal, May 5, 1993. San Francisco— As a young actress in summer stock, Patricia A. McColm gave a memorable performance . . . in *The Imaginary Invalid*, Moliere's farcical look at 17th-century medicine. For the better part of the last 15 years, however, she has been playing a far more demanding role, making a farce of the American judicial system. . . .

Since 1977, Ms. McColm, who has a law degree, . . . has filed more than 30 lawsuits on her own behalf, many of them personal injury claims, and pursued numerous additional complaints. . . . The tale of woe that Ms. McColm recounts in her 30 lawsuits is extraordinary. She alleges more than a dozen personal injuries, resulting from automobile accidents, assaults, batteries, defamation, and false imprisonment. She has filed nine suits against tenants who over the years have rented rooms in her San Francisco home . . . she sued one for failing to properly care for her pets and plants, and another for . . . persuading a third tenant to move out. Among the other cases is a 1987 injunction she won restricting the use of a basketball hoop at a neighbor's house. . . . A number of people who have seen her in action have speculated about her motivation, such as a psychiatrist who suggested that her lawsuits were a "psychotherapeutic" response to one of her accidents. "You have more energy than all of us put together," said one judge. "You should find some other way to channel it. . . . I think you are the most vexatious, vexatious litigant I have ever dealt with."

Thirty lawsuits? Can one person be the victim of so much abuse, mistreatment, and bad luck? Looking at the big picture with respect to Ms. McColm's activities, it is hard to reach this conclusion. On the contrary, it appears that for reasons relating to her own needs and traits, Ms. McColm has decided to become a "professional litigant"—someone who earns a living from filing lawsuits in such a way that it is less costly for the people or companies she sues to settle with her than to defend themselves in court. But what kind of person would choose such a lifestyle? Research on personality traits offers some intriguing answers.

First, it seems reasonable to assume that Ms. McColm is very low on the *agreeableness* dimension of the "big five" dimensions of personality. People who have seen her in action note that she really believes she is in the right, and that others have purposely and consciously tried to harm her. In short, she is deeply suspicious and uncooperative, and she translates these traits into frequent legal actions. Second, given that many of her claims relate to supposed personal injuries she has suffered from falls in various stores and from automobile accidents, it seems possible that she is also low on the *emotional stability* dimension. Complaints about such things as a deviated septum (a portion of the nose) that causes her to "snort" when she catches a cold, and a thumb bent out of shape by the same automobile accident, point to this conclusion.

In essence, then, an unusual combination of traits—high intelligence and acting skill coupled with low agreeableness and emotional stability—may set the stage, so to speak, for Ms. McColm's lawsuits. Of course, in the absence of careful measurements of various aspects of her personality—the kinds of measurements I'll describe in a later section—these suggestions about her are speculative. One thing is clear, however: Her own brand of uniqueness often proves truly disturbing to persons who are on the receiving end of her many legal actions.

Critical Thinking Questions

1. Why do *you* think Ms. McColm files so many lawsuits? Is she the unfortunate victim of circumstances, or do you think these suits stem from her own personality traits?
2. Do you think anything could be done to change her behavior? If so, what?

This is not to imply that the trait approach is perfect, however. On the contrary, it, too, can be criticized in several respects. First, the trait approach is largely *descriptive* in nature. It seeks to describe the key dimensions of personality but does not attempt to determine *how* various traits develop or *how* they influence behavior. Fully developed theories of personality must, of course, address such issues. Second, despite several decades of careful research, there is still no final agreement concerning the traits that are most important or most basic. The "big five" dimensions are widely accepted, but they are far from *universally* accepted, and some psychologists feel that they are not the final answer to these issues (e.g., Block, 1995; Goldberg & Saucier, 1995).

As you can see, these criticisms relate primarily to what the trait approach has not yet accomplished rather than to its findings or proposals. All in all, we can conclude that this approach to personality has generally been a very valuable one. Attempting to understand how people differ appears to be a useful strategy for understanding the uniqueness and the consistency of key aspects of human behavior.

Learning Approaches to Personality

Whatever their focus, all personality theories must ultimately come to grips with two basic questions: What accounts for the *uniqueness* and what underlies the *consistency* of human behavior? Freud's answer focused on *internal* factors—hidden conflicts among the id, ego, and superego and the active struggle to keep unacceptable impulses out of consciousness. At the other end of the continuum are approaches to personality that emphasize the role of learning and experience. While such views were not originally presented as formal theories of personality, they are often described as *learning theories of personality* to distinguish them from other perspectives (Bandura, 1986; Rotter, 1982; Skinner, 1974).

How can a learning perspective account for the uniqueness and consistency of human behavior? Very readily. Uniqueness, the learning approaches contend, merely reflects the fact that we have all had distinctive life (and learning) experiences. Similarly, the learning approaches can explain consistency in behavior over time and across situations by noting that the responses, associations, or habits acquired through learning tend to persist. Moreover, because individuals often find themselves in situations very similar to the ones in which they acquired their characteristic tendencies, their behavior, too, tends to remain quite stable.

Early learning-oriented views of personality took what now seems to be a somewhat extreme position: They denied the importance of *any* internal causes of behavior—such as motives, traits, intentions, or goals (Skinner, 1974). The only things that matter, these early theorists suggested, are external conditions determining patterns of reinforcement (recall the discussion of *schedules of reinforcement* in Chapter 5). At present, few psychologists agree with this position. Most now believe that internal factors play a crucial role in behavior. Moreover, several theorists contend that these internal factors must be carefully considered if we are ever to understand both uniqueness and consistency in human behavior. As an example of these more sophisticated learning approaches, let's consider the *social cognitive theory* proposed by Bandura (1986).

Social Cognitive Theory: A Modern View of Personality

In his **social cognitive theory,** Albert Bandura, a past president of the American Psychological Association, notes that people do indeed acquire many forms of behavior through basic processes of learning—operant conditioning and classical conditioning. He adds, however, that a third form—**observational learning** (recall Chapter 5)—is of special importance. In observational learning individuals acquire both information and new forms of behavior through observing others (*models*) (Bandura, 1977). Such learning plays a role in a very wide range of human activities—everything from learning how to dress and groom in the style of one's own society through learning how to perform new and difficult tasks (see Figure 12.12). In essence, any time that human beings observe others, they can learn from this experience; and such learning can then play an important part in their own behavior. Such models don't have to be present in the flesh for observational learning to occur; as we saw in Chapter 5 and in our discussion of the effects of media violence on aggression in Chapter 10, human beings can also acquire new information and new ways of behaving from exposure to models who are presented symbolically—in films, on television, and so on.

Social Cognitive Theory: A theory of behavior suggesting that human behavior is influenced by many cognitive factors as well as by reinforcement contingencies, and that human beings have an impressive capacity to regulate their own actions.

Observational Learning: The acquisition of new information, concepts, or forms of behavior through exposure to others and the consequences they experience.

Self-Reinforcement: A process in which individuals reward themselves for reaching their own goals.

Self-Efficacy: Individuals' expectations concerning their ability to perform various tasks.

Bandura also calls attention to the fact that learning is far from the entire story where human behavior and personality are concerned. In addition, many cognitive factors play a role. Unlike other species, human beings do not respond passively or automatically to external conditions. Instead, they plan, form expectancies, set goals, imagine possible outcomes, and so on. In short, people's actions are often strongly determined by a wide range of cognitive factors that were totally ignored both by early behaviorists and by early learning theories of personality.

In addition, Bandura (1986) notes, human beings often demonstrate impressive capacity for the *self-regulation* of their own behavior. While people may often respond to external factors such as positive reinforcement and punishment, they sometimes choose to ignore these and to operate in terms of internal standards and values. We set our own goals, and we often provide our own rewards when we reach them—a process Bandura calls **self-reinforcement.** Moreover, these rewards range from a direct pat on our own backs to more generalized feelings of personal accomplishment. For example, consider the hundreds of amateur runners who participate in major marathons. Few believe that they have any chance of winning and obtaining the external rewards offered—status, fame, cash prizes. Why, then, do they run? Because, Bandura would contend, they have *self-determined goals,* such as finishing the race, or merely going as far as they can. Meeting these goals allows them to engage in self-reinforcement, and this is sufficient to initiate what is obviously very effortful behavior.

Another important concept in Bandura's theory is **self-efficacy**—the belief in one's capacity to perform a specific task (Bandura, 1986; Gist & Mitchell, 1992). The higher a person's feelings of self-efficacy, the better that person tends to do at a wide range of tasks. And such success, of course, can ultimately lead to more generalized positive feelings about oneself—changes in the self-concept and in evaluations of it.

I should note that other learning-oriented approaches to personality have much in common with Bandura's views. For example, the *social learning theory*

FIGURE 12.12

Observational Learning in Action

We often learn much from observing the behavior of others—either in the flesh or in movies, tapes, or magazines.

proposed by Julian Rotter (1954, 1982) suggests that the likelihood that a given behavior will occur in a specific situation depends on individuals' *expectancies* concerning the outcomes the behavior will produce and the *reinforcement value* they attach to such outcomes—the degree to which they prefer one reinforcer over another. According to Rotter, individuals form *generalized expectancies* concerning the extent to which their own actions determine the outcomes they experience. Rotter terms persons who strongly believe that they can shape their own destinies **internals** and those who believe their outcomes are largely the result of forces outside their control **externals.** As you can probably guess, internals are often happier and better adjusted than externals. Note again how, in this theory, internal factors such as subjective estimates concerning the likelihood of various outcomes, subjective reactions to these, and generalized expectancies of personal control all combine to influence behavior. Certainly, such suggestions contrast very sharply with the view, stated in early learning approaches to personality, that only external reinforcement contingencies should be taken into account.

Research on the Learning Approaches

Because they are based on well-established principles of psychology, learning theories of personality have been the subject of a great deal of research attention (e.g., Wallace, 1993). (Indeed, as we'll see in Chapter 15, efforts to test these theories have led to the development of several new and highly effective techniques for treating psychological disorders.) As one example of this research, let's briefly consider efforts to investigate the effects of *self-efficacy* (e.g., Burger & Palmer, 1992).

Recall that self-efficacy relates to our beliefs about our ability to perform a specific task or reach a specific goal (Bandura, 1986). Do such cognitions influence performance, as Bandura predicts? Many studies indicate that they do. For instance, high self-efficacy has been related to improved performance on many tasks (Wood, Bandura, & Bailey, 1990). Clearly, then, high self-efficacy offers many benefits.

Given this fact, the next question is obvious: Can anything be done to increase individuals' self-efficacy in various situations? Research on this topic offers an encouraging answer: Self-efficacy *can* be increased through relatively straightforward procedures (e.g., Riskind & Maddux, 1993). For instance, Eden and Aviram (1993) studied people who had become unemployed through "downsizing" and other factors beyond their control and who were trying to find another job. In the study, efforts were made to increase the self-efficacy of participants; the researchers felt this would be useful because after losing their jobs, many people experience reductions in self-efficacy—they begin to wonder how good they are at what they do for a living and whether they will ever get another position. To counter such feelings, Eden and Aviram (1993) had newly unemployed persons participate in workshops designed to enhance their self-efficacy. The workshops sought to accomplish this goal by showing films in which good job-seeking skills were demonstrated. After watching these films, the participants practiced these skills themselves and received feedback and encouragement. Results indicated that these procedures did increase participants' self-efficacy. Did the self-efficacy workshops also help participants get another job? Again, findings were encouraging: Six months later, fully 67 percent of those who took part in the workshops were reemployed; in contrast, only 23 percent of those in a carefully matched control group had found a new job (see Figure 12.13). Findings such as these suggest that self-efficacy is an important aspect of personality but that—like many other traits or characteristics—it can indeed be changed.

Internals: In Rotter's theory, individuals who believe that they exert considerable control over the outcomes they experience.

Externals: In Rotter's terms, individuals who believe that they have little control over the outcomes they experience.

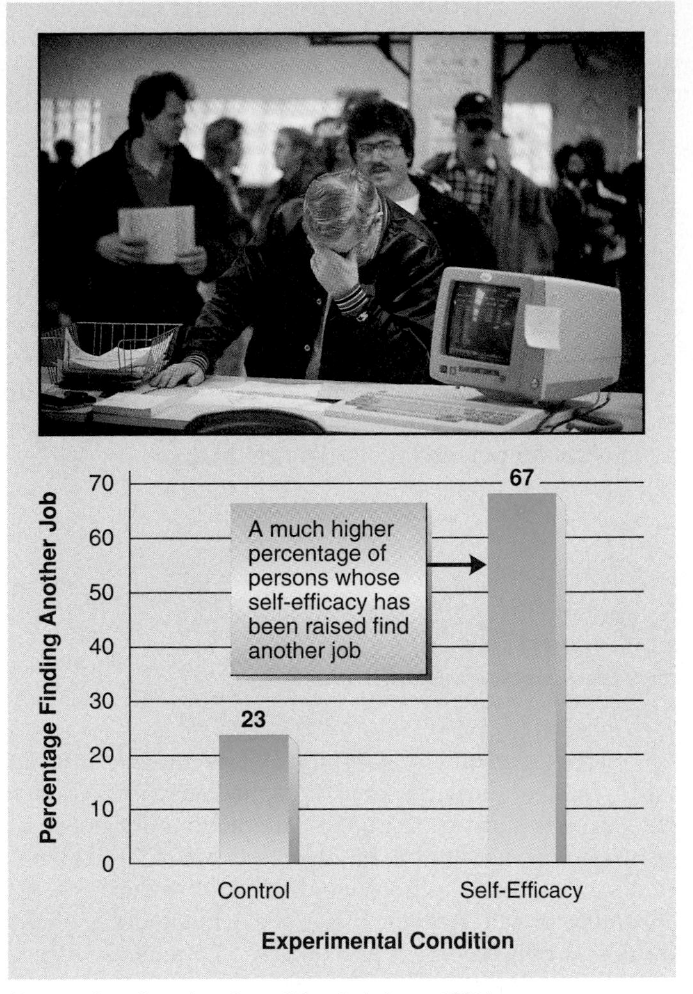

(**Source:** Based on data from Eden & Aviram, 1993.)

FIGURE 12.13

Self-Efficacy and Reemployment

When people lose their jobs through "downsizing" and other factors beyond their control, their feelings of self-efficacy often suffer. Research findings indicate that efforts to restore individuals' beliefs in their own competence can increase their chances of finding another job.

Learning Approaches: An Evaluation

Do all human beings confront an Oedipus conflict? Are peak experiences real, and do they in fact constitute a sign of growing self-actualization? Considerable controversy exists with respect to these and many other aspects of psychoanalytic and humanistic theories of personality. In contrast, virtually all psychologists today agree that behaviors are acquired and modified through basic processes of learning. Moreover, in the late 1990s there is general agreement about the importance of cognitive factors in human behavior. Thus, a key strength of the learning perspective is obvious: It is based on widely accepted and well-documented principles of psychology.

Another positive feature of modern learning approaches to personality is that they have been put to practical use in efforts to modify maladaptive forms of behavior. I'll return to such efforts in Chapter 15, but simply want to indicate here that some of them have proved to be highly effective.

Turning to criticisms, most of these have focused on older approaches rather than on the more sophisticated theories proposed by Bandura (1986) and others. Those early behaviorist theories of personality generally ignored the role of cognitive factors in human behavior, but this is certainly not true of the modern theories. A related criticism centers on the fact that learning theories generally ignore inner conflicts and the influence of unconscious thoughts and impulses on behavior. However, while theories such as Bandura's

Key Questions

- According to learning theories of personality, what accounts for the uniqueness and consistency of human behavior?
- What is Bandura's social cognitive theory?
- What is Rotter's social learning theory?
- What is self-efficacy, and what effects does it have on behavior?

do not explicitly address such issues, these theories do not in any way deny the existence and possible impact of inner and unconscious factors. Rather, modern learning theories would simply insist that such effects be interpreted within the context of modern psychology—for example, as reflecting the impact of subliminal stimuli, as discussed earlier in this chapter.

As you can readily see, these are *not* major criticisms. Thus, it seems fair to state that these social cognitive theories of personality are more in tune with the eclectic, sophisticated approach of modern psychology than were earlier theories. Along with the trait approach, learning approaches are certain to play an important role in continuing efforts to understand the uniqueness and consistency of human behavior that, together, lead us to consider personality in the first place.

Measuring Personality

To study personality scientifically, we must first be able to measure it—or, at least, to measure some of its many aspects. Thus, a key task facing psychologists who want to investigate personality in their research is this basic issue of *measurement.* We have already considered some aspects of this question in Chapter 11, where we discussed several issues relating to the measurement of intelligence. Here, we'll focus on how psychologists measure traits and dimensions of personality. While many different procedures exist, most fall into two major categories often described, respectively, by the terms *objective* and *projective.*

Objective Tests of Personality: Questionnaires and Inventories

Objective tests of personality consist of questions or statements to which individuals respond in various ways. A questionnaire, for example, might ask respondents to indicate the extent to which each of a set of statements is true or false about themselves, how much they agree or disagree with various sentences, or which of a pair of activities they prefer. For instance, here are a few items that are similar to those appearing on one widely used measure of the "big five" dimensions of personality. (I'll describe this measure below.) For each item individuals are asked to indicate the extent to which they agree or disagree with the statement (1 = strongly disagree, 2 = disagree, 3 = neutral, 4 = agree, and 5 = strongly agree).

I am very careful and methodical.

I generally get along well with others.

I cry easily.

Sometimes I feel totally worthless.

I have a lot of trust in other people.

Answers to the questions on these objective tests are scored by means of special keys. The score obtained by a specific person is then compared with those obtained by hundreds or even thousands of other people who have taken the test previously. In this way, an individual's relative standing on the trait being measured can be determined.

MMPI: A widely used objective test of personality based on empirical keying.

On some objective tests, the items included have what is known as *face validity:* Reading the items, it is easy to see that they are related to the trait or traits being measured. For instance, the first statement above seems to be related to the *conscientiousness* dimension of personality, while the second is related to the *agreeableness* dimension. On other tests, however, the items do not necessarily appear to be related to personality traits or characteristics. Rather, a procedure known as *empirical keying* is used. The items are given to hundreds of persons belonging to groups known to differ from one another—for instance, psychiatric patients with specific forms of mental illness and normal persons—and the answers given by the two groups are compared. Items answered differently by these groups are included on the test, *regardless of whether they seem to be related to the traits being measured.* The reasoning is as follows: As long as a test item differentiates between the groups in question, the specific content of the item itself is unimportant.

One widely used test designed to measure various types of psychological disorders, the **MMPI** (short for *Minnesota Multiphasic Personality Inventory*), uses precisely this method. The MMPI was first developed during the 1930s but underwent a major revision in the 1980s. The current version, the MMPI–2, contains ten *clinical scales* and several *validity scales.* The clinical scales, which are summarized in Table 12.2, relate to various forms of psychological disorders. Items included in each of these scales are answered differently by persons who have been diagnosed as having this particular disorder and by persons in a comparison group who do *not* have the disorder. The validity scales are designed to determine whether and to what extent people are trying to fake their answers—for instance, whether the test takers are trying to seem bizarre or, conversely, to give the impression that they are extremely "normal" and well-adjusted. If responses on these validity scales suggest that a person is faking, then that person's responses on the clinical scales must be interpreted with special caution.

TABLE 12.2

Clinical Scales of the MMPI–2

The MMPI–2 is designed to measure many aspects of personality related to psychological disorders.

Clinical Scale	Description of Disorder
Hypochondriasis	Excessive concern with bodily functions
Depression	Pessimism; hopelessness; slowing of action and thought
Hysteria	Development of physical disorders such as blindness, paralysis, and vomiting as an escape from emotional problems
Psychopathic Deviance	Disregard for social customs; shallow emotions
Masculinity–Femininity	Possessing traits and interests typically associated with the opposite sex
Paranoia	Suspiciousness; delusions of grandeur or persecution
Psychasthenia	Obsession; compulsions; fears; guilt; indecisiveness
Schizophrenia	Bizarre, unusual thoughts or behavior; withdrawal; hallucinations; delusions
Hypomania	Emotional excitement; flight of ideas; overactivity
Social Introversion	Shyness; lack of interest in others; insecurity

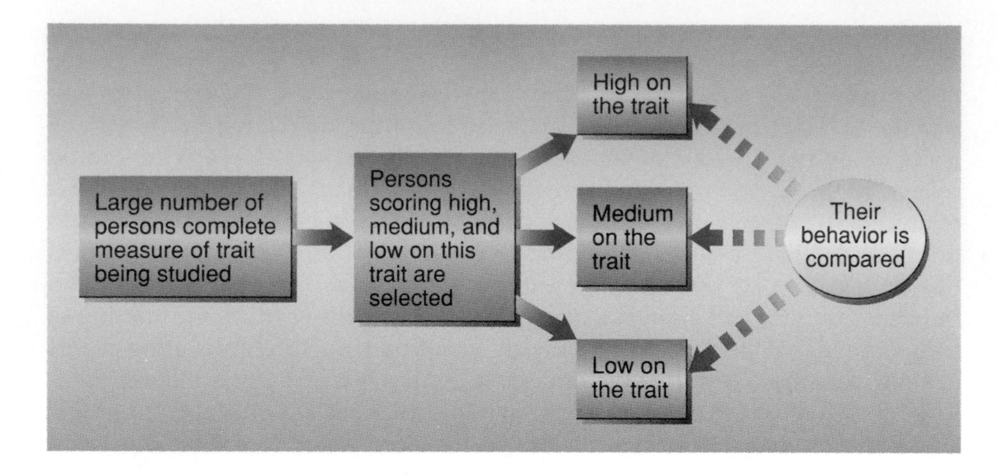

FIGURE 12.14

Studying the Effects of Personality: One Basic Approach

In order to study the effects on behavior of a specific personality trait, a large number of persons complete a measure of this trait. Then researchers select persons scoring high, medium, and low on the trait for further study, and compare their behavior. If it differs, the researchers obtain evidence that this trait is related to the form of behavior being studied.

Another widely used objective measure of personality is the **Millon Clinical Multiaxial Inventory (MCMI)** (Millon, 1987). Items on this test correspond more closely than those on the MMPI to the categories of psychological disorders currently used by psychologists (we'll discuss these in detail in Chapter 14). This makes the test especially useful to clinical psychologists, who must first identify individuals' problems before recommending specific forms of therapy for them.

A third objective test, the **NEO Personality Inventory** (NEO–PI); Costa & McCrae, 1989), is used to measure aspects of personality that are *not* directly linked to psychological disorders. Specifically, it assesses individuals' standing on the "big five" dimensions of personality described earlier. These dimensions appear to represent basic aspects of personality. Thus, the NEO–PI has been widely used in research.

Objective tests of personality are generally used to identify and measure specific aspects of personality—specific traits. How are such measurements used in research? Often, in the following manner. A psychologist interested in studying behavior related to a specific aspect of personality gives a test that measures this trait to a large number of persons. Then the psychologist chooses individuals scoring very low and very high on the test (and perhaps also those in between) to participate in the study. If the behavior of these groups does indeed differ, the psychologist obtains evidence that this particular trait is related to certain forms of behavior (see Figure 12.14).

Projective Tests of Personality: Of Inkblots and Images

In contrast to objective tests, *projective tests* of personality adopt a very different approach. They present individuals with ambiguous stimuli—stimuli that can be interpreted in many different ways. For instance, these can be inkblots like the one shown in Figure 12.15, or ambiguous scenes of the type described in our discussion of achievement motivation in Chapter 10. Persons taking the test are asked to indicate what they see in the inkblot, to make up a story about the scene, and so on. Since the stimuli themselves are ambiguous, it is assumed that the answers given by respondents will reflect various facets of their personality. In other words, different persons "see" different things in these stimuli because these persons differ from one another with respect to various aspects of personality.

Do such tests really work—do they meet the criteria of reliability and validity discussed in Chapter 11? For some projective tests, such as the *TAT*,

Millon Clinical Multiaxial Inventory (MCMI): An objective test of personality specifically designed to assist psychologists in diagnosing various psychological disorders.

NEO Personality Inventory (NEO-PI): An objective measure of personality designed to assess individuals' relative standing on each of the "big five" dimensions of personality.

which is used to measure achievement motivation and other social motives (see Chapter 10), the answer appears to be *yes;* such tests do yield reliable scores and do seem to measure what they are intended to measure. For others, such as the famous **Rorschach test,** which uses inkblots like the one in Figure 12.15, the answer is more doubtful. Responses to this test are scored in many different ways. For instance, one measure involves responses that mention *pairs* of objects or a *reflection* (e.g., the inkblot is interpreted as showing two people, or one person looking into a mirror). Such responses are taken as a sign of self-focus—excessive concern with oneself. Other scoring considers the number of times individuals mention movement, color, or shading in the inkblots. The more responses of this type people make, the more sources of stress they supposedly have in their lives.

FIGURE 12.15

The Rorschach Test: One Projective Measure of Personality

Persons taking the *Rorschach test* describe what they see in a series of inkblots. Supposedly, individuals' responses reveal much about their personality. However, recent findings cast doubt on the validity of this test.

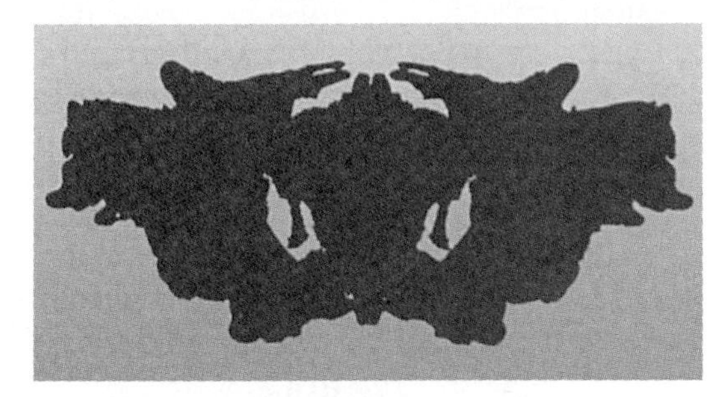

Are such interpretations accurate? Psychologists disagree about this point. The Rorschach test, like other projective tests, has a standard scoring manual (Exner, 1993) that tells psychologists precisely how to score various kinds of responses. Presumably, this manual is based on careful research designed to determine just what the test measures. Recent findings, however, indicate that the scoring advice provided by the manual may be flawed in several respects and does not rest on the firm scientific foundations psychologists prefer (Wood, Nezwonsky, & Stejskal, 1996). Such findings suggest the need for caution with respect to use of this particular test. More generally, they suggest that projective tests of personality, like objective tests, may vary in validity. Only tests that meet high standards of validity, of course, can provide us with useful information about personality.

In sum, while many tools for measuring personality—and thus for conducting systematic research on it—exist, these must be chosen and used with care. Only to the extent these tests meet the criteria of reliability and validity applied to all psychological tests can they assist us in the task of adding to our knowledge of personality.

Key Questions

- What are objective tests of personality?
- What are projective tests of personality?

Key Aspects of Personality: A Sample of Recent Research

In recent decades, efforts to understand personality have undergone a major shift. As I mentioned earlier, rather than attempting to construct grand theories, psychologists have focused on efforts to identify and study key aspects of personality. To give you a fuller idea of the nature of this modern approach, I'll now summarize some intriguing research findings relating to several important aspects of personality.

Two Aspects of the Self: Self-Esteem and Self-Monitoring

Many different theorists—Rogers is perhaps the prime example—believe that our *self-concept* plays a crucial role in our total personality (Benesch & Page, 1989). Reflecting this view, much current research on personality is concerned with various aspects of the self. Here, we'll explore two aspects of the self that have been the focus of a great deal of attention: *self-esteem* and *self-monitoring.*

Rorschach Test: A widely used projective test of personality in which individuals are asked to describe what they see in a series of inkblots.

Self-Esteem: The extent to which our self-evaluations are favorable or unfavorable.

Social Comparison: A process in which we compare ourselves with others.

Self-Monitoring: A personality trait involving the extent to which one's behavior is regulated by internal factors such as attitudes and values, or by external factors such as requirements of a given situation.

Self-Esteem: Some Effects of Feeling Good—or Bad—about Ourselves How do you feel about yourself? Generally good or satisfied? Generally bad or dissatisfied? Most people tend to hold relatively favorable views of themselves; they realize that they aren't perfect, but they conclude that overall, their good points outweigh their bad ones. Large individual differences exist with respect to such self-evaluations, though, so one important aspect of the self is **self-esteem**—the extent to which our self-evaluations are favorable or unfavorable (e.g., Marsh, 1993).

As you can probably guess, self-esteem is related to many forms of behavior. Persons who are high in self-esteem tend to be more confident in social situations (e.g., Jex, Cvetanovski, & Allen, 1994) and to report fewer negative emotions than persons who are low in self-esteem (Strauman, Lemieux, & Coe, 1993). In addition, they tend to perform better on many tasks—perhaps because high self-efficacy is often a part of high self-esteem (e.g., Baumeister, Heatherton, & Tice, 1993). Moreover, they tend to *believe* that they have done well on various tasks, even if this is not true (Martin & Murberger, 1994).

Other findings indicate that high self-esteem may actually be beneficial to our physical as well as our emotional health. Persons high in self-esteem appear to be more resistant to disease than persons low in self-esteem. That is, their immune systems seem to operate more effectively. Why? Some recent findings indicate that self-esteem may be linked to biochemical changes within the body; for instance, high self-esteem is associated with increased levels of *serotonin* in the blood, and this neurotransmitter may play a role in effective functioning of the immune system (e.g., Wright, 1995). Whatever the specific mechanisms involved, having high self-esteem does seem to be beneficial in many different ways.

How do differences in self-esteem arise? One major factor seems to involve **social comparison**—a process in which we compare ourselves with others. Depending on the persons we choose for such comparison and the conclusions we reach about how we compare with them, our self-esteem can receive a boost—or a battering.

Self-Monitoring: Self-Image versus Private Reality At the start of this chapter, I noted that the extent to which individuals show consistent behavior across situations and over time may itself be an important aspect of personality. Some people remain much the same in all contexts, while others are what psychologists have described as "social chameleons"—they change their behavior to match each given situation. These differences in the tendency to be consistent are part of another aspect of personality known as **self-monitoring.** More precisely, self-monitoring refers to the relative tendency of individuals to regulate their behavior on the basis of internal factors such as their own beliefs, attitudes, and values or, instead, on the basis of external factors such as the reactions of others or the requirements of a given situation (Snyder, 1987). Low self-monitors, such as the person shown in Figure 12.16, are on the "internal factor" side of this dimension, while high self-monitors are on the "external factor" side. And low self-monitors tend to show greater consistency across different situations than do high self-monitors (Koestner, Bernieri, & Zuckerman, 1992).

FIGURE 12.16

Self-Monitoring: An Important Dimension of Personality

Like the character shown here, persons low in *self-monitoring* tend to show a high degree of consistency in their behavior across many situations. In contrast, persons high in self-monitoring are sometimes described as being "social chameleons"—they act very differently in different contexts.

"I work hard and I play hard."

(**Source:** Drawing by C. Barsotti; ©1980 The New Yorker Magazine, Inc.)

Self-monitoring involves more than differences in consistency, however. Persons high in self-monitoring are generally better than low self-monitors both at reading others' emotional reactions and at managing their own nonverbal cues. Thus, they are generally more successful at making a good first impression (e.g., Paulhus, Bruce, & Trapnell, 1995). As a result, high self-monitors tend to be more successful in their careers than low self-monitors (Kilduff & Day, 1994). This is hardly surprising; high self-monitors seem to be image-conscious and to approach new situations by asking themselves, "How can I best please the people I have to deal with?" In contrast, low self-monitors ask themselves, "How can I best be *me* in this situation?"

Differences also exist with respect to intimate relationships. First, high self-monitors tend to have a greater number of different romantic partners than low self-monitors. Given their adaptability, this is not surprising (e.g., Snyder, Simpson, & Gangestad, 1986). In addition, high and low self-monitors seem to choose their romantic partners on different grounds. Low self-monitors want dating partners and lovers who share their values and attitudes. In contrast, high self-monitors express greater concern with choosing partners who will make them look good (e.g., because they are so attractive) or who have the right connections (Jones, 1993).

Because they are so changeable, high self-monitors may be viewed by others as unreliable, inconsistent, or even manipulative (Turban & Dougherty, 1994). In short, as is true of virtually every aspect of personality, there is no single point on this dimension that is always best. (To find out where you stand on the self-monitoring dimension, see the Making Psychology Part of Your Life section at the end of this chapter.)

Sensation Seeking: The desire to seek out novel and intense experiences.

Sensation Seeking: The Desire for Stimulation

Do you recall our discussion of adolescent recklessness in Chapter 9? If so, you may remember that adolescents tend to be higher than adults in a characteristic known as **sensation seeking**—the desire to seek out novel and intense experiences (e.g., Zuckerman, 1990). This leads teenagers to engage in high-risk behaviors such as driving fast, experimenting with drugs, and engaging in unprotected sex. This dimension of personality also plays a role in adult behavior. Research on sensation seeking indicates that compared to low sensation seekers, high sensation seekers are more likely to engage in substance abuse (Teichman, Barnea, & Rahav, 1989); more likely to participate in high-risk sports such as skydiving (Humbaugh & Garrett, 1974); and—like teenagers—more likely to drive fast (Zuckerman & Neeb, 1980). In short, they often lead lives in which they actively seek adventure and excitement wherever and however they can find them (see Figure 12.17).

What accounts for this preference for dangerous behavior and high levels of arousal? Miron Zuckerman (1990, 1995), the psychologist who first called attention to this aspect of personality, believes that it has important roots in biological processes. High sensation seekers, he suggests, are persons whose nervous systems operate best at high levels of arousal.

Considerable evidence offers support for this view. High sensation seekers show stronger *orienting responses* than other people to the initial presentation of an unfamiliar auditory or visual stimulus (Zuckerman, Simons, & Como, 1988); in other words, they seem to pay more attention to such stimuli. In addition, high sensation seekers show greater ability to ignore irrelevant information (Martin, 1986). As a result, they are better able to zero in on new stimuli and give them their full

FIGURE 12.17

Sensation Seeking: In Quest of Stimulation—and Excitement!

Sensation seeking is one important aspect of personality; it relates to the desire to seek out novel and intense experiences. Persons high on this dimension often engage in activities like the one shown here.

attention (e.g., Ball & Zuckerman, 1992) than are low sensation seekers. These differences between high and low sensation seekers are consistent with the view that they differ with respect to activation systems within the brain.

Does high sensation seeking always have negative implications for personal health or safety? Not necessarily. Perhaps people high in sensation seeking are better able to tolerate the emotional arousal produced by stressful life events, and so can cope with stress more effectively than persons low in sensation seeking. A study by Smith, Ptacek, and Smoll (1992) provides support for this reasoning. These psychologists found that high school athletes high in sensation seeking were actually *less* likely than athletes low in sensation seeking to experience injuries following stressful experiences, such as strong criticism from their coaches. As is true of other aspects of personality, therefore, the effects of high sensation seeking are neither uniformly negative nor uniformly positive.

Before concluding, we should address one final question about personality: Do cultural factors play a role in personality traits, or in the measurement of them?

Key Questions

- How do persons high in self-esteem differ from those low in self-esteem?
- What are the characteristics of low self-monitors and high self-monitors?
- What is sensation seeking, and how does it influence behavior?
- How can cultural factors influence responses to personality inventories?

EXPLORING GENDER & DIVERSITY

Cultural Differences in Personality: Avoiding the Extremes

Does culture shape personality? In one sense, the answer must be *yes.* The society in which we live, or the ethnic group to which we belong, shapes many of our beliefs, values, and behaviors—and these, as we have seen, play important roles in producing the uniqueness and consistency that are the hallmarks of personality. Do you recall our discussion of national differences in achievement motivation (see Chapter 10)? That is one dramatic example of research findings suggesting that there may be at least some differences in measurable, lasting traits across various cultures. Several other differences have also been uncovered. In relation to the self, for example, persons in Western nations seem to have an *individualistic* orientation; their self-concept focuses on their own traits as unique individuals. In contrast, persons from Asian and African cultures often show a more *collectivistic* orientation than is found in Western cultures; their self-concept is more strongly linked to their membership in various groups, and this colors much of their thinking and many of their judgments (e.g., Kashima et al., 1995). For instance, one of my former graduate students is from the Ivory Coast, an African nation. He explained to me that he could never think only of himself when making decisions—even ones affecting his career; he had to take the reactions of all his family members into account.

That cultural factors influence not only specific aspects of personality but also efforts to measure them is suggested by the findings of a study conducted by Chen, Lee, and Stevenson (1995). These researchers examined the possibility that persons from different cultures would react differently to one standard format used in many personality inventories—a format in which individuals indicate their reactions to various statements by choosing a number ranging from 1 ("strongly disagree") to 5 ("strongly agree"). Different reactions to this questionnaire format had already been found within the United States: African American adolescents were shown to be more likely than white adolescents to choose the extreme numbers (Bachman & O'Malley, 1984). Would members of Asian cultures, where making extreme statements is considered to be impolite, show a similar tendency? To find out, Chen, Lee, and Stevenson asked several thousand high school students living in Taiwan, Japan, Canada, and two parts of the United States (Virginia and Minnesota) to respond to questionnaires using the "strongly agree–strongly disagree" format. Results were clear: Across a wide range of items dealing with many different issues (e.g., the value of higher education, the importance of having many friends, self-confidence), cultural differences emerged. Specifically, students from the United States were more likely to make extreme judgments than those from the other countries. Why was this the case? Other findings indicated that U.S. students scored higher on *individualism*—on "doing their own thing"—than students in the other cultures.

These findings, and those of many other studies, indicate that in our efforts to study personality, we should not overlook cultural factors and differences. Basic dimensions of personality do seem to be the same all over the world; the "big five" dimensions, for instance, appear over and over again in studies of personality no matter where they are conducted. However, differences between cultural groups along these dimensions may well exist, and ignoring such differences could well give us an incomplete picture of the nature of personality and the factors that affect it.

Making Psychology Part of Your Life

Are You a High or a Low Self-Monitor?

Self-monitoring appears to be an important aspect of personality related to many outcomes, from making good impressions on others to succeeding in one's career.

To find out where *you* stand on this dimension, indicate whether each of the statements below is true (or mostly true) or false (or mostly false) about you. If a statement is true (or mostly true) write the letter *T* in the blank space. If it is false (or mostly false), enter the letter *F.*

1. It is difficult for me to imitate the actions of other people.
2. My behavior usually reflects my true feelings, attitudes, or beliefs.
3. At parties, I always try to say and do things others will like.
4. I can give a speech on almost any topic.
5. I would probably make a very poor actor.
6. Sometimes I put on a show to impress or entertain people.
7. I find it difficult to argue for ideas in which I don't believe.
8. In different situations and with different people I often act in very different ways.
9. I would not change my attitudes or my actions in order to please others.
10. Sometimes other people think I am experiencing stronger emotions than I really am.
11. I am not very good at making other people like me.
12. If I have a strong reason for doing so, I can look others in the eye and lie with a straight face.
13. I make up my own mind about movies, books or music; I don't rely on others' opinions in this respect.
14. At a party, I usually let others keep the jokes going.
15. I'm not always the person I seem to be.

To obtain your score, use the following key:

1 F, 2 F, 3 T, 4 T, 5 F, 6 T, 7 F, 8 T, 9 F, 10 T, 11 F, 12 T, 13 F, 14 F, 15 T

Give yourself one point for each of your answers that agrees with this key.

If you scored eight or higher, you are probably a high self-monitor. If you scored four or lower, you are probably a low self-monitor. (But remember: Scores on self-tests such as this are highly subject to error.) Can you think of situations in your own life where being a low or high self-monitor can be helpful to you? How about situations in which it might be harmful?

Summary and Review of Key Questions

Personality: Is It Real?

- **What is personality, and does it really exist?** Personality consists of the unique and stable patterns of behavior, thoughts, and emotions shown by individuals. Research evidence suggests that people do show a high degree of consistency in their behavior, so personality does appear to exist.
- **What role do personality traits and situational factors play in influencing human behavior?** Behavior is influenced by both situational factors and personal dispositions. Traits influence overt behavior only when situational conditions permit such expression.

KEY TERM

personality, p. 466

The Psychoanalytic Approach: Messages from the Unconscious

- **According to Freud, what are the three levels of consciousness?** According to Freud, three levels of consciousness exist: the conscious, the preconscious, and the unconscious.
- **In Freud's theory, what are the three basic parts of personality?** The three basic parts of personality are id, ego, and superego, which correspond roughly to desire, reason, and conscience.
- **According to Freud, what are the psychosexual stages of development?** Freud believed that all human beings move through a series of psychosexual stages during which the id's search for pleasure is focused on different regions of the body: the oral stage, the anal stage, the phallic stage, the latency stage, and finally the genital stage.
- **Do research findings support Freud's views about the unconscious?** Research findings indicate that our behavior can sometimes be influenced by stimuli or information we can't describe verbally. Thus, in this limited sense, there does appear to be some support for Freud's suggestions.
- **According to Jung, what is the collective unconscious?** Jung believed that all human beings share memories of our collective experience as a species. These are expressed when our conscious mind is distracted or inactive, often through archetypes.
- **To what aspects of Freud's theory did Horney object?** Horney rejected Freud's suggestion that females experience penis envy, and his theory that psychological disorders stem only from fixation.
- **According to Adler, what is the role of feelings of inferiority in personality?** Adler believed that human beings experience strong feelings of inferiority during early life and must struggle to overcome these through compensation.

KEY TERMS

psychoanalysis, p. 470 • id, p. 470 • pleasure principle, p. 470 • ego, p. 470 • reality principle, p. 470 • superego, p. 470 • anxiety, p. 471 • defense mechanisms, p. 471 • sublimation, p. 472 • psychosexual stages of development, p. 472 • libido, p. 472 • fixation, p. 472 • oral stage, p. 473 • anal stage, p. 473 • phallic stage, p. 473 • Oedipus complex, p. 473 • latency stage, p. 473 • genital stage, p. 473 • neo-Freudians, p. 476 • collective unconscious, p. 477 • archetypes, p. 477 • anima, p. 477 • animus, p. 477 • introverts, p. 477 • extroverts, p. 477 • striving for superiority, p. 478

Humanistic Theories: Emphasis on Growth

- **How does the view of human beings proposed by humanistic theories of personality differ from that of psychoanalytic theories?** Humanistic theories of personality suggest that human beings strive for personal development and growth; in contrast, psychoanalytic theories view human beings as constantly struggling to control the sexual and aggressive impulses of the id.
- **According to Rogers, why do many individuals fail to become fully functioning persons?** Rogers believed that many individuals fail to become fully functioning persons because distorted self-concepts interfere with personal growth.
- **In Maslow's theory, what is self-actualization?** Self-actualization is a state in which an individual has reached his or her maximum potential and become the best human being he or she can be.
- **What is the self-concept?** The self-concept consists of all of our beliefs and knowledge about ourselves.

KEY TERMS

humanistic theories, p. 478 • fully functioning persons, p. 479 • self-concept, p. 479 • unconditional positive regard, p. 480 • self-actualization, p. 480 • peak experiences, p. 480

Trait Theories: Seeking the Key Dimensions of Personality

- **What are central traits? Source traits?** Allport suggested that human beings possess a small number of central traits that account for much of their uniqueness as individuals. According to Cattell, there are sixteen source traits: basic dimensions that underlie many specific differences between individuals.
- **What are the "big five" dimensions of personality?** Research findings point to the conclusion that there are only five basic dimensions of personality: extraversion, agreeableness, conscientiousness, emotional stability, and openness to experience.
- **What do research findings indicate about the effects of the big five dimensions?** Research indicates that where an individual stands on several of the big five dimensions is readily apparent even during a brief first meeting. In addition, the big five dimensions are related to important life outcomes, ranging from personal adjustment to career success.

KEY TERMS

personality traits, p. 482 • trait theories, p. 482 • secondary traits, p. 483 • central traits, p. 483 • cardinal trait, p. 483 • functional autonomy, p. 483 • source traits, p. 484 • extraversion, p. 484 • agreeableness, p. 484 • conscientiousness, p. 484 • emotional stability, p. 484 • openness to experience, p. 484

Learning Approaches to Personality

- **According to learning theories of personality, what accounts for the uniqueness and consistency of human behavior?** Learning theories of personality suggest that uniqueness derives from the distinctive pattern of learning experiences in each individual's life. Such approaches explain consistency by noting that patterns of behavior, once acquired, tend to persist.
- **What is Bandura's social cognitive theory?** Bandura's social cognitive theory assumes that behavior is influenced by cognitive factors and personal dispositions as well as by reinforcement contingencies and the social and physical environment.
- **What is Rotter's social learning theory?** Rotter's social learning theory stresses the importance of generalized expectancies concerning the internal or external control of outcomes.
- **What is self-efficacy, and what effects does it have on behavior?** Self-efficacy is belief in one's ability to perform a specific task. Self-efficacy influences actual performance on many tasks; it may also affect individuals' self-concept and self-esteem.

KEY TERMS

social cognitive theory, p. 489 • observational learning, p. 489 • self-reinforcement, p. 489 • self-efficacy, p. 489 • internals, p. 490 • externals, p. 490

Measuring Personality

- **What are objective tests of personality?** Objective tests of personality consist of questions or statements to which individuals respond in various ways. Examples are the MMPI and the MCMI (Millon Clinical Multiaxial Inventory).
- **What are projective tests of personality?** Such tests present individuals with ambiguous stimuli—stimuli such as inkblots or scenes interpreted in many different ways. People's responses to these stimuli are assumed to reflect various aspects of their personalities.

KEY TERMS

MMPI, p. 493 • Millon Clinical Multiaxial Inventory (MCMI), p. 494 • NEO Personality Inventory (NEO-PI), p. 494 • Rorschach test, p. 495

Key Aspects of Personality: A Sample of Recent Research

- **How do persons high in self-esteem differ from those low in self-esteem?** Persons high in self-esteem often perform better on many tasks, are healthier, and are more confident in social situations.
- **What are the characteristics of low self-monitors and high self-monitors?** Low self-monitors tend to regulate their behavior on the basis of internal factors such as attitudes and values; they are highly consistent across situations. In contrast, high self-monitors tend to regulate their behavior to match the requirements of each new situation; as a result, they tend to show lower consistency.
- **What is sensation seeking, and how does it influence behavior?** Sensation seeking involves individual differences in the tendency to seek out intense and novel experiences. High sensation seekers engage in more high-risk behaviors than low sensation seekers. In addition, they show stronger orienting responses, are better able to focus their attention to new stimuli, and may handle stressful life events better than low sensation seekers.
- **How can cultural factors influence responses to personality inventories?** Individuals from different cultures have been found to differ in their tendency to use the extreme responses to items on such inventories—the "strongly agree" or "strongly disagree" responses.

KEY TERMS

self-esteem, p. 496 • social comparison, p. 496 • self-monitoring, p. 496 • sensation seeking, p. 497

Critical Thinking Questions

Appraisal

While many people do tend to show consistency in their behavior, some do not. Does this mean that the concept of personality is applicable only to people who show consistency in their behavior over time and across situations?

Controversy

Growing evidence indicates that some aspects of personality are influenced by genetic factors. Does this mean that personality can't be changed? Or, even if genetic factors *do* play a role, do you think that personality remains open to change throughout life?

Making Psychology Part of Your Life

Different jobs and careers seem to require different traits for success. For example, being a successful salesperson seems to require a high degree of sensitivity to others, so high self-monitors might be more successful in this kind of job than low self-monitors. Similarly, being a good accountant requires a high degree of neatness and organization, so people high on these dimensions would probably excel. Taking your own personality into account, can you think of careers for which you are, or are not, personally suited? How do your current career plans fit with your conclusions?

CHAPTER OUTLINE

Health, Stress, and Coping

In health, behavior counts. So say scientists responsible for the *Human Capital Initiative*—an ambitious research agenda proposed by behavioral researchers and aimed at developing solutions to significant health-related problems in this country (American Psychological Society, 1996). The main point of this statement, of course, is that the actions that people take—or fail to take—contribute to whether they remain healthy or, potentially, develop a serious illness. Thus, getting people to embrace healthy behaviors can help them protect their health and can reduce the effects of diseases they cannot avoid. In a sense, then, our health is intimately linked to our behavior and the choices we make.

The recognition that the health of its citizens is, in certain respects, its most valuable asset led the U.S. government to announce a set of health-related goals for the nation in a document entitled *Healthy People 2000* (United States Department of Health and Human Services, 1991). This report outlined three broad national health goals for the United States during the 1990s: (1) increasing the span of healthy life among Americans; (2) reducing disparities in health status that currently exist among certain groups, such as children, the poor, and the elderly; and (3) making preventive health care services accessible to all Americans. Although we have not yet achieved these goals, people are becoming aware of the importance of good health and the value of taking the necessary steps to ensure it (National Center for Health Statistics, 1996). Many of us try to eat healthy foods, refrain from smoking, drink alcohol only in moderation, and engage in regular physical exercise. Psychologists, too, have become increasingly interested in the issue of personal health and have made it the focus of a growing volume of research. This certainly seems appropriate. After all, mental health has always been a central topic in psychology, and it is increasingly clear that mental and physical health are intimately linked.

Our health is intimately linked to our behavior and the choices we make.

In this chapter we'll explore important ways in which we can apply our knowledge of mind–body interactions to promote health and wellness. We'll begin by considering the exciting branch of psychology known as *health psychology.* The primary aim of health psychology is to identify important relationships between psychological variables and health (Gatchel, Baum, & Krantz, 1989; Matarazzo, 1980). We'll also discuss the methods health psychologists use to study these relationships. Second, we'll consider the nature of *stress,* a major health-related problem in the hectic 1990s. We'll focus on both the causes of stress and some of its major effects—how it influences health and performance. Next, we'll consider how some of our *beliefs and attitudes* influence the way we interpret certain health symptoms—and thus affect our willingness to seek medical assistance. Fourth, we'll look at *behaviors* that can directly affect our risk of contracting certain lifestyle-related illnesses, such as cancer, cardiovascular diseases, and AIDS. Finally, we'll consider various ways in which psychologists work to promote personal health by encouraging healthy lifestyles.

Health Psychology: An Overview

Health Psychology: The study of the relation between psychological variables and health; reflects the view that both mind and body are important determinants of health and illness.

Health psychology, the branch of psychology that studies the relation between psychological variables and health, reflects the view that both mind and body are important determinants of health and illness (Feuerstein, Labbé, & Kuczmierczyk, 1986). Specifically, health psychologists believe that our beliefs, attitudes, and behavior contribute significantly to the onset or prevention of illness (Engel, 1980). A closely related field, known as *behavioral medicine,* combines behavioral and biomedical knowledge for the prevention and treatment of disorders ordinarily thought of as being within the domain of medicine (Epstein, 1992).

Health psychology and behavioral medicine have experienced tremendous growth since their beginnings in the early 1970s. Perhaps the most fundamental reason for the increased interest in health psychology and behavioral medicine is the dramatic shift observed in the leading causes of death during this century. In 1900, many of the leading causes of death in the United States could be traced to infectious diseases such as influenza, and tuberculosis. However, the development of antibiotics and vaccines and improved sanitation practices have significantly reduced these health threats, at least in this country.

Lifestyle: In the context of health psychology, the overall pattern of decisions and behaviors that determine health and quality of life.

As shown in Table 13.1, the current leading causes of death are attributable to **lifestyle** factors: the overall pattern of decisions and behaviors that determine a person's health and quality of life (Lalonde, 1974). This fact suggests that psychologists, now more than ever, can make a difference in people's quality of life by helping them to eliminate behaviors that lead to illness and to adopt behaviors that lead to wellness. Indeed, a majority of the conditions that now constitute the leading causes of death (Table 13.1) could be prevented if people would eat nutritious foods, reduce their alcohol consumption, practice safe sex, eliminate smoking, and exercise regularly. One encouraging sign is the observation that death rates from lifestyle-related diseases—with the exception of deaths from smoking—actually decreased during the 1980s (United States Department of Health and Human Services, 1991). In the Research Methods section on page 506, we'll consider the research methods that health psychologists use to study important aspects of health-related behaviors.

Key Questions

- What is health psychology?
- What is the field of behavioral medicine?
- To what can we attribute today's leading causes of death in the United States?
- What are epidemiological studies? (see p. 506)

Table 13.1

Leading Causes of Death in the United States in 1990

As shown here, many important causes of death are related to lifestyle. Thus, healthy life can be extended by changes in behavior.

Causes of Death	Number of Yearly Deaths
Heart Disease	720,058
Cancer	550,322
Cerebrovascular Disease (e.g., stroke)	144,088
Unintentional Injuries	92,983
Chronic Lung Disease	86,679
Pneumonia and Influenza	79,513
Diabetes	47,664
Suicide	30,906
Liver Disease/Cirrhosis	25,815
HIV Infection	25,188

(**Source:** Based on information from McGinnis, 1994.)

RESEARCH METHODS

How Psychologists Study Health-Related Behavior

Interest in health psychology has increased dramatically during the past decade, fueled in part by the exciting discovery that basic psychological concepts help us understand how people deal with health challenges. By applying these basic concepts, psychologists have learned a great deal about how people's knowledge, beliefs, and actions contribute to good health. As you might expect, health psychologists devote much of their efforts to designing interventions to encourage behaviors that make people healthy and to discourage ones that make them sick. These efforts have paid off. Now more than ever, people are aware of the important links between their behavior and their health. And more importantly, they are taking the necessary steps to improve their health.

Much of the basic knowledge that we have obtained about the factors that lead to good or poor health has emerged from **epidemiological studies**—large-scale attempts to identify *risk factors* that predict the development of certain diseases (Winett, 1995). Why are epidemiological studies important? There are actually several reasons. One has to do with the complexity of certain forms of illness; lifestyle diseases often have multiple causes. For example, a large body of evidence has confirmed that the development of heart disease—the single biggest killer of people in the United States—results from a combination of biological, behavioral, and environmental factors.

A second reason epidemiological studies are important has to do with their scope. Epidemiological research often involves the study of thousands of people across lengthy periods of time. Data obtained through this approach help explain why certain groups are more at risk for acquiring some diseases than others. For example, it was epidemiological studies that first alerted scientists that the groups most likely to engage in unprotected sex and intravenous drug use are also most at risk of acquiring HIV, the virus that causes AIDS.

Finally, and perhaps most importantly, the results of epidemiological studies have highlighted patterns of correlation that exist between people's behaviors and important health outcomes. The clues provided by these patterns are useful in the development of interventions that promote good health.

One of the best-known examples of this kind of research was a classic decade-long study conducted in Alameda County, California (Wiley & Camacho, 1980). In this study the researchers asked a large group of adults whether they followed certain health practices, including sleeping seven to eight hours each night, eating breakfast regularly, refraining from smoking, drinking alcohol in moderation or not at all, maintaining their weight within normal limits, and exercising regularly. The Alameda county study yielded the following results: Participants who reported practicing all or most of these behaviors were much less likely to die during the study period than those who practiced few or none of these behaviors. Please note that these results are based on correlations and therefore are not conclusive (refer to Chapter 1). However, they are important in that they highlight the intimate connection between lifestyle and good health. As you proceed through this chapter, I hope that you'll note that many of the findings you'll encounter have emerged from basic epidemiological research.

Stress: Its Causes, Effects, and Control

Epidemiological Studies: Large-scale research conducted to identify risk factors that predict the development of certain diseases.

Stress: Our response to events that disrupt, or threaten to disrupt, our physical or psychological functioning.

Have you ever felt that you were right at the edge of being overwhelmed by negative events in your life? Or felt so overwhelmed that you just gave up? If so, you are already quite familiar with **stress:** our response to events that disrupt, or threaten to disrupt, our physical or psychological functioning (Lazarus & Folkman, 1984; Taylor, 1991). Unfortunately, stress is a common part of life in the 1990s—something few of us can avoid altogether. Partly for this reason, and partly because it seems to exert negative effects on both physical health and psychological well-being, stress has become an important topic of research in psychology. Let's examine the basic nature of stress and some of its major causes.

Stress: Its Basic Nature

Stress is a many-faceted process that occurs in reaction to events or situations in our environment termed **stressors.** An interesting feature of stress is the wide range of physical and psychological reactions that different people have to the same event; some may interpret an event as stressful, whereas others simply take it in stride. Moreover, a particular person may react quite differently to the same stressor at different points in time.

Stressors: The Activators of Stress What are stressors? Although we normally think of stress as stemming from negative events in our lives, positive events such as getting married or receiving an unexpected job promotion can also produce stress (Brown & McGill, 1989). Despite the wide range of stimuli that can potentially produce stress, it appears that many events we find stressful share several characteristics: (1) They are so intense that they produce a state of overload—we can no longer adapt to them. (2) They evoke incompatible tendencies in us, such as tendencies both to approach and to avoid some object or activity. (3) They are uncontrollable—beyond our limits of control. Indeed, a great deal of evidence suggests that when people can predict, control, or terminate an aversive event or situation, they perceive it to be less stressful than when they feel less in control (Karasek & Theorell, 1990; Rodin & Salovey, 1989).

Physiological Responses to Stressors When exposed to stressors, we generally experience many physiological reactions. If you've been caught off-guard by someone who appears out of nowhere and grabs you while yelling "Gotcha," then you are probably familiar with some common physical reactions to stress. Initially, your blood pressure soars, your pulse races, and you may even begin to sweat. These are part of a general pattern of reactions referred to as the *fight-or-flight syndrome,* a process controlled through the sympathetic nervous system. As we saw in Chapter 2, the sympathetic nervous system prepares our bodies for immediate action. Usually these responses are brief, and we soon return to normal levels. When we are exposed to chronic sources of stress, however, this reaction is only the first in a longer sequence of responses activated by our efforts to adapt to a stressor. This sequence, termed by Hans Selye (1976) the **general adaptation syndrome (GAS)**, consists of three stages, as shown in Figure 13.1 on page 508.

The first stage of the GAS is *alarm,* in which the body mobilizes itself for immediate action; arousal of the sympathetic nervous system releases hormones that help prepare the body to meet threats or dangers (Selye, 1976). If stress is prolonged, however, the *resistance* stage begins. During this second stage, arousal is lower than during the alarm stage, but our bodies continue to draw on resources at an above-normal rate in order to cope effectively with the stressor. But continued exposure to the same stressor or additional stressors drains the body of its resources and leads to the third stage, *exhaustion* (refer to Figure 13.1). During this stage our capacity to resist is depleted, and our susceptibility to illness increases. In severe cases of prolonged physical stress, the result can be death.

Cognitive Appraisal of Our Stressors Selye's general adaptation syndrome provides a framework for understanding our physiological responses to stressful events and suggests at least one reasonable explanation for the relation between stress and illness. Few experts would disagree that chronic stress can lead to a lowered resistance to disease. However, a critical weakness with Selye's model is that it fails to consider how cognitive processes help determine whether we *interpret* a specific event as stressful.

Stressors: Events or situations in our environment that cause stress.

General Adaptation Syndrome (GAS): A three-stage profile of response to stress: (1) alarm, or general mobilization; (2) resistance, during which an organism makes efforts to cope; and (3) if the organism fails to overcome the threat and depletes its coping resources, exhaustion.

FIGURE 13.1

Selye's General Adaptation Syndrome Model

According to Hans Selye (shown here), the body's reaction to prolonged stress progresses through three stages: alarm, resistance, and finally exhaustion.

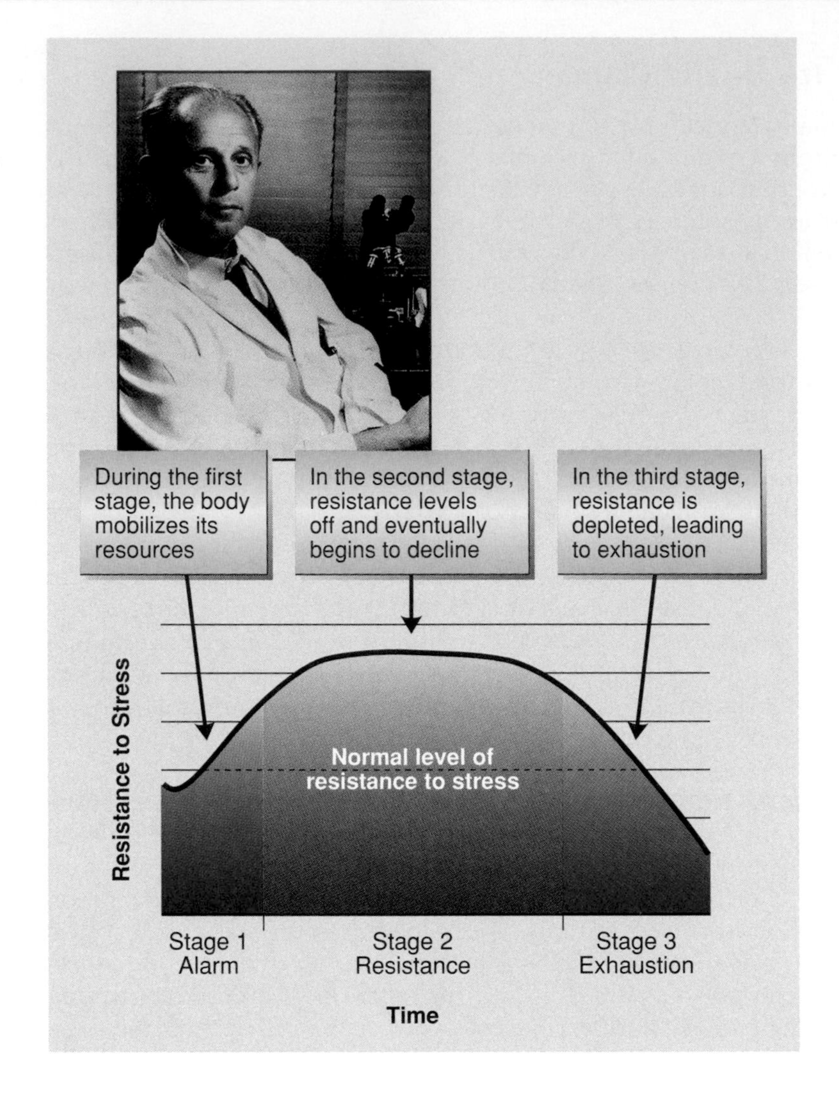

The importance of these processes is made clear by the following fact: When confronted with the same potentially stress-inducing situation, some persons experience psychological stress, whereas others do not. Why? One reason involves individuals' cognitive appraisals (see Figure 13.2). In simple terms, psychological stress occurs only to the extent that the persons involved perceive (1) that the situation is somehow threatening to their important goals (often described as *primary appraisal*) and (2) that they will be unable to cope with these dangers or demands (often described as *secondary appraisal*) (Croyle, 1992; Lazarus & Folkman, 1984).

A study of the cognitive appraisal process by Tomaka and his colleagues (1993) may help illustrate this point. Participants in this study were told that the researchers were interested in measuring their physiological responses (heart rate, pulse) while they performed a mental task: counting backward from 2,737 by sevens—that is, 2,730, 2,723, 2,716, and so on. Just before the participants began counting, the researchers assessed their primary and secondary appraisals of the task. They assessed primary appraisals by asking them, "How threatening do you expect the upcoming task to be?" They assessed secondary appraisals by asking, "How able are you to cope with this task?" The researchers predicted that persons who felt they could *not* successfully perform the task would perceive it as threatening ("threat group") and would therefore experience psychological stress. In contrast, they reasoned, persons who were more confident in their abilities might perceive the task as a challenge ("challenge group"); while these persons would

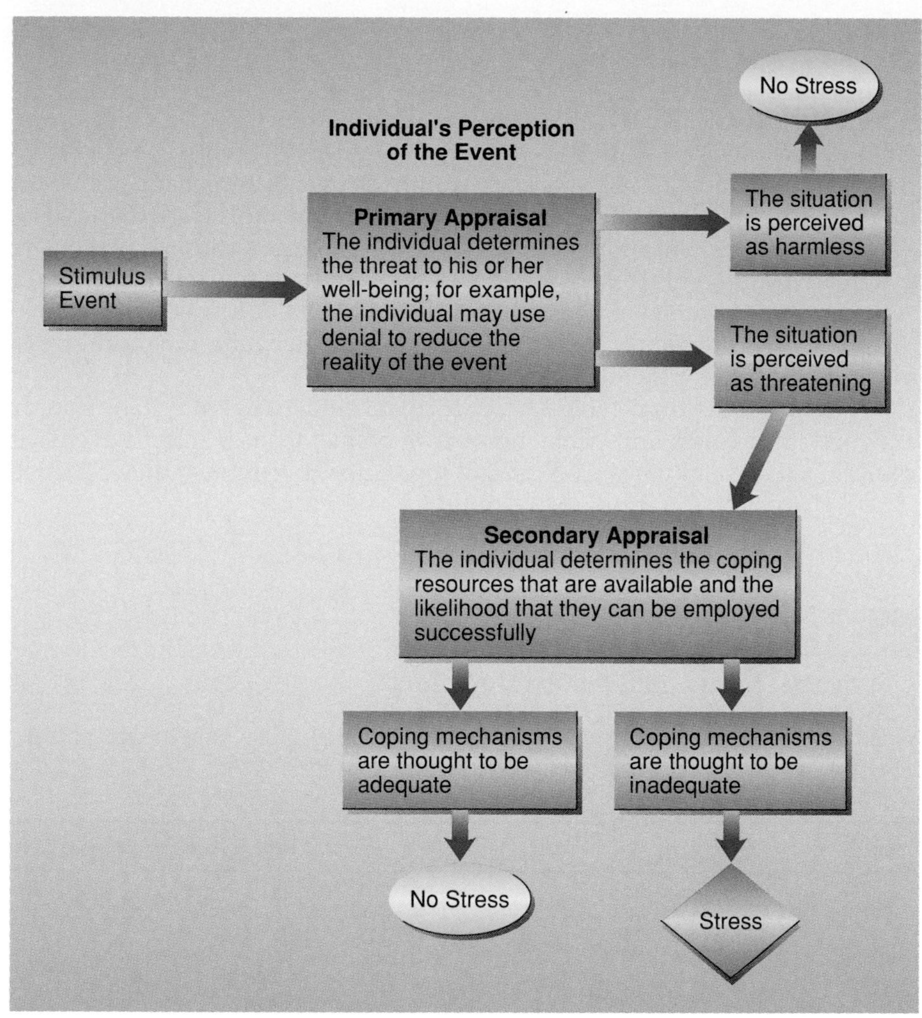

(**Source**: Based on data from Hingson et al., 1990.)

FIGURE 13.2

Stress: The Role of Cognitive Appraisals

The amount of psychological stress you experience depends in part on your cognitive appraisals of the event or situation—the extent to which you perceive it as threatening and perceive that you will be unable to cope with it.

not experience psychological stress, they would in fact exhibit greater *physiological* arousal as they prepared to meet the challenge. All predictions were confirmed. Participants in the threat group reported *feeling* greater stress, while participants in the challenge group actually showed greater physiological arousal. Moreover, the challenge group scored higher on both perceived and actual measures of performance.

Additional research suggests that other cognitive factors also play a role in our interpretation of potentially stressful events, including our observation of the reactions of those around us and the extent of our memories of similar situations (Mendolia & Kleck, 1993; Tomaka et al., 1993). In short, these results and the results of related research provide evidence for the important role of cognitive and social processes in shaping our responses to stress. We'll turn next to some of the causes of stress.

Key Questions

- What is stress, and what are stressors?
- What is the GAS model?
- What determines whether we will interpret an event as stressful or as a challenge?

Stress: Some Major Causes

What factors contribute to stress? Unfortunately, the list is a long one. A wide range of conditions and evènts seem capable of generating such feelings. Among the most important stressors are major negative life events, such as the death of a loved one or a painful divorce; the all-too-frequent minor hassles of everyday life; and conditions and events relating to one's job or career.

Stressful Life Events Death of a spouse, injury to one's child, war, failure in school or at work, an unplanned pregnancy—unless we lead truly charmed lives, most of us experience traumatic events and changes at some time or other. What are their effects on us? This question was first investigated by Holmes and Rahe (1967), who asked a large group of persons to assign arbitrary points (to a maximum of one hundred) to various life events according to how much readjustment each had required. It was reasoned that the greater the number of points assigned to a given event, the more stressful the event was for the persons experiencing it.

As you can see from Table 13.2, participants in Holmes and Rahe's study assigned the greatest unit value (number of points) to such serious events as death of a spouse, divorce, and marital separation. In contrast, they assigned

Table 13.2

Life Events, Stress, and Personal Health

When individuals experience stressful life events such as those near the top of this list, their health often suffers. The greater the unit value (number of points) assigned to each event, the more stressful it is perceived as being.

Rank	Life Event	Life Change Unit Value
1	Death of spouse	100
2	Divorce	73
3	Marital separation	65
4	Jail term	63
5	Death of close family member	63
6	Personal injury or illness	53
7	Marriage	50
8	Getting fired at work	47
9	Marital reconciliation	45
10	Retirement	45
11	Change in health of family member	44
12	Pregnancy	40
13	Sex difficulties	39
14	Gain of new family member	39
15	Business readjustment	39
16	Change in financial state	38
17	Death of close friend	37
18	Change to different line of work	36
19	Change in number of arguments with spouse	35
20	Taking out mortgage for major purchase (e.g., home)	31
21	Foreclosure of mortgage or loan	30
22	Change in responsibilities at work	29

(Continued)

much fewer points to such events as change in residence, vacation, and minor violations of the law, such as a parking ticket.

Holmes and Rahe (1967) then related the total number of "stress points" accumulated by individuals during a single year to changes in their personal health. The results were dramatic—and did much to stir psychologists' interest in the effects of stress. The greater the number of stress points people accumulated, the greater was their likelihood of becoming seriously ill.

In a related study, Cohen, Tyrrell, and Smith (1993) asked volunteers to report stressful events that had affected them negatively during the previous year. Then the researchers gave one group of these persons nose drops containing a virus that causes the common cold. (A control group received uncontaminated nose drops.) The results? Volunteers who reported two or more negative life events during the previous year and felt that they were under a lot of stress were more likely to develop a cold than less stressed volunteers who had experienced fewer than two negative life events.

This picture is complicated, however, by the existence of large differences in individuals' ability to withstand the impact of stress (Oulette-Kobasa & Puccetti, 1983). While some persons suffer ill effects after exposure to a few mildly stressful events, others remain healthy even after prolonged exposure to high levels of stress; they are described as being *stress-resistant* or *hardy.* I'll return to such differences later in this chapter. For the moment, I wish merely to emphasize the fact that in general, the greater the number of stressful life

Rank	Life Event	Life Change Unit Value
23	Son or daughter leaving home	29
24	Trouble with inlaws	29
25	Outstanding personal achievement	28
26	Wife beginning or stopping work	26
27	Beginning or ending school	26
28	Change in living conditions	25
29	Revision of personal habits	24
30	Trouble with boss	23
31	Change in work hours or conditions	20
32	Change in residence	20
33	Change in schools	20
34	Change in recreation	19
35	Change in church activities	19
36	Change in social activities	18
37	Taking out a loan for a lesser purchase (e.g., car or TV)	17
38	Change in sleeping habits	16
39	Change in number of family get-togethers	15
40	Change in eating habits	15
41	Vacation	13
42	Christmas	12
43	Minor violation of the law	11

(**Source**: Based on data from Holmes & Masuda, 1974.)

Hassles: Annoying minor events of everyday life that cumulatively can affect psychological well-being.

events experienced by an individual, the greater the likelihood that the person's subsequent health will be adversely affected (Rowlison & Felner, 1988).

The Hassles of Daily Life While certain events, such as the death of someone close to us, are clearly stressful, they occur relatively infrequently. Does this mean that people's lives are mostly a serene lake of tranquility? Hardly. As you know, daily life is filled with countless minor sources of stress—**hassles**—that seem to make up for their relatively low intensity by their high frequency. That such daily hassles are an important cause of stress is suggested by the findings of several studies by Lazarus and his colleagues (DeLongis, Folkman, & Lazarus, 1988; Kanner et al., 1981; Lazarus et al., 1985). These researchers developed a Hassles Scale on which individuals indicate the extent to which they have been "hassled" by common events during the past month. The items included in this scale deal with a wide range of everyday events, such as having too many things to do at once, shopping, and concerns over money. While such events may seem relatively minor when compared with the life changes studied by Holmes and Rahe (1967), they appear to have important effects. When scores on the Hassles Scale are related to reports of psychological symptoms, strong positive correlations are obtained (Lazarus et al., 1985). In short, the more stress people report as a result of daily hassles, the poorer their psychological well-being.

Some research on this topic indicates that while major life events can exert adverse effects on health, the more minor hassles of everyday life—perhaps because of their frequent, repetitive nature—may actually prove more important in this respect for many people. New evidence, however, suggests that certain major life events may actually be more harmful than was previously suspected. Highly stressful events may exert their harmful effects by creating a ripple effect of minor problems. In other words, after the initial distress attributable to the major event has subsided, a series of minor stressors may lie in its wake. Additional evidence suggests that major life events may also sensitize people to minor hassles, further increasing their potentially harmful effects (Wagner, Compas, & Howell, 1988).

To illustrate how this might work, let's consider a recent study conducted by Pillow, Zautra, and Sandler (1996). These researchers interviewed people who had and who had not recently experienced a traumatic life event, such as the death of a spouse, a divorce, or a health problem with their child. They interviewed each participant to determine the numbers and types of minor stressors they experienced subsequent to the traumatic event. The results indicated that a greater number of minor stressors were reported by participants who had recently experienced a traumatic life event than by participants who had not (see Figure 13.3). Further, each type of life event was associated with a consistent pattern of hassles. For example, divorced participants seemed to experience stress over finances, transportation, personal relationships, and work. In contrast, participants who had recently lost their spouse were more likely to report problems with their health. Let's turn now to a discussion of the effects of work-related stress.

Work-Related Stress Most adults spend more time at work than in any other single activity. It is not surprising, then, that jobs or careers are a central source of stress. Some of the factors producing stress in work settings are obvious; for example, blatant sexual harassment, discrimination, or extreme *overload*—being asked to do too much in too short a time. Interestingly, being asked to do too little can also cause stress. Such *underload* produces intense feelings of boredom, and these, in turn, can be very stressful.

Several other factors that play a role in work-related stress may be less apparent. One of these is *role conflict*—being the target of conflicting demands or expectations from different groups of people. For example, consider the

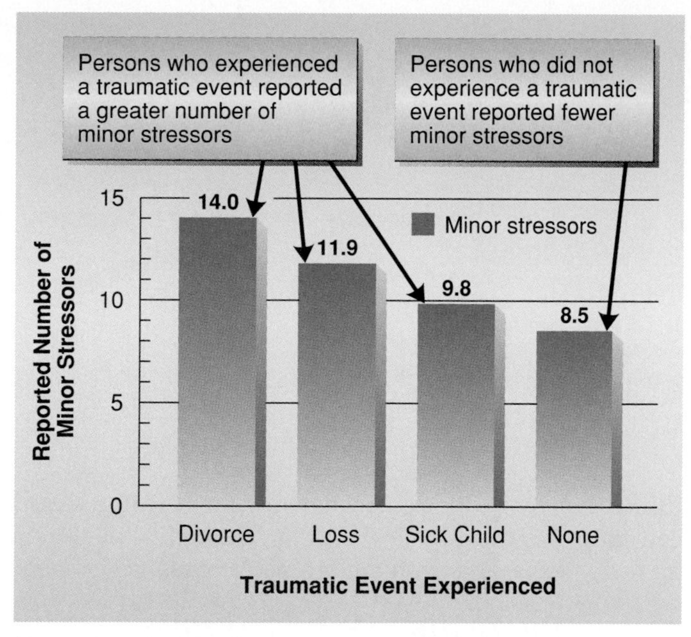

(**Source:** Based on data from Pillow et al., 1996.)

FIGURE 13.3

Sensitization to Daily Hassles

A greater number of minor stressors (hassles) were reported by participants who had recently experienced a traumatic life event than by participants who had not.

plight of many beginning managers. Their subordinates often expect such persons to go to bat for them with the company to improve their work assignments, pay, and conditions. In contrast, the managers' own bosses often expect them to do the opposite: somehow to induce the employees to work harder for fewer rewards. The result: a stressful situation for the managers.

Another work-related factor that can sometimes generate intense levels of stress involves *performance appraisals,* the procedures used for evaluating employees' performance. If employees perceive these as fair, employee stress tends to be low; if employees view them as arbitrary or unfair, stress is almost certain to be high. After all, no one wants to feel that rewards such as raises, promotions, or bonuses are being distributed in an unjust manner. Additional factors that have been found to contribute to stress at work are summarized in Figure 13.4 on page 514.

Can anything be done to reduce stress at work? Fortunately, several lines of research suggest that the answer is yes. First, employers can reduce workplace stress by considering the **person–environment (P–E) fit** (Edwards & Harrison, 1993)—the match between a person and his or her work environment. Mismatches between characteristics of workers and characteristics of their jobs or work environments are associated with increases in stress-related illnesses (Harrison, 1985). Second, sources of social support—the advice and help of others, both on and off the job—can serve as a buffer against stressful situations at work (Landsbergis et al., 1992; Uchino et al., 1996). Finally, companies can help reduce the potential negative effects of unavoidable workplace stress by implementing interventions to improve their employees' ability to cope with workplace stress and change unhealthy practices that can intensify the effects of stress (Maturi, 1992).

Key Questions

- What are some of the most important stressors?
- What are some sources of work-related stress?
- What is the person–environment fit, and why is it important?

Person–Environment (P–E) Fit: The appropriateness of the fit, or match, between a person and his or her work environment; a poor P–E fit may produce stress.

Stress: Some Major Effects

By now you may be convinced that stress stems from many different sources and exerts important effects on persons who experience it. What is sometimes

FIGURE 13.4

Sources of Work-Related Stress

Many factors contribute to stress at work. Several of the most important are summarized here.

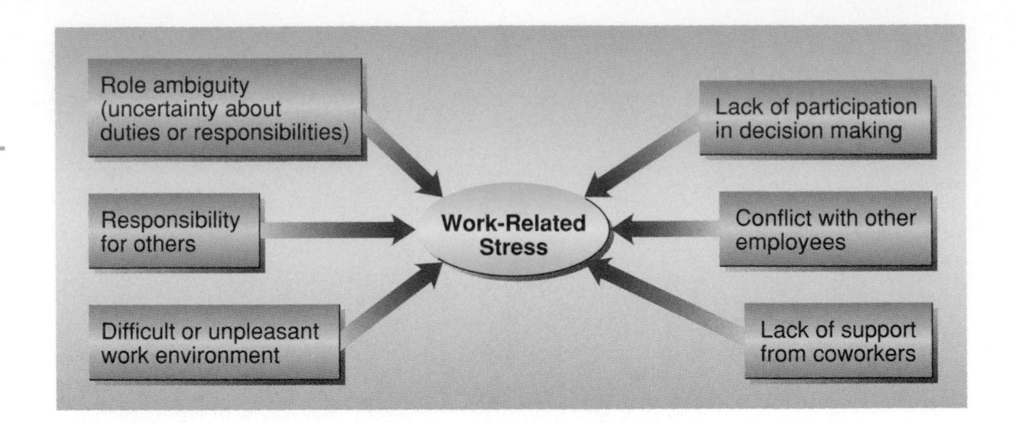

difficult to grasp, though, is just how far-reaching these effects can be. Stress can influence our physical and psychological well-being, our performance on many tasks, and even the ultimate course of our careers.

Stress and Health: The Silent Killer The link between stress and personal health, according to medical experts, is very strong (Kiecolt-Glaser & Glaser, 1992). Some authorities estimate that stress plays some role in 50 to 70 percent of all physical illness (Frese, 1985). Moreover, included in these percentages are some of the most serious and life-threatening ailments known to medical science. To list just a few, stress has been implicated in the occurrence of heart disease, high blood pressure, hardening of the arteries, and even diabetes.

How does stress produce such effects? The mechanisms involved remain to be determined precisely, but growing evidence suggests that the process goes something like this: By draining our resources and keeping us off balance physiologically, stress upsets our complex internal chemistry. In particular, it may interfere with efficient operation of our *immune system*—the mechanism through which our bodies recognize and destroy potentially harmful substances and intruders such as bacteria, viruses, and cancerous cells. Foreign substances that enter our bodies are known as *antigens.* When they appear, certain types of white blood cells (lymphocytes) begin to multiply. These attack the antigens, often destroying them by engulfing them. Other white blood cells produce antibodies, chemical substances that combine with antigens and so neutralize them. When functioning normally, the immune system is nothing short of amazing: Each day it removes or destroys many potential threats to our health.

Unfortunately, prolonged stress seems to disrupt this system. In studies with animals, subjects exposed to inescapable shocks demonstrate reduced production of lymphocytes relative to subjects exposed to shocks from which they could escape (Ader & Cohen, 1984). Studies of the effects of stress on animals and humans suggest that a variety of stressors, including disruptions in interpersonal relationships, loneliness, academic pressure, daily hassles, and the lack of social support, can interfere with our immune systems (Cohen et al., 1992; Jemmott & Magloire, 1988; Levy et al., 1989).

For example, in one study, Cohen and his colleagues (1992) assessed the effects of social support on the immune systems of monkeys. During the year preceding the study, a group of monkeys lived in stable (unchanging) social conditions. When the study began, however, they were randomly assigned to live in either a stable or an unstable social condition for the next twenty-six months. Monkeys in the stable group lived in the same environment through the entire study period. In the unstable condition, however, social groups were disrupted and reorganized frequently. The researchers then observed and assessed the amount of time the monkeys in each group spent in various forms of social interaction, including affiliative behaviors such as engaging in passive physical contact and grooming with other group members. Why were the researchers interested in observing affiliative behaviors? They reasoned that if social support serves as a stress buffer, then the monkeys in the unstable group that engaged in the least amount of affiliative behaviors would experience the greatest negative impact on measures of immune functions. The results of the experiment confirmed these predictions. In short, social support may be an important buffer against the adverse effects of chronic stress.

These results are relevant to people, too. Persons who are divorced or separated from their spouses often experience reduced functioning in certain aspects of their immune system, compared to individuals who are happily married (Kiecolt-Glaser et al., 1987, 1988). Additionally, some recent evidence suggests that the effects of stress on our immune system may be less for people who have effective ways of dealing with their stressors than for those who do not. Some research shows that optimism, regular exercise, and feelings of control over stressful events are associated with reduced suppression of our immune system under stress (Taylor, 1991). All in all, findings on stress and health are both unsettling and encouraging. On the one hand, they suggest that our complex, high-stress lifestyles may be undermining our ability to resist many serious forms of illness, at least to a degree. On the other hand, they indicate that reducing stress through various strategies and coping methods may be beneficial to our health.

Stress and Task Performance Psychologists once believed that stress actually improves performance on a wide range of tasks. They held that the relationship between stress and task performance takes the form of an upside-down U: At first, performance improves as stress increases, presumably because the stress is arousing or energizing. Beyond some point, though, stress becomes distracting and performance actually drops.

While this relationship may hold true under some conditions, growing evidence suggests that even low or moderate levels of stress can interfere with task performance (Motowidlo, Packard, & Manning, 1986; Steers, 1984). There are several reasons why this is so. First, even relatively mild stress can be distracting. People experiencing stress may focus on the unpleasant feelings and emotions it involves, rather than on the task at hand. Second, prolonged or repeated exposure to even mild levels of stress may exert harmful effects on health, and this may interfere with effective performance. Finally, a large body of research indicates that as arousal increases, task performance may rise at first, but that at some point it falls (Berlyne, 1967). The precise location of this turning, or *inflection,* point seems to depend to an important extent on the complexity of the task performed. The greater the complexity, the lower the level of arousal at which the downturn in performance occurs. Many observers believe that the tasks performed by today's working people are more complex than those in the past (Mitchell & Larson, 1987). For this reason, even relatively low levels of stress may interfere with performance in today's complex work world.

However, stress does not always produce adverse effects. For example, people sometimes do seem to rise to the occasion and turn in sterling performances at times when stress is intense. Perhaps the most reasonable conclusion, then, is that while stress can interfere with task performance in many situations, its precise effects depend on many different factors, such as the complexity of the task being performed and personal characteristics of the individuals involved. As a result, generalizations about the impact of stress on work effectiveness should be made with considerable caution.

Burnout: When Stress Consumes Most jobs engender at least some stress. Yet somehow the persons performing them manage to cope; they continue to function despite their daily encounters with various stressors. Some individuals, though, are not so lucky. Over time, they seem to be worn down (or out) by repeated stress. Such persons are said to be suffering from *burnout*, and they show several distinctive characteristics (Maslach, 1982; Lee & Ashforth, 1996).

First, people experiencing burnout often suffer from *physical exhaustion*. They have low energy and always feel tired. In addition, they report symptoms of physical strain, such as frequent headaches, nausea, poor sleep, and changes in eating habits. Second, they experience *emotional exhaustion*. Depression, feelings of hopelessness, and feelings of being trapped in their job are all part of the picture. Third, persons suffering from burnout often show *mental* or *attitudinal exhaustion*, often known as depersonalization. They become cynical, hold negative attitudes toward others, and tend to derogate themselves, their jobs, and life in general. Finally, they often report feelings of *low personal accomplishment* (Maslach & Jackson, 1984)—feelings that they haven't been able to accomplish much in the past and probably won't be successful in the future, either. Studies conducted in work settings (Lee & Ashforth, 1990, 1996) seem to confirm that these factors, summarized in Figure 13.5, provide an accurate description of burnout.

What are the causes of burnout? The primary factor is prolonged stress; but other factors, too, seem to play a role. Burnout seems to occur when certain valued resources are lost, and/or when existing resources are inadequate to meet demands or do not yield the anticipated returns (Lee & Ashforth, 1996). Job conditions implying that one's efforts are useless, ineffective, or unappreciated also contribute to burnout (Jackson, Schwab, & Schuler, 1986). In particular, such conditions contribute to the feelings of low personal accomplishment that are an important part of burnout. Finally, poor opportunities for promotion and the presence of inflexible rules and procedures often lead individuals to feel that they are trapped in an unfair system and to develop negative views of their jobs (Gaines & Jermier, 1983).

Whatever the precise causes of burnout, burned-out people generally seem either to change jobs or to withdraw psychologically, marking time until

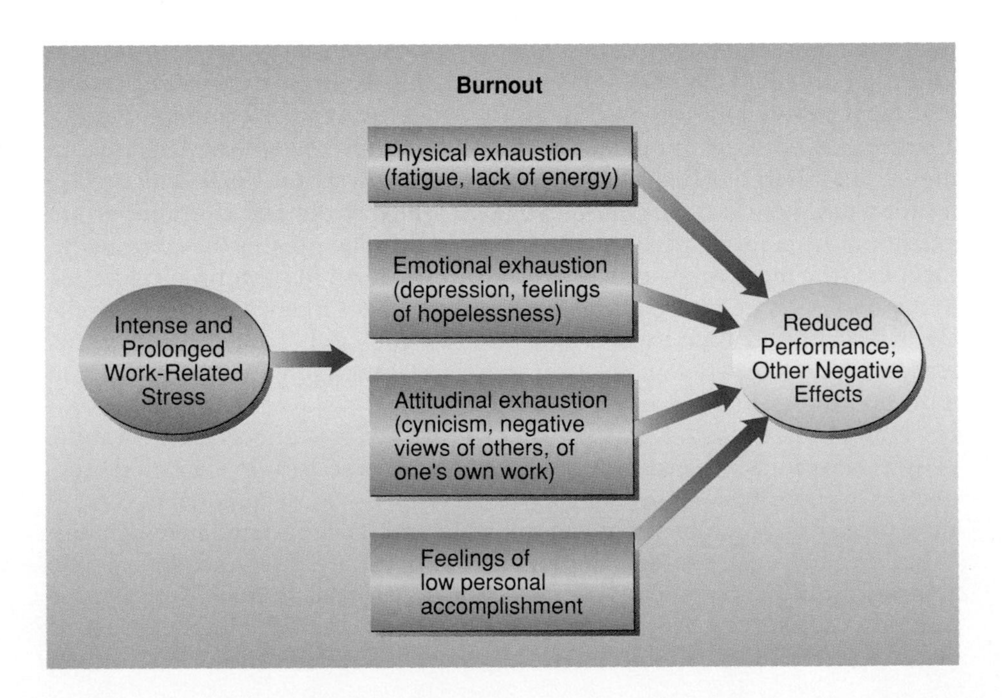

FIGURE 13.5

Burnout: An Overview

Individuals who experience high levels of work-related stress over long periods of time may suffer from burnout. This state involves physical, mental, and attitudinal exhaustion as well as feelings of low personal accomplishment.

retirement. Fortunately, however, the effects of burnout can be overcome. With appropriate help, burned-out individuals can recover from their physical and psychological exhaustion. If ongoing stress is reduced, if people gain added support from friends and coworkers, and if they cultivate hobbies and other outside interests, some people can return to positive attitudes and high levels of productivity.

Individual Differences in Resistance to Stress: Optimism, Pessimism, and Hardiness It is clear that individuals differ in their resistance to stress. Some people seem to be disease-prone—they suffer ill effects from even mild levels of stress. Other people, sometimes referred to as *self-healers*, are able to function effectively even in the face of intense, ongoing stress (Friedman, Hawley, & Tucker, 1994). How do such persons differ?

One answer involves the dimension of *optimism–pessimism*. Optimists are people who see the glass as half full; pessimists are those who see it as half empty. Some evidence indicates that optimists—people who have general expectancies for good outcomes (Scheier & Carver, 1988)—seem to be much more stress-resistant than pessimists—people who have general expectancies for poor outcomes. For example, optimists are much less likely than pessimists to report physical illnesses and symptoms during highly stressful periods such as final exams. Additional evidence helps explain why this is the case. Briefly, optimists and pessimists seem to adopt different tactics for coping with stress (Scheier & Carver, 1992). Optimists concentrate on problem-focused coping: making and enacting specific plans for dealing with sources of stress. They also seek and obtain social support (Carver et al., 1993). In contrast, pessimists tend to adopt different strategies, such as giving up the goal with which stress is interfering or denying that the stress exists (Scheier, Weintraub, & Carver, 1986). Needless to say, the former strategies are often more effective than the latter—although *flexibility* seems to be the key. That is, problem-focused coping is associated with more positive outcomes when the source of the stress is controllable, but with poorer outcomes when it is not (Lester, Smart, & Baum, 1994). Table 13.3 on page 518 presents different strategies adopted by optimists and pessimists.

Some evidence indicates that men and women, too, differ in their choices of coping strategies. Studies have reported that men engage in more problem-focused coping and that females tend more to seek social support from friends or to engage in emotion-focused strategies. These findings have been attributed to the different ways men and women are taught to cope with stress (Ptacek, Smith, & Dodge, 1994). A recent study by Porter and Stone (1995), however, seems to cast doubt on these conclusions. Their results instead indicate that men and women differ very little in the amount of stress they report or in the strategies they use to cope with the stress. They do differ, however, in terms of the content of their respective problems—men are more likely to report work-related problems, whereas women tend to report problems relevant to themselves, parenting, and interactions with others.

People from different cultures may also differ in the ways they handle stress. In one recent study, Chang (1996) examined whether Asian students and students of European descent differed in terms of optimism, pessimism, and their preferences for coping strategies. The results indicated that the Asian students were more pessimistic and tended to use more problem avoidance and social withdrawal as coping strategies.

A characteristic that seems to distinguish stress-resistant people from those who are more susceptible to its harmful effects is **hardiness** (Kobasa, 1979). Actually, this term refers to a cluster of characteristics, rather than just one. Hardy persons seem to differ from less stress-resistant people in three respects. First, they show higher levels of *commitment*—deeper involvement

Hardiness: A personality style characterized by high levels of commitment, a strong sense of control over life events, and the view that change is an opportunity for growth and development.

Table 13.3

Optimists and Pessimists: Contrasting Strategies for Coping with Stress

Optimists and pessimists employ different strategies in coping with stress. The strategies used by optimists often seem to be more effective than those adopted by pessimists.

Strategies Preferred	Description
by Optimists	
Problem-focused coping	Making specific plans for dealing with the source of stress; implementing such plans
Suppressing competing activities	Refraining from other activities until the problem is solved and stress is reduced
Seeking social support	Obtaining the advice of others; talking the problem over with others
by Pessimists	
Denial/distancing	Ignoring the problem or source of stress; refusing to believe that it exists or is important
Disengaging from the goal	Giving up on reaching the goal that is being blocked by the stressor
Focusing on the expression of feelings	Letting off steam instead of working on the problem directly

in whatever they do and stronger tendencies to perceive such activities as worth doing. Second, they tend to view change as a *challenge*—as an opportunity for growth and development, rather than as a threat or a burden. Third, hardy persons have a stronger sense of *control* over events in their lives and over the outcomes they experience. Research findings indicate that persons high in hardiness report better physical and mental health than those low in hardiness, even when they encounter major stressful life changes (Florian, Mikulincer, & Taubman, 1995; Oulette-Kobasa & Puccetti, 1983).

These and other findings indicate that individuals differ greatly in terms of their ability to deal with stress. Understanding the reasons for such differences can be of considerable practical value. We'll return to various techniques for coping with stress in Making Psychology Part of Your Life at the end of this chapter.

Key Questions

- What role does stress play in physical illness?
- What are the effects of low levels of stress? High levels?
- What is burnout? What are its causes?
- Why are some people better able to cope with the effects of stress than others?

Understanding and Communicating Our Health Needs

There is no doubt that modern medicine has provided us with the means to alleviate many types of disease and illness considered incurable until this century. Yet all the available medicine and technology still does not ensure that we will seek proper treatment when necessary, or that we possess the knowledge or skills necessary to realize when help is required.

Moreover, because of the beliefs and attitudes we hold, it's often difficult for health professionals to get us to comply with health-promoting advice.

Consider, for example, the results of an Australian study in which people were asked to identify the behavior patterns responsible for health problems in their country (Hetzel & McMichael, 1987). The patterns people cited most frequently were alcohol and drug abuse, poor diet, lack of exercise, and smoking—a clear indication that respondents were aware of the health risks associated with these behaviors. Similarly, when asked to name the changes that would most likely improve their own health, respondents cited better diet, more exercise, stopping or reducing smoking, reducing alcohol consumption, and coping better with their worries—again, proof that they knew what they were supposed to do to improve their health. Yet when the respondents were asked why they had not made changes in the behaviors they considered most essential to improving their own health, their answers—including "laziness," "lack of time," "not worthwhile," "too difficult or expensive," or "lack of social support"—indicated that sufficient motivation to change was simply not there. This suggests an important role for health psychologists: not only to help people achieve a better understanding of their health needs and to inform them about the risks of specific unhealthy behaviors, but also to identify techniques to reduce or eliminate unhealthy behaviors and to promote the adoption of healthy lifestyles (see Figure 13.6).

CLOSE TO HOME JOHN McPHERSON

"And this indicator tells you how many miles you need to run before you should attend a high school reunion."

(**Source**: CLOSE TO HOME copyright 1993 & 1996 John McPherson. Reprinted with permission of UNIVERSAL PRESS SYNDICATE. All rights reserved.)

FIGURE 13.6

Promoting Healthy Lifestyles

As illustrated by this cartoon, people differ in many ways, including their motivations for taking steps to return to good health. Psychologists and other health professionals can provide the support and guidance necessary to get them back on track.

Symptom Perception: How Do We Know When We're Ill?

As noted in Chapter 3, we all experience bodily sensations, such as the steady beating of our heart or the rush of air flowing in and out of our lungs as we breathe. Certain sensations—such as irregularities in heartbeat, tiny aches and pains, a slight queasiness, or a backache—are often termed *symptoms,* because they may reflect an underlying medical problem. But what factors determine how people experience symptoms?

Important factors, research seems to indicate, are individual differences in attention to our bodies and certain situational factors that influence our attention (Taylor, 1991). People who focus attention on themselves tend to notice symptoms more quickly than those who focus on the external environment. People who live with others, have interesting jobs, and lead exciting lives may be less likely to notice symptoms than are less active people who have boring jobs and/or who live alone (Pennebaker, 1983). In other words, we are most likely to notice symptoms when there are few distractions. Situational factors, such as our moods, can also determine the direction of our attention and thus affect whether we notice symptoms. People who are in a good mood report fewer symptoms and rate themselves as healthier than people who are in a bad mood (Leventhal et al., 1996). Note, however, that some symptoms are difficult or almost impossible to notice on one's own, regardless of one's attention level or mood.

Psychological factors also determine how we *interpret* symptoms. We often interpret the meaning of our current symptoms by comparing them with those we have experienced in the past. We recognize a runny nose, watery eyes, and tiredness as symptoms of the onset of a cold. In these instances our experience, or the experience of others, tells us that the underlying illness is probably not fatal and that the treatment of choice may include lots of rest, plenty of water, and staying dry and warm. Finally, expectations can influence our interpretation of symptoms—by causing us to focus on symptoms we are expecting and to ignore those we are not expecting. After you visit a sick friend, a barely noticeable tickle in your throat may lead you to believe you are catching her cold. Because you expect to get sick, you interpret the tickle as a sign of illness.

Health Beliefs: When Do We Seek Medical Advice?

How do we decide that a symptom is severe enough to require medical attention? Several factors may help determine the conditions under which we actually go to a doctor, clinic, or emergency room. Sometimes people report symptoms or seek out medical attention because something is clearly wrong. But—as you've probably experienced in your own life—people may also complain simply because the cost of doing so is low and the chances of achieving desired interpersonal goals are high (Kowalski, 1996). Also, surprisingly, some evidence suggests that people sometimes do not seek help even when they know that something is seriously wrong (Locke & Slaby, 1982). Why is this so?

The **health belief model,** initially developed to help explain why people don't use medical screening services, may help us to understand the reasons. This model suggests that our willingness to seek medical help depends on: (1) the extent to which we perceive a threat to our health; and (2) the extent to which we believe that a particular behavior will effectively reduce that threat (Rosenstock, 1974). The perception of a personal threat is influenced by our health values, our specific beliefs about our susceptibility to a health problem, and our beliefs concerning the seriousness of the problem. For example, we may decide to stop smoking if we value our health, if we feel that our smoking might lead to fatal lung cancer, and if we don't like what we hear about death from lung cancer.

Our perceptions that our behavior will be effective in reducing a health threat—in this case the risk of lung cancer—depend on whether we believe that a particular practice will reduce the chances we will contract a particular illness and whether the perceived benefits of the practice are worth the effort. For example, whether a smoker concerned about developing cancer will actually quit depends on two beliefs: that giving up smoking will reduce the risk of cancer, and that the benefits of reducing cancer risk will outweigh the pleasures of smoking.

The health belief model helps explain why certain people, especially young persons and adults who have never experienced a serious illness or injury, often fail to engage in actions that would be effective in preventing illness or injury—such as wearing a condom during sexual intercourse or using a safety belt when driving a car (Taylor & Brown, 1988). These people don't engage in such preventive, health-protecting actions because, in their minds, the likelihood of experiencing illness or injury is very low—so why bother? (See the discussion of adolescent recklessness in Chapter 9 for more information on this topic.)

Health Belief Model: A theory of health behaviors; the model predicts that whether or not a person practices a particular health behavior may depend on the degree to which the person perceives a personal health threat and believes that practicing the behavior will reduce that threat.

The health belief model also suggests that if people believe that their actions will be ineffective in changing their health status, they will be less likely to seek help or engage in healthy behaviors. For example, suppose you are overweight and have a family history of high blood pressure. Because you do not believe that anything can be done to lessen your genetic predisposition for heart attacks, you may refuse to adhere to a recommended diet and exercise program, even when you begin to experience symptoms.

Doctor–Patient Interactions: Why Can't We Talk to Our Doctors?

Imagine the following situation: You have waited in a crowded doctor's office for forty-five minutes beyond your scheduled appointment time. Just before you reach the end of your rope, the nurse finally calls your name. Relieved finally to get away from the congestion of the waiting room, you swallow the choice words you've been saving for the doctor. But then, adding insult to injury, she sticks her head in the door of the examining room, says, "Please be seated, I'll be right back"—and leaves! Fully twenty minutes pass before she returns. She offers no apology for the delay. After a rapid succession of questions, pokes, and prods, the doctor scribbles a prescription on a piece of paper and says, "Take two of these four times a day, and call my office in a week if you have further problems." Then she promptly leaves once more.

If aspects of the preceding example sound familiar, then you may recognize the frustration that stems from ineffective doctor–patient interactions. Research has repeatedly documented the existence of communication problems between physicians and their patients (Roter & Ewart, 1992; Waitzkin, 1984). Although health care experts have long recognized the need for improving this situation, it is only since the 1970s that researchers have systematically examined the doctor–patient communication process (Roter & Hall, 1989).

Research has shown that the communication skills most frequently exhibited by doctors during actual medical examinations are those dealing with the mechanics of a patient's illness; for example, direct physical examination of relevant areas of the body and explanation of the nature of prescribed medication and therapy (Duffy, Hamerman, & Cohen, 1980). In contrast, the skills observed least frequently are those related to the psychosocial aspects of patients' problems, such as asking patients what they know or how they feel about their illnesses.

A recent study by Ford, Fallowfield, and Lewis (1996) found similar results during "bad news" consultations between physicians and newly referred cancer patients in a London hospital. These researchers' observations revealed that the doctor–patient interactions were typically clinician-dominated rather than patient-centered. For example, the physicians tended to use closed rather than open questions and seldom gave patients the opportunity to initiate discussion or offer comments. In addition, discussions of psychosocial issues were rare. This was surprising, given the fact that these conversations typically centered on the painful nature of cancer treatments and the possibility that the patients might die. Results like these suggest that it may be important for physicians to receive communication skills training as part of their medical education. Growing evidence on this topic suggests that rapport and the quality of information communicated are often critical factors in successful treatment of the disease and the person (Bonsing, Schreurs, & DeRijk, 1996; Roter & Ewart, 1992).

What do doctors perceive as their role during medical examinations? A recent study by Wechsler and his colleagues (1996) suggests that even among doctors, opinions seem to change over time. In 1994 these researchers surveyed physicians to learn their opinions regarding (1) the forms of health-promoting behavior they felt were important to explain to their patients; and (2) the extent to which they considered certain health-promotion behaviors as part of their responsibilities. Then the researchers compared the results of the survey to one administered thirteen years earlier. First, the results showed that compared to the physicians surveyed in 1981, a greater percentage of those surveyed in 1994 felt that discussing health risk factors with their patients, such as the dangers of smoking or the risk of fatty foods, was an important part of their job. Second, when the researchers asked which of several behaviors the doctors considered to be "definitely" part of their responsibilities, an interesting pattern emerged: The 1994 respondents were more likely to endorse medically relevant behaviors as "definitely" part of their role than the 1981 respondents (see Figure 13.7). In contrast, the 1981 respondents were more likely to endorse psychosocial, or supportive, behaviors as "definitely" part of their role.

In order to be effective in treating patients and promoting their wellness, doctors, nurses, and other health professionals need to know how to get their message across—how to communicate effectively with the persons who come to them for help. The important benefits include a more active role for patients and improved quality of diagnostic information (Macguire, Fairburn, & Fletcher, 1986; McCann & Weinman, 1996). These factors, together with the studies we've examined, underscore the importance of training in communication skills for health care professionals.

Key Questions

- Why are symptoms and sensations important?
- What is the health belief model?
- What factors determine our willingness to make lifestyle changes or seek medical help?
- Why is it important for psychologists to study aspects of doctor–patient interactions?

Behavioral and Psychological Correlates of Illness: *The Effects of Actions and Thoughts on Health*

We are frequently exposed to media accounts of miraculous remissions or even cures of cancer or other serious illnesses. Although one should be extremely skeptical of such reports, a possible basis for these events is becoming clear: Mounting evidence suggests that not only behavioral but psychological variables interact in important ways with physical conditions to determine the progression of many diseases. In other words, aspects of our behavior, perceptions, and personality contribute to the disease process.

Cancer, a group of illnesses in which proliferating abnormal cells overwhelm normal tissue, is often viewed as a physical illness with a definite genetic component; individuals from families with high cancer rates, for example, often show a diminished efficiency of their natural killer cells—those cells designed specifically for the surveillance and destruction of cancerous tumor cells (Kiecolt-Glaser & Glaser, 1992). In most cases, however, whether we actually develop a cancer or other illness is moderated by **risk factors**—aspects of our environment or behavior that affect our chances of developing or contracting a particular disease, within the limits established by our genes (American Cancer Society, 1989).

A deadly class of risk factors are the behaviors within our lifestyle that increase our exposure to **carcinogens**—cancer-producing agents. Tobacco and

Cancer: A group of illnesses in which abnormal cells are formed that are able to proliferate, invade, and overwhelm normal tissues and to spread to distant sites in the body.

Risk Factors: Aspects of our environment or behavior that influence our chances of developing or contracting a particular disease, within the limits set by our genetic structure.

Carcinogens: Cancer-producing agents.

FIGURE 13.7

The Changing Role of Physicians in Health Promotion: Then and Now

Physicians surveyed in 1994 were more likely to endorse medically relevant tasks as "definitely" part of their responsibilities than physicians surveyed in 1981. In contrast, physicians in the 1981 sample were more likely to endorse psychosocial, or supportive, behaviors as "definitely" part of their role.

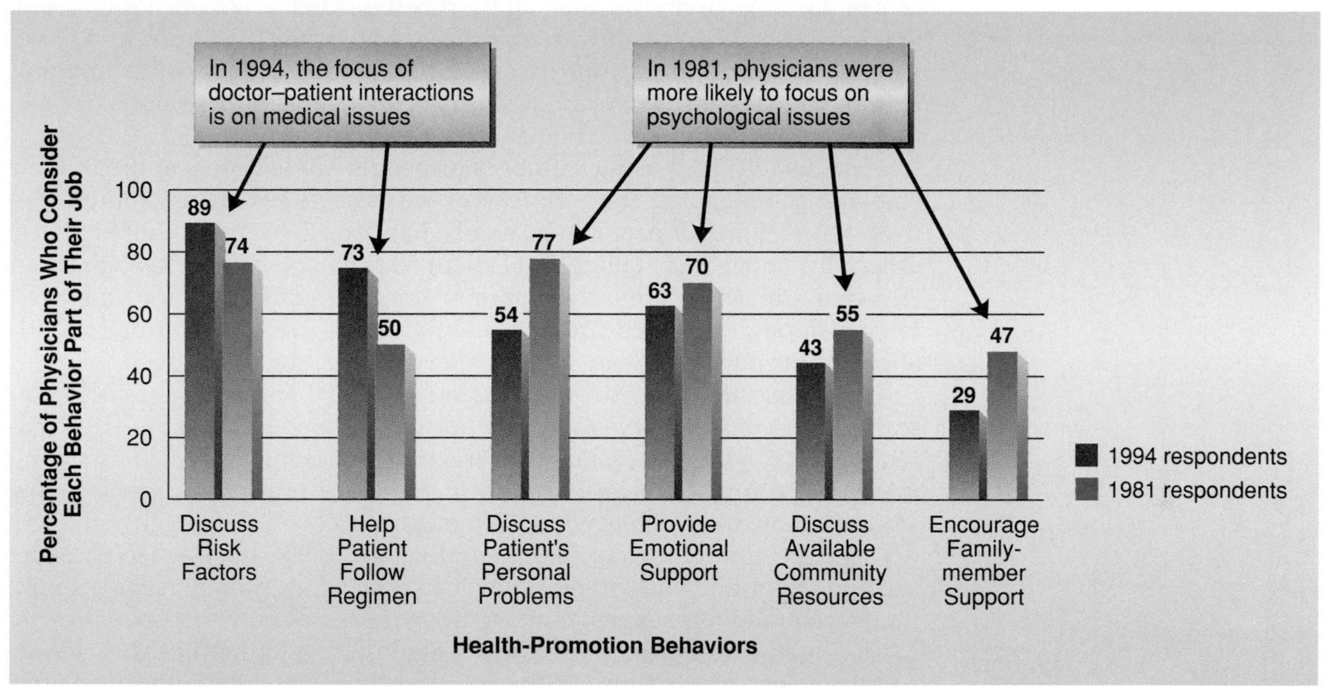

(**Source**: Based on data from Wechsler et al., 1996.)

the smoke it produces, chemicals in the food that we eat and the air that we breathe, alcohol in the beverages we drink, and the radiation we receive from overexposure to the sun have all been implicated to some extent as carcinogens. It was because of concerns about exposure to such substances that in 1994 many people in the United States protested about plans to sell milk from cows fed large amounts of growth hormones: The protesters didn't want such substances in their milk. A more recent example is the public outcry that occurred in response to reports that the regular use of cellular phones could lead to cancers of the brain.

Are such concerns warranted? Even the experts cannot agree. On the one hand, a large body of research demonstrates that long-term exposure to certain carcinogens increases the risk of getting cancer. For other suspected carcinogens, however, critics argue that "carcinogen" designations are premature, and that they are often based on animal studies that use concentrations of substances many times greater than their occurrence under natural conditions.

Still, people do create risks through their behaviors. At a recent world conference, cancer experts estimated that nearly half of all types of cancers are preventable—if people would simply avoid getting too much sun, avoid tobacco use or excessive alcohol, and improve their diet (Hill & Iverson, 1997). Psychologists can play a crucial role in preventing cancer and other health problems by developing interventions that reduce our exposure to harmful substances and promote healthy behaviors like exercise and proper diet. We'll now consider several behavioral risk factors that may contribute to the development of certain illnesses.

Smoking: Risky for You and Everyone around You

Smoking is the largest preventable cause of illness and premature death (before age sixty-five) in the United States, accounting for about 434,000 deaths annually in the United States alone (Lando et al., 1995). Exposure to tobacco smoke is the leading cause of several types of cancers, including cancers of the lung, larynx, bladder, and cervix (Fry, Menck, & Winchester, 1996). Smoking also causes **cardiovascular disease** (disease of the heart and blood vessels). And secondhand smoke causes disease and death in both adults and children. More than 25 percent of adults in the United States smoke (Blume, 1993), and the figure is even higher elsewhere.

Fortunately, increasing numbers of people are learning to break their smoking habit (United States Bureau of the Census, 1991). For example, the overall percentage of people who smoke has decreased in the United States, especially among men, falling from about 50 percent overall in 1965 to about 30 percent in 1989. Similarly, cigarette smoking among adolescents aged twelve through nineteen dropped continuously from 1974 through 1991, although the rate of decrease slowed after 1985 (Nelson et al., 1995).

One cause for alarm, however, is our failure to discover ways to help persons most at risk—heavy smokers who smoke more than twenty-five cigarettes per day—to stop smoking. Several intensive community wide smoking intervention projects have failed to increase quitting rates among heavy smokers, and have achieved only modest success among light smokers (COMMIT Research Group, 1995; Lando et al., 1995). Even when smokers succeed in quitting, the battle isn't over, and many eventually resume smoking. Recent findings suggest that cognitive processes may help explain why relapse occurs. In one study, Gibbons, Eggleston, and Benthin (1997) measured smokers' perceptions of the health risks of smoking before and after they had kicked the habit. Interestingly, a significant change in risk perceptions was evident among persons who had resumed smoking: Compared to their initial views, they now saw smoking as *less* risky. In other words, they convinced themselves that smoking was less risky in order to be consistent with their decision to resume smoking. Alerting smokers to these tendencies as they are quitting may help prevent smoking relapse.

Another source of concern is the observed increase in smoking among certain subgroups—especially young women in the United States and people in developing nations (Rothenberg & Koplan, 1990). We'll explore this intriguing trend further in the Exploring Gender and Diversity section.

Given the overwhelming evidence against smoking, why do people smoke? Genetic, psychosocial, and cognitive factors all seem to play a role. Individual differences in our reaction to **nicotine,** the addictive substance in tobacco, suggest that some people are biologically predisposed to become addicted to nicotine, whereas others remain unaffected—evidence that our genes play a role in determining who will become a smoker (Pomerleau & Pomerleau, 1984). Nicotine enhances the availability of certain neurotransmitter substances, such as acetylcholine, norepinephrine, dopamine, and endogenous opioids. As you may recall from Chapter 2, these substances produce temporary improvements in concentration, recall, alertness, arousal, and psychomotor performance that can be extremely pleasurable for some people.

Cardiovascular Disease: All diseases of the heart and blood vessels.

Nicotine: The addictive substance in tobacco.

Other evidence suggests that psychosocial factors play a role in establishing smoking behavior, especially among young persons. Adolescents are more likely to begin smoking if their parents or other role models smoke, or if they experience peer pressure to do so (Aloise-Young, Graham, & Hanson, 1994). A report by the U.S. Surgeon General (United States Department of

EXPLORING GENDER & DIVERSITY

Smoking around the Globe

There are many ways in which people around the globe differ, but one way in which they appear to be the same is in their susceptibility to the adverse health effects of smoking. As I noted earlier, recent evaluations of smoking prevalence show that the number of smokers worldwide—and hence the incidence of heart disease and of lung and other forms of cancer—continues to climb (LaVecchia et al., 1992, 1993). For example, since 1950 deaths from lung cancer in Japan have increased by a factor of ten among men and by a factor of eight among women. In addition, smoking-related deaths among men in Central and Eastern Europe are expected to exceed the highest rates ever recorded (Boyle, 1993).

The percentage of deaths attributable to smoking has traditionally been higher for males than for females in many parts of the world (Peto et al., 1992). However, this disparity is quickly disappearing—especially for female smokers in the United States. Scientists anticipate that over the next few years the percentage of deaths due to smoking among U.S. men and women will become increasingly similar. What is the reason for this dramatic rise in smoking-related deaths among women? Part of the reason is almost certainly the dramatic rise in the number of women who smoke, both in the United States and throughout the world (Boyle, 1993). A related reason is that more women in the United States are entering high-pressure occupations—ones that may lead some people to smoke. Unfortunately, this trend is expected to continue.

The dangers of smoking, however, are not limited to the smoker. Secondhand smoke, referred to as **passive smoke,** can also increase the incidence of respiratory disease and cardiovascular disease in persons in regular close contact with smokers, such as family members and coworkers (Environmental Protection Agency, 1992). Persons who are subjected to secondhand smoke are at significantly greater risk of developing lung cancer than persons who are not (Stockwell et al., 1992). A recent study by Emmons, Hammond, and Abrams (1994) suggests that people can sharply reduce the harmful effects of passive smoke by taking steps to eliminate smoking at home. These researchers obtained measures of tobacco smoke exposure at home and at other locations from a group of nonsmokers both before and after their spouses quit smoking. Interestingly, these measures revealed that by far the greatest part of the nonsmokers' exposure to passive smoke occurred at home. After their spouses stopped smoking at home, the nonsmokers' overall exposure to tobacco smoke dropped dramatically, despite the fact that their exposure to passive smoke outside the home increased (see Figure 13.8 on page 526).

Smoking is indeed the great equalizer. As smoking rates continue to soar in countries throughout the world, increases in the rates of cancer and cardiovascular diseases can be expected to follow—both among smokers and, unfortunately, among those around them.

Health and Human Services, 1994) suggests that about 90 percent of smokers smoke their first cigarette by age eighteen, but that very few people begin to smoke after age twenty. These data highlight the urgent need for prevention programs targeting adolescents.

Finally, most smokers recognize that smoking is harmful to their health, yet many continue to smoke, a fact that may indicate that they are not yet prepared mentally to quit. Some research appears to support this possibility. According to Prochaska and his colleagues (1994), when attempting to change

Passive Smoke: The smoke that we inhale from the smokers around us.

FIGURE 13.8

Reducing Exposure to Passive Smoke

Research participants' exposure to passive smoke from cigarettes dropped sharply after their spouses stopped smoking at home. Although not depicted here, nicotine concentrations in participants' homes also fell sharply.

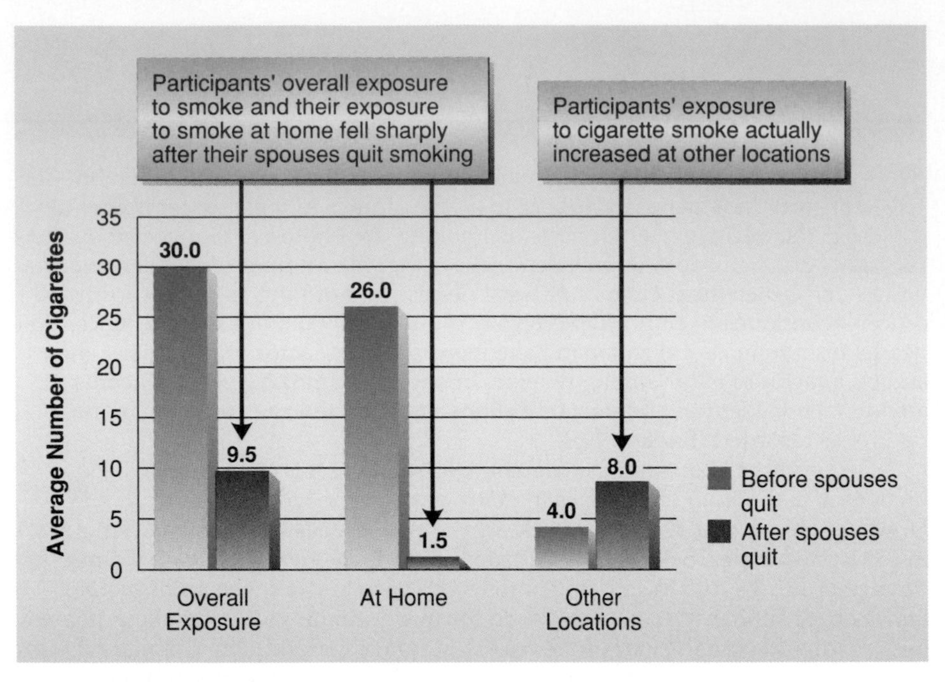

(**Source**: Based on data from Emmons et al., 1994.)

addictive behaviors such as smoking, people proceed through a series of stages that reflect increasing levels of motivation or *readiness to quit*. In the first stage, *precontemplation,* a smoker has no interest in quitting. During the *contemplation* stage smokers begin to think about quitting smoking, but do not take concrete steps toward doing so. In the *preparation* stage smokers prepare plans to quit; they then execute them during the *action* stage. Finally, during the *maintenance* stage, former smokers direct their efforts toward maintaining their nonsmoking status.

In one study, Lichtenstein, Lando, and Nothwehr (1994) examined whether readiness to quit would predict which smokers would benefit from their participation in the *Minnesota Heart Health Program*—a community-based intervention aimed at modifying risk factors that cause cardiovascular disease, including smoking. These researchers assessed each participant's readiness to quit before the program and then compared this measure to the participant's smoking status several years later. The results seemed to support the stage model: Readiness to quit predicted whether participants of the program were still smoking seven years later. While these results are preliminary, they do seem to suggest that assessment of readiness to quit may be a useful tool for predicting which persons are most likely to benefit from interventions designed to help them eliminate unhealthy behaviors.

Diet and Nutrition: What You Eat May Save Your Life

Poor dietary practices can dramatically increase people's risk of developing chronic diseases. A poor diet has been most closely linked with cancer of the colon and rectum (colorectal cancer). Nearly 45,000 cases of colon cancer were reported in the United States in 1993 alone (Jessup et al., 1996). Fortunately, regular consumption of certain foods, such as broccoli and cauliflower, may *reduce* the risk of developing these cancers. Similarly, vitamin A—found in many foods, including carrots, spinach, and cantaloupe—facilitates proper cell division and inhibits the destruction of healthy cells by carcinogens (Willett & MacMahon, 1984). Dietary fiber has also been proposed as a possible inhibitor of colorectal cancer (Graham, 1983).

Diet is also a significant risk factor in the development of *cardiovascular disease,* or diseases of the heart and blood vessels. Cardiovascular diseases include arteriosclerosis (hardening of the arteries), coronary heart disease (reduced blood flow to the heart), and stroke (bursting of a blood vessel in the brain) (McGinnis & Meyers, 1995). Most cardiovascular diseases affect the amount of oxygen and nutrients that reach organs and other tissues; prolonged oxygen and nutrient deficiency can result in permanent damage to the organs or tissues and even death. *Arteriosclerosis,* the major cause of heart failure in the United States, is caused by the buildup of cholesterol and other substances on arterial walls, which leads to a narrowing of those blood vessels.

High levels of a certain type of **serum cholesterol,** or blood cholesterol, are strongly associated with increased risk of cardiovascular diseases (Allred, 1993; Klag et al., 1993). "Bad" or *LDL cholesterol* clogs arteries and is therefore the kind that places us most at risk of heart disease. "Good" or *HDL cholesterol* helps clear LDL from the arteries and escorts it to the liver for excretion. In other words, the more LDL you have, the more HDL you need. The amount of cholesterol in our blood is affected by the amount of fat, especially saturated fat, and cholesterol in our diets. Serum cholesterol can be greatly reduced, however, through a diet that is low in fats, cholesterol, and calories, and high in fiber, fruits, and vegetables (Carmody, Matarazzo, & Istvan, 1987).

Although the link between dietary practices and good health is clear, it is difficult to get people to adhere to a healthy diet (Brownell & Cohen, 1995). In addition, many Americans simply eat *too much.* Statistics indicate that more than 58 million American adults are overweight and face significant health risks because of their weight (McGinnis & Meyers, 1995). Research indicates that poor dietary practices, particularly high fat intake and too much alcohol, increase the risk of heart disease and several types of cancers. Although most interventions designed to help people lose weight work initially, the weight loss achieved through these programs does not typically last (Garner & Wooley, 1991). Why is maintaining weight loss a continuous struggle for many people? Actually, a variety of factors have been shown to play a role, including genetic, behavioral, and environmental ones (Grilo & Pogue-Geile, 1991). However, recent evidence on this topic indicates that the *type* of motivation behind the decision to lose weight may also play a key role in predicting who will be successful at maintaining weight loss over time (Williams et al., 1996).

According to **self-determination theory** (Deci & Ryan, 1985), long-term maintenance of weight loss depends on whether the motivation for doing so is perceived by the dieter as autonomous or externally controlled. Overweight persons frequently begin dieting on the advice of their doctor or at the insistence of concerned family members. Under these circumstances, people may feel coerced into losing weight; this is an example of *controlled motivation.* On the other hand, persons who begin a weight-loss program because they want to do it for themselves may experience the same activity (dieting) quite differently; this is an example of *autonomous motivation.* Self-determination theory predicts that autonomously motivated weight loss will be maintained over time, whereas maintenance of weight loss achieved at the urging of others is less likely. In a recent study, Williams and his colleagues (1996) explored whether self-determination theory would predict long-term success among a group of overweight persons entering a six-month weight-loss program. The results of their study provided support for the theory: Participants who reported entering the program for themselves (autonomous motivation)

Serum Cholesterol: The cholesterol in our blood.

Self-Determination Theory: In relation to health and lifestyle, theory suggesting that motivation for health-promoting behaviors is highest when it is autonomous and lowest when it is prompted by others.

Key Questions

- What is cancer?
- What are the potential consequences of smoking and exposure to secondhand smoke?
- What determines who will become addicted to smoking?
- What are the effects of poor dietary practices?
- What is self-determination theory?

attended the program more regularly, lost more weight during the program, and were more likely to maintain the weight loss nearly two years later than persons who reported joining the program because of other people's wishes (controlled motivation). These results indicate that the type of motivation underlying a decision to lose weight may be an important predictor of successful weight loss—and more importantly, of weight-loss maintenance over time.

Alcohol Consumption: Here's to Your Health?

Some evidence shows that moderate alcohol consumption—typically defined as a daily glass of red wine—may be associated with health benefits. For example, the results of several large-scale studies suggest that moderate alcohol consumption can reduce the risk of coronary heart disease.

Intriguing new evidence on this topic suggests an unexpected benefit of moderate alcohol consumption: increased earnings. In one study, Heien (1996) found that, on average, moderate drinkers have greater earnings than either abstainers or abusers. Recent medical findings concerning the relationship between moderate drinking and cardiovascular problems may help explain this finding; as mentioned above, compared to heavy drinking or abstaining from alcohol, moderate drinking may reduce people's risk of heart attack. Assuming that, on average, healthy people are more productive than unhealthy ones, it is possible that the health benefits afforded by moderate drinking allow people to generate greater income through additional hard work. In other words, the relationship between income and alcohol consumption is indirect; it does *not* mean that drinking alcohol will cause your income to rise.

On the other hand, too much alcohol is harmful and can lead to numerous social and physical disorders. The consequences of alcohol abuse can include stomach disease; cirrhosis of the liver; cancer; impaired sexual functioning; cognitive impairment; and, as we saw in Chapter 8, *fetal alcohol syndrome,* a condition of retardation and physical abnormalities that occurs in children of mothers who are heavy drinkers. Heavy drinking has also been implicated as a risk factor for suicide and suicide attempts, and college students who drink heavily are seven to ten times more likely to engage in unsafe sex, damage property, and drive while drunk (Borges & Rosovsky, 1996; Corey & Correia, 1977). Finally, drinking alcohol may interact with smoking to increase cancer risk. Drinkers of alcohol who are also heavy smokers have twenty-two times greater risk of developing cancer than individuals who neither smoke nor drink (Rothman et al., 1980).

Emotions: Mood and Health

Inadequate emotional expression—especially of unhappy feelings—can have an adverse effect on the progression of certain types of illnesses, such as cancer (Levy et al., 1985, 1988). Individuals who cope with stress by keeping their worries to themselves are likely to experience suppressed immune systems, greater recurrence of cancer, and higher mortality rates.

In contrast, open expression of distress and a willingness to fight illness are sometimes associated with greater immune function, decreased recurrence rates, and increased survival time, even among patients at advanced stages of cancer. Interestingly, combative individuals—those who express anger about getting cancer and hostility toward their doctors and family members—often live longer than patients who passively accept their fate and quietly undergo treatment (Levy, 1990). And patients who demonstrate positive affect—especially joy, well-being, and happiness—also increase the likelihood of recovery.

Emotion can also play a role in the progression of **hypertension,** or high blood pressure, a condition in which the pressure within the blood vessels is abnormally high. Prolonged hypertension, when untreated, can result in extensive damage to the entire circulatory system. Indeed, about 30 percent of cardiovascular disease deaths each year are attributable to hypertension. While poor dietary practices and obesity are the main causes of hypertension, some evidence suggests that emotional stressors can affect the regulation of blood pressure through neurohormonal mechanisms (Krakoff et al., 1985). For example, anxiety and hostility can increase general arousal and facilitate the release of *catecholamines*—a class of neurotransmitters that plays an important role in the sympathetic nervous system. The release of the catecholamine epinephrine has the effect of boosting the body's overall readiness to act, including the blood pressure. Although the effects of emotional stressors are usually brief, extreme reactivity to anxiety, hostility, and anger may indicate a predisposition to develop hypertension (Rosenman, 1988). Not surprisingly, the strongest relations between emotions and blood pressure have been found for unexpressed anger and hostility, a possibility we'll consider next.

Personality and Health: The Type A Behavior Pattern

Think about the people you know. Can you name someone who always seems to be in a hurry, is extremely competitive, and is often hostile and irritable? Now, in contrast, can you name someone who shows the opposite pattern—someone who is relaxed, relatively uncompetitive, and easygoing in relations with others? If you succeeded, you now have in mind two people who could be described as showing Type A and Type B behavior patterns, respectively.

Interest in the **Type A behavior pattern** was first stimulated by medical research. Several physicians (Jenkins, Zyzanski, & Rosenman, 1979, and their colleagues) noticed that many patients who had suffered heart attacks seemed to share certain personality traits (see Chapter 12). These patients tended to be competitive, aggressive, hostile, and impatient; in other words, they displayed the pattern of behaviors that came to be termed Type A. Type A people are likely to be hard workers and tend to seek out the most challenging and stressful work conditions. Often, their efforts are rewarded with additional work from their superiors and coworkers (Feather & Volkmer, 1988).

Researchers now believe that only one facet of the Type A pattern may be related to increased risk of heart disease; specifically, *hostility* (Miller et al., 1996). A particular type of hostility—*cynical hostility,* characterized by suspiciousness, resentment, anger, antagonism, and distrust of others—may be especially detrimental (Barefoot et al., 1989). Some research has shown that this tendency may develop early in life (see Figure 13.9 on page 530). For example, Matthews and her colleagues (1996) examined the development of hostile traits in a group of twelve-year-old boys by observing the quality of interactions of each boy and his parents as they attempted to resolve disagreements in a laboratory setting. The results indicated that high frequencies of negative behaviors exhibited by both parents and sons, and low frequencies of positive behaviors exhibited by the father and son, were predictive of hostility on measures obtained three years later.

The discovery that cynical hostility—not the Type A behavior pattern as a whole—leads to heart disease provided researchers with an important clue to aid them in the design of treatment for this "toxic" component. But is it possible to modify hostility? Fortunately, new evidence suggests that the

Hypertension: High blood pressure, a condition in which the pressure within the blood vessels is abnormally high.

Type A Behavior Pattern: A cluster of traits (including competitiveness, urgency, and hostility) related to important aspects of health, social behavior, and task performance.

FIGURE 13.9

Cynical Hostility: A Dangerous Behavior?

Cynical hostility, the "toxic" component of the Type A behavior pattern, is characterized by suspiciousness, resentment, anger, antagonism, and distrust of others.

answer is yes. In one study, Gidron and Davidson (1996) identified a group of participants who scored high on measures of cynical hostility. Half of these persons were assigned to an eight-week intervention that was specifically designed to modify cynical hostility, while the other half (the control group) received information about the link between hostility and heart disease and ways to reduce the risk. Participants assigned to the intervention condition attended weekly meetings, monitored their hostility daily, and received instruction in the use of specific coping skills; for example, they learned to use relaxation exercises and practiced alternative ways to vent their angry feelings. The results indicated that the intervention was effective: Participants in the intervention group showed significant improvement on measures of cynical hostility, while participants assigned to the control group did not. Please note that these results are preliminary and require confirmation by additional research. However, they do offer hope to persons who exhibit this tendency, and who are therefore at risk for developing cardiovascular problems. The final section of Chapter 11 describes some of the kinds of techniques they learned.

AIDS: A Major Assault on Public Health

AIDS (acquired immune deficiency syndrome) is a viral disease that reduces the immune system's ability to defend the body against the introduction of foreign substances (antigens). The process by which *HIV (human immunodeficiency virus)* produces AIDS symptoms is complex, but essentially involves the devastation of aspects of the infected person's immune system; this makes the person extremely vulnerable to diseases, such as tuberculosis and pneumonia. The first cases of AIDS in the United States were reported in 1981, although we now know there were cases that occurred before that date. It was not until 1984 that the cause of AIDS was isolated—the HIV virus—and an antibody test was developed to detect infection.

Acquired Immune Deficiency Syndrome: The Facts about AIDS Since 1981 researchers have discovered a number of frightening facts about AIDS. First, the estimated incubation period—the time it takes for the disease to develop—can be as long as ten years (Bachetti, 1990). This means that infected individuals can spread the disease to others without even realizing that they are infected. Thus, it is not surprising that HIV has spread to more than 190 countries. The World Health Organization estimates that about 28 million people worldwide are infected with HIV and that nearly 6 million people have died from AIDS (Mertens & Low-Beer, 1996). As shown in Figure 13.10, AIDS is most prevalent in parts of Africa and in other developing nations, although the incidence of AIDS has increased rapidly in the United States as well—from 250 cases documented in the early 1980s to an estimated 535,000 cases at the end of 1994 (Centers for Disease Control, 1993).

AIDS (Acquired Immune Deficiency Syndrome): A viral infection that reduces the immune system's ability to defend the body against the introduction of foreign substances.

Second, AIDS is virtually always fatal, and research shows that most—although not all—individuals infected with HIV will eventually develop AIDS. Many scientists are now optimistic that they will eventually find a cure. This prediction, of course, comes on the heels of recent clinical trials showing that a new class of drugs called *protease inhibitors,* in combination with an older set

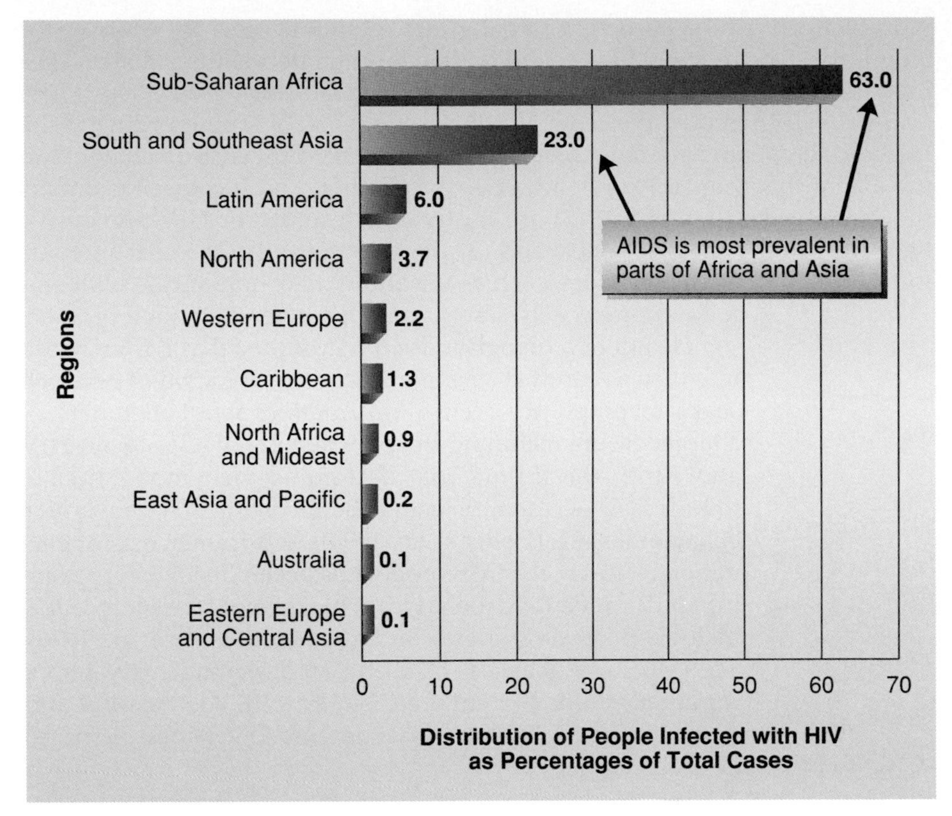

(**Source:** Based on information from UNAIDS.)

FIGURE 13.10

Estimated Distribution of HIV Infections Worldwide

The World Health Organization estimates that nearly 28 million persons have become infected with HIV. Here is a breakdown of different regions' percentages (rounded) of total worldwide cases.

of medicines, can significantly reduce levels of HIV in the blood (Collier et al., 1996; Waldholz, 1996). Public health officials are quick to point out, however, that even if a cure is eventually found, the possibility of providing these drugs to all infected persons in developing countries—which at present account for about 90 percent of the world's AIDS cases—is remote. Therefore, the need for interventions that help prevent the spread of AIDS is crucial.

Third, an individual can be infected only if the virus is introduced directly into the bloodstream. This means that the disease cannot be contracted through such actions as shaking hands with or hugging an infected person. Most HIV infections are acquired through unprotected sexual intercourse, infected needles used for injecting intravenous drugs, and infected blood or blood products. Unfortunately, women can pass the disease to their unborn children during pregnancy or delivery or through breast feeding. It is estimated that about 1.5 million children are currently infected with HIV worldwide (Mertens & Low-Beer, 1996).

How Psychologists Can Help Prevent the Spread of AIDS

Why are psychologists relevant to the AIDS epidemic? One reason, aside from the tragic consequences of this disease, is that most people contract HIV as a result of their behavior. Although AIDS was initially believed to be restricted to homosexuals and intravenous drug users, AIDS is currently being spread worldwide mainly through unprotected *heterosexual* rather than homosexual intercourse. Another reason for psychologists' interest in this problem is that the only effective means of preventing AIDS is through changing people's behaviors—risky behaviors such as injecting drugs with previously used needles, engaging in unprotected sex, and having sex with multiple partners (Longshore, Anglin, & Hsieh, 1997; Reinecke, Schmidt, & Ajzen, 1996).

Health psychologists recognize that developing effective AIDS prevention programs is a complicated business. They know, for example, that techniques effective for a particular target group are not necessarily effective for all groups. One model that is useful in developing interventions that accommodate individual and group differences is the *information–motivation–behavioral skills (IMB)* model (Fisher et al., 1994; see Figure 13.11). According to the IMB model, people are more likely to perform HIV-preventive behaviors to the extent that they: (1) know how HIV is acquired and the specific actions they must take to avoid it; (2) are motivated to perform HIV-preventive behaviors and omit risky ones; and (3) possess the skills necessary to perform HIV-preventive behaviors, such as the ability to communicate with and to be appropriately assertive with a potential sexual partner.

Health psychologists use the IMB model as a framework in which to conduct *elicitation research.* This kind of research seeks to pinpoint specific information about members of a target group, including their current knowledge about HIV and AIDS; the factors that determine their motivation to reduce their personal risk; and their existing HIV-preventive behavioral skills (Fisher et al., 1994). As a framework for elicitation research, the IMB model has been effective in predicting HIV-preventive behaviors in several at-risk groups, including college students and gay men (Fisher et al., 1996). The IMB model may also be useful for designing interventions for other groups currently at risk, as well. We'll explore this possibility in the Exploring Gender and Diversity section.

Key Questions

- What are the health consequences of heavy consumption of alcohol?
- How is the way in which we express our emotions related to our health?
- What are the characteristics of Type A persons? What diseases have been linked to Type A?
- What is AIDS? How is AIDS transmitted?
- What is the IMB model and why is it relevant to AIDS?

EXPLORING GENDER & DIVERSITY

Women and AIDS: A Rapidly Expanding Health Crisis

Clearly, elicitation research and the IMB model are powerful tools to guide the development of effective behavior-change programs. Why? Because they can help researchers uncover the reasons why certain groups of people do not perform AIDS-preventive behavior. One group in the United States that is currently at risk with regard to HIV and AIDS is women. Growing evidence shows that HIV infection rates among U.S. women are growing at an alarming rate (Centers for Disease Control, 1993). What is the reason for this increase? Several factors seem to play a role.

First, in many respects, the mode of transmission of HIV among men and women is similar (Amaro, 1995). Like their male counterparts, most HIV-infected women in the United States (67 percent) acquire HIV as a result of intravenous drug use. Women who use drugs add to their risk of contracting HIV if they have unprotected sex with male partners who may also use drugs or have multiple sexual partners. However, research has uncovered a risk factor unique to women: The chances of male-to-female transmission of HIV through sex are about twelve times greater than those of female-to-male transmission (Padian, Shiboski, & Jewell, 1990).

Second, gender role differences between men and women may also play a role. For example, adherence to traditional gender roles may increase the chances that some women will succumb to pressure to engage in unprotected sex (Amaro, 1995). Some evidence suggests that these cultural pressures may be particularly strong among women of color (Mays & Cochran, 1988). A related problem has to do with differences in the skills required to ensure safe sex. Consider, for example, the skills necessary to ensure the use of a condom during sex. For the man, this simply means putting on the condom. For the woman, however, it means persuading her partner to use a condom or, perhaps, refusing to have sex if he won't. Clearly, each of these actions requires social skills very different from those involved in putting on a condom.

Finally, fear may be an important factor, especially among inner-city women and women in abusive relationships marked by physical violence (Hobfall et al., 1994). Under conditions like these, in which the potential for personal injury is high, it is understandable that women are reluctant to negotiate safe sex with their partners, let alone refuse to have sex with them.

Can anything be done to reverse the rise in HIV infection among U.S. women? The results of one study suggest that the answer is yes. In their study, Hobfoll and his colleagues (1994) compared the relative impacts of two training programs on measures of HIV-preventive behaviors. Participants in the study, a group of inner-city women, were assigned randomly to one of the programs or to a no-training control group. The interventions differed in terms of their content (HIV-specific information versus general health information) but were otherwise identical. Consistent with the IMB model described earlier, the HIV-specific training program was designed to (1) increase the women's knowledge of HIV transmission and prevention; (2) motivate them to perform HIV-preventive behaviors by highlighting their specific risks of acquiring HIV; and (3) provide them with behavioral skills necessary to convince their sexual partners to adopt HIV-preventive behaviors, such as wearing a condom during sex. The results showed that the HIV-prevention group outperformed both the general health group and the no-treatment control group on knowledge measures and in terms of self-reported HIV-preventive behaviors. These results highlight the value of models like IMB in guiding development of more effective interventions.

FIGURE 13.11

AIDS-Preventive Behaviors: A Model

Growing evidence suggests that prevention programs are more effective when they are tailored to meet the needs of specific target groups and when they provide people with the knowledge, motivation, and behavioral skills necessary to perform AIDS-preventive behaviors.

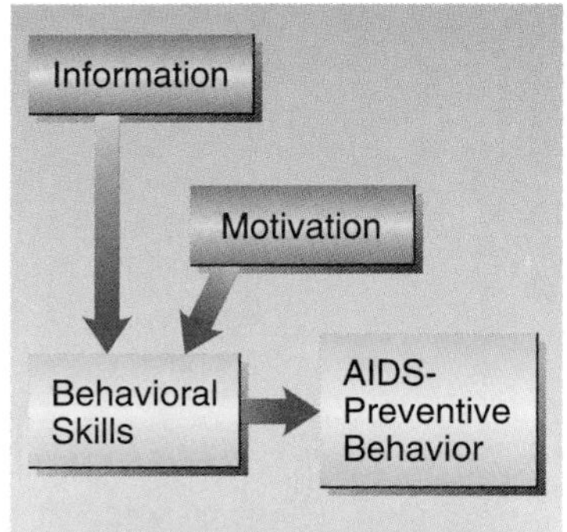

(**Source**: Based on Fisher et al., 1996.)

Promoting Wellness: Developing a Healthier Lifestyle

Have you ever wondered why some individuals live to be more than one hundred years old, while most people live only sixty or seventy years? Studies of persons who live for more than a century indicate that several factors may play a role in their extended life spans. One of these factors is diet; long-lived persons often show a pattern involving greater-than-average consumption of grains, leafy green and root vegetables, fresh milk, and fresh fruits, and they tend to eat low to moderate amounts of meat and animal fat. In addition, they maintain low to moderate levels of daily caloric intake (1,200 to 3,000 calories) and consume only moderate amounts of alcohol each day. Physical activity is perhaps the most important factor contributing to longevity and good health among long-lived people. Many work outdoors and walk a great deal. That is, regular physical activity is an integral part of their lives, continuing well into old age. Additional factors that may contribute to their extended life span are continued sexual activity, personality characteristics, family stability, and continued involvement in family and community affairs during advanced years. (Chapter 9 also addressed many issues relevant to the lifestyles of older adults.)

In sum, while genetic factors certainly play a role in determining life span, a growing body of evidence suggests that people may be able to extend their lives significantly by adhering to a lifestyle that includes a balanced, low-fat, low-calorie diet; regular exercise; and continued activity during later years (Pelletier, 1986).

On the basis of such findings, a growing number of health professionals and psychologists have adopted an approach to health and wellness that is

Prevention Strategies: Techniques designed to reduce the occurrence of physical and psychological problems.

based on **prevention strategies:** techniques designed to reduce the occurrence of illness and other physical and psychological problems. (We'll return to a discussion of prevention strategies again in Chapter 15.) *Primary prevention* is considered the optimal prevention approach. Its goal is to reduce or eliminate the incidence of preventable illness and injury. As we'll see in the discussion below, primary prevention strategies usually involve one or more of the following components: educating people about the relation between their behaviors and their health, promoting motivation and skills to practice healthy behaviors, and directly modifying poor health practices through intervention. (See the Beyond the Headlines section for information on the alarming increase in the incidence of skin cancers during the past several decades—a worldwide health problem that cries out for primary prevention.)

Secondary prevention focuses on decreasing the severity of illness that is already present by means of early detection. Thus, individuals learn about their health status through medical tests that screen for the presence of disease. Although early detection of certain diseases is traditionally carried out by health professionals and often requires sophisticated medical tests, exciting research is under way to teach patients methods of self-examination; the discussion below will expand on this theme.

Beyond the Headlines

As Psychologists See It

Health Psychologists Help Sunworshippers See the Light

Just Catchin' Some Rays? . . . Or—Perhaps More Than You Bargained For

Melbourne, Australia—Public officials in Australia are rallying the health care troops to get the word out: Stay out of the sun! The latest public health figures show that Australia has the highest rate of skin cancer in the world. Indeed, an estimated two out of every three people there are expected to develop skin cancer during their lifetime. At present, nearly one thousand people in Australia die each year from skin cancers, and officials worry that this figure will go higher. They also express concern over the fact that their efforts to inform the Australian public about the dangers of overexposure to the sun have apparently gone largely unheeded. Australians continue to flock to resorts and public beaches in record numbers.

What's going on here? Are these people crazy? In light of the overwhelming evidence that overexposure to the sun causes cancer, why would rational people continue to accept this risk? One reason is that knowledge doesn't always translate into action, a point I've made repeatedly throughout this chapter (and others). The initial efforts aimed at preventing overexposure to the sun consisted of mass-media campaigns in many Western countries. Their purpose was to increase people's knowledge of the links between overexposure to the sun and skin cancer, and to remind people of the need for sun protection, such as appropriate clothing and/or sun-screening agents (see Figure 13.12). Were these campaigns effective? In one sense they were: Studies in the United States and elsewhere consistently show that most adults and many children are generally knowledgeable about the risks of overexposure to sunlight. On the other hand, though, many people still do not take the necessary steps to avoid getting too much sun. So why do people ignore these warnings? Actually there are many possibilities; we'll consider several here.

One obvious reason is that a suntan makes many people feel better about their appearance and themselves. More importantly, they believe that a suntan makes them more attractive to *other* people. Does this description fit you? For many people, especially adolescents and young adults, this belief is a power-

FIGURE 13.12

The Harmful Effects of the Sun

Although it is unlikely that suntanning will produce the dramatic effects depicted here, scientists are alarmed by the rapid increase in the incidence of skin cancers.

"I think you missed a spot with the sunscreen."

(**Source**: CLOSE TO HOME copyright 1993 & 1996 John McPherson. Reprinted with permission of UNIVERSAL PRESS SYNDICATE. All rights reserved.)

ful source of motivation, and thus a difficult one to combat. As you are no doubt aware, the fact of this belief has not been lost on advertisers.

The optimistic bias that people tend to have concerning themselves may also play a role. *Optimistic bias* refers to a person's belief that something negative is less likely to happen to them than it is to other similar persons. Some evidence seems to suggest that people do exhibit this tendency. In one study, Miller, Shoda, and Hurley (1996) asked a group of participants with varying degrees of suntan to rate their chances of developing skin cancer. The results showed that, independent of their suntan level (light, medium, dark), an optimistic bias was apparent in participants' ratings of their chances of developing skin cancer. A final reason for people's tendency to ignore warnings about overexposure to the sun has to do with their beliefs. One commonly held belief is that skin cancer is a disease that affects older people. Adolescents and young adults frequently interpret this to mean that they won't get skin cancer for at least another twenty or thirty years. Their conclusion? Why worry about it? In other words, the time frame involved in the development of many forms of skin cancer simply exceeds their grasp. Thus, it is not surprising that interventions based on education alone have been ineffective as a means of motivating young people to adopt sun-protective behaviors.

Are sun lovers justified in their reasoning? Experts on skin cancers are quick to issue an emphatic *no.* They maintain that overexposure to the sun during youth is one of several important factors that determine the risk of developing skin or other forms of cancer later in life. They add that the consistent use of sunscreens during the first eighteen years of a child's life can potentially reduce the lifetime incidence of some forms of skin cancer by nearly 80 percent. Of course, it is a good idea to continue to practice sun-preventive behaviors throughout life. I should also note that other factors, including heredity and other lifestyle factors, help to determine whether we will develop skin cancer.

So can anything be done to reverse the worldwide increases in skin cancers? Armed with tools like the IMB model and the health belief model described earlier in this chapter, many health psychologists believe the answer is a cautious yes. Indeed, they are currently hard at work developing interventions that they hope will be effective in getting people to "lighten up."

Critical Thinking Questions

1. In this discussion I've mentioned several reasons why people do not take precautions to avoid overexposure to the sun. Can you think of others? Do the reasons differ by age group? By gender?
2. If you were asked to develop an intervention to increase sun-preventive behaviors among college students, what would it look like? What techniques would you use? How would you ensure that any improvements would be maintained over time?

Primary Prevention: Decreasing the Risks of Illness

In most instances, our initial attempts to change our health behaviors are unsuccessful. Typically, we become aware of the need to change behaviors, we initiate change—and we experience a series of failed attempts at change. Only sometimes do we actually succeed in changing our behaviors. The nature of this process indicates that we need help: a variety of intervention programs to meet our varied needs and purposes.

Health Promotion and the Mass Media: Marketing Healthy Lifestyles in the Community We are constantly bombarded with messages about health risks. Numerous nonprofit organizations use television commercials, newspaper articles, magazine ads, and radio advertising to warn us about unhealthy behaviors like smoking, unprotected sex, and alcohol and drug abuse and their associated risks, including cancer, heart disease, and AIDS. These campaigns typically provide information about symptoms that may indicate the presence of a health problem, such as shortness of breath or chest pains in the case of heart attacks. And they often give information about the relation between specific behaviors and disease; for example, "Smoking is the number one cause of heart disease."

But can mass-media campaigns alone produce widespread changes in behavior? There is little evidence that they can (Meyer, Maccoby, & Farquhar, 1980). One reason for the limited success of these programs may be the media's depiction and promotion of unhealthy habits, which counteract health-promotion messages. An analysis of food and beverage commercials presented during prime-time television indicates that their messages are inconsistent with recommended dietary guidelines. For example, Story and Faulkner (1990) computed the frequency of commercials advertising healthy versus unhealthy food and beverages. Most of the prime-time commercials are for unhealthy foods and beverages. The clearest example is the difference in numbers of commercials for fast-food versus family-style restaurants. Despite these findings, it is interesting that many companies use health messages to sell their products.

Therefore, psychologists may need to improve the techniques they use to market good health (Winett, 1995). The mass media can be a very effective tool for promoting behavior change when combined with other intervention programs. For example, the Stanford Heart Disease Prevention Project investigated the combined effects of a media campaign and a program designed to change health-related behaviors (Farquhar, Maccoby, & Solomon, 1984). Three communities were chosen for the study. One community received an intense media campaign focusing on the risk factors associated with heart disease; a second group received the same media campaign plus a personal instruction program on modifying health habits for people in high-risk groups; a third community served as a control. Although the media campaign alone produced modest changes in health behavior, the program that included both a media campaign and personal instruction was most effective. Another successful program, which used a combination of mass media, community antismoking programs, and physician intervention—termed the Quit for Life Project—was able to reduce smoking prevalence in two major Australian cities by 6.5 percentage points over a four-year period (Pierce, Macaskill, & Hill, 1990).

Some evidence suggests that our beliefs may affect our responses to advertisements. This suggests that the way in which health messages are framed is important (Rothman & Solovey, 1997). For example, individuals with high fear of contracting AIDS rate advertisements about AIDS as more effective than people with low fear of contracting AIDS (Struckman-Johnson et al., 1990). These findings suggest that organizations can enhance the effectiveness of ad campaigns regarding AIDS by playing to people's fear of contracting this disease. The results of a recent study by David and Cindy Struckman-Johnson (1996) seem to support this view. These researchers predicted that the addition of a fear-arousing message to AIDS public service announcements (PSAs) about condom use would increase participants' attention to the announcements. The results confirmed these predictions: Participants exposed to the fear-arousing messages indicated a greater willingness to use condoms in the future and took a greater number of the free condoms offered at the end of the experiment than did participants exposed to PSAs without the fear message. These findings are consistent with the health belief model I described earlier, which predicts that people who believe they are susceptible to a disease will be more likely to accept an advertisement's intended message.

The Work of Staying Healthy: Motivating the Couch Potato

Research indicates that only one in five Americans exercises regularly and intensely enough to reduce his or her risk for chronic disease and premature death (Dubbert, 1992). This is surprising, since it is now very well known that regular and vigorous exercise can significantly reduce coronary heart disease, even in the presence of other health risk factors such as smoking, obesity, high blood pressure, and high blood cholesterol (Dishman, 1988; Slattery et al. 1977). Moreover, a recent U.S. Surgeon General's Report on Physical Activity and Health (1996) concludes that even less vigorous forms of activity can be beneficial if done consistently. According to this report, healthful benefits can be obtained from modest levels of exercise—*if* exercise is performed regularly (see Figure 13.13). What does this mean? Apparently fifteen minutes of running or thirty minutes of brisk walking each day will produce measurable benefits. For example, people who walk regularly have less than half the incidence of elevated cholesterol of those who do not (Tucker & Friedman, 1990).

Exercise can also affect our mental health. For example, exercise has been found to improve self-concept, alleviate feelings of depression, and reduce anxiety (Dubbert, 1992). These effects are particularly apparent just after a workout, but there may also be some long-term benefits from regular participation in exercise. Changes in mood following exercise may result partly from socializing and being involved with others (Plante & Rodin, 1990); running with a friend, for instance, provides both companionship and exercise. Mood may also improve because of exercise's effect on self-efficacy—enhanced confidence in our ability to perform a behavior, such as running a mile or completing an aerobics workout (Rodin & Plante, 1989).

So how can we get the rest of the couch potatoes off the couch? Some research suggests that starting and then maintaining an exercise program requires that people arrange their environment so that it supports the desired exercise behavior and weakens competing behaviors. First, it is important to arrange effective cues that become a signal to exercise. Working out in the same location, doing a similar warm-up routine, and recording and posting the results of one's physical activity can be effective in cueing future exercise behavior. It is also important to arrange when exercise occurs, to minimize the effects of the cues for competing behaviors. For example, individuals who have a tendency to work late should establish a morning training routine to minimize competition with a busy work schedule. Second, it is also important to arrange for consequences that maintain exercise behavior. Initially, it is critical for new exercisers to seek out sources of rewards for their exercise behavior and to avoid potential sources of punishment—including muscle soreness, fatigue, and injury. Unfortunately, those most in need of consistent exercise, such as obese or extremely out-of-shape persons or older individuals, may be those most subject to punishing consequences—including the possibility of a heart attack if they overdo it (Curfman, 1993; Knapp, 1988). Finally, the presence of a strong social support network can greatly increase adherence to a lifelong exercise habit.

FIGURE 13.13

Motivating the Couch Potato

A large body of research confirms that regular, moderately vigorous forms of exercise such as walking can be beneficial, if these activities are performed consistently.

Secondary Prevention: The Role of Early Detection in Disease and Illness

Psychologists are taking an increasingly active role in developing motivational strategies to get people to take part in *early detection* procedures—techniques used to screen for the presence of high blood pressure, high blood cholesterol, and some forms of cancer. The identification of these conditions at an early stage can make an enormous difference in the chances for treatment success—in some cases the difference between life and death.

Screening for Disease: Seeking Information about Our Health Status The fact that early detection and treatment of an illness is more effective than later detection and treatment is the foundation for screening programs. Evidence suggests that the widespread use of available screening techniques could decrease the incidence of cardiovascular disease through the early detection of high blood pressure and cholesterol, and could significantly reduce the number of cervical, colon, and prostate cancer deaths (Rothenberg et al., 1987).

Many companies, colleges, community organizations, and hospitals have screening programs to test for high blood pressure and serum cholesterol. Unfortunately, many people either do not take advantage of screening programs at all or fail to get screened regularly. Forgetting and underestimating the time since the last test are the primary reasons people wait too long between screenings. Interventions that heighten awareness or serve a reminder function, such as physician reminder systems and local advertising campaigns, can increase the frequency of screening visits (Mitchell, 1988).

The most significant factors that predict the use of screening, as indicated by the health belief model, are beliefs about the possible benefits of screening, the perceived severity of possible illnesses, perceived vulnerability to disease, and beliefs about what other people (friends, family) think about screening (Hennig & Knowles, 1990).

Self-Examination: Detecting the Early Signs of Illness Self-examination can be instrumental for the early detection of both testicular and breast cancer. The cure rate associated with testicular cancer is extremely high—if the cancer is detected early (Dahl, 1985). Unfortunately, in nearly half of the testicular cancers diagnosed, the presence of the disease is not detected until it has spread from the testes to the abdomen and other organs (Cummings et al., 1983), and the chances of a full recovery are significantly less (Bosl et al., 1981). Despite the fact that testicular self-examination techniques are available and are effective in detecting the early signs of cancer, many males remain unaware of their existence (Goldenring & Purtell, 1984; Steffen, 1990). In one recent study, Finney, Weist, and Friman (1995) compared the effectiveness of two self-examination training techniques: a pamphlet with a step-by-step checklist on how to perform testicular self-examination versus two commercially available films, each depicting a model doing a testicular self-examination. Participants in the study (college students) were trained by means of one of the methods and were then videotaped (from the waist down) while performing a testicular self-exam. Interestingly, the results—assessment of the number of self-examination steps performed correctly—indicated that the checklist was more effective than either of the films.

The dangers associated with undiagnosed breast cancer present a similar challenge for females. Some researchers suggest that breast cancers detected early through secondary prevention programs, such as breast self-examination, clinical breast examination, and mammography, have an 85 to 90 percent chance of being cured (American Cancer Society, 1989). Women are most likely to obtain mammography screening when their physician recommends it, highlighting the critical role these professionals play in promoting the importance of early detection. Programs designed to change certain beliefs are also effective in getting women to obtain mammography screening; for example, beliefs concerning their susceptibility to breast cancer, the severity of breast cancer, and the potential benefits of mammography screening (Aiken et al., 1994; S. M. Miller et al., 1996). For a summary of steps you can take to improve your personal health, see the **Ideas to Take with You** feature on page 541.

Key Questions

- What role do the mass media play in our health?
- What are the effects of regular exercise on our health?
- What is primary prevention? Secondary prevention?
- What is optimistic bias?

Making Psychology Part of Your Life

Managing Stress: Some Useful Tactics

Stress is a fact of life. Stressors are all around us—at work, in our environment, and in our personal lives. Because stress arises from so many different factors and conditions, it's probably impossible to eliminate it completely. But we can apply techniques to lessen its potentially harmful effects (Carver, Scheier & Weintraub, 1989; Folkman et al., 1986). Let's consider several of these techniques, dividing them into three major categories: physiological, behavioral, and cognitive.

Physiological Coping Techniques Common physiological responses to stress include tense muscles, racing pulse, pounding heart, dry mouth, queasy stomach, and sweating. But several coping techniques can be effective.

One of the most effective procedures is learning to reduce the tension in our own muscles through **progressive relaxation** (Jacobson, 1938). To use this technique, begin by alternately flexing and relaxing your muscles to appreciate the difference between relaxed and tense muscles. Next, you might shake out your arms and then let them flop by your sides. Then relax your shoulders by slowly rolling them up and down. Now, relax your neck. Step by step, extend this process until your body is completely relaxed from head to toe. Controlled breathing is also important. When you are tense, you tend to take in relatively short, shallow breaths. However, as your body slows down during relaxation, notice that your breathing changes to deeper, longer breaths. Relaxation procedures are effective in reducing emotional as well as physical tension. A related technique that is often effective for achieving a relaxed state is meditation, described in detail in Chapter 4.

Regular vigorous exercise is another important technique to reduce stress. I've been using this technique myself for many years, mainly through running. Although it does not eliminate the problems that sometimes lead to stress, it certainly increases my capacity to cope with stress, and it definitely makes me feel better.

Behavioral Coping Techniques We're all guilty of behaving in ways that bring stress on ourselves. We overload our schedules with too many responsibilities; we procrastinate; it all adds up to stress. There are plenty of things we can do to reduce the stress in our lives. One method is time management: learning how to make time work for us instead of against us. Adhering to a well-planned schedule can help us make more efficient use of our time and eliminate behaviors that interfere with our main goals. An important—but often ignored—principle of time management is to balance work time and play time. Table 13.4 on page 540 offers several important time-management principles.

Cognitive Coping Techniques We don't always have control over all the stressors in our lives. We can, however, gain some control over our cognitive reactions to them. In other words, when exposed to a stressful situation, we can think about it in different ways—and some of these are much more beneficial than

Table 13.4

Getting the Most out of Your Day: Psychology in Action

One behavioral strategy for reducing stress is time management. Here are some tips to help you get the most out of your day.

Basic Principles of Time Management
1. Each day, make a list of things you want to accomplish.
2. Prioritize your list. Plan to do the toughest things first, and save the easier tasks for later in the day when you are low on energy.
3. Arrange your work schedule to take best advantage of the hours when you work best.
4. Always set aside a block of time when you can work without any interruptions.
5. Be flexible about changes in your schedule so that you can handle unexpected events.
6. Set aside time in your daily schedule for exercise such as jogging, aerobics, or brisk walking. You'll find that the time spent is well worth it and may even increase your productivity.
7. Set aside some times each day or week in which you always do some planned leisure activity—everybody needs a break.

others. The process of replacing negative appraisals of stressors with more positive ones is called **cognitive restructuring** (Meichenbaum, 1977). To use this technique successfully, begin by monitoring your "self-talk"—what you say to yourself during periods of stress. Begin to modify your self-talk by thinking more adaptive thoughts. For example, try to discover something humorous about the situation, or imagine creative ways to reduce or eliminate the source of stress. Also, social support is important. Family, friends, or associates can often help you to "restructure" stressors (Bruhn & Phillips, 1987); that is, these persons can help you to perceive stressful events as less threatening and more under control than you might otherwise do. As you may recall, cognitive appraisal plays a crucial role in the way we interpret stressors. It's a good idea to be in contact with people who can suggest strategies for dealing with stressors that you might not generate yourself. Such strategies can often help reduce the negative feelings that frequently accompany stressful events or situations (Constanza, Derlega, & Winstead, 1988).

Ideas to Take with You

Enhancing Your Own Health

If the field of *health psychology* has a theme, it is this: There are many steps each of us can take to enhance our personal health—to reduce the chances that we will experience serious illness, and to raise the odds that we will enjoy good health and vigor throughout much of our life. Here is an overview of some of the most important of these actions. None will be a surprise; but together, they can add years—and much good health—to your life.

Don't Smoke—and If You Do, Quit Now, and Get the People You Care About to Do the Same

Eat as Healthy a Diet as You Can, and Don't Gain Weight

Drink Alcohol in Moderation!

Exercise!

Don't Take Risks Where Sex Is Concerned

Limit Your Time in the Sun

Engage in Primary Prevention—Check Your Own Body and Get Regular Checkups

Remember: The Health You Will Protect and Enhance by These Steps Is Your Own!

Summary and Review of Key Questions

Health Psychology: An Overview

- **What is health psychology?** Health psychology is the study of the relation between psychological variables and health.
- **What is the field of behavioral medicine?** Behavioral medicine, a field closely related to health psychology, combines behavioral and biomedical science knowledge to prevent and treat disorders.
- **To what can we attribute today's leading causes of death in the United States?** Many of today's leading causes of death can be attributed to illnesses caused by people's lifestyles.
- **What are epidemiological studies?** Epidemiological studies are large-scale research efforts focused on identifying risk factors that predict development of certain diseases, such as heart disease and cancer.

KEY TERMS

health psychology, p. 504 • lifestyle, p. 505 • epidemiological studies, p. 506

Stress: Its Causes, Effects, and Control

- **What is stress, and what are stressors?** Stress is the process that occurs in response to stressors; stressors are situations or events that disrupt, or threaten to disrupt, our physical or psychological functioning.
- **What is the GAS model?** The GAS (general adaptation syndrome) model, first reported by Hans Selye, describes how our bodies react to sources of stress and includes three distinct stages: alarm, resistance, and exhaustion.
- **What determines whether we will interpret an event as stressful or as a challenge?** Cognitive appraisals play an important role in determining whether we interpret potential stressors as stressful or as a challenge.
- **What are some of the most important stressors?** Among the most important stressors are major life events, such as the death of a spouse; daily hassles of everyday life, such as receiving a parking ticket or having to wait in a line at the grocery store; and work-related situations or events.
- **What are some sources of work-related stress?** Sources of work-related stress include work overload and underload, role conflict, and performance appraisals.
- **What is the person–environment fit, and why is it important?** The person–environment (P–E) fit is the match between characteristics of workers and characteristics of their jobs or work environments. Mismatches between these characteristics can lead to increases in stress-related illnesses.
- **What role does stress play in physical illness?** Stress may play a role in 50 to 70 percent of all physical illness, primarily through its effect on the immune system.
- **What are the effects of low levels of stress? High levels?** Even relatively low levels of stress may interfere with task performance. Prolonged exposure to high levels of stress may cause burnout.
- **What is burnout? What are its causes?** Burnout is the physical and psychological exhaustion that some people experience after prolonged stress. Burnout occurs when valued resources are lost or when existing resources are inadequate to meet demands or do not yield the expected returns. Job conditions implying that one's efforts are useless, ineffective, or unappreciated also contribute to the feelings of low personal accomplishment that are an important part of burnout.
- **Why are some people better able to cope with the effects of stress than others?** Individual differences in optimism and hardiness help explain the greater ability of some people to cope with stress. Optimists generally have problem-focused ways of coping with stress and actively seek out social support. Hardy people generally show high levels of commitment, view change as an opportunity for growth, and have a sense of control over events in their lives.

KEY TERMS

stress, p. 506 • stressors, p. 507 • general adaptation syndrome, p. 507 • hassles, p. 512 • person–environment (P–E) fit, p. 513 • hardiness, p. 517

Understanding and Communicating Our Health Needs

- **Why are symptoms and sensations important?** Symptoms and sensations, such as irregularities in heartbeat, are useful because they may help alert us to underlying health problems.
- **What is the health belief model?** The health belief model, initially developed to help explain why people don't use medical screening services, suggests that willingness to seek medical help depends on the extent to which we perceive a threat to our health and the extent to which we believe that a particular behavior will effectively reduce that threat.
- **What factors determine our willingness to make lifestyle changes or seek medical help?** According to the health belief model, our willingness to make lifestyle changes or seek medical help depends on our beliefs concerning our susceptibility to an illness, the severity of the illness, and the effectiveness of steps taken to deal with the illness.
- **Why is it important for psychologists to study aspects of doctor–patient interactions?** Physicians are often more effective in dealing with the technical aspects of medicine than in handling the psychosocial aspects. Because of this fact, psychologists have begun to develop interventions aimed at improving doctor–patient interactions; better interactions, in turn, can have a beneficial impact on important medical outcomes.

KEY TERM

health belief model, p. 520

Behavioral and Psychological Correlates of Illness: The Effects of Actions and Thoughts on Health

- **What is cancer?** Cancer is a group of diseases characterized by a loss of some cells' ability to function normally. Cancerous cells multiply rapidly, generating tumors, and may spread to distant sites in the body.
- **What are the potential consequences of smoking and exposure to secondhand smoke?** Both smoking and exposure to secondhand smoke (passive smoke) have been implicated in many types of cancers, in cardiovascular disease, and in a host of pathologies in children.
- **What determines who will become addicted to smoking?** Individual differences in people's reactions to nicotine, the addictive substance in tobacco, help determine who will become a smoker.
- **What are the effects of poor dietary practices?** Poor dietary practices can increase the risks of obesity, colon and rectal cancer, breast cancer, and cardiovascular disease.
- **What is self-determination theory?** Self-determination theory predicts that autonomously motivated health-preventive behavior is more likely to be maintained over time than behavior achieved at the urging of others.
- **What are the health consequences of heavy consumption of alcohol?** Heavy drinking can cause a variety of health problems that include stomach, liver, and intestinal cancer. It can also impair mental and sexual functioning, and it can result in fetal alcohol syndrome.
- **How is the way in which we express our emotions related to our health?** Failure to express our emotions can adversely affect the progression of cancer and other illnesses. Emotions can also lead to an increase in a person's blood pressure.

- **What are the characteristics of Type A persons? What diseases have been linked to Type A?** Type A persons tend to be competitive, aggressive, hostile, and impatient. Persons who are high in cynical hostility, in particular, are at risk of cardiovascular disease.
- **What is AIDS? How is AIDS transmitted?** AIDS (acquired immune deficiency syndrome) is a reduction in the immune system's ability to defend the body against invaders and is caused by the HIV virus. AIDS is transmitted primarily through unprotected sex, contaminated IV drug needles, and infected blood.
- **What is the IMB model and why is it relevant to AIDS?** According to the information–motivation–behavioral skills (IMB) model, people are more likely to avoid contracting HIV if they know how it is acquired and are motivated to perform HIV-preventive behaviors and omit risky ones.

KEY TERMS

cancer, p. 522 • risk factors, p. 522 • carcinogens, p. 522 • cardiovascular disease, p. 524 • nicotine, p. 524 • passive smoke, p. 525 • serum cholesterol, p. 527 • self-determination theory, p. 527 • hypertension, p. 529 • Type A behavior pattern, p. 529 • AIDS (acquired immune deficiency syndrome), p. 530

Promoting Wellness: Developing a Healthier Lifestyle

- **What role do the mass media play in our health?** The mass media, when combined with other health-promotion programs, can have a beneficial impact on health behaviors.
- **What are the effects of regular exercise on our health?** Regular, moderately vigorous exercise promotes both physical and psychological health. Starting and maintaining an exercise habit requires that people arrange their environment in a way that supports the desired exercise behaviors and weakens competing behaviors.
- **What is primary prevention? Secondary prevention?** In the context of health, primary prevention emphasizes disease prevention through education of people about the relation between their behavior and their health, promotion of healthy behavior, and direct modification of poor health practices. Secondary prevention emphasizes early detection of disease to decrease the severity of illness that is already present.
- **What is optimistic bias?** Optimistic bias refers to a person's belief that something negative is less likely to happen to them than to other persons like them.

KEY TERMS

prevention strategies, p. 534 • progressive relaxation, p. 539 • cognitive restructuring, p. 540

Critical Thinking Questions

Appraisal

Throughout this chapter we've seen that lifestyle factors—what we choose to eat, drink, or smoke, and whether we choose to exercise regularly—greatly influence our health. If one can achieve good health simply by changing one's own behaviors, then why aren't more people doing so?

Controversy

The number of persons infected with HIV in the United States and throughout the world is increasing at an alarming rate. Since it is clear that many infections result from unprotected sex with an infected person, behavioral researchers have developed interventions that effectively promote the use of condoms—particularly among high-risk populations. Others argue, however, that these interventions simply promote promiscuity and thereby worsen the problem. Which perspective is correct? What are your views on this issue?

Making Psychology Part of Your Life

Now that you know something about the many practices that can improve physical and psychological health, will you be more likely to follow these practices yourself? Why or why not?

CHAPTER OUTLINE

Psychological Disorders

Their Nature and Causes

Think back over all the people you have known. Can you remember ones who experienced any of the following problems?

- Deep feelings of depression that did not seem to be related to any events in their lives
- Unusual preoccupation with illness, health, and a large array of symptoms—some of which, at least, were of doubtful reality
- Tremendous concern about being overweight, coupled with either a near-starvation diet or repeated cycles of binging and purging
- Heavy dependence on alcohol, cigarettes, or various drugs, coupled with an inability to stop using these substances

If you *haven't* known someone who experienced one or more of these problems, then you have led a charmed life, because problems like these

Psychological Disorders: Maladaptive patterns of behavior and thought that cause the persons experiencing them considerable distress.

are experienced by many millions of persons every year. In fact, they are so common that as many as half of all human beings experience one or more of these difficulties at some point during their lives (e.g., Blazer et al., 1994; Kessler, 1994). It is on these **psychological disorders**—maladaptive patterns of behavior and thought that cause the persons experiencing them considerable distress—that we will focus in this chapter and the next one.

But what, precisely, are such disorders? I have just offered a brief definition, but it is far from complete. In fact, psychologists and other professionals concerned with such disorders have debated this question for decades. Why? Because *normal* behavior and *abnormal* behavior lie on a continuum, and there is no simple way of distinguishing one from the other. Most psychologists agree, however, that psychological disorders (and, by extension, all forms of behavior described by the term "abnormal") share some, if not all, of the following features.

Ideas about what is and is not acceptable behavior change over time and vary between cultures.

First, these disorders usually generate *distress*—negative feelings and reactions—in the persons who experience them. To this, some experts (e.g., Wakefield, 1992) add "*unexpected* distress," to distinguish between the negative feelings stemming from psychological disorders and those stemming from such events as failing an exam or losing a valuable possession. Only when personal distress is unexpected is it one aspect of a psychological disorder. Why do I say that these disorders "usually" generate distress? Because, as we'll soon see, some persons with psychological disorders are not disturbed by them; in fact, they may even take pleasure in their symptoms (see Figure 14.1).

Second, such disorders involve patterns of behavior or thought that are judged to be unusual or *atypical* in their society. People with these disorders don't behave or think like most others, and these differences are often apparent to the people around them. Third, psychological disorders involve behaviors that are *maladaptive*—ones that interfere with individuals' ability to function normally and meet the demands of daily life. Finally, psychological disorders are associated with behavior that is evaluated negatively by members of a person's society. Ideas about what is and is not acceptable behavior change over time and vary between cultures, however. For example, when I

FIGURE 14.1

Psychological Disorders: Not Always Disturbing to the People Who Have Them

As suggested by this cartoon, not all persons who have psychological disorders are disturbed by them; in fact, some seem to enjoy their symptoms.

"Please, Doc—nothing too aggressive. I'm kind of attached to my symptoms."

(**Source:** Drawing by Koren; ©1996 The New Yorker Magazine, Inc.)

was in college in the early 1960s, wearing a baseball cap to class or in a store would have been viewed as weird, not to mention downright rude. Now, of course, such behavior is widely accepted and would not be labeled as strange.

Taking these points into account, we can define psychological disorders as patterns of behavior and thought that are atypical, viewed as undesirable or unacceptable in a given culture, are maladaptive, and that usually (although not always) cause the persons who experience them considerable distress.

In the remainder of this chapter, we'll examine several different categories of psychological disorders and some of the factors that lead to their occurrence. Before turning to the disorders, however, we'll focus on two preliminary topics. First, we'll take a brief look at how ideas concerning the nature of psychological disorders changed over the centuries and gradually evolved into the science-based modern view held by today's psychologists. Second, we'll examine a widely used system for identifying various psychological disorders. This system is important because it is used by many professionals interested in mental health—including psychiatrists and psychiatric nurses as well as psychologists.

Changing Conceptions of Psychological Disorders

The pendulum of history swings, and like other pendulums, it does not move in only one direction. Over the course of the centuries and in different societies, abnormal behavior has been attributed to natural factors or forces—for example, imbalances within our bodies—or, alternatively, to supernatural ones, such as possession by demons or gods. Let's take a look at a few of these shifts, and at the modern view of abnormal behavior.

The Ancient World: Of Demons and Humors

The earliest view of abnormal behavior emphasized supernatural forces. In societies from China to ancient Babylon, "weird" behavior (remember—that means "weird" in a given society) was generally attributed to possession by evil spirits or other forces outside our everyday experience. Ancient Greece, however, provided an exception to this picture. Several centuries before the start of the common era, Hippocrates, a famous Greek physician, suggested that all forms of disease, including mental illness, had natural causes. He attributed psychological disorders to such factors as brain damage, heredity, and the imbalance of body *humors*—four essential fluids that, he believed, influenced our health and shaped our behavior. Hippocrates even suggested treatments for these disorders that sound impressively modern: rest, solitude, and good food and drink. The Romans generally accepted this view of psychological disorders; and because the Romans spread their beliefs all around what was then the known world, the idea of psychological disorders as the result of natural rather than supernatural causes enjoyed widespread acceptance, too.

The Middle Ages and the Renaissance: The Pendulum Swings

But then came the fall of Rome and what historians term the *middle ages*. At this time religion came to dominate Western societies in a way it had not done

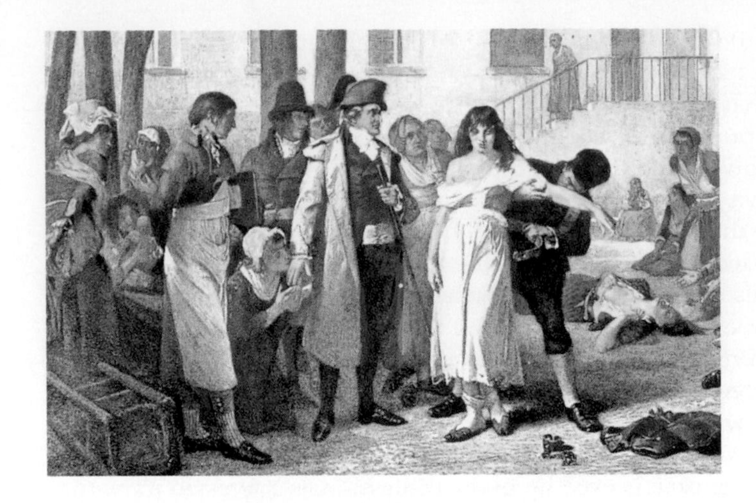

FIGURE 14.2

Humane Treatment of People with Psychological Disorders

Until the eighteenth century, people suffering from psychological disorders were exposed to harsh conditions. Philippe Pinel was a reformer who introduced more humane procedures in a large Paris hospital; he is shown here removing the chains from a patient.

in ancient times. The result was that abnormal behavior was once more attributed largely to supernatural forces. This was not always the case—some physicians suggested that strange behavior might stem from natural causes; but those physicians were ignored, or worse. The results of this shift in views was that persons with serious psychological disorders were seen as being punished for their sins by demons and devils. Thus, they were subjected to often painful *exorcisms*—efforts to remove these demons—and were often beaten, starved, or worse.

With the Renaissance, which began in Europe in the 1400s, the pendulum began to swing again. For instance, the Swiss physician Paracelsus (1493–1541) suggested that abnormal behavior might stem, at least in part, from the influence of natural forces such as the moon—hence the term *lunatic* to describe bizarre behavior. As the Renaissance continued and knowledge of anatomy and biology increased, the view that abnormal behavior was a disease—a kind of illness—began to take hold. Up until the 1700s, many mentally ill persons were kept in madhouses designed as much to keep these disturbed persons out of society as to protect them from harm. Conditions in these so-called *asylums* were brutal. Patients were shackled to walls in dark, damp cells, were never permitted outside, and were often beaten and abused by their guards. Indeed, the public sometimes bought tickets to view the inmates and their strange antics, just as people would pay to visit zoos.

Change, however, was in the wind. As early as the 1700s, a series of reformers—for instance, Jean-Baptiste Pussin and Philippe Pinel, physicians in charge of a large mental hospital in Paris—began arguing that patients with psychological disorders were suffering from a kind of illness, and that they would do much better if freed from their chains, moved to bright, sunny rooms, and permitted to go outside for exercise (see Figure 14.2). These changes *did* produce beneficial effects, so these ideas soon spread and did much to reduce the suffering of patients in such "hospitals." The result, ultimately, was the development of the **medical perspective** on abnormal behavior—the view that psychological disorders are a form of illness, produced, like other illnesses, by natural causes. This perspective is the basis for the field of **psychiatry,** a branch of modern medicine specializing in the treatment of psychological disorders.

Medical Perspective: The view that psychological disorders are a form of illness, produced, like other illnesses, by natural causes.

Psychiatry: A branch of modern medicine specializing in the treatment of psychological disorders.

Within psychology, there is currently less emphasis on abnormal behavior as a disease and more on its potential *biological* or *biochemical* roots (e.g., Heinrichs, 1993). Current evidence suggests that changes in the structure or functioning of the brain may play an important role in several forms of abnormal behavior (Raz, 1993). It also appears that genetic factors, too, may play a role in some psychological disorders (e.g., Gottesman, 1993; McGue, 1993).

So, while many psychologists prefer to avoid describing psychological disorders in strictly medical terms, they do accept the view that such disorders often involve biological causes.

The Psychodynamic Perspective

A very different view of abnormal behavior was offered by Freud and several other important figures in the history of psychology. According to this *psychodynamic perspective,* which we discussed in detail in Chapter 12, many mental disorders can be traced to unconscious urges or impulses and to the struggle over their expression that takes place in the hidden depths of human personality. Remember that in Freud's theory, the *id* demands instant gratification while the *superego* (conscience) denies it. The *ego* (consciousness) must strive to maintain a balance between these forces. According to Freud, mental disorders arise when the ego, sensing that it may soon be overwhelmed by the id, experiences *anxiety*. To cope with such anxiety, the ego uses many different *defense mechanisms*, as described in Chapter 12. These serve to disguise the nature of the unacceptable impulses and so reduce the anxiety experienced by the ego, but they may also lead to maladaptive behavior.

While few psychologists currently accept Freud's views about the origins of psychological disorders, his suggestion that unconscious thoughts or impulses can play a role in abnormal behavior remains influential; in fact, we'll consider the role of these unconscious factors in one psychological disorder, *depression,* in a later section (e.g., Watkins et al., 1996).

The Modern Psychological Approach: Recognizing the Multiple Roots of Abnormal Behavior

Mental illness is a term that makes some psychologists uneasy. Why? Because it implies acceptance of the medical perspective described above. Labeling an individual as "mentally ill" implies that her or his problems are a kind of disease that can be cured through appropriate medical treatment. In one respect, this view makes sense: Many psychological disorders *do* seem to have a biological basis. In another sense, though, the medical view is somewhat misleading. Decades of research suggest that full understanding of many psychological disorders requires attention to *psychological* processes such as learning, perception, and cognition, *plus* recognition of the complex interplay between environmental influences and heredity that is one of the "grand issues" of psychology we examined in Chapter 1.

For example, consider what is perhaps the most common form of psychological disorder, *depression*. This disorder is generally defined as involving intense sadness, lack of energy, and feelings of hopelessness and despair. What are the roots of this complex problem? Current evidence suggests that biochemical and genetic factors probably play an important role (e.g., Henriques & Davidson, 1990). But so, too, do cognitive factors, such as what people think about and how they interpret various events in their lives (e.g., Watkins et al., 1996); and so do social factors, such as how much support and encouragement people receive from important others in their lives (e.g., Terry, Mayocchi, & Hynes, 1996). In order to understand fully the nature of depression as well as its origins, we must take careful account of such factors.

Finally, psychologists also attach considerable importance to *cultural factors*. Some disorders—especially those that are quite severe—appear to be universal, occurring in all or most cultures (Al-Issa, 1982). Others, however,

Key Questions

- What are psychological disorders?
- To what factors were such disorders attributed in the past?
- What is the modern psychological view of such disorders?

vary greatly across cultures in terms of frequency, severity, and precise form. For instance, later in this chapter we'll consider *eating disorders*—disorders in which individuals experience disturbances such as starving themselves until they become dangerously thin (e.g., Garner, 1993). Such disorders occur mainly in Western cultures, where, as I noted in Chapter 10, "thin is in." But as Western pop culture spreads throughout the world, such problems are appearing in other cultures too—everywhere that Western magazines, films, and television programs reach (see Figure 14.3; Chun et al., 1992; Mumford, Whitehouse, & Choudry, 1992). Findings such as these suggest that psychological disorders do often have important roots in cultural beliefs and practices, and that these too should not be overlooked.

In sum, the modern psychological perspective on abnormal behavior suggests that such problems can best be understood in terms of complex and often subtle interactions among biological, psychological, and sociocultural factors. This perspective is more complex than one that views such disorders as "mental illnesses" produced solely by biological causes. However, most psychologists believe that it is also considerably more accurate.

Identifying Psychological Disorders: The DSM–IV

No competent physician would attempt to treat a common cold through surgery or internal injuries with a Band-Aid. The first and often most crucial step in medical practice is *diagnosis*—identifying the nature of the problem that brought the patient to the doctor's office in the first place. Even if we do not choose to view psychological disorders as medical illnesses, the

FIGURE 14.3

Effects of the Spread of Western Pop Culture around the World

Growing numbers of persons around the world—even those in developing countries—are being exposed to Western pop culture. One result is the spread of psychological disorders once known only in developed countries.

need to identify such problems in a clear and reliable manner remains. Without an agreed-upon system of *classification*, different psychologists or psychiatrists might refer to the same disorder with different terms or might use the same terms to describe very different problems (Millon, 1991).

The need for an agreed-upon system for diagnosing such disorders is addressed by the **Diagnostic and Statistical Manual of Mental Disorders–IV** (or *DSM–IV* for short; American Psychiatric Association, 1994). Although this manual is published by the American Psychiatric Association, psychologists have long contributed to its development—and increasingly so in recent years. Thus, it is designed to help all mental health practitioners to recognize and correctly identify (diagnose) specific disorders.

Diagnostic and Statistical Manual of Mental Disorders–IV: A manual designed to help all mental health practitioners to recognize and correctly diagnose specific psychological disorders.

The major diagnostic categories of the DSM–IV are shown in Table 14.1, and among them are all the major kinds of disorders we will discuss in this chapter.

TABLE 14.1

Major Diagnostic Categories of the DSM–IV

The DSM–IV classifies psychological disorders according to the categories listed here.

Diagnostic Category	Examples
Disorders usually first diagnosed in infancy, childhood, or adolescence	Mental retardation, learning disorders, disruptive behavior
Delirium, dementia, and other cognitive disorders	Disturbance of consciousness
Mental disorders due to a general medical condition	Delirium due to a high fever
Substance-related disorders	Alcohol dependence, amphetamine dependence, cocaine-use disorders
Schizophrenia and other psychotic disorders	Schizophrenia, delusional disorders
Mood disorders	Depression, bipolar disorders
Anxiety disorders	Panic attacks, agoraphobia
Somatoform disorders	Somatization disorder, conversion disorders
Factitious disorders	Intentional feigning of symptoms
Dissociative disorders	Dissociative amnesia, dissociative fugue, dissociative identity disorder (multiple personality disorder)
Sexual and gender identity disorders	Sexual desire disorders, sexual arousal disorders, paraphilias
Eating disorders	Anorexia nervosa, bulimia nervosa
Sleep disorders	Primary insomnia, nightmare disorder
Impulse control disorders not elsewhere classified	Intermittent explosive disorder, kleptomania, pathological gambling
Adjustment disorders	Development of emotional or behavioral symptoms in response to an identifiable stressor
Personality disorders	Paranoid personality disorder, schizoid personality disorder, antisocial personality disorder
Other conditions that may be a focus of clinical attention	Medication-induced movement disorders, problems related to abuse or neglect

Assessment Interviews: Interviews conducted by psychologists in which they seek information about individuals' past and present behaviors, current problems, interpersonal relations, and personality.

Halstead–Reitan Neuropsychological Battery: A battery of tests of auditory, visual, and psychomotor functioning (e.g., eye–hand coordination). Individuals' patterns of scores can point to the existence of specific forms of brain damage.

Behavioral Assessment: Observation of specific aspects of an individual's behavior that led the person to seek help—troubled interpersonal relationships, poor social skills, feelings of despair and hopelessness, seemingly irrational fears.

The manual itself describes hundreds of specific disorders—many more than we'll consider here. These descriptions focus on observable features and include *diagnostic features*—symptoms that must be present before an individual is diagnosed as suffering from a particular problem. In addition, the manual also provides much additional background information on each disorder; for instance, information about biological factors associated with the condition and about age-related, culture-related, and gender-related features—variations in each disorder that may be related to age, cultural background, and/or gender.

Another important feature of the DSM–IV is that it classifies disorders along five *axes,* rather than merely assigning them to a given category. One of these (Axis I) relates to major disorders themselves. Another (Axis II) relates to *mental retardation* (recall our discussion of this topic in Chapter 11) and to *personality disorders*—extreme and inflexible personality traits that are distressing to the person or that cause problems in school, work, or interpersonal relationships. A third axis pertains to general medical conditions relevant to each disorder, while a fourth axis considers psychosocial and environmental factors, including specific sources of stress. Finally, the fifth axis relates to a global assessment or current functioning. By enabling mental health practitioners to evaluate people along these various axes, the DSM–IV offers a fuller picture of people's current state and psychological functioning.

How does this newest version of the DSM differ from earlier versions? In several important respects. Perhaps most important, the role of psychologists in developing this new version was greater than ever before (Barlow, 1991). As a result, the DSM–IV is based more firmly than ever before on empirical evidence concerning the nature and prevalence of psychological disorders. Thus, the psychiatrists, psychologists, and other professionals who worked on this new version drew heavily on published studies and reanalysis of existing data in order to refine descriptions of each disorder. The task force also conducted special *field trials* in which they compared new descriptions and categories with existing ones to determine if proposed changes would indeed improve the reliability of diagnosis—the consistency with which specific disorders could be identified (e.g., Widiger et al., 1996).

Additional changes in the DSM–IV reflect efforts to take fuller account of the potential role of cultural factors in psychological disorders. For example, in the DSM–IV, the description of each disorder contains a new section that focuses on *culturally related features*—aspects of each disorder that are related to, and may be affected by, culture. Symptoms specific to a given culture and unique ways of describing distress in various cultures are included whenever available. This information is designed to help professionals recognize the many ways in which an individual's culture can influence the form of psychological disorders.

In these and other ways, the DSM–IV does seem to represent an improvement over earlier versions. However, it's important to note that the manual is still largely *descriptive* in nature: It describes psychological disorders, but it makes no attempt to explain them. This is deliberate; the DSM–IV was specifically designed to assist in diagnosis. It remains neutral with respect to various theories about the origins of psychological disorders. But because psychology, as a science, seeks *explanation,* not simply description, many psychologists view this aspect of the DSM–IV as a shortcoming that limits its value. For information on other tools psychologists use to assess individuals' functioning and the extent to which they are experiencing psychological disorders, please see the Research Methods section.

Key Questions

- What is the DSM–IV?
- In what ways is the latest revision of the DSM an improvement over earlier versions?
- What tools other than the DSM–IV do psychologists use to identify psychological disorders?

Having examined the pros and cons of the DSM–IV—and having covered our two preliminary topics—it's time to turn to the various disorders themselves. In discussing these, I'll generally follow the order in which they are described in the

DSM–IV, with one exception: I'll reserve discussion of what is in some ways the most serious and disturbing disorder, *schizophrenia*, for last.

▪ RESEARCH METHODS ▪

How Psychologists Study Psychological Disorders

Earlier, I noted that an agreed-upon system for identifying psychological disorders is a necessary first step for effective treatment of them. This is not the only reason why accurate diagnosis is necessary, though; in addition, diagnosis is also a crucial step for conducting systematic research on various disorders. Why do they occur? What effects do they have on the persons experiencing them? How can they best be alleviated? These are the kinds of questions *clinical psychologists* address in their research (e.g., Chassin et al., 1996; Vernberg et al., 1996). The DSM–IV is one important guide to identifying various psychological disorders, but it is not the only tool psychologists use for this purpose. Here are some other important diagnostic approaches:

Assessment Interviews As experts in human behavior, psychologists realize that much can be learned from direct interactions with individuals who seek their help. Thus, they often conduct **assessment interviews** in which they seek information about individuals' past and present behaviors, current problems, interpersonal relations, and personality (see Figure 14.4). Such interviews can be *structured,* in which case psychologists follow a detailed set of questions prepared in advance and known to get at the information they want, or *semistructured,* in which practitioners follow an outline of major topics but do not have a list of specific questions. Through such procedures psychologists can learn much about specific persons; they can also formulate interesting hypotheses concerning the origins of various psychological disorders. These hypotheses can then be tested in systematic research of the kind I'll describe throughout this chapter.

Personality Measures Personality is closely related to certain psychological disorders, so psychologists often use various measures of personality as a means of studying such disorders. Since we have already examined such measures in Chapter 12—both *projective tests* such as the Rorschach and TAT and *objective tests* such as the MMPI—I won't repeat that information here.

Assessment of Brain Functioning Some psychological disorders are linked to, or are the result of, damage to portions of the brain. Thus, psychologists sometimes use measures that are specifically designed to assess such damage, and brain functioning generally, in their research. One such measure is the **Halstead–Reitan Neuropsychological Battery.** This consists of many tests of auditory, visual, and psychomotor functioning (e.g., eye–hand coordination). The pattern of scores obtained by a given individual can point to the existence of specific forms of brain damage. More direct evidence on brain functioning can be obtained through various *neuroimaging techniques,* as discussed in Chapter 2—for instance, *magnetic resonance imaging,* and *positron emission tomography.* These tools are often used by psychologists to study the biological bases of various psychological disorders.

Behavioral Assessment Finally, psychologists often focus on specific aspects of an individual's behavior that led the person to seek help—troubled interpersonal relationships, poor social skills, feelings of despair and hopelessness, seemingly irrational fears. **Behavioral assessment** may mean observing individuals in specific situations, ones in which the *target behaviors*—those causing distress—occur. It may also involve gathering information on the *antecedents* of such behaviors—events or stimuli that precede their occurrence and may serve to trigger them—and on their *consequences* or effects.

In sum, psychologists use many different tools, not simply the DSM–IV, in identifying psychological disorders and planning systematic research on them. We'll encounter many examples of these methods as we now discuss various psychological disorders and efforts by psychologists to uncover the factors that lead to their occurrence.

FIGURE 14.4

Assessment Interviews: One Technique for Identifying Psychological Disorders

Psychologists often conduct *assessment interviews* with individuals seeking their help. These interviews are designed to provide information to help practitioners identify psychological disorders and other problems experienced by these persons.

Mood Disorders: The Downs and Ups of Life

Have you ever felt truly "down in the dumps"—sad, blue, and dejected? How about "up in the clouds"—happy, elated, excited? Probably you can easily bring such experiences to mind, for everyone has swings in mood or emotional state. For most of us, these swings are usually moderate in scope; periods of deep despair and wild elation are rare. Some persons, however, experience swings in their emotional states that are much more extreme and prolonged. Their highs are higher, their lows are lower, and they spend more time in these states than most people. Such persons are described as suffering from **mood disorders,** which the DSM–IV divides into two major categories—*depressive disorders* and *bipolar disorders*.

Depressive Disorders: Probing the Depths of Despair

Unless we lead a truly charmed existence, our daily lives bring some events that make us feel sad or disappointed. A poor grade, breaking up with a romantic partner, failure to get a promotion or a raise—these and many other events tip our emotional balance toward sadness. When do such reactions constitute depression? Most psychologists agree that several criteria are useful for reaching this decision.

First, persons suffering from **depression** experience truly profound unhappiness, and they experience it much of the time. Second, persons experiencing depression report that they have lost interest in the usual pleasures of life. Sex, sports, hobbies—all fail to provide the enjoyment they did at other times. Third, persons suffering from depression experience major loss of energy. Everything becomes an effort, and feelings of exhaustion are common. Additional symptoms of depression may include loss of appetite; disturbances of sleep; difficulties in thinking—depressed people find that they cannot think, concentrate, or remember; recurrent thoughts of death; and feelings of worthlessness or excessive guilt. When individuals experience five or more of these symptoms at once, they are classified by the DSM–IV as showing a *major depressive episode*.

Unfortunately, depression is very common. In fact, it is experienced by 21.3 percent of women and 12.7 percent of men at some time during their lives (Kessler et al., 1994). This nearly two-to-one gender difference in rate of experiencing depression has been reported in many studies (e.g., Culbertson, 1997), especially those conducted in wealthy, developed countries, so it appears to be a real one. Why does it exist? As noted by Strickland (1992), probably for several reasons. Situational factors that may contribute to depression in women include the fact that females have traditionally had lower status, power, and income than males, must worry more than males about their personal safety, and are subject to sexual harassment and assaults much more often than males. In addition, research findings indicate that the differences in rates of depression may also stem, at least to a degree, from the fact that females are more willing to admit to such feelings than males, or from the fact that women are more likely than men to remember depressive episodes (Wilhelm & Parker, 1994). I'll return to additional causes of depression experienced uniquely by females in the Exploring Gender and Diversity section on page 558.

How can you tell when you or another person is depressed? For information on this important issue please see the **Ideas to Take with You** feature.

Mood Disorders: Psychological disorders in which individuals experience swings in their emotional states that are much more extreme and prolonged than is true of most people.

Depression: A mood disorder in which individuals experience extreme unhappiness, lack of energy, and several related symptoms.

Ideas to Take with You

How to Recognize Depression

Depression is the most common psychological disorder; about 10 to 20 percent of all adults report having experienced one or more episodes in their lives that meet the clinical definition of depression. Unfortunately, once it starts, depression tends to continue to worsen over time: It places people in an emotional trap from which it is increasingly difficult to escape. So a key task is to recognize depression when it starts and seek help.

How can you recognize the onset of depression in yourself or in others? Here are some of the warning signs:

Feeling Down, Sad, and Blue Every Day of the Week

Most people's moods fluctuate during the week, rising to their best levels on Friday and over the weekend. If you or someone you know is down even at these times, it may be a sign of depression.

Ongoing Lack of Interest in All Pleasurable Activities Including Ones Previously Enjoyed

Most people's interest in various activities—from eating and sex to reading and sports—rises and falls over time. If you or someone you know never enjoys these activities anymore, this can be a sign of depression.

Significant Weight Loss When a Person Is Not Dieting

Some people lose interest in food and eating when they are seriously depressed. If you or someone you know is losing weight without trying to do so (and is not physically ill), this can be a sign of depression.

Fatigue and Loss of Energy Every Day

Again, for most people, feelings of energy and fatigue vary from day to day. But, if you or someone you know feels drained and weary all the time, this can be a sign of depression.

Insomnia or Sleeping Too Much

If you find that you can't sleep at night—or, conversely that you are sleeping much more in the past (partly because you feel so tired)—this can be a sign of depression.

Persistent Inability to Think or Concentrate, or Constant Feelings of Indecisiveness

Most of us feel more decisive, focused, and mentally alert on some days than others; but, if you or someone you know is experiencing reduced ability to think or make decisions all the time, this can be a sign of depression.

Bipolar Disorders: Riding the Emotional Roller Coaster

If depression is an emotional sinkhole, then **bipolar disorder** is an emotional roller coaster. People suffering from bipolar disorder experience wide swings in mood. They move, over varying periods of time, between deep depression and an emotional state known as *mania,* in which they are extremely excited, elated, and energetic. During manic periods, such persons speak rapidly, show a sharply decreased need for sleep, jump from one idea or activity to another, and show excessive involvement in pleasurable activities that have a high potential for harmful consequences. For example, they may engage in wild buying sprees or make extremely risky investments. Clearly, bipolar disorders are very disruptive not only to the individuals who experience them but to other people in their lives as well.

The Causes of Depression: Its Biological and Psychological Roots

Depression and other mood disorders tend to run in families (Egeland et al., 1987). Thus, if one identical twin experiences depression, the other has a substantial chance (perhaps as much as 40 percent) of developing a similar disorder. In contrast, among nonidentical twins, this figure drops to 20 percent (Kolata, 1986).

Other findings suggest that mood disorders may involve abnormalities in brain biochemistry. For example, it has been found that levels of two neurotransmitters, *norepinephrine* and *serotonin,* are lower in the brains of depressed persons than in those of nondepressed persons. Similarly, levels of such substances are higher in the brains of persons showing mania. Further, when persons who have recovered from depression undergo procedures that reduce the levels of serotonin in their brains, their depressive symptoms return within twenty-four hours (Delgado et al., 1990).

Unfortunately, this relatively neat picture is complicated by the following facts: Not all persons suffering from depression show reduced levels of norepinephrine or serotonin; and not all persons demonstrating mania have increased levels of these neurotransmitters. In addition, drugs used to treat both types of disorders produce many effects in addition to changing the presence or activity of these neurotransmitters. At present, then, it is clear that biological factors play a role in depression, but the precise nature of these effects remains to be determined.

While biochemical factors clearly play an important role in depression, *psychological mechanisms,* too, are involved. One such mechanism is *learned helplessness* (Seligman, 1975), beliefs on the part of individuals that they have no control over their own outcomes (we discussed this topic in Chapter 5). Learned helplessness often develops after exposure to situations in which such lack of control is present, but then generalizes to other situations where individuals' fate *is* at least partly in their hands. As you can imagine, feelings of learned helplessness are often associated with depression (e.g., Seligman et al., 1988).

Another psychological mechanism that plays a key role in depression is the negative views that depressed persons seem to hold about themselves (Beck, 1976; Beck et al., 1979). Individuals suffering from depression seem to possess negative *self-schemas*—negative conceptions of their own traits, abilities, and behavior. As a result, depressed persons tend to notice and remember negative information about themselves, such as criticism from others (Joiner, Alfano, & Metalsky, 1993). Because of this sensitivity to negative information, their feelings of worthlessness strengthen—and so does their depression.

Bipolar Disorder: A mood disorder in which individuals experience very wide swings in mood, from deep depression to wild elation.

Finally, depressed persons are prone to several types of faulty or distorted thinking (e.g., Persad & Polivy, 1993). Since they often experience negative moods, the kind of *mood-dependent memory* described in Chapter 6 tends to operate against them. Specifically, depressed persons tend to notice, store, and remember information consistent with their negative moods—negative information (e.g., Mason & Graf, 1993; Roediger & McDermott, 1992). They tend to bring unhappy thoughts and memories to mind, to dwell on them, and to enter new negative information into memory. Needless to say, this pattern sets up a self-perpetuating cycle in which the possibility of escape from depressing thoughts—or depression itself—decreases over time.

A dramatic illustration of such effects is provided by research conducted recently by Watkins and his colleagues (Watkins et al, 1996). These researchers suggested that the tendency of depressed persons to think negative thoughts is so strong that it occurs on an unconscious as well as a conscious level. In other words, depressed persons may tend to bring negative thoughts and information to mind without even being aware that they are doing so. To test this possibility, Watkins and his colleagues (1996) exposed individuals who were depressed and persons who were not depressed to lists of positive words (e.g., admired, optimistic, talented), neutral words (e.g., dresser, flannel, propane, turtles), or negative words (e.g., punished, hopeless, failure, rejected). As each word was shown on a screen, participants in the study were told to imagine themselves in a scene that involved this word. After studying the words in this fashion, the participants were presented with *cue words* that were related to the words they previously studied (e.g., adored for admired, furniture for dresser, and blamed for punished), and were asked to think of as many associations to these cues as possible in thirty seconds. The researchers reasoned that unconscious tendencies for depressed persons to bring negative information to mind would be shown by a greater likelihood on their part than on the part of nondepressed persons to remember negative words they had previously studied in response to the cue words. As you can see from Figure 14.5, this is precisely what happened. Moreover, and also as expected, the opposite was true with respect to positive words: Nondepressed persons remembered more of these than did depressed persons.

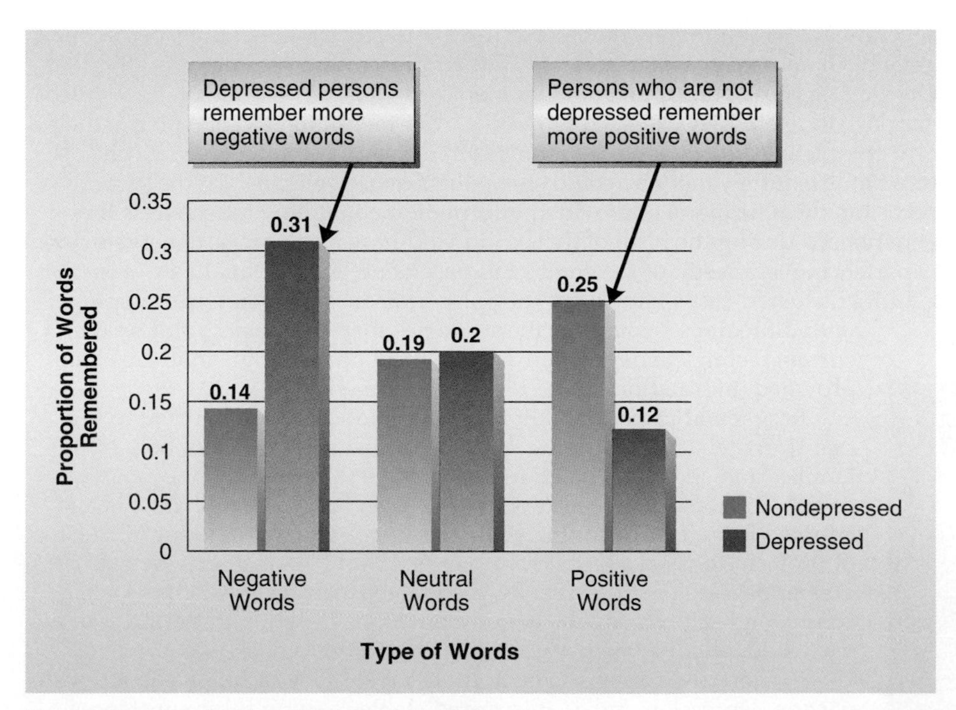

(**Source:** Based on data from Watkins et al., 1996.)

FIGURE 14.5

Unconscious Memory Bias among Depressed Persons

When exposed to cue words related to words they had previously studied, depressed individuals remembered more negative words than persons who were not depressed. In contrast, nondepressed persons remembered more positive words. These findings suggest that depressed persons are more likely than nondepressed persons to bring negative information to mind in many situations.

Postpartum Depression: Depression experienced by new mothers shortly after giving birth.

As indicated by Watkins and his colleagues (1996, p. 39), these findings have important implications for understanding the cognitive roots of depression. Since depressed persons seem to bring negative information to mind without trying to do so, their tendency to perceive the world through "dark gray glasses" is intensified, and they have little opportunity to engage in activities that might boost their mood—after all, they don't even *think* of such activities! Regardless of whether this reasoning is correct, there can be little doubt that cognitive factors play an important role in depression.

In the Exploring Gender and Diversity section below, we'll examine another potential cause of depression—one that affects primarily females.

EXPLORING GENDER & DIVERSITY

Postpartum Depression: Why New Mothers Sometimes Get the Blues

Earlier, I noted that depression is more common among females than males, and indicated that many different factors may contribute to this finding (e.g., Strickland, 1992). One factor I didn't mention has to do with pregnancy and childbirth: Many females experience feelings of depression shortly after giving birth (see Figure 14.6). Such **postpartum depression** is far from rare; indeed, between 20 and 30 percent of new mothers report symptoms of depression (e.g., Gotlib & Whiffen, 1991). Why does this happen? Research findings suggest that these reactions may stem, to a large extent, from the stress to which new mothers are exposed (Terry, 1991). Giving birth is often a draining and difficult experience; and after it is over, new mothers find themselves with many added responsibilities. If these seem overwhelming, and if women don't have adequate support from family and spouses to help them deal with the overload, they may begin to doubt their own ability to handle all the new demands. The result? New mothers may experience feelings of helplessness and resulting depression.

If this reasoning is correct, then it would be expected that several factors relating to stress and efforts to cope with it on the part of new mothers should predict the extent to which the women experience postpartum depression. Evidence indicating that this is indeed the case has recently been reported by Terry, Mayocchi, and Hynes (1996). These researchers gathered information on several variables from new mothers at three different points in time: before they gave birth, four weeks after the birth of their babies, and four months after that. On the first occasion, the pregnant women provided information on how much support and help they expected to receive from their families and spouse; they also completed a questionnaire that measured their beliefs in personal control—to what extent they felt they could shape their own outcomes. On the second occasion, the new mothers provided information about how much stress they experienced during the birth of their child, and how much stress they were now experiencing as a result of the child's temperament: Was the infant an "easy" or a "difficult" child (see Chapter 8)? They also indicated how they were coping with difficulties—what specific strategies they were using; and on their current feelings of depression. On the third occasion, the mothers again provided information on their level of depression.

FIGURE 14.6

Postpartum Depression: A Common Experience for New Mothers

About 20 to 30 percent of new mothers experience feelings of depression shortly after giving birth. Recent findings indicate that such depression stems from many factors relating to the level of stress experienced by new mothers.

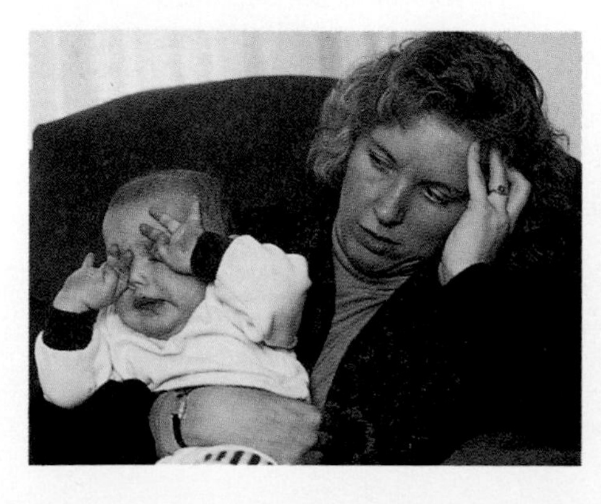

Results indicated that depression was indeed closely linked to several stress-related and coping factors. For instance, the more help from families and spouses women received, the less depression they experienced. Conversely, to the extent that women had "difficult" infants and adopted less effective coping strategies (e.g., "wishful thinking" instead of problem-focused coping; see Chapter 13), the women experienced greater degrees of stress. Finally, the greater their feelings of personal control and self-esteem, the better the women coped with the stress of a new child, and the less depression they experienced.

In short, there seems to be nothing mysterious or unique about postpartum depression; rather, it is a predictable reaction to circumstances that cause new mothers to feel overwhelmed by the burdens and responsibilities they face. If steps to improve these circumstances are taken—for instance, if new mothers are given additional help by family and spouses, and if their beliefs in their own ability to cope are strengthened—then the likelihood or intensity of such depression can be reduced.

Suicide: The act of taking one's own life.

Suicide: When Life Becomes Unbearable

Hopelessness, despair, negative views about oneself—these are some of the hallmarks of depression. Given such reactions, it is not surprising that many persons suffering from this disorder seek a drastic solution—**suicide,** or the taking of their own lives. In the United States, for instance, about 30,000 people commit suicide each year; and ten times that many attempt suicide but don't succeed (Andreason & Black, 1991; see Figure 14.7). About twice as many women as men attempt suicide; but men are three to four times more likely to succeed in ending their own lives mainly because men use no-fail methods such as jumping from high places, guns, or hanging, whereas women tend to use less certain tactics such as poison or drug overdose (Kaplan & Sadock, 1991). Suicide is the tenth or eleventh most frequent cause of death in the United States—and among young persons aged fifteen to twenty-four, it actually ranks *second,* behind only accidents. Suicide rates vary with age and by nation. The highest rates occur among older people, but suicide has been on the rise among young people and is now, disturbingly, high even among teenagers. Why do people seek suicide? Notes left by such persons, and information provided by suicide attempters, suggest that they do so for many different reasons. However, problems with relationships seem to head the list.

FIGURE 14.7

Suicide: The Ultimate Response to Depression

More than 300,000 people attempt to commit suicide each year in the United States alone; about 10 percent of these persons succeed in ending their own lives. Depression plays an important role in these tragic events.

Can suicide be predicted? There appear to be several important warning signs. First, suicide often seems to occur not when individuals are in the depths of despair—at their most depressed—but rather when they show some improvement. Deeply depressed persons lack the energy or will to commit suicide; when they feel somewhat better, however, they become capable of this act. Another clue to suicidal plans is a period of calm following considerable agitation; the person may have made his or her decision and now feels calm or even relieved that an end to the suffering is in sight. For example, consider the case of Sinedu Tadesse, an Ethiopian student at Harvard University who, after suffering from deep depression for years, finally decided to kill her roommate, Trang Ho, and take her own life. Shortly before doing so, she arranged to meet one of her friends, who described their meeting as follows (Thernstrom, 1996):

> When she arrived, her appearance was transformed. She was wearing makeup, high patent-leather heels, and shorts—a change from her Ethiopian self, where wearing shorts is considered disrespectful. There was a profound change in the way she looked and moved and carried herself. There was an air of happiness . . . about her. She seemed lighter. This was the happiest he had ever seen her. He is certain now that she was saying goodbye. (p.66)

Additional clues to potential suicide are provided by cognitive factors. For example, persons who are seriously thinking about suicide report fewer and weaker reasons for living than others (Steede & Range, 1989). Perhaps even more surprising, they also report different patterns of thought about death and its effects. When people contemplate their own deaths, they report several distinct types of fear relating to this event: fear of loss of self-fulfillment (death will bring an end to their plans); fear of loss of social identity (they will be forgotten by others); fear of the consequences to their family; and fear of the unknown. Research findings indicate that persons who have actually attempted suicide report roughly equal fear of each of these outcomes (Orbach et al., 1993). In contrast, individuals who have not attempted suicide report different levels of fear: They are most frightened of loss of self-fulfillment and of the unknown, and least frightened about loss of social identity.

Key Questions

- What are the major symptoms of depression? Of bipolar disorder?
- What factors play a role in the occurrence of mood disorders?
- What are the causes of postpartum depression?
- What are the important warning signs of suicide?

Anxiety Disorders: When Dread Debilitates

At one time or another, we all experience **anxiety**—increased arousal accompanied by generalized feelings of fear or apprehension. If such feelings become very intense and persist for long periods of time, however, they can produce harmful effects. Such **anxiety disorders** take several different forms, but recent findings indicate that they are all related to a generalized feeling of anxiety and worry (Zinberg & Barlow, 1995).

Anxiety: Increased arousal accompanied by generalized feelings of fear or apprehension.

Anxiety Disorders: Psychological disorders that take several different forms, but which are all related to a generalized feeling of anxiety.

Panic Attack Disorder: An anxiety disorder in which individuals experience high levels of physiological arousal coupled with intense fear of losing control.

Panic Attack: The Body Signals "Danger!" But Is It Real?

Have you experienced *panic*—very high levels of physical arousal coupled with the intense fear of losing control? If you have, don't worry; almost everyone has had this experience at some time or other. But persons who suffer from a psychological condition known as **panic attack disorder** experience such reactions often, and sometimes without any specific triggering event. As defined by DSM–IV, such attacks involve a discrete period of fear or discomfort in which at least four of the following symptoms occur suddenly and rise to a peak within ten minutes: palpitations, pounding heart, sweating, trembling or shaking, sensations of shortness of breath, feeling of choking, chest pain or discomfort, nausea, feelings of dizziness or lightheadedness, feelings of unreality, fear of losing control, fear of dying, numbness or tingling sensation, chills or hot flashes.

For some people, panic attacks occur out of the blue, without any apparent cause. For others, however, they are linked with specific situations. In that case, panic disorder is associated with **agoraphobia**—intense fear of specific situations in which individuals suspect that help will not be available should they experience an incapacitating or embarrassing event. Common patterns for agoraphobia include fear of being in a crowd; standing in a line; being on a bridge; traveling in a bus, plane, train, or car; or merely leaving home (American Psychiatric Association, 1994). Persons suffering from such disorders often experience anticipatory anxiety—they are terrified of becoming afraid. I have a good friend who suffers from one form of agoraphobia: He is totally unwilling to travel by airplane. Since he has an active career, this condition causes him great difficulties. He has to drive or take trains even to distant locations. Yet he resists all suggestions that he seek professional help. Apparently the mere thought of discussing his problems is so anxiety-provoking that he prefers to leave matters as they are.

What causes panic attacks? Existing evidence indicates that both biological and cognitive factors play a role. With respect to biological factors, it has been found that there is a genetic component in this disorder: About 50 percent of people with panic disorder have relatives with this problem (Barlow, 1988). In addition, PET scans of the brains of persons who suffer from panic attacks suggest that even in the nonpanic state, their brains may function differently, in subtle ways, from those of other persons (e.g., Reiman et al., 1989).

With respect to cognitive factors, persons suffering from panic attack disorder tend to show a pattern including the following key elements:

1. They tend to interpret bodily sensations as being more dangerous than they really are: for instance, they perceive palpitations as a sign of a heart attack.
2. As a result, they experience anxiety, which itself induces further bodily changes and sensations.
3. These sensations elicit more **catastrophic thinking**—more thoughts about impending disaster—and the result may be a full-blown panic attack (e.g., Barlow, 1988, 1991).

Phobias: Fear That Is Focused

Most people express some fear of snakes, heights, violent storms, and buzzing insects such as bees or wasps. Since all of these can pose real threats to our safety, such reactions are adaptive, up to a point. Some persons, though, experience intense anxiety in the presence of those objects or situations—or even when they merely think about them. Such *phobias* can be so strong that they interfere with everyday activities. Thus, persons suffering from animal phobias may avoid visiting friends who own dogs or may cross the street to avoid passing a person walking a pet. Similarly, those with social phobias—fear of social situations—may avoid a wide range of settings in which they fear they will be exposed to and scrutinized by other persons.

What accounts for such strong fears? One possibility involves the process of *classical conditioning,* described in Chapter 5. Through such learning, stimuli that could not initially elicit strong emotional reactions can often come to do so. For example, a person may acquire an intense fear of bees or wasps after seeing a friend or relative stung by such an insect. The intense pain shown by the victim may serve as an unconditioned stimulus for similar reac-

Agoraphobia: Intense fear of specific situations in which individuals suspect that help will not be available should they experience an incapacitating or embarrassing event.

Catastrophic Thinking: Thoughts about impending disaster that may result in a full-blown panic attack.

FIGURE 14.8

Social Phobias: A Devastating Form of Anxiety Disorder

Persons suffering from social phobias experience strong fear of social situations. This may cause them to lead a life of loneliness and despair, lacking in the human contacts they strongly desire but are unable to obtain.

tions on the part of the person witnessing the scene, with the result that bees or wasps, which were previously quite neutral stimuli for this person, now come to evoke strong fear. Similarly, intense fear of spiders may be related to observation of the strong feelings of disgust they arouse in some people (e.g., Mulkens, deJong, & Merckelbach, 1996).

Among the phobias, *social phobias* are perhaps the most devastating. Persons with these phobias are afraid of a wide range of social settings and interactions—parties, eating in public, giving speeches, using public rest rooms (see Figure 14.8). Their intense fear of such situations often dooms them to a restricted social life, and sometimes to painful loneliness (e.g., Schneider et al., 1992). What are the causes of such phobias? Existing evidence indicates that several factors may play a role: childhood shyness, certain aspects of personality (e.g., being low in extraversion), and an early traumatic experience—a social situation in which the individual felt uncomfortable and something negative happened (e.g., being laughed at, making a mistake). In one study, individuals who had a history of childhood shyness and a traumatic early experience were much more likely to experience social phobias than individuals for whom neither of these factors was present (Stemberger et al., 1995). Recent findings indicate that cultural factors, too, may play a role in social phobias (or in more generalized social anxiety). For example, it has been found that social anxiety is more common among Asian Americans than among Americans of European descent (e.g., Uba, 1994). A recent study by Okazaki (1997) suggests that this may be due, at least in part, to the fact that among Asian Americans, the self-concept and feelings of self-worth are closely linked to social relationships—to being able to maintain harmony with others. Among Americans of European descent, in contrast, the self-concept is linked to being independent and autonomous. The result: Asian Americans may be more likely to experience social anxiety in many situations.

Obsessive–Compulsive Disorder: Behaviors and Thoughts Outside One's Control

Have you ever left your home, gotten halfway down the street, and then returned to see if you really locked the door or turned off the stove? Most of us have had such experiences, and they are completely normal. But for some persons, such anxieties are so intense that the individuals become trapped in

ROBOTMAN® by Jim Meddick

(**Source:** ROBOTMAN reprinted by permission of Newspaper Enterprise Association, Inc.)

FIGURE 14.9

Obsessive Behavior: A Key Component of Obsessive–Compulsive Disorder

Robotman can't prevent himself from attempting to straighten the crooked sign. If he repeats such actions many times a day, this may suggest that he is suffering from *obsessive–compulsive disorder.*

repetitious behaviors known as *compulsions* that they seem unable to prevent (see Figure 14.9) and/or in recurrent modes of thought called *obsessions.* Consider the following description of a person suffering from an **obsessive–compulsive disorder** (Rachman & Hodgson, 1980):

> When George wakes in the morning . . . he feels that his hands are contaminated so he cannot touch his clothing. He won't wash in the bathroom because he feels that the carpet is contaminated. . . . I have to dress him, having first cleaned his shoes and got out a clean shirt, underclothes, socks, and trousers. He holds his hands above his head . . . to make sure that he doesn't contaminate the outside of his clothing. Any error . . . and he will have to have clean clothes. . . . George then goes downstairs, washes his hands in the kitchen and thereafter spends about twenty minutes in the toilet. . . . Basically he has to be completely sure that there is no contamination around because if he is not then he will start to worry about it later on. (pp. 66–67)

What is the cause of such reactions? We all have repetitious thoughts occasionally. For example, after watching a film containing disturbing scenes of violence, we may find ourselves thinking about these over and over again. Most of us soon manage to distract ourselves from such unpleasant thoughts. But individuals who develop obsessive–compulsive disorder are unable to do so. They are made anxious by their obsessional thoughts, yet they can't dismiss them readily from their minds. As a result, they become even more anxious, and the cycle builds. Only by performing specific actions can they ensure their "safety" and reduce this anxiety. Therefore, they engage in complex repetitive rituals (e.g., hand washing or checking things over and over again) that can gradually grow to fill most of their day. Since these rituals do generate reductions in anxiety, the tendency to perform them grows stronger. Unless such persons receive effective outside help, they have little chance of escaping from their anxiety-ridden self-constructed prisons.

Obsessive–Compulsive Disorder: An anxiety disorder in which individuals become trapped in repetitious behaviors known as compulsions that they seem unable to prevent, and/or in recurrent modes of thought called obsessions.

Posttraumatic Stress Disorder: A disorder in which people persistently reexperience traumatic events in their thoughts or dreams, feel as if they are reliving these events from time to time, and persistently avoid stimuli associated with the traumatic events, along with several other symptoms.

Posttraumatic Stress Disorder

Imagine what it is like to be sleeping in your own bed and then suddenly to be thrown out onto the floor as the ground under your home heaves and shakes. Once awakened, you find yourself surrounded by the sounds of objects, walls, and even entire buildings crashing to the ground—and perhaps by shrieks of fear and cries of pain from your neighbors or even your own family. This is precisely the kind of experience reported by many persons during the California earthquake of 1994.

Such experiences are described as *traumatic* by psychologists because they are extraordinary in nature—and extraordinarily disturbing. It is not surprising, then, that some persons exposed to them experience **posttraumatic stress**

FIGURE 14.10

Factors Related to Posttraumatic Stress Disorder in Children

Children exposed to hurricane Andrew (which struck Florida in 1992) were most likely to experience *posttraumatic stress disorder* if they perceived this event as life-threatening; did not receive adequate support from parents, friends, and teachers; and adopted negative coping strategies (e.g., engaging in wishful thinking, blaming themselves for this natural event).

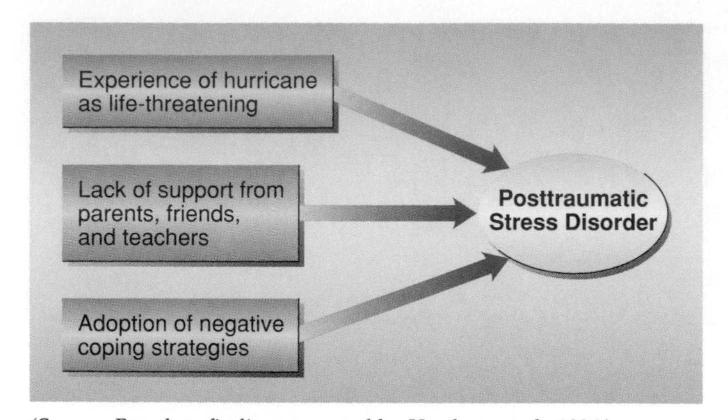

(**Source:** Based on findings reported by Vernberg et al., 1996.)

disorder—a disorder in which people persistently reexperience traumatic events in their thoughts or dreams; feel as if they are reliving these events from time to time; persistently avoid stimuli associated with the traumatic events (places, people, thoughts); and persistently experience symptoms of increased arousal, such as difficulty falling asleep, irritability or outbursts of anger, and difficulty in concentrating. Posttraumatic stress disorder can stem from a wide range of traumatic events—natural disasters, accidents, rape and other assaults, torture, or the horrors of wartime combat (Basoglu et al., 1996; Layman, Gidycz, & Lynn, 1996; Vernberg et al., 1996).

Since not all persons exposed to traumatic events experience this disorder, a key question about posttraumatic stress disorder is this: What factors lead to its occurrence? The results of a recent study by Vernberg and his colleagues (Vernberg et al., 1996) offer revealing findings about this issue. These researchers questioned children living in an area of south Florida that had been devastated in 1992 by hurricane Andrew. They predicted that whether each child would develop posttraumatic stress disorder would be influenced by four groups of factors: whether the child had been exposed to a traumatic event (the extent to which he or she had felt threatened by the hurricane); the child's age and gender; the extent to which the child's parents, teachers, and friends provided emotional support during the stressful period; and the ways in which the child attempted to cope with the traumatic event—whether through effective, positive coping strategies (e.g., trying to see the good side of things, trying to keep calm) or through ineffective, negative coping strategies (e.g., engaging in wishful thinking, blaming himself or herself for the hurricane, or becoming angry). When information on these factors was related to the extent to which children showed posttraumatic stress disorder, three of these factors—exposure to the hurricane, social support, and coping strategies—were indeed found to play a role. Specifically, children who felt that their lives or safety had been threatened by the hurricane, who did not receive adequate social support from parents, teachers, or friends, and who adopted negative coping strategies were most likely to experience this disorder (see Figure 14.10).

In sum, it appears that whether individuals experience posttraumatic stress disorder after exposure to a frightening event depends on several factors. However, other findings suggest that cognitive factors—such as individuals' interpretation of the traumatic event—may be especially important. Only to the extent that individuals define an event as traumatic—dangerous and frightening—are they likely to expe-

Key Questions

- What are anxiety disorders?
- What are panic attacks?
- What are phobias?
- What is obsessive–compulsive disorder?
- What is posttraumatic stress disorder?

rience the symptoms of posttraumatic stress disorder. For instance, victims of date rape who do not define their experience as rape are much less likely to experience this disorder than those who do (Layman et al., 1996). Thus, as is true with many aspects of life, the way in which we perceive events plays a key role in determining how we react to them.

Somatoform Disorders: Physical Symptoms without Physical Causes

Several of Freud's early cases, ones that played an important role in his developing theory of personality, involved the following puzzling situation. An individual would show some physical symptom (such as deafness or paralysis of some part of the body); yet careful examination would reveal no underlying physical causes for the problem. Such disorders are known as **somatoform disorders**—disorders in which individuals have symptoms typically associated with physical diseases or conditions, but in which no known organic or physiological basis for the symptoms can be found. The DSM–IV recognizes several distinct somatoform disorders.

One of these is known as **somatization disorder,** a condition in which an individual has a history of many physical complaints, beginning before age thirty, that occur over a period of years and result in treatment being sought for significant impairments in social, occupational, or other important areas of life. The symptoms reported may include pain in various parts of the body (e.g., head, back, abdomen), gastrointestinal problems (e.g., nausea, vomiting, bloating), sexual symptoms (e.g., sexual indifference, excessive menstrual bleeding), and neurological symptoms not related to pain (e.g., impaired coordination or balance, paralysis, blindness).

Another somatoform disorder is **hypochondriasis**—preoccupation with fears of disease. Hypochondriacs do not actually have the diseases they fear, but they persist in worrying about them, despite repeated reassurance by their doctors that they are healthy. Many hypochondriacs are not simply faking; they feel the pain and discomfort they report and are truly afraid that they are sick or will soon become sick. (Other persons who seek medical help *are* faking, however; please see the Beyond the Headlines section on page 566 for information on this pattern.)

Yet another type of somatoform disorder is known as **conversion disorder.** In hypochondria, there are no apparent physical disabilities—just the worry that they will develop. In conversion disorders, however, there are actual impairments. Individuals suffering from such disorders may experience blindness, deafness, paralysis, or loss of sensation in various body parts. Yet, while these disabilities are quite real to the persons involved, there are no underlying medical conditions that would produce them. Another feature that distinguishes conversion disorders from other somatoform disorders is the presence of psychological factors that seem to play a role in the initiation or intensification of the symptoms—factors such as interpersonal conflicts or other stressors.

What are the causes of somatoform disorders? Freud suggested that persons experiencing unacceptable impulses or conflicts converted these into various symptoms. By doing so, they reduced the anxiety generated by the impulses and at the same time gained much sympathy and attention. While psychologists generally reject this view, it does seem accurate in one respect:

Somatoform Disorders: Disorders in which individuals have symptoms typically associated with physical diseases or conditions, but in which no known organic or physiological basis for the symptoms can be found.

Somatization Disorder: A somatoform disorder in which an individual has a history of many physical complaints, beginning before age thirty, that occur over a period of years and result in treatment being sought for significant impairments in social, occupational, or other important areas of life.

Hypochondriasis: A somatoform disorder involving preoccupation with fears of disease or illness.

Conversion Disorder: A somatoform disorder in which individuals experience actual physical impairment such as blindness, deafness, or paralysis for which there is no underlying medical cause.

Beyond the Headlines

As Psychologists See It

Medical Masqueraders Unmasked

People who seem to devote their entire lives to visiting doctors and having painful medical procedures—-including operations—when they are not ill: how bizarre. How can we account for such actions? As you can see, **Munchausen's syndrome** appears to be related to hypochondriasis, especially when we realize that this latter disorder sometimes achieves important goals for the persons who have it. However, there is one crucial difference: Persons suffering from hypochondriasis are usually not faking; they really experience their symptoms and fears about illness. In contrast, persons with Munchausen's syndrome know that there's nothing actually wrong with them, and set about—quite brazenly—manufacturing their symptoms. Why would anyone engage in such behavior? Perhaps because they enjoy the attention they get from doctors, nurses, and others. Or perhaps they like fooling trained physicians, convincing them that they have serious ailments when in fact they don't. Whatever the reason, such persons generally refuse therapy when their tricks are discovered. They may not actually enjoy their disorder, but they are certainly not willing to give it up without a struggle—and that in itself suggests that the disorder serves important functions for them. In any case, such persons do waste precious medical resources and often run up huge bills that must be paid by insurance companies or government programs; so there's more involved than their own psychological health. For this reason alone, Munchausen's syndrome, no matter how strange, is no laughing matter. On the contrary, it seems to be a pattern of behavior worthy of careful further study.

Munchausen's Sufferers Use Ills to Get Attention

Wall Street Journal, April 22, 1996—A medical masquerade made news last week when a Florida woman with a sick child was charged with inducing the girl's illness, resulting in a medical history that encompassed 40 surgeries and 200 hospital stays. . . .

Behind the alleged abuse is a bizarre condition known to doctors as Munchausen's syndrome, in which people travel from doctor to doctor claiming symptoms of a feigned ailment to get attention for themselves. . . .

Many Munchausen's cases came to light in National Institutes of Health studies of fevers of unknown origin. . . . One such case involved a nurse who was injecting milk into her veins. . . . In another study, researchers analyzed kidney stones passed at home and brought to the hospital. They found some of the rocks were geological—such as quartz . . . rather than biological in origin. . . . Perhaps the most famous medical impostor of the 1990s is known as "the Red Baron," a man in his early thirties who visited at least 14 hospitals from New Orleans to New Haven, seeking treatment for a rare disorder of the lungs and kidneys. . . . He altered medical records and had a command of medical terminology. . . . He claimed to have been a fighter pilot in the Gulf War who was exposed to solvent vapors while painting his jet. In this guise, he underwent repeated kidney biopsies and extensive treatment. When Yale University hematologist Thomas Duffy finally unmasked the baron, he simply left the hospital. . . .

Critical Thinking Questions

1. Do you think that Munchausen's syndrome qualifies as being a psychological disorder? If so, why? If not, why?
2. Why do you think people who show this syndrome adopt it? In other words, what do they get out of their strange behavior?
3. Assuming persons with Munchausen's syndrome could be induced to accept help, what could be done to change this costly and potentially dangerous behavior?

People suffering from somatoform disorders do often seem to benefit from these disorders in terms of eliciting sympathy from important people in their lives such as spouses, parents, or children. In addition, research by one team of psychologists (Lecci et al., 1996) suggests that persons suffering from hypochondria have more health-related goals than most people—such as trying to maintain or lose weight, managing stress, and coping with chronic illnesses. Having these goals permits hypochondriacs to focus much of their thinking on health-related issues, an activity they seem to find rewarding. In addition, of course, this focus on personal health feeds directly into their hypochondria and makes it likely that, like the character shown in Figure 14.1, they will be reluctant to give up their preoccupation without outside assistance.

Key Questions

- What are somatoform disorders?
- What is Munchausen's syndrome, and how is it related to hypochondriasis?

Dissociative Disorders: When Memory Fails

Have you ever awakened during the night and, just for a moment, been uncertain about where you were? Such temporary disruptions in our normal cognitive functioning are far from rare; many persons experience them from time to time as a result of fatigue, illness, or the use of alcohol or other drugs. Some individuals, however, undergo much more profound and lengthy losses of identity or memory. These are known as **dissociative disorders** and, like other psychological disorders, can take several different forms.

In Chapter 6 we saw that *amnesia,* loss of memory, can sometimes be produced by illnesses or injuries to the brain. Sometimes, however, amnesia seems to occur in the absence of such physical causes. This **dissociative amnesia** appears to stem from the active motivation to forget. After experiencing some traumatic event, violating their own standards, or undergoing intense stress, individuals sometimes go blank with respect to these events and cannot recall them. Such amnesia can involve all events within a particular period of time *(localized amnesia)*, or only some events occurring during this period *(selective amnesia)*. Alternatively, it can erase memories for a person's entire life prior to a specific date *(generalized amnesia)*. While individuals suffering from such disorders truly cannot remember past events, many aspects of their behavior remain intact: habits, tastes, previously learned skills. Musicians can continue to play their instruments, computer programmers can still write programs, and hairstylists can still cut and style hair.

A second type of dissociative disorder is known as **dissociative fugue.** This is a sudden and extreme disturbance of memory in which individuals wander off, adopt a new identity, and are unable to recall their own past. Newspapers often report accounts of individuals who simply vanish one day, only to reappear years later in a new location living a new life—often with a new spouse and family.

Such disorders can truly be described as *dissociative* in nature, for they seem to represent reactions in which some portion of memory is split off, or dissociated, from conscious awareness.

Perhaps the most dramatic type of dissociative disorder is **dissociative identity disorder,** the condition formerly labeled as *multiple personality disorder*. In this rare disorder, a single person seems to possess two or more distinct identities or personality states, and these take control of the person's behavior at different times. Another feature of the disorder is the inability to

Munchausen's Syndrome: A syndrome in which individuals pretend to have various medical problems in order to get attention from health practitioners.

Dissociative Disorders: Disorders involving prolonged loss of memory or identity.

Dissociative Amnesia: Profound amnesia stemming from the active motivation to forget specific events or information.

Dissociative Fugue: A sudden and extreme disturbance of memory in which individuals wander off, adopt a new identity, and are unable to recall their own past.

Dissociative Identity Disorder: The condition formerly labeled as *multiple personality disorder,* in which a single person seems to possess two or more distinct identities or personality states, and these take control of the person's behavior at different times.

FIGURE 14.11

Multiple Personality: Real or Fraud?

William Milligan, a convicted rapist, appeared to possess more than ten different personalities, including the one whose writing appears below his photo. Although many cases of multiple personality (now termed *dissociative identity disorder*) appear to involve faking, others seem to involve a genuine psychological disorder.

recall important personal information that is too extensive to be forgotten by ordinary forgetfulness.

A dramatic illustration of dissociative identity disorder is the case of William Milligan, a man arrested in 1977 for the rapes of three women. Milligan was identified by two of the victims, and his fingerprints matched those at the scene of one of the crimes, so it appeared to be an open-and-shut case (see Figure 14.11). Only when he twice attempted suicide was he examined by psychiatrists. The results of their examinations were remarkable. Milligan appeared to possess not one or two distinct personalities but at least *ten*. One was "Billy" Arthur, an emotionless Englishman who dominated the others. A second was Ragen, a powerful Yugoslavian. Additional personalities included Tommy, a belligerent teenager; Christene, a three-year-old English girl; and Christopher, her disturbed thirteen-year-old brother. On the basis of psychiatric testimony concerning his disorder, Milligan was found not guilty by reason of insanity—a legal category suggesting that he was not responsible for his actions. Thus, he was sent for treatment to a mental health center, where it was discovered that he had still more personalities, including a thug with a Brooklyn accent, a practical joker, and even a social snob! Milligan underwent treatment in a state facility for several years and was released when his separate personalities appeared to fuse. After his release he worked for a child abuse–prevention agency and later developed a career as an artist (Kihlstrom, Tataryn, & Hoyt, 1993).

Another bizarre case of dissociative identity disorder came to light some years ago when a multiple-personality patient accused a man she had dated, Mark Peterson, of rape. She claimed that only one of her personalities had given consent. Another had watched the event, and still another went to the police to report the assault. Peterson was convicted under a law that makes having sexual relations with a mental patient equivalent to rape (Kihlstrom et al., 1993).

These and other striking cases of dissociative identity disorder raise an intriguing question: Is multiple identity disorder real? Or are persons like William Milligan merely clever fakers? No final answer currently exists; but this disorder *is* included in the DSM–IV, so clearly many psychiatrists and psychologists do assume that it really exists. What kind of evidence supports this view? Findings such as these: Persons with this disorder sometimes show a distinctive pattern of brain activity when each of their supposedly separate personalities appears (Kaplan & Sadock, 1993). Moreover, in many cases each personality scores differently on widely used personality tests. Such findings suggest that perhaps dissociative identity disorder is related in some way to the "splitting of consciousness" described by the neodissociation theory of hypnosis (discussed in Chapter 4). As you may recall, that theory suggests that hypnosis somehow divides consciousness so that parts of the mind become split or separated from other parts. This view is controversial and is not widely accepted by psychologists; but, as I noted in Chapter 4, some recent findings do seem to provide support for the view that hypnosis involves *some* kind of effects of this type (e.g., Noble & McConkey, 1995). Perhaps dissociative identity disorder involves such processes, but in this case they are generated by internal factors relating to brain function or biochemistry, rather than by hypnosis.

Pending the completion of additional research on this fascinating type of disorder, it is probably best to view it with a degree of caution. It may be possible for more than one personality to exist in one body; but at present too few cases have been studied—and there is too much room for faking—to permit firm conclusions about this issue one way or the other.

Key Questions

- What are dissociative disorders, and what is dissociative amnesia?
- What is dissociative identity disorder?

Sexual and Gender Identity Disorders

As we saw in Chapter 12, Freud believed that many psychological disorders can be traced to disturbances in *psychosexual development*. While Freud's theory is not widely accepted in psychology, there is little doubt that problems relating to sexuality and gender identity form an important group of psychological disorders. Several of these are discussed below.

Sexual Dysfunctions: Disturbances in Desire and Arousal

Sexual dysfunctions include disturbances in sexual desire and/or sexual arousal, disturbances in the ability to attain orgasms, and disorders involving pain during sexual relations. In **sexual desire disorders** people lack interest in sex or have an active aversion to sexual activity. Persons suffering from these disorders report that they rarely have the sexual fantasies most persons generate, that they avoid all or almost all sexual activity, and that these reactions cause them considerable distress.

In contrast, **sexual arousal disorders** involve the inability to attain or maintain an erection (males) or the absence of vaginal swelling and lubrication (females). Among *orgasm disorders* are the delay or absence of orgasms in both sexes and *premature ejaculation* (reaching orgasm too quickly) in males. Needless to say, these problems are often extremely upsetting to the persons who experience them (e.g., Rowland, Cooper, & Slob, 1996).

Paraphilias: Disturbances in Sexual Object or Behavior

What is sexually arousing? For most people, the answer usually includes the sight or touch of another human being. But many people find other stimuli arousing, too. The large volume of business done by Victoria's Secret and other companies specializing in alluring lingerie for women stems, at least in part, from the fact that many men find such garments mildly sexually arous-

Sexual Desire Disorders: Disorders involving a lack of interest in sex or active aversion to sexual activity.

Sexual Arousal Disorders: The inability to attain or maintain an erection (males) or the absence of vaginal swelling and lubrication (females).

FIGURE 14.12

Sadism and Masochism: Two Paraphilias

The items shown here are used by persons suffering from two paraphilias: *sadism*—a disorder in which individuals become sexually aroused only by inflicting pain or humiliation on others, and *sexual masochism*—in which individuals are aroused by receiving such treatment.

ing. Other persons find either inflicting or receiving some slight pain during lovemaking increases their arousal and sexual pleasure. Do such reactions constitute sexual disorders? According to most psychologists, and the DSM–IV, they do not. Only when unusual or bizarre imagery or acts are *necessary* for sexual arousal (that is, when arousal cannot occur without them) do such preferences qualify as disorders. Such disorders are termed **paraphilias,** and they take many different forms.

In *fetishes* individuals become aroused exclusively by inanimate objects. Often these are articles of clothing; in more unusual cases they can involve animals, dead bodies, or even human waste. *Frotteurism,* another paraphilia, involves fantasies and urges focused on touching or rubbing against a nonconsenting person. The touching, not the coercive nature of the act, is what persons with this disorder find sexually arousing. Perhaps more disturbing is *pedophilia,* in which individuals experience sexual urges and fantasies involving children, generally ones younger than thirteen. When such urges are translated into overt actions, the effects on the young victims can, as we noted in Chapter 9, be devastating (e.g., Ambuel, 1995). Two other paraphilias are *sexual sadism* and *sexual masochism* (see Figure 14.12). In sexual sadism individuals become sexually aroused only by inflicting pain or humiliation on others. In sexual masochism people are aroused by receiving such treatment. See Table 14.2 for a description of these and other paraphilias.

Gender Identity Disorders

Have you ever read about a man who altered his gender to become a woman, or vice versa? Such individuals feel, often from an early age, that they were born with the wrong sexual identity. They identify strongly with the other sex and show preferences for cross-dressing (wearing clothing associated with the other gender) and for stereotypical games and pastimes of the other gender. They are displeased with their own bodies and request—again, often from an early age—that they receive medical treatment to alter their primary and secondary sex characteristics. In the past, there was little that medicine could do to satisfy these desires on the part of persons suffering from **gender identity disorder.** Advances in surgical techniques, however, have now made it possible for such persons to undergo *sex-change operations,* in which their sexual organs are actually altered to approximate those of the other gender. Several thousand individuals have undergone such operations, and existing evidence indicates that most report being satisfied with the results and happier than they were before (Green & Fleming, 1990). However, follow-up studies suggest that some persons who undergo such operations experience regrets and continued unhappiness, sometimes to the point that they commit suicide (Abramowitz, 1986). So it appears that such operations have a serious potential downside that should be carefully considered.

Key Questions

- What are sexual dysfunctions and paraphilias?
- What is gender identity disorder?

Paraphilias: Disorders in which sexual arousal cannot occur without the presence of unusual imagery or acts.

Gender Identity Disorder: A disorder in which individuals believe that they were born with the wrong sexual identity.

Eating Disorders

When I was in high school, female figures that can only be described as well-rounded were in vogue. Beginning in the mid-1960s, however, this standard of beauty changed drastically, shifting toward a much slimmer

TABLE 14.2
Paraphilias

Disorders in which unusual or bizarre imagery or acts are necessary for sexual arousal are known as *paraphilias*. Some of the more common types are described here.

Description	Symptoms
Exhibitionism	Sexual urges or arousing fantasies involving exposure of one's genitals to an unsuspecting stranger
Voyeurism	Recurrent sexual urges or arousing fantasies involving the act of observing an unsuspecting person who is naked, disrobing, or engaging in sexual activity
Fetishism	Sexual arousal or persistent fantasies about or actual use of nonliving objects
Sadism and Masochism	Sadism: Sexual arousal or fantasies about or from engaging in actions of dominating or beating another person. Masochism: Sexual arousal or fantasies about or from engaging in the act of being dominated, humiliated, or even beaten
Transvestic Fetishism	Intense sexual urges and arousing fantasies involving cross-dressing (dressing in the clothing of the other sex)
Other Paraphilias	Frotteurism: Sexual urges involving touching or rubbing against a nonconsenting person Necrophilia: Sexual obsession with corpses Klismaphilia: Sexual excitement from having enemas Coprophilia: Sexual interest in feces Zoophilia: Sexual gratification from having sexual activity with animals

shape (see Figure 14.13 on page 572). Puzzling as this is to me personally (like you, I have my own preferences), the "thin is beautiful" image has persisted—and is delivered over and over again by television, films, and magazines. Despite this fact, a growing proportion of adults in the United States and other countries are actually overweight, as I pointed out in Chapter 10. Many of these persons are, of course, unhappy about the shape they are in and would prefer to be slimmer. Even persons classified as being of normal weight, however, feel the pressure of the saying "You can never be too rich or too thin." Given this gap between the image of personal beauty portrayed by the mass media and physical reality, it is not surprising that **eating disorders**—disturbances in eating behavior that involve maladaptive and unhealthy efforts to control body weight—are increasingly common. Among these, two—*anorexia nervosa* and *bulimia nervosa*—are most common.

Anorexia Nervosa: Carrying the Ideal of Being Slim to Extremes

Persons suffering from **anorexia nervosa** refuse to maintain body weight at or above a minimal normal level; this means that they literally starve themselves, sometimes until their weight drops to dangerously low levels. For instance, consider the case of Christy Henrich, a nationally famous gymnast in the 1980s. At a height of 4 feet 10 inches, she weighed about 95 pounds when at the peak of her career. After she developed anorexia nervosa, however, her weight dropped to a low of 47 pounds before she was hospitalized. Why do persons suffering from this disorder starve themselves in this manner? Partly because they have an intense fear of gaining weight or becoming

Eating Disorders: Disturbances in eating behavior that involve maladaptive and unhealthy efforts to control body weight.

Anorexia Nervosa: An eating disorder in which individuals starve themselves until they lose dangerous amounts of weight.

FIGURE 14.13

Changing Ideals of Feminine Beauty: Do They Play a Role in Eating Disorders?

In the 1950s, being attractive was equated with having a figure like that of Marilyn Monroe (left photo). After the mid-1960s, however, standards of feminine beauty shifted greatly, so that being thin—even extremely thin—was seen as the ideal. Research findings indicate that this shift may be linked to the emergence of certain eating disorders during the 1970s.

fat, even though in many cases they are of normal weight or less. In addition, anorexics tend to perceive their own bodies in distorted ways; for instance, such persons often see themselves as much heavier than they are.

Anorexia nervosa is far more common among females than males, probably because the emphasis on having a beautiful body is much stronger for females than males. Interestingly, many young women suffering from anorexia nervosa are convinced that they will not be attractive unless they are extremely thin. Actually, this idea is out of touch with reality, because research findings indicate that few men prefer the extremely thin figures that female anorexics *believe* they prefer (e.g., Williamson, Cubic, & Gleaves, 1993). Whatever its precise origins, anorexia nervosa poses a serious threat to the physical as well as the psychological health of the persons who experience it.

Bulimia: The Binge–Purge Cycle

If you found anorexia nervosa disturbing, you may find a second eating disorder—**bulimia nervosa**—even more unsettling. In this disorder, individuals engage in recurrent episodes of binge eating—eating huge amounts of food within short periods of time—followed by some kind of compensatory purging behavior designed to prevent weight gain. This can involve self-induced vomiting, the misuse of laxatives, fasting, or excessive exercise, to the point where the purging is potentially harmful to their health. Amazing as it may seem, persons suffering from bulimia nervosa (again, mainly young women) report purging about twelve times per week; and many purge even more often than this. My daughter once had a roommate who was a recovered bulimic, and I met her several times. She was of normal weight, as are most bulimics, but her repeated binge–purge cycles had done permanent harm to her digestive system, and she had to stick primarily to a spice-free diet of boiled or steamed foods. As someone who truly loves to eat, I considered that to be the ultimate warning to persons suffering from bulimia: Seek help quickly, or the digestion you ruin may be your own!

A factor that helps explain how persons with bulimia nervosa can engage in repeated cycles of binge eating and vomiting is that over time repeated self-induced vomiting damages their taste receptors, so that they show reduced sensitivity to many tastes (e.g., Rodin et al., 1990). The result: They can tolerate the unpleasant experiences involved in purging.

Bulimia Nervosa: An eating disorder in which individuals engage in recurrent episodes of binge eating following by some form of purging.

Why do so many young women develop this disorder? Again, the "thin is beautiful" ideal seems to play an important role (e.g., Thompson, 1992; Williamson, Cubic, & Gleaves, 1993). Another, and related factor, is the desire to be perfect in all respects, including those relating to physical beauty. Recent findings indicate that women who rate high on this trait are at risk for developing bulimia, especially if they perceive themselves to be overweight (Joiner et al., 1997). And in fact, bulimics—like anorexics—do tend to perceive themselves as much heavier than they really are. This fact is illustrated clearly by a study conducted by Williamson, Cubic, and Gleaves (1993). These researchers asked three groups of young women—ones diagnosed as bulimic, ones diagnosed as anorexic, and ones who had no eating disorder—to rate silhouettes of women ranging from ones that were very skinny to ones that were very obese. First, participants selected the silhouette that most accurately matched their own *current* body size; then they rated the silhouette that represented the body size they most preferred (their *ideal*). Results indicated that when current body size was held constant statistically, both bulimic and anorexic persons rated their current body size as larger than did control participants, and both rated their ideal as smaller than did controls (see Figure 14.14 on page 574). In other words, when current body weight was taken into account (anorexics were, of course, the thinnest), both groups with eating disorders viewed themselves as farther from their ideal than persons who did not suffer from an eating disorder.

While I am certainly not against the mass media—they are a valuable source of information, entertainment, and change—I think it's reasonable to suggest that to the extent they promote the "thin is beautiful" image, they may do serious harm to the health and well-being of many persons, primarily young women, who are the victims of eating disorders.

Fortunately, it appears that the frequency of eating disorders tends to decrease with age. For instance, one recent study reported that the incidence of such disorders among female college students had decreased sharply when they were tested again ten years later. While more than forty percent showed some signs of eating disorders while in college (e.g., dieting frequently, showing the symptoms of anorexia or bulimia), only fifteen percent reported such symptoms ten years later (Heatherton et al., 1997). Interestingly, while the incidence of eating disorders was much lower among men, they experienced larger weight gains during this ten-year period than women and an *increased* tendency to diet. So, eating disorders are certainly not restricted to females.

Key Questions

- What are anorexia nervosa and bulimia nervosa?
- What factors play a role in the occurrence of these eating disorders?

Personality Disorders: Traits That Harm

Have you ever known someone who was highly suspicious and mistrustful of others in virtually all situations? How about someone who "fell in love" frequently, but couldn't maintain a long-term relationship? Someone who always wanted to be the center of attention and did things like dressing in a bizarre manner or getting wild tattoos in order to reach this goal? If so, these may well have been people with specific **personality disorders.** These disorders are defined by the DSM–IV, as extreme and inflexible personality traits that are distressing to the persons who have them or cause them problems in school, work, or interpersonal relations. The emphasis should probably be on "cause them problems" rather than on "distress," because many people with these kinds of traits are *not* disturbed by them: They view their behavior, strange as it may seem to others, as perfectly normal and beneficial, at least to them.

Personality Disorders: Disorders involving extreme and inflexible personality traits that are distressing to the persons who have them or cause them problems in school, work, or interpersonal relations.

FIGURE 14.14

Dissatisfaction with One's Own Body: An Important Factor in Eating Disorders

When actual body size was held constant statistically, both anorexics and bulimics rated their own current body size as larger than did controls (persons not suffering from these disorders); and both rated their ideal body size as smaller than did controls.

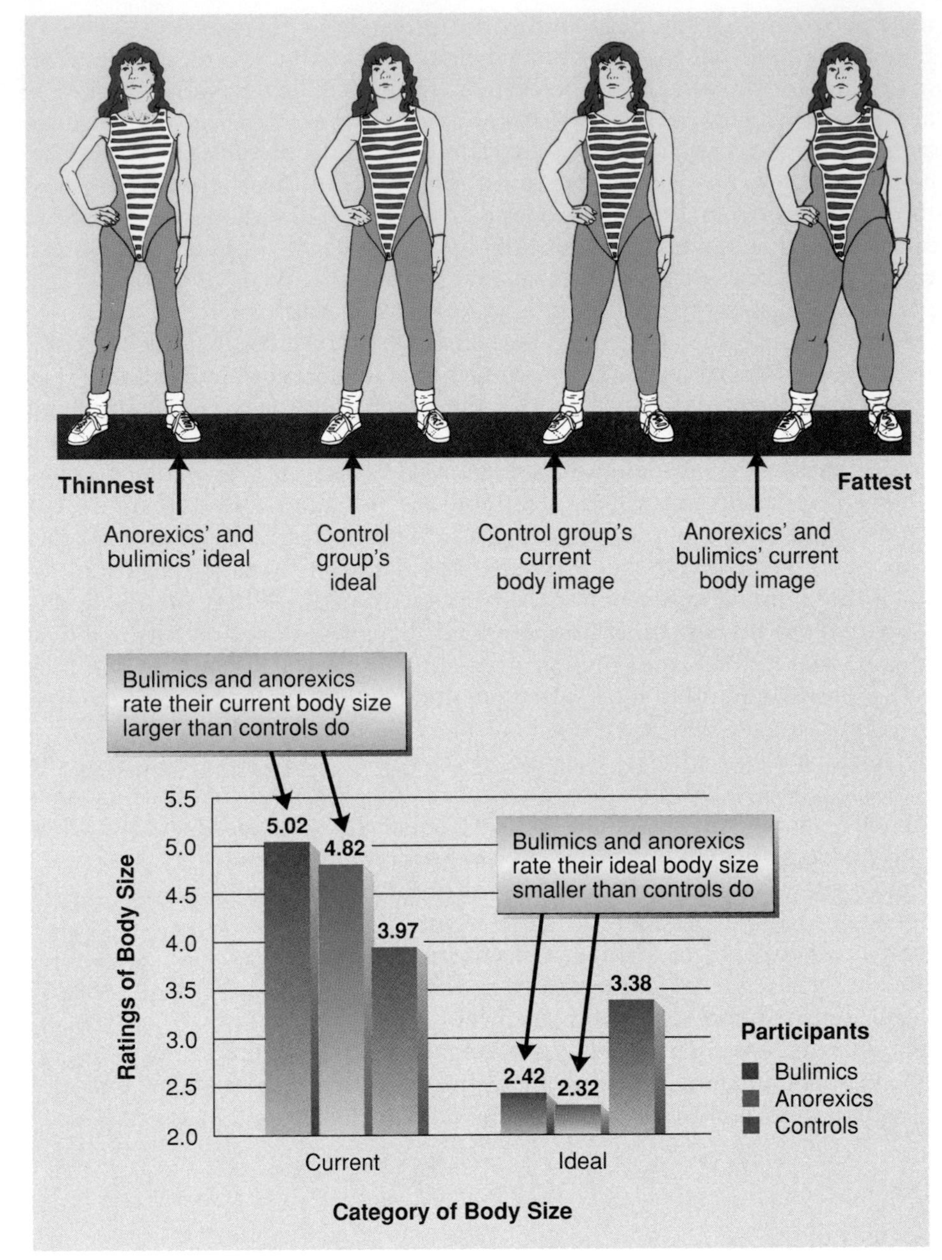

(**Source:** Based on data from Williamson, Cubic, & Gleaves, 1993.)

The DSM–IV divides personality disorders into three distinct clusters, so let's take a look at some of the disorders that fit under these categories. The first cluster is described as involving *odd, eccentric* behavior or traits, and includes three personality disorders: *paranoid, schizoid,* and *schizotypal*. Persons suffering from *paranoid personality disorders* fit the "suspicious and mistrustful"description suggested above; they believe that everyone is out to get them, deceive them, or take advantage of them in some way. In contrast, persons suffering from the *schizoid personality disorder* show another pattern. They have few if any social relationships and live an almost totally solitary life. They can form stable relationships in a few cases, but none of these are close—not even with immediate family members. *Schizotypal personality disorder* involves a pattern in which individuals are very uncomfortable in interpersonal relationships and, at the same time, suffer from cognitive or perceptual distortions and eccentric behavior. For instance, they may wear strangely out-of-date or mismatched clothes, or may show up in a wool sweater in August.

They are often superstitious, and they often believe in mysterious forces that can't be seen but are affecting their behavior.

The second major cluster of personality disorders described by the DSM–IV includes disorders involving *dramatic, emotional,* and *erratic* forms of behavior. People with the *borderline personality disorder* show tremendous instability in their interpersonal relationships, self-image, and moods. Did you ever see the movie *Fatal Attraction*? It depicts a highly unstable woman who has a brief affair with a married man. When he indicates that he does not want to continue the relationship, she goes off the deep end and behaves in very erratic and dangerous ways. That is the kind of pattern shown by persons with borderline personality disorder. For these persons, mood swings are huge, love often changes quickly to hate, and best friends become enemies overnight.

In contrast, people with the *histrionic personality disorder* show a tremendous need for attention from others. They want to be the center of attention, and they will do almost anything to attain this goal—dressing in extremely unusual ways, piercing their bodies in many places, behaving seductively in many contexts (see Figure 14.15).

FIGURE 14.15

Signs of the Histrionic Personality Disorder

Persons suffering from the *histrionic personality disorder* will do almost anything to satisfy their intense craving for attention from others.

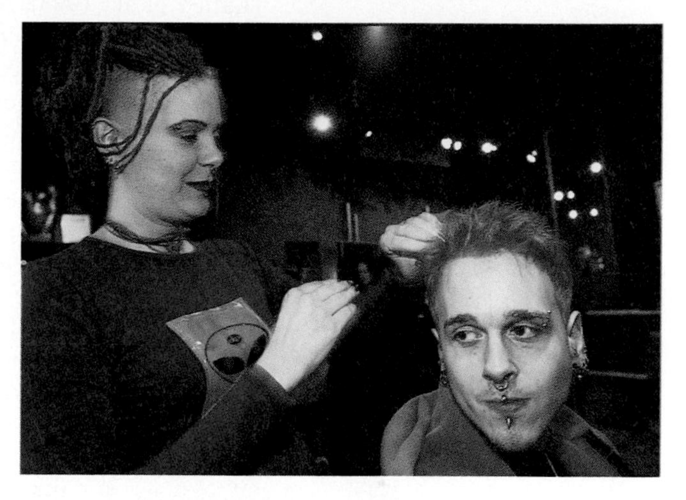

Also included in this cluster of personality disorders is the one that is in some ways the most important and most disturbing—the **antisocial personality disorder.** Have you ever read about confidence artists who swindle elderly people out of their life's savings? About petty criminals who have been arrested for theft or vandalism dozens of times? They might well be diagnosed as showing the antisocial personality disorder. Characteristics of this disorder include:

- Deceitfulness—a willingness to lie anytime, to anyone, about anything.
- Impulsivity and failure to plan ahead.
- Irritability and aggressiveness—such persons often fly off the handle in response to what seem to be trivial provocations or annoyances.
- Reckless disregard for their own safety and that of others—people with this disorder are truly high risk takers.
- Lack of remorse; if such persons hurt others or do harm, it doesn't phase them.
- Failure to conform to social norms—rules and regulations are not for these individuals, and they needlessly disobey them.
- Little or no concern for the rights or welfare of others—persons with this disorder view other people as conveniences to be used for their own purposes.

Together, this combination of traits produces individuals who engage in antisocial behavior without hesitation, often in a seemingly random manner. For example, consider the following statement by Gary Gilmore, a convicted multiple murderer:

> I pulled up near a gas station. . . . I told the service station guy to give me all his money. I then took him to the bathroom and told him to kneel down and then I shot him in the head twice. The guy didn't give me any trouble but I just felt like I had to do it.

Why did Gilmore kill this innocent victim? He had no idea—and he didn't care. Because of their almost total lack of feelings of responsibility or concern for others, persons with the antisocial personality disorder are often truly dangerous. When these destructive traits are coupled with high intelli-

Antisocial Personality Disorder: A personality disorder involving deceitfulness, impulsivity, callous disregard for the safety or welfare of others, and a total lack of remorse for actions that harm others.

gence, good looks, or a charming manner, they can be devastating. Confidence artists, serial killers who lure numerous victims to their doom—many such predators have been diagnosed as showing the antisocial personality disorder.

What are the origins of this disorder? Several factors seem to play a role. The impulsivity and aggression shown in the disorder may be linked to deficits in the ability to delay gratification—a skill most people acquire during childhood (e.g., Sher & Trull, 1994). Biological factors, too, may play a role. Some findings suggest that persons with this disorder show disturbances in brain function, including abnormalities in the neurotransmitter serotonin (Lahey et al., 1993). Additional evidence indicates that such persons show reduced reactions to negative stimuli—for instance, ones that are related to unpleasant experiences such as punishment (Patrick, Bradley, & Lang, 1993). This suggests that persons with the antisocial personality disorder may be less capable than others of experiencing negative emotions and less responsive to stimuli that serve as warnings to most people to "back off"—for example, angry facial expressions on the part of others (Ogloff & Wong, 1990). Whatever the origins of this disorder, one point is clear: Persons with the antisocial personality disorder often pose a serious threat to themselves and to others.

The third major cluster described by the DSM–IV includes disorders involving *anxious* and *fearful* behavior. Included in this cluster are the *avoidant personality disorder,* in which people are socially inhibited and feel inadequate; the *obsessive compulsive disorder* in which people are preoccupied with orderliness and perfectionism; and, lastly, the *dependent personality disorder,* which involves an excessive need to be cared for.

Key Questions

- What are personality disorders?
- What are the three major clusters of personality disorders identified by the DSM–IV?
- What characteristics are shown by persons who have the antisocial personality disorder?

Substance-Related Disorders

Do you know a heavy smoker who has tried, over and over again, to quit this habit? Or do you know someone who can't get through the day without several drinks or beers? If so, you already have firsthand experience with another major category on the DSM–IV: **substance-related disorders.** These are disorders involving maladaptative use of various substances or drugs (recall our discussion in Chapter 4) that leads to significant impairment or distress. Such disorders are generally divided into **substance abuse** and **substance dependence,** depending on the kind of problems involved. *Substance abuse* is diagnosed when individuals show one or more of the following problems: recurrent substance use resulting in failure to fulfill major role obligations at work, school, or home; recurrent substance use in situations where such use is physically hazardous; and repeated legal problems stemming from the use of substances. In contrast, *substance dependence* is diagnosed when individuals require increasing amounts of a substance to achieve the desired effect, experience withdrawal symptoms when they do not take the substance, are unable to cut down on or control use of the substance, and/or spend a great deal of time in activities aimed at securing the substance.

Substance-Related Disorders: Disorders involving maladaptive patterns of substance use leading to clinically significant impairment.

Substance Abuse: A disorder involving one or more of the following: recurrent substance use resulting in failure to fulfill major role obligations at work, school, or home; recurrent substance use in situations in which such use is physically hazardous; and/or recurrent substance-related legal problems.

Substance Dependence: A disorder involving one or more of the following: the need for increasing amounts of a substance to achieve the desired effect, withdrawal symptoms when the substance isn't taken, an inability to cut down on or control use of the substance, and the dedication of a great deal of time to activities aimed at securing the substance.

Unfortunately, both substance abuse and substance dependence are far from rare. In the United States, for instance, it is estimated that between 5 and 7 percent of the population shows alcohol abuse or dependence (National Institute of Alcohol Abuse and Alcoholism, 1993). Similarly, tens of millions of persons smoke cigarettes and—more recently—cigars. Smokers often develop nicotine dependence, which makes it extremely difficult for them to stop smoking, despite the fact that such behavior is clearly harmful to personal health. While the proportion of adults who smoke decreased in the United States in recent decades, the proportion of teenagers who acquire this habit, which dropped through 1990, has recently begun to increase (Horgan, 1993). This has raised a heated controversy over the charge that tobacco companies are engaged in an active advertising campaign to hook young smokers (see Figure 14.16). Finally, as noted in Chapter 13, smoking appears to be on the increase in many countries.

FIGURE 14.16

Smoking by Teenagers: A Growing Problem

Smoking among teenagers appears to be on the rise in the United States and many other countries. This finding has led to charges that tobacco companies are directing their ads at teenagers in an effort to hook young smokers.

The harmful effects of substance-related disorders, coupled with the very large numbers of persons involved, suggest that these are among the most damaging psychological disorders. Moreover, because they stem from many different factors—biological, social, and personal—they are often very difficult to treat. However, several forms of therapy do seem at least moderately effective in treating such problems; we'll examine these in Chapter 15.

Returning briefly to the question of substance abuse among teenagers, recent findings suggest that a combination of factors may place many young people at serious risk for such disorders. These include high levels of stress in adolescents' lives; a tendency to cope with problems in maladaptive ways (e.g., by avoiding them or using substances to feel better); exposure to peers who smoke, drink, or use drugs; and a low degree of support from their parents (Wills et al., 1996). Understanding the factors that place teenagers at risk, of course, may prove very helpful in the design of programs to help young people avoid the profound risks of substance-related disorders.

Key Questions

- What are substance-related disorders?
- What factors place teenagers at risk for developing substance-related disor-

Schizophrenia: *Out of Touch with Reality*

In an important sense, I've saved the most devastating psychological disorder for last. This is **schizophrenia,** which can be defined as a complex disorder characterized by hallucinations (e.g., hearing voices), delusions (beliefs with no basis in reality), disturbances in speech, and several other symptoms. Schizophrenia is so serious, and so disruptive to the persons who develop it, that often schizophrenics must be removed from society, at least temporarily, for their own protection and to undergo treatment. What is the nature of this disorder? What are its major causes? These are the questions on which psychologists who study schizophrenia have focused.

Schizophrenia: A complex disorder characterized by hallucinations (e.g., hearing voices), delusions (beliefs with no basis in reality), disturbances in speech, and several other symptoms.

The Nature of Schizophrenia

Schizophrenia involves severe disruptions in virtually all aspects of psychological functioning. As noted by Heinrichs (1993, p. 221), schizophrenia

Delusions: Firmly held beliefs that have no basis in reality.

Hallucinations: Vivid sensory experiences that have no basis in physical reality.

depletes the mind's resources, just as severe brain damage depletes these resources. But while persons suffering from brain damage experience a world that is stripped of its meaning in many respects, those suffering from schizophrenia experience a world that has become, in Heinrich's words, "excessively, terrifyingly rich." Let's look more closely at the major symptoms of this serious disorder. But first, one important point: Although I'll discuss schizophrenia as though it is a single disorder, many experts believe that it may actually involve several different—and distinct—disturbances (Bellak, 1994). Please keep this point in mind when we return to potential causes of schizophrenia below.

Disturbances of Language or Thought First, and perhaps foremost, schizophrenics do not think or speak like others. Their words jump about in a fragmented and disorganized manner. There is a loosening of associations so that one idea does not follow logically from another; indeed, ideas often seem totally unconnected. In addition, schizophrenics often create words of their own—words that resemble real words but do not exist in their native language; for instance, "littlehood" for childhood or "crimery" for bad actions. Their sentences often begin with one thought and then shift abruptly to another, and may include *incompetent references*—it's impossible to tell to what their words refer (e.g., Barch & Berenbaum, 1996). In extreme cases, schizophrenics' words seem to be totally jumbled into what are sometimes termed a *word salad*.

These problems, and several others, seem to stem from a breakdown in the capacity for *selective attention*. Normally, we can focus our attention on certain stimuli while largely ignoring others. This is not true for schizophrenics. They are easily distracted by anything and everything. Even the sound of their own words may disrupt their train of thought and send them wandering off into a mysterious world of their own creation.

Schizophrenics also frequently suffer from **delusions**—firmly held beliefs that have no basis in reality. Such delusions can take many forms. One common type is *delusions of persecution*—the belief that one is being plotted against, spied on, threatened, or otherwise mistreated. Another common type is *delusions of grandeur*—the belief that one is extremely famous, important, or powerful. Persons suffering from such delusions may claim that they are the president, a famous movie star, or even Jesus, Mohammed, or Buddha. A third type of delusion involves *delusions of control*—the belief that other people, evil forces, or even beings from another planet are controlling one's thoughts, actions, or feelings. As you can see, schizophrenics' ties to reality are tenuous at best.

Disturbances of Perception Schizophrenics also show many signs of disturbed perceptions. Simply put, they do not perceive the world as other people do. Many experience **hallucinations**—vivid sensory experiences that have no basis in physical reality. The most common types of hallucinations are auditory. Schizophrenics "hear" voices, music, or other sounds that aren't present. Visual hallucinations are also quite frequent; and again, these experiences can be quite intense. Hallucinations of smells and tastes are sometimes also reported.

Disturbances of Emotion or Mood A third key symptom of schizophrenia involves inappropriate or unusual emotional reactions. Some schizophrenics show almost no emotion at all; they show no reaction to events to which most people respond strongly, such as the news that a close relative has died or been involved in a serious accident. Others do show emotion, but their reactions are inappropriate. They may giggle when describing a painful childhood experience, or cry after hearing a joke. In sum, schizophrenics' disturbed patterns of thought, perception, and emotion weaken their grip on reality and virtually ensure that they will live in a private world largely of their own creation.

Disturbances of Behavior A fourth symptom of schizophrenia involves unusual actions (see Figure 14.17). These can take an incredible range of forms, as the following description (Hagen, 1993) of a hospital ward for schizophrenics suggests:

> Lou stands hour after hour . . . just rubbing the palm of his hand around the top of his head. Jerry spends his days rubbing his hand against his stomach and running around a post. . . . Helen paces back and forth . . . mumbling about enemies who are coming to get her, while Vic grimaces and giggles over in the corner. . . . Nick tears up magazines, puts bits of paper in his mouth and then spits them out. . . . Bill sits immobile for hours, staring at the floor. . . .

FIGURE 14.17

Bizarre Behavior: One Symptom of Schizophrenia

Persons suffering from schizophrenia often engage in bizarre behaviors that make little sense to outside observers.

Disturbances in Social Functions Given the difficulties outlined above, it is far from surprising that schizophrenics also frequently show seriously impaired social functioning. Their relationships with others deteriorate, and they experience increasing social isolation and withdrawal (Bellack et al., 1990). Further, they show severe deficits in basic social skills, such as solving problems through conversation, compromising with others, and negotiating with them (Bellack et al., 1994).

Positive versus Negative Symptoms As you can readily see, schizophrenia is a complex disorder. Are there any underlying dimensions that can help us make sense out of this vast range of symptoms? One dimension that has proved useful divides symptoms into two types. *Positive symptoms* involve the presence of something that is normally absent, such as hallucinations and delusions. *Negative symptoms* involve the absence of something that is normally present and include withdrawal, apathy, absence of emotion, and so on. (These two groups of symptoms are sometimes referred as Type I and Type II schizophrenia, respectively.) Patients with negative symptoms generally have a poorer prognosis: They remain hospitalized longer and are less likely to recover than patients with positive symptoms (Fenton & McGlashan, 1991). In addition, patients with positive and negative symptoms appear to experience different kinds of cognitive deficits. Those with negative symptoms do worse on tests that measure visual and spatial skills—for example, they have more difficulty in recognizing visual stimuli. In contrast, patients with positive symptoms do worse on tests of short-term memory (Braff, 1989). These findings, as well as many others, indicate that there may be two distinct types of schizophrenia; in fact, many experts believe that there may be several types (Heinrichs, 1993.)

Phases and Types of Schizophrenia

Schizophrenia is a *chronic* disorder, as defined by the DSM–IV: It lasts at least six months. For most people, however, the disease lasts far longer, and symptoms come and go. They have periods when they appear almost normal, and long periods when their symptoms are readily apparent.

Catatonic Type (of schizophrenia): A dramatic type of schizophrenia in which individuals show marked disturbances in motor behavior; many alternate between total immobility and wild, excited behavior in which they rush madly about.

Diathesis–Stress Model: A model suggesting that genetic factors may predispose a person to develop schizophrenia but that this disorder will develop only if the person is exposed to certain kinds of stressful environmental conditions.

Some experts describe schizophrenia as involving three phases: the *prodromal phase,* when the functioning of persons with this disorder begins to deteriorate and they withdraw more and more from others; the *active* or *acute phase,* when they exhibit many positive symptoms; and the *residual phase,* during which they again show fewer symptoms but withdraw and continue to have bizarre thoughts.

Schizophrenia is also divided into five distinct types. The most dramatic of these is the **catatonic type,** in which individuals show marked disturbances in motor behavior. Many alternate between total immobility—they may sit for days or even weeks frozen in a single posture—and wild, excited behavior in which they rush madly about. Other types are described in Table 14.3.

The Origins of Schizophrenia

Schizophrenia is one of the most bizarre, and serious, psychological disorders. It is also more common than you might guess, afflicting 1 to 2 percent of all people in the United States (Wilson et al., 1996). Schizophrenia does not strike all age groups equally, however; on the contrary, it usually doesn't appear until between the ages of sixteen and twenty-five, and occurs much less frequently after age thirty-five (Mueser & Gingerich, 1994). What are the causes of the disorder? Research findings point to roles for many factors.

Genetic Factors Schizophrenia, like several other psychological disorders, tends to run in families. The closer the family tie between two individuals, the higher the likelihood that if one develops schizophrenia, the other will show this disorder too (e.g., Gottesman, 1993). Schizophrenia does not appear to be traceable to a single gene, however; on the contrary, research findings suggest that many genes and many environmental factors operate together to produce a tendency toward this disorder (e.g., Fowles, 1994). For example, one model of the origins of schizophrenia, the **diathesis–stress model,** suggests that genetic factors may predispose a person to develop schizophrenia in the presence of certain kinds of stressful environmental conditions; if these environmental conditions are absent, schizophrenia may not actually occur. However, it does seem clear that genetic factors play some role.

TABLE 14.3

Types of Schizophrenias

Schizophrenia is often divided into the types shown here, each marked by a different pattern of symptoms.

Type	Symptoms
Catatonic	Unusual patterns of motor activity, such as rigid postures; also show speech disturbances such as repetitive chatter
Disorganized	Absence of affect, poorly developed delusions, verbal incoherence
Paranoid	Preoccupation with one or more sets of delusions, often centering around the belief that others are "out to get" the schizophrenic in some way
Undifferentiated	Many symptoms, including delusions, hallucinations, incoherence
Residual	Withdrawal, minimal affect, and absence of motivation; occurs after prominent delusions and hallucinations are no longer present

Family Factors The fact that schizophrenia seems to run in families provides evidence for the role of genetic factors in this disorder. It also raises the possibility that some families create social environments that place their children at risk—environments that increase the likelihood of their developing schizophrenia. What are such environments like? Research findings suggest that they involve high levels of conflict between parents, or situations in which one parent completely dominates the family (e.g., Arieti, 1974). These environments also involve patterns of communication that are confusing and inconsistent. In such families, children are exposed to what is known as the *double bind*: They are encouraged to form intense relationships with one or both parents and are urged to be affectionate; but when they are, their advances are rejected (e.g., Miklowitz et al., 1989). This creates emotional turmoil for children, and places them at risk for schizophrenia if other factors such as genetic ones predispose them to this illness.

Cognitive Factors Schizophrenics is also show important deficits in cognitive functioning, and this may contribute to the development of this disorder. Schizophrenics with positive symptoms often show reduced ability to ignore irrelevant or distracting stimuli—they simply can't concentrate, and they try to pay attention to everything around them (e.g., Elkins, Cromwell, & Asarnow, 1992; Grillon et al., 1990). In contrast, schizophrenics with negative symptoms seem to have the opposite problem: They are *under*attentive to external stimuli. For example, they often show weaker than normal *orienting responses* (reactions indicative of attention) when unfamiliar stimuli are presented (Bernstein, 1987).

Brain Dysfunction Additional evidence suggests that persons suffering from schizophrenia show several types of brain dysfunctions. For instance, some findings indicate that some ventricles (fluid-filled spaces within the brain) are larger in schizophrenics than in normal persons and that this increased size may produce abnormalities in the cerebral cortex (e.g., Weinberger, 1994). In fact, the decreased brain volume resulting from enlarged ventricles has been found, in research using MRI (magnetic resonance imaging), to be related to increased hallucinations and reduced emotion among schizophrenics (e.g., Gur & Pearlson, 1993; Klausner et al., 1992). Schizophrenics also show reduced activity in the frontal lobes relative to normal persons during tasks involving memory or abstract thought (Gur & Pearlson, 1993). Together, all these findings suggest that schizophrenia is related to cognitive deficits and several types of abnormalities in brain functioning.

Biochemical Factors As we'll see in Chapter 15, *antipsychotic drugs* have been highly effective in treating schizophrenia—or, at least, in reducing some of the more bizarre symptoms of this disorder. It seems reasonable to suggest that if we could understand how these drugs were producing these beneficial effects, we might obtain valuable evidence on the biochemical causes of schizophrenia. The fact that many antipsychotic drugs produce muscle tremors like those seen in Parkinson's disease provided one clue to these biochemical factors: Persons suffering from Parkinson's disease have abnormally low levels of the neurotransmitter *dopamine*. This led some researchers to speculate that perhaps schizophrenics had abnormally *high* levels of dopamine, and that antipsychotic drugs reduced these levels—thus reducing some symptoms of schizophrenia but producing side effects such as muscle tremor. Some findings are indeed consistent with this **dopamine hypothesis** (e.g., Julien, 1995). However, other findings seem to contradict this view; for instance, direct comparisons of dopamine levels in schizophrenic patients and in other persons do not reveal the expected differences (Lieberman & Koreen, 1993). As a

Dopamine Hypothesis: The hypothesis that schizophrenia stems, at least in part, from excessively high levels of dopamine.

FIGURE 14.18

The Homeless: Many Are Suffering from Psychological Disorders

Many homeless people suffer from schizophrenia, mood disorders, and other serious psychological problems. Such persons are sometimes described as showing *chronic mental illness.*

result, the current scientific status of the dopamine hypothesis is best reflected in a publication of the National Institute of Mental Health, which stated: "Clearly, no consensus exists about dopamine's role in schizophrenia" (Shore, 1993). Many researchers remain convinced that biochemical factors *do* play an important role in schizophrenia, however, so the search for these factors is certainly continuing at the present time.

In sum, it appears that genetic factors, certain types of home environments, cognitive factors, brain dysfunctions, and biochemical factors may all play roles in schizophrenia. It remains for future research to determine the precise manner in which such factors combine to place specific persons at risk for this serious psychological disorder.

Chronic Mental Illness and the Homeless

In the late 1990s a visit to the downtown area of almost any large American city can be a shock. Huddled in doorways, sprawled on park benches, clustered around open fires in winter are the *homeless*—people who live on the street without any permanent home (see Figure 14.18). Such persons are there for many reasons, including economic dislocation and lack of affordable housing, but one important factor is certainly psychological disorders. Many homeless persons are suffering from schizophrenia, mood disorders, and other serious psychological problems (Caton et al., 1993). Perhaps as many as one third of the homeless were previously hospitalized but were released when drug therapy reduced their symptoms. With nowhere to go, they turned to the streets, where they frequently yielded to the temptations of alcohol and other drugs. Given the number of persons released from large state institutions in recent decades (see Chapter 15), it is hardly surprising that the ranks of the homeless—and of the *chronically mentally ill* among them—have swelled immensely.

Of course, not all homeless persons are chronically mentally ill; but enough are to suggest the need for new programs designed to get those in need of psychological help into settings where they can receive it. The cost of doing so may be high, but ignoring this problem in the hope that it will go away does not seem to be either a humane solution or a viable one.

Key Questions

- What is schizophrenia?
- What are positive and negative symptoms of schizophrenia?
- What are the major types of schizophrenia?
- What factors play a role in the occurrence of schizophrenia?
- What is the relationship between schizophrenia and homelessness?

Making Psychology Part of Your Life

Preventing Suicide: How You Can Help

When terminally ill persons choose to end their lives rather than endure continued pain, their actions seem understandable, even if we disapprove of them on moral or religious grounds. But when young persons whose lives have just begun follow this route, nearly everyone would agree that their death is tragic. Can *you* do anything to help prevent suicides among people you know? Research findings suggest that you can, if you pay careful attention to several warning signs and take appropriate action if this seems necessary.

- **Take all suicide threats seriously.** One common myth about suicide is that people who threaten to kill themselves rarely do—only those who tell no one about their plans commit suicide. *This is untrue!* Approximately 70 percent of all suicides tell others about their intentions. So when someone talks about suicide, *take it seriously*.
- **If someone mentions suicide, don't be afraid to discuss it.** Another common myth about suicide is that this topic should never be discussed with another person—talking about it will only make matters worse. This, too, is false. Encouraging people to talk about suicidal thoughts gets their problems out into the open and can be helpful. So don't ignore it if someone you know mentions suicide; talking about it is usually better.
- **Recognize the danger signs.** These include (a) statements by someone that he or she has no strong reasons for living; (b) agitation or excitement followed by a period of calm resignation; (c) sudden efforts to give valued possessions away to others; (d) direct statements such as "I don't want to be a burden anymore" or "I don't really want to go on living"; (e) revival from a deeply depressed state, coupled with apparent leave-taking. If you observe these changes in others, they may well be danger signs worth considering carefully.
- **Discourage others from blaming themselves for failure to attain unrealistic goals.** Many people who attempt suicide do so because they feel they have failed to measure up to their own standards—even if these are unrealistically high. If you know someone who is prone to this pattern, try to get him or her to focus on the good points and to realize that his or her standards *are* unrealistic—ones no one could hope to attain.
- **If a friend or family member shows the danger signs described here, don't leave this person alone.** With rare exceptions, suicide is a solitary act. So if you are concerned that someone might attempt suicide, don't leave this person alone. If you can't stay with the person, get others to help—or bring the depressed friend or relative with you wherever it is you have to go.
- **Most important of all: Get help!** Remember signal detection theory (see Chapter 3)? Where preventing suicide is concerned, many false alarms are better than one miss—it's far better to get worried or concerned for nothing than to look the other way while a tragedy occurs. So if you are concerned about someone you know, *get professional help.* Call a local suicide hot line, discuss your concerns with someone in the campus counseling center, see a physician or a member of the clergy. Help *is* available. If you have any concerns at all, seek it!

Summary and Review of Key Questions

Changing Conceptions of Psychological Disorders

- **What are psychological disorders?** These are patterns of behavior and thought that are atypical, viewed as undesirable or unacceptable in a given culture, are maladaptive, and that usually (although not always) cause the persons who experience them considerable distress.
- **To what factors were such disorders attributed in the past?** At different times in the past, psychological disorders were attributed to supernatural causes (e.g., evil spirits) or natural causes (e.g., injuries to the brain).
- **What is the modern psychological view of such disorders?** The modern psychological view suggests that psychological disorders involve biological, psychological, social, and cultural factors.

KEY TERMS

psychological disorders, p. 546 • medical perspective, p. 548 • psychiatry, p. 548

Identifying Psychological Disorders: The DSM–IV

- **What is the DSM–IV?** The DSM–IV (*Diagnostic and Statistical Manual of Mental Disorders–IV*) is a widely used guide to various psychological disorders. It provides a description of each disorder, plus information about biological factors associated with the condition and about its age-related, culture-related, and gender-related features.
- **In what ways is the latest revision of the DSM an improvement over earlier versions?** The DSM–IV rests on a firmer basis of published research than did earlier versions and directs increased attention to the role of cultural factors.
- **What tools other than the DSM–IV do psychologists use to identify psychological disorders?** Psychologists also use assessment interviews, personality tests, assessments of brain functioning, and behavioral assessments in their efforts to identify and study psychological disorders.

KEY TERMS

Diagnostic and Statistical Manual of Mental Disorders–IV, p. 551 • assessment interviews, p. 552 • Halstead–Reitan Neuropsychological Battery, p. 552 • behavioral assessment, p. 552

Mood Disorders: The Downs and Ups of Life

- **What are the major symptoms of depression? Of bipolar disorders?** Major symptoms of depression include negative mood, reduced energy, feelings of hopelessness or despair, loss of interest in previously satisfying activities, and difficulties in sleeping. Bipolar disorders involve wide swings in mood between deep depression and mania.
- **What factors play a role in the occurrence of mood disorders?** Mood disorders are influenced by genetic factors and by disturbances in brain activity. Psychological factors that also play a role in such disorders include learned helplessness, negative perceptions of oneself, and tendencies to bring negative thoughts and memories to mind.
- **What are the causes of postpartum depression?** Postpartum depression, depression among new mothers, seems to stem from women's feelings that they will not be able to cope with their new responsibilities, lack of adequate help from families and spouses, a "difficult" temperament on the part of the new child, and adoption of ineffective coping strategies.
- **What are the important warning signs of suicide?** Important warning signs of suicide include recovery from deep depression, a period of calm following periods of agitation, and statements indicative of fewer and weaker reasons for living.

KEY TERMS

mood disorders, p. 554 • depression, p. 554 • bipolar disorders, p. 556 • postpartum depression, p. 558 • suicide, p. 559

Anxiety Disorders: When Dread Debilitates

- **What are anxiety disorders?** These are disorders involving increased arousal accompanied by intense, persistent, generalized feelings of fear or apprehension.
- **What are panic attacks?** Panic attacks involve symptoms of arousal coupled with intense fear—often of losing control in some specific situation.
- **What are phobias?** Phobias are excessive fears focused on specific objects or situations.
- **What is obsessive–compulsive disorder?** This is a disorder in which individuals have repetitious thoughts or engage in repetitious behaviors they can't seem to control.
- **What is posttraumatic stress disorder?** This is a disorder in which people persistently reexperience traumatic events in their thoughts or dreams; feel as if they are reliving these events from time to time; persistently avoid stimuli associated with the traumatic events; and persistently experience symptoms such as difficulty falling asleep, irritability, and difficulty in concentrating.

KEY TERMS

anxiety, p. 560 • anxiety disorders, p. 560 • panic attack disorder, p. 560 • agoraphobia, p. 561 • catastrophic thinking, p. 561 • obsessive–compulsive disorder, p. 563 • posttraumatic stress disorder, p. 563

Somatoform Disorders: Physical Symptoms without Physical Causes

- **What are somatoform disorders?** These are disorders in which individuals have symptoms typically associated with physical diseases or conditions, but in which no known organic or physiological basis for the symptoms can be found.
- **What is Munchausen's syndrome, and how is it related to hypochondriasis?** Munchausen's syndrome is a pattern of behavior in which individuals devote their entire lives to visiting doctors—even having painful medical procedures, including operations—when they are not ill. Although it is not classified as a psychological disorder, Munchausen's syndrome may be related to hypochondriasis, a disorder in which individuals are preoccupied with fears of disease.

KEY TERMS

somatoform disorders, p. 565 • somatization disorder, p. 565 • hypochondriasis, p. 565 • conversion disorder, p. 565 • Munchausen's syndrome, p. 567

Dissociative Disorders: When Memory Fails

- **What are dissociative disorders, and what is dissociative amnesia?** Dissociative disorders involve profound losses of memory or identity. In one such disorder, dissociative amnesia, individuals are unable to remember various events, especially ones they found traumatic or disturbing.
- **What is dissociative identity disorder?** In dissociative identity disorder (formerly known as multiple personality disorder), individuals seem to possess several distinct personalities that take turns controlling their behavior.

KEY TERMS

dissociative disorders, p. 567 • dissociative amnesia, p. 567 • dissociative fugue, p. 567 • dissociative identity disorder, p. 567

Sexual and Gender Identity Disorders

- **What are sexual dysfunctions and paraphilias?** Sexual dysfunctions involve disturbances in sexual desire and/or sexual arousal, disturbances in the ability to attain orgasm, or pain during sexual relations. In paraphilias, unusual imagery or acts are necessary for sexual arousal.

- **What is gender identity disorder?** In gender identity disorder, individuals feel that they were born with the wrong sexual identity and strongly desire to change this identity through medical treatment or other means.

KEY TERMS

sexual desire disorders, p. 569 • sexual arousal disorders, p. 569 • paraphilias, p. 570 • gender identity disorder, p. 570

Eating Disorders

- **What are anorexia nervosa and bulimia nervosa?** In anorexia nervosa, individuals literally starve themselves until their body weight falls dangerously low. In bulimia nervosa, individuals maintain a normal weight but engage in repeated cycles of binge eating and purging.
- **What factors play a role in the occurrence of these eating disorders?** Eating disorders seem to stem, to an important degree, from the "thin is beautiful" image promoted heavily by the mass media—an image that makes many people, especially young women, unhappy with their body shape, and leads them to try extreme methods of weight control.

KEY TERMS

eating disorders, p. 571 • anorexia nervosa, p. 571 • bulimia nervosa, p. 572

Personality Disorders: Traits That Harm

- **What are personality disorders?** Personality disorders are extreme and inflexible personality traits that are distressing to the persons who have them or cause them problems in school, work, or interpersonal relations.
- **What are the three major clusters of personality disorders identified by the DSM–IV?** The first cluster involves odd, eccentric behavior (e.g., paranoid disorder). The second cluster involves dramatic, emotional, and erratic forms of behavior (e.g., the antisocial personality disorder). The third cluster includes disorders involving anxious, fearful behavior.
- **What characteristics are shown by persons who have the antisocial personality disorder?** Persons who have the antisocial personality disorder show such characteristics as deceitfulness, impulsivity, irritability and aggressiveness, reckless disregard for their own safety and that of others, lack of remorse, failure to conform to social norms, and little or no concern for the rights of others.

KEY TERMS

personality disorders, p. 573 • antisocial personality disorder, p. 575

Substance-Related Disorders

- **What are substance-related disorders?** Substance-related disorders involve maladaptive patterns of substance use, leading to significant impairment or distress.
- **What factors place teenagers at risk for developing substance-related disorders?** These factors include high levels of life stress and nonadaptive ways of coping with it, exposure to substance use by peers, and low parental support.

KEY TERMS

substance-related disorders, p. 576 • substance abuse, p. 576 • substance dependence, p. 576

Schizophrenia: Out of Touch with Reality

- **What is schizophrenia?** Schizophrenia is a very serious psychological disorder characterized by hallucinations (e.g., hearing voices), delusions (beliefs with no basis in reality), and disturbances in speech, behavior, and emotion.
- **What are positive and negative symptoms of schizophrenia?** Positive symptoms involve the presence of something that is normally absent, such as hallucinations and delusions. Negative symptoms involve the absence of something that is normally present—withdrawal, apathy, absence of emotion, and so on.
- **What are the major types of schizophrenia?** Major types of schizophrenia include catatonic, paranoid, disorganized, undifferentiated, and residual.
- **What factors play a role in the occurrence of schizophrenia?** Schizophrenia has complex origins involving genetic factors, certain aspects of family environment, cognitive deficits, brain dysfunction, and biochemical factors.
- **What is the relationship between schizophrenia and homelessness?** Many homeless persons appear to be individuals suffering from serious psychological disorders such as schizophrenia or mood disorders.

KEY TERMS

schizophrenia, p. 577 • delusions, p. 578 • hallucinations, p. 578 • catatonic type, p. 580 • diathesis–stress model, p. 580 • dopamine hypothesis, p. 581

Critical Thinking Questions

Appraisal

Psychologists generally agree that only patterns of behavior and thought that are unusual, viewed as undesirable in a given culture, and that cause the persons who experience them distress should be labeled as "abnormal." This suggests that if, for instance, *cannibalism* is viewed as acceptable within a culture and causes the persons who engage in it little or no distress, it can be described as "normal." What are your reactions to this conclusion?

Controversy

The DSM–IV is designed to identify various forms of psychological disorders. This means that when it is used, individuals are labeled as having one or more disorders. Some psychologists object to this, noting that such labels may then shape the way in which mental health professionals—and other people, too—perceive the individuals who have been so labeled. Do you think this is a serious problem? If so, what can be done to reduce it?

Making Psychology Part of Your Life

Now that you know something about the major kinds of psychological disorders, do you think this will help you to recognize these problems in yourself or other persons? And if you do, will this knowledge increase the chances that you will seek help yourself, or recommend it to others who seem to need it?

C H A P T E R O U T L I N E

Therapy

Diminishing the Pain of Psychological Disorders

"The art of life," Thomas Jefferson wrote in a letter in 1786, "is the art of avoiding pain." If that's the case, then most of us are not very accomplished at the art of life; for *pain,* in the form of emotional distress and various psychological disorders, is a common part of the human experience. As I noted in Chapter 14, as many as half of all human beings experience one or more painful periods at some point during their life (Blazer et al., 1994; Kessler et al., 1994). So, yes, there certainly is a lot of pain out there—pain we seem unable to avoid. But—and this is the crucial point—*there is also lots of help for coping with it.* Many techniques for alleviating psychological disorders exist; and when used by skilled professionals, they can be highly effective (e.g., Seligman, 1995). In this chapter we'll examine a wide range of such techniques. Since psychological disorders take many differ-

Psychotherapies: Procedures in which a trained person establishes a special kind of relationship with an individual seeking help, in order to remove or modify existing symptoms, change disturbed patterns of behavior and thought, and promote personal growth.

Psychodynamic Therapies: Therapies based on the idea that psychological disorders stem primarily from the kind of hidden inner conflicts first described by Freud.

ent forms, it is not surprising that methods for dealing with them, too, vary greatly. To acquaint you with the broad spectrum of therapeutic procedures, our discussion will proceed as follows.

First, we'll examine several **psychotherapies**—procedures in which a trained person establishes a special kind of relationship with an individual seeking help, in order to remove or modify existing symptoms, change disturbed patterns of behavior and thought, and promote personal growth (e.g., Wolberg, 1977). As you'll soon see, many forms of psychotherapy exist, ranging from the famous procedures devised by Freud, through modern techniques that rest firmly on basic principles of learning and cognition. Next, we'll explore forms of therapy that involve several persons rather than a single individual—group therapies. Third, we'll consider therapies that focus on interpersonal relations—marital and family therapy. After examining these varied types of therapies, we'll turn to several current issues in psychotherapy: (1) Does psychotherapy really work? (2) Are some kinds of therapies more effective than others? (3) Should psychologists seek prescription privileges—the legal right to write prescriptions? (4) How can all forms of therapy take cultural differences into account? Next, we'll examine therapies that focus on biological factors—biological therapies. Finally, we'll conclude with a discussion of efforts to prevent psychological disorders from occurring in the first place.

Many techniques for alleviating psychological disorders exist; and when used by skilled professionals, they can be highly effective.

Psychotherapies: Psychological Approaches to Psychological Disorders

Say the word *psychotherapy* and many people quickly conjure up the following image: A "patient" lies on a couch in a dimly lit room, while a therapist sits in the background. The therapist urges the patient to reveal the deepest secrets of her or his mind—hidden urges, frustrated desires, traumatic early experiences. As these painful thoughts and images are dredged out of the unconscious, the patient, suffering tremendous emotional turmoil, moves toward improved "mental health" (see Figure 15.1).

This popular image, however, has little to do with many modern forms of psychotherapy. In fact, it applies primarily to only one type, an approach developed by Freud that is rarely used by psychologists and is even fading rapidly from psychiatry, where it was a mainstay for many years (e.g., Hymowitz, 1995). Psychotherapy, as it is currently practiced by psychologists and other professionals, actually takes many different forms, uses a tremendously varied range of procedures, and can be conducted with groups as well as with individuals. What are these procedures like? Let's take a closer look at several important forms of psychotherapy—including, of course, the methods used by Freud.

FIGURE 15.1

Psychotherapy: How Many People Perceive It

When they hear the word *psychotherapy,* many people imagine a scene like this one. In fact, there are many forms of therapy, and most do *not* use the kinds of procedures shown here.

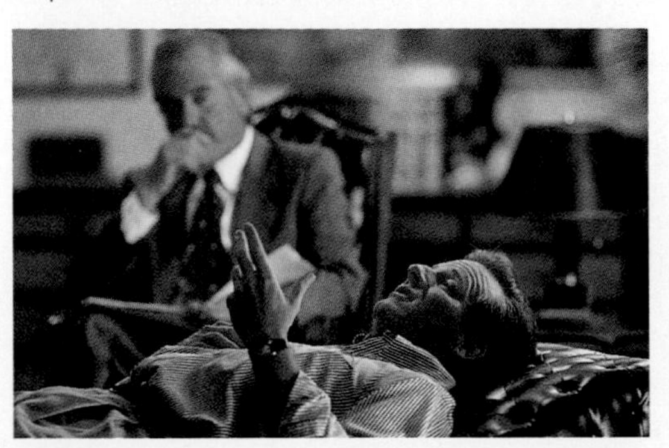

Psychodynamic Therapies: From Repression to Insight

Psychodynamic therapies are based on the idea that psychological disorders stem primarily from the kinds of hidden inner conflicts first described by Freud. More specifically, psychodynamic therapies assume that psychological disorders occur because something has gone seriously wrong with the balance between the inner forces in an individual's personality. While several forms of therapy are based on these assumptions, the most famous is certainly *psychoanalysis,* the approach developed by Freud.

Free Association: A verbal reporting by persons undergoing psychoanalysis of everything that passes through their minds, no matter how trivial it may appear to be.

Psychoanalysis If Freud had known how many movies, television shows, and even cartoons would be based on his method of psychotherapy, he just might have changed it in several respects. He was a serious person who viewed himself as scientific in orientation, and he would probably have found popular representations of his ideas objectionable. What were the methods of therapy he devised? To understand them, it's important to begin with a brief review of the reasoning on which they are based.

As you may recall from Chapter 12, Freud believed that personality consists of three major parts: *id, ego,* and *superego,* which correspond roughly to desire, reason, and conscience. Freud believed that psychological disorders stem from the fact that many of the primitive sexual and aggressive impulses of the id are unacceptable to the ego or the superego and are therefore *repressed*—driven into the depths of the unconscious. There they persist, and individuals must devote a considerable portion of their psychic energy to keeping them in check and out of consciousness. In fact, people often use various *defense mechanisms* to protect the ego from feelings of anxiety generated by these inner conflicts and clashes.

How can such problems be relieved? Freud felt that the crucial task was for people to overcome repression and come face to face with their hidden feelings and impulses. Having gained such insight, he believed, they would experience a release of emotion known as *abreaction.* Then, with their energies at last freed from the task of repression, they could direct these into health growth. Figure 15.2 summarizes these views.

These ideas concerning the causes and cure of mental illness are reflected in the specific procedures used in *psychoanalysis,* the type of therapy developed by Freud. As popular images suggest, the patient undergoing psychoanalysis lies on a couch in a partly darkened room and engages in **free association**—a verbal reporting of *everything* that passes through her or his mind, no matter how trivial it may appear to be (see Figure 15.3 on page 590).

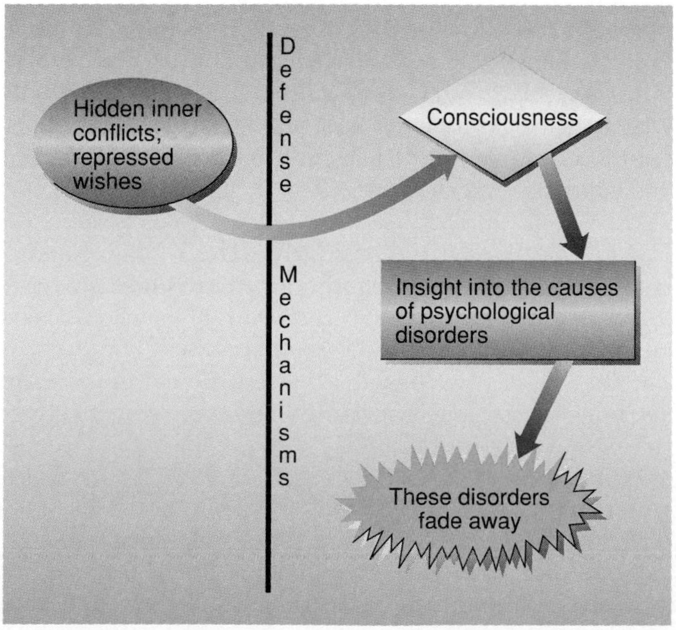

FIGURE 15.2

Psychoanalysis: An Overview

Psychoanalysis, the kind of therapy developed by Freud, is primarily designed to provide individuals with insight into their hidden inner conflicts and repressed wishes. Freud assumed that once awareness of these conflicts penetrated patients' *defense mechanisms* and moved into consciousness, psychological disorders would fade away. In fact, there is little support for these views.

FIGURE 15.3

Freud's Famous Couch: The First Home of Free Association

Lying on this couch, Freud's patients engaged in *free association*, telling him everything that passed through their minds. On the basis of the information patients provided, Freud identified the supposed causes of their disorders and planned their treatment.

Freud believed that the repressed impulses and inner conflicts present in the unconscious would ultimately be revealed by these mental wanderings, at least to the trained ear of the analyst. As we saw in Chapter 4, Freud felt that dreams were especially useful in this respect; he saw dreams as representing inner conflicts and hidden impulses in disguised form. As psychoanalysis progresses and the analyst gains insight into the patient's problems, he or she asks questions and offers suggestions—*interpretations*—designed to enhance the patient's growing awareness of inner conflicts.

During the course of psychoanalysis, Freud reported, several intriguing events often occur. The first of these is **resistance**—a patient's stubborn refusal to report certain thoughts, motives, and experiences or overt rejection of the analyst's interpretations (Strean, 1985). Presumably, resistance occurs because patients wish to avoid the anxiety they experience as threatening or painful thoughts come closer and closer to consciousness.

Another aspect of psychoanalysis is **transference**—intense emotional feelings of love or hate toward the analyst on the part of the patient. Often, Freud held, patients react toward their analyst as they did toward someone who played a crucial role in their early life—for example, one of their parents. Freud believed that transference could be an important tool for helping individuals work through conflicts regarding their parents, this time in a setting where the harm done by undesirable early relationships could be effectively countered. As patients' insight increases, transference gradually decreases and ultimately fades away.

Psychoanalysis: An Evaluation Psychoanalysis is probably the best-known form of psychotherapy. Early efforts by psychologists to ignore it and, later, to discredit it largely failed: Psychoanalysis gained great popularity and refused to vanish, no matter how fervently psychologists pointed out that it was *not* based on scientific findings (Hornstein, 1992). What accounts for its fame? Certainly not its proven effectiveness. In fact, it is fair to say that the reputation of psychoanalysis far exceeds its success in alleviating psychological disorders. In the form proposed by Freud, this procedure suffers from several major and obvious weaknesses that lessen its value. First, psychoanalysis is a costly and time-consuming process. Several years and a large amount of money are usually required for its completion—assuming it ever ends. Second, it is based largely on Freud's theories of personality and psychosexual development. As I noted in Chapter 12, these theories are

Resistance: In psychoanalysis, a patient's stubborn refusal to report certain thoughts, motives, and experiences or overt rejection of the analyst's interpretations.

Transference: Intense emotional feelings of love or hate toward the analyst on the part of patients undergoing psychoanalysis.

provocative but difficult to test scientifically, so psychoanalysis rests on shaky scientific ground. Third, Freud designed psychoanalysis for use with highly educated persons with impressive verbal skills—persons who could describe their inner thoughts and feelings with ease. This limits its usefulness to what some psychologists term YAVIS patients—young, attractive, verbal, intelligent, and successful (Schofield, 1964). Perhaps most important, psychoanalysis has often adopted the posture of a closed logical system. You don't believe in psychoanalysis? That's a clear sign that you are suffering from serious psychological disorders that prevent you from seeing the truth!

Finally, Freud's major assumption—that once insight is acquired, mental health will follow automatically—is contradicted by research findings. Over and over again, psychologists have found that insight into one's thoughts and feelings does *not* necessarily change them or prevent them from influencing behavior (e.g., Rozin, 1996). For instance, consider the following demonstration: Would you eat a piece of chocolate shaped exactly like a cockroach? Many people recoil from consuming such an item—*even though they fully realize that these reactions are irrational.* In fact, many will turn away in disgust, while laughing at their own behavior. In this and many more serious instances, Freud was wrong: Gaining insight into our behavior does *not* guarantee that it will change or become "healthier."

Beyond Psychoanalysis: Psychodynamic Therapy Today

Because of such problems, classical psychoanalysis is a relatively rare type of therapy today. However, modified versions introduced by Freud's students and disciples, including the neo-Freudians we discussed in Chapter 12, are used more frequently. For instance, Alfred Adler, one famous neo-Freudian, emphasized the importance of feelings of inferiority in psychological disorders. He developed a form of therapy that focused on what he termed **basic mistakes**—false beliefs held by individuals that interfere with their mental health, such as "Life is very dangerous" or "I have to please everybody" (Mosak, 1995). Adler developed procedures for changing these beliefs that are similar in some ways to more modern forms of therapy we'll consider below.

While many forms of therapy based on Freud's ideas exist, all adaptations of psychoanalysis in use today share these features: (1) They focus more on patients' present life and personal relationships than on the past; (2) they require less time than did the original version—usually a few months rather than years; and (3) the therapist plays a more active role, commenting and advising patients rather than merely listening most of the time. Despite these differences, however, the basic goal remains the same: helping patients to gain insight into their hidden motives and inner conflicts.

Key Questions

- What is psychoanalysis, and what are its major assumptions?
- What is the role of free association in psychoanalysis?
- How are psychodynamic therapies practiced today?

Humanistic Therapies: Emphasizing the Positive

Freud was something of a pessimist about basic human nature. He felt that we must constantly struggle with primitive impulses from the id. But, as we saw in Chapter 12, many psychologists reject this view. *Humanistic* psychologists contend that people are basically good and that our strivings for growth, dignity, and self-control are just as strong as—perhaps stronger than—the powerful aggressive and sexual urges Freud described. According to these psychologists, psychological disorders do not stem from unresolved inner conflicts. Rather, they arise because the environment somehow interferes with personal growth and fulfillment.

Basic Mistakes: False beliefs held by individuals that interfere with their mental health; a concept in psychotherapy devised by Adler.

Humanistic Therapies: Therapies that focus on helping clients (not "patients") to become more truly themselves—to find meaning in their lives and to live in ways truly consistent with their own values and traits.

Client-Centered Therapy: A form of psychotherapy that seeks to eliminate irrational conditions of worth in the client's mind by providing unconditional positive regard in a caring, empathetic environment.

Conditions of Worth: In Rogers's client-centered therapy, individuals' beliefs that they must be something other than what they really are in order to be loved and accepted by others.

Gestalt Therapy: A humanistic therapy that focuses on helping individuals to come to terms with hidden, "disowned" aspects of their thoughts and feelings.

Such views lead to **humanistic therapies,** which focus on the task of helping *clients* (not "patients") to become more truly themselves—to find meaning in their lives and to live in ways truly consistent with their own values and traits. Unlike psychoanalysts, humanistic therapists believe that clients, not they, must take essential responsibility for the success of therapy. The therapist is mainly a guide and facilitator, *not* the one who runs the show. Let's take a closer look at two forms of humanistic therapy.

Client-Centered Therapy: The Benefits of Being Accepted

Perhaps the most influential humanistic approach is **client-centered therapy,** developed by Carl Rogers (1970, 1980). Rogers strongly rejected Freud's view that psychological disorders stem from conflicts over the expression of primitive, instinctive urges. On the contrary, he argued, such problems arise mainly from a distorted *self-concept*. According to Rogers, individuals often acquire what he terms unrealistic **conditions of worth** early in life. That is, they learn that they must be something other than what they really are in order to be loved and accepted. For example, they come to believe that they will be rejected by their parents if they harbor hostility toward their siblings. In response to such beliefs, people refuse to recognize large portions of their experience and emotions—portions that violate their implicitly accepted conditions of worth. This, in turn, interferes with normal development of the self and causes them to suffer from various forms of maladjustment.

Client-centered therapy (also known as *person-centered therapy*) focuses on eliminating such unrealistic conditions of worth through creation of a psychological climate in which clients feel valued as persons. Client-centered therapists offer *unconditional positive regard,* or *unconditional acceptance,* of the client and her or his feelings; a high level of *empathetic understanding;* and accurate reflection of the client's feelings and perceptions. In this warm, caring environment, freed from the threat of rejection, individuals can come to understand their own feelings and accept even previously unwanted aspects of their own personalities. As a result, they come to see themselves as unique human beings with many desirable characteristics. To the extent such changes occur, Rogers suggests, many psychological disorders disappear and individuals can resume their normal progress toward self-fulfillment (see Figure 15.4).

FIGURE 15.4

Client-Centered Therapy: An Overview

Rogers believed that psychological disorders stem from unrealistic *conditions of worth* acquired early in life. Client-centered therapy seeks to change such beliefs, primarily by placing individuals in an environment where they receive *unconditional acceptance* from the therapist.

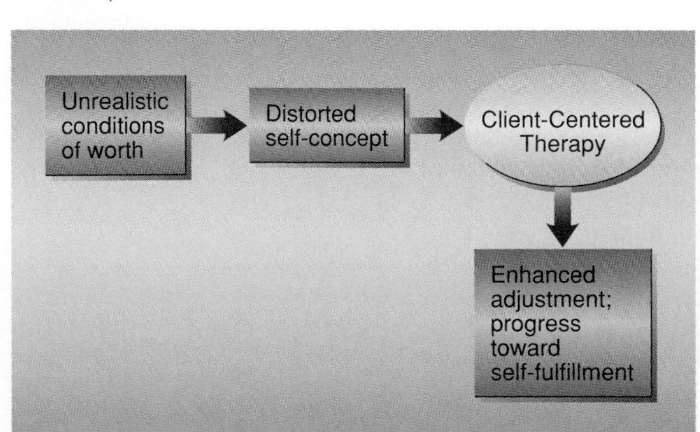

Gestalt Therapy: Becoming Whole

The theme of faulty or incomplete self-awareness so prominent in client-centered therapy is echoed in a second humanistic approach, **Gestalt therapy** (Perls, 1969). As noted in Chapter 3, the German word *Gestalt* means "whole," and this word captures the essence of Gestalt therapy. According to Fritz Perls, originator of this form of psychotherapy, individuals often experience difficulties because key aspects of their thoughts and feelings are not acknowledged in their consciousness, and not related to current conditions in the world around them that are generating such reactions. In short, such people have disowned parts of their own being; to become healthy, they must recapture and come to terms with these lost parts.

How can this be accomplished? Gestalt therapists use many different tactics. They often ask their clients questions such as "What are you doing now?" "How are you feeling now?" If the client reports a painful or anxiety-provoking thought or feeling, he or she is encouraged to "stay with it" and experience it fully. Other techniques are even more dramatic. In the *two-chair technique,* for instance, clients move back and forth between two chairs. While sitting in one, they play themselves; in the other, they assume the role of some important person in their life—wife, husband, mother, father. This helps them to *take care of unfinished business*—to get in touch with part of their self they have not yet fully experienced and accepted, and by doing so to resolve inner conflicts.

Humanistic Therapies: An Overview While humanistic psychotherapies differ in many respects, they share a basic orientation: All reject the views, so powerfully stated by Freud, that psychological disorders stem from repressed urges and hidden conflicts, and that a therapist's key task is to force unwilling patients to gain insights into these conflicts. Further, all assume that human beings have the capacity to reflect on their own problems, to change their own behavior and thoughts, and to make choices that will lead them toward more satisfying lives. Finally, all these therapies suggest that gaps in our self-concepts—flaws in our understanding of ourselves, our feelings, and our experiences—lie at the heart of much psychological distress.

Humanistic therapies have been criticized for their lack of a unified theoretical base and for being vague about precisely what is supposed to happen between clients and therapists. They have, however, helped to alter the dismal picture of human nature painted by Freud. In addition, several techniques devised by humanistic therapists are now widely used, even by psychologists who do not share this perspective. For instance, Carl Rogers was one of the first psychotherapists to tape-record sessions with clients so that the therapists could study the tapes at a later time. This tactic not only helps therapists to assist their clients; it also provides information about which techniques are most effective during therapy. In a similar manner, while most psychologists don't practice Gestalt therapy, they do often use procedures such as the two-chair technique (e.g., Lazarus, 1989). Finally, some of the assumptions underlying humanistic therapies have been subjected to scientific testing and found to be valid. For instance, research findings tend to confirm Rogers's view that the gap between an individual's self-image and his or her "ideal self" plays a crucial role in maladjustment (e.g., Bootzin, Acocella, & Alloy, 1993). In these ways, then, humanistic therapies have made lasting contributions to the practice of psychotherapy.

Key Questions

- According to humanistic therapies, what is the cause of psychological disorders?
- What is the major goal of Rogers's client-centered therapy?
- What is the major goal of Gestalt therapy?

Behavior Therapies: Psychological Disorders and Faulty Learning

While psychodynamic and humanistic therapies differ in many ways, they both place importance on early events in clients' lives as a key source of current disturbances. In contrast, another major group of therapies, known collectively as **behavior therapies,** focus primarily on individuals' current behavior. These therapies are based on the belief that many psychological disorders stem from faulty learning. Either the persons involved have failed to acquire the skills and behaviors they need for coping with the problems of daily life, or they have acquired *maladaptive* habits and reactions—ones that cause them considerable distress. Within this context, the key task for therapy is to change current behavior, not to correct faulty self-concepts or to resolve hidden inner conflicts.

In addition, behavior therapies seek to provide individuals with behaviors and strategies they can use to overcome their problems when they are not in the presence of the therapist—through guided *self-care* (Marks, 1994). Self-care is obviously important in the treatment of many medical conditions; for example, persons with some forms of diabetes must inject themselves with insulin every day. Similarly, many behavior therapists believe that in

Behavior Therapies: Therapies based on the belief that many psychological disorders stem from faulty learning.

Systematic Desensitization: A form of behavior therapy in which individuals first learn how to induce a relaxed state in their own bodies. Then, while in a relaxed state, they are exposed to stimuli that elicit fear.

order to obtain lasting benefits, persons with psychological disorders must practice in their daily lives the skills they acquire during therapy.

What kinds of learning play a role in behavior therapy? As we saw in Chapter 5, three basic kinds of learning exist. Reflecting this fact, behavior therapy employs techniques based on all three major kinds of learning.

Therapies Based on Classical Conditioning *Classical conditioning,* as you will remember, is a process in which organisms learn that the occurrence of one stimulus will soon be followed by the occurrence of another. As a result, reactions that are at first produced only by the second stimulus gradually come to be evoked by the first as well. (Remember the popcorn example from Chapter 5? Because of classical conditioning, you gradually learn to salivate to the beep of your microwave, even without the smell of cooking popcorn.)

What does classical conditioning have to do with psychological disorders? According to behavior therapists, quite a bit (Bandura, 1969). Behavior therapists suggest, for example, that many *phobias* are acquired in this manner. Stimuli that happen to be present when real dangers occur may acquire the capacity to evoke intense fear because of this association. The result? An individual may experience intense anxiety in situations in which a conditioned stimulus is present, but which actually poses no threat to the person's well-being. To eliminate such reactions, behavior therapists sometimes use the technique of *flooding*. This involves exposure to the feared stimulus, or to mental representations of it, under conditions where the person with the phobia can't escape from it. As a result, *extinction* of fear can occur, and the phobias fade away (Levis, 1985).

Another technique based in part on principles of classical conditioning is known as **systematic desensitization.** This procedure too is often used to treat phobias; but, as shown by the cartoon in Figure 15.5, it is sometimes used in connection with other kinds of maladaptive emotional reactions as well. In systematic desensitization, individuals first learn how to induce a relaxed state in their own bodies—often by learning how to relax their muscles. Then, while in a relaxed state, they are exposed to stimuli that elicit fear. Since they are now experiencing relaxation, which is incompatible with fear (or anger, as shown in Figure 15.5), the conditioned link between these stimuli and fear is weakened.

FIGURE 15.5

Behavior Therapy in Action

In *systematic desensitization,* one technique of behavior therapy, individuals learn to relax and then, while relaxed, are exposed to stimuli that cause them to experience intense fear or (as here) intense anger. Since feelings of relaxation are incompatible with fear or anger, the tendency to have such reactions in the presence of certain stimuli is weakened.

"Now relax.... Just like last week, I'm going to hold the cape up for the count of 10. ... When you start getting angry, I'll put it down."

(**Source**: THE FAR SIDE copyright 1987 & 1990 FARWORKS, INC. Used with permission of UNIVERSAL PRESS SYNDICATE. All rights reserved.)

Therapies Based on Operant Conditioning Behavior is often shaped by the consequences it produces; actions are repeated if they yield positive outcomes or if they permit individuals to avoid or escape from negative ones. In contrast, actions that lead to negative results are suppressed. These are the underlying principles incorporated in several forms of therapy based on *operant conditioning*. These therapies differ considerably in their details, but all include the following steps, similar to the "DO-IT" model described in Chapter 5: (1) clear identification of undesirable or maladaptive behaviors currently shown by individuals;

(2) identification of events that reinforce and so maintain such responses; (3) efforts to change the environment so that these maladaptive behaviors are no longer followed by reinforcement.

Operant principles have sometimes been used in hospital settings, where a large degree of control over patients' reinforcements is possible (Kazdin, 1982). Several projects have involved the establishment of **token economies**—systems under which patients earn tokens they can exchange for rewards, such as television-watching privileges, candy, or trips to town. These tokens are awarded for various forms of adaptive behavior such as keeping one's room neat, participating in group meetings or therapy sessions, coming to meals on time, and eating neatly. The results have often been impressive. When individuals learn that they can acquire rewards by behaving in adaptive ways, they often do so, with important benefits to them as well as to hospital staff (e.g., Paul, 1982; Paul & Lentz, 1977).

Token Economies: A form of behavior therapy in which patients in hospital settings earn tokens they can exchange for various rewards by engaging in desirable forms of behavior.

Modeling: Benefiting from Exposure to Others Suppose an individual comes to a psychologist seeking help for an all-too-common problem: lack of *assertiveness*. In other words, this individual is one who can't stand up for her or his own rights, is often pushed around by others, and can't say no in many situations. How can the psychologist help? One answer involves the use of *modeling*—techniques based on *observational learning*. As we saw in Chapter 5, human beings have a tremendous capacity to learn from observing others (e.g., Bandura, 1986). Behavior therapists put this fact to use in treating a wide range of personal problems.

For instance, persons like the one described above are often given *assertiveness training,* in which they are taught the basic social skills they are lacking. How do therapists accomplish this? Often by exposing clients to others who demonstrate (model) appropriate ways of standing up for one's rights. Clients may watch live demonstrations or videotapes in which the actors show very clearly how to respond effectively to such situations as having another push ahead of you in line or being served food you didn't order in a restaurant. Such demonstrations focus on adaptive reactions to such situations: responding firmly, but without excess anger or aggression. After watching such demonstrations, individuals practice the adaptive behaviors themselves and so, quite quickly, acquire new and more appropriate ways of behaving in many situations (Wilson et al., 1996).

Modeling techniques have been used effectively for treating many kinds of problems, ranging from sexual dysfunctions (Kelley & Byrne, 1992) through the inability to control one's temper (Bandura, 1986). Perhaps the most impressive applications have been in the treatment of phobias. Many carefully conducted studies indicate that individuals who experience intense fear of relatively harmless objects can be helped to overcome these fears through exposure to appropriate social models who demonstrate lack of fear and show that no harm occurs in the presence of these objects (e.g., Bandura, 1974). What kinds of phobias are reduced in this manner? A wide range—including powerful, debilitating fears of dogs, snakes, and spiders (Bandura, 1986).

Modeling techniques have also been used successfully to modify the behavior of highly aggressive children and adolescents (Schneider & Byrne, 1987). These youngsters often behave aggressively because they are lacking in basic social skills: They don't know how to ask for what they want in a nonaggressive manner, how to refuse a request without angering the requester, and so on (see Figure 15.6 on page 596). Research findings indicate that modeling can be used to teach such skills quickly and efficiently (Bienert & Schneider, 1993; Schneider, 1991).

Key Questions

- According to behavior therapies, what is the primary cause of psychological disorders?
- On what basic principles of learning are behavior therapies based?
- What is modeling, and how can it be used in treating psychological disorders?

FIGURE 15.6

Improving Social Skills: One Goal of Modeling Therapy

Many highly aggressive children are lacking in basic social skills. For instance, they don't know how to make a request in a polite manner. Modeling therapy can be highly effective in equipping such youngsters with these skills.

Cognitive Therapies: Changing Disordered Thought

A central theme in modern psychology, and one I've emphasized throughout this book, is this: Cognitive processes exert powerful effects on emotions and behavior. In other words, what we *think* strongly influences how we *feel* and what we *do*. This principle forms the basis for another major group of approaches to psychotherapy, **cognitive therapies.** The basic idea behind cognitive therapies is that many psychological disorders stem from faulty or distorted modes of thought. Change these, it is reasoned, and the disorders, too, can be alleviated. Let's examine several forms of cognitive therapy.

Rational–Emotive Therapy: Overcoming Irrational Beliefs

Everyone I meet should like me.

I should be perfect (or darn near perfect) in every way.

Because something once affected my life, it will always affect it.

I can't bear it when things are not the way I would like them to be.

It is impossible to control my emotions; I can't help feeling the way I do about certain things or in certain situations.

Be honest: Do such ideas ever influence *your* thinking? While you may strongly protest that they do not, one psychologist—Albert Ellis (1987)—believes that they probably do. Moreover, he contends that such *irrational thoughts* play a key role in many psychological disorders. Why do we have such thoughts? Not, Ellis contends, because we consciously choose to do so. Rather, these are often automatic reactions stemming from our strong desires for love, success, and a safe, comfortable existence. We *want* to be liked by everyone, to be perfect, and so on—so we let these powerful desires color our perceptions and our thinking.

Other psychologists have traced the origins of such thinking to early childhood experiences. For instance, Blatt (1995) contends that the desire to be perfect may stem from behavior by our parents suggesting that they will love and accept us only if we meet their standards and expectations—which are often unrealistically high.

Whatever their origins, irrational beliefs generally serve to escalate reasonable desires into "musts," as in "I *must* be loved by everyone" or "I *must* experience continuous success to be happy." Closely linked to such ideas are patterns of thought Ellis describes as *awfulizing* or *catastrophizing*—beliefs that if a certain event occurs or fails to occur, it will be a disaster of unbearable proportions from which one can never hope to recover. Examples: "If I don't get that promotion, *my career will be completely over*," or "If I don't get an A in that course after working so hard, *I just won't be able to stand it*."

Ellis maintains that people who hold these irrational beliefs are often their own worst enemies. They cause their own problems—by worrying about their inability to reach impossible goals and by convincing themselves that they simply cannot tolerate the normal frustrations and disappointments of everyday life. To make matters worse, once such thoughts take hold, negative feelings and maladaptive behaviors soon follow. How can this self-defeating cycle be broken? Ellis suggests that the answer involves forcing disturbed individuals to recognize the irrationality of their thoughts.

Cognitive Therapies: Forms of therapy focused on changing distorted and maladaptive patterns of thought.

Rational–emotive therapy (RET) is designed to accomplish this task. During this form of therapy, the therapist attempts first to identify the client's irrational thoughts and then to persuade the client to recognize them for what they are. For example, imagine that a therapist practicing RET is confronted with a client who says, "My girlfriend just dumped me for another guy; *I'll never find anyone else who will love me like she once did!*" The therapist might reply, "So your girlfriend dumped you; why does that mean that no one else will ever love you? Is she really the only woman in the world with whom you could have a relationship?" By challenging the irrationality of clients' beliefs, therapists practicing RET get their clients to see how ridiculous and unrealistic some of their ideas are; in this way, they can help them stop being their own worst enemies.

Rational–Emotive Therapy: A form of therapy that focuses on persuading individuals to recognize and change irrational assumptions that underlie their thinking.

Cognitive Behavior Therapy: A form of cognitive therapy that focuses on changing illogical patterns of thought that underlie depression.

Beck's Cognitive Behavior Therapy for Depression In discussing depression in Chapter 14, I noted that this extremely common but serious psychological disorder has an important cognitive component: It stems, at least in part, from distorted and often self-defeating modes of thought. Recognizing this important fact, Aaron Beck (1985) has devised a **cognitive behavior therapy** for alleviating depression. Like Ellis, Beck assumes that depressed individuals engage in illogical thinking and that this is at the root of their difficulties. Moreover, he contends, the illogical ideas people hold are often maintained even in the face of evidence that contradicts them. What are the cognitive tendencies that may lead to depression? Among the most important are these:

- A tendency to overgeneralize on the basis of limited information—for example, to see oneself as totally worthless because of a few setbacks.
- A tendency to explain away any positive occurrences as exceptions to the general rule of failure and incompetence.
- A tendency to perceive the world as a dangerous, threatening place.
- A tendency to magnify the importance of undesirable events—to perceive them as the end of the world and unchangeable.
- A tendency to engage in absolutist, all-or-none thinking—for example, to interpret a mild rejection as final proof of one's undesirability.

Central to Beck's therapy is the idea that such tendencies lead individuals to have negative moods, which increase the probability of negative thinking. Negative thoughts contribute to depression; and depression, in turn, strengthens illogical thinking (see Figure 15.7). In other words, Beck empha-

Beck's Therapy Focuses on Changing This Kind of Thinking
Illogical Ideas
E.g., tendency to overgeneralize setbacks
E.g., tendency to explain away positive outcomes or experiences
E.g., tendency to magnify the importance of negative events
Negative affect
Negative thoughts, memories, ideas
Depression

FIGURE 15.7

Beck's Cognitive Behavior Therapy: An Overview

Beck's cognitive behavior therapy is designed to change cognitive tendencies that contribute to depression. Such patterns of thought often produce negative affect (mood), which increases the likelihood of further negative thoughts. Beck's cognitive behavior therapy attempts to break this cycle and so to reduce depression.

sizes the importance of mood-dependent memory—how our current moods influence what we remember and what we think about (see Chapters 6 and 14). How can this vicious circle be broken? In contrast to rational–emotive therapy, Beck's cognitive approach does not attempt to disprove the ideas held by depressed persons. Rather, the therapist and client work together to identify the individual's irrational assumptions, beliefs, and expectations, and to formulate ways to test them. For example, if a client states that she is a total failure, the therapist may ask how she defines failure, and whether some experiences she defines this way may actually be only partial failures. If that's so, the therapist inquires, aren't they also partial successes? Continuing in this manner, the therapist might then ask the client whether there are any areas of her life where she *did* experience success and did reach her goals. Recent studies indicate that as a result of these procedures, individuals learn to reinterpret negative events in ways that help them cope with such outcomes *without* becoming depressed (e.g., Bruder et al., 1997). So, while the specific techniques used are different from those used in RET, the major goal is much the same: helping people to recognize, and reject, the false assumptions and conclusions that are central to their difficulties. (For information about another technique for countering depression, please see the Beyond the Headlines section.)

Cognitive Therapies: An Evaluation Do cognitive therapies work? Growing evidence indicates that they may be highly effective in treating several psychological disorders. Many studies indicate that changing or eliminating irrational beliefs, such as the unstated desire to be perfect, can be very effective in countering depression and other personal difficulties (e.g., Blatt et al., 1996). Similarly, the procedures outlined by Beck have been found to be extremely helpful in treating depression (e.g., Bruder, et al., 1997; Hollon & Beck, 1994). These findings suggest that there is a considerable grain of truth to the old belief that the problems experienced by many depressed persons are "all in their minds." Depression, it seems, often does stem from distorted patterns of thought. For this reason, forms of therapy focused on changing such patterns can often prove highly effective.

Key Questions

- According to cognitive therapies, what are the primary causes of psychological disorders?
- What is the major goal of rational–emotive therapy?
- What is the major goal of Beck's cognitive behavior therapy for depression?
- Is there any evidence for a beneficial effect of laughter with respect to psychological disorders?

Group Therapies: *Working with Others to Solve Problems*

Group Therapies: Therapies in which treatment takes place in groups.

Incompatible Response Hypothesis: A hypothesis suggesting that if individuals who are angry and ready to engage in aggression are exposed to stimuli (such as humor) that induce emotional states or response tendencies incompatible with anger, both anger and aggression will be reduced.

All of the therapies we have considered so far are conducted on a one-on-one basis. As you may already know, however, this is not the only approach to helping individuals deal with psychological problems. In recent decades **group therapies,** in which treatment takes place in groups, have grown tremendously in popularity. We'll now examine several important types of group therapy, beginning with ones that are closely linked to the individual therapies considered earlier.

Psychodynamic Group Therapies

Techniques developed by Freud for individual therapy have also been modified for use in group settings. Perhaps the most popular of these is *psy-*

Beyond the Headlines

As Psychologists See It

Nursing the Funny Bone: Carol O'Flaherty Goes from Giving Shots to Needling Audiences

Boston Globe, April 29, 1996—Carol O'Flaherty remembers the day well: "So *you're* the nurse who's supposed to be so funny," the doctor told her. . . . "I've never met a funny nurse in my life. . . ."

Obviously, he had never met O'Flaherty, a self-described "Nurse–humorist. . . ." While she no longer sees patients in the traditional sense, she does practice her own brand of preventive health care. She travels all over New England, talking to groups of people . . . about the importance of humor and laughter in everyday life. "Everyone is a victim today. . . . I mean, you say to someone, 'How are you doing?' and they say, 'Oh God, just terrible.' And their tragedy is that their cat is coughing up furballs."

But O'Flaherty doesn't just tell jokes. She also explains why laughter is so important to health. For instance, she says, laughter boosts the immune system. She points out that while the average 4-year-old child may laugh 400 times a day, the average adult laughs about 4 times a day. . . . O'Flaherty also believes that laughter is the best medicine where depression is concerned. As she puts it: "My grandmother used to say that laughter will help you through a time when you have no money, but money won't help you through a time when you have no laughter. I firmly believe that we need to learn to put our lives in perspective."

Laughter—The Best Medicine?

Ms. O'Flaherty is not alone in her belief that laughter can have important health benefits; other self-styled "humor consultants" have recommended using humor to improve on-the-job productivity (Arnold, 1996) and even to combat the fear and anxiety that accompanies a trip to the dentist (Lopez, 1996). Is laughter, as the old saying suggests, really "the best medicine"? Some research findings do suggest that there may be some truth in the claims of humor advocates, exaggerated though these may be. In fact, I actually provided some of this evidence myself some years ago, when I was investigating a technique for reducing anger and aggression based on the **incompatible response hypothesis.** This hypothesis suggests that it is very difficult, if not impossible, to experience two incompatible emotional states at once; thus, if angry persons can be made to experience some emotion incompatible with their anger, they may be less likely to feel angry or engage in overt aggression. I found that humor worked very well in this respect: Angry persons exposed to humorous materials—funny cartoons, comedy routines, funny films (e.g., Baron, 1978; Baron & Ball, 1974)—did report less anger and engage in less aggression against persons who had annoyed them than angry persons who were *not* exposed to humorous materials. Not all types of humor were successful in this respect; for instance, hostile humor did *not* produce mollifying effects. But most other types were quite effective in reducing anger and aggression.

Can humor also help reduce depression? Additional findings suggest that it can indeed give people a mild mood boost (e.g., Zillmann, 1996). And since being in a negative mood increases the likelihood of remembering negative information and thinking unhappy thoughts, exposure to humor may give depressed persons just the extra help they need to escape from the downward spiral shown in Figure 15.7 on page 597. So Nurse O'Flaherty, and other practitioners who are currently using humor in medical settings, may be onto something real: Perhaps humor can help. However, only systematic further research can help answer such questions as: "What kinds of humor are best?" "How long do the mood-enhancing effects of humor last?" "Can such procedures work with people who are deeply depressed, or only with those who are experiencing milder forms of depression?"

Critical Thinking Questions

1. Large cultural differences in humor exist, so the same jokes don't always translate from one culture

to another. Given this fact, do you think that humor might be more effective in countering depression in some cultures than in others? Why?

2. When people are very angry, they sometimes resent efforts to get them to laugh. Do you think the same might be true of deeply depressed persons?

chodrama—a form of therapies in which group members act out their problems in front of other members, often on an actual stage. Psychodrama also involves such techniques as *role reversal,* in which group members switch parts, and *mirroring,* in which they portray one another on the stage. In each case the goal is to show clients how they actually behave and to help them understand *why* they behave that way—what hidden inner conflicts lie behind their overt actions (Olsson, 1989). While psychodrama is highly appealing to many people—perhaps we all want the opportunity to take center stage at least occasionally—it is subject to the same criticism as all psychodynamic therapies; so its potential benefits may be overstated by its often fervent supporters.

Behavioral Group Therapies

In contrast, there is very compelling evidence for the effectiveness of *behavioral group therapies*—group approaches in which basic principles of learning are applied to solving behavioral problems. Such therapy has been found to be especially useful in teaching individuals basic *social skills,* such as how to communicate their wishes to others and how to stand up for their rights without being aggressive (the kind of *assertiveness training* described earlier). Behavioral group therapy has also proved helpful in teaching individuals *self-control*—the capacity to regulate their own behavior. Many persons experience serious problems in life because they lack this basic skill. They can't force themselves to get up in the morning so as to get to work on time; they can't stop themselves from buying things they can't afford (see Figure 15.8); they can't hold their tempers in check when annoyed (e.g., Bandura, 1986).

Group therapy based on behavioral principles can be highly effective in teaching people these skills. In such sessions, group members describe how they are currently behaving in situations requiring self-control. Then they receive suggestions from other group members about how they can do a better job in this respect. Because different members of the group have different problems with respect to self-control, they can serve one another as models of more effective behavior. They can also serve as sources of positive reinforcement; praising each other when they make progress toward appropriate goals.

FIGURE 15.8

Learning Self-Control: Behavioral Group Therapy Can Help

Many people have difficulty in regulating their own behavior; for instance, like the individual shown here, they can't resist the impulse to buy things they can't afford. Behavioral group therapy is often helpful for such persons.

Humanistic Group Therapies

Psychologists who practice humanistic therapies have been by far the most enthusiastic about adapting their techniques to group settings. In fact, interest in group therapy first originated among humanistic therapists, who developed two forms of such therapy—*encounter groups* and *sensitivity-training groups.* Both of these techniques focus on the goals of personal growth, increased understanding of one's own behavior, and increased honesty and openness in personal relations. In both types of groups, members are encouraged to talk about the problems they encounter in their lives. The reactions they receive from other group members are then crucial in helping them understand their own responses to these problems. The major difference between encounter groups and sensitivity-training groups lies in the fact that encounter groups carry the goal of open exchange of views to a greater extreme; members in these groups are encouraged to yell, cry, touch each other, and generally to act in a completely uninhibited manner. Sensitivity-training groups, in contrast, are somewhat more subdued.

Self-Help Groups: Groups of persons who are experiencing the same kinds of problems and who meet to help each other in their efforts to cope with these difficulties.

To get the process of open exchange of views started, humanistic group therapies often use several ingenious warm-up exercises. For instance, in one sensitivity-training group I attended (it was part of a schoolwide retreat called by our dean), we formed a circle and then, one at a time, let ourselves fall backwards into the waiting arms of the person behind us. This process was repeated until everyone had this experience. I must admit that after this exercise the atmosphere in the room *did* change, and inhibitions were reduced (see Figure 15.9).

FIGURE 15.9

Breaking the Ice in a Sensitivity-Training Group

In order to "prime" the process of open communication, sensitivity-training groups often use warm-up exercises such as the one shown here.

Do such groups really produce beneficial changes? Many persons who have participated in them attest that they do; but most research on this issue has been informal in nature, so it is difficult to reach firm conclusions (Kaplan, 1982).

Self-Help Groups: Help from Our Peers

When we are anxious, upset, or otherwise troubled, we often seek comfort and support from others. Long before there were psychologists and psychiatrists, people sought informal help with personal difficulties from family members, friends, or clergy. This tendency to seek help from people we know, even if they are not professionals, has taken a new form in **self-help groups** (Christensen & Jacobson, 1994). These are groups of persons who are experiencing the same kinds of problems and who meet to help each other in their efforts to cope with these difficulties. Self-help groups are a fact of life in the late 1990s; indeed, it has been estimated that more than 5 percent of all adults in the United States are or have been involved in such groups.

What kinds of problems do these groups address? Almost everything you can imagine—and then some. Self-help groups have been formed to help their members cope with alcoholism (Alcoholics Anonymous is perhaps the most famous of all self-help groups), gambling, the death of a spouse, rape, AIDS, childhood sexual abuse, being a single parent, divorce, stuttering, breast cancer—the list is almost endless.

A guiding principle behind these groups is that people who share a problem have a unique understanding of it and can offer one another a level of empathy that those who have not experienced the problem cannot provide. Do self-help groups succeed? Few scientific studies have been conducted

Key Questions

- What is the major focus of psychodynamic group therapies such as psychodrama?
- What is the major focus of behavioral group therapies?
- What is the major focus of humanistic group therapies?
- What are self-help groups, and what do they provide?

on this question, but there is some indication that they can indeeed yield benefits (Christensen & Jacobson, 1994). In any case, these groups do provide their members with emotional support and help them to make new friends. These outcomes alone may justify their existence.

Therapies Focused on Interpersonal Relations: *Marital and Family Therapy*

While group therapies take place in settings where several people are present, they resemble individual therapies in one crucial respect: Group therapies, too, search for the roots of psychological disorders in processes operating largely *within* individuals.

In contrast, another type of therapy focuses on the potential role of *interpersonal relations* in psychological problems and disorders (Gurman, Kniskern, & Pinsof, 1986). In other words, therapies in this category assume that individuals experience personal problems because their relations with important persons in their lives are ineffective, unsatisfying, or worse. Let's now examine two important forms of therapy that adopt this interpersonal perspective.

Marital Therapy: Spouses as the Intimate Enemy

In the United States and many other countries, more than 50 percent of all marriages now end in divorce; moreover, because many people remarry—and hope seems to spring eternal—growing numbers of persons have been married three or more times (Brody, Neubaum, & Forehand, 1988). Keeping people in joyless marriages where each spouse is destructive to the other's psychological health is definitely *not* a goal of therapy (see Figure 15.10). However, it appears that many marriages that fail could be saved and con-

FIGURE 15.10

When Marital Therapy Might Not Be Appropriate

Marital therapy is appropriate for couples who want to save their marriage and for whom remaining together would not be harmful to the psychological health of either partner. In cases where basic incompatibilities that can't be changed exist, the best solution may be divorce.

"Sometimes I'm sorry I ever ran away with you."

(**Source:** Drawing by Leo Cullum; ©1992 The New Yorker Magazine, Inc.)

verted into loving, supporting relationships if the persons involved sought help before the downward spiral went too far (Hendrick, 1989). Further, marital problems often appear to be closely linked to psychological disorders such as depression and drug dependency (Gotlieb & McCabe, 1990). For these reasons, **marital therapy** (sometimes known as *couple therapy*)—therapy designed to help couples improve the quality of their relationship—can often be highly valuable.

Marital Therapy: Therapy designed to help couples improve the quality of their relationship.

Before turning to the goals and procedures of marital therapy, let's first consider a very basic question: What, in your opinion, is the number one reason why couples seek professional help in the first place? If you guessed "sexual problems," guess again; such difficulties are a distant second in the list (see Figure 15.11). Problems relating to *communication* are far and away the number one cause of marital difficulties. People entering therapy often state that their spouse "never talks to them" or "never tells them what she/he is thinking." Or they complain that the only thing their spouse ever does is *complain*. "He/she never tells me that he/she loves me," they remark. "All he/she does is tell me about my faults, and what I'm doing wrong." Given that couples begin their relationships with frequent statements of mutual esteem and love, the pain of such faulty communication patterns is doubled: Each partner wonders what went wrong—and then generally blames her or his spouse or partner!

A key goal of marital therapy, then, is to improve communication between spouses or partners. Therapists work to foster such improvements in many different ways, including having each partner play the role of the other person so as to see their relationship as the other does. Other techniques involve having couples watch videotapes of their own interactions. This procedure is often truly an eye-opener; "Wow, I never realized that's how I come across!" is a common reaction when people see themselves interacting with their spouse. As communication between partners improves, many other beneficial changes occur. The couple stop criticizing each other in destructive ways (e.g., Baron, 1993), express positive sentiments toward each other more frequently, and stop attributing each other's actions to internal causes or stable

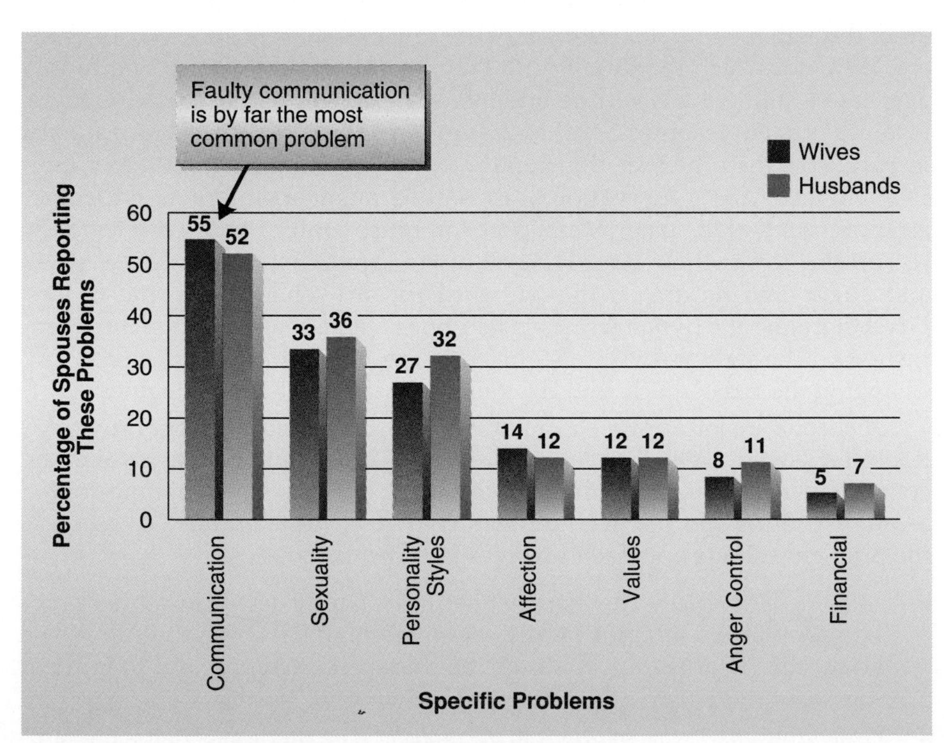

(**Source:** Based on data from O'Leary, Vivian, & Malone, 1992.)

FIGURE 15.11

Why Couples Seek Marital Therapy

As shown here, the number one reason why couples seek help from trained therapists involves faulty communication. Other problems are important, too, but are mentioned less frequently.

traits. In other words, they stop assuming that anything the partner does that annoys them is done on purpose, or that such actions can't be changed because they stem from the partner's basic personality traits (e.g., Kubany et al., 1995). Once communication is reestablished, couples may also find it easier to resolve other sources of friction in their relationships: conflicts over sexuality, money, attitudes, and values. The result may then be a happier and more stable relationship and one that enhances, rather than reduces, the psychological well-being of both partners.

Family Therapy: Changing Environments That Harm

Let's begin with a disturbing fact: When individuals who have been hospitalized for the treatment of serious psychological disorders and who have shown marked improvements return home, they often experience a relapse. All the gains they have made through individual therapy seem to vanish. This fact points to an unsettling possibility: Perhaps the problems experienced by such persons stem, at least in part, from their families—or, more specifically, from disturbed patterns of interaction among family members (Hazelrigg, Cooper, & Borduin, 1987). To the extent this is true, attempting to help one member of a family is not sufficient; unless changes are also made in the family environment, any benefits a patient has experienced may disappear once she or he returns home.

Recognition of this important fact spurred the development of several types of **family therapy**—therapy designed to change the interactions among family members in constructive ways. Perhaps the most common approach to such therapy involves what is known as **family systems therapy**—an approach that treats the family as a dynamic system in which each member has a major role. Within this framework, it is assumed that relations *between* family members are more important in producing psychological disorders than aspects of personality or other factors operating largely *within* individuals (Minuchin & Fishman, 1981). It is also assumed that all members of the family influence each other through the complex network of their relationships.

How does such therapy work? Take, for instance, the case of a highly aggressive child who is getting into lots of trouble in school and elsewhere. A family systems therapist would assume that his difficulties stem, at least in part, from disturbed relationships between this youngster and other family members. Close observation of the family members interacting together might reveal that the parents are locked in bitter conflict, with each trying to recruit the boy to their side. The result: He experiences tremendous stress and anger, and he directs this outward toward schoolmates and others. Understanding the dynamics of his family, in short, could provide the therapist—and the family—with insights into the causes of the boy's problem. Changing these dynamics, in turn, could help to reduce his difficulties.

Family Therapy: Therapy designed to change the interactions among family members in constructive ways.

Family Systems Therapy: A form of family therapy that treats the family as a dynamic system in which each member has a major role.

Problem-Solving Therapy: A form of family therapy that focuses on instituting specific, well-defined changes within a family in order to eliminate specific problems.

A second major approach in known as **problem-solving therapy** (e.g., Robbin & Foster, 1988). This approach focuses not so much on analyzing the complex dynamics within families—although it views these as important—as on instituting specific, well-defined changes within a family. In essence, the problem-solving approach involves four distinct phases:

- *Defining the problem:* The therapist helps the family decide just what problem they face. Different family members may have contrasting views about this, so it is important for the therapist to step in and help them see the underlying pattern, not merely their own views.
- *Generating alternative solutions to the problem:* The therapists helps the family come up with various ways of solving the problem. Again, different

family members may have contrasting perspectives, and it is important for all of these to be represented in the discussion.

- *Evaluating the alternative solutions:* Each possible solution is examined by the family, and a consensus is reached on which one is best or which to try first.
- *Implementing the solution:* Plans for putting the solution to work are made and used.

For example, consider a family in which the teenage daughter is threatening to run away from home. The parents may view the problem as their daughter's rebelliousness and her boyfriend's bad influence on her. She, in turn, may view the friction as stemming from unrealistic restrictions placed on her by her parents: "You treat me like a child!" The therapist might step in and define the basic problem as one of faulty communication in which the parents and their daughter primarily exchange angry criticisms rather than discussing important issues clearly. Possible solutions might include the daughter's agreeing to do her homework and to come home by a specified hour if her parents will treat her more as an adult and be pleasant to her boyfriend. The family would then select one or more possible solutions and try them out, reporting to the therapist on the results. Through this kind of process—which involves open discussion and a healthy chunk of trial and error—the family would move toward solving their basic problems and attaining a happier relationship (see Figure 15.12).

Does family therapy work? Research findings indicate that in many cases it is quite successful. After undergoing such therapy, family members are rated by therapists, teachers, and other observers as showing more adaptive behavior and better relations with each other than was true before the therapy (Hazelrigg, Cooper, & Borduin, 1987). And family therapy also seems to help reduce problems experienced by individual members. For example, consider a study that Henggler, Melton, and Smith (1992) conducted with juvenile offenders in Charleston, South Carolina. The youths involved had an average of 3.5 previous arrests and seemed headed for a life of serious crime. Instead of the usual "treatment"—monthly meetings with the parole officer—family therapy was used. Therapists conducted sessions in the teenagers' homes, over a period of about four months, and involved all available family members. Many serious problems within these families were uncovered in these meetings, and the therapists worked hard at resolving them, using a problem-solving approach. Results were encouraging: Youngsters who received family therapy experienced fewer arrests and reported engaging in fewer crimes than those who received the typical visits-to-the-probation-officer approach.

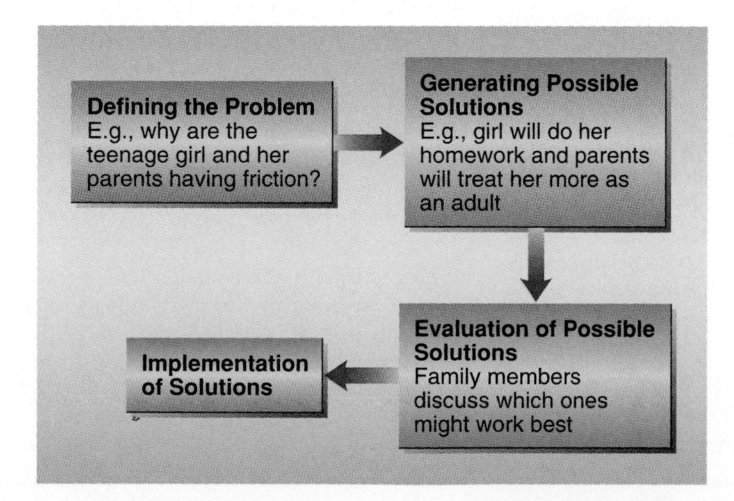

FIGURE 15.12

Problem-Solving Family Therapy: An Overview

Problem-solving therapy focuses on instituting specific changes that will help family members to cope with a specific problem. It involves the four steps shown here.

Key Questions

- What is the major focus of marital or couple therapy?
- What is family systems therapy?
- What is family problem-solving therapy?
- What are efficacy studies?

Findings like these suggest that family therapy may well be a useful approach to dealing with at least some psychological disorders. However, as has been the case with many forms of therapy involving several persons, most research on the effectiveness of family therapy has been somewhat informal in nature. The Research Methods section below describes a more systematic approach—the one most psychologists view as the best way of evaluating the effectiveness of various forms of therapy.

RESEARCH METHODS

How Psychologists Study the Effectiveness of Various Forms of Therapy

Does psychotherapy really work? That's a question we'll discuss in detail in the next section. Another, even more basic issue must be addressed first: How can we tell whether any given form of therapy is effective? In other words, what research strategy (or strategies) will allow us to answer this question? Several different approaches exist, but most psychologists would agree that by far the most powerful, from a scientific view, is one known as the **efficacy study** (e.g., Seligman, 1995).

What is an efficacy study? One that applies the basic methods of experimentation described in Chapter 1 to find out whether a specific form of therapy really works; that is, whether the therapy produces beneficial outcomes for the persons who undergo it. Efficacy studies involve the following basic requirements—which, as you'll see, are very similar to the ones I outlined in Chapter 1 as criteria for valid experimentation on virtually *any* topic in psychology:

- Inclusion in the study of at least one experimental group (persons with a given psychological disorder who are exposed to the therapy) and at least one control group (persons with the same disorder who are not exposed to the therapy).
- Random assignment of participants to these two conditions: All participants must have an equal chance of being assigned to the control (no therapy) or experimental (therapy) condition.
- Rigorous controls: Individuals receiving therapy may seem to improve not because of the therapy but because they are receiving attention from the therapist, expect to get better, and have a friendly relationship with the therapist; so these potential confounding factors must be eliminated by additional control groups. These are groups in which such factors are present, but the key aspects of the therapy under examination are not present.
- Standardization of the experimental treatment: Persons delivering the therapy must be thoroughly trained in it and must know precisely what to do; sessions should be videotaped to ensure that the therapists are doing what the therapy requires—and nothing else that might influence participants' behavior.
- A fixed number of sessions: Participants in the control and experimental conditions must receive the same number of sessions.
- Clear definition of the dependent measures: How will changes in behavior be measured? This must be specified in advance.
- Participants must have only one psychological disorder—the one for which the therapy is designed. If they have several disorders, changes in one may influence changes in others, thus making it impossible to clearly assess effectiveness of the therapy.
- Well-trained "blind" raters: If the dependent variables involve ratings of participants' behavior, the raters must be thoroughly trained and must not know whether participants were assigned to the experimental or the control condition.

Research using such methods, psychologists believe, provides a very rigorous test of the potential effects of any form of therapy. If, in such research, participants who receive therapy *do* show greater improvement than those who do not, we can have high confidence in the conclusion that "this form of therapy works—it is significantly better than no treatment." Of course, this kind of research is not the only way to answer the question; and, as I'll soon point out, it is not a perfect way of answering it. But efficacy studies are a powerful tool of research. They allow psychologists to go far beyond the informal methods, such as personal testimonials from satisfied patients or impassioned praise from true believers, that are sometimes offered as "evidence" for the value of psychotherapy.

Efficacy Study: A study that applies basic methods of experimentation to find out whether a specific form of therapy really works—that is, whether the therapy produces beneficial outcomes for the persons who undergo it.

Psychotherapy: Some Current Issues

Psychotherapy has definitely arrived. While some people continue to view therapy with skepticism, ever-growing numbers of distressed individuals seek it out. Perhaps the magnitude of this shift is best illustrated by the following fact: In the 1950s only 1 percent of the population of the United States had ever had contact with a trained therapist; currently this figure is about 10 percent.

What accounts for this change? Part of the answer involves shifting attitudes toward the idea of participating in psychotherapy. Once, there was a stigma attached to this process. People spoke about it in hushed tones and did their best to conceal the fact that someone in their family—or they themselves—had received therapy. This was certainly true in my own family when my grandmother, suffering from deep depression, received prolonged medical care. I was ten years old at the time and knew quite well that something important was happening; but my parents refused to discuss it with me and brought the topic up only when they thought I couldn't hear them.

While negative attitudes about psychotherapy have not entirely vanished, they have certainly weakened greatly. As a result, growing numbers of people are now willing to seek assistance in dealing with problems that threaten their happiness and well-being. Another factor is the growing sophistication—and effectiveness—of psychotherapy itself. Many new forms of therapy have been introduced in recent decades, and these are applicable to a wider range of disorders and a broader range of people than was true in the past. These trends, too, have contributed to the boom in psychotherapy.

This is not to suggest, however, that important questions about psychotherapy—and about the role of psychologists in it—no longer exist. On the contrary, as psychotherapy has grown in popularity, and as the number of psychologists has increased, such questions have received more and more attention. Several of these issues are considered below.

Does Psychotherapy Really Work? Evidence from Efficacy and Effectiveness Studies

In 1952 Hans Eysenck, a prominent psychologist, dropped a bombshell on his colleagues: He published a paper indicating that psychotherapy is ineffective. In his article, Eysenck reported that about 67 percent of patients with a wide range of psychological disorders improve after therapy, but that *about the same proportion of persons receiving no treatment also improve*. This was a disturbing conclusion for psychologists and quickly led to a great deal of research on this issue. After all, if the same proportion of people recover from psychological disorders with and without therapy, why bother?

As you can probably guess from my earlier comments throughout this chapter, the findings of later studies pointed to a very different conclusion: Contrary to what Eysenck suggested, psychotherapy *is* helpful (Bergin & Lambert, 1978; Clum & Bowers, 1990). Apparently, Eysenck overestimated the proportion of persons who recover without any therapy, and also *under*-estimated the proportion who improve after receiving therapy. In fact, several reviews of existing evidence—more than five hundred separate studies on the effects of therapy—suggest that therapy *does* work. Many of the studies included in these reviews are *efficacy studies* of the type described in the

Research Methods section on page 606, and the results of such work point to the following conclusion: More people who receive psychotherapy show improvements with respect to their psychological disorders than persons who do not receive therapy (e.g., Elkin et al., 1989). Further, the more treatment people receive, the more they improve, the fewer symptoms they show, and the less distress they report (Howard et al., 1986; Orlinsky & Howard, 1987).

Such effects are not restricted to adults; they have also been found with children and adolescents (e.g., Kazdin, 1993; Weisz et al., 1992). As is the case with adults, children and teenagers who receive therapy show greater improvements than those who do not. In sum, psychotherapy is not perfect—it doesn't produce improvements for everyone—but, yes, it *does* work. Therapy helps many people suffering from psychological disorders to recover from their problems.

Results of a Large-Scale Effectiveness Study: Additional Evidence for an Optimistic Conclusion Earlier, I noted that many psychologists view efficacy studies as the most powerful way to obtain evidence relating to the value of therapy. If the findings of such studies indicate that psychotherapy works, then we are on very firm scientific ground in concluding that it is effective. While there is no doubt that efficacy studies *are* very valuable in this respect, it is also clear that they are not totally conclusive, and that they are not the only kind of evidence that might be useful. As noted by Martin Seligman (1995), a president of the American Psychological Association, efficacy studies have certain drawbacks. The most important of these have to do with the fact that in such studies, psychotherapy is *not* practiced as it is in the real world. Thus, it is impossible to tell whether forms of therapy found to be effective in these studies would also succeed under natural conditions. What are the differences between efficacy studies and the actual practice of psychotherapy? Here are some of the most important:

- In efficacy studies, psychotherapy continues for a fixed number of sessions; in actual practice, this is rarely the case—therapy continues until people improve.
- In efficacy studies, only one type of therapy is used; in natural conditions, therapists switch between techniques until they find one that works.
- Participants in efficacy studies are assigned to a type of therapy they have not necessarily sought; in actual practice, individuals actively shop for and choose therapists.
- In efficacy studies, participants have a single psychological disorder; in field settings, patients often have several disorders.
- Efficacy studies focus on improvements with respect to specific symptoms or disorders; in actual practice, psychotherapy is directed toward producing more general improvements in functioning.

Because of these differences, Seligman (1995) concludes, efficacy studies do not necessarily tell us whether a given form of therapy succeeds under natural conditions. To answer that question, we need a different kind of study that Seligman terms *effectiveness research*—research that examines how individuals do under actual conditions of treatment in real-life settings. Such research must, of necessity, lack some of the rigor of efficacy research; therefore, in order to be useful, it should be large-scale in scope—hundreds or even thousands of persons should participate. Fortunately, one major study of this type has been conducted by an organization with no ax to grind in the field of mental health: *Consumer Reports,* a magazine that tests and compares a wide range of products for its subscribers.

I have been a subscriber to *Consumer Reports* since 1963, and I can testify that this magazine takes no advertising and uses rigorous scientific methods to compare competing brands of products—everything from automobiles to electric razors and from lawnmowers to raincoats. Once a year, *Consumer Reports* sends out a questionnaire to its 180,000 subscribers, asking for information about their experience with various products. In 1994 the survey included questions about subscribers' experiences with mental health professionals. The survey asked individuals whether they had sought help with an emotional problem during the past three years; and, if so, who had helped them—friends, clergy, family doctors, self-help groups, or any of a wide range of mental health professionals (psychiatrists, psychologists, social workers, marriage counselors, and so on). The survey asked readers about the duration and frequency of therapy they had received, and—perhaps most important of all—asked how much help they gained from the therapy. Results, which were based on the replies of more than seven thousand persons, pointed to clear conclusions.

First, therapy did help: Most respondents to the survey indicated that it did make them feel much better and helped eliminate the problems and symptoms, especially if therapy continued for six months or more. Second, such improvements were greatest when respondents received therapy from psychologists, psychiatrists, and social workers; improvements were somewhat less when they received therapy from physicians and marriage counselors (see Figure 15.13). Third, the longer therapy continued, the greater the improvement.

Needless to add, this study was far from perfect. Results were based entirely on self-report—what participants *said* happened as a result of therapy. Further, the measures of change were somewhat informal, relying on questions such as "How much did therapy help you with the specific problems that led you to therapy?" Psychologists prefer more specific and more readily quantified questions. Third, there was no control group: All participants were people who had received therapy. What happened to people with similar problems who didn't receive therapy? We can't tell.

Despite these important flaws, however, Seligman (1995) notes that this study *does* tell us much about the experience of several thousand people with

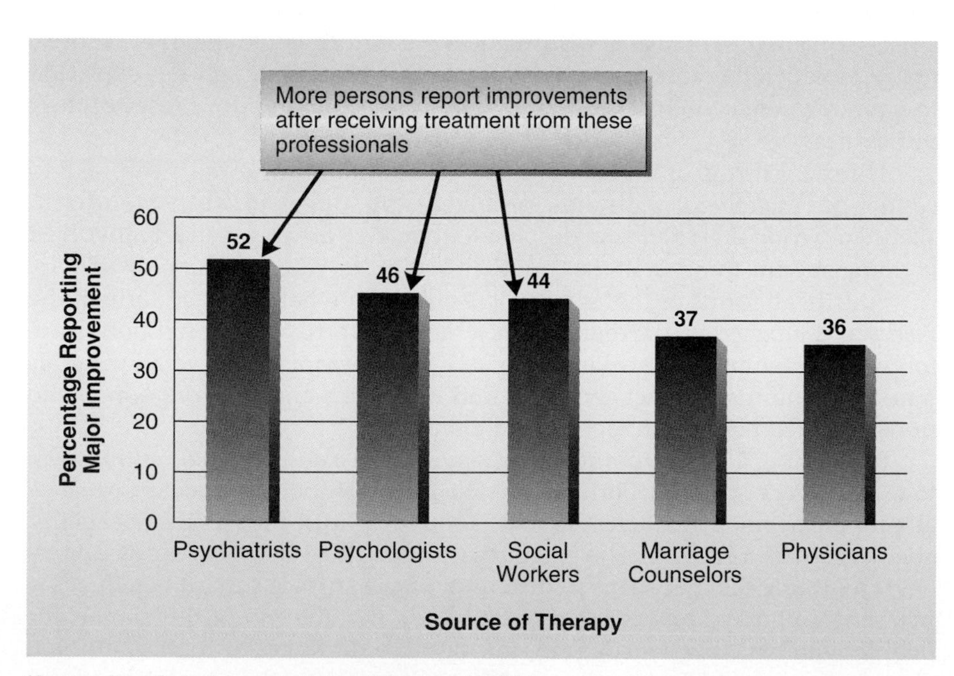

(**Source:** Based on data reported by Seligman, 1995.)

FIGURE 15.13

Evidence for the Effectiveness of Psychotherapy

As shown here, large proportions of persons who received psychotherapy from professionals (psychiatrists, psychologists, social workers) reported feeling much better as a result of such treatment. Somewhat smaller proportions reported major improvement after visiting marriage counselors or physicians.

therapy as it is actually delivered. Thus, he believes that it provides evidence that complements and helps complete the picture provided by efficacy research. In any case, putting these fine points of scientific design aside, it seems clear that evidence from two important sources combines to suggest a straightforward answer to the question "Does therapy help?" It appears that we can answer with some confidence: Yes!

Under what conditions should you seek psychotherapy for yourself? Please see the **Ideas to Take with You** feature for some suggestions.

Are Some Forms of Therapy More Successful Than Others?

The procedures used in various forms of therapy differ sharply. It seems only reasonable, then, to expect that some types of therapies will be more effective than others. But get ready for a surprise: Comparisons among therapies have generally yielded inconclusive results. Like the *Consumer Reports* survey described above, research on this topic has generally indicated that despite the many differences among them, all forms of therapy seem to yield roughly equivalent benefits (Hollon, DeRubeis, & Evans, 1987; Hollon, Shelton, & Loosen, 1991). How can therapies employing sharply different procedures yield similar results? The answer that has emerged in recent years goes something like this. Various forms of therapy do differ in their rationale and in their procedures, but under the surface, all share common crucial features. It is this shared core that accounts for their effectiveness. What is this common core? It may include the following features.

First, all major forms of psychotherapy provide troubled individuals with a special type of setting—one in which they interact closely, usually one-on-one, with a highly trained and empathetic professional. For many clients, this exposure to another person who seems to understand their problems and genuinely to care about them may be a unique experience, or at least one they have rarely encountered. This experience is very reassuring and may play an important role in the benefits of many forms of therapy.

Second, every form of therapy provides individuals with an explanation for their problems. No longer do these seem to be mysterious. Rather, as therapists explain, psychological disturbances stem from understandable causes, many of which lie outside the individual. This is something of a revelation to many persons who have sought in vain for a clue as to the causes of their difficulties.

Third, all forms of therapy specify actions that individuals can take to cope more effectively with their problems. No longer must they suffer in silence or wring their hands in despair. Rather, they are now actively involved in doing specific things that the confident, expert therapist indicates will help.

Fourth, all forms of therapy involve clients in what has been termed the *therapeutic alliance*—a partnership in which powerful emotional bonds are forged between persons seeking help and their therapist. This relationship is marked by mutual respect and trust, and it can be a big plus for people who previously felt helpless, hopeless, and alone.

Combining all these points, the themes of *hope* and *personal control* seem to emerge very strongly. Perhaps diverse forms of therapy succeed because all provide people with increased hope about the future plus a sense of heightened personal control. To the extent that this is the case, it is readily apparent why therapies that seem so different on the surface can all be effective. In a sense, all may provide the proverbial "light at the end of the tunnel" for people who have been struggling through the darkness of their emotional despair (see Figure 15.14 on page 612 for a summary of these points).

Ideas to Take with You

When Should You Seek Therapy?

At the very start of our discussion of psychological disorders, in Chapter 14, I noted that such problems are very common. In fact, some findings indicate that a majority of all persons have at least one period during their lives when they experience at least some of the symptoms of one or more psychological disorders. This raises an important question: How long must symptoms last and how severe must they be for any person—including *you*—to seek professional help? While there are no hard-and-fast answers, here are some guidelines that can help you make this decision.

- First, if a psychological problem is causing *you serious emotional discomfort,* you should consider seeking professional help. What is "serious discomfort"? Feelings of distress, depression, embarrassment, or anxiety that interfere with your ability to live your daily life as you would like to live it, and that seriously reduce your personal happiness.

- Second, if a problem you have had in the past has suddenly worsened, you should consider seeking help. A change for the worse is an important warning sign, and you should *not* ignore it.
- Third, if you have had a relatively minor psychological problem for months or even years, it may be time to seek help. Yes, you can probably continue to cope; but given that psychotherapy really is effective, why should you continue to suffer needlessly? Ask yourself, "Would I put up with this kind of irritation if the problem were purely physical—for instance, an aching tooth?" If the answer is no, then do seriously consider seeking psychological help.
- Fourth, if you have recently experienced some traumatic or disturbing event in your life and you find that you continue to think about it, to dream about it, or to relive it, you should consider professional help. Yes, we are adaptive, and we can recover psychologically from many unpleasant experiences, just as our bodies can recover from many injuries. But occasionally we need help in coping with such emotion-provoking events. If you find that weeks or months after a disturbing event it is still affecting you strongly, it may be time to seek professional help.

- Fifth, if you find that you think constantly about your weight and sometimes get into a binge–purge cycle, please do seek help. Disturbances in eating can have devastating long-term effects on your physical health, so this is *not* a symptom you should choose to live with.

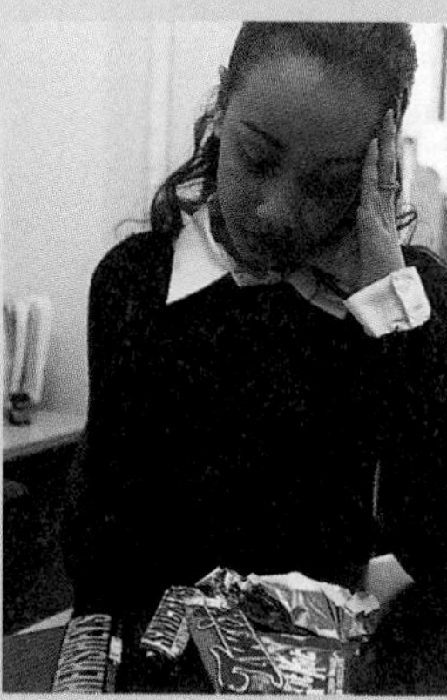

- Finally, if you ever hear voices telling you what to do, or if you ever feel that someone or some force is controlling your thoughts or behavior, please do seek help at once. These are serious symptoms that should *never* be ignored.

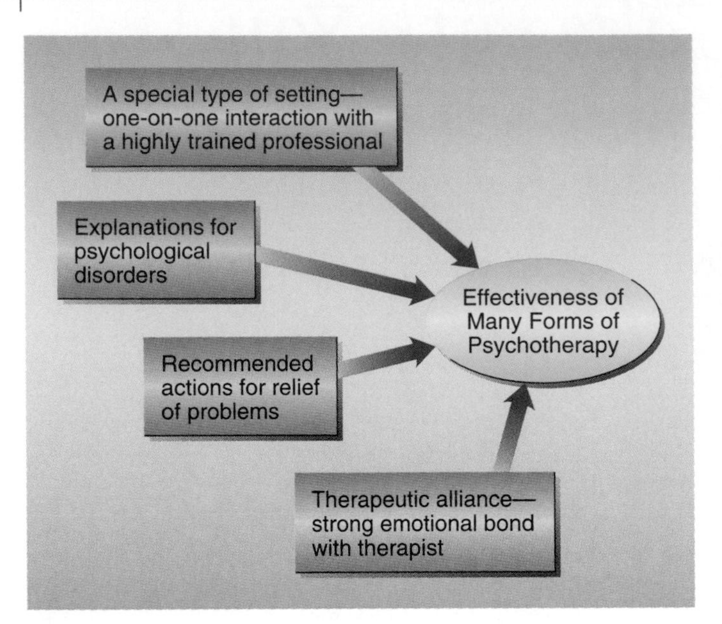

FIGURE 15.14

Factors Common to Many Forms of Therapy

These factors appear to play a role in many forms of therapy. Together, they may explain why numerous and widely differing kinds of psychotherapy are about equal in overall effectiveness.

Given the apparent fact that many forms of therapy are roughly equal in effectiveness, which ones do psychologists choose? Surveys suggest that many pschotherapists describe their approach as *eclectic* (e.g., Norcross, Alford, & DeMichele, 1994): They combine elements from several different forms of therapy in their efforts to help distressed persons. In short, psychologists have many tools available to get the job done, and they tend to use whichever ones seem most appropriate for, and most effective with, individual clients. Because of their scientific training in the basic principles of psychology, however, most psychologists who perform therapy tend to emphasize the role of new learning experiences that occur during therapy and the role of cognitive factors in various psychological disturbances (Goldfried & Castonguay, 1992) rather than the hidden inner conflicts emphasized in psychodynamic approaches.

To Prescribe or Not to Prescribe: Psychology's "Drug Problem"

In the next section of this chapter, we will examine *biologically based therapies*—forms of therapy that attempt to treat psychological disorders through biological means. As we'll soon see, the most important form of biological therapy involves the use of drugs—substances that reduce the symptoms of many psychological disorders. Many drugs are used for this purpose, and some are highly effective. This raises an important question: Should psychologists, as well as medical doctors, be permitted to prescribe such drugs? At the present time there is a strong movement among psychologists to seek this right, generally known as **prescription privileges.** The rationale behind this movement is obvious: If drugs can help, then psychologists should be able to prescribe them; drugs would simply be one more tool available to therapists in their efforts to help distressed persons.

While this certainly makes some sense and has been endorsed by at least a portion of the American Psychological Association (Martin, 1995), many psychologists have taken a strong position *against* prescription privileges (e.g., DeNelsky, 1996; Hayes & Heiby, 1996). What are the reasons behind this opposition? The most important of these relate to the fact that psychology is, first and foremost, a *science,* and that granting psychologists prescription privileges might well change or even weaken this focus. Instead of dedicating themselves to the task of understanding human behavior, psychologists might, if they could write prescriptions, be tempted to adopt a more medical perspective. That is, they might shift from trying to help their patients acquire more adaptive patterns of thought and behavior to simply prescribing appropriate pills. While such drugs *do* often help, it is clear that they are sometimes overused. In other words, psychiatrists and physicans sometimes use drugs to treat the symptoms of psychological disorders without reducing or eliminating the *causes* of such problems.

In all fairness, pressures to use drugs for "quick fixes" are very strong at the present time. *Managed care,* an increasingly common approach to patient care that emphasizes reducing medical costs, often strictly limits the number of therapy sessions individuals can have. This system pushes psychiatrists (who are medical doctors) toward prescribing drugs rather than conducting therapy with patients—therapy that might continue for months. If psycholo-

Prescription Privileges: The legal right to write prescriptions.

gists could write prescriptions, it is argued (e.g., DeNelsky, 1996), they too might be urged to adopt such procedures. It is better, critics of prescription privileges contend, for psychologists to stand fast and do what they do best as experts on human behavior: conducting therapy based solidly on the principles and findings of their field.

Other objections to prescription privileges for psychologists focus on potential effects on the training of psychologists. If psychologists were to be authorized to write prescriptions, their graduate education would have to change to provide training in this complex field. This in itself would change the nature of psychology and push it in the direction of becoming more like medicine. Similarly, the public's perception of the field might also be affected; psychology might come to be viewed either as identical with psychiatry or as a kind of "junior branch" of psychiatry. Finally, prescription privileges might also produce internal splits within psychology. Would all practicing psychologists want to go back to school for additional training to allow them to write prescriptions? Probably not. This would then result in two groups within the field: those who were able to write prescriptions and those who were not.

In sum, many psychologists believe that prescription privileges are neither necessary nor beneficial to the practice of psychology. Others, however, continue to strongly support this change. What will be the final outcome of this debate? Only time will tell, so please stay tuned—and in touch with psychology—for further developments.

The Necessity for Culturally Sensitive Psychotherapy

Despite improvements in the DSM–IV designed to make it more sensitive to cultural differences, existing evidence indicates that race, sex, ethnic background, and social class may all affect the process of diagnosing of psychological disorders (e.g., Lopez, 1989). For instance, African Americans are more likely to be diagnosed as schizophrenic and less likely to be diagnosed as showing affective (mood) disorders than persons of European descent (Snowden & Cheung, 1990).

If racial and ethnic factors can influence diagnosis, it is not surprising to learn that they can also play a role in psychotherapy. For example, therapists and clients may find it difficult to communicate with one another across substantial culture gaps, with the result that the effectiveness of therapy is reduced. Even worse, most forms of psychotherapy were originally developed for, and tested with, persons of European descent. As a result, they may not be entirely suitable for use with individuals from very different backgrounds. Concern over these issues has led many psychologists to call for efforts to make various forms of therapy more *culturally sensitive*. This suggestion implies that all forms of therapy should take careful account of the values and traditions of minority cultures, because ignoring these can lead to situations in which the words or actions of therapists run counter to these factors. To mention just one example, therapists working with people of Hispanic or Asian descent should be sensitive to the fact that views concerning the roles of males and females can be quite different in these cultural groups than they are in other groups living in the United States (Rogler et al., 1987).

In addition, in choosing a form of therapy for use with a specific person, a therapist should consider the cultural, economic, and educational background of the individual. For instance, using a form of therapy developed for highly verbal and highly educated persons (such as psychoanalysis) with persons from disadvantaged backgrounds makes little sense—and will prob-

Key Questions

- Is psychotherapy effective?
- Are some types of psychotherapies more effective than others?
- What are effectiveness studies, and what conclusions do they reach about the success of psychotherapy?
- What arguments have been offered against prescription privileges for psychologists?
- What is culturally sensitive psychotherapy?

ably be ineffective. Through attention to these and related factors, psychologists can help ensure that psychotherapy is sensitive to the varied needs of persons from different cultures, and so also increase the chances that therapy will accomplish its major goal: helping to lessen the pain of psychological disorders (e.g., Hammond & Yung, 1993).

Biologically Based Therapies

Now that I've introduced the issue of using drugs to treat psychological disorders, it's certainly time to discuss this and other **biologically based therapies**—forms of therapy that attempt to reduce psychological disorders through biological means. Efforts along these lines have continued for centuries, perhaps for thousands of years. Indeed, skulls from early civilizations often show neatly drilled holes, suggesting that some persons, at least, may have received surgery on their brains as a means of eliminating psychological disorders. And even in the nineteenth century, many physicians kept devices like the one shown in Figure 15.15 in their offices—devices they used to treat a wide range of "nervous disorders" by means of electric shocks!

Biologically Based Therapies: Forms of therapy that attempt to reduce psychological disorders through biological means.

Drug Therapy: Therapy based on the administration of psychotropic drugs.

As we'll soon see, both of these forms of treatment—*psychosurgery* and the use of electric shock—continue today. But by far the most popular form of biologically based therapy involves the use of various *psychotropic drugs*—drugs that alter feelings, thoughts, and behavior.

FIGURE 15.15

One Early Form of Biological Therapy

Electrical devices such as this one (from the author's collection of antiques) were widely used by physicians in the late nineteenth and early twentieth centuries to "treat" many psychological disorders.

Drug Therapy: The Pharmacological Revolution

In 1955, almost 600,000 persons were full-time resident patients in psychiatric hospitals in the United States. Twenty years later, this number had dropped below 175,000. Were Americans achieving mental health at a dizzying pace? Absolutely not. What happened in those years was something many describe as a *pharmacological revolution:* A wide range of drugs effective in treating many psychological disorders were developed and put to use. So successful was **drug therapy** in reducing major symptoms that hundreds of thousands of persons who had previously been hospitalized for their own safety (and that of others) were now sent home and treated as outpatients. What are these drugs, and how do they produce their effects?

Antipsychotic Drugs If you had visited the wards of a psychiatric hospital for seriously disturbed persons before about 1955, you would have witnessed some pretty wild scenes—screaming, bizarre actions, nudity. If you had returned just a year or two later, however, you would have seen a dramatic change: peace, relative tranquillity, and many patients now capable of direct, sensible communication. What accounted for this startling change? Largely, the development of *antipsychotic drugs*, sometimes known as the *major tranquilizers*.

The most important group of antipsychotic drugs, *phenothiazines,* were discovered by accident. In the early 1950s a French surgeon, Henri Laborit, used a drug in this chemical family, *Thorazine* (chlorpromazine) to try to reduce blood pressure in patients before surgery. He found that their blood pressure didn't drop, but that they became much less anxious. French psychiatrists tried the drug with their patients, and found that it worked: It reduced anxiety—and, even more important, it also reduced hallucinations and delusions among schizophrenic patients. Chemists quickly analyzed chlorpromazine and developed many others drugs that are related to it but are even more effective in reducing psychotic symptoms (e.g., clozapine, haloperidol). By the way, throughout this discussion I'll present brand names of drugs; chemical or generic names will appear in parentheses.

Tardive Dyskinesia: A common side effect produced by antipsychotic drugs, in which individuals experience loss of motor control, especially in the face.

How do the antipsychotics produce such effects? Apparently by blocking *dopamine* receptors in the brain. As noted in Chapter 14, the presence of an excess of this neurotransmitter, or increased sensitivity to it, may play a role in schizophrenia. Whatever the precise mechanism, however, it is clear that antipsychotic drugs are very helpful in reducing the bizarre symptoms of schizophrenia.

The use of antipsychotics, however, is not without drawbacks. They often produce fatigue and apathy as well as calming effects. And after receiving antipsychotic drugs for prolonged periods of time, many patients develop a side effect called **tardive dyskinesia:** loss of motor control, especially in the face. As a result, they show involuntary muscle movements of the tongue, lips, and jaw. These often decrease when persons stop taking the drug, but continue unchanged in at least some individuals (Yudofsky, Hales, & Ferguson, 1991). Unfortunately, since there is no known cure for schizophrenia, persons with this disorder often take antipsychotic drugs throughout life (Mueser & Glynn, 1995); thus, they stand a very good chance of developing this side effect. One relatively new antipsychotic drug, Clozaril (clozapine), appears to be effective without producing tardive dyskinesia; but it causes other side effects, so it is not a final answer to this problem.

While the antipsychotic drugs are clearly of great value and do reduce the most bizarre symptoms of schizophrenia, it should be emphasized that they do *not* cure this disorder. Persons on antipsychotic drugs often remain somewhat withdrawn and continue to show the reduced levels of affect that is often part of schizophrenia. So it is important that patients receive psychotherapy as well as drug therapy. Otherwise they may remain incapable of functioning adequately on their own and, if released from the hospital, may soon join the ranks of homeless people, as discussed in Chapter 14.

Antidepressant Drugs Shortly after the development of chlorpromazine, drugs effective in reducing depression made their appearance. There are three basic types of such compounds: *tricyclics, selective serotonin reuptake inhibitors* (SSRIs), and *MAO inhibitors*. All three types seem to exert their antidepressant effects by influencing neurotransmitters, especially *serotonin*. It has been suggested that SSRIs affect only the reuptake of serotonin, while tricyclics may affect both norepinephrine and serotonin. Both serotonin and norepinephrine levels are low in depressed individuals, so it seems possible that these drugs make serotonin more available by reducing the reuptake or reabsorption of these neurotransmitters (Julien, 1995).

Among the SSRIs, *Prozac* (fluoxetine) is by far the most famous—and also the most commonly prescribed. Depressed persons taking this drug often report that they feel better than they have in their entire lives. Like other antidepressant drugs, however, Prozac appears to have serious side effects. A small number of patients report suicidal thoughts (Teicher, Glod, & Cole, 1990), although these risks seem relatively slight. Other patients report loss of sexual desire; but again, the proportion of persons who experience such side effects seems small (Walker et al., 1993). In contrast, MAO inhibitors can produce more dangerous side effects, such as severe headaches, heart palpitations, stroke, or even death. (These are most likely to occur when individuals using the drugs consume certain foods, such as chocolate, beer, or wine.) For this reason, MAO inhibitors are used less often than the other two types of antidepressants. Tricyclics also produce side effects, such as disturbances in sleep and appetite, but these tend to decrease within a few weeks. Widely prescribed tricyclics include Elavil (amitriptyline) and Tofranil (imipramine).

One final point: While these drugs *are* often effective in treating depression, research evidence suggests that they are not necessarily more effective than several forms of psychotherapy, especially cognitive and cognitive behavior therapies (Bruder et al., 1997; Hollon, Shelton, & Loosen, 1991; Robinson, Berman, & Neimeyer, 1990;). Since psychotherapy avoids the potential dangers involved in the use of any drug, it appears to be the more conservative form of treatment.

Lithium An entirely different kind of antidepressant drug is *lithium* (usually administered as *lithium chloride*). This drug has been found to be quite effective in treating persons with bipolar (manic–depressive) disorder, and is successful with 60 to 70 percent of these patients (Julien, 1995). Since persons with bipolar disorder are often quite agitated and even psychotic, lithium is generally administered along with antipsychotic or antidepressant medications. Unfortunately, lithium has serious potential side effects—excessive doses can cause convulsions, delirium, and even death. Thus, it has a very small "therapeutic window" or dose level that is effective without being dangerous. Exactly how lithium exerts its effects is not known; one possibility is that it alters brain levels of serotonin. Whatever its mechanism, it is one of the few drugs effective in treating manic–depressive disorders, so its continued use seems likely.

Antianxiety Drugs Alcohol, a substance used by many people to combat anxiety, has been available for thousands of years. Needless to say, however, it has important negative side effects. Synthetic drugs with antianxiety effects—sometimes known as *minor tranquilizers*—have been manufactured for several decades. The most widely prescribed at present are the *benzodiazepines*. This group includes drugs whose names you may already know: Valium, Ativan, Xanax, and Librium.

The most common use for antianxiety drugs, at least ostensibly, is as an aid to sleep. They are safer for this purpose than *barbiturates* (see Chapter 4), because they are somewhat less addicting. However, substances derived from the benzodiazepines remain in the body for longer periods of time than those from barbiturates, and can cumulate until they reach toxic levels. Thus, long-term use of these drugs can be quite dangerous. In addition, when antianxiety drugs are taken with alcohol, their effects may be magnified; this is definitely a combination to avoid. Finally, the benzodiazepines do tend to produce dependency; individuals experience withdrawal symptoms when they are abruptly stopped. It is better, therefore, to withdraw from them gradually (Yudofsky et al., 1991). Antianxiety drugs seem to inhibit the central nervous system by acting on specific receptor sites in the brain (Hayward, Wardle, & Higgitt, 1989).

One additional antianxiety drug is not related to the benzodiazepines: BuSpar (buspirone). It seems to be effective, and does not appear to lead to dependency as the benzodiazepines often do (Long & Rybacki, 1994). It does cause other side effects in some persons, however, including dizziness, faintness, and mild drowsiness. Also, there is a lag of one to three weeks before BuSpar produces its antianxiety effects. However, this drug does seem to be a useful alternative to the benzodiazepines.

Do people in all cultural and ethnic groups respond the same to psychotropic drugs? For information on this issue, see the Exploring Gender and Diversity section.

Are There Ethnic Differences in Reactions to Psychotropic Drugs?

EXPLORING GENDER & DIVERSITY

That all groups should have equal rights and equal opportunities is a basic principle that cannot be seriously (or even rationally) challenged. But this principle does not imply that all ethnic groups are identical in every respect; on the contrary, I've called attention to ethnic differences throughout this book. In some cases these differences are biological in nature. True, we are all one species; but different groups of human beings do differ from each other with respect to subtle biological processes. For instance, a large majority of persons of European descent produce an enzyme, lactase, that allows them to digest milk sugar (lactose). As a result, they can consume dairy products (milk, cheese, ice cream) without experiencing any digestive problems. In contrast, more than 90 percent of persons of Asian descent and about 75 percent of persons of African descent are lacking in this enzyme; thus, they may experience problems in digesting dairy products.

Given such differences in basic bodily functions, it makes sense to ask: Do persons belonging to different ethnic groups also differ in their reactions to various drugs used to treat psychological disorders? The answer seems to be yes. For example, where antipsychotic drugs are concerned, physicians practicing in Asian countries seem to prescribe much lower doses than those prescribed in the United States and Europe. Why? Perhaps because lower doses are effective for persons in these Asian countries (e.g., Chien, 1993).

Similar findings have been reported for antidepressant drugs: A survey of ten Asian countries indicated that daily doses of such drugs are about half of what is generally prescribed to Americans of European descent, yet the effects produced by these lower doses were equivalent. Results such as these suggest that cultural and ethnic factors must be taken carefully into account not only in psychotherapy but drug therapies as well.

Electroconvulsive Therapy (ECT): A form of therapy in which strong electric shocks are delivered to the brain.

Electroconvulsive Therapy

Remember my comments about my grandmother's suffering from deep depression? She did, and at that time—the early 1950s—the *psychopharmacological revolution* had not taken place. Because effective drugs for treating my grandmother's depression did not exist, she was given another kind of treatment—**electroconvulsive therapy (ECT).** In the modern form of ECT (somewhat different from what my grandmother received), physicians place electrodes on the patient's temples and deliver shocks of 70 to 130 volts for brief intervals (less than one second). These shocks are continued until the patient has a seizure, a muscle contraction of the entire body, lasting at least thirty seconds. In order to prevent broken bones and other injuries, a muscle relaxant and a mild anesthetic are usually administered before the start of the shocks. Patients typically receive three treatments a week for several weeks (see Figure 15.16).

FIGURE 15.16

Electroconvulsive Therapy Today

In electroconvulsive therapy, an electric current passes through the brain for less than one second, causing a brief seizure. This treatment seems to be effective in alleviating severe depression.

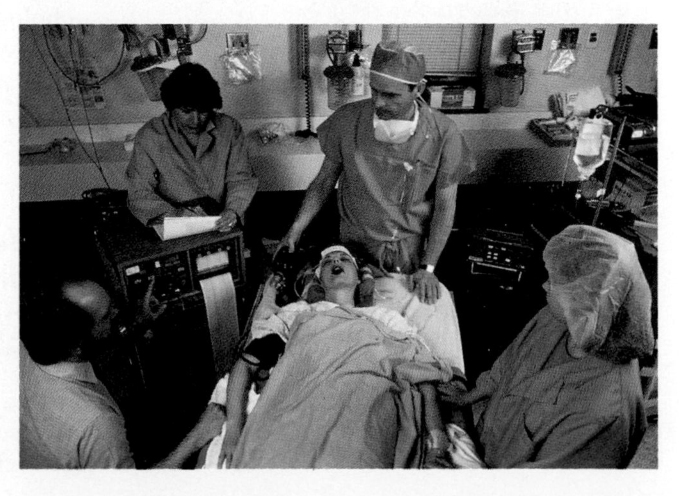

Surprisingly, ECT seems to work, at least for some disorders. For severe depression, ECT is effective and may help many persons who have failed to respond to other forms of therapy (Effective Treatment, 1994).

Unfortunately, there are important risks connected with ECT. It is designed to alter the brain—and it does, apparently producing irreversible damage in at least some cases. Further, although the shocks themselves are painless, many patients find the procedure extremely frightening; some, like my grandmother, are terrified of it. I remember her saying to me, "I only pray, Bobby, that it never happens to *you*!" These facts have led some researchers to criticize the use of ECT and to call for its elimination as a form of therapy. However, the fact that it helps some severely depressed persons who have not responded to other forms of therapy has led to its continued use (e.g., Fink, 1994).

Psychosurgery

In 1935 a Portuguese psychiatrist, Egas Moniz, attempted to reduce aggressive behavior in psychotic patients by severing neural connections between the prefrontal lobes and the remainder of the brain. The operation, known as *prefrontal lobotomy,* seemed to work: Aggressive behavior was reduced. Moniz received the 1949 Nobel Prize in Medicine for his work—but, in one of those strange twists of history, he was later shot and killed by one of his lobotomized patients!

Encouraged by Moniz's findings, psychiatrists all over the world rushed to treat psychological disorders through various forms of **psychosurgery**—brain operations designed to change abnormal behavior. Tens of thousands of patients were given prefrontal lobotomies and related operations. Unfortunately, it soon became apparent that results were not always positive. While some forms of objectionable or dangerous behavior did decrease, serious side effects sometimes occurred. Some patients became highly excitable and impulsive; others slipped into profound apathy and a total absence of emotion.

In view of these outcomes, most physicians stopped performing prefrontal lobotomies, and few are done today. However, other, more limited operations on the brain continue. In one modern procedure, for instance, connections between a very small area of the brain and the limbic system are severed. Results indicate that this limited kind of psychosurgery may be effective with individuals suffering from obsessive–compulsive disorder who have not responded to any other type of treatment (e.g., Jenike et al., 1991). Even newer procedures, involving the insertion of tiny video cameras into the brain to guide laser surgery for repair of blood vessels, have sometimes yielded beneficial results; but it is too early to tell whether such psychosurgery—known as *videolaseroscopy*—will yield long-term gains.

One final point: Even if brain operations are successful, they raise important ethical questions. Is it right to destroy healthy tissue in a person's brain in the hopes that this will relieve symptoms of psychological disorders? Given that the benefits are uncertain, should such irreversible procedures be permitted? These and related issues have led most psychologists to conclude that psychosurgery should be viewed as a very drastic form of treatment—something to be tried only when everything else has failed.

Key Questions

- What types of drugs are used in the treatment of psychological disorders?
- What is electroconvulsive therapy?
- What is psychosurgery?

The Prevention of Psychological Disorders: Bringing Psychology to the Community

Psychosurgery: Brain operations designed to change abnormal behavior.

During the 1950s and 1960s, hundreds of thousands of persons were released from large state hospitals, largely as a result of the development of the drugs described earlier. Where did they go? While some became homeless people, most went back to their families and continued to receive care as *outpatients*—persons who live at home but receive regular care at **community mental health centers.** These are facilities for the delivery of mental health services that are located in the communities where the people they serve live. Such centers are often relatively small, but they provide a wide range of services, especially *aftercare*—treatment for persons newly released from the hospital. In addition, many centers offer *emergency services*—quick response to cries for help that arrive late at night or over the weekend.

One of the most important things such community mental health centers, do, however, is to focus on *prevention*—interventions of various kinds designed to prevent psychological disorders from developing in the first place, or to limit the harmful effects of such disorders by identifying and treating them early on. Let's be a bit more specific by examining three different prevention strategies (first introduced in Chapter 13) as they relate to psychological disorders.

Primary Prevention

Primary prevention consists of efforts to prevent new psychological problems from occurring. Most such efforts focus on *education;* for example, teaching children about the risks of drug use, alerting them to the potential dangers of sexual abuse by adults, or even preventing unwanted teenage pregnancies. This latter problem is not in itself a psychological disorder. However, when girls who are little more than children themselves are faced with the sudden responsibilities of parenthood, they often experience depression, anxiety, and other feelings that can quickly develop into psychological disorders.

Other primary prevention programs are directed at adults. For example, special classes may help couples improve their communication skills. A growing body of evidence indicates that when individuals suppress their emotions and attempt to hide their feelings, it can have negative consequences for both of them—increasing their physiological arousal and stress—and for their partners—making it difficult for them to understand their feelings or needs (e.g., Gross & Levenson, 1997). This, in turn, can have negative consequences for their relationship. Programs focused on these and many other potential problems can often yield handsome dividends in terms of "heading off trouble before it actually starts" (e.g., Avery-Leaf et al., 1995).

Secondary Prevention

Another type of prevention, **secondary prevention,** involves efforts to detect psychological problems early, before they escalate in intensity. For example, consider *diversion programs,* which focus on juvenile offenders in the criminal justice system. It is a well-established fact that once young offenders are placed in prisons, the chances increase that they will continue their dangerous, antisocial behaviors. In diversion programs, young offenders are steered away (diverted) from such institutions and are given another chance to learn social skills and patterns of behavior that may help them lead happier and more productive lives.

For instance, in one diversion program (e.g., Davidson et al., 1987), college students worked one-on-one with juvenile offenders for several hours each week, helping them learn communication skills. Results were encouraging: Teenagers who went through this program were much less likely to engage in further delinquent behaviors than those who were sent to juvenile detention facilities in the normal manner.

Community Mental Health Centers: Facilities for the delivery of mental health services that are located in the communities where the people they serve live.

Primary Prevention: Efforts to prevent new problems from occurring.

Secondary Prevention: Efforts to detect problems early, before they have escalated in intensity.

Tertiary Prevention: Efforts to minimize the long-term harm stemming from problems and disorders.

Tertiary Prevention

In **tertiary prevention,** efforts are made to minimize the long-term harm stemming from psychological disorders. Such programs are especially helpful for persons who are released from state facilities after long years of confinement. One tertiary prevention program, *Training in Community Living,* attempts to repair the damage done by long years of what may amount to custodial care, by teaching former mental-hospital patients the skills they need to live out in the community. The former patients are provided with living quarters and are visited every week by program staff. In other words, they are out in the community but are living in a protected environment, where they can learn the skills they need for an independent life (Levine, Toro, & Perkins, 1993).

In sum, efforts at preventing or minimizing the harm of psychological disorders do often seem to be quite effective. Their goal—like that of all forms of therapy—is to reduce human suffering; but by operating *before* serious disorders occur, they take full advantage of the wisdom in the old saying "an ounce of prevention is worth a pound of cure."

Key Questions

- What are community mental health centers?
- What are primary, secondary, and tertiary prevention in the context of psychological health?

Making Psychology Part of Your Life

How to Choose a Therapist: A Consumer's Guide

The odds are quite high that at some time in your life, you or someone close to you will experience a psychological disorder. Depression, phobias, anxiety—these are very common patterns. If there's one point I hope this chapter has made clear, it is this: Effective help *is* available. When psychological problems occur, don't hesitate to seek assistance. But how should you go about obtaining such help—choosing a therapist? Here are some basic pointers.

1. **Getting Started.** The first step is usually the hardest in any task, and searching for a therapist is no exception. While you are a student, this task is fairly simple. Virtually every college or university has a department of psychology and a student health center. Both are good places to start. Visit them and ask for help. Don't be shy; the people there *want* to help, but they can't approach you—you have to take the first step.

   If you are no longer a student and don't have any contact with a college or university, you can still call your nearest psychology department and ask for help: The chances are that someone there will refer you to one or more excellent therapists. But if for some reason this is not practical for you, you can ask your physician or a member of the clergy to direct you to the help you need. Both will almost certainly know someone you can contact. If you have no local physician and don't know any clergy, contact your local Mental Health Association; it is probably listed in your phone book, and is another good place to start.
2. **Choosing a Therapist.** Let's assume that by following one of the routes above, you have obtained the names of several therapists. How can you choose among them? Several guidelines are useful.

   First, always check for *credentials.* Therapists should be trained professionals. Before you consult one, be sure that this person has a Ph.D. in psychology, an M.D. degree plus a residency in psychiatry, or other equivalent training.

Second, try to find out something about the kind of disorders in which each therapist specializes. Most will readily give you this information; what you are looking for is a good *match* between your needs and the therapist's expertise.

3. **Signs of Progress: How Long Should Therapy Last?** If therapy is going well, both you and the therapist will know it. You'll be able to see beneficial changes in your behavior, your thoughts, and your feelings. But what if it is not going well? When and how should you decide to go elsewhere? This is a difficult decision, but a rough rule of thumb is this: If you have been visiting a therapist regularly (once a week or more) for three months and see no change, it may be time for you, like the woman in Figure 15.17, to ask the therapist whether she or he is satisfied with your progress.

4. **Danger: When to Quit.** Therapy is designed to help; unfortunately, though, there are instances in which it can hurt. How can you tell that you are in danger of such outcomes? There are several basic signals to which you should be alert.

   First, if you or the people around you notice that you are actually becoming more distressed—more depressed, more anxious, more nervous—you should ask yourself whether you are satisfied with what is happening. At the very least, discuss these feelings with your therapist.

   Second, never under any circumstances should you agree to performing activities during therapy that run counter to your own moral or ethical principles. A great majority of therapists would never dream of suggesting such activities; but, sad to relate, there are a few who will take advantage of the therapeutic relationship to exploit their patients. The most common forms of such exploitation are sexual in nature. Unprincipled therapists may suggest that their clients engage in sexual relations with them as part of their "treatment." *This is never appropriate.* So, if your therapist makes such suggestions, *get out of there fast.*

   Third, beware of exaggerated claims. If a therapist tells you that she or he can guarantee to remake your life, to turn you into a powerhouse of human energy, or to assure you of total happiness, be cautious. This is a good sign that you are dealing with an unprincipled—and probably poorly trained—individual. Again, beat a hasty retreat.

These guidelines should help you to avoid some of the pitfalls that exist with respect to finding a competent, caring therapist. Most important of all, always remember this: *Effective help is definitely out there if you take the trouble to look for it.*

FIGURE 15.17

Gauging the Progress of Therapy

If, like the woman in this cartoon, you are not satisfied with your progress in therapy, you should definitely raise this issue with your therapist. If you are unhappy with the answer, it may be time to seek help elsewhere.

"Well, I do have this recurring dream that one day I might see some results."

(**Source**: Drawing by Bruce Eric Kaplan; ©1994 The New Yorker Magazine, Inc.)

Summary and Review of Key Questions

Psychotherapies: Psychological Approaches to Psychological Disorders

- **What is psychoanalysis, and what are its major assumptions?** Psychoanalysis is the form of therapy developed by Freud. It assumes that psychological disorders stem from hidden internal conflicts and that bringing these conflicts and hidden wishes into consciousness is crucial.
- **What is the role of free association in psychoanalysis?** Free association supposedly brings hidden urges and conflicts into consciousness.
- **How are psychodynamic therapies practiced today?** At present psychodynamic therapies are shorter in duration than in the past, and focus more on the patient's current life than on events in her or his distant past.
- **According to humanistic therapies, what is the cause of psychological disorders?** Humanistic therapies assume that psychological disorders stem from factors in the environment that block or interfere with personal growth.
- **What is the major goal of Rogers's client-centered therapy?** Client-centered therapy focuses on eliminating unrealistic conditions of worth in a therapeutic environment of unconditional positive regard.
- **What is the major goal of Gestalt therapy?** Gestalt therapy focuses on helping individuals acknowledge and come to terms with parts of their own feelings or thoughts that are not currently conscious and so to achieve personal "wholeness."
- **According to behavior therapies, what is the primary cause of psychological disorders?** Behavior therapies see psychological disorders as stemming from faulty learning.
- **On what basic principles of learning are behavior therapies based?** Behavior therapies are based on principles of classical conditioning, operant conditioning, and observational learning.
- **What is modeling, and how can it be used in treating psychological disorders?** Modeling is a process through which individuals are helped to acquire new information or learn new behaviors by observing the actions of others. Modeling is effective in treating several disorders, including phobias and sexual dysfunctions.
- **According to cognitive therapies, what are the primary causes of psychological disorders?** Cognitive therapies assume that the major causes of psychological disorders are distorted patterns of thought.
- **What is the major goal of rational–emotive therapy?** The major goal of rational–emotive therapy is to persuade individuals to recognize and reject irrational assumptions in their thinking.
- **What is the major goal of Beck's cognitive behavior therapy for depression?** Beck's cognitive behavior therapy seeks to persuade depressed individuals to recognize and change irrational patterns of thought that induce negative affect and so contribute to their depression.
- **Is there any evidence for a beneficial effect of humor with respect to psychological disorders?** Some research findings indicate that inducing people to laugh can reduce anger, and that it can enhance their current moods and so help to reduce depression.

KEY TERMS

psychotherapies, p. 588 • psychodynamic therapies, p. 588 • free association, p. 589 • resistance, p. 590 • transference, p. 590 • basic mistakes, p. 591 • humanistic therapies, p. 592 • client-centered therapy, p. 592 • conditions of worth, p. 592 • Gestalt therapy, p. 592 • behavior therapies, p. 593 • systematic desensitization, p. 594 • token economies, p. 595 • cognitive therapies, p. 596 • rational–emotive therapy, p. 597 • cognitive behavior therapy, p. 597 • incompatible response hypothesis, p. 598

Group Therapies: Working with Others to Solve Problems

- **What is the major focus of psychodynamic group therapies such as psychodrama?** Psychodynamic group therapies are designed to help individuals bring inner conflicts into consciousness.
- **What is the major focus of behavioral group therapies?** Behavioral group therapies focus on changing specific aspects of behavior, such as social skills or assertiveness.
- **What is the major focus of humanistic group therapies?** Humanistic group therapies focus on enhancing personal growth and improving self-knowledge.
- **What are self-help groups, and what do they provide?** Self-help groups consist of persons who share a problem and who provide one another with social and emotional support as each member tries to cope with the problem.

KEY TERMS

group therapies, p. 598 • self-help groups, p. 601

Therapies Focused on Interpersonal Relations: Marital and Family Therapy

- **What is the major focus of marital or couple therapy?** Marital or couple therapy focuses on improving the relationship between partners, often by enhancing their communication skills.
- **What is family systems therapy?** Family systems therapy is an approach in which therapists view the family as a dynamic system in which each member has a major role.
- **What is family problem-solving therapy?** Family problem-solving therapy focuses on instituting specific changes within a family to help it solve specific problems.
- **What are efficacy studies?** Efficacy studies are research studies designed to assess the effects of a specific form of therapy through the use of rigorous experimental controls.

KEY TERMS

marital therapy, p. 603 • family therapy, p. 604 • family systems therapy, p. 604 • problem-solving therapy, p. 604 • efficacy study, p. 607

Psychotherapy: Some Current Issues

- **Is psychotherapy effective?** Existing evidence suggests that psychotherapy is indeed effective: Most people who undergo it are helped by it.
- **Are some types of psychotherapies more effective than others?** Research findings indicate that many types of therapy are roughly equal in their effectiveness.
- **What are effectiveness studies, and what conclusions do they reach about the success of psychotherapy?** Effectiveness studies investigate the effectiveness of forms of therapy as they are used in actual practice. One large-scale effectiveness survey found that therapy did help; that psychiatrists, psychologists, and social workers were most helpful; and that longer therapy brought greater improvement.
- **What arguments have been offered against prescription privileges for psychologists?** Arguments against prescription privileges include the suggestion that such privileges will lead psychologists to prescribe pills rather than therapy, will change the nature of graduate education in psychology, and will lead to divisions within the field.
- **What is culturally sensitive psychotherapy?** This is psychotherapy that takes careful account of the values and traditions of persons from minority groups and attempts to match forms of therapy to the cultural, educational, and economic backgrounds of clients.

KEY TERM

prescription privileges, p. 612

Biologically Based Therapies

- **What types of drugs are used in the treatment of psychological disorders?** Many different drugs are used to treat many psychological disorders. Antipsychotic drugs reduce symptoms such as hallucinations and delusions. Antidepressant drugs counter depression. Antianxiety drugs reduce anxiety.
- **What is electroconvulsive therapy?** Electroconvulsive therapy (ECT) involves the delivery of strong shocks to the brain. It is used to treat severe depression when all other approaches have failed.
- **What is psychosurgery?** Psychosurgery involves surgery performed on the brain in order to reduce or eliminate psychological disorders.

KEY TERMS

biologically based therapies, p. 614 • drug therapy, p. 614 • tardive dyskinesia, p. 615 • electroconvulsive therapy, p. 617 • psychosurgery, p. 618

The Prevention of Psychological Disorders: Bringing Psychology to the Community

- **What are community mental health centers?** Community mental health centers are facilities for the delivery of mental health services located in the communities they serve.
- **What are primary, secondary, and tertiary prevention in the context of psychological health?** Primary prevention involves efforts to prevent the occurrence of psychological disorders. Secondary prevention involves efforts to detect psychological problems early, before they escalate in intensity. Tertiary prevention involves efforts to minimize long-term harm from psychological disorders.

KEY TERMS

community mental health centers, p. 619 • primary prevention, p. 619 • secondary prevention, p. 619 • tertiary prevention, p. 620

Critical Thinking Questions

Appraisal

If, as existing evidence suggests, many forms of therapy are quite effective, why do so many people continue to suffer from psychological disorders? Why don't more people seek out professional help for their problems?

Controversy

Psychologists are currently divided about whether they should or should not have prescription privileges. What do you think? Should psychologists be allowed to write prescriptions? Or should this privilege be restricted to physicians?

Making Psychology Part of Your Life

Now that you know about the various forms of therapy and the principles on which they are based, do you think you are more likely to seek the help of a trained psychologist (or other professional) if you experience psychological distress? If so, what form of therapy would you prefer?

CHAPTER OUTLINE

Social Thought and Social Behavior

How much time do you spend alone each day? If you are like most people, very little. We work with others, enjoy leisure-time activities with them, eat our meals with them—and, if we have a lover or spouse, sleep with them, too. And even when we are alone, we often think about other persons, wondering what they are like, how they feel about us, and what they will do or say the next time we see them. Clearly, then, the social side of life—our relations with and our thoughts about other people—is a crucial part of our existence.

Recognizing this basic fact, the field of **social psychology** has long specialized in the task of studying all aspects of social thought and social behavior (e.g., Baron & Byrne, 1997). In this chapter, we'll examine a broad sample of the many fascinating—and often surprising—findings social psy-

Social Psychology: The branch of psychology that studies all aspects of social thought and social behavior.

chologists have uncovered. Specifically, we'll begin by considering several aspects of social thought—how, and what, we think about other persons. Included here will be discussions of three important topics: attribution—our efforts to understand the causes behind others' behavior—why they act as they do; social cognition—how we process social information, remember it, and use it in making judgments or decisions about others; and attitudes—our evaluations of various features of the social world.

After considering these aspects of social thought, we'll turn to important aspects of social behavior—how we interact with other people. Among the topics we'll examine are prejudice—negative attitudes and actions toward the members of various social groups; social influence—the many ways in which we attempt to change others' behavior and they attempt to change ours; prosocial behavior—actions we perform that help or benefit others; and attraction and love—why we like or dislike other people, why we fall in (and out) of love with them, and how we form and maintain close personal relationships. Additional aspects of social behavior are covered elsewhere in this book: aggression in Chapter 10, leadership in Chapter 17, and some aspects of group decision making in Chapter 7.

The social side of life—our relations with and our thoughts about other people—is a crucial part of our existence.

Social Thought: Thinking about Other People

How many times each day do you think about other people? Your answer may well be "Who can count?"—because such thoughts are frequent indeed. Anytime you try to figure out why other people have acted in various ways, or attempt to make judgments about them (for example, will someone make a good roommate?), you are engaging in *social thought.* Let's take a closer look at several important aspects of this process.

Attribution: Understanding the Causes of Others' Behavior

Imagine the following situation. You're standing at a counter in a store waiting your turn when suddenly another customer walks up and hands the clerk an item she wishes to purchase. How do you react? While your first response may be "With anger!" a more accurate answer is "It depends." And what it depends upon is your perceptions of *why* this other person cut in front of you. Did she do it on purpose? In that case, you probably *would* get angry. But perhaps she just didn't see you. In that case, you might clear your throat or otherwise indicate your presence to see what would happen next. So it's not just what the person did that matters; your perception of *why* she did it matters too.

This question of *why* others act as they do is one we face every day in many different contexts. The process through which we attempt to answer this question—to determine the causes behind others' behavior—is known as **attribution.** In general, attribution is a fairly

FIGURE 16.1

The Social Side of Life

We spend much of our time every day interacting with others and thinking about them.

orderly process. We examine others' behavior for clues as to the causes behind what they say and do, and then reach our decision. What kind of information do we consider? This depends on the specific question we want to answer. For instance, one basic issue is: Did another person's actions stem from *internal* causes (e.g., their own traits, intentions, or motives) or from *external* causes (e.g., luck or factors beyond their control in a given situation). To answer this question, we often focus on information about (1) whether other people behave in the same way this person does **(consensus),** (2) whether this person behaves in the same manner over time **(consistency),** and (3) whether this person behaves in the same way in different situations **(distinctiveness).** If very few people act like this person (consensus is low), and this person behaves in the same way over time (consistency is high), and this person behaves in much the same manner in many situations (distinctiveness is low), we conclude that the behavior stemmed from internal causes: This is the kind of person he or she is, and will probably remain. In contrast, if all three of these factors are high (consensus, consistency, and distinctiveness), we are more likely to conclude that this person behaved as he or she did because of external causes—for instance, there may have been no choice (Kelley, 1972; see Figure 16.2).

Attribution: The processes through which we seek to determine the causes behind others' behavior.

Consensus: The extent to which behavior by one person is shown by others as well.

Consistency: The extent to which a given person responds in the same way to a given stimulus across time.

Distinctiveness: The extent to which a given person reacts in the same manner to different stimuli or situations.

Attribution: Some Basic Sources of Bias While attribution often involves the logical kind of reasoning described above, this is not always the case. In fact, attribution is frequently subject to several kinds of errors, ones that can lead us to false conclusions about other persons. Let's consider some of these here.

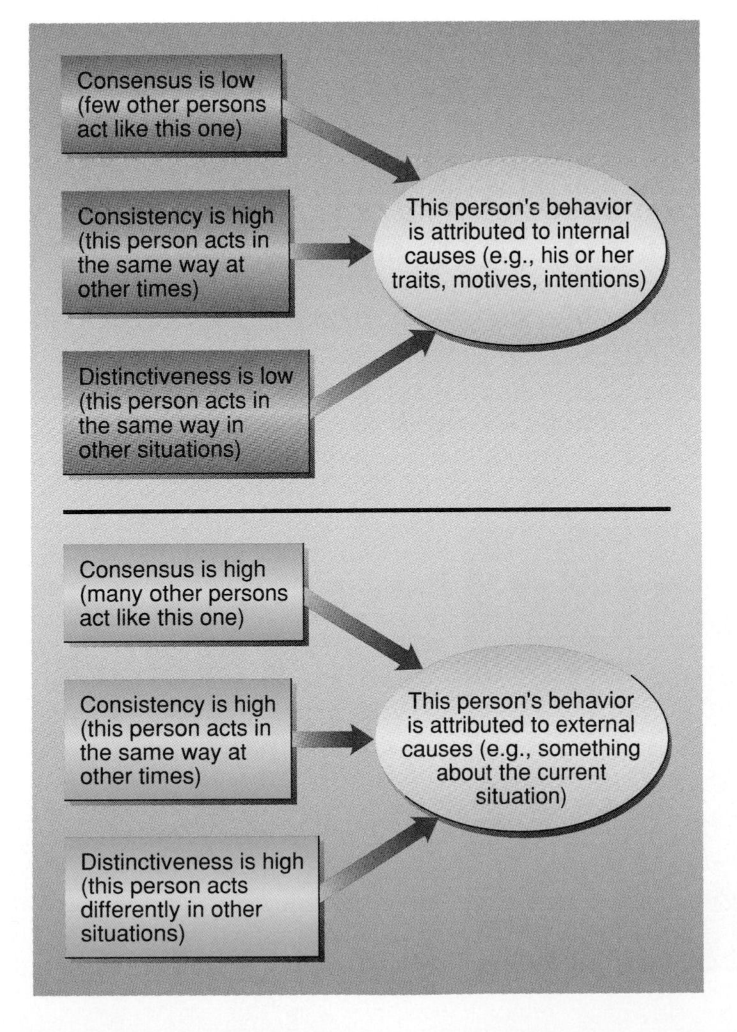

FIGURE 16.2

Causal Attribution

Research findings suggest that when consensus and distinctiveness are low but consistency is high, we tend to attribute others' behavior to internal causes (upper diagram). When consensus, consistency, and distinctiveness are all high, in contrast, we attribute their behavior to external causes (lower diagram).

Fundamental Attribution Error: The tendency to attribute others' behavior to internal causes to a greater extent than is actually justified.

Self-Serving Bias: The tendency to attribute positive outcomes to our own traits or characteristics (internal causes) but negative outcomes to factors beyond our control (external causes).

The Fundamental Attribution Error: Overestimating the Role of Dispositional Causes Suppose you witness the following scene. A man arrives at a meeting thirty minutes late. On entering the room he drops his notes on the floor. While trying to pick them up, he falls over and breaks his glasses. How would you explain these events? Probably by concluding that the man is disorganized and clumsy. In other words, you would emphasize *internal* causes in your explanation. Would you be correct? Perhaps. But it is also possible that you would be jumping to a false conclusion. It might be that this individual was late because of circumstances beyond his control (for instance, a major traffic jam), that he dropped his notes because they were printed on very slick paper, and that he fell down because the floor had just been waxed. The fact that you would be less likely to think of such *external* potential causes reflects one important source of error in attribution—an effect so powerful that it is sometimes termed the **fundamental attribution error** (another term for it is *overattribution bias;* Fiske, 1993). The fundamental attribution error is our strong tendency to explain others' actions in terms of internal (dispositional) causes rather than external (situational) causes. In sum, we tend to perceive that others behave as they do because they are "that kind of person" rather than because of situational factors that may well have affected their behavior.

Why do we show this tendency? The explanation currently accepted by most social psychologists goes something like this. When we focus on others' behavior, we tend to begin by assuming that their actions reflect their underlying characteristics. Then we attempt to correct for any possible effects of the external world—the current situation—by taking these into account. This correction, however, is often insufficient; we don't make enough allowance for the impact of external factors. We may not give enough weight to the possibility of a traffic jam or a slippery floor, for example, when reaching our conclusions (Leyens, Yzerbyt, & Corneille, 1996). Whatever the precise explanation for the fundamental attribution error, however, it has important implications. For example, it suggests that even if individuals are made aware of the situational forces that adversely affect disadvantaged groups in society—forces such as poor diet, disrupted family life, exposure to violent peer models—they may still perceive such persons as "bad" and responsible for their own troubles (see Figure 16.3). In such cases, the fundamental attribution error can have important social consequences (e.g., Burger & Pavelich, 1993).

FIGURE 16.3

The Fundamental Attribution Error in Action

Why are the people shown here dependent on government aid? Because of the *fundamental attribution error,* many persons tend to perceive that people get into this situation only because of their own traits—for instance, because they are lazy, irresponsible, and so on. While this may be true for some welfare recipients, many others are the victims of circumstances beyond their control. In situations like this, the fundamental attribution error can lead us to false conclusions about others and the causes of their behavior.

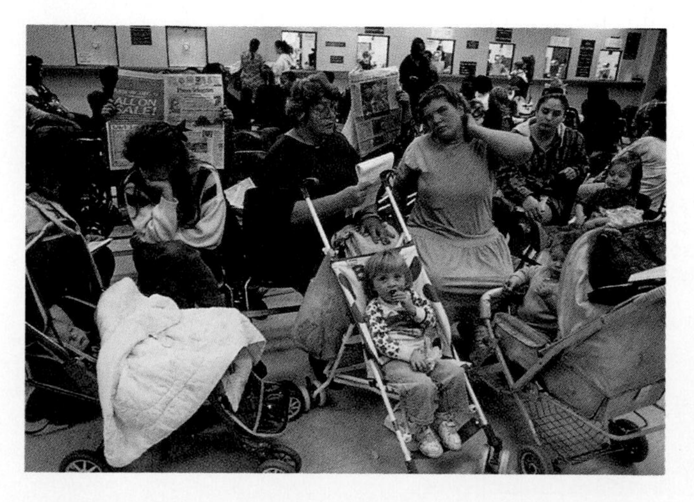

The Self-Serving Bias: "I Can Do No Wrong; You Can Do No Right" Suppose that you write a term paper for one of your classes. After reading it, your professor gives you an A. To what will you attribute your success? If you are like most people, the chances are good that you will explain it in terms of *internal* causes—your own talent or hard work.

Now, in contrast, imagine that your professor gives you a D. How will you explain *this* outcome? Here, there is a real possibility that you will focus mainly on *external* causes—the fact that you didn't have enough time for the project, your professor's unrealistically high standards, and so on. In situations like this one, you are showing another attributional error known as the **self-serving bias** (Brown & Rogers, 1991; Miller & Ross, 1975). This is our tendency to take credit for positive behaviors or outcomes by attributing them to internal causes, but to blame negative ones on external causes, especially on factors beyond our control.

Why does this slant in our attributions occur? The most important factors seem to involve our need to protect and enhance our self-esteem, or the related desire to look good to others (e.g., Greenberg, Pysczynski, & Solomon, 1982). Attributing our successes to internal causes while attributing failures to external causes permits us to accomplish these ego-protective goals (see Figure 16.4). Whatever the precise origins of the self-serving bias, it can be the cause of much interpersonal friction. It often leads each of the persons who work together on a joint task to perceive that *they,* not their partners, have made the major contributions. Similarly, it leads individuals to perceive that negative actions on their part are justified and excusable, while identical actions by others are irrational and unjustified (Baumeister, Stillwell, & Wotman, 1990). If I lose my temper, in other words, I have good reason for doing so; if you lose yours, that's just more evidence for your tendency to fly off the handle for no good reason!

FIGURE 16.4

Attribution as a Technique for Protecting Our Self-Esteem

By attributing negative outcomes or behavior to external causes, but positive ones to internal causes, we protect or boost our self-esteem. These attributional tendencies are known as the *self-serving bias.*

(**Source:** Drawing by Bruce Eric Kaplan; ©1992 The New Yorker Magazine, Inc.)

While the self-serving bias appears to be a common aspect of attribution—it has, for instance, been observed in many different cultures (e.g., Al-Zahrani & Kaplowitz, 1993)—recent evidence suggests that it does have some limits. In an ingenious study, Rosech and Amirkhan (1997) examined statements by athletes appearing in newspapers, to see if the self-serving bias would be visible in the athletes' explanation for why they, or their teams, won or lost. Results indicated that across many hundreds of quotations, the athletes did tend to attribute wins to internal factors—their own skill or abilities. However, this tendency was stronger for "rookies" than for experienced players, and athletes performing alone, for instance, golfers or tennis players, were more likely to show the self-serving bias than athletes playing on teams. So, in sum, the self-serving bias is not an all-powerful tendency where explaining success or failure is concerned. (For information on an especially disturbing kind of attributional error, please see the Exploring Gender and Diversity section.)

Attribution and Rape: Blaming the Victim

EXPLORING GENDER & DIVERSITY

Kurt Lewin, one of the founders of social psychology, once remarked: "There's nothing as practical as a good theory." By this he meant that once we obtain scientific understanding of some aspect of human behavior, we can often put this knowledge to practical use. Where attribution theory is concerned, this has definitely been the case. Social psychologists have applied their knowledge of attribution to practical problems and issues (e.g., Graham & Folkes, 1990) ranging from treatments for depression (see Chapter 15; Alloy, Abramson, & Dykman, 1990) through the causes of marital dissatisfaction (e.g., Kubany et al., 1995). Among the most dramatic—and unsettling—of these applications, however, has been research relating attribution to certain aspects of rape.

In the United States, it has been estimated that a rape (defined as forced sexual intercourse) occurs every eleven minutes (Baron & Richardson, 1994). This statistic is frightening enough; but perhaps even more disturbing is the fact that rape victims are often held responsible for this crime. "She must have led him on," "What was she doing in a bar at that hour of the night, anyway?" These are the kinds of comments frequently heard in conversations concerning media reports of rapes.

FIGURE 16.5

Attributing Blame to Rape Victims

Both males and females assigned considerable blame to the victim of a rape. In addition, they tended to blame her more when she knew the rapist than when this person was a stranger.

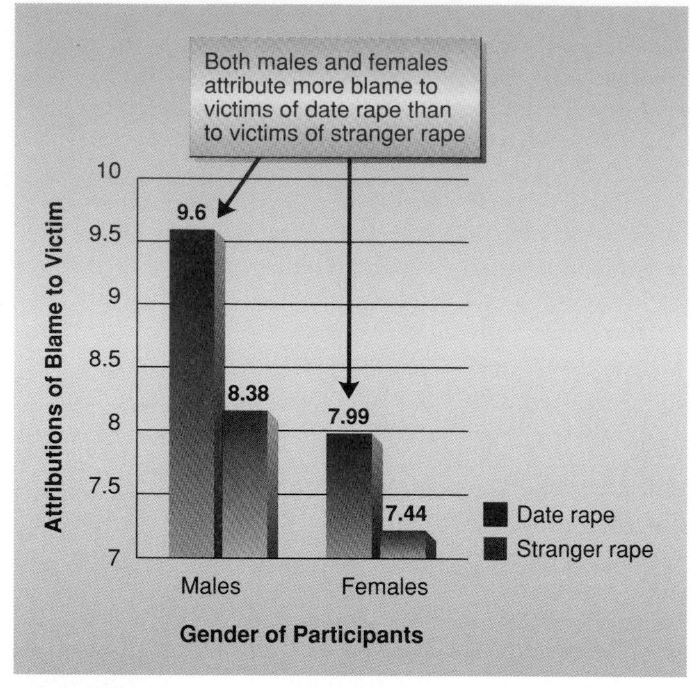

(**Source:** Based on data from Bell, Kuriloff, & Lottes, 1994.)

From the perspective of attribution theory, then, blame is attached to victims as much as, or even more than, to rapists. As you might guess, males are more likely to make such attributions than females (Cowan & Curtis, 1994); but women, too, often show a tendency to attribute responsibility for rape to its victims.

What accounts for this tendency? One possibility involves *belief in a just world*—our desire to assume that the world is basically a fair place where people get what they deserve (Lerner, 1980). According to this reasoning, if a woman is sexually assaulted, then she must have done something to deserve it. Thinking the opposite—that she is a completely blameless victim—is just too painful an idea for most of us to entertain. To avoid such thoughts, we tend to blame the victim, assuming that she must have somehow "asked" for this kind of trouble.

Evidence for this view is provided by the findings of a study by Bell, Kuriloff, and Lottes (1994). These researchers asked male and female college students to read one of two descriptions of a rape. In one case, the woman was attacked by a stranger. In another, she was raped by a date. After reading one of these accounts, participants were asked to rate the extent to which the victim was to blame for the crime. First, as you can see from Figure 16.5, both males and females attributed considerable blame for the rape to the victim. Second, both genders blamed the victim to a greater extent when she knew the rapist (when he was someone she dated) than when the rapist was a stranger. Third, males tended to blame the victim to a greater extent than females.

These findings, and those of related studies, have important implications. First, they help explain why so many victims of date rape—an alarmingly common event (Koss & Harvey, 1991)—are reluctant to report this crime: They realize that they are likely to be blamed for it. Second, the fact that men tend to blame rape victims to a greater extent than women suggests that certain myths about rape—for instance, the belief that some women secretly desire to be raped—are still accepted to some extent by some males. Clearly, such views must be changed if the incidence of this appalling crime is to be reduced from its current frightening levels.

Key Questions

- What is the fundamental attribution error?
- What is the self-serving bias?
- What role does attribution play in perceptions of rape victims?

Social Cognition: How We Process Social Information

Identifying the causes behind others' behavior is an important aspect of social thought; yet it is far from the entire picture. **Social cognition**—our efforts to interpret, analyze, and use information about the social world—involves many other tasks as well. We must decide what information is most important, and so worthy of our attention. We must enter such information into long-term memory, and be able to retrieve it at later times. And we must be able to combine this previously stored information about others in various ways in order to make judgments about them and predict their future actions (Fiske, 1993). It is only by accomplishing these tasks that we can make sense out of the social world in which we live—a world that, we soon learn, is anything but simple.

How do we accomplish these tasks? We have already encountered part of the answer in our earlier discussions of memory and schemas (see Chapter 6) and of *heuristics*—cognitive rules of thumb for making judgments or decisions very quickly (see Chapter 7). Here, we'll focus on additional aspects of social thought—and especially on aspects reflecting the theme (see Chapter 6) that as human beings, we are definitely *not* computers. On the contrary, in our efforts to understand others and make sense out of the social world, we are subject to a wide range of tendencies that together can lead us into serious error. In this section I'll consider several of these "tilts" in social cognition. First, however, let me carefully emphasize the following point: While these aspects of social thought do sometimes result in errors, they are also quite adaptive. They often help us to focus on the kinds of information that are usually most useful, and they reduce the effort required for understanding the social world.

The False Consensus Effect: The Tendency to Assume That Others Think as We Do Be honest: On a scale ranging from 1 (strongly oppose) to 7 (strongly favor) what is your view about marriage for homosexuals? Now, out of one hundred other students at your school, how many do you think share your view, whatever it is? That is, how many students are on the same side of the neutral point (4) on this scale as you are? If you are like most people, the number you will indicate is higher than what would be found in an actual survey. In other words, you assume that people agree with you to a greater extent than is actually true. This tendency is known as the **false consensus effect,** and it is a basic fact of social thought (e.g., Gilovich, 1990; Suls, Wan, & Sanders, 1988).

What is the basis for this tendency? Several factors seem to play a role, but the most important involves the *availability heuristic* described in Chapter 7. As you may recall, this mental rule of thumb suggests that the easier it is to bring information to mind, the more important we judge it to be. Applying this principle to the false consensus effect, it appears that most people find it easier to remember instances in which others have agreed with them than instances in which others have disagreed. The result: They overestimate the extent to which others share their views.

While the false consensus effect is common, it's also important to note that it doesn't occur in all situations. Where highly *desirable* attributes are concerned, people wish to see themselves as unique—more different from others, in a positive direction, than they actually are (Suls & Wan, 1987). As a result, we tend to perceive ourselves as happier, more intelligent, more ethical, and less prejudiced than the people around us (Miller & McFarland, 1987). If you'd like to demonstrate this for yourself, just ask ten of your friends to rate themselves on leadership ability; chances are that most of them will rate themselves as above average on this dimension.

Social Cognition: The processes through which we notice, store, remember, and later use social information.

False Consensus Effect: The tendency to believe that other persons share our attitudes to a greater extent than is true.

Dealing with Inconsistent Information: Paying Attention to What Doesn't Fit Imagine the following situation: You are watching an evening talk show on television. One of the guests is Newt Gingrich, Speaker of the House of Representatives in the United States Congress. You only half listen as he makes a number of, for him, unsurprising comments about taxes, welfare reform, and government generally. Then, in a quiet voice, he says something totally unexpected: He has lost interest in politics and has decided to retire to grow roses at the end of his current two-year term. You sit up straight in disbelief. Can you believe your ears? Did he really say *that?*

This somewhat bizarre example illustrates an important fact about social cognition: In general, we tend to pay much more attention to information that is *unexpected* or somehow *inconsistent* with our expectations than to information that is expected or consistent. Thus, a statement by Newt Gingrich to the effect that he has lost interest in politics would literally leap out at you, demanding close attention.

This tendency to pay greater attention to information inconsistent with our expectations than to information consistent with them is an important and basic aspect of social cognition. It is apparent in a wide range of contexts (e.g., Belmore & Hubbard, 1987; Hilton, Klein, & von Hippel, 1991); and it seems to stem from the fact that inconsistent information is unexpected and surprising, with the result that we work harder to understand it (e.g., Srull, 1994). And because the more attention we pay to information, the better its chance of entering into long-term memory and influencing our later social judgments (Bardach & Park, 1996; Fiske & Neuberg, 1990). This tendency to notice what's inconsistent has important implications.

One final point: While it is usually the case that information to which we pay particular attention exerts stronger effects on our social thought and judgments than other information, this is not always so. Sometimes, although we readily *notice* information that is inconsistent with our expectations, we tend to discount it or downplay it: It's simply too unexpected to accept. For example, you probably can't help noticing the weird headlines on the tabloid newspapers displayed near the checkout lines in supermarkets ("Teen marries monster from outer space!" "Drug turns boy into fish!" "Woman gives birth to dinosaur!"). They are unexpected and inconsistent with views you already hold. But the chances of these stories' influencing your thinking in any serious way are slight, because they are *so* bizarre that you discount them. So the fact that we often pay careful attention to information inconsistent with our current views or thinking does not mean that such information is necessarily more influential with respect to social thought.

Magical Thinking: Does Imagining Make It So? Answer each of these questions quickly and truthfully:

> Suppose someone with AIDS bought a sweater sealed in a plastic bag and put it away in a drawer for a year; would you wear it?
>
> Imagine that someone handed you a cake that looked very much like human vomit—a cake you knew would taste delicious; would you eat it?
>
> If you think about a dangerous or harmful event, does that increase the likelihood that it will happen?

On the basis of purely rational considerations, you know what your answers should probably be: Yes, yes, and no. But are those the answers you actually gave? If you are like most persons, perhaps not. In fact, research findings indicate that as human beings we are quite susceptible to what has been termed **magical thinking** (Rozin & Nemeroff, 1990). Such thinking makes assumptions that don't hold up to rational scrutiny, but which are compelling nonetheless. One principle embodied in magical thinking is known as the

Magical Thinking: Thinking that makes assumptions that don't hold up to rational scrutiny.

principle of *contagion:* This notion holds that when two objects touch, they pass properties to one another, and that the effects of contact may last well beyond the termination of such contact (Zusne & Jones, 1989). Another is the principle of *similarity,* which suggests that things that resemble one another share fundamental properties. Still a third, which might be termed the *"thinking-makes-it-so" principle,* assumes that one's thoughts can achieve specific physical effects in a manner not governed by the laws of physics. Have you ever tried to avoid thinking about some negative event or outcome because of the feeling that if you thought about it, it might be more likely to occur? If so, you are already familiar with this principle (see Figure 16.6).

FIGURE 16.6

Does Thinking Make It So?

One form of *magical thinking* involves the belief that if we think about something, it is more likely to happen. One example: A study found that during the Gulf War in the early 1990s, many Israelis reported that they believed that missiles launched by Iraq were more likely to hit houses if occupants were home than if they were not.

Can you see how these assumptions relate to the questions above? Contagion is linked to the question about the sweater; similarity relates to the unpleasantly shaped cake; and the third principle is connected to the possibility of inviting catastrophes by thinking about them.

Surprising as it may seem, our thought processes in many situations—including social ones—are often influenced by magical thinking. For example, in one study, Rozin, Markwith, and Nemeroff (1992) asked individuals to rate a sweater owned either by a person with AIDS or by a healthy person, given that the sweater had been left in a sealed plastic bag and never touched by its owner. Consistent with the principle of contagion, participants rated the sweater less favorably when it had been owned by the person with AIDS, even though they knew that there was no chance they could catch this fatal disease from the sweater.

Additional evidence suggests that our thinking is often influenced by the similarity and "thinking-makes-it-so" principles, too (e.g., Keinan, 1994). So, the next time you are tempted to make fun of someone's superstitious beliefs (e.g., fear of the number thirteen or of black cats crossing one's path), think again. You may not accept such superstitions yourself, but this does not necessarily mean that your own thinking is completely free from the kinds of magical assumptions described above.

Counterfactual Thinking: The Effects of Considering "What Might Have Been" Imagine the following events:

> *Ms. Caution never picks up hitchhikers. Yesterday, however, she broke her rule and gave a stranger a lift. He repaid her kindness by robbing her.*

Now, in contrast, consider the following events:

> *Ms. Risk frequently picks up hitchhikers. Yesterday, she gave yet another stranger a ride. He repaid her kindness by robbing her.*

Which of these two persons will experience greater regret? If you answered, "Ms. Caution, of course," your thinking in this instance is very much like that of an overwhelming majority of respondents (Kahneman & Miller, 1986). Why is this the case? From a totally rational point of view, there should be no difference. Both Ms. Caution and Ms. Risk have suffered precisely the same negative outcome: They have been robbed. Why, then, do we perceive Ms. Caution as experiencing greater regret? The answer involves some intriguing facts about social thought and the judgments resulting from it. In the most general terms, it appears that our reactions to events depend not only on the events themselves, but also on what these events bring to mind (Miller & McFarland, 1987). When we have some experience, we do not think only about the experience itself; we also engage in what social psychologists describe as **counterfactual thinking**—bringing alternative events and outcomes to mind. In this particular instance, we think, "If only Ms. Caution had not broken her rule against picking up hitchhikers, she'd be okay." Alternatively, we may imagine that "If Ms. Risk had read the papers and thought about what she was doing, she would probably have acted differently."

Why does such counterfactual thinking lead us to believe that Ms. Caution will experience more regret? In part, because it is easier to imagine alternatives to *unusual* behavior (such as Ms. Caution's picking up the hitchhiker) than it is to imagine alternatives to usual, normal behavior (such as Ms. Risk's picking up the hitchhiker). So we conclude that Ms. Caution experienced more regret, because it is easier to imagine her acting in a different way—sticking to her standard rule—than it is to imagine Ms. Risk acting differently.

This reasoning leads to the interesting prediction that negative outcomes that follow unusual behavior will generate more sympathy for the persons who experience them than ones that follow usual behavior. And in fact this prediction has been confirmed in many different studies (e.g., Miller & McFarland, 1987; Macrae, 1992). So counterfactual thinking does occur, and it does influence social judgments and reactions in predictable ways.

Now, before you read on, try this:

List the three biggest regrets in your life—the things that you wish most strongly you could change.

What were they? If you are like most people, they probably related to things you *did not do,* but wish you had: the opportunities you didn't pursue, the school you didn't attend, the romance you didn't have. It is less likely that your regrets involved things you *did do* that yielded negative outcomes—the opportunity you took that didn't work out, the school you attended but didn't like, the romance you had that ended badly.

Now, try this:

List the three biggest regrets in your life during the last week*—the things you wish most strongly you could change.*

Is your answer this time any different? The findings of several studies (e.g., Gilovich & Medvec, 1994) suggest that it may well be: You are probably more likely to mention things you *did* that turned out badly. In short, it seems that the things about which we feel regret change over time. But why, precisely, is this the case? Psychologists who have studied such effects offer several explanations. First, consider regrets for actions we took. We can reduce such regret, over time, by actually reversing the action—by changing our decision or behavior. Similarly, we are quite good at *rationalizing*—at finding good reasons for why we *had* to act in this way; and the more time that passes, the more rationalizations we can generate. In contrast, we cannot reverse or rationalize the past to reduce regrets over actions we didn't take: Missed opportunities may never come again, and we do not find it easier to explain away failure to act as time passes.

Moreover, as time passes, other factors tend to increase regrets about actions we didn't take. For instance, we often fail to act because of fears or lack of confidence; as we look back from a later time, these fears may seem less significant, leaving us with the feeling that we *should have* acted. Similarly, once we have performed an action, we are faced with its consequences: We

Counterfactual Thinking: The tendency to evaluate events by thinking about alternatives to them—"What might have been."

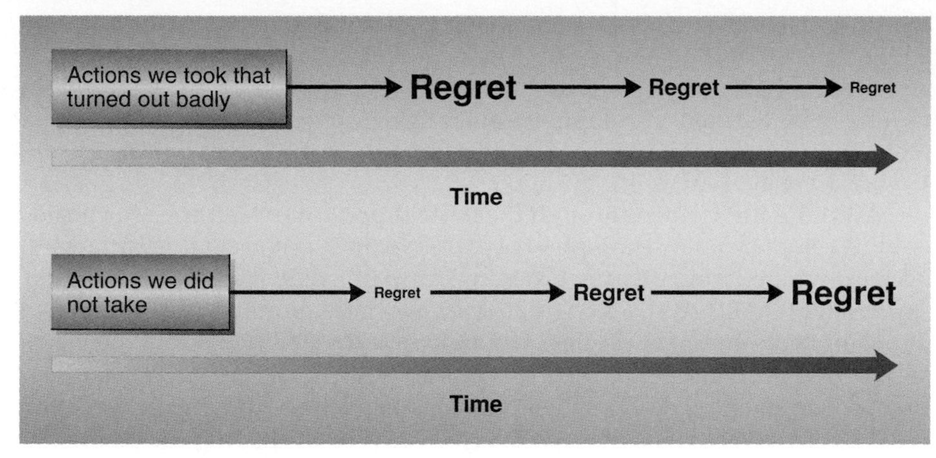

(**Source**: Based on suggestions by Gilovich & Medvec, 1994.)

FIGURE 16.7

Regrets: Why They Change with the Passage of Time

Actions we took that turned out badly can be reversed; even if they are not, we tend to think of many good reasons why we *had* to act the way we did. As a result, regret over such actions decreases over time. In contrast, regrets over actions we didn't take may increase with time, because we continue to wonder what the results of such actions would have been, and because the factors that prevented us from acting (fear, lack of confidence) tend to seem less important with the passage of time.

know what these are. In contrast, if we fail to act, we can continue to speculate—indefinitely!—about what might have happened if we *had* acted. In sum, there are many reasons why the pattern of our regrets for action and inaction may shift over time (see Figure 16.7).

Clear evidence for the occurrence of such effects has been reported by Gilovich and Medvec (1994). The researchers asked a large number of individuals to describe the single action or inaction they regretted most from the past week, and the single action or inaction they regretted most in their entire lives. For regrets from the past week, actions and failures to act were mentioned about equally by participants. For regrets from their entire lives, however, a large majority of participants (84 percent) focused on failures to act. So, as expected, there was a major shift in the pattern of regrets over time.

What factors lead us to engage in counterfactual thinking? A theory proposed recently by Roese (1997) suggests that we are most likely to engage in such thinking—to imagine "what might have been"—in situations where we experience negative outcomes. By engaging in counterfactual thinking at such times, we think of ways of avoiding such outcomes in the future, and this can be comforting.

In sum, it appears that when we think about various events in our lives, we often engage in counterfactual thinking: We imagine what might have been or should have been in these situations. And such thoughts, in turn, can strongly influence our judgments about these events or situations, our current moods, and our plans for the future.

Key Questions

- What is the false consensus effect?
- How do we deal with social information that is inconsistent with our expectations?
- What is magical thinking?
- What is counterfactual thinking? How does it change over time?

Attitudes: Evaluating the Social World

Consider the following list:

Michael Jackson	Whoopi Goldberg
AIDS	fraternities and sororities
Rice Krispies	Saddam Hussein

Do you have any reactions to each item? Unless you have been living a life of total isolation, you probably do. You may like or dislike Michael Jackson, be worried or unconcerned about AIDS, find Rice Krispies tasty or unappealing, find Whoopi Goldberg funny or not funny, and approve or disapprove of fraternities and sororities. Such reactions, which social psychologists call

Attitudes: Lasting evaluations of various aspects of the social world that are stored in memory.

Persuasion: The process through which one or more persons attempt to alter the attitudes of one or more others.

attitudes, generally involve an emotional or affective component (for instance, liking or disliking), a cognitive component (beliefs), and a behavioral component (tendencies to act toward these items in various ways). More simply, attitudes can be defined as lasting evaluations of various aspects of the social world—evaluations that are stored in memory (Fazio & Roskos-Ewoldsen, 1994; Judd et al., 1991).

Attitudes are formed through the basic processes of learning we considered in Chapter 5. For example, they often stem from *operant conditioning,* because we are frequently rewarded by our parents, teachers, or friends for expressing the "correct views"—the ones *they* hold. Similarly, attitudes also derive from *observational learning.* Throughout life we tend to adopt the views and preferences expressed by people we like or respect, because we are exposed to those views and want to be like those persons. Even *classical conditioning* plays a role; in fact, it may be especially influential in shaping the emotional or affective aspect of attitudes (e.g., Betz & Krosnick, 1993; Cacioppo, Priester, & Berntson, 1993).

Whatever their precise origins, attitudes are an important aspect of social thought and have long been a central topic of research in social psychology. In this discussion, we'll focus on two key aspects of attitudes: *persuasion*—how attitudes can sometimes be changed; and *cognitive dissonance*—a process through which we sometimes actually change our own attitudes.

Persuasion: The Process of Changing Attitudes

As the twentieth century draws to a close, the business of changing attitudes—or at least trying to change them—seems to grow ever bigger and more intense. Television commercials, magazine ads, billboards, political campaigns, labels on products warning about the dangers of using them—the messages vary, but the goal remains the same: changing people's attitudes and so, ultimately, their behavior (see Figure 16.8). To what extent are such efforts at **persuasion**—efforts to change attitudes—really effective? And how does persuasion actually occur? Let's see what research findings indicate.

Persuasion: Some Basic Findings

In most cases, efforts at persuasion involve the following elements: Some *scurce* directs some type of *message* to some target *audience.* Early research on persuasion, therefore, focused on these three basic components. It addressed various aspects of the question "*Who* says *what* to *whom* and with what *effect?*" (Hovland, Janis, & Kelley, 1953). The findings of such research were complex, but among the most important were these (Shavitt & Brock, 1994):

1. Experts are more persuasive than nonexperts (Hovland & Weiss, 1951). The same arguments carry more weight when delivered by people who seem to know what they are talking about and to have all the facts than when they are made by people lacking expertise.
2. Messages that do not appear to be designed to change our attitudes are often more successful than ones that seem intended to reach this goal (Walster & Festinger, 1962). In other words, we generally don't trust—and generally refuse to be influenced by—persons who overtly set out to persuade us. This is one reason why the soft sell is so popular in advertising—and in politics.
3. Attractive sources are more effective in changing attitudes than unattractive ones (Kiesler & Kiesler, 1969). This helps explain why the models featured in many ads are highly attractive, and why advertisers engage in a perpetual search for new faces.

FIGURE 16.8

The Business of Persuasion

At the present time, it is virtually impossible to avoid efforts to change our attitudes.

4. People are sometimes more susceptible to persuasion when they are distracted by some extraneous event than when they are paying full attention to what is being said (Allyn & Festinger, 1961). I'll explain why this is so shortly.
5. When an audience holds attitudes contrary to those of a would-be persuader, it is often more effective for the communicator to adopt a *two-sided approach*—to present both sides of the argument—than to take a *one-sided approach.* Apparently, strongly supporting one side of an issue while acknowledging that the other side has a few good points in its favor serves to disarm the audience and makes it harder for them to resist the source's major conclusions.
6. People who speak rapidly are often more persuasive than persons who speak more slowly (Miller et al., 1976). So, contrary to popular belief, we do not always distrust fast-talking politicians and salespersons.
7. Persuasion can be enhanced by messages that arouse strong emotions (especially fear) in the audience, particularly when the persuasive argument provides specific recommendations about how a change in attitudes or behavior will prevent the negative consequences described in the fear-provoking messages (Leventhal, Singer, & Jones, 1965).

One word of caution: Changing attitudes is a complex and tricky business. Many different factors play a role, so simple generalizations are risky at best. However, the findings listed above have generally stood the test of time and repeated testing (that is, replication). For this reason, they appear to constitute an important part of our basic knowledge about persuasion.

Persuasion: The Cognitive Approach The traditional approach to understanding persuasion has certainly been useful. It provided a wealth of information about the "when" and "how" of persuasion—when such attitude change is most likely to occur and how, in practical terms, it can be produced. The traditional approach did not, however, address the *why* of persuasion—why people change their attitudes in response to persuasive messages.

This issue has been brought sharply into focus by a more modern approach to understanding the nature of persuasion—an approach that rests firmly on social psychology's increasingly sophisticated understanding of the nature of social thought. This *cognitive perspective* on persuasion (Petty et al., 1994) does not concentrate on the question of "Who says what to whom and with what effect?" Rather, it focuses on the cognitive processes that determine when individuals are persuaded—what people think about when they are exposed to persuasive messages, and how these thoughts and basic cognitive processes determine whether, and to what extent, people change their attitudes (Petty & Cacioppo, 1986; Petty, Unnava, & Strathman, 1991).

Let's examine what is perhaps the most influential cognitive theory of persuasion: the *elaboration likelihood model* of persuasion. The model asks: What happens when a person receives a persuasive message? According to Petty, Cacioppo, and their colleagues (Petty et al., 1994; Petty & Cacioppo, 1986), the person thinks about the message, the arguments it makes, and (perhaps) the arguments it has left out. It is these thoughts—not the message itself—that then lead either to attitude change or to resistance to such change.

But how does persuasion actually occur? According to the **elaboration likelihood model (ELM),** two different processes, reflecting different amounts of cognitive effort on the part of message recipients, can occur. The first, known as the **central route** to persuasion, occurs when recipients find a message interesting, important, or personally relevant (Zuwerink & Devine, 1996), and when nothing else (such as distraction or prior knowledge of the message) prevents them from devoting careful attention to it. In such cases, individuals may examine the message in a careful and thoughtful manner, evaluating

Elaboration Likelihood Model (ELM): A cognitive model of persuasion suggesting that persuasion can occur through distinct routes.

Central Route (to persuasion): Attitude change resulting from systematic processing of information contained in persuasive messages.

the strength of the arguments it contains. If their reactions are favorable, their attitudes and other existing cognitive structures may be changed, and persuasion occurs.

In contrast, if recipients find the message uninteresting or uninvolving, they are not motivated to process it carefully. This doesn't mean that it can't affect them, however. On the contrary, in such cases persuasion can still occur, according to the ELM—but this time through what is known as the **peripheral route.** Perhaps the message contains something that induces positive feelings, such as a very attractive model or a scene of breathtaking natural beauty (see Figure 16.9). Or perhaps the source of the message is very high in status, prestige, or credibility. Under these conditions, attitude change may occur in the absence of a critical analysis of the contents of the message. Needless to say, advertisers, political promoters, salespersons, and others wishing to change our attitudes are well aware of this peripheral route to persuasion, and often try to use it when they realize that the arguments they can marshal in support of their products or candidates are not strong or convincing.

A growing body of evidence indicates that the ELM analysis is accurate (e.g., DeBono, 1992; Zuwerink & Devine, 1996). For example, the ELM predicts that if weak arguments are added to strong ones in a persuasive appeal, they may actually *reduce* the amount of persuasion produced, especially for issues that are important or involving to individuals. Can you see why this is so? For important issues, individuals tend to scrutinize message arguments very carefully. Such careful processing leads to unfavorable thoughts in response to weak arguments—thoughts that might not occur if the message contained only strong arguments. The result: Persuasion is reduced by the presence of the weak arguments (e.g., Friedrich et al., 1996). Several other predictions based on the ELM have been verified, too (e.g., Roskos-Ewoldsen & Fazio, 1992); so it appears that this model does indeed provide important insights into the nature of persuasion and the cognitive processes that underlie it. In other words, it helps us to understand not just when persuasion is likely to occur, but also *why* and *how* this process takes place.

For an unusual real-life illustration of persuasion, see the Beyond the Headlines section.

FIGURE 16.9

Persuasion through the Peripheral Route

Many ads contain beautiful people or beautiful scenes. The goal is to wow us with these stimuli so that persuasion occurs through the *peripheral route;* that is, without our analyzing in a careful or rational manner the arguments being presented.

Cognitive Dissonance: How We Sometimes Change Our Own Attitudes

There are many occasions in everyday life when we feel compelled to say or do things inconsistent with our true attitudes. A couple of examples: Your friend shows you her new sweater and asks how you like it. You think that the color is horrible, but you don't say that. Instead you say, "Nice . . . really nice." Your boss describes his new idea for increasing sales. You think that it is totally idiotic, but you don't tell him that. Instead you respond: "Sounds really interesting."

The reasons for behaving in these polite but slightly dishonest ways are so obvious that social psychologists describe such situations as involving **forced compliance**—that is, as situations in which we feel compelled to say or do things inconsistent with our true attitudes. Now, here's the most interesting part: When we behave in this way—when we engage in what social psychologists term *attitude-discrepant behavior*—this may sometimes produce

Peripheral Route (to persuasion): Attitude change that occurs in response to persuasion cues—information concerning the expertise, status, or attractiveness of would-be persuaders.

Forced Compliance: A situation in which we feel compelled to say or do things inconsistent with our true attitudes.

Beyond the Headlines

As Psychologists See It

Fantasy: Women Say Man Fooled Them into Sex

Associated Press, April 16, 1996, Nashville, Tenn.—The phone rings late at night. In a sexy whisper, a man persuades a woman to unlock her door, undress, put on a blindfold and wait for him in bed.

At least three women did so, thinking he was their boyfriend, and had sex with the so-called Fantasy Man—one woman twice a week for two months. Now they want police to charge Raymond Mitchell III with rape. The 45-year-old businessman says he was just fulfilling the women's fantasies and the sex was consensual. . . .

Persuasion through Sexual Fantasies

Amazing, eh? How could these women permit a total stranger to talk them into allowing him into their homes—and into their beds? Talk about persuasion! And since they did unlock their doors, undress, put on a blindfold, and get into bed, is it rape? This is a complex legal question that only the courts can answer. But social psychologists also have a lot to say about situations like this one.

First, they would note that Raymond Mitchell III was indeed an expert at persuasion. For instance, he didn't choose his victims at random. Rather, they were women he had met, or women he had observed interacting with their boyfriends. From his observations, he concluded that they would be susceptible to his approach—which was also carefully planned. He didn't just call the women and suggest sex;on the contrary, he used persuasive appeals rich in the kind of fantasies Mitchell suspected would arouse the passions of the women he called. With one victim, for instance, he asked whether she had seen the movie *9 1/2 Weeks.* Then he described it in detail—including a scene in which a woman's sexual fantasies are being fulfilled while she is blindfolded. He suspected that she would find this image highly arousing—and he was right. She had sex with him several times before calling the police.

With another woman, Mitchell pretended to be a man she had met a week earlier and whom she had found highly attractive. Wearing a ski mask, and with his victim sitting blindfolded in a dark room, he was able to convince her that he was indeed this man of her dreams. In short, he did everything in his power to ensure that his victims did not respond to his persuasive appeals by analyzing them carefully. Rather, he tried to put them into a state where they would respond to his statement in a much less systematic and careful manner—through the peripheral route.

While advertisers are generally after our money rather than our love, they often use similar emotion-laden and fantasy-rich techniques to induce us to suspend careful analysis of their claims. Their hope, like that of Fantasy Man, is that we will then respond with our hearts rather than our heads—to the advertiser's benefit and, perhaps, our loss. So watch out: Fantasy Man may be out of action, but the kind of persuasive appeals he used are very much a part of modern advertising—and woe to us if we respond to these appeals in the way these would-be persuaders desire!

Critical Thinking Questions

1. Do you think that Raymond Mitchell's actions constitute rape?
2. How can individuals protect themselves against the kinds of persuasive appeals used by Mitchell—appeals designed to put them into an emotional state in which they will be unable to resist?
3. Do you think that only some people would be susceptible to the kinds of techniques used by Mitchell? If so, what would such people be like? (Refer to the discussion of personality in Chapter 12.)

changes in the attitudes we hold. In fact, our attitudes may now shift in the direction of what we felt compelled to do or say.

Such effects were first predicted by a very famous theory known as the theory of **cognitive dissonance** (Festinger, 1957). The term *cognitive dissonance* (or *dissonance* for short) refers to the unpleasant feelings we experience when

Cognitive Dissonance: The state experienced by individuals when they discover inconsistency between two attitudes they hold or between their attitudes and their behavior.

FIGURE 16.10

Why, Where Attitude Change Is Concerned, "Less" Sometimes Leads to "More"

When individuals have strong reasons for engaging in attitude-discrepant behavior (e.g., when they receive large rewards for doing so), they experience little or no dissonance and show little attitude change. When they have weak reasons for engaging in attitude-discrepant behavior (e.g., when they receive small rewards for doing so), dissonance is much greater; and attitude change, too, is increased. In such cases, "less" does indeed lead to "more."

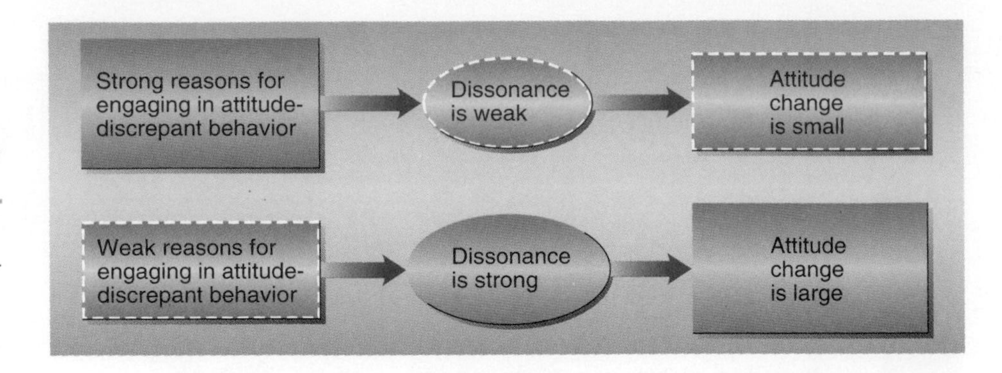

we notice a gap between two attitudes we hold, or between our attitudes and our behavior. Dissonance, it appears, is quite unpleasant (e.g., Elliot & Devine, 1994); so when we experience it, we attempt to reduce it. This can be accomplished in three different ways. First, we can change our attitudes or behavior so that these are more consistent with each other. For example, we can become more favorable toward our boss's plan. Second, we can acquire new information that supports our attitude or our behavior. For instance, we can seek out information indicating that the color of our friend's sweater is all the rage. Third, we can engage in *trivialization*—concluding that the attitudes or behaviors in question are not important (e.g., Simon, Greenberg, & Brehm, 1995). Which of these tactics do we use? As you might guess, whichever requires the least effort. In situations involving forced compliance, however, it is often the case that changing our own attitudes is the easiest step to take; so it is not surprising that in such situations our attitudes often shift so as to match more closely what we have actually said or done. In other words, we actually change our own attitudes because doing so helps us to reduce cognitive dissonance.

Dissonance and the Less-Leads-to-More Effect The prediction that people sometimes change their own attitudes is surprising enough. But now get ready for an even bigger surprise: Dissonance theory also predicts that the weaker the reasons we have for engaging in attitude-discrepant behavior, the greater the pressure to change these attitudes. Why is this so? Because when we have strong reasons for engaging in attitude-discrepant behavior, we realize that these are responsible for our saying or doing things inconsistent with our true attitudes. As a result, we experience very little dissonance. When we have only weak reasons for engaging in attitude-discrepant behavior, however, dissonance is stronger, and so is the pressure to change our attitudes (see Figure 16.10).

Social psychologists refer to this unexpected state of affairs as the **less-leads-to-more effect:** the fact that the stronger the reasons for engaging in attitude-discrepant behavior, the weaker the pressures toward changing the underlying attitudes. Surprising as it may seem, this effect has been confirmed in many different studies (e.g., Riess & Schlenker, 1977). In all these studies, people provided with a small reward for stating attitudes contrary to their own views changed these attitudes so that they became closer so the views they had expressed.

Less-Leads-to-More Effect: The fact that rewards just barely sufficient to induce individuals to state positions contrary to their own views often generate more attitude change than larger rewards.

The less-leads-to-more effect doesn't occur in all cases, however. In order for it to take place, people must feel that they had a choice as to whether to perform the attitude-discrepant behavior and must believe that they were personally responsible both for the chosen course of action and any negative effects it produced (Cooper & Scher, 1990; Goethals, Cooper, & Naficy, 1979). When these conditions exist—and they often do—then the less-leads-to-more effect occurs, and offering individuals small rewards for saying or doing what they don't believe will provide greater attitude change than offering them larger rewards.

Putting Dissonance to Work: Hypocrisy and Safe Sex Many attempts to change our attitudes stem from selfish motives—someone's desire to sell us something, win our vote, and so on. But others stem from more benevolent goals. For example, public service organizations try to get us to stop smoking, wear our safety belts, and to use sunblock when outdoors. Since most people already agree with these suggestions, at least in principle, dissonance would seem to have little bearing on the success of such campaigns. In fact, however, social psychologists believe that dissonance *can* be used to promote these beneficial changes in behavior (e.g., Aronson, 1992). Let's take a closer look at one study that investigated this possibility with respect to promoting safe sexual practices.

In this experiment, Stone and his colleagues (1994) reasoned that most sexually active persons were already in favor of reducing the risk of catching AIDS or other sexually transmitted diseases through safe sexual practices. Despite this fact, however, the researchers felt that they could still use the principle of dissonance to increase actual adoption of these practices, as opposed to mere lip-service endorsement of them. One way of doing this, they reasoned, would be to induce feelings of *hypocrisy* among sexually active persons—feelings that they had said one thing but done another. The researchers sought to produce feelings of hypocrisy by (1) inducing individuals to make a public commitment to some course of action (in this case, using condoms), and (2) reminding them that they had sometimes failed to comply with this commitment. Such feelings, the experimenters believed, would cause a high level of dissonance, and therefore greater willingness to engage only in safe sex.

To test their predictions, Stone and his colleagues (1994) exposed sexually active college students to four conditions. One group—the *commitment* condition—was simply asked to prepare a videotape advocating safe sex. Another—the *mindfulness* condition—was asked only to recall situations in which they had failed to use condoms. Participants in a third group—the *hypocrisy* condition—received both of these treatments: They made a public commitment to safe sex *and* remembered times when they had had not done so. Participants in a control group—the *information only* condition—made no commitment about safe sex and were not asked to recall times when they failed to follow such practices.

After exposure to one of these conditions, each student was given an opportunity to purchase condoms at a reduced price with the money he or she had been paid for taking part in the study. This opportunity was a private one: The experimenter left the room, supposedly to do an errand, leaving each participant alone with the condoms and money for making change. Results indicated that, as predicted, a much higher proportion of participants in the hypocrisy condition than those in the other conditions actually bought condoms (see Figure 16.11 on page 642).

These findings, and those of several related studies (e.g., Aronson, 1992), indicate that inducing individuals to experience hypocrisy—and the strong dissonance this produces—can be an effective means for changing both attitudes and behavior in a desirable direction. In short, it appears, we can sometimes change our own attitudes by saying or doing things we *believe* as well as by saying or doing things we don't believe.

Key Questions

- What are attitudes?
- What factors were found to influence persuasion in early research?
- What is the elaboration likelihood model, and how does it explain persuasion?
- What is cognitive dissonance, and how can it be reduced?
- What is forced compliance? The less-leads-to-more effect?
- How can hypocrisy be used to change behavior?

FIGURE 16.11

Hypocrisy as a Means of Changing Behavior

Individuals who experienced feelings of hypocrisy, because they both made a public commitment to safe sex and were reminded of instances in which they didn't behave in this way, were more likely to buy condoms than individuals who did not experience such feelings. Thus, feelings of hypocrisy produced an important change in their behavior.

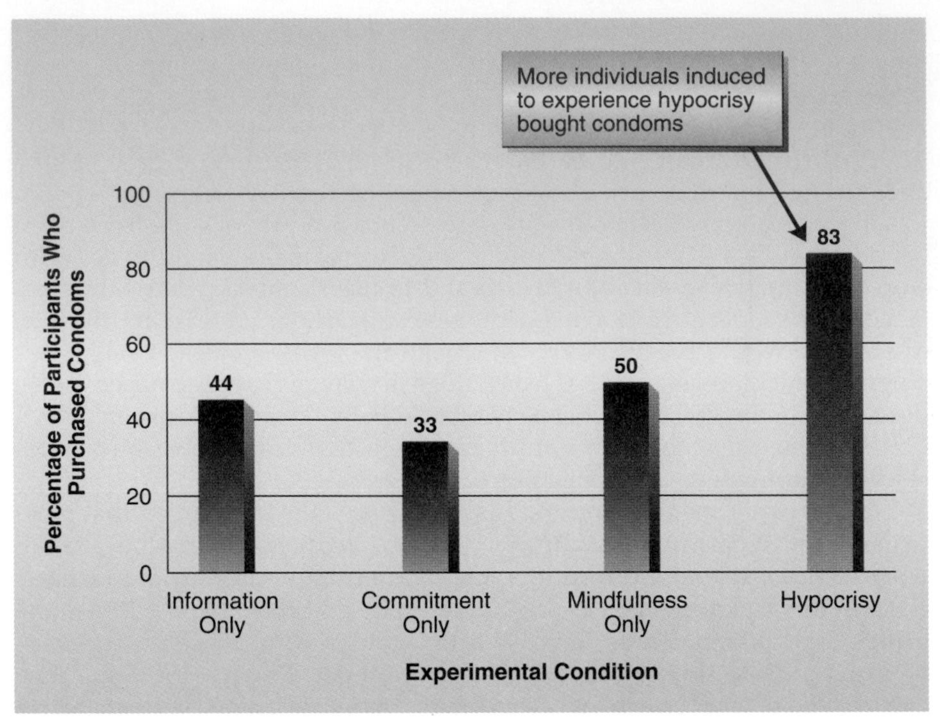

(**Source:** Based on data from Stone et al., 1994.)

Social Behavior: Interacting with Others

Thinking about other people is an important aspect of our social existence; but as you know from your own life, we also *interact* with others in many ways. We work with them on various tasks; we offer them assistance and receive help from them; we attempt to influence others and are on the receiving end of *their* efforts at influence; we fall in and out of love, form and end relationships—the list goes on and on. In this section, we'll consider several important aspects of *social interaction.*

Prejudice: Distorted Views of the Social World . . . and Their Effects

"Ethnic cleansing" in Bosnia; "suicide bombers" who kill themselves and many innocent victims in Israel; mass murder of one ethnic group by another in Africa . . . there seems to be no end to the atrocities stemming from racial, ethnic, and religious hatred. Such actions often stem from **prejudice**—powerful negative attitudes toward the members of a specific social group based solely on their membership in that group (Dovidio & Gaertner, 1986). Where do such attitudes come from? And what can be done to reduce their impact? These are the issues we'll now examine.

Prejudice: Negative attitudes toward the members of some social group based on their membership in this group.

The Origins of Prejudice: Contrasting Perspectives Many different explanations for the origins of prejudice have been proposed. Here are four that have been especially influential.

Direct Intergroup Conflict: Competition as a Source of Bias

It is sad but true that many of the things we value most—a good job, a nice home, high status—are in short supply; there are never enough to go around. This fact serves as the basis for one view of prejudice—**realistic conflict theory** (Bobo, 1983). According to this view, prejudice stems from competition between social groups over valued commodities or opportunities. The theory further suggests that as such competition persists, the members of the groups involved come to view each other in increasingly negative ways (White, 1977). They label members of the other group as enemies, view their own group as superior, and draw the boundaries between themselves and their opponents ever more firmly. As a result, what starts out as economic competition gradually turns into full-scale prejudice, with the hatred and anger this usually implies. Of course, competition between groups does not always produce such effects; but it *does* produce them in enough cases that this factor can be viewed as one important cause of prejudice.

The Us-versus-Them Effect: Social Categorization as a Basis for Prejudice A second perspective on the origins of prejudice begins with a basic fact: We all tend to divide the social world into two distinct categories—*us* and *them* (Turner et al., 1987). We view other persons as belonging either to our own social group, usually termed the *in-group,* or to another group, an *out-group.* We make such distinctions on the basis of many dimensions, including race, religion, sex, age, ethnic background, occupation, and even the town or neighborhood where we live.

If this process of **social categorization**—dividing the world into distinct social categories—stopped there, it would have little connection to prejudice. Unfortunately, it does not. Sharply contrasting feelings and beliefs are usually attached to members of one's in-group and to members of various out-groups. Persons in the "us" category are viewed in favorable terms while those in the "them" category are perceived negatively. Out-group members are seen as being more alike (homogeneous) than members of the in-group, are assumed to possess more undesirable traits, and are often disliked (e.g., Lambert, 1995; Linville & Fischer, 1993). The in-group–out-group distinction also affects *attribution*—explanations for people's behaviors. We tend to attribute desirable behaviors by members of our in-group to stable, internal causes such as their admirable traits, but to attribute desirable behaviors by members of out-groups to temporary factors or to external ones, such as luck (e.g., Hewstone, Bond, & Wan, 1983). So, in sum, our strong tendency to divide the social world into distinct categories of "us" and "them" can be an important basis for prejudice.

The Role of Social Learning A third perspective on the origins of prejudice begins with the obvious fact that prejudice is *learned:* We acquire such attitudes from the people around us through the process of *social learning.* Prejudice emerges out of countless experiences in which children hear or observe their parents, friends, teachers, and others expressing prejudiced views. Because children want to be like these persons, and because they are often rewarded for expressing the "right" views (those held by adults), they quickly adopt such attitudes themselves.

While persons with whom children interact play a key role in this process, the mass media, too, are important. If television, films, and other media present members of various social groups in an unflattering light, these messages may contribute to the development of prejudice on the part of children exposed to them. And in fact African Americans, Asians, Hispanics, and many other minority groups were indeed presented unflatteringly in films and on television in the United States in past decades (see Figure 16.12 on page 644).

Realistic Conflict Theory: A theory proposing that prejudice stems, at least in part, from economic competition between social groups.

Social Categorization: Our tendency to divide the social world into two distinct categories: "us" and "them."

Fortunately, this situation has changed greatly in recent years (e.g., Weigel, Kim, & Frost, 1995); members of these groups are now being shown in a much more favorable manner, for the most part. So at least one important source of prejudiced attitudes seems to be decreasing.

FIGURE 16.12

Minorities and Television: Some Change for the Better

In the past, members of various minority groups were often shown in an unflattering light on television and in films. Recently, however, this situation has changed; today such persons are sometimes shown in a much more favorable manner.

Cognitive Sources of Prejudice: The Role of Stereotypes The final source of prejudice we'll consider is in some ways the most disturbing. It involves the possibility that prejudice stems at least in part from basic aspects of social cognition—from basic ways in which we think about others and process social information (e.g., Kunda & Oleson, 1995). While several processes seems to play a role in this regard, perhaps the most important of these involves **stereotypes.** These are cognitive frameworks consisting of knowledge and beliefs about specific social groups—frameworks suggesting that by and large, all members of these groups possess certain traits, at least to a degree (Judd, Ryan, & Park, 1991). Like other cognitive frameworks (schemas), stereotypes exert strong effects on the ways in which we process social information. For instance, information relevant to a particular stereotype is processed more quickly than information unrelated to it (e.g., Dovidio, Evans, & Tyler, 1986). Similarly, stereotypes lead us to pay attention to specific types of information—usually information consistent with the stereotypes. And when information inconsistent with stereotypes does manage to enter consciousness, it may be actively refuted or simply denied (O'Sullivan & Durso, 1984). In fact, recent findings indicate that when individuals encounter persons who behave in ways contrary to stereotypes, they often perceive them as a new "subtype" rather than as an exception to their existing stereotype (Kunda & Oleson, 1995).

What is the relevance of such effects to prejudice? Together, they tend to make stereotypes somewhat self-confirming. Once an individual has acquired a stereotype about some social group, she or he tends to notice information that fits into this cognitive framework and to remember "facts" that are consistent with it more readily than "facts" inconsistent with it. As a result, the stereotype strengthens with time and may ultimately become invulnerable—new information or experiences simply can't change it.

Given that stereotypes often lead us to serious errors and misjudgments in our social thought, why do they persist? One answer is that they are a kind of labor-saving device where social cognition is concerned (Macrae, Milne, & Bodenhausen, 1994). In other words, they allow us to make quick-and-dirty judgments about others without engaging in complex, effortful thought (e.g., Forgas & Fiedler, 1996). Another possible reason is that they allow us to protect and bolster our social identity (e.g., Brewer, 1993). By perceiving all members of out-groups as alike, and as possessing more negative traits than members of our own in-group, we can boost our own group and our identification with it. Presumably, the greater the threat to our in-group, the stronger such tendencies, and therefore the stronger the relevant stereotypes. One recent study (Ryan, 1996) provides support for these suggestions. Results indicated that African American college students showed stronger stereotypes of white Americans than vice versa, and also tended to show a stronger bias in favor of their own group than did whites. Given the fact that African Americans have often been the target of strong racial prejudice, these findings are hardly surprising. In any case, it appears that stereotypes may serve several different functions; this fact helps account for their persistence.

Stereotypes: Cognitive frameworks suggesting that all members of specific social groups share certain characteristics.

Challenging Prejudice: Techniques That Can Help Whatever the precise roots of prejudice, there can be no doubt that it is a negative, brutal force in human affairs. Reducing prejudice and countering its effects, therefore, are important tasks. What steps can be taken to reach these goals? Here is what the findings of careful research indicate.

Breaking the Cycle of Prejudice: Learning Not to Hate Bigots are clearly made, not born: They acquire their prejudices as a result of learning. Given this fact, one useful way to reduce prejudice involves discouraging the transmission of bigoted views while encouraging more positive attitudes toward others. But how can we induce parents, teachers, and other adults to encourage unbiased views among children in their care? One possibility involves calling the attention of such persons to their own prejudiced views. Few people actually see themselves as prejudiced. Instead, they view *their* negative attitudes toward others as justified. A key initial step, therefore, is convincing caregivers that the problem exists. Once they realize that it does, many are willing to modify their words and actions. True, some die-hard bigots *want* to turn children into hate-filled fanatics. Most people, though, realize that we live in a world of increasing diversity and that attitudes of tolerance are, in the long run, much more adaptive. Thus, campaigns designed to enhance awareness of prejudice and its harmful effects can sometimes be effective (Aronson, 1990).

Another argument that can be used to shift parents and other caregivers in the direction of teaching children tolerance lies in the fact that prejudice harms not only those who are its victims but those who hold such views (Dovidio & Gaertner, 1993). Growing evidence suggests that persons who are prejudiced live in a world filled with needless fears, anxieties, and anger. As a result, they experience needless emotional turmoil that can adversely affect their health (Jussim, 1991). Since most parents and teachers want to do everything possible to further children's well-being, calling these potential costs to their attention may help to persuade them to transmit tolerance rather than prejudice.

Direct Intergroup Contact: The Potential Benefits of Becoming Acquainted Prejudice tends to build social walls between people. Once it exists, members of different ethnic, racial, or religious groups have restricted contact with one another. Such limited contact, in turn, makes it easier for stereotypes to persist. Can this pattern be broken by direct intergroup contact? The **contact hypothesis** suggests that it can (e.g., Schwarzwald, Amir, & Crain, 1992; Stephan, 1987). In order for these beneficial effects to be obtained, contact between groups must occur under the following conditions:

- The groups must be roughly equal in social or task-related status.
- The contact situation must involve cooperation and interdependence so that the groups work toward shared goals.
- Contact between the groups must be informal so they can get to know one another on a one-to-one basis.
- Contact must occur in a setting in which existing norms (generally accepted rules) favor group equality.
- The persons involved must view one another as typical of their respective groups.

When contact between initially hostile groups occurs under these conditions, friendships often form between persons in these groups, and prejudice, in turn, is reduced. Moreover, such reductions in prejudice seem to generalize, so that reduced prejudice toward one group is extended to other groups as well (Pettigrew, 1997). Clearly, then, increased contact between social groups can be one effective means for reducing prejudice.

Contact Hypothesis: The suggestion that increased contact between members of different social groups will reduce prejudice between them.

FIGURE 16.13

Recategorization: Moving the Boundary between "Us" and "Them"

In general, we divide the social world into two categories: "us" and "them." The fans shown here clearly have this division in mind as they cheer for *their* team. This boundary is not fixed, however; it can be moved so as to include groups that were previously viewed as "them."

Recategorization: A technique for reducing prejudice that involves inducing people to shift the boundary between "us" and "them" so that it now includes groups previously viewed as "them."

Sexism: Prejudice based on gender.

Glass Ceiling: A final barrier against female advancement in some organizations that prevents women from attaining top positions.

Social Influence: Efforts by one or more persons to change the attitudes or behavior of one or more others.

Recategorization: Resetting the Boundary between "Us" and "Them" Suppose that a team from your college played against a team from a rival college: Which would be "us" and which would be "them"? The answer is obvious: Your own school's team would constitute your in-group, while the other school's team would be the out-group (see Figure 16.13). But now imagine that the team from the other school had won many games and was chosen to represent your state in a national tournament. When it played against a team from another state, would you now perceive it as "us" or "them"? Probably you would shift your view; now you would see this former "enemy" team as part of your own in-group. Situations like this suggest that the boundary between "us" and "them" is not fixed. On the contrary, it can be shifted so as to include—or exclude—various groups of people. This fact suggests another technique for reducing prejudice, one known as **recategorization** (e.g., Gaertner et al., 1989, 1990). This involves somehow inducing individuals to shift the boundary between "us" and "them" so that it now includes groups they previously viewed as "them." The result: Their prejudice toward these persons is reduced.

Evidence for such effects has been obtained in several research studies (e.g., Dovidio et al., 1995). In one, for example, Gaertner and his colleagues (1993) investigated the attitudes of students at a multicultural high school in the United States. Students came from many different backgrounds—African American, Chinese, Hispanic, Japanese, Korean, Vietnamese, and Caucasian. More than 1,300 students completed a survey designed to measure their perceptions of the extent to which the student body at the school was a single group, consisted of distinct groups, or was composed of separate individuals. Results indicated that the greater the extent to which the students felt that they belonged to a single group, the more positive were their feelings toward persons from backgrounds other than their own. These findings, and those of several related studies (e.g., Gaertner et al., 1990), suggest that recategorization may be a very useful technique for reducing many forms of prejudice.

How do psychologists study prejudice—and, in particular, *sexism,* or prejudice based on gender? For information on this topic, please see the Research Methods section.

Key Questions

- What are some of the major causes of prejudice?
- How can prejudice be reduced?
- What do research findings indicate about the "glass ceiling"?

RESEARCH METHODS

How Psychologists Study Sexism—and the "Glass Ceiling"

Females constitute more than half the world's population. Yet despite this fact, they have been treated like a minority group in many cultures (Fisher, 1992; Heilman, Block, & Lucas, 1992). In the late 1990s this situation is changing to some degree, at least in some countries. Overt discriminatory practices have been banned by laws in many nations, and there has been at least some weakening of negative gender-based stereotypes. Yet **sexism**—prejudice based on gender—persists, often in subtle and hidden forms, such as lower expectations for pay and other benefits among females (e.g., Desmarais & Curtis, 1997). How do psychologists study the nature and impact of concealed forms of prejudice toward women? To answer this question, let's examine how researchers have recently sought to investigate one controversial form of sexism, the **glass ceiling,** which is often defined as a final barrier against female advancement in some organizations that prevents women from attaining top positions (United States Depart-ment of Labor, 1992).

One way of studying the glass ceiling, of course, would be to look for evidence of its existence in labor statistics. Between 1970 and 1992, the proportion of managers who are female rose from 16 percent to more than 42 percent (U.S. Department of Labor, 1992). Yet the proportion of top managers who are women increased only from 3 percent to 5 percent (Fisher, 1992). Is this conclusive evidence for the existence of the glass ceiling? Not really. Several other factors might have contributed to these findings. For instance, it often takes many years for individuals to move up to the top of the ladder in their companies; and the recent trend toward downsizing in many companies may well have increased the length of this period. Since women didn't assume managerial jobs in large numbers until the 1970s and 1980s, it may be simply that not enough time has yet passed for them to have gained representation in top-level jobs. Similarly, it has been found that people in some fields—for instance, finance—generally have a better opportunity to rise to top positions than those in others—for instance, marketing or human resource management (Greenberg & Baron, 1997) and women tend to work in the lower-opportunity fields. This factor too may play a role.

So research to find out whether the glass ceiling is real can't rely solely on such methods. How, then, can it proceed? One approach used in many recent studies involves the *survey method* described in Chapter 1. Investigators have asked thousands of men and women working in many different jobs to complete questionnaires dealing with the nature and causes of the glass ceiling. For example, let's consider a study conducted by Ohlott, Ruderman, and McCauley (1994).

These researchers reasoned that in order to advance their careers, future executives must have a wide range of *developmental opportunities*—job-related experiences that help prepare them for top-level positions (Van Velsor & Hughes, 1990). They then hypothesized that perhaps women receive fewer developmental opportunities than men and that this accounts, at least in part, for their underrepresentation in top-level jobs. To test this reasoning, the researchers had nearly 600 men and women working in many different organizations complete a survey designed to measure the extent to which they had experienced a wide range of developmental opportunities in their jobs—opportunities such as being given new responsibilities different from their previous ones, or being asked to create some kind of change in their company.

Results indicated that in general, males and females did not differ significantly in terms of the developmental opportunities measured. However, a few differences did emerge, and these were ones that the researchers viewed as especially costly to women. Specifically, females reported fewer developmental opportunities that increased their visibility or widened the scope of their responsibilities. In short, they tended *not* to be given key assignments perceived as crucial by their companies—assignments that would teach them the skills they needed and at the same time allow them to demonstrate their competence.

These findings suggest that the glass ceiling is indeed real, and that it stems from factors suggestive of lingering, if subtle, forms of prejudice toward females. While the glass ceiling is not present in all organizations—for example, it has been found to be entirely lacking in some government agencies (Powell & Butterfield, 1994)—its presence in at least some work settings appears to pose an important barrier to female achievement.

Social Influence: Changing Others' Behavior

How many times each day do others try to change your behavior in some way? And how often do *you* try to do this to other persons? If you stop and count, you'll probably come up with a surprisingly large number, for efforts at **social influence**—attempts by one or more persons to change the attitudes or behavior of one or more others—are very common. Social influence takes many different forms. We've already considered one important type—*persuasion*—in our discussion of attitudes. Here, we'll briefly examine three other important forms of influence: *conformity, compliance,* and *obedience.*

Conformity: To Get Along, Often, We Must Go Along Have you ever been in a situation where you felt that you stuck out like a sore thumb? If so, you know how unpleasant the experience can be. In these circumstances we encounter powerful pressures to act or think like those around

FIGURE 16.14

Injunctive Norms: Telling Us What Should Be Done

Injunctive norms indicate what should (or should not) be done in a given situation; they usually leave little room for interpretation.

us. Such pressures toward **conformity**—toward thinking or acting like most other persons—stem from the fact that in many contexts there are spoken or unspoken rules indicating how we *should* behave. These rules are known as **social norms,** and they seem to take two basic forms (Cialdini, Kallgren, & Reno, 1991; Reno, Cialdini, & Kallgren, 1993). *Descriptive norms* tell us what most people do in a given situation; they inform us about what is generally seen as appropriate or adaptive behavior in that situation. In contrast, *injunctive norms* specify what *should* (or should not) be done, not merely what most people do. For instance, suppose you find yourself in a park where there are many people picnicking, but not one shred of paper is blowing around; instead, all the trash cans are filled. The descriptive norm is clear: Most people don't litter in that park. But now suppose that you encounter a sign like the one in Figure 16.14. Clearly, this presents an injunctive norm: It tells you that littering is forbidden and that if you do it, you may be punished with a stiff fine. Some injunctive norms can be explicit and precise—for example, written constitutions, athletic rule books, traffic signs. Others, in contrast—such as "Don't stare at strangers on the street"—are implicit; yet they exert powerful effects on us. Whatever form they take, most social norms are obeyed by most persons most of the time (Cialdini, 1988).

Is this necessarily bad? Not at all; if most people didn't follow such rules on most occasions, we would live in social chaos. Persons waiting to pay for their purchases in stores would not form lines; motorists would drive on whichever side the road they preferred; people would come to work or meetings whenever they felt like it. So norms and the conformity they produce are a necessary part of social life. Only when they enforce needless uniformity do they seem objectionable. For instance, when I was a graduate student in the mid-1960s, most universities had dress codes requiring female students to wear skirts or dresses to class. Winters were severe in Iowa (where I did my graduate studies), so you can imagine the discomfort this caused to many young women who would have preferred to wear pants. In cases in which the norms (rules) in question seem to serve no purpose, many people object to conformity—and well they should.

Compliance: To Ask—Sometimes—Is to Receive Suppose you wanted someone to do something for you; how would you go about getting them to do it? If you think about this question for a moment, you'll soon realize that you probably have quite a few tricks up your sleeve for getting the other person to say yes—for gaining what social psychologists term **compliance.** What are these techniques like? Which ones work best? To gain insight into these questions, one social psychologist, Robert Cialdini, decided that he would study what he termed *compliance professionals*—people who make getting others to say yes their life's work. Who are such persons? They include salespeople, advertisers, lobbyists, fund-raisers, politicians, and con artists, to name a few. To study these people, Cialdini concealed his identity and took temporary jobs in several of these fields. On the basis of this research, he concluded that although there are many different techniques for gaining compliance with our wishes, they all rest to some extent on the basic principles shown in Table 16.1 (Cialdini, 1994). Please examine this table carefully, because I'll be referring to these principles in the rest of this discussion, as I describe a small sample of the many tactics people use for gaining compliance.

Tactics Based on Friendship or Liking: Ingratiation Several tactics we use for gaining compliance from others involve causing them to have positive feelings toward or about us. Among these, **ingratiation**—causing others to like us—is perhaps the most common (e.g., Liden & Mitchell, 1988). How do we accomplish this task? In general, in two basic ways. First, we may engage in various *self-enhancing tactics,* ones designed to enhance our personal

Conformity: A type of social influence in which individuals change their attitudes or behavior in order to adhere to existing social norms.

Social Norms: Rules indicating how individuals ought to behave in specific situations.

Compliance: A form of social influence in which one or more persons acquiesce to direct requests from one or more others.

Ingratiation: A technique for gaining compliance by causing others to like us before we attempt to influence them.

TABLE 16.1

Basic Principles behind Compliance

Research findings indicate that most techniques for gaining compliance rest, to some extent, on the principles shown here.

Principle	Description
Friendship/Liking	In general, we are more willing to comply with requests from friends or from people we like than with requests from strangers or people we don't like.
Commitment/ Consistency	Once we have committed ourselves to a position or action, we are more willing to comply with requests for behaviors that are consistent with that position.
Reciprocity	We are generally more willing to comply with a request from someone who has previously provided a favor or concession to us than with a request from someone who has not.
Scarcity	We value and try to secure opportunities, people, or objects that are scarce or decreasing. As a result, we are more likely to comply with requests that focus on the scarcity of such items than with ones that do not.
Authority	We value authority, so are usually more willing to comply with requests from someone who is a legitimate authority or who simply seems to be one.

(**Source**: Based on suggestions by Cialdini, 1994.)

appeal. These tactics include making ourselves as physically attractive as possible, showing friendliness toward the target person, and associating ourselves with positive events or people the target person already likes. Second, we often engage in *other-enhancing tactics,* such as flattering target persons, agreeing with them, or showing interest in them. All these tactics seem to work—they induce increased liking for us and therefore greater compliance (e.g., Wayne & Liden, 1995). However, if they are obvious or overdone, they may fail or even backfire, causing others to *dislike* us rather than to like us.

Foot-in-the-Door Technique: A technique for gaining compliance in which a small request is followed by a much larger one.

Tactics Based on Commitment or Consistency: The Foot in the Door and the Lowball Cialdini (1994) observed that experts in compliance (such as salespersons and fund-raisers) often start with a trivial request and then, when this is accepted, move on to a larger request—the one they really wanted all along. This is known as the **foot-in-the-door technique,** and the chances are good that you have encountered it, or even used it yourself (see Figure 16.15 for an example). Research findings indicate that it really works (e.g., Beaman et al., 1983), and that one reason it does is that people want to be consistent. Once they have said yes to the first request, they feel

(**Source:** Reprinted with permission of King Features Syndicate.)

FIGURE 16.15

The Foot in the Door in Action

The foot-in-the-door technique involves starting with a small request and then, when this is granted, shifting to a much larger one. The teenager shown here is well aware of this tactic!

it is inconsistent to say no to the second, and so they experience subtle pressure to comply.

Another technique based on this principle of consistency or commitment is known as the **lowball procedure.** In this technique, a salesperson offers a very attractive deal to a customer. After this person accepts, something happens that makes it "necessary" for the salesperson to change the deal—for example, the sales manager rejects it. The rational thing for the customer to do in such situations is to walk away. Yet people often agree to changes in the deal they have accepted—because by agreeing to the deal they made an initial commitment, which they now find hard to change.

Tactics Based on Reciprocity: The Door-in-the-Face and the That's-Not-All Approach Reciprocity is a basic rule of social life: We tend to treat other people as they have treated us. Several tactics for gaining compliance are based on this fact. One of these, known as the **door-in-the-face technique,** is the opposite of the foot-in-the-door technique. Instead of beginning with a small request and then escalating to a larger one, a person employing this tactic starts with a very large request. After that request is refused, a much smaller one is made—the one the requester wanted all along. The target person then feels a subtle pressure to reciprocate by saying yes. After all, the requester made a concession by scaling down the first request. This tactic is often successful, and its success seems to rest largely on the principle of reciprocity (Cialdini, 1994).

A related procedure for gaining compliance, known as the **that's-not-all technique,** uses the following approach. An initial request is followed, before the target person can make up her or his mind, by something that sweetens the deal—a little "extra" from the person using this tactic. For example, auto dealers sometimes throw in a small additional option like floor mats in order to close a deal. The option is usually tiny in comparison to the total value of the car, but it works: Customers feel compelled to reciprocate for this "extra" by saying yes.

Tactics Based on Scarcity: Playing Hard to Get and the Fast-Approaching-Deadline Technique In general, the rarer or the harder to obtain something is, the more valuable it is perceived to be. This basic fact serves as the underlying principle for several tactics for gaining compliance. Perhaps the most common of these is **playing hard to get**—a tactic in which individuals try to create the impression that they are very popular or very much in demand. This puts pressure on romantic partners and employers, for example, to say yes to requests from the person using this tactic. The requests can range from "Let's get engaged" to "Pay me a high salary," but the underlying principle is the same: The persons on the receiving end feel that if they don't agree, they may lose a valuable partner or employee—so they often say yes (e.g., Williams et al., 1993).

A related technique based on the same "what's-scarce-is-valuable" principle is the **fast-approaching-deadline technique.** Here, a deadline is established after which, presumably, it will be impossible for the target person to obtain something—an item for sale, the company of a romantic partner, or the services of a prospective employee, for instance. Each spring I see this technique in operation in local department stores. The stores run ads stating "Final Sale" or "Final Clearance," and imply that winter merchandise now on sale will be gone in a matter of days. In fact, the merchandise is often there long after the announced date for the end of the sale, but this doesn't prevent the tactic from working.

I could go on to discuss other means for gaining compliance, but by now the main point should be clear: Many of these procedures seem to rest on basic principles long studied and well understood by psychologists. The suc-

Lowball Procedure: A tactic for gaining compliance in which, after a deal or arrangement is made, the terms are changed by the person using this tactic.

Door-in-the-Face Technique: A technique for gaining compliance in which a large request is followed by a smaller one.

That's-Not-All Technique: A technique for gaining compliance in which a small extra incentive is offered before target persons have agreed to or rejected a request.

Playing Hard to Get: A tactic for gaining compliance in which individuals try to create the impression that they are very popular or very much in demand.

Fast-Approaching-Deadline Technique: A technique for gaining compliance in which a "deadline" is established after which it will be impossible for the target person to obtain something.

Obedience: A form of social influence in which one or more individuals behave in specific ways in response to direct orders from someone.

cess of crack salespeople, fund-raisers, and others in getting us to say yes to their requests is, therefore, no mystery: These people are simply good applied psychologists, whether they realize it or not!

Obedience: Social Influence by Demand Perhaps the most direct way in which one person can attempt to change the behavior of another is through *direct orders*—simply telling the target person what to do. This approach is less common than either conformity pressure or compliance tactics, but it is far from rare; it occurs in many situations where one person has clear authority over another—in the military, in sports, and in business, to name a few. **Obedience** to the commands of sources of authority is not surprising; superior officers, coaches, and executives have powerful means for enforcing their commands. More surprising, though, is the fact that even persons lacking in such authority can sometimes induce high levels of obedience in others. Unsettling evidence for such effects was first reported by Stanley Milgram in a series of famous—and controversial—experiments (Milgram, 1963, 1974).

FIGURE 16.16

Milgram's Research on Obedience

The photo on the left shows the apparatus used by Milgram in his famous studies. The photo on the right shows the experimenter and a participant (rear) attaching electrodes to the learner's (accomplice's) wrists. Results of the research, shown in the graph, indicated that fully 65 percent of all the participants were fully obedient to the experimenter's commands—they advanced to the highest shock level.

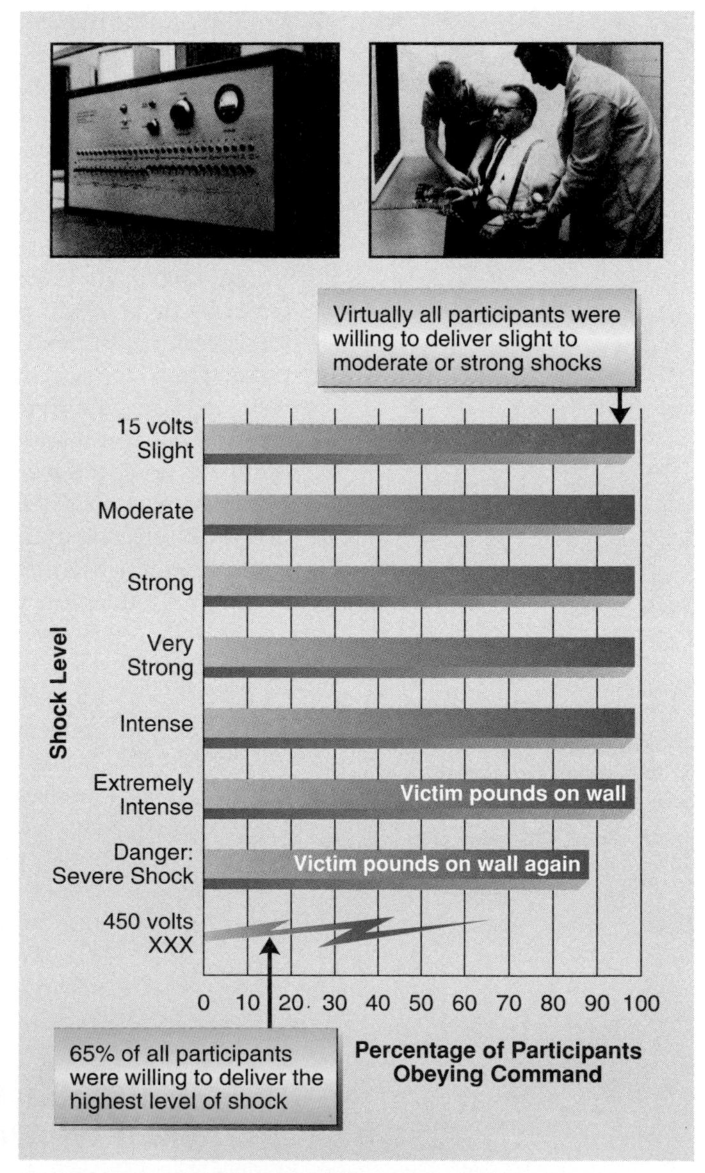

(**Source:** Photos from the film *Obedience*, Copyright 1965 by Stanley Milgram; data based on Milgram, 1963.)

Destructive Obedience: Basic Findings In order to find out whether individuals would obey commands from a relatively powerless stranger, Milgram designed ingenious procedures. Participants were told that they were taking part in a study on the effects of punishment on learning. Their role was to deliver electric shocks to a male "learner" (actually, an accomplice of the researcher) each time he made an error in a simple learning task. These shocks were delivered by means of switches on a special device, and participants were told to move to the next higher switch each time the learner made an error. The first switch purportedly delivered a shock of 15 volts, the second a shock of 30, and so on up to the last switch, which supposedly delivered a shock of 450 volts—one that might well prove fatal to some people. In reality, of course, *the accomplice never received any shocks during the study.* The only real shock was a mild pulse from button number three used to convince participants that the equipment was real.

During the session, the learner made many prearranged errors, so participants soon faced a dilemma: Should they continue delivering increasingly strong shocks to this person, or refuse to continue? The experimenter didn't make this decision easy: He pressured them to continue at several points. Since participants were volunteers and were paid in advance, you might predict that most would quickly refuse such "orders." In reality, though, *fully 65 percent were fully obedient,* continuing through the entire series to the final 450-volt shock (see Figure 16.16).

Of course, many persons protested and expressed concern over the learner's welfare. When ordered to proceed, however, most yielded to the experimenter's social influence and continued to obey. In fact, they did so even when the victim pounded on the wall as if in protest against the shocks he was receiving. Similar findings have been obtained in studies conducted around the world (Jordan, Germany, Australia) and with children as well as adults; so the tendency to obey commands from even a powerless source of authority appears to be frighteningly general in scope (e.g., Kilham & Mann, 1974; Shanab & Yahya, 1977).

Destructive Obedience: Why Does It Occur, and How Can It Be Resisted? Milgram's results are very disturbing. The parallels between the behavior of participants in his studies and atrocities against civilians during time of war are clear. In fact, Milgram conducted his research, in part, to try to determine how seemingly normal German soldiers could have obeyed commands from their officers to murder helpless civilians during World War II. Why were the participants in these experiments so ready to yield to the commands of an experimenter—a person who in reality had little or no power over them? Several factors probably played a role.

First, the experimenter began by explaining that he, not the participants, would be responsible for the learner's well-being. So, just as in many real-life situations where soldiers or police commit atrocities, participants could say "I was only following orders" (e.g., Hans, 1992; Kelman & Hamilton, 1989). Second, the experimenter possessed clear signs of authority; and in most societies, people learn that persons holding authority are to be obeyed (Bushman, 1984, 1988). Third, the experimenter's commands were gradual in nature. He didn't request that participants jump to the 450-volt shock immediately; rather, he moved toward this request one step at a time. This is similar to many real-life situations in which police or military personnel are initially ordered merely to arrest or question people. Only later are they ordered to beat, torture, or even kill them.

In sum, several factors probably contributed to the high levels of obedience observed in Milgram's research and related studies. Together, these factors produced a powerful force—one that most persons found difficult to resist. This does not imply that the commands of authority figures cannot be resisted, however. In fact, history is filled with cases in which brave persons resisted the commands—and the power—of entrenched dictators and governments and, in the end, triumphed over them. The United States, of course, began with an act of rebellion against the British government. And the events of the past decade in the former Soviet Union and throughout Eastern Europe provide clear illustrations of the fact that even powerful regimes can be resisted. What factors contribute to the ability of people to disobey authority figures? Careful research on the nature of obedience indicates that important factors include clear evidence that the persons in authority are pursuing purely selfish goals (Saks, 1992); feelings of increased personal responsibility for the outcomes produced on the part of those who disobey (Hamilton, 1978); and exposure to *disobedient models*—persons who lead others by taking the dangerous first steps. When such conditions exist, persons in authority may lose their capacity to command—and may quickly find themselves on the outside looking in. For an overview of steps *you* can take to protect yourself against various tactics of social influence, see the **Ideas to Take with You** feature.

Key Questions

- What is conformity, and what role do social norms play in it?
- What are some of the basic principles on which many different tactics for gaining compliance are based?
- What is obedience, and how can it be reduced?

Prosocial Behavior: When We Help . . . and When We Don't

In Chapter 10 we examined *aggression*, a form of social behavior in which individuals attempt to harm others (Baron & Richardson, 1994). Here, to balance

Ideas to Take with You

Resisting Social Influence: Some Useful Steps

Keeping these points in mind may help you to resist attempts at social influence in many different situations.

Resisting Persuasion

1. Determine whether the people trying to persuade you have something to gain from doing so. If they do, watch out—and be skeptical.
2. Beware of appeals that are designed to arouse strong emotions in you—these are usually a setup for persuasion.
3. As the would-be persuader presents her or his arguments, think of reasons why they may not be true—in other words, don't listen passively: Counterargue in your own mind.

Resisting Conformity Pressure

1. Ask yourself: Do I really *have* to act like everyone else? What happens if I don't?
2. Ask yourself: Is there any benefit to conforming in this situation or context? Or am I just going along because it's easier?
3. Ask: Do the norms make sense—or do they cause me and others discomfort, inconvenience, or worse?

Resisting Compliance

1. Be on guard against committing yourself too quickly; and if you do make a commitment, be ready to change it if the other person tries to change the deal or arrangement.
2. Watch out for false friendliness or for someone who always seems to agree with you—they may be using ingratiation.
3. Don't reciprocate trivial concessions; they may be setups.
4. Just because you agreed to a small request doesn't mean that you must feel obligated to agree to a larger one.
5. Be on guard when someone mentions a deadline—it may be phony!

Resisting False Sources of Authority

1. Always ask: Is this person *really* a source of authority? Or is he or she just pretending to be one?
2. Ask yourself: What happens if I disobey? Does this person really have any authority over me—or just the image of authority?
3. Ask yourself: *Why* does this person want me to obey—for purely selfish reasons, or for better ones?

the picture, we'll focus on behavior that is in some respects the opposite: **prosocial behavior.** Such behavior involves actions that benefit others without necessarily providing any direct benefit to the persons performing them (e.g., Batson & Weeks, 1996). Why does prosocial behavior occur? In other words, what motives underlie it? What factors tend to enhance or reduce its occurrence? And how do people react to being helped? These are the kinds of questions social psychologists have asked about such behavior, and the ones we'll now consider.

Why Does Prosocial Behavior Occur? Possible Motives for Helping Others Helping others is a common aspect of everyday life. Yet, if you take a step back from this fact, it is also a puzzling form of behavior. Why, after all, should we help others in situations where we expect little or nothing in return? This is a complex issue, and one to which there is as yet no final answer. However, research findings have identified three possible motives as the ones most likely to play a role.

The first of these involves the unselfish motive to help others who are in need of our help. This is known as the **empathy–altruism hypothesis,** and it suggests that when we encounter people who need help, we experience *empathy*—we somehow share their feelings or needs—and so are motivated to help them. Their needs, not our own, are of primary importance, and we act accordingly: We help them (e.g., Batson, 1991).

A second, and sharply contrasting, possibility is known as the **negative state relief hypothesis** (e.g., Fultz, Schaller, & Cialdini, 1988). According to this view, when we see another person in need of help, this induces negative feelings in us. To relieve these, we help the person. Notice that although the result is the same—we offer our assistance—the motivation underlying this action is very different. We are concerned with *our* feelings, and we help not because we care about or empathize with the other person, but simply because helping them makes us feel better.

Finally, a third view emphasizes the role of genetic factors. According to this **genetic determinism hypothesis,** we help others because doing so increases the likelihood that our genes—or ones similar to them—will be passed on to the next generation (e.g., Browne, 1992; Burnstein, Crandall, & Kitayama, 1994). According to this view, then, we will offer help only to others who are somehow similar to ourselves and therefore likely to share some of our genes. Thus, we are especially likely to offer help to people who are related to us rather than to total strangers.

Figure 16.17 provides an overview of these three explanations for helping. Which of these views is most accurate? While existing evidence is mixed, it seems fair to state that there is more support for the empathy–altruism hypothesis than for the others. In many cases, it seems, we help others in need of assistance because we empathize with them and experience an unselfish motivation to help them (e.g., Batson & Weeks, 1996; Shaw, Batson, & Todd, 1994). However, some findings do support each of the other views, too (e.g., Burnstein et al., 1994; Cialdini et al., 1987). Thus, the most reasonable conclusion is that helping does often stem from empathy toward others and an unselfish desire to aid them, but that it may also sometimes stem from more selfish motives as well.

Prosocial Behavior: Actions that benefit others without necessarily providing any direct benefit to the persons who perform them.

Empathy–Altruism Hypothesis: A view suggesting that when we encounter someone who needs help, we experience empathy and as a result are motivated to help them in an unselfish manner.

Negative State Relief Hypothesis: A view suggesting that we sometimes help others in order to relieve the negative feelings that their plight arouses in us.

Genetic Determinism Hypothesis: The view that we help other persons who are similar or related to us because this increases the likelihood of our genes, or related genes, being passed on to the next generation.

Factors That Increase or Reduce the Tendency to Help Others Now that we've examined some of the potential motives behind prosocial behavior, let's consider some of the situational factors that have been found to increase or reduce the likelihood that it will occur.

The Bystander Effect: Why There's Not Always Safety in Numbers Suppose that one night you heard through your open window

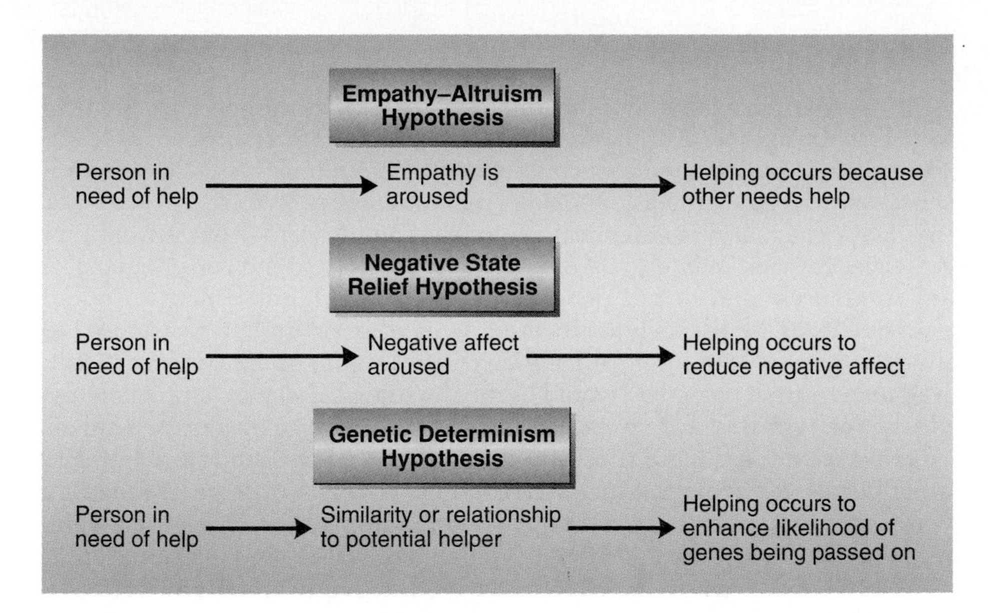

FIGURE 16.17

Three Possible Motives for Prosocial Behavior

As shown here, prosocial behavior may potentially stem from very different motives.

the voice of a young woman calling for help—"Help me! Someone help me! He's killing me!" What would you do? While it's easy to say, "I'd call the police," or "I'd go outside to see what was happening," this is *not* what happened in one famous incident that occurred in New York City in the mid-1960s. A young woman was returning home from her job when she was attacked by a man with a knife. She ran; he caught her and stabbed her repeatedly. She screamed for help; but although lights came on in many windows of nearby buildings, no one actually came to her aid. The result: Her attacker, who at first fled, returned and finished murdering his victim.

Why did no one help or even phone the police? What invisible barriers prevented all those witnesses from offering their help? Two social psychologists, John Darley and Bibb Latané, offered an answer (1968). They reasoned that no one came to the victim's aid because all the witnesses assumed that *someone else would do it.* In other words, in this case there was *danger,* not safety, in numbers. Darley and Latané termed this the **bystander effect.** They reasoned that it occurred, in part, because of *diffusion of responsibility* among the many witnesses: The responsibility for helping was shared, and in this case it was shared with so many other potential helpers that no one acted.

This reasoning was soon confirmed in many different experiments in which participants were exposed to various kinds of staged emergencies—fires, the collapse of another participant, an accident (e.g., Darley & Latané, 1968; Cramer et al., 1988). In these studies the number of apparent bystanders or witnesses was systematically varied; and in every case, the more bystanders present, the less likely were participants in the research to offer help.

Further support for the view that diffusion of responsibility plays a key role in such situations is the finding that the higher the population density in various cities, the lower the incidence of spontaneous helping behavior in them (Levine et al., 1994). And it is not the size of the city that matters; rather, its *population density*—the number of people per square mile—is crucial. So, to repeat, in many cases there appears to be danger, not safety, in numbers; because when many potential helpers witness an emergency, the responsibility for helping is shared—or, in at least some instances, totally dissipated.

Bystander Effect: A reduced tendency of witnesses to an emergency to help when they believe that there are other potential helpers present.

Mood and Prosocial Behavior

Are you more likely to help or do a favor for someone when you are in a good mood or in a bad mood? Common sense offers a simple answer: when you are in a good mood. But in fact the situation is somewhat more complex than this. Yes, people in a good mood *are* often more willing to help others than persons in a neutral or bad mood (e.g., Isen, 1987). For example, in one of my own recent studies (Baron, 1997), we went to a large shopping mall and measured shoppers' willingness to help a stranger who approached them and asked for change for a dollar. This request was made in parts of the mall where pleasant smells were present in the air—the aromas of baking bread or cookies or roasting coffee—or in other areas that were identical except that no pleasant aromas were present. Previous research (e.g., Baron & Thomley, 1994) had indicated that pleasant fragrances tend to put people in a good mood, and when we asked participants in the research to rate their own current mood, those exposed to the pleasant smells did report feeling significantly happier. Given this fact, we predicted that passersby would be more willing to help the stranger when pleasant fragrances were present than when they were absent, and this is what we found (see Figure 16.18). Similar results have been found in many other studies, in which participants have been placed in a good mood by watching a comedy, finding a coin in a phone booth, or receiving a small gift: In each case, persons in a good mood were more helpful (e.g., Wilson, 1981).

But there are some complications in this seemingly straightforward picture. What about situations in which helping involves something more than giving person change for a dollar or picking up some papers a stranger has dropped? What if, instead, it involves helping someone who is covered with blood, or someone who is being sick all over themselves? In such cases, will people in a good mood actually be less likely to help because they don't want to do anything to disturb their happy feelings? In fact, the findings of some studies indicate that this is so: When helping might spoil a good mood, people in a good mood are less likely to help than those in a neutral or negative mood (Shaffer & Graziano, 1983).

Finally, what about being in a bad mood—what effects does this have on helping? Common sense suggests that being in a bad mood would reduce prosocial behavior, and research findings confirm this prediction—but again, only under some conditions. When potential helpers focus on their own needs or misfortunes, they are indeed less likely to help others than persons in a good mood. But when helping another has the potential for making the helpers feel good—for countering their current negative mood by, for example, boosting their self-image—then the opposite may be true: People in a bad mood may actually be more helpful (e.g., Cialdini, Kenrick, & Bauman, 1982; Cunningham et al., 1990).

In sum, the tendency to engage in prosocial behavior is often strongly influenced by our current moods. The direction of such effects, however, depends on several factors, so that under various circumstances helping can be increased by both good and bad moods, or reduced by these same emotional states.

FIGURE 16.18

Mood and Helping: Some Recent Evidence

Shoppers who were approached by a stranger and asked for change for a dollar were more willing to help when there were pleasant smells in the air (e.g., baked bread or cookies) than when such smells were absent. These findings are consistent with the view that being in a good mood sometimes increases our willingness to help others.

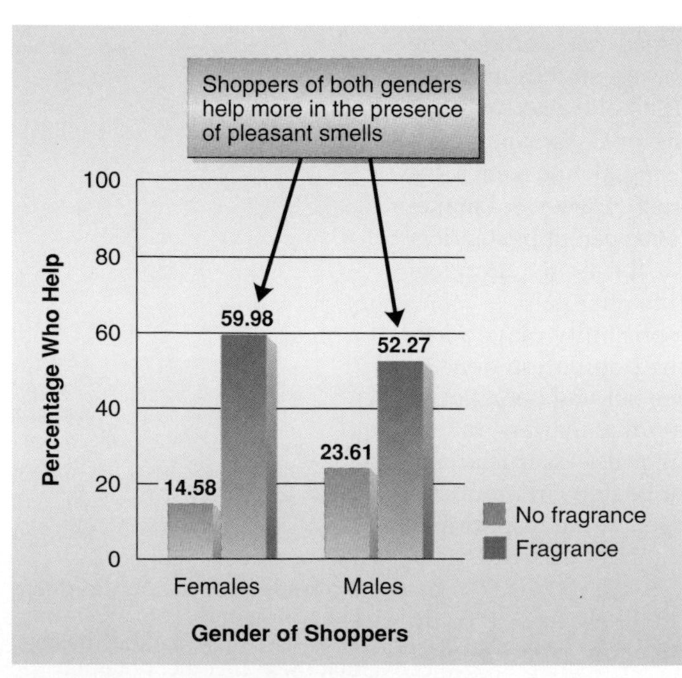

(**Source:** Based on data from Baron, 1997.)

Reactions to Being Helped: Not Always Positive

Do you find it easy to ask others for help? Many people do not, for two important reasons. First, in many Western cultures there is a strong emphasis on being independent: on doing your own thing without interference—or help—from others. Asking for help runs counter to that value and makes many people uneasy (Baron & Byrne, 1997). Second, when we ask another person for help, this puts us in an unfavorable light: It subtly implies that we can't cope with the current situation, or that the other person is somehow smarter, stronger, or more knowledgeable than we are (Nadler, 1987; Yates, 1992). For this reason, too, many people are often reluctant to ask for help.

What about reactions to the help itself? Are these always positive? Again, the answer is no. Help may sometimes be offered to us in a completely unselfish way, with no strings attached. But often there *are* such strings, and we are well aware of them. At the least, being helped by another person places us in their debt: We know we should reciprocate in the future. In addition, we are aware of the fact that help from others may sometimes stem from motives even worse than wanting to put us in their debt. In fact, as noted recently by Gilbert and Silvera (1996), other persons sometimes offer us help in order to undermine our image—to make us look less competent than we really are. Gilbert and Silvera term this tactic **overhelping** and suggest that it is sometimes used by persons who want to make another individual "look bad."

Here's how it works: A person offers help that won't really be beneficial to the person who receives it, but that will be seen as potentially helpful by observers. As a result, if the recipient performs well, observers attribute part of this success to the "help" this person received. Thus, the recipient of the unwanted and unneeded help gets less credit for a good performance than would otherwise have been true. Gilbert and Silvera (1996) demonstrated such effects in a study where participants received information about the performance of a stranger on an anagrams (scrambled letters) task. The participants also learned that the test taker had been given either lots of help or very little help on the task. Then participants were asked to indicate their impressions of the test taker. As predicted, they down-rated the abilities of the test taker who was overhelped.

In sum, receiving help from others seems to be something of a mixed blessing. On the one hand, assistance from others can meet genuine needs and be of great value. On the other, it can carry unwanted obligations, and can reduce both recipients' self-esteem and their social image.

Key Questions

- How do the empathy–altruism, negative state relief, and genetic determinism hypotheses explain prosocial behavior?
- What is the bystander effect, and why does it occur?
- How does mood affect helping?
- How do people react to being helped by others?

Attraction and Love

According to the lyrics of one old song, "Love makes the world go round." And most people agree: **love**—an intense emotional state involving attraction, sexual desire, and deep concern for another person—exerts a profound influence on our lives (Hecht, Marston, & Larkey, 1994; Hendrick & Hendrick, 1993). In this section, we'll examine what psychologists have discovered about love. Before turning to love, however, we'll first consider the nature of *interpersonal attraction*—our degree of liking or disliking for the many people we meet.

Interpersonal Attraction: Why We Like or Dislike Others

Think of someone you like very much, someone you strongly dislike, and someone you'd place in the middle on this dimension. Now, ask yourself this question: *Why* do you have these reactions? Revealing answers are provided by research on the nature and causes of liking and disliking, or **interpersonal attraction.**

Overhelping: Helping others when they don't really need it in order to make them appear less competent than they really are.

Love: An intense emotional state involving attraction, sexual desire, and deep concern for another person.

Interpersonal Attraction: The extent to which we like or dislike other persons.

Propinquity: Nearness Makes the Heart Grow Fonder Many friendships and romances start when individuals are brought into contact with one another, often by chance. We tend to form relationships with people who sit nearby in class, live in our dorm or in our neighborhood, or work in the same office. So *propinquity*—proximity or physical closeness to others—is an

Repeated Exposure Effect: The fact that the more frequently we are exposed to various stimuli (at least up to a point), the more we tend to like them.

important factor in interpersonal attraction. In one sense, this *has* to be true because we can't form relationships with people we never meet! But there seems to be much more to the effects of propinquity than this. Many studies indicate that the more frequently we are exposed to a given stimulus, the more—in general—we tend to like it. This is known as the **repeated exposure effect,** and it seems to extend to people as well as to objects (e.g., Moreland & Beach, 1992; Zajonc, 1968). So the more often we encounter other people, the more we tend to like them—assuming that everything else is equal.

Why does this occur? Apparently because the more frequently we encounter a stimulus, the more familiar it becomes, and therefore the more comfortable or pleasant we feel in its presence. For this reason, propinquity is one important basis for interpersonal attraction.

Similarity: Liking Others Who Are Like Ourselves You've probably heard both of the following proverbs: "Birds of a feather flock together" and "Opposites attract." Which is true? Existing evidence leaves little room for doubt: similarity wins hands down (e.g., Alicke & Largo, 1995; Byrne, 1971). Moreover, this is so whether such similarity relates to attitudes and beliefs, to personality traits, to personal habits such as drinking and smoking, to sexual preferences, to whether people accept traditional or less-traditional gender roles, or even to whether they are morning or evening persons (see Chapter 4; Joiner, 1994; Pilkington & Lydon, 1997).

Why do we like others who are similar to ourselves? The most plausible explanation is that such persons provide validation for our views or our personal characteristics (Goethals, 1986). That is, if another person agrees with us or is similar to us in behavior, this indicates that our views, preferences, and actions are correct—or at least that they are shared by someone else. This makes us feel good, and our liking for the other person increases. Whatever the precise mechanisms involved, similarity is certainly one powerful determinant of attraction.

Physical Attractiveness: Beauty May Be Only Skin Deep, but We Pay Lots of Attention to Skin Perhaps the most obvious factor affecting interpersonal attraction is *physical beauty.* Research findings indicate that, alas, we are indeed suckers for a pretty or handsome face (e.g., Collins & Zebrowitz, 1995; Sprecher & Duck, 1994). Moreover, this is true for both women and men, although the effects seem to be somewhat stronger for males (Feingold, 1990; Pierce, 1992). Why is this the case? One reason is that physically attractive people make us feel good—and this may be one important ingredient in liking (Kenrick et al., 1993). Another, suggested by evolutionary psychology (e.g., Buss, 1997), is that physical attractiveness is associated with good health and good reproductive capacity; choosing attractive mates, therefore, is one strategy for increasing our chances of contributing our genes to the next generation.

Whatever the causes, we do tend to like physically attractive persons more than physically unattractive ones. Moreover, such effects occur across the entire life span (Singh, 1993). Indeed, even one-year-old infants show a preference for attractive rather than unattractive strangers (Langlois, Roggman, & Riser-Danner, 1990). But what, precisely, makes other persons physically attractive? Clearly, concepts of beauty vary from culture to culture—but, surprisingly, less than you might guess. People tend to agree on what is or is not attractive even when judging other persons who differ from themselves in terms of race or ethnic background (Cunningham et al., 1995). So, to repeat, what makes another person physically attractive? An intriguing study conducted recently by Ashmore, Solomon, and Longo (1996) provides some revealing insights into this issue.

These researchers gave male and female college students ninety-six photos of fashion models—young women who, as the authors put it, earn their living by being beautiful—and asked the students to sort these into piles on the basis of similarity of looks. Because participants were free to sort the photos in any way they chose, the researchers reasoned that by examining the photos placed in the different piles, they could learn much about the key dimensions people use in judging beauty. Ashmore and his colleagues predicted that physical beauty would be found to involve several different dimensions, and results strongly supported this view. Three dimensions were present in the sortings of both males and females: sexy–not sexy, cute–not cute, and trendy–not trendy. In addition, males' sortings revealed an additional dimension, one involving judgments of intelligence or elegance. Further analysis of participants' sortings of the photos suggested that these dimensions were related both to specific physical attributes and to behaviors shown, although such patterns were clearer for females than for males. For instance, the "sexy" dimension was related to lack of clothes and to suggestive poses in the photos shown; the "cute" dimension was related to smiling and being shown in a comfortable, relaxed pose; and "trendy" was associated with dark hair and wearing lots of accessories. Overall, the findings obtained by Ashmore and his colleagues (1996) suggest that physical beauty is not a unitary characteristic; rather, in judging others' attractiveness, we tend to focus on several different dimensions. One final point: These findings apply only to judgments of females' physical beauty; further research is needed to identify the dimensions females and males use in judging the physical attractiveness of males.

Other, and perhaps more surprising, findings suggest that faces are perceived as attractive when they don't depart in any pronounced way from the "typical" face in their culture. To test this assertion, Langlois and Roggman (1990) constructed composite faces from photos of different individuals. They found that the more faces they used in constructing the composites—that is, the more "average" the composites became—the more attractive the faces were rated as being.

Judgments of attractiveness do not depend solely on facial features, however. They are also influenced by other aspects of people's appearance. For example, there is currently a strong bias against being overweight in many Western cultures; in view of this fact, it's not surprising that *physique* is another important determinant of attraction, at least among young people. Persons whose physique matches the popular model—currently, slim but muscular—tend to receive higher evaluations than do persons who depart from this model (e.g., Ryckman et al., 1995). Such effects appear to be independent of other aspects of appearance. For example, in one ingenious study, Gardner and Tockerman (1994) used a computer to vary the apparent physique (as shown in photos) of several men and women. Results indicated that when these persons were made to appear overweight, they were rated as less attractive than when they were shown to be of normal weight or very slim.

In sum, physical attractiveness plays an important role in our liking or disliking for others, and several features—facial and otherwise—enter into our judgments of what is and what is not attractive.

Love: The Most Intense Form of Attraction Are you currently in love? In a recent survey of 1,000 American adults, nearly 75 percent indicated that they were (Baron & Byrne, 1997). What did they mean by this statement? In other words, what *is* love, and how do we know that we are experiencing it? These questions have been pondered by countless poets, philosophers, and ordinary human beings for thousands of years—but only recently has love become the subject of systematic research by psychologists

Romantic Love: A form of love in which feelings of strong attraction and sexual desire toward another person are dominant.

Companionate Love: A form of love involving a high degree of commitment and deep concern for the well-being of the beloved.

(e.g., Hendrick & Hendrick, 1993). Let's take a look at the answers that have emerged from this work.

Romantic Love: Its Nature I should begin by noting that in this discussion I'll focus primarily on **romantic love**—a form of love involving feelings of strong attraction and sexual desire toward another person. However, there are several other kinds of love too. One is the love of parents for their children. Another is the kind of love one can observe among couples who reach their fiftieth wedding anniversary, known as **companionate love**—a form of love that involves deep commitment and concern for the well-being of the beloved. Such relationships lack the "flames of passion" we typically think of in relation to love; but most psychologists agree that it is a very important form of love (e.g., Hatfield, 1988; Sternberg, 1988). (See Figure 16.19.)

So what, precisely, does romantic love involve? Most experts agree that several components are central. First, before we can say that we are "in love," the idea of romantic love must be present in our culture. Not all cultures have this concept; and when it is lacking, it is difficult if not impossible for people to say, "I'm in love." Second, we must experience intense emotional arousal when in the presence of an appropriate person—someone defined by our culture as a suitable object for such feelings. And third, these feelings must be mixed with the desire to be loved by the object of our affection, coupled with fears that the relationship might end. Only if all of these conditions are present can we state with certainty, "I'm in love."

Love: How and Why It Occurs Although it is a powerful reaction—one of the strongest we ever experience—romantic love often develops quite suddenly. Many people report that, as countless songs state, they fall in love quite suddenly—as if they were struck by emotional lightning (Murray & Holmes, 1994). How can such powerful reactions develop so quickly? One explanation is that we are prepared to fall in love by our earlier relationships. As we saw in Chapter 8, infants form a powerful *attachment* to their parents or other caregivers; and such attachment is, in a sense, the forerunner of love. It prepares us for forming powerful bonds with other people when we are adults (e.g., Hatfield & Rapson, 1993).

Another, and very different, explanation for the sudden emergence of love relates to evolutionary theory (Buss, 1997; Buss & Schmitt, 1993). According to this view, the reproductive success of our species in the past depended on two factors: (1) a desire on the part of both men and women to engage in sexual intercourse, and (2) an interest in investing the time and effort required to feed and protect their offspring. According to this reason-

FIGURE 16.19

Major Types of Love

Psychologists recognize that there are several different forms of love. Two of these are romantic love, which involves strong feelings of attraction and sexual desire *(left)*, and companionate love, which involves strong feelings of mutual respect and friendship *(right)*.

ing, love enhances both tendencies, because it leads to a lasting bond between males and females—a bond that is necessary for prolonged child care. Pure lust, which would ensure only sexual behavior, was not sufficient; so over time human beings with a propensity to form long-term relationships—to fall in love—were more successful in passing their genes on to the next generation. The result: We are, in a sense, genetically programmed to fall in love.

Which of these views is more accurate? At present there is evidence for both; so the most reasonable conclusion is that both early experiences and our genetic heritage play a role in our tendency to fall in love, and so to form social relationships that sometimes last an entire lifetime.

Love: Why It Sometimes Dies "... And they lived happily ever after." This is the way many fairy tales—and movies from the 1940s and 1950s—end, with the characters riding off into a glowing, love-filled future. If only life could match these high hopes! Some romantic relationships do blossom into lifelong commitment; my own parents, for example, recently celebrated their fifty-fourth anniversary. But for many couples, the glow of love fades and leaves behind relationships from which one or both partners soon seek escape. In fact, for couples marrying today, the chances are less than one in three that they will remain together permanently. What causes such unhappy outcomes? Research on love and on other close relationships suggests that many factors are at work.

We have already considered one of these in Chapter 10: *sexual jealousy* (e.g., Buunk, 1995). If one or both partners in a romantic relationship experience intense jealousy on a regular basis, the relationship is definitely in trouble. Another factor involves the increasing discovery by the partners that they are *dissimilar* in important ways. During the first flames of love, such differences tend to be overlooked; but as passion subsides, basic differences can come increasingly sharply into focus—sometimes with disastrous results. For a person who is neat in his or her personal habits, a lover's relative sloppiness may have seemed charming—a breath of fresh air—when the relationship was new. As time passes, however, it begins to grate, perhaps unbearably. Dissimilarities that weren't present initially may also emerge with the passage of time as the two partners change—and perhaps diverge.

Another, and potentially serious, problem is simple *boredom.* Over time, the unchanging routines of living together may lead people to feel that they are in a rut and are missing out on the excitement of life—including, perhaps, new romantic partners (Fincham & Bradbury, 1992). Such reactions can have important consequences for the relationship.

Finally, as relationships continue, patterns of behavior that can only be described as *self-defeating* sometimes emerge. Dating couples and newlyweds frequently express positive evaluations and feelings to one another. As time passes, however, these supportive statements sometimes give way to negative ones: "You're so inconsiderate!" "I should never have married you!" These kinds of sentiments, either stated overtly or merely implied, become increasingly frequent. The result is that people who began by seeing each other as perfect (or nearly perfect; Murray & Holmes, 1994) and who frequently praised each other may shift to criticizing one another in the harshest terms imaginable (Miller, 1991). Further, their attributions about their partner's behavior change. Instead of giving the partner the benefit of the doubt, they begin to attribute every action of which they disapprove or which causes them irritation as one that is done on purpose: "It's all your fault!" "You are so selfish!" When these patterns develop, love doesn't simply die; it is murdered by caustic, hurtful remarks.

Of course, many relationships *do* succeed. Couples who stay together, or stay married, for decades show a more positive pattern, in which they manage to avoid—or at least minimize—these pitfalls. Partners in such couples

Key Questions

- What factors influence interpersonal attraction?
- Under what conditions do people conclude that they are in love?
- What factors cause love to fade and perhaps disappear?

actively *work* at maintaining and strengthening their relationships: They practice the art of compromise, express positive feelings and sentiments toward their partners, and take each other's wishes and preferences into account on a daily basis. True, this is a lot of effort; but given the rewards of maintaining a long-term intimate relationship with someone we love and who loves us, it would appear to be well worthwhile.

Making Psychology Part of Your Life

Are You in Love? One Way of Telling

One question almost everyone has pondered is this: "Am I really in love?" This is a difficult question to answer, we each set our own criteria for defining reactions to another person as "love," and because we do not all experience passionate feelings of love—some people report that they have never had this kind of experience (Hendrick & Hendrick, 1993).

Despite these difficulties, however, most experts agree that romantic love has several different components that can be described and—perhaps—measured. This conclusion has led to the development of several different scales for measuring love. One of these (in modified form) is printed below. Follow the instructions to obtain a rough measure of your own love for any person you wish to consider. (Remember: Interpret the results of all such self-tests with caution!)

INSTRUCTIONS:

Think of a person with whom you believe you are or have been in love. Insert that person's name in each of the statements below and then respond to each item by writing a number in the space next to it. Responses to each item are made along the following scale:

Not at all true			Moderately true			Definitely true		
1	2	3	4	5	6	7	8	9

For example, if you feel that a statement is definitely true, enter a 9; if you feel that it is completely false, enter a 1. After responding, add the numbers you have entered. The highest score—indicating very intense love—is 135; the lowest is 15.

The items on this scale are based on one developed by Hatfield and Sprecher (1986). They are designed to measure romantic or passionate love.

____ 1. I would feel deep despair if __________ left me.

____ 2. Sometimes I feel I can't control my thoughts, they are obsessively on __________.

____ 3. I feel happy when I am doing something to make __________ happy.

____ 4. I would rather be with __________ than anyone else.

____ 5. I'd get jealous if I thought __________ were falling in love with someone else.

____ 6. I want to know all about __________.

____ 7. I want __________ physically, emotionally, mentally.

____ 8. I have an endless appetite for affection from __________.

____ 9. For me, __________ is the perfect romantic partner.

____ 10. I sense my body responding when __________ touches me.

____ 11. __________ always seems to be on my mind.

____ 12. I want __________ to know me—my thoughts, my fears, and my hopes.

____ 13. I eagerly look for signs indicating __________'s desire for me.

____ 14. I possess a powerful attraction for __________.

____ 15. I get extremely depressed when things don't go right in my relationship with __________.

Summary and Review of Key Questions

Social Thought: Thinking about Other People

- **What is the fundamental attribution error?** The fundamental attribution error (also known as overattribution bias) is our tendency to overestimate the importance of internal (dispositional) causes of others' behavior.
- **What is the self-serving bias?** The self-serving bias is our tendency to attribute our own positive outcomes to internal causes and our own negative outcomes to external factors—including other people.
- **What role does attribution play in perceptions of rape victims?** Rape victims are often blamed for this crime against them because people attribute responsibility for the rape to traits or behaviors on the part of the victim.
- **What is the false consensus effect?** The false consensus effect is our tendency to assume that others share our views to a greater extent than is really true.
- **How do we deal with social information that is inconsistent with our expectations?** In general, we tend to pay greater attention to such information than to information that is consistent with our expectations; but we also sometimes reject it as useless.
- **What is magical thinking?** Magical thinking is thinking that is based on assumptions that don't hold up to rational scrutiny.
- **What is counterfactual thinking? How does it change over time?** Counterfactual thinking involves imagining events and outcomes that didn't occur. Over time, we shift from focusing on things we did that didn't turn out well, to focusing on things we didn't do but should have done.
- **What are attitudes?** Attitudes are lasting evaluations of various aspects of the social world—evaluations that are stored in memory.
- **What factors were found to influence persuasion in early research?** Early research on persuasion found that the success of persuasion was strongly affected by characteristics of the sources (e.g., their attractiveness and expertise), characteristics of the persuasive messages sent (e.g., whether they were one-sided or two-sided), and characteristics of the audience.
- **What is the elaboration likelihood model, and how does it explain persuasion?** The ELM is a cognitive model of persuasion. It focuses on the degree of care with which people think about a persuasive communication—whether persuasion takes the central or the peripheral role.
- **What is cognitive dissonance, and how can it be reduced?** Cognitive dissonance is an unpleasant state we experience when we notice that two attitudes we hold or our attitudes and our behavior are somehow inconsistent. The easiest way to reduce cognitive dissonance is often to change our attitudes.
- **What is forced compliance? The less-leads-to-more effect?** Forced compliance occurs in situations where we feel compelled to say or do something inconsistent with our true attitudes. The less-leads-to-more effect is the fact that the weaker the reasons we have for engaging in attitude-discrepant behavior, the more likely we are to change these attitudes.
- **How can hypocrisy be used to change behavior?** Awareness of hypocrisy can lead individuals to change their behavior by causing them to recognize gaps between their attitudes and their behavior, thereby generating high levels of cognitive dissonance; in order to reduce the dissonance, they may change their behavior.

KEY TERMS

social psychology, p. 626 • attribution, p. 627 • consensus, p. 627 • consistency, p. 627 • distinctiveness, p. 627 • fundamental attribution error, p. 628 • self-serving bias, p. 628 • social cognition, p. 631 • false consensus effect, p. 631 • magical thinking, p. 632 • counterfactual thinking, p. 634 • attitudes, p. 636 • persuasion, p. 636 • elaboration likelihood model (ELM), p. 637 • central route, p. 637 • peripheral route, p. 638 • forced compliance, p. 638 • cognitive dissonance, p. 639 • less-leads-to-more effect, p. 640

Social Behavior: Interacting with Others

- **What are some of the major causes of prejudice?** Prejudice stems from direct competition between social groups, social categorization, social learning, and cognitive factors such as stereotypes.
- **How can prejudice be reduced?** Societies can reduce prejudice by socializing children to be tolerant of others, through increased intergroup contact, and through recategorization—shifting the boundary between "us" and "them" so as to include previously excluded groups.
- **What do research findings indicate about the "glass ceiling"?** Research findings indicate that the glass ceiling is real, and that it stems primarily from the fact that women do not have the opportunity for as many on-the-job experiences beneficial to their careers as do men.
- **What is conformity, and what role do social norms play in it?** Conformity is the tendency to behave like others—to act in accordance with existing descriptive or injunctive social norms.
- **What are some of the basic principles on which many different tactics for gaining compliance are based?** Tactics for gaining compliance are based on the principles of liking or friendship (e.g., ingratiation), commitment or consistency (e.g., the foot-in-the-door technique), reciprocity (e.g., the door-in-the-face technique), and scarcity (e.g., playing hard to get).
- **What is obedience, and how can it be reduced?** Obedience is a form of social influence in which individuals obey the commands of persons in authority. It can be reduced if the persons involved realize that authorities are pursuing selfish goals, if they are exposed to disobedient models, and if they take increased personal responsibility.
- **How do the empathy–altruism, negative state relief, and genetic determinism hypotheses explain prosocial behavior?** The empathy–altruism hypothesis proposes that we help others out of the unselfish desire to assist them. The negative state relief hypothesis suggests that we help them because this makes us feel better. The genetic determinism hypothesis suggests that we help others who are similar to ourselves in order to get our genes into the next generation.
- **What is the bystander effect, and why does it occur?** The bystander effect has to do with the fact that the more persons present at the scene of an emergency, the less likely the victim is to receive aid. This occurs because of diffusion of responsibility among all bystanders.
- **How does mood affect helping?** Being in a good mood can enhance helping unless the costs of helping are so high that they will interfere with this mood. Being in a bad mood can enhance helping by making the helper feel better.
- **How do people react to being helped by others?** People sometimes react to being helped with feelings of gratitude; but they may also fear the strings attached to such help, and they may realize that unnecessary helping (overhelping) can harm their public image.
- **What factors influence interpersonal attraction?** Interpersonal attraction is influenced by propinquity, similarity, and physical attractiveness, plus many other factors as well.
- **Under what conditions do people conclude that they are in love?** Individuals conclude that they are in love when their culture has the concept of romantic love and when they experience strong emotional arousal in the presence of a person defined as appropriate for love by their culture.
- **What factors cause love to fade and perhaps disappear?** Love can be weakened by such factors as sexual jealousy, increased dissimilarity (or increased recognition of existing dissimilarity),

boredom, and a pattern in which negative statements and attributions replace positive ones.

KEY TERMS

prejudice, p. 642 • realistic conflict theory, p. 643 • social categorization, p. 643 • stereotypes, p. 644 • contact hypothesis, p. 645 • recategorization, p. 646 • sexism, p. 646 • glass ceiling, p. 646 • social influence, p. 646 • conformity, p. 648 • social norms, p. 648 • compliance, p. 648 • ingratiation, p. 648 • foot-in-the-door technique, p. 649 • lowball procedure, p. 650 • door-in-the-face technique, p. 650 • that's-not-all technique, p. 650 • playing hard to get, p. 650 • fast-approaching-deadline technique, p. 650 • obedience, p. 650 • prosocial behavior, p. 654 • empathy–altruism hypothesis, p. 654 • negative state relief hypothesis, p. 654 • genetic determinism hypothesis, p. 654 • bystander effect, p. 655 • overhelping, p. 657 • love, p. 657 • interpersonal attraction, p. 657 • repeated exposure effect, p. 658 • romantic love, p. 660 • companionate love, p. 660

Critical Thinking Questions

Appraisal

Social thought and social interaction occur together in everyday life. Do you think that studying them separately makes sense? Or should they be studied together, as they occur in most situations?

Controversy

Do you think that racial, ethnic, and religious prejudices can ever be completely eliminated? Or does our tendency to divide the social world into "us" and "them" mean that we will always have such attitudes?

Making Psychology Part of Your Life

Now that you know what psychologists have discovered about the factors that cause us to like or dislike other persons, can you think of any ways in which you might be able to put this knowledge to use—for example, to try to increase others' liking for you? In what kind of situations would you be most likely to do this? How would you benefit if your efforts succeeded?

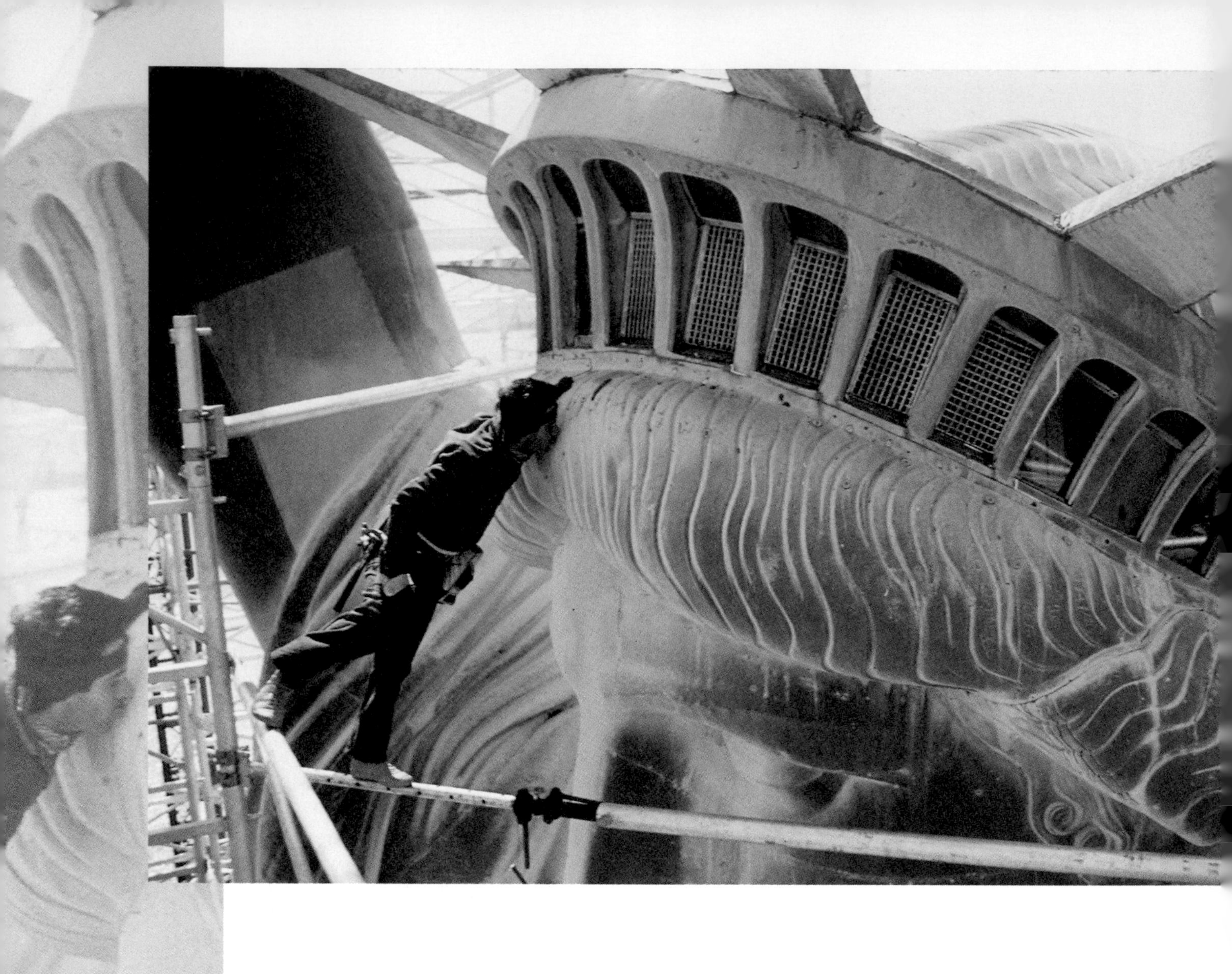

CHAPTER OUTLINE

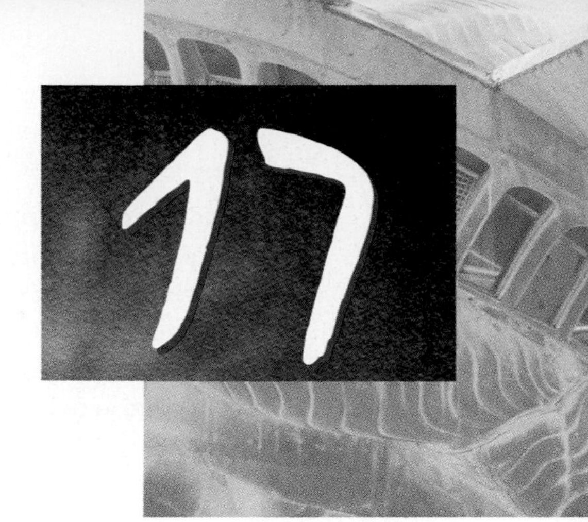

Psychology and the World of Work

Industrial/Organizational Psychology and Human Factors

What activity occupies more of your waking time than any other? The answer for most adults is simple: *work*. Once we leave school and launch our careers, we spend more time on work-related activities—commuting, doing our jobs, working on projects we have brought home with us—than on anything else in our lives. Further, for many of us, our job or occupation becomes a key part of our self-concept (Meyer, Allen, & Smith, 1993). When asked "Who are you?" many people respond in terms of their job or career: "I'm an engineer," "a secretary," "a salesperson" (Greenberg & Baron, 1997). And while many people complain about the necessity of working, most simply can't imagine life without a job or some form of productive work (see Figure 17.1 on page 668).

Given the importance of work in our lives, it is not at all surprising that

While many people complain about the necessity of working, most simply can't imagine life without a job or some form of productive work.

this topic has long been of major interest to psychologists. In fact, work is the focus of two important subfields of psychology. One of these, **industrial/organizational psychology** (I/O psychology for short), focuses on all aspects of behavior in work settings and on the nature of work settings themselves. Thus, I/O psychology studies such issues as the recruitment, selection, and training of employees; techniques for increasing employees' motivation; systems for recognizing and rewarding good performance; and the attitudes people hold toward their jobs or companies.

The second subfield, known as **human factors,** studies what has sometimes been described as the *person–machine* or *person–system interface:* ways in which human beings interact with the tools and systems they use in their work and in other aspects of their daily lives. (The field of human factors is often referred to as *ergonomics* outside the United States.) *Human factors psychologists* relate basic knowledge about human abilities and limitations—for example, our sensory abilities and cognitive capacities—to the design of tools, systems, tasks, and work environments. Their goal is to increase the safety, productivity, and comfort of people while they are at work or using various tools or equipment. If you find the controls on your VCR confusing or have trouble remembering which knob on your stove controls which burner, you can readily understand how important it is for manufacturers to consider human abilities and limitations in designing *anything* people will use.

Because both I/O psychology and human factors psychology represent important aspects of *applied psychology*—efforts to apply the principles and findings of psychology to solving practical problems—we'll review them in this chapter. We'll start by examining five important topics studied by I/O psychologists: *work motivation*—motivation relating to the performance of a job or task; *performance appraisal*—techniques for evaluating people's performance and providing them with feedback about it; *work-related attitudes*—attitudes people hold toward their jobs and organizations; *career-related issues*—factors that influence the course and success of individuals' careers; and finally *leadership*—a process studied by both I/O psychologists and social psychologists.

After exploring these topics, we'll turn to the field of *human factors*. Here, we'll look at the design of *displays*—ways in which information about equipment or systems can be provided to the persons using them—

FIGURE 17.1

Work: A Central Part of Our Self-Concept

When asked "Who are you?" many people reply in terms of their occupations. This fact underscores the central role that work plays in most of our lives.

and the design of *controls* for various tools or systems. Then we'll consider some concrete examples of how human factors psychologists have contributed to improving the design of many kinds of tools and equipment.

Industrial/Organizational Psychology: A branch of psychology that focuses on all aspects of behavior in work settings.

Human Factors: A branch of psychology that focuses on the ways in which human beings interact with the tools, equipment, and systems they use in their work and daily lives.

Industrial/Organizational Psychology: *Studying Behavior in Work Settings*

Although I had various part-time jobs from the time I was fourteen, my first full-time job was one I held during the summer after I graduated from high school. It was a clerical job in the office of a large labor union, and it was, in a word, *boring*. Because I was a summer fill-in for regular staff members who were on vacation, I was given only the most tedious tasks to perform. This was long before the invention of personal computers, so what I did most of the day was stand in front of filing cabinets, inserting letters and forms into various drawers. I soon found that I could finish all my assigned work in about two hours. If I did, though, there was nothing else for me to do the rest of the day. The result? I had to learn to turn off my brain and work in slow motion. Hour after hour I'd stand there, trying to look busy and to occupy my mind with various thoughts. But believe me, it was *pain*, as intense boredom usually is (e.g., Melamed et al., 1995) The only relief was two fifteen-minute breaks, one in the morning and one in the afternoon, and my half-hour lunch. I needed my wages for college, so I stuck it out for the entire summer. But after that, my classes and homework assignments in school seemed like a pleasure in comparison.

What was wrong with that job? From the point of view of I/O psychology, practically everything. It's as though the job had been designed to reduce my motivation, undermine my performance in every conceivable way, and create negative attitudes toward the organization. Let's take a closer look at each of these effects to see how, from the perspective of I/O psychology, the situation could have been improved.

Work Motivation: Theories and Techniques

Every organization, from Microsoft to your local ice-cream stand, wants and needs a motivated workforce. Unless employees are willing to expend effort in performing their jobs, little or nothing will get done, and what *is* accomplished will be low in quality. A basic question relating to work and work settings, then, is this: How can individuals be motivated to expend such effort—to work hard at their jobs, whatever these are?

I/O psychologists believe that in order to answer this question, we must first understand the basic nature of *work motivation*—people's willingness to expend effort in performing various tasks. As in all branches of psychology, this quest for understanding involves efforts to construct and test theories of work motivation. We have already considered several theories related to this issue in Chapter 10. You may recall that in that chapter I described *need theories*, such as the one proposed by Maslow, and *expectancy theory*. Both of these theories have been applied to understanding work motivation. In fact, expectancy theory (Mitchell, 1983; Schuster & Zingheim, 1992) is currently one of the most important approaches to understanding work motivation. As

FIGURE 17.2

Expectancy Theory

According to *expectancy theory,* work motivation is strongly affected by three factors: expectancy, instrumentality, and valence.

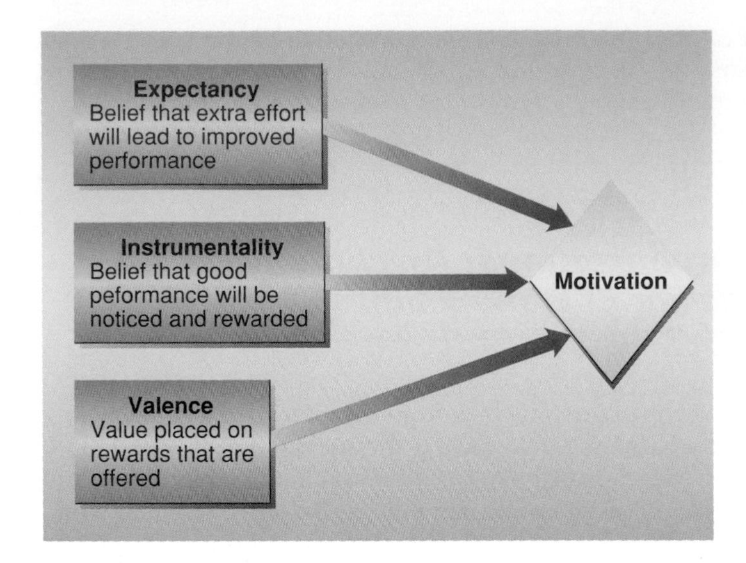

I hope you recall, this theory suggests that the motivation to engage in any activity is a function of *expectancy*—the belief that effort will result in improved performance; *instrumentality*—the belief that good performance will be recognized and rewarded; and *valence*—the perceived value of the rewards available (see Figure 17.2)

Expectancy theory has been tested in many different studies (e.g., Tubbs, Boehne, & Dahl, 1993; Van Eerde & Thierry, 1996); and in general, results confirm its accuracy. People *do* seem to work hardest when they believe that doing so will improve their performance, when they expect that good performance will be rewarded, and when they value the rewards offered. Predictions from the theory are more strongly supported with respect to individuals' stated intentions to work hard and their preferences for working on certain tasks, but the theory is also successful (although to a somewhat lesser degree) in predicting actual task performance and effort (Van Eerde & Thierry, 1996).

From the point of view of expectancy theory, of course, my summer job was a disaster. I knew that working harder would *not* improve my performance—it would simply lead to more boredom. Further, if I did improve my performance, there was little chance that I would be rewarded for doing so: My salary was fixed, and I would get no additional benefits. The result: My motivation sank to extremely low levels.

Now that I've refreshed your memory about expectancy theory, let's turn to two other approaches to work motivation that have received attention from I/O psychologists.

Goal-Setting Theory Suppose that you are studying for a big exam. Do you ever tell yourself in advance that you won't stop until you have read a certain number of pages, memorized some specific number of definitions, or solved a fixed number of problems? The chances are good that you do, because most people realize that they often accomplish more when they have a concrete goal in mind than when they do not. This basic fact lies at the center of another major approach to work motivation, **goal-setting theory** (e.g., Locke & Latham, 1990).

Goal-Setting Theory: A theory of motivation that focuses on the effects on motivation and performance of setting specific, challenging goals.

Actually, goal-setting theory did not begin as a theory; rather, this was one of those cases in which an interesting finding occurred first, and then a theory was constructed to help explain it. The finding was simple but impressive: On a wide variety of tasks, people performed better when they were given specific goals than when they were simply told to "do your best" (e.g., Wood

& Locke, 1990). The term *impressive* is appropriate, because people often did *much* better when working toward specific goals than when such goals were absent. For example, consider a famous study by Latham and Baldes (1975).

The participants in this project were lumber-camp crews who hauled logs from forests to a nearby sawmill. Before the study began, it was found that crews loaded the huge log-hauling trucks to only about 60 percent of capacity. This was very wasteful, because the trucks used tremendous amounts of fuel—gallons per mile, not miles per gallon! To change this situation, Latham and Baldes discussed the problem with the loggers and, together with them, set a specific goal: to load trucks to 94 percent of capacity before driving them to the mill. What happened? The crews quickly improved their performance to this level and then maintained it (see Figure 17.3). In fact, a follow-up study seven years later indicated that crews were still loading the trucks to near capacity, because this goal had now become a regular part of the job.

Notice that in this study, as in many others, the goals set met several criteria:

- They were highly *specific*—people knew just what they were trying to accomplish.
- They were *challenging*—meeting them required increased effort.
- They were *attainable*—they were *not* outside people's reach.
- Employees were *committed* to the goals—they committed themselves to reaching them.

(**Source**: Based on data from Latham & Baldes, 1975.)

FIGURE 17.3

Goal Setting: Some Classic Findings

As shown here, performance improved sharply after a specific, challenging goal was set for workers loading giant logging trucks. Further, improved performance persisted in a follow-up study conducted seven years later.

Research findings indicate that when these conditions are met, goal setting can be a highly effective way of increasing motivation and performance (e.g., Mento, Locke, & Klein, 1992; Wright et al., 1994). In contrast, goals that are not specific and not challenging and to which individuals are not committed may be quite ineffective in these respects (see Figure 17.4).

Why is goal setting so effective? A theory proposed by Locke and Latham (1990) provides an answer. According to this theory, goals increase motivation by increasing (1) attention to the task at hand, (2) effort expended on it, and (3) persistence—there is less temptation to quit once a clear goal has been established. According to Locke and Latham (1990), these effects are fairly automatic: They occur without much intervening conscious thought once a goal has been set. In addition, goal setting also increases performance indirectly, by encouraging the development of specific *task strategies*—ways of performing the task. A growing body of evidence offers support for this theory, and suggests that goal setting does indeed increase performance in these ways (e.g., Weldon, Jehn, & Prahadan, 1991). In one well-conducted study, for example, Audia and his colleagues (1996) observed individuals' performance as they worked on a simple construction task (producing a teaching aid for elementary school students). Before working on the task, participants were given either a quantity goal (e.g., make ten of the products within a specific amount of time) or a quality goal (e.g., make the products with no defects). Results indicated that the quantity goal (but not the quality goal) increased participants' tendencies to use task strategies that would allow them to reach this goal of rapid production—for instance, using an assembly-line method of folding and cutting the various pieces of paper used in the project. So, as predicted by goal-setting theory, establishing specific goals does seem to strongly influence the way in which individuals go about performing a task.

The theory also calls attention to the important role of *self-efficacy*—individuals' beliefs about their ability to perform at given levels. If people conclude that no matter what they do, they lack the capacity to reach a goal, then effort and performance will decrease. In contrast, if they conclude that they *can* reach the goal, motivation and performance are enhanced.

In sum, goal-setting theory suggests that specific, challenging, but realistic goals can and often will increase motivation. Indeed, since literally hun-

FIGURE 17.4

Goal Setting in Action

The individual shown here has made progress toward a specific goal, but has not yet reached it. The feedback he is receiving may well prove helpful.

"Well, that was much better than yesterday, but you're still using your salad fork for the entrée."

(**Source**: Drawing by Cheney; © 1996 The New Yorker Magazine, Inc.)

dreds of studies on goal setting confirm this conclusion, many I/O psychologists believe that it is the single most effective means of attaining *that* goal.

Equity Theory: Fairness and Motivation When I described my first full-time job, I left out one important detail. There was another student working there that summer—and I soon noticed that he seemed to have many special privileges I didn't share. He rarely arrived on time in the morning and often left early. He sometimes disappeared for more than two hours around lunch time, and he also spent lots of time on the phone—mainly on personal calls. When I learned that he was being paid much more than I was, that was the last straw. Why should he get so much better treatment than I did? As you can guess, any remaining motivation I might have had to perform that job well flew right out the window.

This was my first brush with unfairness at work—what I/O psychologists term *inequity*. And it bring us to another important theory of work motivation, **equity theory** (Greenberg, 1993a; Tyler, 1994). The central issue in equity is *perceived fairness*—individuals' beliefs about whether they are being treated fairly or unfairly by others. The theory suggests that people care deeply about this issue and pay a great deal of attention to it. How do we decide whether we are being treated fairly or unfairly? Equity theory proposes that we begin by engaging in *social comparison:* We compare ourselves with others. Specifically, we compare the ratio of our own *inputs*—everything we contribute to a relationship—and our *outcomes*—everything we receive—to the others' ratios of inputs and outcomes (Kulik & Ambrose, 1992). We don't choose just anyone for such comparisons, of course. Rather, we select people we view as similar to ourselves in various ways. Thus, as a summer employee, I didn't compare my inputs and outcomes with those of the head of the department. Rather, I compared myself with someone I viewed as similar—the other student.

Equity theory suggests that if the ratios of inputs provided to outcomes obtained are about equal for ourselves and these others (the ones to whom we compare ourselves), we view our treatment as basically fair. If these ratios are out of balance, however, we conclude that we are being treated unfairly, and a state known as *inequity* develops. Feelings of inequity are uncomfortable and negative, and we try to eliminate them in several ways, as I'll soon describe. When these feelings occur, we also experience a sharp drop in motivation. This is what happened to me in my summer job. As shown in Figure 17.5 on page 674, my inputs were larger than those of the other student, yet his outcomes were much larger than mine. Talk about unfairness!

Two more points are worth noting. First, such judgments are very much in the eye of the beholder: *We* do the comparing, and *we* decide whether our share of available rewards is fair relative to that of others. Second, as you can probably guess, we are much more sensitive to receiving *less* than we feel we deserve than to receiving *more* than we feel we deserve (Greenberg, 1993a). In other words, the *self-serving bias* that we encountered in Chapter 16 operates strongly in this context.

Why do feelings of inequity (or other forms of injustice) interfere with work motivation? Equity theory provides the following answer. When individuals perceive themselves as receiving less than they deserve and experiencing inequity, they can take any one of several steps to reduce such feelings. One possibility is to try to increase their outcomes—to ask for a raise, bonus, or other benefit. Another is to leave the relationship: to quit and find another job. Still a third is to reduce their inputs—to expend less effort on the job. Many studies indicate that this last tactic is a very common one; persons who conclude that they are receiving less than they deserve—that they are being *underrewarded*—reduce their effort relative to persons who feel that they are

Equity Theory: A theory that focuses on perceived fairness—individuals' beliefs about whether they are being treated fairly or unfairly.

FIGURE 17.5

Feelings of Inequity: How They Often Arise

Because my inputs were larger than those of the other student, yet my outcomes were smaller, I experienced strong feelings of inequity in my first summer job.

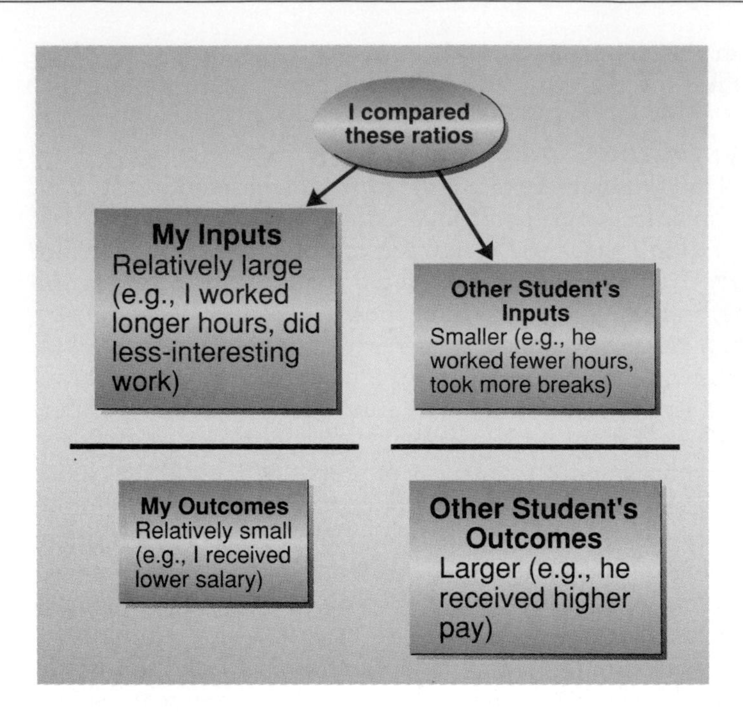

being treated fairly (e.g., Harder, 1992; Pritchard, Dunnette, & Jorgenson, 1972).

Reduced performance is not the only way in which employees can demonstrate lowered work motivation, however. In addition, they can attempt to balance the scales by engaging in hidden actions that provide them with extra benefits. Perhaps the most revealing evidence on such effects is provided by research conducted by Greenberg and his colleagues (e.g., Greenberg & Scott, 1995).

Biting the Hand That Feeds You: Employee Theft as a Reaction to Perceived Unfairness Greenberg (1993b) suggests that one way in which employees deal with the belief that they have been treated unfairly by their companies is simple: They engage in *employee theft*—they take things belonging to the company. Have you ever brought home a pencil or some envelopes from a place where you worked? If so, you have engaged in employee theft. While such actions seem trivial, they are theft, in the legal sense of this term. And in fact, growing evidence indicates that when employees feel unfairly treated, they engage in such behavior on a much larger scale than they do otherwise. For instance, consider the following statement, made by one employee after he learned that the typical person in his company was stealing about $300 worth of merchandise a year: "Heck, I'm behind schedule . . . there's only three months left in the year and I don't have my $300!" (Altheide et al., 1978, p. 108).

In a clear demonstration of the "perceived unfairness leads to theft" equation, Greenberg (1993b) conducted a laboratory study in which students who had been promised $5 per hour for working in a study were told either that they would receive this pay, or that they would receive a much lower rate—$3 per hour. The experimenter announced this cut in pay and provided either a full explanation for why the cut was necessary or no explanation. Then, the experimenter either expressed a great deal of regret about the pay cut, or made no such statements. It was predicted that students who received both a full explanation and a statement of regret about the pay cut would feel the most fairly treated, and so would be least likely to try to "even the score" by engaging in theft when provided with an opportunity to do so. Those who received only an explanation *or* a statement of regret would feel less unfairly treated and would be less likely to try to get even. Finally, those who received neither explanation nor a statement of remorse would feel most unfairly treated and would be the most likely to try to get even.

To test this prediction, the researcher departed at the end of each student's participation, leaving a pile of money on the table. As the researcher left, he said, "I don't know how much money is here, but . . . just take the amount you are supposed to be paid and leave the rest." As expected, students paid the amount of money they were promised ($5) did not engage in any theft; they took precisely what was coming to them. However, among participants who were paid less than expected, those given no explanation and no apology stole the most; those given information *or* statements of regret stole less; and those given both these treatments stole the least (see Figure 17.6).

In sum, when individuals conclude that they are being treated unfairly, their work motivation decreases sharply, and they may engage in actions designed to even the score—to let them get back what they feel they deserve. This suggests that there are important practical, as well as ethical, reasons for ensuring that fairness is standard practice in all work settings.

As a group, theories of work motivation offer important insights into the conditions under which people will—and won't—work hard. Please see the **Ideas to Take with You** feature on page 676 for a summary of these theories.

Key Questions

- According to expectancy theory, what conditions are necessary for high levels of work motivation?
- What kinds of goals are most likely to result in increased motivation and performance?
- What factors do people consider in deciding whether they are being treated fairly or unfairly?
- When individuals decide that they have not been treated fairly, what actions do they sometimes take to correct this situation?

Techniques for Increasing Work Motivation: From Job Design to the "Big Brother" Tactic How can work motivation be enhanced? This is a key question investigated by I/O psychologists. The findings of their research indicate that several techniques based on the theories of motivation we have considered can be highly effective in this regard.

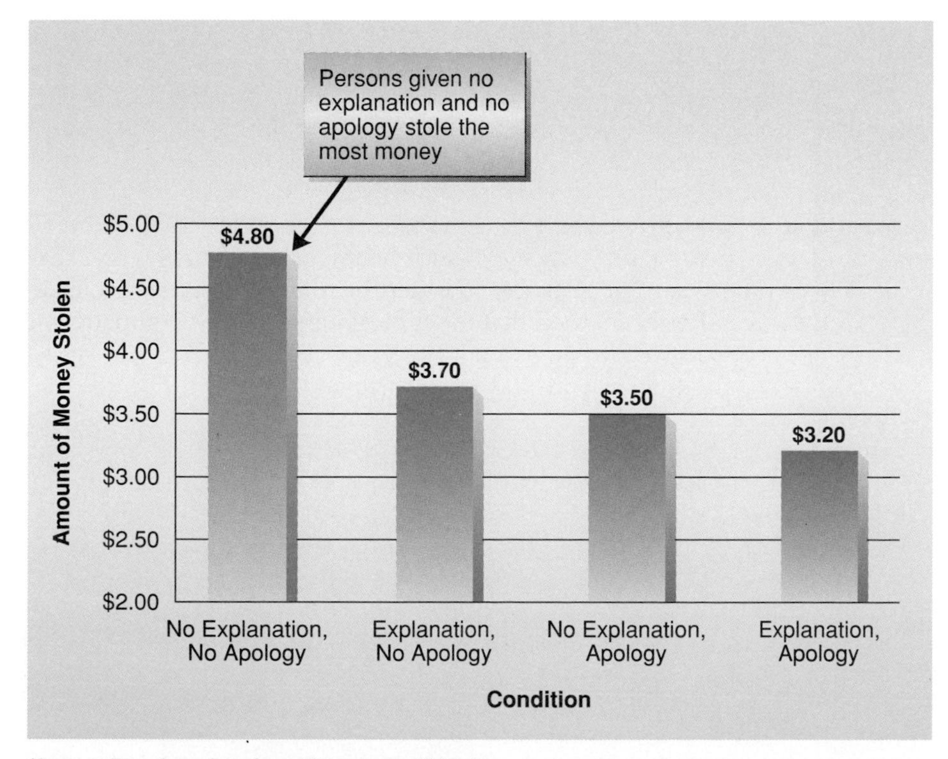

(**Source**: Based on data from Greenberg, 1993b.)

FIGURE 17.6

Reactions to Unfairness: Evening the Score through Theft

Individuals who were given no explanation for why they were paid less than they were promised and no apology for this underpayment stole more money than individuals who were given an explanation and/or an apology. Persons who received both an explanation and an apology stole the least money.

Ideas to Take with You

When Will People Work Hard—or Goof Off?

Theories of work motivation offer important insights into the question of when people will work hard, and when they won't.

Expectancy Theory

Suggests that people will work hard only when three conditions are met:

- People believe that extra effort will improve their performance.
- Good performance will be noticed and rewarded.
- The rewards offered are ones they want.

Equity Theory

Suggests that people will work hard only when they feel they have been treated fairly—when they have received the rewards they deserve, the methods for dividing available rewards are fair, and they have been treated with courtesy and respect.

Goal-Setting Theory

Suggests that people will work hard when they have specific and challenging (but attainable) goals, and when they receive feedback about their progress toward these goals.

For instance, as we've already seen, *goal setting* can greatly increase motivation and performance in many different settings (e.g., Stern & Stewart, 1993).

Other techniques aimed at enhancing work motivation focus, instead, on the task of **job design**—efforts to make jobs more interesting and appealing to the persons who perform them (Griffin & McMahan, 1995). One such approach is **job enlargement**. This involves expanding jobs—especially dull, repetitious ones—to include a larger variety of tasks, all at the same level of skill. For instance, if my summer job had been enlarged to include other simple tasks such as typing and perhaps filling out various forms, it would have been more interesting to me—or at least more bearable.

Another job-design technique, known as **job enrichment,** involves giving employees not only more tasks to perform, but ones at higher levels of skill and responsibility. Thus, if my summer job had involved answering letters from customers, dealing with problems over the phone, or perhaps even developing a better filing system, it would have been more appealing. Many studies indicate that through job enlargement and job enrichment, jobs that are viewed as tedious and meaningless by the persons who perform them can be made more interesting and more meaningful, often with corresponding improvements in motivation and performance (e.g., Campion & McClelland, 1993; Johns, Xie, & Fang, 1992).

Techniques such as goal setting, job enlargement, and job enrichment are often greeted with enthusiasm—or at least acceptance—by employees. Another technique, however, is far more controversial and often runs into stiff resistance. This technique is known as **electronic performance monitoring** (or, sometimes, **computer-based monitoring**), and involves procedures in which companies monitor employees' performance through access to their computer terminals and telephones. Such procedures can be used by employers only when their employees use computers or telephones; but, as you already know, an enormous number of jobs involve these devices. Thus, by 1990 the performance of more than 26 million workers in the United States alone was being monitored by their companies electronically and today the number is even higher (DeTienne, 1993).

Does such monitoring improve performance? Psychologists have only recently begun to study this issue, so it is too early for firm conclusions (e.g., Aiello & Svec, 1993). However, a growing body of evidence suggests that electronic performance monitoring may exert effects on behavior similar to those produced by the presence of an *audience*—of other persons who watch an individual's performance in more traditional ways, such as looking over the person's shoulder (see Figure 17.7). Psychologists refer to such effects by the term **social facilitation,** but don't be misled: The effects of an audience are *not* always positive. In fact, a large body of research on social facilitation indicates that while sometimes the presence of an audience facilitates performance, sometimes it impairs it. Specifically, the presence of an audience seems to improve performance when individuals are highly skilled or practiced on a given task, but it can worsen performance when individuals are not highly skilled or are just learning to perform the task (e.g., Geen, 1989; Zajonc, 1968).

Direct evidence for the conclusion that electronic performance monitoring produces such effects has been reported by Aiello and Kolb (1995). These researchers had student volunteers perform a data-entry task under several different conditions. In one, the *individual monitoring* condition, the students were told that the supervisor might monitor their individual performance electronically as they worked. In another, the *work-group monitoring* condition, they were told that the supervisor could observe only the performance of their entire work group—their individual performance could not be identified (they worked in groups of three to six persons). Finally, students in a *control* condition received no information about monitoring of their performance.

Job Design: Efforts to make jobs more interesting and appealing to the persons who perform them.

Job Enlargement: Expansion of jobs to include a larger variety of tasks, all at the same level of skill.

Job Enrichment: Expansion of jobs to include tasks at higher levels of skill and responsibility.

Electronic Performance Monitoring (computer-based monitoring): Procedures in which companies monitor employees' performance through their computer terminals or telephones; sometimes referred to as computer-based monitoring.

Social Facilitation: The effects of an audience on performance. Contrary to what this term suggests, such effects are not always beneficial.

FIGURE 17.7

Effects of an Audience

A large body of research findings indicates that the presence of an audience—others who actively watch while an individual performs some task—can have important effects on behavior.

As you might guess, some individuals began at a relatively high level of performance—they were good at the data-entry task right from the start. For such persons, electronic monitoring improved performance: Those in both the individual and group monitoring conditions performed better than those in the no-monitoring control group. For persons who initially performed at a low level, however, the opposite was true; those in the two monitoring conditions actually performed worse than those in the no-monitoring condition.

In sum, the findings reported by Aiello and Kolb (1995) and other researchers (e.g., Nebeker & Tatum, 1993) suggest that electronic monitoring of performance *can* sometimes increase performance—but that it can sometimes reduce performance, too. One factor that may play an important role in determining which of these effects occurs is the design of the computer monitoring system itself. For instance, such systems can be designed so as to provide employees with the option of delaying or preventing monitoring at a given point in time, if they so wish. A recent study by Stanton and Barnes-Farrel (1996) varied such conditions, and found that when employees could prevent monitoring of their performance, they experienced greater feelings of personal control and performed better than when they could not prevent monitoring. Such findings indicate that before companies adopt computer monitoring, they should devote careful thought to the nature of such monitoring, to the skills of their employees, and several other factors. Only if they do can the potential benefits of this controversial procedure be maximized and its potential costs be minimized.

Key Questions

- What are job enlargement and job enrichment?
- What is electronic performance monitoring, and what effects does it have on performance?
- What is social facilitation, and what role does it play in electronic performance monitoring?

Performance Appraisal: Tying Rewards to Performance

Suppose that you worked for a company where, year after year, everyone received the same raise. How would you react to these conditions? If you are like most people, you would probably get somewhat discouraged and lose much of your motivation to work hard. After all, why bother, if no one cares—or, at least, if no one rewards you for good performance? To avoid such situations, most organizations have a set of procedures for evaluating employees' performance and for linking these evaluations—known as **performance appraisals**—to rewards (e.g., Balzer & Sulsky, 1990; Murphy & Cleveland, 1991). If such procedures operate effectively, then persons who do the best work and make the largest contribution will receive the largest raises (or other benefits). Moreover, if performance appraisal procedures are viewed as fair by employees, this can be a major plus for their motivation (e.g., Greenberg & Scott, 1995).

The task of evaluating performance, however, is far from simple. In most organizations, performance appraisals usually occur once a year, or at most twice a year. This means that the individuals who must make such evaluations have to try to remember the performance of several persons in many situations and over long periods of time. And then they must use this information to form judgments or make decisions about these people. As we saw in Chapters 6, 7, and 16, our abilities to perform such tasks are impressive, but they are also far from perfect. There is lots of room for errors to enter into the process, and so to distort the decisions and judgments we reach (e.g., Sanchez & De La Torre, 1996; Woehr & Feldman, 1993). What are these errors like? And what steps can be taken to hold them to a minimum? These two questions are among the issues on which I/O psychologists have focused, so let's take a closer look at both.

Performance Appraisals: Procedures for evaluating employees' performance so that this can be linked to the rewards they receive.

Performance Appraisal: Potential Sources of Error Suppose one day *you* faced the task of evaluating the performance of several persons. Would you allow yourself to be influenced by your liking or dislike for these persons? By the extent to which they were similar to you? By their race, ethnic background, or gender? Your answer is almost certainly "Of course not! That wouldn't be fair!" And in fact most persons charged with the task of evaluating others' performance *do* try to eliminate the impact of such factors. Unfortunately, however, a large body of evidence indicates that people are not entirely successful in this respect. On the contrary, the process of performance appraisal appears to be subject to many different sources of potential error. Here, in summary form, are a few of the most important.

- *Halo effects*. Have you ever heard the saying "Love is blind?" It refers to the fact that when we love another person (or even like them very much), we can no longer evaluate them in an objective manner. Sad to relate, such effects sometimes influence performance appraisal. Once we have formed a positive overall impression of someone, the "halo effect" means that we tend to perceive everything the person does in a favorable manner; conversely, once we have formed a negative overall impression, we tend to perceive everything in an *un*favorable manner (e.g., Murphy & Cleveland, 1991; Robbins & DeNisi, 1994). This is why the advice to "hit the ground running" when you take a new job makes a lot of sense: If you start out strong and generate a positive first impression in others, this may work in your favor for a long, long time.
- *Leniency errors*. In my department, faculty are called upon to evaluate secretaries every year. The overall ratings are made on a scale ranging from "unacceptable" through "outstanding." What rating do you think most secretaries receive from most professors? You guessed it: *outstanding*. The result, of course, is that the whole appraisal system is useless. If everyone receives the highest (or at least very high) ratings, how can raises and promotions be linked to performance? Why do such *leniency errors*—the tendency to evaluate everyone favorably—occur? In part because secretaries are told their ratings and, if they disagree with them, must discuss them with faculty members. Most professors want to avoid such embarrassing situations, so they take the easy way out and give their secretaries very high scores (e.g., Hauenstein, 1993; Murphy, Jako, & Anhalt, 1993). Whatever their source, leniency errors can greatly reduce the value of any performance appraisal system.
- *Affective reactions*. Suppose you have to evaluate the performance of two persons, one you like very much and one you dislike. In principle, you should try to eliminate these personal feelings from this task, and rate only each person's performance. Can you do this? Perhaps, but a large body of evidence indicates that despite your best efforts, you may still be influenced by your liking or disliking for these two people (e.g., Robbins & DeNisi, 1994). Yes, your ratings will certainly reflect their performance—we do pay careful attention to such factors (Borman, White, & Dorsey, 1995). But your ratings will also probably be influenced, at least to a degree, by your affective (emotional) reactions to these persons (Robbins & DeNisi, 1994).
- *Attributional errors*. Suppose, again, that you face the task of evaluating the performance of two persons. In your judgment, both have performed at the same level. But you believe that one has "coasted" to this performance—he or she is very talented, but is loafing along at half speed. The other person, in contrast, is less talented but has worked very hard. Would you give these two persons the same rating? Perhaps. But perhaps your attributions concerning the *causes* behind their performance would

Behaviorally Anchored Rating Scales: Rating scales that provide raters with examples of excellent to poor performance on key dimensions of job performance.

also influence your judgment. In fact, research findings indicate that most people would assign higher ratings to the second person, who has limited talent but has worked very hard (e.g., Mitchell, Green, & Wood, 1982). In one sense, this is reasonable: Effort should count. But from another standpoint, it is an error in performance appraisal, because in this process the emphasis should be on *performance*—on what people have accomplished. Being human, however, we often let our attributions influence our judgments about others, as we saw in Chapter 16.

These potential errors, and several others, are summarized in Table 17.1. When these potential pitfalls are combined, it is clear that the task of evaluating others' performance in a fair and accurate way is definitely far from easy (e.g., Ganzach, 1995; Sulsky & Balzer, 1988).

Performance Appraisal: Techniques for Improving Its Accuracy The fact that performance appraisals are subject to many different potential errors raises an important practical question: How can the accuracy of such ratings be improved? I/O psychologists have identified several procedures that can prove helpful in this regard (e.g., Mero & Motowidlo, 1995). One such technique involves keeping very careful records of employees' performance. Memory, as we saw in Chapter 6, is far from perfect. Since evaluations of others' performance rest to an important extent upon what we remember about their performance, it is crucial for raters to keep accurate records to which they can refer when formulating performance appraisals. Such records are often termed *diary notes,* and they should be entered into employees' records soon after each important performance-related event occurs (Balzer & Sulsky, 1990).

Another useful procedure for improving the accuracy of performance appraisals involves providing raters with rating scales or formats that make their job of being accurate easier (e.g., Hartel, 1993). For example, **behaviorally anchored rating scales,** or *BARS* for short (Landy & Farr, 1983), provide raters with examples of excellent, average, and poor performance on

TABLE 17.1

Potential Errors in Performance Appraisal

As shown here, ratings of others' performance can be influenced by many extraneous factors.

Potential Error	Description
Halo Effects	A tendency to evaluate all aspects of an individual's performance in a manner consistent with our overall impression of this person
Leniency Error	A tendency to inflate ratings of all the persons rated
Affective Reactions	Effects of liking or disliking for others on ratings of their performance
Attributional Error	A tendency to assign higher ratings to persons who show high levels of effort than to persons who show lower levels of effort, even if their performance is identical
Similar-to-Me Error	A tendency to assign higher ratings to persons who are similar to the rater on various dimensions than to ones who are dissimilar
Stereotypes	A tendency to rate others on the basis of their membership in a given social group

key job-related dimensions—the important dimensions along which job performance can vary. Raters then compare employees' behavior with these examples, and so come up with accurate ratings of the employees' performance on each important job-related dimension. How are the key dimensions identified and examples of excellent, average, and poor performance for a given job chosen? Primarily from information provided by persons who actually hold the job in question. Such persons, who are usually quite expert concerning the requirements of their own job (e.g., Richman & Quinones, 1996), are asked to sort many written descriptions of on-the-job behavior by placing them in piles that, in their view, involve related activities. Then they are asked to sort the behaviors in each pile in terms of whether they demonstrate excellent, average, or poor performance. Perhaps a concrete example of how BARS are used will help clarify matters. Let's consider a job with which you are probably quite familiar: that of university professor.

What are the key dimensions of performance for a professor? One, of course, involves teaching. Can you now imagine examples of excellent, average, and poor teaching you have experienced as a student? I'm sure that you can. Another dimension of performance for a professor might involve research activities. What would constitute excellent performance on *this* dimension? Perhaps publishing several articles each year, or obtaining a research grant from a government agency to fund such activities. Poor performance, in contrast, might involve no publications and no efforts to secure research funding. Other dimensions of professors' performance might include counseling of students and service to the department and university; again, examples of excellent, average, and poor performance could be generated for each of these dimensions.

Can you see why behaviorally anchored rating scales can often be useful to persons who must evaluate others' performance? The key point is this: Instead of being left to formulate their own ideas about what are the key dimensions of performance for this particular job and what constitutes excellent, average, or poor performance, raters are provided with such information—with *anchors* linked directly to examples of on-the-job behavior. While BARS do not guarantee perfectly accurate ratings, they do seem to represent an important advance over informal scales in which raters are simply asked to rate employees' performance on dimensions that may or may not be the key ones for their jobs without any concrete examples of different levels of performance (e.g., Hartel, 1993).

A third technique for improving the accuracy of performance appraisals—and one that is related to certain aspects of BARS—involves what I/O psychologists term **frame-of-reference training** (e.g., Pulakos, 1986; Sulsky & Day, 1992). This procedure recognizes the fact that in many cases different raters have contrasting ideas about the two issues mentioned above: about what the key dimensions of performance are for a given job, and what constitutes good or poor performance on each of these dimensions. In frame-of-reference training, persons who will evaluate others' performance on a given job meet and together examine various examples of on-the-job performance. They discuss these until they agree on the key dimensions for evaluating performance on this job, and on what represents good and poor performance on each of these dimensions. As a result of such training, all raters come to share a common frame of reference. Then they can all use the same criteria for evaluating employees' performance—an outcome that increases the fairness of performance appraisal systems in any organization where many different persons perform the task of evaluating others' performance. The results of many studies indicate that frame-of-reference training is indeed useful from the point of view of increasing the accuracy of performance appraisals (e.g., Day & Sulsky, 1995), perhaps because it helps raters form accurate overall impressions of the persons they must rate.

Frame-of-Reference Training: Procedures designed to ensure that all performance raters share a common frame of reference—that they agree as to what constitutes excellent, average, or poor performance.

Key Questions

- What are some of the most important potential causes of errors in appraisals of others' performance?
- What are diary notes, and how can they improve rating accuracy?
- What are behaviorally anchored rating scales and frame-of-reference training? How can they improve rating accuracy?

In sum, several techniques for improving the accuracy of performance appraisal exist, and these are now being used in many work settings. To the extent they contribute to employees' beliefs that they are being treated fairly and that there is a strong link between their performance and their outcomes, such procedures can increase both performance and job satisfaction—the topic we'll consider next.

Before turning to job satisfaction, however, please see the Beyond the Headlines section for a discussion of a very different aspect of employees' behavior.

Beyond the Headlines

As Psychologists See It

Sleeping on the Job: Can It Have Potential Benefits?

Shh! Napping Is Trying to Tiptoe into the Workplace

Wall Street Journal, June 26, 1996—Sleeping on the job may boost your mood, if not your career. . . . Michael K. Lorelli, president of Tambrands, Inc., knows some people might be embarrassed to do what he does. But in time, he thinks, it will become accepted. . . . What he—along with others not inhibited by stereotypes—likes to do is nap. Grabbing 40 winks at work sounds like a great idea to a lot of people, but most employers have yet to appreciate napping's rejuvenating effects. Now snooze fans, backed by a growing body of evidence. . . are nudging the once-taboo subject onto the job site. . . .

"Napping on the job—what next?" I can almost hear you saying. But an increasing number of companies are experimenting with this practice. For instance, the Federal Aviation Administration has found that pilots who nap for thirty minutes during flights are better at landing than ones who don't. And there is some indication that short naps improve the driving of long-distance truck drivers.

In France, Framatome S.A., France's nuclear power company, is currently testing the effects of short naps for employees who must work the night shift. Preliminary findings indicate that the employees wake from their short snoozes refreshed and more alert (see Figure 17.8). Surprisingly, many celebrities take naps. For instance, Jim Lehrer, of public television's *The NewsHour with Jim Lehrer,* takes a nap every day at 12:30 p.m. He claims that this greatly increases his alertness.

Is there any scientific basis for this practice? Some sleep researchers believe that there is. Almost everyone has a "down" period sometime between 2:00 and 5:00 p.m., largely in response to normal circadian rhythms, which we discussed in Chapter 4. As Claudio Stampi, one psychologist who studies sleep, puts it: "We've found that you get tremendous recovery of alertness—-several hours' worth—out of a fifteen-minute nap. . . You can get temporary help through stimulation—coffee, exercise, brighter light, cooler temperatures—but you're actually fixing the problem by taking a nap" (*Wall Street Journal,* June 26, 1996).

So will napping really catch on as a technique for improving alertness and performance in many jobs? Perhaps. And if so, it may be helped by a device, designed by several psychologists and known as the Relax and Refresh Chair, that I actually saw at a recent convention of the American Psychological Association. This chair, which is manufactured by Japan's Matsushita Electric Industrial Company (Matsushita owns Panasonic, for example), combines massage with a light-blocking hood and a control panel that allows users to program the length of their nap. The effect is relaxing—until the wake-up cycle starts and nappers are hit with flashing lights and blasts of cold air!

FIGURE 17.8

Napping: Can It Improve Job Performance?

Growing evidence suggests that when employees take short naps, they awake refreshed and feeling more alert. The result: Their performance often improves.

Critical Thinking Questions

1. What do *you* think: Is napping an "idea whose time has come" so that it will soon be accepted in many work settings?
2. Considering what you learned about morning people and night people in Chapter 4, do you think that napping may be more helpful to some persons than to others?
3. In view of our discussion of circadian rhythms in Chapter 4, do you think there are times of the day when napping may be most useful? If so, why?

Work-Related Attitudes: The Prevalence, Causes, and Effects of Job Satisfaction

In Chapter 16 I defined *attitudes* as lasting evaluations of various aspects of the social world—evaluations that are stored in memory (Fazio & Roskos-Ewoldsen, 1994; Judd et al., 1991). Since work plays such an important role in most adults' lives, it is only natural to expect that people will hold many work-related attitudes—for example, attitudes toward their jobs (Gutek & Winter, 1992), their company (Hackett, Boycio, & Hausdorf, 1994), and the people with whom they work. This is certainly the case, and such *work-related attitudes* have long been a topic of research in I/O psychology. Here, we'll focus on one important type of work-related attitude—**job satisfaction,** the attitude a person holds toward his or her job (e.g., Hulin, 1991).

The Prevalence of Job Satisfaction: Do People Like Their Work? Remember my first full-time job? I truly hated it and couldn't wait for it to end. Is this a common experience? Or do most people hold more positive attitudes about their jobs? The results of large-scale surveys conducted in many countries across several decades offer a fairly encouraging conclusion: Most people report being quite satisfied with their jobs and the work they perform (e.g., Page & Wiseman, 1993). In fact, about 80 to 90 percent of survey respondents report high levels of job satisfaction—figures quite similar to those reported for personal happiness in Chapter 9.

The total picture is a bit more complex than this, however. First, people are not equally satisfied with all aspects of their jobs. While they may report a high level of satisfaction overall, they tend to be more satisfied with some aspects than with others. For example, they may be comfortable with their pay but be less happy about their working conditions. Second, some groups of people report higher levels of job satisfaction than others. Who tends to be the most satisfied? Here are some key findings:

Job Satisfaction: Individuals' attitudes toward their work or jobs.

- White-collar employees (persons holding managerial, technical, or professional jobs) tend to be more satisfied than blue-collar workers.
- Older people with more job seniority tend to be more satisfied than younger, less experienced people (Eichar, Brady, & Fovtinsky, 1991).
- Women and members of minority groups tend to be less satisfied with their jobs than men and members of majority groups (Lambert, 1991).
- There are large, consistent individual differences in job satisfaction—some people tend to be satisfied in almost any job, while others tend to be dissatisfied no matter what job they hold (Arvey et al., 1989; Gutek & Winter, 1992).

In sum, it appears that while most persons tend to report fairly high levels of satisfaction with their current jobs, considerable variation exists on this dimension. Let's now examine some of the factors responsible for these differences.

The Causes of Job Satisfaction Research on job satisfaction indicates that in fact, it is influenced by many different variables. These tend to fall into two major groups: factors relating to *jobs* themselves and the context in which they are performed, and factors relating to *personal characteristics* of employees.

Work-Related Influences on Job Satisfaction One key determinant of job satisfaction has do with the *reward system* adopted by an organization. Job satisfaction tends to be higher when employees believe that the reward system is fair than when they believe it is unfair and shows favoritism (Miceli & Lane, 1991). Another factor that has a major impact on job satisfaction is the *perceived quality of supervision*—the extent to which employees believe that their bosses are competent, have their best interests at heart, and treat them with respect and consideration. A third important factor in job satisfaction is the extent to which individuals feel that they can participate in decisions that affect them—the greater such participation, the higher job satisfaction tends to be. Fourth, the level of *work and social stimulation* provided by jobs themselves is important. When people feel rushed and overloaded, satisfaction tends to decrease (Gardell, 1987). Similarly, job satisfaction also declines when we are bored or have too little to do—as I discovered in my first full-time job.

What makes a job boring? Evidence on this issue has recently been reported by Melamed and his colleagues (1995). These researchers asked almost 1,300 blue-collar workers holding a wide range of jobs to report on their feelings of monotony and on their job satisfaction. In addition, the researchers studied records of the workers' sick days. Results indicated that two kinds of jobs are monotonous and boring to employees: jobs in which the same activities are repeated over and over again on a short cycle (within one hour or less), and jobs that involve work *underload*—tasks that demand long periods of careful vigilance and monitoring of work-related activities, despite the fact that usually nothing happens. For instance, workers at nuclear plants must monitor gauges for long periods of time, during which there is usually no important change. Similarly, persons who check products for quality have to examine each passing unit carefully, despite the fact that there may be long periods between defective items. As shown in Figure 17.9, the greater the extent to which jobs showed these characteristics, the greater the subjective monotony reported by employees, and the lower their reported job satisfaction. In addition, among women—but not among men—the greater employees' subjective monotony, the more sick days they took. The reasons for this gender difference are unclear, but it may stem at least in part

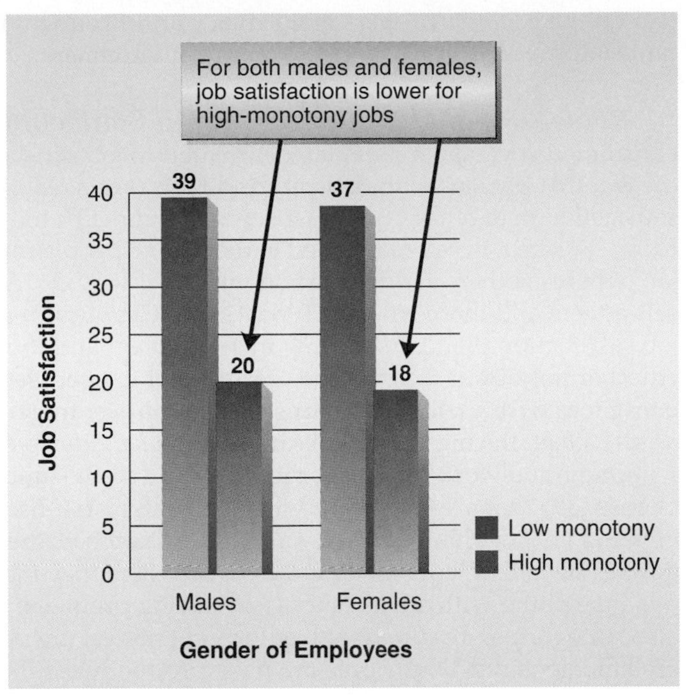

(**Source**: Based on data from Melamed et al., 1995.)

FIGURE 17.9

Subjective Monotony and Job Satisfaction

The greater the subjective monotony (the monotony experienced by employees) of various jobs, the lower employees' job satisfaction. What makes jobs monotonous? Repetitive activities that have to be done over and over again on short cycles (one hour or less), and the requirement that employees pay close attention to their work, even though nothing much is happening.

from the fact that women, more than men, may tend to use sick days as a means of coping with high levels of work-related stress (Zaccaro, Craig, & Quinn, 1991).

Finally, individuals tend to report higher levels of satisfaction when they do their jobs in *pleasant work settings* than when they work in unpleasant ones. What makes a work setting pleasant? Many aspects of the physical environment do, including comfortable temperatures, adequate lighting, absence of noise, fresh as opposed to stale air, and adequate space and privacy (e.g., Baron, 1994). While ensuring such conditions is generally the task of organizations, individuals can improve their own work settings in many ways. For instance, the device shown in Figure 17.10, which I invented and patented, is designed to clean and refresh the air and remove unwanted noise in a room. It also increases privacy by making it more difficult for anyone outside the room to overhear what is being said or done inside it. Therefore, this device—

FIGURE 17.10

The P.P.S.™—One Device for Improving Work Environments

The product shown here—known as the P.P.S.™—filters and refreshes the air in work settings (or any other room), reduces external noise, and increases privacy.

named the P.P.S.™ (for personal Privacy and Productivity System)—can be quite effective in improving the physical environment.

Person-Related Influences on Job Satifaction We have already considered several personal factors related to job satisfaction—for instance, the fact that persons with seniority and high status report higher levels of job satisfaction than others. Some aspects of personality, too, appear to be linked to job satisfaction; as I mentioned earlier, some people find satisfaction in any job, whereas others are dissatisfied whatever they do. Also, persons high in self-esteem and those who are Type As (see Chapter 13) tend to report higher job satisfaction than persons low in self-esteem and those who are Type Bs. Another important factor is the extent to which people are performing jobs consistent with their own interests and abilities. In general, the closer this *person–job fit*, the higher the job satisfaction (e.g., Fricko & Beehr, 1992).

One framework for measuring this kind of fit—and for helping people choose jobs that are consistent with their interests—has been developed by Holland (1973). This approach, sometimes known as the *Holland Scales*, categorizes people in terms of the types of activities they most enjoy—for example, interacting with others (social) or solving problems (investigative)—and also categorizes occupational environments on these same dimensions. Holland contends that people are most productive and happiest when there is a good fit between their interests and the requirements of their jobs, and this idea has been confirmed by many research findings.

In sum, a wide range of factors influence job satisfaction. Thus, there are many concrete steps that organizations can take to enhance their employees' positive evaluations of their work.

Job Satisfaction: Its Major Effects

Attitudes often are reflected in overt actions, so it is only reasonable to expect job satisfaction to influence work-related behavior. And it does; but the relationship is more complex, and perhaps more subtle, than you might imagine. Let's consider the impact of job satisfaction on two important aspects of work-related behavior: employee withdrawal (absenteeism, quitting) and task performance.

Job Satisfaction and Employee Withdrawal When people are dissatisfied with their jobs, they find ways to minimize contact with them—they *withdraw*. This can involve *absenteeism*—not showing up for work (see Figure 17.11)—and *quitting* (sometimes known as *voluntary withdrawal*). But while job satisfaction is related to both of these outcomes, the link is quite weak. Why? Probably because low job satisfaction is just one factor influencing employees' decisions about whether to come to work and whether to seek another job (e.g., Tett & Meyer, 1993). Economic necessity may often outweigh even very low levels of job satisfaction where both absenteeism and quitting are concerned. In other words, if an individual needs the income provided by a job and knows that absences may lead to being fired, this person may come to work regularly—even though he or she hates the job. Similarly, if an individual knows that few other jobs are available, he or she may stay in a job, even if highly dissatisfied with it: There is little choice. Because of such factors, people often can't act on the basis of their low job satisfaction, and so the link between such work-related attitudes and their behavior is weak.

FIGURE 17.11

Low Job Satisfaction in Action

When people dislike their jobs (i.e., when they have low job satisfaction), they may, like the character shown here, try to avoid contact with work.

"I'll be a little late for work today because I hate my job."

(**Source**: FROM THE WALL STREET JOURNAL—PERMISSION, CARTOON FEATURES SYNDICATE.)

Job Satisfaction and Task Performance It is often assumed that "happy employees are productive employees"—that persons who have positive attitudes toward their jobs will work harder and do better work than those who hold negative attitudes. Surprisingly, though, this relationship, too, appears to be quite weak. In other words, it is difficult to predict individuals' performance at work from their job satisfaction. Why? Again, the explanation may involve several factors.

Organizational Citizenship Behavior: Actions by individuals that help other employees in their organization, or the organization itself, and that are "beyond the call of duty."

First, many jobs are structured so that there is little room for variation in performance. On the one hand, the persons holding them must maintain a minimum level of performance just to remain in the job; on the other hand, they can't exceed this minimum by much, because they are just a small cog in a much larger wheel. For instance, production workers have to work at a minimum speed; but they can't go much faster than this, no matter how satisfied they are, because the work arrives at a fixed and steady pace.

Second, task performance and job satisfaction may not be causally linked. Rather, any apparent relationship between them may actually stem from the fact that both are related to a third factor—receipt of various rewards. As suggested by Porter and Lawler (1968), both job satisfaction and high levels of performance may stem from the receipt of rewards. When these are high and are perceived as fair, both performance and job satisfaction increase—but there may be no direct link between these two factors.

Finally, while the link between job satisfaction and *individual* performance may be quite weak, research evidence indicates that the link between employees' job satisfaction and an *organization's* level of performance may be somewhat stronger (Ostroff, 1992). Why would this be so? Perhaps because when individuals have high levels of job satisfaction, they are willing to engage in actions that are "beyond the call of duty"—actions that are not part of their job, but which help the company overall. Such actions are known as **organizational citizenship behavior** (e.g., Morrison, 1994; Organ, 1988). They can take many different forms, such as offering help to a coworker who needs assistance; never missing a day of work; overlooking problems and sources of irritation; speaking well of the company to others, thus making it easier for the company to recruit good employees; and showing courtesy to coworkers and customers (Konovsky & Pugh, 1994). There is considerable evidence that such actions contribute to a pleasant working environment and to the overall level of performance and success attained by an organization. Thus, job satisfaction can have beneficial effects on performance in this relatively indirect—but important—way.

How do I/O psychologists study job satisfaction? To find out, see the Research Methods section.

Key Questions

- What is job satisfaction? Do most individuals report high or low levels of job satisfaction?
- What are some key work-related and person-related factors that influence job satisfaction?
- What are the major effects of low or high job satisfaction?
- What is organizational citizenship behavior, and how does it relate to links between job satisfaction and job performance?

■ *RESEARCH METHODS* ■

How Psychologists Study Job Satisfaction

Attitudes are very real; but, as we saw in Chapter 16, they can't be "seen" directly. Rather, they can only be assessed indirectly, through various aspects of people's behavior. This is certainly true with respect to job satisfaction, which is simply one kind of attitude. How, then, do I/O psychologists study job satisfaction? There are several different methods.

By far the most common approach to measuring job satisfaction involves the use of questionnaires, or rating scales, specifically designed to measure various aspects of people's attitudes toward their jobs. Several different scales for measuring job satisfaction have been developed, and some of these have been used for several decades. One of the most popular is the **Job Descriptive Index (JDI).** In this questionnaire, individuals indicate whether or not each of several adjectives describes a particular aspect of their work (Smith, Kendall, & Hulin, 1969). Questions on the JDI deal with five distinct aspects of job: the work itself, pay, promotional opportunities, supervision, and coworkers.

Another widely used measure is the **Minnesota Satisfaction Questionnaire (MSQ).** Here, people completing the scale rate the extent to which they are satisfied or dissatisfied with various aspects of their jobs—their pay, chances for advancement, and so on (Weiss et al., 1967). Although these and other measures of job satisfaction were developed as long as thirty years ago, they have been found to be highly reliable and valid, so they continue in use today (e.g., Melamed et al., 1995). A major benefit of rating scales is that they can be completed quickly and efficiently by large numbers of people. Another is that when the same questionnaire is used in many different companies, it is possible to determine whether job satisfaction varies across these companies. Items similar to those on the JDI and MSQ are shown in Table 17.2.

Questionnaires are not the only techniques through which I/O psychologists measure job satisfaction, however. Another approach is the **critical incident technique,** in which employees describe events relating to their work that they have found especially satisfying or dissatisfying. I/O psychologists then closely examine their answers to see if there any common themes. For instance, if many employees mention situations in which they were harshly criticized by their supervisors as producing dissatisfaction, this would suggest that the way negative feedback is delivered may be one important factor in job satisfaction (e.g., Baron, 1996).

Finally, I/O psychologists sometimes measure job satisfaction by means of *confrontation meetings*, in which employees are asked to "lay it on the line" and discuss their major complaints and concerns. If such sessions are conducted in a skillful manner, much can be learned about the factors that cause employees to experience high or low levels of job satisfaction.

In sum, I/O psychologists use several different methods in their efforts to measure, and study, job satisfaction. And their efforts in this respect have certainly paid off: Such research has added greatly to our knowledge of the factors that influence job satisfaction, and to the effects of such attitudes on many aspects of behavior.

Careers: New Forms, New Strategies

What kind of job do you want when you finish school? What kind of career do you see yourself having in the years ahead? These are questions nearly everyone considers in college—I certainly did, back in the early 1960s, when I decided to become a psychologist. But in several respects answers to these questions have become harder and harder to come by, and less and less certain, with the passing years. When I was in college, most people assumed that they would go to work for a large company after graduation and might well remain with the same organization for the rest of their careers. As you probably know, such single-job careers are now largely a thing of the past. As I noted in Chapter 9, large companies are the ones that have downsized most in recent years, so opportunities with them have been increasingly limited. The result is that individuals now starting their **careers**—their lifelong series of employment experiences—need new strategies and approaches if they are to attain success. I/O psychologists are well aware of this fact and, as a result, have devoted increasing attention to the study of careers (e.g., Cascio, 1995). What have they learned from this research? That while many factors play a role in career success, the three described below seem to be among the most crucial.

Job Descriptive Index (JDI): A widely used measure of job satisfaction in which individuals indicate whether or not each of several adjectives describes a particular aspect of their work.

Minnesota Satisfaction Questionnaire (MSQ): A widely used measure of job satisfaction in which individuals rate the extent to which they are satisfied or dissatisfied with various aspects of their jobs.

Critical Incident Technique: A technique for measuring job satisfaction in which individuals describe events relating to their work that they found especially satisfying or dissatisfying.

Careers: Individuals' lifelong series of employment experiences.

Career Goals: The Value of Lifetime Learning Outside of Japan, which seems to be a major exception, few companies offer lifetime employment to their employees (Fingleton, 1995). This means that young people today should give up the dream of climbing ever upward on the corporate ladder. What should replace this dream? Primarily, a new perspective that views jobs or assignments as a means of gaining valuable skills. In short, people entering their career today should view it as a series of opportunities for gaining new skills that will increase their value on the job market. The

TABLE 17.2

Widely Used Measures of Job Satisfaction

The items shown here are similar to those in two widely used measures of job satisfaction—the JDI and the MSQ.

Job Descriptive Index (JDI)	Minnesota Satisfaction Questionnaire (MSQ)
Enter "Yes," "No," or "?" for each description or word below to indicate whether they describe an aspect of your job.	Indicate the extent to which you are satisfied with each aspect of your present job. Enter one number next to each aspect.
Work itself:	
_____ Routine	1 = Extremely dissatisfied
_____ Satisfactory	2 = Not satisfied
_____ Good	3 = Neither satisfied nor dissatisfied
Promotions:	4 = Satisfied
_____ Dead-end job	5 = Extremely satisfied
_____ Few promotions	_____ Utilization of your abilities
_____ Good opportunity for promotion	_____ Authority
	_____ Company policies and practices
	_____ Independence
	_____ Supervision–human relations

basic idea is simple: As individuals acquire these skills, they become more desirable as employees and so expand the scope of their future careers. This means that when one is contemplating a job, it is probably better to ask "What will I learn?" rather than "How long will it last?" or "What will it pay?" When individuals view jobs mainly as learning experiences, they can map out a career strategy that will help them become what they ultimately want to be: a highly desirable commodity where employers are concerned. (For some advice on how to succeed in job interviews, see the Making Psychology Part of Your Life section at the end of this chapter.)

Job Rotation: An Important Way to Build a Career One of my uncles owned a pie-baking company. Although he was quite wealthy, he insisted that my cousins work in the factory making pies, and serve as delivery drivers, before they could assume executive positions. As he put it: "You've got to know this business from the ground up—all the jobs in it—before you can run it." This is actually sound advice for young people seeking to advance their own careers. Consistent with the "learn as much as you can" theme I mentioned previously, it is useful to move from job to job within a single company. Such transfers involve what is known as **job rotation**—lateral moves between jobs in a given organization—and they can do much to build individuals' skills. Research findings indicate that job rotation is expe-

Job Rotation: Lateral moves between jobs within a given organization.

rienced mainly by high-performing employees relatively early in their careers, and that it is related to positive outcomes such as high promotion rates and salary growth (Campion, Cheraskin, & Stevens, 1994). So it is definitely one important goal individuals should seek in their efforts to build their own careers. The moral: If you are offered job rotation, accept it. The benefits of doing so can be substantial.

Having a Mentor: "With a Little Help from my Friends . . ."

Consider fifty new college graduates hired by a large company to do pretty much the same job. All start out at the same level; but if you return in one year to see how they are doing, you may already notice large differences. Some will be gone, others will be falling behind, and a few will clearly be out front—already on the fast track to success. Why? Many factors play a role, but one of the most important involves having a *mentor*. As we saw in Chapter 9, a mentor is a more experienced (and usually older) individual who advises and helps new employees in many ways (e.g., Fagenson, 1992; Tepper, 1995).

How do mentors advance the careers of the younger persons they help—their *protégés?* In many different ways. For instance, they provide much-needed emotional support and confidence for those who are just starting out. In addition, they nominate protégés for promotions, provide them with opportunities to demonstrate their competence, and call them to the attention of higher management. They also suggest effective ways for reaching various work goals—shortcuts younger employees probably wouldn't devise themselves. Finally, mentors protect protégés from the effects of errors, and help them avoid various pitfalls that might damage their careers. Overall, the effect is very beneficial; in fact, many studies indicate that having a mentor early in one's career is an important predictor of later success (e.g., Whitely, Dougherty, & Dreher, 1991).

What do mentors get in return for all this help? For one thing, the respect and support of their protégés, who are often very grateful for the help they have received. In addition, having successful protégés often boosts the status of mentors: After all, they have attracted and helped train the very best! Finally, of course, mentors experience the rewards of helping the next generation—the kind of *generativity* that is an important stage of adult development in Erikson's theory (see Chapter 9). So mentoring is definitely not a one-way street.

Who becomes a mentor and for whom? These are complex questions, but, as we saw in Chapter 16, it is a basic fact of social life that people tend to like and feel more comfortable around persons who are similar to themselves than around persons who are different (e.g., Dovidio et al., 1995). Thus, it seems reasonable to expect that similarity along several dimensions will be the rule in mentor–protégé relationships; and in fact this appears to be the case (e.g., Thomas, 1993). As you can readily see, this raises an important—and unsettling—issue: Since senior employees at most companies tend to be male and white, to the extent similarity influences the formation of mentor–protégé relationships, this similarity rule may create problems for women and minorities. For information on this important issue, please see the Exploring Gender and Diversity section.

> *Key Questions*
>
> - How have careers changed in recent decades?
> - What is job rotation, and what effect does it have on careers?
> - What are the benefits of having a mentor?
> - Do women and minorities experience difficulties in obtaining mentors?

Leadership: Patterns of Influence within Groups

Try this simple demonstration with your friends. Ask them to rate themselves, on a seven-point scale ranging from 1 (very low) to 7 (very high), in terms of

EXPLORING GENDER & DIVERSITY

Race, Gender, and Mentoring

Are women and minorities really at a disadvantage where obtaining a mentor is concerned? Unfortunately, some research findings indicate that they are. In general, women and members of minority groups (e.g., African Americans) seem to find it more difficult to obtain mentors than do white males (e.g., Fagenson, 1992; Thomas, 1993). Such difficulties seem to stem, at least in part, from the effects of similarity, as described previously: Most managers in the United States and other Western countries are white males, and such persons feel most comfortable around individuals of the same gender and similar background. However, other factors also play a role. In recent surveys, women have reported less willingness than males to serve as mentors (Noe, 1988). Conversely, many male managers express concerns about serving as a mentor for female employees: They fear that the close relationships that develop may be misperceived as romantic entanglements (see Figure 17.12; Pierce, 1995).

Whatever the precise reasons, it seems clear that women and minorities do experience difficulties in obtaining mentors and that this, in turn, can have adverse effects on their careers. Clear evidence for such effects is provided by a study conducted recently by Dreher and Cox (1996). These researchers mailed questionnaires to thousands of graduates of M.B.A. programs—males and females, minority and nonminority persons—asking them to report on whether they had a mentor early in their careers, and on one important measure of career success: total earnings. Results indicated that as expected, white male graduates were more likely to have mentors than women or members of various minority groups. An additional, and perhaps even more unsettling, finding was that these contrasting experiences with mentoring translated into large differences in salary: White males with mentors reported salaries fully $22,454 higher on average than women or minority-group members who did not have mentors.

These findings were based solely on responses to a survey, so it is impossible to rule out the potential impact of other factors that may have contributed to these results; for instance, the fact that white males plug more easily into informal communication networks—the infamous "old-boy network." However, when this research is combined with other studies suggesting that having a mentor is often very beneficial for one's career, it does seem reasonable to conclude that difficulties in establishing such relationships may be one more barrier faced by women and minorities on the road to career success.

FIGURE 17.12

One Reason Why Males Are Reluctant to Mentor Females

Some males who could serve as mentors for females are reluctant to do so because of their concern that the relationship will be perceived as a romantic one.

leadership potential. What do you think you will find? Probably most of your friends will rate themselves as *average or above* on this characteristic. This suggests that they view leadership in very favorable terms; but what, precisely, *is* leadership? Psychologists define it as *the process through which one member of a group (its leader) influences other group members toward the attainment of specific group goals* (Yukl, 1994). In other words, being a **leader** has to do with *influence*—who exerts the most influence in a given group.

Research on leadership has been a part of psychology for many years and has been studied from many different perspectives. In this discussion, however, we'll focus our attention on three basic issues: *traits versus situations* in the mak-

Leader: The person within a group who exerts the most influence.

Great Person Theory: A theory suggesting that all great leaders possess certain traits that set them apart from other persons.

ing of a leader; contrasting *styles* of leadership; and, finally, perhaps the most dramatic form of leadership—*transformational* or *charismatic* leadership.

Who Becomes a Leader: Traits, Situations, or Both? Are some people born to lead? Common sense suggests that this is so. Eminent leaders of the past such as Alexander the Great, Queen Elizabeth I, and Abraham Lincoln seem to differ from ordinary human beings in several respects. Such observations led early researchers to formulate a view of leadership known as the great person theory. According to this theory, great leaders possess certain traits that set them apart from most human beings. Further, the theory suggests that these traits remain stable over time and across different cultures—so that *all* great leaders, no matter when or where they live, resemble one another in certain respects.

These are intriguing ideas, but until about 1980 research designed to test them generally failed to yield positive findings. Try as they might, researchers could not formulate an agreed-upon short list of the key traits shared by all leaders (Yukl, 1994). In recent years, however, this situation has altered greatly. More sophisticated research methods, coupled with a better understanding of the basic dimensions of human personality, have led many researchers to conclude that leaders do indeed differ from other persons in several important ways (see Figure 17.13; Kirkpatrick & Locke, 1991).

What, then, are the key traits of leaders—the characteristics that suit them for this important role? The findings of research on this topic are summarized in Table 17.3. As you can see from this table, leaders appear to rate higher than most people in such characteristics as *drive*—the desire for achievement coupled with high energy and resolution; *self-confidence; creativity;* and *leadership motivation*—the desire to be in charge and exercise authority over others. Perhaps the most important single characteristics of leaders, however, is a high level of *flexibility:* the ability to recognize what actions or approaches are required in a given situation, and then to act accordingly (Zaccaro, Foti, & Kenny, 1991).

While certain traits do seem to be related to leadership, however, it is also clear that leaders do *not* operate in a social vacuum. On the contrary, different groups, facing different tasks and problems, seem to require different types of leaders—or at least leaders who demonstrate different styles. This basic fact is recognized in all modern theories of leadership, which take careful note of the fact that leadership is a complex role, involving not only influence but

FIGURE 17.13

Great Leaders: Do They Share Certain Traits?

The *great person* theory of leadership suggests that all great leaders, no matter where or when they live, share certain traits. While the extreme view proposed by the great person theory is not supported by existing evidence, some research findings indicate that leaders do differ from other persons in some respects.

TABLE 17.3

Traits Associated with Leadership

Research findings indicate that successful leaders show the traits listed here to a greater extent than do other persons.

Trait	Description
Drive	Desire for achievement; ambition; high energy; tenacity; initiative
Honesty and Integrity	Trustworthiness; reliability; openness
Leadership Motivation	Desire to exercise influence over others in order to reach shared goals
Self-Confidence	Trust in own abilities
Cognitive Ability	Intelligence; ability to integrate and interpret large amounts of information
Expertise	Knowledge of the group's activities; knowledge of relevant technical matters
Creativity	Originality
Flexibility	Ability to adapt to needs of followers and to changing requirements of the situation

(Source: Based on suggestions by Kirkpatrick & Locke, 1991.)

many other kinds of interactions between leaders and followers (Bass, 1990; House & Podsakoff, 1994; Locke, 1991). So, *yes,* traits do matter where leadership is concerned, but they are only part of the total picture. Leadership, like all forms of social behavior, can be understood only in terms of complex interactions between social situations and individual traits. Approaches that focus entirely on one of these aspects tend to be quite inaccurate.

How Leaders Operate: Contrasting Styles and Approaches

All leaders are definitely *not* alike. On the contrary, they differ greatly in terms of personal *style* or approach to leadership (e.g., George, 1995). While there are probably as many different styles of leadership as there are leaders, research on leader behavior suggests that in fact a relatively small number of dimensions play a key role in shaping the kinds of relationships leaders have with their followers.

One of these dimensions has to do with the extent to which leaders permit their followers to have any say in decision making—the *autocratic–democratic* dimension. Autocratic leaders make decisions unilaterally, whereas democratic leaders invite input and participation in decision making from their followers. Another important dimension involves the extent to which leaders dictate how followers should carry out their assigned tasks versus giving them the freedom to work in any way they wish. This is referred to as the *directive–permissive* dimension, and it cross-cuts the autocratic–democratic dimension; thus, leaders tend to show one of the four different patterns summarized in Figure 17.14 on page 694 (Muczyk & Reimann, 1987).

Finally, leaders' styles also differ with respect to two other important dimensions, sometimes known as *task orientation* and *person orientation*. Task orientation is the extent to which a given leader focuses on getting the task

FIGURE 17.14

Two Key Dimensions of Leader Behavior

Leaders differ in their behavior or style along the two dimensions shown here, as well as on other dimensions.

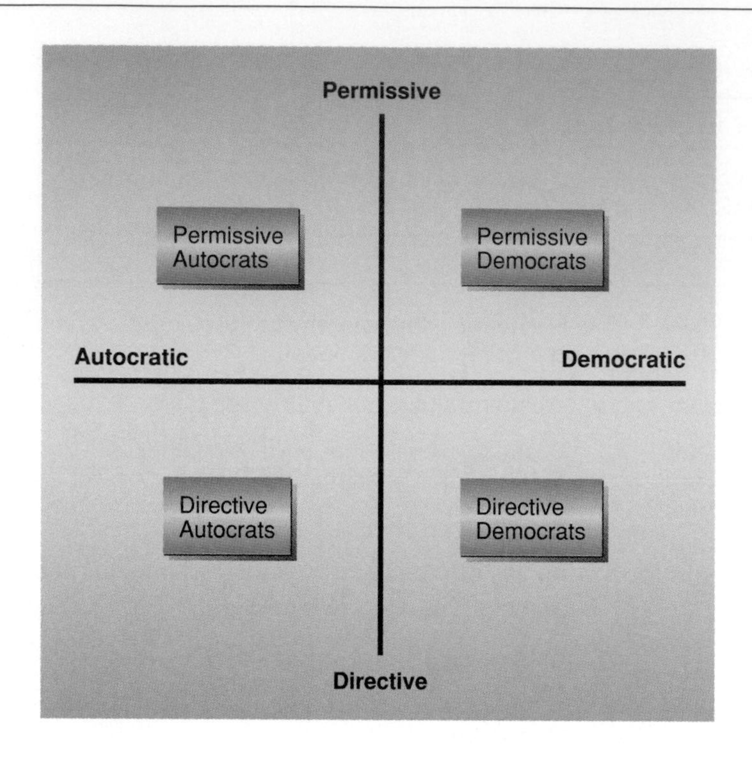

done—whatever it happens to be. Person orientation, in contrast, is a leader's interest in maintaining good, friendly relations with his or her followers. Leaders can be high or low on each of these dimensions; for instance, a given leader can be high on both, low on both, high on one and low on the other, or moderate on both. Task orientation and person orientation appear to be very basic dimensions of leader style: They have been observed among thousands of different leaders in many different contexts (e.g., business groups, military groups, sports teams), and in several different countries (Bass, 1990). Interestingly, no single style seems to be best; rather, which one is most effective depends on the specific circumstances. For example, when leaders are high on person orientation, they often have friendly relations with their followers—who may then be reluctant to give them any bad news. The result: The leaders can get into serious trouble because they are not receiving vital feedback from followers (Baron, 1996). In contrast, leaders high in task orientation often wring high levels of performance out of their followers. The followers may feel that their leader has no interest in them, however, and this may weaken their commitment to the group.

In sum, leaders do appear to differ greatly with respect to personal style—how they go about fulfilling the leadership role—and these differences have important effects on their groups. However, because leaders' styles are only one of many factors influencing leadership, it would be misleading to suggest that one style is always—or even usually—best.

Transformational Leadership: Leadership through Vision and Charisma Have you ever seen films of John F. Kennedy? Franklin Roosevelt? Martin Luther King Jr.? If so, you may have noticed that there seemed to be something special about these leaders. As you listened to their speeches, you may have found yourself being moved by their words and stirred by the vigor with which they delivered their messages. You are definitely not alone in such reactions: These leaders exerted powerful effects on many millions of persons and by doing so, changed their society—and perhaps even the entire world. Leaders who accomplish such feats are often termed **transformational** or **charismatic leaders;** and these terms (which are often used interchangeably) seem fitting, for such people often do transform the world they live in. What characteristics make certain leaders charismatic? And how do these leaders exert such dramatic influence on their followers? Let's see what research findings have to say about these issues.

Transformational or Charismatic Leaders: Leaders who exert exceptionally powerful effects on large numbers of followers or, sometimes, on their entire societies.

The Basic Nature of Charisma: Traits or Relationships? At first glance, it is tempting to assume that transformational leaders are special because they possess certain traits; in other words, that such leadership can be understood in terms of the great person theory described earlier. But while traits may play a role in transformational leadership, there is growing consensus that it makes more sense to understand such leadership as involving a special type of *relationship* between leaders and their followers (House, 1977). Charismatic leadership, it appears, rests more on specific types of reactions on the part of followers than on traits possessed by charismatic leaders. Such reactions include: (1) high levels of devotion and loyalty toward the leader, (2) enthusiasm for the leader and the leader's ideas, (3) willingness among followers to sacrifice their own interests for the sake of a larger group goal, and (4) levels of performance beyond those that would normally be expected. In short, transformational leadership involves a special kind of leader–follower relationship, one in which the leader can, in the words of one author, "make ordinary people do extraordinary things" (Conger, 1991).

The Behavior of Transformational Leaders But what, precisely, do transformational leaders do to generate this kind of relationship with followers? Studies designed to answer this question point to the following conclusion: Such leaders gain the capacity to exert profound influence over others because of many different factors. One of the most important of these is the fact that such leaders propose a *vision* (Howell & Frost, 1989): They describe, usually in vivid, emotion-provoking terms, an image of what their nation or group can—and should—become. Consider the following words, uttered by Martin Luther King Jr. in his famous "I have a dream" speech:

> So I say to you, my friends, that even though we must face the difficulties of today and tomorrow, I still have a dream. It is a dream deeply rooted in the American dream that one day this nation will rise up and live out the true meaning of its creed—we hold these truths to be self-evident, that all men are created equal. This will be the day when all of God's children will be able to sing with new meaning, "My country, 'tis of thee, sweet land of liberty. . . ."

Transformational leaders do more than merely describe a dream or vision; in addition, they offer a route for reaching it. They tell their followers, in straightforward terms, how to get from here to there. This too seems to be crucial, for a vision that seems perpetually out of reach is unlikely to motivate people to try to attain it.

Third, transformational leaders engage in what Conger (1991) terms *framing:* They define the goals of their movement or organization in a way that gives meaning and purpose to whatever actions they are requesting from followers. Perhaps the nature of framing is best illustrated by the well-known story of two stonecutters working on a cathedral in the Middle Ages. When asked what they are doing, one replied, "Why, cutting this stone, of course." The other answered, "Building the world's most beautiful temple to the glory of God." Which person would be more likely to expend great effort on this task? The answer is obvious.

Other behaviors shown by transformational leaders include high levels of self-confidence and confidence in their followers, a high degree of concern

FIGURE 17.15

Transformational Leaders: How They Operate

Research findings indicate that transformational leaders exert their profound effects because of the factors shown here.

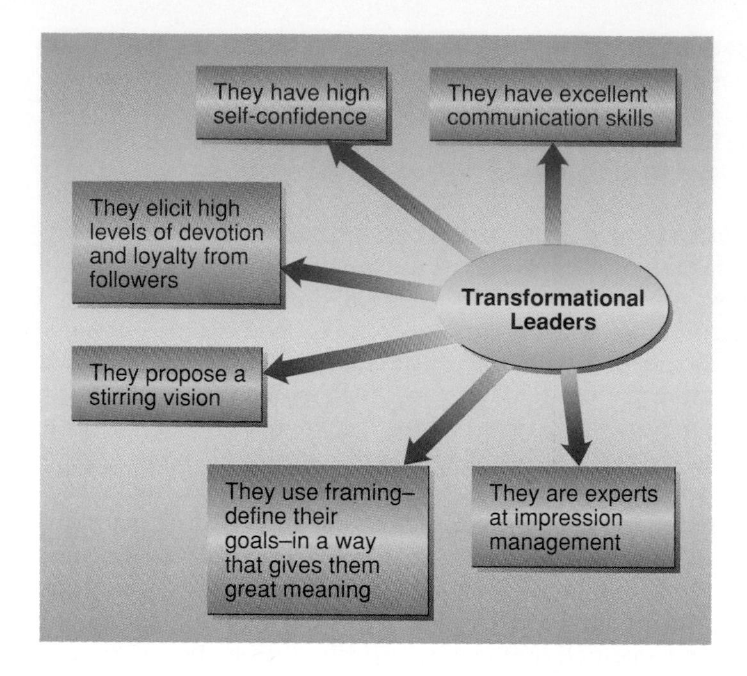

for their followers' needs, excellent communication skills, and a stirring personal style (House, Spangler, & Woycke, 1991). Finally, transformational leaders are often masters of *impression management,* engaging in many actions designed to make a good impression on others. When these forms of behavior are added to the exciting visions they promote, the tremendous impact of transformational leaders loses most of its apparent mystery. In fact, it rests firmly on principles and processes well understood by social psychologists (see Figure 17.15).

The Effects of Transformational Leaders: A Very Mixed Bag

Are transformational or charismatic leaders always a plus for their groups or societies? As you probably already realize, definitely not. Many charismatic leaders use their skills for what they perceive to be the good of their group or society—people like Martin Luther King Jr., Franklin Roosevelt, and Indira Gandhi, to name just a few. Moreover, such leaders seem to emerge at times of crisis—just when their special skills are most needed (Pillai, 1996). But others use this leadership style for purely selfish ends (Howell & Avolio, 1992). For example, Michael Milken, formerly of the brokerage firm Drexel Burnham Lambert, was described by colleagues and clients as being extremely charismatic. Yet he used people's trust and loyalty for illegal ends: stock fraud that cost innocent investors millions of dollars. Similarly, David Koresh, charismatic leader of a religious cult in Waco, Texas, used his position to reserve all females in the group for himself—girls as young as ten years old—while insisting that the other males remain celibate. Ultimately, Koresh's leadership resulted in his death and that of many of his followers when the cult's headquarters was attacked by federal officials.

In short, charismatic or transformational leadership is definitely a two-edged sword. It can be used to promote beneficial social change consistent with the highest principles and ethical standards; or it can be used for selfish, illegal, and immoral purposes. Whether transformational leadership exerts its influence for good or for bad depends on the personal conscience and moral code of the person who wields it.

Key Questions

- What is the current status in psychology of the great person theory of leadership?
- What are the key dimensions of leadership behavior or style?
- How do transformational leaders influence their followers so strongly?

Human Factors: Designing for Efficiency, Health, and Safety

Have you ever made a mistake while trying to program a video recorder so that you didn't get the program you wanted? Have you ever cut your hand on a jagged, unfinished edge inside some electric appliance? Have your wrists ever ached after typing for hours at the keyboard of a computer? If you've had these experiences, or ones like them, you will probably agree with the following principle: *All tools, equipment, and systems used by human beings should be designed to maximize the ease, safety, and efficiency with which they can be utilized.* This principle is central to the field of *human factors,* or *ergonomics* as it is sometimes known (e.g., Sanders & McCormick, 1993). Psychologists specializing in this field use their knowledge about human behavior—especially their knowledge of human abilities and limitations—to help design tools and equipment that are both convenient and safe for human use. In this section we'll examine some of the findings of human factors psychology, focusing especially on issues relating to the *display of information,* effective *controls,* and the effective design of specific tools and equipment.

Visual Displays: Principles and Applications

One year in the mid-1980s, I set out to buy a new car. That year many models featured a new kind of speedometer. Instead of the standard round gauge with a pointer, many cars had a digital display in which bars of light moved across the screen. The bars changed color from green to amber to red, as speed increased. I test-drove many cars with this new kind of display and found it to be distracting. The result? I bought a car with the standard speedometer. Evidently millions of drivers agreed with me, because today this "improvement" has largely vanished.

This example underscores an important fact: Some kinds of **visual displays**—displays that present information visually—are easier to notice and understand than others. What kinds of displays are best? Research findings point to the following conclusions:

- Pointers that move against a fixed scale, as used in most speedometers, are usually easier to read than the reverse—a moving scale and a fixed pointer.
- Displays in which increases in the units being measured (e.g., speed) are shown on the display in a manner we naturally interpret as *up* or *higher* are easier to read than ones in which this "natural" relationship is absent. For instance, since we generally interpret clockwise movement as indicating "higher," standard speedometers make sense in this respect, too, and so are easy to read.
- Displays in which the scale markings are clear and easy to read are more effective than ones in which such markings are small or hard to read. If you have ever tried to tell the time with a watch that showed only four dots (at the 12, 3, 6, and 9 positions) and had no numbers on it, you've had firsthand experience with this fact.
- Displays that include different colors for important ranges or zones (e.g., one color for "normal," another for "caution," and a third for "danger") are easier to read than displays lacking such visual cues.

Visual Displays: Displays that present information visually.

Compatibility: In human factors, the degree to which controls operate in a manner consistent with human expectations.

In short, there appear to be better and worse ways to design visual displays, and careful attention to such principles can result in gauges and other visual displays that are easy to read and interpret. This is an important point in situations in which individuals must use the information provided by gauges as a basis for making quick decisions or taking rapid actions—as is the case, for instance, for airline pilots and employees in nuclear power plants, who must monitor processes occurring in complex aircraft or deep within reactors in terms of the readings on many visual displays.

Effective Controls: "What Happens When I Turn This Dial . . . ?"

Look at the remote controls shown in Figure 17.16. Would they vary in their ease of use? Probably so. The ones with different-shaped or different-sized controls for different functions would probably be easiest to use. The ones in which all the controls are virtually identical would be less effective, for obvious reasons.

Unfortunately, confusing or misleading controls are far from rare. In fact, one famous accident—the Three Mile Island incident, in which a major nuclear-powered electric plant came very close to a meltdown—stemmed, in part, from such problems (Seminara, 1993). Some controls in that ill-fated plant had three positions labeled "Off," "Auto," and "On." This sounds straightforward, but there was one major problem: These controls were spring-loaded so that after being set to "Off," they moved back to the "Auto" position. Thus, some employees assumed that the controls were in the correct "Auto" position when in fact they were not. The result? Near catastrophe.

Dramatic instances such as this highlight the importance of effective *controls* in the design of tools, equipment, and systems. What principles should guide the design of controls? Human factors psychologists have found that the most important principle is **compatibility**—the degree to which controls operate in a manner consistent with human expectations. For example, most people expect that when they turn a knob in a clockwise direction, it will increase whatever function is being controlled: the volume on a radio or CD player goes up, the temperature in an oven rises, and so on. Similarly, people seem naturally to expect that moving a lever forward will increase the function being controlled, whereas pulling it back will reduce it. So a basic rule of design where controls are concerned is this: Make sure that they follow the compatibility principle—that they do what most people expect them to do.

This sounds so simple and natural that you may be wondering why complications ever arise. One answer is that in some situations we don't have clear-cut expectations about the operation of controls. For instance, look at

FIGURE 17.16

Effective—and Ineffective—Controls

Would you find some of these remotes easier to use than others? Probably you would, because the controls on these devices vary in terms of their effectiveness.

the front of any stove. Which control regulates which burner? People differ in their expectations—and the result is that even after owning a stove for several years, you may still turn the wrong knob when you want a particular burner to come on.

In other situations, we *do* have expectations about how controls will operate, but they are out of synch with the way the controls actually do operate. A dramatic illustration of this kind of problem is provided by *antilock brakes,* designed to prevent skids on wet or icy pavements. When these braking systems were introduced, it was expected that they would prevent many automobile accidents, and insurance companies offered reduced premiums for cars equipped with such brakes. Millions of automobiles now have such brakes in the United States alone, so it has become possible to compare accident rates and repair costs for cars with and without them. The result? No difference! How can this be so? The field of human factors provides a ready answer—and one that was largely overlooked by safety experts without training in human factors (Miller, 1994). When most drivers feel their vehicle beginning to skid, they pump the brakes—the correct response with regular brakes. But that's precisely the *wrong* thing to do when a car has antilock brakes. In that case, the correct action is to apply steady pressure. Before the potential benefits of antilock brakes can be realized, therefore, it will be necessary either to change the way they operate so that pumping the brake *is* correct, or to retrain many millions of drivers to use the brake pedals on their cars in a new way.

Designing Tools and Equipment: Two Concrete Examples

Different jobs require different tools and equipment—that's a basic fact of life. For this reason, human factors psychologists are often called upon to assist in the design of specific tools or systems. In such cases, they apply their basic knowledge of such topics as perception, learning, fatigue, and many other aspects of human behavior to the task at hand. To illustrate such work, let's take a look at the contributions of human factors psychologists to the design of two pieces of equipment that seem about as different as they can be: the mailbags used by letter carriers, and computer keyboards.

Designing a Better Mailbag: Human Factors to the Rescue

The sight of a letter carrier strolling down the street, leather mailbag slung over her or his shoulder, is a familiar one to many people. In fact, the design of mailbags hasn't changed much in centuries; and why should it, you may be wondering. What could be simpler? In fact, however, letter carriers report that these mailbags are a cause of considerable discomfort. They are designed to carry heavy loads—a minimum of thirty-five pounds, and often much more. And because they rest on one shoulder, they are also the cause of many muscle and back injuries (e.g., Holewijn & Lotens, 1992). This fact led a group of human factors psychologists (Bloswick et al., 1994) to investigate whether a better mailbag could in fact be designed.

They began their research by talking to post office managers in order to get their suggestions about how the conventional mailbag could be improved. This preliminary work led to two alternative possibilities: a mailbag supported at the waist by a belt, and a mailbag with two pouches, supported by both shoulders.

The researchers then compared these three designs in a study where male volunteers were tested for muscle fatigue both before and after using each mailbag for an hour. Results were clear: While all three bags produced some fatigue, the conventional one produced significantly more fatigue than the other two models. The conclusion? The standard mailbag can definitely be improved so as to reduce fatigue and injuries for millions of postal workers throughout the world.

Designing a Better Keyboard: Taking the Pain Out of Computing If you visit almost any modern office, you are likely to see some employees sitting in front of computers wearing wrist splints or typing with their wrists supported by special devices. Why? Because each year millions of persons who spend their days typing on computer keyboards experience strain and injuries to their wrists and hands. Indeed, so common are such problems that they are currently estimated to account for more than 50 percent of occupational injuries (e.g., Rempel, Harrison, & Barnhart, 1992). These problems develop because when using standard keyboards, people often bend their hands upward at the wrist—a movement known as *extension*. Such extension compresses the *carpal tunnel* of the wrist, through which the tendons that control the fingers and several important nerves must pass. Compressing the carpal tunnel places great force on these tendons and nerves and often results in injuries and associated pain.

Key Questions

- What basic principles govern the design of effective visual displays?
- What basic design principles are fundamental to effective controls?
- How have human factors psychologists contributed to the design of improved mailbags for letter carriers and improved computer keyboards?

Can anything be done to reduce such problems? Human factors psychologists believe something can. After studying the movements involved in typing on computer keyboards, they have found that wrist *flexion*—a movement in which the hand is bent downward, not upward, at the wrist—places much less pressure on the carpal tunnel. Presumably, then, a keyboard that promotes wrist flexion should be less likely to produce fatigue and injury. To test this possibility, one group of researchers (Hedge et al., 1996) recently designed such a keyboard—one on which the surface with the keys tilts downward. They then compared this keyboard with a standard keyboard—and with a keyboard to which a wrist support had been added—by asking employees at a large company to use the three designs in their daily work (see Figure 17.17). Careful measurements of the pressures on employees' wrists, made by means of special wrist-monitoring devices, indicated that these pressures were indeed lower when the employees used the new tilt-downward keyboard. Moreover, almost all users reported that they found the system comfortable and preferred it to the standard one and to the wrist-support keyboard. While such findings are far from conclusive, they agree with the results of other studies indicating that people also improve their overall

FIGURE 17.17

Designing a Better Computer Keyboard

The keyboard on the left tilts downward, thus reducing the necessity for wrist extension. Most people found this keyboard more comfortable to use than the standard keyboard on the right. Careful studies of the effects of these two designs on users' wrists also indicate that the new design shown on the left produces less potentially harmful pressure on the wrist.

(**Source**: from Hedge et al., 1996. Courtesy Dr. A. Hedge.)

body posture when using a tilt-downward keyboard (e.g., Rudakewych, Valent, & Hedge, 1994). Thus, it seems possible that with further development, keyboards designed to take account of human anatomy and human comfort may well replace the standard version so familiar to most of us. If this results in a sharply reduced incidence of wrist-related strains and injuries, it will constitute yet another important contribution to human health and well-being by psychologists who focus on the interface between human beings and the tools and equipment they use (e.g., Dempsey & Leamon, 1995).

Making Psychology Part of Your Life

Impression Management in Job Interviews: The Fine Art of Looking Good

Getting the right job—one consistent with your interests and abilities—is an important step toward personal happiness and fulfillment. Yet it's not easy in today's competitive world. Can psychology help in this respect? Absolutely. Psychologists have studied in detail the process of *impression management*—how to make a good first impression on others. Many organizations use employment interviews as the basis for choosing employees, so knowing something about this process can be very helpful to you in your job search. Here are some tips for successful interviewing based on the findings of this research.

- Do your homework. Because interviewers often care deeply about their companies, they often ask questions designed to find out whether an applicant knows anything about the business. Before you interview, do your homework. Find out about the company, what it does, and how it operates. Demonstrating such knowledge can get you off to a good start in many interviews.
- Dress and groom appropriately. Casual is definitely in as a style of dress—but don't assume that it's appropriate for a job interview. Some organizations have loosened their dress codes for employees with "dress-down Fridays," but interviewers still expect job candidates to be well groomed. Typically, standard business attire is best for both men and women. It's also helpful to avoid too much makeup, too much perfume or cologne, and flashy jewelry; interviewers often make negative attributions about applicants who go to excess in these respects.
- Engage in self-enhancing tactics, but don't overdo it. Among the most useful *self-enhancement* tactics are positive statements about your experience and competence (backed up by solid evidence) and positive nonverbal cues (smiling, a reasonably high level of eye contact with the interviewer, and an upright, alert posture). Indicating that you know you're not perfect can help, too. But whatever tactics you use, don't overdo it.
- Engage in other-enhancing techniques—again, in moderation. The other side of the coin, where increasing interviewers' liking for you is concerned, is *other enhancement:* actions that put *interviewers* in a favorable light or cause them to feel good. When people are in a good mood, they tend to evaluate everything around them—including other persons—more favorably. How can you boost interviewers' moods? Through such steps as agreeing with the interviewer, showing a high degree of interest in what this person says, and offering a touch of flattery here and there. Again, be careful; it's all too easy to overdo these tactics, with disastrous results.
- Concentrate on jobs for which you are really qualified. Interviewers typically have very busy schedules, so they truly dislike wasting their time talking to people who aren't qualified for the job they are trying to fill. Going to interviews that are really long shots, therefore, is pointless in most cases. Don't rule out jobs that are a bit of a stretch for you, but do avoid applying for ones for which you lack the necessary credentials or experience.
- Practice, practice, practice. None of the procedures described above is very complex, but using them effectively requires practice. So get some friends to help by playing the roles of interviewers, and conduct a number of "rehearsals." Few of us are naturals where interviewing is concerned; the more you practice, within reason, the better.
- Good luck!

Summary and Review of Key Questions

Industrial/Organizational Psychology: Studying Behavior in Work Settings

- **According to expectancy theory, what conditions are necessary for high levels of work motivation?** Expectancy theory suggests that motivation will be high when expectancy, instrumentality, and valence are all high.
- **What kinds of goals are most likely to result in increased motivation and performance?** Effective goals are ones that are specific and challenging (but attainable) and ones to which individuals are personally committed.
- **What factors do people consider in deciding whether they are being treated fairly or unfairly?** People compare the ratios of their own inputs—everything they contribute to a relationship—and their outcomes—everything they receive—with other persons' ratios of inputs and outcomes.
- **When individuals decide that they have not been treated fairly, what actions do they sometimes take to correct this situation?** They may reduce their inputs, attempt to increase their outcomes, withdraw from the relationship, or seek to "even the score" by taking what they feel they deserve.
- **What are job enlargement and job enrichment?** Job enlargement involves giving employees more tasks at the same level, while job enrichment involves giving them tasks requiring higher levels of skill or responsibility.
- **What is electronic performance monitoring, and what effects does it have on performance?** This technique involves monitoring employees' performance through their computer terminals or telephones. It has been found to increase performance in many, but not all, situations.
- **What is social facilitation, and what role does it play in electronic performance monitoring?** *Social facilitation* refers to the effects on behavior of the presence of an audience. Electronic performance monitoring seems to produce effects similar to those of an audience; it increases performance on well-learned tasks, but reduces performance on tasks people have not yet mastered. Another important factor is the extent to which employees can control monitoring of their performance.
- **What are some of the most important potential causes of errors in appraising others' performance?** Important sources of error in performance appraisals include halo effects, leniency errors, affective reactions, and attributional errors.
- **What are diary notes, and how can they improve rating accuracy?** Diary notes are records of individuals' performance to which raters can refer when formulating performance appraisals.
- **What are behaviorally anchored rating scales and frame-of-reference training?** Behaviorally anchored rating scales are scales that provide raters with examples of excellent, average, and poor performance on key job-related dimensions. Frame-of-reference training involves procedures designed to assure that different raters agree about what constitutes good or poor performance on key dimensions of job performance.
- **What is job satisfaction? Do most individuals report high or low levels of job satisfaction?** Job satisfaction refers to employees' attitudes toward their jobs or work. Most people report fairly high levels of job satisfaction.
- **What are some key work-related and person-related factors that influence job satisfaction?** Work-related causes of job satisfaction include reward systems, quality of supervision, the nature of the work itself, and physical working conditions. Personal factors include seniority, several aspects of personality, and degree of person–job fit.
- **What are the major effects of low or high job satisfaction?** Levels of job satisfaction have been found to exert relatively modest effects on employee absence and turnover, and on job performance.
- **What is organizational citizenship behavior, and how does it relate to links between job satisfaction and job performance?** Organizational citizenship behavior consists of actions taken by employees that are "beyond the call of duty" and that benefit either other employees or the organization. An increased frequency of such behaviors is related to high levels of job satisfaction.
- **How have careers changed in recent decades?** In the past, individuals often worked for one company throughout their careers. Currently, this pattern is quite rare.
- **What is job rotation, and what effect does it have on careers?** Job rotation involves moving from one job to another job within an organization, at the same level of responsibility or authority. It often enhances career progress.
- **What are the benefits of having a mentor?** Mentors assist their protégés in many ways—giving them advice, helping them avoid pitfalls, calling them and their accomplishments to the attention of top management.
- **Do women and minorities experience difficulties in obtaining mentors?** Recent findings indicate that women and minorities often find it more difficult to obtain a mentor than do white males.
- **What is the current status in psychology of the great person theory of leadership?** While not all great leaders seem to share certain traits, recent findings suggest that leaders and followers do differ in some respects.
- **What are the key dimensions of leadership behavior or style?** Key dimensions of leadership behavior or style include variations along the autocratic–democratic and directive–permissive dimensions. In addition, leaders differ greatly in the extent to which they are person-oriented or task-oriented.
- **How do transformational leaders influence their followers so strongly?** Transformational leaders establish special kinds of relationships with their followers. In addition, they have high self-confidence and excellent communication skills; and they are expert in impression management, in framing, and in presenting a stirring vision.

KEY TERMS

industrial/organizational psychology, p. 669 • human factors, p. 669 • goal-setting theory, p. 670 • equity theory, p. 673 • job design, p. 677 • job enlargement, p. 677 • job enrichment, p. 677 • electronic performance monitoring, p. 677 • social facilitation, p. 677 • performance appraisals, p. 678 • behaviorally anchored rating scales, p. 680 • frame-of-reference training, p. 681 • job satisfaction, p. 683 • organizational citizenship behavior, p. 687 • Job Descriptive Index (JDI), p. 688 • Minnesota Satisfaction Questionnaire (MSQ), p. 688 • critical incident technique, p. 688 • careers, p. 688 • job rotation, • p. 689 • leader, p. 691 • great person theory, p. 692 • transformational or charismatic leaders, p. 695

Human Factors: Designing for Efficiency, Health, and Safety

- **What basic principles govern the design of effective visual displays?** Effective visual displays should incorporate such features as pointers that move against a fixed background, pointers that indicate increases in the units measured by clockwise movements, and clear markings or scale ranges.
- **What basic design principles are fundamental to effective controls?** Effective controls should follow the principle of compatibility—they should operate in ways most people expect. In addition, switches, levers, and so on that control different functions should be clearly labeled and easy to distinguish.
- **How have human factors psychologists contributed to the design of improved mailbags for letter carriers and improved computer keyboards?** Research has demonstrated that mail-

bags that are supported at the waist or that hang from both shoulders (rather than one shoulder) produce less fatigue than the standard mailbag now in widespread use. Psychologists have found that computer keyboards that tilt downward, and so place less pressure on the carpal tunnel, reduce wrist strain and injuries.

KEY TERMS

visual displays, p. 697 • compatibility, p. 698

Critical Thinking Questions

Appraisal

Work plays an extremely important role in most people's lives. Yet the field of industrial/organizational psychology has often been omitted from introductory psychology texts. Why do you think this was true in the past? Do you think that coverage of this field should be included in all textbooks like this one?

Controversy

Electronic performance monitoring is definitely here—it is currently being used to monitor the performance of millions of employees. Do you think such procedures are fair? Or do you consider them to be an invasion of employees' privacy and rights?

Making Psychology Part of Your life

Now that you know more about such topics as work motivation, performance appraisal, and careers, can you think of ways in which you can use this information to increase your own success? For instance, will this information change your ideas about what kinds of jobs you should accept or whether you should seek a mentor?

Appendix

Statistics: Uses—and Potential Abuses

At many points in this text, I've noted that one benefit you should gain from your first course in psychology is the ability to think about human behavior in a new way. This appendix will expand on that theme by offering a basic introduction to one essential aspect of psychological thinking: statistics.

What does this special form of mathematics have to do with psychology or thinking like a psychologist? The answer involves the fact that all fields of science require two major types of tools. First, scientists need various kinds of equipment to gather the data they seek. Obviously, this equipment differs from field to field.

Second, all scientists need some means for interpreting the findings of their research—for determining the *meaning* of the information they have acquired and its relationship to important theories in their field. Again, this varies from one science to another. In most cases, though, some type of mathematics is involved. To understand the findings of their research, psychologists make use of *statistics*—or, more accurately, *statistical analysis* of the data they collect.

As you'll soon see, statistics are a flexible tool and can be used for many different purposes. In psychology, however, they are usually employed to accomplish one or more of the following tasks: (1) *summarizing* or *describing* large amounts of data; (2) *comparing* individuals or groups of individuals in various ways; (3) determining whether certain aspects of behavior are *related* (whether they vary together in a systematic manner); and (4) *predicting* future behavior from current information.

Descriptive Statistics: Summarizing Data

Suppose that a psychologist conducts an experiment concerned with the effects of staring at others in public places. The procedures of the study are simple. He stares at people in stores, airports, and a variety of other locations, and he records the number of seconds until they look away—or until they approach to make him stop! After carrying out these procedures twenty times, he obtains the data shown in Table A.1. Presented in this form, the scores seem meaningless. If they are grouped together in the manner shown in Figure A.1, however, a much clearer picture emerges. Now we can see at a glance that the most frequent score is about 4 seconds; that fewer people look away after 3 or 5 seconds; and that even fewer look away very quickly (after 2 seconds) or after a longer delay (6 seconds). This graph presents a **frequency distribution**: It indicates the number of times each score occurs within an entire set of scores.

A graph such as the one in Figure A.1 on page 706 provides a rough idea of the way a set of scores is distributed. In science, however, a rough idea is not sufficient: More precision is required. In particular, it would be useful to have an index of (1) the middle score of the distribution of scores (their **central tendency**) and (2) the extent to which the scores spread out around this point (their **dispersion**). Such measures are provided by **descriptive statistics.**

Frequency Distribution: The frequency with which each score occurs within an entire distribution of scores.

Central Tendency: The middle (center) of a distribution of scores.

Dispersion: The extent to which scores in a distribution spread out or vary around the center.

Descriptive Statistics: Statistics that summarize the major characteristics of an array of scores.

Mean: A measure of central tendency derived by adding all scores and dividing by the number of scores.

Mode: A measure of central tendency indicating the most frequent score in an array of scores.

Median: A measure of central tendency indicating the midpoint of an array of scores.

Measures of Central Tendency: Finding the Center

You are already familiar with one important measure of central tendency: the **mean,** or average. We calculate a mean by adding all scores and then dividing by the total number of scores. The mean represents the typical score in a distribution and in this respect is often quite useful. Sometimes, though, it can be misleading. This is because the mean can be strongly affected by one or a few extreme scores. To see why this is so, consider the following example. Ten families live on a block. The number of children in each family is shown in Table A.2 on page 706. Adding these numbers together and dividing by ten yields a mean of four. Yet, as you can see, *not one family actually has four children.* Most have none or two, but one has eight and another has nineteen.

In cases such as this, it is better to refer to other measures of central tendency. One of these is the **mode**—the most frequently occurring score. As you can see, the mode of the data in Table A.2 is 2: More families have two children than have any other number. Another useful measure of central tendency is the **median**—the midpoint of the distribution. Fifty percent of the scores fall at or above the median, while 50 percent fall at or below this value. Returning to the data in Table A.2, the median also happens to be 2: Half the scores fall at or below this value, while half fall at or above it.

As you can readily see, both the mode and the median provide more accurate descriptions of the data than does the mean in this particular example. However, this is true only in instances where extreme scores distort the mean. In fact, there is no single rule for choosing among these measures. The decision to employ one over the others should be made only after careful study of frequency distributions such as the one shown in Figure A.1.

Measures of Dispersion: Assessing the Spread

The mean, median, and mode each tell us something about the center of a distribution, but they provide no indication of its shape. Are the scores bunched together? Do they spread out over a wide range? This issue is addressed by measures of *dispersion.*

TABLE A.1

Raw Data from a Simple Experiment

When a psychologist stares at strangers in a public place, these persons either look away or approach him in the number of seconds shown. Note that more people look away or approach after 4 seconds than any other value.

	Number of Seconds Until Person Either Looks Away or Approaches
Person 1	4
Person 2	4
Person 3	1
Person 4	4
Person 5	3
Person 6	2
Person 7	5
Person 8	3
Person 9	6
Person 10	5
Person 11	4
Person 12	4
Person 13	3
Person 14	3
Person 15	5
Person 16	4
Person 17	4
Person 18	2
Person 19	6
Person 20	5

FIGURE A.1

A Frequency Distribution

In a frequency distribution, scores are grouped together according to the number of times each occurs. This one suggests that most persons react to being stared at within about 4 seconds.

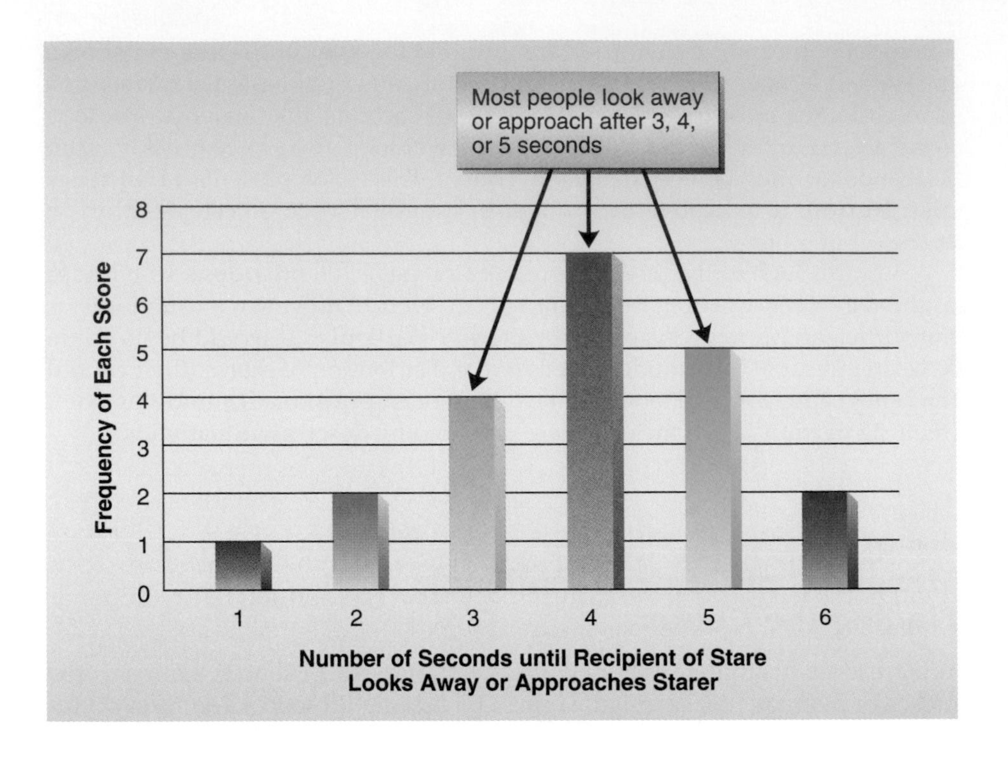

The simplest measure of dispersion is the **range**—the difference between the highest and lowest scores. For example, the range for the data in Table A.2 is 19 (19 – 0 = 19). Although the range provides some idea of the extent to which scores vary, it does not indicate how much the scores spread out around the center. Information on this important issue is provided by the **variance** and **standard deviation**.

The *variance* provides a measure of the average distance between scores in a distribution and the mean. It indicates the extent to which, on average, the scores depart from (vary around) the mean. Actually, the variance refers to the average *squared* distance of the scores from the mean; squaring eliminates negative numbers. The *standard deviation* then takes account of this operation of squaring by calculating the square root of the variance. So the standard deviation represents the average distance between scores and the mean in any distribution. The larger the standard deviation, the more the scores are spread out around the center of the distribution.

TABLE A.2

How the Mean Can Sometimes Be Misleading

Ten families have a total of 40 children among them. The mean is 4.0; but, as you can see, not one family has this number of children. This illustrates the fact that the mean, while a useful measure of central tendency, can be distorted by a few extreme scores.

	Number of Children
Family 1	0
Family 2	0
Family 3	2
Family 4	2
Family 5	2
Family 6	2
Family 7	2
Family 8	3
Family 9	19
Family 10	8
	Total = 40 children
	Mean = 40/10 = 4.0

The Normal Curve: Putting Descriptive Statistics to Work

Despite the inclusion of several examples, this discussion so far has been somewhat abstract. As a result, it may have left you wondering about the following question: Just what do descriptive statistics have to do with understanding human behavior or thinking like a psychologist? One important answer involves their relationship to a special type of frequency distribution known as the **normal curve**.

While you may never have seen this term before, you are probably quite familiar with the concept it describes. Consider the following characteristics: height, size of vocabulary, strength of motivation to attain success. Suppose you obtained measurements of each among thousands of persons. What would be the shape of each of these distributions?

If you guessed that they would all take the form shown in Figure A.2, you are correct. In fact, on each dimension most scores would pile up in the middle, and fewer and fewer scores would occur farther away from this value.

What does the normal curve have to do with the use of descriptive statistics? A great deal. One key property of the normal curve is as follows: Specific proportions of the scores within it are contained in certain areas of the curve; moreover, these portions can be defined in terms of the standard deviation of all of the scores. Therefore, once we know the mean of a normal distribution and its standard deviation, we can determine the relative standing of any specific score within it. Perhaps a concrete example will help clarify both the nature and the value of this relationship.

Figure A.3 on page 708 presents a normal distribution with a mean of 5.0 and a standard deviation of 1.0. Let's assume that the scores shown are those on a test of desire for power. Suppose that we now encounter an individual with a score of 7.0. We know that she is high on this characteristic, but *how* high? On the basis of descriptive statistics—the mean and standard deviation—plus the properties of the normal curve, we can tell. Statisticians have found that 68 percent of the scores in a normal distribution fall within one standard deviation of the mean, either above or below it. Similarly, fully 96 percent of the scores fall within two standard deviations of the mean. Given this information, we can conclude that a score of 7 on this test is very high indeed: Only 2 percent of persons taking the test attain a score equal to or higher than this one (refer to Figure A.3).

In a similar manner, descriptive statistics can be used to interpret scores in any other distribution, providing it approaches the normal curve in form. Because a vast array of psychological characteristics and behaviors do seem to be distributed in this manner, we can readily determine an individual's relative standing on any of these dimensions from just two pieces of information: the mean of all scores in the distribution and the standard deviation.

For one final example, imagine that your first psychology test contains fifty multiple-choice items. You obtain a score of 40. Did you do well or poorly? If your instructor provides two additional pieces of information—the mean of all the scores in the class and the standard deviation—you can tell. Suppose the mean is 35, and the standard deviation is 2.50. The mean indicates that most people got a lower score than you did. The relatively small standard deviation indicates that most scores were quite close to the mean—only about twice this distance *above* the mean. Further—and here is a key point—this

Range: The difference between the highest and lowest scores in a distribution of scores.

Variance: A measure of dispersion reflecting the average squared distance between each score and the mean.

Standard Deviation: A measure of dispersion reflecting the average distance between each score and the mean.

Normal Curve: A symmetrical, bell-shaped frequency distribution. Most scores are found near the middle, and fewer and fewer occur toward the extremes. Many psychological characteristics are distributed in this manner.

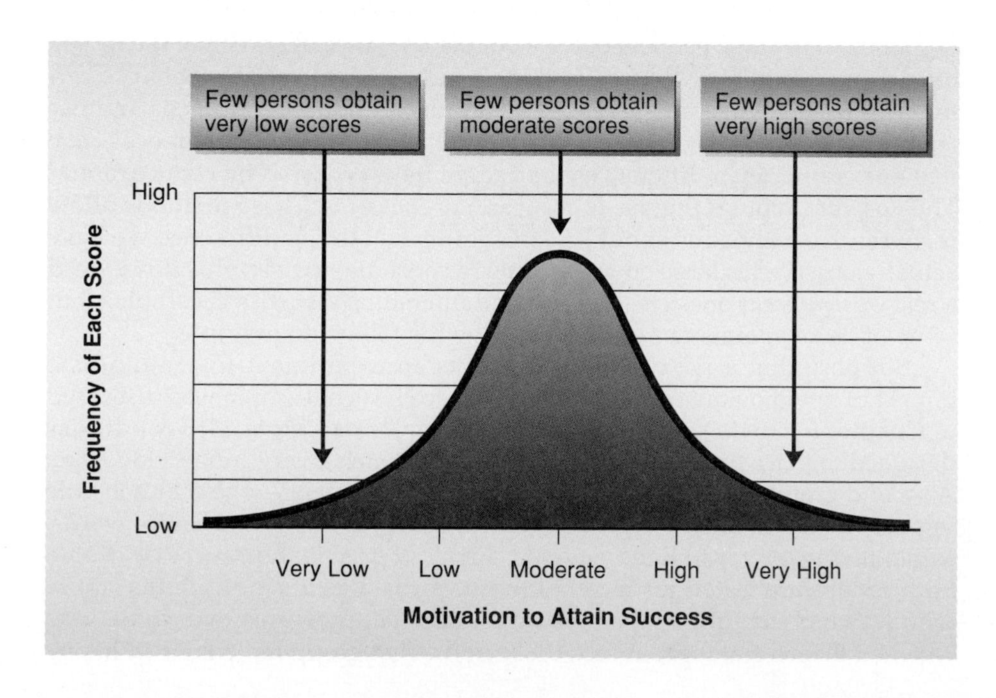

FIGURE A.2

The Normal Curve

On many dimensions relating to behavior, scores show the kind of frequency distribution illustrated here: the *normal curve.* Most scores pile up in the middle, and fewer and fewer occur toward the extremes. Thus, most people are found to be average height, to have average vocabularies, and to show average desire for success.

FIGURE A.3

Interpreting Scores by Means of the Normal Distribution

Sixty-eight percent of the scores in a normal distribution fall within one standard deviation of the mean (above or below it). Similarly, fully 96 percent of the scores fall within two standard deviations of the mean. Thus, on a test with a mean of 5.0 and a standard deviation of 1.0, only 2 percent of persons attain a score of 7.0 or higher.

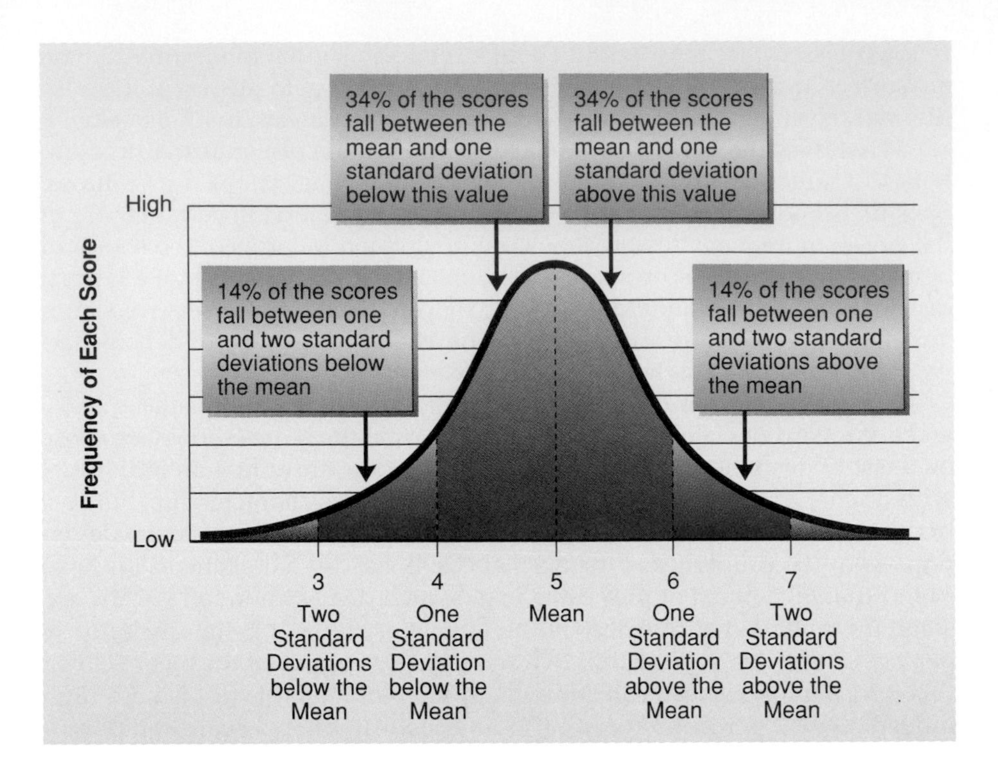

conclusion would be accurate whether there were 30, 100, or 500 students in the class, assuming the mean and standard deviation remained unchanged. It is precisely this type of efficiency that makes descriptive statistics so useful for summarizing even large amounts of information.

Inferential Statistics: Determining Whether Differences Are or Are Not Real

Throughout this book, the results of many experiments have been described. When these studies were discussed, differences between various conditions or groups were often mentioned. For example, we saw that participants exposed to one set of conditions or one level of an independent variable behaved differently from participants exposed to another set of conditions or another level of an independent variable. How did we know that such differences were real ones rather than differences that might have occurred by chance alone? The answer involves the use of inferential statistics. These methods allow us to reach conclusions about just this issue: whether a difference we have actually observed is large enough for us to conclude (to *infer)* that it is indeed a real or *significant* one. The logic behind inferential statistics is complex, but some of its key points can be illustrated by the following example.

Inferential Statistics: Statistical procedures that permit us to determine whether differences between individuals or groups are ones that are likely or unlikely to have occurred by chance.

Suppose that a psychologist conducts an experiment to examine the impact of mood on memory. (As you may recall, such research was discussed in Chapter 6.) To do so, he exposes one group of participants to conditions designed to place them in a good mood: They watch a very funny videotape. A second group, in contrast, is exposed to a neutral tape—one that has little impact on their mood. Both groups are then asked to memorize lists of words, some of which refer to happy events, such as "party" and "success." Later, both groups are tested for recall of these words. Results indicate that those who watched the funny tape remember more happy words than those who watched the neutral tape; in fact, those in the first group remember 12 happy words, while those in the second remember only 8—a difference of 4.0. Is this difference a real one?

One way of answering this question would be to repeat the study over and over again. If a difference in favor of the happy group were obtained consistently, our confidence that it is indeed real (and perhaps due to differences in subjects' mood) would increase. As you can see, however, this would be a costly procedure. Is there any way of avoiding it? One answer is provided by inferential statistics. These methods assume that if we repeated the study over and over again, the size of the difference between the two groups obtained each time would vary; moreover, these differences would be normally distributed. Most would fall near the mean, and only a few would be quite large. When applying inferential statistics to the interpretation of psychological research, we make a very conservative assumption: We begin by assuming that there is no difference between the groups—that the mean of this distribution is zero. Through methods that are beyond the scope of this discussion, we then estimate the size of the standard deviation. Once we do, we can readily evaluate the difference obtained in an actual study. If an observed difference is large enough that it would occur by chance only 5 percent (or less) of the time, we can view it as significant. For example, assume that in the study we have been discussing, this standard deviation (a standard deviation of mean differences) is 2.0. This indicates that the difference we observed (4.0) is two standard deviations above the expected mean of zero (please refer to Figure A.4). As you'll recall from our discussion of the normal curve, this means that the difference is quite large and would occur by chance less than 2 percent of the time. Our conclusion: The difference between the two groups in our study is *probably* real. Thus, mood does indeed seem to affect memory.

Please note the word *probably* above. Since the tails of the normal curve never entirely level off, there is always some chance—no matter how slight—that even a huge observed difference is due to chance. If we accept a difference that really occurred by chance as being real, we make what statisticians describe as a Type I error. If, in contrast, we interpret a real difference as being one that occurred by chance, we make a Type II error. Clearly, both kinds can lead us to false conclusions about the findings of a research project.

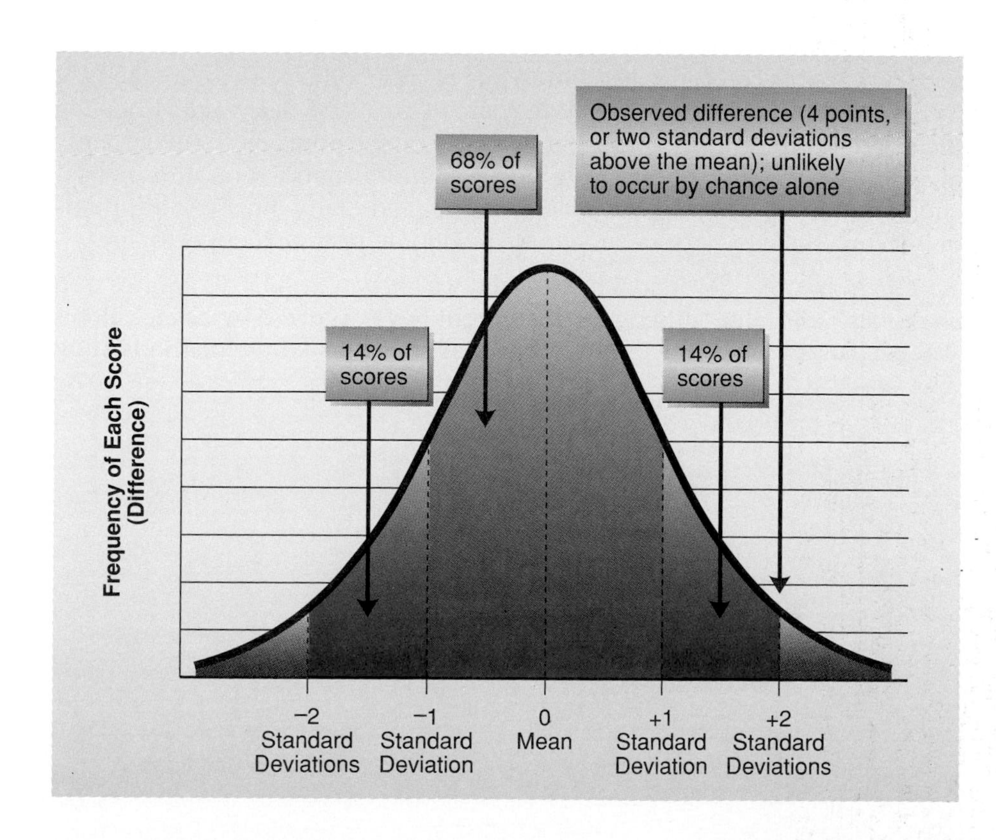

FIGURE A.4

Using Inferential Statistics to Determine Whether an Observed Difference Is a Real One

Two groups in a study concerned with the effects of mood on memory attain mean scores of 12.0 and 8.0, respectively. Is this difference significant (real)? Through inferential statistics, we can tell. If the study were repeated over and over, and the two groups did not really differ, the mean difference in their scores would be zero. Assuming that the standard deviation is 2.0, we know that the probability of a difference this large is very small—less than 2 percent. In view of this fact, we conclude that this finding is indeed significant.

Correlation and Prediction

Does crime increase as temperatures rise? Does a candidate's chance of winning elections increase with his or her height? Does our ability to solve certain kinds of problems change with age? Psychologists are often interested in whether two or more variables are *related*, so that changes in one are associated with changes in the other. Remember: This is quite different from the issue of whether changes in one variable *cause* changes in another.

In order to answer such questions, we must gather information on each variable. For example, assume that we wanted to find out if political fortunes are indeed related to height. To do so, we might obtain information on (1) the height of hundreds of candidates and (2) the percentage of votes they obtained in recent elections. Then we'd plot these two variables, height against votes, by entering a single point for each candidate on a graph such as those in Figure A.5. As you can see, the first graph in this figure indicates that tallness is positively associated with political success; the second points to the opposite conclusion; and the third suggests that there is no relationship at all between height and political popularity.

Correlation Coefficient: A statistic indicating the degree of relationship between two or more variables.

While such graphs, known as *scatterplots*, are useful, they don't by themselves provide a precise index of the strength of the relationship between two or more variables. To obtain such an index, we often calculate a statistic known as a **correlation coefficient**. Such coefficients can range from –1.00 to +1.00. Positive numbers indicate that as one variable increases, so does the other. Negative numbers indicate that as one factor increases, the other decreases. The greater the departure from 0.00 in either direction, the stronger the relationship between the two variables. Thus, a correlation of +0.80 is stronger than one of +0.39. Similarly, a correlation of –0.76 is stronger than one of –0.51.

Once we've computed a correlation coefficient, we can test its significance; we can determine whether it is large enough to be viewed as unlikely to occur by chance alone. Further, we can also compare correlations to determine if, in fact, one is significantly larger or smaller than another.

In addition to determining the extent to which two or more variables are related, statistical procedures also exist for determining the degree to which a specific variable can be *predicted* from one or more others. These methods of *regression analysis* are complex, but they are of great practical value. Knowing the extent to which individuals' performance can be predicted from currently available information—such as grades, past performance, or scores on psychological tests—can aid companies, schools, and many other organizations in selecting the best persons for employment or educational opportunities.

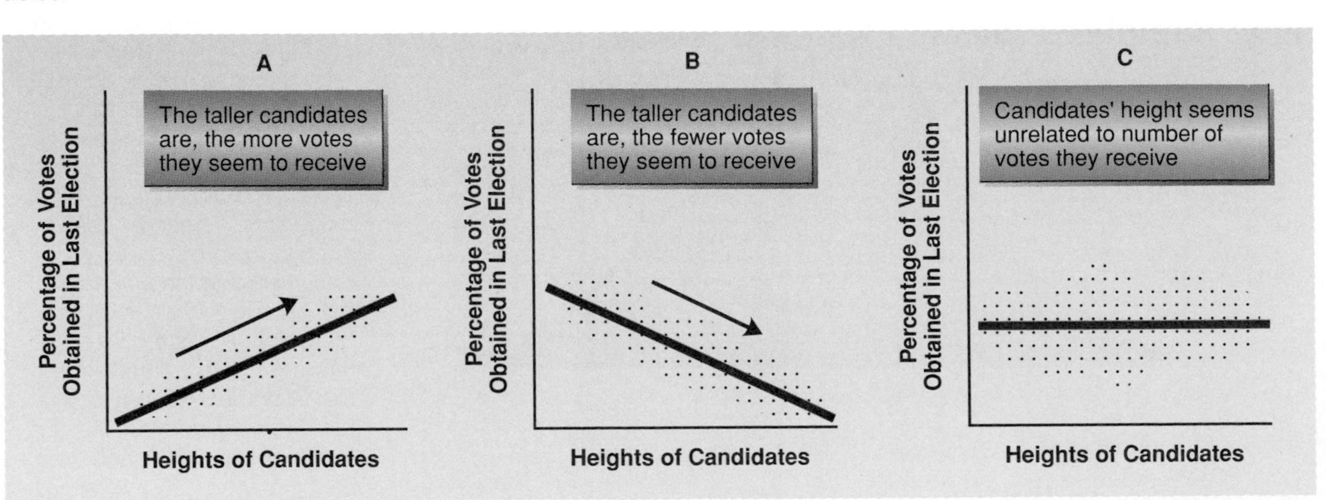

FIGURE A.5

Illustrating Relationships through Scatterplots

Is height related to success in politics? To find out, we measure the height of many candidates and obtain records of the percentage of votes they obtained. We then plot height against votes in a scatterplot. Plot A indicates a positive relationship between height and political success. Plot B indicates a negative relationship between these variables. Plot C suggests that there is no relationship between these variables.

The Misuse of Statistics: Numbers Don't Lie . . . or Do They?

A public figure once remarked that there are three kinds of lies: "lies, damned lies, and statistics"! By this he meant that statistics are often used for purposes quite different from the ones we've discussed here. Instead of helping us understand scientific data, interpret test scores, or make predictions about behavior, statistics are sometimes employed to confuse, deceive, or mislead their intended victims. To make matters worse, in the wrong hands statistics can be quite effective in this role. The reason for such success lies in the fact that most of us firmly accept another popular saying: "Numbers don't lie." Thus, when confronted with what appear to be mathematical data and facts, we surrender our usual skepticism and readily accept what we are told. Since the costs of doing so can be quite high, let's conclude this brief discussion of statistics by examining some of the more common—and blatant—*mis*uses of statistics.

Random Events Don't Always Seem Random

You pick up the paper and read an account of a young woman who won more than one million dollars at a gambling casino. She placed sixteen bets in a row at a roulette table and won on every spin of the wheel. Why? Was she incredibly lucky? Did she have a system? If you are like many people, you may jump to the conclusion that there is indeed something special about her. After all, how else can this incredible series of events be explained?

If you do jump to such conclusions, you are probably making a serious mistake. Here's why. For any single player, the odds of winning so many times in succession are indeed slight. But consider the vast number of players and the number of occasions on which they play; some casinos remain open around the clock. Also, remember the shape of the normal curve. The mean number of wins in a series of sixteen bets is indeed low—perhaps one or two. But the tails of the curve never level off, so there is some probability, however slight, of even sixteen wins occurring in a row. In short, even events that would be expected to occur very rarely by chance *do* occur. The moral is clear: Don't overinterpret events that seem, at first glance, to border on impossible. They may actually be rare chance occurrences with no special significance of their own.

Large Samples Provide a Better Basis for Reaching Conclusions Than Small Ones

Many television commercials take the following form. A single consumer is asked to compare three unlabeled brands of facial tissue or to compare the whiteness of three loads of wash. She then makes the "right" choice, selecting the sponsor's product as softest, brightest, or whitest. The commercial ends with a statement of the following type: "Here's proof. Our brand is the one most shoppers prefer." Should you take such evidence seriously? I doubt it. In most cases, it is not possible to reach firm statistical conclusions on the basis of the reactions of a single individual, or even of several individuals. Rather, a much larger number of cooperative participants is necessary. After watching such a commercial, then, you should ask what would happen if the same procedures were repeated with 20, 50, or 500 shoppers. Would the sponsor's brand actually be chosen significantly more often than the others? The commercials leave the impression that it would; but, as I'm sure you now realize, jumping to such conclusions is risky. So be skeptical of claims based on very small samples. They are on shaky grounds at best, and they may be purposely designed to be misleading.

Unbiased Samples Provide a Better Basis for Reaching Conclusions Than Biased Ones

Here's another popular type of commercial, and another common misuse of statistics. An announcer, usually dressed in a white coat, states: "Three out of four dentists surveyed recommend *Jawbreak* sugarless gum." At first glance, the meaning of this message seems clear: Most dentists prefer that their patients chew a specific brand of gum. But look more closely; there's an important catch. Notice that the announcer says, "Three out of four dentists *surveyed*. . . ." Who were these people? A fair and representative sample of all dentists? Major stockholders in the Jawbreak company? Close relatives of the person holding the patent on this product? From the information given, it's impossible to tell. To the extent these or many other possibilities are true, the dentists surveyed represent a *biased* sample; they are *not* representative of the population to which the sponsor wishes us to generalize: all dentists.

So whenever you encounter claims about the results of a survey, ask two questions: (1) Who were the persons surveyed? (2) How were they chosen? If these questions can't be answered to your satisfaction, be on guard: Someone may be trying to mislead you.

Unexpressed Comparisons Are Often Meaningless

Another all-too-common misuse of statistics involves what might be described as "errors of omission." Persons using this tactic mention a comparison but then fail to specify all of the groups or items involved. For example, consider the following statement: "In recent laboratory tests, *Plasti-spred* was found to contain fully 82 percent less cholesterol! So, if you care about your family's health, buy Plasti-spred, the margarine for modern life." Impressive, right? After all, Plasti-spred seems to contain much less of a dangerous substance than—what? There, in fact, is the rub: We have no idea as to the identity of the other substances in the comparison. Were they other brands of margarine? Butter? A jar of bacon drippings? A beaker full of cholesterol?

The lesson offered by such claims is clear. Whenever you are told that a product, candidate, or anything else is better or superior in some way, always ask the following question: Better than *what*?

Some Differences Aren't Really There

Here's yet another type of commercial you've probably seen before. An announcer points to lines on a graph that diverge before your eyes and states, "Here's proof! *Gasaway* neutralizes stomach acid twice as fast as the other leading brand." And in fact, the line labeled Gasaway does seem to rise more quickly, leaving its poor competitor in the dust. Should you take such claims seriously? Again, the answer is no. First, such graphs are usually unlabeled. As a result, we have no idea as to what measure of neutralizing acids or how much time is involved. It is quite possible that the curves illustrate only the first few seconds after the medicine is taken and that beyond that period the advantage for the sponsor's product disappears.

Second, and even more important, there are no grounds for assuming that the differences shown are *significant*—that they could not have occurred by chance. Perhaps there is no difference whatsoever in the speed with which the two products neutralize acid, but the comparison was run over and over again until—by chance—a seemingly large difference in favor of the sponsor's brand occurred. This is not to say that all advertisers, or even most, engage in such practices. Perhaps the differences shown in some commercials are indeed real. Still, given the strong temptation to stress the benefits of one's own product, the following policy is probably best: Assume that all differences reported in ads and similar sources are *not* significant—that is, not real—unless specific information to the contrary is provided.

Graphs May Distort (or at Least Bend) Reality

The results of psychological research are often represented in graphs; graphs can communicate major findings efficiently and can readily present complex relationships that are difficult to describe verbally. Unfortunately, however, graphs are often used for another purpose: to alter the conclusions drawn from a given set of data. There are many ways to do this, but the most common involves altering the meaning of the axes—the horizontal or vertical boundaries of the graph. A specific example may help clarify this process.

Consider how two groups—one in favor of strong government actions to prevent teenagers from smoking and the other a lobbying group for the tobacco industry—might present data relating to the percentage of teenagers who smoke. The first group might make its case with Graph A in Figure A.6, while the second would present *its* side with the Graph B. As you can see, both graphs show the same data: The proportion of teenagers smoking increased from 12 percent in the first year to 16 percent in the third year. But this change seems much more dramatic—and potentially more important—in Graph A than in Graph B. Why? Because of the different calibrations of the vertical axes used in the two versions. People looking at these two graphs could easily be led to opposite conclusions about the scope of the teen smoking problem *unless they paid careful attention to the numbers on the vertical axes.*

Sad to relate, such fine-tuning of graphs is common; you will probably encounter it in magazines, political mailings, and many other sources. The moral is clear: It is important to pay careful attention to the scale employed in any graph, the precise quantities being measured, and all labels employed. If you overlook such factors, you may be a sitting duck for those who wish to lead you to the conclusions *they* favor.

FIGURE A.6

Misleading Graphs: One Common Technique

Depending on the scale on the vertical axis, the same trends can seem small and trivial or large and impressive. In Graph A the growth in teenage smoking seems very large, while in Graph B it seems tiny. You should always be on guard against graphs that are fine-tuned in order to lead you to certain conclusions.

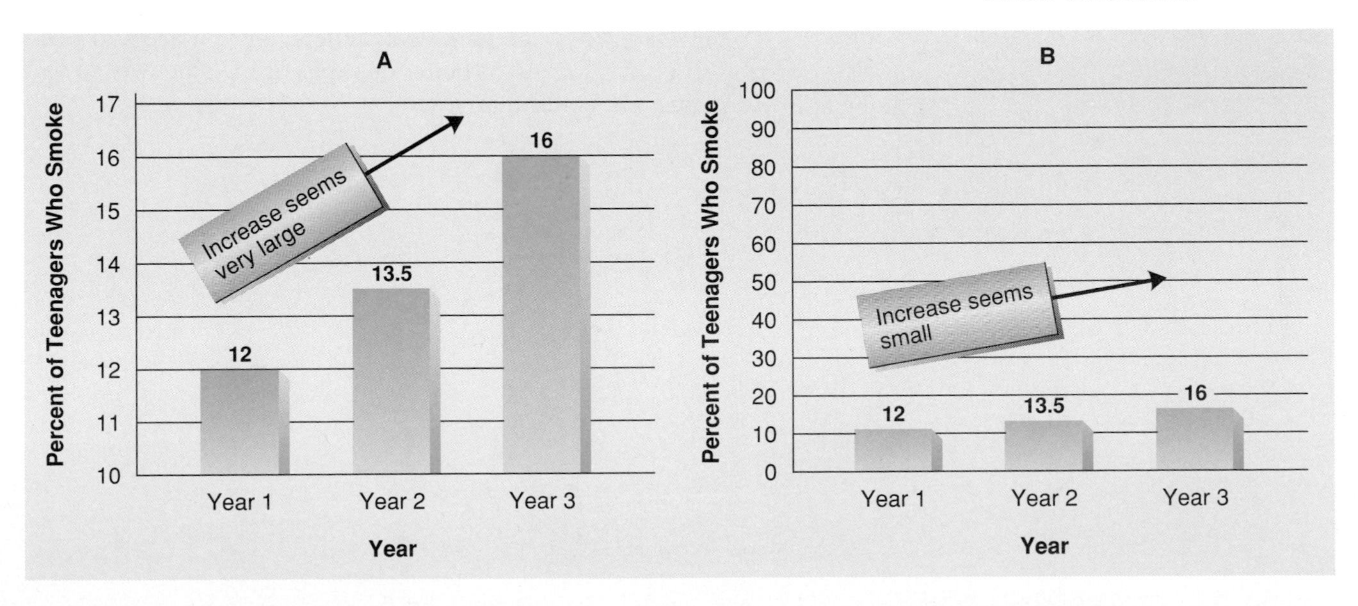

Summary and Review of Key Questions

Descriptive Statistics

KEY TERMS:

frequency distribution, p. 705 • central tendency, p. 705 • dispersion, p. 705 • descriptive statistics, p. 705 • mean, p. 705 • mode, p. 705 • median, p. 705 • range, p. 707 • variance, p. 707 • standard deviation, p. 707 • normal curve, p. 707

- All scientists require two types of tools in their research: equipment for collecting data and some means of interpreting their findings. In psychology statistics are often used for the latter purpose.
- Large quantities of data can be grouped into frequency distributions indicating the number of times each score occurs. Two important facts about any frequency distribution are its central tendency—its center—and its dispersion, or the extent to which scores spread out around this value.
- Common measures of central tendency include the mean, mode, and median. Dispersion is often measured in terms of variance and the standard deviation. This latter term refers to the average distance of each score from the mean.
- The frequency distributions for many behavioral characteristics show a bell-shaped form known as the normal distribution or normal curve. Most scores fall near the middle, and fewer occur at increasing distances from this value. Specific proportions of the scores are found under certain parts of the curve.

Inferential Statistics

KEY TERM:

inferential statistics, p. 708

- Psychologists use inferential statistics to determine whether differences between individuals or groups are significant, or real. Inferential statistics assume that the mean difference in question is zero and that observed differences are distributed normally around this value.
- If an observed difference is large enough that it would occur by chance only 5 percent of the time, it is viewed as significant.

Correlation and Prediction

KEY TERM:

correlation coefficient, p. 710

- To determine whether two or more variables are related, psychologists compute correlation coefficients. These range from –1.00 to +1.00. The larger the departure from 0.00, the stronger the correlation between the variables in question.
- Correlations, and statistics derived from them, can be used to predict future behavior from current information. Such predictions are of great practical benefit to schools, companies, and others wishing to predict future performance from individuals' current behavior.

Misuse of Statistics

- Although statistics have many beneficial uses, they are often employed to deceive or mislead.
- Misuse of statistics can involve the use of extremely small or biased samples, unexpressed comparisons, and misleading graphs and presentations.

Glossary

Absolute Threshold: The smallest amount of a stimulus that we can detect perfect ly 50 percent of the time.
Accommodation: In Piaget's theory, the modification of existing mental frameworks to take account of new information.
Acquisition: The process by which a conditioned stimulus acquires the ability to elicit a conditioned response through repeated pairings of an unconditioned stimulus with the conditioned stimulus.
Action Potential: A rapid shift in the electrical charge across the cell membrane of neurons. This disturbance along the membrane communicates information within neurons.
Acuity: The visual ability to see fine details.
Adaptation: In Piaget's theory of cognitive development, a process in which individuals build mental representations of the world through direct interaction with it.
Adolescence: A period beginning with the onset of puberty and ending when individuals assume adult roles and responsibilities.
Adolescent Recklessness: The tendency for adolescents to engage in forms of behavior that are dangerous or reckless.
Affect: A person's current mood.
Afferent Nerves: Nerve cells that carry information from receptors throughout the body toward the brain.
Aggression: Behavior directed toward the goal of harming another living being who wishes to avoid such treatment.
Aggressive Motivation: The desire to harm or injure others in some manner.
Agonist: A chemical substance that facilitates the action of a neurotransmitter at a receptor site.
Agoraphobia: Intense fear of specific situations in which individuals suspect that help will not be available should they experience an incapacitating or embarrassing event.
Agreeableness: One of the "big five" dimensions of personality; ranges from good-natured, cooperative, trusting at one end to irritable, suspicious, uncooperative at the other.
AIDS (Acquired Immune Deficiency Syndrome): A viral infection that reduces the immune system's ability to defend the body against the introduction of foreign substances.
Algorithm: A rule that guarantees a solution to a specific type of problem.
Alpha Waves: Rapid, low-amplitude brain waves that occur when individuals are awake but relaxed.
Alzheimer's Disease: An illness primarily afflicting individuals over the age of sixty-five and involving severe mental deterioration, including retrograde amnesia.
Amnesia: Loss of memory stemming from illness, accident, drug abuse, or other causes.
Amphetamines: Drugs that act as stimulants, increasing feelings of energy and activation.
Amygdala: A limbic-system structure involved in aspects of emotional control and formation of emotional memories.
Anal Stage: In Freud's theory, a psychosexual stage of development in which pleasure is focused primarily on the anal zone.
Analogy: A strategy for solving problems based on applying solutions that were previously successful with other problems similar in underlying structure.
Anchoring-and-Adjustment Heuristic: A cognitive rule of thumb for decision making in which existing information is accepted as a reference point but then adjusted in light of various factors.
Anima: According to Jung, the archetype representing the feminine side of males.
Animus: According to Jung, the archetype representing the masculine side of females.
Anorexia Nervosa: An eating disorder in which individuals starve themselves until they lose dangerous amounts of weight.
Antagonist: A chemical substance that inhibits the impact of a neurotransmitter at a receptor site.
Anterograde Amnesia: The inability to store in long-term memory information that occurs after an amnesia-inducing event.
Antisocial Personality Disorder: A personality disorder involving deceitfulness, impulsivity, callous disregard for the safety or welfare of others, and a total lack of remorse for actions that harm others.
Anxiety: In Freudian theory, unpleasant feelings of tension or worry experienced by individuals in reaction to unacceptable wishes or impulses; increased arousal accompanied by generalized feelings of fear or apprehension.
Anxiety Disorders: Psychological disorders that take several different forms, but which are all related to a generalized feeling of anxiety.
Apnea: A sleep disorder in which sleepers stop breathing several times each night, and thus wake up.
Applied Behavior Analysis: A field of psychology that specializes in the application of operant conditioning principles to solve problems of everyday life.
Archetypes: According to Jung, inherited manifestations of the collective unconscious that shape our perceptions of the external world.
Arousal Theory: A theory of motivation suggesting that human beings seek an optimal level of arousal, not minimal levels of arousal.
Artificial Concepts: Concepts that can be clearly defined by a set of rules or properties.
Artificial Intelligence: A branch of science that studies the capacity of computers to demonstrate performance that, if it were produced by human beings, would be described as showing intelligence.
Assessment Interviews: Interviews conducted by psychologists in which they seek information about individuals' past and present behaviors, current problems, interpersonal relations, and personality.
Assimilation: In Piaget's theory, the tendency to understand new information in terms of existing mental frameworks.
Attachment: A strong affectional bond between infants and their caregivers.
Attention-Deficit Hyperactivity Disorder: A psychological disorder in which children are unable to concentrate their attention on any task for more than few minutes.
Attitudes: Lasting evaluations of various aspects of the social world that are stored in memory.
Attribution: The processes through which we seek to determine the causes behind others' behavior.
Autobiographical Memory: Memory for information about events in our own lives (also known as episodic memory).

Automatic Processing: Processing of information with minimal conscious awareness.
Autonomic Nervous System: The part of the peripheral nervous system that connects internal organs, glands, and involuntary muscles to the central nervous system.
Availability Heuristic: A cognitive rule of thumb in which the importance or probability of various events is judged on the basis of how readily they come to mind.
Avoidant Attachment: A pattern of attachment in which babies don't cry when their caregiver leaves in the strange situation test, and are slow to greet their caregiver when this person returns.
Axon: The part of the neuron that conducts the action potential away from the cell.
Axon Terminals: Structures at the end of axons that contain transmitter substances.

Babbling: An early stage of speech development in which infants emit virtually all known sounds of human speech.
Backward Conditioning: A type of conditioning in which the presentation of the unconditioned stimulus (UCS) precedes the presentation of the conditioned stimulus (CS).
Barbiturates: Drugs that act as depressants, reducing activity in the nervous system and behavior output.
Basic Mistakes: False beliefs held by individuals that interfere with their mental health; a concept in psychotherapy devised by Adler.
Behavior Therapies: Therapies based on the belief that many psychological disorders stem from faulty learning.
Behavioral Assessment: Observation of specific aspects of an individual's behavior that led the person to seek help-troubled interpersonal relationships, poor social skills, feelings of despair and hopelessness, seemingly irrational fears.
Behaviorally Anchored Rating Scales: Rating scales that provide raters with examples of excellent to poor performance on key dimensions of job performance.
Behaviorism: The view that only observable, overt activities that can be measured scientifically should be studied by psychology.
Bereavement: The process of grieving for the persons we love who die.
Binocular Cues: Cues to depth or distance provided by the use of both eyes.
Biofeedback: A technique that enables people to monitor and self-regulate certain bodily functions through the use of specialized equipment.
Biological Constraints on Learning: Tendencies of some species to acquire some forms of conditioning less readily than other species do.
Biological Rhythms: Cyclic changes in bodily processes.
Biologically Based Therapies: Forms of therapy that attempt to reduce psychological disorders through biological means.
Biopsychology: A branch of psychology interested in discovering the biological bases of our thoughts, feelings, and behaviors.
Bipolar Disorder: A mood disorder in which individuals experience very wide swings in mood, from deep depression to wild elation.
Bisexual (Sexual Orientation): A sexual orientation in which individuals seek and enjoy sexual contact with members of both sexes.
Blind Spot: The point in the back of the retina through which the optic nerve exits the eye. This exit point contains no rods or cones and is therefore insensitive to light.
Blindsight: A rare condition, resulting from damage to the primary visual cortex, in which individuals report being blind yet respond to certain aspects of visual stimuli as if they could see.
Body Language: Nonverbal cues involving body posture or movement of body parts.
Brightness: The physical intensity of light.
Brightness Constancy: The tendency to perceive objects as having a constant brightness even when they are viewed under different conditions of illumination.
Bulimia Nervosa: An eating disorder in which individuals engage in recurrent episodes of binge eating following by some form of purging.
Bystander Effect: A reduced tendency of witnesses to an emergency to help when they believe that there are other potential helpers present.

Cancer: A group of illnesses in which abnormal cells are formed that are able to proliferate, invade, and overwhelm normal tissues and to spread to distant sites in the body.
Cannon-Bard Theory: A theory of emotion suggesting that various emotion-provoking events simultaneously produce subjective reactions labeled as emotion and physiological arousal.
Carcinogens: Cancer-producing agents.
Cardinal Trait: According to Allport, a single trait that dominates an individual's entire personality.
Cardiovascular Disease: All diseases of the heart and blood vessels.
Careers: Individuals' lifelong series of employment experiences.
Case Method: A method of research in which detailed information about individuals is used to develop general principles about behavior.
Catastrophic Thinking: Thoughts about impending disaster that may result in a full-blown panic attack.
Catatonic Type (of schizophrenia): A dramatic type of schizophrenia in which individuals show marked disturbances in motor behavior; many alternate between total immobility and wild, excited behavior in which they rush madly about.
Central Nervous System: The brain and the spinal cord.
Central Route (to persuasion): Attitude change resulting from systematic processing of information contained in persuasive messages.
Central Traits: According to Allport, the five or ten traits that best describe an individual's personality.
Cerebellum: A part of the brain concerned with the regulation of basic motor activities.
Cerebral Cortex: The outer covering of the cerebral hemispheres.
Chaining: A procedure that establishes a sequence of responses, which lead to a reward following the final response in the chain.
Childhood: The period between birth and adolescence.
Chromosomes: Threadlike structures containing genetic material, found in nearly every cell of the body.
Circadian Rhythms: Cyclic changes in bodily processes occurring within a single day.
Classical Conditioning: A basic form of learning in which one stimulus comes to serve as a signal for the occurrence of a second stimulus. During classical conditioning, organisms acquire information about the relations between various stimuli, not simple associations between them.
Climacteric: A period during which the functioning of the reproductive system and various aspects of sexual activity change greatly.
Cocaine: A powerful stimulant that produces pleasurable sensations of increased energy and self-confidence.
Cochlea: A portion of the inner ear containing the sensory receptors for sound.
Cognition: The mental activities associated with thought, knowledge, and memory.
Cognitive Behavior Therapy: A form of cognitive therapy that focuses on changing illogical patterns of thought that underlie depression.

Cognitive Dissonance: The state experienced by individuals when they discover inconsistency between two attitudes they hold or between their attitudes and their behavior.
Cognitive Restructuring: A method of reducing stress by adjusting cognitive appraisals of stressors; clients learn to monitor and modify their self-talk and coping strategies.
Cognitive Therapies: Forms of therapy focused on changing distorted and maladaptive patterns of thought.
Cohort Effects: Differences between persons of different ages stemming from the fact that they have experienced contrasting social or cultural conditions.
Collective Unconscious: In Jung's theory, a portion of the unconscious shared by all human beings.
Community Mental Health Centers: Facilities for the delivery of mental health services that are located in the communities where the people they serve live.
Companionate Love: A form of love involving a high degree of commitment and deep concern for the well-being of the beloved.
Compatibility: In human factors, the degree to which controls operate in a manner consistent with human expectations.
Complex Cells: Neurons in the visual cortex that respond to stimuli moving in a particular direction and having a particular orientation.
Compliance: A form of social influence in which one or more persons acquiesce to direct requests from one or more others.
Concepts: Mental categories for objects or events that are similar to one another in certain respects.
Concrete Operations: In Piaget's theory, a stage of cognitive development occurring roughly between the ages of seven and eleven. It is at this stage that children become aware of the permanence of objects.
Concurrent Schedule of Reinforcement: A situation in which behaviors having two or more different reinforcement schedules are simultaneously available.
Conditioned Response (CR): In classical conditioning, the response to the conditioned stimulus.
Conditioned Stimulus (CS): In classical conditioning, the stimulus that is repeatedly paired with an unconditioned stimulus.
Conditioned Taste Aversion: A type of conditioning in which the UCS (usually internal cues associated with nausea or vomiting) occurs several hours after the CS (often a novel food) and leads to a strong CS-UCS association in a single trial.
Conditions of Worth: In Rogers's client-centered therapy, individuals' beliefs that they must be something other than what they really are in order to be loved and accepted by others.
Cones: Sensory receptors in the eye that play a crucial role in sensations of color.
Confirmation Bias: The tendency to pay attention primarily to information that confirms existing views or beliefs.
Confluence Approach: A view of creativity suggesting that for creativity to occur, multiple factors must converge.
Conformity: A type of social influence in which individuals change their attitudes or behavior in order to adhere to existing social norms.
Conscientiousness: One of the "big five" dimensions of personality; ranges from well-organized, careful, responsible at one end to disorganized, careless, unscrupulous at the other.
Consensus: The extent to which behavior by one person is shown by others as well.
Conservation: Understanding of the fact that certain physical attributes of an object remain unchanged even though its outward appearance changes.
Consistency: The extent to which a given person responds in the same way to a given stimulus across time.
Constancies: Our tendency to perceive physical objects as unchanging despite shifts in the pattern of sensations these objects induce.
Contact Hypothesis: The suggestion that increased contact between members of different social groups will reduce prejudice between them.
Content Validity: The extent to which items on a test are related in a straightforward way to the characteristic the test aims to measure.
Context-Dependent Memory: The fact that information entered into memory in a particular context or setting is easier to recall in that context, or in a similar context, than in others.
Continuous Reinforcement Schedule: A schedule of reinforcement in which every occurrence of a particular behavior is reinforced.
Controlled Processing: Processing of information with relatively high levels of conscious awareness.
Conventional Level (of morality): According to Kohlberg, a stage of moral development during which individuals judge morality largely in terms of existing social norms or rules.
Conversion Disorder: A somatoform disorder in which individuals experience actual physical impairment such as blindness, deafness, or paralysis for which there is no underlying medical cause.
Cornea: The curved, transparent layer through which light rays enter the eye.
Corpus Callosum: A band of nerve fibers connecting the two hemispheres of the brain.
Correlation: A tendency for one aspect of the world (or one variable) to change with another aspect of the world (or variable).
Correlational Method: A research method in which researchers attempt to determine whether, and to what extent, different variables are related to each other.
Counterfactual Thinking: The tendency to evaluate events by thinking about alternatives to them—"What might have been."
Crack: A derivative of cocaine that can be smoked. It acts as a powerful stimulant.
Creativity: The ability to produce work that is both novel and appropriate.
Criterion-Related Validity: The extent to which scores on a test are related to behaviors (criteria) that are relevant to the characteristics the test purports to measure.
Critical Incident Technique: A technique for measuring job satisfaction in which individuals describe events relating to their work that they found especially satisfying or dissatisfying.
Critical Thinking: Thinking that avoids blind acceptance of conclusions or arguments and instead closely examines all assumptions, evidence, and conclusions.
Cross-Sectional Research: Research comparing groups of persons of different ages in order to determine how certain aspects of behavior or cognition change with age.
Cross-Tolerance: Increased tolerance for one drug that develops as a result of taking another drug.
Crystallized Intelligence: Aspects of intelligence that draw on previously learned information as a basis for making decisions or solving problems.
Cultural Bias: The tendency of items on a test of intelligence to require specific cultural experience or knowledge.

Dark Adaptation: The process through which our visual system increases its sensitivity to light under low levels of illumination.
Daydreams: Imaginary scenes and events that occur while an individual is awake.
Debriefing: Providing research participants with full information about

all aspects of a study after they have participated in it.
Deception: The temporary withholding of information about a study from participants.
Decision Making: The process of choosing among various courses of action or alternatives.
Deep Structure: Information that underlies the form of a sentence and is crucial to its meaning.
Defense Mechanisms: Techniques used by the ego to keep threatening and unacceptable material out of consciousness and so to reduce anxiety.
Delayed Conditioning: A form of forward conditioning in which the presentation of the unconditioned stimulus (UCS) begins while the conditioned stimulus (CS) is still present.
Delta Waves: High-amplitude, slow brain waves that occur during several stages of sleep, but especially during Stage 4.
Delusions: Firmly held beliefs that have no basis in reality.
Dendrites: The parts of neurons that conduct action potentials toward the cell body.
Dependence: Strong need for a particular drug and inability to function without it.
Dependent Variable: The variable that is measured in an experiment.
Depressants: Drugs that reduce activity in the nervous system and therefore slow many bodily and cognitive processes. Depressants include alcohol and barbiturates.
Depression: A mood disorder in which individuals experience extreme unhappiness, lack of energy, and several related symptoms.
Developmental Psychology: The branch of psychology that focuses on the many ways we change throughout life.
Diagnostic and Statistical Manual of Mental Disorders-IV: A manual designed to help all mental health practitioners to recognize and correctly diagnose specific psychological disorders.
Diary Approach: A method of research in which individuals report on various aspects of their behavior on a regular basis for several days, weeks, or even months.
Diathesis-Stress Model: A model suggesting that genetic factors may predispose a person to develop schizophrenia but that this disorder will develop only if the person is exposed to certain kinds of stressful environmental conditions.
Difference Threshold: The amount of change in a stimulus required before a person can detect the shift.
Discriminative Stimulus: Stimulus that signals the availability of reinforcement if a specific response is made.
Disorganized or Disoriented Attachment: A pattern of attachment in which infants show contradictory reactions to their caregiver after being reunited with the caregiver in the strange situation test.
Dissociative Amnesia: Profound amnesia stemming from the active motivation to forget specific events or information.
Dissociative Disorders: Disorders involving prolonged loss of memory or identity.
Dissociative Fugue: A sudden and extreme disturbance of memory in which individuals wander off, adopt a new identity, and are unable to recall their own past.
Dissociative Identity Disorder: The condition formerly labeled as multiple personality disorder, in which a single person seems to possess two or more distinct identities or personality states, and these take control of the person's behavior at different times.
Distinctiveness: The extent to which a given person reacts in the same manner to different stimuli or situations.
Door-in-the-Face Technique: A technique for gaining compliance in which a large request is followed by a smaller one.
Dopamine Hypothesis: The hypothesis that schizophrenia stems, at least in part, from excessively high levels of dopamine.
Double-Blind Procedure: Procedure in which the researchers who have contact with participants do not know the hypothesis under investigation.
Down Syndrome: A genetically caused condition that results in mental retardation.
Dream: In Levinson's theory of adult development, a vision of future accomplishments—what a person hopes to achieve in the years ahead.
Dreams: Cognitive events, often vivid but disconnected, that occur during sleep. Most dreams take place during REM sleep.
Dreams of Absent-Minded Transgression: Dreams in which persons attempting to change their own behavior, as in quitting smoking, see themselves slipping into the unwanted behavior in an absent-minded or careless manner.
Drive Theory: A theory of motivation suggesting that behavior is "pushed" from within by drives stemming from basic biological needs.
Drug Abuse: Instances in which individuals take drugs purely to change their moods, and in which they experience impaired behavior or social functioning as a result.
Drug Therapy: Therapy based on the administration of psychotropic drugs.
Drugs: Chemical compounds that change the functioning of biological systems.
Dysfunctional Families: Families that do not meet the needs of children and in fact do them serious harm.

Eating Disorders: Disturbances in eating behavior that involve maladaptive and unhealthy efforts to control body weight.
Efferent Nerves: Nerve cells that carry information from the brain to muscles and glands throughout the body.
Efficacy Study: A study that applies basic methods of experimentation to find out whether a specific form of therapy really works—that is, whether the therapy produces beneficial outcomes for the persons who undergo it.
Ego: In Freud's theory, the part of personality that takes account of external reality in the expression of instinctive sexual and aggressive urges.
Egocentrism: The inability of young children to distinguish their own perspective from that of others.
Elaboration Likelihood Model (ELM): A cognitive model of persuasion suggesting that persuasion can occur through distinct routes.
Elaborative Rehearsal: Rehearsal in which the meaning of information is considered and the information is related to other knowledge already present in memory.
Electroconvulsive Therapy: A form of therapy in which strong electric shocks are delivered to the brain.
Electroencephalogram (EEG): A record of electrical activity within the brain. EEGs play an important role in the scientific study of sleep.
Electroencephalography (EEG): A technique for measuring the electrical activity of the brain via electrodes placed at specified locations on the skull.
Electronic Performance Monitoring: Procedures in which companies monitor employees' performance through their computer terminals or telephones; sometimes referred to as computer-based monitoring.
Embryo: The developing child during the second through the eighth week of prenatal development.
Emotional Intelligence: A form of intelligence relating to the emotional side of life such as the ability to recognize and manage one's own and others' emotions, to motivate oneself and restrain impulses, and to handle interpersonal relationships effectively.
Emotional Stability: One of the "big five" dimensions of personality;

ranges from poised, calm, composed at one end to nervous, anxious, excitable at the other.
Emotions: Reactions consisting of physiological reactions, subjective cognitive states, and expressive behaviors.
Empathy-Altruism Hypothesis: A view suggesting that when we encounter someone who needs help, we experience empathy and as a result are motivated to help them in an unselfish manner.
Encoding: The process through which information is converted into a form that can be entered into memory.
Endocrine Glands: Glands that secrete hormones directly into the bloodstream.
Epidemiological Studies: Large-scale research conducted to identify risk factors that predict the development of certain diseases.
Episodic Memory: Memories of events that we have experienced personally (sometimes termed autobiographical memory).
Equity Theory: A theory that focuses on perceived fairness—individuals' beliefs about whether they are being treated fairly or unfairly.
Escalation of Commitment: The tendency to become increasingly committed to bad decisions even as losses associated with them increase.
Expectancy Theory: A theory of motivation suggesting that behavior is "pulled" by expectations of desirable outcomes.
Expected Utility: The product of the subjective value of an event and its predicted probability of occurrence.
Experimentation (the experimental method): A research method in which researchers systematically alter one or more variables in order to determine whether such changes influence some aspect of behavior.
Experimenter Effects: Unintended effects, caused by researchers, on participants' behavior.
Explicit Memory: Memory for information that has been stored as a result of previous learning-information that we actively try to bring to mind and that we can express verbally.
Externals: In Rotter's terms, individuals who believe that they have little control over the outcomes they experience.
Extinction: The process through which a conditioned stimulus gradually loses the ability to evoke conditioned responses when it is no longer followed by the unconditioned stimulus.
Extrasensory Perception: Perception without a basis in sensory input.
Extraversion: One of the "big five" dimensions of personality; ranges from sociable, talkative, fun-loving at one end to sober, reserved, cautious at the other.
Extroverts: In Jung's theory, individuals who are open and confident and make friends readily.
Eyewitness Testimony: Information provided by witnesses to crimes or accidents.

Facial Feedback Hypothesis: A hypothesis indicating that facial expressions can influence as well as reflect emotional states.
False Consensus Effect: The tendency to believe that other persons share our attitudes to a greater extent than is true.
Family Systems Therapy: A form of family therapy that treats the family as a dynamic system in which each member has a major role.
Family Therapy: Therapy designed to change the interactions among family members in constructive ways.
Fantasies: Intense and vivid daydreams.
Farsightedness: A condition in which the visual image entering our eye is focused behind rather than directly on the retina. Therefore close objects appear out of focus, while distant objects are in clear focus.
Fast-Approaching-Deadline Technique: A technique for gaining compliance in which a "deadline" is established after which it will be impossible for the target person to obtain something.
Feature Detectors: Neurons at various levels within the visual cortex that respond primarily to stimuli possessing certain features.
Fetus: The developing child during the last seven months of prenatal development.
Figure-Ground Relationship: Our tendency to divide the perceptual world into two distinct parts: discrete figures and the background against which they stand out.
Fixation: Excessive investment of psychic energy in a particular stage of psychosexual development; this results in various types of psychological disorders.
Fixed-Interval Schedule: A schedule of reinforcement in which a specific interval of time must elapse before a response will yield reinforcement.
Fixed-Ratio Schedule: A schedule of reinforcement in which reinforcement occurs only after a fixed number of responses have been emitted.
Flashbulb Memories: Vivid memories of what we were doing at the time of an emotion-provoking event.
Flooding: Procedures for eliminating conditioned fears based on principles of classical conditioning. During flooding an individual is exposed to fear-inducing objects or events. Since no unconditioned stimulus then follows, extinction of fears eventually takes place.
Fluid Intelligence: Aspects of intelligence that involve forming concepts, reasoning, and identifying similarities.
Foot-in-the-Door Technique: A technique for gaining compliance in which a small request is followed by a much larger one.
Forced Compliance: A situation in which we feel compelled to say or do things inconsistent with our true attitudes.
Formal Operations: In Piaget's theory, the final stage of cognitive development, during which individuals may acquire the capacity for deductive or propositional reasoning.
Fovea: The area in the center of the retina in which cones are highly concentrated.
Frame-of-Reference Training: Procedures designed to ensure that all performance raters share a common frame of reference—that they agree as to what constitutes excellent, average, or poor performance.
Framing: Presentation of information concerning potential outcomes in terms of gains or in terms of losses.
Free Association: A verbal reporting by persons undergoing psychoanalysis of everything that passes through their minds, no matter how trivial it may appear to be.
Frequency Theory: A theory of pitch perception suggesting that sounds of different frequencies (heard as differences in pitch) induce different rates of neural activity in the hair cells of the inner ear.
Friendships: Relationships involving strong mutual affective (emotional) ties between two persons.
Frontal Lobe: The portion of the cerebral cortex that lies in front of the central fissure.
Frustration: The blocking of ongoing, goal-directed behavior.
Fully Functioning Persons: In Rogers's theory, psychologically healthy persons who enjoy life to the fullest.
Functional Autonomy: In Allport's theory, maintenance of patterns of behavior by motives other than the ones originally responsible for the behavior's occurrence.
Functional Fixedness: The tendency to think of using objects only as they have been used in the past.
Fundamental Attribution Error: The tendency to attribute others' behavior to internal causes to a greater extent than is actually justified.

Gate-Control Theory: A theory of pain suggesting that the spinal cord contains a mechanism that can block transmission of pain to the brain.
Gender: The supposed traits and behavior of males and females as defined by a given society.
Gender Constancy: The stability of gender over time.
Gender Differences: Differences between females' and males' behavior. Often, perceptions of these differences are exaggerated by gender stereotypes.
Gender Identity: Children's understanding of the fact that they are male or female.
Gender Identity Disorder: A disorder in which individuals believe that they were born with the wrong sexual identity.
Gender Roles: Beliefs about how males and females are expected to behave in many situations.
Gender Schema Theory: A theory that children develop a cognitive framework reflecting the beliefs of their society concerning the characteristics and roles of males and females; this gender schema then strongly affects the processing of new social information.
Gender Stereotypes: Cultural beliefs about differences between women and men.
General Adaptation Syndrome: A three-stage profile of response to stress: (1) alarm, or general mobilization; (2) resistance, during which an organism makes efforts to cope; and (3) if the organism fails to overcome the threat and depletes its coping resources, exhaustion.
Genes: Biological "blueprints" that shape development and all basic bodily processes.
Genetic Determinism Hypothesis: The view that we help other persons who are similar or related to us because this increases the likelihood of our genes, or related genes, being passed on to the next generation.
Genetic Hypothesis: The view that group differences in intelligence are due, at least in part, to genetic factors.
Genetic Theories of Aging: Theories that attribute physical aging primarily to genetic programming.
Genital Stage: In Freud's theory, the final psychosexual stage of development—one in which individuals acquire the adult capacity to combine lust with affection.
Gestalt Psychologists: German psychologists intrigued by our tendency to perceive sensory patterns as well-organized wholes, rather than as separate, isolated parts.
Gestalt Therapy: A humanistic therapy that focuses on helping individuals to come to terms with hidden, "disowned" aspects of their thoughts and feelings.
Gestures: Movements of various body parts that convey a specific meaning to others.
Glass Ceiling: A final barrier against female advancement in some organizations that prevents women from attaining certain top positions.
Glial Cells: Cells in the nervous system that surround, support, and protect neurons.
Goal Setting Theory: A theory of motivation that focuses on the effects on motivation and performance of setting specific, challenging goals.
Gonads: The primary sex glands.
Graded Potential: A basic type of signal within neurons that results from external physical stimulation of the dendrite or cell body. Unlike the all-or-nothing nature of action potentials, the magnitude of graded potentials varies in proportion to the size of the stimulus.
Grammar: Rules within a given language indicating how words can be combined into meaningful sentences.
Great Person Theory: A theory suggesting that all great leaders possess certain traits that set them apart from other persons.
Group Therapies: Therapies in which treatment takes place in groups.

Hallucinations: Vivid sensory experiences that have no basis in physical reality.
Halstead-Reitan Neuropsychological Battery: A battery of tests of auditory, visual, and psychomotor functioning (e.g., eye-hand coordination). Individuals' patterns of scores can point to the existence of specific forms of brain damage.
Hardiness: A personality style characterized by high levels of commitment, a strong sense of control over life events, and the view that change is an opportunity for growth and development.
Hassles: Annoying minor events of everyday life that cumulatively can affect psychological well-being.
Health Belief Model: A theory of health behaviors, the model predicts that whether or not a person practices a particular health behavior may depend on the degree to which the person perceives a personal health threat and believes that practicing the behavior will reduce that threat.
Health Psychology: The study of the relation between psychological variables and health; reflects the view that both mind and body are important determinants of health and illness.
Heredity: Biologically determined characteristics passed from parents to their offspring.
Heritability: The proportion of the variance in a trait within a given population that is attributable to genetic factors.
Heterosexual (sexual orientation): A sexual orientation in which individuals prefer sexual relations with members of the other sex.
Heuristics: Mental rules of thumb that permit us to make decisions and judgments in a rapid and efficient manner.
Hierarchy of Needs: In Maslow's theory of motivation, an arrangement of needs from the most basic to those at the highest levels.
Hindsight Effect: The tendency to assume that we would have been better at predicting actual events than is really true.
Hippocampus: A structure of the limbic system that plays a role in the formation of certain types of memories.
Homeostasis: A state of physiological balance within the body.
Homosexual (sexual orientation): A sexual orientation in which individuals prefer sexual relations with members of their own sex.
Hormones: Substances secreted by endocrine glands that regulate a wide range of bodily processes.
Hue: The color that we experience due to the dominant wavelength of a light.
Human Factors: A branch of psychology that focuses on the ways in which human beings interact with the tools, equipment, and systems they use in their work and daily lives.
Humanistic Theories: Theories of personality emphasizing personal responsibility and innate tendencies toward personal growth.
Humanistic Therapies: Therapies that focus on helping clients (not "patients") to become more truly themselves—to find meaning in their lives and to live in ways truly consistent with their own values and traits.
Hunger Motivation: The motivation to obtain and consume food.
Huntington's Disease: A genetically based fatal neuromuscular disorder characterized by the gradual onset of jerky, uncontrollable movements.
Hypercomplex Cells: Neurons in the visual cortex that respond to complex aspects of visual stimuli, such as width, length, and shape.
Hypersomnias: Disorders involving excessive amounts of sleep or an overwhelming urge to fall asleep.
Hypertension: High blood pressure, a condition in which the pressure within the blood vessels is abnormally high.
Hypnosis: An interaction between

two persons in which one (the hypnotist) induces changes in the behavior, feelings, or cognitions of the other (the subject) through suggestions. Hypnosis involves expectations on the part of subjects and their attempts to conform to social roles (e.g., the role of hypnotized person).

Hypochondriasis: A somatoform disorder involving preoccupation with fears of disease or illness.

Hypothalamus: A small structure deep within the brain that plays a key role in the regulation of the autonomic nervous system and of several forms of motivated behavior such as eating and aggression.

Hypotheses: Testable predictions derived from theories.

Hypothetico-Deductive Reasoning: In Piaget's theory, a type of reasoning first shown by individuals during the stage of formal operations. It involves formulating a general theory and deducing specific hypotheses from it.

Id: In Freud's theory, the portion of personality concerned with immediate gratification of primitive needs.

Illusions: Instances in which perception yields false interpretations of physical reality.

Implicit Memory: Memory for information that we cannot express verbally. (See also procedural memory.)

Incentives: Rewards individuals seek to attain.

Incompatible Response Hypothesis: A hypothesis suggesting that if individuals who are angry and ready to engage in aggression are exposed to stimuli (such as humor) that induce emotional states or response tendencies incompatible with anger, both anger and aggression will be reduced.

Independent Variable: The variable that is systematically changed in an experiment.

Industrial/Organizational Psychology: A branch of psychology that focuses on all aspects of behavior in work settings.

Infantile Amnesia: Our inability to remember experiences during the first two or three years of life, probably because we do not possess a well-developed self-concept during this period.

Inferential Statistics: A special form of mathematics that allows us to evaluate the likelihood that a given pattern of findings is due to chance alone.

Information-Processing Approach: An approach to understanding human memory that emphasizes the encoding, storage, and later retrieval of information.

Informed Consent: A principle requiring that research participants be provided with information about all the events and procedures a study will involve before they agree to participate in it.

Ingratiation: A technique for gaining compliance by causing others to like us before we attempt to influence them.

Insomnia: The inability to fall asleep or to maintain sleep once it is attained.

Inspection Time: The minimum amount of time a particular stimulus must be exposed for individuals to make a judgment about it that meets some preestablished criterion of accuracy.

Instinct Theory: A theory of motivation suggesting that many forms of behavior stem from innate urges or tendencies.

Instincts: Patterns of behavior assumed to be universal in a species.

Intelligence: Individuals' abilities to understand complex ideas, to adapt effectively to the environment, to learn from experience, to engage in various forms of reasoning, to overcome obstacles by careful thought.

Intentional Forgetting: Efforts to remove, or at least ignore, information in long-term memory that is inaccurate or no longer important to us.

Interchannel Discrepancies: Inconsistencies between cues from different basic channels of nonverbal communication.

Internals: In Rotter's theory, individuals who believe that they exert considerable control over the outcomes they experience.

Interpersonal Attraction: The extent to which we like or dislike other persons.

Intrinsic Motivation: Motivation to perform activities because they are rewarding in and of themselves.

Introverts: In Jung's theory, individuals who are hesitant and cautious and do not make friends easily.

IQ: Originally, "intelligence quotient," a number that examiners derived by dividing an individual's "mental age" by his or her chronological age. Now IQ simply indicates an individual's level of performance on an intelligence test relative to those of other persons their age.

Iris: The colored part of the eye; adjusts the amount of light that enters by constricting or dilating the pupil.

James-Lange Theory: A theory of emotion suggesting that emotion-provoking events produce various physiological reactions and that recognition of these is responsible for subjective emotional experiences.

Job Descriptive Index: A widely used measure of job satisfaction in which individuals indicate whether or not each of several adjectives describes a particular aspect of their work.

Job Design: Efforts to make jobs more interesting and appealing to the persons who perform them.

Job Enlargement: Expansion of jobs to include a larger variety of tasks, all at the same level of skill.

Job Enrichment: Expansion of jobs to include tasks at higher levels of skill and responsibility.

Job Rotation: Lateral moves between jobs within a given organization.

Job Satisfaction: Individuals' attitudes toward their work or jobs.

Just Noticeable Difference (JND): The smallest amount of change in a physical stimulus necessary for an individual to notice a difference in the intensity of a stimulus.

Kinesthesia: The sense that gives us information about the location of our body parts with respect to each other and allows us to perform movement.

Korsakoff's Syndrome: An illness caused by long-term abuse of alcohol; often involves profound retrograde amnesia.

Language: A system of symbols, plus rules for combining them, used to communicate information.

Late-Adult Transition: In Levinson's theory of adult development, a transition in which individuals must come to terms with their impending retirement.

Latency Stage: In Freud's theory, the psychosexual stage of development that follows resolution of the Oedipus complex. During this stage sexual desires are relatively weak.

Lateralization of Function: Specialization of the two hemispheres of the brain for the performance of different functions.

Laws of Grouping: Simple principles describing how we tend to group discrete stimuli together in the perceptual world.

Leader: The person within a group who exerts most influence.

Learned Helplessness: Feelings of helplessness that develop after exposure to situations in which no effort succeeds in affecting outcomes.

Learning: Any relatively permanent change in behavior (or behavior potential) resulting from experience.

Lens: A curved structure behind the pupil that bends light rays, focusing them on the retina.

Less-Leads-to-More Effect: The fact that rewards just barely sufficient to induce individuals to state positions contrary to their own views often generate more attitude change than larger rewards.

Levels of Processing View: A view of memory suggesting that the greater the effort expended in processing information, the more readily it will be recalled at later times.
Libido: According to Freud, the psychic energy that powers all mental activity.
Life Structure: In Levinson's theory of adult development, the underlying pattern or design of a person's life.
Lifestyle: In the context of health psychology, the overall pattern of decisions and behaviors that determine health and quality of life.
Limbic System: Several structures deep within the brain that play a role in emotional reactions and behavior.
Linguistic Relativity Hypothesis: The view that language shapes thought.
Localization: The ability of our auditory system to determine the direction of a sound source.
Long-Term Memory: A memory system for the retention of large amounts of information over long periods of time.
Longitudinal Research: Research in which the same individuals are studied across relatively long periods of time.
Longitudinal-Sequential Design: A research method in which several groups of individuals of different ages are studied across time.
Love: An intense emotional state involving attraction, sexual desire, and deep concern for another person.
Lowball Procedure: A tactic for gaining compliance in which, after a deal or arrangement is made, the terms are changed by the person using this tactic.

Magical Thinking: Thinking that makes assumptions that don't hold up to rational scrutiny.
Magnetic Resonance Imaging (MRI): A method for studying the intact brain in which technicians obtain images by exposing the brain to a strong magnetic field.
Make-Believe Play: Play in which children pretend to be engaging in various familiar activities, such as eating or going to sleep.
Marital Therapy: Therapy designed to help couples improve the quality of their relationship.
Means-Ends Analysis: A technique for solving problems in which the overall problem is divided into parts and efforts are made to solve each part in turn.
Medical Perspective: The view that psychological disorders are a form of illness, produced, like other illnesses, by natural causes.
Medulla: A brain structure concerned with the regulation of vital bodily functions such as breathing and heartbeat.
Memory: The capacity to retain and later retrieve information.
Menopause: Cessation of the menstrual cycle.
Mental Retardation: Considerably below-average intellectual functioning combined with varying degrees of difficulty in meeting the demands of everyday life.
Mental Set: The impact of past experience on present problem solving; specifically, the tendency to retain methods that were successful in the past even if better alternatives now exist.
Mentor: Older and more experienced individual who helps guide young adults.
Meta-Analysis: A statistical procedure for combining the results of many different studies in order to estimate both the direction and the magnitude of the effects of independent variables studied in these experiments.
Metacognition: Awareness and understanding of our own cognitive processes.
Metacognitive Processing: An expanded level of awareness that allows us, in a sense, to observe ourselves in the problem-solving process.
Microexpressions: Fleeting facial expressions that occur very quickly and may reveal individuals' true emotional reactions to events or situations.
Midbrain: A part of the brain containing primitive centers for vision and hearing. It also plays a role in the regulation of visual reflexes.
Midlife Transition: In Levinson's theory of adult development, a turbulent transitional period occurring between the ages of forty and forty-five.
Millon Clinical Multiaxial Inventory (MCMI): An objective test of personality specifically designed to assist psychologists in diagnosing various psychological disorders.
Minnesota Satisfaction Questionnaire: A widely used measure of job satisfaction in which individuals rate the extent to which they are satisfied or dissatisfied with various aspects of their jobs.
Mitosis: Cell division in which chromosome pairs split and then replicate themselves so that the full number is restored in each of the cells produced by division.
MMPI: A widely used objective test of personality based on empirical keying.
Monocular Cues: Cues to depth or distance provided by one
Mood Congruence Effects: Our tendency to notice or remember information congruent with our current mood.
Mood-Dependent Memory: The finding that what we remember while in a given mood may be determined in part by what we learned when previously in that same mood.
Mood Disorders: Psychological disorders in which individuals experience swings in their emotional states that are much more extreme and prolonged than is true of most people.
Moral Development: Changes that occur with age in the capacity to reason about the rightness or wrongness of various actions.
Morning Person: Individual who experiences peak levels of energy and physiological activation relatively early in the day.
Morphemes: The smallest units of speech that convey meaning.
Motivation: Internal processes that activate, guide, and maintain behavior over time.
Multicultural Perspective: In psychology, an approach that pays careful attention to the effects of ethnic and cultural factors on behavior.
Munchausen's Syndrome: A syndrome in which individuals pretend to have various medical problems in order to get attention from health practitioners.

Narcolepsy: A sleep disorder in which individuals are overcome by uncontrollable periods of sleep during waking hours.
Natural Concepts: Concepts that are not based on a precise set of attributes or properties, do not have clear-cut boundaries, and are often defined by prototypes.
Naturalistic Decision Making: A movement toward studying decision making as it occurs in applied or real-world settings.
Naturalistic Observation: A research method in which behavior is studied in the settings where it usually occurs.
Nature-Nurture Controversy: Argument regarding the relative contributions of genetic factors (nature) and environmental factors (nurture) to aspects of behavior and cognitive processes.
Nearsightedness: A condition in which the visual image entering our eye is focused slightly in front of our retina rather than directly on it. Therefore near objects can be seen clearly, while distant objects appear fuzzy or blurred.
Negative Afterimage: A sensation of complementary color that we experience after staring at a stimulus of a given hue.
Negative Reinforcers: Stimuli that

strengthen responses that permit an organism to avoid or escape from their presence.
Negative State Relief Hypothesis: A view suggesting that we sometimes help others in order to relieve the negative feelings that their plight arouses in us.
Neo-Freudians: Personality theorists who accepted basic portions of Freud's theory but rejected or modified other portions.
Neodissociation Theory of Hypnosis: A theory suggesting that hypnotized individuals enter an altered state of consciousness in which consciousness is divided.
Nervous System: The complex structure that regulates bodily processes and is responsible, ultimately, for all aspects of conscious experience.
Neural Networks: Computer systems modeled after the brain and made up of highly interconnected elementary computational units that work together in parallel.
Neurons: Cells specialized for communicating information, the basic building blocks of the nervous system.
Neurotransmitters: Chemicals, released by neurons, that carry information across the synapse.
Nicotine: The addictive substance in tobacco.
Night (Evening) Person: Individual who experiences peak levels of energy and physiological activation relatively late in the day.
Night Terrors: Extremely frightening dreamlike experiences that occur during non-REM sleep.
Nodes of Ranvier: Small gaps in the myelin sheath surrounding the axons of many neurons.
Nonverbal cues: Outward signs of others' emotional states. Such clues involve facial expression, eye contact, and body language.

Obedience: A form of social influence in which one or more individuals behave in specific ways in response to direct orders from someone.
Object Permanence: The fact that objects continue to exist when they pass from view.
Observational Learning: The acquisition of new forms of behavior, information, or concepts through exposure to others and the consequences they experience.
Obsessive-Compulsive Disorder: An anxiety disorder in which individuals become trapped in repetitious behaviors known as compulsions that they seem unable to prevent, and/or in recurrent modes of thought called obsessions.
Occipital Lobe: The portion of the cerebral cortex involved in vision.
Oedipus Complex: In Freud's theory, a crisis of psychosexual development in which children must give up their sexual attraction for their opposite-sex parent.
Openness to Experience: One of the "big five" dimensions of personality; ranges from imaginative, sensitive, intellectual at one end to down-to-earth, insensitive, crude at the other.
Operant Conditioning: A process through which organisms learn to repeat behaviors that yield positive outcomes or permit them to avoid or escape from negative outcomes.
Opiates: Drugs that induce a dreamy, relaxed state and, in some persons, intense feelings of pleasure. Opiates exert their effects by stimulating special receptor sites within the brain.
Opponent-Process Theory: Theory that describes the processing of sensory information related to color at levels above the retina. The theory suggests that we possess six different types of neurons, each of which is either stimulated or inhibited by red, green, blue, yellow, black, or white.
Opponent-Process Theory of Emotion: A theory suggesting that an emotional reaction is followed automatically by an opposite reaction.
Optic Nerve: A bundle of nerve fibers that exit the back of the eye and carry visual information to the brain.
Oral Stage: In Freud's theory, a psychosexual stage of development during which pleasure is centered in the region of the mouth.
Organizational Citizenship Behavior: Actions by individuals that help other employees in their organization, or the organization itself, and that are "beyond the call of duty."
Overhelping: Helping others when they don't really need it in order to make them appear less competent than they really are.

Panic Attack Disorder: An anxiety disorder in which individuals experience high levels of physiological arousal coupled with intense fear of losing control.
Paraphilias: Disorders in which sexual arousal cannot occur without the presence of unusual imagery or acts.
Parapsychologists: Individuals who study psi and other paranormal events.
Parasympathetic Nervous System: The portion of the autonomic nervous system that readies the body for restoration of energy.
Parietal Lobe: A portion of the cerebral cortex, lying behind the central fissure, that plays a major role in the skin senses: touch, temperature, pressure.
Parkinson's Disease: A progressive and ultimately fatal disorder, caused by a deterioration of dopamine-producing neurons in the brain.
Passive Smoke: The smoke that we inhale from the smokers around us.
Peak Experiences: According to Maslow, intense emotional experiences during which individuals feel at one with the universe.
Perception: The process through which we select, organize, and interpret input from our sensory receptors.
Performance Appraisals: Procedures for evaluating employees' performance so that this can be linked to the rewards they receive.
Peripheral Nervous System: The portion of the nervous system that connects internal organs and glands, as well as voluntary and involuntary muscles, to the central nervous system.
Peripheral Route (to persuasion): Attitude change that occurs in response to persuasion cues—information concerning the expertise, status, or attractiveness of would-be persuaders.
Personality Disorders: Disorders involving extreme and inflexible personality traits that are distressing to the persons who have them or cause them problems in school, work, or interpersonal relations.
Personality: An individual's unique and relatively stable patterns of behavior, thoughts, and feelings.
Personality Traits: Specific dimensions along which individuals' personalities differ in consistent, stable ways.
Person-Environment (P-E) Fit: The appropriateness of the fit, or match, between a person and his or her work environment; a poor P-E fit may produce stress.
Persuasion: The process through which one or more persons attempt to alter the attitudes of one or more others.
Phallic Stage: In Freud's theory, a psychosexual stage of development during which pleasure is centered in the genital region. It is during this stage that the Oedipus complex develops.
Phenylketonuria (PKU): A genetically based disorder in which persons lack the enzyme to break down phenylalanine, a substance present in many foods. The gradual buildup of phenylalanine contributes to subsequent outcomes that include retardation.
Phobias: Intense, irrational fears of objects or events.
Phonemes: A set of sounds basic to a given language.
Phonological Development: Development of the ability to produce recognizable speech.

Physiological Dependence: Strong urges to continue using a drug based on organic factors such as changes in metabolism.
Pinna: The external portion of the ear.
Pitch: The characteristic of a sound that is described as high or low. Pitch is mediated by the frequency of a sound.
Pituitary Gland: An endocrine gland that releases hormones to regulate other glands and several basic biological processes.
Place Theory: A theory suggesting that sounds of different frequency stimulate different areas of the basilar membrane, the portion of the cochlea containing sensory receptors for sound.
Placenta: A structure that surrounds, protects, and nourishes the developing fetus.
Playing Hard to Get: A tactic for gaining compliance in which individuals try to create the impression that they are very popular or very much in demand.
Pleasure Principle: The principle on which the id operates, according to which immediate pleasure is the sole motivation for behavior.
Pons: A portion of the brain through which sensory and motor information passes and which contains structures relating to sleep, arousal, and the regulation of muscle tone and cardiac reflexes.
Positive Reinforcers: Stimuli that strengthen responses that precede them.
Positron Emission Tomography (PET): An imaging technique that detects the activity of the brain by measuring glucose utilization or blood flow.
Postconventional Level (of morality): According to Kohlberg, the final stage of moral development, in which individuals judge morality in terms of abstract principles.
Postpartum Depression: Depression experienced by new mothers shortly after giving birth.
Posttraumatic Stress Disorder: A disorder in which people persistently reexperience traumatic events in their thoughts or dreams, feel as if they are reliving these events from time to time, and persistently avoid stimuli associated with the traumatic events, along with several other symptoms.
Practical Intelligence: Intelligence useful in solving everyday problems.
Preconventional Level (of morality): According to Kohlberg, the earliest stage of moral development, in which individuals judge morality in terms of the effects produced by various actions.
Prejudice: Negative attitudes toward the members of some social group based on their membership in this group.
Premack Principle: The principle that a more preferred activity can be used to reinforce a less preferred activity.
Preoperational Stage: In Piaget's theory, a stage of cognitive development during which children become capable of mental representations of the external world.
Prescription Privileges: The legal right to write prescriptions.
Prevention Strategies: Techniques designed to reduce the occurrence of physical and psychological problems.
Primary Aging: Changes in our bodies caused by the passage of time and, perhaps, genetic factors.
Primary Prevention: Efforts to prevent new problems from occurring.
Proactive Interference: Interference with the learning or storage of current information by information previously entered into memory.
Problem Solving: Efforts to develop or choose among various responses in order to
Problem-Solving Therapy: A form of family therapy that focuses on instituting specific, well-defined changes within a family in order to eliminate specific problems.
Procedural Memory: Information we cannot readily express verbally—for example, information necessary to perform various skilled motor activities such as riding a bicycle.
Processing Speed: The speed with which a person can process information.
Progressive Relaxation: A stress-reduction technique in which people learn to reduce tension by flexing and relaxing, one by one, muscle groups throughout the body.
Propositions: Sentences that relate one concept to another and can stand as separate assertions.
Prosocial Behavior: Actions that benefit others without necessarily providing any direct benefit to the persons who perform them.
Prosopagnosia: A rare condition in which brain damage impairs a person's ability to recognize faces.
Prospective Memory: Remembering to perform certain activities at specific times.
Prototypes: Representations in memory of various objects or stimuli in the physical world; the best or clearest examples of various objects or stimuli in the physical world.
Psi: Unusual processes of information or energy transfer that are currently unexplained in terms of known physical or biological mechanisms. Included under the heading of psi are such supposed abilities as telepathy (reading others' thoughts) and clairvoyance (perceiving unseen objects or unknown events).
Psychiatry: A branch of modern medicine specializing in the treatment of psychological disorders.
Psychoanalysis: A method of therapy based on Freud's theory of personality, in which the therapist attempts to bring repressed unconscious material into consciousness.
Psychological Dependence: Strong desires to continue using a drug even though it is not physiologically addicting.
Psychological Disorders: Maladaptive patterns of behavior and thought that cause the persons experiencing them considerable distress.
Psychology: The science of behavior and cognitive processes.
Psychosexual Stages of Development: According to Freud, an innate sequence of stages through which all human beings pass. At each stage, pleasure is focused on a different region of the body.
Psychosurgery: Brain operations designed to change abnormal behavior.
Psychotherapies: Procedures in which a trained person establishes a special kind of relationship with an individual seeking help, in order to remove or modify existing symptoms, change disturbed patterns of behavior and thought, and promote personal growth.
Puberty: The period of rapid change during which individuals reach sexual maturity.
Punishment: The application or removal of a stimulus so as to decrease the strength of a behavior.
Pupil: An opening in the eye, just behind the cornea, through which light rays enter the eye.

Random Assignment of Participants to Experimental Conditions: Assuring that all research participants have an equal chance of being exposed to each level of the independent variable (that is, of being assigned to each experimental condition).
Rational-Emotive Therapy: A form of therapy that focuses on persuading individuals to recognize and change irrational assumptions that underlie their thinking.
Raven Progressive Matrices: A popular test of intelligence that was designed to be relatively free of cultural bias.
Realistic Conflict Theory: A theory proposing that prejudice stems, at least in part, from economic competition between social groups.
Reality Principle: The principle according to which the ego operates,

in which the external consequences of behavior are considered in the regulation of expression of impulses from the id.
Reasoning: Cognitive activity that transforms information in order to reach specific conclusions.
Recategorization: A technique for reducing prejudice that involves inducing people to shift the boundary between "us" and "them" so that it now includes groups previously viewed as "them."
Reconditioning: The rapid recovery of a conditioned response to a CS-UCS pairing following extinction.
Reinforcement: The application or removal of a stimulus to increase the strength of a specific behavior.
Relative Size: A visual cue based on comparison of the size of an unknown object to objects of known size.
Reliability: The extent to which any measuring device (including a psychological test) yields the same result each time it is applied to the same quantity.
REM (Rapid Eye Movement) Sleep: A state of sleep in which brain activity resembling waking restfulness is accompanied by deep muscle relaxation and movements of the eyes. Most dreams occur during periods of REM sleep.
Repeated Exposure Effect: The fact that the more frequently we are exposed to various stimuli (at least up to a point), the more we tend to like them.
Replication: A basic scientific principle requiring that the results of an experiment be repeated before they are accepted with confidence.
Representativeness Heuristic: A mental rule of thumb suggesting that the more closely an event or object resembles typical examples of some concept or category, the more likely it is to belong to that concept or category.
Repression: The active elimination from consciousness of memories or experiences we find threatening.
Resilience in Development: The capacity of some adolescents raised in harmful environments to somehow rise above these disadvantages and achieve healthy development.
Resistance: In psychoanalysis, a patient's stubborn refusal to report certain thoughts, motives, and experiences or overt rejection of the analyst's interpretations.
Resistant Attachment: A pattern of attachment in which infants reject and refuse to be comforted by their caregiver after the caregiver leaves them in the strange situation test.
Reticular Activating System: A structure within the brain concerned with sleep, arousal, and the regulation of muscle tone and cardiac reflexes.
Retina: The surface at the back of the eye containing the rods and cones.
Retrieval: The process through which information stored in memory is located.
Retrieval Cues: Stimuli associated with information stored in memory that can aid in its retrieval.
Retroactive Interference: Interference with retention of information already present in memory by new information being entered into memory.
Retrograde Amnesia: Loss of memory of events that occurred before an amnesia-inducing event.
Risk Factors: Aspects of our environment or behavior that influence our chances of developing or contracting a particular disease, within the limits set by our genetic structure.
Rods: One of the two types of sensory receptors for vision found in the eye.
Romantic Love: A form of love in which feelings of strong attraction and sexual desire toward another person are dominant.
Rorschach Test: A widely used projective test of personality in which individuals are asked to describe what they see in a series of inkblots.

Saccadic Movements: Quick movements of the eyes from one point of fixation to another.
Sampling: In the survey method, the methods used to select persons who respond to the survey.
Saturation: The degree of concentration of the hue of light. We experience saturation as the purity of a color.
Schachter-Singer Theory: A theory of emotion suggesting that our subjective emotional states are determined, at least in part, by the cognitive labels we attach to feelings of arousal; also known as two-factor theory.
Schedules of Reinforcement: Rules determining when and how reinforcements will be delivered.
Schemas: Cognitive frameworks representing our knowledge and assumptions about specific aspects of the world.
Schizophrenia: A complex disorder characterized by hallucinations (e.g., hearing voices), delusions (beliefs with no basis in reality), disturbances in speech, and several other symptoms.
Secondary Aging: Physical changes due to disease, disuse, or abuse of our bodies.
Secondary Prevention: Efforts to detect problems early, before they have escalated in intensity.
Secondary Traits: According to Allport, traits that exert relatively weak effects upon behavior.
Secure Attachment: A pattern of attachment in which infants actively seek contact with their caregiver, and take comfort from the caregiver's presence when he or she returns in the strange situation test.
Selective Attention: Our ability to pay attention to only some aspects of the world around us while largely ignoring others.
Self-Actualization: In Maslow's theory, a state of personal development in which individuals reach their maximum potential.
Self-Concept: All the information and beliefs individuals have about their own characteristics and themselves.
Self-Determination Theory: In relation to health and lifestyle, theory suggesting that motivation for health-promoting behaviors is highest when it is autonomous and lowest when it is prompted by others.
Self-Efficacy: Individuals' expectations concerning their ability to perform various tasks.
Self-Esteem: The extent to which our self-evaluations are favorable or unfavorable.
Self-Help Groups: Groups of persons who are experiencing the same kinds of problems and who meet to help each other in their efforts to cope with these difficulties.
Self-Monitoring: A personality trait involving the extent to which one's behavior is regulated by internal factors such as attitudes and values, or by external factors such as requirements of a given situation.
Self-Reinforcement: A process in which individuals reward themselves for reaching their own goals.
Self-Serving Bias: The tendency to attribute positive outcomes to our own traits or characteristics (internal causes) but negative outcomes to factors beyond our control (external causes).
Semantic Development: Development of understanding of the meaning of spoken or written language.
Semantic Memory: General, abstract knowledge about the world.
Sensation: Input about the physical world provided by our sensory receptors.
Sensation Seeking: The desire to seek out novel and intense experiences.
Sensorimotor Stage: In Piaget's theory, the earliest stage of cognitive development.
Sensory Adaptation: Reduced sensitivity to unchanging stimuli over time.
Sensory Memory: A memory system that retains representations of sensory input for brief periods of time.
Sensory Receptors: Cells specialized for the task of transduction—convert-

ing physical energy (light, sound) into neural impulses.
Serial Position Curve: The greater accuracy of recall of words or other information early and late in a list than of words or information in the middle of the list.
Serum Cholesterol: The cholesterol in our blood.
Sexism: Prejudice based on gender.
Sexual Abuse: Sexual contact or activities forced on children or adolescents by other persons, usually adults.
Sexual Arousal Disorders: The inability to attain or maintain an erection (males) or the absence of vaginal swelling and lubrication (females).
Sexual Desire Disorders: Disorders involving a lack of interest in sex or active aversion to sexual activity.
Sexual Fantasies: Mental images that are sexually arousing or erotic to the individual who has them.
Sexual Jealousy: A negative state aroused by a perceived threat to a sexual relationship with another person.
Sexual Motivation: Motivation to engage in various forms of sexual relations.
Shape Constancy: The tendency to perceive a physical object as having a constant shape even when the image it casts on the retina changes.
Shaping: A technique in which closer and closer approximations of desired behavior are required for the delivery of positive reinforcement.
Short-Term Memory: A memory system that holds limited amounts of information for relatively short periods of time.
Signal Detection Theory: A theory suggesting that there are no universal absolute thresholds for sensations. Rather, detection of a stimulus depends on its physical energy and on internal factors such as the relative costs and benefits associated with detecting the stimulus.
Simple Cells: Cells within the visual system that respond to specific shapes presented in certain orientations (horizontal, vertical, etc.).
Simultaneous Conditioning: A form of conditioning in which the conditioned stimulus (CS) and the unconditioned stimulus (UCS) begin and end at the same time.
Size Constancy: The tendency to perceive a physical object as having a constant size even when the size of the image it casts on the retina changes.
Sleep: A process in which important physiological changes (e.g., shifts in brain activity, slowing of basic bodily functions) are accompanied by major shifts in consciousness.
Social Categorization: Our tendency to divide the social world into two distinct categories: "us" and "them."
Social Cognition: The processes through which we notice, store, remember, and later use social information.
Social Cognitive Theory: A theory of behavior suggesting that human behavior is influenced by many cognitive factors as well as by reinforcement contingencies, and that human beings have an impressive capacity to regulate their own actions.
Social Comparison: A process in which we compare ourselves with others.
Social Facilitation: The effects of an audience on performance. Contrary to what this term suggests, such effects are not always beneficial.
Social Influence: Efforts by one or more persons to change the attitudes or behavior of one or more others.
Social Norms: Rules indicating how individuals ought to behave in specific situations.
Social Psychology: The branch of psychology that studies all aspects of social thought and social behavior.
Social Referencing: Using others' reactions to appraise an uncertain situation or experience.
Social-Cognitive or Role-Playing View of Hypnosis: A view suggesting that effects produced by hypnosis are the result of hypnotized persons' expectations about and their social role as "hypnotized subject."
Somatic Nervous System: The portion of the peripheral nervous system that connects the brain and spinal cord to voluntary muscles.
Somatization Disorder: A somatoform disorder in which an individual has a history of many physical complaints, beginning before age thirty, that occur over a period of years and result in treatment being sought for significant impairments in social, occupational, or other important areas of life.
Somatoform Disorders: Disorders in which individuals have symptoms typically associated with physical diseases or conditions, but in which no known organic or physiological basis for the symptoms can be found.
Somnambulism: A sleep disorder in which individuals actually get up and move about while still asleep.
Source Traits: According to Cattell, key dimensions of personality that underlie many other traits.
Split-Half Reliability: The correlation between an individual's scores on two equivalent halves of a test.
Spontaneous Recovery: Following extinction, return of a conditioned response upon reinstatement of CS-UCS pairings.
SQUID (Superconducting Quantum Interference Device): An imaging technique that captures images of the brain through its ability to detect tiny changes in magnetic fields in the brain.
Stage Theory: Any theory proposing that all human beings move through an orderly and predictable series of changes.
Stanford-Binet Test: A widely used individual test of intelligence.
State-Dependent Retrieval: The greater ease of retrieval of information stored in long-term memory when our internal state is the same as it was when the information was first acquired.
Stereotypes: Cognitive frameworks suggesting that all members of specific social groups share certain characteristics.
Stimulants: Drugs that increase activity in the nervous system (e.g., amphetamines, caffeine, nicotine).
Stimulus: A physical event capable of affecting behavior.
Stimulus Control: Consistent occurrence of a behavior in the presence of a discriminative stimulus.
Stimulus Discrimination: The process by which organisms learn to respond to certain stimuli but not to others.
Stimulus Generalization: The tendency of stimuli similar to a conditioned stimulus to evoke conditioned responses.
Storage: The process through which information is retained in memory.
Strange Situation Test: A procedure for studying attachment in which a caregiver leaves a child alone with a stranger for several minutes and then returns.
Stress: Our response to events that disrupt, or threaten to disrupt, our physical or psychological functioning.
Stressors: Events or situations in our environment that cause stress.
Striving for Superiority: Attempting to overcome feelings of inferiority. According to Adler, this is the primary motive for human behavior.
Subjective Well-Being: Personal happiness.
Sublimation: A defense mechanism in which threatening unconscious impulses are channeled into socially acceptable forms of behavior.
Subliminal Perception: The presumed ability to perceive a stimulus that is below the threshold for conscious experience.
Substance Abuse: A disorder involving one or more of the following: recurrent substance use resulting in failure to fulfill major role obligations at work, school, or home; recurrent substance use in situations in which

such use is physically hazardous; and/or recurrent substance-related legal problems.
Substance Dependence: A disorder involving one or more of the following: the need for increasing amounts of a substance to achieve the desired effect, withdrawal symptoms when the substance isn't taken, an inability to cut down on or control use of the substance, and the dedication of a great deal of time to activities aimed at securing the substance.
Substance-Related Disorders: Disorders involving maladaptive patterns of substance use leading to clinically significant impairment.
Suicide: The act of taking one's own life.
Superego: According to Freud, the portion of human personality representing the conscience.
Suprachiasmatic Nucleus: A portion of the hypothalamus that seems to play an important role in the regulation of circadian rhythms.
Surface Structure: The actual words of which sentences consist.
Survey Method: A research method in which large numbers of people answer questions about aspects of their views or their behavior.
Syllogistic Reasoning: A type of formal reasoning in which two premises are used as the basis for deriving logical conclusions.
Symbolic Play: Play in which children pretend that one object is another object.
Sympathetic Nervous System: The portion of the autonomic nervous system that readies the body for expenditure of energy.
Synapse: A region where the axon of one neuron closely approaches other neurons or the cell membrane of other types of cells such as muscle cells.
Synaptic Vesicles: Structures in the axon terminals that contain various neurotransmitters.
Syntax: Rules about how units of speech can be combined into sentences in a given language.
Systematic Desensitization: A form of behavior therapy in which individuals first learn how to induce a relaxed state in their own bodies. Then, while in a relaxed state, they are exposed to stimuli that elicit fear.
Systematic Observation: A basic method of science in which events or processes in the world are observed and measured in a very careful manner.

Tacit Knowledge: Knowledge that plays an important role in practical intelligence. Such knowledge is action-oriented and goal-directed, and is usually acquired without direct help from others.
Tardive Dyskinesia: A common side effect produced by antipsychotic drugs, in which individuals experience loss of motor control, especially in the face.
Teleomeres: Strips of DNA that cap the ends of chromosomes, and which seem to regulate the number of times a cell can divide.
Temperament: Stable individual differences in the quality and intensity of emotional reactions.
Templates: Specific patterns stored in our memories for various visual stimuli that we encounter.
Temporal Lobe: The lobe of the cerebral cortex that is involved in hearing.
Teratogens: Factors in the environment that can harm the developing fetus.
Tertiary Prevention: Efforts to minimize the long-term harm stemming from problems and disorders.
Test-Retest Reliability: A measure of the extent to which individuals' scores on a test remain stable over time.
Thalamus: A structure deep within the brain that receives sensory input from other portions of the nervous system and then transmits this information to the cerebral hemispheres and other parts of the brain.
That's-Not-All Technique: A technique for gaining compliance in which a small extra incentive is offered before target persons have agreed to or rejected a request.
Theories: In science, frameworks for explaining various events or processes.
Timbre: The quality of a sound, resulting from the complexity of a sound wave; timbre helps us distinguish the sound of a trumpet from that of a saxophone.
Tip-of-the-Tongue Phenomenon: The feeling that we can almost remember some information we wish to retrieve from memory.
Token Economies: A form of behavior therapy in which patients in hospital settings earn tokens they can exchange for various rewards by engaging in desirable forms of behavior.
Tolerance: Habituation to a drug, causing larger and larger doses to be required to produce effects of the same magnitude.
Trace Conditioning: A form of forward conditioning in which the onset of the conditioned stimulus (CS) precedes the onset of the unconditioned stimulus (UCS) and the CS and UCS do not overlap.
Trait Theories: Theories of personality that focus on identifying the key dimensions along which people differ.
Transduction: The translation of physical energy into electrical signals by specialized receptor cells.
Transference: Intense emotional feelings of love or hate toward the analyst on the part of patients undergoing psychoanalysis.
Transformational or Charismatic Leader: Leaders who exert exceptionally powerful effects on large numbers of followers or, sometimes, on their entire societies.
Trial and Error: A method of solving problems in which possible solutions are tried until one succeeds.
Triarchic Theory: A theory suggesting that there are three basic forms of intelligence: componential, experiential, and contextual (practical) intelligence.
Trichromatic Theory: A theory of color perception suggesting that we have three types of cones, each primarily receptive to particular wavelengths of light.
Type A Behavior Pattern: A cluster of traits (including competitiveness, urgency, and hostility) related to important aspects of health, social behavior, and task performance.

Unconditional Positive Regard: In Rogers's theory, a therapeutic atmosphere that communicates that a person will be respected or loved regardless of what he or she says or does.
Unconditioned Response (UCR): In classical conditioning, the response evoked by an unconditioned stimulus.
Unconditioned Stimulus (UCS): In classical conditioning, a stimulus that can evoke an unconditioned response the first time it is presented.

Validity: The extent to which a test actually measures what it claims to measure.
Variable-Interval Schedule: A schedule of reinforcement in which a variable amount of time must elapse before a response will yield reinforcement.
Variable-Ratio Schedule: A schedule of reinforcement in which reinforcement is delivered after a variable number of responses have been performed.
Verbal Protocol Analysis: A technique for studying cognitive processes in which participants are asked to talk aloud while making a decision or solving a problem.
Vestibular Sense: Our sense of balance.
Visual Display: Displays that present information visually.
Visual Images: Mental pictures or representations of objects or events.

Wavelength: The peak-to-peak distance in a sound or light wave.
Wear-and-Tear Theories of Aging: Theories suggesting that aging results from the continual use of cells and organs in our bodies.
Wernicke-Geschwind Theory: A theory of how the brain processes information relating to speech and other verbal abilities.
Work Motivation: The tendency to expend energy and effort on one's job or on a specific task.
Workplace Violence: Violent outbursts in which employees attack and even kill other persons with whom they work.
Yerkes-Dodson Law: The suggestion that the level of arousal beyond which performance begins to decline is a function of task difficulty.

References

Anderson, C. A., Anderson, K. B., & Deuser, W. E. (1996). Examining an affective aggression framework: Weapon and temperature effects on aggressive thoughts, affect, and attitudes. *Personality and Social Psychology Bulletin, 22,* 366–376.

Abramowitz, S. I. (1986). Psychosocial outcomes of sexual reassignment surgery. *Journal of Consulting and Clinical Psychology, 54,* 183–189.

Adams, R. J. (1987). An evaluation of color preference in early infancy. *Infant Behavior and Development, 10,* 143–150.

Abram, S. E. (1993). Advances in chronic pain management since gate control. *Regional Anesthesia, 18,* 66–81.

Ader, R., & Cohen, N. (1984). Behavior and the immune system. In W. D. Gentry (Ed.), *Handbook of behavioral medicine.* New York: Guilford.

Ader, R., Kelly, K., Moynihan, J. A., Grota, L. J., & Cohen, N. (1993). Conditioned enhancement of antibody production using antigen as the unconditioned stimulus. *Brain, Behavior, and Immunity, 7,* 334–343.

Adler, N. J., & Bartholomew, S. (1992). Managing globally competent people. *Academy of Management Executive, 6,* 52–65.

Aiello, J. R. (1993). Computer-based work monitoring: Electronic surveillance and its effects. *Journal of Applied Social Psychology, 23,* 499–507.

Aiello, J. R., & Kolb, K. J. (1995). Electronic performance monitoring and social context: Impact on productivity and stress. *Journal of Applied Psychology, 80,* 339–353.

Aiello, J. R., & Svec, C. M. (1993). Computer monitoring of work performance: Extending the social facilitation framework to electronic presence. *Journal of Applied Social Psychology, 23,* 537–548.

Aiken, L. R. (1991). *Psychological testing and assessment* (7th ed.). Boston: Allyn and Bacon.

Aiken, L. S., West, S. G., Woodward, C. K., Reno, R. R., & Reynolds, K. D. (1994). Increasing screening mammography in asymptomatic women: Evaluation of a second-generation, theory-based program. *Health Psychology, 13,* 526–538.

Ainsworth, M. D. S. (1973). The development of infant-mother attachment. In B. Caldwell & H. Riciutti (Eds.), *Review of child development research* (Vol. 3, pp. 1–94). Chicago: University of Chicago Press.

Ainsworth, M. D. S., Blehar, M. C., Waters, E., & Wall, S. (1978). *Patterns of attachment.* Hillsdale, NJ: Erlbaum.

Akerstedt, T., & Froberg, J. E. (1976). Interindividual differences in circadian pattern of catecholamine excretion, body temperature, performance, and subjective arousal. *Biological Psychology, 4,* 277–292.

Al-Issa, I. (1982). Does culture make a difference in psychopathology? In I. Al-Issa (Ed.), *Culture and psychopathology.* Baltimore: University Park Press.

Al-Zahrani, S. S., & Kaplowitz, S. A. (1993). Attributional biases in individualistic and collective cultures: A comparison of Americans with Saudis. *Social Psychology Quarterly, 56,* 223–233.

Alagna, F. J., Whitcher, S. J., & Fisher, J. D. (1979). Evaluative reactions to interpersonal touch in a counseling interview. *Journal of Counseling Psychology, 26,* 465–472.

Alberts-Corush, J., Firestone, P., & Goodman, J. T. (1986). Attention and impulsivity characteristics of the biological and adoptive parents of hyperactive and normal control children. *American Journal of Orthopsychiatry, 56,* 413–423.

Alicke, M. D., & Largo, E. (1995). The role of the self in the false consensus effect. *Journal of Experimental Social Psychology, 31,* 28–47.

Allen, C. (1995, March 23). Fighting over more than just spilled coffee. *Los Angeles Times,* Sec. B., p. 7.

Alloy, L. B., Abramson, L. Y., & Dykman, B. M. (1990). Depressive realities and nondepressive optimistic illusions: The role of the self. In R. E. Ingram (Ed.), *Contemporary psychological approaches to depression: Treatment, research, and theory.* New York: Plenum.

Allport, G. W. (1965). *Letters from Jenny.* New York: Harcourt, Brace & World.

Allport, G. W., & Odbert, H. S. (1936). Trait names: A psycholexical study. *Psychological Monographs, 47,* 211.

Allred, J. B. (1993). Lowering serum cholesterol: Who benefits? *Journal of Nutrition, 123,* 1453–1459.

Allyn, J., & Festinger, L. (1961). The effectiveness of unanticipated persuasive communications. *Journal of Abnormal and Social Psychology, 62,* 35–40.

Aloise-Young, P. A., Graham, J. W., & Hansen, W. B. (1994). Peer influence on smoking initiation during early adolescence: A comparison of group members and group outsiders. *Journal of Applied Psychology, 79,* 281–287.

Altheide, D. L., Adler, P. A., Adler, P., & Altheide, D. A. (1978). The social meanings of employee theft. In J. M. Johnson & J. D. Douglas (Eds.), *Crime at the tip: Deviance in business and the professions* (pp. 90–124). Philadelphia: J. B. Lippincott.

Altshuler, J. L., & Ruble, D. N. (1989). Developmental changes in children's awareness of strategies for coping with uncontrollable stress. *Child Development, 60,* 1337–1349.

Alvarez-Borda, B., Ramirez-Amaya, V., Perez-Montfort, R., & Bermudez-Rattoni, F. (1995). Enhancement of antibody production by a learning paradigm. *Neurobiology of Learning and Memory, 64,* 103–105.

Amabile, T. M. (1983). *The social psychology of creativity.* New York: Springer-Verlag.

Amaro, H. (1995). Love, sex, and power: Considering women's realities in HIV prevention. *American Psychologist, 50,* 437–447.

Amato, P. R. (1990). Parental divorce and attitudes toward marriage and family life. *Journal of Marriage and the Family, 50,* 453–461.

Ambuel, B. (1995). Adolescents, unintended pregnancy, and abortion: The struggle for a compassionate social policy. *Current Directions in Psychological Science, 4,* 1–5.

American Cancer Society. (1989). *Cancer facts and figures—1989.* Atlanta, GA: Author.

American Psychiatric Association (1994). *Diagnostic and statistical manual of mental disorders* (4th ed.). Washington, DC: American Psychiatric Association.

American Psychological Association (1992). Ethical principles of psychologists and code of conduct. *American Psychologist, 47,* 1597–1611.

American Psychological Association. (1993a). *1993 Membership register.* Washington, D.C.: American Psychological Association.

American Psychological Association. (1993b). Guidelines for providers of psychological services to ethnic, linguistic, and culturally diverse populations. *American Psychologist, 48,* 45–48.

American Psychological Association. (1994). Office of Demographic Employment, and Educational Research. Washington, D.C.: American Psychological Association.

American Psychologist Society. (April, 1996). Doing the right thing: A research plan for healthy living. *APS Observer Special issue: Human Capital Initiative Report 4—Healthy Living.* Washington, D.C.: Author.

Amoore, J. (1970). *Molecular basis of odor.* Springfield, IL: Thomas.

Amoore, J. (1982). Odor theory and odor classification. In E. Theimer (Ed.), *Fragrance chemistry-the science of the sense of smell.* New York: Academic Press.

Anderson, C. A., & Bushman, B. J. (1997). External validity of "trivial" experiments: The case of laboratory aggression. *Review of General Psychology, 1,* 19–41.

Anderson, C. A., Deuser, W. E., & DeNeve, K. M. (1995). Hot temperatures, hostile affect, hostile cognition, and arousal: Tests of a general theory of affective aggression. *Personality and Social Psychology Bulletin, 21,* 434–448.

Andre, A. D., & Segal, L. D. (1993, April). Design functions. *Ergonomics in Design,* pp. 5–7.

Andreason, N. C., & Black, D. (1995). *Introductory textbook of psychiatry* (2nd ed.) Washington, DC: American Psychiatric Press.

Andreasen, N. C., Flaum, M., Swayze, V., II, O'Leary, D. S., Alliger, R., Cohen, G., Ehrhardt, J., & Yuhn, W. T. C. (1993). Intelligence and brain structure in normal individuals. *American Journal of Psychiatry, 150,* 130–134.

Andrews, J. D. W. (1967). The achievement motive and advancement in two types of organization. *Journal of Personality and Social Psychology, 6,* 163–168.

Antrobus, J. (1991). Dreaming: Cognitive processes during cortical activation and high afferent thresholds. *Psychological Review, 98,* 96–212.

Arena, J. G., Bruno, G. M., Hannah, S. L., & Meador, J. K. (1995). A comparison of frontal electromyographic biofeedback training, trapezius electromyographic biofeedback training, and progressive muscle relaxation therapy in the treatment of tension headache. *Headache, 35,* 411–419.

Arieti, S. (1974). *Interpretation of schizophrenia.* New York: Basic Books.

Armstrong, C. (1991). Emotional changes following brain injury: Psychological and neurological components of depression, denial and anxiety. *Journal of Rehabilitation, 2,* 15–22.

Arnett, J. (1992). Reckless behavior in adolescence: A developmental perspective. *Developmental Review, 12,* 391–409.

Arnett, J. (1995). The young and the reckless: Adolescent reckless behavior. *Current Directions in Psychological Science, 4,* 67–70.

Arnold, D. (1996, April 29). He hopes to tickle world's funny bone. *Boston Globe,* pp. 22, 24.

Aronoff, J., Woike, B. A., & Hyman, L. M. (1992). Which are the stimuli in facial displays of anger and happiness? Configurational bases of emotional recognition. *Journal of Personality and Social Psychology, 62,* 1050–1066.

Aronoff, S. R., & Spilka, B. (1984–1985). Patterning of facial expressions among terminal cancer patients. *Omega, 15,* 101–108.

Aronson, E. (1990). Applying social psychology to desegregation and energy conservation. *Personality and Social Psychology Bulletin, 16,* 118–132.

Aronson, E. (1992). The return of the repressed: Dissonance theory makes a comeback. *Psychological Inquiry, 3*(4), 303–311.

Arthey, S., & Clarke, V. A. (1995). Suntanning and sun protection: A review of the psychological literature. *Social Science Medicine, 40,* 265–274.

Arvey, R. D., Bouchard, T. J., Jr., Segal, N. L., & Abraham, L. M. (1989). Job satisfaction: Genetic and environmental components. *Journal of Applied Psychology, 74,* 187–192.

Ashmore, R. D., Solomon, M. R., & Longo, L. C. (1996). Thinking about fashion models' looks: A multidimensional approach to the structure of perceived physical attractiveness. *Personality and Social Psychology Bulletin, 22,* 1083–1104.

Aspendorf, J. B., Warkentink, V., & Baudonniere, P. M. (1996). Self-awareness and other-awareness II: Mirror self-recognition, social contingency awareness, and synchronic imitation. *Developmental Psychology, 32,* 313–321.

Astley, S. J., Claaren, S. K., Little, R. E., Sampson, P. D., & Daling, J. R. (1992). Analysis of racial shape in children gestationally exposed to marijuana, alcohol, and/or cocaine. *Pediatrics, 89,* 67–77.

Audia, G., Kristof-Brown, A., Brown, K. G., & Locke, E. A. (1996). Relationship of goals and microlevel work processes to performance on a multipath manual task. *Journal of Applied Psychology, 81,* 483–497.

Avery-Leaf, S., Cano, A., Cascardi, M., & O'Leary, K. D. (1995). Evaluation of a dating violence prevention program. Paper presented at the fourth International Family Violence Research Conference, Durham, New Hampshire.

Azar, B. (1996, August). Why men lose keys—and women find them. *American Psychological Association Monitor,* p. 32.

Babcock, R. L., & Salthouse, T. A. (1990). Effects of increased processing demands on age differences in working memory. *Psychology and Aging, 5,* 421–428.

Bachetti, P. (1990). Estimating the incubation period of AIDS by comparing population infection and diagnosis patterns. *Journal of the American Statistical Association, 85,* 1002–1008.

Bachman, J. G. (1987, February). An eye on the future. *Psychology Today,* pp. 6–7.

Backman, L., Hill, R. D., & Forsell, Y. (1996). The influence of depressive symptomatology on episodic memory functioning among clinically nondepressed older adults. *Journal of Abnormal Psychology, 105,* 97–105.

Baddeley, A. (1990). *Human memory: Theory and practice.* Boston: Allyn and Bacon.

Baddeley, A. D. (1992). Working memory. *Science, 255,* 556–559.

Baghurst, P. A., McMichael, A. J., Wigg, N. R., Vimpahni, G. V., Robertson, E. F., Roberts, R. J., & Tongs, S. L. (1992). Environmental exposure to lead and children's intelligence at the age of seven years: The Port Pirie cohort study. *New England Journal of Medicine, 327,* 1279–1284.

Bahrick, H. P. (1984). Memory for people. In J. E. Harris & P. E. Morris (Eds.), *Everyday memory actions and absent-mindedness* (pp. 19–34). London: Academic Press.

Bailey, M. J., & Pillard, R. C. (1991). A genetic study of male sexual orientation. *Archives of General Psychiatry, 48,* 1089–1096.

Bailey, M. J., Pillard, R. C., Neale, M. C., & Agyei, Y. (1993). Heritable factors influence sexual orientation in women. *Archives of General Psychiatry, 50,* 217–223.

Baillargeon, R. (1987). Object permanence in 3.5– and 4.5–month-old infants. *Developmental Psychology, 23,* 655–664.

Baker, A. G., & Mackintosh, N. J. (1977). Excitatory and inhibitory conditioning following uncorrelated presentations of CS and US. *Animal Learning and Behavior, 5*(3), 315–319.

Baker-Ward, L., Ornstein, P. A., & Holden, D. J. (1984) The expression of memorization in early childhood. *Journal of Experimental Child Psychology, 37,* 555–575.

Ball, S. A., & Zuckerman, M. (1992). Sensation seeking and selective attention: Focused and divided attention on a dichotic listening task. *Journal of Personality and Social Psychology, 63,* 825–831.

Balogh, R. D., & Porter, R. H. (1986). Olfactory preferences resulting from mere exposure in human neonates. *Infant Behavior and Development, 9,* 395–401.

Balzer, W. K., & Sulsky, L. M. (1990). Performance appraisal effectiveness. In K. Murphy & F. Saal (Eds.), *Psychology in organizations: Integrating science and practice* (pp. 133–156). Hillsdale, NJ: Erlbaum.

Bandura, A. (1969). *Principles of behavior modification.* New York: Holt, Rinehart & Winston.

Bandura, A. (1974). Analysis of modeling processes. In A. Bandura (Ed.), *Modeling: Conflicting theories* (pp. 1–36). New York: Lieber-Atherton.

Bandura, A. (1977). *Social learning theory.* Englewood Cliffs, NJ: Prentice-Hall.

Bandura, A. (1986). *Social foundations of thought and action: A social cognitive theory.* Englewood Cliffs, NJ: Prentice-Hall.

Bandura, A., Ross, D., & Ross, S. (1963). Imitation of film-mediated aggressive models. *Journal of Abnormal and Social Psychology, 66,* 3–11.

Banich, M. T., & Belger, A. (1990). Inter-hemispheric interaction: How do the hemispheres divide and conquer a task? *Cortex, 26,* 77–94.

Barbur, J. L., Watson, J. D. G., Frackowiak, R. S. J., & Zeki, S. (1993). Conscious visual perception without V1. *Brain, 116,* 1293.

Barch, D. M., & Berenbaum, H. (1996). Language production and thought disorder in schizophrenia. *Journal of Abnormal Psychology, 105,* 81–88.

Bardach, A. L., & Park, B. (1996). The effect of in-group/out-group status on memory for consistent and inconsistent behavior of an individual. *Personality and Social Psychology Bulletin, 22,* 169–178.

Barefoot, J. C., Dodge, K. A., Peterson, B. L., Dahlstrom, W. G., & Williams, R. B. (1989). The Cook-Medley hostility scale: Item content and ability to predict survival. *Psychosomatic Medicine, 51,* 46–57.

Bargones, J. Y., & Werner, L. A. (1994). Adults listen selectively; infants do not. *Psychological Science, 5,* 170–174.

Barkley, R. A. (1990). *Attention deficit hyperactivity disorder: A handbook for diagnosis and treatment.* New York: Guilford.

Barlow, D. H. (1988). *Anxiety and its disorders: The nature and treatment of anxiety and panic.* New York: Guilford Press.

Barlow, D. H. (1991). Disorders of emotion. *Psychological Inquiry, 2,* 58–71.

Barlow, D. H. (1991). Introduction to the special issue on diagnoses, dimensions, and DSM-IV: The science of classification. *Journal of Abnormal Psychology, 100,* 243–244.

Baron, J. (1988). *Thinking and deciding.* Cambridge, England: Cambridge University Press.

Baron, J., & Brown, R. (Eds.). (1991). *Teaching decision making to adolescents.* Hillsdale, NJ: Erlbaum.

Baron, R. A, & Byrne, D. (1997). *Social psychology: Understanding human interaction* (8th ed.). Boston: Allyn & Bacon.

Baron, R. A. (1970). Attraction toward the model and model's competence as determinants of adult imitative behavior. *Journal of Personality and Social Psychology, 14,* 335–344.

Baron, R. A. (1978). Aggression-inhibiting influence of sexual humor. *Journal of Personality and Social Psychology, 36,* 189–197.

Baron, R. A. (1983). The "sweet smell of success"? The impact of pleasant artificial scents (perfume or cologne) on evaluations of job applicants. *Journal of Applied Psychology, 68,* 709–713.

Baron, R. A. (1983). The control of human aggression: A strategy based on incompatible responses. In R. G. Geen & E. I. Donnerstein (Eds.), *Aggression: Theoretical and empirical reviews.* New York: Academic Press.

Baron, R. A. (1987). Mood of interviewer and the evaluation of job candidates. *Journal of Applied Social Psychology, 17,* 911–926.

Baron, R. A. (1993). Criticism (informal negative feedback) as a source of perceived unfairness in organizations: Effects, mechanisms, and countermeasures. In R. Cropanzano (Ed.), *Justice in the workplace: Approaching fairness in human resource management* (pp. 155–170). Hillsdale, NJ: Erlbaum.

Baron, R. A. (1993). Interviewers' moods and evaluations of job applicants: The role of applicant qualifications. *Journal of Applied Social Psychology, 23,* 253–271.

Baron, R. A. (1993). Reducing aggression and conflict: The incompatible response approach. Or: Why people who feel good usually won't be bad. In G. G. Brannigan & M. R. Merrens (Eds.), *The undaunted psychologist* (pp. 203–218). Philadelphia: McGraw-Hill.

Baron, R. A. (1994). The physical environment of work settings: Effects on task performance, interpersonal relations, and job satisfaction. In M. Staw & L. L. Cummings (Eds.), *Research in organizational behavior* (Vol. 16, pp. 1–46). Greenwich, CT: JAI Press.

Baron, R. A. (1996). "La vie en rose" revisited: Contrasting perceptions of informal upward feedback among managers and subordinates. *Management Communication Quarterly, 9,* 338–348.

Baron, R. A. (1997). The sweet smell of . . . helping: Effects of pleasant ambient odors on helping in shopping malls. *Personality and Social Psychology Bulletin, 2,* 498–503.

Baron, R. A., & Ball, R. L. (1974). The aggression-inhibiting influence of nonhostile humor. *Journal of Experimental Social Psychology, 10,* 23–33.

Baron, R. A., & Bronfen, M. I. (1994). A whiff of reality: Empirical evidence concerning the effects of pleasant fragrances on work-related behavior. *Journal of Applied Social Psychology, 13,* 1179–1203.

Baron, R. A., & Byrne, D. (1997). *Social psychology: Understanding human interaction* (8th ed.). Boston: Allyn & Bacon.

Baron, R. A., & Kalsher, M. J. (1996). The sweet smell of . . . safety? *Proceedings of the Human Factors and Ergonomics Society, 40,* 1282.

Baron, R. A., & Neuman, J. H. (1996). Workplace violence and workplace aggression: Evidence on their relative frequency and potential causes. *Aggressive Behavior, 22,* 161–173.

Baron, R. A., & Richardson, D. (1994). *Human aggression* (2nd ed.). New York: Plenum.

Baron, R. A., & Thomley, J. (1994). A whiff of reality: Positive affect as a potential mediator of the effects of pleasant fragrances on task performance and helping. *Environment and Behavior, 26,* 766–784.

Barr, H. M., Streissguth, A. P., Darby, B. I., & Sampson, P. D. (1990). Prenatal exposure to alcohol, caffeine, tobacco, and aspirin: Effects on fine and gross motor performance in 7–year-old children. *Developmental Psychology, 26,* 339–348.

Barrera, M. E., & Maurer, D. (1981a). Discrimination of strangers by the three-month-old. *Child Development, 52,* 559–563.

Basoglu, M., Paker, M., Ozmen, E., Tasdemir, O., Sahin, D., Ceyhanli, A., & Incesu, C. (1996). Appraisal of self, social environment, and state authority as a possible mediator of posttraumatic stress disorder in tortured political activists. *Journal of Abnormal Psychology, 105,* 232–236.

Bass, B. M. (1990). *Bass and Stogdill's handbook of leadership* (3rd ed.). New York: Free Press.

Batson, C. D. (1991). *The altruism question: Toward a social-psychological answer.* Hillsdale, NJ: Erlbaum.

Batson, C. D., & Weeks, J. L. (1996). Mood effects of unsuccessful helping: Another test of the empathy-altruism hypothesis. *Personality and Social Psychology Bulletin, 22,* 148–157.

Baum, D. R., & Jonides, J. J. (1979). Cognitive maps: Analysis of comparative judgments of distance. *Memory and Cognition, 7,* 462–468.

Baumeister, R. F. (Ed.). (1993). *Self-esteem: The puzzle of low self-regard.* New York: Plenum.

Baumeister, R. F., & Leary, M. R. (1995). The need to belong: Desire for interpersonal attachments as a fundamental human motivation. *Psychological Bulletin, 117,* 497–529.

Baumeister, R. F., Heatherton, T. F., & Tice, D. M. (1993). When ego threats lead to self-regulation failure: Negative consequences of high self-esteem. *Journal of Personality and Social Psychology, 64,* 141–156.

Baumeister, R. F., Stillwell, A., & Wotman, S. R. (1990). Victim and perpetrator accounts of interpersonal conflict: Autobiographical narratives about anger. *Journal of Personality and Social Psychology, 59,* 994–1003.

Baumrind, D. (1984). A developmental perspective on adolescent drug use. Unpublished manuscript, University of California, Berkeley.

Beaman, A. L., Cole, N., Preston, M., Glentz, B., & Steblay, N. M. (1983). Fifteen years of the foot-in-the-door research: A meta-analysis. *Personality and Social Psychology Bulletin, 9,* 181–186.

Beck, A. T. (1976). *Cognitive therapy and the emotional disorders.* New York: International Universities Press.

Beck, A. T. (1985). *Anxiety disorders and phobias: A cognitive perspective.* New York: Basic Books.

Beck, A. T., Rush, A. J., Shaw, B. F., & Emery, G. (1979). *Cognitive theory of depression.* New York: Guilford Press.

Becklen, R., & Cerone, D. (1983). Selective looking and the noticing of unexpected events. *Memory & Cognition, 11,* 601–608.

Beckstead, J. W. (1991). Psychological factors influencing judgments and attitude regarding animal research: An application of functional measurement and structural equation modeling. Unpublished doctoral dissertation, State University of New York, Albany.

Behrend, D.A., Rosengren, K. S., & Perlmutter, M. (1992). The relation between private speech and parental interactive style. In R. M. Diaz & L. E. Berk (Eds.), *Private speech: From social interaction to self-regulation* (pp. 85–100). Hillsdale, NJ: Erlbaum.

Békésy, G. von. (1960). *Experiments in hearing.* New York: McGraw-Hill.

Bell, M. A., & Fox, N. A. (1992). The relationship between frontal brain electrical activity and cognitive development during infancy. *Child Development, 63,* 1142–1163.

Bell, P. A. (1992). In defense of the negative affect escape model of heat and aggression. *Psychological Bulletin, 111,* 342–346.

Bell, S. T., Kuriloff, P. J., & Lottes, I. (1994). Understanding attributions of blame in stranger rape and date rape situations: An examination of gender, race, identification, and students' social perceptions of rape victims. *Journal of Applied Social Psychology, 24,* 1719–1734.

Bellack, A. S., Morrison, R. L., Mueser, K. T., Wade, J. H. & Sayers, S. L. (1990). Role play for assessing the social competence of psychiatric patients. *Psychological Assessment: A Journal of Consulting and Clinical Psychology, 2,* 248–255.

Bellack, A. S., Sayers, M., Mueser, K. T., & Bennett, M. (1994). Evaluation of social problem solving in schizophrenia. *Journal of Abnormal Psychology, 103,* 371–378.

Bellak, L. (1994). The schizophrenic syndrome and attention deficit disorder. *American Psychologist, 49,* 25–29.

Belmore, S. M., & Hubbard, M. L. (1987). The role of advance expectancies in person memory. *Journal of Personality and Social Psychology, 53,* 61–70.

Belsky, J., & Cassidy, J. (1995). Attachment: Theory and evidence. In M. Rutter & D. Hay (Eds.), *Development through life: A handbook for clinicians* (pp. 373–402). Oxford, England: Blackwell.

Belsky, J., Spritz, B., & Crnic, K. (1996). Infant attachment security and affective-cognitive information processing at age 3. *Psychological Science, 7,* 111–114.

Bem, D. J. (1996). Exotic becomes erotic: A developmental theory of sexual orientiaton. *Psychological Review, 103,* 320–335.

Bem, D. J., & Honorton, C. (1994). Does psi exist? Replicable evidence for an anomalous process of information transfer. *Psychological Bulletin, 115,* 4–18.

Bem, S. L. (1984). Adrogyny and gender schema theory: A conceptual and empirical integration. In R. A. Dientsbier & T. B. Sondregger (Eds.), *Nebraska Symposium on Motivation* (Vol. 34, pp. 179–226). Lincoln: University of Nebraska Press.

Benesch, K. F., & Page, M. M. (1989). Self-construct systems and interpersonal congruence. *Journal of Personality, 57,* 139–173.

Benjamin, L. T., Jr., & Dixon, D. N. (1996). Dream analysis by mail: An American woman seeks Freud's advice. *American Psychologist, 51,* 461–468.

Bensing, J., Schreurs, K., & De Rijk, A. (1996). The role of the general practitioner's affective behavior in medical encounters. *Psychology and Health, 11,* 825–838.

Benson, D. F. (1985). Aphasia. In K. M. Heilman & E. Valenstein (Eds.), *Clinical neuropsychology* (pp. 17–47). New York: Oxford University Press.

Benson, H., & Friedman, R. (1985). A rebuttal to the conclusions of David S. Holmes's article: "Meditation and somatic arousal reductions." *American Psychologist, 40,* 725–728.

Berardi-Coletta, B., Buyer, L. S., Dominowski, R. L., & Rellinger, E. R. (1995). Metacognition and problem solving: A process-oriented approach. *Journal of Experimental Psychology: Learning, Memory, and Cognition, 21,* 205–223.

Berenbaum, S. A., & Hines, M. (1992). Early androgens are related to childhood sex-typed toy preferences. *Psychological Science, 3,* 203–206.

Bergin, A. E., & Lambert, M. J. (1978). The evaluation of therapeutic outcomes. In S. L. Garfield & A. E. Bergin (Eds.), *Handbook of psychotherapy and behavior change: An empirical analysis* (2nd ed., pp. 139–190). New York: Wiley.

Berglas, S., & Jones, E. E. (1978). Drug choice as a self-handicapping strategy in response to noncontingent success. *Journal of Personality and Social Psychology, 36,* 405–417.

Berkowitz, L. (1984). Some effects of thoughts on anti- and pro-social influences of media events: A cognitive-neoassociation analysis, *Psychological Bulletin, 95,* 410–427.

Berkowitz, L. (1989). Frustration-aggression hypothesis: Examination and reformulation. *Psychological Bulletin, 106,* 59–73.

Berkowitz, L. (1990). On the formation and regulation of anger and aggression. *American Psychologist, 45,* 494–503.

Berkowitz, L. (1993). *Aggression: Its causes, consequences, and control.* New York: McGraw-Hill.

Berkowitz, L., & Donnerstein, E. (1982). External validity is more than skin deep: Some answers to criticism of laboratory experiments. *American Psychologist, 37,* 245–257.

Berlyne, D. E. (1967). Arousal and reinforcement. In D. Levine (Ed.), *Nebraska Symposium on Motivation* (Vol. 15, pp. 279–286). Lincoln: University of Nebraska Press.

Berndt, T. J. (1992). Friendship and friends' influence in adolescence. *Current Directions in Psychological Science, 1,* 156–159.

Berndt, T. J., & Savin-Williams, R. C. (1993). Peer relations and friendships. In B. Tolan & B. Cohler (Eds.), *Handbook of clinical research and practice with adolescents* (pp. 203–219). New York: Wiley.

Bernstein, A. S. (1987). Orienting response research in schizophrenia: Where we have come and where we might go. *Schizophrenia Bulletin, 13,* 623–641.

Bernstein, I. L. (1978). Learned taste aversion in children receiving chemotherapy. *Science, 200,* 1302–1303.

Berry, D. C., & Broadbent, D. E. (1984). On the relationship between task performance and associated verbal knowledge. *Quarterly Journal of Experimental Psychology, 36,* 209–231.

Berry, D. S. (1991). Attractive faces are not all created equal: Joint effects of facial babyishness and attractiveness on social perception. *Personality and Social Psychology Bulletin, 17,* 523–531.

Berry, D. S., & McArthur, L. Z. (1986). Perceiving character in faces: The impact of age-related craniofacial changes on social perception. *Psychological Bulletin, 100,* 3–18.

Berry, D. T. R., & Webb, W. B. (1985). Mood and sleep in aging women. *Journal of Personality and Social Psychology, 49,* 1724–1727.

Besson, J., & Chaouch, A. (1987). Peripheral spinal mechanisms of nociception. *Psychological Review, 67,* 67–186.

Bettancourt, B. A., & Miller, N. (1996). Gender differences in aggression as a function of provocation: A meta-analysis. *Psychological Bulletin, 119,* 422–447.

Betz, A. I., & Krosnick, J. A. (1993). *A test of the primacy of affect: Does detection of the affective tone of a stimulus precede detection of stimulus presence or content?* Unpublished manuscript, Ohio State University.

Betz, E. L. (1982). Need fulfillment in the career development of women. *Journal of Vocational Behavior, 20,* 53–66.

Biederman, I. (1987) Recognition-by-components: A theory of human image understanding. *Psychological Review, 94,* 115–147.

Biederman, J., Faraone, S. V., Keenan, K., Benjamin, J., Krifcher, B., Steingard, R., Spencer, T., Norman, D., Kolodny, R., Kraus, I., Perrin, J., Keller, M. B., & Tsuagn, M. T. (1992). Further evidence for family-genetic risk factors in attention-deficit/hyperactivity disorder. *Archives of General Psychiatry, 49,* 728–738.

Bienert, H., & Schneider, B. H. (1993). Diagnosis-specific social skill: Training with peer-nominated aggressive-disruptive and sensitive-isolated preadolescents. *Journal of Applied Developmental Psychology.*

Bigler, R. S. (1995). The role of classification skill in moderating environmental influences on children's gender attitudes: A study of the functional use of gender in the classroom. *Child Development, 66,* 1072–1087.

Birnbaum, I. M., & Parker, E. D. (Eds.). (1977). *Alcohol and human memory.* Hillsdale, NJ: Erlbaum.

Bishop, J. E. (1996, April 11). Sixth-sense therapy path to be reported. *Wall Street Journal,* p. 4.

Bivens, J. A., & Berk, L. E. (1990). A longitudinal study of the development of elementary school children's private speech. *Merrill-Palmer Quarterly, 36,* 443–463.

Bixler, E. O., Kales, A., Soldatos, C. R., Kales, J. D., & Healey, S. (1979). Prevalence of sleep disorders in the Los Angeles metropolitan area. *American Journal of Psychiatry, 136,* 1257–1262.

Bjorklund, D. F. (1987). How age changes in knowledge base contribute to the development of children's memory: An interpretive review. *Developmental Review, 7,* 93–130.

Bjorkqvist, J., Osterman, K., & Layerspectz, M. J. (1994). Sex differences in covert aggression among adults. *Aggressive Behavior, 20,* 27–33.

Bjorkqvist, K., Lagerspetz, & Kaukiainen, A. (1992). Do girls manipulate and boys fight? Developmental trends in regard to direct and indirect aggression. *Aggressive Behavior, 18,* 117–127.

Bjorkqvist, K., Osterman, K., & Kaukianainen, A. (1992). The development of direct and indirect aggressive strategies in males and females. In K. Bjorkqvist & P. Niemela (Eds.), *Of mice and women: Aspects of female aggression* (pp. 51–64). San Diego: Academic Press.

Black, J. S., & Mendenhall, M. (1990). Cross-cultural training effectivness: A review and a theoretical framework for future research. *Academy of Management Review, 15,* 113–136.

Blackmore, S. (1986). A critical guide to parapsychology. *Skeptical Inquirer, 11*(1), 97–102.

Blake, R. R., & Mouton, J. S. (1985). *The managerial grid III.* Houston: Gulf.

Blakemore, C., & Cooper, G. F. (1970). Development of the brain depends on the visual environment. *Nature, 228,* 477–478.

Blakeslee, S. (1993, September 7). Human nose may hold an additional organ for a real sixth sense: Odorless skin chemicals may draw or repel other people. *New York Times,* pp. C1, C3.

Blaney, P. H. (1986). Affect and memory: A review. *Psychological Bulletin, 99,* 229–246.

Blatt, S. J. (1995). The destructivness of perfectionism: Implications for the treatment of depression. *American Psychologist, 50,* 1003–1020.

Blatt, S. J., Zuroff, D. C., Quinlan, D. M., & Pilkonis, P. (1996). Interpersonal factors in brief treatment of depression: Further analysis of the NIMH Treatment of Depression Collaborative Research Program. *Journal of Consulting and Clinical Psychology, 64,* 162–171.

Blazer, D. G., Kessler, R. C., McGonagle, K. A., & Swartz, M. S. (1994). The prevalence and distribution of major depression in a national community sample: The National Comorbidity Survey. *American Journal of Psychiatry, 151,* 979–986.

Blessing, S. B., & Ross, B. H. (1996). Content effects in problem categorization and problem solving. *Journal of Experimental Psychology: Learning, Memory, and Cognition, 22,* 792–810.

Block, J. (1995). A contrarian view of the five-factor approach to personality description. *Psychological Bulletin, 117,* 187–215.

Bloswick, D. S., Gerber, A., Sebesta, D., Johnson, S., & Mecham, W. (1994). Effect of mailbag design on musculoskeletal fatigue and metabolic load. *Human Factors, 36,* 210–218.

Blumberg, M. S., & Wasserman, E. A. (1995). Animal mind and the argument from design. *American Psychologist, 50,* 133–144.

Blume, E. (1993). Smoking control effort moves to second phase. *Journal of the National Cancer Institute, 85,* 1720.

Blyth, D. A., Bulcroft, R., & Simmons, R. G. (1981, August). *The impact of puberty on adolescents: A longitudinal study.* Paper presented at the annual meetings of the American Psychological Association, Los Angeles.

Bobo, L. (1983). Whites' opposition to busing: Symbolic racism or realistic group conflict? *Journal of Personality and Social Psychology, 45,* 1196–1210.

Bobocel, D. R., & Meyer, J. P. (1994). Escalating commitment to a failing course of action: Separating the roles of choice and justification. *Journal of Applied Psychology, 79,* 360–363.

Boehm, L. E. (1994). The validity effect: A search for mediating variables. *Personality and Social Psychology Bulletin, 20,* 285–293.

Bohannon, J., & Stanowicz, L. (1988). The issue of negative evidence: Adult responses to children's language errors. *Developmental Psychology, 24,* 684–689.

Boles, D. B. (1992). Factor analysis and the cerebral hemispheres: Temporal, occipital and frontal functions. *Neuropsychologia, 30,* 963–988.

Boles, D. B., & Law, M. B. (1992). *Orthogonal lateralized processes have orthogonal attentional resources.* Paper presented at the annual meeting of the Psychonomic Society, St. Louis, MO.

Bonardi, C., Honey, R. C., & Hall, G. (1990). Context specificity of conditioning in flavor-aversion learning: Extinction and blocking tests. *Animal Learning & Behavior, 18,* 229–237.

Bond, R., & Smith, P. B. (1996). Culture and conformity: A meta-analysis of studies using Asch's (1952b, 1956) line judgment task. *Psychological Bulletin, 119,* 111–137.

Bond, S. B., & Mosher, D. L. (1986). Guided imagery of rape: Fantasy, reality, and the willing victim myth. *Journal of Sex Research, 22,* 162–183.

Bookstein, F. L., Sampson, P. D., Streissgarth, A. P., & Barr, H. M. (1996). Exploiting redundant measurement of dose and developmental outcome: New methods from the behavioral teratology of alcohol. *Developmental Psychology, 32,* 404–415.

Bootzin, R. R., Acocella, J. R., & Alloy, L. B. (1993). *Abnormal psychology* (6th ed.). New York: McGraw-Hill.

Borbely, A. A., Achermann, P., Trqachsel, L., & Tobler, I. (1989). Sleep initiation and initial sleep intensity: Interactions of homeostatic and circadian mechanisms. *Journal of Biological Rhythms, 4,* 149–160.

Borges, G., & Rosovsky, H. (1996). Suicide attempts and alcohol consumption in an emergency room sample. *Journal of Studies on Alcohol, 57,* 543–548.

Borman, W. C., White, L. A., & Dorsey, D. W. (1995). Effects of ratee task performance and interpersonal factors on supervisor and peer performance ratings. *Journal of Applied Psychology, 80,* 168–177.

Bornstein, R. F. (1992). Subliminal mere exposure effects. In R. Bornstein & T. S. Pittman (Eds.), *Perception without awareness: Cognitive, clinical, and social perspectives* (pp. 191–210). New York: Guilford Press.

Bosl, G. J., Vogelzang, N. J., Goldman, A., Fraley, E. E., Lange, P. H., Lewitt, S. H., & Kennedy, B. J. (1981). Impact of delay in diagnosis on clinical stage of testicular cancer. *Lancet, 2,* 970–973.

Bouchard, T. J., Jr. (1987). *Information about the Minnesota Center for Twin and Adoption Research.* Minneapolis: University of Minnesota.

Bouchard, T. J., Jr., & McGue, M. (1981). Familial studies of intelligence: A review. *Science, 212,* 1055–1059.

Bouchard, T. J., Jr., Lykken, D. T., McGue, M., Segal, N. L. & Tellegen, A. (1990). Sources of human psychological differences: The Minnesota Study of Twins Reared Apart. *Science, 250,* 223–228.

Bower, G. H., Clark, M. C., Lesgold, A. M., & Winzenz, D. (1969). Hierarchical retrieval schemes in recall of categorized word lists. *Journal of Verbal Learning and Verbal Behavior, 8,* 323–343.

Bowers, K. S. (1992). Imagination and dissociation in hypnotic responding. *International Journal of Clinical and Experimental Hypnosis, 40,* 253–275.

Bowers, K. S., & Farvolden, P. (1996). Revisiting a century-old Freudian slip: From suggestion disavowed to the truth repressed. *Psychological Bulletin,* 119, 355–380.

Bowlby, J. (1969). *Attachment and loss: Vol. 1. Attachment.* New York: Basic Books.

Bowlby, J. (1988). *A secure base: Clinical applications of attachment theory.* London: Routledge.

Bowles, N., & Hynds, F. (1978). *Psy search: The comprehensive guide to psychic phenomena.* New York: Harper & Row.

Boyes, M. C., & Walker, L. J. (1988). Implications of cultural diversity for the universality claims of Kohlberg's theory of moral reasoning. *Human Development, 31,* 44–59.

Boykin, A. W. (1994). Harvesting talent and culture: African-American children and educational reform. In R. Rossi (Ed.), *Schools and students at risk* (pp. 116–138). New York: Teachers College Press.

Boyle, P. (1993). The hazards of passive-and active-smoking. *New England Journal of Medicine, 328,* 1708–1709.

Bozarth, M. A. (1987). Intracranial self-administration procedures for the assessment of drug reinforcement. In M. A. Bozarth (Ed.), *Methods of assessing the reinforcing properties of abused drugs* (pp. 173–187). Berlin: Springer-Verlag.

Braff, D. L. (1989). Sensory input deficits and negative symptoms in schizophrenic patients. *American Journal of Psychiatry, 146,* 1006–1011.

Brainerd, C. J. (1996). Piaget: A centennial celebration. *Psychological Science, 7,* 191–195.

Brainerd, C. J., Reyna, V. F., & Brandse, E. (1995). Are children's false memories more persistent than their true memories? *Psychological Science, 6,* 359–364.

Braungart, M. M., & Braungart, R. G. (1990). The life course development of left- and right-wing youth activist leaders from the 1960s. *Political Psychology, 11,* 242–282.

Braverman, N. S., & Bronstein, P. (Eds.). (1985). Experimental assessments and clinical applications of conditioned food aversions. *Annals of the New York Academy of Sciences, 443,* 1–41.

Brean, H. (1958, March 31). What hidden sell is all about. *Life,* pp.104–114.

Breland, K., & Breland, M. (1961). The misbehavior of organisms. *American Psychologist, 16,* 681–684.

Brewer, M. B. (1993). Social identity, distinctiveness, and in-group homogeneity. *Social Cognition, 11,* 150–154.

Brockner, J., & Rubin, J. Z. (1985). *Entrapment in escalating conflicts.* New York: Springer-Verlag.

Brody, G. H., Neubaum, E., & Forehand, R. (1988). Serial marriage: A heuristic analysis of an emerging family form. *Psychological Bulletin, 103,* 211–222.

Brody, L. R., & Hall, J. A. (1993). Gender and emotion. In M. Lewis and J. Haviland (Eds.), *Handbook of emotions.* New York: Guilford Press.

Brody, N. (1992). Intelligence (2nd ed.). San Diego, CA: Academic Press.

Brown, J. D., & McGill, K. L. (1989). The cost of good fortune: When positive life events produce negative health consequences. *Journal of Personality and Social Psychology, 57,* 1103–1110.

Brown, J. D., & Rogers, R. J. (1991). Self-serving attributions: The role of physiological arousal. *Personality and Social Psychology Bulletin, 17,* 501–506.

Brown, R. (1973). *A first language: The early stages.* Cambridge, MA: Harvard University Press.

Brown, R. W., & Kulik, J. (1977). Flashbulb memories. *Cognition, 5,* 73–99.

Brown, R. W., & McNeill, D. (1966). The "tip of the tongue" phenomenon. *Journal of Verbal Learning and Verbal Behavior, 5,* 325–337.

Browne, M. W. (1992, April 14). Biologists tally generosity's rewards. *New York Times,* pp. C1, C8.

Brownell, K. D., & Cohen, L. R. (1995). Adherence to dietary regimens 1: An overview of research. *Behavioral Medicine, 20,* 149–154.

Bruck, M., Ceci, S. J., & Francoeur, E. (1994). *Anatomically detailed dolls do not facilitate preschoolers' reports of touching.* Paper presented at the annual meeting of the Canadian Pediatric Society, St. John's, Newfoundland, Canada.

Bruder, G. E., Stewart, M. W., Mercier, M. A., Agosti, V., Leite, P., Donovan, S., & Quitkin, F. M. (1997). Outcome of cognitive-behavioral therapy for depression: Relation to hemispheric dominance for verbal processing. *Journal of Abnormal Psychology, 106,* 138–144.

Bruhn, J. G., & Phillips, B. U. (1987). A developmental basis for social support. *Journal of Behavioral Medicine, 10,* 213–229.

Bryden, J. P., Ley, R. G., & Sugarman, J. H. (1982). A left ear advantage for identifying the emotional quality of tonal sequences. *Neuropsychologia, 20,* 83–87.

Burger, J. M., & Palmer, M. L. (1992). Changes in and generalization of unrealistic optimism following experiences with stressful events: Reactions to the 1989 California earthquake. *Personality and Social Psychology Bulletin, 18,* 39–43.

Burger, J. M., & Pavelich, J. L. (1993). *Attributions for presidential elections: The situational shift over time.* Unpublished manuscript, Santa Clara University.

Burish, T. G., & Carey, M. P. (1986). Conditioned aversive response in cancer chemotherapy patients: Theoretical and developmental analysis. *Journal of Consulting and Clinical Psychology, 54,* 593–600.

Burns, B. D. (1996). Meta-analogical transfer: Transfer between episodes of analogical reasoning. *Journal of Experimental Psychology: Learning, Memory, and Cognition, 22,* 1032–1048.

Burnstein, E., Crandall, C., & Kitayama, S. (1994). Some neo-Darwinian rules for altruism: Weighing cues for inclusive fitness as a function of the biological importance of the decision. *Journal of Personality and Social Psychology, 67,* 773–789.

Burrell, C. (1996, March 23). Number of fatherless children in U.S. quadruples in 45 years. Associated Press, *Albany Times Union,* p. B1.

Burt, D. B., Zembar, M. J., & Niederehe, G. (1995). Depression and memory impairment: A meta-analysis of the association, its pattern, and specificity. *Psychological Bulletin, 117,* 285–305.

Bushman, B. J. (1984). Perceived symbols of authority and their influence on compliance. *Journal of Applied Social Psychology, 14,* 501–508.

Bushman, B. J. (1988). The effects of apparel on compliance: A field experiment with a female authority figure. *Personality and Social Psychology Bulletin, 14,* 459–467.

Buss, D. H. (1997). *Evolutionary psychology.* Boston: Allyn and Bacon.

Buss, D. M., & Schmitt, D. P. (1993). Sexual strategies theory: An evolutionary perspective on human mating. *Psychological Review, 100,* 204–232.

Buss, D. M., Larsen, R. J., Westen, D., & Semmelroth, J. (1992). Sex differences in jealousy: Evolution, physiology, and psychology. *Psychological Science, 3,* 251–258.

Butler, S., Gross, J., & Hayne, H. (1995). The effect of drawing on memory performance in young children. *Developmental Psychology, 31,* 597–608.

Buunk, B. P. (1995). Sex, self-esteem, dependency and extradyadic sexual experiences as related to jealousy responses. *Journal of Social and Personal Relationships, 12,* 147–153.

Byne, W. (1995). Science and belief: Psychobiological research on sexual orientation. *Journal of Homosexuality, 3/4,* 303–344.

Byrne, D. (1971). *The attraction paradigm.* New York: Academic Press.

Byrne, D. (1982). Predicting human sexual behavior. In A. G. Kraut (Ed.), *The G. Stanley Hall Lecture Series* (Vol. 2, pp. 363–364, 368). Washington, DC: American Psychological Association.

Byrne, D. (1992). Personal communication.

Cacioppo, J. T., Petty, R. E., & Quintanar, L. R. (1982). Individual differences in relative hemisphere alpha abundance and cognitive responses persuasive communications. *Journal of Personality and Social Psychology, 43,* 623–626.

Cacioppo, J. T., Petty, R. E., Feinstein, J. A., & Jarvis, W. B. G. (1996). Dispositional differences in cognitive motivation: The life and times of individuals varying in need for cognition. *Psychological Bulletin, 119,* 197–253.

Cacioppo, J. T., Priester, J. R., & Berntson, G. G. (1993). Rudimentary determinants of attitude: II. Arm flexion and extension have differential effects on attitudes. *Journal of Personality and Social Psychology, 65,* 5–17.

Campbell, F. A., & Ramey, C. T. (1994). Effects of early intervention on intellectual and academic achievement: A follow-up study of children from low-income families. *Child Development, 65,* 694–698.

Campbell, J. N., & LaMotte, R. H. (1983). Latency to detection of first pain. *Brain Research, 266,* 203–208.

Campion, M. A., & McClelland, C. L. (1993). Follow-up and extension of the interdisciplinary costs and benefits of enlarged jobs. *Journal of Applied Psychology 78,* 339–351.

Campion, M. A., Cheraskin, L., & Stevens, M. J. (1994). Career-related antecedents and outcomes of job rotation. *Academy of Management Journal, 37,* 1518–1542.

Cannon-Bowers, J. A., Salas, E., & Pruitt, J. S. (1996). Establishing the boundaries of a paradigm for decision-making research. *Human Factors, 38,* 193–205.

Capaldi, E. J. (1978). Effects of schedule and delay of reinforcement on acquisition speed. *Animal Learning and Behavior, 6,* 330–334.

Capaldi, E. J. (in press). The discriminative stimulus and response enhancing properties of reward produced memories. In S. B. Fountain, M. D. Bunnsey, J. H. Danks, & M. K. McBeath (Eds.), *Sequential and temporal organization: Behavioral and biological perspectives.*

Capaldi, E. J., Birmingham, K. M., & Alptekin, S. (1995). Memories of reward events and expectancies of reward events may work in tandem. *Animal Learning & Behavior, 23,* 40–48.

Carlo, G., Koller, S. H., Eisenberg, N., Da Silva, M. S., & Frohlich, C. B. (1996). A cross-national study on the relations among prosocial moral reasoning, gender role orientations, and prosocial behavior. *Developmental Psychology, 32,* 231–240.

Carlson, N. R. (1994). *Physiology of behavior* (5th ed.). Boston: Allyn and Bacon.

Carmody, T. P., Matarazzo, J. D., & Istvan, J. A. (1987). Promoting adherence to heart-healthy diets: A review of the literature. *Journal of Compliance in Health Care, 2,* 105–124.

Carnevale, A. P., & Stone, S. C. (1995). *The American mosaic: An in-depth report on the future of diversity at work.* New York: McGraw-Hill.

Carpendale, J. L. M., & Krebs, D. L. (1995). Variations in moral judgment as a function of type of dilemma and moral choice. *Journal of Personality, 63,* 289–313.

Carroll, J. M., & Russell, J. A. (1996). Do facial expressions signal specific emotions? Judging emotion from the face in context. *Journal of Personality and Social Psychology, 70,* 205–218.

Carver, C. S., & Scheier, M. F. (1992). *Perspectives on personality* (2nd ed.). Boston: Allyn and Bacon.

Carver, C. S., Pozo, C., Harris, S. D., Noriega, V., Scheier, M. F., Robinson, D. S., Ketcham, A. S., Moffat, F. L., & Clark, K. C. (1993). How coping mediates the effect of optimism on distress: A study of women with early stage breast cancer. *Journal of Personality and Social Psychology, 65,* 375–390.

Carver, C. S., Scheier, M. F., & Weintraub, J. K. (1989). Assessing coping strategies: A theoretically based approach. *Journal of Personality and Social Psychology, 56,* 267–283.

Cascio, W. F. (1995). *Managing human resources: Productivity, quality of work life, profits* (4th ed.). New York: McGraw-Hill.

Case, R. (1991). *The mind's staircase: Exploring the conceptual underpinnings of children's thought and knowledge.* Hillsdale, NJ: Erlbaum.

Catania, A. C. (1992). *Learning* (3rd ed.). Englewood Cliffs, NJ: Prentice-Hall.

Caton, C. L. M., Wyatt, R. J., Felix, A., Grunberg, J., & Dominguez, M. S. (1993). Follow-up of chronically homeless mentally ill men. *American Journal of Psychiatry, 150,* 1639–1642.

Cattell, R. B., & Dreger, R. M. (Eds.). (1977). *Handbook of modern personality theory.* Washington, DC: Hemisphere.

Ceci, S. J. (1991). How much does schooling influence general intelligence and its cognitive components? A reassessment of the evidence. *Developmental Psychology, 27,* 703–723.

Ceci, S. J., Baker, J. E., & Bronfenbrenner, U. (1988). Prospective remembering, temporal calibration, and context. In M. M. Gruneberg, P. E. Morris, & R. N. Sykes (Eds.), *Practical aspects of memory: Current research and issues* (pp. 360–365). Chichester, England: John Wiley & Sons.

Centers for Disease Control and Public Health Service. (1993). *HIV/AIDS surveillance.* Atlanta, GA: Centers for Disease Control.

Centerwall, B. S. (1989). Exposure to television as a cause of violence. In G. Comstock (Ed.), *Public communication and behavior* (Vol. 2). San Diego: Academic Press.

Cerelli, E. (1989). *Older drivers, the age factor in traffic safety* (DOT HS-807–402). Washington, DC: National Highway Traffic and Safety Administration.

Chang, E. C. (1996). Cultural differences in optimism, pessimism, and coping: Predictors of subsequent adjustment in Asian American and Caucasian American college students. *Journal of Counseling Psychology, 43,* 113–123.

Chase, W. G., & Simon, H. A. (1973). The mind's eye in chess. In W. G. Chase (Ed.), *Visual information processing* (pp. 215–281). New York: Academic Press.

Chasnoff, I. J., Griffith, D. R., MacGregor, S., Dirkes, K., & Burns, K. S. (1989). Temporal patterns of cocaine use in pregnancy: Perinatal outcome. *Journal of the American Medical Association, 261,* 1741–1744.

Chassin, L., Curran, P. J., Hussong, A. M., & Colder, C. R. (1996). The relation of parent alcoholism to adolescent substance use: A longitudinal follow-up study. *Journal of Abnormal Psychology, 105,* 70–80.

Chaves, J. F., & Brown, J. M. (1987). Spontaneous cognitive strategies for the control of clinical pain and stress. *Journal of Behavioral Medicine, 10,* 263–276.

Chen, C., Lee, S. Y., & Stevenson, H. W. (1995). Response style and cross-cultural comparisons of rating scales among East Asian and North American students. *Psychological Science, 6,* 170–175.

Cherry, E. C. (1953). Some experiments on the recogniton of speech with one and with two ears. *Journal of Acoustical Society of America, 25,* 975–979.

Chess, S., & Thomas, A. (1984). *Origins and evolution of behavior disorders.* New York: Brunner/Mazel.

Chi, M. T. H., Feltovich, P. J., & Glaser, R. (1981). Categorization and representation of physics problems by experts and novices. *Cognitive Science, 5,* 121–152.

Chien, C. (1993). Ethnopsychopharmacology. In A. G. Gaw (Ed.), Culture, ethnicity, and mental illness (pp. 413–430). Washington, DC: American Psychiatric Association.

Chomsky, N. (1968). *Language and mind.* New York: Harcourt Brace.

Christenfeld, N. (1995). Choices from identical options. *Psychological Science, 6,* 50–55.

Christensen, A., & Jacobson, N. S. (1994). Who (or what) can do psychotherapy: The status and challenge of nonprofessional therapies. *Psychological Science, 5,* 8–14.

Christensen-Szalanski, J. J. J., & Willham, C. F. (1991). The hindsight bias: A meta-analysis. *Organizational Behavior and Human Decision Processes, 48,* 147–168.

Cialdini, R. B. (1988). *Influence: Science and practice* (2nd ed.). Glenview, IL: Scott, Foresman.

Cialdini, R. B. (1994). Interpersonal influence. In S. Shavitt & T. C. Brock (Eds.), *Persuasion* (pp. 195–218). Boston: Allyn & Bacon.

Cialdini, R. B., Kallgren, C. A., & Reno, R. R. (1991). A focus theory of normative conduct. *Advances in Experimental Social Psychology, 24,* 201–234.

Cialdini, R. B., Kenrick, D. T., & Bauman, D. J. (1982). Effects of mood on prosocial behavior in children and adults. In N. Eisenberg-Berg (Ed.), *Development of prosocial behavior.* New York: Academic Press.

Cialdini, R. B., Schaller, M., Houlainhan, D., Arps, K., Fultz, J., & Beaman, A. L. (1987). Empathy-based helping: Is it selflessly or selfishly motivated? *Journal of Personality and Social Psychology, 52,* 749–758.

Clark, E. V. (1973). Nonlinguistic strategies and the acquisition of word meanings. *Cognition, 2,* 161–182.

Clark, H. H., & Chase, W. G. (1972). On the process of comparing sentences against pictures. *Cognitive Psychology, 3,* 472–517.

Clark, H., & Clark, E. (1977). *Psychology and language: An introduction to psycholinguistics.* New York: Harcourt Brace Jovanovich.

Clark, W., & Clark, S. (1980). Pain response in Nepalese porters. *Science, 209,* 410–412.

Clarke, S., Kraftsik, R., Van der Loos, H., & Innocenti, G. M. (1989). Forms and measures of adult and developing human corpus callosum: Is there sexual dimorphism? *Journal of Comparative Neurology, 280,* 213–230.

Clarke-Stewart, A., Friedman, S., & Koch, J. (1985). *Child development: A topical approach.* New York: John Wiley & Sons.

Clum, G. A., & Bowers, T. G. (1990). Behavior therapy better than placebo treatments: Fact or artifact? *Psychological Bulletin, 107,* 110–113.

Cohen, S. H., & Reese, H. W. (1994). *Life-span developmental psychology: Methodological contributions.* Hillsdale, NJ: Erlbaum.

Cohen, S., Kaplan, J. R., Cunnick, J. E., Manuck, S. B., & Rabin, B. S. (1992). Chronic social stress, affiliation, and cellular immune response in nonhuman primates. *Psychological Science, 3,* 301–304.

Cohen, S., Tyrrell, D. A., & Smith, A. P. (1993). Negative life events, perceived stress, negative affect, and susceptibility to the common cold. *Journal of Personality and Social Psychology, 64,* 131–140.

Colborn, T., Dumanoski, D., & Myers, J. P. (1996). *Our stolen future: How we are threatening our fertility, intelligence, and survival—a scientific detective story.* New York: Penguin Books.

Colby, A., Kohlberg, L., Feonton, E., Speicher-Dubin, B., & Lieberman, M. (1983). A longitudinal study of moral judgment. *Monographs of the Society for Research in Child Development, 48,* (1–2, Serial No. 200).

Cole, J. D., & Jacobs, M. R. (1993). The role of social context in the preventions of conduct disorders. *Development and Psychopathology, 5,* 263–275.

Coleman, B.C. (1997). Puberty starts earlier than thought for U.S. girls. Associated Press, April 8th.

Collaer, M. L., & Hines, M. (1995). Human behavioral sex differences: A role for gonadal hormones during early development? *Psychological Bulletin, 118,* 55–107.

Collier, A. C., Coombs, R. W., Schoenfeld, D. A., Bassett, R. L., Timpone, J., Baruch, A., Jones, M., Facey, K., Whitacre, C., McAuliffe, V. J., Friedman, H. M., Merigan, T. C., Reichman, R. C., Hooper, C., & Corey, L. (1996). Treatment of human immunodeficiency virus infection with saquinavir, zidovudine, and zalcitabine. *New England Journal of Medicine, 334,* 1011–1017.

Collins, M. A., & Zebrowitz, L. A. (1995). The contributions of appearance to occupational outcomes in civilian and military settings. *Journal of Applied Social Psychology, 25,* 129–163.

Colwill, R. M. (1993). An associative analysis of instrumental learning. *Current Directions in Psychological Science, 2,* 111–116.

Colwill, R. M., & Rescorla, R. A. (1985). Postconditioning devaluation of a reinforcer affects instrumental responding. *Journal of Experimental Psychology, 11,* 120–132.

Colwill, R. M., & Rescorla, R. A. (1988). Associations between the discriminative stimulus and the reinforcer in instrumental learning. *Journal of Experimental Psychology, 14,* 155–164.

COMMIT Research Group. (1995). Community intervention trial for smoking cessation (COMMIT). *American Journal of Public Health, 85,* 183–200.

Conger, J. A. (1991). Inspiring others: The language of leadership. *Academy of Management Executive, 5,* 31–45.

Constanza, R. S., Derlega, V. J., & Winstead, B. A. (1988). Positive and negative forms of social support: Effects of conversational tactics on coping with stress among same-sex friends. *Journal of Experimental Social Psychology, 24,* 182–193.

Conte, J., Sorenson, M. A., Fogarty, L., & Rosa, J. D. (1991). Evaluating children's reports of sexual abuse: Results from a survey of professionals. *American Journal of Orthopsychiatry, 61,* 428–437.

Cook, R. G. (1993). The experimental analysis of cognition in animals. *Psychological Science, 4,* 174–178.

Cooper, J., & Scher, S. J. (1990). Actions and attitude: The role of responsibility and aversive consequences in persuasion. In T. Brock & S. Shavitt (Eds.), *The psychology of persuasion.* San Francisco: Freeman.

Cooper, M. L., Frone, M. R., Russell, M., & Mudar, P. (1995). Drinking to regulate positive and negative emotions: A motivational model of alcohol use. *Journal of Personality and Social Psychology, 69,* 990–1005.

Coppola, R., Myslobodasky, M., & Weinberger, D. R. (1995). Midline abnormalities and psychopathology: How reliable is the midsagittal magnetic resonance "window" into the brain? *Psychiatry-Research-Neuroimaging, 61,* 33–42.

Coren, S., & Girgus, J. S. (1978). *Seeing is deceiving: The psychology of visual illusion.* Hillsdale, NJ: Lawrence Erlbaum.

Coren, S., & Ward, L. M. (1989). *Sensation and perception* (3rd ed.). San Diego: Harcourt Brace Jovanovich.

Coren, S., Girgus, J. S., Erlichman, H., & Hakstean, A. R. (1976). An empirical taxonomy of visual illusions. *Perception & Psychophysics, 20,* 129–137.

Corey, K. B., & Correia, C. J. (1997). Drinking motives predict alcohol-related problems in college students. *Journal of Studies in Alcohol, 58*(1), 100–105.

Corso, J. F. (1977). Auditory perception and communication. In J. E. Birren & K. W. Schaie (Eds.), *Handbook of the psychology of aging* (pp. 535–553). New York: Van Nostrand Reinhold.

Costa, P. T., Jr., & McCrae, R. R. (1989). *The NEO-PI/NEO-FFI manual supplement.* Odessa, FL: Psychological Assessment Resources.

Costa, P. T., Jr., & McCrae, R. R. (1994). The Revised NEO Personality Inventory (NEO-PI-R). In R. Briggs & J. M. Cheek (Eds.), *Personality measures: Development and evaluation* (Vol. 1.). Greenwich, CT: JAI Press.

Cottrell, N., Eisenberg, R., & Speicher, H. (1992). Inhibiting effects of reciprocation wariness on interpersonal relationships. *Journal of Personality and Social Psychology, 62,* 658–668.

Court, J. H., & Raven, J. (1982). Manual for Raven's progressive matrices and vocabulary scales. (Research Supplement No. 2, P. 3., Sect. 7). London: H. K. Lewis.

Cowan, G., & Curtis, S. R. (1994). Predictors of rape occurrence and victim blame in the William Kennedy Smith case. *Journal of Applied Social Psychology, 24,* 12–20.

Cowan, N. (1984). On short and long auditory stores. *Psychological Bulletin, 96,* 341–370.

Cowan, N., Wood, N. L., & Borne, D. N. (1994). Reconfirmation of the short-term storage concept. *Psychological Science, 5,* 103–106.

Cowell, P. E., Turetsky, B. I., Gur, R. C., & Grossman, R. I. (1994). Sex differences in aging of the human frontal and temporal lobes. *Journal of Neuroscience, 14,* 4748–4755.

Coyle, J. T. (1987). Alzheimer's disease. In G. Adelman (Ed.), *Encyclopedia of neuroscience* (pp. 29–31). Boston: Birkhauser.

Coyle, J. T., Price, D. L., & DeLong, M. R. (1983). Alzheimer's disease: A disorder of cortical cholinergic innervation. *Science, 219,* 1184–1190.

Craik, F. I. M., & Lockhart, R. S. (1972). Levels of processing: A framework for memory research. *Journal of Verbal Learning and Verbal Behavior, 11,* 671–684.

Craik, F. I. M., & Tulving, E. (1975). Depth of processing and the retention of words in episodic memory. *Journal of Experimental Psychology: General, 104,* 268–294.

Cramer, R. E., McMaster, M. R., Bartell, P. A., & Dragna, M. (1988). Subject competence and minimization of the bystander effect. *Journal of Personality and Social Psychology, 55,* 588–598.

Crespi, L. P. (1942). Quantitative variation of incentive and performance in the white rat. *American Journal of Psychology, 55,* 467–517.

Croyle, R. T. (1992). Appraisal of health threats: Cognition, motivation, and social comparison. *Cognitive Therapy and Research, 16,* 165–182.

Crusco, A. H., & Wetzel, C. G. (1984). The Midas touch: The effects of interpersonal touch on restaurant tipping. *Personality and Social Psychology Bulletin, 10,* 512–517.

Crutcher, R. J. (1994). Telling what we know: The use of verbal report methodologies in psychological research. *Psychological Science, 5,* 241–244.

Csikszentmihalyi, M., & Larson, R. (1984). *Being adolescent: Conflict and growth in the teenage years.* New York: Basic Books.

Culberton, F. M. (1997). Depression and gender: An international review. *American Psychologist, 52,* 25–31.

Cummings, M. K., Lampone, D., Mettlin, C., & Pontes, J. E. (1983). What young men know about testicular cancer. *Preventive Medicine, 12,* 326–330.

Cunningham, M. R., Roberts, A. R., Wu, C. H., Barbee, A. P., & Druen, P. B. (1995). "Their ideas of beauty are, on the whole, the same as ours": Consistency and variability in the cross-cultural perception of female physical attractiveness. *Journal of Personality and Social Psychology, 68,* 261–279.

Cunningham, M. R., Shaffer, D. R., Barbee, A., Wolff, P. L., & Kelley, D. J. (1990). Separate processes in the relation of elation and depression to helping: Social versus personal concerns. *Journal of Experimental Social Psychology, 26,* 13–33.

Curfman, G. O. (1993). Is exercise beneficial-or hazardous-to your heart? *The New England Journal of Medicine, 329,* 173.

Czeisler, C. A., Moore-Ede, M. C., & Coleman, R. M. (1982). Rotating shift work schedules that disrupt sleep are improved by applying Circadian principles. *Science, 217,* 460–462.

Dabbs, J. M., Jr. (1992). Testosterone measurements in social and clinical psychology. *Journal of Social and Clinical Psychology, 11,* 302–321.

Dabbs, J. M., Jr., Carr, T. S., Frady, R. L., & Riad, J. K. (1995). Testosterone, crime, and misbehavior among 692 male prison inmates. *Personality and Individual Differences, 18,* 627–633.

Dahl, O. (1985). Testicular carcinoma: A curable malignancy. *Acta Radiology and Oncology, 24,* 3–15.

Daniel, J., & Potasova, A. (1989). Oral temperature and performance in 8 hour and 12 hour shifts. *Ergonomics, 32,* 689–696.

Darley, J. M., & Latane, B. (1968). Bystander intervention in emergencies: Diffusion of responsibility. *Journal of Personality and Social Psychology, 8,* 377–383.

Daro, D., & McCurdy, K. (1992). *Current trends in child abuse reporting and fatalities: The results of the 1990 annual fifty-state survey.* Chicago: National Center on Child Abuse Prevention Research.

Datan, N., Antonovsky, A., & Moaz, B. (1984). Love, war, and the life cycle of the family. In K. A. McCluskey & H. W. Reese (Eds.), *Life-span developmental psychology: Historical and generational effects* (pp. 143–159). New York: Academic Press.

Daum, I., Ackermann, H., Schugens, M. M., Reimold, C., Dichgans, J., & Birbaumer, N. (1993). The cerebellum and cognitive functions in humans. *Behavioral Neuroscience, 104,* 411–419.

Daum, I., & Schugens, M. M. (1996). On the cerebellum and classical conditioning. *Current Directions in Psychological Science, 5,* 58–61.

Davey, G. C. L. (1992). Classical conditioning and the acquisition of human fears and phobias: A review and synthesis of the literature. *Advances in Behavior Research Therapy, 14,* 29–66.

Davidson, K., & Hopson, J. L. (1988). Gorilla business. *Image* (San Francisco Chronicle), 14–18.

Davidson, R. J. (1992). Emotion and affective style: Hemispheric substrates. *Psychological Science, 3,* 39–43.

Davidson, W. S., II, Redne, R., Blakely, C. H., Mitchell, C. M., & Emshoff, J. G. (1987). Diversion of juvenile offenders: An experimental comparison. *Journal of Consulting and Clinical Psychology, 55,* 68–75.

Davies, M. F. (1987). Reduction of hindsight bias by restoration of foresight perspective. *Organizational Behavior and Human Decision Processes, 40,* 50–68.

Davison, G. C., Navarre, S. G., & Vogel, R. S. (1995). The articulated thoughts in simulated situations paradigm: A think-aloud approach to cognitive assessment. *Current Directions in Psychological Science, 4,* 29–33.

Day, D. V., & Sulsky, L. M. (1995). Effects of frame-of-reference training and information configuration on memory organization and rating accuracy. *Journal of Applied Psychology, 80,* 158–167.

De Villiers, J. G., & De Villiers, P. A. (1978). *Language acquisition.* Cambridge, MA: Harvard University Press.

de Weerth, C., & Kalma, A. P. (1993). Female aggression as a response to sexual jealousy: A sex role reversal? *Aggressive Behavior, 19,* 265–279.

Deary, I. J. (1995). Auditory inspection time and intelligence: What is the direction of causation? *Developmental Psychology, 31,* 237–250.

Deary, I. J., & Stough, C. (1996). Intelligence and inspection time. *American Psychologist, 51,* 599–608.

Deaux, K. (1993). Commentary: Sorry, wrong number—a reply to Gentile's call. *Psychological Science, 4,* 125–126.

DeBono, K. G. (1992). Pleasant scents and persuasion: An information processing approach. *Journal of Applied Social Psychology, 22,* 910–919.

DeCasper, A. J., & Fifer, W. P. (1980). Of human bonding: Newborns prefer their mothers' voices. *Science, 208,* 991–1004.

DeCasper, A. J., & Spence, M. J. (1986). Prenatal maternal speech influences newborns' perception of speech sounds. *Infant Behavior and Development, 9,* 133–150.

Deci, E. L. (1975). *Intrinsic motivation.* New York: Plenum.

Deci, E. L., & Ryan, R. M. (1985). *Intrinsic motivation and self-determination in human behavior.* New York: Plenum Press.

Delgado, P. L., Charney, D. S., Price, L. H., Aghajanian, G. K., Landis, H., & Heninger, G. R. (1990). Serotonin function and mechanism of antidepressant action: Reversal of antidepressant-induced remission by rapid depletion of plasma atryptophan. *Archives of General Psychiatry, 47,* 411–418.

DeLoache, J. S. (1995). Early understanding and use of symbols: The model model. *Current Directions in Psychological Science, 4,* 109–113.

DeLongis, A., Folkman, S., & Lazarus, R. S. (1988). The impact of daily stress on health and mood: Psychological and social resources as mediators. *Journal of Personality and Social Psychology, 54,* 486–495.

Delvenne, V., Lotstra, F., Goldman, S., & Biver, F. (1995). Brain hypometabolism of glucose in anorexia nervosa: A PET scan study. *Biological Psychiatry, 37,* 161–169.

Dembo, Y., Levin, I., & Siegler, R. S. (1997). A comparison of the geometric reasoning of students attending Israeli ultraorthodox and mainstream schools. *Developmental Psychology, 33,* 92–103.

Dement, W. C. (1975). *Some must watch while some must sleep.* San Francisco: W. H. Freeman.

Dement, W. C., & Kleitman, N. (1957). The relation of eye movement during sleep to dream activity: An objective method for the study of dreaming. *Journal of Experimental Psychology, 53,* 339–353.

Dement, W. C., & Wolpert, E. A. (1958). The relation of eye movements, body mobility and external stimuli to dream content. *Journal of Experimental Psychology, 55,* 543–553.

Dempsey, P. G., & Leamon, T. B. (1995, October). Implementing bent-handled tools in the workplace. *Ergonomics in Design,* pp. 15–21.

DeNelsky, G. Y. (1996). The case against prescription privileges for psychologists. *American Psychologist, 51,* 207–212.

Denning, P. J. (1992). Neural networks. *American Scientist, 80,* 426–429.

DePaulo, B. M. (1992). Nonverbal behavior and self-presentation. *Psychological Bulletin, 111,* 230–243.

DePaulo, B. M., Epstein, J. A., & Wyer, M. M. (1993). Sex differences in lying: How women and men deal with the dilemma of deceit. In M. Lewis & C. Saarni (Eds.), *Lying and deception in everyday life* (pp. 126–147). New York: Guilford Press.

DePaulo, B. M., Kashy, D. A., Kirkendol, S. E., Wyer, M. M., & Epstein, J. A. (1996). Lying in everyday life. *Journal of Personality and Social Psychology, 70,* 979–995.

Deppe, R. K., & Harackiewicz, J. M. (1996). Self-handicapping and intrinsic motivation: Buffering intrinsic motivation from the threat of failure. *Journal of Personality and Social Psychology, 70,* 868–876.

Desmarais, S., & Curtis, J. (1997). Gender and perceived pay entitlement: Testing for effects of experience with income. *Journal of Personality and Social Psychology, 72,* 141–150.

DeTienne, K. B. (1993). Big brother or friendly coach? Computer monitoring in the 21st century. *The Futurist, 27,* 33–37.

DeValois, R. L., & DeValois, K. K. (1975). Neural coding of color. In E. C. Carterette & M. P. Friedman (Eds.), *Handbook of perception* (pp. 117–166). New York: Academic Press.

Diekmann, K. A., Tenbrunsel, A. E., Shah, P. P., Schroth, H. A., & Bazerman, M. H. (1996). The descriptive and prescriptive use of previous purchase price in negotiations. *Organizational Behavior and Human Decision Processes, 66,* 179–191.

Diener, E., & Diener, C. (1996). Most people are happy. *Psychological Science, 7,* 181–185.

Diener, E., Wolsic, B., & Fujita, F. (1995). Physical attractiveness and subjective well-being. *Journal of Personality and Social Psychology, 69,* 120–129.

Dinges, N. G., & Hull, P. (1992). Personality, culture, and international studies. In D. Lieberman (Ed.), *Revealing the world: An interdisciplinary reader for international studies.* Dubuque, IA: Kendall-Hunt.

Dishman, R. K. (1988). *Exercise adherence: Its impact on public health.* Champaign, IL: Human Kinetic Books.

Dittman, R. W., Kappes, M. H., Kappes, M. E., Borger, D., Meyer-Bahlburg, H. F. L., Stegner, H., Willig, R. H., & Wallis, H. (1990). Congenital adrenal hyperplasia II: Gender-related behavior and attitudes in female salt-wasting and simple-virilizing patients. *Psychoneuroendocrinology, 15,* 421–434.

Dollard, J., Doob, L., Miller, N., Mowrer, O. H., & Sears, R. R. (1939). *Frustration and aggression.* New Haven, CT: Yale University Press.

Dominowski, R. L. (1990). Problem solving and metacognition. In K. J. Gilhholy, M. T. G. Keane, R. H. Logie, & G. Erdos (Eds.), *Lines of thinking.* New York: Wiley.

Douek, E. (1988). Olfaction and medicine. In S. Van Toller & G. Doll (Eds.), *Perfumery: The psychology and biology of fragrance.* London: Chapman Hall.

Dovidio, J. F., Evans, N., & Tyler, R. B. (1986). Racial stereotypes: The contents of their cognitive representations. *Journal of Experimental Social Psychology, 22,* 22–37.

Dovidio, J. F., & Gaertner, S. L. (1993). Stereotype and evaluative intergroup bias. In D. M. Mackie & D. L. Hamilton (Eds.), *Affect, cognition, and stereotyping: Interactive processes in group perception.* Orlando, FL: Academic Press.

Dovidio, J. F., & Gaertner, S. L. (Eds.). (1986). *Prejudice, discrimination, and racism.* Orlando, FL: Academic Press.

Dovidio, J. F., Gaertner, S. L., Isen A. M., & Lawrance, R. E. (1995). Group representations and intergroup bias: Positive affect, similarity, and group size. *Personality and Social Psychology Bulletin, 21,* 856–865.

Dreher, G. F., & Cox, T. H., Jr. (1996). Race, gender, and opportunity: A study of compensation attainment and the establishment of mentoring relationships. *Journal of Applied Psychology, 81,* 297–308.

Dubbert, P. M. (1992). Exercise in behavioral medicine. *Journal of Consulting and Clinical Psychology, 60,* 613–618.

Dubbert, P. M. (1995). Behavioral (lifestyle) modification in the prevention and treatment of hypertension. *Clinical Psychology Review, 15*(3), 187–216.

Duff, C. (1996, July 8). Passing the bucks: Aging boomers cut the cord but can't let go of the wallet. *Wall Street Journal,* pp. A1, A2.

Duffy, D. L., Hamerman, D., & Cohen, M. A. (1980). Communication skills of house officers: A study in a medical clinic. *Annals of Internal Medicine, 93,* 354–357.

Duncan, L. E., & Agronick, G. S. (1995). The intersection of life stage and social events: Personality and life outcomes. *Journal of Personality and Social Psychology, 69,* 558–658.

Duncker, K. (1945). On problem solving. *Psychological Monographs* (whole No. 270).

Dutton, D. G., & Aron, A. P. (1974). Some evidence for heightened sexual attraction under conditions of high anxiety. *Journal of Personality and Social Psychology, 30,* 510–517.

Dweck, C. S., & Licht, B. G. (1980). Learned helplessness and intellectual achievement. In M. E. P. Seligman & J. Garber (Eds.), *Human helplessness: Theory and application.* New York: Academic Press.

Dyer, F. C. (1991). Bees acquire route-based memories but not cognitive maps in a familiar landscape. *Animal Behaviour, 41,* 239–246.

Eckerman, C. O. (1993). Imitation and toddler's achievement of coordinated action with others. In J. Nadel & L. Camaioni (Eds.), *New perspectives in early communicative development* (pp. 116–156). New York: Routledge.

Eckerman, C. O., & Didow, S. M. (1996). Nonverbal imitation and toddlers' mastery of verbal means of achieving coordinated action. *Developmental Psychology, 32,* 141–152.

Eden, D., & Aviram, A. (1993). Self-efficacy training to speed reemployment: Helping people to help themselves. *Journal of Applied Psychology, 78,* 352–360.

Edwards, J. R., & Harrison, R. V. (1993). Job demands and worker health: Three-dimensional reexamination of the relationship between person-environment fit and strain. *Journal of Applied Psychology, 78,* 628–648.

Effective treatment for treating depression (1994, April). *Johns Hopkins Medical Letter, 6*(2), 6–7.

Egeland, J. A., Gerhard, D. S., Pauls, D. L., Sussex, J. N., Kidd, K. K., Allen, C. R., Hostetter, A. M., & Housman, D. E. (1987). Bipolar affective disorders linked to DNA markers on chromosome 11. *Nature, 325,* 783–787.

Ehrhardt, A. A., & Meyer-Bahlberg, H. F. L. (1981). Effects of prenatal sex hormones on gender-related behavior. *Science, 211,* 1312–1317.

Ehrman, R. N., Robbins, S. J., Childress, A. R., & O'Brien, C. P. (1992). Conditioned responses to cocaine-related stimuli in cocaine abuse patients. *Psychopharmacology, 107,* 523–529.

Eich, E. (1995). Searching for mood dependent memory. *Psychological Science, 6,* 67–75.

Eich, E., Macaulay, D., & Ryan, L. (1994). Mood dependent memory for events of the personal past. *Journal of Experimental Psychology: Learning, Memory, and Cognition, 15,* 443–455.

Eich, J. E. (1985). Levels of processing, encoding specificity, elaboration, and CHARM. *Psychological Review, 92,* 1–38.

Eichar, D. M., Brady, E. M., & Fortinsky, R. H. (1991). The job satisfaction of older workers. *Journal of Organizational Behavior, 12,* 609–620.

Eichenbaum, H., & Bunsey, M. (1995). On the binding of associations in memory: Clues from studies on the role of the hippocampal region in paired-associate learning. *Current Directions in Psychological Science, 4,* 19–23.

Eimas, P. D., & Tarter, V. C. (1979). The development of speech perception. In H. W. Reese & L. P. Lipsitt (Eds.), *Advances in child development and behavior* (Vol. 13, pp. 155–193). New York: Academic Press.

Ekman, P. (1985). *Telling lies.* New York: Norton.

Ekman, P. (1992). Facial expressions of emotion: New findings, new questions. *Psychological Science, 3,* 34–38.

Ekman, P., & Friesen, W. V. (1975). *Unmasking the face.* Englewood Cliffs, NJ: Prentice Hall.

Ekman, P., Davidson, R. J., & Friesen, W. V. (1990). The Duchenne smile: Emotional expression and brain physiology II. *Journal of Personality and Social Psychology, 58,* 342–353.

Elkin, J., Shea, T., Watkins, J. T., Imber, S. D., Stotsky, S. M., Collins, J. F., Glass, D. R., Pilkonis, P. A., Leber, W. R., Docherty, J. P., Fiester, S. J., & Parloff, M. B. (1989). National Institutes of Mental Health treatment of depression and collaborative research program. *Archives of General Psychiatry, 46,* 971–982.

Elkind, D. (1967). Egocentrism in adolescence. *Child Development, 38,* 1025–1034.

Elkins, I. J., Cromwell, R. L., & Asarnow, R. F. (1992). Span of apprehension in schizophrenic patients as a function of distracter masking and laterality. *Journal of Abnormal Psychology, 101,* 53–60.

Elliot, A. J. (1981) *Child language.* Cambridge, England: Cambridge University Press.

Elliot, A. J., & Devine, P. G. (1994). On the motivational nature of cognitive dissonance: Dissonance as psychological discomfort. *Journal of Personality and Social Psychology, 67,* 382–394.

Ellis, A. (1987). The impossibility of achieving consistently good mental health. *American Psychologist, 42,* 364–375.

Elsmore, T. F., & McBride, S. A. (1994). An eight-alternative concurrent schedule: Foraging in a radial maze. *Journal of Applied Behavior Analysis, 28,* 236.

Emmons, K. M., Hammond, S. K., & Abrams, D. B. (1994). Smoking at home: The impact of smoking cessation on nonsmokers' exposure to environmental tobacco smoke. *Health Psychology, 13,* 516–520.

Empson, J. A. C. (1984). Sleep and its disorders. In R. Stevens (Ed.), *Aspects of consciousness.* New York: Academic Press.

Engel, G. L. (1980). The clinical application of a biopsychosocial model. *American Journal of Psychiatry, 137,* 535–544.

Engen, T. (1982). *The perception of odors.* New York: Academic Press.

Engen, T. (1986). *Remembering odors and their names.* Paper presented at the First International Conference on the Psychology of Perfumery, University of Warwick, England.

Engen, T. (1987). Remembering odors and their names. *American Scientist, 75,* 497–503.

Engen, T., & Ross, B. M. (1973). Long-term memory of odors with and without verbal descriptions. *Journal of Experimental Psychology, 100,* 221–227.

Environmental Protection Agency. (1992). *Respiratory health effects of passive smoking: Lung cancer and other disorders.* Washington, DC: Author.

Epstein, L. H. (1992). Role of behavior theory in behavioral medicine. Special Issue: Behavioral medicine: An update for the 1990s. *Journal of Consulting and Clinical Psychology, 60,* 493–498.

Ericsson, K. A., & Simon, H. A. (1993). *Protocol analysis: Verbal reports as data.* Cambridge, MA: MIT Press.

Erikson, E. H. (1950). *Childhood and society.* New York: Norton.

Erikson, E. H. (1987). *A way of looking at things: Selected papers from 1930 to 1980* (S. Schlein, Ed.). New York: Norton.

Erlenmeyer-Kimling, L., & Jarvik, L. F. (1963). Genetics and intelligence. *Science, 142,* 1477–1479.

Eron, L. D. (1987). The development of aggressive behavior from the perspective of a developing behaviorist. *American Psychologist, 42,* 435–442.

Estrada, C. A., Isen, A. M., & Young, M. J. (1995). Positive affect improves creative problem solving and influences reported source of practice satisfaction in physicians. *Motivation and Emotion, 388,* 385–300.

Etaugh, C., & Liss, M. B. (1992). Home, school, and playroom: Training grounds for adult gender roles. *Sex Roles, 26,* 129–147.

Evans, C. (1985). *Landscapes of the night.* New York: Viking.

Exner, J. E. (1993). *The Rorschach: A comprehensive system: Vol. 1. Basic Foundations* (3rd ed.). New York: Wiley.

Eysenck, H. J. (1952). The effects of psychotherapy: An evaluation. *Journal of Consulting Psychology, 16,* 319–324.

Fagenson, E. A. (1992). Mentoring-who needs it? A comparison of protégés' and nonprotégés' need for power, achievement, affiliation, and autonomy. *Journal of Vocational Behavior, 41,* 48–60.

Farquhar, J. W., Maccoby, N., & Solomon, D. S. (1984). Community applications of behavioral medicine. In W. D. Gentry (Ed.), *Handbook of behavioral medicine.* New York: Guilford Press.

Fazio, R. H., & Roskos-Ewoldsen, D. R. (1994). Acting as we feel: When and how attitudes guide behavior. In S. Shavitt & T. C. Brock (Eds.), *Persuasion* (pp. 71–93). Boston: Allyn & Bacon.

Feather, N. T., & Volkmer, R. E. (1988). Preference for situations involving effort, time pressure, and feedback in relation to Type A behavior, locus of control, and test anxiety. *Journal of Personality and Social Psychology, 55,* 266–271.

Feingold, A. (1992). Cognitive gender differences: A developmental perspective. *Sex Roles, 29,* 91–112.

Feingold, A. J. (1990). Gender differences in the effects of physical attractiveness on romantic attraction: A comparison across five research paradigms. *Journal of Personality and Social Psychology, 59,* 981–993.

Feldman, D. C., & Tompson, H. B. (1993). Entry shock, culture shock: Socializing the new breed of global managers. *Human Resource Management, 31,* 345–362.

Felleman, D. J., & Van Essen, D. C. (1991). Distributed hierarchical processing in the primate cerebral cortex. *Cerebral Cortex, 1,* 1–47.

Fenton, W. S., & McGlashan, T. H. (1991). Natural history of schizophrenia subtypes: II. Positive and negative symptoms and long-term course. *Archives of General Psychiatry, 48,* 978–986.

Ferster, C. B., & Skinner, B. F. (1957). *Schedules of reinforcement.* New York: Appleton-Century-Crofts.

Festinger, L. (1957). *A theory of cognitive dissonance.* Evanston, IL: Row, Peterson.

Feuerstein, M., Labbé, E. E., & Kuczmierczyk, A. R. (1986). *Health psychology: A psychobiological perspective.* New York: Plenum.

Fibiger, H. C., Lepiane, F. G., Jakubovick, A., & Phillips, A. G. (1987). The role of dopamine in intracranial self-stimulation of the ventral tegmental area. *Journal of Neuroscience, 7,* 3888–3896.

Fibiger, H. C., Murray, C. L., & Phillips, A. G. (1983). Lesions of the nucleus basalis magnocellularis impair long-term memory in rats. *Society for Neuroscience Abstracts, 9,* 332.

Fielder, F. E., Mitchell, T., & Triandis, H. C. (1971). The culture assimilator: An approach to cross-cultural training. *Journal of Applied Psychology, 55,* 95–102.

Fields, H. L., & Basbaum, A. (1984). Endogenous pain control mechanisms. In P. D. Wall & R. Melzack (Eds.), *Textbook of pain* (pp. 142–152). Edinburgh: Churchill Livingstone.

Fierman, J. (1995, August 21). It's 2:00 A.M., let's go to work. *Fortune,* pp. 82–86.

Fincham, F. D., & Bradbury, T. N. (1992). Assessing attributions in marriage: The relationship attribution measure. *Journal of Personality and Social Psychology, 62,* 457–468.

Fincham, F. D., & Bradbury, T. N. (1993). Marital satisfaction, depression and attributions: A longitudinal analysis. *Journal of Personality and Social Psychology, 64,* 442–452.

Fingleton, E. (1995, March 20). Jobs for life: Why Japan won't give them up. *Fortune,* pp. 119–120, 121–123, 125.

Fink, M. (1994). Can ECT be an effective treatment for adolescents? *Harvard Mental Health Letter, 10,* 8.

Finney, J. W., Weist, M. D., & Friman, P. C. (1995). Evaluation of two health education strategies for testicular self-examination. *Journal of Applied Behavior Analysis 28,* 39–46.

Fischoff, B. (1975). Hindsight–foresight: The effect of outcome knowledge on judgment under uncertainty. *Journal of Experimental Psychology: Human Perception and Performance, 1,* 288–299.

Fischhoff, B. (1996). The real world: What good is it? *Organizational Behavior and Human Decision Processes, 65,* 232–248.

Fisher, H. (1992). *Anatomy of love.* New York: Norton.

Fisher, J. D., Fisher, W. A., Misovich, S. J., Kimble, D. L, & Malloy, T. E. (1996). Changing AIDS risk behavior: Effects of an intervention emphasizing AIDS risk reduction information, motivation, and behavioral skills in a college population. *Health Psychology, 15,* 114–123.

Fisher, J. D., Fisher, W. A., Williams, S. S., & Malloy, T. E. (1994). Empirical tests of an information-motivation-behavioral skills model of AIDS preventive behavior with gay men and heterosexual university students. *Health Psychology 13,* 238–250.

Fiske, S. T. (1993). Social cognition and social perception. In L. W. Porter & M. R. Rosenzweig (Eds.), *Annual Review of Psychology, 44,* 155–194.

Fiske, S. T., & Neuberg, S. L. (1990). A continuum model of impression formation, from category based to individuating processes: Influences of information and motivation in attention and interpretation. In M. P. Zanna (Ed.), *Advances in experimental social psychology* (Vol. 23). New York: Academic Press.

Flaherty, C. F., & Largen, J. (1975). Within-subjects positive and negative contrast effects in rats. *Journal of Comparative and Physiological Psychology, 88,* 653–664.

Flavell, J. H. (1985). *Cognitive development* (2nd ed.). Englewood Cliffs, NJ: Prentice-Hall.

Flin, R., Slaven, G., & Stewart, K. (1996). Emergency decision making in the offshore oil and gas industry. *Human Factors, 38,* 262–277.

Florian, V., Mikulincer, M., & Taubman, O. (1995). Does hardiness contribute to mental health during a stressful real-life situation? The roles of appraisal and coping. *Journal of Personality and Social Psychology, 68,* 687–695.

Flynn, J. R. (1987). Massive IQ gains in 14 nations: What IQ tests really measure. *Psychological Bulletin, 101,* 171–191.

Flynn, J. R. (1991). *Asian-Americans: Achievement beyond IQ.* Hillsdale, NJ: Erlbaum.

Foderaro, L. W. (1988, February 4). The fragrant house: An expanding market for every mood. *The New York Times,* pp. C1, C10.

Folger, R., & Baron, R. A. (1996). Violence and hostility at work: A model of reactions to perceived injustice. In C. VandenBos & E. Q. Bulato (Eds.), pp. 51–86. *Workplace violence.* Washington, DC: American Psychological Association.

Folkman, S., Chesney, M., Collette, L., Boccellari, & Cook, M. (1996). Postbereavement depressive mood and its prebereavement predictors in HIV+ and HIV-gay men. *Journal of Personality and Social Psychology, 70,* 336–348.

Folkman, S., Lazarus, R. S., Dunkel-Schetter, C., DeLongis, A., & Gruen, R. J. (1986). Dynamics of a stressful encounter: Cognitive appraisal, coping, and encounter outcomes. *Journal of Personality and Social Psychology, 50,* 992–1003.

Ford, S., Fallowfield, L., & Lewis, S. (1996). Doctor-patient interactions in oncology. *Social Science Medicine, 12,* 1511–1519.

Forgas, J. P. (1995). Mood and judgment: The affect infusion model (AIM). *Psychological Bulletin, 21,* 747–765.

Forgas, J. P. (1995). Mood and judgment: The affect infusion model (AIM). *Psychological Bulletin, 117,* 39–66.

Forgas, J. P. (1995). The role of emotion in social judgments: An introductory review and an affect infusion model (AIM). *European Journal of Social Psychology.*

Forgas, J. P., & Bower, G. H. (1988). Affect in social and personal judgments. In K. Fiedler & J. P. Forgas (Eds.), *Affect, cognition, and social behavior.* Toronto: Hogrefe.

Forgas, J. P., & Fiedler, K. (1996). Us and them: Mood effects on intergroup discrimination. *Journal of Personality and Social Psychology, 70,* 28–40.

Forsell, Y., Jorm, A. F., Fratiglioni, L., Grut, M., & Winblad, B. (1993). Application of DSM-III-R criteria for major depressive episode to elderly subjects with and without dementia. *American Journal of Psychiatry, 150,* 1199–1202.

Foulkes, D. (1985). *Dreaming: A cognitive-psychological analysis.* Hillsdale, NJ: Erlbaum.

Fowler, R. D. (1993). 1992 report of the chief executive officers. *American Psychologist, 48,* 726–735.

Fowles, D. C. (1994). A motivational theory of psychopathology. In W. Spaulding (Ed.), *Nebraska symposium on motivation: Integrated views of motivation and emotion* (Vol. 41, pp. 181–238). Lincoln: University of Nebraska Press.

Frankenburg, W. K., & Dodds, J. B. (1992). *Denver II Training Manual.*

Franks, J. J., & Bransford, J. D. (1971). Abstraction of visual patterns. *Journal of Experimental Psychology, 90,* 65–74.

Frederick, D., & Libby, R. (1986). Expertise and auditors' judgments of conjunctive events. *Journal of Accounting Research, 24,* 270–290.

Freedman, J. L. (1986). Television violence and aggression: A rejoinder. *Psychological Bulletin, 100,* 372–378.

Frese, M. (1985). Stress at work and psychosomatic complaints: A causal interpretation. *Journal of Applied Psychology, 70,* 314–328.

Fricko, M. A. M., & Beehr, T. A. (1992). A longitudinal investigation of interest congruence and gender concentration as predictors of job satisfaction. *Personnel Psychology, 45,* 99–117.

Friedman, H. S., Hawley, P. H., & Tucker, J. S. (1994). Personality, health, and longevity. *Current Directions in Psychological Science, 3,* 37–41.

Friedman, H. S., & Miller-Herringer, T. (1991). Nonverbal display of emotion in public and private: Self-monitoring, personality, and expressive cues. *Journal of Personality and Social Psychology, 62,* 766–775.

Friedman, H. W., Tucker, J. S., Schwartz, J. E., Tomlinson-Keasey, C., Martin, L. R., Wingart, D. L., & Criqui, M. H. (1995). Psychosocial and behavioral predictors of longevity: The aging and death of the "termites." *American Psychologist, 50,* 69–78.

Friedman, H. W., Tucker, J. S., Tomlinson-Keasey, C., Schwartz, J. E., Wingard, D. L., & Criqui, M. H. (1993). Does childhood personality predict longevity? *Journal of Personality and Social Psychology, 65,* 176–185.

Friedrich, J., Featherstonhaugh, D., Casey, S., & Gallagher, D. (1996). Argument integration and attitude change: Suppression effects in the integration of one-sided arguments that vary in persuasiveness. *Personality and Social Psychology Bulletin, 22,* 177–191.

Fry, A. F., & Hale, S. (1996). Processing speed, working memory, and fluid intelligence. *Psychological Science, 7,* 237–241.

Fry, W. A., Menck, H. R., & Winchester, D. P. (1996). The national cancer data base report on lung cancer. *Cancer, 77,* 1947–1955.

Fuchs, I., Eisenberg, N., Herz-Lazarowitz, R., & Sharabany, R. (1986). Kibbutz, Israeli city, and American children's moral reasoning about prosocial moral conflicts. *Merrill-Palmer Quarterly, 32,* 37–50.

Fultz, J., Shaller, M., & Cialdini, R. B. (1988). Empathy, sadness, and distress: Three related but distant vicarious affective responses to another's suffering. *Personality and Social Psychology Bulletin, 14,* 312–325.

Funder, D. C., & Colvin, C. R. (1991). Explorations in behavioral consistency: Properties of persons, situations, and behavior. *Journal of Personality and Social Psychology, 60,* 773–794.

Funder, D. C., & Sneed, C. D. (1993). Behavioral manifestations of personality: An ecological approach to judgmental accuracy. *Journal of Personality and Social Psychology, 64,* 479–490.

Furnham, A., Kirkcaldy, B. D., & Lynn, R. (1994). National attitudes to competitiveness, money, and work among young people: First, second, and third world differences. *Human Relations, 47,* 119–132.

Gabrieli, J. D. D., Fleischman, D. A., Keane, M., Reminger, S. L., & Morrell, F. (1995). Double dissociation between memory systems underlying explicit and implicit memory in the human brain. *Psychological Science, 6,* 76–82.

Gaertner, S. L., Dovidio, J. F., Anastasio, P. A., Bachman, B. A., & Rust, M. C. (in press). The common ingroup identity model: Recategorization and the reduction of intergroup bias. In W. Stroebe & H. Hewstone (Eds.), *European Review of Social Psychology.*

Gaertner, S. L., Mann, J. A., Dovidio, J. F., & Murrell, J. A. (1990). How does cooperation reduce intergroup bias? *Journal of Personality and Social Psychology, 57,* 239–249.

Gaertner, S. L., Mann, J., Murrell, A., & Dovidio, J. F. (1989). Reducing intergroup bias: The benefits of recategorization. *Journal of Personality and Social Psychology, 57,* 239–249.

Gaertner, S. L., Rust, M. C., Dovidio, J. F., Bachman, B. A., & Anastasio, P. A. (1993). The contact hypothesis: The role of common ingroup identity on reducing intergroup bias. *Small Groups Research, 25,* 224–249.

Gaines, J., & Jermier, J. M. (1983). Emotional exhaustion in a high stress organization. *Academy of Management Journal, 26,* 567–586.

Gainotti, G. (1993). Emotional and psychosocial problems after brain injury. *Neuropsychological Rehabilitation, 3,* 259–277.

Galambos, N. I. (1992). Parent–adolescent relations. *Current Directions in Psychological Science, 1,* 146–149.

Galanter, E. (1962). Contemporary psychophysics. In R. Brown, E. Galanter, E. G. Hess, & G. Mandler (Eds.), *New Directions in Psychology.* New York: Holt, Rinehart, & Winston.

Gannon, L., Luchetta, T., Rhodes, K., Pardie, L., & Segrist, D. (1992). Sex bias in psychological research: Progress or complacency? *American Psychologist, 47,* 389–396.

Ganzach, Y. (1995). Negativity (and positivity) in performance evaluation: Three field studies. *Journal of Applied Psychology, 80,* 491–499.

Garcia, J., Hankins, W. G., & Rusiniak, K. W. (1974). Behavioral regulation of the milieu interne in man and rat. *Science, 185,* 824–831.

Garcia, J., & Koelling, R. A. (1966). Relation of cue to consequence in avoidance learning. *Psychonomic Science, 4,* 123.

Garcia, J., Rusiniak, K. W., & Brett, L. P. (1977). Conditioning food-illness aversions in wild animals: Caveat Canonici. In H. Davis & H. M. B. Hurwitz (Eds.), *Operant-Pavlovian interactions.* Hillsdale, NJ: Erlbaum.

Gardell, B. (1987). Efficiency and health hazards in mechanized work. In J. C. Quick, R. S. Bhagat, J. E. Dalton, & J. D. Quick (Eds.), *Work stress* (pp. 10–71). New York: Praeger.

Gardner, B. T., & Gardner, R. A. (1975). Evidence for sentence constituents in the early utterances of child and chimpanzee. *Journal of Experimental Psychology: General, 4,* 244–267.

Gardner, H. (1983). *Frames of mind: The theory of multiple intelligences.* New York: Basic Books.

Gardner, R. M., & Tockerman, Y. R. (1994). A computer–TV methodology for investigating the influence of somatotype on perceived personality traits. *Journal of Social Behavior and Personality, 9,* 555–563.

Garland, H., & Newport, S. (1991). Effects of absolute and relative sunk costs on the decision to persist with a course of action. *Organizational Behavior and Human Decision Processes, 48,* 55–69.

Garner, D. M. (1993). Binge eating in anorexia nervosa. In G. C. Fairburn & G. T. Wilson (Eds.), *Binge eating: Nature, assessment, and treatment* (pp. 750–786). New York: Guilford Press.

Garner, D. M., & Wooley, S. C. (1991). Confronting the failure of behavioral and dietary treatments for obesity. *Clinical Psychology Review, 11,* 729–780.

Gatchel, R. J., Baum, A., & Krantz, D. S. (1989). *An introduction to health psychology* (2nd ed.). New York: Random House.

Gauvain, M., & Rogoff, B. (1989). Collaborative problem solving and children's planning skills. *Developmental Psychology, 25,* 139–151.

Gazzaniga, M. S. (1984). Right hemisphere language: Remaining problems. *American Psychologist, 39,* 1494–1495.

Gazzaniga, M. S. (1985, November). The social brain. *Psychology Today,* pp. 29–38.

Gazzaniga, M. S., Fendrich, R., & Wessinger, C. M. (1994). Blindsight reconsidered. *Current Directions in Psychological Science, 3,* 93–96.

Ge, X., Conger, R. D., Lorenz, F. O., Shanahan, M., & Elder, G. H., Jr. (1995). Mutual influences in parent and adolescent psychological distress. *Developmental Psychology, 2,* 406–419.

Geen, R. G. (1989). Alternative conceptions of social facilitation. In P. B. Paulus (Ed.), *Psychology of group influence* (2nd ed., pp. 1–37). New York: Academic Press.

Geen, R. G., Beatty, W. W., & Arkin, R. M. (1984). *Human motivation.* Boston: Allyn and Bacon.

Gehring, R. E., & Toglia, M. P. (1989). Recall of pictorial enactments and verbal descriptions with verbal and imagery study strategies. *Journal of Mental Imagery, 13,* 83–98.

Geller, E. S. (1988). A behavioral science approach to transportation safety. *Bulletin of the New York Academy of Medicine, 64*(7), 632–661.

Geller, E. S. (1995). Integrating behaviorism and humanism for environmental protection. *Journal of Social Issues, 4,* 179–195.

Geller, E. S. (1996). Managing the human element of occupational health and safety. In R. W. Lack (Ed.), *Essentials of safety and health management.* Boca Raton, FL: Lewis Publishers.

Gentner, D. (1982). Why nouns are learned before verbs: Linguistic relativity versus natural partitioning. In S.A. Kuczaj (Ed.), *Language development, Vol. 2. Language, thought, and culture* (pp. 301–334). Hillsdale, NJ: Erlbaum.

George, J. M. (1995). Leader positive mood and group performance: The case of customer service. *Journal of Applied Social Psychology, 25,* 778–794.

George, J. T., & Hopkins, B. L. (1989). Multiple effects of performance-contingent pay for waitpersons. *Journal of Applied Behavior Analysis, 22,* 131–142.

Geschwind, N. (1972). Language and the brain. *Scientific American, 226,* 76–83.

Gibbons, B. (1986). The intimate sense of smell. *National Geographic, 170,* 324–361.

Gibbons, F. X., Eggleston, T. J., & Benthin, A. C. (1997). Cognitive reactions to smoking relapse: The reciprocal relation between dissonance and self-esteem. *Journal of Personality and Social Psychology, 72*(1), 184–195.

Gibson, E. J., & Rader, N. (1979). Attention: the perceiver as performer. In G. A. Hale & M. Lewis (Eds.), *Attention and cognitive development.* New York: Plenum.

Gibson, E. J., & Walk, R. D. (1960). The "visual cliff." *Scientific American, 202,* 64–71.

Gidron, Y., & Davidson, K. (1996). Development and preliminary testing of a brief intervention for modifying CHD-predictive hostility components. *Journal of Behavioral Medicine, 19*(3), 203–220.

Gilbert, A. N., & Wysocki, C. J. (1987). The smell survey results. *National Geographic, 172,* 514–525.

Gilbert, D. T., & Malone, P. S. (1995). The correspondence bias. *Psychological Bulletin, 117,* 21–38.

Gilbert, D. T., & Silvera, D. H. (1996). Overhelping. *Journal of Personality and Social Psychology, 70,* 678–690.

Gill, J. (1985, August, 22). Czechpoints. *Time Out,* p. 15.

Gilligan, C. F. (1982). *In a different voice.* Cambridge, MA: Harvard University Press.

Gilovich, T. (1990). Differential construal and the false consensus effect. *Journal of Personality and Social Psychology, 59,* 623–634.

Gilovich, T., & Medvec, V. H. (1994). The temporal pattern to the experience of regret. *Journal of Personality and Social Psychology, 67,* 357–365.

Giordani, B., Berent, S., Boivin, M. J., & Penney, J. B. (1995). Longitudinal neuropsychological and genetic linkage analysis of persons at risk for Huntington's disease. *Archives of Neurology, 52,* 59–64.

Giovannucci, E., Colditz, G. A., Stampfer, M. J., Hunter, D., Rosner, B. A., Willett, W. C., & Speizer, F. E., (1994). A prospective study of cigarette smoking and risk of colorectal adenoma and colorectal cancer in U.S. women. *Journal of the National Cancer Institute, 86,* 192–199.

Gisiner, R., & Schusterman, R. J. (1992). Sequence, syntax, and semantics: Responses of a language-trained sea lion (*Zalophus californianus*) to novel sign combinations. *Journal of Comparative Psychology, 106,* 78–91.

Gist, M. E., & Mitchell, T. R. (1992). Self-efficacy: A theoretical analysis of its determinants and malleability. *Academy of Management Review, 17,* 183–211.

Gladue, B. A. (1994). The biopsychology of sexual orientation. *Current Directions in Psychological Science, 3,* 150–154.

Gladwell, M. (1996, September 30). The new age of man. *The New Yorker,* pp. 56–67.

Glick, P. (1989). Remarried families, stepfamilies, and stepchildren: A brief demographic analysis. *Family Relations, 38,* 24–27.

Gluck, M. A., & Myers, C. E. (1995). Representation and association in memory: A neurocomputational view of hippocampal function. *Current Directions in Psychological Science, 4,* 23–29.

Gobet, F., & Simon, H. A. (1996a). The roles of recognition processes and look-ahead search in time-constrained expert problem solving: Evidence from grand-master-level chess. *Psychological Science, 7,* 52–55.

Gobet, F., & Simon, H. A. (1996b). Recall of random and distorted chess positions: Implications for the theory of expertise. *Memory & Cognition, 24,* 493–503.

Godden, D., & Baddeley, A. D. (1975). Context-dependent memory in two natural environments: On land and under water. *British Journal of Psychology, 66,* 325–331.

Goeders, N. E., Lane, J. D., & Smith, J. E. (1984). Self-administration of methionine enkephalin into the nucleus accumbens. *Pharmacology, Biochemistry and Behavior, 20,* 451–455.

Goethals, G. R., (1986). Fabricating and ignoring social reality: Self-serving estimates of consensus. In J. Olson, C. P. Herman, & N. P. Zanna (Eds.), *Relative deprivation and social comparison: The Ontario symposium on social cognition IV.* Hillsdale, NJ: Erlbaum.

Goethals, G. R., Cooper, J., & Naficy, A. (1979). Role of foreseen, foreseeable, and unforeseeable behavioral consequences in the arousal of cognitive dissonance. *Journal of Personality and Social Psychology, 37,* 1179–1185.

Goldberg, L. R., & Saucier, G. (1995). So what do you propose we use instead? A reply to Block. *Psychological Bulletin, 117,* 221–225.

Goldenring, J. M., & Purtell, E. (1984). Knowledge of testicular cancer risk and need for self-examination in college students: A call for equal time for men in teaching early cancer detection techniques. *Pediatrics, 74,* 1093–1096.

Goldfried, M. R., & Castonguay, L. C. (1992). The future of psychotherapy integration. *Psychotherapy, 29,* 4–10.

Goleman, D. (1995). *Emotional intelligence.* New York: Bantam.

Goodman, G. S., Hirschman, J. E., Hepps, D., & Rudy, L. (1991). Children's memory for stressful events. *Merrill-Palmer Quarterly, 37,* 109–158.

Gopnik, A. (1996). The post-Piaget era. *Psychological Science, 7,* 221–225.

Gordon, P. (1990). Learnability and feedback: A commentary on Bohannon and Stanowicz. *Developmental Psychology, 26,* 215–218.

Gordon, W. C. (1989). *Learning and memory.* Belmont, CA: Brooks/Cole Publishing Company.

Gotlieb, I. H., & McCabe, S. B. (1990). Marriage and psychopathology. In F. F. Fincham & T. N. Brabury (Eds.), *The psychology of marriage* (pp. 226–257). New York: Guilford Press.

Gotlieb, I. H., & Whiffen, V. E. (1991). The interpersonal context of depression: Implications for theory and research. In W. H. Jones & D. Perlman (Eds.), *Advances in personal relationships* (Vol. 3, pp. 177–206). London: Jessica Kingsley.

Gottesman, I. I. (1993). Origins of schizophrenia: Past as a prologue. In R. Plomin & G. E. McClearn (Eds.), *Nature, nurture, and psychology* (pp. 2231–2344). Washington, DC: American Psychological Association.

Gottfried, A. W. (Ed.). (1984). *Home environment and early cognitive development.* San Francisco: Academic.

Gottman, J. (1993). *What predicts divorce: The relationsip between marital processes and marital outcomes.* Hillsdale, NJ: Erlbaum.

Gould, R. L. (1978). *Transformations, growth, and change in adult life.* New York: Simon & Schuster.

Graf, P., & Schachter, D. L. (1985). Implicit and explicit memory for new associations in normal and amnesic subjects. *Journal of Experimental Psychology: Learning, Memory, and Cognition, 11,* 501–518.

Graham, C. H., & Hsia, Y. (1958). Color defect and color theory. *Science, 127,* 675–682.

Graham, S. (1983). Diet and cancer: Epidemiologic aspects. *Review of Cancer Epidemiology, 2,* 2–45.

Graham, S. (1992). "Most of the subjects were white and middle class." Trends in published research on African Americans in selected APA journals, 1970–1989. *American Psychologist, 47,* 629–639.

Graham, S., & Folkes, V. (Eds.). (1990). *Attribution theory: Applications to achievement, mental health, and interpersonal conflict.* Hillsdale, NJ: Erlbaum.

Granchrow, J. R., Steiner, J. E., & Daher, M. (1983). Neonatal facial expressions in response to different qualities and intensities of gustatory stimuli. *Infant Behavior and Development, 6,* 189–200.

Graziano, W. G., Jensen-Campbell, L. A., Shebilske, L. J., & Lundgren, S. R. (1993). Social influence, sex differences, and judgments of beauty: Putting the interpersonal back in interpersonal attraction. *Journal of Personality and Social Psychology, 65,* 522–531.

Green, J. P., & Lynn, S. J. (1995). Hypnosis, dissociation, and simultaneous task performance. *Journal of Personality and Social Psychology, 69,* 728–735.

Green, L., Fry, A. F., & Myerson, J. (1994). Discounting of delayed rewards: A life-span comparison. *Psychological Science, 5,* 33–36.

Green, R., & Fleming, D. T. (1990). Transsexual surgery follow-up: Status in the 1990s. *Annual Review of Sex Research, 1,* 163–174.

Greenberg, J. (1993a). The social side of fairness: Interpersonal and informational classes of organizational justice. In R. Cropanzano (Ed.), *Justice in the workplace* (pp. 79–103). Hillsdale, NJ: Erlbaum.

Greenberg, J. (1993b). Stealing in the name of justice: Informational and interpersonal moderators of theft reactions to underpayment inequity. *Organizational Behavior and Human Decision Processes, 54,* 81–103.

Greenberg, J., & Baron, R. A. (1997). *Behavior in organizations* (6th ed). Englewood Cliffs, NJ: Prentice-Hall.

Greenberg, J., & Scott, K. S. (1995). Why do workers bite the hands that feed them? Employee theft as a social exchange process. In B. M. Staw & L. L. Cummings (Eds.), *Research in organizational behavior* (Vol. 18). Greenwich, CT: JAI Press.

Greenberg, J., Pyszczynski, T., & Solomon, S. (1982). The self-serving attributional bias: Beyond self-presentation. *Journal of Experimental Social Psychology, 18,* 56–67.

Greene, B. F., Winett, R. A., Van Houten, R., Geller, E. S., & Iwata, B. A. (1987). Behavior analysis in the community: Readings from the *Journal of Applied Behavior Analysis.* Lawrence, KS: University of Kansas.

Greenwald, A. G. (1992). New look 3: Unconscious cognition reclaimed. *American Psychologist, 47,* 766–779.

Greenwald, A. G., & Pratkanis, A. R. (1988). On the use of "theory" and usefulness of theory. *Psychological Review, 95,* 575–579.

Greenwald, A. G., Spangenberg, E. R., Pratkanis, A. R., & Eskenazi, J. (1991). Double-blind tests of subliminal self-help audiotapes. *Psychological Science, 2,* 119–122.

Greist-Bousquet, S., Watson, M., & Schiffman, H. R. (1990). *An examination of illusion decrement with inspection of wings-in and wings-out Müller-Lyer figures: The role of corrective and contextual information perception.* New York: Wiley.

Griffin, R. W., & McMahan, G. C. (1995). Motivation through job design. In J. Greenberg (Ed.), *Organizational behavior: The state of the science* (pp. 23–44). Hillsdale, NJ: Erlbaum.

Grillon, C., Courchesne, E., Ameli, R., Geyer, M. A., & Braff, D. L. (1990). Increased distractibility in schizophrenic patients: Electrophysiologic and behavioral evidence. *Archives of General Psychiatry, 47,* 171–179.

Grilly, D. M. (1989). *Drugs and human behavior.* Boston: Allyn and Bacon.

Grilo, C. M., & Pogue-Geile, M. F. (1991). The nature of environmental influences on weight and obesity: A behavior genetic analysis. *Psychological Bulletin, 110,* 520–537.

Grissmer, D. W., Kirby, S. N., Berends, M., & Willamson, S. (1994). *Student achievement and the changing American family.* Santa Monica, CA: RAND Corporation.

Gross. J. J., & Levenson, R. W. (1997). Hiding feelings: The acute effects of inhibiting negative and positive emotion. *Journal of Abnormal Psychology, 106,* 95–103.

Gruneberg, M. M., Morris, P., & Sykes, R. N. (1988). *Practical aspects of memory: Current research and issues* (Vols. 1 & 2). Chichester, England: John Wiley & Sons.

Guilford, J. P. (1950). Creativity. *American Psychologist, 5,* 444–454.

Gully, K. J., & Dengerink, H. A. (1983). The dyadic interaction of persons with violent and nonviolent histories. *Aggressive Behavior, 9,* 13–20.

Gur, R. E., & Pearlson, G. D. (1993). Neuroimaging in schizophrenia research. In *Schizophrenia 1993: Special report* (pp. 163–179). Washington, DC: National Institute of Mental Health, Schizophrenia Research Board.

Gurman, A. S., Kniskern, D. P., & Pinsof, W. M. (1986). Research on marital and family therapies. In S. L. Garfield & A. E. Bergin (Eds.), *Handbook of psychotherapy and behavior change* (pp. 565–626). New York: Wiley.

Gustavson, C. R., Garcia, J., Hawkins, W. G., & Rusiniak, K. W. (1974). Coyote predation control by aversive conditioning. *Science, 184,* 581–583.

Gutek, B. A., & Winter, S. J. (1992). Consistency of job satisfaction across situations: Fact or framing artifice? *Journal of Vocational Behavior, 41,* 61–78.

Guthrie, J. P., Ash, R. A., & Bendapudi, V. (1995). Additional validity evidence for a measure of Morningness. *Journal of Applied Psychology, 80,* 186–190.

Hackett, R. D., Boycio, P., & Hausdorf, P. A. (1994). Further assessments of Meyer and Allen's (1991) three-component model of organizational commitment. *Journal of Applied Psychology 79,* 15–23.

Hahn, G., Charlin, V. L., Sussman, S., Dent, C. W., Manzi, J., Stacy, A. W., Flay, B., Hansen, W. B., & Burton, D. (1990). Adolescents' first and most recent use situations of smokeless tobacco and cigarettes: Similarities and differences. *Addictive Behaviors, 15,* 439–448.

Haier, R. J. (1993). Cerebral glucose metabolism and intelligence. In P. A. Vernon (Ed.), *Biological approaches to the study of human intelligence* (pp. 317–332). Norwood, NJ: Ablex.

Hales, D. (1996, August 18). How teenagers see things. *Parade,* pp. 4, 5.

Hall, J. A., & Veccia, E. M. (1991). More "touching" observations: New insights on men, women, and interpersonal touch. *Journal of Personality and Social Psychology, 59,* 1155–1162.

Hamer, D. H., Hu, S., Magnuson, V. L., Hu, N., & Pattatucci, A. J. (1993). A linkage between DNA markers on the X chromosome and male sexual orientation. *Science, 261,* 321–327.

Hamilton, G. V. (1978). Obedience and responsibility: A jury simulation. *Journal of Personality and Social Psychology, 36,* 126–146.

Hammond, W. R., & Yung, B. (1993). Psychology's role in the public health response to assaultive violence among young African-American men. *American Psychologist, 48,* 142–154.

Hampson, E., Rovet, J. F., & Altmann, D. (1994, August). *Spatial reasoning in children with congenital adrenal hyperplasia due to 21–hydroxylase deficiency.* Paper presented at the meeting of the International Society of Psychoneuroendocrinology, Seattle, WA.

Hanisch, K. A. (1995). Behavioral families and multiple causes: Matching the complexity of responses to the complexity of antecedents. *Current Directions in Psychological Science, 4,* 156–161.

Hans, V. P. (1992). Obedience, justice, and the law: PS reviews recent contributions to a field ripe for new research efforts by psychological scientists. *Psychological Science, 3,* 218–221.

Harder, J. W. (1992). Play for pay: Effects of inequity in a pay-for-performance context. *Administrative Science Quarterly, 37,* 321–335.

Hardy, Q. (1996, July 8). Idaho county tests a new way to curb teen sex: Prosecute. *Wall Street Journal,* pp. A1, A4.

Harlow, H. F., & Harlow, M. H. (1966). Learning to love. *American Scientist, 54,* 244–272.

Harrigan, J. A., Luci, K. S., Kay, D., McLaney, A., & Rosenthal, R. (1991). Effects of expresser role and type of self-touching on observers' perceptions. *Journal of Applied Social Psychology, 21,* 585–609.

Harris Poll. (1995). Reported in "America gets some heavy news," *Associated Press,* March 23, 1996.

Harris, J., & Wilkins, A. J. (1982). Remembering to do things: A theoretical framework and illustrative experiment. *Human Learning, 1,* 1–14.

Harris, P. L. (1991). The work of the imagination. In A. Whiten (Ed.), *Natural theories of mind* (pp. 283–304). Oxford: Blackwell.

Harris, P. R. (1979, March). Cultural awareness training for human resource development. *Training and Development Journal,* 64–74.

Harrison, J. K. (1992). Individual and combined effects of behavior modeling and the cultural assimilator in cross-cultural management training. *Journal of Applied Psychology, 77,* 952–962.

Harrison, R. V. (1985). The person-environment fit model and the study of job stress. In T. A. Beehr & R. S. Bhagat (Eds.), *Human stress and cognition in organizations* (pp. 23–55). New York: Wiley.

Hart, D., Stinson, C., Field, N., Ewert, M., & Horowitz, M. (1995). A semantic space approach to representations of self and other in pathological grief: A case study. *Psychological Science, 6,* 96–100.

Hartel, C. E. (1993). Rating format research revisited: Format effectiveness and acceptability depend on rater characteristics. *Journal of Applied Psychology, 78,* 212–217.

Hartmann, E. L. (1973). *The functions of sleep.* New Haven: Yale University Press.

Hassett, J. (1978). Sex and smell. *Psychology Today, 11,* 40, 42, 45.

Hatch, T. (1990). Social intelligence in young children. Paper presented at the meeting of the American Psychological Association.

Hatfield, E. (1988). Passionate and companionate love. In R. J. Sternberg & M. I. Barnes (Eds.), *The psychology of love* (pp. 191–217). New Haven, CT: Yale University Press.

Hatfield, E., & Rapson, R. L. (1993). *Love, sex, and intimacy: Their psychology, biology, and history.* New York: HarperCollins.

Hatfield, E., & Sprecher, S. (1986). *Mirror, mirror . . . The importance of looks in everyday life.* Albany, NY: SUNY Press.

Hauenstein, N. A. (1992). An information-processing approach to leniency in performance judgments. *Journal of Applied Psychology, 77,* 485–493.

Haugaard, J. J., Repucci, N. D., Laurd, J., & Nauful, T. (1991). Children's definitions of the truth and their competency as witnesses in legal proceedings. *Law and Human Behavior, 15,* 253–273.

Hawkins, J. D., Catalano, R. F., & Miller, J. Y. (1992). Risk and protective factors for alcohol and other drug problems in adolescence and early adulthood: Implications for substance abuse prevention. *Psychological Bulletin, 112,* 64–105.

Hawkins, S. A., & Hastie, R. (1990). Hindsight: Biased judgments of past events after the outcomes are known. *Psychological Bulletin, 107,* 311–327.

Hayes, S. C., & Heiby, E. (1996). Psychology's drug problem: Do we need a fix or should we just say no? *American Psychologist, 51,* 198–206.

Hayward, P., Wardle, J., & Higgitt, A. (1989). Benzodiazepine research: Current findings and practical consequences. *British Journal of Psychiatry, 28,* 307–327.

Hazan, C., & Shaver, P. R. (1990). Love and work: An attachment-theoretical perspective. *Journal of Personality and Social Psychology, 59,* 270–280.

Hazelrigg, M. D., Cooper, H. M., & Borduin, C. M. (1987). Evaluating the effectiveness of family therapies: An integrative review and analysis. *Psychological Bulletin, 101,* 428–442.

Heatherton, T. F., Mahamedi, F., Striepe, M., & Field, A. E. (1997). A 10–year longitudinal study of body weight, dieting, and eating disorder symptoms. *Journal of Abnormal Psychology, 106,* 117–125.

Heatherton, T., & Weinberger, J. L. (1994). *Can personality change?* Washington, DC: American Psychological Association.

Hecaen, H., & Angelergues, R. (1964). Localization of symptoms in aphasia. In A. V. S. de Reuck & M. O'Connor (Eds.), *CIBA foundation symposium on the disorders of language* (pp. 222–256). London: Churchill Press.

Hecht, M. L., Marston, P. J., & Larkey, L. K. (1994). Love ways and relationship quality in heterosexual relationships. *Journal of Social and Personal Relationships, 11,* 25–43.

Heckhausen, J. (1997). Developmental regulation across adulthood: Primary and secondary control of age-related challenges. *Developmental Psychology, 33,* 176–187.

Heckhausen, J., & Schulz, R. (1995). A life-span theory of control. *Psychological Review, 102,* 284–304.

Hedge, A., McCrobie, D., Morimoto, S., Rodriquez, S., & Land, B. (1996, January). Toward pain-free computing. *Ergonomics in Design,* pp. 4–10.

Heilman, M. E., Block, C. J., & Lucas, A. (1992). Presumed incompetent? Stigmatization and affirmative action efforts. *Journal of Applied Psychology, 77,* 536–544.

Heinrichs, R. W. (1993). Schizophrenia and the brain: Conditions for a neuropsychology of madness. *American Psychologist, 48,* 221–233.

Helen, D. (1996). The relationship between alcohol consumption and earnings. *Journal of Studies on Alcohol, 57,* 536–542.

Heller, M. A., Calcaterra, J. A., Burson, L. L., & Tyler, L. A. (1996). Tactual picture identification by blind and sighted people: Effects of providing categorical information. *Perception & Psychophysics, 38,* 310–232.

Hellige, J. B. (1993). Unity of thought and action: Varieties of interaction between the left and right cerebral hemispheres. *Current Directions in Psychological Sciences, 2,* 21–25.

Hellmich, N. (1995, June 9). Optimism often survives spinal cord injuries. *USA Today,* p. 40.

Helms, J. E. (1989). Oral and literate traditions among black Americans living in poverty. *American Psychologist, 44,* 367–373.

Helms, J. E. (1992). Why is there no study of cultural equivalence in standardized cognitive ability testing? *American Psychologist, 47,* 1083–1101.

Hendrick, C. (Ed.). (1989). *Close relationships.* Newbury Park, CA: Sage.

Hendrick, C., & Hendrick S. S. (1993). Lovers as friends. *Journal of Social and Personal Relationships, 10,* 459–466.

Hendricks, C. F. (1992). *The rightsizing remedy.* Homewood, IL: Business One Irwin.

Henggler, S. W., Melton, G. B., & Smith, L. A. (1992). Family preservation using multisystematic therapy: An effective alternative to incarcerating juvenile offenders. *Journal of Consulting and Clinical Psychology, 60,* 953–961.

Henker, B., & Whalen, C. K. (1989). Hyperactivity and attention deficits. *American Psychologist, 44,* 216–223.

Hennig, P., & Knowles, A. (1990). Factors influencing women over 40 years to take precautions against cervical cancer. *Journal of Applied Social Psychology, 20,* 1612–1621.

Henriques, J. B., & Davidson, R. J. (1990). Regional brain electrical asymmetries discriminate between previously depressed and healthy control subjects. *Journal of Abnormal Psychology, 99,* 22–31.

Henriques, J. B., & Davidson, R. J. (1991). Left frontal hypoactivation in depression. *Journal of Abnormal Psychology, 100,* 535–545.

Herdt, G. H., & Davidson, J. (1988). The Sambia "Turnim-Man": Sociocultural and clinical aspects of gender formation in male pseudohermaphrodites with 5–alpha-reductase deficiency in Papua New Guinea. *Archives of Sexual Behavior, 17,* 33–56.

Herman, L. M., Kuczaj, S. A., & Holder, M. D. (1993). Responses to anomalous gestural sequences by a language-trained dolphin: Evidence for processing of semantic relations and syntactic information. *Journal of Experimental Psychology: General, 122,* 184–194.

Herman, L. M., Richards, D. G., & Wolz, J. P. (1984). Comprehension of sentences by bottlenosed dolphins. *Cognition, 16,* 129–219.

Hermann, C., Kim, M., & Blanchard, E. B. (1995). Behavioral and prophylactic pharmacological intervention studies of pediatric migraine: An exploratory meta-analysis. *Pain, 60,* 239–255.

Herrnstein, R. J. (1961). Relative and absolute strength of response as a function of frequency of reinforcement. *Journal of Experimental Analysis of the Behavior 4,* 267–272.

Herrnstein, R. J. (1970). On the law of effect. *Journal of the Experimental Analysis of Behavior, 13,* 243–266.

Herrnstein, R. J., & Murray, C. (1994). *The bell curve.* New York: The Free Press.

Herrnstein, R. J., Nickerson, R. S., deSanchez, M., & Swets, J. A. (1986). Teaching thinking skills. *American Psychologist, 41,* 1279–1289.

Hershberger, S. L., Lichtenstein, P., & Knox, S. S. (1994). Genetic and environmental influences on perceptions of organizational climate. *Journal of Applied Psychology, 79,* 24–33.

Hetzel, B., & McMichael, T. (1987). *The LS factor: Lifestyle and health.* Ringwood, Victoria: Penguin.

Hewstone, M., Bond, M. H., & Wan, K. C. (1983). Social factors and social attributions: The explanation of intergroup differences in Hong Kong. *Social Cognition, 2,* 142–157.

Higgins, A. T., & Turnure, J. E. (1984). Distractibility and concentration of attention in children's development. *Child Development, 55,* 1799–1810.

Hilgard, E. R. (1979). Divided consciousness in hypnosis: Implications of the hidden observer. In E. Fromm & R. E. Shor (Eds.), *Hypnosis: Developments in research and new perspectives* (2nd ed). Chicago: Aldine.

Hilgard, E. R. (1986). *Divided consciouseness: Multiple controls in human thought and action* (2nd ed.). New York: Wiley.

Hilgard, E. R. (1993). Dissociation and theories of hypnosis. In E. Fromm & M. R. Nash (Eds.), *Contemporary hypnosis research* (pp. 69–101). New York: Guilford Press.

Hill, D., & Iverson, D. (1997). World conference for Cancer Organisations, March 3–7, 1996, Melbourne, Australia. *Cancer, 79*(3), 619–625.

Hilton, D. J. (1995). The social context of reasoning: Conversational inference and rational judgment. *Psychological Bulletin, 118,* 248–271.

Hilton, J. L., Klein, J. G., & von Hippel, W. (1991). Attention allocation and impression formation. *Personality and Social Psychology Bulletin, 17,* 548–559.

Hines, M., Chiu, L., McAdams, L. A., Bentler, P. M., & Lipcamon, J. (1992). Cognition and the corpus callosum: Verbal fluency, visuospatial ability, and language lateralization related to midsagittal surface areas of callosal subregions. *Behavioral Neuroscience, 106,* 3–14.

Hingson, R., Strunin, L., Berlin, B., & Heeren, T. (1990). Beliefs about AIDS, use of alcohol and drugs, and unprotected sex among Massachusetts adolescents. *American Journal of Public Health, 80,* 295–299.

Hirsch, A. R. (1992). Nostalgia: A neuropsychiatric understanding. *Advances in Consumer Research, 19,* 390–395.

Hobfoll, S. E., Jackson, A. P., Lavin, J., Britton, P. J., & Shepherd, J. B. (1994). Reducing inner-city women's AIDS risk activities: A study of single, pregnant women. *Health Psychology, 13,* 397–403.

Hobson, J. A. (1988). *The dreaming brain.* New York: Basic Books.

Hoffman, J. E., & Subramaniam, B. (1995). The role of visual attention in saccadic eye movements. *Perception & Psychophysics, 57,* 787–795.

Hogan, R., Hogan, J., & Roberts, B. W. (1996). Personality measurement and employment decisions: Questions and answers. *American Psychologist, 51,* 469–477.

Holland, J. L. (1973). *Making vocational choices: A theory of careers.* Englewood Cliffs, NJ: Prentice-Hall.

Hollon, S. D., & Beck, A. T. (1994). Cognitive and cognitive-behavioral therapies. In A. E. Bergin & S. L. Garfield (Eds.), *Handbook of psychotherapy and behavior change* (4th ed.). New York: Wiley.

Hollon, S. D., DeRubeis, R. J., & Evans, M. D. (1987). Causal mediation of change in treatment for depression: Discriminating between nonspecificity and noncausality. *Psychological Bulletin, 102,* 139–149.

Hollon, S. D., Shelton, R. C., & Loosen, P. T. (1991). Cognitive therapy and pharmacotherapy for depression. *Journal of Consulting and Clinical Psychology, 59,* 88–99.

Holm, A., & Dodd, B. (1996). The effect of first written language on the acquisition of English literacy. *Cognition, 59,* 119–147.

Holmes, D. (1990). The evidence for repression: An examination of sixty years of research. In J. Singer (Ed.), *Repression and dissociation: Implications for personality theory, psychopathology, and health* (pp. 85–102). Chicago: University of Chicago Press.

Holmes, T. H., & Masuda, M. (1974). Life change and illness susceptibility. In B. S. Dohrenwend and B. P. Dohrenwend (Eds.), *Stressful life events: Their nature and effects.* New York: Wiley.

Holmes, T. H., & Rahe, R. H. (1967). The social readjustment rating scale. *Journal of Psychosomatic Research, 11,* 213–218.

Holstein, C. B. (1976). Irreversible, stepwise sequence in the development of moral judgment: A longitudinal study of males and females. *Child Development, 47,* 51–61.

Holwijn, M., & Lotens, W. A. (1992). The influence of backpack design on physical performance. *Ergonomics, 35,* 149–157.

Honig, W. K., & Staddon, J. E. R. (Eds.). (1977). *Handbook of operant behavior.* Englewood Cliffs, NJ: Prentice-Hall.

Honig, W. K., & Urcuioli, P. J. (1981). The legacy of Guttman and Kalish: Twenty-five years of research on stimulus generalization. *Journal of the Experimental Analysis of Behavior, 36,* 405–445.

Honts, C. R. (1994). Psychophysiological detection of deception. *Current Direction in Psychological Science, 3,* 77–82.

Hoppe, R. B. (1988). In search of a phenomenon: Research in parapsychology. *Contemporary Psychology, 33,* 129–130.

Hoptman, M. J., & Davidson, R. J. (1994). How and why do the two cerebral hemispheres interact? *Psychological Bulletin, 116,* 195–219.

Horgan, C. (1993). *Substance abuse: The nation's number one health problem: Key indicators for policy.* Princeton, NJ: Robert Wood Johnson Foundation.

Hornstein, G. A. (1992). The return of the repressed: Psychology's problematic relations with psychoanalysis, 1909–1960. *American Psychologist, 47,* 254–263.

Horvath, J. A., Forsythe, G. B., Sweeney, P. J., McNally, J. A., Wattendorf, J. A., Williams, W. M., & Sternberg, R. J. (in press). *Tacit knowledge in military leadership: Evidence from officer interviews* (Technical Report). Alexandria, VA: U.S. Army Research Institute for the Behavioral and Social Sciences.

Houfman, L. G., House, M., & Ryan, J. B. (1981). Dynamic visual acuity: A review. *Journal of the American Optometric Association, 52,* 883–887.

House, R. J. (1977). A theory of charismatic leadership. In J. G. Hunt & L. L. Larson (Eds.), *Leadership: The cutting edge* (pp. 189–207). Carbondale, IL: Southern Illinois University Press.

House, R. J., & Podsakoff, P. M. (1994). Leadership effectiveness: Past perspectives and future directions for research. In J. Greenberg (Ed.), *Organizational behavior: The state of the sceince* (pp. 45–82). Hillsdale, NJ: Erlbaum.

House, R. J., Spangler, W. D., & Woycke, J. (1991). Personality and charisma in the U.S. presidency: A psychological theory of leader effectiveness. *Administrative Science Quarterly, 36,* 263–296.

Hovland, C. I., & Weiss, W. (1951). The influence of source credibility on communication effectiveness. *Public Opinion Quarterly, 1,* 635–650.

Hovland, C., Janis, I. L., & Kelley, H. H. (1953). *Communication and Persuasion: Psychological studies of one on one.* New Haven, CT: Yale University Press.

Howard, K. I., Kopta, S. M., Krause, M. S., & Orlinsky, D. E. (1986). The dose-effect relationship in psychotherapy. *American Psychologist, 41,* 159–164.

Howe, M. L., & Courage, M. L. (1993). On resolving the enigma of infantile amnesia. *Psychological Bulletin, 113,* 305–326.

Howell, J. M. & Frost, P. J. (1989). A laboratory study of charismatic leadership. *Organizational Behavior and Human Decision Processes, 43,* 243–269.

Howell, J. M., & Avolio, B. J. (1992). The ethics of charismatic leadership: Submission or liberation? *Academy of Management Executive, 6,* 43–54.

Hubbell, C. L., & Reid, L. D. (1995). Antagonism at delta opioid receptors blocks cocaine's, but not morphine's, enhancement of responding for intracranial stimulation. *Experimental and Clinical Psychopharmacology, 3,* 123–128.

Hubel, D. H., & Wiesel, T. N. (1979). Brain mechanisms of vision. *Scientific American, 241,* 150–162.

Huesmann, L. R. (Ed.). (1994). *Aggressive behavior: Current perspectives.* New York: Plenum.

Hughes, J. R., Smith, T. W., Kosterlitz, H. W., Fothergill, L. A., Morgan, B. A., & Morris, H. R. (1975). Identification of two related pentapeptides from the brain with potent opiate agonist activity. *Nature, 258,* 577–581.

Hulin, C. I. (1991). Adaptation, persistence, and commitment in organizations. In M. D. Dunnette & L. M. Hough (Eds.), *Handbook of industrial and organizational psychology* (2nd ed., Vol. 2, pp. 445–506). Palo Alto, CA: Consulting Psychologists Press.

Hulse, S. H. (1993). The present status of animal cognition: An introduction. *Psychological Science, 4,* 154–155.

Hultsch, D. F., & Dixon, R. A. (1990). Learning and memory in aging. In J. E. Birren & K. W. Schaie (Eds.), *Handbook of the psychology of aging* (3rd ed., pp. 359–374). San Diego: Academic Press.

Humbaugh, K., & Garrett, J. (1974). Sensation seeking among skydivers. *Perceptual and Motor Skills, 38,* 103–111.

Hummell, J. E. (1994). Reference frames and relations in computational models of object recognition. *Current Directions in Psychological Science, 3,* 111–116.

Hura, S. L., & Echols, C. H. (1996). The role of stress and articulatory difficulty in children's early productions. *Developmental Psychology, 32,* 165–176.

Hurvich, L. M. (1981). *Color vision.* Sunderland, MA: Sinauer Associates.

Husband, A. J., Lin, W., Madsen, G., & King, M. G. (1993). A conditioning model for immunostimulation: Enhancement of the antibody response to ovalbumin by behavioral conditioning in rats. In A. J. Husband (Ed.), *Psychoimmunology: CNS-Immune Interactions* (pp. 139–147). Boca Raton, FL: CRC Press.

Hwang, K. (1986). Behavior of Swedish primary and secondary caretaking fathers in relation to mother's presence. *Developmental Psychology, 22,* 739–751.

Hyde, J. S., & Plant, E. A. (1995). Magnitude of psychological gender differences: Another side to the story. *American Psychologist, 3,* 159–161.

Hyde, J. S., Fennema, E., & Lamon, S. J. (1990). Gender differences in mathematics performance: A meta-analysis. *Psychological Bulletin, 107,* 130–155.

Hyman, R. (1994). Anomaly or artifact? Comments on Bem and Honorton. *Psychological Bulletin, 115,* 19–24.

Hymowitz, C. (1995, December 21). High anxiety: In the name of Freud, why are psychiatrists complaining so much? *Wall Street Journal,* pp. A1, A6.

Ijzendoorn, M. H. (1995). Adult attachment representations, parental responsiveness, and infant attachment: A meta-analysis on the predictive validity of the adult attachment interview. *Psychological Bulletin, 117,* 387–403.

Inglehart, R. (1990). *Culture shift in advanced industrial society.* Princeton, NJ: Princeton University Press.

Intons-Peterson, M. J., & Roskos-Ewoldsen, B. (1988). Sensory/perceptual qualities of images. Paper presented at the 29th annual meeting of the Psychonomics Society, Chicago.

Isabella, R. (1993). Origins of attachment: Maternal interactive behavior across the first year. *Child Development, 64,* 605–621.

Isen, A. M. (1987). Positive affect, cognitive processes, and social behavior. In L. Berkowitz (Ed.), *Advances in experimental social psychology* (Vol. 20, pp. 203–253). New York: Academic Press.

Isen, A. M. (1993). Positive affect and decision making. In M. Lewis & J. M. Haviland (Eds.), *Handbook of emotion* (pp. 216–277). New York: Guilford Press.

Isen, A. M., & Baron, R. A. (1991). Positive affect and organizational behavior. In B. M. Staw & L. L. Cummings (Eds.), *Research in organizational behavior* (Vol. 14, pp. 1–48). Greenwich, CT: JAI Press.

Ittelson, W. H. (1996). Visual perception of markings. *Psychonomic Bulletin & Review, 3,* 171–187.

Iwahashi, M. (1992). Scents and science. *Vogue,* pp. 212–214.

Izard, C. E. (1992). *Human emotions* (2nd ed.). New York: Plenum.

Izard, C. E. (1992). *The psychology of emotion.* New York: Plenum.

Izard, C. E., Hembree, E. A., & Huebner, R. R. (1987). Infants' emotion expressions to acute pain. *Developmental Psychology, 23,* 105–113.

Izard, C. E., Huebner, R. R., Risser, D., McGinnes, G., & Dougherty, L. (1980). The young infant's ability to produce discrete emotion expressions. *Developmental Psychology, 16,* 132–140.

Jacobson, S., Fein, G., Jacobson, J., Schwartz, P., & Dowler, J. (1984). Neonatal correlates of prenatal exposure to smoking, caffeine, and alcohol. *Infant Behavior and Development, 7,* 253–265.

James, W. J. (1890). *Principles of psychology.* New York: Holt.

Jameson, D., & Hurvich, L. M. (1989). Essay concerning color constancy. *Annual Review of Psychology, 40,* 1–22.

Jamieson, D. W., Lydon, J. E., & Zanna, M. P. (1987). Attitude and activity preference similarity: Different bases of interpersonal attraction for low and high self-monitors. *Journal of Personality and Social Psychology, 53,* 1052–1060.

Jarvinen, D. W., & Nicholls, J. G. (1996). Adolescents, social goals, beliefs about the causes of social success, and satisfaction in peer relations. *Developmental Psychology, 32,* 434–441.

Jefferson, D. J. (1993, August 12). Dr. Brown treats what ails the rides at amusement parks. *The Wall Street Journal,* p. 1.

Jemmott, J. B., III, & Magloire, K. (1988). Academic stress, social support, and secretory immunoglobulin A. *Journal of Personality and Social Psychology, 55,* 803–810.

Jencks, D. (1972). *Inequality: A reassessment of the effect of family and school in America.* New York: Basic Books.

Jenike, M. A., Baer, L., Ballantine, H. T., Martuza, R. L., Tynes, S., Giriunas, I., Buttolph, M. L., & Cassem, N. H. (1991). Cingulotomy for refractory obsessive compulsive disorder: A long-term follow-up of 33 cases. *Archives of General Psychiatry, 48,* 548–557.

Jenkins, C. D., Zyzanski, S. J., & Rosenman, R. H. (1979). *Jenkins Activity Survey.* Cleveland, OH: Psychological Corp.

Jenkins, J. G., & Dallenbach, K. M. (1924). Obliviscence during sleep and waking. *American Journal of Psychology, 35,* 605–612.

Jessor, R. (1993). Successful adolescent development among youth in high-risk settings. *American Psychologist, 48,* 117–126.

Jessup, J. M., McGinnis, L. S., Steel, G. D., Menck, H. R., & Winchester, D. P. (1996). The National Cancer database report on colon cancer. *Cancer, 88*(4), 918–926.

Jex, S. M., Cvetanovski, J., & Allen, S. J. (1994). Self-esteem as a moderator of the impact of unemployment. *Journal of Social Behavior and Personality, 9,* 69–80.

Johns, G., Xie, J. L., & Fang, Y. (1992). Mediating and moderating effects in job design. *Journal of Management, 18,* 657–676.

Johnson, B. T., & Eagly, A. H. (1989). Effects of involvement on persuasion: A meta-analysis. *Psychological Bulletin, 106,* 290–314.

Johnson, D. F., & Pittenger, J. B. (1984). Attribution, the attractiveness stereotypes, and the elderly. *Developmental Psychology, 20,* 1168–1172.

Johnson, E. J. (1985). Expertise and decision under uncertainty: Performance and process. In M. Chi, R. Glasse, & M. Farr (Eds.), *The nature of expertise.* Columbus, OH: National Center for Research in Vocational Education.

Johnson, H. M. (1994). Processes of successful intentional forgetting. *Psychological Bulletin, 116,* 274–292.

Johnson-Laird, P. N., Byrne, R. M. J., Tabossi, P. (1989). Reasoning by model: The case of multiple quantification. *Psychological Review, 96,* 658–673.

Johnston, J. C., McCann, R. S., & Remington, R. W. (1995). Chronometric evidence for two types of attention. *Psychological Science, 6,* 365–369.

Johnston, M. W., & Bell, A. P. (1995). Romantic emotional attachment: Additional factors in the development of the sexual orientation of men. *Journal of Counseling and Development, 73,* 621–625.

Johnston, W., & Dark, V. (1986). Selective attention. *Annual Review of Psychology, 37,* 43–75.

Joiner, T. E., Jr. (1994). The interplay of similarity and self-verification in relationship formation. *Social Behavior and Personality, 22,* 195–200.

Joiner, T. E., Jr., Alfano, M. S., & Metalsky, G. I. (1993). When depression breeds contempt: Reassurance seeking, self-esteem, and rejection of depressed college students by their roommates. *Journal of Abnormal Psychology, 101* 165–173.

Joiner, T. E., Jr., Heatheton, T. F., Rudd, M. D., & Schmidt, N. B. (1997). Perfectionism, perceived with status, and bulimic symptoms: Two studies testing a diathesis-stress model. *Journal of Abnormal Psychology, 106,* 145–153.

Jones, J. C., & Barlow, D. H. (1990). Self-reported frequency of sexual urges, fantasies, and masturbatory fantasies in heterosexual males and females. *Archives of Sexual Behavior, 19,* 269–279.

Jones, M. (1993). Influence of self-monitoring on dating motivations. *Journal of Research in Personality, 27,* 197–206.

Jou, J., Shanteau, J., & Harris, R. J. (1996). An information processing view of framing effects: The role of causal schemes in decision making. *Memory & Cognition, 24,* 1–15.

Judd, C. M., Drake, R. A, Downing, J. W., & Krosnick, J. A. (1991). Some dynamic properties of attitude structures: context-induced response facilitation and polarization. *Journal of Personality and Social Psychology, 60,* 193–202.

Judd, C. M., Ryan, C. N., & Park, B. (1991). Accuracy in the judgment of in-group and outgroup variability. *Journal of Personality and Social Psychology, 61,* 366–379.

Julien, R. M. (1995). *A primer of drug action* (7th ed.). New York: Freeman.

Jussim, L. (1991). Interpersonal expectations and social reality: A reflection-construction model and reinterpretation of evidence. *Psychological Review, 98,* 54–73.

Just, M. A., & Carpenter, P. A. (1987). *The psychology of reading and language comprehension.* Newton, MA: Allyn and Bacon.

Kaempf, G. L., Klein, G. A., Thordsen, M. L., & Wolf, S. (1996). Decision making in complex naval command-and-control environments. *Human Factors, 38,* 220–231.

Kagan, J., & Snidman, N. (1991). Temperamental factors in human development. *American Psychologist, 46,* 856–862.

Kagan, J., Snidman, N., & Arcus, D. M. (1992). Initial reactions to unfamiliarity. *Current Directions in Psychological Science, 1,* 171–174.

Kahneman, D., & Tversky, A. (1982). Judgment under uncertainty: Heuristics and biases. In D. Kahneman, P. Slovic, & A. Tversky (Eds.), *Judgment under uncertainty: Heuristics and biases* (pp. 3–22). Cambridge, England: Cambridge University Press.

Kahnemann, D., & Miller, D. T. (1986). Norm theory: Comparing reality to its alternatives. *Psychological Review, 93,* 136–153.

Kalichman, S. (1996). Bringing our work to the community. *APA Monitor,* 33.

Kalivas, P. W., & Samson, H. H. (Eds.). (1992). *The neurobiology of drug and alcohol addiction.* Annals of the New York Academy of Sciences, Vol. 654. New York: Academy of Sciences.

Kamin, L. J. (1965). Temporal and intensity characteristics of the conditioned stimulus. In W. F. Prokasy (Ed.), *Classical conditioning: A symposium.* New York: Appleton-Century-Crofts.

Kaneda, M., Izuka, H., Ueno, H., Hiramatsu, M., Taguchi, J., & Tsukino, J. (1994, May). *Development of a drowsiness warning system.* Paper presented at the 14th International Technical Conference on the Enhanced Safety of Vehicles, Munich, Germany.

Kanner, A. D., Coyne, J. C., Schaefer, C., & Lazarus, R. S. (1981). Comparison of two modes of stress measurement: Daily hassles and uplifts versus major life events. *Journal of Behavioral Medicine, 4,* 1–39.

Kaplan, F. (May 12, 1997). It's computer checkmate for chess master. *Albany Times Union,* p. 1, 5.

Kaplan, H. I., & Sadock, B. J. (1991). *Synopsis of psychiatry: Behavioral sciences and clinical psychiatry* (6th ed.). Baltimore, MD: Williams & Wilkins.

Kaplan, R. E. (1982). The dynamics of injury in encounter groups: Power, splitting, and the mismanagement of resistance. *International Journal of Group Psychotherapy, 32,* 163–187.

Karasek, R., & Theorell, T. (1990). *Healthy work: Job stress, productivity, and the reconstruction of working life.* New York: Basic Books.

Kashima, Y., Yamaguchi, S., Kim, U., Choi, S. C., Gelfand, M. J., & Yuki, M. (1995). Culture, gender, and self: A perspective from individualism-collectivism research. *Journal of Personality and Social Psychology, 69,* 925–937.

Kassin, S. M., & Kiechel, K. L. (1996). The social psychology of false confessions: Compliance, internalization, and confabulation. *Psychological Science, 7,* 125–128.

Kaufman, A. S., & Kaufman, N. L. (1993). Kaufman adolescent and adult intelligence test. Circle Pines, MN: American Guidance.

Kaufman, A., Baron, A., & Kopp, R. E. (1966). Some effects of instructions on human operant behavior. *Psychonomic Monographs Supplement, 1,* 243–250.

Kavanagh, R. D., Zimmerberg, B., & Fein, S. (1996). (Eds). *Emotion: Interdisciplinary perspectives.* Mawhah, NJ: Erlbaum.

Kazdin, A. E. (1982). The token economy: A decade later. *Journal of Applied Behavior Analysis, 15,* 431–446.

Kazdin, A. E. (1993). Psychotherapy for children and adolescents: Current progress and future research directions. *American Psychologist, 48,* 644–657.

Keary, K., & Fitzpatrick, C. (1994). Children's disclosure of sexual abuse during formal investigation. *Child Abuse and Neglect, 18,* 543–548.

Keenan, K., & Shaw, D. (1997). Developmental and social influences on young girls' early problem behavior. *Psychological Bulletin, 121,* 95–113.

Keinan, G. (1994). Effects of stress and tolerance of ambiguity on magical thinking. *Journal of Personality and Social Psychology, 67,* 48–55.

Kelly, D. D. (1981). Disorders of sleep and consciousness. In E. Kandel & J. Schwartz (Eds.), *Principles of neural science.* New York: Elsevier-North Holland.

Kelley, H. H. (1972). Attribution in social interaction. In E. E. Jones et al. (Eds.), *Attribution: Perceiving the causes of behavior.* Morristown, NJ: General Learning Press.

Kelley, K., & Byrne, D. (1992). *Exploring human sexuality.* Englewood Cliffs, NJ: Prentice Hall.

Kelley, K., & Byrne, D. (1992). *Human sexual behavior.* Englewood Cliffs, NJ: Prentice Hall.

Kelman, H. C., & Hamilton, V. L. (1989). *Crimes of obedience.* New Haven, CT: Yale University Press.

Kelsey, F. O. (1969). Drugs and pregnancy. *Mental Retardation, 7,* 7–10.

Kendall-Tackett, K. A. (1991). Characteristics of abuse that influence when adults molested as children seek treatment. *Journal of Interpersonal Violence, 6,* 486–493.

Kendall-Tackett, K. A., Williams, L. M., & Finkelhor, D. (1993). Impact of sexual abuse on children: A review and synthesis of recent empirical studies. *Psychological Bulletin, 113,* 164–180.

Kendziora, K. T., & O'Leary, S. G. (1993). Dysfunctional parenting as a focus for prevention and treatment of child behavior problems. In T. H. Oliendick & R. J. Prinz (Eds.), *Advances in child clinical psychology* (Vol. 15). New York: Plenum.

Kenney, D. A. (1994). *Interpersonal perception: A social relations analysis.* New York: Guilford Press.

Kenrick, D. T., Groth, G. E., Trost, M. R., & Sadalla, E. K. (1993). Integrating evolutionary and social exchange perspectives on relationships: Effects of gender, self-appraisal, and involvement level on mate selection criteria. *Journal of Personality and Social Psychology, 64,* 951–969.

Kessler, C. R. (1994). Incidence of mental disorders in a non-institutionalized population. *Archives of General Psychiatry, 50,* in press.

Kessler, R. C., McGonagle, K. A., Zhao, S., Nelson, C. B., Hughes, M., Eshleman, S., Witchen, H-U., & Kendler, K. S. (1994). Lifetime and 12–month prevalence of DSM-III-R psychiatric disorders in the United States. *Archives of General Psychiatry, 5,* 8–19.

Kiecolt-Glaser, J. K., & Glaser, R. (1992). Psychoneuroimmunology: Can psychological interventions modulate immunity? *Journal of Consulting and Clinical Psychology, 60,* 569–575.

Kiecolt-Glaser, J. K., Kennedy, S., Malkoff, S., Fisher, L., Speicher, C. E., & Glaser, R. (1988). Marital discord and immunity in males. *Psychosomatic Medicine, 50,* 213–229.

Kiesler, C. A., & Kiesler, S. B. (1969). *Conformity.* Reading, MA: Addison-Wesley.

Kihlstrom, J. F. (1994). Hypnosis, delayed recall, and the principles of memory. *International Journal of Clinical and Experimental Hypnosis, 42,* 337–345.

Kihlstrom, J. F., Tataryn, D. J., & Hoyt, I. P. (1993). Dissociative disorders. In P. B. Sutker & H. E. Adams (Eds.), *Comprehensive handbook of psychopathology* (2nd ed.). New York: Plenum Press.

Kilduff, M., & Day, D. V. (1994). Do chameleons get ahead? The effects of self-monitoring on managerial careers. *Academy of Management Journal, 37,* 1047–1060.

Kilham, W., & Mann, L. (1974). Level of destructive obedience as function of transmitter and executant roles in the Milgram obedience paradigm. *Journal of Personality and Social Psychology, 29,* 696–702.

Kinnunen, T., Zamansky, T., & Block, M. (1994). Is the hypnotized subject lying? *Journal of Abnormal Psychology, 103,* 184–191.

Kinsey, A. C., Pomeroy, W., & Martin, C. (1984). *Sexual behavior in the human male.* Philadelphia: W. B. Saunders.

Kinsey, A. C., Pomeroy, W., Martin, C., & Gebhard, P. (1953). *Sexual behavior in the human female.* Philadelphia: W. B. Saunders.

Kirby, K. N., & Herrnstein, R. J. (1995). Preference reversals due to myopic discounting of delayed reward. *Psychological Science, 6,* 83–89.

Kirkpatrick, S. A., & Locke, E. A. (1991). Leadership: Do traits matter? *Academy of Management Executive, 5*(2), 48–60.

Klag, M. J., Ford, D. E., Mead, L. A., He, J., Whelton, P. K., Liang, K., & Levine, D. M. (1993). Serum cholesterol in young men and subsequent cardiovascular disease. *New England Journal of Medicine, 328,* 313–318.

Klatzky, R. L., & Lederman, S. J. (1995). Identifying objects from a haptic glance. *Perception & Psychophysics, 37,* 1111–1123.

Klausner, J., Sweeney, J., Deck, M., Hass, G., & Kelly, A. B. (1992). Clinical correlates of cerebral ventricular enlargement on schizophrenia. Further evidence for frontal lobe disease. *Journal of Nervous and Mental Disease, 180,* 407–412.

Klayman, J., & Ha, Y. W. (1987). Confirmation, disconfirmation, and information in hypothesis testing. *Psychological Review, 94,* 211–228.

Klein, S. B., & Loftus, J. (1988). The nature of self-reference encoding: The contributions of elaborative and organizational processes. *Journal of Personality and Social Psychology, 55,* 5–11.

Kleinke, C. L. (1986). Gaze and eye contact: A research review. *Psychological Bulletin, 100,* 78–100.

Klinger, E. (1990). *Daydreaming: Using waking fantasy and imagery for self-knowledge and creativity.* Los Angeles: Tarcher.

Knapp, D. N. (1988). Behavioral management techniques and exercise promotion. In R. K. Dishman (Ed.), *Exercise adherence: Its impact on public health.* Champaign, IL: Human Kinetics Books.

Knowles, J. B., Coulter, M., Wahnon, S., Reitz W., & MacLean, A. W. (1990). Variation in process S: Effects on sleep continuity and architecture. *Sleep, 13,* 97–107.

Knowlton, B. J., Ramus, S. J., & Squire, L. R. (1992). Intact artificial grammar learning in amnesia: Dissociation of classification learning and explicit memory for specific instances. *Psychological Science, 3,* 172–179.

Kobasa, S. C. (1979). Stressful life events, personality, and health: An inquiry into hardiness. *Journal of Personality and Social Psychology, 37,* 1–11.

Kochanska, G. (1993). Toward a synthesis of parental socialization and child temperament in early development of conscience. *Child Development, 65,* 325–347.

Koehler, J. J. (1996). The base rate fallacy reconsidered: Descriptive, normative, and methodological challenges. *Behavioral and Brain Sciences, 19,* 1–53.

Koestner, R., Bernieri, F., & Zuckerman, M. (1992). Self-regulation and consistency between attitudes, traits, and behaviors. *Personality and Social Psychology Bulletin, 18,* 52–59.

Kohlberg, L. (1984). *Essays on moral development: Vol. 2. The Psychology of moral development.* San Francisco: Harper & Row.

Kohler, I. (1962, May). Experiments with goggles. *Scientific American,* pp. 62–72.

Kolata, G. (1985). Obesity declared a disease. *Science, 227,* 1019–1020.

Kolata, G. B. (1986). Manic depression: Is it inherited? *Science, 232,* 448–450.

Konovsky, M. A., & Brockner, J. (1993). Managing victim and survivor layoff reactions: A procedural justice perspective. In R. Cropanzano (Ed.), *Justice in the workplace* (pp. 133–155). Hillsdale, NJ: Erlbaum.

Konovsky, M. A., & Pugh, S. D. (1994). Citizenship behavior and social exchange. *Academy of Management Journal, 37,* 656–696.

Koocher, G. P., Goodman, G. S., White, C. S., Friedrich, W. N., Sivan, A. B., & Reynolds, C. R. (1995). Psychological science and the use of anatomically detailed dolls in child sexual-abuse assessments. *Psychological Bulletin, 118,* 119–222.

Koss, M. P., & Harvey, M. R. (1991). *The rape victim: Clinical and community interventions* (2nd ed.). Newbury Park, CA: Sage.

Kosslyn, S. M. (1980). *Image and mind.* Cambridge, MA: Harvard University Press.

Kosslyn, S. M., Segar, C., Pani, J., & Hilger, L. A. (1991). When is imagery used? A diary study. *Journal of Mental Imagery.*

Kowalski, R. M. (1996). Complaints and complaining: Functions, antecedents, and consequences. *Psychological Bulletin, 119,* 179–196.

Krakoff, L. R., Dziedzic, S., Mann, S. J., Felton, K., & Yeager, K. (1985). Plasma epinephrine concentrations in healthy men: Correlation with systolic blood pressure and rate-pressure product. *Journal of American College of Cardiology, 5,* 352.

Kranzler, J., & Jensen, A. R. (1989). Inspection time and intelligence: A meta-analysis. *Intelligence, 13,* 329–247.

Kring, A. M., Smith, D. A., & Neale, J. M. (1994). Individual differences in dispositional expressiveness: Development and validation of the emotional expressivity scale. *Journal of Personality and Social Psychology, 66,* 934–949.

Kritch, K. M., Bostow, D. E., & Dedrick, R. F. (1995). Level of interactivity of videodisc instruction on college students' recall of AIDS information. *Journal of Applied Behavior Analysis, 28,* 85–86.

Krosnick, J. A., Beta, A. L., Jussim, L. J., & Lynn, A. R. (1992). Subliminal conditioning of attitudes. *Personality and Social Psychology Bulletin, 18,* 152–162.

Kubany, E. S., Bauer, G. B., Muraoka, M. Y., Richard, D. C., & Read, P. (1995). Impact of labeled anger and blame in intimate relationships. *Journal of Social and Clinical Psychology, 14,* 53–60.

Kübler-Ross, E. (1974). *Questions and answers on death and dying.* New York: Macmillan.

Kuczmarski, R. J. (1992). Prevalence of overweight and weight gain in the United States. *American Journal of Clinical Nutrition, 55,* 4955–5025.

Kuhn, D. (1989). Children and adults as intuitive scientists. *Psychological Review, 96,* 674–689.

Kulik, C. T., & Ambrose, M. L. (1992). Personal and situational determinants of referent choice. *Academy of Management Review, 17,* 212–237.

Kunda, Z., & Nisbett, R. E. (1986). The psychometrics of everyday life. *Cognitive Psychology, 18,* 195–224.

Kunda, Z., & Oleson, K. C. (1995). Maintaining stereotypes in the face of disconfirmation: Construction grounds for subtyping deviants. *Journal of Personality and Social Psychology, 68,* 565–579.

Kunzinger, E. L., III. (1985). A short-term longitudinal study of moral development during early grade school. *Developmental Psychology, 21,* 642–646.

Kurdek, L. A. (1993). Predicting marital dissolution: A 5-year longitudinal study of newlywed couples. *Journal of Personality and Social Psychology, 64,* 221–242.

Kutchinsky, B. (1992). The child sexual abuse panic. *Nordisk Sexologist, 10,* 30–42.

Lahey, B. B., Hart, E. L., Pilszka, S., & Applegate, B. (1993). Neurophysiological correlates of conduct disorder: A rationale and a review of research. *Journal of Clinical Child Psychology, 22,* 141–153.

Lamb, M. E. (1977). Father-infant and mother-infant interactions in the first year of life. *Child Development, 48,* 167–181.

Lambert, A. J. (1995). Stereotypes and social judgment: The consequences of group variability. *Journal of Personality and Social Psychology, 68,* 388–403.

Lambert, S. (1991). The combined effect of job and family characteristics on the job satisfaction, job involvement, and intrinsic motivation of men and women workers. *Journal of Organizational Behavior, 12,* 341–363.

Landau, S., Milich, R., & Lorch, E. P. (1992). Visual attention to and comprehension of television in attention-deficit hyperactivity disordered and normal boys. *Child Development, 63,* 928–937.

Lando, H. A., Pechacek, T. F., Pirie, P. L., Murray, D. M., Mittelmark, M. B., Lichtenstein, E., Nothwehr, F., & Gray, C. (1995). Changes in adult cigarette smoking in the Minnesota Heart Health Program. *American Journal of Public Health, 85,* 201–208.

Landsbergis, P. A., Schnall, P. L., Deitz, D., Friedman, R., & Pickering, T. (1992). The patterning of psychological attributes and distress by job strain and social support in a sample of working men. *Journal of Behavioral Medicine, 15,* 379–405.

Landy, F. J., & Farr, J. L. (1983). *The measurement of work performance: Methods, theory, and applications.* New York: Academic Press.

Lange, J. D., Brown, W. A., Wincze, J. P., & Zwick W. (1980). Serum testosterone concentration and penile tumescence changes in men. *Hormones and Behavior, 14,* 267–270.

Langlois, J. H., & Roggman, L. A. (1990). Attractive faces are only average. *Psychological Science, 1,* 115–121.

Langlois, J. H., Roggmann, L. A., & Reisser-Danner, L. A. (1990). Infants' differential social responses to attractive and unattractive faces. *Developmental Psychology, 26,* 153–159.

Larrick, R. P. (1993). Motivational factors in decision theories: The role of self-protection. *Psychological Bulletin, 113,* 440–450.

Lassiter, G. D., Briggs, M. A., & Slaw, R. D. (1991). Need for cognition, causal processing, and memory for behavior. *Personality and Social Psychology Bulletin, 17,* 694–700.

Latham, G., & Baldes, J. (1975). The practical significance of Locke's theory of goal setting. *Journal of Applied Psychology, 60,* 122–124.

Lauer, J., & Lauer, R. (1985, June). Marriages made to last. *Psychology Today,* pp. 22–26.

LaVecchia, C., Lucchini, F., Negri, E., Boyle, P., & Levi, F. (1993). Trends in cancer mortality in the Americas, 1955–1989. *European Journal of Cancer, 29,* 431–470.

LaVecchia, C., Lucchini, F., Negri, E., Boyle, P., Maisonneuve, P., & Levi, F. (1992). Trends of cancer mortality in Europe, 1955–1989: II, Respiratory tract, bone, connective and soft tissue sarcomas, and skin. *European Journal of Cancer, 23,* 514–599.

Law, D. J., Pellegrino, J. W., & Hunt, E. B. (1993). Comparing the tortoise and the hare: Gender differences and experience in dynamic spatial reasoning tasks. *Psychological Science, 4,* 35–40.

Lawless, H., & Engen, T. (1977). Associations to odors: Interference, mnemonics, and verbal labeling. *Journal of Experimental Psychology: Human Learning and Memory, 3,* 52–59.

Layman, J., Gidycz, C. A., & Lynn, S. J. (1996). Unacknowledged versus acknowledged rape victims: Situational factors and posttraumatic stress. *Journal of Abnormal Psychology, 105,* 124–131.

Lazarus, A. A. (1989). Why I am an eclectic (not an integrationist). *British Journal of Guidance and Counseling, 17,* 248–258.

Lazarus, R. S., & Folkman, S. (1984). *Stress, appraisal, and coping.* New York: Springer.

Lazarus, R. S., Opton, E. M., Nomikos, M. S., & Rankin, N. O. (1985). The principle of short-circuiting of threat: Further evidence. *Journal of Personality, 33,* 622–635.

Lecci, L., Kzroly, P., Suehlman, L. S., & Lanyon, R. I. (1996). Goal-relevant dimensions of hypochondriacal tendencies and their relation to symptom manifestation and psychological distress. *Journal of Abnormal Psychology, 105,* 42–52.

Lee, G. R., Seccombe, K., & Shehan, C. L. (1991). Marital status and personal happiness: An analysis of trend data. *Journal of Marriage and the Family, 53,* 839–844.

Lee, P. C., Senders, C. W., Gantz, B. J., & Otto, S. R. (1985). Transient sensorineural hearing loss after overuse of portable headphone cassette radios. *Otolaryngology, 93,* 622–625.

Lee, R. T., & Ashforth, B. E. (1990). On the meaning of Maslach's three dimensions of burnout. *Journal of Applied Psychology, 75,* 743–747.

Lee, R. T., & Ashforth, B. E. (1996). A meta-analytic examination of the correlates of the three dimensions of job burnout. *Journal of Applied Psychology, 81,* 123–133.

Leichtman, M. D., & Ceci, S. J. (1995). The effects of stereotypes and suggestions on preschoolers' reports. *Developmental Psychology, 31,* 568–578.

Leitenberg, H., & Henning, K. (1995). Sexual fantasy. *Psychological Bulletin, 117,* 469–496.

Leonard, K. E. (1989). The impact of explicit aggressive and implicit nonaggressive cues on aggression in intoxicated and sober males. *Personality and Social Psychology Bulletin, 15,* 390–400.

Lepper, M., & Green, D. (Eds.). (1978). *The hidden costs of reward.*

Lerner, R. M. (1990). Plasticity, person-context relations, and cognitive training in the aged years: A developmental contextual perspective. *Developmental Psychology, 26,* 911–915.

Lerner, M. J. (1980). *The belief in a just world: A fundamental delusion.* New York: Plenum.

Lerner, R. M. (1993). The demise of the nature-nurture dichotomy. *Human Development, 36,* 119–124.

Lester, N., Smart, L., & Baum, A. (1994). Measuring coping flexibility. *Psychology and Health, 9,* 409–424.

LeVay, S. (1991). A difference in hypothalamic structure between heterosexual and homosexual men. *Science, 253,* 1034–1037.

Levenson, R. W. (1992). Autonomic nervous system differences among emotions. *Psychological Science, 3,* 23–27.

Leventhal, E. A., Hansell, S., Diefenbach, M., Leventhal, H., & Glass, D. C. (1996). Negative affect and self-report of physical symptoms: Two longitudinal studies of older adults. *Health Psychology, 15*, 193–199.

Leventhal, H., Singer, R., & Jones, S. (1965). The effects of fear and specifying of recommendation upon attitudes and behavior. *Journal of Personality and Social Psychology, 2*, 20–29.

Levine, D. S. (1991). *Introduction to neural and cognitive modeling.* Hillsdale, NJ: Erlbaum.

Levine, M., Toro, P. A., & Perkins, D. V. (1993). Social and community interventions. *Annual Review of Psychology, 44*, 525–558.

Levine, R. V., Martinez, T. S., Brase, G., & Sorenson, K. (1994). Helping in 36 U.S. cities. *Journal of Personality and Social Psychology, 67*, 69–82.

Levinger, G. (1988). Can we picture "love"? In R. J. Sternberg & M. I. Barnes (Eds.), *The psychology of love* (pp. 139–158). New Haven, CT: Yale University Press.

Levinson, D. J. (1986). A conception of adult development. *American Psychologist, 41*, 3–13.

Levis, D. J. (1985). Implosive theory: A comprehensive extension of conditioning theory of fear/anxiety to psychology. In S. Reiss & R. R. Bootzin (Eds.), *Theoretical issues in behavior therapy.* New York: Academic Press.

Levy, S. M. (1990). Psychosocial risk factors and cancer progression: Mediating pathways linking behavior and disease. In K. D. Craig & S. M. Weiss (Eds.), *Health enhancement, disease prevention, and early intervention: Biobehavioral perspectives.* New York: Springer.

Levy, S. M., Herberman, R. B., Simons, A., Whiteside, T., Lee, J., McDonald, R., & Beadle, M. (1989). Persistently low natural killer cell activity in normal adults: Immunological, hormonal and mood correlates. *Natural Immune Cell Growth Regulation, 8*, 173–186.

Levy, S. M., Herberman, R., Maluish, A., Achlien, B., & Lippman, M. (1985). Prognostic risk assessment in primary breast cancer by behavioral and immunological parameters. *Health Psychology, 4*, 99–113.

Levy, S. M., Lee, J., Bagley, C., & Lippman, M. (1989). Survival hazards analysis in first recurrent breast cancer patients: Seven-year follow-up. *Psychosomatic Medicine, 50*, 520–528.

Lewis, M., Sullivan, M. W., Stanger, C., & Weiss, M. (1989). Self-development and self-consciousness emotions. *Child Development, 60*, 146–156.

Lewkowicz, D. J. (1996). Infants' response to the audible and visible properties of the human face 1. Role of lexical-syntactic content, temporal synchrony, gender, and manner of speech. *Developmental Psychology, 32*, 347–366.

Lewy, A. J., Sack, R. I., & Singer, C. M. (1992). Bright light, melatonin, and biological rhythms in humans. In J. Montplaisir & R. Godbout (Eds.), *Sleep and biological rhythms: Basic mechanisms and applications to psychiatry.* New York: Oxford University Press.

Ley, P. (1988). *Communicating with patients.* London: Croom Helm.

Leyens, J. P., Yzerbyt, V., & Corneille, O. (1996). The role of applicability in the emergence of the overattribution bias. *Journal of Personality and Social Psychology, 70*, 291–229.

Lichtenstein, E., Lando, H. A., & Nothwehr, F. (1994). Readiness to quit as a predictor of smoking changes in the Minnesota Heart Health Program. *Health Psychology, 18*, 393–396.

Liddell, F. D. K. (1982). Motor vehicle accidents (1973–6) in a cohort of Montreal drivers. *Journal of Epidemiological Community Health, 36*, 140–145.

Liden, R. C., & Mitchell, T. R. (1988). Ingratiatory behaviors in organizational settings. *Academy of Management Review, 13*, 572–587.

Lieberman, D. A. (1990). *Learning: Behavior and cognition.* Belmont, CA: Wadsworth Publishing Company.

Lieberman, J. A., & Koreen, A. R. (1993). Neurochemistry and neuroendocrinology of schizophrenia. In *Schizophrenia 1993: Special report* (pp. 197–256). Washington, DC: National Institute of Mental Health, Schizophrenia Research Board.

Linden, E. (1992). Chimpanzees with a difference: Bonobos. *National Geographic, 181*(3), 46–53.

Lindman, R. E., & Lang, A. R. (1994). The alcohol-aggression stereotype: A cross-cultural comparison of beliefs. *International Journal of the Addictions, 29*, 1–13.

Linville, P. W., & Fischer, G. W. (1993). Exemplar and abstraction models of perceived group variability and stereotypicality. *Social Cognition, 11*, 92–125.

Lipshitz, R., & Bar-Ilan, O. (1996). How problems are solved: Reconsidering the phase theorem. *Organizational Behavior and Human Decision Processes, 65*, 48–60.

Locke, B. Z., & Slaby, A. E. (1982). Preface. In D. Mechanic (Ed.), *Symptoms, illness behavior, and help-seeking* (pp. xi-xv). New York: Prodist.

Locke, E. A. (1991). *The essence of leadership.* New York: Lexingon Books.

Locke, E. A., & Latham, G. P. (1990). *A theory of goal setting and task performance.* Englewood Cliffs, NJ: Prentice-Hall.

Loehlin, J. C., Lindzey, G., & Spuhle, J. N. (1975). Race differences in intelligence. New York: Freeman.

Loftus, E. F. (1991). The glitter of everyday memory . . . and the gold. *American Psychologist, 46*, 16–18.

Loftus, E. F. (1992). When a lie becomes memory's truth: Memory distortion after exposure to misinformation. *Current Directions in Psychological Science, 1*, 121–123.

Loftus, E. F. (1993). The reality of repressed memories. *American Psychologist, 48*, 518–537.

Loftus, E. F., & Coan, D. (1995). The construction of childhood memories. In D. Peters (Ed.), *The child in context: Cognitive, social and legal perspectives.* New York: Kluwer.

Loftus, E. F., & Herzog, C. (1991). Unpublished data, University of Washington. Cited in Loftus, E. F. (1993). The reality of repressed memories. *American Psychologist, 48*, 518–537.

Logan, G. D. (1985). Skill and automaticity: Relations, implications, and future directions. *Canadian Journal of Psychology, 39*, 367–386.

Logan, G. D. (1988). Toward an instance theory of automotization. *Psychological Review, 95*, 492–527.

Logue, A. W. (1988). Research on self-control: An integrating framework. *Behavioral and Brain Sciences, 11*, 665–679.

Logue, A. W., Logue, K. R., & Strauss, K. E. (1983). The acquisition of taste aversion in humans with eating and drinking disorders. *Behavioral Research and Therapy, 21*, 275–289.

Logue, A. W., Ophir, I., & Strauss, K. E. (1981). The acquisition of taste aversion in humans. *Behavior Research and Therapy, 19*, 319–333.

Long, G. M., & Crambert, R. F. (1990). The nature and basis of age-related change in dynamic visual acuity. *Psychology and Aging, 5*, 138–143.

Long, J. W., & Rybacki, J. J. (1994). *The essential guide to prescription drugs.* New York: HarperCollins.

Longoni, A. M., Richardson, J. T., & Aiello, A. (1993). Articulatory rehearsal and phonological storage in working memory. *Memory & Cognition, 21*, 11–22.

Longshore, D., Anglin, M. D., & Hsieh, S. (1997). Intended sex with fewer partners: An empirical test of the AIDS risk reduction model among injection drug users. *Journal of Applied Social Psychology, 27*(3), 187–208.

Lopez, M. (1996, April 4). Laughter's the best medicine. Virtual video technology visor takes the pain out of periodontics for patients. *Albany Times Union*, pp. C-1, C-5.

Lopez, S. R. (1989). Patient variable biases in clinical judgment: Conceptual overview and methodological considerations. *Psychological Bulletin, 106*, 184–203.

Lubart, T. I. (1994). Creativity. In R. J. Sternberg (Ed.), *Thinking problem solving* (pp. 289–332). San Diego, CA: Academic Press.

Lubart, T. T., & Sternberg, R. J. (1995). An investment approach to creativity: Theory and data. In S. M. Smith, T. B. Ward, & R. A. Finke (Eds.), *The creative cognition approach* (pp. 269–302). Cambridge, MA: MIT Press.

Luchins, A. S. (1942). Mechanization in problem solving. *Psychological Monographs, 54* (whole No. 248).

Luthans, F., Paul, R., & Baker, D. (1981). An experimental analysis of the impact of a contingent reinforcement intervention on salespersons' performance behaviors. *Journal of Applied Psychology, 66*, 314–323.

Lykken, D. T. (1985). The probity of the polygraph. In S. M. Kassin & L. S. Wrightsman (Eds.), *The psychology of evidence and trial procedure.* Beverly Hills, CA: Sage.

Lykken, D. T., Bouchard, T. J., McGue, M., & Tellegen, A. (1993). Heritability of interests: A twin study. *Journal of Applied Psychology, 78*, 649–661.

Lykken, D. T., McGue, M., Tellegen, A., & Bouchard, T. J. (1992). Emergenesis: Genetic traits that may not run in families. *American Psychologist, 47*, 1565–1577.

Lyman, B. J., & McDaniel, M. A. (1986). Effects of encoding strategy on long-term memory for odours. *Quarterly Journal of Experimental Psychology, 38A*, 753–765.

Lyman, B. J., & McDaniel, M. A. (1987, April). *Effects of experimenter and subject provided verbal and visual elaborations on long-term memory for odors.* Paper presented at the annual meeting of the Eastern Psychological Association, Arlington, VA.

Lynn, M., & Mynier, K. (1993). Effects of server posture on restaurant tipping. *Journal of Applied Social Psychology, 23*, 678–685.

Lynn, R. (1990). The role of nutrition in secular increases in intelligence. *Personality and Individual Differences, 11*, 273–285.

Lynn, R. (1993). Oriental Americans: Their IQ, educational attainment, and socio-economic status. *Personality and Individual Differences, 15*, 237–242.

Lynn, R. (1994). Sex differences in intelligence and brain size: A paradox resolved. *Personality and Individual Differences, 17*, 257–271.

Lynn, R. (1996). Racial and ethnic differences in intelligence in the United States on the Difference Ability Scale. *Personality and Individual Differences, 20*, 271–273.

Lynn, S. J., Rhue, J. W., & Weekes, J. R. (1990). Hypnotic involuntariness: A social cognitive analysis. *Psychological Review, 974*, 169–184.

MacNichol, E.F. (1964). Retinal mechanisms of color vision. *Vision Research*, vol. 4.

Macrae, C. N., Milne, A. B., & Bodenhausen, G. V. (1994). Stereotypes as energy-saving devices: A peek inside the cognitive toolbox. *Journal of Personality and Social Psychology, 66*, 37–47.

Maier, S. F., & Jackson, R. L. (1979). Learned helplessness: All of us were right (and wrong): Inescapable shock has multiple effects. In G. H. Bower (Ed.), *The psychology of learning and motivation* (Vol. 13). New York: Academic Press.

Malandro, L. A., Barker, L., & Barker, D. A. (1994). *Nonverbal communication* (3rd ed.). New York: Random House.

Mandel, D. R., Jusczyk, P. W., & Pisoni, D. B. (1995). Infants' recognition of the sound patterns of their own names. *Psychological Science, 6*, 314–317.

Mann, T. (1994). Informed consent for psychological research: Do subjects comprehend consent forms and understand their legal rights? *Psychological Science, 5*, 140–143.

Mannheim, K. (1972). The problem of generations. In P. G. Altbach & R. S. Laufer (Eds.), *The new pilgrims: Youth protest in transition* (pp. 101–138). New York: David McKay.

Manuzza, S., Klein, R. G., Bessler, A., Malloy, P. l, & LaPadula, A. (1993). Adult outcome of hyperactive boys: Educational Achievement, occupational rank, and psychiatric status. *Archives of General Psychiatry, 50,* 565–576.

Marcus, G. F. (1996). Why do children say "breaked"? *Current Directions in Psychological Science, 3,* 81–85.

Marks, I. (1994). Behavior therapy as an aid to self-care. *Current Directions in Psychological Science, 3,* 19–22.

Markus, H. M. & Nurius, P. (1986). Possible selves. *American Psychologist, 41,* 954–969.

Marlatt, G. A., Baer, J. S., Donovan, D. M., & Kivlahan, D. R. (1988). Addictive behaviors: Etiology and treatment. *Annual Review of Psychology, 58,* 265–272.

Marr, D. (1982). *Vision: A computational investigation into the human representation and processing of visual information.* San Francisco: W. H. Freeman.

Marsh, H. W. (1993). Relations between global and specific domains of self: The importance of individual importance, certainty, and ideal. *Journal of Personality and Social Psychology, 65,* 975–992.

Martin, C. L., & Little, J. K. (1990). The relation of gender understanding to children's sex-typed preferences and gender stereotypes. *Child Development, 61,* 1427–1439.

Martin, C. L., & Murbergber, M. A. (1994). Effects of self-esteem and assigned goals on actual and perceived performance. *Journal of Social Behavior and Personality, 9,* 81–87.

Martin, M. (1986). Individual differences in sensation seeking and attentional ability. *Personality and Individual Differences, 6,* 637–649.

Martin, S. (1995, September). APA to pursue prescriptions privileges. *APA Monitor,* p. 6.

Maslach, C. (1982). *Burnout: The cost of caring.* Englewood Cliffs, NJ: Prentice-Hall.

Maslach, C., & Jackson, S. E. (1984). Burnout in organizational settings. In S. Oskamp (Ed.), *Applied social psychology annual* (Vol. 5, pp. 135–154). Beverly Hills: Sage.

Maslow, A. H. (1970). *Motivation and personality* (2nd ed.). New York: Harper & Row.

Mason, M. E., & Graf, P. (1993). Introduction: Looking back and into the future. In P. Graf & E. J. Masson (Eds.), *Implicit memory: New directions in cognition, development, and neuropsychology* (pp. 1–11). Hillsdale, NJ: Erlbaum.

Masters, W. H., & Johnson, V. E. (1966). *Human sexual response.* Boston: Little, Brown.

Matarazzo, J. D. (1980). Behavioral health and behavioral medicine: Frontiers for a new health psychology. *American Psychologist, 35,* 807–817.

Matarazzo, J. D. (1992). Psychological testing and assessment in the 21st century. *American Psychologist, 47,* 1007–1018.

Matlin, M. W., & Foley, H. J. (1992). *Sensation and perception* (3rd ed.). Needham Heights, MA: Allyn and Bacon.

Matsumoto, D. (1994). *People: Psychology from a cultural perspective.* Pacific Groves, CA: Brooks/Cole Publishing.

Matsumoto, D., & Assar, M. (1992). The effects of language on judgments of universal facial expressions of emotion. *Journal of Nonverbal Behavior, 16,* 85–99.

Matthews, K. A., Woodall, K. L., Kenyon, K., & Jacob, T. (1996). Negative family environment as a predictor of boys' future status on measures of hostile attitudes, interview behavior, and anger expression. *Health Psychology 15,* 30–37.

Maturi, R. (1992, July 20). Stress can be beaten. *Industry Week,* pp. 23–26.

Maupin, H. E., & Fisher, R. J. (1989). The effects of superior female performance and sex-role orientation on gender conformity. *Canadian Journal of Behavioral Science, 21,* 55–69.

Maurer, D., & Barrera, M. (1981). Infants' perception of natural and distorted arrangements of a schematic face. *Child Development, 52,* 196–202.

Maurer, D., & Young, R. E. (1983). Newborn's following of natural and distorted arrangements of facial features. *Infant Behavior and Development, 6,* 127–131.

May, C. P., Hasher, L., & Stoltzfus, E. R. (1993). Optimal time of day and the magnitude of age differences in memory. *Psychological Science, 4,* 326–330.

Mays, V. M., & Cochran, S. D. (1988). Issues in the perception of AIDS risk and risk reduction by black and Hispanic/Latino women. *American Psychologist, 43,* 949–957.

Mazur, J. E. (1987). An adjusting procedure for studying delayed reinforcement. In M. L. Commons, J. E. Mazur, J. A. Nevin, & H. Rachlin (Eds.), *Quantitative analyses of Behavior: Vol. 5. The effect of delay and of intervening events on reinforcement value* (pp. 44–73). Hillsdale, NJ: Erlbaum.

Mazur, J. E. (1996). Procrastination by pigeons: Preference for larger, more delayed work requirements. *Journal of the Experimental Analysis of behavior, 65,* 159–171.

Mazursky, D., & Ofir, C. (1996). "I knew it all along, under all conditions? Or possibly, I could not have expected it to happen" under some conditions? *Organizational Behavior and Human Decision Processes, 66,* 237–240.

McCall, R. B. (1994). Academic underachievers. *Current Directions in Psychological Science, 3,* 15–19.

McCann, S., & Weinman, J. (1996). Encouraging patient participation in general practice consultations: Effect on consultation length and content, patient satisfaction, and health. *Psychology and Health, 11,* 857–869.

McCanne, T. R., & Anderson, J. A. (1987). Emotional responding following experimental manipulation of facial electromyographic activity. *Journal of Personality and Social Psychology, 52,* 759–768.

McClearn, G. E., Plomin, R., Gora-Maslak, G., & Crabbe, J. C. (1991). The gene chase in behavioral science. *Psychological Science, 2,* 222–229.

McClelland, D. C. (1985). *Human motivation.* New York: Cambridge University Press.

McClelland, D. C. (1995). Achievement motivation in relation to achievement-related recall, performance, and urine flow, a marker associated with release of vasopressin. *Motivation and Emotion, 19,* 59–76.

McConkey, K. M. (1991). The construction and resolution of experience and behavior in hypnosis. In S. J. Lynn & J. W. Rhue (Eds.), *Theories of hypnosis: Current models and perspectives* (pp. 542–563). New York: Guilford Press.

McConkie, G. W., & Zola, D. (1984). Eye movement control during reading. The effect of word units. In W. Prinz & A. F. Sanders (Eds.), *Cognition and motor processes* (pp. 63–74). Berlin: Springer-Verlag.

McDaniel, M. A., & Frei, R. L. (1994). *Validity of customer service measures in personnel selection: A review of criterion and construct evidence.* Manuscript submitted for publication.

McDonald, H. E., & Hirt, E. R. (1997). When expectancy meets desire: Motivational effects in reconstructive memory. *Journal of Personality and Social Psychology, 72,* 5–23.

McGinnis, J. M. (1994). The role of behavioral research in national health policy. In S. Blumenthal, K. Matthews, & S. Weiss (Eds.), *New research frontiers in behavioral medicine: Proceedings of the national conference* (p. 219). Washington, D. C.: NIH Publications.

McGinnis, J. M., & Meyers, L. D. (1995). Dietary change and health: Policy implications. *Behavioral Medicine, 20,* 165–169.

McGue, M. (1993). From proteins to cognitions: The behavioral genetics of alcoholism. In R. Polmin & G. E. McClearn (Eds.), *Nature, nurture and psychology* (pp. 245–268). Washington DC: American Psychological Association.

McGue, M., Bouchard, T. J., Jr., Iaconon, W. G., & Lykken, D. T. (1993). Behavioral genetics of cognitive ability: A life-span perspective. In R. Plomin & G. E. McClearn (Eds.), *Nature, nurture, and psychology* (pp. 59–76). Washington, DC: American Psychological Association.

McGue, M., & Lykken, D. T. (1992). Genetic influence on risk of divorce. *Psychological Science, 3,* 368–373.

McIlwraith, R. D., Jacobvitz, R. S., Kubey, R., & Alexander, A. (1991). Television addiction: Theories and data behind the ubiquitous metaphor. *American Behavioral Scientist, 35,* 104–121.

McKenna, S. P., & Glendon, A. I. (1985). Occupational first aid training: Decay in cardiopulmonary resuscitation (CPR) skills. *Journal of Occupational Psychology, 58,* 109–117.

McKenry, P. C., Kotch, J. B., & Browne, D. H. (1991). Correlates of dysfunctional parenting attitudes among low-income adolescent mothers. *Journal of Adolescent Research, 6,* 212–234.

McReynolds, W. T. (1980). Learned helplessness as a schedule-shift effect. *Journal of Research in Personality, 14,* 139–157.

Medin, D. L., & Ross, B. H. (1992). *Cognitive psychology.* Fort Worth, TX: Harcourt Brace Jovanovich.

Mednick, M. T., Mednick, S. A., & Mednick, E. V. (1964). Incubation of creative performance and specific associative priming. *Journal of Abnormal and Social Psychology, 69,* 84–88.

Meichenbaum, D. H. (1977). *Cognitive-behavior modification.* New York: Plenum.

Meijmann, T., van der Meer, O., & van Dormolen, M. (1993). The after-effects of night work on short-term memory performance. *Ergonomics, 36,* 37–42.

Melamed, S., Ben-Avi, I., Luz, J., & Green, M. S. (1995). Objective and subjective work monotony: Effects on job satisfaction, psychological distress, and absenteeism in blue-collar workers. *Journal of Applied Psychology, 80,* 29–42.

Meltzoff, A. N. (1990). Towards a developmental cognitive science: The implications of crossmodal matching and imitation for the development of representation and memory in infancy. In A. Diamond (Ed.), *Annals of the New York Academy of Sciences: Vol 608. The development and neural bases of higher cognitive functions* (pp. 1–37). New York: New York Academy of Sciences.

Meltzoff, A. N., & Moore, M. K. (1977). Imitation of facial and manual gestures by human neonates. *Science, 198,* 75–78.

Meltzoff, A. N., & Moore, M. K. (1989). Imitation in newborn infants: Exploring the range of gestures imitated and the underlying mechanisms. *Developmental Psychology, 25,* 954–962.

Melzack, R. (1976). Pain: Past, present, and future. In M. Weisenberg & B. Tursky (Eds.), *Pain: New perspectives in therapy and research.* New York: Plenum.

Melzack, R. (1993). Pain: Past, present, and future. *Canadian Journal of Experimental Psychology, 47,* 615–629.

Mendolia, M., & Kleck, R. E. (1993). Effects of talking about a stressful event on arousal: Does what we talk about make a difference? *Journal of Personality and Social Psychology, 64,* 283–292.

Mento, A. J., Locke, E. A., & Klein, H. J. (1992). Relationship of goal level to valence and instrumentality. *Journal of Applied Psychology, 77,* 395–405.

Merikle, P. M. (1992). Perception without awareness. *American Psychologist, 47,* 792–795.

Mero, N. P., & Motowidlo, S. J. (1995). Effects of rater accountability on the accuracy and the favorability of performance ratings. *Journal of Applied Psychology, 80,* 517–524.

Mertens, T. E., & Low-Beer, D. (1996). HIV and AIDS: Where is the epidemic going? *WHO Bulletin OMS, 74,* 121–128.

Metcalfe, J., Funnell, M., & Gazzaniga, M. S. (1995). Right-hemisphere memory superiority: Studies of a split-brain patient. *Psychological Science, 6,* 157–163.

Meter, R. P. (1991). Language acquisition by deaf children. *American Scientist, 79,* 60–76.

Metzger, A. M. (1980). A methodological study of the Kübler-Ross stage theory. *Omega, 10,* 291–301.

Meyer, A. J., Maccoby, N., & Farquhar, J. W. (1980). Skills training in a cardiovascular health education campaign. *Journal of Consulting and Clinical Psychology, 48,* 129–142.

Meyer, J. P., Allen, J. J., & Smith, C. A. (1993). Commitment to organizations and occupations: Extension and test of a three-component conceptualization. *Journal of Applied Psychology, 78,* 538–551.

Miceli, M. P., & Lane, M. C. (1991). Antecedents of pay satisfaction: A review and extensions. In K. Rowland & O. R. Ferris (Eds.), *Research in personnel and human resources management* (Vol. 9, pp. 235–309). Greenwich, CT: JAI Press.

Miklowitz, D. J., Goldstein, M. J., Doane, J. A., Neuchterlein, K. H., Strachan, A. M., Snyder, K. S., & Magana-Amato, A. (1989). Is expressed emotion an index of a transactional process? I. Parents' affective style. *Family Process, 22,* 153–167.

Miles, D. R., & Carey, G. (1997). Genetic and environmental architecture of human aggression. *Journal of Personality and Social Psychology, 72,* 207–217.

Milgram, S. (1963). Behavioral study of obedience. *Journal of Abnormal and Social Psychology, 67,* 371–378.

Milgram, S. (1974). *Obedience to authority.* New York: Harper.

Millenson, J. R., & Leslie, J. C. (1979). *Principles of behavioral analysis* (2nd ed.). New York: Macmillan.

Miller, C. L., Miceli, P. J., Whitman, T. L., & Borkowski, J. G. (1996). *Developmental Psychology, 32,* 533–541.

Miller, D. T., & McFarland, C. (1987). Counterfactual thinking and victim compensation: A test of norm theory. *Personality and Social Psychology Bulletin, 12,* 513–519.

Miller, D. T., & Ross, M. (1975). Self-serving biases in attribution of causality: Fact or fiction? *Psychological Bulletin, 82,* 313–325.

Miller, K. (1994, March 17). Safety quiz: Insurance-claims data don't show advantage of some auto devices. *Wall Street Journal,* pp. Al, A7.

Miller, K. F., Smith, C. M., Zhu, J., & Zhang, H. (1995). Preschool origins of cross-national differences in mathematical competence: The role of number-naming systems. *Psychological Science, 6,* 56–60.

Miller, L. (1987). The emotional brain. *Psychology Today, 22,* 35–42.

Miller, M. E., & Bowers, K. S. (1993). Hypnotic analgesia: Dissociated experience or dissociated control? *Journal of Abnormal Psychology, 102,* 29–38.

Miller, N. E. (1985). The value of behavioral research on animals. *American Psychologist, 40,* 423–440.

Miller, N., Maruyama, G., Beaber, R. J., & Valone, K. (1976). Speed of speech and persuasion. 615–624.

Miller, P. H., & Zalenski, R. (1982). Preschoolers' knowledge about attention. *Developmental Psychology, 18,* 871–875.

Miller, R. S. (1991). On decorum in close relationships: Why aren't we polite to those we love? *Contemporary Social Psychology, 15,* 63–65.

Miller, S. M., Shoda, Y., & Hurley, K. (1996). Applying cognitive-social theory to health-protective behavior: Breast self-examination in cancer screening. *Psychological Bulletin, 119,* 70–94.

Miller, T. Q., Smith, T. W., Turner, C. W., Guijarro, M. L., & Hallet, A. J. (1996). A meta-analytic review of research on hostility and physical health. *Psychological Bulletin. 119,* 322–348.

Millon, T. (1987). *Millon clinical multiaxial inventory-II: Manual for MCMI-II* (2nd ed.). Minneapolis, MN: National Computer System.

Millon, T. (1991). Classification psychopathology: Rationale, alternatives, and standards. *Journal of Abnormal Psychology, 100,* 245–261.

Milner, B. (1974). Hemispheric specialization: Scope and limits. In F. O. Schmitt & F. G. Worden (Eds.), *The neurosciences: Third study program* (pp. 75–89). Cambridge, MA: MIT Press.

Milner, B., Corkin, S., & Teuber, H. L. (1968). Further analysis of the hippocampal amnesic syndrome; 14–year follow-up study of H. M. *Neuropsychologia, 6,* 317–338.

Minami, H., & Dallenbach, K. M. (1946). The effect of activity upon learning and retention in the cockroach. *American Journal of Psychology, 59,* 1–58.

Minkoff, H., Deepak, N., Menez, R., & Fikrig, S. (1987). Pregnancies resulting in infants with acquired immunodeficiency syndrome or AIDS-related complex: Follow-up of mothers, children, and subsequently born siblings. *Obstetrics and Gynecology, 69,* 288–291.

Minor, T. R. (1990). Conditioned fear and neophobia following inescapable shock. *Animal Learning & Behavior, 18,* 212–226.

Minor, T. R., Dess, N. K., Ben-David, E., & Chang, W. (1994). Individual differences in vulnerability to inescapable shock in rats. *Journal of Experimental Psychology 20,* 401–412.

Minuchin, S., & Fishman, H. C. (1981). *Family therapy techniques.* Cambridge, MA: Harvard University Press.

Mischel, W. (1977). On the future of personality measurement. *American Psychologist, 32,* 246–254.

Mischel, W. (1985). *Personality: Lost or found? Identifying when individual differences make a difference.* Paper presented at the meetings of the American Psychological Association, Los Angeles.

Mistler-Lachman, J. L. (1975). Queer sentences, ambiguity, and levels of processing. *Memory and Cognition, 3,* 395–400.

Mistry, J., & Rogoff, B. (1994). Remembering in cultural context. In W. J. Lonner & R. Malpass (Eds.), *Psychology and culture* (pp. 139–144). Boston: Allyn & Bacon.

Mitchell, D. J., Russo, J. E., & Pennington, N. (1989). Back to the future: Temporal perspective in the explanation of events. *Journal of Behavioral Decision Making. 2,* 25–38.

Mitchell, H. (1988, February). Why are women still dying of cervical cancer? *Australian Society,* pp. 34–35.

Mitchell, T. R. (1983). Expectancy-value models in organizational psychology. In N. Feather (Ed.), *Expectancy, incentive, and action* (pp. 293–314). Hillsdale, NJ: Erlbaum.

Mitchell, T. R., & Larson, J. R., Jr. (1987). *People in organizations: An introduction to organizational behavior* (3rd ed.). New York: McGraw-Hill.

Mitchell, T. R., Green, S. G., & Wood, R. S. (1982). An attributional model of leadership and the poor performing subordinate: Development and validation. In B. M. Staw and L. L. Cummings (Eds.), *Research in organizational behavior* (Vol. 3). Greenwich, CT: JAI Press.

Miura, I., & Okamoto, Y. (1989). Comparisons of U.S. and Japanese first graders' cognitive representation of number and understanding of place value. *Journal of Educational Psychology, 81,* 109–113.

Money, J., & Ehrhardt, A. A. (1972). *Man and woman, boy and girl.* Baltimore: Johns Hopkins University Press.

Montgomery, G., & Kirsch, I. (1996). Mechanisms of placebo pain reduction: An empirical investigation. *Psychological Science, 7,* 174–176.

Moore, B. C. J. (1982). *An introduction to the psychology of hearing* (2nd ed.). New York: Academic.

Moore, R. Y., & Card, J. P. (1985). Visual pathways and the entrainment of circadian rhythms: The medical and biological effects of light. In R. J. Wurtman, M. J. Baum, J. T. Potts, Jr. (Eds.), *Annals of the New York Academy of Science, 453,* 123–133.

Moore-Ede, M. C., Sulzman, F. M., & Fuller, C. A. (1982). *The clocks that time us.* Cambridge, MA: Harvard University Press.

Moray, N. (1959). Attention in dichotic listening: Affective cues and the influence of instruction. *Quarterly Journal of Experimental Psychology, 11,* 59–60.

Moreland, R. L., & Beach, S. R. (1992). Exposure effects in the classroom: the development of affinity among students. *Journal of Experimental Social Psychology, 28,* 255–276.

Morgan, H. J., & Janoff-Bulman, R. (1994). Positive and negative self-complexity: Patterns of adjustment following traumatic versus non-traumatic life experiences. *Journal of Social and Clinical Psychology, 13,* 63–85.

Morganstern, K. P. (1973). Implosive therapy and flooding procedures: A critical review. *Psychological Bulletin, 79,* 318–334.

Morrison, E. W. (1994). Role definitions and organizational citizenship behavior: The importance of employees' perspective. *Academy of Management Journal, 37,* 1543–1567.

Morrongiello, B. A., & Clifton, R. K. (1984). Effects of sound frequency on behavioral and cardiac orienting in newborn and five-month-old infants. *Journal of Experimental Child Psychology, 38,* 429–446.

Morrow, K. B., & Sorell G. T. (1989). Factors affecting self-esteem, depression, and negative behaviors in sexually abused female adolescents. *Journal of Marriage and the Family, 51,* 677–686.

Morse, J. M., & Morse, R. M. (1988). Cultural variation in the inference of pain. *Journal of Cross Cultural Psychology, 19,* 232–242.

Mosak, H. H. (1995). Adlerian psychotherapy. In R. J. Corsini & D. Wedding (Eds.), *Current psychotherapies* (5th ed., pp. 51–94). Itasca, IL: F. E. Peacock.

Moscovitch, M. (1985). Memory from infancy to old age: Implications for theories of normal and pathological memory. *Annals of the New York Academy of Sciences, 444,* 79–96.

Motowidlo, S. J., Packard, J. S., & Manning, M. R. (1986). Occupational stress: Its causes and consequences for job performance. *Journal of Applied Psychology, 71,* 618–629.

Mowrer, O. H., & Jones, H. M. (1945). Habit strength as a function of the pattern of reinforcement. *Journal of Experimental Psychology, 35,* 293–311.

Muczyk, J. P., & Reimann, B. C. (1987). The case for directive leadership. *Academy of Management Review, 12,* 637–647.

Mueser, K. T., & Gingerich, S. (1994). *Coping with schizophrenia: A guide for families.* Oakland, CA: Harbinger Publications.

Mueser, K. T., & Glynn, S. M. (1995). *Behavioral family therapy for psychiatric disorders.* Boston: Allyn & Bacon.

Mulkens, S. A. N., deJong, P. J., & Merckelbach, H. (1996). Disgust and spider phobia. *Journal of Abnormal Psychology, 105,* 464–468.

Mullaney, D. J., Johnson, L. C., Naitoh, P., Friedman, J. K., & Globus, G. G. (1977). Sleep during and after gradual sleep reduction. *Psychophysiology, 14,* 237–244.

Mumford, D. B., Whitehouse, A. M., & Choudry, I. Y. (1992). Survey of eating disorders in English-medium schools in Lahore, Pakistan. *International Journal of Eating Disorders, 11,* 173–184.

Munsinger, H. A. (1978). The adopted child's IQ: A crucial review. *Psychological Bulletin, 82,* 623–659.

Murphy, K. R., & Cleveland, J. N. (1991). *Performance appraisal: An organizational perspective.* Boston: Allyn & Bacon.

Murphy, K. R., Jako, R. A., & Anhalt, R. L. (1993). Nature and consequences of halo error: A critical analysis. *Journal of Applied Psychology, 78,* 218–225.

Murray, S. L., & Holmes, J. G. (1994). Storytelling in close relationships: The construction of confidence. *Personality and Social Psychology Bulletin, 20,* 650–663.

Murrey, G. J., Cross, H. J., & Whipple, J. (1992). Hypnotically created pseudomemories: Further investigation into the "memory distortion or response bias" question. *Journal of Abnormal Psychology, 101,* 75–77.

Myers, C. E., Ermita, B. R., Harris, K., Hasselmo, M., Solomon, P., & Gluck, M. A. (1996). A computational model of cholinergic disruption of septohippocampal activity in classical eyeblink conditioning. *Neurobiology of Learning and Memory, 66,* 51–66.

Myers, D. G., & Diener, E. (1995). Who is happy? *Psychological Science, 6,* 10–19.

Nadis, S. (1992, February). The energy-efficient brain: PET scans reveal how the brain delegates mental tasks. *Omni,* p. 16.

Nadler, A. (1987) Determinants of help-seeking behaviour: The effects of helper's similarity, task centrality, and recipient's self-esteem. European *Journal of Social Psychology, 17,* 57–67.

Naeser, M. A., Hayward, R. W., Laughlin, S. A., & Zatz, L. M. (1981). Quantitative CT scan studies in aphasia. *Brain and Language, 12,* 140–164.

Nagayama Hall, G. C., & Barongan, C. (1997). Prevention of sexual aggression: Sociocultural risk and protective factors. *American Psychologists, 52,* 5–14.

Naglieri, J. A. (1997). IQ: Knowns and unknowns, hits and misses. *American Psychologist, 52,* 75–76.

Nakajima, S., Kobayashi, Y., & Imada, H. (1995). Contextual control of taste aversion in rats: The effects of context extinction. *The Psychological Record, 45,* 309–318.

Nash, J. E., & Persaud, T. V. N. (1988). Embryopathic risks of cigarette smoking. *Experimental Pathology, 33,* 65–73.

Nathans, J. (1989). The genes for color vision. *Scientific American, 260,* 42–49.

Nathans, J., Thomas, D., & Hogness, D. S. (1986). Molecular genetics of human color vision: The genes encoding blue, green, and red pigments. *Science, 232,* 193–202.

National Association of Independent Insurers (1996). Kids, cars, and crashes. Associated Press release carried in many newspapers.

National Center for Health Statistics. (1996). *Healthy people 2000 review, 1995–1996.* Hyattsville, MD: NCHS.

National Institute of Alcohol Abuse and Alcoholism (NIAAA). (1993). *Eighth special report to the U.S. Congress on alcohol and health.* Washington, DC: U.S. Department of Health and Human Services.

Navarro, R. (1990). *Sound pressure levels of portable stereo headphones.* Indianapolis: Ear Institute of Indiana.

Neale, M. A., & Bazerman, M. H. (1985). The effects of framing and negotiator overconfidence on bargaining behaviors and outcomes. *Academy of Management Journal, 28,* 34–49.

Nebeker, D. M., & Tatum, B. C. (1993). The effects of computer monitoring, standards, and rewards on work performance, job satisfaction, and stress. *Journal of Applied Social Psychology, 23,* 508–536.

Needleman, H. L., Schell, A., Bellinger, D., Leviton, A., & Allred, E. N. (1990). The long term effects of exposure to low dosages of lead in childhood: An 11–year follow-up report. *New England Journal of Medicine, 322,* 83–88.

Neher, A. (1991). Maslow's theory of motivation: A critique. *Journal of Humanistic Psychology, 31,* 89–112.

Neher, A. (1996). Jung's theory of archetypes: A critique. *Journal of Humanistic Psychology, 36,* 61–91.

Neisser, U. (1991). A case of misplaced nostalgia. *American Psychologist, 46,* 34–36.

Neisser, U. (1997). Never a dull moment. *American Psychologist, 52,* 79–81.

Neisser, U., Boodoo, G., Bouchard, T. J., Jr., Bykin, A. W., Brody, N., Ceci, S. J., Halpern, D. F., Loehlin, J. C., Perloff, R., Sternberg, R.J., & Urbina, S. (1996). Intelligence: Knowns and unknowns. *American Psychologist, 51,* 77–101.

Nelson, C. A. (1995). The ontogeny of human memory: A cognitive neuroscience perspective. *Developmental Psychology, 31,* 723–738.

Nelson, D. E., Giovino, G. A., Shopland, D. R., Mowery, P. D., Mills, S. L., & Eriksen, M. P. (1995). Trends in cigarette smoking among U.S. adolescents, 1974 through 1991. *American Journal of Public Health, 85,* 34–39.

Nelson, L. J., & Miller, D. T. (1995). The distinctiveness effect in social categorization: You are what makes you unusual. *Psychological Science, 6,* 246–249.

Nelson, M. J., Lamke, T. A., & French, J. L. (1973). *The Henmon-Nelson Tests of Mental Ability.* Riverside, CA: Riverside Publishing.

Neugarten, B. L. (1987). The changing meaning of age. *Psychology Today, 21,* 29–33.

Newcomb, A. F., & Bagwell, C. L. (1995). Children's friendship relations: A meta-analytic review. *Psychological Bulletin, 117,* 306–347.

Newton, J., Toby, O., Spence, S. H., & Schotte, D. (1995). Cognitive-behavioral therapy versus EMG biofeedback in the treatment of chronic low back pain. *Behaviour Research and Therapy, 33,* 691–697.

Nisan, M., & Kohlberg, L. (1982). Universality and variation in moral judgment: A longitudinal and cross-sectional study in Turkey. *Child Development, 53,* 865–876.

Noble, J., & McConkey, K. M. (1995). Hypnotic sex change: Creating and challenging a delusion in the laboratory. *Journal of Abnormal Psychology, 104,* 69–74.

Noe, R. A. (1988). Women and mentoring: A review and research agenda. *Academy of Management Review, 13,* 65–78.

Noelman-Hoeksema, S. (1990). *Sex differences in depression.* Stanford, CA: Stanford University Press.

Norcross, J. C., Alford, B. A., & DeMichele, J. T. (1994). The future of psychotherapy: Delphi data and concluding observation. *Psychotherapy, 29,* 150–158.

Norman, D. A., & Shallice, T. (1985). Attention to action: Willed and automatic control of behavior. In R. J. Davidson, G. E. Schwartz, & D. Shapiro (Eds.), *Consciousness and self-regulation: Vol. 4. Advances in research and theory* (pp. 2–18). New York: Plenum Press.

Norris, F. H., & Murrell, S. A. (1990). Social support, life events, and stress as modifiers of adjustment to bereavement by older adults. *Psychology and Aging, 5,* 429–436.

Northcraft, G. B., & Neale, M. A. (1987). Experts, amateurs, and real estate: An anchoring-and-adjustment perspective on property pricing in decision. *Organizational Behavior and Human Decision Processes, 39,* 94–97.

Norton, A., & Moorman, J. E. (1987). Current trends in marriage and divorce among American women. *Journal of Marriage and the Family, 49,* 3–14.

Novick, B. E. (1989). Pediatric AIDS: A medical overview. In J. M. Seibert & R. A. Olson (Eds.), *Children, adolescents, and AIDS* (pp. 1–23). Lincoln: University of Nebraska Press.

Novy, D. M., Nelson, D. V., Francis, D., & Turk, D. C. (1995). Perspectives of chronic pain: An evaluative comparison of restrictive and comprehensive models. *Psychological Bulletin, 118,* 238–247.

Nyhan, W. L. (1987). Phenylalanine and mental retardation (PKU). In G. Adelman (Ed.), *Encyclopedia of neuroscience* (Vol. 2, pp. 940–942). Boston: Birkhauser.

O'Connor, K., Gareau, D., & Borgeat, F. (1995). *Biofeedback and Self-Regulation, 20,* 111–122.

O'Leary, K. D., Vivian, D., & Malone, J. (1992). Assessment of physical aggression in marriage: The need for multimodal assessment. Behavior *Research and Therapy, 14,* 1–10.

O'Leary, S. G. (1995). Parental discipline mistakes. *Current Directions in Psychological Science, 4,* 11–13.

O'Sullivan, C. S., & Durso, F. T. (1984). Effects of schema-incongruent information on memory for stereotypical attributes. *Journal of Personality and Social Psychology, 47,* 55–70.

Oaksford, M., Morris, F., Grainger, B., & Williams, J. M. G. (1996). Mood, reasoning, and central executive processes. *Journal of Experimental Psychology: Learning, Memory and Cognition, 22,* 476–492.

Ogbu, J. U. (1994). From cultural differences to differences in cultural frames of reference. In P. M. Greenfield & R. R. Cocking (Eds.), *Cross-cultural roots of minority child development* (pp. 365–391). Hillsdale, NJ: Erlbaum.

Ohbuchi, K. I., & Ogura, S. (1984). The experience of anger (1): The survey for adults and university students with Averill's questionnaire (Japanese). *Japanese Journal of Criminal Psychology, 22,* 1–35.

Ohbuchi, K. I., Kameda, M., & Agarie, N. (1989). Apology as aggression control: Its role in mediating appraisal of and response to harm. *Journal of Personality and Social Psychology, 56,* 219–227.

Ohlott, P. J., Ruderman, M. N., & McCauley, C. D. (1994). Gender differences in managers' developmental job experiences. *Academy of Management Journal, 37,* 46–67.

Okazaki, S. (1997). Sources of ethnic differences between Asian American and White American college students on measures of depression and social anxiety. *Journal of Abnormal Psychology, 106,* 52–60.

Oldham, G. R., Cummings, A., Mischel, L. J., Schmidtke, J. M., & Zhou, J. (1995). Listen while you work? Quasi-experimental relations between personal-stereo headset use and employee work responses. *Journal of Applied Psychology, 80,* 547–564.

Olds, J. (1973). Commentary. In E. S. Valenstein (Ed.), *Brain stimulation and motivation.* Glenview, IL: Scott Foresman.

Olds, J., & Milner, P. (1954). Positive reinforcement produced by electrical stimulation of septal area and other regions of rat brain. *Journal of Comparative and Physiological Psychology, 47,* 419–227.

Olsson, P. A. (1989). Psychodrama and group therapy approaches to alexithymia. In D. A. Halperin (Ed.), *Group Psychodynamics: New paradigms and new perspectives.* Chicago: Year Book Medical.

Olweus, D. (1995). Bullying or peer abuse at school: Facts and intervention. *Current Directions in Psychological Science, 4,* 196–200.

Orasanu, J., & Connolly, T. (1993). The reinvention of decision making. In G. A. Klein, J. Orasanu, R. Calderwood, & C. E. Zsambok (Eds.), *Decision making in action: Models and methods* (pp. 3–20). Norwood, NJ: Ablex.

Orbach, I., Kedem, P., Gorchover, O., Apter, A., & Tyano, S. (1993). Fears of death in suicidal and nonsuicidal adolescents. *Journal of Abnormal Psychology, 102,* 553–558.

Organ, D. W. (1988). *Organizational citizenship behavior: The good soldier syndrome.* Lexington, MA: Lexington Books.

Orlinsky, D. E., & Howard, K. E. (1987). The relation of process to outcome in psychotherapy. In S. L. Garfield & A. E. Bergin (Eds.), *Handbook of psychotherapy and behavior change* (3rd ed.). New York: Wiley.

Osterman, K., Björkqvist, K., Lagerspetz, K., Kaukianainen, A., Hauesmann, L. W., & Fraczek, A. (1994). Peer and self-estimated aggression and victimization in 8-year-old children from five ethnic groups. *Aggressive Behavior, 20,* 411–428.

Ostroff, C. (1992). The relationship between satisfaction, attitudes and performance: An organizational level analysis. *Journal of Applied Psychology, 77,* 963–974.

Otis, A. S., & Lennon, R. T. (1967). *The Otis-Lennon mental ability tests.* Los Angeles: Psychological Corp.

Oulette-Kobasa, S. C., & Puccetti, M. C. (1983). Personality and social resources in stress resistance. *Journal of Personality and Social Psychology, 45,* 836–850.

Padian, N. S., Shiboski, S., & Jewell, N. (1990). The effect of the number of exposures on the risk of heterosexual HIV transmission. *Journal of Infectious Diseases. 161,* 883–887.

Palace, E. M. (1995). Modification of dysfunctional patterns of sexual response through autonomic arousal and false physiological feedback. *Journal of Consulting and Clinical Psychology, 63*(4), 604–615.

Paller, K. A., Kutas, M., & McIsaac, H. K. (1995). Monitoring conscious recollection via the electrical activity of the brain. *Psychological Science, 6,* 107–111.

Parrott, W. G. (1991). The emotional experiences of envy and jealousy. In P. Salovey (Ed.), *The psychology of jealousy and envy* (pp. 2–20). New York: Guilford Press.

Passman, R. H., & Weisberg, P. (1975). Mothers and blankets as agents for promoting play and exploration by young children in a novel environment: The effects of social and nonsocial attachment objects. *Developmental Psychology, 11,* 170–177.

Pastor, D. L. (1981). The quality of mother-infant attachment and its relationship to toddlers' initial sociability with peers. *Developmental Psychology, 17,* 326–335.

Patrick, C. J., Bradley, M. M., & Lang, P. J. (1993). Emotion in the criminal psychopath: Startle reflex modulation. *Journal of Abnormal Psychology, 102,* 83–92.

Patterson, F. (1978). Conversations with a gorilla. *National Geographic, 154,* 438–465.

Paul, G. L. (1982). *The development of a "transportable" system of behavioral assessment for chronic patients.* Invited address, University of Minnesota, Minneapolis.

Paul, G. L., & Lentz, R. J. (1977). *Psychosocial treatment of chronic mental patients: Milieu versus social-learning programs.* Cambridge, MA: Harvard University Press.

Paul, L., Foss, M. A., & Galloway, J. (1993). Sexual jealousy in young women and men: Aggressive responsiveness to partner and rival. *Aggressive Behavior, 19,* 401–420.

Paulhus, D. L., Bruce, M. N., & Trapnell, P. D. (1995). Effects of self-presentation on the validity of personality impressions: A longitudinal study. *Personality and Social Psychology Bulletin, 21,* 100–108.

Paulseu, E., Frith, C. D., & Frackowiak, R. S. J. (1993). The neural correlates of the verbal component of working memory. *Nature, 362,* 342–343.

Pavlov, I. P. (1927). *Conditioned reflexes.* (G. V. Anrep, Trans.). London: Oxford University Press.

Payne, D. G. (1987). Hyperamnesia and reminiscence in recall: A historical and empirical review. *Psychological Bulletin, 101,* 5–27.

Payne, J. W. (1994). Thinking aloud: Insights into information processing. *Psychological Science, 5,* 241–248.

Pearce, J. M. (1986). A model for stimulus generalization in Pavlovian conditioning. *Psychological Review, 94,* 61–73.

Pelham, W. E. (1993). Pharmacotherapy for children with attention-deficit hyperactivity disorder. *School Psychology Review, 22,* 199–227.

Pelletier, K. R. (1986). Longevity: What can centenarians teach us? In K. Dychtwald (Ed.), *Wellness and health promotion for the elderly.* Rockville, MD: Aspen Publishers.

Pelletier, L. A., & Herold, E. S. (1988). The relationship of age, sex guilt, and sexual experience with female sexual fantasies. *Journal of Sex Research, 24,* 250–256.

Pennebaker, J. W. (1983). Accuracy of symptom perception. In A. Baum, S. E. Taylor, & J. Singer (Eds.). *Handbook of psychology and health* (Vol. 4, pp. 189–218). Hillsdale, NJ: Erlbaum.

Pennington, N., & Hastie, R. (1993). A theory of explanation-based decision making. In G. A. Klein, J. Orasanu, R. Calderwood, & C. E. Zsambok (Eds.), *Decision making in action: Models and methods* (pp. 188–201). Norwood, NJ: Ablex.

Pepler, D. J., & Craig, W. M. (1995). A peek behind the fence: Naturalistic observations of aggressive children with remote audiovisual recording. *Developmental Psychology, 31,* 548–553.

Pepperberg, I. M. (1990). Conceptual abilities of some nonprimate species, with an emphasis on an African grey parrot. In S. T. Parker & K. R. Gibson (Eds.), *"Language" and intelligence in monkeys and apes* (pp. 469–507). New York: Cambridge University Press.

Persad, S. M., & Polivy, J. (1993). Differences between depressed and nondepressed individuals in the recognition of and response to facial emotional cues. *Journal of Abnormal Psychology, 102,* 358–368.

Peters, R. D., Kloeppel, E., Alciandri, E., Fox, J. E., Thomas, M. L., Thorne, D. R., Sing, H. C., & Baliwinski, S. M. (1995). Effects of partial and total sleep deprivation on driving performance. *Proceedings of the Human Factors Society,* 39th Annual Meeting, 935.

Peterson, A. C. (1987, September). Those gangly years. *Psychology Today,* pp. 28–34.

Peterson, I. (1996). The soul of a chess machine: Lessons learned from a contest pitting man against computer. *Science News, 149,* 200–201.

Peterson, L., & Brown, D. (1994). Integrating child injury and abuse-neglect research: Common histories, etiologies, and solution. *Psychological Bulletin, 116,* 293–315.

Peterson, L. R., & Peterson, M. J. (1959). Short-term retention of individual verbal items. *Journal of Experimental Psychology, 58,* 193–198.

Peto, R., Lopez, A. D., Boreham, J., Thun, M., & Heath, C. (1992). Mortality from tobacco in developed countries: Indirect estimation from national vital statistics. *Lancet, 339,* 1268–1278.

Pettigrew, T. E. (1997). Generalized intergroup contact effects on prejudice. *Personality and Social Psychology Bulletin, 23,* 175–185.

Petty, M. M., Singleton, B., & Connell, D. W. (1992). An experimental evaluation of an organizational incentive plan in the electric utility industry. *Journal of Applied Psychology, 77,* 427–436.

Petty, R. E., & Cacioppo, J. T. (1986). The elaboration likelihood model of persuasion. In L. Berkowitz (Ed.), *Advances in experimental social psychology* (Vol. 19, pp. 123–205). New York: Academic Press.

Petty, R. E., Cacioppo, J. T., Strathman, A. J., & Priester, J. R. (1994). To think or not to think; Exploring two routes to persuasion. In S. Shavitt & T. C. Brock (Eds.), *Persuasion* (pp. 113–147). Boston: Allyn and Bacon.

Petty, R. E., & Jarvis, B. G. (1996). An individual difference perspective on assessing cognitive processes. In N. Schwarz & S. Sudman (Eds.), *Answering questions: Methodology for determining cognitive and communicative processes in survey research* (pp. 221–257). San Francisco: Jossey-Bass.

Petty, R. E., Unnava, R., & Strathman, A. J. (1991). Theories of attitude change. In T. S. Robertson & H. H. Kassarjian (Eds.), *Handbook of consumer behavior* (pp. 241–280). Englewood Cliffs, NJ: Prentice-Hall.

Pfaffman, C. (1978). The vertebrate phylogeny, neural code, and integrative processes of taste. In E. C. Carterrette & M. P. Friedman (Eds.), *Handbook of perception* (vol. 6A). New York: Academic.

Pfiffner, L. J., & O'Leary, S. G. (1993). School-based psychological treatment. In J. L. Matson (Ed.), *Handbook of hyperactivity in children* (pp. 234–255). Boston: Allyn & Bacon.

Phillips, A. G., & Fibiger, H. C. (1989). Neuroanatomical bases of intracranial self-stimulation: Untangling the Gordian knot. In J. M. Leibman & S. J. Cooper (Eds.), *The neuropharmacological bases of reward* (pp. 66–105). Oxford, England: Clarendon Press.

Phillips, A. G., Spyraki, C., & Fibiger, H. C. (1982). Conditioned place preference with amphetamine and opiates as reward stimuli: Attenuation by haloperidol. In B. G. Hoebel & D. Movin (Eds.), *The neural basis of feeding and reward* (pp. 455–464). Brunswick, MN: Haer Institute.

Piaget, J. (1965). *The moral judgment of the child.* New York: Free Press. (Original work published 1932.)

Piaget, J. (1975). *The child's conception of the world.* Totowa, NJ: Littlefield, Adams. (Originally published in 1929.)

Pierce, C. A. (1992). *The effects of physical attractiveness and height on dating choice: Meta-analysis.* Unpublished masters thesis, University at Albany, State University of New York, Albany.

Pierce, C. A. (1995). *Attraction in the workplace: An examination of antecedents and consequences of organizational romance.* Unpublished doctoral dissertation, SUNY-Albany.

Pierce, J. P., Macaskill, P., & Hill, D. (1990). Long-term effectiveness of mass media led antismoking campaigns in Australia. *American Journal of Public Health, 80,* 565–569.

Pierce, P. F. (1996). When the patient chooses: Describing unaided decisions in health care. *Human Factors, 38,* 278–287.

Pierce, W. D., & Epling, W. F. (1994). The applied importance of research on the matching law. *Journal of Applied Behavior Analysis, 28,* 237–241.

Pilkington, N. W., & Lydon, J. E. (1997). The relative effect of attitude similarity and attitude dissimilarity on interpersonal attraction: Investigating the moderating roles of prejudice and group membership. *Personality and Social Psychology Bulletin, 23,* 107–122.

Pillai, R. (1996). Crisis and the emergence of charismatic leadership in groups: An experimental investigation. *Journal of Applied Social Psychology, 26,* 543–562.

Pillow, D. R., Zautra, A. J., & Sandler, I. (1996). Major life events and minor stressors: Identifying mediational links in the stress process. *Journal of Personality and Social Psychology, 70,* 381–394.

Pinel, J. P. J. (1993). *Biopsychology* (2nd ed.). Boston: Allyn and Bacon.

Pinker, S. (1984). Visual cognition: An introduction. *Cognition: International Journal of Cognitive Science, 18,* 1–63.

Pinker, S. (1989). *Learnability and cognition.* Cambridge, MA: MIT Press.

Plante, T. G., & Rodin, J. (1990). Physical fitness and enhanced psychological health. *Current Psychology: Research & Reviews, 9,* 3–24.

Plomin, R., & Bergeman, C. S. (1991). The nature of nurture: Genetic influence on "environmental" measures. *Behavioral and Brain Sciences, 14,* 373–427.

Polich, J. (1993). Cognitive brain potentials. *Current Directions in Psychological Science, 3,* 175–178.

Pomerleau, O. F., & Pomerleau, C. S. (1984). Neuro-regulators and the reinforcement of smoking: Towards a biobehavioral explanation. *Neuroscience and Biobehavioral Reviews, 8,* 503–513.

Poole, D. A., (1996). Strolling fuzzy-trace theory through eyewitness testimony (or vice versa). *Learning and Individual Differences, 7,* 87–93.

Poon, L. W., & Fozard, J. L. (1980). Age and word frequency effects in continuous recognition memory. *Journal of Gerontology, 35,* 77–86.

Pope, K. S., & Vetter, V. A. (1992). Ethical dilemmas encountered by members of the American Psychological Association. *American Psychologist, 47,* 397–411.

Porter, L. S., & Stone, A. A. (1995). Are there really gender differences in coping? A reconsideration of previous data and results from a daily study. *Journal of Social and Clinical Psychology. 14,* 184–202.

Porter, L. W., & Lawler, E. E., III. (1968). *Managerial attitudes and performance.* Homewood, IL: Dorsey Press.

Posner, M. I., & Petersen, S. E. (1990). The attention system of the human brain. *Annual Review of Neuroscience,* 13, 25–42.

Powell, G. N., & Butterfield, D. A. (1994). Investigating the "glass ceiling" phenomenon: An empirical study of actual promotions to top management. *Academy of Management Journal, 37,* 68–86.

Pratt, C., & Garton, A. (Eds.) (1993). *The development and use of representation in children.* Chichester, England: Wiley.

Priester, J., & Petty, R. E. (1995). Source attributions and persuasion: Perceived honesty as a determinant of message scrutiny. *Personality and Social Psychology Bulletin, 21,* 637–654.

Prigatano, G. P. (1992). Personality disturbances associated with traumatic brain injury. *Journal of Consulting and Clinical Psychology, 3,* 360–368.

Prior, M., Smart, M. A., Sanson, A., & Oberklaid, F. (1993). Sex differences in psychological adjustment from infancy to 8 years. *Journal of the American Academy of Child and Adolescent Psychiatry, 32,* 291–304.

Pritchard, R. D., Dunnette, M. D., & Jorgenson, D. O. (1972). Effects of perceptions of equity and inequity on work performance and satisfaction. *Journal of Applied Psychology, 57,* 75–94.

Prochaska, J. O., Velicer, W. F., Rossi, J. S., Goldstein, M. G., Marcus, B. H., Rakowski, W., Fiore, C., Harlow, L. L., Bedding, C. A., Rosenbloom, D., & Rossi, R. R. (1994). Stages of change and decisional balance for 12 problem behaviors. *Health Psychology, 13,* 39–46.

Pruitt, D. G., & Rubin, J. Z. (1986). *Social conflict: Escalation, stalemate, settlement.* New York: Random House.

Ptacek, J. T., Smith, R. E, & Dodge, K. L. (1994). Gender differences in coping with stress: When stressor and appraisals do not differ. *Personality and Social Psychology Bulletin, 20,* 421–430.

Pulakos, E. D. (1986). The development of training programs to increase accuracy with different rating tasks. *Organizational Behavior and Human Decision Processes, 38,* 76–91.

Pulkinen, L. (1996). Female and male personality styles: A typological and developmental analysis. *Journal of Personality and Social Psychology, 70,* 1288–1306.

Pylyshyn, Z. W. (1981). The imagery debate: Analogue media versus tacit knowledge. *Psychological Review, 88,* 16–45.

Rachlin, H. (1995). The value of temporal patterns in behavior. *Current Directions in Psychological Science, 4,* 188–192.

Rachman, S. J., & Hodgson, R. J. (1980). *Obsessions and compulsions.* Englewood Cliffs, NJ: Prentice-Hall.

Raphael, B., Cubis, J., Dunne, M., Lewin, T., & Kelly, B. (1990). The impact of parental loss on adolescents' psychosocial characteristics. *Adolescence, 25,* 689–700.

Rasmussen, T., & Milner, B. (1975). Excision of Broca's area without persistent aphasia. In K. J. Zulch, O. Creutzfeldt, & G. C. Gailbraith (Eds.), *Central localization* (pp. 258–263). New York: Springer-Verlag.

Rauschecker, J. P. (1995). Compensatory plasticity and sensory substitution in the cerebral cortex. *Trends in Neuroscience, 18,* 36–43.

Raven, J. C. (1977). *Raven Progressive Matrices.* Los Angeles: Psychological Corp.

Rayner, K., & Raney, G. E. (1996). Eye movement control in reading and visual search: Effects of word frequency. *Psychonomic Bulletin & Review, 3,* 245–248.

Raynor, J. O. (1970). Relationships between achievement-related motives, future orientation, and academic performance. *Journal of Personality and Social Psychology, 15,* 28–33.

Raz, S. (1993). Structural cerebral pathology in schizophrenia: Regional or diffuse? *Journal of Abnormal Psychology, 102,* 445–452.

Reason, J. T., & Lucas, D. (1984). Using cognitive diaries to investigate naturally occurring memory blocks. In J. E. Harris & P. E. Morris (Eds.), *Everyday memory actions and absent-mindedness* (pp. 53–70). London: Academic Press.

Rechtschaffen, A., Gilliland, M. A., Bergmann, B. M., & Winter, J. B. (1983). Physiological correlates of prolonged sleep deprivation in rats. *Science, 221,* 182–184.

Reed, S. B., Kirsch, I., Wickless, C., Moffitt, K. H., & Taren, P. (1996). Reporting biases in hypnosis: Suggestion or compliance? *Journal of Abnormal Psychology, 105,* 142–145.

Reed, T. E., & Jensen, A. R. (1993). Choice reaction time and visual pathway conduction velocity both correlate with intelligence but appear not to correlate with each other: Implications for information processing. *Intelligence, 17,* 191–203.

Reeder, G. D., Fletcher, G. J. O., & Furman, K. (1989). The role of observers: Expectations in attitude attribution. *Journal of Experimental Social Psychology, 25,* 168–188.

Reeves, A., & Sperling, G. (1986). Attention gating in short-term retention of individual verbal items. *Psychological Review, 93,* 180–206.

Reid, L. D. (1990). Rates of cocaine addiction among newborns. Personal communication, Rensselaer Polytechnic Institute.

Reid, L. D. (1996). Endogenous opioids and alcohol dependence: Opioid alkaloids and the propensity to drink alcoholic beverages. *Alcohol, 13,* 5–11.

Reid, L. D. (Ed.). (1990). *Opioids, bulimia, and alcohol abuse and alcoholism.* New York: Springer-Verlag.

Reid, L. D., Hubbell, C. L., Tsai, J., Fishkin, M. D., & Amendola, C. A. (1996). Naltrindole, a delta-opioid antagonist, blocks MDMA's ability to enhance pressing for rewarding brain stimulation. *Pharmacology Biochemistry and Behavior, 53,* 477–480.

Reiman, E. M., Fusselman, M. J., Fox, P. T., & Raichle, M. E. (1989). Neuroanatomical correlates of anticipatory anxiety. *Science, 243,* 1071–1074.

Reinecke, J., Schmidt, P., & Ajzen, I. (1996). Application of the theory of planned behavior to adolescents' condom use: A panel study. *Journal of Applied Social Psychology, 26,* 749–772.

Reisenzein, R. (1983). The Schachter theory of emotion: Two decades later. *Psychological Bulletin, 94,* 239–264.

Reissland-Berghart, N. (1988). Neonatal imitation in the first hour of life: Observations in rural Nepal. *Developmental Psychology, 24,* 464–469.

Rempel, D. M., Harrison, R. J., & Barnhart, S. (1992). Work-related cumulative trauma disorders of the upper extremity. *Journal of the American Medical Association, 267,* 838–843.

Reno, R. R., Cialdini, R. B., & Kallgren, C. A. (1993). The transsituational influence of social norms. *Journal of Personality and Social Psychology, 64,* 104–112.

Rensberger, B. (1993, May 3). The quest for machines that not only listen, but also understand. *Washington Post,* p.3.

Rentsch, J. R., & Heffner, T. S. (1994). Assessing self-concept: Analysis of Gordon's coding scheme using "Who am I?" responses. *Journal of Social Behavior and Personality, 9,* 283–300.

Repacholi, B. M., & Gopnik, A. (1997). Early reasoning about desires: Evidence from 14– and 18–month-olds. *Developmental Psychology, 33,* 12–21.

Rescorla, R. A. (1988). Pavlovian conditioning: It's not what you think it is. *American Psychologist, 43,* 151–160.

Rescorla, R. A., & Wagner, A. R. (1972). A theory of Pavlovian conditioning: Variations in the effectiveness of reinforcement and nonreinforcement. In A. Black & W. F. Prokasy (Eds.), *Classical conditioning: II. Current research and theory.* New York: Appleton.

Rest, J. R. (1986). *Moral development: Advances in research and theory.* New York: Preager.

Reyna, V. F., & Titcomb, A. (1996). Constraints on the suggestibility of eyewitness testimony: A fuzzy-trace theory analysis. In D. Payne & F. Conrad (Eds.), *Intersections in basic and applied memory research.* Hillsdale, NJ: Erlbaum.

Rhodewalt, F., & Fairfield, M. (1991). Claimed self-handicaps and the self-handicapper: The relations of reduction in intended effort to performance. *Journal of Research in Personality, 245,* 402–417.

Rice, C. G., Breslin, M., & Roper, R. G. (1987). Sound levels from personal cassette players. *British Journal of Audiology, 21,* 273–278.

Rice, F. P. (1992). *Intimate relationships, marriages, and families.* Mountain View, CA: Mayfield.

Richardson, J. T. E., & Zucco, G. M. (1989). Cognition and olfaction: A review. *Psychological Bulletin, 105,* 352–360.

Richman, W. L., & Quinones, M. A. (1996). Task frequency rating accuracy: The effect of task engagement and experience. *Journal of Applied Psychology, 81,* 512–524.

Riess, M., & Schlenker, B. R. (1977). Attitude changes and responsibility avoidance as modes of dilemma resolution in forced-compliance situations. *Journal of Personality and Social Psychology, 35,* 21–30.

Rigby, C. S., Deci, E. L., Patrick, B. C., & Ryan, R. M. (1992). Beyond the intrinsic-extrinsic dichotomy: Self-determination in motivation and learning. *Motivation and Emotion, 16,* 165–185.

Rind, B., & Bordia, P. (1996). Effect on restaurant tipping of male and female servers drawing a happy, smiling face on the backs of customers' checks. *Journal of Applied Social Psychology, 26,* 218–225.

Riskind, J. H., & Maddux, J. E. (1993). Loomingness, helplessness, and fearfulness: An integration of harm-looming and self-efficacy models of fear. *Journal of Social and Clinical Psychology, 12,* 73–89.

Rissman, E. F. (1995). An alternative animal model for the study of female sexual behavior.

Current Directions in Psychological Science, 4, 6–10.

Robbin, A. L., & Foster, L. (1988). *Negotiating adolescence: A behavioral family systems approach to parent/teen conflict.* New York: Guilford Press.

Robbins, T. L., & DeNisi, A. S. (1994). A closer look at interpersonal affect as a distinct influence on cognitive processing in performance evaluations. *Journal of Applied Psychology, 79,* 341–353.

Roberts, T. A., & Nolen-Hoeksema, S. (1990). *Gender differences in construals of and responsiveness to evaluations in an achievement situation.* Unpublished manuscript, Stanford University.

Robinson, L. A., Berman, J. S., & Neimeyer, R. A. (1990). Psychotherapy for the treatment of depression: A comprehensive review of controlled outcome research. *Psychological Bulletin, 108,* 30–49.

Robinson, R. G., Kubos, K. L., Starr, L. B., Rao, K., & Price, T. R. (1984). Mood disorders in stroke patients: Importance of location of lesion. *Brain, 107,* 81–93.

Rodin, J. (1984, April). A sense of control. *Psychology Today,* 38–45.

Rodin, J., Bartoshuk, L., Peterson, C., & Schank, D. (1990). Bulimia and taste: Possible interactions. *Journal of Abnormal Psychology, 99,* 32–39.

Rodin, J., & Plante, T. (1989). The psychological effects of exercise. In R. S. Williams & A. Wellece (Eds.), *Biological effects of physical activity.* Champaign, IL: Human Kinetics.

Rodin, J., & Salovey, P. (1989). Health psychology. *Annual Review of Psychology, 40,* 533–580.

Rodin, J., & Slochower, J. (1976). Externality in the nonobese: Effects of environmental responsiveness on weight. *Journal of Personality and Social Psychology, 33,* 338–344.

Roediger, H. I., & McDermott, K. B. (1992). Depression and implicit memory: A commentary. *Journal of Abnormal Psychology, 101,* 587–591.

Roesch, S. C., & Amirkhan, J. H. (1997). Boundary condition for self-serving attributions: Another look at the sports pages. *Journal of Applied Social Psychology, 27,* 245–261.

Roese, N. J. (1997). Counterfactual thinking. *Psychological Bulletin, 121,* 133–148.

Rogers, C. R. (1970). *Carl Rogers on encounter groups.* New York: Harper & Row.

Rogers, C. R. (1977). *Carl Rogers on personal power: Inner strength and its revolutionary impact.* New York: Delacorte.

Rogers, C. R. (1980). *A way of being.* Boston: Houghton Mifflin.

Rogers, C. R. (1982, August). Nuclear war: A personal response. *American Psychological Association,* pp. 6–7.

Rogler, L. H., Malgady, R. G., Constantino, G., & Blumenthal, R. (1987). What do culturally sensitive mental health services mean? The case of Hispanics. *American Psychologist, 42,* 565–570.

Rogoff, B. (1990). *Apprenticeship in thinking: Cognitive development in social context.* Oxford, England: Oxford University Press.

Rogoff, B., & Mistry, J. (1985). Memory development in cultural contexts. In M. Pressley & C. Brainerd (Eds.), *The cognitive side of memory development.* New York: Springer-Verlag.

Rosch, E. H. (1973). Natural categories. *Cognitive Psychology, 4,* 328–349.

Rosch, E. H. (1975). The nature of mental codes for color categories. *Journal of Experimental Psychology: Human Perception and Performance, 1,* 303–322.

Rosen, K. S., & Rothbaum, F. (1993). Quality of parental caregiving and security of attachment. *Developmental Psychology, 29,* 358–367.

Rosenberg, E. L., & Ekman, P. (1995). Conceptual and methodological issues in the judgment of facial expressions of emotion. *Motivation and Emotion, 19,* 111–138.

Rosenblith, J. F. (1992). *In the beginning: Development from conception to age two.* Newbury Park, CA: Sage.

Rosenfield, D., Folger, R., & Adelman, H. F. (1980). When rewards reflect competence: A qualification of the overjustification effect. *Journal of Personality and Social Psychology, 39,* 368–376.

Rosenman, R. H. (1988). The impact of certain emotions in cardiovascular disorders. In M. P. Janisse (Ed.), *Individual differences, stress, and health psychology* (pp. 1–23). New York: Springer-Verlag.

Rosenstock, I. M. (1974). The health belief model and preventive health behavior. *Health Education Monographs, 2,* 354–386.

Rosensztein, D., & Oster, H. (1988). Differential facial responses to four basic tastes in newborns. *Child Development, 59,* 1555–1568.

Rosenzweig, M. R. (1992). Psychological science around the world. *American Psychologist, 47,* 718–722.

Roskies, E. (1987). *Stress management for the healthy Type A.* New York: Guilford Press.

Roskos-Ewoldsen, D. R., & Fazio, R. H. (1992). The accessibility of source likabilty as a determinant of persuasion. *Personality and Social Psychology Bulletin, 18,* 19–25.

Ross, L. L., & McBean, D. (1995). A comparison of pacing contingencies in classes using a personalized system of instruction. *Journal of Applied Behavior Analysis, 28,* 87–88.

Roter, D. L., & Ewart, C. K. (1992). Emotional inhibition in essential hypertension: Obstacle to communication during medical visits? *Health Psychology, 11,* 163–169.

Roter, D. L., & Hall, J. A. (1989). Studies of doctor–patient interaction. *Annual Review of Public Health, 10,* 163–180.

Rothbart, M. K., & Ahadi, S. A. (1994). Temperament and the development of personality. *Journal of Abnormal Psychology, 103,* 55–66.

Rothenberg, R. B., & Koplan, J. P. (1990). Chronic disease in the 1990s. *Annual Review of Public Health, 11,* 267–296.

Rothenberg, R., Nasca, P., Mikl, J., Burnett, W., & Reynolds, B. (1987). In R. W. Amler & H. B. Dull (Eds.), *Closing the gap: The burden of unnecessary Illness.* New York: Oxford University Press.

Rothland, J. C., Brandt, J., Zee, D., & Codori, A. M. (1993). Unimpaired verbal memory with oculomotor control in asymptomatic adults with the genetic marker for Huntington's disease. *Archives of Neurology, 50,* 799–802.

Rothman, A. J., & Salovey, P. (1997) Shaping perceptions to motivate healthy behavior. The role of message framing. *Psychological Bulletin, 121*(1), 3–19.

Rothman, K. R., Cristina, I. C., Flanders, D., & Fried, M. P. (1980). Epidemiology of laryngeal cancer. In P. E. Sartwell (Ed.), *Epidemiologic reviews* (Vol. 2, pp. 195–209). Baltimore: Johns Hopkins University Press.

Rotter, J. B. (1954). *Social learning and clinical psychology.* Englewood Cliffs, NJ: Prentice-Hall.

Rotter, J. B. (1982). *The development and applications of social learning theory: Selected papers.* New York: Praeger.

Rovee-Collier, C. K. (1987). Learning and memory. In J. D. Osofky (Ed.), *Handbook of infant development* (2nd ed., pp. 98–148). New York: Wiley.

Rowe, D. C., Vazsonyi, A. T., & Flannery, D. J. (1995). Ethnic and racial similarity in developmental process: A study of academic achievement. *Psychological Science, 6,* 33–38.

Rowland, D. L., Cooper, S. E., & Slob, A. K. (1996). Genital and psychoaffective response to erotic stimulation in sexually functional and dysfunctional men. *Journal of Abnormal Psychology, 105,* 194–203.

Rowlison, R. T., & Felner, R. D. (1988). Major life events, hassles, and adaptation in adolescence: Confounding in the conceptualization and measurement of life stress and adjustment revisited. *Journal of Personality and Social Psychology, 55,* 432–444.

Rozin, P. (1996). Toward a psychology of food and eating: From motivation to module to model to marker, morality, meaning, and metaphor. *Current Directions in Psychological Science, 6,* 18–20.

Rozin, P., Markwith, M., & Nemeroff, C. (1992). Magical contagion beliefs and fear of AIDS. *Journal of Applied Social Psychology, 22,* 1081–1092.

Rozin, P., & Michener, L. (1996, April 8). Cited in "Is it the chocolate talking or are you really in love?" *Wall Street Journal,* p. B1.

Rozin, P., & Nemeroff, C. (1990). The laws of sympathetic magic: A psychological analysis of similarity and contagion. In W. Stigler, R. A. Shweder, & G. Herdt (Eds.), *Cultural psychology: Essays in comparative human development* (pp. 205–232). Cambridge, England: Cambridge University Press.

Rubin, J. Z. (1985). Deceiving ourselves about deception: Comment on Smith and Richardson's "Amelioration of deception and harm in psychological research." *Journal of Personality and Social Psychology, 48,* 252–253.

Rudakewych, M., Valent, L., & Hedge, A. (1994). Field evaluation of a negative slope keyboard system designed to minimize postural risks to computer workers. In A. Grieco, G. Molteni, E. Occhipinti, & B. Piccoli (Eds.), *Work and display units '94* (pp. C17–C19). London: Taylor & Francis.

Rushton, J. P. (1989a). Genetic similarity, human altruism, and group selection. *Behavioral and Brain Sciences, 12,* 503–559.

Rushton, J. P. (1989b). Genetic similarity in male friendships. *Ethology and Sociobiology, 10,* 361–373.

Rushton, J. P. (1997). Race, IQ, and the APA report on The Bell Curve. *American Psychologist, 52,* 69–71.

Rushton, W. A. H. (1975). Visual pigments and color blindness. *Scientific American, 232,* 64–74.

Russell, G. A. (Ed.). (1994). *Violence in intimate relationships.* New York: PMA Publishing.

Russell, J. A. (1994). Is there universal recognition of emotion from facial expression? A review of the cross-cultural studies. *Psychological Bulletin, 115,* 102–141.

Russell, J. A. (1995). Facial expressions and emotion: What lies beyond minimal universality? *Psychological Bulletin, 118,* 379–391.

Ryan, C. S. (1996). Accuracy of black and white college students' in-group and out-group stereotypes. *Personality and Social Psychology Bulletin, 22,* 1114–1127.

Ryan, R. M. (1982). Control and information in the intrapersonal sphere: An extension of cognitive evaluation theory. *Journal of Personality and Social Psychology, 43,* 450–561.

Ryckman, R. M., Butler, J. C., Thornton, B., & Lindner, M. A. (1995, April). Identification and assessment of physique subtype stereotypes. Paper presented at the meeting of the Eastern Psychological Association, Boston.

Saarni, C. (1993). Socialization of emotion. In M. Lewis & J. Haviland (Eds.), *Handbook of emotions* (pp. 435–446).

Sacks, O. (1993, May 10). To see and not see: A neurologist's notebook. *The New Yorker,* pp. 59–73.

Saks, M. J. (1992). Obedience versus disobedience to legitimate versus illegitimate authorities issuing good versus evil directions. *Psychological Science, 3,* 221–223.

Samson, L. F. (1988). Perinatal viral infections and neonates. *Journal of Perinatal and Neonatal Nursing, 1,* 56–65.

Sanchez, J. I., & De La Torre, P. (1996). A second look at the relationship between rating and behavioral accuracy in performance appraisal. *Journal of Applied Psychology, 81,* 3–10.

Sanders, M. S., & McCormick, E. J. (1993). *Human factors in engineering and design.* New York: McGraw-Hill.

Sanna, L. J., & Pusecker, P. A. (1994). Self-efficacy, valence of self-evaluation, and performance. *Personality and Social Psychology Bulletin, 20,* 82–93.

Sansavini, A., Bertoncini, J., & Giovanelli, G. (1997). Newborns discriminate the rhythm of multisyllabic stressed words. *Developmental Psychology, 33,* 3–11.

Sargent, C. (1984). Between death and shame: Dimensions in pain in Bariba culture. *Social Science Medicine, 19,* 1299–1304.

Sarter, M., Berntson, G. G., & Cacioppo, J. T. (1996). Brain imaging and cognitive neuroscience. *American Psychologist, 51,* 13–21.

Savage-Rumbaugh, E. S., Sevcik, R. A., Brakke, K. E., & Rumbaugh, D. M. (1992). Symbols: Their communicative use, communication, and combination by bonobos (*Pan paniscus*). In L. P. Lipsitt & C. Rovee-Collier (Eds.), *Advances in infancy research* (Vol. 7, pp. 221–278). Norwood, NJ: Ablex.

Savage-Rumbaugh, S., Romski, M. A., Hopkins, W. D., & Sevcik, R. A. (1989). Symbol acquisition and use by *Pan troglodytes, Pan paniscus, Homo sapiens.* In P. G. Heltne, & L. A. Marquardt (Eds.), *Understanding chimpanzees* (pp. 266–295). Cambridge, MA: Harvard University Press.

Saxby, E., & Peniston, E. G., (1995) Alpha-theta brainwave neurofeedback training: An effective treatment for male and female alcoholics with depressive symptoms. *Journal of Clinical Psychology, 51*(5), 685–693.

Saxe, L. (1994). Detection of deception: Polygraph and integrity tests. *Current Directions in Psychological Science, 3,* 69–73.

Saywitz, K. J., Geiselman, A., & Bornstein, G. K. (1992). Effects of cognitive interviewing and practice on children's recall performance. *Journal of Applied Psychology, 77,* 744–756.

Scarr, S., & Weinberg, R. A. (1976). IQ test performance of black children adopted by white families. *American Psychologist, 31,* 726–739.

Schab, F. R. (1991). Odor memory: Taking stock. *Psychological Bulletin, 109,* 242–251.

Schachter, D. L., & Kihlstrom, J. F. (1989). Functional amnesia. In F. Boller & J. Grafman (Eds.), *Handbook of neuropsychology* (Vol. 3, pp. 209–230). New York: Elsevier.

Schachter, S., & Singer, J. E. (1962). Cognitive, social, and physiological determinants of emotional states. *Psychological Review, 69,* 379–399.

Schaie, K. W. (1974). Translations in gerontology-from lab to life: Intellectual functioning. *American Psychologist, 29,* 802–807.

Schaie, K. W. (1986). *Adult development and aging* (2nd ed.). Boston: Little, Brown.

Schaie, K. W. (1990). Intellectual development in adulthood. In J. E. Birren & K. W. Schaie (Eds.), *Handbook of the psychology of aging* (3rd ed., pp. 291–309). San Diego: Academic Press.

Schaie, K. W. (1993). The Seattle longitudinal studies of adult intelligence. *Current Directions in Psychological Science, 2,* 171–175.

Scheier, M. F., & Carver, C. S. (1988). *Perspectives on personality.* Boston: Allyn and Bacon.

Scheier, M. F., & Carver, C. S. (1992). Effects of optimism on psychological and physical wellbeing: Theoretical overview and empirical update. *Cognitive Therapy and Research, 16,* 201–228.

Scheier, M. F., Weintraub, J. K., & Carver, C. S. (1986). Coping with stress: Divergent strategies of optimists and pessimists. *Journal of Personality and Social Psychology, 51,* 1257–1264.

Schiffman, H. R. (1990). *Sensation and perception: An integrated approach* (3rd ed). New York: John Wiley & Sons.

Schiller, P. H. (1994). Area V4 of the primate visual cortex. *Current Directions in Psychological Science, 3,* 89–92.

Schneider, B. H. (1991). A comparison of skill-building and desensitization strategies for intervention with aggressive children. *Aggressive Behavior, 17,* 301–311.

Schneider, B. H., & Byrne, B. M. (1987). Individualizing social skills training for behaviour-disordered children. *Journal of Consulting and Clinical Psychology, 55,* 444–445.

Schneider, F. R., Johnson, J., Hornig, C. D., Oliebowitz, M. R., & Weissman, M. M. (1992). Social phobia: Comorbidity and morbidity in an epidemiologic sample. *Archives of General Psychiatry, 49,* 282–288.

Schofield, W. (1964). *Psychotherapy: The purchase of friendship.* Englewood Cliffs, NJ: Prentice-Hall.

Schulze, C., Karie, T., & Dickens, W. (1996). *Does the bell curve ring true?* Washington, DC: Brookings Institution.

Schunn, C. D., & Dunbar, K. (1996). Priming, analogy, and awareness in complex reasoning. *Memory & Cognition, 24,* 271–284.

Schuster, J. R., & Zingheim, P. K. (1992). *The new pay: Linking employee and organizational performance.* New York: Lexington Books.

Schwarz, N., Bless, H., Strack, F., Klumpp, G., Rittenauer-Schatka, G., & Simons, A. (1991). Ease of retrieval as information: Another look at the availability heuristic. *Journal of Personality and Social Psychology, 61,* 195–202.

Schwarzwald, J., Amir, Y., & Crain, R. L. (1992). Long-term effects of school desegregation experiences on interpersonal relations in the Israeli defense forces. *Personality and Social Psychology Bulletin, 18,* 357–368.

Schweikert, R., Guentert, L., & Hersberger, L. (1990). Phonological similarity, pronunciation rate, and memory span. *Psychological Science, 1,* 74–77.

Schweinberger, S. R., Klos, T., & Sommer, W. (1995). Covert face recognition in prosopagnosia: A dissociable function? *Cortex, 31,* 517–529.

Schyns, P. G., & Oliva, A. (1994). From blobs to boundary edges: Evidence for time- and spatial-scale-dependent scene recognition. *Psychological Science, 5,* 195–200.

Scott, J. P. (1992). Aggression: Functions and control in social systems. *Aggressive Behavior, 18,* 1–20.

Scribner, S. (1977). Recall of classical syllogisms: A cross-cultural investigation of error on logical problems. In R. J. Falmagne (Ed.), *Reasoning: Representation and process.* Hillsdale, NJ: Erlbaum.

Scribner, S. (1986). Thinking in action: Some characteristics of practical thought. In R. J. Sternberg & R. K. Wagner (Eds.), *Practical intelligence: Nature and origins of competence in the everyday world* (pp. 13–30). New York: Cambridge University Press.

Searle, J. (1980). Minds, brains, and programs. *Behavioral and Brain Science, 3,* 417–457.

Sedvall, G. (1992). The current status of PET scanning with respect to schizophrenia. *Neuropsychopharmacology, 7,* 43–54.

Segal, N. L., & Bouchard, T. J. (1993). Grief intensity following the loss of a twin and other relatives: Test of kinship-genetic hypotheses. *Human Biology, 65,* 87–105.

Seifer, R., & Schiller, M. (in press). The role of parenting sensitivity, infant temperament, and dyadic interaction in young children: A survey of research issues. In N. L. Wolraich & D. Routh (Eds.), *Advances in developmental and behavioral pediatrics* (Vol. 7, pp. 1–43). Greenwich, CT: JAI Press.

Seifer, R., Sameroff, A. J., Barrett, L. C., & Krafchuk, E. (1994). Infant temperament measured by multiple observations and mother report. *Child Development, 65,* 1478–1490.

Seifer, R., Schiller, M., Sameroff, A. J., Resnick, S., & Riordan, K. (1996). Attachment, maternal sensitivity, and infant temperament during the first year of life. *Developmental Psychology, 32,* 12–25.

Sekuler, R., & Blake, R. (1990). *Perception.* New York: Alfred A. Knopf.

Seligman, M. E. P. (1975). *Helplessness: On depression, development, and death.* San Francisco: W. H. Freeman.

Seligman, M. E. P. (1995). The effectiveness of psychotherapy: The Consumer Reports study. *American Psychologist, 50,* 965–974.

Seligman, M. E. P., Castellon, C., Cacciola, J., Schulman, P., Luborsky, L., Ollove, M., & Downing, R. (1988). Explanatory style change during cognitive therapy for unipolar depression. *Journal of Abnormal Psychology, 97,* 13–18.

Seligman, M. E. P., & Hager, J. L. (1972). *Biological boundaries of learning.* New York: Appleton-Century-Crofts.

Selye, H. (1976). *The stress of life* (2nd ed.). New York: McGraw-Hill.

Seminara, J. L. (1993, July). Taking control of controls. *Ergonomics in Design,* pp. 5–7.

Seta, C. E., Hayes, N. S., & Seta, J. J. (1994). Mood, memory, and vigilance: The influence of distraction on recall and impression formation. *Personality and Social Psychology Bulletin, 20,* 170–177.

Sewitch, D. E. (1987). Slow wave sleep deficiency insomnia: A problem in thermo-downregulation at sleep onset. *Psychophysiology, 24,* 200–215.

Sexton, M., Fox, N. L., & Hebel, HJ. R. (1990). Prenatal exposure to tobacco: II. Effects on cognitive functioning at age three. *International Journal of Epidemiology, 19,* 72–77.

Shaffer, D. R., & Graziano, W. G. (1983). Effects of positive and negative moods on helping tasks having pleasant or unpleasant consequences. *Motivation and Emotion, 7,* 269–278.

Shanab, M. E., & Spencer, R. E. (1978). Positive and negative contrast effects obtained following shifts in delayed water reward. *Bulletin of the Psychonomic Society, 12,* 199–202.

Shanab, N. E., & Yahya, K. A. (1977). A behavioral study of obedience in children. *Journal of Personality and Social Psychology, 35,* 530–536.

Shapiro, D. H. (1980). *Meditation: Self-regulation strategy and altered states of consciousness.* New York: Aldine.

Sharp, M. J., & Getz, J. G. (1996). Substance use as impression management. *Personality and Social Psychology Bulletin, 22,* 60–67.

Sharpe, D., Adair, J. G., & Roese, N. J. (1992). Twenty years of deception research: A decline in subjects' trust? *Personality and Social Psychology Bulletin, 18,* 585–590.

Sharpsteen, D. J. (1991). The organization of jealousy knowledge: Romantic jealousy as a blended emotion. In P. Salovey (Ed.), *The psychology of jealousy and envy* (pp. 31–51). New York: Guilford Press.

Shaver, P. R., & Brennan, K. A. (1992). Attachment styles and the "big five" personality traits: Their connections with each other and with romantic relationship outcomes. *Personality and Social Psychology Bulletin, 18,* 536–545.

Shaver, P. R., & Hazan, C. (1994). Attachment. In A. L. Weber & J. H. Harvey (Eds.), *Perspectives on close relationships* (pp. 110–130). Boston: Allyn & Bacon.

Shavitt, S., & Brock, T. C. (Eds.). (1994). *Persuasion.* Boston: Allyn & Bacon.

Shaw, L. L., Batson, C. D., & Todd, R. M. (1994). Empathy avoidance: Forestalling feeling for another in order to escape the motivational consequences. *Journal of Personality and Social Psychology, 67,* 879–887.

Shepard, R. N. (1964). Circularity in judgments of relative pitch. *Journal of the Acoustical Society of America, 36,* 2346–2353.

Shepard, R. N., & Metzler, J. (1971). Mental rotation of three-dimensional objects. *Science, 171,* 701–703.

Sher, K. J., & Trull, T. J. (1994). Personality and disinhibitory psychopathology: Alcoholism and antisocial personality disorder. *Journal of Abnormal Psychology, 103,* 92–102.

Shettleworth, S. J. (1993). Where is the comparison in comparative cognition? *Psychological Science, 4,* 179–183.

Shiffrin, R. M., & Dumais, S. T. (1981). The development of automatism. In J. R. Anderson (Ed.), *Cognitive skills and their acquisition.* Hillsdale, NJ: Erlbaum.

Shiffrin, R. M., & Schneider, W. (1977). Controlled and automatic human information processing. II: Perceptual learning, automatic attending, and a general theory. *Psychological Review, 84,* 127–190.

Shimamura, A. P., & Jurica, P. J. (1994). Memory interference effects and aging: Findings from a test of frontal lobe function. *Neuropsychology, 8,* 408–412.

Shimamura, A. P., Berry, J. M., Mangela, J. A., Rusting, C. L., & Jurica, P. J. (1995). Memory and cognitive abilities in university professors: Evidence for successful aging. *Psychological Science, 6,* 271–277.

Shoda, Y., Mischel, W., & Peake, P. K. (1990). Predicting adolescent cognitive and self-regulatory competencies from preschool delay of gratification. *Developmental Psychology, 26,* 978–986.

Shore, D. (1993). *Special report: Schizophrenia 1993.* Rockville, MD: U.S. Department of Health and Human Services.

Siegal, M., & Peterson, C. C. (1996). Breaking the mold: A fresh look at children's understanding of questions about lies and mistakes. *Developmental Psychology, 32,* 322–334.

Siegel, S. (1975). Evidence from rats that morphine tolerance is a learned response. *Journal of Comparative and Physiological Psychology, 89,* 598–606.

Siegel, S. (1983). Classical conditioning, drug tolerance, and drug dependence. In R. G. Smart, F. B. Glaser, Y. Israel, H. Kalant, R. E. Popham, & W. Schmidt (Eds.), *Research advances in alcohol and drug problems* (Vol. 7). New York: Plenum.

Siegel, S. (1984). Pavlovian conditioning and heroin overdose: Reports by overdose victims. *Bulletin of the Psychonomic Society, 22,* 428–430.

Siegel, S., Hinson, R. E., Krank, M. D., & McCully, J. (1982). Heroin "overdose" death: The contribution of drug-associated environmental cues. *Science, 216,* 436–437.

Siegler, R. S., & Ellis, S. (1996). Piaget on childhood. *Psychological Science, 7,* 211–215.

Sigman, M. (1995). Nutrition and child development: More food for thought. *Current Directions in Psychological Science, 4,* 52–55.

Silva, C. E., & Kirsch, I. (1992). Interpretive sets, expectancy, fantasy proneness, and dissociation as predictors of hypnotic response. *Journal of Personality and Social Psychology, 63,* 847–856.

Simon, L., Greenberg, J., & Brehm, J. (1995). Trivialization: The forgotten mode of dissonance reduction. *Journal of Personality and Social Psychology, 68,* 247–260.

Simon, S. J., & Werner, J. M. (1996). Computer training through behavior modeling, self-paced, and instructional approaches: A field experiment. *Journal of Applied Psychology, 81*(6), 648–659.

Simonton, D. K. (1990). Creativity and wisdom in aging. In J. E. Birren & K. W. Schaie (Eds.), *Handbook of the psychology of aging* (3rd ed., pp. 320–329). San Diego: Academic Press.

Simonton, D. K. (1994). Individual differences, developmental changes, and social context. *Behavioral and Brain Sciences, 17,* 552–563.

Simonton, D.K. (1990). Creativity and wisdom in aging. In J.E. Birren, & K.W. Schaie (Eds.), *Handbook of the psychology of aging,* 3rd ed. (pp. 320–329). San Diego: Academic Press.

Simpson, E. (1974). Moral development research: A case study of scientific cultural bias. *Human Development, 17,* 81–105.

Sinclair, R. C., Hoffman, C., Mark, M. M., Martin, L. L., & Pickering, T. L. (1994). Construct accessibility and the misattribution of arousal: Schachter and Singer revisited. *Psychological Science, 5,* 15–19.

Singer, J. L. (1975). Navigating the stream of consciousness: Research in daydreaming and related inner experience. *American Psychologist, 30,* 727–738.

Singer, J. L., Singer, D. G., & Rapaczynski, W. S. (1984). Children's imagination as predicted by family patterns and television viewing: A longitudinal study. *Genetic Psychology Monographs, 110,* 43–69.

Singh, D. (1993). Adaptive significance of female's physical attractiveness: Role of waist-to-hip ratio. *Journal of Personality and Social Psychology, 65,* 293–307.

Siquelande, E. R., & Lipsitt, L. P. (1996). Conditioned head-turning in human newborns. *Journal of Experimental Child Psychology, 3,* 356–376.

Skeels, H. M. (1938). Mental development of children in foster homes. *Journal of Consulting Psychology, 2,* 33–43.

Skeels, H. M. (1966). Ability status of children with contrasting early life experience. *Society for Research in Child Development Monographs, 31*(3), 1–65.

Skinner, B. F. (1938). *The behavior of organisms.* New York: Appleton-Century-Crofts.

Skinner, B. F. (1971). *Beyond freedom and dignity.* New York: Alfred A. Knopf.

Skinner, B. F. (1974). *About behaviorism.* New York: Vintage Books.

Slattery, M. L., Potter, J., Caan, B., Edwards, S., Coates, A., Ma, K., & Berry, T. D. (1997). Energy balance and colon cancer-beyond physical activity. *Cancer Research, 57,* 75–80.

Slobin, D. I. (1979). *Psycholinguistics* (2nd ed.). Glenview, IL: Scott, Foresman.

Slovic, P., Fischoff, B., & Lichtenstein, S. (1977). Behavioral decision theory. *Annual Review of Psychology, 28,* 1–39.

Smith, C. P. (Ed.). (1992). *Motivation and personality: Handbook of thematic content analysis.* New York: Cambridge University Press.

Smith, D. E., Gier, J. A., & Willis, F. N. (1982). Interpersonal touch and compliance with a marketing request. *Basic and Applied Social Psychology, 3,* 35–38.

Smith, E. R., & Henry, S. (1996). An in-group becomes part of the self: Response time evidence. *Personality and Social Psychology Bulletin, 22,* 635–642.

Smith, J. F., & Kida, T. (1991). Heuristics and biases: Expertise and task realism in auditing. *Psychological Bulletin, 109,* 472–489.

Smith, K. H., & Rogers, M. (1994). Effectiveness of subliminal messages in television commercials: Two experiments. *Journal of Applied Psychology, 79,* 866–874.

Smith, P. C., Kendall, L. M., & Hulin, C. L. (1969). *The measurement of satisfaction in work and retirement.* Chicago: Rand McNally.

Smith, R. E., Ptacek, J. T., & Smoll, F. L. (1992). Sensation seeking, stress, and adolescent injuries: A test of stress-buffering, risk-taking, and coping skills hypotheses. *Journal of Personality and Social Psychology, 62,* 1016–1024.

Smith, S. M. (1979). Remembering in and out of context. *Journal of Experimental Psychology: Human Learning and Memory, 5,* 460–471.

Smith, S. M., & Shaffer, D. R. (1991). Celerity and cajolery: Rapid speech may enhance or inhibit persuasion through its impact on message elaboration. *Personality and Social Psychology Bulletin, 17,* 663–669.

Smith, S. S., & Richardson, D. (1983). Amelioration of deception and harm in psychological research: The important role of debriefing. *Journal of Personality and Social Psychology, 44,* 1075–1082.

Smotherman, W. P., & Robinson, S. R. (1996). The development of behavior before birth. *Developmental Psychology, 32,* 425–434.

Snowden, L. R., & Cheung, F. K. (1990). Use of inpatient mental health services by members of ethnic minority groups. *American Psychologist, 45,* 347–355.

Snyder, M., & Gangestad, S. (1987). On the nature of self-monitoring: Matters of assessment, matters of validity. *Journal of Personality and Social Psychology, 51,* 125–139.

Snyder, M., Simpson, J. A., & Gangestad, S. (1986). Personality and sexual relations. *Journal of Personality and Social Psychology, 51,* 181–190.

Snyder, S. (1991). Movies and juvenile delinquency: An overview. *Adolescence, 26,* 121–132.

Solomon, R. L. (1982). The opponent-process in acquired motivation. In D. W. Pfaff (Ed.), *The physiological mechanisms of motivation.* New York: Springer-Verlag.

Sommers, K., Whitman, T. L., Borkowski, J. G., Schellenbach, C., Maxwell, S., & Keogh, D. (1993). Cognitive readiness and adolescent parenting. *Developmental Psychology, 29,* 389–398.

Spanos, N. P. (1991). A sociocognitive approach to hypnosis. In S. J. Lynn & J. R. Rhue (Eds.), *Hypnosis theories: Current models and perspectives* (pp. 324–361). New York: Guilford Press.

Spanos, N. P., Burgess, C. A., & Perlini, A. H. (1992). Compliance and suggested deafness in hypnotic and nonhypnotic subjects. *Imagination, Cognition, and Personality, 11,* 211–223.

Spanos, N. P., Perlini, A. H., Patrick, L., Bell, S., & Gwynne, M. I. (1990). The role of compliance in hypnotic and nonhypnotic analgesia. *Journal of Research in Personality, 24,* 433–453.

Spearman, C. E. (1927). *The abilities of man.* London: Macmillan.

Spence, A. P. (1989). *Biology of human aging.* Englewood Cliffs, NJ: Prentice-Hall.

Sperling, G. (1960). The information available in brief visual presentations. *Psychological Monographs: General and Applied, 74,* 1–29.

Sperry, R. W. (1968). Hemisphere deconnection and unity of conscious experience. *American Psychologist, 29,* 723–733.

Spirduso, W. W., & MacRae, P.G. (1990). Motor performance and aging. In J. E. Birren & K. W. Schaie (Eds.), *Handbook of the psychology of aging* (3rd ed., pp. 184–200). San Diego: Academic Press.

Sprecher, S., & Duck, S. (1994). Sweet talk: The importance of perceived communication for romantic and friendship attraction experienced during a get-acquainted date. Personality and *Social Psychology Bulletin, 20,* 391–400.

Springer, S. P., & Deutsch, G. (1985). *Left brain, right brain.* San Francisco: Freeman.

Squire, L. R. (1987). *Memory and brain.* New York: Oxford University Press.

Squire, L. R. (1991). Closing remarks. In L. R. Squire & E. Lindenlaub (Eds.), *The biology of memory* (pp. 643–644). Stuttgart, Germany: F. K. Schattauer Verlag.

Squire, L. R., & Spanis, C. W. (1984). Long gradient of retrograde amnesia in mice: Continuity with the findings in humans. *Behavioral Neuroscience, 98,* 345–348.

Sroufe, L. A., & Waters, E. (1976). The ontogenesis of smiling and laughter on the organization of development in infancy. *Psychological Review, 83,* 173–189.

Standing, L. G., Canezio, J., & Haber, N. (1970). Perception and memory for pictures: Single-trial learning of 2500 visual stimuli. *Psychonomic Science, 19,* 73–74.

Stangor, C., & Ruble, D. N. (1989). Strength of expectancies and memory for social information: What we remember depends on how much we know. *Journal of Experimental Social Psychology, 39,* 1408–1423.

Stanley, J. (1993). Boys and girls who reason well mathematically. In G. R. Bock & K. Ackrill

(Eds.), *The origins and development of high ability.* Chichester, England: Wiley.

Stanton, J. M., & Barnes-Farerell, J. L. (1996). Effects of electronic performance monitoring on personal control, task satisfaction, and task performance. *Journal of Applied Psychology, 81,* 738–745.

Staw, B. M., & Ross, J. (1987). Behavior in escalation situations: Antecedents, prototypes, and solutions. In L. L. Cummings & B. M. Staw (Eds.), *Research in organizational behavior* (Vol. 9, pp. 29–78). Greenwich, CT: JAI Press.

Staw, B. M., & Ross, J. (1989). Understanding behavior in escalation situations. *Science, 246,* 216–220.

Steede, K. C., & Range, L. M. (1989). Does television induce suicide contagion with adolescents? *Journal of Community Psychology, 15,* 24–28.

Steele, C. M., & Josephs, R. A. (1990). Alcohol myopia: Its prized and dangerous effects. *American Psychologist, 45*(8), 921–933.

Steele, C. M., & Josephs, R. A. (1990). Alcohol myopia: Its prized and dangerous effects. *American Psychologist, 45,* 921–933.

Steers, R. M. (1984). *Organizational behavior* (2nd ed.). Glenview, IL: Scott Foresman.

Steffen, V. J. (1990). Men's motivation to perform the testicular self-exam: Effect of prior knowledge and an educational brochure. *Journal of Applied Social Psychology, 20,* 681–702.

Stellar, E. (1985, April). *Hunger in animals and humans.* Lecture to the Eastern Psychological Association, Boston.

Stemberger, R. T., Turner, S. M., Beidel, D. C., & Calhoun, K. S. (1995). Social phobia: An analysis of possible developmental factors. *Journal of Abnormal Psychology, 104,* 526–531.

Stephan, W. G. (1987). The contact hypothesis in intergroup relations. In C. Hendrick (Ed.), Group processes and intergroup relations. *Review of Personality and Social Psychology, 9,* 41–67.

Stern, J. M., & Stewart, G. G., III. (1993, June). Pay for performance: Only the theory is easy. *HR Magazine,* pp. 48–49.

Sternberg, R. J. (1985). *Beyond IQ.* Cambridge: Cambridge University Press.

Sternberg, R. J. (1986). *Intelligence applied.* New York: Harcourt Brace Jovanovich.

Sternberg, R. J. (1988). *The triangle of love.* New York: Basic Books.

Sternberg, R. J. (1988). Triangulating love. In R. J. Sternberg & H. J. Barnes (Eds.), *The psychology of love* (pp. 119–138). New Haven, CT: Yale University Press.

Sternberg, R. J. (1995). For whom the bell curve tolls: A review of The Bell Curve. *Psychological Science, 6,* 257–261.

Sternberg, R. J., & Lubart, T. I. (1996). Investing in creativity. American Psychologist, 51, 677–688.

Sternberg, R. J., & Williams, M. W. (1997). *How to develop student creativity.* Alexandria, VA: Association for Supervision and Curriculum Development.

Sternberg, R. J., Conway, B. E., Ketron, J. L., & Bernstein, M. (1981). People's conception of intelligence. *Journal of Personality and Social Psychology, 41,* 37–55.

Sternberg, R. J., Wagner, R. K., Williams, W. M., & Horvath, J. A. (1995). Testing common sense. *American Psychologist, 50,* 912–927.

Stevenson, H. W., & Stigler, J. W. (1992). *The learning gap.* New York: Summit.

Stewart, T. A. (1995, March 20). Planning a career in a world without managers. *Fortune,* pp. 72–74, 75, 77, 79.

Stice, E., & Barrera, M., Jr. (1995). A longitudinal examination of the reciprocal relations between perceived parenting and adolescents' substance use and externalizing behaviors. *Developmental Psychology, 31,* 332–334.

Stiff, J. B., Miller, G. R., Sleight, C., Mongeau, P. I., et al. (1989). Explanations for visual cue primacy in judgments of honesty and deceit. *Journal of Personality and Social Psychology, 56,* 555–564.

Stifter, C. A., & Fox, N. A. (1990). Infant reactivity: Physiological correlates of newborn and 5–month temperament. *Developmental Psychology, 26,* 582–588.

Stipp, D. (1990, May 17). Einstein bird has scientists atwitter over mental feats. *Wall Street Journal,* pp. 1, 7.

Stockwell, H. G., Goldman, A. L., Lyman, G. H., Noss, C. I., Armstrong, A. W., Pinkham, P. A., Candelora, E. C., & Brusa, M. R. (1992). Environmental tobacco smoke and lung cancer risk in nonsmoking women. *Journal of the National Cancer Institute, 18,* 1417–1422.

Stone, J., Aronson, E., Crain, A. L., Winslow, M. P., & Fried, C. B. (1994). Inducing hypocrisy as a means of encouraging young adults to use condoms. *Personality and Social Psychology Bulletin, 20,* 116–128.

Stoppard, J. M., & Gruchy, C. D. G. (1993). Gender, context, and expression of positive emotion. *Personality and Social Psychology Bulletin, 19,* 143–150.

Story, M., & Faulkner, P. (1990). The prime time diet: A content analysis of eating behavior and food messages in television program content and commercials. *American Journal of Public Health, 80,* 738–740.

Strauman, T. J., Lemieux, A. M., & Coe, C. L. (1993). Self-discrepancy and natural killer cell activity: Immunological consequences of negative self-evaluation. *Journal of Personality and Social Psychology, 64,* 1042–1052.

Strean, H. S. (1985). *Resolving resistances in psychotherapy.* New York: Wiley Interscience.

Strickland, B. R. (1992). Women and depression. *Current Directions in Psychological Science, 1,* 132–134.

Struckman-Johnson, C. J., Gilliland, R. C., Struckman-Johnson, D. L., & North, T. C. (1990). The effects of fear of AIDS and gender on responses to fear-arousing condom advertisements. *Journal of Applied Social Psychology, 20,* 1396–1410.

Struckman-Johnson, D., & Struckman-Johnson, C. (1996). Can you say condom? It makes a difference in fear-arousing AIDS prevention public service announcements. *Journal of Applied Social Psychology. 26,* 1068–1083.

Suh, E., Diener, E., & Funita, F. (1996). Events and subjective well-being: Only recent events matter. *Journal of Personality and Social Psychology, 70,* 1091–1102.

Sullivan, M. J. L., Bishop, S. R., & Pivik, J. (1995). The pain catastrophizing scale: Development and validation. *Psychological Assessment, 7,* 524–532.

Suls, J., & Wan, C. K. (1987). In search of the false uniqueness phenomenon: Fear and estimates of social consensus. *Journal of Personality and Social Psychology, 52,* 211–217.

Suls, J., Wan, C. K., & Sanders, C. L. (1988). False consensus and false uniqueness in estimating the prevalence of health-protective behaviors. *Journal of Applied Social Psychology, 19,* 66–79.

Sulsky, L. M., & Balzer, W. K. (1988). Meaning and measurement of performance rating accuracy: Some methodological and theoretical concerns. *Journal of Applied Psychology, 73,* 497–506.

Sulsky, L. M., & Day, D. V. (1992). Frame-of-reference training and cognitive categorization: An empirical investigation of rater memory issues. *Journal of Applied Psychology, 77,* 501–510.

Sulsky, L. M., & Day, D. V. (1994). Effects of frame-of-reference training on rater accuracy under alternative time delays. *Journal of Applied Psychology, 79,* 535–543.

Sundstrom, E. (1986). *Work places.* Cambridge, England: Cambridge University Press.

Swaab, D. F., Gooren, L. J. G., & Hofman, M. A. (1995). Brain research, gender, and sexual orientation. *Journal of Homosexuality, 3/4,* 283–301.

Swartzentruber, D. (1991). Blocking between occasion setters and contextual stimuli. *Journal of Experimental Psychology: Animal Behavior Processes, 12,* 163–173.

Swerzgold, J. (1993, December). Downsizing: Down, but not out. *Management Review,* p. 6.

Swets, J. A. (1992). The science of choosing the right decision threshold in high-stakes diagnostics. *American Psychologist, 47,* 522–532.

Symons, C. S., & Johnson, T. B. (1997). The self-reference effect in memory: A meta-analysis. *Psychological Bulletin, 12,* 371–394.

Tangney, J. P., Miller, R. S., Flicker, L., & Barlow, D. H. (1996). Are shame, guilt, and embarrassment distinct emotions? *Journal of Personality and Social Psychology, 70,* 1256–1269.

Tardif, T. (1996). Nouns are not always learned before verbs: Evidence from Mandarin speakers' early vocabularies. *Developmental Psychology, 32,* 492–504.

Teasley, S. D. (1995). The role of talk in children's peer collaborations. *Developmental Psychology, 31,* 207–220.

Teicher, M. H., Glod, C., & Cole, O. J. (1990). Emergence of intense suicidal preoccupation during fluoxetine treatment. *American Journal of Psychiatry, 147,* 207–210.

Teichman, M., Barnea, Z., & Rahav, G. (1989). Sensation seeking, state and trait anxiety, and depressive mood in adolescent substance abusers. *International Journal of the Addictions, 24,* 87–99.

Tennen, H., & Eller, S. J. (1977). Attributional components of learned helplessness. *Journal of Personality and Social Psychology, 35,* 265–271.

Tepper, B. J. (1995). Upward maintenance tactics in supervisory mentoring and nonmentoring relationships. *Academy of Management Journal, 38,* 1191–1205.

Terman, L. M. (1954). The discovery and encouragement of exceptional talent. *American Psychologist, 9,* 221–230.

Terrace, H. S. (1985). In the beginning was the "name." *American Psychologist, 40,* 1011–1028.

Terry, D. J. (1991). Stress, coping, and adaptation to new parenthood. *Journal of Social and Personal Relationships 8,* 527–547.

Terry, D. J., Mayocchi, L., & Hynes, G. J. (1996). Depressive symptomatology in new mothers: A stress and coping perspective. *Journal of Abnormal Psychology, 105,* 220–231.

Tett, R. P., & Meyer, J. P. (1993). Job satisfaction, organizational commitment, turnover intention, and turnover: Path analyses based on meta-analytic findings. *Personnel Psychology, 46,* 259–293.

Teyler, T. J., & DiScenna, P. (1984). Long-term potentiation as a candidate mnemonic device. *Brain Research Reviews, 7,* 15–28.

Thernstrom, M. (1996, June 6). Diary of a murder. pp. 61–71.

Thoma, S. J. (1986). Estimating gender differences in the comprehension and preference of moral issues. *Developmental Review, 6,* 165–180.

Thomas, A., & Chess, S. (1977). *Temperament and development.* New York: Brunner/Mazel.

Thomas, A., & Chess, S. (1989). Temperament and development. In G. A. Kohnstamm, J. E. Bates, & M. K. Rothbart (Eds.), *Temperament in childhood.* New York: Wiley.

Thomas, D. A. (1993). Racial dynamics in cross-race developmental relationships. *Administrative Science Quarterly 38,* 169–194.

Thomas, J. L. (1992). *Adulthood and aging.* Boston: Allyn and Bacon.

Thomas, M. H. (1982). Physiological arousal, exposure to a relatively lengthy aggressive film, and aggressive behavior. *Journal of Research in Personality, 16,* 72–181.

Thompson, J. K. (1992). Body image: Extent of disturbance, associated features, theoretical models, assessment methodologies, intervention strategies, and a proposal for a new DSM-IV diagnostic category-Body Image Disorder. In M. Hesen, R. M. Eisler, & P. M. Miller (Eds.), *Progress in behavior modification* (pp. 3–54). Sycamore, IL: Sycamore Publishing.

Thompson, R. F. (1989). A model system approach to memory. In P. R. Solomon, G. R. Goethals, C. M. Kelley, & B. R. Stephens (Eds.), *Memory: Interdisciplinary approaches.* New York: Springer-Verlag.

Thompson, R. F., & Krupa, D. J. (1994). Organization of memory traces in the mammalian brain. *Annual Review of Neuroscience, 17,* 519–549.

Thorndike, R. L., & Hagen, E. (1982). *Ten thousand careers.* New York: Wiley.

Thurstone, E. L. (1938). *Primary mental abilities.* Chicago: University of Chicago Press.

Tice, D. M. (1989). Metatraits: Interitem variance as personality assessment. In D. M. Buss & N. Cantor (Eds.), *Personality psychology: Recent trends and emerging directions* (pp. 194–200). New York: Springer-Verlag.

Tice, D., & Baumeister, R. F. (1993). Anger control. In D. Wegner and J. Pennebaker (Eds.), *Handbook of mental control.* Englewood Cliffs, NJ: Prentice-Hall.

Tiffany, S. T. (1990). A cognitive model of drug urges and drug-use behavior: Role of automatic and nonautomatic processes. *Psychological Review, 97,* 147–168.

Tisserand, R. B. (1977). *The art of aromatherapy.* Rochester, VT: Healing Arts Press.

Tolman, E. C., & Honzik, C. H. (1930). Introduction and removal of reward, and maze performance in rats. *University of California Publications in Psychology, 4,* 257–275.

Tomaka, J., Blascovich, J., Kelsey, R. M., & Leitten, C. L. (1993). Subjective, physiological, and behavioral effects of threat and challenge appraisal. *Journal of Personality and Social Psychology, 65,* 248–260.

Tomarken, A. J., Davidson, R. J., & Henriques, J. B. (1990). Resting frontal brain asymmetry predicts affective responses to films. *Journal of Personality and Social Psychology, 59,* 791–801.

Topka, H., Valls-Sole, J., Massaquoi, S. G., & Hallett, M. (1993). Deficit in classical conditioning in patients with cerebellar degeneration. *Brain, 116,* 961–969.

Torrance, E. P. (1974). *Torrance tests of creative thinking.* Lexington, MA: Personnel Press.

Totterdell, P., Spelten, E., Smith, L., Barton, J., & Folkard, S. (1995). Recovery from work shifts: How long does it take? *Journal of Applied Psychology, 80,* 43–57.

Treffinger, D. J. (1995). Creative problem solving: Overview and educational implications. *Educational Psychology Review, 7,* 301–312.

Tronick, E. Z. (1989). Emotions and emotional communication in infants. *American Psychologist, 44,* 112–119.

Tubbs, M. E., Boehne, D., & Dahl, J. G. (1993). Expectancy, valence, and motivational force functions in goal-setting research: An empirical test. *Journal of Applied Psychology, 78,* 361–373.

Tucker, L. A., & Friedman, G. M. (1990). Walking and serum cholesterol in adults. *American Journal of Public Health, 80,* 1111–1113.

Tulving, E. (1993). What is episodic memory? *Current Directions in Psychological Science, 2,* 67–70.

Tulving, E., & Psotka, L. (1971). Retroactive inhibition in free recall: Inaccessibility of information available in the memory store. *Journal of Experimental Psychology, 87,* 1–8.

Turban, D. B., & Dougherty, T. M. (1994). Role of protégé personality in receipt of mentoring and career success. *Academy of Management Journal, 37,* 688–702.

Turban, D. B., & Keon, T. O. (1993). Organizational attractiveness: An interactionist perspective. *Journal of Applied Psychology, 78,* 184–193.

Turk, D. C. (1994). Perspectives on chronic pain: The role of psychological factors. *Current Directions in Psychological Science, 3,* 45–48.

Turk, D. C., & Rudy, T. E. (1992). Cognitive factors and persistent pain: A glimpse into Pandora's box. *Cognitive Therapy and Research, 16,* 99–122.

Turner, J. A., & Clancy, S. (1986). Strategies for coping with chronic low back pain: Relationship to pain and disability. *Pain, 24,* 355–362.

Turner, J. C., Hogg, M. A., Oakes, P. J., Richer, S. D., & Wetherell, M. S. (1987). *Rediscovering the social group: A self-categorization theory.* Oxford, England: Blackwell.

Turner, W. J. (1995). Type 1: An Xq28 phenomenon. *Archives of Sexual Behavior, 24,* 109–134.

Turtle, J. W., & Yuille, J. C. (1994). Lost but not forgotten details: Repeated eyewitness recall leads to reminiscence but not hypermnesia. *Journal of Applied Psychology, 79,* 260–271.

Tversky, A., & Kahneman, D. (1974). Judgment under uncertainty: Heuristics and biases. *Science, 185,* 1124–1131.

Tversky, A., & Kahneman, D. (1981). The framing of decisions and the psychology of choice. *Science, 211,* 453–458.

Tyler, T. R. (1994). Psychological models of the justice motive: Antecedents of distributive and procedural justice. *Journal of Personality and Social Psychology, 67,* 850–863.

Tyler, T. R., & Cook, F. L. (1984). The mass media and judgment of risk: Distinguishing impact on personal and societal level judgments. *Journal of Personality and Social Psychology, 47,* 693–708.

Uba, L. (1994). *Asian Americans: Personality patterns, identity, and mental health.* New York: Guilford Press.

Uchino, B. N., Cacioppo, J. T., & Kiecolt-Glaser, J. K. (1996). The relationship between social support and physiological processes: A review with emphasis on underlying mechanisms and implications for health. *Psychological Bulletin, 119,* 488–531.

Uhrbock, R. S. (1961). Music on the job: Its influence on worker morale and production. *Personnel Psychology, 14,* 9–38.

United States Bureau of the Census. (1991). *Statistical Abstract of the United States, 1991.* Washington, DC: U.S. Government Printing Office.

United States Department of Health and Human Services. (1989). *Aging in the eighties: The prevalence of comorbidity and its associations with disability* (DHHS Publication No. PHS 89–1250). Washington, DC: U.S. Government Printing Office.

United States Department of Health and Human Services. (1991). *Healthy people 2000. National health promotion and disease prevention objectives.* Washington, DC: DHHS publication PHS 91–50212.

United States Department of Health and Human Services. (1994). *Preventing tobacco use among young people: A report of the Surgeon General.* Atlanta, GA: Government Printing Office.

United States Department of Justice (1994). *Criminal victimization in the United States, 1992.* Washington, DC: Office of Justice Programs, Bureau of Justice Statistics.

United States Department of Labor. (1992). *Employment and earnings* (Vol. 39, No. 5, Table A-22). Washington, DC: U.S. Department of Labor.

Urban, M. J. (1992) Auditory subliminal stimulation: A reexamination. *Perceptual and Motor Skills, 74,* 515–541.

Urberg, K. A., Degirmencioglu, S. M., Tolson, J. M., & Halliday-Scher, K. (1995). The structure of adolescent peer networks. *Developmental Psychology, 31,* 540–547.

Usher, J. A, & Neisser, U. (1995). Childhood amnesia and the beginnings of memory for four early life events. *Journal of Experimental Psychology: General.*

Valkenburg, P. M., & van der Voort, T. H. A. (1994). Influence of TV on daydreaming and creative imagination: A review of research. *Psychological Bulletin, 116,* 316–339.

Valleroy, L. A., Harris, J. R., & Way, P. O. (1990). The impact of HIV infection on child survival in the developing world. *AIDS, 4,* 667–672.

Van Eerde, W., & Thierry, H. (1996). Vroom's expectancy models and work-related criteria: A meta-analysis. *Journal of Applied Psychology, 81,* 575–586.

Van Velsor, E., & Hughes, M. W. (1990). *Gender differences in the development of managers: How women managers learn from experience.* Technical report no. 145, Center for Creative Leadership, Greensboro, NC.

Vauclair, J., Fagot, J., & Hopkins, W. D. (1993). Rotation of mental images in baboons when the visual input is directed to the cerebral hemisphere. *Psychological Science, 4,* 99–103.

Veenhoven, R. (1993). *Happiness in nations.* Rotterdam, Netherlands: Risbo.

Vernberg, E. M., LaGreca, A. M., Silverman, W. K., & Prinstein, M. J. (1996). Prediction of posttraumatic stress symptoms in children after hurricane Andrew. *Journal of Abnormal Psychology, 105,* 237–248.

Vernon, P. A. (1987). *Speed of information processing and intelligence.* Norwood, NJ: Ablex.

Vernon, P. A. (1993). *Biological approaches to the study of human intelligence.* Norwood, NJ: Ablex.

Vernon, P. A., Jan, K. L., Harris, J. A., & McCarthy, J. M. (1997). Environmental predictors of personality differences: A twin and sibling study. *Journal of Personality and Social Psychology, 72,* 177–183.

Viemero, V., & Pajanen, S. (1992). The role of fantasies and dreams in the TV viewing-aggression relationship. *Aggressive Behavior, 18,* 106–116.

Volpicelli, J. R., Alterman, A. I., Hayashida, M., & O'Brien, C. P. (1992). Naltrexone in the treatment of alcohol dependence. *Archives of General Psychiatry, 49,* 876–880.

Von Senden, M. (1960). *Space and sign.* Trans. by P. Heath. New York: Free Press.

Voyer, D., Voyer, S., & Bryden, M. P. (1995). Magnitude of sex differences in spatial abilities: A meta-analysis and consideration of critical variables. *Psychological Bulletin, 117,* 250–270.

Vygotsky, L. S. (1987). Thinking and speech. In R. W. Rieber, A. S. Carton (Eds.), & N. Minick (Trans.), *The collected works of L. S. Vygotsky: Vol 1. Problems of general psychology* (pp. 37–285). New York: Plenum. (Original work published in 1934.)

Wagenaar, W. A., (1986). My memory: A study of autobiographical memory over six years. *Cognitive Psychology, 18,* 225–252.

Wagner, B. M., Compas, B. E., & Howell, D. C. (1988). Daily and major life events: A test of an integrative model of psychological stress. *American Journal of Community Psychology, 16,* 189–205.

Waitzkin, H. (1984). Doctor–patient communication: Clinical implications of social scientific research. *Journal of the American Medical Association, 252,* 2441–2446.

Wakefield, J. C. (1992). The concept of mental disorder: On the boundary between biological facts and social values. *American Psychologist, 47,* 373–388.

Walden, T. A., & Ogan, T. A. (1988). The development of social referencing. *Child Development, 29,* 1230–1240.

Waldholz, M. (1996, July 8). Combined-drug therapy being hailed as promising weapon in AIDS battle, *The Wall Street Journal.*

Walker, L. J. & DeVries, B. (1985). *Moral stages/moral orientations: Do the sexes really differ?* Paper presented at the meetings of the American Psychological Association, Los Angeles.

Walker, L. J. (1989). A longitudinal study of moral reasoning. *Child Development, 60,* 157–166.

Walker, L. J. (1991). Sex differences in moral reasoning. In W. M. Kurtines & J. L. Gewirtz (Eds.), *Handbook of moral behavior and develop-*

ment, Vol. 2 (pp. 164–193). Hillsdale, NJ: Erlbaum.

Walker, P. W., Cole, J. O., Gardner, E. A., Hughes, A. R., Johnston, J. A., & Batey, S. R. (1993). Improvement in fluoxetine-associated sexual dysfunction in patients switched to bupropion. *Journal of Clinical Psychiatry, 54,* 549–465.

Wallace, B. (1993). Day persons, night persons, and variability in hypnotic susceptability. *Journal of Personality and Social Psychology, 64,* 827–833

Wallace, R. K., & Benson, H. (1972). The physiology of meditation. *Scientific American, 236,* 84–90.

Wallace, R. K., & Fisher, L. E. (1987). *Consciousness and behavior* (2nd ed.). Boston: Allyn and Bacon.

Walsh, S. (1993). Cited in Toufexis, A. (1993, February 15), *Time,* pp. 49–51.

Walster, E., & Festinger, L. (1962). The effectiveness of "overheard" persuasive communication. *Journal of Abnormal and Social Psychology, 65,* 395–402.

Walton, G. E., & Bower, T. G. R. (1993). Newborns form "prototypes" in less than 1 minute. *Psychological Science, 4,* 203–205.

Wang, X. T. (1996). Framing effects: Dynamics and task domains. *Organizational Behavior & Human Decision Processes, 68*(2), 145–157.

Wark, G. R., & Krebs, D. L. (1996). Gender and dilemma differences in real-life moral judgment. *Developmental Psychology, 32,* 220–230.

Wasserman, D., Lempert, R. O., & Hastie, R. (1991). Hindsight and causality. *Personality and Social Psychology Bulletin, 17,* 30–35

Wasserman, E. A. (1993). Comparative cognition: Toward a general understanding of cognition in behavior. *Psychological Science, 4,* 156–161.

Waters, L. K., & Zakarajsek, T. (1990). Correlates of need for cognition total and subscale scores. *Education and Psychological Measurement, 50,* 210–217.

Watkins, P. C., Vache, K., Verney, S. P., Mathews, A., & Muller, S. (1996). Unconscious mood-congruent memory bias in depression. *Journal of Abnormal Psychology, 105,* 34–41.

Watson, D. (1989). Strangers' ratings of the five robust personality factors: Evidence of a surprising convergence with self-report. *Journal of Personality and Social Psychology, 57,* 120–128.

Watson, J. B., & Raynor, R. (1920). Conditioned emotional reactions. *Journal of Experimental Psychology, 3,* 1–14.

Watson, J. S., & Ramey, C. T. (1972). Reactions to response-contingent stimulation in early infancy. *Merrill-Palmer Quarterly, 18,* 219–229.

Watson, T. S. (1996). A prompt plus delayed contingency procedure for reducing bathroom graffiti. *Journal of Applied Behavior Analysis, 29,* 121–124.

Watts, B. L. (1982). Individual differences in circadian activity rhythms and their effects on roommate relationships. *Journal of Personality, 50,* 374–384.

Wayne, S. J., & Liden, R. C. (1995). Effects of impression management on performance ratings: A longitudinal study. *Academy of Management Journal, 38,* 232–260.

Webb, W. (1975). *Sleep: The gentle tyrant.* Englewood Cliffs, NJ: Prentice-Hall.

Webb, W., & Agnew, H. W. (1967). Sleep cycling within the twenty-four hour period. *Journal of Experimental Psychology, 74,* 167–169.

Weber, B. (Feb. 18, 1996). It's man over machine as chess champion beats computer he calls tough opponent. *The New York Times,* p. 24.

Wechsler, H., Levine, S., Idelson, R. K., Schor, E. L., & Coakley, E. (1996). The physicians' role in health promotion revisited: A survey of primary care practitioners. *The New England Journal of Medicine, 334,* 996–998.

Weekes, J. R., Lynn, S. J., Green, J. P., & Brentar, J. T. (1992). Pseudomemory in hypnotized and task-motivated subjects. *Journal of Abnormal Psychology, 101,* 356–360.

Wehner, R., & Menzel, R. (1990). Do insects have cognitive maps? *Annual Review of Neuroscience, 13,* 403–414.

Weigel, R. H., Kim, E. L., & Frost, J. L. (1995). Race relations on prime time television reconsidered: Patterns of continuity and change. *Journal of Applied Social Psychology, 25,* 223–236.

Weinberger, D. R. (1994). Biological basis of schizophrenia: Structural/functional considerations relevant to potential for antipsychotic drug reasons. *Journal of Clinical Psychiatry, Monograph Series, 12,* 4–7.

Weiner, B. (1989). *Human motivation.* Hillsdale, NJ: Erlbaum.

Weingartner, H., Miller, H., & Murphy, D. L. (1977). Mood-state-dependent retrieval of verbal associations. *Journal of Abnormal Psychology, 86,* 276–286.

Weisberg, R., & Suls, J. M. (1973). An information-processing model of Duncker's candle problem. *Cognitive Psychology, 4,* 255–276.

Weisenberg, M. (1982). Cultural and ethnic factors in reaction to pain. In I. Al-Issa (Ed.), *Culture and psychopathology.* Baltimore: University Park Press.

Weiskrantz, L. (1995). Blindsight—not an island unto itself. *Current Directions in Psychological Science, 4,* 146–150.

Weiss, D. J., Dawis, R. V., England, G. W., & Loftquist, L. H. (1967). *Manual for the Minnesota Satisfaction Questionnaire* (Minnesota Studies on Vocational Rehabilitation, Vol. 22). Minneapolis, MN: Industrial Relations Center, Work Adjustment Project, University of Minnesota.

Weisz, J. R., Weiss, B., Morton, T., Granger, D., & Han, S. (1992). *Meta-analysis of psychotherapy outcome research with children and adolescents.* Unpublished manuscript, University of California, Los Angeles.

Weldon, E., Jehn, K. A., & Prahaden, P. (1991). Processes that mediate the relationship between a group goal and improved group performance. *Journal of Personality and Social Psychology, 61,* 555–569.

Wellman, H. M., Ritter, K., & Flavell, J. H. (1975). Deliberate memory behavior in the delayed reactions of very young children. *Developmental Psychology, 11,* 780–787.

Wellman, H. M., Somerville, S. C., & Haake, R. J. (1979). Development of search procedures in real-life spatial environments. *Developmental Psychology, 15,* 530–542.

Wells, G. L. (1993). What do we know about eyewitness identification? *American Psychologist, 48,* 553–571.

Wen, S. W., Goldenberg, R. L., Cutter, G. R., Hoffman, H. J., Cliver, S. P., Davis, R. O., & DuBard, M. B. (1990). Smoking, maternal age, fetal growth, and gestational age at delivery. *American Journal of Obstetries and Gynecology, 162,* 53–58.

Werker, J. F., & Desjardins, R. N. (1995). Listening to speech in the 1st year of life: Experiential influences on phoneme perception. *Current Directions in Psychological Science, 4,* 76–80.

Werner, E. E. (1995). Resilience in development. *Current Directions in Psychological Science, 44,* 81–84.

Werts, M. G., Caldwell, N. K., & Wolery, M. (1996). Peer modeling of response chains: Observational learning by students with disabilities. *Journal of Applied Behavior Analysis, 29,* 53–66.

White, R. K. (1977). Misperception in the Arab-Israeli conflict. *Journal of Social Issues, 25,* 41–78.

Whitely, W., Dougherty, T. M., & Dreher, G. F. (1991). Relationship of career mentoring and socioeconomic origin to managers' and professionals' early career progress. *Academy of Management Journal, 34,* 331–351.

Whorf, B. L. (1956). Science and linguistics. In J. B. Carroll (Ed.), *Language, thought, and reality: Selected writings of Benjamin Whorf.* Cambridge, MA: MIT Press.

Whyte, G. (1991). Diffusion of responsibility: Effects on the escalation tendency. *Journal of Applied Psychology, 76,* 408–415.

Widiger, T. A., Cadoret, R., Hare, R., Robins, L., Rutherford, M., Zanarini, M., Alterman, A., Apple, M., Corbitt, E., Forth, A., Hart, S., Jultermann, J., Woody, G., & Frances, A. (1996). DSM-IV antisocial personality disorder field trial. *Journal of Abnormal Psychology, 105,* 3–16.

Widom, C. S. (1989). Does violence beget violence? A critical examination of the literature. *Psychological Bulletin, 106,* 3–28.

Wielkiewicz, R. M., & Calvert, C. R. X. (1989). *Training and habilitating developmentally disabled people: An introduction.* Newbury Park, CA: Sage.

Wiesel, T. N. (1982). Postnatal development of the visual cortex and the influence of environment. *Nature, 299,* 583–591.

Wilcoxon, H. C., Dragoin, W. B., & Kral, P. A. (1971). Illness-induced aversions in rats and quail: Relative salience of visual and gustatory cues. *Science, 171,* 826–828.

Wiley, J. A., & Camacho, T. C. (1980). Life-style and future health: Evidence from the Alameda County study. *Preventive Medicine, 9,* 1–21.

Wilhelm, K., & Parker, G. (1994). Sex differences in lifetime depression rates: Fact or artifact? Psychological Medicine, 24, 97–111.

Willett, W. C., & MacMahon, B. (1984). Diet and cancer—an overview. *New England Journal of Medicine, 310,* 633–638.

Williams, D. E., & Page, M. M. (1989). A multidimensional measure of Maslow's hierarchy of needs. *Journal of Research in Personality, 23,* 192–213.

Williams, G. C., Grow, V. M., Freedman, Z. R., Ryan, R. M., & Deci, E. I. (1996). Motivational predictors of weight loss and weight-loss maintenance. *Journal of Personality and Social Psychology, 70,* 115–126.

Williams, K. B., Radefeld, P. A. Binning J. F., & Suadk, J. R. (1993). When job candidates are "hard" versus "easy-to-get": Effects of candidate availability on employment decisions. *Journal of Applied Social Psychology, 23,* 169–198.

Williams, W. M., & Sternberg, R. J. (in press). *Success acts for managers.* Orlando, FL: Harcourt Brace.

Williamson, D. A., Cubic, B. A., & Gleaves, D. H. (1993). Equivalence of body image disturbances in anorexia and bulimia nervosa. *Journal of Abnormal Psychology, 102,* 177–180.

Willis, S. L., & Nesselroade, C. S. (1990). Long-term effects of fluid ability training in old-old age. *Developmental Psychology, 26,* 905–910.

Willis, W. D. (1985). *The pain system. The neural basis of nociceptive transmission in the mammalian nervous system.* Basel: Karger.

Wills, T. A., McNamara, G., Vaccaro, D., & Hirky, A. E. (1996). Escalated substance use: A longitudinal grouping analysis from early to middle adolescence. *Journal of Abnormal Psychology, 105,* 166–180.

Wilson, D. W. (1981). Is helping a laughing matter? *Psychology, 18,* 6–9.

Wilson, G. T., Nathan, P. E., O'Leary, K. D., & Clark, L. A. (1996). *Abnormal psychology: Integrating perspectives.* Boston: Allyn & Bacon.

Wilson, M. I., & Daly, M. (1996). Male sexual proprietariness and violence against wives. *Current Directions in Psychological Science, 5,* 2–7.

Wilson, T. D., Houston, C. E., Etling, K. M., & Brekke, N. (1996). A new look at anchoring effects: Basic anchoring and its antecedents. *Journal of Experimental Psychology: General, 125*(4), 387–402.

Wilson, T. D., & Klaaren, K. J. (1992). *Effects of affective expectations on willingness to relive pleasant and unpleasant events.* Unpublished data. Cited in Wilson, T. D., & Klaaren, K. J., "Expectation whirls me round": The role of affective expectations in affective experience. In M. S. Clark (Ed.), *Emotion and social behavior* (pp. 1–31). Newbury Park, CA: Sage.

Wilson, T. D., Lisle, D. J., Kraft, D., & Wetzel, C. G. (1989). Preferences as expectation-driven inferences: Effects of affective expectations on affective experience. *Journal of Personality and Social Psychology, 56*, 519–530.

Winefield, A. H., & Tiggemann, M. (1991). Employment status and psychological well-being: A longitudinal study. *Journal of Applied Psychology, 75*, 455–459.

Winett, R. A. (1995). A framework for health promotion and disease prevention programs. *American Psychologist, 50*, 341–350.

Winett, R. A., & Neale, M. S. (1981). Flexible work schedules and family time allocation: Assessment of a system change on individual behavior using self-report logs. *Journal of Applied Behavior Analysis, 14*, 39–46.

Winn, P. (1995). The lateral hypothalamus and motivated behavior: An old syndrome reassessed and a new perspective gained. *Current Directions in Psychological Science, 4*, 182–187.

Winograd, E. (1988). Some observations on prospective remembering. In M. M. Gruneberg, P. E. Morris, & R. N. Sykes (Eds.), *Practical aspects of memory: Current research and issues: Vol. 1* (pp. 348–353). Chichester, England: John Wiley & Sons.

Winter, D. G. (1983). *Development of an integrated system for scoring motives in verbal running text.* Unpublished manuscript, Wesleyan University.

Wise, R. A., & Bozarth, M. A. (1987). A psychomotor stimulant theory of addiction. *Psychological Review, 94*, 469–492.

Woehr, D. J., & Feldman, J. (1993). Processing objective and question order effects on the causal relation between memory and judgment in performance appraisal: The tip of the iceberg. *Journal of Applied Psychology, 78*, 232–241.

Wogalter, M. S., & Laughery, K. R. (1996). WARNING! Sign and label effectiveness. *Current Directions in Psychological Science, 5*, 33–37.

Wogalter, M. S., & Young, S. L. (1991). Behavioral compliance to voice and print warnings. *Ergonomics, 34*, 79–89.

Wogalter, M. S., & Young, S. L. (1993). Using warnings to increase safe behavior: A process approach. *Best's safety directory.* Oldwick, NJ: A. M. Best Company.

Wolberg, L. R. (1977). *The technique of psychotherapy.* New York: Grune & Stratton.

Wolfe, B. M., & Baron, R. A. (1971). Laboratory aggression related to aggression in naturalistic social situations: Effects of an aggressive model on the behavior of college student and prisoner observers. *Psychonomic Science, 24*, 193–194.

Wolpe, J. (1958). *Psychotherapy by reciprocal inhibition.* Stanford, CA: Stanford University Press.

Wolpe, J. (1969). *The practice of behavior therapy.* Oxford: Pergamon Press.

Wood, J. M., Nezworski, M. T., & Stejskal, W. J. (1996). The comprehensive system for the Rorschach: A critical examination. *Psychological Science, 7*, 3–10.

Wood, R. A., & Locke, E. A. (1990). Goal setting and strategy effects on complex tasks. In B. M. Staw & L. L. Cummings (Eds.), *Research in organizational behavior* (Vol. 12, pp. 73–110). Greenwich, CT: JAI Press.

Wood, R., Bandura, A., & Bailey, T. (1990). Mechanisms governing organizational performance in complex decision-making environments. *Organizational Behavior and Human Decision Processes, 46*, 181–201.

Wood, W., Wong, F. Y., & Chachere, J. G. (1991). Effects of media violence on viewers' aggression in unconstrained social interaction. *Psychological Bulletin, 109*, 373–383.

Woodall, K. L., & Matthews, K. A. (1993). Changes in and stability of hostile characteristics: Results from a 4–year longitudinal study of children. *Journal of Personality and Social Psychology, 64*, 491–499.

Woodcock, R. W., & Johnson, M. B. (1989). Woodcock-Johnson Tests of Cognitive Ability: Standard and Supplemental Batteries.

Woodruff-Pak, D. S., & Thompson, R. F. (1988). Classical conditioning of the eyeblink response in the delay paradigm in adults aged 18–83 years. *Psychology and Aging, 3*, 219–229.

Woody, E. Z., & Bowers, K. S. (1994). A frontal assault on dissociated control. In S. J. Lynn & J. W. Rhue (Eds.), *Dissociation: Theoretical and clinical perspectives* (pp. 52–79). New York: Guilford Press.

World-wide: The Navy recovered. (1996). *The Wall Street Journal*, p. 2, col. 1.

Wortman, C. B., Carnelley, K. B., & Kessler, R. C. (1994). *Impact of widowhood on depression: Findings from a prospective national survey.* Manuscript submitted for publication.

Wright, P. M., O'Leary-Kelly, A. M., Cortinak, J. M., Klein, H. J., & Hollenbeck, J. R. (1994). On the meaning and measurement of goal commitment. *Journal of Applied Psychology, 79*, 795–803.

Wright, R. (1995, March 13). The biology of violence. *The New Yorker*, pp. 68–77.

Wright, R. W. (1982). *The sense of smell.* Boca Raton, FL: CRC Press.

Wrightsman, L. S. (1988). *Personality development in adulthood.* Newbury Park, CA: Sage.

Wyer, R. S. Jr., & Srull, T. K. (Eds.). (1994). *Handbook of social cognition* (2nd ed., Vol. 1). Hillsdale, NJ: Erlbaum.

Wylie, R. (1974). *The self-concept* (Vol. 1). Lincoln: University of Nebraska Press.

Yankner, J., Johnson, S. T., Menerdo, T., Cordell, B., & Firth, C. L. (1990). Relations of neural APP-751/APP-695 in RNA ratio and neuritic plaque density in Alzheimer's disease. *Science, 248*, 854–856.

Yates, S. (1992). Lay attributions about distress after a natural disaster. *Personality and Social Psychology Bulletin, 18*, 217–222.

Yonas, A., Arterberry, M. E., & Granrud, C. E. (1987). Four-month-old infants' sensitivity to binocular and kinetic information for three-dimensional object shape. *Child Development, 58*, 910–927.

Young, A. M., & Herling, S. (1986). Drugs as reinforcers: Studies in laboratory animals. In S. R. Goldberg & I. P. Stolerman (Eds.), *Behavioral analysis of drug dependence* (pp. 9–67). New York: Academic Press.

Yudofsky, S., Hales, R. E., & Ferguson, T. (1991). *What you need to know about psychiatric drugs.* New York: Grove Weidenfeld.

Yuille, J. C., & Tollestrup, P. A. (1990). Some effects of alcohol on eyewitness memory. *Journal of Applied Psychology, 75*, 268–273.

Yukl, G. (1994). *Leadership in organizations* (3rd ed.). Englewood Cliffs, NJ: Prentice-Hall.

Zaccaro, S. J., Craig, B., & Quinn, J. (1991). Prior absenteeism, supervisory style, job satisfaction, and personal characteristics: An investigation of some mediated and moderated linkages to work absenteeism. *Organizational Behavior and Human Decision Processes, 50*, 24–44.

Zaccaro, S. J., Foti, R. J., & Kennedy, D. A. (1991). Self-monitoring and trait-based variance in leadership: An investigation of leader-flexibility across multiple group situations. *Journal of Applied Psychology, 76*, 308–315.

Zaidel, D. W. (1994). Worlds apart: Pictorial semantics in the left and right cerebral hemispheres. *Current Directions in Psychological Science, 3*, 5–8.

Zajonc, R. B. (1968). Attitudinal effects of mere exposure. *Journal of Personality and Social Psychology Monograph Supplement, 9*, 1–27.

Zajonc, R. B., & McIntosh, D. N. (1992). Emotions research: Some promising questions and some questionable promises. *Psychological Science, 3*, 70–74.

Zajonc, R. B., Murphy, S. T., & Inglehart, M. (1989). Feeling and facial efference: Implications of the vascular theory of emotion. *Psychological Review, 96*, 395–416.

Zatzick, D. F., & Dimsdale, J. E. (1990). *Psychosomatic Medicine*, 52, 544–557.

Zeki, S. (1992, September). The visual image in mind and brain. *Scientific American*, pp. 69–76.

Zeman, J., & Shipman, K. (1996). Children's expression of negative affect: Reasons and method. *Developmental Psychology, 32*, 842–849.

Zillmann, D. (1993). Mental control of angry aggression. In D. M. Wegner & J. W. Pennebaker (Eds.), *Handbook of mental control.* Englewood Cliffs, NJ: Prentice-Hall.

Zillmann, D. (1996). Anger. In *Encyclopedia of Mental Health.* New York: Harcourt Brace.

Zillmann, D., Schweitzer, K. J., & Mundorf, N. (1994). Menstrual cycle variation in women's interest in erotica. *Archives of Sexual Behavior, 23*, 579–597.

Zinberg, R. E., & Barlow, D. H. (1996). Structure of anxiety and the anxiety disorders: A hierarchical model. *Journal of Abnormal Psychology, 105*, 181–193.

Zuckerman, M. (1990). The psychophysiology of sensation seeking. *Journal of Personality, 58*, 313–345.

Zuckerman, M. (1994). *Behavioral expressions and biosocial bases of sensation seeking.* New York: Cambridge University Press.

Zuckerman, M. (1995). Good and bad humors: Biochemical bases of personality and its disorders. *Psychological Science, 6*, 325–332.

Zuckerman, M., DePaulo, B. M., & Rosenthal, R. (1981). Verbal and nonverbal communication of deception. In L. Berkowitz (Ed.), *Advances in experimental social psychology* (Vol. 14, pp. 1–59). New York: Academic Press.

Zuckerman, M., & Neeb, M. (1980). Demographic influences in sensation seeking and expression of sensation seeking in religion, smoking, and driving habits. *Personality and Individual Differences, 1*, 197–206.

Zuckerman, M., Simons, R. F., & Como, P. (1988). Sensation seeking and stimulus intensity as modulators of cortical, cardiovascular, and electrodermal responses: A cross-modality study. *Personality and Individual Differences, 9*, 361–372.

Zusne, L., & Jones, W. H. (1989). *Anomalistic psychology: A study of magical thinking* (2nd ed.). Hillsdale, NJ: Erlbaum.

Zuwerink, J. R., & Devine, P. G. (1996). Attitude importance and resistance to persuasion: It's not just the thought that counts. *Journal of Personality and Social Psychology, 70*, 931–944.

Name Index

Subject Index

Photo Credits: **Chapter One:** p. 2: Stuart Dee/The Image Bank; p. 6 (left): Mark Antman/The Image Works; (right): Michael J. Howell/Rainbow; p. 7: Lyrl Ahern; p. 8: Gary Gold/Gamma Liaison; p. 10: Desmond Boylan/Reuters/Archive Photo; p. 15: Wedgworth/Custom Medical Stock Photo, Inc.; p. 22: Dan McCoy/Rainbow; p. 23: Howard Bluestein/Photo Researchers, Inc.; p. 24: Robert Harbison; p. 25: Bob Daemmrich/Stock Boston; p. 28 (left): Barbara Alper/Stock Boston; p. 28 (right): Tom McCarthy/The Picture Cube; p. 36: Kerbs/Monkmeyer; p. 39: Clark/Monkmeyer. **Chapter Two:** p. 42: Raphael Gaillarde/Gamma Liaison; p. 52 (left): Grunnitus/Monkmeyer; p. 52 (right): Will Hart; p. 58: Photosynthesis Archives; p. 59 (left): Leonard Lessin/Peter Arnold, Inc.; p. 59 (right): Peter Menzel; p. 64: Custom Medical Stock Photo, Inc.; p. 75: Science Photo Library/Photo Researchers, Inc.; p. 79: Stephen Marks. **Chapter Three:** p. 82: Robert Frerck/Woodfin Camp; p. 85 (left): Dallas & John Heaton/Stock Shop-Medichrome; p. 85 (right): Tony Neste; p. 88: Peter Menzel/Stock Boston; p. 90: J. & L. Weber/Peter Arnold, Inc.; p. 101: Willie Hill/Stock Boston; p. 102: Culver Pictures; p. 108: MacDonald/The Picture Cube; p. 113: Ullman/Monkmeyer; p. 116 (top center): Robert E. Daemmrich/Tony Stone Images; p. 116 (bottom left): Bill Ross/Tony Stone Images; p. 116 (bottom right): J. & M. Ibbotson/Tony Stone Images; p. 117 (bottom left): Tommy L. Thompson/Black Star; p. 117 (bottom right): Steve Mats/Tony Stone Images; p. 118 (left & right): Rob Pretzer; p. 121: Digi-Rule Inc. **Chapter Four:** p. 130: Tony Freeman/Photo Edit; p. 135: Will Hart; p. 136: Jeff Greenberg/Photo Researchers, Inc.; p. 138: Robert Harbison; p. 140: Robert Harbison; p. 143: Michal Heron/Woodfin Camp & Assoc.; p. 144 (top right): Forsyth/Monkmeyer; p. 144 (bottom right): Suzanne Szasz/Photo Researchers, Inc.; p. 150: Bob Daemmrich/Stock Boston; p. 155: Courtesy of Robert A. Baron; p. 156 (left): David Parker/Science Photo Library/Photo Researchers; p. 156 (top right): Culver Pictures; p. 156 (bottom right): Kolvoord/The Image Works; p. 165: Tony Neste. **Chapter Five:** p. 168: Marc F. Bernheim/Woodfin Camp & Assoc.; p. 171: The Image Works; p. 172: National Library of Medicine/Photosynthesis Archive; p. 179: Roger Tully/Medichrome; p. 181: Photosynthesis Archive; p. 184: David Weintraub/Science Source/Photo Researchers, Inc.; p. 186 (left): John Coletti; p. 186 (right): Will Faller; p. 180: A. Reininger/Woodfin Camp & Assoc.; p. 192: Will Faller; p. 195: Will Hart; p. 200: Brian Smith; p. 202: Will Hart; p. 205: Will Faller; p. 206: David Austen/Tony Stone Images. **Chapter 6:** p. 212: Marc A. Auth/New England Stock Photo; p. 218 (left): Will Hart; p. 218 (center): Will Hart; p. 218 (right): Walter Bibikow/The Picture Cube; p. 230: Bob Krist/Tony Stone Images; p. 233: Robert Harbison; p. 234:

Spencer Grant/Photo Researchers, Inc.; p. 237: Will Faller; p. 240: Will Hart; p. 243 (left): David Young-Wolff/Tony Stone Images; p. 243 (right): Jerome Tisne/Tony Stone Images. **Chapter Seven:** p. 254: J. Gerald Smith/Photo Researchers, Inc.; p. 257 (top left): Rick Rusing/Tony Stone Images; p. 257 (bottom left) Courtesy of NASA; p. 257 (right): M. Jacob/The Image Works; 265 (left): David Simson/Stock Boston; 265 (top right): Billy Barnes/Stock Boston; p. 265 (bottom right): Win McNamee/Reuters/Archive Photos; p. 282: Barbara Johnston/Reuters/Archive Photos; p. 284: Eastcott/Momatiuk/The Image Works; p. 292: Courtesy H. S. Terrace, Columbia University. **Chapter Eight:** p. 296: Scott Barrow; p. 298: Will Faller; p. 300 (top left): Neil Harding/Tony Stone Images; p. 300 (bottom left): Axel Bartel/The Picture Cube; p. 300 (right): Medichrome; p. 304: Dr. Nadja Eissland-Burghart; p. 306: Courtesy of J. Campos, B. Bertenthal & R. Kermoian; p. 310: Will Faller; p. 312: Courtesy Judy DeLoache; p. 314: Will Faller; p. 322: Pauline Cutler/Tony Stone Images; p. 328 (top left): Martin Rogers/Woodfin Camp & Assoc.; p. 328 (right): Martin Rogers/Tony Stone; p. 328 (bottom left): Will Faller; p. 330 (left): Robert Harbison; p. 330 (right): Kagan/Monkmeyer; p. 334 (top left): Will Faller; p. 334 (bottom left): Stephen Marks; p. 334 (right): Art Stein/Photo Researchers. **Chapter Nine:** p. 340: Scott Barrow; p. 343 (left): Cary Wolinsky/Tony Stone Images; p. 343 (right): Annerino/Gamma Liaison; p. 350: Robert Yager/Tony Stone Images; p. 353: Frank Siteman/The Picture Cube; p. 356: David Young-Wolff/Tony Stone Images; p. 358 (both): Library of Congress; p. 359 (all): Courtesy of Robert A. Baron; p. 365 (left): Chip Henderson/Tony Stone Images; 365 (top right): Will & Deni McIntyre/Photo Researchers, Inc.; p. 365 (bottom right): Popperfoto/Archive Photos; p. 369: Jodi Buren/Woodfin Camp & Assoc.; p. 370: Andy Saks/Tony Stone Images; p. 374: Reuters/Corbis-Bettmann. **Chapter Ten:** p. 380: Ed Lallo/The Picture Cube; p. 383 (left): Joseph McBride/Tony Stone Images; p. 383 (right): Will Faller; p. 385: William R. Sallaz/Duomo; p. 391 (left): Penny Tweedie/Tony Stone Images; p. 391 (top right): M. Antman/The Image Works; p. 391 (bottom right): Will Hart; p. 392: Billy Barnes/Stock Boston; p. 395: Hronn Axelsdottir, Brooklyn; p. 396: James Wilson/Woodfin Camp & Assoc.; p. 398: Photofest; p. 401: Courtesy of Robert A. Baron; p. 402: John Coletti; p. 412: Mike Abramson/Woodfin Camp & Assoc.; p. 414: Courtesy of Robert A. Baron; p. 418: Jon Riley/The Stock Shop. **Chapter Eleven:** p. 422: SuperStock Inc.; p. 425 (left): Kaluzny/Thatcher/Tony Stone Images; p. 425 (right): Tim Brown/Tony Stone Images; p. 427: Steven E. Sutton/Duomo; p. 434: Culver Pictures; p. 441 (top left): Paul Chesley/Tony Stone Images; p. 441 (bottom left): UPI/Corbis-Bettmann; p. 441 (top right): Robert E. Daemmrich/Stock Boston; p. 441 (bottom right): Culver Pictures; p. 444: Martha Bates/Stock Boston; p. 445: Arnold Zann/Black Star; p.446: David Hiser/Tony Stone Images; p. 449: Robert Harbison; p. 455: Pedrick/The Image Works. **Chapter Twelve:** p. 464: Bob Daemmrich/Stock Boston; p. 468: The Granger Collection, New York; p. 473: M. Grecco/Stock Boston; p. 477: Photofest; p. 483: Jim Pickerell/Tony Stone Images; p. 485: Christopher Brown/Stock Boston; p. 486 (left): Jon Riley/Tony Stone Images; p. 486 (right): Paul Meredith/Tony Stone Images; p. 489: Robert Harbison; p. 491: Andy Sacks/Tony Stone Images; p. 497: Patrick Ward/Stock Boston. **Chapter Thirteen:** p. 502: Catherine Karnow/Woodfin Camp & Assoc.; p. 508: AP/Wide World Photos; p. 530: Defleur/Photo Researchers, Inc.; p. 533: Stephen Marks; p. 537: Will Hart; p. 541 (left): Barbara Alper/Stock Boston; p. 541 (right): Will Hart. **Chapter Fourteen:** p. 544: Hronn Axelsdottir, Brooklyn; p. 548: North Wind Picture Archives; p. 550: Christine Osborne/Photo Researchers, Inc.; p. 553: Will Hart; p. 555 (left): Jeff Persons/Stock Boston; p. 555 (right): Timothy Shonnard/Tony Stone Images; p. 558: Henry Schleichkorn/Custom Medical Stock Photo, Inc.; p. 559: UPI/Bettmann; p. 562: Bob Daemmrich/Stock Boston; p. 568 (both): UPI/Bettmann; p. 572 (left): Corbis-Bettmann; p. 572 (right): Big Pictures/Archive Photos; p. 575: Sylvain Grandadam/Tony Stone Images; p. 577: Will Hart; p. 579: Mary Ellen Mark; p. 582: Chromosohm/Sohm/Photo Researchers, Inc. **Chapter Fifteen:** p. 586: Dennis Brack/National Gallery of Art/Black Star; p. 588: Bruce Ayres/Tony Stone Images; p. 590: AP/Wide World Photos; p. 596: Gale Zucker/Stock Boston; p. 600: The Stock Shop; p. 601: W. Hill/The Image Works; p. 611 (left): Will Hart; p. 611 (top right): John Giordano/SABA; p. 611 (bottom right): Ullman/Monkmeyer; p. 614: Courtesy of Robert A. Baron; p. 617: James Wilson/Woodfin Camp & Assoc. **Chapter Sixteen:** p. 624: Phyllis Picardi/Stock Boston; p. 626: David Young-Wolff/Tony Stone Images; p. 628: A. Ramey/Woodfin Camp & Assoc.; p. 633: Roberto Thoni/Corbis-Bettmann; p. 636: Kevin Horan/Tony Stone Images; p. 638: Courtesy of DDB Needham for Phillips Petroleum Company; p. 644: Culver Pictures; p. 646: Geo. Rose/Gamma Liaison; p. 648: Coco McCoy/Rainbow; p. 653 (left): Paula Bronstein/Tony Stone Images; p. 653 (right): Bob Daemmrich/Stock Boston; p. 660 (both): Tony Neste. **Chapter Seventeen:** p. 666: Koni Nordman/Woodfin Camp & Associates; p. 668 (top): Robert Harbison; p. 668 (bottom left): John Coletti; p. 668 (bottom right): Will Hart; p. 671: Zigy Kaluzny/Tony Stone Images; p. 676 (left): Peter Langone/Tony Stone Images; p. 676 (right): Charles Gupton/Tony Stone Images; p. 677: Mitch Kezar/Tony Stone Images; pp. 683 & 685: Courtesy of Robert A. Baron; p. 691: Bruce Ayres/Tony Stone Images; p. 692 (left and center): North Wind Picture Archives; p. 692 (right): Library of Congress; p. 698: Courtesy of Robert A. Baron.

Figure Credits p. 94: Fig. 3.7 adapted from MacNichol, E. F. (1964). Retinal mechanisms of color vision. *Vision Research, 4,* 119–133. Copyright 1964. Used with kind permission from Elsevier Science Ltd., The Boulevard, Langford Lane, Kidlington OX5 1GB, UK. p. 106: Fig. 3.15 from Pfaffmann, C. (1978). The vertebrate phylogeny, neural code, and integrative processes of taste. In E.C. Carterrette & M.P. Friedman (Eds.), *Handbook of perception* (Vol. 6A). Reprinted by permission of Academic Press, Inc. and the author. p. 116: Fig. 3.22 from Palmer, S.E. (1992). Common region: A new principle of perceptual grouping. *Cognitive Psychology, 24,* 436–447. Reprinted by permission of Academic Press, Inc. and the author. p. 118: Fig. 3.26 from Coren, S. & Girgus, J.S. (1978). *Seeing is deceiving: The psychology of visual illusion.* Reprinted by permission of Lawrence Erlbaum Associates, Inc. p. 143: Fig. 4.6 from Hartmann, E.L. (1973). *The functions of sleep.* Reprinted by permission of Yale University Press. p. 149: Fig. 4.8 based on suggestions in Antrobus (1991). Dreaming: Cognitive processes during cortical activation and high afferent thresholds. *Psychological Review, 98,* 96–212. Copyright © 1991 by the American Psychological Association. Adapted by permission. p.173: Fig. 5.3 from Baker, A.G., & Mackintosh, N.J. (1977). Excitatory and inhibitory conditioning following uncorrelated presentations of CCS and US. *Animal Learning and Behavior, 5,* (3), 315–319. Reprinted by permission of Psychonomic Society, Inc. p. 178: Fig. 5.5 from Garcia, J. & Koelling, R.A. (1966). Relation of cue to consequence in avoidance learning. *Psychonomic Science, 4,* 123–124. Reprinted by permission of Psychonomic Society, Inc. p. 193: Fig 5.14 from Mowrer, D.H., & Jones, H.M. (1945). Habit strength as a function of the pattern of reinforcement. *Journal of Experimental Psychology, 35,* 293–311. Reprinted by permission of the American Psychological Association. p. 216: Fig. 6.2 from Atkinson, R.C., & Shiffrin, R.M. (1968). Human memory: A proposed system and its control processes. In K.W. Spence (Ed.), *The psychology of learning and motivation: Advances in research and theory* (Vol. 2: 89–195). Reprinted by permission of Academic Press, Inc. p. 220: Fig 6.4 from Postmann, L., & Phillips, L.W. (1965). Short-term temporal changes in free recall. *Quarterly Journal of Experimental Psychology, 17,* 132–138. Reprinted by permission of The Experimental Psychology Society. p. 232: Fig. 6.9 Adapted in part from Tulving, E. and Psotka, L. (1971). Appeared in *Journal of Experimental Psychology, 87,* 1–8. © 1971 by the American Psychological Association. Adapted with permission. And adapted in part from Gruneberg, M.M., Morris, P., & Sykes, R.N. (1988). *Practical aspects of memory: Current research and issues* (Vols. 1&2). Copyright John Wiley & Sons Limited. Reproduced with permission. p. 259: Fig. 7.2 adapted from Kosslyn, S.M. (1980). *Image and mind.* Cambridge, Mass.: Harvard University Press. p. 264: Fig. 7.3 adapted in part from Baron, J. (1988). *Thinking and deciding.* Used by permission of Cambridge University Press. And adapted in part from Klayman, J., & Ha, Y.W. (1987). Confirmation, disconformation and information in hypothesis testing. *Psychological Review, 94,* 211–228. Copyright © 1988 by the American Psychological Association. Adapted with permission. p. 272: Fig. 7.6 Adapted in part from Staw, B.M. & Ross, J. (1989). Understanding behavior in escalation situations. *Science, 246,* 216–220. And adapted in part from Garland, H., & Newport, S., (1991). Effects of absolute and relative sunk costs on the decision to persist with a course of action. *Organizational Behavior and Human Decision Processes, 48,* 55–67. Used by permission of Academic Press, Inc. and the authors. p. 303: Fig. 8.3 based in part of Frankenburg, W.K., Dodds, J., Archer, P., et al. *Denver II Training Manual.* By permission of W.K. Frankenburg. p. 384: Fig. 10.2 adapted in part from Geen, R.G., Beatty, W.W., & Arkin, R.M. (1984). Human motivation. Boston: Allyn and Bacon. And adapted in part from Brehm, J.R. & Self, E.A. (1989). The intensity of motivation. *Annual Review of Psychology, 40,* 109–131. Adapted by permission of Annual Reviews Inc. p. 385: Fig. 10.3 from Weiner, B. (1989). Human motivation. Reprinted by permission of Lawrence Erlbaum Associates, Inc. p. 433: Fig. 11.5 adapted from Wielkiewicz, R.M. & Calvert, C.R.X. (1989). *Training and habilitating developmentally disabled people: An introduction.* Adapted by permission of Sage Publications, Inc. p. 509: Fig. 13.2 based on data from Hingson, R., Strunin, L., Berlin, B. & Heeren, T. (1990). Beliefs about AIDS, use of alcohol and drugs, and unprotected sex among Massachusetts adolescents. *American Journal of Public Health, 80,* 295–299. Copyright © 1990 American Public Health Association. Reprinted by permission. p. 516: Fig, 13.5 adapted from Lee, R.T. & Ashforth, B.E. (1990). On the meaning of Maslach's three dimensions of burnout. *Journal of Applied Psychology, 75,* 734–747. Copyright © by the American Psychological Association. Adapted by permission. p. 574: Fig. 14.14 from Williamson, D.A., Cubic, B.A., & Gleaves, D.H. (1993). Equivalence of body image disturbances in anorexia and bulimia nervosa. *Journal of Abnormal Psychology, 102,* 177–180. © 1993 by the American Psychological Association. Adapted with permission. p. 592: Fig. 15.4 adapted from Rogers, C. (1970). *Carl Rogers on encounter groups.* Copyright © 1970 by Carl Rogers. Adapted by permission of HarperCollins Publishers, Inc. p. 651: Fig. 16.16 photos from the film *Obedience,* copyright © 1965 by Stanley Milgram and distributed by Penn State Media Sales; data from Milgram, S. (1974). *Obedience to authority.* New York: Harper & Row Publishers. Used by permission of the Estate of Stanley Milgram. p. 670: Fig. 17.2 from Katzell & Thompson (1964). p. 671: Fig. 17.3 based on data from Latham, G. and Baldes, J. (1975). The practical significance of Licke's theory of goal setting. Appeared in *Journal of Applied Psychology, 60,* 120–124. Copyright © 1975 by the American Psychological Association. Adapted with permission.